About the author

Respected wine critic and vigneron James Halliday AM has a career that spans 48 years, but he is most widely known for his witty and informative writing about wine. As one of the founders of Brokenwood in the Hunter Valley and thereafter of Coldstream Hills in the Yarra Valley, James is an unmatched authority on every aspect of the wine industry, from the planting and pruning of vines through to the creation and marketing of the finished product. His winemaking has led him to sojourns in Bordeaux and Burgundy, and he had a long career as a wine judge in Australia and overseas. In 1995 he received the wine industry's ultimate accolade, the Maurice O'Shea Award. In 2010 James was made a Member of the Order of Australia for his services to the wine industry.

James has written or contributed to nearly 80 books on wine since he began writing in 1970. His books have been translated into Japanese, French, German, Danish, Icelandic and Polish, and have been published in the United Kingdom and the United States, as well as in Australia. He is the author of *Varietal Wines*, *James Halliday's Wine Atlas of Australia*, *The Australian Wine Encyclopedia* and *A Life in Wine*.

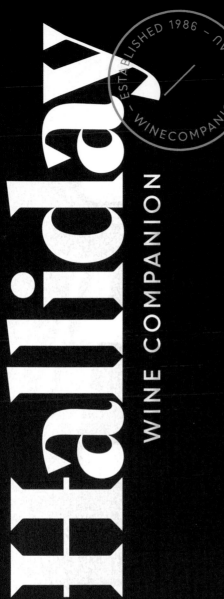

ESTABLISHED 1986 – WINECOMPANION.COM.AU

Halliday

WINE COMPANION

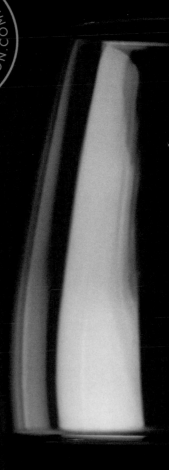

The bestselling
and definitive guide
to Australian wine

2019

Hardie Grant

BOOKS

Wine zones and regions of Australia

NEW SOUTH WALES			
WINE ZONE		**WINE REGION**	
Big Rivers	(A)	Murray Darling	1
		Perricoota	2
		Riverina	3
		Swan Hill	4
Central Ranges	(B)	Cowra	5
		Mudgee	6
		Orange	7
Hunter Valley	(C)	Hunter	8
		Upper Hunter	9
Northern Rivers	(D)	Hastings River	10
Northern Slopes	(E)	New England	11
South Coast	(F)	Shoalhaven Coast	12
		Southern Highlands	13
Southern New South Wales	(G)	Canberra District	14
		Gundagai	15
		Hilltops	16
		Tumbarumba	17
Western Plains	(H)		

SOUTH AUSTRALIA			
WINE ZONE		**WINE REGION**	
Adelaide Super Zone includes Mount Lofty Ranges, Fleurieu and Barossa wine regions			
Barossa		Barossa Valley	18
		Eden Valley	19
Fleurieu	(J)	Currency Creek	20
		Kangaroo Island	21
		Langhorne Creek	22
		McLaren Vale	23
		Southern Fleurieu	24
Mount Lofty Ranges		Adelaide Hills	25
		Adelaide Plains	26
		Clare Valley	27
Far North	(K)	Southern Flinders Ranges	28
Limestone Coast	(L)	Coonawarra	29
		Mount Benson	30
		Mount Gambier	31
		Padthaway	32
		Robe	33
		Wrattonbully	34
Lower Murray	(M)	Riverland	35
The Peninsulas	(N)	Southern Eyre Peninsula*	36

VICTORIA			
WINE ZONE		**WINE REGION**	
Central Victoria	(P)	Bendigo	37
		Goulburn Valley	38
		Heathcote	39
		Strathbogie Ranges	40
Gippsland	(Q)	Upper Goulburn	41
		Alpine Valleys	42
North East Victoria	(R)	Beechworth	43
		Glenrowan	44
		King Valley	45
		Rutherglen	46
North West Victoria	(S)	Murray Darling	47
		Swan Hill	48
Port Phillip	(T)	Geelong	49
		Macedon Ranges	50
		Mornington Peninsula	51
		Sunbury	52
		Yarra Valley	53
Western Victoria	(U)	Ballarat*	54
		Grampians	55
		Henty	56
		Pyrenees	57

* For more information see page 50.

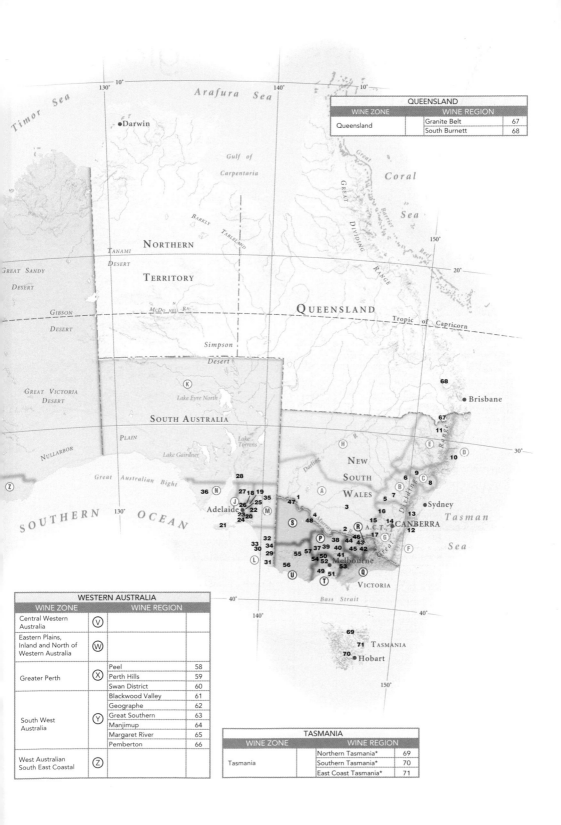

QUEENSLAND		
WINE ZONE	WINE REGION	
Queensland	Granite Belt	67
	South Burnett	68

WESTERN AUSTRALIA			
WINE ZONE		WINE REGION	
Central Western Australia	V		
Eastern Plains, Inland and North of Western Australia	W		
Greater Perth	X	Peel	58
		Perth Hills	59
		Swan District	60
South West Australia	Y	Blackwood Valley	61
		Geographe	62
		Great Southern	63
		Manjimup	64
		Margaret River	65
		Pemberton	66
West Australian South East Coastal	Z		

TASMANIA		
WINE ZONE	WINE REGION	
Tasmania	Northern Tasmania*	69
	Southern Tasmania*	70
	East Coast Tasmania*	71

Published in 2018 by Hardie Grant Books,
an imprint of Hardie Grant Publishing

Hardie Grant Books (Melbourne)
Building 1, 658 Church Street
Richmond, Victoria 3121

Hardie Grant Books (London)
5th & 6th Floors
52–54 Southwark Street
London SE1 1UN

hardiegrantbooks.com

The *Australian Wine Companion* is a joint venture between James Halliday and
Explore Australia Pty Ltd.

The map in this publication incorporates data copyright © Commonwealth of
Australia (Geoscience Australia) 2004. Geoscience Australia has not evaluated
the data as altered and incorporated within this publication and therefore gives
no warranty regarding accuracy, completeness, currency or suitability for any
particular purpose.

Australian wine zones and wine regions data copyright © Australian Wine
and Brandy Corporation, April 2005

ISBN 978 1 74379 420 3

10 9 8 7 6 5 4 3 2 1

Cover design by Tristan Ceddia, Never Now
Typeset by Megan Ellis
Author photograph by Julian Kingma
Printed by McPherson's Printing Group, Maryborough, Victoria

Contents

Introduction

It is decidedly curious that the picture most frequently painted is of a vibrant export market and flat domestic sales in a tough, competitive environment. Dealing with the latter first up, in the 2017 financial year sales volume rose 2% to 500 million litres, with value up 6% to $3.3 billion. Consumers are paying more for each litre sold, and buying more. The budget, and the various reports of consumer confidence, suggest the market should be in fine fettle. But talk to sales reps and independent retailers, and they all say it's tough out there.

There are few frowns on the faces of exporters, and only broad smiles on the faces of Treasury Wine Estates' shareholders, with the share price almost touching $20 at the time of going to print. The People's Republic of China insists that Hong Kong and Macau are part of its territory; combined sales in these three regions reached $1 billion for the 12 months to 31 March 2018.

While the value per litre of Australian wines is the highest of the top five exporters to China, with France in second place, there has been solid growth across all price sectors. Research conducted by Wine Intelligence on behalf of Wine Australia shows that the number of Chinese drinkers of Australian wine has doubled since 2013.

This increase reflects the solid growth in entry level and commercial wines retailing for less than ¥60 (approximately AUD13) per bottle. The increased accessibility of imported wine in China means that it is becoming a mainstream beverage enjoyed by a much broader base of consumers, and a beverage of choice for informal meals and relaxing at home. A further indication of this is the increase in sales of white wines, up 33% to $30 million for the 12 months to 31 March 2018. Chardonnay is the number one variety, but riesling was up 77% at twice the rate of increase as chardonnay.

	Australian wine exports					
	Total		PR China		Hong Kong	
	Volume (litres)	Value AUD	Volume (litres)	Value AUD	Volume (litres)	Value AUD
	million	billion	million	million	million	million
2000	284	$1.34	0.3	$1.2	2	$13
2005	661	$2.75	4	$13	4	$23
2010	777	$2.16	55	$164	6	$44
2015	724	$1.89	68	$370	10	$132
2017	778	$2.31	117	$607	8	$114
MAT Mar '18	884	$3.14	171	$932	8	$107

The market share of each of the major exporters to China for the moving annual total (MAT) February 2018 shows that Australia continues to narrow the gap between itself and France, and widen the gap between itself and Chile. France and Australia supplied 65% of all wine imported by China in the 12 months to February 2018.

How to use this book

Wineries

Seville Estate

65 Linwood Road, Seville, Vic 3139 **Region** Yarra Valley
T (03) 5964 2622 **www**.sevilleestate.com.au **Open** 7 days 10-5
Winemaker Dylan McMahon **Est.** 1972 **Dozens** 8000 **Vyds** 12ha
Seville Estate was founded by Dr Peter and Margaret McMahon in 1972.
It underwent several changes in ownership up to 2006, when wealthy Chinese
businessman Yiping Wang, with a background of wine shops in China, acquired
outright ownership. Throughout the changes, Peter McMahon's grandson Dylan
McMahon remained as winemaker, and has been appointed general manager/
winemaker. Significant investments have been made, including the purchase of the
neighbouring vineyard and property (formerly Ainsworth Estate), which has lifted
the property size to 20ha, with 12ha under vine. The extra land has allowed for
replanting original vine material grafted onto rootstock, in an effort to preserve
the original 1972 clones and safeguard the future of the precious property. Seville
Estate also has luxury accommodation, with the original homestead and three
self-contained apartments. Exports to the US, Canada and China. *Wine Companion
2019* Winery of the Year.

Winery name   Seville Estate

The name of the producer, as it appears on the front label, is used throughout the book.

Winery rating   ★★★★★

I look at the ratings for this year and the previous two years; if the wines tasted this
year achieved a higher rating than last year, that higher rating has been given. If, on
the other hand, the wines are of lesser quality, I take into account the track record
over the past two years (or longer where the winery is well known) and make a
judgement call on whether it should retain its ranking or be given a lesser one. In
what I call the mercy rating, in most instances a demotion is no more than half a
star. Where no wines were submitted by a well-rated winery with a track record of
providing samples, I may use my discretion to roll over last year's rating.

While there are (only) 1216 wineries profiled in this edition, there are more than
2800 wineries to be found on www.winecompanion.com.au.

The percentage at the end of each rating on page 10 refers to the number of
wineries achieving that rating within the total number of wineries in the *Wine
Companion* database at the time of going to print. Two caveats: first, I retain a
discretionary right to depart from the normal criteria; second, the basis of the ratings
are best understood on the website, where all wine ratings appear.

Some may think my ratings are too generous, but less than half (42.9%) of the
wineries in our database that are believed, or known to be, active are given ratings in

this book, spread across the categories shown below. Moreover, if I were to reduce the number of wineries in each category by (say) 50% the relative ranking would not change, other than a massive increase in the NR category, providing no useful guidance for the reader.

★★★★★   Outstanding winery regularly producing wines of exemplary quality and typicity. Will have at least two wines rated at 95 points or above, and has had a 5-star rating for the previous two years. 232 wineries, 8.2%

Where the winery name is itself is printed in red, it is a winery generally acknowledged to have had a long track record of excellence in the context of its region – truly the best of the best. 101 wineries, 3.6%

★★★★★   Outstanding winery capable of producing wines of very high quality, and did so this year. Also will usually have at least two wines rated at 95 points or above. 220 wineries, 7.8%

★★★★☆   Excellent winery able to produce wines of high to very high quality, knocking on the door of a 5-star rating. Will normally have one wine rated at 95 points or above, two (or more) at 90 or above, and others 87–89. 224 wineries, 7.9%

★★★★   Very good producer of wines with class and character. Will have two (or more) wines rated at 90 points or above (or possibly one at 95 or above). 317 wineries, 11.2%

★★★☆   A solid, usually reliable, maker of good, sometimes very good, wines. Will have one wine rated at 90 points or above, others 86–89. 103 wineries, 3.6%

★★★   A typically good winery, but often has a few lesser wines. Will have wines rated at 86–89 points. 19 wineries, 0.7%

NR   The NR rating mainly appears on www.winecompanion.com.au. The rating is given in a range of circumstances: where there have been no tastings in the 12-month period; where there have been tastings, but with no wines scoring more than 88 points; or where the tastings have, for one reason or another, proved not to fairly reflect the reputation of a winery with a track record of success. NR wineries in the book are generally new wineries with no wine entries. 0 wineries.

Contact Details 65 Linwood Road, Seveille, Vic 3139 **T** (03) 5964 2622

The details are usually those of the winery and cellar door, but in a few instances may simply be a postal address; this occurs when the wine is made at another winery or wineries, and is sold only through the website and/or retail outlets.

Region Yarra Valley

A full list of zones, regions and subregions appears on pages 50–53. Occasionally you will see 'Various' as the region. This means the wine is made from grapes purchased from a number of regions, often by a winery without a vineyard of its own.

www.sevilleestate.com.au

An important reference point, normally containing material not found (for space reasons) in this book.

Open 7 days 10-5

Although a winery might be listed as not open or only open on weekends, many may in fact be prepared to open by appointment. A telephone call will establish whether it is possible or not. For space reasons we have simplified the open hours listing; where the hours vary each day, or for holidays, etcetera, we refer the reader to the website.

Winemaker Dylan McMahon

In all but the smallest producers, the winemaker is simply the head of a team; there may be many executive winemakers actually responsible for specific wines in the medium to large companies (80000 dozens and upwards). Once again, space constraints mean usually only one or two winemakers are named, even if they are part of a larger team.

Est. 1972

Keep in mind that some makers consider the year in which they purchased the land to be the year of establishment, others the year in which they first planted grapes, others the year they first made wine, and so on. There may also be minor complications where there has been a change of ownership or break in production.

Dozens 8000

This figure (representing the number of 9-litre (12-bottle) cases produced each year) is merely an indication of the size of the operation. Some winery entries do not feature a production figure: this is either because the winery (principally, but not exclusively, the large companies) regards this information as confidential.

Vyds 12ha

Shows the hectares of vineyard(s) owned by the winery.

Summary Seville Estate was founded by Dr Peter and Margaret McMahon in 1972. It underwent several changes in ownership up to 2006, when wealthy Chinese businessman Yiping Wang, with a background of wine shops in China, acquired outright ownership.

Surely self-explanatory, except that I have tried to vary the subjects I discuss in this part of the winery entry.

New wineries

 The vine leaf symbol indicates the 67 wineries that are new entries in this year's *Wine Companion*.

Tasting notes

There has been a progressive adoption of the 100-point system in wine shows and in reviews by other commentators. The majority follow the system outlined below, and which I used in precisely this form in the *Wine Companion* 2018. Space constraints mean that only 3864 notes are printed in full in this book, with points, drink-to dates and prices included for a further 2906 wines. Tasting notes for all wines receiving 84 points or above appear on www.winecompanion.com.au. Also see page 26.

Ratings

97–99	**G O L D**	♀♀♀♀♀	**Exceptional.** Wines that have won a major trophy/trophies in important wine shows, or are of that standard.
95–96		♀♀♀♀♀	**Outstanding.** Wines of gold medal standard, usually with a great pedigree.
94	**S I L V E R**	♀♀♀♀♀	Wines on the cusp of gold medal status, virtually indistinguishable from those wines receiving 95 points.
90–93		♀♀♀♀♀	**Highly Recommended.** Wines of silver medal standard, wines of great quality, style and character, and worthy of a place in any cellar.
89	**B R O N Z E**	♀♀♀♀	**Recommended.** Wines on the cusp of silver medal standard, the difference purely a judgement call.
86–88		♀♀♀♀	Wines of bronze medal standard; well produced, flavoursome wines, usually not requiring cellaring.
		✪	**Special Value.** Wines considered to offer special value for money within the context of their glass symbol status.
84–85		♀♀♀♀	**Acceptable.** Wines of good commercial quality, free from significant fault.
80–83		♀♀♀	**Over to You.** Everyday wines without much character and/or somewhat faulty.
75–79		♀♀♀	**Not Recommended.** Wines with one or more significant winemaking faults.

♀♀♀♀♀ **Old Vine Reserve Yarra Valley Pinot Noir 2017** Vines planted '72; 70% whole berry/30% whole bunches, wild yeast–open ferment, 23 days on skins, matured in French oak (30% new) for 10 months. Vivid crimson-purple; a majestic pinot, unrolling its beautiful tapestry of wild strawberry and forest berries, accompanied by feather-light, but persistent, tannins. I checked its quality by swallowing some at 8.30am. Screwcap. 13.8% alc. **Rating** 99 **To** 2032 $70 ✪

The tasting note opens with the vintage of the wine tasted. This tasting note will have been written within the 12 months prior to publication. Even that is a long time, and during the life of this book the wine will almost certainly change. More than this, remember that tasting is a highly subjective and imperfect art. The price of the wine is listed where information is available. Tasting notes for wines rated 95 points or above are printed in red.

The initials CM, DB, JF, NG, SC or TS, sometimes appearing at the end of a tasting note, signify that Campbell Mattinson, David Bicknell, Jane Faulkner, Ned Goodwin, Steven Creber or Tyson Stelzer tasted the wine and provided the tasting note and rating. Short biographies for each member of the tasting team can be found on page 63.

Screwcap

This is the closure used for this particular wine. The closures in use for the wines tasted are (in descending order): screwcap 87.9% (last year 90%), one-piece natural cork 5.8% (last year 5.3%), Diam 4.7% (last year 3.1%). The remaining 1.6% (in approximate order of importance) are Crown Seal, Vino-Lok, ProCork, Zork and Twin Top. I believe the percentage of screwcap-closed wines will continue to rise for red wines; 97.3% of white wines tasted are screwcapped, leaving little room for any further increase.

13.8% alc.

As with closures, I have endeavoured to always include this information, which is in one sense self-explanatory. What is less obvious is the increasing concern of many Australian winemakers about the rise in alcohol levels, and much research and practical experimentation (picking earlier, higher fermentation temperatures in open fermenters, etcetera) is occurring. Reverse osmosis and yeast selection are two of the options available to decrease higher than desirable alcohol levels. Recent changes to domestic and export labelling mean the stated alcohol will be within a maximum of 0.5% difference to that obtained by analysis.

To 2032

Rather than give a span of drinking years, I have simply provided a (conservative) 'drink-to' date. Modern winemaking is such that, even if a wine has 10 or 20 years during which it will gain greater complexity, it can be enjoyed at any time over the intervening months and years.

$70

I use the price provided by the winery. It should be regarded as a guide, particularly if purchased retail.

Winery of the year

Seville Estate

Seville Estate was established in 1972 by Dr Peter McMahon and wife Margaret. It was the pioneer in planting on the red volcanic soils of the Upper Yarra, at a time when the climate was wetter and cooler than it is today. It was a courageous decision, amplified by the choice of cabernet sauvignon, shiraz and riesling to accompany chardonnay and pinot noir.

The riesling bore mute testimony to the challenges of the vineyard, with some spectacular botrytised wines bearing the sweetness required for trockenbeerenauslese in Germany. The problem was that the botrytis spores rained down on the adjoining block of shiraz, and the riesling had to go. And then there was Peter's decision to keep the shiraz in the faces of Dr John Middleton (of Mount Mary), who condemned shiraz as 'a weed', and of Guill de Pury (of Yeringberg), who in 1991 pulled out his shiraz because 'no one will buy it'.

With picking then very much a family affair, grandson Dylan McMahon grew up helping with the vintage every year. In 2000 he started working full-time on the estate while remotely undertaking the wine science degree at CSU. Between '02 and '03 he worked in Europe, returning home in '04 to become Seville Estate's winemaker.

Fast-forwarding to today, Seville Estate is very different after several changes in ownership, culminating in the present control of Mr Yiping Wang, a wealthy Chinese businessman with a chain of wine shops in China. He has invested heavily in the enterprise, buying the adjoining vineyard and property (formerly Ainsworth Estate), and establishing luxury accommodation in the original homestead and in three self-contained apartments. Dylan has been encouraged to replant original material (grafted onto rootstock) to preserve the 1972 clones, which Dylan regards as essential for the future of Seville Estate's distinctive style.

A consistent winner of gold medals and trophies at the Yarra Valley Wine Show and further afield, Seville Estate is a red 5-star winery, its name also printed in red. Only Australia's top 100 wineries (out of 2835) are thus identified. When I was proofreading the pages for this book, the Seville Estate entry – in particular, its tasting notes – hit me in the face. With its absolutely dazzling array of great wines made over the 2015, '16 and '17 vintages, I instantly knew that it had to be the Winery of the Year.

For the record, their wines come in four ranges: Sewn – entry point wines made from contract-grown grapes; The Barber – made for early consumption; Estate – wines made using a combination of the old 1972 vines and the younger 1996 vines; and Reserve – its wines speak for themselves, made in tiny quantities, mainly from the 1972 plantings. At the very top is the Dr McMahon label, the best of the best, with typically only one varietal release each vintage.

Previous 'Winery of the Year' recipients were Paringa Estate (2007), Balnaves of Coonawarra (2008), Brookland Valley (2009), Tyrrell's (2010), Larry Cherubino Wines (2011), Port Phillip Estate/Kooyong (2012), Kilikanoon (2013), Penfolds (2014), Hentley Farm Wines (2015), Tahbilk (2016), Mount Pleasant (2017) and Mount Mary (2018).

Winemaker of the year

Julian Langworthy

My selection of Julian Langworthy as Winemaker of the Year caused me to ponder on the three greatest winemakers of the 20th century, Maurice O'Shea of Mount Pleasant Wines, Colin Preece of Seppelt's Great Western and Max Schubert of Penfolds (Schubert's masterwork, Grange). They plied their trade in a market where fortified wines, largely sold in saloons and hotels, reigned supreme. The one thing they had in common was the balance of their wines underlying their extreme longevity.

Each had a substantial winery that provided support, although that support had its limits. Schubert was able to make the epic voyage to Spain and France in 1950 to study firsthand the making of sherry – it was from that journey that Grange, a Penfolds-banned wine during '51–'61, saw its almost accidental birth; Preece had personal issues with some of the numerous members of the Seppelt family, with relations souring to the point where he felt compelled to resign; O'Shea was rescued by a number of members of the McWilliam clan – the McWilliams first buying half the shares in Mount Pleasant, and ultimately the other half in the aftermath of the Great Depression. If you take a broad view, these hugely talented winemakers were incidental to their employers' financial needs, but left in limbo for much of their careers (Schubert was brought out of retirement when the marketing gurus belatedly realised his value). There was no expectation that any one of these winemakers would have any knowledge of, let alone responsibility for, the commercial value or the financial cost of their wines. How different to the wine world of today.

Julian Langworthy is chief winemaker for the Fogarty Wine Group (FWG), the fastest growing wine business in Western Australia. He reports to the Group General Manager, and is responsible for the stylistic direction of all of the FWG wineries and their individual brands. He mentors and manages a team of 10 winemakers and, in conjunction with the Group Chief Viticulturist, is responsible for all fruit purchases – this is in addition to more than 300ha of estate vineyards spread from Hunter Valley in New South Wales to Margaret River in Western Australia.

Julian has particular responsibilities for Deep Woods, with an extensive promotional role for its profile interstate and internationally. He plays a lead role in brand planning, providing wine business acumen and general support for the marketing team. He has broad-based human resources responsibilities, including coordination for all site compliance issues, and others too many to mention.

Are his winemaking skills and palate on par with the greats of the 20th century? It's a question without an answer. But if he is to be compared with the best of today, the answer is an emphatic yes. His wine show successes (and the team he has led) have gold medals flying around the room like confetti, with trophies (including the biggest of all, the Jimmy Watson) equally plentiful. And most of all, he is universally admired and liked by all who have had contact with him and/or the great wines he makes.

Previous 'Winemaker of the Year' recipients were Robert Diletti (2015), Peter Fraser (2016), Sarah Crowe (2017) and Paul Hotker (2018).

Wine of the year

Duke's Vineyard Magpie Hill Reserve Riesling 2017

Selling their successful clothing manufacturing business in Perth didn't leave Hilde and Ian (Duke) Ransom wondering what they would do next. Hilde is an artist of some note, so her views were of prime importance. Duke's vision was even more focused – he says, 'I have drunk wine for 60 years, good wine for 40 years and very good wine for 20 years', and goes on to explain, 'I took Hilde for some long drives in the Australian countryside, mostly wine regions.' They wended their way through South Australia, Victoria, Tasmania and Canberra, finally slowing down as they reached the Western Australia's Great Southern region. Having looked at more than 50 properties, they bought the tranquil Magpie Hill Farm.

They set about creating a large dam, but – despite the Department of Agriculture and Food having given it a glowing report – the dam builder and a local water guru agreed the property could never catch or hold water. A week later the property was back on the market. Duke went for a drive to clear his mind and saw a for sale sign being erected on a site 2km down the road. Duke drove into the beautiful property and made an offer, which was soon accepted.

Time has shown that Duke's belief the vineyard would be ideal for riesling ('Our wine of choice and the wine of the region.') was correct. Rob Diletti (of Castle Rock) makes the wines with infinite skill and sensitivity. Duke and Hilde have the Duke's Vineyard Magpie Hill property on the market at the time of going to print, and have purchased a 2-acre block on the water's edge in Albany. I wish them well for their second-time-around retirement, and warn the local fish that there are two strangers in town.

I leave you with excerpts from the 11 tasting notes covering the 2006–17 vintages. 'A celebration of the purity, elegance, drive, and length of a wine … that will outlive your patience' ('17); 'Its blossom-filled bouquet a short introduction to a wine that takes the palate in an instant and refuses to let go … its array of lemon and lime flavours remorselessly building intensity from start to finish' ('15); 'Exceptional clarity, purity and intensity, a long exciting life ahead; lime, apple and mineral characters coalesce on the palate and aftertaste' ('10).

Previous 'Wine of the Year' recipients are Bass Phillip Reserve Pinot Noir 2010 (2014), Xanadu Stevens Road Cabernet Sauvignon 2011 (2015), Serrat Shiraz Viognier 2014 (2016), Best's Thomson Family Shiraz 2014 (2017) and Henschke Hill of Grace 2012 (2018).

Best value winery

Provenance Wines

Scott Ireland's journey through wine started in 1981 when he left the nest in Melbourne and travelled to Adelaide without any clear idea of what he wanted to do, other than earn enough money to keep body and soul together. He managed to get a vintage job at Peter Lehmann in the Barossa Valley. 'I couldn't have found a better starting point in the industry: a whole new world opened,' remembers Scott.

In '83 he was offered employment by Hunter Valley winemaker Ian Scarborough, who also had a mobile bottling plant (Scarmac) servicing wineries in the Hunter Valley, Barossa Valley and Coonawarra. There are few – if any – more demanding wine businesses. You work to a series of fixed appointments stretching out for months ahead, with wineries entirely reliant on the service. Delays are unacceptable, the days long.

In '88 Scott ran a parallel Scarmac mobile wine filtration operation, starting in the Hunter Valley, then Mudgee, Clare Valley, the Yarra Valley and Tasmania. While social activities are limited, there is close contact with the small wineries and makers who use the services, giving rise to insights otherwise unavailable.

Scott's first full-time winemaking job was with Gary Crittenden at Dromana Estate on the Mornington Peninsula between '90 and '94. 'I learnt so much in those five years,' he says. He was witness to the perils (for others) of winery ownership between '95 and 2004. In the latter year he was finally able to clear the decks, and he became the owner and operator of Provenance, which was an established contract winemaker (its roots dating back to '97). Scott set up its business on Austins & Co.'s vineyard, the largest in Geelong, and it became Provenance's principal client.

In 2016 he had to make a major decision: to downsize and relocate his business to Ballarat, or find a permanent home elsewhere in Geelong. Through good fortune, and beyond his wildest dreams, Provenance now has a combined 150-tonne winery and its first cellar door (opened in '17) in part of a restored bluestone paper mill on the banks of the Barwon River.

In May '11 Scott married his partner, Jen Lilburn, in a marquee on their Provenance vineyard at Scotsburn on their joint 50th birthday; their two daughters (aged 15 and 17) were bridesmaids. In '17 he offered his loyal assistant winemaker, Sam Vogel, a share in the business to celebrate the long-term lease of the new premises. 'It's all due to Sam that the wines are as good as they are,' he modestly says. And Scott has long-term management of 15ha of vineyards in Geelong, Ballarat, Henty and Macedon, the latter three the coolest regions of the Australian mainland.

And the wines? They are brilliant.

Previous 'Best Value Winery' recipients were Hoddles Creek Estate (2015), West Cape Howe (2016), Larry Cherubino Wines (2017), and Grosset (2018).

Best new winery

Mewstone Wines

Without wishing in any way to denigrate past recipients of the Best New Winery award, this year's recipient has achieved a level of success we haven't seen before, and are unlikely to see again. The winery is owned by Tasmanian-born brothers Matthew (Matt) and Jonathan (Jonny) Hughes and their respective wives Cathie and Margie. Each couple has two children.

Matt is a banker, having worked successively with Macquarie Bank, JP Morgan and Morgan Stanley; he is in the process of retiring to become CFO of Mewstone. In 2000 younger brother Jonny (now 38) obtained an economics degree from the University of Tasmania, but decided that he would rather make wine than money. A one-year post-graduate degree in wine science from Lincoln University in New Zealand was the best option for his purposes.

Duly armed with his degrees, in '03 Jonny returned to Australia to undertake vintage work at Bleasdale before going back to New Zealand's Felton Road for its (later) '03 vintage (thwarted by frost). In '04 he worked at Stonier for the southern hemisphere vintage, then at Barolo during a magnificent northern hemisphere vintage, completing his flying winemaker career in the Hunter Valley, followed by Canada's Okanagan Valley.

On returning to Tasmania in '06, he jumped the employment fence to work in a Hobart wine bar succinctly called Grape; after one year he moved to a distributor with a who's-who list of mainland producers. Having covered all the bases, he then became assistant winemaker at Moorilla Estate for seven years.

In '11 the brothers purchased the land on which to plant the estate vineyard, which will eventually increase to 5ha from its present (April 2018) 2.65ha. Both now and in the future Mewstone will purchase grapes from growers in all parts of Tasmania to build a mosaic of wines under the Hughes & Hughes brand. There are no preconceptions for any of the wines in this portfolio although, as the years pass, some regional blends may establish an ongoing part of the portfolio.

At the present time, the Hughes & Hughes wines may make use of innovations in the winery drawing upon Jonny's experiences overseas. He has also learnt much from Moorilla's winemaker, Conor van der Reest, who has made his reputation handling small amounts of many wines involving varietal and vinification practices that have successfully challenged orthodoxy.

There were 12 wines submitted for this edition of the *Wine Companion*, four from the '16 vintage and eight from the '17 vintage. They are a brilliant group, led by the '17s, all showing a sure, delicate, precisely weighted touch. There is only one way forward for Mewstone: up.

Previous 'Best New Winery' recipients are Rob Dolan Wines (2014), Flowstone (2015), Bicknell fc (2016), Bondar Wines (2017) and Dappled (2018).

FATTO A MANO
by Riedel

OLD WORLD PINOT NOIR

CO OUR YOUR TABLE
RIEDEL.COM

RIEDEL
THE WINE GLASS COMPANY

GRAPE 🍇 VARIETAL SPECIFIC®

Ten of the best new wineries

Each one of these wineries making its debut in the *Wine Companion* has earned a 5-star rating. They are thus the leaders of the 67 new wineries in this edition, although a number of other first-up wineries also achieved five stars. The ultimate selection criteria included the number of wines earning 95 points or above, and also value for money. Without disparaging selections in prior years, this was a hot field, with some fascinating careers ahead for many.

BEST NEW WINERY
Mewstone Wines Southern Tasmania / PAGE 426
The story of Mewstone Wines appears on page 18; further details appear in its winery entry on page 426.

Brave Souls Wine Barossa Valley / PAGE 123
It's abundantly clear that if Julia Weirich decides to do anything, it will happen no matter how improbable it may seem. She possesses a formidable intelligence, but it's her person-to-person lightness of touch, not a Germanic force of intellectual arms, that wins the day. The name of the winery is derived from the 1859 shipwreck of the SS Admella, with their label design illustrating the bravery of three men who risked their lives to save those on board.

Dune Wine McLaren Vale / PAGE 225
I am smitten by their wines. I writhe in agony about not having given them higher points and not buying more – the latter purely due to a cellar full of wine and only a brief time left to drink more than a token quantity of it. This isn't a Coriole brand per se, but it certainly has the commitment of the Lloyd family, as well as its sense of humour.

Levrier by Jo Irvine Various South Australia / PAGE 394
What do Jo Irvine and I have in common? The only person in the world able to answer that question is myself, and not – as you might guess – Jo. Because I'm sure that she doesn't know 50 years ago I was a part-owner of two greyhounds, neither of which were as fast as those they raced against. We share another thing, too; I was a practising lawyer before writing about or making wine, and Jo was a theatre nurse.

Nick Spencer Wines Gundagai / PAGE 469
Gundagai has long been in need of a Pied Piper calling experienced winemakers to cross its borders and put down their roots – and Nick Spencer has finally taken the plunge after an exotic flying winemaking career (including Kakheti in Georgia). Spencer also has a side bet on the much cooler nearby Tumbarumba region.

Rikard Wines Orange / **PAGE 541**

William Rikard-Bell made national headlines in 2008 for all the wrong reasons when an explosion at Drayton's Family Wines in the Hunter Valley killed two and left William with life-threatening burns to 70% of his body. His first job had been in Orange and, after a prolonged recovery, it was to there that he returned in '11 with wife Kimberley and two young daughters.

Sherrah Wines McLaren Vale / **PAGE 594**

There's a strong Irish overtone to Alex Sherrah's journey to wine. Having gained a Bachelor of Science in organic chemistry and pharmacology, he set off to see the world. Returning broke, he managed to secure various jobs at Tatachilla – at one stage he worked each Friday until knock-off time for the weekly barbecue, earning him the nickname 'Boy Friday'.

SubRosa Grampians/Pyrenees / **PAGE 632**

When Adam Louder and partner Nancy Panter were in their many discussions trying to come up with a name for their winery-to-be, a dictionary fell open at the page reading, 'happening or done in secret – origin Latin "under the rose" (the rose an emblem of secrecy)'. Cryptic crossword fare, and more wines like those of their first release will steal the limelight.

Turon Wines Adelaide Hills / **PAGE 689**

Winemaker Turon White has upturned the usual pattern of new entrants finding a place to make their wines in a packing shed or a come-and-go shared space in an existing winery. He has designed and built a winery on the vineyard site for his wines, and for those of other small makers.

Walsh & Sons Margaret River / **PAGE 707**

I cannot resist comparing Walsh & Sons with Burgundy where families intermingle – and through marriage, death or other reasons, split or agglomerate parcels of vineyards during the lifetime of all those directly or indirectly involved. Also in true Burgundy fashion, the hows and wherefores may be difficult to discern.

Ten of the best value wineries

The 10 wineries featured this year basically selected themselves from the 2836 wineries, shutting out any discussion of a different result simply because these showed a clean pair of heels in a totally convincing fashion. Points and price are automatically assessed in the database by a miniature algorithm. The geographical pattern of the wines this year is very different to that of last year. Six of the 10 wineries come from the Barossa Valley, Adelaide Hills, the Adelaide zone and McLaren Vale. The other four are spread across Geelong, Canberra District, Margaret River and Great Southern.

BEST VALUE WINERY
Provenance Wines Geelong / **PAGE 528**
The story of Provenance Wines appears on page 17; further details appear in its winery entry on page 528.

Castelli Estate Great Southern / **PAGE 149**
Castelli Estate led the way alphabetically with 19 wines (14 given the value rosette), led by the 2017 Great Southern Riesling (97 points), followed by the 2016 Frankland River Cabernet Sauvignon (96 points). Then followed three on 95, five on 94, and eight rated 90–93 points.

Chain of Ponds Adelaide Hills / **PAGE 154**
Chain of Ponds opened up with a clash of cymbals with their 2013 The Cachet and 98 points. Then followed five 95-point wines, the three with the value rosette being the 2017 Black Thursday Sauvignon Blanc, 2017 Corkscrew Road Chardonnay and 2016 Graves Gate Syrah.

Mandoon Estate Margaret River / **PAGE 412**
Mandoon Estate set the scene with three wines on 97 points (and the value rosette): 2015 Reserve Margaret River Chardonnay, 2014 Reserve Frankland River Shiraz and 2014 Reserve Research Station Margaret River Cabernet Sauvignon. Then followed the sole wine, 2017 Swan Valley Verdelho, on 96 (something you rarely see), three three wines on 95 and one on 94. Mandoon's primary base of its best wines is Margaret River.

Nick O'Leary Wines Canberra District / **PAGE 468**
The 2017 Tumbarumba Riesling, 2017 White Rocks Riesling and 2016 Bolaro Shiraz all received 96 points, followed by two wines each on 95 and 94 points respectively. All seven wines received the value rosette. The brightness of the fruit flavours of his wines are the key.

Patritti Wines Adelaide zone / **PAGE 494**

Patritti has 10ha of grenache at Aldinga North, and 10ha of shiraz in Blewitt Springs. Thus two single vineyard wines on 96 points, the 2016 JPB Shiraz and 2016 Lot Three Shiraz, followed by three wines each on 95 points. In all, 11 of the 12 wines in this year's submission received the value rosette. Patritti isn't well known in the eastern states, and deserves a wider audience there.

Rudderless McLaren Vale / **PAGE 560**

What Rudderless has in quality makes up for the very small production. They have one wine on 97 points, one on 96, and six on 95, all with the value rosette. Leading the way is the 2015 Sellicks Hill Grenach, hotly followed by the 2015 Sellicks Hill Grenache Mataro Graciano. The wines are chiefly sold through Doug Govan's iconic Victory Hotel.

Scott Adelaide Hills / **PAGE 582**

Sam Scott had a long career in retailing and winemaking in Australia and California before breaking out on his own in 2009. Eight out of 10 wines from Scott's *Wine Companion* 2019 submission have received the value rosette. The 2016 The Denizen Chardonnay and, the outsider, 2017 La Prova Fiano (both with value rosettes) lead the way on 95 points, followed by three wines on 94 points.

Teusner Barossa Valley / **PAGE 657**

Teusner is no stranger to the Best Value Winery field, this year with two wines on 96 points, the 2017 Joshua and 2015 Avatar, both grenache mataro shiraz blends. Three wines on 95 points, one wine on 94 points and four wines on 93 points also received the value rosette.

Turkey Flat Barossa Valley / **PAGE 687**

Turkey Flat only knows how to make very good wines at very good prices, led by its outstanding 2016 Shiraz on 98 points, and pursued by the Jimmy Watson Memorial Trophy–breaking mould of their 2016 Grenache on 96 points. They have three wines on 95 points, all from old vines, and two wines on 94 points. If ever wines are made in the vineyard, Turkey Flat leads the way with the infinite care of its old vines.

Ten dark horses

To qualify for this award, each winery has to have received a 5-star rating for the first time, and have a history of at least four lesser ratings. Principia is Dark Horse of the Year, and accordingly heads the list; the remaining wineries are in alphabetical order.

DARK HORSE OF THE YEAR
Principia Mornington Peninsula / PAGE 526

Darrin Gaffy has been knocking on the door of 5 stars since records have been kept for this purpose (1996 the first year). In that time, Principia has received 4 stars or, on eight occasions, 4.5. This year he triumphed with the four wines submitted all receiving 95 or 96 points. Making wines with a self-imposed strict discipline eschewing many pieces of equipment and/or additions isn't easy, and achieving this outcome must be doubly satisfying – particularly when, as here, three were pinot noirs from a vintage that required extra skill from the winemaker.

Brini Estate Wines McLaren Vale / PAGE 127

Sebastiano Brini arrived in McLaren Vale from Italy with no English, £5 in his pocket, a suitcase and a passion for growing grapes. By 1953 he had saved enough money to buy a property in Blewitt Springs; he used two-thirds to run dairy cows, while the other third had established grape vines (shiraz, grenache and mataro). It's hard to imagine that Sebastiano purchased the property knowing the quality of the soil, which is unlike anything in Italy. It's the deep sand and sandy loam soils of Blewitt Springs that make it so special. Sebastiano's sons, John and Marcello, inherited the property, expanding the plantings in the '60s and again in the '90s.

Byrne Vineyards South Australia / PAGE 137

The extensive Byrne family has been through some tough times and some good times – none better than those of today. The merging of production from the Riverland with that from the Clare Valley has seen production soar from 35 000 dozen to 150 000 dozen bottles, much of it headed to export markets. The other adroit move has been the making of an in-vogue Pinot Noir Shiraz (treading where others fear to tread) in the Clare Valley, and a luscious, oaky but full-flavoured Barossa Shiraz: in both instances just what the doctor ordered.

Laurel Bank Southern Tasmania / PAGE 387

Laurel Bank was established by Kerry Carland in 1986, but deliberately kept a low profile by withholding release of most of its early wines. When the time came, in '95, Kerry entered the Royal Hobart Wine Show and won the Most Successful Tasmanian Exhibitor trophy. Since then Laurel Bank has produced many very attractive wines, but not enough in any one year before this to regain their 2010 5-star rating.

Lonely Vineyard Eden Valley / PAGE 399

Whoever is responsible for the website in the family of Michael Schreurs and Karina Ouwens (and I suspect it's the latter) has a superb sense of humour, and a love of cats.

Michael is the winemaker, and Karina is a commercial lawyer working in Adelaide. The five wines in the current release are particularly impressive. Not so lonely in the future, I suspect.

Schild Estate Wines Barossa Valley / PAGE 577

Founded by Ed Schild in 1952, when he planted a small vineyard at Rowland Flat. It's no exaggeration to say he has flown under the radar like few others, given the estate's present vineyard holding of 163ha, and an infinitely valuable and rare block of 170-year-old shiraz on the Moorooroo Vineyard. In '15 all of the estate wines flew high, but none more so than the Moorooroo Shiraz.

Tim McNeil Wines Clare Valley / PAGE 674

When Tim and Cass McNeil established Tim McNeil Wines, Tim had long since given up his teaching career, graduating with a degree in oenology from Adelaide University in 1999. He then spent 11 years honing his craft at important wineries in the Barossa and Clare valleys before Tim McNeil Wines became his full-time job in August 2010. The McNeils's 16ha property at Watervale includes mature dry-grown riesling, and the cellar door overlooks the riesling, with panoramic views of Watervale and beyond. This vineyard provided the grapes from the great '17 vintage, which Tim has made into two quite wonderful wines that propelled the winery to 5 stars.

The Willows Vineyard Barossa Valley / PAGE 664

The story of the Scholz family dates back to 1845, when Johann Gottfried Scholz fled from religious persecution in Silesia. He came with skills in healing broken bones, and his original cottage became the site of the Barossa's first private hospital. His great-great-grandson, Bert, turned his attention to the small family vineyard, planted in 1936. Further plantings followed, only to be greeted by the shiraz glut of the late '70s. Bert's son Peter undertook his first winemaking job with Peter Lehmann at Saltram in '79, and 10 years later opened a cellar door adjacent to the hospital. The wines' names reflect the family history, including the icon wine, Bonesetter Barossa Shiraz.

Three Dark Horses McLaren Vale / PAGE 670

It would be unthinkable that Three Dark Horses could miss selection even though it is qualified through the five-year rule. Moreover, I'm very confident that Matt Broomhead's venture is destined for greater things in coming years, as its newly acquired vineyard and onsite winery (in time for the 2019 vintage) come on-stream.

Windance Wines Margaret River / PAGE 722

In 1998 Drew and Rosemary Brent-White came from a farming family background to establish this winery 5km south of the beautiful Yallingup beach. They practised sustainable land management and organic farming practices where possible, and did so very successfully. As at 2018 the winery had won 16 trophies and 52 gold medals in regional and Western Australian wine shows. Daughter Billie and her husband, Tyke Wheatley, now own the business: Billie, a qualified accountant, was raised at Windance, and manages the business and the cellar door, and Tyke (with winemaking experience at Picardy, Happs and Burgundy) has taken over the winemaking and manages the vineyard.

Best of the best by variety

As usual, the number of wines in each group is limited. The varietal categories are the same as in previous years, as is the link of each wine with its region, so only the best are listed in full. That said, the cut-off point does reflect the strength of the particular category. Where the list would be unacceptably long, the wines printed in black are grouped by region and their names shortened while still enabling the exact wine to be identified in the tasting notes for the winery in question. In looking at the points, remember these are the best of the 9289 wines tasted for this edition.

Riesling

This year saw the unprecedented award of Wine of the Year to Duke's 2017 Magpie Hill Reserve Riesling from Great Southern's Porongurup subregion.

RATING	WINE	REGION
99	2017 Duke's Vineyard Magpie Hill Reserve	Porongurup
98	2017 Grosset Polish Hill	Clare Valley
98	2012 Leasingham Classic Clare	Clare Valley
98	2017 Seppelt Drumborg Vineyard	Henty
98	2017 Ottelia	Mount Gambier
97	**Adelaide Hills** 2017 Ochota Barrels Kids of the Black Hole **Clare Valley** 2017 Jim Barry The Florita Clare Valley, 2017 Naked Run The First Clare Valley, 2017 Pikes The Merle Clare Valley, 2017 Rieslingfreak No. 2 Clare Valley, 2017 Wines by KT Churinga Vineyard Clare Valley, 2017 Wines by KT Peglidis Vineyard **Grampians** 2017 Fallen Giants Fallen Giants Vineyard Block 1 **Great Southern** 2017 Castelli Estate Great Southern, 2014 Forest Hill Vineyard Block 1 Great Southern, 2017 Forest Hill Vineyard Block 1 Great Southern, 2017 Kerrigan + Berry **Porongurup** 2010 Abbey Creek Vineyard Museum Release Porongurup, 2017 Castle Rock Estate Porongurup, 2017 Duke's Vineyard Single Vineyard **Tasmania** 2016 Kate Hill	

Chardonnay

The field of 1025 chardonnays (with 46 at 97 points or above) was represented by both sides of the continent. There's no disputing it: Margaret River has walked away the winner.

RATING	WINE	REGION
98	2015 Singlefile The Vivienne	Denmark
98	2015 Devil's Lair 9th Chamber	Margaret River
98	2016 Evoi Reserve	Margaret River
98	2016 Watershed Premium Awakening Single Block A1	Margaret River
98	2017 Yabby Lake Vineyard Single Block Release Block 6	Mornington Peninsula
98	2017 Seville Estate Reserve	Yarra Valley
97	**Adelaide Hills** 2016 Penfolds Reserve Bin A, 2016 Petaluma Tiers Piccadilly Valley, 2016 Shaw + Smith Lenswood Vineyard, **Blend** 2016 Hardys Eileen Hardy, 2015 Penfolds Bin 144 Yattarna **Eden Valley** 2016 Mountadam High Eden Estate **Geelong** 2017 Clyde Park Vineyard Single Block B3 Bannockburn, 2015 GC by Farr, 2015 Provenance Regional Selection, 2016 Scotchmans Hill Bellarine Peninsula, **Henty** 2015 Provenance Regional Selection **Margaret River** 2016 Cape Mentelle, 2016 Clairault, 2016 Deep Woods Estate Reserve, 2016 Domaine Naturaliste Artus, 2017 Driftwood Estate Single Site, 2015 Evans &	

Tate Redbrook Reserve, 2014 Evans & Tate Redbrook Reserve, 2016 Flametree S.R.S. Wallcliffe, 2015 Flowstone, 2015 Flowstone Queen of the Earth, 2014 Heydon Estate The Willow Single Vineyard, 2017 House of Cards The Royals Single Vineyard, 2015 Mandoon Estate Reserve 2013 Robert Oatley Vineyards The Pennant, 2016 Vasse Felix Heytesbury, 2015 Windows Estate Petit Lot, 2016 Xanadu Reserve, 2016 Xanadu Stevens Road **Mornington Peninsula** 2015 Garagiste Tuerong, 2016 Kooyong Faultline Single Vineyard, 2016 Ten Minutes by Tractor Wallis **Orange** 2016 Rowlee Single Vineyard **Tasmania** 2015 Dawson & James **Yarra Valley** 2016 Giant Steps Lusatia Park Vineyard, 2016 Hoddles Creek Estate Syberia, 2016 Oakridge Local Vineyard Series Willowlake Vineyard, 2017 Rochford Premier, 2017 Serrat, 2017 Seville Estate

Semillon

Nothing much to say except that the Hunter Valley had had another excellent year in 2017 for semillon.

RATING	WINE	REGION
97	2010 Mount View Estate Museum Release Flagship	Hunter Valley
97	2017 Silkman Reserve	Hunter Valley
97	2013 Tyrrell's Museum Release Vat 1 Hunter	Hunter Valley
96	**Hunter Valley** 2017 Audrey Wilkinson The Ridge, 2009 Audrey Wilkinson The Ridge Reserve, 2014 Chateau Francois Pokolbin, 2012 Drayton's Family Susanne, 2011 Keith Tulloch Museum Release, 2014 Leogate Estate Creek Bed Reserve, 2013 McLeish Estate Cellar Reserve, 2013 Meerea Park Alexander Munro Individual Vineyard, 2007 Mistletoe Museum Release Reserve, 2017 Mount Pleasant 1946 Vines Lovedale Vineyard, 2010 Mount Pleasant Elizabeth, 2013 Mount Pleasant Lovedale, 2006 Mount View Estate Museum Release Reserve, 2009 Pokolbin Estate Phil Swannell, 2014 Silkman Reserve, 2014 Silkman Single Vineyard Blackberry, 2012 Simon Whitlam & Co, 2014 Tempus Two Uno, 2017 Thomas Braemore Individual Vineyard, 2012 Thomas Cellar Reserve Braemore Individual Vineyard, 2017 Thomas The O.C. Individual Vineyard, 2017 Tulloch Limited Release Julia, 2013 Two Rivers Museum Release Stone's Throw, 2017 Tyrrell's Johnno's, 2012 Tyrrell's Museum Release Vat 1, 2013 Tyrrell's Single Vineyard Belford, 2017 Whispering Brook Single Vineyard, **Margaret River** 2016 Cape Mentelle	

Sauvignon Blanc

In the blink of an eye, the Marlborough version of sauvignon blanc has become everyone's whipping boy. Serious sauvignon blancs have a range of aromas and flavours, but are equally dependent upon texture and structure – this possibly simply coming from the region (à la Adelaide Hills), a subtle injection of oak, or some clever lees work and warm fermentation.

RATING	WINE	REGION
97	2017 Michael Hall Piccadilly	Adelaide Hills
97	2017 Larry Cherubino Cherubino	Pemberton
96	2015 Geoff Weaver Ferus Lenswood	Adelaide Hills
96	2017 Shaw + Smith	Adelaide Hills
96	2016 Scotchmans Hill Cornelius Single Vineyard Sauvignon	Geelong
96	2017 Deep Woods Estate	Margaret River
96	2015 Flowstone	Margaret River
96	2016 Flowstone	Margaret River
95	**Adelaide Hills** 2017 Catlin Cheese & Kisses Single Vineyard Fume Blanc, 2017 Chain of Ponds Black Thursday, 2017 Geoff Weaver Single Vineyard, 2017 Patritti, 2017 Sidewood Estate, 2017 Wirra Wirra Hiding Champion Single Vineyard **Denmark** 2017 Apricus Hill Single Vineyard **Geelong** 2017 Oakdene	

Bellarine Peninsula, 2017 Oakdene Jessica Single Vineyard Bellarine Peninsula Sauvignon **King Valley** 2017 Simão & Co **Macedon Ranges** 2017 Hanging Rock Jim Jim **Margaret River** 2016 Domaine Naturaliste Sauvage Wallcliffe, 2017 Evans & Tate Breathing Space, 2017 Heydon Estate Chin Music Single Vineyard, 2017 House of Cards Three Card Monte, 2017 McHenry Hohnen Vintners Burnside Vineyard, 2017 Passel Estate, 2017 Preveli Wild Thing, 2017 Stella Bella, 2017 Windows Estate Estate Grown **Orange** 2017 Colmar Estate, 2017 Gilbert Family gilbert by Simon Gilbert **Pemberton** 2017 Castelli Estate The Sum, 2017 Larry Cherubino The Yard Channybearup **Tasmania** 2016 Moorilla Estate Muse St Matthias Vineyard Sauvignon **Wrattonbully** 2017 Terre à Terre Down to Earth **Yarra Valley** 2017 Gembrook Hill, 2017 Greenstone Vineyards Estate Series, 2017 Out of Step Willowlake Vineyard

Semillon Sauvignon Blends

Margaret River is absolutely dominant, Great Southern sweeping up the rest of this underpriced category.

RATING	WINE	REGION
97	2015 Stella Bella Suckfizzle Sauvignon Blanc Semillon	Margaret River
96	2017 Larry Cherubino Cherubino Beautiful South	WA blend
96	2015 Cullen Vineyard Sauvignon Blanc Semillon	Margaret River
96	2015 Domaine Naturaliste Sauvage SSB	Margaret River
96	2017 Evoi River Sauvignon Blanc Semillon	Margaret River
96	2017 Fraser Gallop Estate Parterre SSB	Margaret River
96	2016 Juniper Estate Aquitaine Blanc	Margaret River
96	2017 Xanadu DJL Sauvignon Blanc Semillon	Margaret River
95	**Great Southern** 2017 Trevelen Farm Sauvignon Blanc Semillon **Margaret River** 2016 Streicker Bridgeland Block Sauvignon Semillon, 2016 Cullen Mangan Vineyard Sauvignon Blanc Semillon, 2017 Driftwood Estate Artifacts Sauvignon Blanc Semillon, 2017 Fire Gully Sauvignon Blanc Semillon, 2016 Flying Fish Cove Sauvignon Blanc Semillon, 2017 Fraser Gallop Estate Semillon Sauvignon Blanc, 2017 Hamelin Bay Five Ashes Vineyard Semillon Sauvignon Blanc, 2016 Happs Three Hills Eva Marie, 2017 Higher Plane Semillon Sauvignon Blanc, 2013 Leeuwin Estate Art Series Sauvignon Blanc Semillon, 2015 Lenton Brae Wilyabrup Semillon Sauvignon Blanc, 2017 Snake + Herring Perfect Day Sauvignon Blanc Semillon, 2017 Stella Bella Semillon Sauvignon Blanc, 2017 Windows Estate Estate Grown Semillon Sauvignon Blanc.	

Other White Wines and Blends

The usual spread of regions and varieties, with quality being the determining factor, but also with an offering of some high quality alternative varieties.

RATING	WINE	REGION
97	2015 Castagna Growers Selection Roussanne	Beechworth
97	2015 Arlewood Estate La Bratta Bianco	Margaret River
97	2016 Mount Mary Triolet	Yarra Valley
96	**Adelaide Hills** 2017 Deviation Road Gruner Veltliner Adelaide Hills, 2015 Hahndorf Hill Winery GRU 2 Gruner Veltliner Adelaide Hills, 2017 Hahndorf Hill Winery GRU Gruner Veltliner **Beechworth** 2016 Castagna Ingenue Viognier **Blend** 2015 Hardys HRB Pinot Gris **Margaret River** 2016 Flowstone Gewurztraminer **Mornington Peninsula** 2013 Crittenden Estate Cri de Coeur Savagnin **New England** 2017 Symphony Hill Gewurztraminer **Swan Valley** 2017 Mandoon Estate Verdelho	

Sparkling

Tasmania is not a surprise here. We will see an ever-growing percentage of sparkling wines from Tasmania, quality going alongside regional origin.

White and Rose

RATING	WINE	REGION
97	2012 Barringwood Recently Disgorged Blanc de Blanc	Tasmania
97	2008 House of Arras Blanc de Blancs	Tasmania
97	2003 House of Arras EJ Carr Late Disgorged	Tasmania
97	2007 House of Arras Grand Vintage	Tasmania
97	2001 House of Arras Museum Release Blanc de Blancs	Tasmania
97	2006 House of Arras Rose	Tasmania
97	2011 Jansz Single Vineyard Vintage Chardonnay	Tasmania
96	**Adelaide Hills** 2012 Terre à Terre Daosa Blanc de Blancs **Blend** 2014 Chandon Cygnet Pinot Meunier Rose Blend, 2013 Chandon Vintage Blanc de Blancs, 2017 Sassafras Chardonnay Savagnin Ancestral **Tasmania** 2014 Barringwood Classic Cuvee	

Sparkling red

The big three – two sparkling shirazs and a blend (the Primo Estate Joseph). Nothing much changes here.

RATING	WINE	REGION
97	2007 Seppelt Show Sparkling Limited Release Shiraz	Grampians
96	NV Rockford Black Shiraz	Barossa Valley
96	NV Primo Estate Joseph Sparkling Red	McLaren Vale

Sweet

Riesling now has the game by its whiskers, holding sway over almost all the others. It gets to this position because it achieves intensity of flavour without loss of varietal character. De Bortoli Noble One (semillon) is, of course, a distinguished exception.

RATING	WINE	REGION
97	2017 Grosset Alea Riesling	Clare Valley
97	2015 Derwent Estate Late Harvest Riesling	Southern Tasmania
96	2017 Frankland Estate Smith Cullam Riesling	Frankland River
96	2017 Lethbridge Dr Nadeson Riesling	Geelong
96	2017 Josef Chromy Botrytis Riesling	Northern Tasmania
96	2015 De Bortoli Noble One Botrytis Semillon	Riverina

Rose

Many consumers won't treat rose as seriously as it deserves. It really is a happy hunting ground these days, as winemakers across the country look at each other's efforts and become thoroughly intrigued by what is possible.

RATING	WINE	REGION
96	2017 Guthrie Sleepless Nights Pinot Rose	Adelaide Hills
96	2017 Spinifex Luxe	Barossa Valley
96	2017 Preveli Wild Thing Pinot Rose	Margaret River
96	2016 Delamere Vineyards Hurlo's Rose	Northern Tasmania

Pinot Noir

Put these at twice the price alongside burgundies, and the pinot noirs won't yield any ground. But the journey still has a long way to go, with new clones slotting in alongside MV6, an old clone unique to Australia. The average age of vines is also rising – the oldest are now more than 40 years old.

RATING	WINE	REGION
99	2015 Tout Pres by Farr	Geelong
99	2017 Seville Estate Old Vine Reserve	Yarra Valley
98	2016 Chatto Isle Black Label Huon Valley	Tasmania
98	2017 Giant Steps Applejack Vineyard	Yarra Valley
98	2017 Rochford Premier	Yarra Valley
98	2017 Serrat	Yarra Valley
97	**Adelaide Hills** 2016 Shaw + Smith Lenswood Vineyard **Central Victoria zone** 2015 Mount Terrible Jamieson **Geelong** 2017 Clyde Park Vineyard Single Block D, 2016 Sangreal by Farr **Henty** 2015 Provenance Regional Selection **Macedon Ranges** 2016 Bindi Wine Growers Original Vineyard, 2016 Lane's End Vineyard **Mornington Peninsula** 2015 Foxeys Hangout Kentucky Rd 777, 2016 Foxeys Hangout Scotsworth Farm, 2015 Paringa Estate The Paringa Single Vineyard , 2016 Portsea Estate Estate , 2016 Ten Minutes by Tractor Wallis, 2017 Yabby Lake Vineyard Single Block Release Block 6 **Tasmania** 2016 Bay of Fires, 2014 Bream Creek Reserve, 2016 Chatto White Label Huon Valley, 2014 Dawson & James, 2016 Dawson & James, 2017 Dr Edge, 2016 Home Hill Kelly's Reserve, 2017 Meadowbank, 2016 Pooley Butcher's Hill Single Vineyard, 2015 Pooley Clarence House Vineyard Single Vineyard, 2016 Pooley Cooinda Vale Single Vineyard, 2015 Tolpuddle Vineyard **Yarra Valley** 2017 Coldstream Hills Deer Farm Vineyard, 2016 De Bortoli The Estate Vineyard Dixons Creek, 2017 Giant Steps, 2016 Mount Mary, 2015 Punch Lance's Vineyard, 2017 Seville Estate, 2016 Yarra Yering, 2015 Yering Station Scarlett	

Shiraz

A total of 78 wines made the cut-off at 97 points. Shiraz represented 26% of the total 2017 crush, far ahead of cabernet sauvignon and merlot.

RATING	WINE	REGION
99	2014 Rockford Basket Press	Barossa
99	2015 Schild Estate Moorooroo	Barossa Valley
99	2013 Penfolds Bin 95 Grange	SA Blend
99	2015 Seville Estate Dr McMahon Yarra Valley	Yarra Valley
98	2012 Grant Burge Meshach	Barossa Valley
98	2012 Hentley Farm Museum Release Clos Otto	Barossa Valley
98	2013 Hentley Farm Museum Release The Creation	Barossa Valley
98	2016 Turkey Flat	Barossa Valley
98	2015 Giaconda Estate Vineyard	Beechworth
98	2016 Clonakilla Murrumbateman Syrah	Canberra District
98	2015 Wendouree	Clare Valley
98	2012 Henschke Hill of Roses	Eden Valley
98	2016 Fallen Giants Block 3	Grampians
98	2016 Fallen Giants Vineyard	Grampians
98	2007 Pepper Tree Museum Release Single Vineyard Reserve Coquun	Hunter Valley
98	2017 Giant Steps Known Pleasures	McLaren Vale

98	2015 Cape Mentelle Single Vineyard	Margaret River
98	2016 Seville Estate Old Vine Reserve	Yarra Valley
98	2016 Yarra Yering Carrodus	Yarra Valley

97 **Adelaide Hills** 2016 Shaw + Smith, 2015 Wicks Estate Eminence **Adelaide zone** 2015 Penfolds Magill Estate **Barossa Valley** 2016 Head The Brunette Moppa, 2015 Hewitson Monopole Mother Vine, 2016 John Duval Entity, 2013 Landhaus Estate Rare, 2015 Langmeil Winery The Freedom 1843, 2015 Penfolds Bin 798 RWT, 2016 Soul Growers Gobell Single Vineyard, 2016 Soul Growers Hoffman 100 Year Old Block Single Vineyard, 2016 Thistledown Bachelor's Block Ebenezer, 2015 Torbreck RunRig, 2015 Torbreck The Factor, 2012 Torbreck The Laird, 2016 Torbreck The Struie, 2015 Two Hands Holy Grail Single Vineyard Seppeltsfield **Barossa zone** 2016 Henschke Tappa Pass Vineyard Selection, 2015 John Duval Eligo The Barossa, 2014 Kellermeister Wild Witch, 2017 Spinifex Syrah **Beechworth** 2015 Castagna Genesis Syrah **Eden Valley** 2012 Gibson Australian Old Vine Collection, 2015 Heirloom Vineyards A'Lambra, 2013 Henschke Hill Of Grace, 2013 Henschke Mount Edelstone, 2016 Stage Door Wine Co, 2015 Woods Crampton Phillip Patrick Old Vines Single Vineyard **Frankland River** 2015 Kerrigan + Berry, 2014 Mandoon Estate Reserve **Geelong** 2016 Austins & Co. Custom Collection Spencer, 2016 By Farr **Grampians** 2016 Circe Utopies, 2016 Lindenderry at Red Hill Reserve **Hunter Valley** 2013 Leogate Estate The Basin Reserve, 2009 Meerea Park Aged Release Alexander Munro Individual Vineyard, 2016 Tyrrell's Vat 9 **McLaren Vale** 2016 Bekkers Syrah, 2015 Gemtree Ernest Allan, 2015 Gemtree Obsidian, 2016 Hardys Tintara Sub Regional Upper Tintara, 2015 Mitolo Savitar, 2015 Oliver's Taranga Vineyards HJ, 2014 Oliver's Taranga Vineyards M53, 2016 Richard Hamilton Centurion, 2017 Rouleur, 2014 Shottesbrooke Eliza Reserve, 2016 2 Mates The Perfect Ten, 2015 Ulithorne Frux Frugis, 2016 Wirra Wirra Chook Block, 2016 Yangarra Estate Vineyard, 2015 Yangarra Estate Vineyard Ironheart **Mornington Peninsula** 2015 Jones Road, 2016 Paringa Estate Peninsula **Mudgee** 2014 Lowe Block 5 **Western Victoria** 2016 Norton Estate Wendy's Block **Yarra Valley** 2016 Pimpernel Vineyards Grouch, 2015 Punt Road Napoleone Vineyard Block 8, 2016 Tarrahill.

Shiraz and/or Grenache

This category brings grenache and its siblings into the frame, either as a variety or as a two or three-way blend. I am hugely excited by the changing approach to grenache, particularly by appropriate vineyard management and a clear vision of the winemaking style. The result of this approach has been, and will continue to be, more elegant, perfumed versions of the varieties. McLaren Vale is presently the chief custodian of the best shiraz blends, but it shouldn't rest on its laurels and assume that others can't play the same game – because they can.

RATING	WINE	REGION
98	2015 Kellermeister Rocamora Ancestor Vine Stonegarden Vineyard Grenache	Eden Valley
98	2015 Yangarra Estate Vineyard High Sands Grenache	McLaren Vale
97	2013 Hentley Farm Museum Release H-Block Shiraz Cabernet	Barossa Valley
97	2015 Wendouree Shiraz Mataro	Clare Valley
97	2017 Silkman Reserve Shiraz Pinot	Hunter Valley
97	2016 Angove Warboys Vineyard Shiraz Grenache	McLaren Vale
97	2016 Bekkers Syrah Grenache	McLaren Vale
97	2014 Hewitson Old Garden Vineyard Mourvedre	Barossa Valley
97	2016 Soul Growers 106 Vines Mourvedre	Barossa Valley
97	2016 John Duval Annexus Grenache	Barossa zone

97	2016 John Duval Annexus Valley Mataro	Barossa zone
97	2016 Clos Clare The Hayes Boy Grenache	Clare Valley
97	2016 Head Ancestor Vine Springton Grenache	Eden Valley
97	2016 Bekkers Grenache	McLaren Vale
97	2016 Chapel Hill Bush Vine Grenache	McLaren Vale
97	2014 Clarendon Hills Romas Grenache	McLaren Vale
97	2016 Hither & Yon Grenache	McLaren Vale
97	2016 Kay Brothers Amery Vineyards Griffon's Key Reserve Grenache	McLaren Vale
97	2016 Reynella Basket Pressed Grenache	McLaren Vale
97	2015 Rudderless Sellicks Hill Grenache	McLaren Vale
97	2016 Evoi Malbec	Margaret River
97	2017 Yarra Yering Light Dry Red Pinot Shiraz	Yarra Valley

Shiraz Viognier

Shiraz viognier is now an accepted wine in its own right. The malleability of shiraz isn't diminished by the inclusion of 5% (give or take) of co-fermented viognier.

RATING	WINE	REGION
98	2016 Clonakilla	Canberra District
98	2016 Boireann	Granite Belt
98	2017 Serrat	Yarra Valley
97	2014 Torbreck Descendant	Barossa Valley
97	2015 Torbreck Descendant	Barossa Valley
97	2016 Yarra Yering Dry Red No. 2	Yarra Valley
97	2015 Yering Station Reserve	Yarra Valley

Cabernet Sauvignon

As if to prove a point, cabernet sauvignon had two wines at 99 points and three at 98 points, a fair return on the number of cabernets crushed in the regions most suited for them.

RATING	WINE	REGION
99	2015 Cullen Vanya	Margaret River
99	2016 Yarra Yering Carrodus	Yarra Valley
98	2015 Penley Estate Helios	Coonawarra
98	2013 Juniper Estate The Tribute	Margaret River
98	2015 De Bortoli Melba Vineyard	Yarra Valley
97	2014 Katnook Coonawarra Odyssey	Coonawarra
97	2016 Penley Estate Helios	Coonawarra
97	2016 Wynns Coonawarra Estate The Gables	Coonawarra
97	2012 Robert Oatley The Pennant	Frankland River
97	2013 Robert Oatley The Pennant	Frankland River
97	2015 Singlefile The Philip Adrian	Frankland River
97	2015 Brokenwood Wildwood Road Vineyard	Margaret River
97	2012 Robert Oatley The Pennant	Margaret River
97	2014 Mandoon Estate Reserve Research Station	Swan District
97	2012 De Bortoli Melba Vineyard	Yarra Valley

Cabernet and Family

The spoils for both Cabernet Sauvignon and Cabernet and Family are spread around to a greater degree than in previous editions of the *Wine Companion*. I don't think that this should for one moment be interpreted as a negative for cabernet; there is a genuine style choice between the pure cabernet rendition and those with more than 15% of a variety other than cabernet. The points are as they are, but there is a very strong case to be made for putting the two classes side by side, and giving a fairer view of the grape quality of Australian cabernet and Bordeaux blends.

RATING	WINE	REGION
99	2014 Hardys 165th Anniversary Edition Cabernet Shiraz	Blend
99	2015 Yarra Yering Dry Red No. 1	Yarra Valley
98	2013 Chain of Ponds The Cachet	Adelaide Hills
98	2016 Cullen Diana Madeline	Margaret River
97	2016 Three Kangaroos Hill Side Cabernet Sauvignon Shiraz	Barossa Valley
97	2014 Gaelic Cemetery Premium Cabernet Malbec	Clare Valley
97	2015 Evoi The Satyr Reserve	Margaret River
97	2014 Vasse Felix Tom Cullity Cabernet Sauvignon Malbec	Margaret River
97	2015 Penfolds Bin 389 Cabernet Shiraz	SA blend
97	2013 Yalumba The Caley Cabernet Shiraz	SA blend
97	2016 Mount Mary Quintet	Yarra Valley
97	2016 Woodlands Reserve de la Cave Cabernet Franc	Margaret River
97	2016 Yarra Yering Dry Red No. 1	Yarra Valley
97	2016 Yarra Yering Malbec	Yarra Valley

Etc

RATING	WINE	REGION
98	2017 Best's Original 1860's Vines Pinot Meunier	Great Western
97	2016 Cupitt's Nebbiolo	Hilltops
97	2016 Yarra Yering Dry Red No. 3	Yarra Valley

Fortified

The points speak for themselves. These wines are unique to Australia in terms of their age, complexity, intensity and varietal make-up. They arguably represent the best value of all Australian wines given the cost of production, notably in the amount of working capital tied up for decades.

RATING	WINE	REGION
100	1918 Seppeltsfield 100 Year Old Para Liqueur	Barossa Valley
99	NV Chambers Rosewood Rare Rutherglen Muscadelle	Rutherglen
98	NV Baileys of Glenrowan Winemakers Selection Rare Old Muscat	Glenrowan
98	NV All Saints Estate Museum Rutherglen Muscadelle	Rutherglen
98	NV All Saints Estate Rutherglen Museum Muscat	Rutherglen

Best wineries of the regions

The nomination of the best wineries of the regions has evolved into a three-level classification (further explained on page 9). At the very top are the wineries with their names and stars printed in red; these have been generally recognised for having a long track record of excellence – truly the best of the best. Next are wineries with their stars (but not their names) printed in red, which have had a consistent record of excellence for at least the past three years. Those wineries with black stars have achieved excellence this year (and sometimes longer).

ADELAIDE HILLS
Ashton Hills Vineyard ★★★★★
Bird in Hand ★★★★★
Casa Freschi ★★★★★
Catlin Wines ★★★★★
Chain of Ponds ★★★★★
Charlotte Dalton Wines ★★★★★
Coates Wines ★★★★★
Deviation Road ★★★★★
Geoff Weaver ★★★★★
Guthrie Wines ★★★★★
Hahndorf Hill Winery ★★★★★
Karrawatta ★★★★★
Longview Vineyard ★★★★★
Mike Press Wines ★★★★★
Mt Lofty Ranges Vineyard ★★★★★
Murdoch Hill ★★★★★
Nova Vita Wines ★★★★★
Ochota Barrels ★★★★★
Petaluma ★★★★★
Riposte ★★★★★
Romney Park Wines ★★★★★
Scott ★★★★★
Shaw + Smith ★★★★★
Sidewood Estate ★★★★★
Tapanappa ★★★★★
The Lane Vineyard ★★★★★
Turon Wines ★★★★★
View Road Wines ★★★★★
Wicks Estate Wines ★★★★★

ADELAIDE ZONE
Heirloom Vineyards ★★★★★
Hewitson ★★★★★
Patritti Wines ★★★★★
Penfolds Magill Estate ★★★★★

ALPINE VALLEYS
Mayford Wines ★★★★★

BALLARAT
Eastern Peake ★★★★★
Mitchell Harris Wines ★★★★★
Tomboy Hill ★★★★★

BAROSSA VALLEY
1847 | Yaldara Wines ★★★★★
Bethany Wines ★★★★★
Brave Souls Wine ★★★★★
Brothers at War ★★★★★
Caillard Wine ★★★★★
Charles Melton ★★★★★
Chateau Tanunda ★★★★★
Dorrien Estate ★★★★★
Dutschke Wines ★★★★★
Elderton ★★★★★
First Drop Wines ★★★★★
Gibson ★★★★★
Glaetzer Wines ★★★★★
Grant Burge ★★★★★
Hayes Family Wines ★★★★★
Head Wines ★★★★★
Hemera Estate ★★★★★
Hentley Farm Wines ★★★★★
Jacob's Creek ★★★★★
John Duval Wines ★★★★★
Kaesler Wines ★★★★★
Kalleske ★★★★★
Kellermeister ★★★★★
Landhaus Estate ★★★★★
Langmeil Winery ★★★★★
Laughing Jack ★★★★★
Massena Vineyards ★★★★★

Maverick Wines ★★★★★
Murray Street Vineyards ★★★★★
Penfolds ★★★★★
Peter Lehmann ★★★★★
Purple Hands Wines ★★★★★
Rockford ★★★★★
Rolf Binder ★★★★★
Ruggabellus ★★★★★
St Hallett ★★★★★
St Hugo ★★★★★
Saltram ★★★★★
Schild Estate Wines ★★★★★
Schubert Estate ★★★★★
Schwarz Wine Company ★★★★★
Seppeltsfield ★★★★★
Smallfry Wines ★★★★★
Sons of Eden ★★★★★
Soul Growers ★★★★★
Spinifex ★★★★★
Teusner ★★★★★
The Willows Vineyard ★★★★★
Thorn-Clarke Wines ★★★★★
Three Kangaroos ★★★★★
Torbreck Vintners ★★★★★
Turkey Flat ★★★★★
Two Hands Wines ★★★★★
Wolf Blass ★★★★★
Woods Crampton ★★★★★
Yelland & Papps ★★★★★
Z Wine ★★★★★

BEECHWORTH
A. Rodda Wines ★★★★★
Castagna ★★★★★
Fighting Gully Road ★★★★★
Giaconda ★★★★★
Golden Ball ★★★★★
Piano Piano ★★★★★
Willem Kurt Wines ★★★★★

BENDIGO
Balgownie Estate ★★★★★
Bress ★★★★★

BLACKWOOD VALLEY
Dickinson Estate ★★★★★
Nannup Estate ★★★★★

CANBERRA DISTRICT
Capital Wines ★★★★★

Clonakilla ★★★★★
Eden Road Wines ★★★★★
Helm ★★★★★
Lerida Estate ★★★★★
Mount Majura Vineyard ★★★★★
Nick O'Leary Wines ★★★★★
Ravensworth ★★★★★

CENTRAL OTAGO, NZ
Charteris Wines ★★★★★

CENTRAL VICTORIA
Mount Terrible ★★★★★
Terra Felix ★★★★★

CLARE VALLEY
Artis Wines ★★★★★
Claymore Wines ★★★★★
Clos Clare ★★★★★
Gaelic Cemetery Wines ★★★★★
Grosset ★★★★★
Jim Barry Wines ★★★★★
Kilikanoon Wines ★★★★★
Koerner Wine ★★★★★
Leasingham ★★★★★
Mitchell ★★★★★
Mount Horrocks ★★★★★
Naked Run Wines ★★★★★
O'Leary Walker Wines ★★★★★
Paulett Wines ★★★★★
Pikes ★★★★★
Rieslingfreak ★★★★★
Sevenhill Cellars ★★★★★
Shut the Gate Wines ★★★★★
Steve Wiblin's Erin Eyes ★★★★★
Talbots Block Wines ★★★★★
Taylors ★★★★★
Tim Adams ★★★★★
Tim McNeil Wines ★★★★★
Wendouree ★★★★★
Wilson Vineyard ★★★★★
Wines by KT ★★★★★

COONAWARRA
Balnaves of Coonawarra ★★★★★
Bellwether ★★★★★
Brand's Laira Coonawarra ★★★★★
Katnook Coonawarra ★★★★★
Koonara ★★★★★
Lindeman's ★★★★★

Majella ★★★★★
Parker Coonawarra Estate ★★★★★
Patrick of Coonawarra ★★★★★
Penley Estate ★★★★★
Redman ★★★★★
Rymill Coonawarra ★★★★★
Wynns Coonawarra Estate ★★★★★
Zema Estate ★★★★★

DENMARK
Apricus Hill ★★★★★
Harewood Estate ★★★★★
Rockcliffe ★★★★★
The Lake House Denmark ★★★★★

EDEN VALLEY
Eden Hall ★★★★★
Flaxman Wines ★★★★★
Heggies Vineyard ★★★★★
Henschke ★★★★★
Leo Buring ★★★★★
Lonely Vineyard ★★★★★
Mountadam ★★★★★
Pewsey Vale ★★★★★
Poonawatta ★★★★★
Stage Door Wine Co ★★★★★
Yalumba ★★★★★

FRANKLAND RIVER
Alkoomi ★★★★★
Ferngrove ★★★★★
Frankland Estate ★★★★★
Swinney Vineyards ★★★★★

GEELONG
Austins & Co. ★★★★★
Bannockburn Vineyards ★★★★★
Barrgowan Vineyard ★★★★★
Brown Magpie Wines ★★★★★
Clyde Park Vineyard ★★★★★
Farr | Farr Rising ★★★★★
Lethbridge Wines ★★★★★
Oakdene ★★★★★
Paradise IV ★★★★★
Pettavel ★★★★★
Provenance Wines ★★★★★
Robin Brockett Wines ★★★★★
Scotchmans Hill ★★★★★
Shadowfax ★★★★★

Spence ★★★★★
Yes said the Seal ★★★★★

GEOGRAPHE
Capel Vale ★★★★★
Iron Cloud Wines ★★★★★
Talisman Wines ★★★★★
Whicher Ridge ★★★★★
Willow Bridge Estate ★★★★★

GIPPSLAND
Bass Phillip ★★★★★
Blue Gables ★★★★★
Narkoojee ★★★★★

GLENROWAN
Baileys of Glenrowan ★★★★★

GRAMPIANS
Best's Wines ★★★★★
Fallen Giants ★★★★★
Grampians Estate ★★★★★
Mount Langi Ghiran Vineyards
    ★★★★★
Seppelt ★★★★★
SubRosa ★★★★★

GRANITE BELT
Boireann ★★★★★
Golden Grove Estate ★★★★★
Heritage Estate ★★★★★
Symphony Hill Wines ★★★★★

GREAT SOUTHERN
Byron & Harold ★★★★★
Castelli Estate ★★★★★
Forest Hill Vineyard ★★★★★
Rosenthal Wines ★★★★★
Singlefile Wines ★★★★★
Trevelen Farm ★★★★★
Willoughby Park ★★★★★

GREAT WESTERN
A.T. Richardson Wines ★★★★★

GUNDAGAI
Nick Spencer Wines ★★★★★

HEATHCOTE
Flynns Wines ★★★★★

Heathcote Estate ★★★★★
Jasper Hill ★★★★★
Paul Osicka ★★★★★
Sanguine Estate ★★★★★

HENTY
Crawford River Wines ★★★★★
Henty Estate ★★★★★

HILLTOPS
Freeman Vineyards ★★★★★
Moppity Vineyards ★★★★★

HUNTER VALLEY
Andevine Wines ★★★★★
Audrey Wilkinson ★★★★★
Brokenwood ★★★★★
Chateau Francois ★★★★★
De Iuliis ★★★★★
Drayton's Family Wines ★★★★★
Ernest Hill Wines ★★★★★
Glenguin Estate ★★★★★
Gundog Estate ★★★★★
Hart & Hunter ★★★★★
Keith Tulloch Wine ★★★★★
Lake's Folly ★★★★★
Leogate Estate Wines ★★★★★
McLeish Estate ★★★★★
Meerea Park ★★★★★
Mistletoe Wines ★★★★★
Mount Pleasant ★★★★★
Mount View Estate ★★★★★
Pepper Tree Wines ★★★★★
Pokolbin Estate ★★★★★
Silkman Wines ★★★★★
Sweetwater Wines ★★★★★
Tallavera Grove | Carillion ★★★★★
Thomas Wines ★★★★★
Tulloch ★★★★★
Two Rivers ★★★★★
Tyrrell's Wines ★★★★★
Vinden Estate ★★★★★
Whispering Brook ★★★★★

KANGAROO ISLAND
The Islander Estate Vineyards
★★★★★

KING VALLEY
Brown Brothers ★★★★★
Wood Park ★★★★★

LANGHORNE CREEK
Bleasdale Vineyards ★★★★★
Bremerton Wines ★★★★★
John's Blend ★★★★★
Lake Breeze Wines ★★★★★

MACEDON RANGES
Bindi Wine Growers ★★★★★
Curly Flat ★★★★★
Granite Hills ★★★★★
Hanging Rock Winery ★★★★★
Lane's End Vineyard ★★★★★
Lyons Will Estate ★★★★★

MANJIMUP
Peos Estate ★★★★★

MARGARET RIVER
Amelia Park Wines ★★★★★
Arlewood Estate ★★★★★
Ashbrook Estate ★★★★★
Brookland Valley ★★★★★
Cape Grace Wines ★★★★★
Cape Mentelle ★★★★★
Chapman Grove Wines ★★★★★
Clairault | Streicker Wines ★★★★★
Cloudburst ★★★★★
Credaro Family Estate ★★★★★
Cullen Wines ★★★★★
Deep Woods Estate ★★★★★
Devil's Lair ★★★★★
Domaine Naturaliste ★★★★★
Driftwood Estate ★★★★★
Evans & Tate ★★★★★
Evoi Wines ★★★★★
Fire Gully ★★★★★
Flametree ★★★★★
Flowstone Wines ★★★★★
Flying Fish Cove ★★★★★
Forester Estate ★★★★★
Fraser Gallop Estate ★★★★★
Grace Farm ★★★★★
Hamelin Bay ★★★★★
Happs ★★★★★
Hay Shed Hill Wines ★★★★★

Heydon Estate ★★★★★
Higher Plane ★★★★★
House of Cards ★★★★★
Howard Park ★★★★★
Juniper Estate ★★★★★
Latitude 34 Wine Co ★★★★★
Leeuwin Estate ★★★★★
Lenton Brae Wines ★★★★★
McHenry Hohnen Vintners ★★★★★
Mr Barval Fine Wines ★★★★★
Moss Wood ★★★★★
Palmer Wines ★★★★★
Passel Estate ★★★★★
Peccavi Wines ★★★★★
Pierro ★★★★★
Preveli Wines ★★★★★
Rosily Vineyard ★★★★★
Sandalford ★★★★★
Stella Bella Wines ★★★★★
Thompson Estate ★★★★★
tripe.Iscariot ★★★★★
Twinwoods Estate ★★★★★
Umamu Estate ★★★★★
Vasse Felix ★★★★★
Victory Point Wines ★★★★★
Voyager Estate ★★★★★
Walsh & Sons ★★★★★
Watershed Premium Wines ★★★★★
Windance Wines ★★★★★
Windows Estate ★★★★★
Woodlands ★★★★★
Woody Nook ★★★★★
Xanadu Wines ★★★★★

MCLAREN VALE
Bekkers ★★★★★
Bondar Wines ★★★★★
Brini Estate Wines ★★★★★
Chalk Hill ★★★★★
Chapel Hill ★★★★★
Clarendon Hills ★★★★★
Coriole ★★★★★
d'Arenberg ★★★★★
Dandelion Vineyards ★★★★★
Dodgy Brothers ★★★★★
DOWIE DOOLE ★★★★★
Dune Wine ★★★★★
Fox Creek Wines ★★★★★
Gemtree Wines ★★★★★

Geoff Merrill Wines ★★★★★
Hardys ★★★★★
Haselgrove Wines ★★★★★
Hickinbotham Clarendon Vineyard
    ★★★★★
Hither & Yon ★★★★★
Hugh Hamilton Wines ★★★★★
Hugo ★★★★★
Kangarilla Road Vineyard ★★★★★
Kay Brothers Amery Vineyards
    ★★★★★
McLaren Vale III Associates ★★★★★
Mr Riggs Wine Company ★★★★★
Mitolo Wines ★★★★★
Oliver's Taranga Vineyards ★★★★★
Pirramimma ★★★★★
Primo Estate ★★★★★
Reynella ★★★★★
Richard Hamilton ★★★★★
Rudderless ★★★★★
SC Pannell ★★★★★
Serafino Wines ★★★★★
Sherrah Wines ★★★★★
Shingleback ★★★★★
Shirvington ★★★★★
Shottesbrooke ★★★★★
Smidge Wines ★★★★★
Three Dark Horses ★★★★★
Ulithorne ★★★★★
Vigena Wines ★★★★★
Wirra Wirra ★★★★★
Yangarra Estate Vineyard ★★★★★
Zerella Wines ★★★★★

MORNINGTON PENINSULA
Allies Wines ★★★★★
Circe Wines ★★★★★
Crittenden Estate ★★★★★
Dexter Wines ★★★★★
Eldridge Estate of Red Hill ★★★★★
Elgee Park ★★★★★
Foxeys Hangout ★★★★★
Garagiste ★★★★★
Hurley Vineyard ★★★★★
Jones Road ★★★★★
Kooyong ★★★★★
Lindenderry at Red Hill ★★★★★
Main Ridge Estate ★★★★★
Montalto ★★★★★

Moorooduc Estate ★★★★★
Ocean Eight Vineyard & Winery
 ★★★★★
Paradigm Hill ★★★★★
Paringa Estate ★★★★★
Port Phillip Estate ★★★★★
Portsea Estate ★★★★★
Principia ★★★★★
Scorpo Wines ★★★★★
Stonier Wines ★★★★★
Ten Minutes by Tractor ★★★★★
Tuck's Ridge ★★★★★
Willow Creek Vineyard ★★★★★
Yabby Lake Vineyard ★★★★★

MOUNT BARKER
Plantagenet ★★★★★
Poacher's Ridge Vineyard ★★★★★
3 Drops ★★★★★
West Cape Howe Wines ★★★★★

MOUNT LOFTY RANGES ZONE
Michael Hall Wines ★★★★★

MUDGEE
Eloquesta ★★★★★
Lowe Wines ★★★★★
Robert Oatley Vineyards ★★★★★
Robert Stein Vineyard ★★★★★

NAGAMBIE LAKES
Tahbilk ★★★★★

NORTH EAST VICTORIA
Eldorado Road ★★★★★
Simão & Co ★★★★★

ORANGE
Bloodwood ★★★★★
Colmar Estate ★★★★★
Cooks Lot ★★★★★
Gilbert Family Wines ★★★★★
Philip Shaw Wines ★★★★★
Rikard Wines ★★★★★
Ross Hill Wines ★★★★★
Rowlee ★★★★★
Swinging Bridge ★★★★★

PEMBERTON
Bellarmine Wines ★★★★★

PERTH HILLS
Millbrook Winery ★★★★★

PORONGURUP
Abbey Creek Vineyard ★★★★★
Castle Rock Estate ★★★★★
Duke's Vineyard ★★★★★

PYRENEES
Blue Pyrenees Estate ★★★★★
Dalwhinnie ★★★★★
DogRock Winery ★★★★★
Mount Avoca ★★★★★
Summerfield ★★★★★
Taltarni ★★★★★

QUEENSLAND
Witches Falls Winery ★★★★★

RIVERINA
Calabria Family Wines ★★★★★
De Bortoli ★★★★★
McWilliam's ★★★★★
R. Paulazzo ★★★★★

RUTHERGLEN
All Saints Estate ★★★★★
Campbells ★★★★★
Chambers Rosewood ★★★★★
Morris ★★★★★
Pfeiffer Wines ★★★★★
Stanton & Killeen Wines ★★★★★

SHOALHAVEN COAST
Coolangatta Estate ★★★★★
Cupitt's Winery ★★★★★

SOUTH AUSTRALIA
Angove Family Winemakers ★★★★★
Byrne Vineyards ★★★★★
Levrier by Jo Irvine ★★★★★
RockBare ★★★★★
Thistledown Wines ★★★★★
Wines by Geoff Hardy ★★★★★

SOUTH WEST AUSTRALIA ZONE
Kerrigan + Berry ★★★★★
Snake + Herring ★★★★★

SOUTHERN FLEURIEU
Salomon Estate ★★★★★

SOUTHERN HIGHLANDS
Centennial Vineyards ★★★★★

STRATHBOGIE RANGES
Maygars Hill Winery ★★★★★

SUNBURY
Craiglee ★★★★★
Galli Estate ★★★★★

SWAN DISTRICT
Mandoon Estate ★★★★★

SWAN VALLEY
Faber Vineyard ★★★★★
Houghton ★★★★★
Sittella Wines ★★★★★

TASMANIA
Barringwood ★★★★★
Bay of Fires ★★★★★
Bream Creek ★★★★★
Chatto ★★★★★
Dalrymple ★★★★★
Dawson & James ★★★★★
Delamere Vineyards ★★★★★
Derwent Estate ★★★★★
Devil's Corner ★★★★★
Domaine A ★★★★★
Dr Edge ★★★★★
Freycinet ★★★★★
Frogmore Creek ★★★★★
Ghost Rock Vineyard ★★★★★
Heemskerk ★★★★★
Holm Oak ★★★★★
Home Hill ★★★★★
House of Arras ★★★★★
Jansz Tasmania ★★★★★
Josef Chromy Wines ★★★★★
Kate Hill Wines ★★★★★
Laurel Bank ★★★★★
Meadowbank Wines ★★★★★
Mewstone Wines ★★★★★
Milton Vineyard ★★★★★
Moorilla Estate ★★★★★
Pipers Brook Vineyard ★★★★★
Pooley Wines ★★★★★
Pressing Matters ★★★★★
Sailor Seeks Horse ★★★★★
Sinapius Vineyard ★★★★★

Small Island Wines ★★★★★
Stargazer Wine ★★★★★
Stefano Lubiana ★★★★★
Stoney Rise ★★★★★
Tamar Ridge | Pirie ★★★★★
Tolpuddle Vineyard ★★★★★

UPPER GOULBURN
Delatite ★★★★★

VARIOUS
Ben Haines Wine ★★★★★
Handpicked Wines ★★★★★
Hesketh Wine Company ★★★★★
Ministry of Clouds ★★★★★
Treasury Wine Estates ★★★★★

VICTORIA
Sentio Wines ★★★★★

WESTERN AUSTRALIA
Larry Cherubino Wines ★★★★★

WESTERN VICTORIA
Norton Estate ★★★★★

WRATTONBULLY
Terre à Terre ★★★★★

YARRA VALLEY
Bicknell fc ★★★★★
Chandon Australia ★★★★★
Coldstream Hills ★★★★★
De Bortoli ★★★★★
Denton Viewhill Vineyard ★★★★★
Dominique Portet ★★★★★
Fetherston Vintners ★★★★★
First Foot Forward ★★★★★
Gembrook Hill ★★★★★
Giant Steps ★★★★★
Goodman Wines ★★★★★
Greenstone Vineyards ★★★★★
Helen's Hill Estate ★★★★★
Hillcrest Vineyard ★★★★★
Hoddles Creek Estate ★★★★★
Journey Wines ★★★★★
Mac Forbes ★★★★★
Mayer ★★★★★
Medhurst ★★★★★
Mount Mary ★★★★★

Oakridge Wines ★★★★★
One Block ★★★★★
Pimpernel Vineyards ★★★★★
Punch ★★★★★
Punt Road ★★★★★
Rob Hall Wines ★★★★★
Rochford Wines ★★★★★
Rouleur ★★★★★
St Huberts ★★★★★
Serrat ★★★★★
Seville Estate ★★★★★

Soumah ★★★★★
Stefani Estate ★★★★★
Sutherland Estate ★★★★★
Tarrahill. ★★★★★
TarraWarra Estate ★★★★★
Tokar Estate ★★★★★
Toolangi Vineyards ★★★★★
Warramunda Estate ★★★★★
Yarra Yering ★★★★★
Yering Station ★★★★★
Yeringberg ★★★★★

Regional production 2016–17

The problem with discussing the known 2017 figures in the context of the unknown 2018 figures is obvious. The collection and collation of the '18 production results is a tedious business, and history consistently shows a – give or take – 10% understatement of the tonnes crushed. The solution is pragmatic: inflate the results by 10% across the board, and make it known that this has been done.

Well before the conclusion of vintage for a given region, almost all of the relevant growing season conditions are known, whether frost, fire, drought or flood. Tracking spot prices for grapes grown in the warm inland regions (70% of the total vintage in '17) is a bit like exit polls in elections. These, too, are as much about the past as they are about the future. Only when the results are officially declared will you know how accurate they were.

The vintage snapshot (pages 58–62) is based on responses from 2835 wineries across Australia that depict a vintage with its share of variables (e.g. frost, heat and dry conditions) impacting yields, but not quality. The most likely outcome is a vintage 5–10% lower in yields than '17, but of good to very good quality.

The warm inland regions will see an increase in revenue for entry level shiraz, cabernet sauvignon, merlot and – wait for it – pinot gris. Whatever the demands of the Chinese market may have, it's not more pinot gris. But the latest research carried out by London-based Wine Intelligence (on behalf of Wine Australia) does show an increased demand for lower-priced Australian wines for home and restaurant consumption. This is an early sign of a move towards a mature market, and a broadening of the consumer pool.

The demand for pinot gris, and commercial entry sauvignon blanc and chardonnay, is almost certainly from the US and the UK. Then from Austwine (Australian bulk wine specialists with an in-depth understanding of the entire Australian grape supply channels) comes the biggest surprise of all: results suggest an oversupply of cool drylands premium red wines that will satisfy existing demand for several years.

Were it not for Federal Ministers Julie Bishop (Foreign Affairs) and Steve Ciobo (Trade) making on-the-record comments suggesting tensions between Australia and China (possibly as backwash from Trump's early morning tweets), I might have believed this was simply part of doing business in China (like the ban of ostentatious gifts passed several years ago) or collateral damage from the re-balancing of trade between China and the US. But this doesn't shake my strong-held belief that China is destined to become the world's largest market for wine, with Australia the leader of the pack.

A couple of finishing remarks. The first – the total Chinese market for alcohol-based drinks in 2016 is believed to be USD180 billion, with spirits and rice wine at USD100 billion, beer USD40 billion, wine USD18 billion, and yellow wine (whatever that is) USD4 billion. Generational change will surely see a shift from spirits and rice wine to table wine. A 1% increment in our share would see exports increase from the present AUD1 billion to AUD3.2 billion (at a nominal USD0.70 exchange rate). And my second point – it's high time that more vines are planted in Australia.

STATE/REGIONS	2017 TONNES	2016 TONNES	% CHANGE 2016–17	% OF CRUSH 2017
SOUTH AUSTRALIA	983,538	926,430	6	51
Langhorne Creek	67,332	68,090	-1	3
Barossa Valley	79,884	61,580	30	4
McLaren Vale	50,537	46,433	9	3
Riverland	535,233	517,577	3	28
MURRAY DARLING–SWAN HILL	409,419	416,966	−2	21
NEW SOUTH WALES	397,730	348,441	14	21
Hunter Valley	4,171	3,034	37	0
Mudgee	1,501	1,997	-25	0
Riverina	354,425	311,639	14	18
VICTORIA	87,334	63,933	37	5
Mornigton Peninsula	2,268	3,198	-29	0
Rutherglen	2,355	1,907	23	0
Yarra Valley	9,553	9,378	2	0
WESTERN AUSTRALIA	39,715	39,055	2	2
Greath Southern	8,168	7,615	7	0
Margaret River	23,444	20,639	14	1
Pemberton	1,191	2,805	-58	0
TASMANIA	11,120	10,214	9	1
QUEENSLAND	812	2,168	-63	0
AUSTRALIAN CAPITAL TERRITORY	0	0	0	0
WARM INLAND REGIONS	1,350,741	1,259,180	7	70
COOL/TEMPERATE REGIONS	578,889	548,027	6	30
TOTAL TONNES	1,929,630	1,807,207	7	100

Varietal production 2016–17

The statistics show an interesting contrast between the old brigade and the new, the big end of town and the small. In 2017 there was a record crush of 1.93 million tonnes; shiraz attracted a significant increase in the price per tonne, up 12% on the 2016 crush. Before you rush to the China conclusion, cabernet sauvignon reflected a slight decrease. Compared to shiraz with an average price of $765 per tonne, cabernet sauvignon had an average of $647 per tonne. Merlot, the third-ranked red grape, showed a 5% increase per tonne in a virtually unchanged production scenario.

Merlot was long ago described as cabernet without the pain by US writers looking at the Napa and Sonoma Valleys. We haven't managed to produce cabernet as fearsomely tannic as many of the most expensive Californian icons, merlot much of a muchness in each country. But at a given price point within the commercial and premium red wine styles, shiraz and merlot have broader appeal than cabernet sauvignon. As the price increases, merlot's importance (as a single or dominant varietal wine) decreases.

The other grape of crucial importance is, of course, chardonnay. Small wonder its price rose by 7%, given the fall in tonnage. That said, the price per tonne is substantially reduced by the disproportionate amount grown in the Riverland and Riverina regions, as well as their much higher average yield. This leaves sauvignon blanc (refusing to be browbeaten by Marlborough) and pinot gris, both with huge appeal to those not particularly interested in flavour or texture, thus providing a social lubricant for that cohort.

Riesling and pinot noir each has particular appeal to wine professionals, and each has something to crow about: riesling the second highest increase in price to $871 per tonne; pinot noir's price the second highest overall. Grenache is on everyone's lips these days, and the sharp increase in production had minimal impact on its high price per tonne. Durif fared well; its tonnage not quite doubling, but close thereto, and yet sustaining a 12% price increase to a modest $537 per tonne (held back by the Riverland proportion).

Then comes a string of very different wines and outcomes. Prosecco makes the official list for the first time, with a very useful 6217 tonnes. Tempranillo holds on to its highest price per tonne, flag waving vigorously, but there the good news comes to a shuddering stop. Tempranillo may well be the most expensive variety, but it has significantly declined in production. I still believe that the variety will be an important, ongoing part of the Australian wine landscape. I truly wish I could say the same for sangiovese, but I don't know how to explain the significant decrease in price along with an even more significant decline in production. The same can be said of nero d'Avola, although it's a very small player. There are varieties on the list which have been coming and going, here one year, gone the next. Arneis is one of those, and fiano – hanging on by its fingernails.

	2017 TONNES	2016 TONNES	2017 WEIGHTED AVERAGE PURCHASE VALUE ($)	% CHANGE IN PRICE 2016–17
SHIRAZ	500,938	430,185	765	12
CHARDONNAY	361,047	406,028	411	7
CABERNET SAUVIGNON	279,041	255,074	647	-2
MERLOT	125,487	111,959	455	5
SAUVIGNON BLANC	107,423	100,769	568	3
PINOT GRIS	75,338	73,372	674	9
SEMILLON	70,495	64,066	361	5
PINOT NOIR	50,108	47,860	884	-1
RIESLING	28,288	28,224	871	13
PETIT VERDOT	23,647	20,299	362	4
GRENACHE	17,911	13,235	859	-3
GEWURZTRAMINER	14,176	14,219	369	1
DURIF	9,189	5,758	537	12
VERDELHO	7,755	11,005	467	19
PROSECCO	6,217	NA*	705	-6
TEMPRANILLO	5,129	6,582	926	1
SANGIOVESE	3,897	5,210	700	-16
FIANO	2,641	NA*	230	NA
MARSANNE	2,190	1,621	350	-16
NERO D'AVOLA	796	864	570	-9
MUSCADELLE	420	382	651	-44

* Data not available

Varietal wine styles and regions

For better or worse, there simply has to be concerted action to highlight the link between regions, varieties and wine styles. It's not a question of creating the links: they are already there, and have been in existence for periods as short as 20 years or as long as 150 years. So here you will find abbreviated summaries of those regional styles (in turn reflected in the Best of the Best lists commencing on page 26).

Riesling

Riesling's link with the **Eden Valley** dates back at least to when Joseph Gilbert planted his Pewsey Vale vineyard, and the grape quickly made its way to the nearby **Clare Valley**. These two regions stood above all others for well over 100 years, producing wines that shared many flavour and texture characteristics: lime (a little more obvious in the Eden Valley), apple, talc and mineral, lightly browned toasty notes emerging with five–10 years bottle age. Within the last 20 or so years, the subregions of Western Australia's **Great Southern** have established a deserved reputation for finely structured, elegant rieslings with wonderful length, sometimes shy when young, bursting into song after five years. The subregions are (in alphabetical order) **Albany**, **Denmark**, **Frankland River**, **Mount Barker** and **Porongurup**. **Canberra** is up with the best and **Tasmania**, too, produces high class rieslings, notable for their purity and intensity courtesy of their high natural acidity. Finally, there is the small and very cool region of **Henty** (once referred to as Drumborg), its exceptional rieslings sharing many things in common with those of Tasmania.

Semillon

There is a Siamese-twin relationship between semillon and the **Hunter Valley**, which has been producing a wine style like no other in the world for well over 100 years. The humid and very warm climate (best coupled with sandy soils not common in the region) results in wines that have a median alcohol level of 10.5% and no residual sugar, are cold-fermented in stainless steel and bottled within three months of vintage. They are devoid of colour and have only the barest hints of grass, herb and mineral wrapped around a core of acidity. Over the next five to 10 years they develop a glowing green–gold colour, a suite of grass and citrus fruit surrounded by buttered toast and honey notes. As with rieslings, screwcaps have added decades to their cellaring life. The **Adelaide Hills** and **Margaret River** produce entirely different semillon, more structured and weighty, its alcohol 13–14%, and as often as not blended with sauvignon blanc, barrel fermentation of part or all common. Finally, there is a cuckoo in the nest: Peter Lehmann in the **Barossa/Eden Valley** has adapted Hunter Valley practices, picking early, fermenting in steel, bottling early, and holding the top wine for five years before release – and succeeding brilliantly.

Chardonnay

This infinitely flexible grape is grown and vinified in all 63 regions, and accounts for half of Australia's white wine grapes and wine. Incredibly, before 1970 it was all but unknown, hiding its promise here and there (**Mudgee** was one such place) under a cloak of anonymity. It was in Mudgee and the **Hunter Valley** that the first wines labelled chardonnay were made in 1971 (by Craigmoor and Tyrrell's). Its bold yellow colour, peaches and cream flavour and vanilla oak was unlike anything that had gone before and was accepted by domestic and export markets with equal enthusiasm. When exports took off into the stratosphere between 1985 and '95, one half of Brand Australia was cheerful and cheap oak-chipped chardonnay grown in the **Riverina** and **Riverland**. By coincidence, over the same period chardonnay from the emerging cool climate regions was starting to appear in limited quantities, its flavour and structure radically different to the warm-grown, high-cropped wine. Another 10 years on, and by 2005–6 the wine surplus was starting to build rapidly, with demand for chardonnay much less than its production. As attention swung from chardonnay to sauvignon blanc, the situation became dire. Lost in the heat of battle were supremely elegant wines from most cool regions, **Margaret River** and **Yarra Valley** the leaders of the large band. Constant refinement of the style, and the adoption of the screwcap, puts these wines at the forefront of the gradually succeeding battle to re-engage consumers here and abroad with what are world class wines.

Sauvignon Blanc

Two regions, the **Adelaide Hills** and **Margaret River**, stood in front of all others until recently joined by **Orange**; these three produce Australia's best sauvignon blanc, wines with real structure and authority. It is a matter of record that Marlborough sauvignon blanc accounts for one-third of Australia's white wine sales; all one can say (accurately) is that the basic Marlborough style is very different, and look back at what happened with Australian chardonnay. Margaret River also offers complex blends of sauvignon blanc and semillon in widely varying proportions, and with varying degrees of oak fermentation.

Shiraz

Shiraz, like chardonnay, is by far the most important red variety and, again like chardonnay, is tremendously flexible in its ability to adapt to virtually any combination of climate and soil/terroir. Unlike chardonnay, a recent arrival, shiraz was the most important red variety throughout the 19th and 20th centuries. Its ancestral homes were the **Barossa Valley**, the **Clare Valley**, **McLaren Vale** and the **Hunter Valley**, and it still leads in those regions. With the exception of the Hunter Valley, it was as important in making fortified wine as table wine over the period 1850–1950, aided and abetted by grenache and mourvedre (mataro). In New South Wales the **Hilltops** and **Canberra District** are producing elegant, cool grown wines that usually conceal their power (especially when co-fermented with viognier) but not their silky length. Further north, but at a higher altitude, **Orange** is also producing fine, fragrant and spicy wines. All the other New South Wales regions are capable of producing good shiraz of seriously good character and quality; shiraz ripens comfortably but quite late in the season. Polished, sophisticated wines are the result. Victoria has a cornucopia of regions at the cooler end of the spectrum; the coolest (though not too cool for comfort) are the **Yarra Valley, Mornington Peninsula, Sunbury** and **Geelong**, all producing fragrant, spicy medium-bodied wines. **Bendigo, Heathcote, Grampians** and **Pyrenees**, more or less running east–west across the centre of Victoria, are producing some of the most exciting medium-bodied shirazs in Australia, each with its own terroir stamp, but all combining generosity and elegance. In Western Australia, **Great Southern** and three of its five subregions, **Frankland River, Mount Barker** and **Porongurup**, are making magical shirazs, fragrant and spicy, fleshy yet strongly structured. **Margaret River** has been a relatively late mover, but it, too, is producing wines with exemplary varietal definition and finesse.

Cabernet Sauvignon

The tough-skinned cabernet sauvignon can be, and is, grown in all regions, but it struggles in the coolest (notably **Tasmania**) and loses desirable varietal definition in the warmer regions, especially in warmer vintages. Shiraz can cope with alcohol levels in excess of 14.5%, cabernet can't. In South Australia, **Coonawarra** stands supreme, its climate (though not its soil) strikingly similar to that of Bordeaux, the main difference lower rainfall. Perfectly detailed cabernets are the result, with no need of shiraz or merlot to fill in the mid-palate, although some excellent blends are made. **Langhorne Creek** (a little warmer) and **McLaren Vale** (warmer still) have similar maritime climates, doubtless the reason why McLaren Vale manages to deal with the warmth of its summer–autumn weather. The **Eden Valley** is the most reliable of the inner regions, the other principal regions dependent on a cool summer. From South Australia to Western Australia, where **Margaret River**, with its extreme maritime climate shaped by the warm Indian Ocean, stands tall. It is also Australia's foremost producer of cabernet merlot et al in the Bordeaux mix. The texture and structure of both the straight varietal and the blend is regal, often to the point of austerity when the wines are young, but the sheer power of this underlying fruit provides the balance and guarantees the future development of the wines over a conservative 20 years, especially if screwcapped. The **Great Southern** subregions of **Frankland River** and **Mount Barker** share a continental climate that is somewhat cooler than Margaret River's, and has a greater diurnal temperature range. Here cabernet has an incisive, dark-berry character and firm but usually fine tannins – not demanding merlot, though a touch of it and/or malbec can be beneficial. It is grown successfully through the centre and south of Victoria, but is often overshadowed by shiraz. In the past 20 years it has ceased to be a problem child and become a favourite son of the **Yarra Valley**; the forward move of vintage dates has been the key to the change.

Pinot Noir

The promiscuity of shiraz (particularly) and cabernet sauvignon is in sharp contrast to the puritanical rectitude of pinot noir. One sin of omission or commission, and the door slams shut, leaving the bewildered winemaker on the outside. **Tasmania** is the El Dorado for the variety, and the best is still to come with better clones, older vines and greater exploration of the multitude of mesoclimates that Tasmania has to offer. While it is north of Central Otago (New Zealand), its vineyards are all air conditioned by the Southern Ocean and Tasman Sea, and it stands toe-to-toe with Central Otago in its ability to make deeply-coloured, profound pinot with all the length one could ask for. Once on the mainland, Victoria's Port Phillip zone, encompassing the **Geelong**, **Macedon Ranges**, **Sunbury**, **Mornington Peninsula** and **Yarra Valley** is the epicentre of Australian pinot noir, **Henty** a small outpost. The sheer number of high quality, elegant wines produced by dozens of makers in those regions put the **Adelaide Hills** and **Porongurup** (also capable of producing quality pinot) into the shade.

Other Red Varieties

There are many other red varieties in the *Wine Companion* database, and there is little rhyme or reason for the distribution of the plantings.

Sparkling Wines

The patter is eerily similar to that of pinot noir, **Tasmania** now and in the future the keeper of the Holy Grail, the **Port Phillip** zone the centre of activity on the mainland.

Fortified Wines

Rutherglen and **Glenrowan** are the two (and only) regions that produce immensely complex, long barrel-aged muscat and muscadelle, the latter called tokay for more than a century, now renamed topaque. These wines have no equal in the world, Spain's Malaga nearest in terms of lusciousness, but nowhere near as complex. The other producer of a wine without parallel is Seppeltsfield in the **Barossa Valley**, which each year releases an explosively rich and intense tawny liqueur style that is 100% 100 years old.

Australia's geographical indications

The process of formally mapping Australia's wine regions is all but complete, though it will never come to an outright halt – for one thing, climate change is lurking in the wings.

The division into states, zones, regions and subregions follows; those regions or subregions marked with an asterisk are not yet registered, and may never be, but are in common usage. The bizarre Hunter Valley GI map now has Hunter Valley as a zone, Hunter as the region and the sprawling Upper Hunter as a subregion along with Pokolbin (small and disputed by some locals). Another recent official change has been the registration of Mount Gambier as a Region in the Limestone Coast zone. I am still in front of the game with Tasmania, dividing it into Northern, Southern and East Coast. In a similar vein, I have included Ballarat (with 15 wineries) and the Southern Eyre Peninsula (three wineries).

State/Zone	Region	Subregion
AUSTRALIA		
Australia Australian South Eastern Australia★	★ The South Eastern Australia zone incorporates the whole of the states of NSW, Vic and Tas, and only part of Qld and SA.	
NEW SOUTH WALES		
Big Rivers	Murray Darling Perricoota Riverina Swan Hill	
Central Ranges	Cowra Mudgee Orange	
Hunter Valley	Hunter	Broke Fordwich Pokolbin Upper Hunter Valley

State/Zone	Region	Subregion
Northern Rivers	Hastings River	
Northern Slopes	New England Australia	
South Coast	Shoalhaven Coast Southern Highlands	
Southern New South Wales	Canberra District Gundagai Hilltops Tumbarumba	
Western Plains		

SOUTH AUSTRALIA

Adelaide (super zone, includes Mount Lofty Ranges, Fleurieu and Barossa)		
Barossa	Barossa Valley Eden Valley	High Eden
Far North	Southern Flinders Ranges	
Fleurieu	Currency Creek Kangaroo Island Langhorne Creek McLaren Vale Southern Fleurieu	
Limestone Coast	Coonawarra Mount Benson Mount Gambier Padthaway Robe Wrattonbully	
Lower Murray	Riverland	
Mount Lofty Ranges	Adelaide Hills Adelaide Plains Clare Valley	Lenswood Piccadilly Valley Polish Hill River★ Watervale★
The Peninsulas	Southern Eyre Peninsula★	

State/Zone	Region	Subregion
VICTORIA		
Central Victoria	Bendigo Goulburn Valley Heathcote Strathbogie Ranges Upper Goulburn	Nagambie Lakes
Gippsland		
North East Victoria	Alpine Valleys Beechworth Glenrowan King Valley Rutherglen	
North West Victoria	Murray Darling Swan Hill	
Port Phillip	Geelong Macedon Ranges Mornington Peninsula Sunbury Yarra Valley	
Western Victoria	Ballarat★ Grampians Henty Pyrenees	Great Western
WESTERN AUSTRALIA		
Central Western Australia		
Eastern Plains, Inland and North of Western Australia		
Greater Perth	Peel Perth Hills Swan District	Swan Valley

State/Zone	Region	Subregion
South West Australia	Blackwood Valley	
	Geographe	
	Great Southern	Albany
		Denmark
		Frankland River
		Mount Barker
		Porongurup
	Manjimup	
	Margaret River	
	Pemberton	
West Australian South East Coastal		

QUEENSLAND

Queensland	Granite Belt	
	South Burnett	

TASMANIA

Tasmania	Northern Tasmania★	
	Southern Tasmania★	
	East Coast Tasmania★	

AUSTRALIAN CAPITAL TERRITORY

NORTHERN TERRITORY

Wine and food or food and wine?

It all depends on your starting point: there are conventional matches for overseas classics, such as caviar (Champagne), fresh foie gras (sauternes, riesling or rosé) and new season Italian white truffles (any medium-bodied red). Here the food flavour is all important, the wine merely incidental.

At the other extreme come 50-year-old classic red wines: Grange, or Grand Cru Burgundy, or First Growth Bordeaux, or a Maurice O'Shea Mount Pleasant Shiraz. Here the food is, or should be, merely a low-key foil, but at the same time must be of high quality.

In the Australian context I believe not enough attention is paid to the time of year, which – particularly in the southern states – is or should be a major determinant in the choice of both food and wine. And so I shall present my suggestions in this way, always bearing in mind how many ways there are to skin a cat (but not serve it).

Spring

Sparkling
Oysters, cold crustacea, tapas, any cold hors d'oeuvres

Young riesling
Cold salads, sashimi

Gewurztraminer
Asian cuisine

Young semillon
Antipasto, vegetable terrine

Pinot gris
Crab cakes, whitebait

Verdelho, chenin blanc
Cold smoked chicken, gravlax

Mature chardonnay
Grilled chicken, chicken pasta, turkey, pheasant

Rose
Caesar salad, trout mousse

Young pinot noir
Seared kangaroo fillet, grilled quail

Merlot
Pastrami, warm smoked chicken

Cool-climate medium-bodied cabernet sauvignon
Rack of baby lamb

Light to medium-bodied cool-climate shiraz
Rare eye fillet of beef

Young botrytised wines
Fresh fruits, cake

Summer

Chilled fino
Cold consommé

2–3-year-old semillon
Gazpacho

2–3-year-old riesling
Seared tuna

Young barrel-fermented semillon sauvignon blanc
Seafood or vegetable tempura

Young off-dry riesling
Prosciutto & melon/pear

Cool-climate chardonnay
Abalone, lobster, Chinese-style prawns

10–year-old semillon or riesling
Braised pork neck

Mature chardonnay (5+ years)
Braised rabbit

Off-dry rose
Chilled fresh fruit

Young light-bodied pinot noir
Grilled salmon

Aged pinot noir (5+ years)
Coq au vin, wild duck

Young grenache/sangiovese
Osso bucco

Hunter Valley shiraz (5–10 years)
Beef spare ribs

Sangiovese
Saltimbocca, roast poussin

Medium-bodied cabernet sauvignon (5 years)
Barbecued butterfly leg of lamb

Mature chardonnay
Smoked eel, smoked roe

All wines
Parmagiana

Autumn

Amontillado
Warm consommé

Barrel-fermented mature whites
Smoked roe, bouillabaisse

Complex mature chardonnay
Sweetbreads, brains

Aged (10-year-old) marsanne or semillon
Seafood risotto, Lebanese

Grenache
Grilled calf's liver, roast kid, lamb or pig's kidneys

Mature Margaret River cabernet merlot
Lamb fillet, roast leg of lamb with garlic and herbs

Cool-climate merlot
Lamb loin chops

Fully aged riesling
Chargrilled eggplant, stuffed capsicum

Mature grenache/rhône blends
Moroccan lamb

Rich, full-bodied Heathcote shiraz
Beef casserole

Southern Victorian pinot noir
Peking duck

Young muscat
Plum pudding

Winter

Dry oloroso sherry
Full-flavoured hors d'oeuvres

Sparkling Burgundy
Borscht, wild mushroom risotto

Viognier
Pea and ham soup

Aged (10+ years) semillon
Vichysoisse (hot)

Sauvignon blanc
Coquilles St Jacques (pan-fried scallops)

Chardonnay (10+ years)
Cassoulet

2–4-year-old semillon sauvignon blanc
Seafood pasta

Tasmanian pinot noir
Squab, duck breast

Mature pinot noir
Mushroom ragout, ravioli

Mature cool-grown shiraz viognier
Pot au feu

10-year-old Grampians shiraz
Chargrilled rump steak

15–20-year-old full-bodied Barossa shiraz
Venison, kangaroo fillet

Coonawarra cabernet sauvignon
Braised lamb shanks/shoulder

Muscat (rare)
Chocolate-based desserts

Topaque (rare)
Creme brûlée

Vintage fortified shiraz
Dried fruits, salty cheese

Australian vintage charts

Each number represents a mark out of 10 for the quality of vintages in each region.

red wine   white wine   fortified

2014 2015 2016 2017   2014 2015 2016 2017   2014 2015 2016 2017

NSW

Hunter Valley

2014	2015	2016	2017
10	5	6	8
7	6	7	9

Mudgee

2014	2015	2016	2017
7	9	8	7
9	8	9	6

Orange

2014	2015	2016	2017
5	9	8	7
7	9	7	8

Canberra District

2014	2015	2016	2017
7	10	9	9
8	10	9	8

Hilltops

2014	2015	2016	2017
9	8	9	9
9	8	8	7

Southern Highlands

2014	2015	2016	2017
7	6	8	6
7	8	8	6

Tumbarumba

2014	2015	2016	2017
9	7	8	9
8	9	9	8

Riverina/Griffith

2014	2015	2016	2017
7	8	7	8
8	8	7	8

Shoalhaven

2014	2015	2016	2017
9	7	8	7
9	8	8	8

VIC

Yarra Valley

2014	2015	2016	2017
7	10	7	8
8	9	7	8

Mornington Peninsula

2014	2015	2016	2017
9	10	8	8
9	9	7	9

Geelong

2014	2015	2016	2017
8	10	7	8
7	9	8	7

Macedon Ranges

2014	2015	2016	2017
8	9	8	7
8	8	9	8

Sunbury

2014	2015	2016	2017
9	8	7	x
8	7	7	x

Gippsland

2014	2015	2016	2017
5	9	8	9
9	9	8	9

Bendigo

2014	2015	2016	2017
9	8	8	8
7	8	8	7

Heathcote

2014	2015	2016	2017
8	8	9	7
7	7	8	7

Grampians

2014	2015	2016	2017
9	8	6	9
9	8	7	8

Pyrenees

2014	2015	2016	2017
8	7	7	8
9	8	7	8

Henty

2014	2015	2016	2017
9	10	10	5
10	9	10	8

Beechworth

2014	2015	2016	2017
8	8	8	7
8	9	8	7

Nagambie Lakes

2014	2015	2016	2017
8	8	8	8
8	9	9	7

Upper Goulburn

2014	2015	2016	2017
9	9	8	7
9	7	9	9

Strathbogie Ranges

2014	2015	2016	2017
6	8	7	7
7	8	7	7

King Valley

2014	2015	2016	2017
7	9	7	8
9	8	8	10

Alpine Valleys

2014	2015	2016	2017
7	10	6	9
8	9	6	10

Glenrowan

2014	2015	2016	2017
9	8	8	7
7	7	9	7

Rutherglen

2014	2015	2016	2017
7	9	7	6
x	9	9	6

Murray Darling

2014	2015	2016	2017
8	9	7	7
8	7	8	8

SA

	2014	2015	2016	2017
Barossa Valley				
	7	9	8	7
	7	8	7	8
Eden Valley				
	8	9	8	7
	8	10	9	10
Clare Valley				
	8	9	8	8
	8	9	9	9
Adelaide Hills				
	8	9	8	8
	8	10	7	9
McLaren Vale				
	7	8	8	9
	8	8	7	8
Southern Fleurieu				
	8	7	8	9
	8	6	8	8
Langhorne Creek				
	9	9	9	8
	8	7	7	7
Kangaroo Island				
	8	8	9	8
	9	8	9	9
Adelaide Plains				
	7	8	9	8
	7	8	8	8
Coonawarra				
	8	9	9	7
	8	8	8	9

	2014	2015	2016	2017
Wrattonbully				
	9	9	10	9
	8	9	10	9
Padthaway				
	8	9	x	8
	9	9	x	8
Mount Benson & Robe				
	9	10	8	7
	9	9	9	9
Riverland				
	8	9	8	7
	8	8	7	8

WA

	2014	2015	2016	2017
Margaret River				
	8	8	9	8
	9	9	9	8
Great Southern				
	8	8	8	7
	8	8	9	9
Manjimup				
	9	8	6	7
	8	7	7	8
Pemberton				
	9	6	8	7
	9	8	9	9
Geographe				
	9	7	8	8
	8	7	8	8

	2014	2015	2016	2017
Peel				
	8	x	8	x
	8	x	7	x
Perth Hills				
	8	9	9	9
	10	9	8	9
Swan Valley				
	8	7	6	6
	8	8	7	7

QLD

	2014	2015	2016	2017
Granite Belt				
	9	8	8	6
	8	8	7	9
South Burnett				
	8	8	x	8
	7	8	x	8

TAS

	2014	2015	2016	2017
Northern Tasmania				
	8	8	8	8
	9	8	8	7
Southern Tasmania				
	9	9	8	9
	9	9	8	9

Australian vintage 2018: a snapshot

Vintage 2018 was in two halves, December 31 the turning point. Despite a late budburst (later even than '17), moon watchers pointing to two full moons in March were right in forecasting an early vintage. Rainfall up to December 31 was good, conditions overall mild, and flowering in all regions was good. Thereafter the rain disappeared and the weather became erratic, the potential for large crops seldom achieved. For many regions the second half of the growing season had a start–stop–start pattern, with heat spikes (relatively short but severe) followed by cooler weather, and disease pressure needing vigilance. Once autumn arrived, conditions for late ripening varieties were perfect.

SOUTH AUSTRALIA

The **Barossa Valley** was affected by some protracted hot weather in January and February, causing the vines to shut down, and it took time for ripening to pick up the pace after the conclusion of the heatwaves in early March. Once it did, the second half of March and through to the end of April provided perfect ripening conditions, with shiraz and grenache showing particular promise, with great colour and flavour. **Eden Valley** and **Clare Valley** riesling will be site specific, the higher and/or cooler sites performing best. One conservative vigneron rates 2018 as the fourth consecutive exceptionally good riesling vintage, close in quality to the great '17 vintage. The **Adelaide Hills**, normally a haven, required vigilance to reduce stress and keep a healthy canopy. The Indian summer at the end of March and early April put the ship back on course, and chardonnay, pinot noir and shiraz are the standout varieties. Overall quality is strong, comparable to '13 and '16. **Adelaide Plains** inevitably had to manage some very high temperatures once the new year rolled by. Overall, yields will be 20–30% down, red wines faring best with great colour and depth of flavour. For **McLaren Vale**, the standout was a disappearance of rain after the '17 year. From October to March 30% of the average rainfall was experienced, and there were higher maximum and minimum temperatures compared to normal. The vines managed to survive these challenges, although smaller berry size will be reasonably widespread. One noted producer was honest enough to suggest that red wines will be deeply coloured but may lack richness. The other common feature was periods of heat, followed by cooler weather in which the vines simply remained quasi-dormant. **Langhorne Creek** has its vast water-based air conditioning system that largely buffered the heat spikes that caused problems elsewhere in southeastern Australia. Rainfall was low (no disease pressure) but enough to sustain vine health. Cabernet sauvignon and petit verdot, with moderate yields of excellent quality, are the standouts. From the last few days of December until 13 April, not a single drop of rain fell in **Kangaroo Island**. Combined with 10 days of temperatures peaking over 40°C, things looked pretty desperate until the conditions cooled down at the end of February; thereafter the vines recovered very slowly, coupled with a slow increase in baumes. In the Limestone Coast zone, **Coonawarra** expects the vintage will produce 50% of normal volume, combining fruit losses from the November 4 frost and poor set from the cold conditions. **Mount Benson** and **Robe** think that 10% will be lost overall, some vignerons suffering more than others. Reports from **Padthaway** range form no impact to more than 10%, the latter case depending on frost protection measures being in place. **Wrattonbully** is ecstatic about the vintage. There is, however, uniformity in the expectations of highly aromatic and fresh white varieties (sauvignon blanc and chardonnay standouts), remembering that some regions have negligible plantings of white varieties. The expectation from all is that cabernet sauvignon, cabernet franc and shiraz will all produce intensely coloured and intensely flavoured wines with controlled tannin and extract. The November 4 frost extended as far as the Grampians to the east of the Limestone Coast. **Riverland** had an armchair ride, the weather up to harvest very favourable after a cool and wet spring. The yields are average, with a good balance between berry size and quantit. The best varieties are chardonnay and shiraz, the overall quality very good thanks to very low disease pressure.

VICTORIA

Yarra Valley followed the vintage in two halves: a cool and relatively moist winter and spring needing disease control, thereafter conditions obstinately dry through to the conclusion of vintage. Chardonnay (as ever) was the standout. The **Mornington Peninsula** had a vintage set to show special quality and quantity – the best for the past 30 years, comparable to 2004. Need for shoot and bunch thinning and, if done expeditiously, the result was fruit of great purity and quality. **Geelong** was cool to December 31, with heat rising in a dry January and February. Moderate yields, with very good chardonnay and pinot noir (the latter especially in **Ballarat**, too), shiraz strong in Geelong. In **Gippsland** there was very good fruit set which promised generous yields, and rain fell when needed. A first class outcome across all varieties. The **Macedon Ranges** had average winter and spring rain, then a wet January (twice average) that required strict disease control. February was dry and, through to the end of vintage, had perfect sunny weather (no sunburn issues). Pinot noir was very, very good, with thick skins requiring gentle vinification. **Bendigo** stuck precisely to form for the vintage, the weather in two halves. Shiraz was definitely the standout, overall quality very high, yields variable. **Heathcote** had a mild and wet spring, which led to very good fruit set. There were average yields due to lower than normal bunch weights. Shiraz was the standout with lovely colour and intensity. **Grampians** had a perfect spring, then the November 4 frost caused severe damage on lower altitude vineyards. It was a stop-start January, with some hot days, then cooler in February. Riesling was the standout, with high natural acidity. **Henty** had an utterly exceptional vintage, making it necessary to go back to 1988 to find one comparable. Early Easter (two full moons) provided a warm March and perfect weather to conclusion. A dry, very warm start set the pattern for the **Pyrenees**, thereafter the only issue was applying sufficient water for optimal ripening. Moderate yields, with shiraz and cabernet sauvignon the standouts. **Beechworth** precisely reflected the pre/post change in the weather, with significant rainfall before the new year, thereafter almost none. January provided a relatively brief heatwave, then cool conditions until a very warm beginning to April resulted in exceptional Bordeaux and Italian varieties plus the usual chardonnay. A dry and warm spring with perfect fruit set in **Nagambie Lakes** was followed by two days of rain in early December, leading to a sea of verdant, almost fluorescent, green vineyards. Very good white wines, good to excellent reds. **Strathbogie Ranges** was calm and steady, a complete contrast to the chaos of '17. Winds in late summer and early autumn was the only issue of any kind. Shiraz and cabernet sauvignon did best. Pinot gris and gewurztraminer are the standouts for **Upper Goulburn** in a year with average yield, some disease pressure after December rainfall the only issue. **Alpine Valleys** had sunny days and even temperatures during ripening, which led to an early start, with crops generally down, but overall quality very high and natural acidity excellent. The standouts among many are chardonnay, vermentino, friulano, pinot blanc, arneis, tempranillo and shiraz. Late budburst in the **King Valley** was followed by an early summer catch- up, with December rainfall leading to some disease pressure. January was dry and warm, downy mildew disappeared and vintage from that point on was perfect except for lighter bunch weights. Standouts are cabernet sauvignon, shiraz and prosecco. **Glenrowan** and **Rutherglen** had a trouble-free vintage that ran to a normal timetable, the standout varieties muscat and shiraz, topaque not far behind.

NEW SOUTH WALES

The headline came from one vigneron who said, '**Hunter Valley** vignerons are happy when it doesn't rain, and we certainly haven't had much in the past 10 months'. No surprise then that the flags are being run out for the 2018 shiraz; comparisons to '14 abound. Semillon was more of a mixed bag, with dry weather and high temperatures: '03 a similar vintage. Overall yields were down, just as quality was high. **Upper Hunter** started dry and finished dry, with no rain in between − one of the driest in living memory. Quality good. Yields not. **Orange** had 33% of the long-term average rain for winter, and only 73% of the 12-month average. Irrigation was essential. Vintage followed very warm and generally stable weather right through to the end. Then − in best Australian bush folk speak − apart from a smattering of annoying hailstorms and a major bushfire, everything was fine. Yields were moderate, chardonnay the best white, shiraz, merlot and cabernet sauvignon the reds to stand up. Overall quality 'better than '17'. To say the weather in the **Canberra District** was unsettled from September '17 through to February '18 is an understatement, with periods of drought, heavy rain, hailstorms, etc. A warm, dry March, following the last week of February, was ideal, making harvesting ever so easy. Fruit quality excellent; riesling and shiraz viognier outstanding. One region elder said, 'We're looking at a truly great year, the closest parallel being '09.' Spring in **Hilltops** started with very cool temperatures and, even when summer arrived, the temperature range through December, January, February, March and April ranged between low teens and maximums in the mid-20s. The growing degree days total was low for the region. Rain at the right time helped promote vine growth, but all went well, with harvest conditions ideal with minimum rain. All red varieties, including shiraz and cabernet sauvignon, have intense colour; sangiovese and nebbiolo are the standouts for the vintage. **Tumbarumba** had a warm and dry growing season, which was balanced by some late summer rain to rejuvenate the vines. Moderate yields of high quality chardonnay and pinot noir are the standouts. Alternating periods of dry weather and summer storms in the **Southern Highlands** resulted in low yields and a vintage that was ultimately saved by a dry, warm March. Albarino, pinot gris, pinot noir and tempranillo are the standouts. **Shoalhaven Coast** experienced warm and dry summer conditions to set up one of the best vintages of the last 20 years, with next to no disease pressure in a region usually challenged by humidity. Yields were moderate to high, the quality excellent across the range, with riesling, semillon, savagnin and tannat the standouts. **Riverina** had a trouble-free, high quality vintage, with all fruit picked prior to the end of March, a month earlier than in '17. Quality was equally good for white and red varieties.

WESTERN AUSTRALIA

Margaret River performed as usual so far as the weather was concerned, with rain heavy in winter (20% above average), below average for spring, and with perfect growing conditions through December and on into late February, with only five days above 30°C. One vigneron reported, 'Beautiful clarity and purity of fruit; incredibly expressive wines from [their] site; depth and concentration with power, yet elegance and high natural acidity. Epic vintage.' All subregions within the **Great Southern** reported an outstanding vintage, with fairly consistent growing season conditions across the very large region. Thus all had a wet winter with the soil profile totally full by spring. Once the growing season was in full swing, very good flowering conditions were followed by a vintage virtually free of heat spikes, in stark contrast to the conditions in the eastern half of Australia. Average to slightly above average yields were the outcome, exceptional for all varieties, the cool and dry weather allowing vignerons to pick and choose the days they would harvest. Winter rainfall in **Manjimup** was close to the long-term average, but thereafter was above average, ensuring the dams were full and there was adequate water in the soils to carry the grapes through to maturity. Conditions were cooler than usual, and this, coupled with rainfall, meant that powdery mildew was an ever-present threat needing rigorous control. Botrytis was also an issue as sugar level rose. The situation changed radically with perfect autumn conditions, cool and dry. More elegant varieties, including sauvignon blanc, riesling and pinot noir, are the standouts. **Pemberton** reflected the weather of Manjimup, with rainfall spread throughout the growing season. The weather then changed radically, with conditions through March and April cool and dry, allowing the final ripening process without any threat. The overall quality is very high, the two standouts chardonnay and shiraz. **Geographe** shared in the bounty of a near-perfect growing season: rain when it was needed, warmth when required, and a ceiling on the warmth with few or no heat spikes. The marri blossom was extraordinary, thus birds presented no issues whatsoever. Yields were low to moderate, but exceptional quality made up for the lower yield. Despite all the promise of the vintage stemming from long-term average rainfall through winter and near-perfect spring conditions, the **Swan Valley** experienced a tropical storm with more than 60mm of rain falling on January 16, which changed the outlook dramatically. There was some damage, with chenin blanc in particular suffering from grape splitting and bunch rot, and some vineyards also suffered significant bird damage. Thereafter the summer was mild with an unusual absence of heatwaves, yields were average, and everything ran like clockwork. In the outcome, the general view is this was one of the best vintages in the region for many years, with deep coloured, perfumed red wines that are the best seen in decades. Shiraz, verdelho and chenin blanc also fared well. For **Perth Hills** all the rain fell at precisely the right time, and the growing season through to harvest was mild. Zero heatwaves and zero days above 40°C made this one of the mildest summers on record. Excellent to outstanding viognier, shiraz and petit verdot, yield (down somewhat) the only cause for complaint.

TASMANIA

East Coast Tasmania received 16% of its normal winter rainfall, and barely one-third of its average spring rainfall. A cold start in spring was followed by warming, with flowering occurring quickly under ideal conditions. Well-formed bunches with no hen–and–chicken resulted in moderate to high yields. The rain stayed away until the first week of December, with 115mm of rain, followed by 20mm more not long after. Summer continued warm overall with a cool spell in February, following 31mm of rain at the end of January. Despite the higher yields, all varieties ripened earlier than usual, with excellent flavour intensity, ideal baumes and soft acidities. It seems quite possible the year will disprove the view that high yields are incompatible with high quality. **Northern Tasmania** followed the pattern of the East Coast, with a high yielding year for most producers. The standout varieties are chardonnay and pinot noir, but it's probable that all varieties in all areas will perform well. **Southern Tasmania** also followed suit, with a cold start, then spring rapidly warming up, with no frost threats, and perfect weather for flowering (warm and dry). Apart from some early December rainfall, summer was dry and temperatures mild. Expectations are for an excellent year for chardonnay, and a good year for pinot noir.

QUEENSLAND

Granite Belt's season started well with good spring rainfall and cool days. Vineyards were carrying above average yields, but looked balanced. An early heatwave caused ripening to accelerate, provided water was available. Then a series of small hailstorms hit isolated pockets with varying ferocity; Golden Grove Estate bore the brunt, losing between 10% and 70% in most varieties. Apart from the hail, the vintage looks good, with some gems including vermentino, malbec and tempranillo. **South Burnett** told a similar story, albeit with different causes. Low winter and spring rainfall was no problem, and up to and into the halfway point of vintage, everything was perfect.

The tasting team

Campbell Mattinson
Campbell is an award-winning Australian journalist, author, editor and publisher. He has been a key reviewer for the *Wine Companion* for many years, is the publisher of the WINEFRONT website and the author of *The Big Red Wine Book* and *The Wine Hunter*.

David Bicknell
David is a Roseworthy college graduate with more than 30 vintages of experience in both Australia and France. He is a co-founder of the Victorian Pinot Noir Workshop, a past dux of the Len Evans Tutorial, a *Gourmet Traveller* Winemaker of the Year, and he has judged, panel chaired and chaired at many Australian wine shows. He fills his spare time growing wine for his own family label, Applecross.

Jane Faulkner
Jane is a respected journalist with more than 25 years' experience. She has a special interest in Italian and alternative varieties, chairs several wine shows and is chief of judges for the Australian Alternative Varieties Wine Show. Aside from her love of wine, Jane is an avid traveller and zealous environmentalist.

Ned Goodwin MW
Ned has worn many hats, including show judge, dux of the Len Evans Tutorial, sommelier, educator, TV host, wine buyer, consultant, critic and writer. Born in London, raised in Australia, educated in France and Japan, and now based in Sydney with continued business across Asia, his varied international experience brings a fresh perspective to the *Wine Companion* tasting team.

Steven Creber
Steven's career in wine started in the vineyards and small wineries of the Yarra Valley in the 1970s. Over the next 10 years he worked in North East Victoria, Sunraysia, the Barossa Valley and Coonawarra in various production roles. He then spent 20-odd years, until 2012, as a taster, buyer and copywriter with Dan Murphy's. Since then, he has been a Yarra Valley–based consultant, adviser and writer for a number of retailers, wholesalers and winemakers.

Tyson Stelzer
Tyson is a multi-award winning wine writer, television host and producer, author of 16 wine books, international keynote speaker and wine show chairman and judge. An accomplished presenter, Tyson has 13 years' experience presenting at international events in nine countries. He has been named the International Wine & Spirit Communicator of the Year and the Australian Wine Communicator of the Year.

Acknowledgements

Time waits for no (wo)man, least of all for myself. So I had to pick up my pen to write these words – one-finger typing on iPhone or iPad is incredibly slow, and correcting mistakes on it carries the danger of losing part or all of my painful typing. Dictation used to be my salvation, with mini tapes and simple analog rewind doing exactly what I wanted. But now there are dozens of unwanted, incomprehensible features, reducing me to a gibbering wreck. It's proof positive that I turn 80 within days of the publication of this book.

The passing days, weeks, months, years disappear through my fingers like a stream of sand. And I am unbelievably lucky that I have Paula Grey, who for more than a quarter of a century has been there to pick up phone calls from people with an urgent need to speak to me – after that, they'll instantly no longer need to discuss anything with me. Beth Anthony joined Paula 18 years ago, and has a photographic memory of every one of the thousands of boxes she has opened to enter the wines into the database, and an eagle eye for the discrepancies between winery/wine/winemaker/vintage information supplied and what is on the bottle's label. Beth simultaneously sets up the day's tastings and stewards for me throughout each day.

Ten years ago I crossed the bridge of not personally tasting all the wines, simply because there has to be a team in place that can function without me when the bus in the sky falls on me. Finding tasters to replace me would be difficult, but far from impossible; and the invisible threads that have held the *Wine Companion* team in place for all these years are another thing again. My most sincere thanks to this year's team of Campbell Mattinson, Ned Goodwin, Jane Faulkner and Steven Creber, who collectively tasted 4692 of this year's 9289 wines.

Tasting six days a week, 10 hours a day, for the final three months of the book is immeasurably tiring, but worse is to come. As the book takes form in the office, Paula, Beth and I are variously proofreading, chasing gaps in information across three printouts of the book pages, with non-negotiable deadlines – these are the months of hell.

The team at Hardie Grant is headed by Sandy Grant, who was solely responsible for having the faith to create the joint venture for all platforms of the *Wine Companion*, my heartfelt thanks to him is ever-present.

My special thanks also to soft-spoken Senior Editor Loran McDougall, who weathered my diatribes without complaint, never pointing out she was also dealing with books on the Christmas list with their own deadlines. To Rachel Pitts (Editor) and Geraldine Stallard (Project Editor), who had to deal with the arcane language of grapegrowing and winemaking, as well as the cross-referencing of never-ending facts and figures within each winery's entry. And to Megan Ellis, whose magic wand in typesetting the *Wine Companion* in the blink of an eye continues to amaze me.

My thanks to Tracy and Alan at the Coldstream Post Office, who receive the tsunami of wine boxes every year. And even more do I thank the wineries who sent those boxes in the first place. Without them, there'd be no *Wine Companion*.

Australian wineries
and wines

A note on alphabetical order
Wineries beginning with 'The' are listed under 'T'; for example,
'The Lane Vineyard'. Winery names that include a numeral are treated
as if the numeral is spelt out; for example, '2 Mates'
is listed under 'T'.

A. Rodda Wines

PO Box 589, Beechworth, Vic 3747 **Region** Beechworth
T 0400 350 135 **www**.aroddawines.com.au **Open** Not
Winemaker Adrian Rodda **Est.** 2010 **Dozens** 800 **Vyds** 2ha
Adrian Rodda has been winemaking since 1998, almost entirely working with David Bicknell
at Oakridge. He was involved in the development of the superb Oakridge 864 Chardonnay, his
final contribution to 864 coming in 2009. At the start of 2010 he and wife Christie, a doctor,
decided to move to Beechworth, and it was no coincidence that he was a long-term friend
of viticulturist Mark Walpole. More coincidences came with the Smiths vineyard and winery
being available for lease; he now shares it with Mark, who makes his Beechworth wines there.
Even more propitious was the availability of Smiths vineyard chardonnay, planted in 1974.

🍷🍷🍷🍷🍷 **Willow Lake Vineyard Yarra Valley Chardonnay 2017** Here the intensity of
the wine on the palate is expressed through the mouthwatering grapefruit flavours.
The Smiths Vineyard and Baxendale Vineyard all have unmistakable signatures –
chardonnay isn't being used to do tricks, this is terroir (in the full sense of that
term) speaking loud and clear. Screwcap. 13% alc. **Rating** 96 **To** 2027 $42 ✪
Smiths Vineyard Beechworth Chardonnay 2017 Purity combines with
excellent mouthfeel and varietal fruit – this vineyard is one of Australia's best for
chardonnay. The acidity is slippery, adhering to the roof of the mouth to create a
tension between the tongue and the palate. Screwcap. 13% alc. **Rating** 96 **To** 2027
$42 ✪
Beechworth Cuvee de Chez 2016 66% cabernet sauvignon dominant,
with merlot, malbec, cabernet franc and petit verdot, all fermented and matured
differently, all coming from the celebrated Smiths vineyard. There are rivulets of
delicious red fruits running down the palate, ending with a hosanna of wild herbs
that provide contrast. Screwcap. 14% alc. **Rating** 96 **To** 2031 $38 ✪
Baxendale Vineyard Whitlands Chardonnay 2017 The first impression is
the great length of the wine, its extreme focus next. There is a palpable restraint
that makes it easy to understand why Whitlands grapes have been chiefly used for
sparkling wine, arguably the most reflective of its place. The A. Rodda chardonnays
make a great trio – few comparisons of this nature succeed so well. Screwcap.
13% alc. **Rating** 95 **To** 2027 $42

🍷🍷🍷🍷♀ **Aquila Audax Vineyard Tempranillo 2016 Rating** 92 **To** 2031 $38

A.T. Richardson Wines

103 Hard Hill Road, Armstrong, Vic 3377 **Region** Great Western
T 0438 066 477 **www**.atrichardsonwines.com **Open** Not
Winemaker Adam Richardson **Est.** 2005 **Dozens** 2000 **Vyds** 7ha
Perth-born Adam Richardson began his winemaking career in 1995, working for Normans,
d'Arenberg and Oakridge along the way. He has held senior winemaking roles, ultimately
with TWE America before moving back to Australia with wife Eva and children in late 2015.
In '05 he had put down roots in the Grampians region, establishing a vineyard with shiraz
from old clones from the 19th century, and riesling, extending the plantings with tannat and
nebbiolo. The wines are exceptionally good, no surprise given his experience and the quality
of the vineyard. He has also set up a wine consultancy business, drawing on experience that
is matched by few consultants in Australia. Exports to Europe.

🍷🍷🍷🍷🍷 **Hard Hill Road Great Western Durif 2016** Amazing colour (opaque purple-
red). Dense, ripe black fruit, a faint sauvage note and spice. Concentrated and
controlled with a web of green apple acidity and fine tannin. Whatever oak it has
seen, it has just sucked it up. Big, fresh, maybe brutal, but so well done. Amazing
durif. Screwcap. **Rating** 96 **To** 2035 $50 DB ✪
Chockstone Grampians Riesling 2017 I'm guilty of not always including
the Grampians as a high quality regional producer of riesling in Australia-wide
comparisons. The perfumed bouquet of lime and apple blossom leads into a long,
mouthwatering burst of lime/lemon, with crisp acidity the icing on the cake.
Screwcap. 11.5% alc. **Rating** 95 **To** 2032 $21 ✪

Chockstone Grampians Shiraz 2016 The brooding black fruits, licorice, spice and graphite of the bouquet speak truly of the intense yet elegant, medium to full-bodied palate. The tannins are fine, the oak a servant, the finish long and impeccably balanced. Screwcap. 14.5% alc. **Rating** 95 **To** 2036 $25 ☻

Hard Hill Road Great Western Shiraz 2016 Dark purple-red. There's a real sense of density here. Ripe blackcurrant drifting into cassis and raspberry essence. Ripeness, opulence of fruit, oak support, brightness and line. All the boxes ticked. Screwcap. **Rating** 95 **To** 2030 $50 DB

🍷🍷🍷🍷🍷 **Chockstone Grampians Pinot Gris 2017** **Rating** 93 **To** 2020 $21 ☻
Chockstone Grampians Rose 2017 **Rating** 90 **To** 2020 $21 ☻

Abbey Creek Vineyard   ★★★★★

2388 Porongurup Road, Porongurup, WA 6324 **Region** Porongurup
T (08) 9853 1044 **Open** By appt
Winemaker Castle Rock Estate (Robert Diletti) **Est.** 1990 **Dozens** 1000 **Vyds** 1.6ha
This is the family business of Mike and Mary Dilworth, the name coming from a winter creek that runs alongside the vineyard and the view of The Abbey in the Stirling Range. The vineyard is split between pinot noir, riesling and sauvignon blanc. The rieslings have had significant show success for a number of years.

🍷🍷🍷🍷🍷 **Museum Release Porongurup Riesling 2010** Still pale straw-green, which is amazing; this has the rare marriage of what seems to be youth and limitless power. It has developed to the point that now and over the next 10 years it will relish the challenge of any Chinese or seafood dish you choose to get into (gustatory) bed with. Screwcap. 12.5% alc. **Rating** 97 **To** 2040 $35 ☻

🍷🍷🍷🍷🍷 **Porongurup Riesling 2017** This is a prime example of the ability of riesling to combine ultimate delicacy with intensity. It is glorious now in its vibrant youth, but will have two more lives as adolescent (5-7yo) and adult (10-20+yo). Each will be different, each beautiful. Screwcap. 11% alc. **Rating** 96 **To** 2032 $25 ☻

Museum Release Porongurup Riesling 2013 What has the wine got left in its tank? Look at the tasting note I made after tasting the '10. Screwcap. 12.5% alc. **Rating** 96 **To** 2033 $30 ☻

Porongurup Riesling 2016 Still available (at the same price as when first tasted in Sept '16) and still morphing towards adolescence. If either this wine or its '13 sibling has any time to change for the better, simply look at the last six vintages. Screwcap. 11.8% alc. **Rating** 95 **To** 2031 $25 ☻

Porongurup Pinot Noir 2016 Super bright crimson-purple; a scented bouquet of violets, spice and red flowers leads into a perfectly weighted and structured palate, rich with red cherry and plum fruit. Lovely now, but will grow its aromatics and flavour wheel over the next 10 years, supported by its fine tannins and subtle French oak. Screwcap. 13% alc. **Rating** 95 **To** 2028 $30 ☻

Porongurup Pinot Noir 2013 Still delicious, the colour light but bright; in a holding pattern, or, if you prefer, on the plateau. It won't improve because it doesn't need to, but it's not going to crash. The drink-to date (and points) given by Campbell Mattinson in Jan '15 are still on the money. Screwcap. 13.5% alc. **Rating** 94 **To** 2021 $35

🍷🍷🍷🍷🍷 **Porongurup Sauvignon Blanc 2017** **Rating** 91 **To** 2020 $24
Museum Release Porongurup Pinot Noir 2011 **Rating** 90 **To** 2020 $35

After Hours Wine   ★★★★☆

455 North Jindong Road, Carbunup, WA 6285 **Region** Margaret River
T 0438 737 587 **www.**afterhourswine.com.au **Open** Fri–Mon 10–4
Winemaker Phil Potter **Est.** 2006 **Dozens** 3000 **Vyds** 8.6ha
In 2005 Warwick and Cherylyn Mathews acquired the long-established Hopelands vineyard, planted to cabernet sauvignon (2.6ha), shiraz (1.6ha), merlot, semillon, sauvignon blanc and chardonnay (1.1ha each). The first wine was made in '06, after which they decided to

completely rework the vineyard, which required many hours of physical labour. The vines were retrained, with a consequent reduction in yield and rise in wine quality and value.

ΨΨΨΨΨ **Margaret River Chardonnay 2016** There is an Australian Cool Climate Wine Show founded by the winemakers of Murrumbateman, and a National Cool Climate Wine Show founded by the winemakers of Bathurst, and this wine won a gold medal at each in '17. The wine does in fact have considerable richness, and has been well made, with a display of white peach varietal fruit and citrussy acidity drawing out the long finish. There's a world of difference between this and the 9 to 5 Chardonnay '17. Screwcap. 13% alc. **Rating** 95 **To** 2026 $30 ✪

ΨΨΨΨΨ **Oliver Margaret River Shiraz 2016 Rating** 92 **To** 2029 $28
P.J. Margaret River Cabernet Sauvignon 2016 Rating 90 **To** 2026 $30

Alkimi Wines   ★★★★

11 View Street, Healesville, Vic 3777 (postal) **Region** Yarra Valley
T 0410 234 688 **www.**alkimiwines.com **Open** Not
Winemaker Stuart Dudine **Est.** 2014 **Dozens** 450 **Vyds** 0.5ha
The name is taken from the phonetic spelling of alchemy, the medieval concept of transmuting base metals into gold and similar works of magic. It's somehow appropriate for owner/winemaker Stuart Dudine, because there are unexplained gaps in his wine journey. We do know that he worked with Emmerich Knoll (a particularly gifted winemaker) in Austria, and with Stephane Ogier and Chateau Mont-Redon in France. His love of the Rhône Valley sprang from his time at Henschke, working with syrah, grenache and mourvedre. Since 2012 he has been based in the Yarra Valley, working (inter alia) for Yarra Yering, Oakridge and Mac Forbes. His overall raison d'être is to find vineyard parcels that perform exceptionally well in their patch of soil, year in and year out no matter the season.

ΨΨΨΨΨ **The Good Earth Yarra Valley Syrah Rose 2017** Grown on the Rising vineyard. Juicy pomegranate, blood orange and strawberry flavours create a mouthwatering impression, dry spice and wood smoke notes drifting gently through the finish. It's complex without being in-your-face about it. Dryness is key here. Screwcap. 12.7% alc. **Rating** 93 **To** 2020 $27 CM ✪
Yarra Valley Syrah 2016 This is a tangy, medium-weight-at-most red with cranberry, red cherry, gun smoke and orange-like characters. Indeed the latter notes are quite prominent on the nose; as light as this wine is, it feels exotic, nuanced even. Screwcap. 13.2% alc. **Rating** 92 **To** 2024 $32 CM
Upper Goulburn Grenache 2017 Rose-like, though slightly heavier than that, just. It's dry and spicy with stringy tannin and good length. Cherries, pips, stewed plums, woodsy notes. Some spritz too. Far more length than breadth. It takes a while to get your head around it but for a (very) light style it's good. Screwcap. 13% alc. **Rating** 90 **To** 2023 $32 CM
Geelong Mourvedre 2017 It's light, spicy and firm, and is served super fresh, though savouriness is arguably its main shtick. The general style of the Alkimi range could see them become known as the Fresh Wine People. 'Sinewy' comes to mind as you sip on this. Screwcap. 13.5% alc. **Rating** 90 **To** 2021 $32 CM

Alkoomi   ★★★★★

Wingebellup Road, Frankland River, WA 6396 **Region** Frankland River
T (08) 9855 2229 **www.**alkoomiwines.com.au **Open** 7 days 10–5
Winemaker Andrew Cherry **Est.** 1971 **Dozens** 80 000 **Vyds** 164ha
Established in 1971 by Merv and Judy Lange, Alkoomi has grown from a single hectare to one of Western Australia's largest family-owned and operated wineries. Now owned by daughter Sandy Hallett, and her husband Rod, Alkoomi is continuing the tradition of producing high quality wines which showcase the Frankland River region. Alkoomi is actively reducing its environmental footprint; future plans will see the introduction of new varietals. Alkoomi operates cellar doors in Albany and at the winery (which also has a function centre). Exports to all major markets.

ŶŶŶŶŶ **Black Label Riesling 2017** Has the Frankland River signature of intensely focused fruit flavours in a citrus spectrum girdled by minerally acidity. The impact of the wine is so substantial it is almost painful, albeit in the best way. Screwcap. 12% alc. **Rating** 95 **To** 2032 $24 ✪

Jarrah Shiraz 2012 Alkoomi's top shiraz from 40yo vines. Only just into medium-bodied territory, but making up for any lack of weight by its elegance and balance. Gently savoury/spicy notes are sewn into the fabric of the wine, tannins trimming the very long finish. Screwcap. 14% alc. **Rating** 95 **To** 2037 $45

Black Label Cabernet Sauvignon 2016 Elegance is the byword of this cabernet that brings perfectly ripened flavours of cassis/blackcurrant in a gently flowing stream across the palate, with superfine tannins and cedary oak adding carefully calibrated complexity. Will provide enjoyment when young or mature. Screwcap. 14.5% alc. **Rating** 95 **To** 2031 $24 ✪

Black Label Malbec 2016 A most unexpected, although attractive, bouquet with dark chocolate immediately making its presence felt. It backs off to a degree on the blueberry/blackberry palate, warm spices also having their say. A major strength is the rounded tannin structure and the consequent mouthfeel. Screwcap. 14.5% alc. **Rating** 95 **To** 2031 $24 ✪

White Label Riesling 2017 Classic cool-grown riesling aromas, with blossoms of all kinds. The palate is a revelation, lime and lemon to the fore, coupled by minerally acidity that creates the length and freshness. The aftertaste lingers for an exceptionally long time. Screwcap. 12% alc. **Rating** 94 **To** 2027 $15 ✪

Melaleuca 2017 The highly perfumed, flowery bouquet sings of wild flowers, and it's not auto-suggestion from the name. Sweet and sour lime juice (not the least unpleasant) arrives on the palate, confirming this is indeed riesling, and with all the attitude its unusual personality suggests it should have. Screwcap. 12% alc. **Rating** 94 **To** 2022 $34

Wandoo 2014 Alkoomi has been making this fragrant semillon for many years, the mature vines and experience making this wine special. Vibrant Meyer lemon, lemongrass and integrated oak all sing from the same page, still as fresh as a daisy. Has considerable length. Screwcap. 11.5% alc. **Rating** 94 **To** 2024 $35

Black Label Sauvignon Blanc 2017 Very different from Margaret River sauvignon blanc, with a stainless-steel corset holding all the flavours in place, and indirectly imprinting a powerful message of pink grapefruit that allows herbal/grassy notes some room to play, but draws down the shutters on tropical fruits. Screwcap. 12% alc. **Rating** 94 **To** 2021 $24 ✪

ŶŶŶŶŶ **White Label Sauvignon Blanc 2017** Rating 92 To 2018 $15 CM ✪
White Label Semillon Sauvignon Blanc 2017 Rating 92 To 2019 $15 CM ✪
Black Label Shiraz Viognier 2016 Rating 92 To 2024 $24 ✪
Black Label Cabernet Franc 2016 Rating 92 To 2029 $24 ✪
White Label Cabernet Merlot 2016 Rating 91 To 2029 $15 ✪
White Label Late Harvest 2017 Rating 90 To 2023 $15 ✪

All Saints Estate   ★★★★★

All Saints Road, Wahgunyah, Vic 3687 **Region** Rutherglen
T 1800 021 621 **www**.allsaintswine.com.au **Open** Mon–Sat 9–5.30, Sun 10–5.30
Winemaker Nick Brown, Chloe Earl **Est.** 1864 **Dozens** 25 000 **Vyds** 33.46ha
The winery rating reflects the fortified wines and table wines alike. The one-hat Terrace restaurant makes this a must-stop for any visitor to North East Victoria, as does the National Trust–listed property with its towering castle centrepiece. All Saints and St Leonards are owned and managed by fourth-generation Brown family members Eliza, Angela and Nick. Eliza is an energetic and highly intelligent leader, wise beyond her years, and highly regarded by the wine industry. The Brown family celebrated the winery's 150th anniversary in 2014. Exports to the UK, the US, Canada, Singapore and China.

ΨΨΨΨΨ **Museum Rutherglen Muscadelle NV** Magic. Excellent walnut and plum-pudding colour with an olive-green tinge. What's extraordinary, given the museum release has an average age of 100+ years, is just how fresh it is. Toffee brittle flecked with lemon and orange zest, beautiful balance of tamarind tartness and freshness to the palm sugar sweetness. But the overall effect is not sweet, instead it's an exercise in complexity and depth of flavour. Breathe this, taste this and reflect on the century past. Vino-Lok. 18% alc. **Rating** 98 $1000 JF

Rutherglen Museum Muscat NV Extraordinary colour for its age (100+ years): a dark mahogany. Intense flavours of raisins and salted burnt toffee float across the palate. It's akin to seriously long-aged balsamic vinegar. If you're lucky enough to score a sip, a glass or a bottle, take time to savour every last drop. 500ml. Vino-Lok. 18% alc. **Rating** 98 $1000 JF

Rare Rutherglen Muscadelle NV Everything you could wish for from a rare muscadelle with a 50+ solera age: black tea, pomander, blood orange zest with a slight radicchio bitterness, which is complex, as is the umami flavour of salted caramel. And there's the requisite flavour of plum pudding. Beguiling. 375ml. Vino-Lok. 18% alc. **Rating** 97 $120 JF ◐

ΨΨΨΨΨ **Grand Rutherglen Tawny NV** An exceptional Grand because it balances the complexity of its age with freshness and vitality. Bright mid-amber hue with a touch of ruby to its rim. Offers lemon drops, cardamom, treacle and burnt toffee with more complex influences of freshly rolled tobacco and bitter herbs. It's smooth and lingers long. A treat. 375ml. Vino-Lok. 18% alc. **Rating** 96 $75 JF ◐

Grand Rutherglen Muscadelle NV Deep mahogany with an olive rim; this is a whorl of toffee plus coffee grounds and freshly baked malt loaf studded with raisins, charred chicory and salted chocolate. Very complex, rich, smooth and slippery. Wonderfully fresh. 375ml. Vino-Lok. 18% alc. **Rating** 96 $75 JF ◐

Rare Rutherglen Muscat NV With the solera at 50+yo, the flavours fall into another spectrum. Complex with umami influences of Vegemite, bitter chocolate, Pontefract licorice and panforte, plus currants and plum pudding. Smooth and unctuous. 375ml. Vino-Lok. 18% alc. **Rating** 96 $120 JF

Classic Rutherglen Muscadelle NV Walnut-dark amber; an average age of 15 years, one can really get a sense of what the estate is about with this. Complex flavours of toffee, molasses, cold tea and fruit cake. It is incredibly smooth with everything perfectly in place. Vino-Lok. 18% alc. **Rating** 95 $38 JF

Grand Rutherglen Muscat NV Dark mahogany with a slight olive rim; rich, voluptuous and slinky; layers of flavours from burnt toffee to caramels studded with dark chocolate and raisins, plus a chef's cupboard full of spices and dried herbs. Beautiful balance. 375ml. Vino-Lok. 18% alc. **Rating** 95 $75 JF

ΨΨΨΨΨ **Classic Rutherglen Muscat NV** Rating 93 $38 JF
Rosa 2017 Rating 92 To 2019 $32 JF
Family Cellar Shiraz 2015 Rating 92 To 2029 $62 JF
Durif 2016 Rating 92 To 2024 $32 JF
Rutherglen Muscadelle NV Rating 92 $25 JF ◐
Rutherglen Muscat NV Rating 91 $25 JF

Allandale Winery   ★★★★

132 Lovedale Road, Lovedale, NSW 2325 **Region** Hunter Valley
T (02) 4990 4526 **www.allandalewinery.com.au Open** Mon–Sat 9–5, Sun 10–5
Winemaker Bill Sneddon **Est.** 1978 **Dozens** 20 000 **Vyds** 6.47ha
In January 2016, Allandale was purchased by the Lee and Leung families, who had a long association with Allandale as its Hong Kong distributors. The winery and staff remained unchanged; together they are committed to sustaining the fine quality of wines for which Allandale has gained its reputation over four decades. Exports to the UK and Hong Kong.

ΨΨΨΨΨ **Winemaker's Reserve Hunter Valley Semillon 2014** Showing exceptionally well in the middle of its journey from adolescence to maturity. Citrus, herb and lemongrass are rolled into one totally satisfying stream of flavour, acidity evident but not the least abrasive. Screwcap. 11.5% alc. **Rating** 94 **To** 2029 $50

ΨΨΨΨ♀ Hunter Valley Semillon 2017 Rating 92 To 2029 $22 ○
Hunter Valley Chardonnay 2017 Rating 90 To 2021 $25

Allegiance Wines   ★★★★

Scenic Court, Alstonville, NSW 2477 **Region** Various
T 0434 561 718 **www**.allegiancewines.com.au **Open** Not
Winemaker Contract **Est.** 2009 **Dozens** 40 000
When Tim Cox established Allegiance Wines in 2009, he had the decided advantage of having worked across many facets of the Australian wine industry for almost 30 years – on both the sales and marketing side, and also on the supplier side with Southcorp. He started Cox Wine Merchants to act as distributor for Moppity Vineyards, and successfully partnered with Moppity for over 5 years. This is a virtual wine business, owning neither vineyards nor winery, either having wines made for the business or purchasing as cleanskins or as bulk wine. Exports to Singapore, Hong Kong and NZ.

ΨΨΨΨΨ Unity Margaret River Chardonnay 2017 Matured for 8 months. This is a pretty nifty example of the breed. Varietal character flirts with a 'too fine' criticism, but ultimately doesn't have a case to answer. Oak might have been on the plus side, but it too answers the challenge. You are left with a wine of finesse, length and balance with stone fruit and citrus both on the money. Screwcap. 12.5% alc. Rating 94 To 2025 $60

ΨΨΨΨ♀ Unity Barossa Valley Shiraz 2014 Rating 91 To 2031 $100
The Matron Tumbarumba Chardonnay 2016 Rating 90 To 2020 $25
The Artisan Barossa Valley Shiraz 2016 Rating 90 To 2029 $60
The Artisan Margaret River Cabernet 2013 Rating 90 To 2033 $60
The Fighter McLaren Vale Tempranillo 2016 Rating 90 To 2019 $25

Allies Wines   ★★★★★

15 Hume Road, Somers, Vic 3927 **Region** Mornington Peninsula
T 0412 111 587 **www**.allies.com.au **Open** By appt
Winemaker David Chapman **Est.** 2003 **Dozens** 1000 **Vyds** 3.1ha
A former chef and sommelier, David Chapman began Allies in 2003 while working at Moorooduc Estate. He makes pinot noir, emphasising the diversity of the Mornington Peninsula by making a number of wines sourced from different districts. David spends much of his time in the vineyard, working to ensure well exposed and positioned bunches, to achieve ripe, pure flavours and supple tannins. His winemaking focuses on simple techniques that retain concentration and character: no added yeasts, and no fining or filtration, are standard practices. Production of wines is small and will probably remain that way, given that any expansion will limit the number of vines David can personally tend. Exports to Hong Kong.

ΨΨΨΨΨ Assemblage Mornington Peninsula Pinot Noir 2017 The label text uses the word 'silky' and it couldn't be more right. This is sheer pinot noir, its foresty, cherried flavours made tense by spice, acid and tannin but kept flowing and free thanks to the velvet of its texture. It's a terrific wine. Screwcap. 12.8% alc. Rating 96 To 2025 $30 CM ○

Allinda   ★★★★☆

119 Lorimers Lane, Dixons Creek, Vic 3775 **Region** Yarra Valley
T (03) 5965 2450 **www**.allindawinery.com.au **Open** W'ends & public hols 11–5
Winemaker Al Fencaros **Est.** 1991 **Dozens** 8000 **Vyds** 3ha
Winemaker Al Fencaros has a Bachelor of Wine Science (CSU) and was formerly employed by De Bortoli in the Yarra Valley. Al's grandparents made wine in Hungary and Serbia, and Al's father continued to make wine after migrating to Australia in the early 1960s. The vineyard is now 28 years old, and is managed without the use of chemical fertilisers, herbicides or

pesticides. All of the Allinda wines are produced onsite; all except the Shiraz (from Heathcote) are estate-grown from a little over 3ha of vineyards. Limited retail distribution in Melbourne and Sydney. Exports to China.

🍷🍷🍷🍷🍷 **Reserve Yarra Valley Cabernet Sauvignon 2015** Allinda's wines are understated, scented of vanilla pod, red- to blackcurrant, and green bean. With their savoury guise and medium-bodied astringency, woven sensitively with just the right amount of oak and extraction, they are digestible and highly ageable. Quintessential Yarra Valley. Cork. 13.5% alc. **Rating** 96 **To** 2030 $50 NG ✪
Limited Release Yarra Valley Chardonnay 2016 Estate-grown with no pesticides, herbicides or manufactured fertilisers. Gleaming straw-green, it has the drive and length typical of the Yarra Valley, its energy derived from fruit not oak (although oak is there). Screwcap. 13.5% alc. **Rating** 94 **To** 2024 $29 ✪

🍷🍷🍷🍷🍷 **Yarra Valley Chardonnay 2015 Rating** 93 **To** 2023 $27 NG ✪
Yarra Valley Cabernets 2016 Rating 93 **To** 2028 $30 NG
Limited Release Riesling 2016 Rating 92 **To** 2023 $24 CM ✪
Heathcote Shiraz 2016 Rating 92 **To** 2028 $30 NG
Limited Release Yarra Valley Cabernets 2014 Rating 90 **To** 2025 $40 CM

Amadio Wines   ★★★★

461 Payneham Road, Felixstow, SA 5070 **Region** Adelaide Hills
T (08) 8337 5144 **www.**amadiowines.com **Open** Wed–Sun 10–5.30
Winemaker Danniel Amadio **Est.** 2004 **Dozens** 75 000 **Vyds** 250ha
Danniel Amadio says he has followed in the footsteps of his Italian grandfather, selling wine from his cellar (cantina) direct to the consumer. He also draws upon the business of his parents, built not in Italy, but in Australia. Amadio Wines has substantial vineyards, primarily in the Adelaide Hills and Barossa Valley, and also source contract-grown grapes from the Clare Valley, McLaren Vale and Langhorne Creek, with a strong suite of Italian varieties. Exports to the UK, the US, Canada, Denmark, Russia, India, Indonesia, South Korea, Singapore, Hong Kong and China.

🍷🍷🍷🍷🍷 **Premium Single Vineyard Selection Adelaide Hills Shiraz 2016** Matured in new American oak 'for a little period of time', and a small percentage of French oak. The oak is evident, but sits well with the black fruits – berry and cherry – on the medium-bodied palate. The mouthfeel is built on the excellent balance of fruit, tannins and oak. Screwcap. 14.5% alc. **Rating** 92 **To** 2036 $28
Kangaroo Island Trading Company Single Vineyard Cabernet Sauvignon 2015 Typical young cabernet, holding its cards close to the chest at this stage of its development. Quite brooding in aroma, with herbal, minty notes along with dark blackberry and blackcurrant fruit characters, all reluctant to show themselves fully. Cork. 14.5% alc. **Rating** 92 **To** 2030 $39 SC
Heritage Selection Barossa Valley Aglianico 2014 Deep crimson-purple; this wine certainly makes a bold statement with Eastern spice, dark chocolate, anise and plum fruit supported and balanced by firm tannins, with an intriguing aftertaste of lemon drops. Cork. 14% alc. **Rating** 92 **To** 2029 $45
Heritage Selection Adelaide Hills Montepulciano 2014 Has more depth and presence than the majority of Australian montepulcianos. Black cherry licorice and blackberry are all on parade, and are not interrupted by tannins. Not entirely sure how it will develop. Cork. 14.5% alc. **Rating** 92 **To** 2024 $45
Premium Single Vineyard Selection Adelaide Hills Pinot Grigio 2017 Plenty of richness in the bouquet, crowded with aromas of ripe orchard fruits, lemon myrtle, creamed honey and lime juice. A textural palate, the flavour of soft brown-skinned pears most prominent, and a perceptible level of sweetness. Obvious appeal here. Screwcap. 13.5% alc. **Rating** 91 **To** 2019 $25 SC
Kangaroo Island Trading Company Single Vineyard Shiraz 2015 A very rich and fruity plum pudding style, with condensed black fruit flavours wrapped in dark chocolate and plentiful oak, the tannins adding more flavour. Pleads for more time in barrel. Cork. 14.5% alc. **Rating** 91 **To** 2025 $39

Single Vineyard Selection Adelaide Hills Cabernet Sauvignon 2015
Amadio cabernet from the Adelaide Hills generally presents as a riper style, and no exception here. Good varietal definition, with aromas of cassis leading the charge, and mint, green herb and tobacco leaf in attendance. A solid palate, quite sweet-fruited, medium to full-bodied, a dash of mocha oak and a string of thick tannin all through. Give it some time. Screwcap. 14.5% alc. **Rating** 91 **To** 2027 $28 SC
Premium Single Vineyard Selection Adelaide Hills Merlot 2016 Fleshy, juicy red fruit is the order of the day, with plum, mulberry and cherry at its core. A measure of oak plays a part, adding dimension to the bouquet, and another layer to the palate that shows ample volume of soft and plush flavour. Screwcap. 14% alc. **Rating** 90 **To** 2021 $17 SC ○
Kangaroo Island Trading Company Single Vineyard Merlot 2015 A ripe and plummy bouquet, tending towards plum pudding. More savoury elements in the mix as well, with black olive, mulberry leaf, licorice and seemingly some spicy, cedary oak. Full-bodied, with dense dark fruit flavours; has some improvement to come. Screwcap. 14% alc. **Rating** 90 **To** 2025 $39 SC

ᵀᵀᵀᵀ **Kangaroo Island Trading Company Single Vineyard Sauvignon Blanc 2016 Rating** 89 **To** 2019 $25

Amato Vino   ★★★★

PO Box 475, Margaret River, WA 6285 **Region** Margaret River
T 0409 572 957 **www**.amatovino.com.au **Open** Not
Winemaker Brad Wehr, Contract **Est.** 2003 **Dozens** 5000
Brad Wehr has long walked on the wild side with his wines and his labels. The three brands within his portfolio are: wine by brad, Mantra and Amato Vino (the last based on SA's Riverland). It's not altogether surprising that he has become the Australian importer for California's Bonny Doon Vineyard; some of the quirky humour of Bonny Doon is exemplified by the wine by brad label. Exports to Ireland, Canada, South Korea and Singapore.

ᵀᵀᵀᵀᵀ **Fiano 2017** Wild-fermented in stainless steel before being bottled unfined and unfiltered. It's complex, textural and generously flavoured, the palate a minor powerhouse, the finish warm but rich in spicy impact and indeed character. Screwcap. 13.6% alc. **Rating** 92 **To** 2019 $25 CM ○
Amato Vino Riverland Bianco 2017 Personality is high on the agenda. Honey drizzled over green apple, nashi pear with studs of clove and spice. It's perfumed, right, taut and lively at once. Screwcap. 13.6% alc. **Rating** 92 **To** 2020 $25 CM ○

ᵀᵀᵀᵀ **Amato Nero d'Avola 2017 Rating** 89 **To** 2021 $25 CM

Amelia Park Wines   ★★★★★

3857 Caves Road, Wilyabrup, WA 6280 **Region** Margaret River
T (08) 9755 6747 **www**.ameliaparkwines.com.au **Open** 7 days 10–5
Winemaker Jeremy Gordon **Est.** 2009 **Dozens** 25 000 **Vyds** 9.6ha
Jeremy Gordon had a winemaking career starting with Evans & Tate and Houghton thereafter, before moving to the eastern states to broaden his experience. He returned to Margaret River, and after several years he and wife Daniela founded Amelia Park Wines with business partner Peter Walsh. Amelia Park initially relied on contract-grown grapes, but in 2013 purchased the Moss Brothers site in Wilyabrup, allowing the construction of a new winery and cellar door. Exports to the UK, the US, Canada, India, the Philippines, Singapore, Thailand and China.

ᵀᵀᵀᵀᵀ **Reserve Margaret River Cabernet Sauvignon 2015** Takes a tide of cassis and bay leaf–like flavour and straps it tight to the future. It's powerfully flavoured and textured and prosecutes every point convincingly on the finish. Nothing more needs to be said other than it's absolutely spot on. Screwcap. 14.5% alc. **Rating** 96 **To** 2040 $55 CM ○
Reserve Margaret River Chardonnay 2016 Buoyant chardonnay. Takes quality, if not the world, in its stride. Ripe stone fruit, sweet pears, grapefruit and smoky bacon–like characters. It seduces as it sings. Screwcap. 13% alc. **Rating** 95 **To** 2024 $55 CM

Margaret River Cabernet Merlot 2016 Value here is about as good as it gets. This is a seriously good wine, supple and svelte, not overdone, ripe and generous where it needs to be and balanced and firm where it counts. It flows, it seduces, it lingers. Every input, both ex vineyard and ex winery, has been a positive one. Screwcap. 14.5% alc. **Rating** 95 **To** 2033 $29 CM ✪

Margaret River Semillon Sauvignon Blanc 2017 Balance, composure, just enough tension and plenty of length. Flavour too, naturally, and the texture to go with it. Squeaky clean. Impeccably turned out. Classy. Screwcap. 12.5% alc. **Rating** 94 **To** 2021 $22 CM ✪

Margaret River Chardonnay 2017 Strong oak flavours, but the fruit rises to the task. In many ways this is Margaret River chardonnay in all its glory. Peach, tinned pear, cedar wood and cream characters get the show well and truly on the road, and keep it there. Screwcap. 13% alc. **Rating** 94 **To** 2024 $32 CM

Frankland River Shiraz 2016 Enter the land of licorice. Black cherry, violet and strong vanillan oak characters all put on quite a show, but the licorice flavours play the lead role. It's a generous red in all respects and it's hard to imagine its future as anything other than positive. Screwcap. 14.5% alc. **Rating** 94 **To** 2034 $29 CM ✪

Amherst Winery   ★★★★

285 Talbot-Avoca Road, Amherst, Vic 3371 **Region** Pyrenees
T 0400 380 382 **www.**amherstwinery.com **Open** W'ends & public hols 11–5
Winemaker Luke Jones, Andrew Koerner **Est.** 1989 **Dozens** 1500 **Vyds** 5ha
In 1989 Norman and Elizabeth Jones planted vines on a property with an extraordinarily rich history, commemorated by the name Dunn's Paddock. Samuel Knowles was a convict who arrived in Van Diemen's Land in 1838. He endured continuous punishment until he fled to SA in '46. He changed his name to Dunn and in 1851 married 18-year-old Mary Taaffe. They walked to Amherst, pushing a wheelbarrow of their belongings. The original lease title is in his name. In January 2013, Luke Jones, son of Norman and Elizabeth, and his wife Rachel, acquired the Amherst Winery business; Luke has a wine marketing diploma plus a diploma in wine technology. Exports to China.

ŸŸŸŸŸ **Daisy Creek Pyrenees Shiraz 2016** This is a beautiful shiraz to drink, the word 'seamless' entirely apt. It tastes of plum, licorice, mint and coffee-cream, though the truth is that the flavours pull as a whole and present in delicious unison. Tannin is ripe, fine and perfectly integrated. It will age, surely, but full enjoyment can be had right now. Screwcap. 14% alc. **Rating** 94 **To** 2028 $20 CM ✪

ŸŸŸŸŸ **North-South Shiraz 2015 Rating** 92 **To** 2025 $28 CM
Chinese Gardens Cabernet 2015 Rating 91 **To** 2028 $16 CM ✪
Lachlan's Pyrenees Chardonnay 2016 Rating 90 **To** 2022 $25 CM
Rachel's Pyrenees Rose 2017 Rating 90 **To** 2019 $20 CM ✪

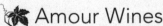 Amour Wines   ★★★★☆

69 Bruce Road, Orange, NSW 2800 **Region** Orange
T 0423 240 720 **www.**amourwines.com.au **Open** By appt
Winemaker Matt Eades **Est.** 2014 **Dozens** 250 **Vyds** 0.6ha
Like others before him, Matt Eades embarked on a career in insurance and law, but the lure of wine was too strong to be kept at bay for long. It all began in 1997 with his first foray to a nearby wine region, and in 2009 he enrolled in the Charles Sturt oenology degree, graduating in '13. His first vintage was in the Yarra Valley in '10, making his first wines from Beechworth shiraz in '12 and '13. Together with wife Katie, he has adopted Orange as his principal home base.

ŸŸŸŸŸ **Orange Shiraz 2015** 20+yo vines from a single vineyard at 830m, matured in used French oak for 24 months. This is an utterly delicious cool-grown shiraz with a warm vinous heart that ticks all the boxes. It's luscious, yet not over the top, with an elegant framework for its red and black cherry fruit provided by superfine tannins and the time in barrel. Screwcap. 14% alc. **Rating** 95 **To** 2035 $42

ŸŸŸŸŸ **Orange Chardonnay 2015 Rating** 92 **To** 2022 $40

Ampel

PO Box 243, Leichhardt, NSW 2040 **Region** Northern Tasmania
T 0418 544 001 **www.**vinous.com.au **Open** Not
Winemaker Jeremy Dineen **Est.** 2010 **Dozens** 1000

Tim Stock's distribution company, Vinous, was the distributor of Josef Chromy's wines until 2010, when the arrangement ended (amicably). Prior to this, Tim had become great friends with Jeremy Dineen, winemaker and general manager of the Chromy business. Jeremy was able to source grapes from a variety of vineyards for the Tasmanian wines that Tim needed for his customers on the mainland. The grapes are sourced from Helen and Gerald Phillips's vineyard in the Tamar Valley. The vineyard was planted on land covered by virgin scrub, reflecting the impoverished quartz gravel soil. With virtually no organic matter present, it took six years for the first small crop to appear, but the vines have now built deep, substantial root systems. The Phillips's farming method is sustainable, with minimal treatments, a benefit of the free-draining soil. The plantings are two-thirds pinot noir and one-third pinot gris; the pinot noir inspiration coming from the Côte Chalonaise in Burgundy (light, fresh and fruity) and pinot gris from Alsace (generous and broadly structured, yet aromatic).

🍷🍷🍷🍷 **Pinot Noir 2016** Light, bright crimson-purple; the fragrant bouquet is at once spicy and flowery, presaging the taut palate of red and purple fruits. While only light to medium-bodied, the intense flavours run through to the finish and aftertaste. Screwcap. 13.5% alc. **Rating** 92 **To** 2022 $26

🍷🍷🍷🍷 **Pinot Gris 2017 Rating** 89 **To** 2019 $27

Amulet Vineyard

1036 Wangaratta Road, Beechworth, Vic 3747 **Region** Beechworth
T (03) 5727 0420 **www.**amuletwines.com.au **Open** 7 days 10–5
Winemaker Ben Clifton, Sue Thornton **Est.** 1997 **Dozens** NA **Vyds** 6ha

Amulet Vineyard, established and owned by Sue and Eric Thornton, was a pioneer of Italian varieties in the region. These, together with French varieties, are planted on the elevated, cool site. The wine is sold under two labels, the scarecrow label representing value, the wood duck label for reserve wines. Amulet hosts a traditional Highland Games each May.

🍷🍷🍷🍷 **Sangiovese Rose 2017** It's fruit-driven with savoury edges and the truth is that it just works. It tastes of tangerine and red cherry, orange rind and clove-studded apples. Length is satisfying without being exceptional but for style and drinkability, it has it going on. Screwcap. 12.1% alc. **Rating** 91 **To** 2019 CM

🍷🍷🍷🍷 **Sangiovese 2015 Rating** 89 **To** 2022 $30 CM
Sparkling Shiraz NV Rating 89 $30 CM

🍇 An Approach to Relaxation

c/- 221 Magnolia Road, Vine Vale, SA 5232 **Region** Barossa Valley
T +31 646 361 2169 **www.**anapproachtorelaxation.com **Open** Not
Winemaker Carla Betts, Richard Betts **Est.** 2014 **Dozens** 900 **Vyds** 5ha

What would two Americans who live in Amsterdam, make wine in Australia and travel 250 days a year, call their wine business? An Approach to Relaxation of course. Carla (nee Rzeszewski) moved from acting to wine, becoming wine director at The Spotted Pig and the John Dory Oyster Bar in New York. Richard nearly became a lawyer, but instead became wine director at the 5-star resort The Little Nell in Aspen, Colorado, a master sommelier, and co-founded Betts & Scholl in Vine Vale, winemaking there 2000–09. Having purchased grenache (their raison d'être) from 120-year-old vines grown on the sandy soils of Vine Vale for their first three vintages, in '17 they purchased a 6.5ha property at Siegersdorf in the centre of the so-called Vine Vale sandpit, with the Rza Block grenache planted 1850–1880 (which forms the core of Suzette). There are also some 20–25-year-old grenache and a few randomly scattered mataro vines. The remaining land is being planted to more grenache. Perhaps they will now find time to relax. Exports to the US, Sweden and the Netherlands.

🍷🍷🍷🍷🍷 **Sucette 2016** Clear colour (apart from cork dust) signals a very good Barossa Valley grenache, which covers all the bases. It refreshingly (and deceptively) sends its message of succulent red fruits of every kind, and no confection to trade off. The palate is very long, as is the lingering aftertaste. Cork. 14.5% alc. **Rating** 95 To 2026 $45

Anderson

1619 Chiltern Road, Rutherglen, Vic 3685 **Region** Rutherglen
T (02) 6032 8111 **www**.andersonwinery.com.au **Open** 7 days 10–5
Winemaker Howard Anderson, Christobelle Anderson **Est.** 1992 **Dozens** 2000 **Vyds** 8.8ha
Having notched up a winemaking career spanning 50 years, including a stint at Seppelt (Great Western), Howard Anderson and family started their own winery, initially with a particular focus on sparkling wine but now extending across all table wine styles. Daughter Christobelle graduated from Adelaide University in 2003 with first-class honours, and has worked in Alsace, Champagne and Burgundy either side of joining her father full-time in '05. The original estate plantings of shiraz, durif and petit verdot (6ha) have been expanded with tempranillo, saperavi, brown muscat, chenin blanc and viognier.

🍷🍷🍷🍷🍷 **Grand Muscat NV** The colour of an olive rim and mahogany heart leaves no doubt about its age. The wine is a luscious blend of muscat grape flavours wrapped in rancio, burnt caramel and Arabian spices, plus dashes of dark chocolate and Christmas pudding. Vino-Lok. 18% alc. **Rating** 94

🍷🍷🍷🍷🍷 **Cellar Block Saperavi 2013** Rating 91 To 2028 $45
Methode Traditionelle Chenin Blanc 2011 Rating 90 $27

Anderson Hill ★★★★

407 Croft Road, Lenswood, SA 5240 **Region** Adelaide Hills
T 0412 499 149 **www**.andersonhill.com.au **Open** W'ends & public hols 11–6
Winemaker Ben Anderson, Brendon Keys **Est.** 1994 **Dozens** 500 **Vyds** 8ha
Ben and Clare Anderson planted their vineyard in 1994. A substantial part of the grape production is sold (Hardys and Penfolds have been top-end purchasers of the chardonnay), but enough is retained to produce their three wines. The cellar door has panoramic views, making the venue popular for functions ranging from weddings to birthdays.

🍷🍷🍷🍷🍷 **Sticks & Stones Pinot Noir 2015** Clear and bright colour; has plenty of character, with a mix of red fruits and wild herb/olive nuances on the finish. Fruit, not oak or tannin-driven, and reflects the good vintage. Screwcap. 12.8% alc. Rating 92 To 2025 $30
Crazy Chook Lady Chardonnay 2016 Unusual to see American oak on contemporary Aussie chardonnay, but here it is. A smidgeon, melded with mostly French. It works well, too, imparting ample texture and a nourishing nuttiness to the core of creamy nougat flavours, all gently massaging the stream of melon and stone fruit notes. A well made, eminently pleasurable drink. Screwcap. 13% alc. Rating 91 To 2022 $30 NG
Down She Goes Pinot Noir 2016 Bright, clear colour; warm spices and talc on the bouquet, then a supple, gently rounded palate with plum and red cherry fruit; good length and balance. Well made. Screwcap. 13.9% alc. Rating 91 To 2024 $30
Vicki Norma Chardonnay 2015 A fresh and complex chardonnay with a slightly reductive bouquet followed by a palate built around classic white peach and grapefruit flavours. Oak has been a means to an end, not an end in itself. Screwcap. 13% alc. Rating 90 To 2020 $28

🍷🍷🍷🍷 **Dorrie Chardonnay 2014** Rating 89 To 2018 $28
Ruby Shiraz 2016 Rating 89 To 2023 $30
Chardonnay Pinot Noir 2017 Rating 89 $28 NG

Andevine Wines

247 Wilderness Road, Rothbury, NSW 2320 **Region** Hunter Valley
T 0427 948 880 **www**.andevinewines.com.au **Open** Fri–Mon 10–5
Winemaker Andrew Leembruggen **Est.** 2012 **Dozens** NFP
Andrew Leembruggen has been a Hunter Valley boy since his cadetship at Mount Pleasant
in 1998, becoming senior winemaker in 2002. He led winemaking operations for Drayton's
Family Wines from '10 to '12 before his departure to create Andevine Wines. Andrew has
also made wine in the Rhône Valley, Bordeaux, Napa Valley and Coonawarra. There are three
ranges of wines: Vineyard Reserve for 100% Hunter Valley (available exclusively from the
cellar door); Hunter Valley varietals (available exclusively through Naked Wines); and Regional
Collection wines, sourced from regions across NSW.

Reserve Hunter Valley Semillon 2017 Made in an uncompromising style, its
sights set almost exclusively on the future. Pristine lemon, talc, saline and mineral
flavours glisten as they shoot through the palate. Floral notes tease at the edges. It
promises to age gorgeously. Screwcap. 10.8% alc. **Rating** 95 **To** 2027 $40 CM
Reserve Canberra Syrah 2016 Buoyant expression of Canberra syrah. Awash
with red cherry and blueberry flavours, almost luxuriously so, before clove and
gun smoke notes chime heartily in. Plenty of juicy fruit, an appropriate level of
fine tannin, and a surge of savoury/nutty character to close. This, deservedly, will
cause many folks to swoon. Screwcap. 14% alc. **Rating** 95 **To** 2028 $45 CM
Reserve Hunter Valley Chardonnay 2015 Enchanting wine. It's floral and
milky with lemon curd, candied citrus and stone fruit flavours shooting through.
Sweet oak plays a positive role, but more importantly the swing of acidity, fruit and
honeysuckle-like top notes is both engaging and distinctive. Screwcap. 12.3% alc.
Rating 94 **To** 2022 $40 CM
Reserve Hilltops Nebbiolo 2016 Whispers of creamy oak, but the variety
dominates, as it should. Flavours of red and black cherries, peppercorn notes
studded throughout, and a clear trail of dry, meaty spice. It's above average quality,
and the future looks bright. Screwcap. 14.5% alc. **Rating** 94 **To** 2030 $35 CM

Hunter Valley Semillon 2017 Rating 93 **To** 2025 $18 CM
Reserve Canberra Syrah 2015 Rating 93 **To** 2027 $45 CM

Andrew Peace Wines ★★★★

Murray Valley Highway, Piangil, Vic 3597 **Region** Swan Hill
T (03) 5030 5291 **www**.apwines.com **Open** Mon–Fri 8–5, Sat 12–4
Winemaker Andrew Peace, David King **Est.** 1995 **Dozens** 180 000 **Vyds** 270ha
The Peace family has been a major Swan Hill grapegrower since 1980, moving into
winemaking with the opening of a $3 million winery in '96. Varieties planted include
chardonnay, colombard, grenache, malbec, mataro, merlot, pinot gris, riesling, sangiovese,
sauvignon blanc, semillon, tempranillo and viognier. The planting of sagrantino is the largest
of only a few such plantings in Australia. Exports to all major markets.

Empress Joanna Vineyard Wrattonbully Shiraz 2016 Well made, even if the
caramel vanillan oak is doing much of the heavy lifting at this stage. The texture
and weight are good, the tannins likewise, the fruits a happy marriage of plum and
blackberry. Screwcap. 14% alc. **Rating** 91 **To** 2030
**Australia Felix Premium Barrel Reserve Wrattonbully Cabernet Shiraz
2016** While minty notes abound, there's fruit weight and richness to carry this
through to a resounding finish. Full-bodied, laden with currants and blackberries,
and of course oak adding its influence with spices and sweetening the palate.
Screwcap. 14% alc. **Rating** 90 **To** 2028 $28 JF

Angas Plains Estate   ★★★★

317 Angas Plains Road, Langhorne Creek, SA 5255 **Region** Langhorne Creek
T (08) 8537 3159 www.angasplainswines.com.au **Open** 7 days 11–5
Winemaker Peter Douglas **Est.** 1994 **Dozens** 3000 **Vyds** 15.2ha
In 1994 Phillip and Judy Cross began the Angas Plains Estate plantings, first with cabernet sauvignon, second shiraz and third a small block of chardonnay predominantly used as a sparkling base. The location, on ancient Angas River floodplains, together with cooling evening breezes from the local Lake Alexandrina, proved ideally suited to the red varieties. Skilled contract winemaking has resulted in some excellent wines from the estate-grown shiraz and cabernet sauvignon. Exports to Singapore, Hong Kong and China.

ΨΨΨΨΨ **Special Reserve Langhorne Creek Shiraz 2016** The far greater impact of oak from 14 months in 75% new French and American hogsheads defines this wine at the present time, and will never cease to dominate, even though it may end up an even contest between the fruit and oak. Diam. 14% alc. **Rating** 94 To 2041 $40

ΨΨΨΨΩ **PJs Langhorne Creek Shiraz 2016** Rating 92 To 2029 $25 ○
PJs Langhorne Creek Cabernet Sauvignon 2016 Rating 90 To 2029 $25

Angelicus   ★★★☆

Lot 9 Catalano Road, Burekup, WA 6227 **Region** Geographe
T 0429 481 425 www.angelicus.com.au **Open** Not
Winemaker John Ward, Sue Ward **Est.** 1997 **Dozens** 850 **Vyds** 2.2ha
Dr John and Sue Ward moved from Sydney to WA with the aim of establishing a vineyard and winery. They moved to the Geographe region, where they purchased a 51ha block of granite-strewn rocky hillside facing north and west, looking towards the Indian Ocean. They began planting vines in 2009, the lion's share to grenache (bushvines, managed biodynamically), five clones of tempranillo, 0.3ha verdelho and 0.1ha vermentino. Exports to the UK.

ΨΨΨΨΩ **Rosa 2017** A wily blend of 44% grenache, the rest tempranillo, wild-yeast fermented in barrel and stirred to broaden texture and mouthfeel. The result is a delicious rose that manages to bridle freshness and flavour with a skein of red berry notes popping through the mouth along a tangy beam of nourishing acidity and herbal lift. Screwcap. 12.5% alc. **Rating** 92 To 2019 $20 NG ○

Angove Family Winemakers   ★★★★★

Bookmark Avenue, Renmark, SA 5341 **Region** South Australia
T (08) 8580 3100 www.angove.com.au **Open** Mon–Fri 10–5, Sat 10–4, Sun 10–3
Winemaker Tony Ingle, Paul Kernich **Est.** 1886 **Dozens** 1 million **Vyds** 480ha
Angove exemplifies the economies of scale achievable in the Riverland without compromising quality. Good technology provides wines that are never poor and sometimes exceed their theoretical station in life. The vast Nanya vineyard has been redeveloped with changes in the varietal mix, row orientation and a partial move to organic growing. Angove's expansion into Padthaway (chardonnay), Watervale (riesling) and Coonawarra (cabernet sauvignon) via long-term contracts, and the purchase of the Warboys vineyard (one of the oldest vineyards in McLaren Vale, planted in the 1930s, now certified organic and biodynamic) in 2008, have resulted in outstanding premium wines. A large cellar door and cafe on the Warboys vineyard at the corner of Chalk Hill Road and Olivers Road, McLaren Vale, is open 10–5 daily. Exports to all major markets.

ΨΨΨΨΨ **Warboys Vineyard McLaren Vale Shiraz Grenache 2016** This is quite simply as good as they come. The fusion of 60% shiraz and 40% grenache is seamless in texture, structure and, most importantly, flavour. That said, it's the shiraz that does all the heavy lifting, its blackberry, licorice and pepper intersecting symbiotically with the contrasting red fruits of the grenache. Screwcap. 14.5% alc. **Rating** 97 To 2035 $44 ○

ŶŶŶŶŶ **Warboys Vineyard McLaren Vale Shiraz 2016** Speaks with a voice very different from its siblings – it's more fragrant and juicy; dark chocolate wrapped around spiced plum and dark cherry fruit, tannins sewn through the intense interplay of the palate. Screwcap. 14.5% alc. **Rating** 96 **To** 2036 $44 ✪

Single Vineyard Blewitt Springs McLaren Vale Shiraz 2016 The wine has a backbone of freshness that runs through the bouquet and palate. It has a complex mainframe, with black and red cherries, spice, earth and dark chocolate flavours to the fore. Blewitt Springs is a special part of McLaren Vale, the wines with unequalled intensity and length. Screwcap. 13.5% alc. **Rating** 95 **To** 2031 $44

Single Vineyard Sellicks Foothills McLaren Vale Shiraz 2016 This has an opulence that is unusual, as it is not only about fruit, but includes a chocolate biscuit textural play at the same time. It fills the mouth, yet doesn't seek to get into your face. Lovely wine. Screwcap. 13.5% alc. **Rating** 95 **To** 2031 $44

Family Crest McLaren Vale Grenache Shiraz Mourvedre 2016 A powerful yet disciplined and focused wine with a treasure trove of spiced fruits on the bouquet, then a palate laced with tannins. This is as close to belligerent as a GSM can come, but it's not bluster, just the real deal for cellaring. Screwcap. 14% alc. **Rating** 95 **To** 2026 $22 ✪

Average Age 15 Years Rare Tawny Port NV It is pungently aromatic, the bouquet and palate with great rancio and a myriad of burnt toffee/butterscotch, fruitcake (especially with a teaspoon of this wine poured over it), roasted almonds, even a little singed bitter chocolate. 500ml. Screwcap. 19.8% alc. **Rating** 95 $45

Single Vineyard Willunga McLaren Vale Shiraz 2016 This wastes no time in taking control of proceedings with its trenchant approach. The flavours are layered and compressed, with blackberry, plum and dark chocolate allowing no penetration of light at this stage. There's no doubt it has the balance needed to justify putting it into the darkest corner of the cellar for 10+ years. Screwcap. 13.5% alc. **Rating** 94 **To** 2029 $44

Warboys Vineyard McLaren Vale Grenache 2016 As with pinot noir, the depth of the colour gives little guide to the quality of the wine; here bright and crystal-clear crimson. The bouquet is highly floral and gently spicy, the juicy red fruits with flecks of herb. The palate continues the red berry/cherry theme, adding plum for good measure. Screwcap. 14.5% alc. **Rating** 94 **To** 2023 $44

ŶŶŶŶŶ **Alternatus McLaren Vale Grenache 2017** Rating 93 To 2022 $23 CM ✪
Grand Tawny Average Age 10 Years NV Rating 92 $25 ✪
Alternatus McLaren Vale Fiano 2017 Rating 91 To 2020 $23 ✪
Duck Shoot Yarra Valley Pinot Noir 2017 Rating 91 To 2023 $17 ✪
Family Crest McLaren Vale Shiraz 2016 Rating 91 To 2028 $22 CM ✪
Family Crest McLaren Vale Chardonnay 2017 Rating 90 To 2023 $22
Family Crest McLaren Vale Cabernet Sauvignon 2016 Rating 90 To 2031 $22
Alternatus McLaren Vale Tempranillo 2017 Rating 90 To 2018 $23

Angullong Wines   ★★★★☆

Victoria Street, Millthorpe, NSW 2798 **Region** Orange
T (02) 6366 4300 **www**.angullong.com.au **Open** 7 days 11–5
Winemaker Jon Reynolds, Liz Jackson **Est.** 1998 **Dozens** 20 000 **Vyds** 216.7ha
The Crossing family (Bill and Hatty, and third generation James and Ben) has owned a 2000ha sheep and cattle station for over half a century. Located 40km south of Orange, overlooking the Belubula Valley, more than 200ha of vines have been planted. In all there are 15 varieties, with shiraz, cabernet sauvignon and merlot leading the way. Most of the production is sold. Exports to Germany and China.

ŶŶŶŶŶ **Fossil Hill Orange Sangiovese 2016** 100% Brunello clones, matured in French oak (20% new). This is a totally delicious sangiovese, with bright red cherry fruits, gentle tannins and a long finish. These are exciting clones. Screwcap. 14.5% alc. **Rating** 96 **To** 2029 $26 ✪

Fossil Hill Orange Tempranillo 2016 Matured in French oak (20% new).
A vibrant tempranillo that should (and does) appreciate the cool climate of
Orange, with juicy red cherry fruits duelling with fine-grained but persistent
tannins. More authentic than most. Screwcap. 14% alc. **Rating** 94 **To** 2029 $26 ○

YYYYY Fossil Hill Orange Shiraz Viognier 2016 Rating 92 To 2029 $26
Orange Merlot 2016 Rating 92 To 2025 $20 ○
Fossil Hill Orange Barbera 2016 Rating 92 To 2026 $26
Fossil Hill Central Ranges Vermentino 2017 Rating 91 To 2020 $24
Fossil Hill Orange Riesling 2017 Rating 90 To 2027 $24
Orange Sauvignon Blanc 2017 Rating 90 To 2018 $20 CM ○
Orange Pinot Grigio 2017 Rating 90 To 2019 $20 ○
Fossil Hill Orange Rosato 2017 Rating 90 To 2019 $24

Angus the Bull ★★★★

PO Box 611, Manly, NSW 1655 **Region** Central Victoria
T (02) 8966 9020 **www**.angusthebull.com **Open** Not
Winemaker Hamish MacGowan **Est.** 2002 **Dozens** 20 000
Hamish MacGowan took the virtual winery idea to its ultimate conclusion, with a single wine
(Cabernet Sauvignon) designed to be drunk with a perfectly cooked steak. Parcels of grapes
are selected from regions across Victoria and South Australia each year, the multi-regional
blend approach designed to minimise vintage variation. In 2012 a second wine, Wee Angus
Cabernet Merlot, was added. Exports to the UK, Canada, Ireland, the Philippines, Fiji, Papua
New Guinea, Vanuatu, Indonesia, Singapore, Thailand, Hong Kong and NZ.

YYYYY Cabernet Sauvignon 2015 Made in its now-familiar style, this could even
surprise given a medium-term stint in the cellar. Boysenberry and blackcurrant
flavours are freshened by florals, gum leaf and cocoa-like notes. Carry of flavour
through the finish is very good. Improves with air; rarely a bad sign. Screwcap.
14% alc. **Rating** 93 **To** 2025 $22 CM ○

Annie's Lane ★★★★

58 Queensbridge Street, Southbank, Vic 3006 (postal) **Region** Clare Valley
T (03) 8533 3000 **www**.annieslane.com.au **Open** Not
Winemaker Alex MacKenzie **Est.** 1851 **Dozens** NFP
The Clare Valley brand of TWE, with the winery name coming from Annie Wayman, a turn-
of-the-century local identity. The brand consistently offers wines that over-deliver against their
price points. Copper Trail is the flagship release, and there are some very worthy cellar door
and on-premise wines.

YYYYY Copper Trail Clare Valley Shiraz 2016 Aromas of blackberry and other dark
fruits are prominent, but the mocha-chocolate character from the oak is also much
in play. In the mouth, it's a wine of density, with a tangy blackberry conserve
flavour seeping into the palate and running into the finish, flanked by the insistent
oak. Screwcap. 14.5% alc. **Rating** 92 **To** 2030 $80 SC
Quelltaler Watervale Shiraz Cabernet 2016 Aromas of chocolate, green leaf
and/or mint (depending on how you see it), earth and spice, the latter perhaps
an oak character. Only medium-bodied, the fruit is bright and buoyant, fresh and
youthful in nature, with both varieties contributing to the spread of flavours. The
tannin feels a touch gummy, but a little more bottle age should see it all come
together. Screwcap. 14.5% alc. **Rating** 92 **To** 2024 $27 SC

Anvers ★★★★☆

633 Razorback Road, Kangarilla, SA 5157 **Region** Adelaide Hills
T (08) 8111 5120 **www**.anvers.com.au **Open** Sun 11–5
Winemaker Kym Milne MW **Est.** 1998 **Dozens** 10 000 **Vyds** 24.5ha

Myriam and Wayne Keoghan's principal vineyard is in the Adelaide Hills at Kangarilla (16ha of cabernet sauvignon, shiraz, chardonnay, sauvignon blanc and viognier), with a second (97-year-old) vineyard at McLaren Vale (shiraz, grenache and cabernet sauvignon). Winemaker Kym Milne has experience gained across many of the wine-producing countries in both northern and southern hemispheres. Exports to the UK and other major markets.

ΨΨΨΨΨ **The Warrior Adelaide Hills Langhorne Creek Shiraz 2016** Intense with fruit, oak and tannin, but all three pull together to ultimately produce a powerhouse red to be reckoned with. Flavours/aromas of coffee, blueberry and sweet plum make it happen on the palate, but jarfuls of spice, cream, potpourri and cool mints are also thrown into the mix along the way. A hedonist's delight. Screwcap. 14.5% alc. **Rating** 94 **To** 2036 $50 CM

ΨΨΨΨΨ **Kingsway Shiraz 2015** Rating 93 To 2025 $30 SC
Razorback Road Sauvignon Blanc 2017 Rating 90 To 2018 $20 CM ✪
Razorback Road Sauvignon Blanc 2016 Rating 90 To 2018 $20 SC ✪
Kingsway Chardonnay 2016 Rating 90 To 2021 $30 SC

Aphelion Wine

18 St Andrews Terrace, Willunga, SA 5172 **Region** McLaren Vale
T 0404 390 840 **www.aphelionwine.com.au** **Open** Not
Winemaker Rob Mack **Est.** 2014 **Dozens** 1200
Aphelion Wine is akin to a miniature painting done with single-hair paintbrushes. But when you consider the credentials of winemaker Rob Mack, supported by co-founder wife Louise Rhodes Mack, great oaks come to mind. Rob has accumulated two degrees (first accounting and management in 2007, then Bachelor of Wine Science from CSU in '16). He scaled the heights of direct marketing as wine buyer and planner for Laithwaites Wine People (June '10–Jan '13), and spent the next 18 months as production manager for Direct Wines in McLaren Vale. Woven through this has been significant employment with five wineries, four in McLaren Vale, a region he obviously knows well.

ΨΨΨΨΨ **The Confluence Grenache 2017** Interesting wine, with a heightened juicy flavour profile, presumably from extended skin contact. The overall mouthfeel has more complexity than its siblings, the flavour profile similar. Screwcap. 14.5% alc. **Rating** 95 **To** 2025 $32 ✪
The Aromat Grenache 2017 Bright, youthful crimson-purple; a perfectly balanced wine, letting the varietal fruit flavour speak for itself. Delicious red fruits, long, juicy and balanced. Screwcap. 14.5% alc. **Rating** 94 **To** 2025 $32
The Verdant McLaren Vale Grenache 2017 The colour is slightly diminished by the use of 100% whole bunches, the very different flavour set also reflecting this. It is unexpectedly richer than its siblings, albeit less pure or fresh. Screwcap. 14.5% alc. **Rating** 94 **To** 2025 $32
The Affinity Grenache Mataro Shiraz 2017 The power of the 80yo grenache stand up to the 60% mataro and shiraz, and the minimal tannin influence (due to the protective rather than extractive fermentation regime). This is a super-juicy wine that should sell and be consumed double-quick. Screwcap. 14.5% alc. **Rating** 94 **To** 2022 $32

ΨΨΨΨΨ **Mataro 2016** Rating 92 To 2026 $32

Apricus Hill

550 McLeod Road, Denmark, WA 6333 **Region** Denmark
T 0427 409 078 **www.apricushill.com.au** **Open** Not
Winemaker James Kellie **Est.** 1995 **Dozens** 800 **Vyds** 8ha
When the then owners of Somerset Hill, Graham and Lee Upson, placed the vineyard on the market, James and Careena Kellie (of Harewood Estate) purchased it with two purposes: first, to secure a critical fruit source for Harewood, and second, to make and market a small range of single vineyard, single varietal wines for sale exclusively through the spectacular cellar door, with its sweeping vista. Thus Somerset Hill is now Apricus Hill. Exports to Japan.

🍷🍷🍷🍷🍷 **Single Vineyard Denmark Semillon 2017** This vineyard has some of the most powerful and rich semillon in Australia, and absolutely doesn't need oak. It's rich in every type of lemon, from sour to sweet, plus lemongrass and high-tensile acidity. This really is exceptional. Screwcap. 12% alc. **Rating** 95 **To** 2032 $27 ✪
Single Vineyard Denmark Sauvignon Blanc 2017 Another wine from Apricus Hill that is right on the money. It is real wine, with tension and drive contributed by French oak, which paradoxically doesn't impart as much flavour as structure and intensity. Screwcap. 12.5% alc. **Rating** 95 **To** 2023 $27 ✪
Single Vineyard Denmark Pinot Noir 2017 Bright crimson-purple; a strikingly rich pinot with a deep well of red and black cherry fruit that will sustain the wine for years to come as it picks up spices and the many other characters of high quality aged pinot. It has the balance and length to ensure the wheels don't fall off with age. Screwcap. 13.5% alc. **Rating** 95 **To** 2029 $27 ✪

Arakoon ★★★★

7/229 Main Road, McLaren Vale, SA 5171 **Region** McLaren Vale
T (08) 8323 7339 **www**.arakoonwines.com.au **Open** By appt
Winemaker Raymond Jones **Est.** 1999 **Dozens** 3500 **Vyds** 3.5ha
Ray and Patrik Jones' first venture into wine came to nothing: a 1990 proposal for a film about the Australian wine industry with myself as anchorman. In 1999 they took the plunge into making their own wine and exporting it, along with the wines of others. As the quality of the wines has improved, so has the originally zany labelling been replaced with simple but elegant labels. Exports to Sweden, Denmark, Germany, Singapore, Malaysia and China.

🍷🍷🍷🍷🍷 **Lighthouse Fleurieu Cabernet Shiraz 2015** Unfined and unfiltered, the cooler soprano tones of Adelaide Hills' cabernet and its currant and mint mesh effortlessly with the baritone of Blewitt Springs shiraz. By far the freshest red of the range, with sappy, juicy tannins embedded with green bean crunch, defining the wine. Long, sinuous, detailed and very persistent, attesting to the versatility of the blend. Screwcap. 14.5% alc. **Rating** 94 **To** 2023 $18 NG ✪

🍷🍷🍷🍷🍷 **Full Bodied Red Grenache Shiraz Mourvedre 2016** **Rating** 92 **To** 2024 $19 NG ✪
Sellicks Beach Shiraz 2016 **Rating** 90 **To** 2025 $20 NG ✪

Aramis Vineyards ★★★★☆

411 Henley Beach Road, Brooklyn Park, SA 5032 **Region** McLaren Vale
T (08) 8352 2900 **www**.aramisvineyards.com **Open** By appt
Winemaker Renae Hirsch, Peter Leske **Est.** 1998 **Dozens** 12 000 **Vyds** 26ha
Aramis Vineyards was founded in 1998 by Lee Flourentzou. Located barely 2km from the Gulf of St Vincent, it is one of the coolest sites in McLaren Vale, planted to shiraz (18ha) and cabernet sauvignon (8ha), the two varieties best suited to the site. This philosophy leads Aramis to source grapes from other regions that best represent each variety, including sauvignon blanc and chardonnay from Adelaide Hills and riesling from Eden Valley. The city-based cellar door also features wines from other boutique producers. Exports to the US, Canada, Singapore, Malaysia, Thailand, Vietnam, Japan, Hong Kong and NZ.

🍷🍷🍷🍷🍷 **Single Vineyard McLaren Vale Shiraz 2015** Excellent dark red-purple; French oak makes its presence felt both with aromas and flavours among the savoury profile of dark chocolate, Dutch licorice and woodsy spices with some satsuma plums. A densely structured wine with plenty of ripe plush tannins and ready now. Screwcap. 14.5% alc. **Rating** 93 **To** 2026 $30 JF

Aravina Estate ★★★★☆

61 Thornton Road, Yallingup, WA 6282 **Region** Margaret River
T (08) 9750 1111 **www**.aravinaestate.com **Open** 7 days 10–5
Winemaker Ryan Aggiss **Est.** 2010 **Dozens** 10 000 **Vyds** 28ha

In 2010 Steve Tobin and family acquired the winery and vineyard of Amberley Estate from Accolade, but not the Amberley brand. Steve has turned the property into a multifaceted business with a host of attractions: a restaurant, sports car collection, wedding venue and so forth. Exports to Indonesia, Malaysia, Hong Kong and China.

ŸŸŸŸŸ **Wildwood Ridge Reserve Chardonnay 2016** Still looking young and tight, the wine has both elegance and intensity. Grapefruit, white peach and citrussy acidity do the heavy lifting, oak a means to an end, not an end in itself. Will continue to cruise along. Screwcap. 13% alc. **Rating** 95 **To** 2026 $50

ŸŸŸŸŸ **Limited Release Tempranillo 2016 Rating** 92 **To** 2026 $30

Arimia Margaret River ★★★★☆

242 Quininup Road, Yallingup, WA 6280 **Region** Margaret River
T (08) 9755 2528 **www**.arimia.com.au **Open** 7 days 10–5
Winemaker Mark Warren **Est.** 1998 **Dozens** 3685 **Vyds** 5.9ha
Ann Spencer purchased the 55ha property overlooking the Indian Ocean in 1997, its northern boundaries marked by Cape Naturaliste National Park. Quininup Creek meanders through the property, providing the water source for its blue-green dam. The name is a combination of daughters Ariann and Mia. The vineyard has a Joseph's coat array of varieties, including semillon, sauvignon blanc, verdelho, chardonnay, cabernet sauvignon, merlot, petit verdot, shiraz, grenache, mourvedre and zinfandel.

ŸŸŸŸŸ **Chardonnay 2016** The pale bright straw-green hue welcomes you to the glass. A very elegant chardonnay, picked at the midpoint between white peach/nectarine and grapefruit/citrus flavours, oak a player in the game, but not a leader. Screwcap. 13% alc. **Rating** 94 **To** 2024 $34

ŸŸŸŸŸ **Grenache Shiraz Mourvedre 2014 Rating** 92 **To** 2029 $35
Mourvedre 2015 Rating 90 **To** 2025 $52
Zinfandel 2014 Rating 90 **To** 2021 $30

Arlewood Estate ★★★★★

Cnr Bussell Highway/Calgardup Road, Forest Grove, WA 6286 **Region** Margaret River
T (08) 9757 6676 **www**.arlewood.com.au **Open** Thurs–Mon 11–5 or by appt
Winemaker Stuart Pym **Est.** 1988 **Dozens** 3000 **Vyds** 6.43ha
The antecedents of today's Arlewood shifted several times; they might interest a PhD researcher, but – with one exception – have no relevance to today's business. That exception was the 1999 planting of the vineyard by the (then) Xanadu winemaker Jurg Muggli. Garry Gossatti purchased the run-down, close-planted vineyard in 2008, and lived in the onsite house from '08–'12, driving to Perth one day per week for his extensive hospitality/hotel business (which paid Arlewood's bills). His involvement in the resurrection of the vineyard was hands-on, and the cool site in the south of Margaret River was, and remains, his obsession. He now drives down every weekend from Perth to talk to viticulturist Russell Oates and contract winemaker Stuart Pym, clearly believing that the owner's footsteps make the best fertiliser. Exports to the UK, Switzerland, Singapore, Malaysia, Hong Kong and China.

ŸŸŸŸŸ **La Bratta Bianco 2015** A wine that brought goose bumps due to my unabashed love of fine white Bordeaux! This is a stunning assemblage of Bordeaux's white varieties with semillon leading the way, a cheeky dash of chardonnay providing some mitigating fill to the herbal scents and racy acidity. This is a tour de force of winemaking, underlain by a profound love and understanding of the fruit and its origins. Waxy, creamy; redolent of candied quince and pungent lemon oil. Textural. Compelling. Screwcap. 13% alc. **Rating** 97 **To** 2027 $40 NG ❂

ŸŸŸŸŸ **Margaret River Cabernet Sauvignon 2015** This is very good, but could be better if hand-picked with the same devotion applied to the superlative whites. The tannin management, still, is superb. A smooth wave of juicy, currant-clad tannins beam across this savoury wine's midriff, directing it long across seams of sensitively appointed oak (30% new French; 2 years). Finishes with a souse of bay leaf and thyme. Screwcap. 14% alc. **Rating** 95 **To** 2030 $40 NG

Margaret River Bianco 2017 Despite the Italian verbage, this is a blend of semillon (47%), sauvignon blanc (45%), and the remaining dollop chardonnay. Lemon drop, quince, candied citrus, together with an undercarriage of verdant herb, lay the platform of scents. Judicious oak work heaves this from the mundane into the texturally intriguing. Ridiculous value, with solid white Bordeaux written all over it! Screwcap. 14% alc. **Rating** 94 **To** 2025 $15 NG ✪

 Margaret River Cabernet Merlot 2015 Rating 93 **To** 2025 $25 NG ✪
Margaret River Rosso NV Rating 92 **To** 2021 $15 NG ✪

Artis Wines

7 Flora Street, Stepney, SA 5069 **Region** Clare Valley/Adelaide Hills
T 0418 802 495 **www**.artiswines.com.au **Open** Not
Winemaker Andrew Miller **Est.** 2016 **Dozens** 450

What do you do after decades working for one of the largest wine groups in Australia (Orlando/Pernod Ricard)? You start your own very small wine business making 450 dozen bottles of Clare Valley Riesling and Adelaide Hills Shiraz. And in doing so, you call upon your experience gained over the years working in France, Spain, the US, NZ, Argentina and Portugal, coupled with travel to many more wine regions.

Single Vineyard Clare Valley Riesling 2016 Complex vinification has invested the wine with an extra level of texture, but left lime-accented varietal expression untouched in a riesling bursting with flavour, the savoury/briny nuances adding complexity. Screwcap. 11.9% alc. **Rating** 96 **To** 2026 $37 ✪

Single Vineyard Adelaide Hills Gruner Veltliner 2017 You can see in the instant you taste this why gruner veltliner should be so long-lived, and also see its affinity to fermentation in used French oak. White pepper is there, as is citrus zest/apple skin, and the acidity will take it though many years. Screwcap. 13.4% alc. **Rating** 95 **To** 2032 $37

Single Vineyard Adelaide Hills Syrah 2016 Both the bouquet and articulate palate have a strong French oak influence, greater than what 20% new would suggest. The wine should come into balance with a few more years in bottle, then settle down on a long-term future. Screwcap. 13.8% alc. **Rating** 94 **To** 2036 $45

Arundel Farm Estate ★★★☆

321 Arundel Road, Keilor, Vic 3036 **Region** Sunbury
T (03) 9338 9987 **www**.arundelfarmestate.com.au **Open** W'ends 10–5
Winemaker Mark Matthews, Claude Ceccomancini **Est.** 1984 **Dozens** 2000 **Vyds** 7.4ha

The first stage of the vineyard in 1984 was 0.8ha of shiraz and cabernet sauvignon. Rick Kinzbrunner of Giaconda made the first vintage in '88 and for some years thereafter, but the enterprise lapsed until it was revived with new plantings in '96 and 2000. Today it is planted solely to shiraz and viognier. In October '11 Claude and Sandra Ceccomancini acquired the business and appointed Mark Matthews as winemaker.

Sunbury Viognier 2016 It stands up straight in the glass; it gives that impression of power. It's all spice and stone fruit, custard apple and honeysuckle, the latter character the barest whisper. It's pretty well done. Screwcap. 14.5% alc. **Rating** 91 **To** 2020 $25 CM

Ashbrook Estate

379 Tom Cullity Drive, Wilyabrup, WA 6280 **Region** Margaret River
T (08) 9755 6262 **www**.ashbrookwines.com.au **Open** 7 days 10–5
Winemaker Catherine Edwards, Brian Devitt **Est.** 1975 **Dozens** 12500 **Vyds** 17.4ha

This fastidious producer of consistently excellent estate-grown table wines shuns publicity and is less well known than deserved, selling much of its wine through the cellar door and to a loyal mailing list clientele. It is very much a family affair: Brian Devitt is at the helm; winemaking is by his daughter Catherine and viticulture by son Richard (also a qualified winemaker). Exports to the US, Canada, Germany, Indonesia, Japan, Singapore, Hong Kong and China.

ŶŶŶŶŶ Gold Label Margaret River Riesling 2017 This is a very good riesling from a region that (with the exception of Leeuwin Estate) by and large eschews the variety. Here pure lime and lemon juicy fruit flavours are artfully lifted by a touch of CO_2. Crisp, minerally acidity puts the seal on the deal of a quality wine. Screwcap. 12.5% alc. **Rating** 95 **To** 2029 $25 ✪

Margaret River Verdelho 2017 Trophy Best White Varietal Wine Perth Wine Show '17. The usual verdelho tinned fruit-salad flavour is balanced by acidity – here it is the other way around, with tight citrus fruit to the fore, tropical to the rear. It will flourish over the next 3 years. Screwcap. 13% alc. **Rating** 95 **To** 2022 $25 ✪

Margaret River Cabernet Sauvignon Merlot 2014 62% cabernet sauvignon, 15% merlot, 12% petit verdot, 11% cabernet franc. Manages to carry its alcohol without any fuss. Indeed, the overall picture is a medium-bodied wine with excellent varietal expression (blackcurrant, plum, redcurrant) and a perfectly balanced palate, the finish long and convincing. Screwcap. 14.8% alc. **Rating** 95 **To** 2034 $30 ✪

Margaret River Semillon 2017 Mature vines and stainless steel fermentation focus maximum attention on the zesty palate, with its mix of lemongrass, cut grass and unsweetened lemon flavours on the very long finish. Screwcap. 13% alc. **Rating** 94 **To** 2032 $25 ✪

Reserve Margaret River Cabernet Sauvignon 2014 Bright, clear crimson-purple; an unapologetically full-bodied cabernet, with blackcurrant, black olive and dried herb aromas and flavours. The tannin structure is also unforgiving; the wine is not yet open for business, needing a decade to do so. Screwcap. **Rating** 94 **To** 2039 $65

ŶŶŶŶŶ Margaret River Chardonnay 2016 **Rating** 93 **To** 2026 $35
Margaret River Sauvignon Blanc 2017 **Rating** 92 **To** 2021 $25 ✪

Ashton Hills Vineyard ★★★★★

126 Tregarthen Road, Ashton, SA 5137 **Region** Adelaide Hills
T (08) 8390 1243 **www.**ashtonhills.com.au **Open** Fri–Mon 11–5
Winemaker Stephen George, Paul Smith **Est.** 1982 **Dozens** 1500 **Vyds** 3ha
Stephen George made Ashton Hills one of the great producers of pinot noir in Australia, and by some distance the best in the Adelaide Hills. With no family succession in place, he sold the business to Wirra Wirra in April 2015. (It had been rumoured for some time that he was considering such a move, so when it was announced, there was a sigh of relief that it should pass to a business such as Wirra Wirra, with undoubted commitment to retaining the extraordinary quality of the wines.) Stephen continues to live in the house on the property and provide ongoing consulting advice. Exports to the US, Hong Kong and China.

ŶŶŶŶŶ Reserve Pinot Noir 2016 The bouquet is very fragrant and no less complex, with its exploration of wild strawberries picked before full ripeness, the full box of exotic spices, and fine but unrelenting tannins. Not an easy vintage for pinot noir, but this is seriously good. Screwcap. 14% alc. **Rating** 96 **To** 2026 $70 ✪

Estate Riesling 2017 The floral, apple blossom-filled bouquet signals a cool-climate riesling with a near unique combination of pure varietal fruit within a gauze dressing of acidity that creates the textures of the wine. Only 150 dozen made. Screwcap. 11% alc. **Rating** 95 **To** 2030 $30 ✪

Piccadilly Valley Chardonnay 2017 The first sign of the new ownership of Wirra Wirra with a variety that Stephen George avoided. Miraculously (or especially), it's a very good wine with X-factor in abundance. There's grip and length to the grapefruit/stone fruit/apple trio. Screwcap. 13% alc. **Rating** 94 **To** 2025 $35

Clare Valley Sparkling Shiraz 2010 50% of the base wine came from Wendouree's 1919 block. It was oak-aged for 4 years before taken to bottle for its second fermentation, spending almost 3 years on lees. The question of dosage is very difficult with sparkling shiraz, needed to balance the tannins – this is a very good wine, but I wonder whether the dosage could have been a little lower. Diam. 13.5% alc. **Rating** 94 $45

ŸŸŸŸŸ **Piccadilly Valley Pinot Noir 2016 Rating** 93 To 2024 $35 CM ○
Estate Pinot Noir 2016 Rating 92 To 2026 $45

 # Athletes Of Wine

19 Soudan Road, West Footscray, Vic 3012 (postal) **Region** Various Victoria
T 0410 273 905 **www.**athletesofwine.com.au **Open** Not
Winemaker Liam O'Brien, Alister Timms, Jo Marsh **Est.** 2009 **Dozens** 1500
The athletes are Melbourne sommeliers, Matt Brooke and Liam O'Brien, who met working at Circa the Prince, and were inspired to endeavour to resuscitate a half-acre block of pinot noir in the Macedon Ranges planted in 2000, but left untouched, unpruned and half dead. They left the first crop for the birds in '08; picked a few grapes in '09; and were exhilarated to harvest half a tonne of pinot in both '10 and '11. In '12 they took over the lease of 0.6ha of chardonnay in Romsey, which involved leaving the pinot block while they built careers and families. Today they lease the chardonnay block in Romsey, and buy pinot from growers in the Macedon region. I crossed paths with both Matt and Liam at Circa, and with Liam at the Len Evans Tutorial. So it comes as no surprise to find that they are persevering with their venture, and that the quality of the wines is as good as it is. Mind you, there's plenty of room to grow without losing the fun of the chase.

ŸŸŸŸŸ **Vino Athletico Macedon Pinot Noir 2016** Excellent depth of colour, the complex flavours based on various types of plum (including poached) and coming from an array of spices. Very good now, but with much more to come as the wine ages. Screwcap. 13.3% alc. **Rating** 94 To 2029 $32

ŸŸŸŸŸ **Vino Athletico Macedon Chardonnay 2016 Rating** 93 $32
Vinero Chardonnay 2015 Rating 90 To 2022 $44
Alto! Alto!! Rose 2017 Rating 90 To 2020 $27

Atlas Wines

PO Box 458, Clare, SA 5453 **Region** Clare Valley
T 0419 847 491 **www.**atlaswines.com.au **Open** Not
Winemaker Adam Barton **Est.** 2008 **Dozens** 3000 **Vyds** 8ha
Owner and winemaker Adam Barton had an extensive winemaking career before establishing Atlas Wines, working in McLaren Vale, the Barossa Valley, the Coonawarra, the iconic Bonny Doon Vineyard in California and, most recently, at Reillys Wines in the Clare Valley. He has 6ha of shiraz and 2ha of cabernet sauvignon grown on a stony ridge on the eastern slopes of the region, and sources small batches from other distinguished sites in the Clare and Barossa. The quality of the wines is extraordinarily good and consistent. Exports to Canada, Singapore, Hong Kong and China.

ŸŸŸŸŸ **172° Watervale Riesling 2017** Rapier-like. A line of flavour runs along the length of a knife edge. Rind of lime, slate, steel and grapefruit. A scintillating style, done very well. Screwcap. 12.7% alc. **Rating** 94 To 2028 $30 CM ○

ŸŸŸŸŸ **Vintage Project Adelaide Hills Chardonnay 2017 Rating** 92 To 2024 CM
Clare Valley Shiraz 2016 Rating 90 To 2024 $27 CM

Attwoods Wines

45 Attwoods Road, Scotsburn, Vic 3352 **Region** Geelong
T 0407 906 849 **www.**attwoodswines.com.au **Open** Not
Winemaker Troy Walsh **Est.** 2010 **Dozens** 650 **Vyds** 2ha

Australian-born winemaker and owner Troy Walsh began his journey into wine as a sommelier in London for 12 years (1990–2002), working his way up to some of the most exalted restaurants. In '10 he began following the Flying Winemaker path of vintages in Australia and France each year. He also quickly ran his colours up the mast by focusing on pinot noir and chardonnay in Burgundy and Geelong. The wineries he worked with here and in France all used whole-bunch fermentation as a significant part of the vinification process, and he uses the practice to a greater or lesser degree in most of his wines. Initially all of the grapes were contract-grown, and Troy continues to purchase grapes from two vineyards near Bannockburn. In 2010 Troy and wife Jane purchased an 18ha property 20km south of Ballarat, and moved the family from Melbourne, establishing a 1.5ha ultra-high density planting (1 × 1.2m spacing) of pinot noir (MV6, 777 and Pommard) and 0.5ha of chardonnay. Attwoods also leases a 27-year-old vineyard at Garibaldi planted to 0.5ha each of pinot noir and chardonnay.

♥♥♥♥♥ **Le Sanglier Geelong Shiraz 2014** It's a painting in watercolours where the paints have been heavily applied. It tastes of black cherry, boysenberry, deli meats, pepper and dried herbs. It's powerful through the palate, refreshing through the finish, assertive of tannin, and long. Diam. 13.3% alc. **Rating** 95 **To** 2029 $50 CM
Garibaldi Farm Ballarat Chardonnay 2016 From a 25yo vineyard near Ballarat. It's all about refreshment in the mouth, quite a nod to complexity too. Nectarine, honey, lime, lactose and toasted wheat flavours do everything they can to bring you around to their view. Diam. 13% alc. **Rating** 94 **To** 2024 $50 CM

Atze's Corner Wines   ★★★★☆

Box 81, Nuriootpa, SA 5355 **Region** Barossa Valley
T 0407 621 989 **www.**atzescornerwines.com.au **Open** By appt
Winemaker Contract, Andrew Kalleske **Est.** 2005 **Dozens** 2000 **Vyds** 30ha
The seemingly numerous members of the Kalleske family have widespread involvement in grapegrowing and winemaking in the Barossa Valley. This venture is that of Andrew, son of John and Barb. In 1975 they purchased the Atze vineyard, which included a small block of shiraz planted in '12, but with additional plantings along the way, including more shiraz in '51. Andrew also purchases grapes from the family vineyard, which has 20ha of shiraz and small amounts of mataro, petit verdot, grenache, cabernet, tempranillo, viognier, petite sirah, graciano, montepulciano, vermentino and aglianico. The wines are all made in the onsite winery. Exports to the US.

♥♥♥♥♥ **The Bachelor Shiraz 2016** This full-bodied, voluptuous shiraz is founded on deft winemaking, layering the smooth sheath of ripe black fruit and gentle licorice to spice flavours with a massaged hand of silken tannins, a clench of reductive tension, judicious oak and a gentle acid breeze. Screwcap. 14.5% alc. **Rating** 94 **To** 2027 $30 NG ✪

♥♥♥♥♀ **Boehm's Black Shiraz 2016** Rating 93 **To** 2030 $45 NG
Secret Drop Cabernet Sauvignon 2015 Rating 93 **To** 2030 $30 NG
Wild Roses Vermentino 2017 Rating 92 **To** 2021 $24 NG ✪
A Label Cabernet Sauvignon 2016 Rating 92 **To** 2024 $24 NG ✪
A Label Shiraz 2016 Rating 91 **To** 2022 $24 NG

Audrey Wilkinson   ★★★★★

750 De Beyers Road, Pokolbin, NSW 2320 **Region** Hunter Valley
T (02) 4998 1866 **www.**audreywilkinson.com.au **Open** 7 days 10–5
Winemaker Jeff Byrne **Est.** 1866 **Dozens** 30 000 **Vyds** 35.33ha
Audrey Wilkinson is one of the most historic and beautiful properties in the Hunter Valley, known for its stunning views and pristine vineyards. It was, in fact, the first vineyard planted in Pokolbin, in 1866. The property was acquired in 2004 by the late Brian Agnew and has been owned and operated by his family since. The wines, made predominantly from estate-grown grapes, are released in three tiers: Audrey Series, Winemakers Selection and Reserve, the latter only available from the cellar door. Exports to the US, Canada, the UK, Finland and the Czech Republic.

ŸŸŸŸŸ **The Ridge Semillon 2017** This vintage was blissful in many parts of eastern Australia, the Hunter Valley as happy as any. The varietal fruit expression has been dialled up to maximum without any suggestion of excess. Semillon can be confused with young (or old for that matter) riesling with its tandem Granny Smith apple and lime, and a feather duster of grass whispering along with the built-in acidity. The future? It's up to you to decide. Screwcap. 12% alc. **Rating** 96 To 2035 $45 ○

The Ridge Reserve Semillon 2009 The glorious straw-green hue announces a wine in the prime of its life, a prime that isn't going to wither any time soon. Indeed, it will add yet further as toasty nuances couple with the flinty acidity. But now (as later), lime-accented fruit fills the long palate and aftertaste, with a whisper of honey. Screwcap. 11.5% alc. **Rating** 96 To 2029 $65 ○

Winemakers Selection Shiraz 2017 Although '17 was the hottest year on record, it 'delivered perfect ripening conditions'. It is a rich and powerful shiraz with some 1965 blood in its vinous veins. Blue and black fruits are foremost, the tannins ripe, and the balance of its full body good. Climate change catastrophe? Gaia has means of defending itself. Screwcap. 14.5% alc. **Rating** 96 To 2047 $40 ○

Winemakers Selection Chardonnay 2017 From the same grape source as The Oakdale, but here using 30% new oak. It's an odd situation, or is it? This wine is fresher, lighter and marginally better balanced than its sibling. Screwcap. 13% alc. **Rating** 95 To 2023 $35 ○

The Oakdale Chardonnay 2017 Fermented and matured in French oak (70% new). Early picking has introduced a zesty element to the white peach, grapefruit and Granny Smith apple fruit flavours that have made light work of the high percentage of new oak. Screwcap. 13% alc. **Rating** 95 To 2024 $45

Winemakers Selection Semillon 2017 Unexpectedly but markedly different in flavour and mouthfeel to The Ridge. It's a good wine, but its structure and texture are loose, wobbling around the mouth, the acidity looking for a place to call home. By rights time should help. Screwcap. 12% alc. **Rating** 94 To 2027 $30 ○

ŸŸŸŸŸ **Semillon 2017** Rating 91 To 2027 $22 JF ○
Shiraz 2017 Rating 91 To 2025 $22 JF ○
Hunter Valley Adelaide Hills Semillon Sauvignon Blanc 2017 Rating 90 To 2020 $22 JF
Tempranillo 2017 Rating 90 To 2022 $22 JF

Austins & Co.   ★★★★★

870 Steiglitz Road, Sutherlands Creek, Vic 3331 **Region** Geelong
T (03) 5281 1799 **www**.austinsandco.com.au **Open** By appt
Winemaker John Durham **Est.** 1982 **Dozens** 25 000 **Vyds** 61.5ha
Pamela and Richard Austin have quietly built their business from a tiny base, and it has flourished. The vineyard has been progressively extended to over 60ha. Son Scott (with a varied but successful career outside the wine industry) took over management and ownership in 2008. The quality of the wines is admirable. Exports to the UK, Canada, Hong Kong, Japan and China.

ŸŸŸŸŸ **Custom Collection Spencer Shiraz 2016** The far greater quality of this wine than its sibling is in part due to fruit selection in the vineyard, and a more complex vinification, the key points being 9 months' maturation in French oak (35% new) preceded by 9 months' maturation in concrete eggs. You skip over the 15% alcohol, the wine finer and more intense, with extreme length to its spice-ridden black cherry and licorice fruits. Screwcap. 15% alc. **Rating** 97 To 2041 $60 ○

ŸŸŸŸŸ **Custom Collection Delilah Pinot Noir 2015** Hand-picked, 100% destemmed, 4 days cold soak, open-fermented, matured in French oak (33% new) for 12 months. Bright, light, clear crimson; the vinification has drawn out every ounce of aroma and flavour in a spicy red fruit palate of exceptional intensity and length. A delicious pinot. Screwcap. **Rating** 96 To 2030 $65 ○

Geelong Chardonnay 2016 Wild-fermented in barrel, a small portion underwent mlf, with extended lees contact. A focused wine, the winemaking sensitive to the fresh fruit blend of white peach, apple and grapefruit. Thoroughly elegant chardonnay. Screwcap. 13.5% alc. **Rating** 95 **To** 2023 $40

Custom Collection Ellyse Chardonnay 2016 Named after Richard and Pamela's first grandchild, Ellyse Chardonnay is only made in the best vintages. Very developed given its youth, although it is bright straw-green; the bouquet and palate dismiss any thought of premature development, the palate in particular elegant and bordering on frisky. The flavours are of lemon curd, white peach, melon and gently toasty oak. Screwcap. 13.5% alc. **Rating** 95 **To** 2021 $60

Custom Collection Delilah Pinot Noir 2016 A perfumed, spicy bouquet leads into a palate with red cherry in all its forms: fresh, poached, sour, spiced. It's undeniably fruity, but still building texture. Screwcap. 13.5% alc. **Rating** 94 **To** 2026 $60

Shiraz 2016 Full purple-red; a complex, layered, full-bodied cool-climate shiraz, its character and quality largely derived from the vineyard. It's at the start of a long life riding on the back of vibrating black fruits and ripe tannins. Screwcap. 14.5% alc. **Rating** 94 **To** 2036 $35

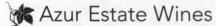 **6Ft6 Rose 2017** Rating 93 To 2019 $25
Riesling 2017 Rating 91 To 2023 $25
6Ft6 Sauvignon Blanc 2017 Rating 90 To 2021 $25
Custom Collection Ruby May Pinot 2015 Rating 90 To 2025 $65

Aylesbury Estate ★★★☆

72 Ratcliffe Road, Ferguson, WA 6236 **Region** Geographe
T (08) 9728 3020 **www**.aylesburyestate.com.au **Open** Not
Winemaker Luke Eckersley **Est.** 2015 **Dozens** 1800 **Vyds** 8.7ha
Ryan and Narelle Gibbs (and family) are the sixth generation of the pioneering Gibbs family in the Ferguson Valley. When the family first arrived in 1883, they named the farm Aylesbury after the town in England whence they came. For generations the family ran cattle on the 200ha property, but in 1998 it was decided to plant 4.2ha of cabernet sauvignon as a diversification of the business. Merlot (2.5ha) followed in 2001, and 1.6ha of sauvignon blanc in '04. In '08 Ryan and Narelle took over ownership and management of the business from Ryan's father, selling the grapes until '15, when the first Aylesbury Estate wines were made.

♥♥♥♥ **Waterfall Gully Ferguson Valley Sauvignon Blanc 2017** It sure doesn't lack fruit intensity. This is a juicy mouthful of flavour tasting of cut grass, green apple and tropical fruits, the length modest but the show entertaining. Screwcap. 13% alc. **Rating** 89 **To** 2019 $25 CM

🍇 Azur Estate Wines ★★★★

PO Box 1243, Aldinga Beach, SA 5173 **Region** McLaren Vale
T 0410 189 841 **www**.azurestate.wordpress.com **Open** Not
Winemaker Fanchon Ferrandi **Est.** 2015 **Dozens** 150
The combination of Old and New World winemaking and philosophies are contributed by Fanchon Ferrandi and Michael Rubenhold. Franchon's childhood was split between southern France and the majestic island of Corsica, which she parlayed into a degree in biochemistry, a graduate diploma in oenology and an MBA in wines and spirits before spending 10 years as chief winemaker at Tatachilla. Michael's training took place at Hardys' Tintara Cellars before he and Fanchon traversed the vineyards of Chile, California, Spain and France. They now have a vineyard with 2.3ha of shiraz and 0.3ha of durif.

♥♥♥♥♡ **Shiraz 2015** Has the McLaren Vale taste profile in spades, with rich purple and black fruits wrapped in Swiss chocolate, the mouthfeel supple thanks to soft, ripe tannins and lengthy maturation in oak. Screwcap. 14.5% alc. **Rating** 93 **To** 2030 $35

Baarmutha Wines

1184 Diffey Road, Beechworth, Vic 3747 **Region** Beechworth
T (03) 5728 2704 **www**.baarmuthawines.com.au **Open** By appt
Winemaker Vincent Webb **Est.** 2006 **Dozens** 300 **Vyds** 2ha
Vincent Webb is a modern-day Renaissance man. He is a graduate of oenology and viticulture
at CSU, but his full-time occupation is scheduler with Ausnet Services. He manages the
vineyard and winery with 'plenty of help' from wife Sharon and their young sons. Family and
friends hand-select the fruit at harvest, and small quantities of wine are made using precisely
what you would expect: a basket press, open vat fermenters, wild yeast fermentation, and
maturation in new and used French oak. One of 10 wineries to open in the Beechworth
region since 2006, which has many attractions for both winemakers and wine consumers.

Beechworth Shiraz 2015 Deeply coloured, immediately staking the ground
with licorice, spice and blackberry on the bouquet. The medium-bodied palate
has bright, juicy fruit underpinned by fine-grained tannins. Well made, good wine.
Screwcap. 13.5% alc. **Rating** 93 **To** 2030 $38
Beechworth Shiraz 2016 Excellent dark crimson hue; the palate full of ripe
dark plums, spiced cherries, cassis, with oodles of licorice, soy sauce and juniper.
Full-bodied with ripe, textured tannins and more explosive fruit and savoury
flavour, with tamarind-like acidity to close. Plenty to like, but there's a hint of
porty-ripe fruit/oxidation. Screwcap. 13.5% alc. **Rating** 91 **To** 2022 $38 JF

BackVintage Wines

2/177 Sailors Bay Road, Northbridge, NSW 2063 **Region** Various
T (02) 9967 9880 **www**.backvintage.com.au **Open** Mon–Fri 9–5
Winemaker Julian Todd, Nick Bulleid MW, Mike Farmilo **Est.** 2003 **Dozens** 10 000
BackVintage Wines is a virtual winery in the fullest sense. Not only does it not own vineyards
or a winery, but it also only sells by phone or through its website. Nick Bulleid says, 'We buy
grapes, manage the fermentation and subsequent maturation. We also blend bulk wine sourced
from some of the best winemakers throughout Australia.' The value for money offered by
these wines is self-evident, and really quite remarkable.

Watervale Riesling 2016 While bright and fresh, there's a just a mite more
colour and toasty notes for a young rizza. It's also laced with lime juice, kaffir lime
leaves, coriander seeds, dry to the very end. Screwcap. 12% alc. **Rating** 92 **To** 2023
$13 JF ✪
Hunter Valley Semillon 2016 The regional thumbprint is firmly planted with
all manner of lemon flavours from zest, juice and curd plus lemongrass. Super
fresh with crunchy acidity on the finish, yet there's body and a slippery texture.
Screwcap. 12% alc. **Rating** 92 **To** 2030 $13 JF ✪
Adelaide Hills Chardonnay 2016 Mid straw-gold; it's built with white stone
fruit, cashews, creamy-lees woven through to a medium-weighted palate, lemony
acidity on the finish. Screwcap. 12.5% alc. **Rating** 92 **To** 2020 $13 JF ✪
Reserve Yarra Valley Pinot Noir 2016 It has a terrific crimson hue, an
enticing nose of spiced cherries, pips and woodsy spices, and a fuller-bodied palate
loaded with flavour, firm tannins and a bitter, tangy finish. A bargain, too. What's
there not to love? Screwcap. 13% alc. **Rating** 92 **To** 2022 $17.50 JF ✪
Adelaide Hills Sauvignon Blanc 2016 Gee this looks good – pale straw and
bright; tastes rather fine too with a mere hint of tropical fruit more in the citrus
spectrum with lemon peel and juice. It's fresh with decent length and a snappy
crisp finish. Screwcap. 12.5% alc. **Rating** 91 **To** 2019 $13 JF ✪
Reserve Yarra Valley Chardonnay 2016 Not sure what makes this a reserve
other than a black label and a $2 price difference compared with the Adelaide
Hills Chardonnay. Full of white and yellow stone fruit, ripe and fleshy on the
palate, creamed honey and nutty, leesy notes with some spiced oak flavours too.
Fuller-bodied with good acidity on the finish. Screwcap. 13% alc. **Rating** 91
To 2021 $15 JF ✪

Badger's Brook

874 Maroondah Highway, Coldstream, Vic 3770 **Region** Yarra Valley
T (03) 5962 4130 **www**.badgersbrook.com.au **Open** Wed–Sun 11–5
Winemaker Michael Warren, David Crawford **Est.** 1993 **Dozens** 2500 **Vyds** 4.8ha
Situated next door to the well known Rochford, the vineyard is planted to chardonnay, sauvignon blanc, pinot noir, shiraz (1ha each), cabernet sauvignon (0.35ha), merlot and viognier (0.2ha each), with a few rows each of roussanne, marsanne and tempranillo. The Badger's Brook wines, made onsite since 2012, are 100% estate-grown; the second Storm Ridge label uses Yarra Valley grapes. Also houses the Tramonto Kitchen & Bar. Exports to Asia.

Yarra Valley Cabernet Sauvignon 2015 Includes 10% merlot. It shows the merit of the vintage clearly. Blackcurrant, bay leaf and cedar-spice oak characters work and play harmoniously together, the end result mid-weight, well sustained and delicious. Screwcap. 13% alc. **Rating** 93 **To** 2029 $28 CM
Yarra Valley Tempranillo 2016 It saw no new oak, and yet oak or oak-like flavours are quite apparent, as is so often the case with tempranillo. It's creamy and vanillan with cola and redcurrant flavours whooshing through the palate in seductive style. Volume, texture, emphasis, it's all here. Screwcap. 13% alc. **Rating** 93 **To** 2025 $30 CM
Yarra Valley Pinot Noir 2016 It sits on the slender side but there's plenty going on; oak has been well applied, the sinewy nature of the tannin is most impressive, and it all lingers nicely. Not a great deal of intensity but all the components here earn their keep. Screwcap. 13.5% alc. **Rating** 92 **To** 2024 $30 CM
Yarra Valley Pinot Rose 2017 Pale crimson. It cracks on with red cherry, citrus and dried herb flavours, some blossomy notes too. Convincing throughout. The aftertaste comes with both candied and savoury aspects, both of which work as positives. Screwcap. 12.5% alc. **Rating** 91 **To** 2020 $20 CM ✪

Baie Wines

120 McDermott Road, Curlewis, Vic 3222 **Region** Geelong
T 0400 220 436 **www**.baiewines.com.au **Open** By appt
Winemaker Robin Brockett **Est.** 2000 **Dozens** 2000 **Vyds** 6ha
Takes its name from the farming property Baie Park, owned by the Kuc family (headed by Anne and Peter) for decades. In 2000 they established 2ha each of sauvignon blanc, pinot gris and shiraz, the first vintage following in '06. The vineyard is planted on north-facing slopes running down to the shore of Port Phillip Bay; the maritime influence is profound. Patriarch Peter is a GP, used to working long hours and with attention to detail, and he and agriculturist son Simon are responsible for the viticulture. Anne greets visitors at the waterfront estate, and Simon's wife Nadine is the marketing force behind the business.

Bellarine Peninsula Pinot Gris 2017 A pale copper blush; some barrel ferment (2 months) has added creamy texture to the ginger spice and poached pear flavours. Neatly composed with fresh acidity to close. Screwcap. 13% alc. **Rating** 91 **To** 2019 $25 JF
Bellarine Peninsula Rose 2017 Pale-cherry pink with an orange hue; made from pinot noir and spent 2 months in seasoned French oak. Aromas of cherry pips, red fruits and spicy nuances lead onto a palate with texture and depth. Screwcap. 12.5% alc. **Rating** 90 **To** 2018 $25 JF

Bailey Wine Co

PO Box 368, Penola, SA 5277 **Region** Coonawarra
T 0417 818 539 **www**.baileywineco.com **Open** Not
Winemaker Tim Bailey **Est.** 2015 **Dozens** 400
After 20 years living and working in Coonawarra, Tim (and Lucille) Bailey decided to take a busman's holiday by establishing their own small wine business. Tim's day job is winemaker at Leconfield, but he has also worked in the Sonoma Valley of California, and travelled through the Napa Valley as well as France. Tim and Lucille say they have a simple philosophy:

'Find great growers in the regions we love and let the vineyard shine through in the bottle.' Thus they sourced Clare Valley riesling and Grampians shiraz in 2016, and Adelaide Hills chardonnay and Coonawarra cabernet sauvignon for '17.

ŸŸŸŸŸ **Bryksy Vineyard Watervale Riesling 2017** Perfumed and inviting from the outset but there's keen intensity of flavour here too; helped along no doubt by a whisper of fruit (if not actual) sweetness. It bounces along with lime and apple blossom–like flavour/aroma and comes across at all times as thoroughly delicious. Screwcap. 11% alc. **Rating** 94 **To** 2024 $25 CM ✪

ŸŸŸŸŸ **Hyde Park Vineyard Grampians Shiraz 2016 Rating** 93 **To** 2028 $30 CM
Punch Down Boys Field Blend 2017 Rating 92 **To** 2025 $30 CM

Baileys of Glenrowan   ★★★★★

779 Taminick Gap Road, Glenrowan, Vic 3675 **Region** Glenrowan
T (03) 5766 1600 **www**.baileysofglenrowan.com.au **Open** 7 days 10–5
Winemaker Paul Dahlenburg **Est.** 1870 **Dozens** 15 000 **Vyds** 143ha
Since 1998 the utterly committed Paul Dahlenburg has been in charge of Baileys and has overseen an expansion in the vineyard and the construction of a 2000t capacity winery. The cellar door has a heritage museum, winery viewing deck, contemporary art gallery and landscaped grounds preserving much of the heritage value. Baileys has also picked up the pace with its muscat and tokay (topaque), reintroducing the Winemakers Selection at the top of the tree, while continuing the larger-volume Founder series. In December 2017 Casella Family brands purchased the brand and the Glenrowan property.

ŸŸŸŸŸ **Winemakers Selection Rare Old Muscat NV** Dark mahogany; essence of raisins and a whisper of orange blossom; it has flavour and texture intensity and complexity even beyond that of the Rare Old Topaque. All the spices in Arabia, Christmas pudding, cognac-soaked plums. Despite all this, has the essential freshness to cleanse the gloriously long finish and vibrating aftertaste. 375ml. Cork. 17.5% alc. **Rating** 98 $75 ✪
Winemakers Selection Rare Old Topaque NV The extreme age is obvious from the colour with its olive rim; the bouquet is voluminous and intensely complex, the palate incredibly luscious with multi-spice, mandarin zest, tea leaf, and Callard & Bowser butterscotch flavours. The palate is like velvet, the rancio and spirit there but not excessive. A micro-sip avoided the obscenity of spitting it (all) out when making this note. 375ml. Cork. 17.5% alc. **Rating** 97 $75 ✪

ŸŸŸŸŸ **1920s Block Shiraz 2015** It's arguable this wine is of the same quality as the 1904 Block, the dry-grown estate vineyard producing intensely coloured and flavoured wine, made in the same way as the 1904. It is medium to full-bodied, with a long palate of blackberry and plum fruit, and firm tannins on the lingering finish. Screwcap. 15% alc. **Rating** 96 **To** 2035 $45 ✪
1904 Block Shiraz 2015 The name of the wine tells you much of the story of this hitherto grossly underpriced shiraz. It was open-fermented, basket-pressed (the press as old as the vines), and matured in high quality French oak. The wine was allowed, indeed encouraged, to speak of its place (and age), but not forced to overstate its full-bodied status. Screwcap. 15% alc. **Rating** 96 **To** 2040 $95
Founder Series Classic Topaque NV Amber with a slight grading to light olive on the rim proclaiming its age; abundant flavour, with Christmas cake, singed toffee and abundant spice; the long finish is well balanced, although the sweetness continues to the mid-palate, until rancio helps dry the finish. Great care at Baileys is being taken to maintain the quality and style of this wine, and this is as great a bargain as any wine on the market today. Vino-Lok. 17% alc. **Rating** 95 $30 ✪
Founder Series Classic Muscat NV The colour has developed past any hint of red (darker and deeper than the Topaque). A good example of the more elegant style that Paul Dahlenburg is seeking to make, with a perfumed rose petal and spice bouquet; the palate beautifully poised without sacrificing fruit intensity or the lusciously sweet, raisined flavour. The spirit is part of the answer, also blending

decisions. Great value. Three gold medals and *Winestate Magazine* Trophy for Best Fortified Wine of the Year '15. Vino-Lok. 17% alc. **Rating** 95 $30 ◎

🍷🍷🍷🍷🍷 **Organic Shiraz 2016 Rating** 90 **To** 2025 $28 SC

Baillieu   ★★★★☆

32 Tubbarubba Road, Merricks North, Vic 3926 **Region** Mornington Peninsula
T (03) 5989 7622 **www**.baillieuvineyard.com.au **Open** At Merricks General Wine Store
Winemaker Geraldine McFaul **Est.** 1999 **Dozens** 2500 **Vyds** 9.2ha
Charlie and Samantha Baillieu have re-established the former Foxwood vineyard, growing chardonnay, viognier, pinot gris, pinot noir and shiraz. The north-facing vineyard is part of the 64ha Bulldog Run property owned by the Baillieus, and is immaculately maintained. The refurbished Merricks General Wine Store is a combined bistro/providore/cellar door.

🍷🍷🍷🍷🍷 **Mornington Peninsula Chardonnay 2016** You can see the smile on
chardonnay's face from a distance. Peach, nectarine, cashew and sweet spice flavours both rush up to meet you, and keep chatting all the way through to the satisfying finish. Full-bodied, full-flavoured chardonnay done well. Screwcap. 13.5% alc.
Rating 94 **To** 2021 $35 CM
Mornington Peninsula Pinot Noir 2016 Such a pretty wine. This is fine, elegant, silken and long with strawberry, chicory and dry spice flavours running pleasantly through the palate. Wood smoke—like notes add an extra highlight. Tannin is perfectly managed; oak plants a light kiss; it all runs artfully along the tongue. Pure pleasure. Screwcap. 13% alc. **Rating** 94 **To** 2023 $40 CM

🍷🍷🍷🍷🍷 **Mornington Peninsula Rose 2017 Rating** 93 **To** 2019 $25 CM ◎
Mornington Peninsula Vintage Brut 2015 Rating 91 $35 CM

Balgownie Estate   ★★★★★

Hermitage Road, Maiden Gully, Vic 3551 **Region** Bendigo
T (03) 5449 6222 **www**.balgownieestatewines.com.au **Open** 7 days 11–5
Winemaker Tony Winspear **Est.** 1969 **Dozens** 10 000 **Vyds** 35.28ha
Balgownie Estate is the senior citizen of Bendigo, having celebrated its 40th vintage in 2012. A $3 million winery upgrade coincided with a doubling of the size of the vineyard. The estate also has a cellar door in the Yarra Valley (Yarra Glen), where operations fit in neatly with the Bendigo wines. Balgownie has the largest vineyard-based resort in the Yarra Valley, with over 65 rooms and a limited number of spa suites. In April '16 Chinese Interactive China Cultural Technology Investments purchased the Balgownie Bendigo and Yarra Valley operations for $29 million. Exports to the UK, the US, Canada, Fiji, Hong Kong, Singapore, China and NZ.

🍷🍷🍷🍷🍷 **Museum Release Bendigo Shiraz 2007** In excellent condition, thanks in part
to the screwcap. A deep, dark-garnet hue belying its age, everything beautifully sewn together, the tannins, acidity, the fruit just a hint of black licorice and unctuous aged balsamic. Pitch-perfect now but still plenty of life ahead. 14.5% alc.
Rating 96 **To** 2027 $95 JF
Old Vine Bendigo Shiraz 2015 Fruit not merely from the original '69 plantings, but just 12 rows that are deemed the best. There's a silkiness on the palate, a richness of fruit flavour, but it's not dense, as the tannins, while ripe, are fine. Complex flavours are laced with licorice, blueberries and splashes of sweet oak. Ultimately a satisfying savoury style. Screwcap. 14.8% alc. **Rating** 95 **To** 2030
$120 JF
Old Vine Bendigo Cabernet Sauvignon 2015 As with its namesake shiraz, fruit comes off the original '69 plantings, open fermenters, 24 days on skins and aged 20 months in French oak barriques (50% new). Well composed and complex with a flood of black fruits, oak spice with coffee grounds and licorice, supple, persistent tannins, and ready now. Screwcap. 13.8% alc. **Rating** 95 **To** 2027 $95 JF
Bendigo Shiraz 2015 Tremendous concentration of fruit without being over-the-top, it's more a whorl of cassis and plums, cherry pips and blueberries. Savoury

but sturdy tannins, both fruit and oak derived, add to the frame of this not-quite full-bodied wine. It starts with an exuberance and brightness, just tapering off with a dry finish. Screwcap. 14% alc. **Rating** 94 To 2030 $45 JF

ŸŸŸŸŸ Yarra Valley Chardonnay 2016 Rating 93 To 2023 $45 JF
Yarra Valley Pinot Noir 2016 Rating 93 To 2026 $45 JF
Bendigo Cabernet Sauvignon 2015 Rating 93 To 2027 $45 JF
Black Label Bendigo Cabernet Merlot 2015 Rating 92 To 2023 $25 JF ❂
Museum Release Bendigo Cabernet 2004 Rating 92 To 2022 $110 JF
Black Label Yarra Valley Chardonnay 2016 Rating 90 To 2021 $25 JF
Bendigo Merlot 2015 Rating 90 To 2023 $45 JF

Ballandean Estate Wines ★★★★

Sundown Road, Ballandean, Qld 4382 **Region** Granite Belt
T (07) 4684 1226 **www.**ballandeanestate.com **Open** 7 days 9–5
Winemaker Dylan Rhymer, Angelo Puglisi **Est.** 1970 **Dozens** 12 000 **Vyds** 34.2ha
A rock of ages in the Granite Belt, owned by the ever-cheerful and charming Angelo Puglisi and wife Mary. Mary has introduced a gourmet food gallery at the cellar door, featuring foods produced by local artisans as well as Greedy Me gourmet products made by Mary herself. Ballandean Estate can't always escape the unpredictable climate of the Granite Belt. Exports to Singapore, Taiwan and China.

ŸŸŸŸŸ Just Red Cabernet Merlot 2016 75/25% blend. Twist the top and the value light turns straight on. It boasts attractive flavour, texture and satisfying length, all at a snip of a price. Currants, chocolate, Ribena and an infusion of bay leaves. No kinks, no wrong notes, just smooth flowing flavour. Screwcap. 13.2% alc. Rating 91 To 2022 $17 CM ❂
Messing About Granite Belt Saperavi 2016 Saperavi has the most extraordinary colour – the deepest, darkest purple-red; wafts of wood smoke, earth and iodine. It's richly flavoured with satsuma plums, licorice, cedar and charcuterie, but a touch astringent on the finish. ProCork. Rating 90 To 2024 $42 JF
Angela's Reserve Liqueur Muscat NV A lovely mid-amber hue with a touch of bronze; incredibly fresh and youthful, it's smoky with wafts of cold tea, sultanas and florals, especially lavender. Quite sweet with a toffee brittle note on the finish. 500ml. Screwcap. 18.2% alc. Rating 90 $65 JF

ŸŸŸŸ Messing About Granite Belt Durif 2016 Rating 89 To 2026 $35 JF

Ballycroft Vineyard & Cellars ★★★★☆

1 Adelaide Road, Greenock, SA 5360 **Region** Barossa Valley
T 0488 638 488 **www.**ballycroft.com **Open** 7 days 11–4 by appt
Winemaker Joseph Evans **Est.** 2005 **Dozens** 500 **Vyds** 3.5ha
This micro-business is owned by Joseph and Sue Evans. Joe's life on the land started in 1984 and he later obtained a viticulture degree from Roseworthy. Between '92 and '99 he worked in various capacities at Rockford Wines, and since then at Greenock Creek Wines. Joe and Sue are a two-person band, so would-be visitors to the cellar door would be wise to make an appointment for a personal tasting with one of them. Groups of up to eight people are welcome.

ŸŸŸŸŸ Small Berry Langhorne Creek Montepulciano 2015 A delicious, jubey wine that pulses with bright acidity, fresh red-berried fruits, flecks of spice, Mediterranean mint and dried herbs. Perfect for the warmer weather, chilling it absolutely acceptable. Screwcap. 13.3% alc. Rating 91 To 2019 $25 JF
Small Berry French Oak Greenock Barossa Valley Shiraz 2015 This is in better shape than its American oak sibling although this, too, is slapped with wood and smelling of whisky barrels. Fruit compote, earth and blackstrap licorice lead onto the full-bodied palate with expansive tannins and oozing richness with every drop. Screwcap. 15.3% alc. Rating 90 To 2025 $47 JF

Small Berry Greenock Barossa Valley Mataro 2015 A rich, dense and big Barossa mataro with oodles of flavour from salty licorice, new leather, game and charcuterie plus aniseed balls. Firm chewy tanninscause this to cry out for char-grilled steak. Screwcap. 14.7% alc. **Rating** 90 **To** 2021 $25 JF

Balnaves of Coonawarra ★★★★★

15517 Riddoch Highway, Coonawarra, SA 5263 **Region** Coonawarra
T (08) 8737 2946 **www**.balnaves.com.au **Open** Mon–Fri 9–5, w'ends 12–5
Winemaker Pete Bissell **Est.** 1975 **Dozens** 10000 **Vyds** 74.33ha
Grapegrower, viticultural consultant and vigneron, Doug Balnaves has over 70ha of high quality estate vineyards. The wines are invariably excellent, often outstanding, notable for their supple mouthfeel, varietal integrity, balance and length; the tannins are always fine and ripe, the oak subtle and perfectly integrated. Coonawarra at its best. Exports to the UK, the US, Canada, Indonesia, Japan, Hong Kong and China.

ŶŶŶŶŶ **Cabernet Sauvignon 2015** Deeply coloured, this is classic Coonawarra cabernet with cassis, mulberry, mint and dried bay leaf coming together with fine but firm tannins to present an intense, earthy wine that doesn't even flick the needle of dead fruit/high alcohol. It thus has a certain austerity of the kind you once found in classed growth Bordeaux from good vintages such as '70. Screwcap. 14.5% alc. **Rating** 96 **To** 2035 $40 ✪
The Tally Reserve Cabernet Sauvignon 2015 The highly expressive bouquet of cassis, mulberry and herbs married with French oak feeds into a powerful palate where savoury tannins brook no argument about their purpose in life. They need petting and soothing for a minimum of 5 years before this comes back into the Balnaves family orbit. ProCork. 14% alc. **Rating** 96 **To** 2045 $90
Chardonnay 2016 A balanced mix of stone fruit, citrus to nougat, creamy lees, lemon curd and oak spices. While there's flavour aplenty, it's finely tuned and almost tight with excellent length. Screwcap. 13% alc. **Rating** 95 **To** 2023 $30 JF ✪
Shiraz 2015 As usual, an immaculately made wine from quality estate grapes. The mix of plum, dark cherry and blackberry is only medium-bodied, but it has swallowed the oak with the ease that you will have in swallowing this wine. One of the style lighthouses in Coonawarra. Screwcap. 14% alc. **Rating** 95 **To** 2035 $28 ✪
Cabernet Merlot 2015 Bright, full crimson-purple; fruit flavours and tannin structure stake their respective claims from the outset, neither admitting defeat. Blackcurrant, mulberry and black olive flavours are in the red corner, ripe tannins from fruit and oak in the blue corner. This isn't a once-only prize fight, it will continue for many years. Screwcap. 14% alc. **Rating** 95 **To** 2035 $28 ✪
The Blend 2015 60% merlot, 33% cabernet sauvignon, 5% cabernet franc, 2% petit verdot. The components were separately vinified, and blended before 14 months' maturation. Balnaves has made this Bordeaux blend its own, defiantly thumbing its nose at Margaret River. It's on the light side of medium-bodied, but ticks all fruit boxes from blue and black, moving on to its supple mouthfeel ex fine tannins and oak. Screwcap. 14% alc. **Rating** 94 **To** 2027 $19 ✪

ŶŶŶŶŶ **Entav Clone Cabernet Petit Verdot 2017 Rating** 93 **To** 2022 $28 JF

Bannockburn Vineyards ★★★★★

Midland Highway, Bannockburn, Vic 3331 **Region** Geelong
T (03) 5281 1363 **www**.bannockburnvineyards.com **Open** By appt
Winemaker Matthew Holmes **Est.** 1974 **Dozens** 7000 **Vyds** 24ha
The late Stuart Hooper had a deep love for the wines of Burgundy, and was able to drink the best. When he established Bannockburn, it was inevitable that pinot noir and chardonnay would form the major part of the plantings, with lesser amounts of riesling, sauvignon blanc, cabernet sauvignon, shiraz and merlot. Bannockburn is still owned by members of the Hooper family, who continue to respect Stuart's strong belief in making wines that reflect the flavours of the vineyard. Exports to Canada, China, Singapore and Hong Kong.

🍷🍷🍷🍷🍷 Serre 2015 A beautiful release, as intriguing as it is delicious. Wild with complex, herb-strewn flavour but has excellent fruit intensity and a matrix of tannin keeping it firmly in place. Spice, meat and tangy rhubarb-like characters flitter about the core of cherry plum. It promises to age quite exquisitely. Screwcap. 13.5% alc. **Rating** 96 **To** 2028 $97 CM

Chardonnay 2016 Powerful. It really pours it on, the throttle open, all cylinders firing. Peach, toast, butter and marzipan, cedary oak flashing throughout. A milkiness verging on condensed milk, and yet slashed with citrussy acidity. There's a wealth of flavour here, fruit and oak, the tension and drive to match. There's no need to wait; it's all go. Screwcap. 14% alc. **Rating** 95 **To** 2023 $62 CM

Shiraz 2015 Dark and serious with spice, meat and soupy herb notes littered through berried fruit. It's a complex show, stemmy, medium in weight, a touch reductive, all round not for the faint-hearted, but it beats with quality in its own way. It will be extremely complex at maturity. Screwcap. 14% alc. **Rating** 95 **To** 2029 $44 CM

1314 a.d. Chardonnay 2017 It's a wine to bring a smile to your face. It has flavour and life, feeling fun and serious at once. It tastes of pear and ginger, slate and a mix of fresh and cooked apples. Flint notes appear too but at all times it feels fluid and juicy. It's a truly lovely wine, freestyling through the mouth. Screwcap. 13.5% alc. **Rating** 94 **To** 2022 $30 CM ❂

🍷🍷🍷🍷🍷 Sauvignon Blanc 2017 **Rating** 93 **To** 2024 $34 CM
Riesling 2017 **Rating** 92 **To** 2022 $32 CM
Pinot Noir 2016 **Rating** 92 **To** 2026 $62 CM
1314 a.d. Pinot Noir 2016 **Rating** 90 **To** 2023 $30 CM

Barmah Park Wines ★★★

945 Moorooduc Road, Moorooduc, Vic 3933 **Region** Mornington Peninsula
T (03) 5978 8049 **www**.barmahparkwines.com.au **Open** 7 days 10–5
Winemaker Ewan Campbell (Contract) **Est.** 2000 **Dozens** 500 **Vyds** 2.75ha
Tony Williams planted pinot gris and pinot noir (using clones, MV6 and G5V15), having the first vintage made in 2003. In '05 a substantial restaurant was opened, offering breakfast in the vines until 11.30am, and lunch from noon to 5pm.

🍷🍷🍷🍷 Pinot Noir 2014 The colour is starting to show development; a firm wine with plum/blue fruits to the fore, on a palate that mixes dusty and savoury characters. '14 was not an easy vintage, the low yields resulting in a slightly tough persona. Screwcap. 13.5% alc. **Rating** 89 **To** 2021 $45

Barnyard1978 ★★★★

12 Canal Rocks Road, Yallingup, WA 6282 **Region** Margaret River
T (08) 9755 2548 **www**.barnyard1978.com.au **Open** 7 days 10.30–5
Winemaker Todd Payne **Est.** 1978 **Dozens** 1250 **Vyds** 4ha
The then Sienna Estate made the first plantings in 1978, but under the new ownership of Raminta and Edidijus Rusilas, a five-year restoration program of the somewhat neglected vineyard, plus new plantings, has paid dividends. So, too, has the opening of a restaurant with two separate tasting decks for different times of day. It's also a winner of an award by the Master Builders Association of Western Australia for its low environmental impact construction.

🍷🍷🍷🍷🍷 Margaret River Chardonnay 2017 A different take on Margaret River chardonnay, more tangy than most, and livelier than some of the heavyweights. It's hard not to be put off by the Barnyard name, on the other hand; a touch of funk is often seen as a positive. Screwcap. 12% alc. **Rating** 94 **To** 2027 $30 ❂

🍷🍷🍷🍷 Margaret River Semillon Sauvignon Blanc 2017 **Rating** 91 **To** 2021 $25

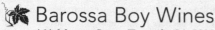 # Barossa Boy Wines

161 Murray Street, Tanunda, SA 5382 **Region** Barossa Valley
T (08) 8563 7550 **www**.barossaboywines.com.au **Open** Not
Winemaker Trent Burge **Est.** 2016 **Dozens** 3500

Sixth generation Barossan Trent Burge is the son of Grant and Helen Burge, a self-styled country boy who liked nothing better than exploring the family's 356ha of vineyards spread across the Barossa on his motorbike. Then cricket intervened, taking him to England on a cricket club program each English summer, returning to Australia each English winter to work as a cellar hand and earn enough to sustain himself for the following six months. The endless summers ceased in 2006 when he joined the Grant Burge wine business full-time, learning every facet of winemaking and marketing. In February '16 Accolade acquired the Grant Burge business, making it inevitable that he would strike out on his own. The slick website, the high quality labelling and packaging of his Barossa Boy Wines bear witness to his experience in marketing. He says his grapes come from vineyards in special sites across the Barossa and Eden valleys, and it's a fair bet the family vineyards will play a large role in that. In '17 he and wife Jessica welcomed their first child, the seventh generation now in place.

🍷🍷🍷🍷🍷 **Double Trouble Shiraz Cabernet 2016** Complex vinification of some very good fruit has produced an ultra-smooth and perfectly balanced medium-bodied blend, with black fruits dominant, but leaving space for splashes of red and purple fruit flavours. Very good value. Screwcap. 14% alc. **Rating** 94 **To** 2036 $30 ✪

🍷🍷🍷🍷🍷 **Young Wisdom Mataro 2016 Rating** 90 **To** 2026 $50

Barratt ★★★★☆

Uley Vineyard, Cornish Road, Summertown, SA 5141 **Region** Adelaide Hills
T (08) 8390 1788 **www**.barrattwines.com.au **Open** W'ends 11.30–5
Winemaker Lindsay Barratt **Est.** 1992 **Dozens** 1000 **Vyds** .5.6ha

This is the venture of Lindsay Barratt. Lindsay has always been responsible for viticulture and, following his retirement as a physician in 2001, he has taken full, hands-on responsibility for winemaking (receiving a graduate diploma in oenology from the University of Adelaide in '02). The quality of the wines is excellent. Exports to Singapore and Taiwan.

🍷🍷🍷🍷🍷 **Uley Vineyard Piccadilly Valley Chardonnay 2016** White peach, fig and cashew lead the way on the bouquet, with a background note of butterscotch, which may be oak, or the beginning of bottle development, or a bit of both. Glides freely along the palate, showing ripe stone fruit flavours, fresh and energetic, the lemony acidity in a supporting role before gathering momentum to provide the thrust on the finish. Screwcap. 13.5% alc. **Rating** 95 **To** 2023 SC
Piccadilly Valley Sauvignon Blanc 2017 Shows the seamless and attractive combination of ripe fruit and herbaceous characters that Adelaide Hills sauvignon blanc achieves with ease in the right conditions. A roll call of all the anticipated aromas fill the bouquet – passionfruit, snow pea, honeydew, etc – which leads to a palate full of equally mouthwatering flavours and lime juice–like acidity. Screwcap. 13% alc. **Rating** 94 **To** 2020 $24 SC ✪

🍷🍷🍷🍷🍷 **Uley Vineyard Piccadilly Valley Pinot Noir 2016 Rating** 93 **To** 2023 SC
Piccadilly Sunrise Rose 2017 Rating 90 **To** 2020 SC

Barrgowan Vineyard ★★★★★

30 Pax Parade, Curlewis, Vic 3222 **Region** Geelong
T (03) 5250 3861 **www**.barrgowanvineyard.com.au **Open** By appt
Winemaker Dick Simonsen **Est.** 1998 **Dozens** 150 **Vyds** 0.5ha

Dick and Dib (Elizabeth) Simonsen began planting their shiraz (with five clones) in 1994, intending to make wine for their own consumption. With all clones in full production, the Simonsens make a maximum of 200 dozen and accordingly release small quantities of shiraz, which sell out quickly. The vines are hand-pruned, the grapes hand-picked, the must basket-pressed, and all wine movements are by gravity. The quality is exemplary.

🍷🍷🍷🍷🍷 **Simonsens Bellarine Peninsula Shiraz 2016** Vivid crimson-purple; in the typically elegant winery style, medium-bodied, fresh and decorated with star bursts of spice and pepper in the red and black cherry fruit. Fine tannins and oak do the rest. Diam. 13.4% alc. **Rating** 95 **To** 2031 $30 ✪

Barringwood ★★★★★

60 Gillams Road, Lower Barrington, Tas 7306 **Region** Northern Tasmania
T (03) 6287 6933 **www**.barringwood.com.au **Open** Thurs–Mon 10–5
Winemaker Josef Chromy Wines (Jeremy Dineen) **Est.** 1993 **Dozens** 3000 **Vyds** 5ha
Judy and Ian Robinson operated a sawmill at Lower Barrington, on the main tourist trail to Cradle Mountain, and when they planted 500 vines in 1993 the aim was to do a bit of home winemaking. The urge to expand the vineyard and make wine on a commercial scale soon occurred, and they embarked on a six-year plan, planting 1ha per year in the first four years and building the cellar and tasting rooms during the following two years. The recent sale of Barringwood to Neville and Vanessa Bagot hasn't seen any significant changes to the business.

🍷🍷🍷🍷🍷 **Recently Disgorged Blanc de Blanc 2012** This is cool-climate Australian sparkling, making sense in terms of its chardonnay makeup, while resounding with drinkability. Orchard fruits, nashi pear gelato and tangerine, all ringing with an urgency across saliva-inducing acidity and a whiff of brioche. Profound. Diam. 11.6% alc. **Rating** 97 $80 NG ✪

🍷🍷🍷🍷🍷 **Classic Cuvee 2014** The gears shift to a stronger pinot role (42%), parlaying with chardonnay (44%), and the rest meunier. Fuelled, too, by a whooping 36 months on lees (top NV Champagne's go-to) and a sensibly assertive 4g/l of dosage. This is exceptional. The mlf (66%) only adds to the bolshie, truffled richness. Buttered toast, marzipan and a choir of orchard fruits barrel along the salacious mineral seams. Acidity is juicy. A strutting sparkling wine, flamboyant and unafraid. Diam. 11.5% alc. **Rating** 96 $48 NG ✪
Pinot Gris 2017 Very good gris here. Pear, apple, honeysuckle, jasmine. Viscous as gris should be, with a faint pumice-like pucker and free-flow of transparent acidity from fore to aft, given further lift by some unresolved spritz. This is richly endowed of texture and yet, fresh and effortless in its showcase of ripe fruit flavours. Screwcap. 13.7% alc. **Rating** 95 **To** 2019 $32 NG ✪
Mill Block Pinot Noir 2016 Compact, juicy and expansive, this single-plot pinot is very good. 15% whole bunches fruit used in the fermentation, before 11 months' maturation in French oak. This approach seems to have attenuated and polymerised the tannins, smoothing away any brittle edges. Cherry notes and candied orange rind amaro, dusted with exotic spices, jitterbug about the mouth. There is still grip, though, but it is silk on a sharp spindle. Screwcap. 13.5% alc. **Rating** 94 **To** 2025 $56 NG

🍷🍷🍷🍷🍷 **Chardonnay 2016 Rating** 93 **To** 2023 $36 NG
Schonburger 2017 Rating 93 **To** 2020 $28 NG
Estate Pinot Noir 2016 Rating 92 **To** 2023 $36 NG
Tasmanian Methode Traditionnelle Cuvee NV Rating 92 $32 NG

Barristers Block ★★★☆

141 Onkaparinga Valley Road, Woodside, SA 5244 **Region** Adelaide Hills
T (08) 8389 7706 **www**.barristersblock.com.au **Open** 7 days 10.30–5
Winemaker Anthony Pearce, Peter Leske **Est.** 2004 **Dozens** 7000 **Vyds** 18.5ha
Owner Jan Siemelink-Allen has over 20 years in the industry, first as a grapegrower of 10ha of cabernet sauvignon and shiraz in Wrattonbully, then as a wine producer from that region. In 2006 she and her family purchased an 8ha vineyard planted to sauvignon blanc and pinot noir near Woodside in the Adelaide Hills. Exports to the UK, Germany, Vietnam, Malaysia, South Korea, Hong Kong, Singapore and China.

ΨΨΨΨ **Adelaide Hills Riesling 2017** It won a bronze medal at the Adelaide Hills Wine Show and that seems pretty right. Lemon sorbet, lime, bath salt and red apple flavours run both directly and impressively through the palate, the finish squeezed tight but the refreshment factor high. It's a lean profile; it needs food. Screwcap. 12.5% alc. **Rating** 89 **To** 2024 $30 CM

Poetic Justice Charlize Rose 2017 Made with pinot noir and tempranillo. Pale copper-crimson. It leans towards the savoury side of the spectrum with tart apple, red cherry, cranberry and a mash of earth and spice notes all trying to get a word in edgeways. It finishes crisp and dry. It works. Screwcap. 13% alc. **Rating** 89 **To** 2019 $30 CM

Barwon Ridge Wines

50 McMullans Road, Barrabool, Vic 3221 **Region** Geelong
T 0418 324 632 **www.**barwonridge.com.au **Open** W'ends, public hols & by appt
Winemaker Leura Park (Nyall Condon) **Est.** 1999 **Dozens** 850 **Vyds** 3.6ha
In 1999 Geoff and Joan Anson and Ken King (of Kings of Kangaroo Ground) planted Barwon Ridge. The vineyard nestles in the Barrabool Hills just to the west of Geelong. Geoff and Joan now operate the vineyard and they are focusing on producing premium fruit, with the wines now made at Leura Park. The vineyard is part of the re-emergence of winemaking in the Barrabool Hills, after the area's first boom through the 1840s to '80s. Barwon Ridge is planted to pinot noir, shiraz, cabernet sauvignon, marsanne and chardonnay.

ΨΨΨΨΨ **Geelong Pinot Noir 2015** Complexity, mouthfeel, flavour and length; all are in this wine's favour. Sour cherry into plum, tangy acidity, sappy herbs and the lightest touch of smoky/cedary oak. Chardonnay and pinot noir are clearly the stars of the range here. Screwcap. 12.8% alc. **Rating** 94 **To** 2024 $38 CM

ΨΨΨΨΨ **Geelong Chardonnay 2015 Rating** 93 **To** 2022 $29 CM
Geelong Chardonnay Pinot Noir 2016 Rating 93 $35 NG

Basedow Wines

161–165 Murray Street, Tanunda, SA 5352 **Region** Barossa Valley
T 0418 847 400 **www.**basedow.com.au **Open** 7 days 10–5
Winemaker Richard Basedow, Rob Gibson **Est.** 1896 **Dozens** 5000 **Vyds** 214ha
Peter, Michael and Richard Basedow are the three 'Brothers Basedow' (B3, as they call themselves), fifth-generation Barossans with distinguished forefathers. Grandfather Oscar Basedow established the Basedow winery in 1896, while Martin Basedow established Roseworthy Agricultural College. As well as retaining consultant winemaker Rob Gibson, the brothers constructed a winery in the old Vine Vale Primary School property in 2008, using the schoolrooms as a cellar door. In '14 B3 Wines purchased the Basedow brand from James Estate, restoring continuity of ownership, and in November '15 the wheel turned full circle when they purchased the old family winery. Exports to the UK, Canada, Denmark, South Korea, Thailand, Singapore and China.

ΨΨΨΨΨ **Eden Valley Riesling 2017** Lime juice creeping into grapefruit territory gives the wine a head start in terms of flavour range and depth, acidity its all-important lynchpin. Has the length and line of riesling that the highest class achieves. Screwcap. 11% alc. **Rating** 95 **To** 2030 $22 ○

🍇 Basils Farm

43–53 Nye Road, Swan Bay, Vic 3225 **Region** Geelong
T (03) 5258 4280 **www.**basilsfarm.com.au **Open** Wed–Mon 9–4
Winemaker Ray Nadeson **Est.** 2005 **Dozens** 1500 **Vyds** 3.86ha
Basils Farm is the venture of Jim and Tina McMeckan, who have had a holiday home on the Bellarine Peninsula for more than 30 years. In 2005 they discovered (and purchased) a property with stunning views across Swan Bay to Queenscliff, and it was on this property that they established Basils Farm. It has 3.86ha under vine (planted to pinot noir, chardonnay

and shiraz), the first full vintage from these plantings occurring in '18, supplemented in the meantime by purchased grapes from the Bellarine Peninsula. Wine is sold through the onsite cafe and cellar door, online, and wholesale in the Melbourne/greater Geelong region. The cafe uses its own farm-grown and locally-sourced produce to create a seasonal menu. There are three brands: Pn2, Basils Farm and Kiltynane. Fruit for the Pn2 Prosecco is sourced from the King Valley, the other wines locally.

🍷🍷🍷🍷🍷 **Kiltynane Bellarine Peninsula Chardonnay 2016** Gleaming straw-green; a good quality chardonnay with plenty to say for itself. Grapefruit zest and juice lead the attack, and white peach and a whisker of green apple have absorbed the French oak without a murmur. Screwcap. 13.5% alc. **Rating** 92 **To** 2021 $55

Bass Phillip ★★★★★

Tosch's Road, Leongatha South, Vic 3953 **Region** Gippsland
T (03) 5664 3341 **www**.bassphillip.com **Open** By appt
Winemaker Phillip Jones **Est.** 1979 **Dozens** 1500
Phillip Jones handcrafts tiny quantities of superlative pinot noir which, at its best, has no equal in Australia. Painstaking site selection, ultra-close vine spacing and the very, very cool climate of South Gippsland are the keys to the magic of Bass Phillip and its eerily Burgundian pinots. One of Australia's greatest small producers. Regrettably, no wines were received for this edition.

Bass River Winery ★★★★

1835 Dalyston-Glen Forbes Road, Glen Forbes, Vic 3990 **Region** Gippsland
T (03) 5678 8252 **www**.bassriverwinery.com **Open** Thurs–Tues 9–5
Winemaker Pasquale Butera, Frank Butera **Est.** 1999 **Dozens** 1500 **Vyds** 4ha
The Butera family has established 1ha each of pinot noir and chardonnay and 2ha split equally to riesling, sauvignon blanc, pinot gris and merlot, with both the winemaking and viticulture handled by the father and son team of Pasquale and Frank. The small production is principally sold through the cellar door, with some retailers and restaurants in the South Gippsland area. Exports to Singapore.

🍷🍷🍷🍷🍷 **1835 Gippsland Chardonnay 2016** A restrained style that offers a balance of flavours tailored to a fine line of acidity. White stone fruit, a dash of citrus with lemon curd, leesy creaminess across the palate. Above all, a really pleasing drink. Screwcap. 12.5% alc. **Rating** 93 **To** 2024 $40 JF
Single Vineyard Heathcote Syrah 2016 In an Australian context, if syrah indicates a cooler climate in which to grow shiraz, Heathcote is not that region. However, there's plenty to like here with its rich ripe mix of black plums injected with flavours of juniper, bay leaves, tar and buckshot. It's full-bodied, and while not aged in new oak, there's still plenty of woodsy spices with the raspy, raw tannins needing time to settle. Screwcap. 14% alc. **Rating** 92 **To** 2029 $25 JF ❂

Battle of Bosworth ★★★★

92 Gaffney Road, Willunga, SA 5172 **Region** McLaren Vale
T (08) 8556 2441 **www**.battleofbosworth.com.au **Open** 7 days 11–5
Winemaker Joch Bosworth **Est.** 1996 **Dozens** 15000 **Vyds** 80ha
Owned and run by Joch Bosworth (viticulture and winemaking) and partner Louise Hemsley-Smith (sales and marketing), this winery takes its name from the battle that ended the War of the Roses, fought on Bosworth Field in 1485. The vineyards were established in the early 1970s in the foothills of the Mt Lofty Ranges. The vines are fully certified A-grade organic. The label depicts the yellow soursob (*Oxalis pes-caprae*), whose growth habits make it an ideal weapon for battling weeds in organic viticulture. Shiraz, cabernet sauvignon and chardonnay account for 75% of the plantings. The Spring Seed wines are made from estate vineyards. Exports to the UK, the US, Canada, Sweden, Norway, Belgium, Hong Kong and Japan.

♟♟♟♟♟ **McLaren Vale Shiraz 2015** Creamy smooth, and with the fruit to match. This will please a lot of folks. Blackberry, licorice, tilled earth and rusty spice notes give this both ample oomph and interest, with texture and length the final clinchers. Screwcap. 14.5% alc. **Rating** 93 **To** 2028 $25 CM ❂

Chanticleer McLaren Vale Shiraz 2015 Quite remarkably for a shiraz at this level, it didn't see any time in oak. It tastes of pure plum, redcurrant, aniseed and mint, bare whispers of both milk chocolate and florals adding to what can only be described as a seductive picture. Pure shiraz velvet. Screwcap. 14% alc. **Rating** 93 **To** 2025 $45 CM

Spring Seed Wine Co. Morning Bride McLaren Vale Rose 2017 This takes the ball and runs with it. It's as textural as it is dry, as aromatic as it is mouthwatering. It's light copper in colour, tastes of redcurrant and herbs, and tries its darndest to keep you coming back for more. Screwcap. 12.5% alc. **Rating** 92 **To** 2019 $20 CM ❂

McLaren Vale Cabernet Sauvignon 2016 Sweet fruit flows through the palate, resiny/creamy oak helping it along its way. Nothing sticks out, nothing is either under- or overdone, nothing is awry, it just gets the job done in soft, harmonious fashion. Screwcap. 14.5% alc. **Rating** 92 **To** 2026 $28 CM

Heretic McLaren Vale Touriga Nacional Graciano Shiraz 2017 Low alcohol but dark colour and no sign of unripeness. Light on its feet but jubey and sweet with herb and dust-like notes as tempering agents. Chewy finish works well. Super fresh. Excellent drink-now option. Screwcap. 12.5% alc. **Rating** 90 **To** 2023 $28 CM

♟♟♟♟ **McLaren Vale Chardonnay 2016 Rating** 89 **To** 2020 $25 CM
Puritan McLaren Vale Shiraz 2017 Rating 89 **To** 2027 $22
Spring Seed Wine Co. Scarlet Runner McLaren Vale Shiraz 2016 Rating 89 **To** 2021 $22 CM

Bay of Fires ★★★★★

40 Baxters Road, Pipers River, Tas 7252 **Region** Northern Tasmania
T (03) 6382 7622 **www.**bayoffireswines.com.au **Open** Mon–Fri 11–4, w'ends 10–4
Winemaker Penny Jones **Est.** 2001 **Dozens** NFP
Hardys purchased its first grapes from Tasmania in 1994, with the aim of further developing and refining its sparkling wines, a process that quickly gave birth to House of Arras (see separate entry). The next stage was the inclusion of various parcels of chardonnay from Tasmania in the 1998 Eileen Hardy, then the development in 2001 of the Bay of Fires brand. Bay of Fires has had outstanding success with its table wines: Pinot Noir was obvious, the other wines typically of gold medal standard. Exports to the US, Asia and NZ.

♟♟♟♟♟ **Pinot Noir 2016** From the East Coast and Derwent Valley, flaunting the expected depth and hue of the colour. It throbs like a high-performance car idling before the flag falls, then awesome in the way it instantly responds to the lightest of touch on the accelerator. Screwcap. 13.5% alc. **Rating** 97 **To** 2036 $48 ❂

♟♟♟♟♟ **Riesling 2017** An impeccable riesling of perfect balance and length, nodding to the Rheingau. The lime-infused flavours are cosseted by crisp acidity and subliminal residual sugar. Showing plenty to enjoy now, yet more in the future. Screwcap. 12.5% alc. **Rating** 95 **To** 2032 $37

Eddystone Point Riesling 2016 From Coal River and Derwent Valley vineyards. It has a gleaming straw-green hue, floral bouquet, then a mid-palate flush with exuberant lime and lemon, reined in by the affirmative action of pebbly acidity on the finish. A long and prosperous life ahead. Screwcap. 12.5% alc. **Rating** 95 **To** 2031 $26 ❂

Chardonnay 2016 A very good example of Tasmanian chardonnay, brimming with life and full of complexity. White and pink grapefruit lead the way, with white peach and nectarine in close attendance. It has focus, effortless precision, and all the length you could ask for. Screwcap. 13% alc. **Rating** 95 **To** 2026 $48

Eddystone Point Pinot Noir 2016 Has the excellent colour expected of Tasmanian pinots. The power and depth of the bouquet and palate are likewise right in the centre of varietal expression with a seamless fusion of cherries and plums of all kinds, oak submerged, tannins so silky they are lost in the folds of the fruit, but are there. Has been amassing gold medals and trophies in virtually every show it's been entered in. Screwcap. 13% alc. **Rating** 95 **To** 2030 $31 ✪

Tasmanian Cuvee Pinot Noir Chardonnay Rose NV A blend of pinot noir and chardonnay that spent 4 years on lees. The cherry blossom and spice-infused bouquet leads into a seductive palate with brioche and dark cherry fruits riding on a lingering finish. A very elegant rose. Cork. 12.5% alc. **Rating** 95 $40

Pinot Gris 2017 Hand-picked, whole-bunch pressed, 20% fermented and matured in used French oak, all parcels having spent 4 months on lees. The result is a wine of complexity and real presence. Whether it is above the line of fire for most pinot gris drinkers is a question that only Bay of Fires can answer. Screwcap. 13.5% alc. **Rating** 94 **To** 2020 $37

Tasmanian Cuvee Pinot Noir Chardonnay Brut NV This spent 3 years on lees, and while no statement is made one way or the other, it was presumably bottle/traditional fermented. Unusual aromas give way to a more familiar palate, albeit very youthful, with hints of honey and the first signs of toast. Will repay time on cork. Cork. 12.5% alc. **Rating** 94 $40

🍷🍷🍷🍷🍷 **Eddystone Point Sauvignon Blanc 2017** **Rating** 93 **To** 2019 $26 ✪
Eddystone Point Pinot Gris 2017 **Rating** 93 **To** 2019 $26 ✪
Sauvignon Blanc 2017 **Rating** 92 **To** 2019 $37
Eddystone Point Chardonnay 2016 **Rating** 90 **To** 2023 $31

Beach Road   ★★★★☆

309 Seaview Road, McLaren Vale, SA 5171 **Region** Langhorne Creek/McLaren Vale
T (08) 8323 7344 **www**.beachroadwines.com.au **Open** 7 days 10–4
Winemaker Briony Hoare **Est.** 2007 **Dozens** 4000 **Vyds** 0.2ha
Briony (winemaker) and Tony (viticulturist) Hoare began their life partnership after meeting while studying wine science at the Roseworthy campus of Adelaide University. Their involvement in the industry dates back to the early 1990s, Briony working around Australia with many of the flagship wines of (then) Southcorp, and Tony gaining extensive experience in Mildura, the Hunter Valley and McLaren Vale (where he spent five years as viticulturist for Wirra Wirra). In 2005 the pair decided to go it alone, setting up a wine consultancy, and in '07 launching Beach Road. The focus on Italian varieties stems from Briony's vintage in Piedmont, where she worked with barbera, nebbiolo, cortese and moscato. Along the way, however, they both had a lot of exposure to grenache, shiraz and mourvedre.

🍷🍷🍷🍷🍷 **Greco 2017** Summer in a glass. It's refreshing and full of saline lemony acidity, wafts of lime blossom and lemon juice; flinty with basil; the savoury twist making it utterly moreish. Screwcap. 13% alc. **Rating** 93 **To** 2019 $35 JF

PX Pedro Ximenez NV An inherited solera with an average age of 30 years, and yet its colour is a youthful pale-mid amber with a rouge rim, looking years younger. Heady with flavours of rum and raisins, prunes dunked in brandy, fruit cake and baking spices, caramel and toffee. It's delicious, and the lively acidity keeps this super fresh, not appearing overly sweet, with the spirit clean and warming. 500ml. Screwcap. 19% alc. **Rating** 93 $42 JF

Bolle Rosso Nero d'Avola Aglianico Montepulciano NV 'Bolle Rosse', Italian for red bubbles, is a mix of 77% primitivo, 13% nero d'Avola, 7% aglianico and a splash of montepulciano. This is cheery stuff. Fresh and bright with plenty of red fruits, spice and tannins – all balanced to make an uncomplicated fizz. Cork. 15% alc. **Rating** 90 $25 JF

Beechworth Wine Estates

Lot 2 Diffey Road, Beechworth, Vic 3477 **Region** Beechworth
T (03) 5728 3340 **www**.beechworthwe.com.au **Open** By appt
Winemaker Mark Kelly **Est.** 2003 **Dozens** 3200 **Vyds** 8.6ha
John and Joanne Iwanuch describe their estate as a family-run and owned business, with their four children participating in all aspects of vineyard life. Situated on the Rail Trail, 4km from Beechworth, they have planted sauvignon blanc, pinot gris, fiano, chardonnay, shiraz, cabernet sauvignon, merlot, tempranillo, sangiovese, tannat, malbec, barbera, nebbiolo and graciano. Exports to Germany.

Reserve Chardonnay 2015 Beguiling chardonnay. Powerful, creamy, floral and long. As soon as you put it near your nose you know you're in for a treat. This is wonderful stuff. Grapefruit, white flowers, fistfuls of spice, smoky bacon, almonds, yellow stone fruits, the full ensemble. Nose, palate, finish: all are top notch. Screwcap. 12.3% alc. **Rating** 96 **To** 2024 $42 CM ✪

Pinot Gris 2017 **Rating** 92 **To** 2019 $20 CM ✪
Fiano 2017 **Rating** 92 **To** 2020 $25 CM ✪
Shiraz 2015 **Rating** 92 **To** 2025 $25 CM ✪
Chardonnay 2016 **Rating** 91 **To** 2023 $35 CM
Pinot Grigio 2017 **Rating** 91 **To** 2019 $19 CM ✪
Tempranillo Graciano 2016 **Rating** 91 **To** 2022 $28 CM

Bekkers

212 Seaview Road, McLaren Vale, SA 5171 **Region** McLaren Vale
T 0408 807 568 **www**.bekkerswine.com **Open** Thurs–Sat 10–4
Winemaker Emmanuelle Bekkers, Toby Bekkers **Est.** 2010 **Dozens** 1000 **Vyds** 5.5ha
This brings together two high-performance, highly experienced and highly credentialled business and life partners. Toby Bekkers graduated with an honours degree in applied science in agriculture from the University of Adelaide, and over the ensuing years has had broad-ranging responsibilities as general manager of Paxton Wines in McLaren Vale, and as a leading exponent of organic and biodynamic viticulture. Emmanuelle was born in Bandol in the south of France, and gained two university degrees, in biochemistry and oenology, before working for the Hardys in the south of France, which led her to Australia and a wide-ranging career, including Chalk Hill. Exports to the UK, Canada, France and China.

McLaren Vale Syrah 2016 Deeply coloured; as usual, a very complex shiraz loaded to the gills with the blackest of black fruits. While tannins and new oak are an essential part of the bouquet and palate, they remain the servants of the fruit. Even in this display of power, there is balance and symmetry that will guarantee a minimum 40-year life. Screwcap. 14.5% alc. **Rating** 97 **To** 2056 $110 ✪
McLaren Vale Syrah Grenache 2016 A 69/31% blend from five vineyards, fermented and matured separately. An exercise in complexity from start to finish in flavour, texture and structure. This has a European touch to the way intensity and elegance dance a pas de deux. It changes shape once again with a magical burst of flavour than lingers forever. Screwcap. 14.5% alc. **Rating** 97 **To** 2041 $80 ✪
McLaren Vale Grenache 2016 If the Syrah Grenache is all about complexity, this is all about stealth. The bright, light crimson hue and fragrant bouquet are seemingly fixed to the flagpole of red berry fruits, but just when you think this may simply be a pretty red wine, the previously hidden fine tannins make their appearance. The result is a wine with great length and great purity. Screwcap. 15% alc. **Rating** 97 **To** 2029 $80 ✪

Bellarmine Wines

1 Balyan Retreat, Pemberton, WA 6260 **Region** Pemberton
T (08) 9842 8413 **www**.bellarmine.com.au **Open** By appt
Winemaker Dr Diane Miller **Est.** 2000 **Dozens** 5000 **Vyds** 20.2ha

This vineyard is owned by German residents Dr Willi and Gudrun Schumacher. Long-term wine lovers, the Schumachers decided to establish a vineyard and winery of their own, using Australia partly because of its stable political climate. The vineyard is planted to merlot, pinot noir, chardonnay, shiraz, riesling, sauvignon blanc and petit verdot. Exports to the UK, the US, Germany and China.

ŶŶŶŶŶ Pemberton Riesling Select 2017 The dainty scale on the front label indicates slightly above 55g/l of residual sugar has been retained on a scale of zero to 100, but thanks to finely tuned acidity, the wine simply tastes dazzlingly fruity and fresh, a lemon-lime sorbet. Leaves the mouth asking for more. Screwcap. 7.5% alc. Rating 95 To 2032 $26 ✪
Pemberton Riesling Dry 2017 A generous and complex mouthfilling riesling with lime, lemon and Granny Smith apple flavours (in that order of importance). Notwithstanding its development potential, it's no sin to share a bottle or two without further delay. Screwcap. 11% alc. **Rating** 94 **To** 2027 $26 ✪
Pemberton Riesling Half-dry 2017 Just under 25g/l of residual sugar has been left in this wine by stopping fermentation and sterile filtering it to ensure fermentation doesn't recommence. It's a pure, delicate mix of lime juice, Granny Smith apple and the residual sugar, all contributing to this utterly seductive riesling. Screwcap. 9% alc. **Rating** 94 **To** 2030 $26 ✪

Bellbrae Estate   ★★★★☆

520 Great Ocean Road, Bellbrae, Vic 3228 **Region** Geelong
T (03) 5264 8480 **www**.bellbraeestate.com.au **Open** 7 days 11–5
Winemaker David Crawford **Est.** 1999 **Dozens** 3500 **Vyds** 8ha
The Surf Coast area of Geelong enjoys a slightly milder climate overall than other areas of the Geelong viticultural region. Being so close to Bass Strait, Bellbrae Estate experiences a maritime influence that reduces the risk of frost in spring and provides more even temperature ranges during summer – ideal growing conditions for producing elegant wines that retain their natural acidity. Wines are released under the Bellbrae Estate and Longboard labels.

ŶŶŶŶŶ Longboard Geelong Chardonnay 2016 Announces its credibility with the first whiff of the bouquet, equally quickly confirmed by the palate. This is very good stuff, fully ripe at 12.5% alc., and not looking to be a wannabe sauvignon blanc. It's white peach first up, then pink grapefruit takes command on the back-palate and finish. Screwcap. **Rating** 95 **To** 2024 $22 ✪
Southside Geelong Sauvignon Blanc 2016 A sauvignon blanc full of attitude, requiring fast thinking (and tasting) to take in the depth and range of tropical fruits, then the way the texture and structure steady the wine on the back-palate and finish. Screwcap. 12.5% alc. **Rating** 94 **To** 2018 $34

ŶŶŶŶŶ Bells Geelong Syrah 2016 Rating 93 **To** 2027 $40 CM
Longboard Geelong Sauvignon Blanc 2017 Rating 91 **To** 2019 $22 CM ✪
Longboard Geelong Chardonnay 2017 Rating 91 **To** 2021 $22 CM ✪
Longboard Bendigo Pinot Gris 2017 Rating 91 **To** 2019 $24 CM
Longboard Geelong Shiraz 2016 Rating 91 **To** 2023 $22 ✪

Bellvale Wine   ★★★☆

95 Forresters Lane, Berrys Creek, Vic 3953 **Region** Gippsland
T 0412 541 098 **www**.bellvalewine.com.au **Open** By appt
Winemaker John Ellis **Est.** 1998 **Dozens** 4000 **Vyds** 22ha
The Ellis family has a rich agricultural heritage that can be traced back to a farm in Nieuw Amsterdam (New York, US) in the late 1600s. Owner/winemaker/viticulturist John Ellis (no relation to John Ellis of Hanging Rock Winery) honed his passion for fine wine and viticulture over an extensive time spent in Europe. This included many trips to Burgundy, France, during his 25-year career as a commercial pilot. Drawn to South Gippsland's cool climate, John migrated to Australia in the 1980s. On his property, he has established pinot

noir (14ha), chardonnay (6ha) and pinot gris (2ha) on the red soils of a north-facing slope. He chose a density of 7150 vines per ha, following as far as possible the precepts of Burgundy. Exports to the UK, Canada, France, Germany, Singapore and Japan.

ŶŶŶŶŶ **Gippsland Pinot Noir 2017** No price, no background and no time to herd cats. It's a great pity, for there's an echo of the resplendent fruit of '17, the dumb waiter bringing the wine to my lips. Nominal/minimal points. Screwcap. 14% alc. **Rating** 90 **To** 2023

ŶŶŶŶ **Quercus Vineyard Gippsland Pinot Noir 2016 Rating** 89 **To** 2023

Bellwether ★★★★★

14183 Riddoch Highway, Coonawarra, SA 5263 **Region** Coonawarra
T 0417 080 945 **www.**bellwetherwines.com.au **Open** Thurs–Mon 11–5
Winemaker Sue Bell, Steve Brown **Est.** 2009 **Dozens** 2000
When Constellation decided to sell (or mothball) its large Padthaway winery, built by Hardys little more than 10 years previously at a cost of $20 million, chief winemaker Sue Bell was summarily retrenched. In quick succession she received a $46000 wine industry scholarship from the Grape & Wine Research Development Council to study the wine industry in relation to other rural industries in Australia and overseas, and its interaction with community and society. She also became Dux of the Len Evans Tutorial, her prize an extended trip through Bordeaux and Burgundy. She decided to stay and live in Coonawarra, and the next stroke of good fortune was that the beautiful stone Glen Roy shearing shed in Coonawarra (built in 1868) came on the market – which is now her winery and cellar door. Exports to the UK, Canada and France.

ŶŶŶŶŶ **Coonawarra Cabernet Sauvignon 2013** What an enticing wine unfurling with aromas of mulberries, boot polish and oak spices. Yes, there's the unmistakable leafy freshness/eucalyptus that's a stamp of the region, but it's like seasoning, adding another layer of complexity. A medium-bodied cabernet with beautiful, fine tannins and refreshing acidity leading onto the seamless palate. Screwcap. 13% alc. **Rating** 96 **To** 2033 $50 JF
Tamar Valley Chardonnay 2013 This is restrained and finely tuned thanks to its natural acidity, yet still packed with flavour. It's smoky with creamed honey, clotted cream and nougat with wafts of white blossom, ginger flower and lavender. The palate is precise, the oak superbly integrated, and more importantly, it's delicious. Screwcap. 12% alc. **Rating** 95 **To** 2025 $50 JF

ŶŶŶŶŶ **Riverland Bianco d'Alessano 2016 Rating** 93 **To** 2019 $25 JF ❸
Wrattonbully Shiraz 2015 Rating 93 **To** 2023 $30 JF
Wrattonbully Tempranillo 2016 Rating 90 **To** 2020 $30 JF

Ben Haines Wine ★★★★★

5 Parker Street, Lake Wendouree, Vic 3350 (postal) **Region** Various
T 0417 083 645 **www.**benhaineswine.com **Open** Not
Winemaker Ben Haines **Est.** 2010 **Dozens** 1800
Ben Haines graduated from the University of Adelaide in 1999 with a degree in viticulture, waiting a couple of years (immersing himself in music) before focusing on his wine career. An early interest in terroir led to a deliberate choice of gaining experience in diverse regions, including the Yarra Valley, McLaren Vale, Adelaide Hills, Langhorne Creek, Tasmania and Central Victoria, as well as time in the US and France. His services as a contract winemaker are in high demand, and his name bobs up all over the place. Exports to the US.

ŶŶŶŶŶ **Volta Brackets Yarra Valley Marsanne 2016** If properly grown (and vinified) on the right site (Tahbilk and Yeringberg notable examples), marsanne can flower brilliantly once 5yo, improving further thereafter. This is Ben Haines' fifth vintage from the Warramunda vineyard (not far from Yeringberg) and he is fine-tuning his approach. Only time required. Screwcap. 12.8% alc. **Rating** 95 **To** 2026 $35 ❸

Raphaella Yarra Valley Syrah 2014 Sourced from the Yeringberg vineyard, where the vines were planted in '99. Two wild ferments, (one whole berries, the other whole bunches), matured for 20 months in French barriques. Good colour; this is a wine of intensity that treads lightly, the acidity and freshness underpinning the fruit important to sophisticated winemaking. Diam. 13.9% alc. **Rating** 95 **To** 2044 $60

Ben Murray Wines

PO Box 781, Tanunda, SA 5352 **Region** Barossa Valley
T 0438 824 493 **Open** Not
Winemaker Dan Eggleton **Est.** 2016 **Dozens** 500 **Vyds** 1ha
'Ben Murray' doesn't exist, but owners Dan Eggleton and Craig Thompson do. Each has had years of experience in various facets of the wine business – Dan with 20 years working for businesses ranging from major corporates to boutique enterprises, and Craig bringing a 1ha old vine grenache vineyard at Lyndoch into the venture, plus experience as a wine importer. The one thing they specifically have in common is a love of drinking wine.

Marananga Barossa Valley Shiraz 2016 A full-bodied shiraz with an elegant twist here and there. It doesn't back off, strongly arguable that it doesn't need to. This is part of the DNA of Barossa Valley shiraz – take it or leave it. Screwcap. 14.5% alc. **Rating** 94 **To** 2041 $70

Bent Creek

13 Blewitt Springs Road, McLaren Flat, SA 5171 **Region** McLaren Vale
T (08) 8383 0414 **www**.bentcreekvineyards.com.au **Open** W'ends 12–4
Winemaker Tim Geddes, Sam Rugari, David Garrick **Est.** 1999 **Dozens** 5000
Established in 1999, today Bent Creek is a partnership between Sam Rugari and David Garrick, collectively with over 40 years' experience in the wine industry. They source premium fruit from vineyards in McLaren Vale (with 70–100-year-old vines) to Piccadilly Valley in the Adelaide Hills, working closely with the growers. There is an overall focus on small parcels of high quality fruit that reflect the variety, vintage and unique terroir each has to offer. Exports to Indonesia, Hong Kong and China.

Black Dog McLaren Vale Shiraz 2016 The dark crimson-ruby hue matches the fruit in this full-bodied wine. Some blackberry essence, with layers of dark chocolate and lashings of oak spice and tannins. Nothing refined here – it's a big wine. Screwcap. 14.5% alc. **Rating** 90 **To** 2024 $25 JF
Black Dog Cabernet Sauvignon 2016 Good concentration of flavour with fresh blackberries and jam. Full-bodied and expansive tannins for cabernet; ripe, but manages to stay upbeat. Screwcap. 14.5% alc. **Rating** 90 **To** 2026 $25 JF

Beresford Wines ★★★★☆

252 Blewitt Springs Road, McLaren Flat, SA 5171 **Region** McLaren Vale
T (08) 8383 0362 **www**.beresfordwines.com.au **Open** 7 days 10–5
Winemaker Chris Dix **Est.** 1985 **Dozens** 25 000 **Vyds** 28ha
This is a sister company to Step Rd Wines in Langhorne Creek, owned and run by VOK Beverages. The estate plantings are of cabernet sauvignon and shiraz (10ha each), chardonnay (5.5ha) and grenache (2.5ha), but they account for only a part of the substantial production. Some of the wines offer excellent value. Exports to the UK, the US, Germany, Denmark, Poland, Singapore, Hong Kong and China.

Estate McLaren Vale Shiraz 2016 Luxuriant of scent and composure: violet, licorice and a cooler climatic stamp of iodine meander amid blueberry, mulberry and satsuma plum, finishing with a lick of five-spice and tapenade. This is strongly regional, generous and delicious. Screwcap. 14.3% alc. **Rating** 93 **To** 2024 $50 NG
Limited Release McLaren Vale Cabernet Sauvignon 2016 Maritime freshness carries a phalanx of currant, bay leaf, anise and black plum across the

palate. This is a rich wine with ample oak tannins, too, but they add a bit of shins and elbow-spike to the richness, providing interest. Trust me, they will be smoothed out with a few years in bottle. Screwcap. 13.3% alc. **Rating** 93 **To** 2028 $80 NG

Estate McLaren Vale Cabernet Sauvignon 2016 Beresford's Estate range is solid. The fruit, intense of flavour; the structural attributes – oak, acidity and grape tannin – well integrated and serving as vectors of line and length, rather than idols of ambition. It is maritime warm–climate cabernet, with brio. Cassis, bouquet garni et al. Screwcap. 13.5% alc. **Rating** 92 **To** 2028 $50 NG

Classic McLaren Vale Chardonnay 2017 A ripe wine displaying the positive attributes of a warm climate: abundance of stone to tropical fruit flavours and palate warmth. More positives manifest in deft winemaking: mineral-clad tension and creamy oak, serving as a conduit of flavour and grip, rather than a scream. Screwcap. 13.3% alc. **Rating** 91 **To** 2022 $28 NG

Classic McLaren Vale Shiraz 2016 Round, juicy and fully loaded. Blue to black fruits all, with lilac floral scents providing lift and an elegance. There is a gentle tannic rasp, serving the wine well, while providing direction across the palate. A punctuation mark of anise, too. Screwcap. 14.3% alc. **Rating** 91 **To** 2022 $30 NG

Limited Release McLaren Vale Shiraz 2016 Matured for 18 months in an arsenal of French and American wood. The oak is far better integrated than in its Grand Reserve sibling. Violet and creamy blue to black fruit allusions all are sluiced with eucalyptus and firm, palate-shaping tannins. Works well in a rustic, oak-driven way. The fruit rises above. Largesse and freshness. Screwcap. 13.5% alc. **Rating** 91 **To** 2028 $80 NG

Estate McLaren Vale Grenache 2016 Unadulterated McLaren Vale grenache in all its giddy glory: Turkish delight, raspberry bonbon and a skein of anise to dried herb, jitterbugging along a line of cranberry acidity. Bit pricey. Screwcap. 13.8% alc. **Rating** 91 **To** 2022 $50 NG

ŸŸŸŸ   **McLaren Vale Grenache Rose 2017** Rating 89 To 2019 $30
Angelique Premium Cuvee NV Rating 89 $25 NG

Berton Vineyard   ★★★★

55 Mirrool Avenue, Yenda, NSW 2681 **Region** Riverina
T (02) 6968 1600 **www.**bertonvineyards.com.au **Open** Mon–Fri 10–4, Sat 11–4
Winemaker James Ceccato, Bill Gumbleton, Glen Snaidero **Est.** 2001 **Dozens** 1 million
Vyds 32.14ha
The Berton Vineyard partners – Bob and Cherie Berton, James Ceccato and Jamie Bennett – have almost 100 years' combined experience in winemaking, viticulture, finance, production and marketing. The 30ha property in the Eden Valley was aquired in 1996 and the vines planted. Wines are released under various labels: Berton Vineyard (Reserve, Winemakers Reserve, Metal Label), Foundstone, Outback Jack and Head Over Heels. Exports to the UK, the US, Sweden, Norway, Russia, Japan and China.

ŸŸŸŸŸ   **High Eden The Bonsai 2015** Shiraz and cabernet, aged (separately) in French oak for 20 months. It's a rich, seductive red with plum, tar and peppercorn flavours sweeping through the palate. There's a firmness to the tannin but it doesn't intrude. Peppermint-cream characters, most likely from the oak, are well integrated. It's satisfying, and it will last. Screwcap. 14.5% alc. **Rating** 92 **To** 2028 $40 CM

High Eden Sauvignon Blanc 2016 Has so much tropical fruit – lychee, passionfruit and gooseberry – that you have to ask when does 'much' become 'too much'. The cultured yeast used has a 100% success rate in amplifying the aroma and flavour of sauvignon blanc, but there has to be the core there in the first place, with the cool High Eden climate the ultimate genesis of what you find in the glass. Screwcap. 13% alc. **Rating** 91 **To** 2018 $20 ●

ŸŸŸŸ   **Winemakers Reserve Fiano 2017** Rating 89 To 2018 $14 CM ●
Reserve Barossa Shiraz 2015 Rating 89 To 2023 $17 ●

Best's Wines

111 Bests Road, Great Western, Vic 3377 **Region** Grampians
T (03) 5356 2250 www.bestswines.com **Open** Mon–Sat 10–5, Sun 11–4
Winemaker Justin Purser **Est.** 1866 **Dozens** 20 000 **Vyds** 34ha

Best's winery and vineyards are among Australia's best-kept secrets. Indeed the vineyards, with vines dating back to 1866, have secrets that may never be revealed: for example, one of the vines planted in the Nursery Block has defied identification and is thought to exist nowhere else in the world. Part of the cellars, too, go back to the same era, constructed by butcher-turned-winemaker Henry Best and his family. The Thomson family has owned the property since 1920, with Ben, the fifth generation, having taken over management from father Viv. Best's consistently produces elegant, supple wines – the Bin No. 0 is a classic; the Thomson Family Shiraz (largely from vines planted in 1867) magnificent (in the *Wine Companion* 2017 it was awarded the mantle of Wine of the Year from a field of almost 9000 wines). Very occasionally a pinot meunier (with 15% pinot noir) is made solely from 1868 plantings of those two varieties; there is no other pinot meunier of this vine age made anywhere else in the world. Justin Purser brings with him a remarkable CV, with extensive experience in Australia, NZ and Burgundy. Exports to the UK, the US, Canada, Sweden, Switzerland, Singapore, Hong Kong and China.

ŸŸŸŸŸ Original 1860's Vines Great Western Pinot Meunier 2017 It's rare that I feel a compulsion to swallow some of a wine I taste in the normal 70 or so wines sampled per day for the *Wine Companion*, but I plead guilty here. Its unique 150+ years of history makes it impossible for this wine to be made anywhere else in the world. Even if you were just tasting history it would have its call, but when you add in a very good vintage and sure hands in the winery, you would likely buy it just for its quality. Light but bright crimson, its length is prodigious, its scented bouquet a siren call, the palate silk. Screwcap. 12.5% alc. **Rating** 98 To 2037 $100 ❂

ŸŸŸŸŸ Foudre Ferment Great Western Riesling 2017 Made with more than a passing nod to the Rheingau, but doesn't forget its place or the exotic vinification. Indeed, to achieve the lime juice lusciousness and complexity of this wine, the Rheingau would have to be in Kabinett territory. Screwcap. 11% alc. **Rating** 96 To 2030 $35 ❂

House Block Great Western Riesling 2017 Gloriously juicy and rich yet also pure. It's going to win the hearts of most who taste it – there is nothing else in Australia with this particular flavour and texture. Screwcap. 10% alc. **Rating** 96 To 2032 $35 ❂

Bin No. 0 Great Western Shiraz 2016 There should be no doubt that this is absolutely of world quality. It ticks each and every box with its deep colour, evocative bouquet smelling of 'old money' (in wine terms), a long and velvety palate, the finish simply wanting you to start the process over again. Screwcap. 14.5% alc. **Rating** 96 To 2046 $85

Great Western Riesling 2017 Bright straw-green, fuller than many of its vintage peers. The length of the palate is exceptional, as is the fluid line of the intertwined citrus fruit and acidity, with lime and Meyer lemon. The result is a riesling that will be drunk before its due time, and I would be happy to join forces tonight. Screwcap. 11% alc. **Rating** 95 To 2032 $25 ❂

Old Clone Great Western Pinot Noir 2017 Excellent colour, and there's a purity to the aroma, flavour and mouthfeel that is striking. Plum, strawberry and cherry are bound tight together by an invisible yet relentless force, at once a single flavour, yet many. Complex? Yes, very, but beautiful. Screwcap. 12.5% alc. **Rating** 95 To 2032 $45

Great Western Pinot Noir 2017 A very impressive pinot noir. It's obvious the cool vintage wasn't too cool, although it also required a sure touch in the winery, letting the wine have its say and not over-extracting it. The spicy, savoury elements are balanced, and held in a sheath of red berry fruits. Screwcap. 13% alc. **Rating** 95 To 2032 $25 ❂

White Gravels Hill Great Western Shiraz 2016 Deep colour; an immediately arresting wine with a complex dark fruit, licorice and spice bouquet that the medium to full-bodied palate takes to another level altogether. The injection of 15% new oak and the 70% whole-bunch ferment are doing all that is expected of them. Screwcap. 14% alc. **Rating** 95. **To** 2041 $45

LSV Great Western Shiraz Viognier 2016 Very good colour; very intense and complex from the word go, reflecting the 15% whole bunch/5% co-fermented viognier, with exotic aromas and a splendidly textured and structured palate. Screwcap. 14.5% alc. **Rating** 95 **To** 2036 $35 ✪

Great Western Cabernet Sauvignon 2016 86% cabernet sauvignon, 4% merlot, and some shiraz and cabernet franc. Strong crimson-purple; pure, intense and long, cassis to the fore, black olive, and firm but ripe tannins. Best's is having a ball. Screwcap. 14% alc. **Rating** 95 **To** 2041 $25 ✪

13 Acre Vineyard Great Western Cabernet Sauvignon Merlot Cabernet Franc 2016 62% cabernet sauvignon, 22% merlot, 12% cabernet franc and 2% each of shiraz and petit verdot. It is positively juicy, with red fruits and fine tannins sewn together by invisible thread. The finish of the wine is spellbinding. Screwcap. 13.5% alc. **Rating** 95 **To** 2036 $45

Great Western Nursery Block Dry Red 2017 14 different varieties plus several unidentified; co-fermented; matured in old American puncheons for 8 months. Is the history of the wine more important than its quality or vice versa? It's a good question, and I will go for history. The wine is as fresh as a spring day with light red fruits akin to pinot noir or grenache in a light mode. Screwcap. 12.5% alc. **Rating** 95 **To** 2030 $45

Great Western The Concongella 2013 1868 old vine pinot meunier, dolcetto and shiraz, matured for 24 months in used French hogsheads. The opposite in style to the Nursery Block Dry Red, only part reflecting the 4-year vintage difference. Time could not reverse the style of the two wines, this one full-bodied, long, savoury and complex, and the '17 Nursery Block light-bodied now and in the future. Cork. 12.5% alc. **Rating** 95 **To** 2043 $150

Great Western Concongella Blanc 2017 Made from 17 varieties, some unidentified; co-fermented and unoaked. This makes drinking history; the flavours range from spicy (à la muscat a petits grains) through to riesling and beyond, and to stone fruit. Screwcap. 11.5% alc. **Rating** 94 **To** 2023 $35

Great Western Cabernet Franc 2016 A blend of 95% cabernet franc, 6% cabernet sauvignon; matured in used French oak for 14 months. The bouquet has a hint of tobacco, and an echo of the luscious dark berry fruits that continue through to the long, balanced finish. Screwcap. 13.5% alc. **Rating** 94 **To** 2041 $45

Great Western Dolcetto 2017 From vines planted in the 1870s, matured for 6 months in old American puncheons. I think the delicious red fruits will still be going in 5+ years' time, but I'm not persuaded they will be better. Terrific value. Screwcap. 12.5% alc. **Rating** 94 **To** 2020 $25 ✪

Great Western Sparkling Shiraz 2014 Fresh blueberry, blackberry and boysenberry, and a hint of chocolate mint as well. Quite plush, the flavours a combination of savoury, spice and generous but restrained fruit – the fine bead a feature. Excellent example of the style. Crown seal. 14.5% alc. **Rating** 94 **To** 2025 $35 SC

♟♟♟♟♟ **Great Western Chardonnay 2017** Rating 93 **To** 2027 $25 ✪
Great Western Pinot Meunier Pinot Noir 2017 Rating 93 **To** 2027 $45
Great Western Rose 2017 Rating 91 **To** 2019 $25 SC
Bin No. 1 Great Western Shiraz 2016 Rating 91 **To** 2029 $25

Bethany Wines ★★★★★

378 Bethany Road, Tanunda, SA 5352 **Region** Barossa
T (08) 8563 2086 **www**.bethany.com.au **Open** Mon–Sat 10–5, Sun 1–5
Winemaker Alex MacClelland **Est.** 1981 **Dozens** 15 000 **Vyds** 38ha

The Schrapel family has been growing grapes in the Barossa Valley for 140 years, and has had this winery since 1981. Nestled high on a hillside on the site of an old bluestone quarry, Geoff and Rob Schrapel produce a range of consistently well made and attractively packaged wines. Bethany has vineyards in the Barossa and Eden valleys. Exports to all major markets.

☆☆☆☆☆ **LE Barossa Shiraz 2016** This is a pointed wine of impeccable ripeness, inherent freshness and deft oak application, guiding the wine's intrinsic qualities to their obvious conclusion: a long, sappy finish. Blueberry, violet, star anise and a whiff of cracked pepper are the conduits. Screwcap. 14% alc. **Rating** 95 **To** 2028 $55 NG

GR15 Reserve Barossa Shiraz 2016 This tastes expensive, with an avalanche of ripe boysenberry and black cherry notes sheathed in a carapace of high quality toasty oak, needing a decade or more to unravel. The grape tannins are plucked and plumed, finely grained and well melded to everything else going on. The acidity on point. Smooth and manicured by a savvy winemaking hand. Cork. 14% alc. **Rating** 95 **To** 2031 $95 NG

LE Barossa Shiraz 2015 Satsuma plum, hoisin sauce and Chinese five-spice notes meander around a juicy, finely wrought tannic spine. The acidity, too, gently dutiful, is far from excessive. The flavours grow sweeter as the wine opens, concluding with a burst of kirsch. This is more red fruit-scented than the Barossan norm. A reaction to the challenges of the vintage and a very apt one at that. Screwcap. 13.5% alc. **Rating** 94 **To** 2023 $55 NG

☆☆☆☆☆ **Reserve Eden Valley Riesling 2017** Rating 93 To 2028 $32 NG
East Grounds Barossa Shiraz 2016 Rating 93 To 2024 $48 NG
Barossa Shiraz 2015 Rating 93 To 2030 $35 NG
Old Vine Barossa Grenache 2016 Rating 93 To 2028 $26 SC ✪
Creek Barossa Shiraz 2015 Rating 92 To 2021 $25 NG ✪
Barossa Cabernet Sauvignon 2016 Rating 92 To 2025 $35 NG
Select Barossa Late Harvest Riesling 2017 Rating 92 To 2025 $28 NG
Eden Valley Riesling 2017 Rating 91 To 2025 $24 NG
East Grounds Barossa Shiraz 2015 Rating 91 To 2023 $48 NG

Between the Vines   ★★★☆

452 Longwood Road, Longwood, SA 5153 **Region** Adelaide Hills
T 0403 933 767 **www**.betweenthevines.com.au **Open** W'ends & public hols 12–5
Winemaker Matt Jackman, Simon Greenleaf **Est.** 2013 **Dozens** 400 **Vyds** 2.1ha
The estate vineyard (2.1ha of chardonnay) was planted in 1995, and purchased by Stewart and Laura Moodie in 2006. Stewart and Laura do all the spraying/netting/wire lifting, pruning, and fruit and shoot thinning, Laura having undertaken a year-long viticulture course. They employ backpackers for labour where needed, and only bring in professional teams for the harvest. In '13 the Moodies created the Between the Vines brand, grafting 0.2ha of tempranillo (on chardonnay rootstock). Output has increased and small quantities of pinot noir and tempranillo are bottled under their label. Matt Jackman makes the wine in consultation with the Moodies, while Simon Greenleaf makes the sparkling varieties.

Bicknell fc

41 St Margarets Road, Healesville, Vic 3777 **Region** Yarra Valley
T 0488 678 427 **www**.bicknellfc.com **Open** Not
Winemaker David Bicknell **Est.** 2011 **Dozens** 455 **Vyds** 2.5ha
This is the busman's holiday for Oakridge chief winemaker David Bicknell and (former viticulturist; present partner) Nicky Harris. It is focused purely on chardonnay and pinot noir, with no present intention of broadening the range; nor, indeed, the volume of production. As from 2014 all the grapes have come from Val Stewart's close-planted vineyard at Gladysdale, established in 1988. The partners have leased this vineyard, which will become the total focus of their business. From 2015 the wines were labelled Applecross, the name of the highest mountain pass in Scotland, a place that David Bicknell's father was very fond of.

ℙℙℙℙℙ **Applecross Yarra Valley Chardonnay 2016** This is a chardonnay with X-factor; pure, mouthwatering, creamy, laced with oyster shell and grapefruit flavour and primped with white peach. It's impressive from the outset but not in a wearying way; exactly the opposite. It's such a stylish wine. 270 dozen made. Screwcap. 13.5% alc. **Rating** 95 **To** 2024 $42 CM

Applecross Yarra Valley Pinot Noir 2016 During retraining of the vineyard it was found that some of the vines were chardonnay. So this pinot noir has a tiny percentage of chardonnay included. It's a lifted, inviting pinot noir where everything seems natural and easy even though its message is complex. It's spicy, bunchy, cherried, alive with rose petal notes, and ever-so-slightly minty. Needless to say, the quality is high. Screwcap. 14% alc. **Rating** 95 **To** 2025 $45 CM

Bike & Barrel

PO Box 167, Myrtleford, Vic 3736 **Region** Alpine Valleys
T 0409 971 235 **Open** Not
Winemaker Jo Marsh, Daniel Balzer **Est.** 2013 **Dozens** 280 **Vyds** 1.5ha
Brian and Linda Lewis have split their vineyard and wine interests in two. One half is a commercial vineyard of 10ha on undulating free-draining slopes above the valley floor, mainly supplying local wineries with chardonnay, prosecco, pinot noir and tempranillo. For Bike & Barrel they have 1.5ha of pinotage, fiano, schioppettino and refosco dal peduncolo rosso.

ℙℙℙℙℙ **House Block Alpine Valleys Schioppettino 2015** Unsurprisingly it's the same vineyard source as Billy Button's version of this grape, also made by Jo Marsh. It offers red berry-into-boysenberry flavours with inflections of gum leaf and black/white pepper, though the main appeal is its fresh, juicy, mid-weight drinkability. Screwcap. 13.6% alc. **Rating** 90 **To** 2020 CM

Billanook Estate ★★★

280 Edward Road, Chirnside Park, Vic 3116 **Region** Yarra Valley
T 0407 354 484 **www.**billanookestate.com.au **Open** W'ends 10–5
Winemaker Domenic Bucci, John D'Aloisio **Est.** 1994 **Dozens** 1200 **Vyds** 14.06ha
The D'Aloisio family has been involved in the agricultural heritage of the Yarra Valley since the late 1960s, and in '94 planted the first vines on their 36ha property. The vineyard is planted to shiraz, sauvignon blanc, cabernet sauvignon, pinot noir, merlot, nebbiolo, tempranillo and barbera. Most of the grapes are sold to various wineries in the valley, leaving a small percentage for the Billanook Estate label.

ℙℙℙℙ **Nebbiolo 2015** A mix of ripe plums and cherries with dried herbs and a slight jubey note. Fleshier on the palate, tannins have decent grip but with the tangy acidity; this is quite approachable. Screwcap. 14% alc. **Rating** 89 **To** 2021 $35 JF

Billy Button Wines

11 Camp Street, Bright, Vic 3741 **Region** Alpine Valleys
T 0418 559 344 **www.**billybuttonwines.com.au **Open** Thurs–Sun 12–6
Winemaker Jo Marsh **Est.** 2014 **Dozens** 3500
Jo Marsh speaks quietly, if not diffidently, making light of the numerous awards she won during her studies for her Degree in Agricultural Science (Oenology) at the University of Adelaide. She continued that habit when she won a contested position in Southcorp's (now Treasury Wine Estates) Graduate Recruitment Program; she was appointed assistant winemaker at Seppelt Great Western in 2003. By '08 she had been promoted to acting senior winemaker, responsible for all wines made onsite. After resigning from Seppelt, she became winemaker at Feathertop, and after another two happy years decided to step out on her own in '14. She has set up a grower network in the Alpine Valleys and makes a string of excellent wines.

ℙℙℙℙℙ **The Torment King Valley Riesling 2017** Jo Marsh's torment was venturing out of her self-set vine enclave of the Alpine Valleys to the Croucher vineyard in the King Valley for her first riesling in '15. Quartz-white, this terrific wine has a rapier thrust of bright acidity running through the palate, shards of citrus and Granny Smith apple flying by its side. Lovely now, but will grow another leg with 5 years in bottle. Screwcap. 12% alc. **Rating** 94 **To** 2027 $25 ✪

The Little Rascal Arneis 2017 Charged with aroma, flavour and texture. This works simply as a crisp dry white but it has the body and indeed complexity to withstand closer inspection. Pour it into a larger-bowled glass and let it stretch its legs a bit; it crackles with spice, is awash with floral perfumes and bursts with red apple–like flavour. Screwcap. 11.5% alc. **Rating** 94 **To** 2019 $25 CM ✪

The Alluring Tempranillo 2016 Tempranillo is clearly thriving in the region and this is yet more proof. Red and black cherries, the sweetness of cola, a splash of ground coffee and modest input from spice add up to a sweet-savoury wine with more than a little drama. We're in 'do yourself a favour' territory here. Screwcap. 14% alc. **Rating** 94 **To** 2023 $30 CM ✪

♟♟♟♟♟ **The Versatile Vermentino 2017** Rating 92 To 2019 $25 CM ✪
2 by 2 Shiraz Tempranillo 2016 Rating 92 To 2021 $25 CM ✪
The Squid Alpine Valleys Saperavi 2016 Rating 92 To 2024 $30 CM
The Socialite Alpine Valleys Prosecco 2016 Rating 92 To 2019 $30
The Classic Alpine Valleys Chardonnay 2016 Rating 91 To 2023 $30
The Chameleon Pinot Gris 2017 Rating 91 To 2019 $25 CM
2 by 2 Nebbiolo Barbera Rose 2017 Rating 91 To 2020 $20 CM ✪
The Affable Barbera 2016 Rating 91 To 2020 $30 CM
The Elusive Nebbiolo 2015 Rating 91 To 2025 $30
The Clandestine Schioppettino 2016 Rating 91 To 2021 $30 CM
The Happy Gewurztraminer 2017 Rating 90 To 2023 $25
2 by 2 Chardonnay Vermentino 2016 Rating 90 To 2019 $20 CM ✪
The Demure Pinot Blanc 2017 Rating 90 To 2022 $25
The Groovy Gruner Veltliner 2017 Rating 90 To 2027 $25
The Feisty Friulano 2016 Rating 90 To 2018 $25 CM
The Delinquent Verduzzo 2016 Rating 90 To 2018 $25 CM
The Mysterious Malvasia 2016 Rating 90 To 2018 $25 CM
The Rustic Sangiovese 2016 Rating 90 To 2020 $30 CM
The Renegade Refosco 2016 Rating 90 To 2020 $30 CM

Bindi Wine Growers   ★★★★★

343 Melton Road, Gisborne, Vic 3437 (postal) **Region** Macedon Ranges
T (03) 5428 2564 **www.bindiwines.com.au Open** Not
Winemaker Michael Dhillon, Stuart Anderson **Est.** 1988 **Dozens** 2000 **Vyds** 6ha
One of the icons of Macedon. The chardonnay is top-shelf, the pinot noir as remarkable (albeit in a very different idiom) as Bass Phillip, Giaconda or any tiny-production, icon wine. The addition of Heathcote-sourced shiraz under the Pyrette label confirms Bindi as one of the greatest small producers in Australia. Exports to the UK, the US and other major markets.

♟♟♟♟♟ **Original Vineyard Pinot Noir 2016** The brightest clarity of colour of the three Bindi pinots, and by some distance the most elegant and nuanced, moving towards red fruits and a lifted, spiced finish. Diam. 13.5% alc. **Rating** 97 **To** 2031 $85 ✪

♟♟♟♟♟ **Block 5 Pinot Noir 2016** Full purple colour; a fragrant bouquet of dark berries/cherries, then a full-bodied palate with earthy tannins intertwined with the dark fruits. Length and power; stylish. Diam. 13.5% alc. **Rating** 96 **To** 2029 $120

Kostas Rind Chardonnay 2016 It's beautifully tight, crisp and youthful, the oak/fruit balance little short of perfect. Melon, green apple and nectarine all swirl quietly behind the shelter of life-giving acidity. Screwcap. 13.5% alc. **Rating** 95 **To** 2026 $60

Quartz Chardonnay 2016 Vinified in the same disciplined way as Kostas Rind. It may seem effortless, but it's not. This is all about purity, length and balance. Screwcap. 13.5% alc. **Rating** 95 **To** 2029 $90

Dixon Pinot Noir 2016 Deep purple hue; multi-plum fruit aromas and flavours; a long, even palate delivering on the promise of the bouquet. Diam. 13.5% alc. **Rating** 95 **To** 2028 $60

Pyrette Heathcote Shiraz 2016 This is ultra full-bodied, not because of alcohol or extract, nor tannins, simply the density of its sultry black fruits, licorice and spices. Pass judgement in a decade from now. Diam. 14% alc. **Rating** 94 **To** 2046 $35

Bird in Hand ★★★★★

Bird in Hand Road, Woodside, SA 5244 **Region** Adelaide Hills
T (08) 8389 9488 **www.**birdinhand.com.au **Open** Mon–Fri 10–5, w'ends 11–5
Winemaker Kym Milne (MW), Dylan Lee, Matteo Malagese **Est.** 1997
Dozens 130 000 **Vyds** 29ha
This very successful business takes its name from a 19th-century goldmine. It is the venture of the Nugent family, headed by Dr Michael Nugent; son Andrew is a Roseworthy graduate. The family also has a vineyard in the Clare Valley providing riesling and shiraz. The estate plantings (merlot, pinot noir, cabernet sauvignon, sauvignon blanc, riesling, shiraz) provide only part of the annual crush, the remainder coming from contract growers. In 2010 a Bird in Hand cellar door was opened in Dalian, in China's northeastern Liaoning province, with a second following in Yingkou. Exports to all major markets.

ŶŶŶŶŶ Adelaide Hills Syrah 2016 Light but bright colour, with juicy red and purple fruits on the elegant bouquet and palate. Syrah usage for this wine, and shiraz for its sibling, is more than often not meaningful – but it certainly is here. Screwcap. 14.5% alc. **Rating** 95 **To** 2026 $40

Lalla Victoria Late Disgorged 2007 Traditional method, only 336 bottles made. After 10 years on lees prior to disgorgement, the spiced red fruits of pinot noir still come through on the very complex palate, allied with hints of marzipan/nougat. There seems to be some low level dosage. Either way, the balance is impeccable. Diam. 12.5% alc. **Rating** 95 $175

Clare Valley Riesling 2017 Quartz-white; a classy wine reflecting the great vintage, the region and the variety in equal measure. There is a brightness to the flavours that is compelling. Screwcap. 12% alc. **Rating** 94 **To** 2030 $27 ❂

Nest Egg Adelaide Hills Chardonnay 2016 The label's expensive silver on dull white paper requires reading with an iPhone torch light, otherwise full daylight. An elegant and fine-boned wine resides within, fruit flavours running from white peach to Granny Smith apple to grapefruit, each courteously acknowledging the contribution of the others. Beautifully detailed, but the X-factor is yet to reveal itself. Screwcap. 13.5% alc. **Rating** 94 **To** 2028 $85

Adelaide Hills Shiraz 2016 A deeply coloured, full-bodied shiraz with a blast of blackberry, licorice and persistent tannins. This is tailor-made for prolonged cellaring, its balance and coherence underlining this future. Screwcap. 14.5% alc. **Rating** 94 **To** 2036 $40

ŶŶŶŶŶ Adelaide Hills Nero d'Avola 2016 Rating 93 **To** 2026 $46
Adelaide Hills Arneis 2017 Rating 90 **To** 2021 $29

BlackJack Vineyards ★★★★

Cnr Blackjack Road/Calder Highway, Harcourt, Vic 3453 **Region** Bendigo
T (03) 5474 2355 **www.**blackjackwines.com.au **Open** W'ends & most public hols 11–5
Winemaker Ian McKenzie, Ken Pollock **Est.** 1987 **Dozens** 4000 **Vyds** 6ha
Established by the McKenzie and Pollock families on the site of an old apple and pear orchard in the Harcourt Valley, BlackJack is best known for some very good shirazs. Despite some tough vintage conditions, BlackJack has managed to produce supremely honest, full-flavoured and powerful wines. Exports to Canada and China.

ŶŶŶŶŶ Chortle's Edge Shiraz 2015 This packs a sizeable punch. Lovers of full-bodied red wine, make hay. It tastes of creamy vanilla, wood spice, blackberry and coffee grounds, and while much of this flavour might sound oak-induced, the weight and impact of fruit here is significant. It's a warm, rich, go-ahead red at a most appetising price. Screwcap. 14.5% alc. **Rating** 92 **To** 2025 $20 CM ❂

Black Range Estate

638 Limestone Road, Yea, Vic 3717 **Region** Upper Goulburn
T (03) 5797 2882 **www**.blackrangeestate.com **Open** Not
Winemaker Paul Evans **Est.** 2001 **Dozens** 360 **Vyds** 24ha
Rogan Lumsden and Jessica Ng were based in Hong Kong, he as a pilot for Dragonair, she
inflight manager for Cathay Pacific, but each was thinking of life after airlines. In 2000 they
purchased the property where they now live and planted the first vines (7ha of shiraz and
2.4ha of merlot), following up with 4.5ha of pinot noir and 10.1ha of pinot gris in '03. The
first vintage of Merlot and Shiraz was made that year. Plan A was to sell the grapes, plus what
they term 'wild ideas of adding accommodation and a restaurant following our retirement
years later'. In '13, following inspiration from running the Medoc Marathon three times after
learning it came complete with wine tasting tables as it wound its way through the vineyards,
they took a step into making wine, asking Paul Evans to make a merlot. In '14 they grafted
an additional 4.5ha of merlot onto their pinot noir vines.

🍷🍷🍷🍷🍷 **Rogan Yea Valley Merlot 2015** Merlots don't come much richer or bigger
than this, but it does have balance in its own fashion, and will certainly be long
lived. Screwcap. 14% alc. **Rating** 90 **To** 2030

Blaxland Vineyards

25 Murray Street, Tanunda, SA 5352 **Region** Barossa Valley
T (08) 8304 8879 **www**.blaxwine.com.au **Open** 7 days 10–5
Winemaker Chris Polymiadis **Est.** 1995 **Dozens** 65 000 **Vyds** 675ha
Founder and owner Ron Collins has prospered mightily given the headwinds that have
buffeted the Australian wine industry over the past decade. Blaxland Vineyards is the
12th largest vineyard proprietor in Australia; it owns the 320ha Tanunda Hill Vineyard in
the Barossa Valley, the 266ha Old Mundulla Vineyard in the Limestone Coast, and the 89ha
St Magnus Vineyard in the Adelaide Hills. It has side-stepped the cost of establishing a winery
by forming ongoing arrangements with leading wineries to make its wines, meeting its
cost criteria, overseen by Chris Polymiadis. The wines have enjoyed considerable success in
overseas wine shows, notably in China, California and Germany. The value for money is self-
evident. Exports to the UK, the US, China and Japan.

🍷🍷🍷🍷🍷 **Barossa Valley Shiraz 2014** Dense and deep but vivid hue of crimson-purple;
an impressive wine at the price, with real aspirations to elegance. French oak plays
a role on both the bouquet and the light to medium-bodied palate. Both black
(predominant) and red fruits are associated with a pinch of spice, supported by fine
tannins. Screwcap. 14.5% alc. **Rating** 92 **To** 2029 $25 ✪

🍷🍷🍷🍷 **Tanunda Hill Barossa Shiraz 2016 Rating** 89 **To** 2032

Bleasdale Vineyards

1640 Langhorne Creek Road, Langhorne Creek, SA 5255 **Region** Langhorne Creek
T (08) 8537 4000 **www**.bleasdale.com.au **Open** Mon–Sun 10–5
Winemaker Paul Hotker, Matt Laube **Est.** 1850 **Dozens** 100 000 **Vyds** 45ha
This is one of the most historic wineries in Australia, celebrating 165 years of continuous
winemaking by the direct descendants of the founding Potts family in 2015. Not so long
before the start of the 21st century, its vineyards were flooded every winter by diversion of the
Bremer River, which provided moisture throughout the dry, cool, growing season. In the new
millennium, every drop of water was counted. The vineyards have been significantly upgraded
and refocused, with shiraz accounting for 45% of plantings, supported by seven other proven
varieties. Bleasdale has completely revamped its labels and packaging, and has headed to the
Adelaide Hills for sauvignon blanc, pinot gris and chardonnay under the direction of gifted
winemaker (and viticulturist) Paul Hotker. Exports to all major markets.

🍷🍷🍷🍷🍷 **Wellington Road Langhorne Creek GSM 2016** Short barrel maturation is
the master stroke in keeping the wine red fruited, fragrant and supple. Chalky fruit

tannins add refreshment and ultimately, drinkability, without sacrificing critical structure. Hard to not keep going back to this wine. Another consistent wine show performer from year to year. Fabulous quality. Screwcap. 14% alc. **Rating** 96 To 2030 $29 DB ✪

The Iron Duke Langhorne Creek Cabernet Sauvignon 2016 A powerful, intense and pure cabernet with great length. Top gold Adelaide Wine Show '17, gold medal Hobart Wine Show '17. Screwcap. 14% alc. **Rating** 96 To 2041 $65 ✪

Frank Potts 2016 A clever cabernet-dominant blend incorporating malbec, franc, merlot and petit verdot to great effect. Red and black fruited, leafy cabernet, fine savoury tannins, line and length to burn. Complexity derived from judicious use of different varieties rather than sheer mass, oak or volume. Gold at the National Wine Show '17 speaks volumes. Screwcap. 14% alc. **Rating** 96 To 2030 $35 DB ✪

Generations Langhorne Creek Malbec 2016 Deep colour; the wine effortlessly takes hold of every aspect of the palate, with layered plum and black forest flavours, just the modest amount of new oak and tannins. Gold medal National and Perth Wine Shows '17. Screwcap. 14% alc. **Rating** 96 To 2029 $35 ✪

Generations Langhorne Creek Shiraz 2016 A nice forward, open fragrance of red and black fruit, hints of cordite, breezy soft tannins that the 22% new oak all but soaked up. Balance and poise. Gold medal Perth Wine Show '17. Screwcap. 14% alc. **Rating** 95 To 2025 $35 DB ✪

Wellington Road Langhorne Creek Shiraz Cabernet Sauvignon 2016 Bright garnet and purple hued. Blackberry, blackcurrant and spice. 25% new oak adds support and structure to the medium-bodied frame, but doesn't intrude. Gold medals across many shows attest to the quality of the wine. Screwcap. 14% alc. **Rating** 95 To 2028 $29 DB ✪

The Riparian Vineyard Langhorne Creek Malbec 2016 The bouquet immediately announces the full-bodied palate that follows. The plummy fruit has excellent structure, and the wine will develop at a leisurely pace. There is far more similarity to the trio of Bleasdale Malbecs than differences, freshness in all preserved by minimal alcohol and hands-off winemaking. Screwcap. 14% alc. **Rating** 95 To 2034 $35 ✪

Adelaide Hills Chardonnay 2017 An articulate and elegant chardonnay with white stone fruit, lemon citrus, yeast-derived complexity and toasty oak, all expertly placed. No single element dominates, and there's a lovely citric tang to the finish that adds length and persistence. Stylish drinking for the price. Screwcap. 12.5% alc. **Rating** 94 To 2023 $25 DB ✪

The Powder Monkey Single Vineyard Langhorne Creek Shiraz 2016 Ripe black fruit, spice, flint and toast and bacon fat from the 27% new French oak. This is deceptively medium-bodied, almost sleek, with fine velvety tannins, a bright redcurrant freshness and a long, persistent finish. The oak level is the only question. Screwcap. 14% alc. **Rating** 94 To 2028 $65 DB

Mulberry Tree Langhorne Creek Cabernet Sauvignon 2016 Made with the same care as a red wine four times its price, the quality embarrassingly good. It's an elegant wine shouting its variety and place from the rooftops, its vibrantly fresh blackcurrant/cassis heart pumping furiously. Screwcap. 14% alc. **Rating** 94 To 2031 $20 ✪

The Islander Estate Vineyard Kangaroo Island Malbec 2016 Deep crimson-purple; still in primordial condition; light to medium-bodied, and will enjoy 24 months to fill out the middle palate. Screwcap. 14% alc. **Rating** 94 To 2033 $35

🍷🍷🍷🍷 **The Iron Duke Cabernet Sauvignon 2015** Rating 93 To 2030 $65
The Mullianna Vineyard Malbec 2016 Rating 93 To 2033 $35
Adelaide Hills Pinot Gris 2017 Rating 92 To 2019 $20 ✪
Adelaide Hills Sauvignon Blanc 2017 Rating 90 To 2020 $20 ✪
Bremerview Langhorne Creek Shiraz 2016 Rating 90 To 2026 $20 ✪

Bloodwood ★★★★★

231 Griffin Road, Orange, NSW 2800 **Region** Orange
T (02) 6362 5631 **www**.bloodwood.biz **Open** By appt
Winemaker Stephen Doyle **Est.** 1983 **Dozens** 4000 **Vyds** 8.43ha
Rhonda and Stephen Doyle are two of the pioneers of the Orange district, with 2013 marking Bloodwood's 30th anniversary. The estate vineyards (chardonnay, riesling, merlot, cabernet sauvignon, shiraz, cabernet franc and malbec) are planted at an elevation of 810–860m, which provides a reliably cool. climate. The wines are sold mainly through the cellar door and by an energetic, humorous and informatively run mailing list. Bloodwood has an impressive track record across the full gamut of wine styles, especially riesling; all of the wines have a particular elegance and grace. Very much part of the high quality reputation of Orange. Exports to Malaysia.

ŸŸŸŸŸ **Riesling 2017** It spends time on lees and has both more body and more texture than you might expect of a young Australian riesling. Indeed the texture here may well be worth the price of admission alone. Orange peel, lime zest, sweet spice, talc – all frolic about here. It's a lovely drinking experience. Screwcap. 12.6% alc. Rating 95 To 2024 $25 CM ✪

ŸŸŸŸỸ **Schubert 2016** Rating 93 To 2023 $32 CM
Shiraz 2015 Rating 93 To 2030 $32 CM
Big Men in Tights 2017 Rating 92 To 2020 $20 CM ✪
Chardonnay 2017 Rating 90 To 2021 $28 CM
Pinot Noir 2017 Rating 90 To 2029 $35

Blue Gables ★★★★★

100 Lanigan Road, Maffra West Upper, Vic 3859 **Region** Gippsland
T (03) 5148 0372 **www**.bluegables.com.au **Open** W'ends 10–5 by appt
Winemaker Alastair Butt, Mal Stewart (sparkling) **Est.** 2004 **Dozens** 1800 **Vyds** 3.7ha
Blue Gables is the culmination of a long-held dream for chemical engineer Alistair Butt and journalist wife Catherine Hicks; they purchased 8ha of a north-facing hillside from Catherine's father's dairy farm, and built a two-storey gabled-roof farmhouse, hence the name. This small vineyard, nestled high above the Macalister Irrigation District in east Gippsland, was established in 2004. The planting continued in '05 with 0.8ha each of sauvignon blanc, pinot gris and shiraz and 0.4ha of chardonnay. The wines have had significant success in the Gippsland Wine Show and Victorian Wines Show.

ŸŸŸŸŸ **East Gippsland Pinot Gris 2016** A very well made gris in the true style; honeyed bouquet and texture and structure to burn. Delicious allspice runs as background music for both the bouquet and palate; there is also pear, ginger and citrus, the last brightening the finish. Gold medal Gippsland Wine Show. Screwcap. 13.7% alc. Rating 95 To 2020 $30 ✪
KT Reserve Shiraz 2015 The difference between this wine and its Hanratty Hill sibling is that only a single new French barrique was used; the wine matured for 11 months. Given the vines were only 12yo, one might have expected this to be overwhelmed by the oak, but that didn't happen. All up, very impressive. Screwcap. 14.8% alc. Rating 95 To 2030 $65

ŸŸŸŸỸ **East Gippsland Sauvignon Blanc 2016** Rating 90 To 2019 $25
Jesse East Gippsland Chardonnay 2016 Rating 90 To 2022 $30

Blue Pyrenees Estate ★★★★★

Vinoca Road, Avoca, Vic 3467 **Region** Pyrenees
T (03) 5465 1111 **www**.bluepyrenees.com.au **Open** 7 days 11–5
Winemaker Andrew Koerner, Chris Smales **Est.** 1963 **Dozens** 60 000 **Vyds** 149ha
Forty years after Remy Cointreau established Blue Pyrenees Estate (then known as Chateau Remy), the business was sold to a small group of Sydney businessmen. Former Rosemount

senior winemaker Andrew Koerner heads the winery team. The core of the business is the very large estate plantings, most decades old, but with newer arrivals, including viognier. Blue Pyrenees has a number of programs designed to protect the environment and reduce its carbon footprint. Exports to Asia, primarily China.

🍷🍷🍷🍷🍷 **Section One Shiraz 2015** From the vineyard block usually responsible for the Reserve wines, planted in the '70s. Elegance doesn't come easily in the Pyrenees, but this wine has it thanks to its medium-bodied and fresh red fruits. Screwcap. 14.5% alc. **Rating** 95 **To** 2029 $42

Estate Red 2015 83% cabernet sauvignon, 12% malbec, 5% merlot. This is a delight – and a surprise. Instead of the usually slightly bony/hard mouthfeel of most of the Blue Pyrenees red wines, this is luscious and round, cassis, redcurrant and plum all intersecting, pliable tannins doing nothing to diminish the pleasure. Screwcap. 14.5% alc. **Rating** 95 **To** 2030 $42

Bone Dry Rose Pinot Noir 2017 Lovely pale tea rose colour. Red berry–scented with notes of cranberry and Turkish delight. It's hard not to fall for its soft, delicate, juicy palate, with just enough savoury notes to maintain freshness and interest. Crowd-pleasing stuff. The lowish alcohol a bonus. Screwcap. 12% alc. **Rating** 94 **To** 2018 $22 DB ✪

🍷🍷🍷🍷 **Midnight Cuvee 2013** **Rating** 91 $32 CM
Methode Traditionnelle Vintage Brut 2013 **Rating** 91 $32 DB
Cabernet Sauvignon 2015 **Rating** 90 **To** 2023 $26
Methode Traditionnelle Dry Sparkling Rose NV **Rating** 90 $22
Methode Traditionnelle Sparkling Shiraz NV **Rating** 90 $28 TS

Blue Rock Wines ★★★★

PO Box 692, Williamstown, SA 5351 **Region** Eden Valley
T 0419 817 017 **www**.bluerockwines.com.au **Open** Not
Winemaker Zissis Zachopoulos **Est.** 2005 **Dozens** 4000 **Vyds** 15ha

This is the venture of the brothers Zachopoulos: Nicholas, Michael and Zissis, the last with a double degree – viticulture and wine science – from CSU. Michael and Nicholas manage the 104ha property, which is situated in the Eden Valley at an elevation of 475m. Most blocks are north-facing, the slopes providing frost protection with their natural air drainage, the soils likewise rich and free-draining. The vineyards have been planted so far to mainstream varieties, with an ongoing planting program extending to 8ha of tempranillo, pinot gris, pinot noir, grenache and mataro. Most of the production is the subject of a sales agreement with Grant Burge, with 75t retained each year to make the Blue Rock wines.

🍷🍷🍷🍷🍷 **Pantelis Barossa Cabernet Sauvignon 2014** Aged for 24 months in 75% new French and Hungarian oak, an adept restraining device to the florals and dark fruit allusions that gush across this full-bodied wine's midriff. These are swept to a long tail by a herbaceous astringency and bitter chocolate tannins, pressing the fruit into a nourishing whole while towing the finish long. Screwcap. 14.5% alc. **Rating** 94 **To** 2029 $50 NG

🍷🍷🍷🍷 **Black Velvet Barossa Shiraz 2014** **Rating** 93 **To** 2022 $40 NG
Eden Valley Cabernet Sauvignon 2015 **Rating** 93 **To** 2023 $20 NG ✪
Eden Valley Riesling 2017 **Rating** 91 **To** 2025 $17 NG ✪
Eden Valley Shiraz 2015 **Rating** 91 **To** 2021 $20 NG ✪

Boat O'Craigo ★★★★☆

458 Maroondah Highway, Healesville, Vic 3777 **Region** Yarra Valley
T (03) 5962 6899 **www**.boatocraigo.com.au **Open** Fri–Sun 10.30–5.30
Winemaker Rob Dolan (Contract) **Est.** 1998 **Dozens** 3000 **Vyds** 21.63ha

When Margaret and Steve Graham purchased a property at Kangaroo Ground, naming it in honour of their Scottish ancestors, they correctly chose to plant shiraz and cabernet sauvignon on the warm site with its black volcanic basalt soil. In 2003 the maiden vintage followed and, with son Travers joining the business, they purchased a vineyard in the foothills of the Black Spur Ranges, with gewurztraminer, sauvignon blanc, chardonnay and pinot noir. The third stage was the '11 acquisition of a substantial winery in Warranwood, equidistant between the vineyards. Exports to Hong Kong and China.

ΨΨΨΨΨ **Reserve Yarra Valley Shiraz 2016** There's some beef on this wine's bones, and a little too much oak, though it remains savoury and cool climate at heart. Coffee-cream and black cherry flavours build a good head of steam before pepper spice and savoury/dry herb notes float in. Tannin is firm and spicy; there's enough substance here to lend the wine a presence; and it finishes with a confident push of flavour. Diam. 14.5% alc. **Rating** 94 **To** 2034 $55 CM

Braveheart Yarra Valley Cabernet Sauvignon 2016 The structural elements are paramount here though there's no lack of fruit or indeed complexity. It's a handsome wine, elegant too you'd argue. It tastes of blackcurrant and olives, bay leaves, mulch and tobacco; tannin mowing through the finish. It will cellar well. Screwcap. 14% alc. **Rating** 94 **To** 2034 $30 CM ✪

ΨΨΨΨΨ **Black Cameron Yarra Valley Shiraz 2016 Rating** 93 **To** 2028 $30 CM
Black Spur Yarra Valley Rose 2017 Rating 90 **To** 2020 $24 CM

Boireann ★★★★★

26 Donnellys Castle Road, The Summit, Qld 4377 **Region** Granite Belt
T (07) 4683 2194 **www**.boireannwinery.com.au **Open** Fri–Sun 10–4
Winemaker Peter Stark **Est.** 1998 **Dozens** 1200 **Vyds** 1.6ha
Peter and Therese Stark have a 10ha property set among the great granite boulders and trees that are so much a part of the Granite Belt. The vineyard is planted to French and Italian varieties: a straight merlot; shiraz and viognier; grenache and mourvedre providing a Rhône blend; four Bordeaux varieties that go to make the Lurnea; and then there also are tannat, pinot noir (French) and sangiovese, barbera and nebbiolo (Italian), making up the viticultural League of Nations. Peter is a winemaker of exceptional talent, producing cameo amounts of red wines that are of a quality equal to Australia's best. After much soul-searching the property was sold in March 2018, with the business now managed by Brad and Metz Rowe.

ΨΨΨΨΨ **Granite Belt Shiraz Viognier 2016** Superb colour; the fragrance of the wine is immediate and powerful, as are the flavours of the palate. This comes before you've really settled down to properly assess this juicy, utterly beguiling, medium-bodied wine. It's the highly unusual serpentine way the flavours accompany every movement in the mouth, never losing their charm. Screwcap. 13.5% alc. **Rating** 98 **To** 2046 $65 ✪

ΨΨΨΨΨ **Granite Belt Shiraz 2016** What a pity Boireann can't make sufficient quantities to enter significant wine shows. This picture-perfect shiraz is another in a long stream of beautifully crafted wines at mouthwatering prices. Blackberry and black cherry fruit is backed by ripe tannins and tailor-made oak. Screwcap. 13% alc. **Rating** 95 **To** 2029 $35 ✪

La Cima Granite Belt Nebbiolo 2016 Excellent colour, particularly for nebbiolo; Peter Stark leaves huge footsteps to be followed. He has effortlessly tamed nebbiolo to produce a rose petal/red blossom bouquet and a silky, supple, red-fruited palate, tannins no more than a whisper. Screwcap. 14% alc. **Rating** 95 **To** 2029 $40

Granite Belt Mourvedre 2016 A full-bodied wine by most standards, including Boireann's. It stands to one side of most of the estate's wines, with black fruits and savoury tannins. But it's so perfectly balanced it will become steadily more graceful as it ages over the decades. Screwcap. 14% alc. **Rating** 95 **To** 2046 $35 ✪

The Lurnea 2016 35% cabernet sauvignon, 22% merlot, 20% tannat, 14% petit verdot, 9% cabernet franc. Boireann's Bordeaux blend. Still in its infancy, but will get there. Screwcap. 13.5% alc. **Rating** 94 **To** 2036 $35

La Cima Granite Belt Sangiovese 2016 While only light to medium-bodied, this brightly coloured wine hits the bullseye with its red fruits refusing to lie down in the face of powdery/savoury tannins. The flavours linger long in the mouth. Screwcap. 13.5% alc. **Rating** 94 **To** 2026 $30 ❂

Granite Belt Tannat 2016 Ah, inky tannat. It's a unique variety with ridiculous amounts of colour and tannins, and Peter Stark hasn't over-extracted it in the winery – it's very well made. The like/dislike votes will be close to 50/50; my points are an indication of respect but not affection for the variety. Screwcap. 14% alc. **Rating** 94 **To** 2046 $35

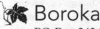 **La Cima Rosso 2016** **Rating** 93 **To** 2030 $40
La Cima Granite Belt Barbera Superiore 2016 **Rating** 91 **To** 2022 $35

Bondar Wines

Rayner Vineyard, 24 Twentyeight Road, McLaren Vale, SA 5171 **Region** McLaren Vale
T 0419 888 303 **www**.bondarwines.com.au **Open** By appt
Winemaker Andre Bondar **Est.** 2013 **Dozens** 3000 **Vyds** 11ha
Husband and wife Andre Bondar and Selina Kelly began a deliberately unhurried journey in 2009, which culminated in the purchase of the celebrated Rayner Vineyard post-vintage '13. Andre had been a winemaker at Nepenthe for seven years, and Selina had recently completed a law degree, but was already somewhat disillusioned about the legal landscape. They changed focus, and began to look for a vineyard capable of producing great shiraz. Rayner had all the answers: a ridge bisecting the land, Blewitt Springs sand on the eastern side, and the 'Seaview' with heavier clay loam soils over limestone on the western side. They are continuing to close-plant counoise, with mataro, carignan and cinsaut to follow. An Adelaide Hills syrah is in their sights. Exports to the UK, the US and China.

 Violet Hour McLaren Vale Shiraz 2016 It takes the fragrant appeal of Blewitt Springs shiraz and builds tannin, texture and complex flavour into the deal, quality taken care of in the process. This spent 6 weeks on skins and the tannin shows it; layers of velvet folded through the finish. Saltbush notes, thyme, rose petals turned dry. It's a modern face of McLaren Vale shiraz (it saw no new oak) but it's still a powerful one. Screwcap. 13.8% alc. **Rating** 95 **To** 2030 $28 CM ❂

Rayner Vineyard Grenache 2017 And so the glory days of Australian grenache roll on. This is A-grade. Lifted, lively, ripe, finessed and finished to perfection. Light in a lovely way. Drink in the scent, drink in the wine. A curl of spice-shot tannin pulls the final strings. It begs the word gorgeous. Screwcap. 14% alc. **Rating** 95 **To** 2025 $38 CM

Junto McLaren Vale Grenache Shiraz Mourvedre 2017 This is light and lifted, bright and buoyant. It's far more about perfume and mouthfeel than it is about density. It trips about with anise and raspberry, fennel and florals, delighting as it goes. Screwcap. 13.5% alc. **Rating** 94 **To** 2024 $28 CM ❂

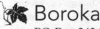 **Adelaide Hills Chardonnay 2017** **Rating** 93 **To** 2023 $35 CM
McLaren Vale Fiano 2017 **Rating** 92 **To** 2020 $28 CM
McLaren Vale Grenache Rose 2017 **Rating** 91 **To** 2020 $25 CM

Boroka
★★★

PO Box 242, Warragul, Vic 3820 **Region** Various
T (03) 5623 3391 **www**.boroka.com.au **Open** Not
Winemaker Hamish Seabrook **Est.** 1968 **Dozens** 500
The Boroka of today bears no resemblance to that of the late 1960s and '70s, when its activities were centred on the foothills of the Grampians mountain range in western Victoria. David McCracken received support from Viv Thomson of Best's and its then winemaker Trevor Mast. While the McCracken family moved from Great Western, and is these days resident elsewhere, the connection with the region has been maintained through Hamish Seabrook, who not only makes the Boroka wines, but was a winemaker for Best's before moving to the

Barossa Valley where he now lives and works. He sources grapes and wines from various parts of South Australia and Victoria for the Boroka brand. Exports to China.

ŸŸŸŸ **The Pinnacle Great Western Shiraz 2013** Inky crimson-purple, still showing little or no colour change. It is full-bodied, and curiously having all the hallmarks of excessive extraction except for the near absence of tannins. The alcohol is the only explanation: where it will head is anyone's guess. Cork. 14.9% alc. **Rating** 89 **To** 2023 $35

Bourke & Travers   ★★★★☆
PO Box 457, Clare, SA 5453 **Region** Clare Valley
T 0400 745 057 **www.**bourkeandtravers.com **Open** Not
Winemaker David Travers, Michael Corbett **Est.** 1998 **Dozens** 350 **Vyds** 6ha
Owner David Travers' family has been continuously farming in Australia for 159 years, chiefly raising sheep and broadacre cereals and legumes. In the 1870s David's great-grandfather, Nicholas Travers, established a vineyard south of Leasingham, between what is now Kilikanoon and O'Leary Walker. However, his son Paul left this property to establish a large sheep and grazing property near Port Lincoln, and Paul's son Gerald (David's father) retains these properties today, David remaining heavily involved in their operation. David established Bourke & Travers on Armagh Creek in 1996, and planted the first grapes (shiraz) in '98. The Bourke in the brand comes from David's mother, Kathleen Bourke (her maiden name). The wine portfolio has been increased with a syrah rose and a single vineyard grenache, while 25% whole-bunch fermentation has been introduced in the shiraz.

ŸŸŸŸŸ **Single Vineyard Clare Valley Shiraz 2016** This shiraz brings its A game. It's ripe, fluid, complex and long; a ripper. Blue and black berries, florals, creamy vanilla and flashes of black pepper. Tannin adds some swagger. Chocolatey aftertaste but freshness and vibrancy are in full flight here. Screwcap. 13.8% alc. **Rating** 96 **To** 2036 $40 CM ✪

ŸŸŸŸŸ **Block 41 Syrah Rose 2017** **Rating** 93 **To** 2020 $26 CM ✪

Bowen Estate   ★★★★
15 459 Riddoch Highway, Coonawarra, SA 5263 **Region** Coonawarra
T (08) 8737 2229 **www.**bowenestate.com.au **Open** 7 days 10–5
Winemaker Emma Bowen **Est.** 1972 **Dozens** 12 000 **Vyds** 33ha
Regional veteran Doug Bowen presides over one of Coonawarra's landmarks, but he has handed over full winemaking responsibility to daughter Emma, 'retiring' to the position of viticulturist. In May 2015 Bowen Estate celebrated its 40th vintage with a tasting of 24 wines (shiraz and cabernet sauvignon) from 1975 to 2014. Exports to the UK, the Maldives, Singapore, China, Japan and NZ.

ŸŸŸŸŸ **Coonawarra Chardonnay 2017** A solid wine with rockmelon, quince and stone fruit flavours directed to a long, gently mineral finish by a signpost of well applied oak. The core of creamy nougat and roasted nuts imparts generosity and complexity. A good drink. Screwcap. 13.5% alc. **Rating** 92 **To** 2022 $28 NG
Coonawarra Cabernet Sauvignon 2016 Bowen, the benchmark of ageable Coonawarra cabs, has seen alcohol soar across more recent vintages. This is no exception. Thankfully, cabernet's stiff-upper-lipped, sage-brushed tannins, bright acidity, synergy with oak and its herbal undercarriage, are all useful restraining devices. These structural bulwarks impose order to the gush of cassis, eucalyptus and black olive. Just. Screwcap. 15% alc. **Rating** 92 **To** 2031 $35 NG

ŸŸŸŸ **Coonawarra Shiraz 2016** **Rating** 89 **To** 2028 $35 NG

Box Grove Vineyard ★★★★☆

955 Avenel-Nagambie Road, Tabilk, Vic 3607 **Region** Nagambie Lakes
T 0409 210 015 **www**.boxgrovevineyard.com.au **Open** By appt
Winemaker Sarah Gough **Est.** 1995 **Dozens** 2500 **Vyds** 27ha

This is the venture of the Gough family, with industry veteran (and daughter) Sarah Gough managing the vineyard, winemaking and marketing. Having started with 10ha each of shiraz and cabernet sauvignon under contract to Brown Brothers, Sarah decided to switch the focus of the business to what could loosely be called 'Mediterranean varieties'. These days, prosecco, vermentino, primitivo and roussanne are the main varieties, plus the original plantings. Osteria (an Italian word meaning a place that serves wine and food) holds tastings and meals prepared by visiting Melbourne chefs by appointment. Exports to Singapore and China.

ŸŸŸŸŸ **Shiraz Roussanne 2015** 97% shiraz and 3% roussanne grown side by side, co-fermented, and matured in French oak (30% new) for 12 months. Has retained excellent colour, and the co-fermentation of the two varieties works well, enhancing the elegant, savoury nature of this medium-bodied wine. The palate is long and harmoniously balanced, the French oak subtle but adding significantly to a most attractive wine. Screwcap. 14.7% alc. **Rating** 95 **To** 2030 $30 ✪

ŸŸŸŸŸ **Late Harvest Viognier 2017 Rating** 93 **To** 2022 $24 ✪
Primitivo 2016 Rating 91 **To** 2029 $30
Vermentino 2017 Rating 90 **To** 2022 $24
Primitivo Saignee 2017 Rating 90 **To** 2021 $24

Brackenwood Vineyard ★★★★

Bishop Road, Hope Forest, SA 5172 (postal) **Region** Adelaide Hills
T 0400 266 121 **www**.brackenwoodvineyard.com.au **Open** Not
Winemaker Damon Nagel, Reg Wilkingson **Est.** 1999 **Dozens** 1500 **Vyds** 7.6ha

Brackenwood Vineyard is situated at the extreme southern end of the Adelaide Hills, skirted by the Old Victor Harbour Road. Damon Nagel has established shiraz (2.65ha), riesling (1.7ha), sauvignon blanc (1.3ha), nebbiolo (1.2ha) and chardonnay (0.75ha), and all wines are estate-grown from these grapes. The vineyard has been managed biodynamically for four years, and the wines are made without the addition of acidity or yeast nutrients, all relying on wild yeast.

ŸŸŸŸŸ **Syrah 2016** A quick smell and taste tells you this is a pretty smart wine, rich in dark cherries, blackberry, spice and crushed pepper. Very good to drink now or in 10 years. Screwcap. 13.2% alc. **Rating** 93 **To** 2029 $30
Fume Blanc 2016 As the intensity of the flavour first hits the mouth, you think it's sweet (off-dry), but the back-palate and finish suggest it is in fact dry, the aftertaste doing nothing to resolve the question one way or the other. Screwcap. 13.4% alc. **Rating** 92 **To** 2020 $25 ✪
Syrah 2015 Light, clear crimson-purple; the fresh, fragrant red-fruited bouquet and palate are unencumbered by tannins, half suggesting pinot noir in ethos. Delicious for drinking now, little to be gained by cellaring. Screwcap. 14.3% alc. **Rating** 90 **To** 2023 $30
Rosso 2017 Light but bright crimson; blends don't come further from left field than this, bringing together pinot noir, shiraz and barbera. It works far better than you might guess, full of fresh red berries, and while only light-bodied, has good presence and length. Ready to drink now. Screwcap. 11.3% alc. **Rating** 90 **To** 2022 $20 ✪

ŸŸŸŸ **Riesling 2017 Rating** 89 **To** 2025 $25
Gamay Pinot Noir 2017 Rating 89 **To** 2020 $25

Brand's Laira Coonawarra ★★★★★

14860 Riddoch Highway, Coonawarra, SA 5263 **Region** Coonawarra
T (08) 8736 3260 **www**.brandslaira.com **Open** Mon–Fri 9–4.30, w'ends 11–4
Winemaker Peter Weinberg, Amy Blackburn **Est.** 1966 **Dozens** NFP **Vyds** 278ha
Three days before Christmas 2015, Casella Family Brands received an early present when it purchased Brand's Laira from McWilliam's. Over the years McWilliam's had moved from 50% to 100% ownership of the winery and had purchased an additional 100ha of vineyards (taking the winery to its present 278ha). Exports to select markets.

ƤƤƤƤƤ **Stentiford's Shiraz 2015** It's not dense but it is powerful. Indeed it's a medium-weight wine of significant presence, aflame with spice, run with redcurrant, flashed with mint and smoothed over by cream and cedar wood. Tight, grainy tannin controls the finish. Screwcap. 13.5% alc. **Rating** 95 **To** 2035 $80 CM
One Seven One Cabernet Sauvignon 2015 Heavy-hitter in flavour terms, but the balance is there and oak has completely melted down into the fruit. Classic Coonawarra cabernet in many ways. Tobacco, cassis, the sweeter side of boysenberry, tips of mint and wafts of cedar wood. A class act. Screwcap. 14% alc. **Rating** 95 **To** 2040 $80 CM
Blockers Cabernet Sauvignon 2015 Archetypal cassis, mint and tobacco flavours flow in tandem with a stream of creamy vanillan oak. The price suggests that this is a drink-early proposition, but this will perform well over at least the medium term, if not (a lot) longer. I came back and retasted this a day later and it was still strutting its stuff. Bargain alert. Screwcap. 14% alc. **Rating** 94 **To** 2035 $25 CM ✪
1968 Vines Cabernet Sauvignon 2015 It has you smiling, it has you impressed. Deep blackcurrant, peppercorn, milk chocolate and mint. It's bold, almost brooding, upfront, but it then sets sail to a more elegant place through the back half. The Brand's Laira reds are in fine form. Screwcap. 14% alc. **Rating** 94 **To** 2035 $40 CM

ƤƤƤƤƤ **Tall Vines Shiraz 2015 Rating** 92 **To** 2033 $40 CM
August Tide Red Blend 2015 Rating 91 **To** 2025 $25 CM

Brangayne of Orange ★★★★

837 Pinnacle Road, Orange, NSW 2800 **Region** Orange
T (02) 6365 3229 **www**.brangayne.com **Open** Mon–Fri 11–4, Sat 11–5, Sun 11–4
Winemaker Simon Gilbert **Est.** 1994 **Dozens** 3000 **Vyds** 25.7ha
The Hoskins family (formerly orchardists) moved into grapegrowing in 1994 and have progressively established high quality vineyards. Brangayne produces good wines across all mainstream varieties, ranging, remarkably, from pinot noir to cabernet sauvignon. It sells a substantial part of its crop to other winemakers. Exports to China.

ƤƤƤƤƤ **Shiraz 2015** The very cool climate comes through loud and clear from the outset; red cherry fruit studded with sequins of spice and black pepper, tannins and oak in the shady background. Attractive cool-climate style. Screwcap. 14% alc. **Rating** 91 **To** 2028 $35
Sauvignon Blanc 2017 Crisp, crunchy and minerally within a lemon sorbet palate (with a lick of passionfruit). Screwcap. 12.7% alc. **Rating** 90 **To** 2019 $22
Rose 2017 Fresh and breezy and, best of all, bone dry. The shiraz base does all expected of it. Well made. Screwcap. 12.7% alc. **Rating** 90 **To** 2019 $22
Cabernet Sauvignon 2015 Until the Chinese dragon came on the scene, wanting Australian cabernet at (almost) any price, cabernet looked in need of life support. Wines such as this may well see a quick turnaround in the supply/demand equation, blackcurrant and bay leaf flavours as ordered. Screwcap. 14% alc. **Rating** 90 **To** 2025 $35

ƤƤƤƤ **Pinot Grigio 2017 Rating** 89 $22

Brash Higgins

California Road, McLaren Vale, SA 5171 **Region** McLaren Vale
T (08) 8556 4237 **www**.brashhiggins.com **Open** By appt
Winemaker Brad Hickey **Est.** 2010 **Dozens** 1000 **Vyds** 7ha
There have been a number of changes in the name of the vineyard and in the ownership structure, none of the prior details of any relevance. Today Brash Higgins is owned by Chris and Anne Carter, Brian and Ann McGuiness, and Rik and Jenny Nitert. The estate-grown grapes are in large part retained for the brand. Exports to the US and Canada.

SHZ Site Specific McLaren Vale Shiraz 2015 It's all about the fruit here; smelling of dark black plums sprinkled with cinnamon, powdered licorice root and dubbin boot polish. Full-bodied and richly flavoured with plump sweet tannins, and with that regional dark chocolate and aged balsamic vinegar fragrance. Screwcap. 14.7% alc. **Rating** 94 **To** 2025 $39 JF

ZBO Ricca Terra Farms Zibibbo 2016 Rating 93 **To** 2022 $39 JF
R/SM Field Blend Riesling Semillon 2016 Rating 93 **To** 2021 $39 JF
GR/M Co-Ferment Grenache Mataro 2016 Rating 93 **To** 2024 $39 JF
MATO Lennon Vineyard Mataro 2016 Rating 93 **To** 2024 $39 JF
FRNC Sommerville Vineyard Cabernet Franc 2016 Rating 92 **To** 2021 $30 JF
NDV Amphora Project Nero d'Avola 2016 Rating 92 **To** 2022 $42 JF
CHN Willamba Hill Vineyard Chenin Blanc 2016 Rating 90 **To** 2019 $39 JF
Omensetter Shiraz Cabernet 2012 Rating 90 **To** 2024 $95 JF

Brave Goose Vineyard

PO Box 852, Seymour, Vic 3660 **Region** Central Victoria
T 0417 553 225 **www**.bravegoosevineyard.com.au **Open** By appt
Winemaker Nina Stocker **Est.** 1988 **Dozens** 200 **Vyds** 6.5ha
The Brave Goose Vineyard was planted in 1988 by former chairman of the Grape & Wine Research and Development Corporation, Dr John Stocker, and his wife Joanne. In '87 they had found the property on the inside of the Great Dividing Range, near Tallarook, with north-facing slopes and shallow, weathered ironstone soils. They established 2.5ha each of shiraz and cabernet sauvignon, and 0.5ha each of merlot, viognier and gamay, but made only small amounts under the Brave Goose label. (The 'brave goose' in question was the sole survivor of a flock put into the vineyard to repel cockatoos and foxes.) Two decades on, Jo and John handed the reins of the operation to their winemaker daughter Nina and son-in-law John Day.

Viognier 2016 It's a tightly wound rendition of this usually textural variety and sure, there is a creaminess and roundness, but there's also lemony acidity reining it in. In the midst, a melange of dried herbs, apricot kernel and some stone fruit with lots of spice. Screwcap. 13% alc. **Rating** 91 **To** 2023 $27 JF
Shiraz 2016 Very good dark garnet; an abundance of ripe and overripe fruit somewhat accentuated by the cedary, clove-like sweet oak. There's a spicy undercurrent with licorice and pepper plus menthol and imperious tannins that need taming with time. Screwcap. 14.5% alc. **Rating** 90 **To** 2024 $28 JF
Cabernet Merlot 2016 The 85/10% blend with 5% malbec has created a concentrated full-bodied style, dense with dark fruit, cassis, cedar, cloves and eucalyptus. While there is a freshness, the 25% new French oak adds to the almost impenetrable persimmon-like fruit tannins, and it's tough. Come back to this in a couple of years. Screwcap. 14.5% alc. **Rating** 90 **To** 2028 $28 JF

Brave Souls Wine

12 Clevedon Street, Botany, NSW, 2019 (postal) **Region** Barossa Valley
T 0420 968 473 **www**.bravesoulswine.com.au **Open** Not
Winemaker Julia Weirich **Est.** 2017 **Dozens** 1500

The story of Brave Souls and its founder Julia Weirich has a strong Australian can-do air about it, albeit with German beginings. Julia obtained her German masters degree in industrial engineering and decided she needed to travel but didn't know where to start. She asked her friends, and they all said Australia. From this point on, the story line twisted and turned, first up her lack of fluency (real or imagined) in English, the second being her foray into wine, about which she knew nothing. From a standing start in 2012, and with her tourist visa about to expire in '13, she noticed a position vacant ad by Fesq & Co. She applied on the basis she had nothing to lose, and three interviews later she was marketing co-ordinator for Fesq. One year earlier she had completed stages WSET 1 to 3. Later she took off for winemaking experience at Bass Phillip, NZ, Burgundy, southern and central Italy and South Africa. Where to next? Back to Australia, where she really wanted to make wine, and to Fesq (which had become like family to her) to take the new role of European Wine Manager, and to Sons of Eden making Brave Souls Wine. And she's studying winemaking with the University of California on its extension program.

ŸŸŸŸŸ **The Whaler Barossa Valley Shiraz 2016** It has a bright, full crimson hue, and the bouquet speaks of fresh, dark berry fruits. The medium-bodied palate is a first-up triumph, with a finely woven texture carrying red and black cherries, pepper, spice and herb that would more often come from cool climates. Screwcap. 14.5% alc. **Rating** 96 **To** 2036 $28 ✪
The Lighthouse Keeper Eden Valley Riesling 2017 Pale straw-green; the aromatic bouquet picks up citrus blossom on the first whiff, the palate seamlessly running with lime/lemon flavours along silvery lines of acidity. A very good example of a very good vintage. Screwcap. 12.5% alc. **Rating** 95 **To** 2027 $28 ✪
The Able Seaman Barossa Valley Grenache Shiraz Mourvedre 2016 The 45/29/26% blend is assembled from vines across the Barossa Valley aged between 15 and 100 years, matured for 16 months in new and used oak. A lot of winemaking IP is on show with this vibrant wine, a light year away from some of the stodgy dead fruit blends of prior times. This will also develop secondary flavours ex the cherry of the grenache. Screwcap. 14.5% alc. **Rating** 95 **To** 2031 $28 ✪

Bream Creek   ★★★★★

Marion Bay Road, Bream Creek, Tas 7175 **Region** Southern Tasmania
T (03) 6231 4646 **www.**breamcreekvineyard.com.au **Open** At Dunalley Waterfront Cafe
Winemaker Glenn James, Pat Colombo **Est.** 1974 **Dozens** 6000 **Vyds** 7.6ha
Until 1990 the Bream Creek fruit was sold to Moorilla Estate, but since then the winery has been independently owned and managed by Fred Peacock, legendary for the care he bestows on the vines under his direction. Fred's skills have seen an increase in production and outstanding wine quality across the range, headed by the pinot noir. The list of trophies and gold, silver and bronze medals is extensive, the quality of wines is exemplary. Fred's expertise as a consultant is in constant demand. Exports to China.

ŸŸŸŸŸ **Reserve Pinot Noir 2014** Fills the senses with its rich purity and clarity of varietal character. It is a pinot that will be very long lived thanks to its balance and length. While it has depth and power, it has not been the least over-extracted; counterintuitively, its supple tannins emphasise its elegance. Screwcap. 13.9% alc. **Rating** 97 **To** 2034 $55 ✪

ŸŸŸŸŸ **Reserve Pinot Noir 2015** The identical vinification of this and its vintage sibling strongly suggests it was a best barrel selection, a belief strengthened by the palate. There is abundant depth and richness, the varietal character underwritten by the fine drive and lingering finish. I suspect this wine will widen the gap between the two wines as time goes by. Screwcap. 13.7% alc. **Rating** 96 **To** 2030 $55 ✪
Riesling 2017 Glinting straw-green; the balance between the high acidity (8.2g/l) and residual sugar (8.2g/l) has been judged with unusual skill, allowing the flavours of Rose's lime juice free play, with none of the screeching acidity in some

Tasmanian rieslings. The similarity with its '16 sibling is a tribute to the vineyard and Fred Peacock's assured touch. Screwcap. 13% alc. **Rating** 95 **To** 2027 $28 ⊙

Riesling 2016 Here the residual sugar was 10.7g/l, and while not threatening the impeccable balance between it and the acidity, it is part of the extra level of depth to the Rose's lime juice quality it shares with its sibling. Its fine tannins are akin to those of German rieslings and the best from Alsace. Trophy Best Tasmanian Riesling Canberra International Riesling Challenge '17. Screwcap. 13.5% alc. **Rating** 95 **To** 2030 $28 ⊙

Chardonnay 2016 Bright pale green; immaculately fashioned from high quality fruit, with seamless balance and length the corner posts of an effortless display of variety and of place. Ripe stone fruit and a touch of grapefruit are the prime movers; oak more an observer than player. Screwcap. 12.5% alc. **Rating** 95 **To** 2026 $34 ⊙

Pinot Noir 2015 Tasted after a string of thin, weedy mainland pinots, underlining the richness and depth of the varietal character of this wine. Black cherry, satsuma plum and spicy/foresty notes are built on a foundation of ripe and persistent tannins. A prosperous future awaits. Screwcap. 13.7% alc. **Rating** 95 **To** 2025 $36

Reserve Chardonnay 2016 Hand-picked, whole-bunch pressed, wild-fermented in French oak (21% new), matured for 9.5 months. Distinctly greater weight and complexity, yet a little more French oak, a few more days in that oak, and 0.3% more alcohol have had a seemingly disproportionate effect (its varietal sibling is effortless and ready to drink). Screwcap. 12.8% alc. **Rating** 94 **To** 2029 $48

Chardonnay 2015 A most attractive Tasmanian chardonnay, which is sometimes a poor relation of Tasmanian riesling, pinot noir and sparkling wines. The bouquet, the supple trifecta of white peach/grapefruit, acidity and integrated French oak hits home base. Screwcap. 13.3% alc. **Rating** 94 **To** 2024 $34

Pinot Rose 2017 Pale scarlet; a distinctly spicy bouquet is followed by an intensely flavoured strawberries-and-cream palate. A striking wine. Screwcap. 12.5% alc. **Rating** 94 **To** 2019 $27 ⊙

Vintage Cuvee Traditionelle 2011 A traditional-method blend of pinot noir and chardonnay that spent over 4 years on lees, the cork hitting the roof a split-second after the cage was removed. Follows in the fruit footsteps of the gold medal–winning '10. Has the power and drive that is the mark of Tasmanian sparkling, the only question being the depth and extent of the stone fruit, apple and wild strawberry. Needs more time. Diam. 11.5% alc. **Rating** 94 $42

Bremerton Wines ★★★★★

Strathalbyn Road, Langhorne Creek, SA 5255 **Region** Langhorne Creek
T (08) 8537 3093 **www**.bremerton.com.au **Open** 7 days 10–5
Winemaker Rebecca Willson **Est.** 1988 **Dozens** 30 000 **Vyds** 120ha
Rebecca Willson (chief winemaker) and Lucy Willson (marketing manager) are the first sisters in Australia to manage and run a winery. With 120ha of premium vineyards (80% of which goes into their own labels), they grow cabernet sauvignon, shiraz, verdelho, chardonnay, sauvignon blanc, malbec, merlot, fiano, graciano and petit verdot. Exports to most major markets.

♀♀♀♀♀ **B.O.V. 2014** Attesting to the quality capacity of cabernet in Langhorne Creek, this is blackcurrant, anise, sage and graphite strung across firm, balancing tannins. The 40% shiraz echoes along riffs of violet and dried seaweed. Pillars of well poised oak help to rein it all in. A quintessential Aussie classic in the making. Cork. 14.5% alc. **Rating** 95 **To** 2028 $85 NG

Special Release Graciano 2016 There is more and more graciano appearing across my tasting spread and for good reason. While a minor chord in Rioja, it is Mediterranean by nature and with that, the variety is sturdy and far from thirsty. Welcome to Australia! Blood plum, bush tomato and a potpourri of herbal notes slink across dried scrubby tannins and a spout of acid freshness. What joy! Screwcap. 14% alc. **Rating** 95 **To** 2021 $24 NG ⊙

Special Release Langhorne Creek Barbera 2016 As good as any New World barbera yet tasted, this is made in a modern style, with 15 months of maturation in second and third-use tier barrels. The result is blackberry, anise and tar, exploding across a swathe of gently toasty oak. A squirt of barbera's lip-smacking acidity keeps it all on the straight and narrow. This is mid-weighted, food-friendly and dangerously gulpable. Screwcap. 13.5% alc. **Rating** 94 **To** 2020 $24 NG ○

Special Release Langhorne Creek Mourvedre 2016 Dried tobacco and strewn herb segue to bright red fruit flavours. Mourvedre's bloody, ferruginous tannins are impeccably mown to a spray of bright acidity. As with most wines at this address, this lies in an idiom of mid-weighted, dangerous drinkability, all founded on superlative tannin management: the estate's opus. Screwcap. 14% alc. **Rating** 94 **To** 2023 $24 NG ○

Special Release Langhorne Creek Malbec 2016 Rebecca Willson has crafted a precise, joyous range across Bremerton's 'Special Release' tier. This is no exception, with a riot of black fruit allusions painted across a beam of toasty oak, a rudder for the cascading flavours. Gritty coffee grind tannins, purple florals and a wee tad of volatility all serve to lift and refresh. Full of flavour and highly drinkable. Screwcap. 14.5% alc. **Rating** 94 **To** 2026 $24 NG ○

♥♥♥♥♀ Batonnage Shiraz Malbec 2016 Rating 93 To 2022 $32 NG
Coulthard Cabernet 2016 Rating 93 To 2026 $22 NG ○
Special Release Tempranillo Graciano 2016 Rating 93 To 2021 $24 NG ○
Batonnage Chardonnay 2016 Rating 92 To 2024 $32 NG
Special Release Fiano 2017 Rating 92 To 2022 $24 NG ○
Selkirk Shiraz 2016 Rating 92 To 2023 $22 NG ○
Old Adam Shiraz 2015 Rating 92 To 2029 $56 NG
Walter's Reserve Cabernet 2014 Rating 92 To 2029 $56 NG
Tamblyn 2016 Rating 92 To 2022 $18 NG ○
Special Release Vermentino 2017 Rating 91 To 2021 $24 NG
Special Release Lagrein 2015 Rating 90 To 2021 $24 NG

Bress ★★★★★

3894 Harmony Way, Harcourt, Vic 3453 **Region** Bendigo
T (03) 5474 2262 www.bress.com.au **Open** W'ends & public hols 11–5 or by chance
Winemaker Adam Marks **Est.** 2001 **Dozens** 5000 **Vyds** 17ha
Adam Marks has made wine in all parts of the world since 1991, making the brave decision (during his honeymoon in 2000) to start his own business. Having initially scoured various regions of Australia for the grapes best suited to those regions, the focus has switched to three Central Victorian vineyards: in Bendigo, Macedon Ranges and Heathcote. The Harcourt vineyard in the Bendigo region is planted to riesling (2ha), shiraz (1ha) and 3ha of cabernet sauvignon and cabernet franc; the Macedon vineyard to chardonnay (6ha) and pinot noir (3ha); and the Heathcote vineyard to shiraz (2ha). Exports to the Philippines, Singapore and Hong Kong.

♥♥♥♥♥ Gold Chook Macedon Pinot Noir 2016 What's striking about this pinot is not the bunchy character, the fresh cherry and raspberry accented fruit, nor the savoury earthy tones (although that all helps), but its vitality. This is spine-tingly fresh, a livewire of energy and purity. It's so moreish and totally satisfying. Screwcap. 12.5% alc. **Rating** 96 **To** 2025 $50 JF ○

Gold Chook Heathcote Shiraz 2016 A ball of spiced fruit rolls across the full-bodied palate taking detailed ripe tannins along with it. A kitchen cupboard full of spices led by juniper, cinnamon and star anise. There's a hint of very ripe fruit saved by a buoyant palate and the fine acidity. Good gear this. Screwcap. 14% alc. **Rating** 95 **To** 2026 $50 JF

♥♥♥♥♀ Gold Chook Harcourt Valley Riesling 2017 Rating 93 To 2022 $30 JF

Brian Fletcher Signature Wines ★★★☆

1142 Kaloorup Road, Kaloorup, WA 6280 **Region** Margaret River
T (08) 9368 4555 **www**.brianfletcherwines.com.au **Open** Not
Winemaker Brian Fletcher **Est.** 2012 **Dozens** 12 000
Brian Fletcher began his winemaking career in 1978, graduating in oenology at CSU. He had an illustrious career in eastern Australia before moving to Margaret River to become chief winemaker for Evans & Tate. He has not left the region since that time, forming a partnership with the Calneggia family, who are major vineyard developers and owners in the region. The wines are made under the Naked Wines umbrella, whereby Naked Wines provides the capital required and takes the wines at a guaranteed price.

ΨΨΨΨ **Margaret River Chardonnay 2017** The juice was 'part fermented in oak', and 15% underwent mlf. Carefully calibrated and constructed for immediate consumption. Good value. Screwcap. 13.5% alc. **Rating** 89 **To** 2021 $20
Shiraz 2015 The full page of background info supplied tells us 'grapes harvested and the wine fermented on skins to extract colour and flavour' – like every red wine made in Australia. Actually it is a fresh and lively mix of red and black fruits with spicy nuances. Great value. Screwcap. 14.5% alc. **Rating** 89 **To** 2022 $15 ✪

Briar Ridge Vineyard ★★★★☆

Mount View Road, Mount View, NSW 2325 **Region** Hunter Valley
T (02) 4990 3670 **www**.briarridge.com.au **Open** 7 days 10–5
Winemaker Gwyneth Olsen **Est.** 1972 **Dozens** 9500 **Vyds** 39ha
Semillon and shiraz have been the most consistent performers, underlying the suitability of these varieties to the Hunter Valley. Briar Ridge has been a model of stability, and has the comfort of substantial estate vineyards from which it is able to select the best grapes. It also has not hesitated to venture into other regions, notably Orange. In 2013 Gwyneth (Gwyn) Olsen was appointed winemaker after an impressive career in Australia and NZ. In '12 she added the distinction of graduating as Dux of the AWRI Advanced Wine Assessment course to her CV. Exports to the UK, Europe and Canada.

ΨΨΨΨΨ **Museum Release Dairy Hill Vineyard Hunter Valley Shiraz 2010** Still plenty of bright brambleberries plus plum compote leading onto some potpourri and more savoury aged nuances; a dusting of spice, brewed tea and leather. Medium-bodied, fine acidity and supple tannins have melded into one. While there's still life ahead of it, it's pitch-perfect now. Screwcap. 14.5% alc. **Rating** 95 **To** 2021 $110 JF

ΨΨΨΨΥ **Signature Series Karl Stockhausen Shiraz 2016** Rating 93 To 2026 $35 JF
Big Bully Cabernet Sauvignon 2015 Rating 93 To 2030 $35 JF
Dairy Hill Semillon 2017 Rating 92 To 2029 $35
Fume Sauvignon Blanc Semillon 2017 Rating 91 To 2020 $23 JF ✪
Stockhausen Semillon 2017 Rating 90 To 2028 $28
Early Harvest Semillon 2017 Rating 90 To 2027 $23

Brini Estate Wines ★★★★★

698 Blewitt Springs Road, McLaren Vale, SA 5171 **Region** McLaren Vale
T (08) 8383 0080 **www**.briniwines.com.au **Open** By appt
Winemaker Adam Hooper (Contract) **Est.** 2000 **Dozens** 8000 **Vyds** 16.4ha
The Brini family has been growing grapes in the Blewitt Springs area of McLaren Vale since 1953. In 2000 John and Marcello Brini established Brini Estate Wines to vinify a portion of the grape production (up to that time it had been sold to companies such as Penfolds, Rosemount Estate and d'Arenberg). The flagship Limited Release Shiraz is produced from dry-grown vines planted in 1947, the other wines from dry-grown vines planted in '64. Exports to Vietnam and China.

ΨΨΨΨΨ **Blewitt Springs Single Vineyard McLaren Vale Shiraz 2015** Blewitt Springs is clearly the best district in McLaren Vale for all red wines, which typically have

an elegance and precision that can't be relegated to second place. Such is the case here, the wine with the elegance of a ballet dancer as it glides across the palate. Fruit (red and black), tannins and oak coalesce into one beautiful mouthful (and mouthfeel). Bargain-plus. Screwcap. 14.5% alc. **Rating** 96 **To** 2030 $24 ✪
Christian Single Vineyard McLaren Vale Shiraz 2013 The wine sings from the word go. It is medium-bodied and exceptionally juicy, with a river of plum, blackberry and dark chocolate fruit flavours, ripe tannins and quality oak forming the banks on either side of the river. Screwcap. 14.5% alc. **Rating** 96 **To** 2033 $45 ✪
Sebastian Single Vineyard McLaren Vale Shiraz 2015 This full-bodied wine showcases the special quality of the '15 vintage with the richness and depth of the purple and black fruits; their pillowy tannins in perfect synchrony. It's a classic now-or-later style. Screwcap. 14.5% alc. **Rating** 94 **To** 2035 $32

🍷🍷🍷🍷🍷 **Single Vineyard McLaren Vale Grenache Shiraz Mourvedre 2014** Rating 92 To 2022 $24 ✪
Estate Single Vineyard Merlot 2015 Rating 91 To 2024 $24
Chenin Blanc 2017 Rating 90 To 2020 $18 ✪
Koota Gra Grenache Mourvedre Shiraz 2015 Rating 90 To 2021 $18 ✪

Brockenchack Wines   ★★★★☆

351 Sawpit Gully Road, Keyneton, SA 5353 **Region** Eden Valley
T 0418 986 289 **www.brockenchack.com.au Open** By appt
Winemaker Shawn Kalleske, Joanne Irvine **Est.** 2007 **Dozens** 5000 **Vyds** 16ha
Trevor (and wife Marilyn) Harch have long been involved in liquor distribution in Queensland, owning one of Australia's leading independent liquor wholesalers. Over the years, Trevor became a regular visitor to the Barossa/Eden Valley, and in 1999 purchased the Tanunda Cellars Wine Store. In 2007, Trevor and Marilyn purchased a vineyard in the Eden Valley and retained Shawn Kalleske as winemaker. The vineyard has 8ha of shiraz, 2ha each of riesling and cabernet sauvignon, and 1.3ha each of pinot noir, pinot gris and chardonnay. The majority of wines released are labelled in honour of one or other member of the Harch family. 'Brockenchack' comes from the first names of the four grandchildren: Bronte, Mackenzie, Charli and Jack. Exports to Germany, Japan, China and NZ.

🍷🍷🍷🍷🍷 **Miss Bronte Eden Valley Cabernet Sauvignon 2016** A rugged beauty. Tannin thunders through the back half of the wine, blueberry and blackcurrant fruit flavours putting their shoulder to the wheel. Mint and violet notes hover expectantly. It's good. Screwcap. 14% alc. **Rating** 94 **To** 2032 $28 CM ✪

🍷🍷🍷🍷🍷 **Mackenzie William 1896 Eden Valley Riesling 2017** Rating 93 To 2027 $17 CM ✪
Zip Line Eden Valley Shiraz 2016 Rating 92 To 2028 $24 CM ✪
Tru-Su Eden Valley Rose 2017 Rating 91 To 2018 $17 CM ✪
Jack Harrison Eden Valley Shiraz 2014 Rating 91 To 2029 $58 CM
Hare Hunter Eden Valley Pinot Noir 2016 Rating 90 To 2024 $35 CM
Great Scott Eden Valley Sparkling Shiraz NV Rating 90 $24 CM

Brokenwood   ★★★★★

401–427 McDonalds Road, Pokolbin, NSW 2321 **Region** Hunter Valley
T (02) 4998 7559 **www.brokenwood.com.au Open** Mon–Sat 9.30–5, Sun 10–5
Winemaker Iain Riggs, Stuart Hordern **Est.** 1970 **Dozens** 100000 **Vyds** 64ha
A deservedly fashionable winery producing consistently excellent wines. Its big-selling Hunter Valley Semillon provides the volume to balance the limited quantities of the flagships ILR Semillon and Graveyard Shiraz. Next there is a range of wines coming from regions including Beechworth (a major resource is the associated Indigo vineyard), Orange, Central Ranges, McLaren Vale, Cowra and elsewhere. In 2017 Iain Riggs celebrated his 35th vintage at the helm of Brokenwood, offering his unique mix of winemaking skills, management of a diverse business, and an unerring ability to keep Brokenwood's profile fresh and newsworthy.

He has also contributed a great deal to various wine industry organisations. Exports to all major markets.

⁹⁹⁹⁹⁹ **Wildwood Road Vineyard Margaret River Cabernet Sauvignon 2015**
Imperious cabernet defined by the assertive, impeccably wrought gauntlet of tannin: a squeegee of pebbly grape tannins, sensitively extracted and nestled in cedar oak (40% new French for 16 months), that impart authority. Blackcurrant, bouquet garni and black olive. This is streamlined but incisive. Savoury but ripe. Assertive but juicy. Screwcap. 14.5% alc. **Rating** 97 **To** 2032 $80 NG ○

⁹⁹⁹⁹⁹ **Four Winds Vineyard Canberra District Riesling 2017** I am coming to admire riesling from Canberra and its periphery more and more. They are the most Germanic in Australia, clad with a mineral armour while pirouetting about the mouth along a beam of peppery acidity, stone fruit flavours and plenty of citrus. There is nothing sour nor abrasive about them. Just nourishing, transparent and refreshing stuff here, with a dollop of fruit sweetness to make the long glide mellifluous. Screwcap. 11.5% alc. **Rating** 96 **To** 2027 $36 NG ○
Tallawanta Vineyard Hunter Valley Shiraz 2016 One's impression after the first sip is that of genetic integrity. The Hunter's fidelitous savoury, leather-varnished tannins are embedded into the wine's spine. Mid-weighted, with root spice and dusty cherry flavours all on song. This is a delicious, moreish wine that will age very well indeed. Screwcap. 13.5% alc. **Rating** 96 **To** 2041 $140 NG
Tallawanta Vineyard Hunter Valley Semillon 2015 From 25yo vines, '15 being the first year Brokenwood took over their management. This has great depth and drive, lime/lemon fruit dancing a pas de deux with talcy acidity. Great now, more so in the future. Screwcap. 11% alc. **Rating** 95 **To** 2032 $46
Beechworth Nebbiolo Rosato 2017 Sour red berry fruits and orange zest — almost ineffable of tang and refreshment — are lifted across a lightweight palate by nebbiolo's mosaic of spindle-thread tannins and bright, crunchy acidity. Moreover, the pale hue of mottled pink is stunning! Among the very best of its class. Drink in copious draughts! Screwcap. 13% alc. **Rating** 95 **To** 2019 $30 NG ○
Mistress Block Vineyard Hunter Valley Shiraz 2016 Mistress Block is more explosive and sweeter of fruit than the restrained, herbal Tallawanta. Slightly less depth, too. The wine is strung across the Hunter's savoury tannic bow, although there are glimpses of the northern Rhône with its kiss of bing cherry brightness, purple florals, iodine and smoked deli meats. The capacity to age is no less, although perhaps enjoyable younger while its fruit is running riot. Screwcap. 13.5% alc. **Rating** 95 **To** 2031 $110 NG
Rayner Vineyard McLaren Vale Shiraz 2016 This rich wine is akin to a Turkish belly dancer infusing rosewater and purple floral scents across a buxom midriff, free-flowing with blue to dark fruits, anise, root spice and swaggering bitter chocolate tannins. A delicious drink already, with promise of more to come. Screwcap. 14.5% alc. **Rating** 95 **To** 2031 $100 NG
Vegas Block Hunter Valley Shiraz 2016 A challenging vintage for many, this is nevertheless one of the more compelling Hunter shirazs tasted in recent memory, meshing syrah's aromatic violet-iodine genetics with a strong regional shiraz voice: saddle leather tannins, cherry and a brusque mid-weighted gait of linger. This is, as the back label notes, in the vein of Hunter 'Light Dry Red' styles of yore. Screwcap. 13.5% alc. **Rating** 95 **To** 2028 $75 NG
Wade Block 2 Vineyard McLaren Vale Shiraz 2015 This is textbook McLaren Vale shiraz, sourced from a 67yo plot in Blewitt Springs, imparting je ne sais quoi freshness and vinosity to the wine's inherent power. A quiver of blackberry, kirsch and soaring violet scents are pulled to an extreme across the senses by a bow of manicured tannins, coffee oak and bright acidity. Screwcap. 14.5% alc. **Rating** 95 **To** 2035 $66 NG
Chardonnay 2016 Comprising 49% Beechworth, 32% Orange, 14% Cowra and 5% Hunter Valley; fermented and matured in French barriques. An uncommon regional blend, but one that works to perfection here. The flavours are in the classic grapefruit/white peach group, the oak subtle. Screwcap. 12.5% alc. **Rating** 94 **To** 2025 $30

ΨΨΨΨ♀ Hunter Valley Shiraz 2016 Rating 93 To 2023 $50 NG
Hunter Valley Semillon 2017 Rating 92 To 2027 $28
Beechworth Pinot Gris 2017 Rating 92 To 2021 $30 NG
Indigo Vineyard Beechworth Pinot Noir 2016 Rating 92 To 2024 $55 NG
Four Winds Vineyard Canberra Shiraz 2016 Rating 92 To 2026 $66 NG
Indigo Vineyard Beechworth Shiraz 2016 Rating 92 To 2024 $66 NG
Cabernet Merlot 2014 Rating 92 To 2025 $36 NG
Shiraz 2015 Rating 91 To 2025 $36 NG

Bromley Wines   ★★★★

PO Box 571, Drysdale, Vic 3222 **Region** Geelong
T 0487 505 367 **www.**bromleywines.com.au **Open** Not
Winemaker Darren Burke **Est.** 2010 **Dozens** 300
In his previous life, Darren Burke worked as an intensive-care nurse in Australia and the UK, but at the age of 30 he fell to the allure of wine and enrolled in the Bachelor of Applied Science (Oenology) at Adelaide University. Thereafter he became graduate winemaker at Orlando, then at Alkoomi, fitting in a vintage in Chianti. With successful vintages in 2005 and '06 completed, and the impending birth of their first child, Darren and wife Tammy decided to move back east. There Darren worked at several wineries on the Bellarine Peninsula before taking up his winemaking post at Leura Park Estate. Says Darren, 'The essence of Bromley is family. All our wines carry names drawn from our family history. Family is about flesh and blood, sweat and tears, love and laughter.' Exports to Singapore.

ΨΨΨΨΨ Eclipse Heathcote Rose 2017 This is pallid of hue yet loquacious of a musk, anise, tangerine and kumquat-led conversation across the palate. Dry, with a needle of crunchy acidity, a smidgeon of oak and unresolved spritz, all driving red fruit flavours long as they snap, crackle and pop. Freezer this to a good chill and drink in gulps! Screwcap. 13% alc. Rating 94 To 2019 $25 NG ✪

ΨΨΨΨ♀ Geelong Chenin Blanc 2017 Rating 93 To 2025 $25 NG ✪
Heathcote Nebbiolo 2016 Rating 93 To 2024 $35 NG
Geelong Riesling 2017 Rating 91 To 2029 $25 NG
Geelong Pinot Noir 2016 Rating 91 To 2024 $35 NG

Brook Eden Vineyard   ★★★★

167 Adams Road, Lebrina, Tas 7254 **Region** Northern Tasmania
T (03) 6395 6244 **www.**brookeden.com.au **Open** 7 days 11–5 Sept–May
Winemaker Winemaking Tasmania **Est.** 1988 **Dozens** 1000 **Vyds** 2.1ha
At 41° south and an altitude of 160m, Brook Eden is one of the coolest sites in Tasmania, and represents 'viticulture on the edge'. While the plantings remain small (1ha pinot noir, 0.8ha chardonnay and 0.3ha pinot gris), yield has been significantly reduced, resulting in earlier picking and better quality grapes.

ΨΨΨΨ♀ Chardonnay 2016 Nothing like Tassie acidity, and with just 4 months in French oak barriques plus mlf, this is fresh as a daisy and linear. Takes its lead with all manner of citrus flavours from grapefruit pith and lemon juice to lemon curd. Zesty, crisp acidity ensuring this stays focused. Screwcap. 13.2% alc. Rating 92 To 2022 $35 JF
Pinot Grigio 2014 Not much information proffered other than fermented on skins for about 10 days, which accounts for the pale-quince hue. It's really dry, refreshing with neat phenolics adding to the texture, and enough nashi pear and spice to make a varietal imprint. Screwcap. 13.2% alc. Rating 91 To 2019 $30 JF
Nero 2015 So, the wine's called Nero, but it is not referring the Sicilian grape variety nero d'Avola; the word simply means 'black' in Italian. Being Tasmanian, it is pinot noir. Tad confusing, perhaps. Thankfully the wine isn't puzzling. It's possible to sit and smell the ebb and flow of the aromas: wildly peppery, incredibly pink grapefruit, orange studded with cloves – a most unusual combination.

The lighter palate is tightly coiled with the jangly acidity and with the tannins, both needing to settle. Screwcap. 13.6% alc. **Rating** 91 **To** 2027 $45 JF

Riesling 2014 The nose and palate start to veer into tertiary territory with baked ricotta, candied lemon rind and glace citrus. Certainly no shortage of acidity keeping it lively, but as the fruit drops out, there's a dryness, a kerosene and burnt character that makes the finish bitter. Drink soon and with food. Screwcap. 11.7% alc. **Rating** 90 **To** 2020 $30 JF

Brookland Valley ★★★★★

Caves Road, Wilyabrup, WA 6280 **Region** Margaret River
T (08) 9755 6042 **www.**brooklandvalley.com.au **Open** 7 days 11–5
Winemaker Courtney Treacher **Est.** 1984 **Dozens** NFP
Brookland Valley has an idyllic setting, plus its cafe and Gallery of Wine Arts, which houses an eclectic collection of wine, food-related art and wine accessories. After acquiring a 50% share of Brookland Valley in 1997, Hardys moved to full ownership in 2004 and it is now part of Accolade Wines. The quality, value for money and consistency of the wines are exemplary.

ŢŢŢŢŢ **Estate Margaret River Chardonnay 2017** Toasty French oak comes through clearly on the bouquet; there's also the power of high quality fruit from the mature estate vineyard with a bell-clear mix of white peach and grapefruit. A label deprived of oxygen. Screwcap. 13.5% alc. **Rating** 96 **To** 2027 $49 ✿

ŢŢŢŢŢ **Verse 1 Margaret River Shiraz 2015** **Rating** 92 **To** 2020 $15 ✿

Brothers at War ★★★★★

16 Gramp Avenue, Angaston, SA 5353 **Region** Barossa Valley
T 0405 631 889 **www.**brothersatwar.com.au **Open** Not
Winemaker Angus Wardlaw **Est.** 2014 **Dozens** 600
David Wardlaw was one of the bastions of the Barossa Valley in the second half of the 20th century, working alongside greats such as Peter Lehmann, John Vickery, Jim Irvine and Wolf Blass. For son Angus, a life in wine was inevitable, working first (in 2009) at Dorrien Estate and after four years starting at Kirrihill Wines in the Clare Valley. He has a love for all things Eden Valley. His brother Sam, with a love of all things Barossa, started in the production side of the business when he worked for Premium Wine Bottlers until '09, after which he was employed by Andrew Seppelt at Murray Street Vineyards, spending the next six years there. Partner Matt Carter's role is mysterious; while he started as a cellar hand at Colonial Wine for a couple of vintages, he has since moved into civil construction, currently running large infrastructure projects but returning from time to time to drink plenty of the Brothers at War wines.

ŢŢŢŢŢ **Fist Fight Barossa Shiraz 2016** A very classy bouquet full of dark berry fruits ex forest or hedgerow, and a stash of velvet to soften the impact. The quality of this magical wine comes from its controlled alcohol that takes any question of the heat of the battle by the scruff of the neck and discards it on the nearest landfill. Screwcap. 14% alc. **Rating** 96 **To** 2031 $35 ✿
Single Vineyard Old Vine Eden Valley Syrah 2015 Bright crimson hue; the fragrant bouquet of spice, pepper and savoury nuances leads into a palate brimming with energy and drive. Polished black cherries, plus notes of raspberries, have the freshness that 13.5% alcohol from the Eden Valley can achieve. A really lovely old vine wine. Screwcap. **Rating** 96 **To** 2040 $80
Single Vineyard Old Vine Barossa Valley Shiraz 2015 Matured for 2 years in French hogsheads (50% new). When you see the colour, assess the bouquet and think about the oak, you expect a full-bodied wine – it's a great (and pleasant) surprise to find a medium-bodied shiraz with blackberry and plum fruits, fine, ripe tannins and a long, well balanced palate. Screwcap. 14% alc. **Rating** 95 **To** 2035 $80
I'm Always Right Eden Valley Cabernet Sauvignon 2016 This has all the trademarks of high quality cabernet: an impressive black-fruited and cedary

bouquet, building to a medium-bodied palate with layers of blackcurrant, bay leaf, firm tannins and subtle cedar/cigar-box oak. Screwcap. 14% alc. **Rating** 94 **To** 2036 $35

♟♟♟♟♀ **Nothing in Common Eden Valley Riesling 2017** Rating 90 To 2025 $25
Mum's Love Eden Valley Rose 2017 Rating 90 To 2018 $25 CM

Brothers in Arms ★★★★

Lake Plains Road, Langhorne Creek, SA 5255 **Region** Langhorne Creek
T (08) 8537 3182 **www**.brothersinarms.com.au **Open** By appt
Winemaker Jim Urlwin **Est.** 1998 **Dozens** 25 000 **Vyds** 85ha
The Adams family has been growing grapes at Langhorne Creek since 1891, when the vines at the famed Metala vineyards were planted. Guy Adams is the fifth generation to own and work the vineyard, and over the past 20 years has both improved the viticulture and expanded the plantings. In 1998 they decided to hold back a small proportion of the production for the Brothers in Arms label, and now they dedicate 85ha to Brothers in Arms (40ha each of shiraz and cabernet sauvignon and 2.5ha each of malbec and petit verdot). Exports to the UK, the US, Canada, Sweden, Denmark, Singapore, South Korea, Malaysia, Hong Kong and China.

♟♟♟♟♀ **Shiraz 2015** Dark garnet; lashings of everything from plums, charry oak, hoisin sauce and extract, asphalt and juniper berries. Full-bodied with bold tannins yet everything comes together – in a big style but it works. Cork. 14.5% alc. **Rating** 90 **To** 2025 $45 JF
Side by Side Malbec 2015 For malbec and Langhorne Creek, this is surprisingly buoyant with its core of plums, black cherries and some freshly roasted coffee grounds. The tamarind-like acidity keeps the medium-bodied palate fresh alongside supple tannins. Screwcap. 14.5% alc. **Rating** 90 **To** 2023 $27 JF

Brown Brothers ★★★★★

Milawa-Bobinawarrah Road, Milawa, Vic 3678 **Region** King Valley
T (03) 5720 5500 **www**.brownbrothers.com.au **Open** 7 days 9–5
Winemaker Joel Tilbrook, Cate Looney, Geoff Alexander, Katherine Brown,
Tom Canning **Est.** 1885 **Dozens** Over 1 million **Vyds** 570ha
Draws upon a considerable number of vineyards spread throughout a range of site climates, ranging from very warm to very cool. An expansion into Heathcote added significantly to its armoury. In 2010 Brown Brothers took a momentous step, acquiring Tasmania's Tamar Ridge for $32.5 million. In May '16 it acquired Innocent Bystander and stock from Giant Steps, and with it a physical presence in the Yarra Valley. The premium quality varietal wines to one side, Brown Brothers has gained two substantial labels: Innocent Bystander Moscato and Innocent Bystander Prosecco. Brown Brothers is known for the diversity of varieties with which it works, and the wines represent good value for money. Deservedly one of the most successful family wineries – its cellar door receives the greatest number of visitors in Australia. A founding member of Australia's First Families of Wine. Exports to all major markets.

♟♟♟♟♟ **Patricia Chardonnay 2015** Still finding its feet (as a 3yo), but the components here are top notch. It's fleshy with flavour but sizzling with acidity; creamy oak doing its best to bring it all together. Peach, citrus, honey and sweet milk flavours put on a seductive show, though another year or two in bottle will lift it a notch higher. Screwcap. **Rating** 95 **To** 2025 $45 CM
Cellar Door Release Arneis 2017 This Yarra Valley arneis is a fine white wine boasting both delicacy and power, its heart filled with pears and stone fruits, its veins run with citrus and splashed with spice. It feels ever-so-elegant and extends ever-so-long through the finish. It's both succulent and dry, and doesn't eschew texture either. Screwcap. 12.5% alc. **Rating** 94 **To** 2020 $25 CM ✪

♟♟♟♟♀ **Patricia Shiraz 2014** Rating 93 To 2032 $62 CM
Methode Traditionelle King Valley Pinot Noir Chardonnay Pinot Meunier NV Rating 92 $25 CM ✪

18 Eighty Nine Chardonnay 2016 Rating 91 To 2022 $19 CM ⊙
Cellar Door Release Albarino 2017 Rating 91 To 2022 $25 CM
Shiraz Mondeuse Cabernet Sauvignon 2013 Rating 91 To 2031 $90
Sparkling Brut Rose NV Rating 91 $27 CM
Cellar Door Banksdale Chardonnay 2016 Rating 90 To 2022 $25 CM
Single Vineyard King Valley Prosecco 2017 Rating 90 To 2019 $25 CM

Brown Hill Estate ★★★★

Cnr Rosa Brook Road/Barrett Road, Rosa Brook, WA 6285 **Region** Margaret River
T (08) 9757 4003 **www.**brownhillestate.com.au **Open** 7 days 10–5
Winemaker Nathan Bailey, Haydn Millard **Est.** 1995 **Dozens** 3000 **Vyds** 22ha
The Bailey family is involved in all stages of wine production, with minimum outside help.
Their stated aim is to produce top quality wines at affordable prices, via uncompromising
viticultural practices emphasising low yields. They have shiraz and cabernet sauvignon
(8ha each), semillon, sauvignon blanc and merlot (2ha each).

🍷🍷🍷🍷 **Oroya Reserve Malbec 2016** Leather, anise and blackberry flavours, and a
touch of chocolatey oak, combine to create a rich, seamless and entirely satisfying
red wine. It's already in fine drinking shape but it will mature over many a year.
Screwcap. 14% alc. **Rating** 93 To 2030 $45 CM
Chaffers Shiraz 2016 It smells ripe, sweet and berried, the palate then following
on faithfully with rich plum and blackberry flavours pressing gently into raisin
territory. There's a musky/vanillan character from oak and a firm finish; it has the
throttle well and truly open but it negotiates the road well. Screwcap. 14% alc.
Rating 92 To 2028 $25 CM ⊙
Charlotte Sauvignon Blanc 2017 The palate builds slowly but surely; its
flavours of pear, lemongrass and blackcurrant are both varietally true and squarely
set to please. Bang on, in short. Screwcap. 12.5% alc. **Rating** 91 To 2019 $24 CM
Lakeview Sauvignon Blanc Semillon 2017 The thistle, the bur, the
passionfruit, the tip of grapefruit. This is a fresh, energetic white wine, at one both
with its region and with the varieties employed. Tasty is the word I'm looking for.
Screwcap. 12.5% alc. **Rating** 91 To 2019 $24 CM
Hannans Cabernet Sauvignon 2016 It's a chocolatey expression of Margaret
River cabernet with concentrated curranty/raisined fruit and gamey, tobacco-like
edges. It has the heft to cellar and the tannin too, though its supple palate has it
ready to be enjoyed any time from now. Screwcap. 14% alc. **Rating** 91 To 2028
$25 CM

Brown Magpie Wines ★★★★★

125 Larcombes Road, Modewarre, Vic 3240 **Region** Geelong
T (03) 5266 2147 **www.**brownmagpiewines.com **Open** W'ends 11–4 Nov–Apr
(7 days 11–4 Jan)
Winemaker Shane Breheny, Loretta Breheny **Est.** 2000 **Dozens** 5000 **Vyds** 9ha
Shane and Loretta Breheny's 20ha property is situated predominantly on a gentle, north-facing
slope, with cypress trees on the western and southern borders providing protection against
the wind. Vines were planted over 2001–02, with pinot noir (4ha) taking the lion's share,
followed by pinot gris and shiraz (2.4ha each) and 0.1ha each of chardonnay and sauvignon
blanc. Viticulture is Loretta's love; winemaking (and wine) is Shane's.

🍷🍷🍷🍷🍷 **Paraparap Reserve Single Vineyard Geelong Pinot Noir 2015** Dark
brick-red. Ripe, black spicy fruit with a ribbon of wild herb running through,
presumably from 10% whole-bunch inclusion. Tannins are really fine and silky
with the wine building in intensity across the palate. Oak more than just a part,
however, the longer the wine sits in the glass, the better it gets. Good fruit from a
good season well handled. Screwcap. 14% alc. **Rating** 95 To 2027 $60 DB
Loretta Blanc de Noir 2013 Disgorged Sept '17. Pale but bright pink; despite
its fragrant, flowery bouquet and initially juicy palate, this quickly changes into a

very complex wine with texture as important as flavour. The later disgorgement (almost 4 years on lees) has added to a sparkling wine of great character. Diam. 12.4% alc. **Rating** 94 $35

♟♟♟♟♀ **Single Vineyard Geelong Pinot Gris 2017** Rating 92 To 2019 $26 DB
Modewarre Mud Reserve Single Vineyard Geelong Shiraz 2015
Rating 92 To 2025 $60 DB

Browns of Padthaway

Glendon Park, 71 McLeons Road, Keppoch, SA 5271 **Region** Padthaway
T (08) 8765 6040 **www**.brownsofpadthaway.com.au **Open** By appt
Winemaker O'Leary Walker Wines **Est.** 1993 **Dozens** 15 000 **Vyds** 150ha
The Brown family has for many years been the largest independent grapegrower in Padthaway, a district in which most of the vineyards were established and owned by Wynns, Seppelt, Lindemans and Hardys respectively. Browns has produced excellent wines and wine production has increased accordingly. The major part of the grape production is sold, and distribution of the wines in Australia has been sporadic. It seems likely that significant amounts are being exported (to the UK, the US, Germany and NZ).

♟♟♟♟♀ **Melba Lillian Family Reserve Chardonnay 2017** Contract-made, and well done at that. Light straw-green; it's a juicy, immediately enjoyable, style with white stone fruit and grapefruit doing the heavy lifting. Screwcap. 13% alc. **Rating** 91 To 2022 $24

♟♟♟♟ **Myra Family Reserve Cabernet Sauvignon 2013** Rating 89 To 2023 $24
Edward Family Reserve Malbec 2015 Rating 89 To 2025 $22

Buckshot Vineyard ★★★★

PO Box 119, Coldstream, Vic 3770 **Region** Heathcote
T 0417 349 785 **www**.buckshotvineyard.com.au **Open** Not
Winemaker Rob Peebles **Est.** 1999 **Dozens** 700 **Vyds** 2ha
This is the venture of Meegan and Rob Peebles, and comes on the back of Rob's 20+ year involvement in the wine industry, including six vintages in Rutherglen starting in 1993, weekend work at Coldstream Hills' cellar door in '93, and 10 years at Domaine Chandon. It is the soils of Heathcote, and a long-time friendship with John and Jenny Davies, that sees the flagship shiraz, and a smaller amount of zinfandel (with some shiraz component) coming from a small block that is part of a 40ha vineyard owned by the Davies southwest of Colbinabbin. Rob continues to make the wines at Domaine Chandon. Exports to the US.

♟♟♟♟♀ **Heathcote Shiraz 2016** There's a flush of red and black fruits mixed with heady regional aromas – think bay leaves, blueberries and ferrous notes. Some dried herbs and spearmint pop out, the tannins have negotiable grip, concluding with bracingly fresh acidity on the finish. Will unfurl in time. Screwcap. 14% alc. **Rating** 93 To 2027 $35 JF

Bull Lane Wine Company

PO Box 77, Heathcote, Vic 3523 **Region** Heathcote
T 0427 970 041 **www**.bulllane.com.au **Open** Not
Winemaker Simon Osicka **Est.** 2013 **Dozens** 400
After a successful career as a winemaker with what is now TWE, Simon Osicka together with viticulturist partner Alison Phillips returned to the eponymous family winery just within the eastern boundary of the Heathcote region in 2010. Spurred on by a decade of drought impacting on the 60-year-old dry-grown vineyard, and a desire to create another style of shiraz, Simon and Alison spent considerable time visiting Heathcote vineyards with access to water in the lead-up to the '10 vintage. After the weather gods gave up their tricks of '11, Bull Lane was in business. Exports to Denmark and China.

♟♟♟♟♟ Heathcote Shiraz 2016 Deeply coloured, it is a super-intense and concentrated, but not tannic, wine. The earliest vintage in 50 years that father Paul Osicka can remember, which might have destroyed the wine, but vineyard vigilance and the non-extractive winery practices saved the day. Screwcap. 14.5% alc. **Rating** 95 To 2041 $27 **☉**

♟♟♟♟♀ Via del Toro Pyrenees Nebbiolo 2016 **Rating** 90 To 2022 $32

Bunkers Margaret River Wines ★★★☆

1142 Kaloorup Road, Kaloorup, WA 6280 **Region** Margaret River
T (08) 9368 4555 **www.**bunkersswines.com.au **Open** Not
Winemaker Brian Fletcher **Est.** 2010 **Dozens** 5500 **Vyds** 34ha
Over the past 20+ years, Mike Calneggia has had his fingers in innumerable Margaret River viticultural pies. He has watched some ventures succeed, and others fail, and while Bunkers Wines (owned by Mike and Sally Calneggia) is only a small part of his viticultural undertakings, it has been carefully targeted from the word go. It has the six mainstream varieties (cabernet, semillon, merlot, chardonnay, sauvignon blanc and shiraz) joined by rising star, tempranillo, in the warm and relatively fertile northern part of the Margaret River. Brian Fletcher is winemaker and Murray Edmonds the viticulturist (both ex Evans & Tate). Mike and his daughter Amy are responsible for sales and marketing. They say, 'The world of wine is full of serious people making serious wines for an ever-decreasing serious market ... Bunkers wines have been created to put the "F" word back into wine: "FUN", that is.' Exports to China.

♟♟♟♟♀ The Box Tempranillo 2015 This has admirable varietal expression, with bright red berry and cherry fruits to the fore, already having sunk the American oak into its fruit swells. Screwcap. 14% alc. **Rating** 90 To 2025 $20 **☉**

Bunnamagoo Estate ★★★★☆

603 Henry Lawson Drive, Mudgee, NSW 2850 **Region** Mudgee
T 1300 304 707 **www.**bunnamagoowines.com.au **Open** 7 days 10–4
Winemaker Robert Black **Est.** 1995 **Dozens** 80 000 **Vyds** 108ha
Bunnamagoo Estate (on one of the first land grants in the region) is situated near the historic town of Rockley. A 6ha vineyard planted to chardonnay, merlot and cabernet sauvignon has been established by Paspaley Pearls, a famous name in the WA pearl industry. The winery and cellar door are located at the much larger (and warmer) Eurunderee Vineyard (102ha) at Mudgee. Exports to the UK, Singapore, Fiji, Papua New Guinea, Indonesia, Hong Kong and China.

♟♟♟♟♟ 1827 Handpicked Cabernet Sauvignon 2015 It's clear there has been rigid selection of high quality grapes, and the wine (just) gets away with 15% alc. – dangerous territory for cabernet. Full-on cassis fruit is neatly braced by tannins and quality French oak, resulting in a medium to full-bodied cabernet that retains balance and lightness of foot. Diam. **Rating** 95 To 2035 $50
Riesling 2017 While Mudgee isn't generally associated with riesling, there were some good wines made from time to time by Ian MacRae prior to Jacob Stein gaining national recognition, and Bunnamagoo Estate winemaker Robert Black showing that the early successes weren't flukes. This is part contract-grown, and is a very good wine. It has the intensity of riesling grown in a cool climate, with lime, lemon and green apple flavours supported by grainy/minerally acidity. Screwcap. 11% alc. **Rating** 94 To 2030 $22 **☉**
Merlot 2016 Very well made, the wine outperforming expectations with its vibrant cassis fruits first and foremost, deft oak handling and ripe tannins also faultless. Screwcap. 14.5% alc. **Rating** 94 To 2031 $24 **☉**

♟♟♟♟♀ Semillon 2017 **Rating** 93 To 2027 $22 **☉**
1827 Handpicked Chardonnay 2016 **Rating** 92 To 2023 $40
Rose 2017 **Rating** 92 To 2020 $22 **☉**
Kids Earth Fund Autumn Semillon 2016 **Rating** 92 To 2020 $25 CM **☉**
Cabernet Sauvignon 2015 **Rating** 90 To 2025 $24

Burge Family Winemakers ★★★★☆

1312 Barossa Way, Lyndoch, SA 5351 **Region** Barossa Valley
T (08) 8524 4644 **www.**burgefamily.com.au **Open** Fri, Sat, Mon 10–5
Winemaker Rick Burge **Est.** 1928 **Dozens** 3500 **Vyds** 10ha
Burge Family Winemakers established itself as an icon producer of exceptionally rich, lush and concentrated Barossa red wines. The year 2013 marked 85 years of continuous winemaking by three generations of the family. At the time of going to print, the future of the winery was in the lap of the gods. Rick Burge has been diagnosed with cancer, and he and wife Bronnie have placed the business on the market as a going concern. The well-wishes of the greater wine community go with Rick and Bronnie at this difficult time. Exports to Canada, Hong Kong and Singapore.

🍷🍷🍷🍷🍷 **Draycott Shiraz 2015** Barossa shiraz in all its glory. Concentrated, sweet-fruited, tickled with savoury complexity and awarded the lightest kiss of smoky oak. Blackberry, coal and anise are the core flavours. An example of how it's done. Pure dark flavour. Cork. 15% alc. **Rating** 95 **To** 2040 $42 CM
Olive Hill Premium Semillon 2017 It lays out its citrus-driven charms from the outset and keeps the show going through to a satisfying finish. If you want to know what high quality Barossa semillon tastes like, here is exhibit A. Floral overtones, fresh herbs and nectarine-like inputs add layers, not to mention drive. Beautiful. Screwcap. 12% alc. **Rating** 94 **To** 2024 $24 CM ⊙

🍷🍷🍷🍷🍷 **Wilsford Founders Reserve Noel's Blend Old Liqueur Muscat NV** **Rating** 93 $36 CM
Garnacha Rose 2017 Rating 91 **To** 2020 $24 CM
Olive Hill Shiraz Grenache Mourvedre 2013 Rating 90 **To** 2024 $28 CM

Burke & Wills Winery ★★★★

3155 Burke & Wills Track, Mia Mia, Vic 3444 **Region** Heathcote
T (03) 5425 5400 **www.**wineandmusic.net **Open** By appt
Winemaker Andrew Pattison, Robert Ellis **Est.** 2003 **Dozens** 1500 **Vyds** 1.6ha
After 18 years at Lancefield Winery in the Macedon Ranges, Andrew Pattison moved his operation a few kilometres north in 2004 to set up Burke & Wills Winery at the southern edge of the Heathcote region. The vineyards at Mia Mia comprise 0.6ha of shiraz, 0.6ha of Bordeaux varieties (cabernet sauvignon, cabernet franc, petit verdot, merlot and malbec) and 0.4ha of gewurztraminer. He still sources a small amount of Macedon Ranges fruit from his former Malmsbury vineyard; additional grapes are contract-grown in Heathcote. In 2017 the winery won the inaugural Premier's Award for Best Victorian Wine with the 2015 Vat 1 Shiraz. Exports to Malaysia.

🍷🍷🍷🍷🍷 **Vat 2 American Oak Shiraz 2013** There's a lot going on in this still very youthful wine, with an aromatic bouquet and juicy black cherry/berry fruits on the palate. Fine-grained tannins are also a positive contribution, the oak functional but not a significant part of the flavour wheel. Strangely and consistently appealing. Screwcap. 14.5% alc. **Rating** 94 **To** 2025 $28 ⊙

🍷🍷🍷🍷🍷 **Camp 5 Shiraz Cabernet Merlot 2013 Rating** 90 **To** 2022 $20 JF ⊙

Bush Track Wines ★★★★

219 Sutton Lane, Whorouly South, Vic 3735 **Region** Alpine Valleys
T 0409 572 712 **www.**bushtrackwines.com.au **Open** By appt
Winemaker Jo Marsh, Eleana Anderson **Est.** 1987 **Dozens** 350 **Vyds** 9.65ha
Bob and Helen McNamara established the vineyard in 1987, planting 5.53ha of shiraz including 11 different clones, and 2ha of chardonnay, 1.72ha of cabernet sauvignon and 0.4ha of sangiovese. They have made small volumes of wines since 2006. Improvement in vineyard practices, and the services of Jo Marsh (Billy Button Wines) and Eleana Anderson (Mayford Wines), should secure the future of Bush Track Wines.

♆♆♆♆♆ **Alpine Valley Chardonnay 2016** A storm of sulphides, a career of stone fruit. This is a wilder, funkier release than previous iterations; a more serious wine, if you like. It leans against boundaries to see where they might break. Importantly it boasts both volume and length, driven by the fruit rather than the winemaking. What it does best though is give a clear view of the outer capabilities of Alpine Valleys chardonnay, and for an extremely modest asking price. Screwcap. 12.5% alc. **Rating** 94 **To** 2023 $25 CM ✪
Ovens Valley Shiraz 2016 70 dozen, made by Jo Marsh. Beautifully crafted. Medium weight with fruit and spice notes working in delicious tandem. Rips of star anise–like flavour really get the juices flowing. The bones are fine, the fruit is ripe, the finish is full and satisfying. Ticks in every box. Screwcap. 14% alc. **Rating** 94 **To** 2028 $25 CM ✪

♆♆♆♆♀ **Grapes of Wrath 2016 Rating** 93 **To** 2025 $25 CM ✪
Alpine Valleys Cabernet Sauvignon 2016 Rating 92 **To** 2026 $25 CM ✪

Buttermans Track ★★★★☆

PO Box 82, St Andrews, Vic 3761 **Region** Yarra Valley
T 0425 737 839 **www.**buttermanstrack.com.au **Open** Not
Winemaker James Lance, Gary Trist **Est.** 1991 **Dozens** 600 **Vyds** 2.13ha
I became intimately acquainted with the Buttermans Track in the latter part of the 1980s when Coldstream Hills, at that stage owned by my wife Suzanne and myself, purchased grapes from the Roberts family's Rising Vineyard. I had to coax a 3t truck with almost no brakes and almost no engine to tackle the hills and valleys of the unsealed Buttermans Track. Louise and Gary Trist began planting their small vineyard in '91 on a small side road just off the track. Between then and 2003 they established 0.86ha of pinot noir, 0.74ha of shiraz and 0.53ha of sangiovese. The Trist family sold the grapes to Yarra Valley wineries until '08. From that year onwards a small parcel of sangiovese was retained for their own label, which has now extended to include the other two estate varieties.

♆♆♆♆♆ **Sangiovese 2015** Excellent dark purple-crimson; wonderful balance of morello and black cherries, new leather, warm earth and a host of spices from cinnamon and star anise to licorice and dried herbs. It's fuller bodied and even on the palate. And for a sangiovese the tannins are astonishingly supple, textural like raw silk, yet powerful, glossy and finishing with pitch-perfect acidity. Screwcap. 13.7% alc. **Rating** 95 **To** 2025 $32 JF ✪
Riesling 2017 A delightful wine that starts off shy and demure with a hint of florals, lemon barley and mandarin peel. Then the chalky acidity kicks in lengthening out the palate to a decisive, dry conclusion. Really mouthwatering. Careful not to dribble. Screwcap. 11.2% alc. **Rating** 94 **To** 2026 $28 JF ✪

Byrne Vineyards ★★★★★

PO Box 15, Kent Town BC, SA 5071 **Region** South Australia
T (08) 8132 0022 **www.**byrnevineyards.com.au **Open** Not
Winemaker Peter Gajewski, Phil Reedman MW **Est.** 1963 **Dozens** 150 000 **Vyds** 384ha
The Byrne family has been involved in the SA wine industry for three generations, with vineyards spanning Clare Valley, Eden Valley, Adelaide Plains and Riverland. The vines vary from 20 to over 50 years of age. Exports to the UK, Canada, France, Germany, Denmark, Sweden, Norway, Thailand, the Philippines, Singapore, Japan and China.

♆♆♆♆♆ **Antiquarian Clare Valley Pinot Noir Shiraz 2016** Silken, floral, pretty and delicious. Pour this into a large-bowled glass and it delights at every turn. Plums, cherries, garden herbs and the polish of cedar wood. It's mid-weight at most but delightful to drink, all ripples and streams. An immaculate red wine. Screwcap. 14.5% alc. **Rating** 95 **To** 2030 $60 CM
Antiquarian Barossa Shiraz 2014 Hulking wine. Muscles rippling, fruit bursting, oak and then more oak, rocks of tannin but smooth-skinned ones. It's stain-the-glass territory in terms of colour, and it has a wealth of berried, jammy

flavour but it still feels fresh; it's big everywhere but manages to get the proportions right. If a big black beauty of a wine is required, this delivers. Diam. 14.5% alc. **Rating** 95 **To** 2034 $60 CM

ΥΥΥΥΩ **Reserve Clare Valley Shiraz 2014** Rating 92 To 2028 $28 CM
Limited Release Clare Valley Grenache 2014 Rating 92 To 2025 $60 CM
Sidney Wilcox Grenache Shiraz 2016 Rating 90 To 2022 $25 CM

Byron & Harold   ★★★★★

351 Herdigan Road, Wandering, WA 6308 **Region** Great Southern
T 0402 010 352 **www**.byronandharold.com.au **Open** Not
Winemaker Kate Morgan **Est.** 2011 **Dozens** 36 000 **Vyds** 18ha
The owners of Byron & Harold make a formidable partnership, covering every aspect of winemaking, sales, marketing, business management and administration. Paul Byron and Ralph (Harold) Dunning together have more than 65 years of experience in the Australian wine trade, working at top levels for some of the most admired wineries and wine distribution companies. Andrew Lane worked for 20 years in the tourism industry, including in a senior role with Tourism Australia, leading to the formation of the Wine Tourism Export Council. More recently he developed the family vineyard (Wandering Lane). Exports to the UK, Canada, China and NZ.

ΥΥΥΥΥ **The Partners Riesling 2017** Crisp. Fresh. Pure. The joy of riesling from a region that produces some of the finest. A classy wine with subtle white blossom, lavender and lemon zest aromas; the palate electrifying with its superfine acidity and length. Screwcap. 12% alc. **Rating** 96 **To** 2029 $35 JF ✪
Rose & Thorns Riesling 2017 A zippy, refreshing, spot-on wine, working off a citrus theme with lemon, lime and tangerine flavours, and aromas of white blossom and green apple. The lime sorbet–like natural acidity takes this for a ride all the way to a long finish. Screwcap. 12.5% alc. **Rating** 95 **To** 2027 $28 JF ✪
The Partners Cabernet Sauvignon 2015 A neat blend of cassis, boysenberries spiced with bay leaves, black olives, cedar and juniper berries. The palate is fuller bodied, yet there's a flow and fineness to it with beautifully orchestrated tannins. Screwcap. 14.5% alc. **Rating** 95 **To** 2030 $45 JF

ΥΥΥΥΩ **Wandering Lane Riesling 2017** Rating 93 To 2026 $22 JF ✪
Wheelabout Spencer Road Riesling 2017 Rating 93 To 2027 $28 JF
The Partners Chardonnay 2016 Rating 93 To 2023 $45 JF
Wandering Lane Shiraz 2015 Rating 90 To 2023 $22 JF

Caillard Wine   ★★★★★

5 Annesley Street, Leichhardt, NSW 2040 (postal) **Region** Barossa Valley
T 0433 272 912 **www**.caillardwine.com **Open** Not
Winemaker Dr Chris Taylor, Andrew Caillard MW **Est.** 2008 **Dozens** 700
Andrew Caillard MW has had a long and varied career in wine, including vintages at Brokenwood and elsewhere. He has also taken the final step of making his own wine with the support of wife Bobby. Andrew says the inspiration to make mataro (and now shiraz) came while writing the background for Penfolds' The Rewards of Patience tastings. He learnt that both Max Schubert and John Davoren had experimented with mataro, and that the original releases of Penfolds' St Henri comprised a fair percentage of the variety. For good measure, Andrew's great (times four) grandfather, John Reynell, planted one of Australia's first vineyards at Reynella, around 1838. Exports to Hong Kong and China.

ΥΥΥΥΥ **Shiraz 2016** What a wonderful hue – the colour of a black baccara rose but smelling of a Mr Lincoln, with spice notes from pepper, licorice and cloves. The palate opens with a flurry of boysenberries and plums; full-bodied but restrained thanks to judicious oak use (French barriques for 15 months with just 10% new). The clincher is the detailed, fine tannins. Screwcap. 13.4% alc. **Rating** 95 **To** 2036 $55 JF

Pinxit 2015 When a mix-up in the cellar results in a barrel of Parker Coonawarra cabernet sauvignon blended with five barriques of Barossa Valley mataro, it's either a stuff-up or serendipity. Thankfully it's the latter. Pale-mid ruby; an intriguing mix of warm earth, ferrous notes, dried herbs and menthol to the satsuma plums and cassis fruit. It's exceptionally savoury with refreshing cranberry-like acidity. Slinky, fine tannins ensure this is a beautifully modulated wine. Screwcap. 13.8% alc. **Rating** 95 **To** 2030 $60 JF

Mataro 2015 With its sour cherry and raspberry fruit profile and a dash of fresh pomegranate juice, it builds with a spice mix of star anise, pepper and cloves; menthol and smoke too. The palate is quite fine and medium-bodied with a tautness between the sinewy, savoury tannins and crunchy acidity. Such a mouthwatering finish. Screwcap. 13.5% alc. **Rating** 95 **To** 2025 $55 JF

ΨΨΨΨΨ **Mataro 2016 Rating** 93 **To** 2026 $55 JF

Calabria Family Wines

1283 Brayne Road, Griffith, NSW 2680 **Region** Riverina/Barossa Valley
T (02) 6969 0800 **www**.calabriawines.com.au **Open** Mon–Fri 8.30–5, w'ends 10–4
Winemaker Bill Calabria **Est.** 1945 **Dozens** NFP **Vyds** 55ha
Calabria Family Wines (until 2014 known as Westend Estate) has successfully lifted both the quality and the packaging of its wines. Its 3 Bridges range is anchored on estate vineyards. The operation is moving with the times, increasing its plantings of durif and introducing aglianico, nero d'Avola and St Macaire (on the verge of extinction, and once grown in Bordeaux, this 2ha is the largest planting in the world). Equally importantly, it is casting its net over the Barossa Valley, Canberra District, Hilltops and King Valley premium regions, taking this one step further by acquiring a 12ha vineyard in the Barossa Valley. Exports to the UK, the US and other major markets, including China.

ΨΨΨΨΨ **St Petri Barossa Valley Shiraz Grenache Mataro 2016** Matured in French (95%) and American oak, which together has quite an impact, yet the beauty of this wine is still clear. Wood smoke, earth, sweet spice and leather flavours give character to the core of raspberry and plum. Tannin is both ultrafine and assertive. Impossible not to be impressed. Screwcap. **Rating** 96 **To** 2028 $70 CM ❸

The Iconic Grand Reserve Barossa Valley Shiraz 2015 This is a big, beautiful wine, its heart of darkness smothered in creamy, smooth oak. It serves richness in one sure, steady pour, the attack no more or less than the finish, the mid-palate not letting anyone or anything down. Seduction here comes fully franked, pure quality not far behind. Tannin swirls through the finish, its own flourish of sorts. Cork. 14.5% alc. **Rating** 95 **To** 2040 $175 CM

ΨΨΨΨΨ **St Petri Barossa Valley Shiraz Carignan 2016 Rating** 93 **To** 2026 $70 CM
3 Bridges Tumbarumba Chardonnay 2017 Rating 92 **To** 2024 $25 CM ❸
3 Bridges Barossa Valley Shiraz 2016 Rating 92 **To** 2026 $25 CM ❸
Cool Climate Series Hilltops Shiraz 2016 Rating 91 **To** 2024 $15 CM ❸
Cellar Collection Barossa Valley Shiraz 2014 Rating 91 **To** 2026 $45 CM
3 Bridges Barossa Valley Cabernet 2016 Rating 90 **To** 2024 $25 CM
Calabria Private Bin Nero d'Avola 2017 Rating 90 **To** 2022 $15 CM ❸

Calneggia Family Vineyards Estate

1142 Kaloorup Road, Kaloorup, WA 6280 **Region** Margaret River
T (08) 9368 4555 **www**.cfvwine.com.au **Open** Not
Winemaker Brian Fletcher **Est.** 2010 **Dozens** 1500 **Vyds** 34ha
The Calneggia family has owned vineyards and been involved in wine in the Margaret River region for over 25 years. The family produces the Rosabrook, Bunkers, Bramble Lane and Brian Fletcher Signature wines, and now their first Calneggia Family Vineyards Estate wines, in conjunction with winemaker Brian Fletcher.

ŸŸŸŸ **Margaret River Rose 2017** A 62/38% blend of shiraz and cabernet sauvignon made by the saignee method (running juice off dry red must) prior to the active commencement of fermentation; the components then starting their own fermentation. A rich wine with a surge of red berry flavours. Screwcap. 13% alc. **Rating** 89 **To** 2019 $25

Campbells   ★★★★★

4603 Murray Valley Highway, Rutherglen, Vic 3685 **Region** Rutherglen
T (02) 6033 6000 **www**.campbellswines.com.au **Open** Mon–Sat 9–5, Sun 10–5
Winemaker Colin Campbell, Julie Campbell **Est.** 1870 **Dozens** 36 000 **Vyds** 72ha
Campbells has a long and rich history, with five generations of the family making wine for over 150 years. There were difficult times: phylloxera's arrival in the Bobbie Burns vineyard in 1898; the Depression of the 1930s; and premature deaths in the Campbell family. But the Scottish blood of founder John Campbell has ensured that the business has not only survived, but quietly flourished. Indeed, there have been spectacular successes in unexpected quarters (white table wines, especially riesling) and expected success with muscat and topaque. Other highs include 99-point scores from Robert Parker and a 100-point score from *Wine Spectator*, putting Campbells in a special position. It is fair to say that the nigh on half-century fourth-generation stewardship of Malcolm and Colin Campbell has been the most important so far, but the five members of the fifth generation all working in the business are well equipped to move up the ladder when Colin and/or Malcolm retire. A founding member of Australia's First Families of Wine. Exports to the UK, the US, China and other major markets.

ŸŸŸŸŸ **Isabella Rare Topaque NV** The dark mahogany and olive rim precedes a mind-blowingly powerful, rich and complex wine at the top of the topaque tree. I'm sure this has become even more intense, and more compellingly textured, than previous tastings, yet isn't the slightest bit stale. I suppose it's just the sheer bliss of tasting these wines that causes me to write as if I have not previously encountered them. 375ml. Screwcap. 18% alc. **Rating** 97 $120 ✪

ŸŸŸŸŸ **Merchant Prince Rare Muscat NV** Wines of this intensity can be a life-changing experience; any thicker or denser and it would be impossible to pour. It has might but it also has glory, packing bags of tarry, toffeed, burnt fruits and honeyed flavours, but still managing to skip through the palate at a speed more youthful wines often cannot manage. Few wines the world over come as guaranteed to impress as this does. 375ml. Screwcap. 18% alc. **Rating** 96 $120 CM
Grand Rutherglen Topaque NV Deep olive-brown; a wonderful example of muscadelle/topaque, with all the cold tea, butterscotch, Christmas cake and burnt toffee expected of the variety at its zenith. I have to admit to a special love of topaque, while recognising the greatness of the muscat that Rutherglen makes. 375ml. Screwcap. 17.5% alc. **Rating** 95 $65
Grand Rutherglen Muscat NV This is for veteran tasters – if you are a P-plate driver you don't get behind the wheel of a Ferrari. Here a sword of rancio brings burnt and sweet flavours of every description into play. 375ml. Screwcap. 17.5% alc. **Rating** 95 $65
Liquid Gold Classic Rutherglen Topaque NV Butterscotch, cold tea and honey all roll around the mouth in a glistening, almost velvety, fashion. It is very sweet, but the rancio cleanses the finish and aftertaste. 500ml. Screwcap. 17.5% alc. **Rating** 94 $38
Rutherglen Topaque NV There's an argument to say that the youngest tier of topaque is the most enjoyable, as it's so immediately compelling (and dangerous). There are shortbread biscuits, spices galore and honey all to be had. 375ml. Screwcap. 17.5% alc. **Rating** 94 $19 ✪
Classic Rutherglen Muscat NV Now you know you are entering the magic hall of Rutherglen muscat, the flavours coming unbidden at such a rate it's hard to record them in any orderly fashion. Singed butterscotch, malt, dried and crystallised fruits, then the vinous masochism of the rancio. 500ml. Screwcap. 17.5% alc. **Rating** 94 $38

🍷🍷🍷🍷🍷 Bobbie Burns Rutherglen Shiraz 2016 Rating 93 To 2025 $23 CM ⊙
Limited Release Rutherglen Durif 2016 Rating 93 To 2026 $28 CM
Rutherglen Muscat NV Rating 92 $19 ⊙

Cannibal Creek Vineyard ★★★★☆

260 Tynong North Road, Tynong North, Vic 3813 **Region** Gippsland
T (03) 5942 8380 **www**.cannibalcreek.com.au **Open** 7 days 11–5
Winemaker Patrick Hardiker **Est.** 1997 **Dozens** 3000 **Vyds** 5ha
Patrick and Kirsten Hardiker moved to Tynong North in 1988, initially grazing beef cattle, but aware of the viticultural potential of the sandy clay loam and bleached subsurface soils weathered from the granite foothills of the Black Snake Ranges. Plantings began in '97 using organically based cultivation methods; varieties include pinot noir, chardonnay, sauvignon blanc, merlot and cabernet sauvignon. The family established the winery in an old farm barn built in the early 1900s by the Weatherhead family, with timber from Weatherhead Hill (visible from the vineyard). In 2016 they opened a new cellar door and restaurant, designed by Enarchitects and hand-built by Patrick, awarded 'Cellar Door With Best Food in Gippsland' by *Gourmet Traveller Wine* in '18.

🍷🍷🍷🍷🍷 Reserve Pinot Noir 2016 Beautifully aromatic with bright cherries and spice plus whole-bunch fragrance and earthy nuances for added interest. A delightfully light mid-frame with fine tannins. Overall, this is an elegant style. Screwcap. 13.4% alc. **Rating** 95 **To** 2026 $60 JF

🍷🍷🍷🍷🍷 Reserve Pinot Noir 2016 Rating 93 To 2024 $60 CM
Merlot 2016 Rating 93 To 2023 $38 JF
Reserve Sauvignon Blanc 2017 Rating 92 To 2022 $35 JF
Pinot Noir 2016 Rating 92 To 2024 $38 CM
Blanc de Blancs 2015 Rating 91 $38 JF
Sauvignon Blanc 2017 Rating 90 To 2021 $32 JF
Cabernet Sauvignon 2016 Rating 90 To 2025 $48 JF
Vin de Liqueur 2016 Rating 90 $45 JF

Cantina Abbatiello ★★★★

90 Rundle Street, Kent Town, SA 5067 (postal) **Region** Adelaide
T 0421 200 414 **Open** Not
Winemaker Contract **Est.** 2015 **Dozens** 600
Luca Abbatiello was born and raised in a small village in the south of Italy. 'Vagabondo' means nomad, and as he grew up the wanderlust took hold, wine and food remaining important wherever he went. And while he worked for Michelin-starred restaurants in England (where he first headed), he says he still missed the homemade food of Italy. This led him and his partner to move to Australia in 2014, gravitating to Adelaide. Here he found the family food that he had missed, and a work environment full of opportunities. The most recent of those has been the creation of his virtual winery Cantina Abbatiello.

🍷🍷🍷🍷🍷 Vagabondo Adelaide Hills Chardonnay 2016 A standard no-frills barrel-fermented chardonnay. It is medium-bodied with neatly balanced stone fruit/citrus flavours, and well integrated oak on the long palate. Screwcap. 13.5% alc. **Rating** 90 **To** 2021 $30

Cape Barren Wines ★★★★

PO Box 738, North Adelaide, SA 5006 **Region** McLaren Vale
T (08) 8267 3292 **www**.capebarrenwines.com **Open** By appt
Winemaker Rob Dundon **Est.** 1999 **Dozens** 17 000 **Vyds** 16.5ha
Cape Barren was founded in 1999 by Peter Matthew. He sold the business in late 2009 to Rob Dundon and Tom Adams, who together have amassed in excess of 50 years' experience in winemaking, viticulture and international sales. The wines, including shiraz and grenache, are sourced from dry-grown vines between 70 and 125 years old. Chardonnay, sauvignon

blanc and gruner veltliner are sourced from the Adelaide Hills. Exports to the US, Canada, Switzerland, China and other markets across Asia.

ՓՓՓՓՓ **Old Vine Reserve McLaren Vale Shiraz 2015** A melange of spicy dark fruit, bitter chocolate and cocoa, blackstrap licorice with a slight radicchio-char and bitterness following the tamarind-like acidity, and oak-infused spices. The palate is full-bodied and buoyant with ripe tannins, some grip and dryness on the finish. Definitely needs protein as a match. Cork. 14.7% alc. **Rating** 93 **To** 2030 $45 JF
Native Goose McLaren Vale Shiraz 2016 Excellent black-red hue; richly flavoured, yet not heavy, as it unfurls onto its medium-bodied palate full of dark fruit dusted with cocoa, fragrant with black licorice and warm earth. It's savoury with its dry tannins a slight hindrance. Screwcap. 14% alc. **Rating** 92 **To** 2024 $24 JF ❂
Native Goose McLaren Vale Grenache Shiraz Mourvedre 2016 A 59/37/4% blend with the grenache and mourvedre coming off a 60yo dry-grown vineyard and the shiraz close behind at 45yo. It's well composed with a savoury thread holding everything in its place from the dark fruits, red licorice and menthol to the supple, slightly drying tannins. Medium-bodied, lithe and one to enjoy in its youth. Screwcap. 14.5% alc. **Rating** 91 **To** 2022 $25 JF

ՓՓՓՓ **Adelaide Hills Sauvignon Blanc 2017 Rating** 89 **To** 2020 $18 JF ❂

Cape Grace Wines   ★★★★★

281 Fifty One Road, Cowaramup, WA 6284 **Region** Margaret River
T (08) 9755 5669 **www**.capegracewines.com.au **Open** 7 days 10–5
Winemaker Dylan Arvidson, Mark Messenger (Consultant) **Est.** 1996
Dozens 2000 **Vyds** 6.25ha
Cape Grace can trace its history back to 1875, when timber baron MC Davies settled at Karridale, building the Leeuwin lighthouse and founding the township of Margaret River. Robert and Karen Karri-Davies planted their vineyard 120 years later, to chardonnay, shiraz and cabernet sauvignon, with smaller amounts of cabernet franc, malbec and chenin blanc. Robert is a self-taught viticulturist; Karen has over 15 years of international sales and marketing experience in the hospitality industry. Winemaking is carried out on the property; consultant Mark Messenger is a veteran of the Margaret River region. Exports to Singapore and China.

ՓՓՓՓՓ **Reserve Margaret River Cabernet Sauvignon 2014** A velour of massaged oak and grape tannins serves as an immaculate platform for billowing dark fruit allusions, all wrapped around a sprig of sage and bouquet garni. The finish is detailed, layered and palate-staining. Yet despite the wine's persistence and penetrative length, it is no behemoth. Screwcap. 13.9% alc. **Rating** 96 **To** 2034 $85 NG
Margaret River Cabernet Franc 2016 A medium-bodied, suave expression of this variety, forsaking what can be an overt leafiness for a sappy meld of ripe red fruits, chilli heat and satsuma plum, flecked with some vanillan oak and Chinese five-spice. The tannins are palate-whetting and finely tuned. Very good cab franc on the just-riper side. Screwcap. 13.6% alc. **Rating** 94 **To** 2024 $40 NG

ՓՓՓՓՓ **Margaret River Cabernet Sauvignon 2015 Rating** 93 **To** 2026 $55 NG
Margaret River Shiraz 2015 Rating 91 **To** 2023 $35 NG
Margaret River Chardonnay 2016 Rating 90 **To** 2024 $38 NG

Cape Jaffa Wines   ★★★★☆

459 Limestone Coast Road, Mount Benson via Robe, SA 5276 **Region** Mount Benson
T (08) 8768 5053 **www**.capejaffawines.com.au **Open** 7 days 10–5
Winemaker Anna and Derek Hooper **Est.** 1993 **Dozens** 10 000 **Vyds** 22.86ha
Cape Jaffa was the first of the Mount Benson estates, its winery made from local rock. Between 800t and 1000t of grapes are crushed each year. Cape Jaffa's fully certified

biodynamic vineyard provides 50% of production, with additional fruit sourced from another biodynamic grower in Wrattonbully. Having received the Advantage South Australia Regional Award in '09, '10 and '11 for its sustainable initiatives in the Limestone Coast, Cape Jaffa is now a Hall of Fame inductee. Exports to the UK, Canada, Thailand, the Philippines, Hong Kong, Singapore and China.

🍷🍷🍷🍷🍷 **Mesmer Eyes Red & White Blend 2016** A new wine and named after the tea tree shrub Mesmer Eyes, a popular nursery variety prized for its distinct red and white flowers. The wine smells and tastes of gewurztraminer (85%) and something else with candied pear, musk, a sprinkling of black pepper, blood orange juice and peel – really complex and heady with depth on the palate. But the colour is light garnet. Screwcap. 15% alc. **Rating** 95 To 2023 $29 JF ✪
Epic Drop Limestone Coast Shiraz 2016 Dark-fruited in character, with a touch of dark chocolate and toasty oak in the background. The flavours sink into the palate without getting 'big', and the tannin builds without becoming intrusive. Absolutely needs time to relax and unfold. Screwcap. 14.5% alc. **Rating** 94 To 2030 $29 SC

🍷🍷🍷🍷🍷 **Samphire Skin Contact White 2016** **Rating** 93 To 2020 $29 CM
Riptide Red Blend 2016 **Rating** 93 To 2022 $29 JF
Anna's Limestone Coast White Blend 2017 **Rating** 92 To 2021 $29 CM
En Soleil Shiraz 2015 **Rating** 91 To 2026 $39 CM

Cape Mentelle ★★★★★

331 Wallcliffe Road, Margaret River, WA 6285 **Region** Margaret River
T (08) 9757 0888 **www**.capementelle.com.au **Open** 7 days 10–5
Winemaker Frederique Perrin Parker **Est.** 1970 **Dozens** 80 000 **Vyds** 150ha
Part of the LVMH (Louis Vuitton Möet Hennessy) group. Cape Mentelle is firing on all cylinders, with the winemaking team fully capitalising on the extensive and largely mature vineyards, which obviate the need for contract-grown fruit. It is hard to say which of the wines is best; the ranking, such as it is, varies from year to year. That said, sauvignon blanc semillon, chardonnay, shiraz and cabernet sauvignon lead the portfolio. Exports to all major markets.

🍷🍷🍷🍷🍷 **Single Vineyard Margaret River Shiraz 2015** Exceptional attention to detail manifested by the very expensive X-ray optical scanning of every berry passing by on a moving belt, and the simultaneous removal of imperfect berries by a tiny jet of air. The wine has remarkable elegance, purity and energy. Screwcap. 14% alc. **Rating** 98 To 2035 $98 ✪
Margaret River Chardonnay 2016 Full-on green-gold; it's exceptionally intense and concentrated, with all manner of stone fruits and a savoury gauze of grapefruit juice and zest. The acidity is important now, and will be so later. Striking. Screwcap. 14% alc. **Rating** 97 To 2026 $45 ✪

🍷🍷🍷🍷🍷 **Margaret River Semillon 2016** Fermented and matured in French oak. It is every bit as complex as its vinification could give, filling the mouth with strands of flavours ranging from lemon to honey. But it's the power of the crunchy acidity on the finish that gives this wine its passport with unlimited rights of re-entry. Screwcap. 13% alc. **Rating** 96 To 2042 $60 ✪
Margaret River Cabernet Sauvignon 2015 This should be the wine least ready to drink of the trio of Cape Mentelle '15 siblings, but is the most ready. It is absolutely delicious now, with all of its flavour, texture and structure ducks in a row. It's the stealthy softness of the tannins, which are there, and will continue to do what is required of them for decades to come. Screwcap. 14% alc. **Rating** 96 To 2035 $98
Trinders Margaret River Cabernet Merlot 2015 An immaculate wine made with the same attention to detail as it was with the first vintage all those years ago. It is vitally fresh and balanced, making it an any-time, every-time, classic Australian blend. Screwcap. 14% alc. **Rating** 95 To 2030 $31 ✪

Wallcliffe Margaret River Merlot Petit Verdot 2015 The undoubted complexity comes from the fine, persistent tannins that run through the length of the palate, providing the structure for the fruit to hang onto. A left-field blend that has worked very well. Screwcap. 13.5% alc. **Rating** 95 **To** 2030 $49

🍷🍷🍷🍷🍷 **Margaret River Sauvignon Blanc Semillon 2017** **Rating** 93 **To** 2022 $26 ✪
Margaret River Rose 2017 **Rating** 90 **To** 2020 $28

Cape Naturaliste Vineyard ★★★★

1 Coley Road (off Caves Road), Yallingup, WA 6282 **Region** Margaret River
T (08) 9755 2538 **www**.capenaturalistevineyard.com.au **Open** 7 days 10.30–5
Winemaker Bruce Dukes, Craig Brent-White **Est.** 1997 **Dozens** 5300 **Vyds** 10.7ha
Cape Naturaliste Vineyard has a long and varied history going back 150 years, when it was a coach inn for travellers journeying between Perth and Margaret River. Later it became a dairy farm, and in 1970 a mining company purchased it, intending to extract nearby mineral sands. The government stepped in and declared the area a national park, whereafter (in '80) Craig Brent-White purchased this property. Bruce Dukes joined Craig as winemaker, initially responsible for the white wines before red wines were added to the roster. Overall, little has changed over the last 20 years. The vineyard is planted to cabernet sauvignon, shiraz, merlot, semillon and sauvignon blanc, and is run on an organic/biodynamic basis.

🍷🍷🍷🍷🍷 **Torpedo Rocks Single Vineyard Cabernet Merlot 2014** A lovely, savoury-infused wine that's medium-bodied and balances the core of cassis and red fruits to the cedary oak. A fling of eucalyptus and mint, with integrated tannins; approachable now. Screwcap. 14.5% alc. **Rating** 92 **To** 2026 $40 JF

Margaret River Sauvignon Blanc 2017 A lively and almost thirst-quenching wine that states its varietal and regional charm – the flurry of citrus, herbs, snow peas and lemongrass. There's zippy and zesty acidity, but it's not all upfront appeal as there's some texture rounding out the palate. Screwcap. 12.3% alc. **Rating** 91 **To** 2019 $20 JF ✪

Torpedo Rocks Reserve Shiraz Cabernet Merlot 2014 Dark ruby with some bricking; there's power to this from the dark, rich fruit to the grainy tannins strutting their stuff across the full-bodied palate. No shortage of flavour, with plenty of oak and its vanillan-woodsy spices that finish warm. Screwcap. 14.7% alc. **Rating** 91 **To** 2025 $60 JF

Torpedo Rocks Shiraz 2014 The colour is advanced. While it has dark plums and cherries laced with cinnamon and other woodsy spices – oak derived too – this has a more savoury profile with salami/prosciutto flavours. Fuller-bodied with firm tannins a little rough around the edges, yet it has that appealing regional bay leaf/wood smoke character. Screwcap. 14.6% alc. **Rating** 90 **To** 2022 $40 JF

Torpedo Rocks Cabernet Sauvignon 2014 This wine could come from nowhere else, so strong is the regional thumbprint of mulberries and boysenberries. There's some riper stewed fruit and a mix of dried herbs and leafy freshness all dutifully following through on the palate. The cedary-clove oak imparts a slight sweetness. Screwcap. 14.6% alc. **Rating** 90 **To** 2025 $40 JF

Capel Vale ★★★★★

118 Mallokup Road, Capel, WA 6271 **Region** Geographe
T (08) 9727 1986 **www**.capelvale.com **Open** 7 days 10–4
Winemaker Daniel Hetherington **Est.** 1974 **Dozens** 50 000 **Vyds** 90ha
Established by Perth-based medical practitioner Peter Pratten and wife Elizabeth in 1974. The first vineyard adjacent to the winery was planted on the banks of the quiet waters of Capel River. The viticultural empire has since been expanded, spreading across Geographe (15ha), Mount Barker (15ha), Pemberton (28ha) and Margaret River (32ha). There are four tiers in the Capel Vale portfolio: Debut (varietals), Regional Series, Black Label Margaret River Chardonnay and Cabernet Sauvignon, and at the top: the Single Vineyard Series. Exports to all major markets.

ṖṖṖṖṖ **Single Vineyard Series Whispering Hill Mount Barker Riesling 2017**
Very well handled, high quality fruit gets the wine off to a top start. It is tightly structured; minerally acidity doing its part; counterintuitively mouthwatering. Lime, Granny Smith apple and Meyer lemon are bound together for life thanks to the overall balance of the wine. Screwcap. 12.5% alc. **Rating** 95 **To** 2032 $32 ❂
Single Vineyard Series Whispering Hill Mount Barker Riesling 2016
Still bright straw-green, with almost no colour change; generously proportioned in terms of fruit depth, but in no way flabby or extractive. Delicious Rose's lime juice runs through the length of the palate, acidity tingling in the background. Screwcap. 12.5% alc. **Rating** 95 **To** 2031 $32 ❂
Single Vineyard Series Whispering Hill Mount Barker Shiraz 2015 Has remarkable intensity, freshness and drive given its medium-bodied weight. Every component of this highly detailed wine has been given assured consideration in the vinification and maturation phases. Red and black cherry/berry fruits sparkle in the mouth, the finish with the clarity of a high quality wine. Screwcap. 14.5% alc. **Rating** 95 **To** 2033 $55

ṖṖṖṖṖ **Regional Series Mount Barker Riesling 2017** Rating 93 To 2027 $25 ❂
Cellar Exclusive Mount Barker Shiraz 2015 Rating 93 To 2030 $27 ❂
Black Label Margaret River Chardonnay 2017 Rating 92 To 2029 $35
Debut Sauvignon Blanc Semillon 2017 Rating 90 To 2020 $18 ❂
Regional Series Margaret River Chardonnay 2017 Rating 90 To 2020 $25
Regional Series Pemberton Pinot Rose 2017 Rating 90 To 2020 $25
Regional Series Margaret River Cabernet 2016 Rating 90 To 2031 $27

Capercaillie Wines   ★★★★
4 Londons Road, Lovedale, NSW 2325 **Region** Hunter Valley
T (02) 4990 2904 **www.**capercailliewines.com.au **Open** 7 days 10–4.30
Winemaker Peter Lane **Est.** 1995 **Dozens** 10000 **Vyds** 8ha
A successful winery in terms of the quality of its wines, as well as their reach outwards from the Hunter Valley. The Capercaillie wines have generous flavour, its fruit sources spread across south-eastern Australia, although the portfolio also includes wines that are 100% Hunter Valley. Exports to Dubai and China.

ṖṖṖṖṖ **The Creel 2017** A graceful young semillon with long, slender lines of flavour and a trill to the finish. You could take this anywhere and serve it in any company. Just enough mouthfeel and just enough breadth, but really it's about the final sprint, where its real quality is revealed. Screwcap. 11% alc. **Rating** 94 **To** 2026 $35 CM
Hunter Valley Semillon 2017 A fine, elegant, lengthy release with a decent grab of youthful flavour but with mid-term, if not longer, cellarability written all over it. Lemongrass, slate, citrus and a flicker of red apple all make positive contributions here. Slightly grippy finish but it doesn't stop the flavours from running onwards. Screwcap. 11.9% alc. **Rating** 94 **To** 2025 $25 CM ❂

ṖṖṖṖṖ **Hilltops Shiraz 2016** Rating 90 To 2023 $25 CM

Capital Wines   ★★★★★
13 Gladstone Street, Hall, ACT 2618 **Region** Canberra District
T (02) 6230 2022 **www.**capitalwines.com.au **Open** Thurs–Sun 10.30–5
Winemaker Andrew McEwin, Phil Scott **Est.** 1986 **Dozens** 3500 **Vyds** 5ha
Capital Wines started as Kyeema Wines, established by Andrew McEwin in 1986. In 2000 he purchased another 4ha vineyard 4km south of Murrumbateman, which was planted in 1984 to shiraz, cabernet sauvignon and chardonnay (Kyeema had in fact sourced fruit from this vineyard since its first vintage); plantings were extended with merlot, shiraz and tempranillo in '02, removing the cabernet in '07. Kyeema became Capital Wines in '08 with a much expanded range of wines, including the highly successful Kyeema Vineyard premium range and the Ministry Series. The Kyeema Vineyard shiraz is from an old SA clone sourced

from vineyards used by Penfolds. Some additional grapes are purchased, mainly from the Canberra District.

🍷🍷🍷🍷 **The Black Rod 2013** Made with merlot and shiraz grown on the Kyeema vineyard. 3 years on lees. Both rich and mellow at once, its flavours of leather, chocolate, briar and black cherry swinging sweetly through the palate. The wine's briary characters play peek-a-boo on the finish, but liqueur notes rush to smooth things over. Crown seal. 14% alc. **Rating** 91 $36 CM

Carlei Estate | Carlei Green Vineyards ★★★★

1 Alber Road, Upper Beaconsfield, Vic 3808 **Region** Yarra Valley/Heathcote
T (03) 5944 4599 **www**.carlei.com.au **Open** W'ends 11–6
Winemaker Sergio Carlei **Est.** 1994 **Dozens** 10 000 **Vyds** 2.25ha
Sergio Carlei has come a long way, graduating from home winemaking in a suburban garage to his own commercial winery that falls just within the boundaries of the Yarra Valley. Along the way Carlei acquired a Bachelor of Wine Science from CSU, and established a vineyard with organic and biodynamic accreditation adjacent to the Upper Beaconsfield winery, plus another parcel of 7ha in Heathcote. Contract winemaking services are now a major part of the business. Exports to the US, Singapore and China.

🍷🍷🍷🍷 **Green Vineyards Cardinia Ranges Pinot Gris 2016** Wild-yeast fermented and left on lees 10 months in a mix of seasoned oak, stainless steel and ceramic eggs. It's textural with a mix of bruised and baked apples, a sprinkling of ginger spice and cream. Appealing phenolics, just a touch broad on the finish. Screwcap. 13.5% alc. **Rating** 90 **To** 2020 $40 JF
Green Vineyards Heathcote Viognier 2017 A deep gold hue – more colour than expected given the vintage. The palate shows restraint, though, with some baked apple and toffee apple, clotted cream, and really citrussy too. Wafts of honeysuckle and spices. Screwcap. 13.5% alc. **Rating** 90 **To** 2019 $50 JF
Carlei Estate Heathcote Viognier 2017 A ripe and voluptuous wine, very textural with lemon essence, dried apricots and lemon barley water. Toasty, nutty and creamy leesy notes add to the volume of the palate. Screwcap. 13.5% alc. **Rating** 90 **To** 2020 $60 JF

Carpe Vinum ★★★★

PO Box 333, Penola, SA 5277 **Region** Limestone Coast
T 0452 408 488 **www**.carpevinum.com.au **Open** Not
Winemaker Tom Carson, Sue Bell **Est.** 2011 **Dozens** 750 **Vyds** 4ha
Carpe Vinum is the venture of Malcolm and Henry Skene. In 2011 Malcolm returned from many years overseas – postgraduate studies and then work in Europe (and the UK) – while Henry had been building his legal practice in Melbourne. Both had a keen interest in wine, and one night over dinner they decided to seize the day and set about making their own cabernet sauvignon, the variety they loved best of all. Not quite by chance, the Skene family had owned the Krongart property near Penola since 1869, and in the mid-1990s their uncle/father planted 4ha of cabernet sauvignon. Its isolation and other distractions meant that it had gone untended for years until they were able to persuade viticulturist Fred Boot to leave Yabby Lake, where he had spent the previous 14.5 years (at the Strathbogie Ranges vineyards) and begin the resuscitation of the vineyard. It's still a work in progress. Tom Carson made the '14 and '15 vintages, and Sue Bell made the '16 vintage.

🍷🍷🍷🍷 **Single Vineyard Limestone Coast Cabernet Sauvignon 2015** The vineyard lies just outside the Coonawarra GI boundary. This is a robust cabernet, its powerful blackcurrant and black olive fruit relegates the oak to a functional role. This will kick on for decades thanks to the balance of the modest alcohol. Screwcap. 13.5% alc. **Rating** 92 **To** 2035 $37

Casa Freschi ★★★★★

159 Ridge Road, Ashton, SA 5137 **Region** Adelaide Hills/Langhorne Creek
T 0409 364 569 **www**.casafreschi.com.au **Open** By appt
Winemaker David Freschi **Est.** 1998 **Dozens** 2000 **Vyds** 7.7ha
Casa Freschi is a small, quality-obsessed vigneron, currently producing 10 single vineyard wines from two vineyards (in the Adelaide Hills and at Langhorne Creek). David Freschi's parents, Attilio and Rosa, first planted 2.5ha of cabernet sauvignon, shiraz and malbec in 1972, David continuing the plantings with 2ha of close-planted nebbiolo and 3.2ha of chardonnay, pinot gris, riesling and gewurztraminer, all grown using organic principles. The wines are made at the gravity-fed micro-winery built in 2007. Exports to the UK, Singapore, the Philippines and Japan.

TTTTT **Adelaide Hills Chardonnay 2016** The selection of small parts of the high density 1.6ha vineyard has given this wine a flying start, the vinification exacting and amplifying the intensity of the fruit. Structure, texture and fruit all combine to provide a palate of great length and urgency. Screwcap. 13% alc. **Rating** 96 To 2029 $55 ❂

Langhorne Creek Malbec 2015 The beautiful hue of crimson rimmed by royal purple underlines the symbiosis between Langhorne Creek and malbec. This sends a silky, sumptuous message of pure plum (damson, blood, satsuma – you name it) flowing across the palate, and no difficult questions about the finish or aftertaste. Cork. 14% alc. **Rating** 96 To 2035 $55 ❂

Ragazzi Langhorne Creek Nebbiolo 2016 The colour is clear, but showing the first signs of development. The vinification is crowding angels onto a pinhead, but this is a pretty snappy nebbiolo, with a rose petal and spice perfume, the palate jauntily picking up the lead of the bouquet. Screwcap. 13% alc. **Rating** 95 To 2026 $28 ❂

Langhorne Creek Nebbiolo 2015 Bombards you with questions from start to finish, but I'm prepared to put my neck on the block here. The perfumed rosewater and spice bouquet sets the path for the finely detailed texture and structure of the palate that cuts across any question about the modest alcohol. Cork. 13.5% alc. **Rating** 95 To 2028 $55

Ragazzi Adelaide Hills Chardonnay 2017 The usual attention to detail has resulted in a complex but perfectly balanced wine with crystal clear varietal expression firmly placed in the driver's seat. Even with the low alcohol, the flavours are of white peach, nectarine and creamy fig, citrus appearing with the acidity. Screwcap. 12.5% alc. **Rating** 94 To 2029 $28 ❂

TTTT♀ **Ragazzi Adelaide Hills Pinot Grigio 2017** Rating 91 To 2020 $28
Langhorne Creek Syrah 2015 Rating 90 To 2025 $55
Profondo Old Vines 2015 Rating 90 To 2040 $55

Cassegrain Wines ★★★★

764 Fernbank Creek Road, Port Macquarie, NSW 2444 **Region** Hastings River
T (02) 6582 8377 **www**.cassegrainwines.com.au **Open** Mon–Fri 9–5, w'ends 10–5
Winemaker John Cassegrain, Alex Cassegrain **Est.** 1980 **Dozens** 50000 **Vyds** 34.9ha
Cassegrain has continued to evolve and develop. It still draws on the original Hastings River vineyard of 4.9ha, where the most important varieties are semillon, verdelho and chambourcin, with pinot noir and cabernet sauvignon making up the numbers. However, Cassegrain also part-owns and manages Richfield Vineyard in the New England region, with 30ha of chardonnay, verdelho, semillon, shiraz, merlot, cabernet sauvignon and ruby cabernet. Grapes are also purchased from Tumbarumba, Orange and the Hunter Valley. Exports to Japan, China and other major markets.

TTTT♀ **Edition Noir Shiraz Pinot 2016** Fruit, spice, structure and length. This is a wine of intrigue and character, its berried flavours overlaid with coffee, dark chocolate, rounds of spice and orange rind. It's frisky, a little exotic and enjoyable now – though its best should be revealed after a short-to-medium stint in a cool, dark place. Screwcap. 14% alc. **Rating** 91 To 2025 $28 CM

Reserve Shiraz 2015 It feels ripe but it also feels tight and sinewy. Firmness is certainly part of its shtick. Red and black cherry, orange rind, a whisper of milk chocolate and woody spice characters. It looks to have a promising future ahead. Cork. 14.5% alc. **Rating** 91 **To** 2024 $50 CM

Edition Noir Gewurztraminer 2016 From Orange. All the varietal hallmarks with good concentration of flavour, especially upfront. Turns dry, almost slatey, through the finish – no bad thing. Screwcap. 13% alc. **Rating** 90 **To** 2019 $25 CM

Edition Noir Sangiovese 2016 Convincing expression of the variety. It emphasises red cherry flavours, but darker plum-like characters play a role, as do dry spice and leather notes. It finishes both clean and complete with a gentle ripple of tannin. Screwcap. 14.5% alc. **Rating** 90 **To** 2020 $28 CM

♀♀♀♀ **Fromenteau Reserve Chardonnay 2016** **Rating** 89 **To** 2020 $35 CM
Spring Rose 2017 **Rating** 89 **To** 2018 $22 CM

Castagna   ★★★★★

88 Ressom Lane, Beechworth, Vic 3747 **Region** Beechworth
T (03) 5728 2888 **www.**castagna.com.au **Open** By appt
Winemaker Julian Castagna, Adam Castagna **Est.** 1997 **Dozens** 1800 **Vyds** 4ha
Julian Castagna is an erudite and totally committed disciple of biodynamic grapegrowing and winemaking. While he acknowledges that at least part of the belief in biodynamics has to be intuitive, he also seeks to understand how the principles and practices enunciated by Rudolf Steiner in 1924 actually work. He purchased two egg-shaped, food-grade concrete tanks, each holding 900 litres. They are, he says, 'the most perfect shape in physics', and in the winery reduce pressure on the lees and deposit the lees over a larger surface area, which, he believes, will eliminate the need for batonnage. He has been joined by son Adam, who is responsible for the 400 dozen or so of Adam's Rib made each year, complementing the production of Castagna. Exports to the UK, France, Spain, Denmark, South Korea, Hong Kong, China and Japan.

♀♀♀♀♀ **Growers Selection Roussanne 2015** The ripe stone-fruited lift and the bitter almond, quince, ginger and bergamot notes are as riveting as they are viscous across the cheeks and energetic down the throat, scurrying along a waft of oak, phenolics and a tensile mineral thread. Impressively long. Bloody compelling! Reminiscent of Beaucastel Vielles Vignes. Diam. 13.5% alc. **Rating** 97 **To** 2023 $45 NG **✪**

Genesis Syrah 2015 Granitic DNA defines this mid-weighted syrah. Of a mineral grind, flirtatious and energetic of ambition and crunch; this is iodine cloaked in dried seaweed and umami; blueberry, tapenade, charcuterie and sour cherry sass. An impeccably detailed weave of transparent acidity and moreish tannins – firm without grate. This flows long and juicy. Among the country's exemplary cool-climate syrah, revelry and sophistication all at once. Diam. 13.5% alc. **Rating** 97 **To** 2027 $75 NG **✪**

♀♀♀♀♀ **Ingenue Viognier 2016** This is sumptuous viognier, bred across an innate comprehension of the variety's ripening patterns. Richly weighted and viscous, with a leesy precision imbuing energy, direction and length. A good waft of phenolics, too, serving as another directive signpost for the flavours: apricot, ginger, honeysuckle and almond milk. Diam. 13.5% alc. **Rating** 96 **To** 2021 $55 NG **✪**

Growers Selection Harlequin 2014 As Julian Castagna once said, 'This is orange wine made by somebody who knows how to make wine'. And right he is too! The secret to the style is honing the inherent tannins that result from the maceration of grape skins and juice. A blend of roussanne, sauvignon, semillon and viognier, this is on point. A mesh of ginger candy, dried apricot and chutney, with perky acidity threaded through a weave of gentle pucker. Nothing too dry; nothing out of place. Plenty of flow. Thrust of fruit and parry of structure. Drinkability in spades! Diam. 13% alc. **Rating** 95 **To** 2022 $40 NG

Sparkling Genesis 2009 Light years away from most sparkling red, this was made in the traditional method with 6 years on tirage and further time in bottle post-disgorgement to settle down. The dosage is 6g/l. The finish is defined as much by a tannic twine as it is by the fizz and acid tow. Aniseed, blackberry and violet notes are sashayed along the mouth by a joyous energy to a savoury, bitter finish. It drinks like an artisanal lambrusco. A serious red, this ... with fizz! Diam. 14% alc. **Rating** 95 $85 NG

Growers Selection Chardonnay 2016 Julian Castagna's obsession with texture and detail is on full display across this plump, generous chardonnay. Toasted hazelnut, peach and nougat shimmy along a mineral-clad bow, taut enough to confer energy, but knit with a suitably loose weave to impart imminent pleasure. This drinks like a Meursault AC. Diam. 13.5% alc. **Rating** 94 **To** 2023 $45 NG

Un Segreto Sangiovese Shiraz 2015 This is delicious! Medium-bodied yet dense. Delicate and fine-boned yet brimming with flavour. Dichotomies such as these make for intriguing drinking while conferring authority and complexity. Violet, cherry, cola, satsuma plum and just the right amount of cinnamon oak pirouette about the mouth. The generosity of shiraz and the flirt of sangiovese do a nice dance along a beam of frisky tannin and transparent acidity. Diam. 13.5% alc. **Rating** 94 **To** 2024 $75 NG

Barbarossa Nebbiolo 2015 A light ruby to garnet, belying the intensity of flavour and the myriad of textures and nuances that await in the glass. Blood and satsuma plum. Orange rind. Wood smoke, rosewater and a dank, carnal underbelly of bushland and mulch combine along a spindle of dry, structural focus: deftly poised, edgy tannins and bright, palate-whetting acidity. Tasted even better the next day, expanding impressively across the palate with an endearing sweetness. Diam. 14% alc. **Rating** 94 **To** 2024 $100 NG

ɥɥɥɥ̧ **Allegro 2017** Rating 93 To 2021 $32 NG
La Chiave Sangiovese 2015 Rating 93 To 2024 $75 NG
Pet-Nat Allegro 2017 Rating 93 $45 NG
Growers Selection King Valley Savagnin 2016 Rating 91 To 2021 $40 NG

Castelli Estate   ★★★★★

380 Mount Shadforth Road, Denmark, WA 6333 **Region** Great Southern
T (08) 9364 0400 **www**.castelliestate.com.au **Open** 7 days 10–5
Winemaker Mike Garland **Est.** 2007 **Dozens** 10 000

Castelli Estate will cause many small winery owners to go green with envy. When Sam Castelli purchased the property in late 2004, he was intending simply to use it as a family holiday destination. But because there was a partly constructed winery he decided to complete the building work and simply lock the doors. However, wine was in his blood courtesy of his father, who owned a small vineyard in Italy's south. The temptation was too much, and in '07 the winery was commissioned. Fruit is sourced from some of the best sites in WA: Frankland River, Mount Barker, Pemberton and Porongurup. Exports to Singapore and China.

ɥɥɥɥɥ **Great Southern Riesling 2017** Night-harvested; some cold maceration pre-pressing, only the free-run juice cool-fermented with cultured yeast. A quite beautiful example of Great Southern riesling, radiating purity and harmony between its fruit and acidity, both running long and clear. It will live for decades. Screwcap. 12% alc. **Rating** 97 **To** 2037 $27 ✪

ɥɥɥɥɥ **Frankland River Cabernet Sauvignon 2016** 10 days' cold soak before warm fermentation; 26 days on skins; matured in French barriques (50% new). This takes you on a serious trip with a wine that over-delivers on its price, with cassis, redcurrant, fresh and dried herbs and spices, and tannins that are remarkably juicy. French oak has proved its affinity with cabernet time and again, but puts an exclamation mark here. Screwcap. 14.1% alc. **Rating** 96 **To** 2036 $38 ✪

The Sum Riesling 2017 This high quality riesling has a floral/blossom bouquet, and a collage of lime and lemon fruit on the palate. The X-factor derives from its tactile qualities that come through clearly on the back-palate and lingering aftertaste, the intensity of the flavours running all the way through to the finish. Screwcap. 12.1% alc. **Rating** 95 **To** 2030 $19 ✪

The Sum Sauvignon Blanc 2017 While this is fresh and vibrant, it has nothing in common with Marlborough sauvignon blanc other than its varietal makeup. It has intricate structure and texture flowing purely from the fruit, minerally acidity providing its backbone. Tropical nuances endeavour to keep grassy notes out of the picture, but fail to do so. I'm not advocating sauvignon blanc's place in the cellar, but this will stroll along for another 3+ years. Screwcap. 12.5% alc. **Rating** 95 **To** 2020 $19 ✪

Great Southern Shiraz 2016 Has a restrained feel to it at this stage, but it's a wine with more to give. Brooding red and black fruit on the bouquet, with cool-climate shiraz 'pepper and spice' and a whiff of oak. Quite a soft, supple palate, with an impression of depth more than obvious weight, underpinned by very fine but gently persistent tannin. Screwcap. 14.5% alc. **Rating** 95 **To** 2030 $34 SC ✪

Empirica Pemberton Fume Blanc 2017 Free-run juice sent directly from press to French oak (new and 1yo), on full solids and fermented naturally to dryness. Captures the smoky fume style to a tee. Savoury, flinty aromas with well matched herbal and grassy characters on the bouquet flow through to the palate, where another dimension of juicy nectarine and melon makes an appearance. Screwcap. 12% alc. **Rating** 94 **To** 2020 $28 SC ✪

Empirica Great Southern Pinot Gris 2017 Aromas and flavours principally in nashi pear/red apple territory, but enhanced by the less fruit-driven characters coming through on the bouquet and palate, and the almost glycerous texture that runs long through the finish. Shows freshness as well – a big plus. Screwcap. 13.3% alc. **Rating** 94 **To** 2022 $28 SC ✪

The Sum Shiraz 2016 The complex yet fresh bouquet draws you into the wine, where dark cherry fruit is riddled with cool-climate spice and black and white pepper. While no more than medium-bodied, it has vibrancy and freshness, and is very hard to resist at this price. Screwcap. 13.7% alc. **Rating** 94 **To** 2031 $19 ✪

Great Southern Shiraz Malbec 2016 There's a lot of enjoyment to be had from a single bottle of this, and I'd be inclined to have several spares. The fusion and synergy between the two varieties is faultless, with plush plum and blackberry fruits anchored by fine tannins. Screwcap. 14.2% alc. **Rating** 94 **To** 2030 $22 ✪

Cabernet Merlot 2016 The aromas throw up the herbs and stones of Provençale, the cassis/blackcurrant fruits from far further north of France. The medium to full-bodied palate has very good texture/mouthfeel and abundant red and black fruits. Seriously over-delivers on its price. Screwcap. 13.7% alc. **Rating** 94 **To** 2029 $22 ✪

♟♟♟♟♟ **Empirica Gewurztraminer 2017** Rating 93 To 2022 $28 SC
Sauvignon Blanc Semillon 2016 Rating 93 To 2022 $22 ✪
The Sum Pinot Noir 2017 Rating 92 To 2029 $22 ✪
Empirica Great Southern Syrah 2016 Rating 92 To 2024 $34 SC
Great Southern Shiraz Malbec 2015 Rating 92 To 2025 $22 ✪
The Sum Cabernet Sauvignon 2016 Rating 92 To 2031 $19 ✪
Denmark Pinot Noir 2015 Rating 90 To 2022 $34
Empirica Geographe Tempranillo 2016 Rating 90 To 2024 $34 SC

Castle Rock Estate   ★★★★★

2660 Porongurup Road, Porongurup, WA 6324 **Region** Porongurup
T (08) 9853 1035 **www**.castlerockestate.com.au **Open** 7 days 10–5
Winemaker Robert Diletti **Est.** 1983 **Dozens** 4500 **Vyds** 11.2ha
A vineyard, winery and cellar door on an exceptionally beautiful 55ha property with sweeping vistas of the Porongurup Range, operated by the Diletti family. The standard of viticulture is very high and the vineyard itself is ideally situated, growing riesling, pinot noir, chardonnay, sauvignon blanc, cabernet sauvignon and merlot. The two-level winery, set on a natural slope, maximises gravity flow. The rieslings have always been elegant and have handsomely repaid

time in bottle; the Pinot Noir is the most consistent performer in the region; the Shiraz is a great cool-climate example; and chardonnay has joined a thoroughly impressive quartet, elegance the common link. Rob Diletti's excellent palate and sensitive winemaking mark Castle Rock as one of the superstars of WA. Exports to China.

♥♥♥♥♥ Porongurup Riesling 2017 Glinting quartz-green; an intriguing mix of flowers/blossom, talc and spice on the bouquet is followed by a finely wrought palate of the highest quality, with citrus fruit and tingling acidity singing to each other in unison. Balance is the key now and in the future. Screwcap. 11.8% alc. **Rating** 97 To 2032 $25 ✪

♥♥♥♥♥ Diletti Chardonnay 2016 A super-elegant style that Rob Diletti is so well known for. Its white peach/grapefruit flavours are supported by subtle oak and clear-cut acidity. It will develop slowly and surely, growing in stature as it does so. Screwcap. 12.5% alc. **Rating** 95 To 2029 $30 ✪
Great Southern Pinot Noir 2016 Castle Rock is consistently producing the best pinot noirs from WA. Estate-grown in Porongurup, the colour is perfect, the bouquet and palate are with the precision of a Swiss watch. The fruit base is predominantly cherry (red, black and sour) with a patina of fine, persistent tannins underwriting its long future. Screwcap. 13.5% alc. **Rating** 95 To 2031 $38
Great Southern Chardonnay 2017 Fermented in 2yo and 3yo barrels, seen as a way to add texture, but not oak flavour. The approach has worked brilliantly, leaving the signature white peach and grapefruit flavours in high relief. Rob Diletti is one of the very best of the group of young(ish) Australian winemakers. Screwcap. 12% alc. **Rating** 94 To 2027 $20 ✪

♥♥♥♥♡ Porongurup Sauvignon Blanc 2017 Rating 93 To 2020 $20 ✪

Catlin Wines ★★★★★
39B Sydney Road, Nairne, SA 5252 **Region** Adelaide Hills
T 0411 326 384 **www.**catlinwines.com.au **Open** Not
Winemaker Darryl Catlin **Est.** 2013 **Dozens** 2000
Darryl Catlin grew up in the Barossa Valley with vineyards as his playground, picking bushvine grenache for pocket money as a child. Various stints with Saltram, the Australian Bottling Company and Vintner Imports followed in his 20s, before he moved on to gain retail experience at Adelaide's Royal Oak Cellar, London's Oddbins and McKay's Macquarie Cellars. The next stage was studying for a winemaking degree while working at Adelaide's East End Cellars. Then followed a number of years at Shaw + Smith, rising from cellar hand to winemaker, finishing up in 2012 and establishing his own business the following year. Exports to the UK.

♥♥♥♥♥ Cheese & Kisses Single Vineyard Adelaide Hills Fume Blanc 2017 Hand-picked, wild-fermented on skins for 3 weeks, then pressed to French oak and matured on lees for 7 months. The vinification details would warm the cockles of lovers of natural wine until they see its pale quartz-green colour and its absence of feral characters on either the bouquet or palate. Yet it has the extra layer of texture and flavour invested by its unorthodox fermentation without diminishing the fruit. Screwcap. 12% alc. **Rating** 95 To 2021 $27 ✪
Adelaide Hills Syrah 2015 From particular rows in the highly regarded Longview vineyard. Whole berries and 40% whole bunches were given a prolonged cold soak before a slow, even fermentation and 1 month on skins, matured in French oak (30% new). The result is a juicy, complex mix of dark fruits and exceptional fine-grained tannins. Screwcap. 14% alc. **Rating** 95 To 2035 $45
The Molly Mae Clare Valley Riesling 2017 From the dry-grown Bimbadeen vineyard; crushed, wild-fermented, 5 months on lees. Flooded with delicious lime and Meyer lemon fruit that rushes along the palate and well into the persistent aftertaste. Natural acidity provides balance and complexity. Terrific wine at the price. Screwcap. 11.5% alc. **Rating** 94 To 2030 $17 ✪

ɪɪɪɪɪ   Adelaide Hills Gruner Veltliner 2016 Rating 93 To 2019 $30 CM
        GB's Single Vineyard Adelaide Hills Rose 2017 Rating 93 To 2021 $20 ❸
        Adelaide Hills Pinot Noir 2016 Rating 92 To 2023 $30 CM
        Maple Ridge Adelaide Hills Pinot Noir 2016 Rating 92 To 2024 $45 CM
        Red Adelaide Hills Shiraz 2015 Rating 92 To 2024 $30 CM
        Adelaide Hills Montepulciano 2015 Rating 92 To 2022 $30 CM
        Lorna Starr Pinot Blanc 2017 Rating 90 To 2021 $27
        Ernest Guy Gruner Veltliner 2017 Rating 90 To 2023 $30

Caudo Vineyard   ★★★☆

River Boat Road, Cadell, SA 5321 **Region** Riverland
T 0427 351 911 **www**.caudovineyard.com.au **Open** 7 days 10–9
Winemaker Contract **Est.** 2011 **Dozens** NFP **Vyds** 120ha
Joe, Christine and Zac Caudo have been supplying grapes to wineries for over 20 years.
The first step towards vertical integration came with a partnership with Cellarmasters, who
created their Caudo brand from grapes coming from their estate vineyard. The Caudos have
now taken the next step, developing their own brands of Desert Edge, Mediterranean Fiesta,
Murraylands, Hogwash Bench and Bubbly Summers. With well made wines at $10, $12 and
$15, those who don't wish to pay more than they have to for easy drinking wines should stop
and take at look.

ɪɪɪɪɪ   **Murraylands Shiraz 2015** Grown on 25yo vines and matured in both French
        and American oak, 20% new. The fruit has a candied aspect but both the colour
        and depth are good, as is the working relationship between the fruit and the oak.
        This is a goodun'. Warm and sweet but well fruited and well made. Screwcap.
        14.5% alc. **Rating** 92 **To** 2024 $30 CM

ɪɪɪɪ   **Cadell Valley Semillon Chardonnay 2015** Rating 89 To 2018 $18 CM ❸
        Murraylands Cabernet Shiraz 2016 Rating 89 To 2021 $20 CM
        Murraylands Sangiovese 2013 Rating 89 To 2020 $30 CM

Centennial Vineyards   ★★★★★

'Woodside', 252 Centennial Road, Bowral, NSW 2576 **Region** Southern Highlands
T (02) 4861 8722 **www**.centennial.net.au **Open** 7 days 10–5
Winemaker Tony Cosgriff **Est.** 2002 **Dozens** 10 000 **Vyds** 28.65ha
Centennial Vineyards, a substantial development jointly owned by wine professional John
Large and investor Mark Dowling, covers 133ha of beautiful grazing land, with the vineyard
planted to pinot noir (6.21ha), chardonnay (7.14ha), sauvignon blanc (4.05ha), tempranillo
(3.38ha), pinot gris (2.61ha) and smaller amounts of savagnin, riesling, arneis, gewurztraminer
and pinot meunier. Production from the estate is supplemented by purchases of grapes from
Orange to meet the challenge of the Southern Highlands' capricious weather. Exports to the
US, Denmark, Singapore, China and South Korea.

ɪɪɪɪɪ   **Reserve Single Vineyard Riesling 115 2017** '115' denotes 11% alcohol and
        5g/l residual sugar. The grapes were grown in Orange and vinified at home base.
        The balance is perfect, so the acidity can be taken for granted. The flavours of lime
        and pink grapefruit are delicate but pure, the wine reaching its optimum from '25
        and onwards. Screwcap. 11.4% alc. **Rating** 95 **To** 2027 $26 ❸
        Reserve Single Vineyard Chardonnay 2016 One of the relatively few
        vintages in which the quality of the estate vineyards in Bowral allowed Tony
        Cosgriff to demonstrate his skills. It has a core of pink grapefruit, with white
        peach and Granny Smith apple in support, the long palate sustained by crisp
        acidity and integrated French oak. Screwcap. 12.5% alc. **Rating** 95 **To** 2024 $35 ❸
        Limited Release Single Vineyard Shiraz 2015 A very smart label facelift
        for the Limited Release range, with this first example from Hilltops. Complex
        vinification has resulted in a polished, supple and elegant medium–bodied shiraz. It
        has blackberry, plum and dark cherry fruit resting in the arms of high quality oak.
        Very restricted release (125 dozen). Screwcap. 14.7% alc. **Rating** 95 **To** 2035 $45

Reserve Single Vineyard Shiraz 2016 A medium-bodied cool-grown wine with the balance Tony Cosgriff commonly achieves. Here black fruits have supple tannins and well handled oak to provide a medium to full-bodied shiraz with a long, harmonious finish. Diam. 14.6% alc. **Rating** 94 **To** 2031 $32

Winery Block Tempranillo 2016 Very well made and poised. A medium-bodied wine with crystal clear varietal definition courtesy of a soft belt of red berry/cherry fruits. Screwcap. 13% alc. **Rating** 94 **To** 2026 $26 ✪

Brut Rose NV A new disgorgement since last tasted in Jul '17. 4% pinot noir, 9.5g/l dosage, 31 months on lees. A very nicely balanced and flavoured rose tasting of wild strawberry with a touch of citrus, the finish long and clean. Diam. 12.5% alc. **Rating** 94 **To** 2021 $35

ᵀᵀᵀᵀ♀ **House Block Pinot Noir 2016** Rating 93 To 2026 $28
Reserve Single Vineyard Shiraz Viognier 2016 Rating 93 To 2031 $35
Winery Block Pinot Grigio 2017 Rating 92 To 2019 $24 ✪
Winery Block Chardonnay 2016 Rating 91 To 2024 $28
Bong Bong Pinot Noir 2016 Rating 91 To 2022 $20 ✪
Single Vineyard Shiraz 2016 Rating 91 To 2029 $25
Pinot Rose 2017 Rating 90 To 2020 $24
Reserve Bridge Creek Rose 2017 Rating 90 To 2019 $27
Brut Traditionelle NV Rating 90 $35
Limited Blanc de Blancs NV Rating 90 $40

Chaffey Bros Wine Co   ★★★★

26 Campbell Road, Parkside, SA 5063 (postal) **Region** Barossa Valley
T 0417 565 511 **www**.chaffeybros.com **Open** Not
Winemaker Daniel Chaffey Hartwig, Theo Engela **Est.** 2008 **Dozens** 7000
Chaffey Bros was co-founded by Daniel Chaffey Hartwig, whose great-uncle Bill Chaffey founded Seaview Wines in McLaren Vale, and who was himself a descendant of the Chaffey brothers who came to Australia to create the Riverina and Riverland agricultural regions by designing and implementing the original irrigation schemes. Daniel, born and raised in the Barossa Valley, picked grapes during school holidays, and later worked at Penfolds' cellar door. After eight years of selling and helping other people create wine labels, he became a bulk wine merchant dealing in both Australian and overseas wines and wineries, and also developing a range of branded wines. Exports to Canada, Denmark, the Netherlands, Singapore, Macau, Hong Kong and China.

ᵀᵀᵀᵀ♀ **Zeitpunkt Eden Valley Riesling 2017** Shows the unusually aromatic perfumed florals and spice the cool vintage bestowed on Eden Valley riesling, in company with the more familiar slate and citrus notes. Beautifully balanced and poised, with delicate fruit sweetness underpinned by minerally and very natural feeling acidity. Hard to resist drinking this now. Screwcap. 11.5% alc. **Rating** 93 **To** 2025 $28 SC

Tripelpunkt Eden Valley Riesling 2017 The bouquet is of lemon sherbet – like opening a packet of Wizz Fizz, a childhood memory – then a swirl of honeysuckle, white flowers and sweet citrus. Flavours of ripe red apple and nectarine, a thread of sweetness just perceptible but skilfully woven into the fabric of the wine. Screwcap. 12% alc. **Rating** 93 **To** 2022 $25 SC ✪

Evangeline Eden Valley Syrah 2016 This might be Eden Valley, but using syrah on the label raises an eyebrow. What's not in question is its drinkability. A fruit basket of berries, a raft of spices; it's juicy and so vibrant. It has tannins and acidity to ensure it'll age but gee, it's too good to wait for, so pour away. Screwcap. 14% alc. **Rating** 93 **To** 2026 $33 JF

Evangeline Eden Valley Syrah 2015 The flavour profile is sweeter than the word 'syrah' might imply, but the wine's quality is never in doubt. Flavours of port-wine jelly, pure plum, sweet raspberry and assorted dry/twiggy spices fill out the palate well; nutty tannin then completes the picture perfectly. Throughout the wine feels fluid and supple, making it a pleasure to spend time with. Screwcap. 14.5% alc. **Rating** 93 **To** 2027 $35 CM

This Is Not Your Grandma's Barossa Valley Rose 2017 In perfect drinking shape. Dry, racy with acidity and flavoursome at once. Raspberry and rosehip with cuts of apple and anise. Gets you in a mind for food. Screwcap. 11.5% alc. **Rating** 92 **To** 2018 $22 CM ✪

Synonymous Barossa = Shiraz 2016 A picture-perfect example of this variety from this region. Rich, ripe aromas of blackberry and blood plum are accented by that familiar tarry earthiness with a sweet seasoning of dark chocolate and vanilla, the latter perhaps an oaky contribution. Enjoyable now in the full flush of youth. Screwcap. **Rating** 92 **To** 2022 $28 SC

This Is Not Your Grandma's Eden Valley Riesling 2017 From 18–40yo vines at the Noack vineyard at Springton. Crisp and fresh, as behoves the vintage. Light, floral and delicate lime. Certain to develop very well. Screwcap. 11.5% alc. **Rating** 91 **To** 2024 $20 ✪

Dufte Punkt 2017 Equal contributions from riesling, gewurztraminer and weißer herold (aka kerner). The bouquet is full of exotic, scented bath powder, lychee and rose petals, the palate nodding in support, and adding acidity. Well worth a nerdy look. Screwcap. 12.5% alc. **Rating** 91 **To** 2025 $25

The Super Barossa is Shiraz + Cabernet 2015 Raw with fruit and oak but generous of both. Coffee cream, blackberry and sweet plum flavours jumble their way through the palate. It doesn't feel seamless but there's plenty here to latch onto. Screwcap. 14% alc. **Rating** 91 **To** 2026 $38 CM

Bluhen Punkt Eden Valley Gewurztraminer 2017 Has above average varietal expression on the bouquet and palate, with exotic spice, berry, rosewater and confection notes. Total of 238 dozen made. Screwcap. 12.5% alc. **Rating** 90 **To** 2022 $28

Pax Aeterna Old Vine Grenache 2017 From 83yo vines from the Kevin Schild Vineyard at Light Pass, fermented with 33% whole bunches. Light and bright to the point of rose; strawberry/raspberry/red cherry flavours and the barest hint of tannins. Screwcap. 13.5% alc. **Rating** 90 **To** 2020 $30

Battle for Barossa La Resistance! Grenache + Shiraz + Mourvedre 2016 Spicy and fruit-driven, with the aromatic qualities of grenache leading the way. Raspberry, strawberry jam and sweet cherry are prominent in the flavour profile within the smoothly textured palate, which glides easily along from start to finish, the lightest touch of tannin keeping it in shape. Screwcap. 14.5% alc. **Rating** 90 **To** 2021 $25 SC

Battle for Barrosa La Conquista! Tempranillo + Garnacha + Graciano 2016 A lifted, perfumed bouquet, with each variety contributing of course – but the whole seems more than the sum of its parts. It's silky and slippery on the palate with flavours of cherry cola and raspberry, and a sweet-fruited finish. Screwcap. 14% alc. **Rating** 90 **To** 2020 $25 SC

🍷🍷🍷🍷 **Funkelpunkt Sparkling 2017** **Rating** 89 $28 SC

Chain of Ponds ★★★★★

c/- 83 Pioneer Road, Angas Plains, SA 5255 (postal) **Region** Adelaide Hills
T (08) 8537 0600 **www**.chainofponds.com.au **Open** Not
Winemaker Greg Clack **Est.** 1993 **Dozens** 20 000

It is years since the Chain of Ponds brand was separated from its then 200ha of estate vineyards, which were among the largest in the Adelaide Hills. It does, however, have long-term contracts with major growers. Prior to the 2015 vintage, Greg Clack came onboard as full-time chief winemaker. In May '16 Chain of Ponds closed its cellar door and moved to Project Wine's small batch processing facility at Langhorne Creek, completing its withdrawal from the Adelaide Hills other than the grape purchasing contracts. Exports to the UK, the US, Canada, Singapore, Hong Kong, the Philippines and China.

🍷🍷🍷🍷🍷 **The Cachet 2013** Deep, healthy colour, still with crimson on the rim. The particularly complex vinification was conceived and implemented without a hitch. 47% cabernet sauvignon, 43% shiraz and 10% merlot from three different vineyards with different canopy management, site aspects and soils; the varieties handled separately and fermented with different procedures. Oak choice and use varied significantly – the sumptuous, black-fruited blend finalised after 20+ months' maturation in barrel, then matured for a further 30 months in bottle prior to release. A very special wine. Cork. 14.5% alc. **Rating** 98 **To** 2033 $100 ❂

🍷🍷🍷🍷🍷 **Black Thursday Adelaide Hills Sauvignon Blanc 2017** A particularly good release from this favourable vintage. Snow pea and mown grass are the first impression, with citrus, green melon and crunchy apple providing the fruit-driven aspect. A touch of smoky/gunflint character adds complexity. Juicy flavours, texture and length are all big ticks on the palate. 8% semillon. Screwcap. 12% alc. **Rating** 95 **To** 2019 $20 SC ❂

Corkscrew Road Single Vineyard Adelaide Hills Chardonnay 2017 Made with the usual skill of Greg Clack, here with the added bonus of quality grapes with a mix of Granny Smith apple, white peach, pear and grapefruit flavours. This will be a long-lived wine. Screwcap. 13% alc. **Rating** 95 **To** 2030 $35 ❂

Graves Gate Adelaide Hills Syrah 2016 Bright hue; an elegant, medium-bodied syrah, its X-factor coming from its east-facing slope that maximises the morning sun and minimises the afternoon sun. It's got a spice and cracked pepper garnish for the red and black fruits, the tannins fine but persistent. A total contrast to its Acquaintance sibling. Screwcap. 14.5% alc. **Rating** 95 **To** 2026 $20 ❂

Ledge Single Vineyard Adelaide Hills Shiraz 2016 Retains its cool-grown ancestry, the magic lying in the rich flavours of red and black cherry/berry fruits peppered by spice, simultaneously filling the mouth with ripe tannins yet retaining line, length and a quicksilver balance. Screwcap. 14.5% alc. **Rating** 95 **To** 2036 $38

Amadeus Single Vineyard Adelaide Hills Cabernet Sauvignon 2016 The completion of fermentation in barrel is a technique I also used in 1973, and continued for as long as I was an executive winemaker. In this wine it has integrated the fruit and oak as expected, and also heightened the varietal cassis component. Screwcap. 14.5% alc. **Rating** 95 **To** 2036 $38

Novello Adelaide Cabernet Merlot 2016 I can't fathom why this has such a low price. It's rich and supple, with layer upon layer of luscious cassis/Ribena fruit offset by a precisely judged framework of savoury herbal fruit and ripe tannins. Will go the distance many times over. 476 dozen made. Screwcap. 14% alc. **Rating** 94 **To** 2031 $16 ❂

🍷🍷🍷🍷🍷 **Section 400 Adelaide Hills Pinot Noir 2017** **Rating** 93 **To** 2025 $20 ❂
Millers Creek Adelaide Hills Chardonnay 2017 **Rating** 92 **To** 2022 $20 ❂
Novello Adelaide Rose 2017 **Rating** 92 **To** 2020 $16 ❂
Acquaintance McLaren Vale Shiraz 2016 **Rating** 92 **To** 2031 $20 ❂
Novello Adelaide Semillon Sauvignon Blanc 2017 **Rating** 90 **To** 2020 $16 ❂
Amelia's Letter Adelaide Hills Pinot Grigio 2017 **Rating** 90 **To** 2019 $20 ❂

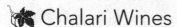
Chalari Wines   ★★★★
14 Slab Gully Road, Roleystone, WA 6111 **Region** Various WA
T 0404 485 137 **www.chalariwines.com.au Open** Not
Winemaker Alexi Christidis **Est.** 2016 **Dozens** NFP
Winemaker and proprietor Alexi Christidis explains that the name 'Chalari' reflects his Greek heritage and his father, who was always one for a cup of coffee or a drink and watching the world go by – the word means 'relaxed'. While studying oenology at CSU Alexi decided to make small batches of wine, exemplified by his purchase of 2t of hand-picked riesling from Frankland River, making it in a 5t 'winery' in the Perth Hills using a low-intervention natural approach.

🍷🍷🍷🍷🍷 **Frankland River Riesling 2017** Immediately on entering the mouth there is the tactile quality I call squeaky or slippery – it's appealing, and I'd like to know what causes it. The wine has good varietal expression, with a mix of lime and Meyer lemon. While its cellaring capacity is not in doubt, there's plenty to enjoy tonight. Screwcap. 12.7% alc. **Rating** 94 **To** 2027 $29 ❂

Chalk Hill

★★★★★

58 Field Street, McLaren Vale, SA 5171 **Region** McLaren Vale
T (08) 8323 6400 **www.**chalkhill.com.au **Open** Not
Winemaker Renae Hirsch **Est.** 1973 **Dozens** 20 000 **Vyds** 89ha
The growth of Chalk Hill has accelerated after passing from parents John and Diana Harvey to grapegrowing sons Jock and Tom. Both are heavily involved in wine industry affairs in varying capacities. Further acquisitions mean the vineyards now span each district of McLaren Vale, planted to both the exotic (savagnin, barbera and sangiovese) and mainstream (shiraz, cabernet sauvignon, grenache, chardonnay and cabernet franc). The Alpha Crucis series is especially praiseworthy. Exports to most markets; to the US under the Alpha Crucis label and to Canada under the Wits End label.

🍷🍷🍷🍷🍷 **Alpha Crucis Winemakers' Series Kerri Thompson McLaren Vale Shiraz 2016** There's a whole lot to love here. The grunt of tannin, the groan of fruit, the bursts of bitumen and licorice, the liquid toast, the way herb and spice notes are at one with the 'everything' of the wine. Everywhere you look here you see authority, power and control. Screwcap. 14.5% alc. **Rating** 96 **To** 2042 $60 CM ○
Alpha Crucis Winemakers' Series Peter Schell McLaren Vale Shiraz 2016 The spiciest release in the series, and the most savoury. Deli meat, dry spice, snapped twig and pepper notes are splashed through pure, dark, gloriously berried fruit. For balance, interest and layers of flavours, this is a champion of a wine. Screwcap. 14.5% alc. **Rating** 96 **To** 2038 $60 CM ○
Alpha Crucis McLaren Vale Shiraz 2016 In the end it's the balance that does it. Saturated plum, saltbush, boysenberry and tar flavours come smeared with coffee grounds and milk chocolate, a wave of tannin rumbling through the back half of the wine. It has grunt, it has scaffolding, it has texture, but it takes it to the next level by keeping everything in appropriate measure. Screwcap. 14.5% alc. **Rating** 96 **To** 2040 $85 CM
Alpha Crucis Winemakers' Series Tim Knappstein McLaren Vale Shiraz 2016 This brings it all together. Fruit, oak, tannin and overall balance; it's all humming along. Asphalt, blackberry, toasted cedar wood and saltbush-like highlights. It's a big, meaty wine with muscles and curves in all the right places. Screwcap. 14.5% alc. **Rating** 95 **To** 2040 $60 CM
Clarendon McLaren Vale Syrah 2016 Almost impossible not to admire this. It has grunt and weight, but nuance and savour-spice are also well and truly in the frame. The syrah tag is apt. Redcurrant and blackberry flavours are equally well represented, the nuance coming via wood smoke, earth, clove and nougat. It will mature handsomely. Screwcap. 14% alc. **Rating** 95 **To** 2035 $40 CM
Luna McLaren Vale Shiraz 2016 Includes a dash of barbera. Starts ticking the boxes with its bright colour, and continues to do so through the fragrant, gently spicy, dark-berry bouquet, thence the medium-bodied palate. It derives its quality through its freshness, the purity of fruit flavours, and the supple mouthfeel. Screwcap. 14% alc. **Rating** 94 **To** 2023 $19 ○
Alpha Crucis Winemakers' Series Corrina Wright McLaren Vale Shiraz 2016 Sweet, custardy oak sits slightly separate from the (berried, tar-like) fruit, but even so, the richness, structure and length of this wine remain undeniable. It will wield its power for decades to come. Screwcap. 15% alc. **Rating** 94 **To** 2040 $60 CM
Alpha Crucis Winemakers' Series Renae Hirsch McLaren Vale Shiraz 2016 Arguably the prettiest wine in the series, its inherent richness lightened by notes of violet, vanilla and blossomy herbs. It's easy to be seduced. Flavours of red and black licorice continue the theme, plum and blackberry notes never far away. Absolutely convincing from start to finish. Screwcap. 14.5% alc. **Rating** 94 **To** 2040 $60 CM

🍷🍷🍷🍷🍷 **Alpha Crucis Winemakers' Series Bec Willson McLaren Vale Shiraz 2016** **Rating** 93 **To** 2031 $60 CM
McLaren Vale Shiraz 2016 Rating 93 **To** 2028 $25 CM ○

Alpha Crucis Titan McLaren Vale Cabernet Sauvignon 2016 Rating 93
To 2028 $30 CM
McLaren Vale Barbera 2016 Rating 92 To 2021 $28
McLaren Vale Fiano 2017 Rating 90 To 2020 $25 CM

Chalmers ★★★★☆

118 Third Street, Merbein, Vic 3505 **Region** Heathcote
T 0400 261 932 **www**.chalmers.com.au **Open** Not
Winemaker Bart van Olphen, Tennille Chalmers, Kim Chalmers **Est.** 1989
Dozens 7000 **Vyds** 27ha
Following the 2008 sale of their very large vineyard and vine nursery propagation business,
the Chalmers family has refocused its wine businesses. All fruit for their individual variety,
single vineyard range comes from the 80ha property on Mt Camel Range in Heathcote
(vermentino, fiano, greco, lambrusco, rosato, nero d'Avola, sagrantino and aglianico). The
entry-level Montevecchio label is based around blends and more approachable styles. A second
vineyard at Merbein is a contract grapegrower, but also has a small nursery block housing the
Chalmers' clonal selections. In '13 a program of micro-vinification of the rarer, and hitherto
unutilised, varieties from the block was introduced. In '17 a new winery at Merbein was
commissioned in time for most of that year's vintage, and from '18 all winemaking was carried
out there. Exports to the UK and Japan.

🍷🍷🍷🍷🍷 **Montevecchio Heathcote Rosato 2017** A co-fermented blend of
77% lambrusco maestri and 23% lagrein. Light vivid puce, exceptional given the
whole-bunch pressing. Intriguing yet intense flavours bring red fruits onto the
same field as a savoury bitterness that has perfect balance, giving the wine the
ability to marry with Chinese duck, pork and vegetable (especially mushroom)
dishes. Screwcap. 11.5% alc. **Rating** 94 To 2021 $24 ○
Arturo Heathcote Malbec 2016 Malbec is on the march in Australia, albeit
with a relatively slow drum beat at this stage. Arturo is the name given to a blend
of six clones imported by Chalmers from Argentina, creating added interest.
Texture provides good mouthfeel and length, the flavours of black fruits and spice
likewise good. No alcohol heat either. Screwcap. 14.5% alc. **Rating** 94 To 2031
$26 ○

🍷🍷🍷🍷🍷 **Heathcote Rosato 2017** Rating 93 To 2020 $27 ○
Dott. Pavana 2017 Rating 92 To 2020 $31
Arturo Heathcote Malbec 2013 Rating 91 To 2022 $26
Heathcote Nero d'Avola 2017 Rating 91 To 2022 $27
Heathcote Vermentino 2017 Rating 90 To 2025 $27
Montevecchio Heathcote Moscato 2017 Rating 90 To 2019 $24 SC

Chambers Rosewood ★★★★★

Barkly Street, Rutherglen, Vic 3685 **Region** Rutherglen
T (02) 6032 8641 **www**.chambersrosewood.com.au **Open** Mon–Sat 9–5, Sun 10–5
Winemaker Stephen Chambers **Est.** 1858 **Dozens** 5000 **Vyds** 50ha
Chambers' rare muscat and rare muscadelle (or topaque or tokay, what's in a name?) are the
greatest of all in the Rutherglen firmament, and the other wines in the hierarchy are also
magnificent. Stephen Chambers comes into the role as winemaker, the sixth generation of the
Chambers family, but father Bill, with his startling light blue eyes, is seldom far away. Exports
to the UK, the US, Canada, Belgium, Denmark, China and NZ.

🍷🍷🍷🍷🍷 **Rare Rutherglen Muscadelle NV** The dark mahogany and olive rim to the
hue turns out to be a sure sign of a wine that is as magnificently complex as it
ever was. It's absolutely certain the wine is being sold in tiny quantities to protect
the quality of the solera. Its viscosity as it slowly pours from the neck of the bottle
is yet another sign. The explosive impact of the first taste is otherworldly as dark
spices, tea, butterscotch and vibrant, mouthwatering acidity carries all the aromas

and flavours that have gone before to a long, lingering finish and aftertaste. 375ml.
Screwcap. 18% alc. **Rating** 99 $250 ✪

Old Vine Rutherglen Muscadelle NV A wine that Stephen Chambers has
placed outside the normal Rutherglen classification system – 'old vine' rather than
'old wine'. Yet this is clearly much older than the entry point wine, now with
edges of brown, the flavours distinctly more complex, with a burnt-spice savoury
edge to the toffee, cold tea and Christmas cake flavours. Exceptional value. 375ml.
Screwcap. 18.5% alc. **Rating** 97 $30 ✪

ΨΨΨΨΨ **Old Vine Rutherglen Muscat NV** A wine that immediately commands
attention and respect with its racy touch of rancio to the liqueur raisins of a deluxe
Christmas pudding, backed by spices of every known kind. 375ml. Screwcap.
18.5% alc. **Rating** 96 $25 ✪

Grand Rutherglen Muscat NV A perfect example of muscat, supple and
smooth in one moment, wildly exotic and energetic the next, playing tricks on
the palate – just an excuse to have another sip, of course. The length of the wine is
prodigious, as is its balance, but the orchestra of Christmas pudding, Turkish delight
and high-toned spices plays on. 375ml. Screwcap. 18.5% alc. **Rating** 95 $55

ΨΨΨΨΨ **Rutherglen Muscadelle NV Rating** 93 $20 ✪
Rutherglen Muscat NV Rating 92 $20 ✪

Chandon Australia   ★★★★★

727 Maroondah Highway, Coldstream, Vic 3770 **Region** Yarra Valley
T (03) 9738 9200 **www**.chandon.com.au **Open** 7 days 10.30–4.30
Winemaker Dan Buckle, Glenn Thompson, Adam Keath **Est.** 1986
Dozens NFP **Vyds** 172.2ha
Established by Möet & Chandon, this is one of the two most important wine facilities in
the Yarra Valley; the tasting room has a national and international reputation, having won
a number of major tourism awards in recent years. The sparkling wine range has evolved,
and there has been increasing emphasis placed on the table wines, now also released under
the Chandon label. An energetic winemaking team under the leadership of Dan Buckle has
maintained the high quality standards. Exports to all major markets.

ΨΨΨΨΨ **Vintage Blanc de Blancs 2013** Made in the traditional method with
38 months on lees. This has great drive and impact to the palate, sweeping away
the more indefinite aromas. The extended time on lees and, of course, chardonnay
from very cool regions, results in a mouthwatering array of lemon, quince and
toasted almonds. Diam. 12.5% alc. **Rating** 96 $41 ✪

Cygnet Pinot Meunier Rose 2014 Sourced mainly from Chandon's Whitlands
vineyard at 780m altitude in the King Valley. Batches tank-fermented before
blending (a little red wine added for colour) and bottling for second fermentation,
held on lees for 36 months. Has a compelling mix of youthful exuberance and
grip, yet retains elegance. Red fruits rule the roost. Diam. 12.5% alc. **Rating** 96
$59 ✪

Vintage Brut 2013 A carefully assembled and constructed brut, disgorged in
Nov '16 after 3 years on lees. It's refined and balanced, with grapefruit and brioche
in opposite corners of the ring, the finish long and controlled. Interesting contrast
in flavour to the Rose. Diam. 12.5% alc. **Rating** 95 $41

Winemaker's Selection Chardonnay Pinot Noir 2008 Made in the
traditional method with over 8 years on lees, which few producers offer (Arras is
the other major player); this wine has the most complex base. Straw colour; fig,
brioche, spice, dried fruits and life-sustaining acidity draw out the finish. Diam.
12.5% alc. **Rating** 95 $59

Late Disgorged Blanc de Blancs 2006 Aged on lees for 10 years, disgorged
Mar '17. It has an effortless drinkability but it's powerful. This is sparkling wine
with both the italics and bold applied. It's nutty and honeyed with lemon curd
and dry pear flavours powering through. Ginger perhaps, red apple even, but the

real drive comes from citrus and nectarine characters. This make a clear statement without every eschewing sheer drinkability. Diam. 12.5% alc. **Rating** 95 $115 CM
Vintage Brut Rose 2013 3 years on lees, disgorged Nov '16. Pale pink, with just a hint of salmon; the bouquet is instantly arresting with its spiced red berry fruits, likely from the pinot table wine used to add colour as much as from the pinot in the cepage. The overall level of flavour is also higher and richer. Diam. 12.5% alc. **Rating** 95 $39
Meunier Cuvee 2014 Made in the traditional method with 36 months on lees. The varietal origin is reflected in the palest pink tint to the expected straw colour. The cabernet sauvignon bouquet has spice, subtle red berry fruits, brioche and pastry aromas. The length is admirable, as is the balance. Diam. 12.5% alc. **Rating** 94 $39

ŢŢŢŢŢ **Whitlands Plateau Blanc de Blancs 2013** Rating 93 $37 CM
Late Disgorged 2006 Rating 93 $105 CM
Blanc de Blancs NV Rating 91 CM
Whitlands Plateau Pinot Gris Cuvee 2016 Rating 90 $35

Chapel Hill

1 Chapel Hill Road, McLaren Vale, SA 5171 **Region** McLaren Vale
T (08) 8323 8429 **www**.chapelhillwine.com.au **Open** 7 days 11–5
Winemaker Michael Fragos, Bryn Richards **Est.** 1973 **Dozens** 60 000 **Vyds** 44ha
A leading medium-sized winery in McLaren Vale. Owned since 2000 by the Swiss Thomas Schmidheiny group, which owns the respected Cuvaison winery in California and vineyards in Switzerland and Argentina. Wine quality is unfailingly excellent. The production comes from estate plantings of shiraz, cabernet sauvignon, chardonnay, verdelho, savagnin, sangiovese and merlot, plus contract-grown grapes. The red wines are not filtered or fined, and there are no tannin or enzyme additions, just SO_2 – natural red wines. Exports to all other major markets.

ŢŢŢŢŢ **Bush Vine McLaren Vale Grenache 2016** The bouquet sings of spices that prostrate themselves at the feet of the flow of cherry, raspberry and strawberry fruits with nary a hint of tough tannins, oak conspicuous by its absence. Takes purity onto a seldom-seen level. Screwcap. 14.5% alc. **Rating** 97 To 2031 $30 ✪

ŢŢŢŢŢ **Road Block McLaren Vale Shiraz 2016** Just like the other type of road block, this will stop you in your tracks, such is its command. It's dense, concentrated, full-bodied and rich. Layers of blackberry essence, dark chocolate and sweet vanillan oak, and masses of tannin. Fans of the style, knock yourselves out. Screwcap. 14.5% alc. **Rating** 95 To 2036 $65 JF
Gorge Block McLaren Vale Cabernet Sauvignon 2016 It has all the power and drive of cabernet from the Vale and yet it's balanced out by the core of cassis, blackcurrants and savoury tannins. Attractive aromatics with a hint of florals and juniper, bay leaves, baking spices and cedary oak. No question it will last some distance. Screwcap. 14.5% alc. **Rating** 95 To 2035 $65 JF
McLaren Vale Mourvedre 2016 Shows why mourvedre has always had a place in McLaren Vale. It is generous and bold, flush with dark fruits of all kinds, plus dashes of earth and dark chocolate, but doesn't lose its line or balance (provided, of course, that it's well made, as it is here). The alcohol is under control. Screwcap. 14.5% alc. **Rating** 95 To 2036 $30 ✪
The Parson McLaren Vale Shiraz 2016 Very good colour; speaks loud and clear of its birthplace, although without bombast. Black fruits, dark chocolate, wisps of licorice and well balanced tannins all play a role on the medium to full-bodied palate. A win-win scenario: drink now or much, much later. Screwcap. 14.5% alc. **Rating** 94 To 2036 $18 ✪

ŢŢŢŢŢ **Sangiovese Rose 2017** Rating 93 To 2019 $16 ✪
The Vinedresser Shiraz 2016 Rating 93 To 2026 $25 CM ✪
House Block Shiraz 2016 Rating 93 To 2036 $65 JF
Grenache Shiraz Mourvedre 2016 Rating 93 To 2026 $25 SC ✪

Cabernet Sauvignon 2016 Rating 93 To 2030 $30 JF
The Vicar Shiraz 2016 Rating 92 To 2036 $75 JF
The Parson Cabernet Sauvignon 2016 Rating 92 To 2026 $18 CM ❍
The Parson Shiraz 2016 Rating 91 To 2023 $18 JF ❍
The Parson Cabernet Sauvignon 2016 Rating 91 To 2031 $18 ❍
Home Grown Gorge Block Chardonnay 2017 Rating 90 To 2020 $15 ❍
Home Grown Shiraz Mourvedre 2017 Rating 90 To 2020 $15 ❍
The Parson Grenache Shiraz Mourvedre 2016 Rating 90 To 2021 $16 ❍
The Vinedresser Cabernet Sauvignon 2016 Rating 90 To 2026 $25 JF

Chapman Grove Wines   ★★★★★

37 Mount View Terrace, Mount Pleasant, WA 6153 **Region** Margaret River
T (08) 9364 3885 **www**.chapmangrove.com.au **Open** Not
Winemaker Richard Rowe (Consultant) **Est.** 2005 **Dozens** 5000 **Vyds** 32ha
A very successful venture under the control of CEO Ron Fraser. The wines come from the estate vineyards planted to chardonnay, semillon, sauvignon blanc, shiraz, cabernet sauvignon and merlot. There are three price levels: at the bottom end, the standard Chapman Grove range; then the Reserve range; and, at the top, ultra-premium wines under the Atticus label. Exports to Canada, Hong Kong, Singapore, the Philippines, Thailand, Taiwan and China.

❦❦❦❦❦ **Atticus Grand Reserve Cabernets 2016** Cabernet sauvignon, merlot, cabernet franc and petit verdot. An unambiguously classy wine, its quality established by the first whiff, and confirmed by the super-elegant, medium-bodied palate. All the cabernet cassis/blackcurrant you could wish for floats along the mouth, with the other members of the Bordeaux family in respectful support. Lovely wine. Cork. 13.8% alc. **Rating** 96 **To** 2041 $120
Aged Release Atticus Margaret River Chardonnay 2006 Now gleaming green-gold, it is, as the colour suggests, fully developed and needing to be enjoyed without delay. There are buttery/toasty notes, the balance and flavour saved by bright acidity (and modest alcohol). Points for the wine and its valour in the fight against the march of time. Screwcap. 13.5% alc. **Rating** 95 **To** 2019 $75

❦❦❦❦❦ **Reserve Margaret River Chardonnay 2016 Rating** 92 **To** 2028 $30
The Lone Quince Margaret River Sauvignon Blanc Semillon 2017
Rating 90 **To** 2020 $15 ❍

Charles Cimicky   ★★★☆

Hermann Thumm Drive, Lyndoch, SA 5351 **Region** Barossa Valley
T (08) 8524 4025 **www**.charlescimickywines.com.au **Open** Tues–Fri 10.30–3.30
Winemaker Charles Cimicky **Est.** 1972 **Dozens** 20000 **Vyds** 25ha
These wines are of good quality thanks to the sophisticated use of good oak in tandem with high quality grapes. Historically, Cimicky has had an ultra-low profile, but he has relented sufficiently to send me some wines. Exports to the US, Canada, Switzerland, Germany, Malaysia and Hong Kong.

❦❦❦❦❦ **Barossa Valley Durif 2015** Dense, inky purple right through to the rim; the palate is as dense as the colour suggests, with a blue-and-black-fruit-smoothie texture and flavour, garnished with dark chocolate and sour cherries. Screwcap. **Rating** 94 **To** 2040 $45

Charles Melton   ★★★★★

Krondorf Road, Tanunda, SA 5352 **Region** Barossa Valley
T (08) 8563 3606 **www**.charlesmeltonwines.com.au **Open** 7 days 11–5
Winemaker Charlie Melton, Krys Smith **Est.** 1984 **Dozens** 15000 **Vyds** 32.6ha
Charlie Melton, one of the Barossa Valley's great characters, with wife Virginia by his side, makes some of the most eagerly sought à la mode wines in Australia. There are 7ha of estate vineyards at Lyndoch, 9ha at Krondorf and 1.6ha at Light Pass, the lion's share shiraz and grenache, and a small planting of cabernet sauvignon. An additional 30ha property was

purchased in High Eden, with 10ha of shiraz planted in 2009, and a 5ha field of grenache, shiraz, mataro, carignan, cinsaut, picpoul and bourboulenc planted in '10. The expanded volume has had no adverse effect on the quality of the rich, supple and harmonious wines. Exports to all major markets.

ŸŸŸŸŸ **Rose of Virginia 2017** Brief skin contact followed crushing, the wine then made from free-run juice. Both the bouquet and palate ride on a magic carpet of exotic red berry fruits that take this rose from the bonds of earthly flavours. Charlie Melton is a master in the dark arts of producing roses that are gorgeous with food if you wish, or for simply having a glass on a spring day. Screwcap. 12% alc. **Rating** 95 **To** 2020 $25 ✪

Pretty Little Thing Eden Valley Adelaide Hills Riesling 2016 An interesting regional blend, perfectly sensible, but why so uncommon? Garbed in a floral pink label, it sends the message that this wine isn't for real, just for fun. It's crisp, crunchy, fresh and distinctly minerally. 'Leave me alone' is its inward cry. Screwcap. 11.8% alc. **Rating** 94 **To** 2029 $25 ✪

Charles Sturt University Winery   ★★★★☆

Mambarra Drive, Wagga Wagga, NSW 2650 **Region** Various
T (02) 6933 2435 **www.**winery.csu.edu.au **Open** Not
Winemaker Campbell Meeks **Est.** 1977 **Dozens** 2500 **Vyds** 25.1ha
CSU, as the university is commonly known, has once again changed its winemaking activities, the changes driven by the difficult task of meeting the aims of making wine for commercial production and sale, while also integrating winemaking into its academic charter of providing a fully fledged oenology degree course. The previously existing winery has been decommissioned with the appropriate removal of equipment, and a new boutique facility has been established within the National Wine & Grape Industry Centre on campus. The focus of the winery is on grapes grown in NSW, many of the growers being CSU alumni or with another connection. The labels are the work of noted artist Tony Curran, who has a PhD in Fine Art from CSU.

ŸŸŸŸŸ **Tumbarumba Chardonnay 2016** Hand-picked from a single vineyard, fermented and matured in new and used French oak. Attractive wine; the fruit base delicate but well balanced by the oak on the juicy palate, with a mix of stone fruit and citrus, the acidity precise. Screwcap. 13.5% alc. **Rating** 95 **To** 2024 $25 ✪

ŸŸŸŸŸ **Canberra District Shiraz 2016 Rating** 93 **To** 2029 $27 ✪
Hilltops Nebbiolo 2016 Rating 92 **To** 2026 $27
Orange Chardonnay 2016 Rating 91 **To** 2021 $25
Riverina Tempranillo Rose 2016 Rating 90 **To** 2019 $22

Charlotte Dalton Wines   ★★★★★

PO Box 125, Verdun, SA 5245 **Region** Adelaide Hills
T 0466 541 361 **www.**charlottedaltonwines.com **Open** Not
Winemaker Charlotte Hardy **Est.** 2015 **Dozens** 700
Charlotte Hardy has been making wines for 15 years, with a star-studded career at Craggy Range (NZ), Chateau Giscours (Bordeaux) and David Abreu (California), but has called SA home since 2007. Her winery is part of her house named the 'Basket Range', which has been through many incarnations since starting life as a pig farm in 1858. Much later it housed the Basket Range Store, and at different times in the past two decades it has been the winery to Basket Range Wines, The Deanery Wines and now Charlotte Dalton Wines.

ŸŸŸŸŸ **Love You Love Me Adelaide Hills Semillon 2017** From the Deanery vineyard at Balhannah. Beautifully fresh aromas with lemon, herbs and a hint of snow pea playing a part. It feels quite light-bodied but there's texture from the oak and lees and a subtle penetration of citrus and green apple that finds its way around every corner of the palate. The fine acidity keeps it all taut and delivers a long and racy finish. Screwcap. 11.7% alc. **Rating** 95 **To** 2027 $39 SC

Ærkeengel Adelaide Hills Semillon 2016 Ærkeengel is Danish for 'archangel', honouring Charlotte's late mother who was half Danish. A complex semillon, correctly having no connection with the Hunter Valley, although it does have barrel-fermented siblings from Margaret River and the Adelaide Hills. Regardless, this wine has been very well made, neatly balancing rich textural flavour components against the unalterable acidity of semillon. Screwcap. 12.6% alc. **Rating** 95 **To** 2026 $42

Love Me Love You Adelaide Hills Shiraz 2017 Jumps out of the glass with youthful exuberance before settling into the groove of spicy, delicious cool-climate shiraz. Black cherry, raspberry and red-fleshed plum provide the fruit-driven aspect, with some sappy whole-bunch elements in the mix. Fresh, juicy and buoyant, there's a lingering astringency of fine tannin and acid, which gives it a bracing but well balanced finish. Screwcap. 13.4% alc. **Rating** 95 **To** 2027 $42 SC

ŶŶŶŶŶ **Grace Chardonnay 2017** Rating 93 **To** 2025 $39 SC
Eliza Broderick Vineyard Pinot Noir 2017 Rating 93 **To** 2027 $42 SC
Beyond the Horizon Shiraz 2016 Rating 93 **To** 2030 $47 SC

Charteris Wines   ★★★★★

PO Box 800, Cessnock, NSW 2320 **Region** Central Otago, NZ
T (02) 4998 7701 **www**.charteriswines.com **Open** Not
Winemaker PJ Charteris **Est.** 2007 **Dozens** 170 **Vyds** 1.7ha

Owners Peter James (PJ) Charteris and partner Christina Pattison met at Brokenwood in the Hunter Valley in 1999. PJ was the chief executive winemaker, Christina the marketing manager. Together they have over three decades of winemaking and wine marketing experience. For NZ-born PJ, finding a top pinot noir site in Central Otago was a spiritual homecoming (they claim to have searched both Australia and NZ for the right match of site to variety). They also have a vineyard with the gold-plated address of Felton Road, Bannockburn, planted to clones 115,777 and Abel. PJ carries on a consultancy business in Australia, with some, though not all, of his focus being the Hunter Valley.

ŶŶŶŶŶ **The Hunt Vineyard Central Otago Riesling 2015** Pale quartz-green; the fragrant citrus blossom bouquet leads into an intense palate, its length increased by acidity, and a certain pleasurable grip ex the unsweetened lemon zest flavour. The wine is not dry, but the residual sugar is masked by the all-important acidity. Screwcap. 12% alc. **Rating** 95 **To** 2029 $35 ❂

Cellar Release The Winter Vineyard Central Otago Pinot Noir 2013 Deep colour; this will require real patience, its dark cherry fruits locked up in the arms of pinot tannins and Central Otago acidity. My original drink to date of '25 may prove short of the mark – a nice problem to have. Screwcap. 14% alc. **Rating** 95 **To** 2028 $70

Central Otago Pinot Noir 2014 Fresh, lively and full of red cherries and berries on the bouquet and palate alike. Less intense than the Winter Vineyard '13, but is far more accessible for early consumption. Screwcap. 13.5% alc. **Rating** 94 **To** 2025 $40

Chateau Francois   ★★★★★

1744 Broke Road, Pokolbin, NSW 2321 **Region** Hunter Valley
T (02) 4998 7548 **Open** Not
Winemaker Don Francois **Est.** 1969 **Dozens** 200

I have known former NSW Director of Fisheries Dr Don Francois for almost as long as I have been involved with wine, which is a very long time indeed. I remember his early fermentations of sundry substances other than grapes (none of which, I hasten to add, was the least bit illegal) in the copper bowl of an antiquated washing machine in his suburban laundry. He established Chateau Francois one year before Brokenwood, and our winemaking and fishing paths have crossed many times since. Some years ago Don suffered a mild stroke and no longer speaks or writes with fluency, but this has not stopped him from producing a range of absolutely beautiful semillons that flourish marvellously with age. I should add that he is even prouder of the distinguished career of his daughter, Rachel Francois, at the NSW bar. The semillon vines are now 49 years old, producing exceptional wine that is sold for the proverbial song year after year. Owing to a serious illness, Don Francois has ceased production, but has substantial amounts of his 2014, '15 and '16 semillons available. I cannot help but emphasise just how good these wines are given their price.

ＰＰＰＰＰ **Pokolbin Semillon 2014** This has a gold-plated 15-year life ahead, but the lemon juice and lemon curd flavours are already evident, acidity providing both balance and length. Strongly, but ever so surely, moving towards its mid-range optimum. Screwcap. 11% alc. **Rating** 96 **To** 2029 $20 ✪

Chateau Tanunda ★★★★★

9 Basedow Road, Tanunda, SA 5352 **Region** Barossa Valley
T (08) 8563 3888 **www**.chateautanunda.com **Open** 7 days 10–5
Winemaker Neville Rowe **Est.** 1890 **Dozens** 130 000 **Vyds** 100ha
This is one of the most historically significant winery buildings in the Barossa Valley, built from bluestone quarried at nearby Bethany in the late 1880s. It has been restored by John Geber and family, and a new small-batch basket press has been installed. Chateau Tanunda owns almost 100ha of vineyards in Bethany, Eden Valley, Tanunda and Vine Vale, with additional fruit sourced from a group of 30 growers covering the panoply of Barossa districts. The wines are made from hand-picked grapes, basket-pressed, and are neither fined nor filtered. There is an emphasis on single vineyard and single district wines under the label Terroirs of the Barossa. The grand building houses the cellar door and the Barossa Small Winemakers Centre, offering wines from boutique winemakers. Exports to all major markets have been a major reason for the increase in production from 50 000 to 130 000 dozen, success due to the unrelenting, market-oriented approach of John Geber.

ＰＰＰＰＰ **Terroirs of the Barossa Marananga Shiraz 2016** A heady mix of black plums and blue fruits, laden with spice and integrated cedary oak. The full-bodied palate takes everything in its stride with supple, velvety tannins and excellent length. It should last some distance but it is under cork, this already showing some leaching. 15% alc. **Rating** 95 **To** 2030 $50 JF
50 Year Old Vines Barossa Shiraz 2015 Everything is in its place from spicy dark fruits and fine tannins to the judicious use of oak. It's quite savoury with umami flavours from licorice to soy sauce, and just manages to stay in the elegant spectrum. Cork. 15.5% alc. **Rating** 95 **To** 2026 $75 JF
The Chateau 100 Year Old Vines Shiraz 2015 It pours on the power, striking blow after blow of thick, sweet, dense flavour. Blackberry, honey, soy and malt, inflections of mint and cloves, a churn of grainy, muscular tannin. There's real flex here, real grunt. You either succumb or you stand out of its way. Red berry flavours add a brighter note; a light on a mountain of flavour. Cork. 15% alc. **Rating** 94 **To** 2030 $150 CM
Noble Baron Shiraz 2014 Mid-garnet hue; enticing aromatics and flavours of black plums, licorice and dried herbs, plus dark cherries dipped in chocolate, a floral quality and some creaminess too. Fittingly seasoned with the right amount of spice, oak and the savoury tannins melding into the structure of the wine. Neatly balanced and overall, impressive. Diam. 14.5% alc. **Rating** 94 **To** 2026 $50 JF
The Chateau 100 Year Old Vines Shiraz Grenache Mourvedre 2015 A soft, mellifluous, highly seductive red, all cream and violets, vanilla and redcurrant, the flavours coming at you in waves, the textures in satiny folds. It feels both bright and deep at once, and will satisfy and please all-comers as a result. Cork. 15% alc. **Rating** 94 **To** 2028 $150 CM

ＰＰＰＰＰ **150 Year Old Vines Barossa Semillon 2017** **Rating** 93 **To** 2030 $59 JF
Grand Barossa Shiraz 2016 **Rating** 93 **To** 2025 $25 JF ✪
The Chateau Single Vineyard Shiraz 2016 **Rating** 93 **To** 2028 $35 JF
Grand Barossa Cabernet Malbec 2016 **Rating** 93 **To** 2026 $25 JF ✪
Grand Barossa Cabernet Sauvignon 2016 **Rating** 90 **To** 2028 $25 JF
Chorus Tempranillo Grenache Graciano 2015 **Rating** 90 **To** 2022 $17 JF ✪

Chatto   ★★★★★

PO Box 54, Cessnock, NSW 2325 **Region** Southern Tasmania
T (02) 4990 8660 **www**.chattowines.com **Open** Not
Winemaker Jim Chatto **Est.** 2000 **Dozens** 300 **Vyds** 1.5ha
Jim Chatto is recognised as having one of the very best palates in Australia, and has proved to
be an outstanding winemaker. He and wife Daisy have long wanted to get a small Tasmanian
pinot business up and running, but having moved to the Hunter Valley in 2000, it took
six years to find a site that satisfied all of the criteria Jim considers ideal. It is a warm, well
drained site in one of the coolest parts of Tasmania, looking out over Glaziers Bay. So far they
have planted nine clones of pinot noir, with a spacing of 5000 vines per ha. This will be a
busman's holiday for some years to come following Jim's appointment as chief winemaker for
McWilliam's Wine Group.

ŸŸŸŸŸ **Isle Black Label Huon Valley Pinot Noir 2016** Clear, full crimson with plenty
happening on the bouquet, cherry and plum both contributing. The palate is
altogether serious, with a remarkable mouthfeel built around the foundation of
precisely engineered tannins and hints of forest. Each time you go back to it the
greater the purity, likewise the intensity. Received too late for the *Wine Companion*
2018, included in the 2019 edition because of its exceptional quality. Screwcap.
13.5% alc. **Rating** 98 **To** 2031 $75

White Label Huon Valley Pinot Noir 2016 The bouquet is still locked up, the
palate anything but: intensely and immediately expressive, dark cherry/berry fruits
held in an embrace of fine but persistent tannins and an airbrush of French oak. Its
balance and length guarantee a long future, with spices bursting through over the
next 5 years. Screwcap. 13.5% alc. **Rating** 97 **To** 2030 $50 ●

ŸŸŸŸŸ **Mania Tamar Valley Chardonnay 2016** Tasmanian chardonnays don't always
develop well; but this will do so with ease. Chatto has managed to make a wine of
exceptional intensity and length, its flavours midway between grapefruit and stone
fruit, oak a bystander. Screwcap. 13.6% alc. **Rating** 96 **To** 2028 $35

Cherry Tree Hill   ★★★★

Hume Highway, Sutton Forest, NSW 2577 **Region** Southern Highlands
T (02) 8217 1409 **www**.cherrytreehill.com.au **Open** 7 days 9–5
Winemaker Anton Balog (Contract) **Est.** 2000 **Dozens** 4000 **Vyds** 14ha
The Lorentz family, then headed by Gabi Lorentz, began the establishment of the Cherry
Tree Hill vineyard in 2000 with the planting of 3ha each of cabernet sauvignon and riesling.
Merlot and sauvignon blanc (3ha each) followed in '01; and, finally, 2ha of chardonnay in '02.
Gabi's inspiration was childhood trips on a horse and cart through his grandfather's vineyard
in Hungary. Gabi's son David is now the owner and manager of the business. Poor vintage
conditions resulted in no wines being available for this edition.

Chris Ringland   ★★★★

Franklin House, 6–8 Washington Street, Angaston, SA 5353 **Region** Barossa
T (08) 8564 3233 **www**.chrisringland.com **Open** By appt
Winemaker Chris Ringland **Est.** 1989 **Dozens** 150 **Vyds** 2.05ha
The wines made by Chris Ringland for his eponymous brand were at the very forefront of
the surge of rich, old vine Barossa shirazs discovered by Robert Parker in the 1980s. As a
consequence of very limited production, and high quality (albeit polarising) wine, it assumed
immediate icon status. The production of 150 dozen does not include a small number of
magnums, double-magnums and imperials that are sold each year. The addition of 0.5ha
of shiraz planted in 1999, joined by 1.5ha planted in 2010, has had little practical impact
on availability. Exports to the UK, France, Germany, Spain, South Korea, Japan, Hong Kong
and China.

⟡⟡⟡⟡⟡ **Reservation Barossa Shiraz 2014** Full-on style; sweet and dense, with floral notes hovering and a combination of clove, suede leather and graphite characters circling the main fruit-packed action. Blackberry and plum – big, bold, pure, exaggerated even, but completely undeniable. Screwcap. 15% alc. **Rating** 94 To 2030 $60 CM

⟡⟡⟡⟡⟡ **CR Sealed Barossa Shiraz 2016 Rating** 93 To 2030 $39 CM
CR Barossa Shiraz 2016 Rating 92 To 2026 $30 CM

Chrismont ★★★★
251 Upper King River Road, Cheshunt, Vic 3678 **Region** King Valley
T (03) 5729 8220 **www**.chrismont.com.au **Open** 7 days 10–5
Winemaker Warren Proft **Est.** 1980 **Dozens** 25 000 **Vyds** 100ha
Arnie and Jo Pizzini's substantial vineyards in the Cheshunt and Whitfield areas of the upper King Valley are planted to riesling, chardonnay, pinot gris, merlot, barbera, sagrantino, marzemino, arneis, prosecco, fiano, petit manseng, tempranillo, sangiovese and nebbiolo. The La Zona wine range ties in the Italian heritage of the Pizzinis and is part of their interest in all things Italian. In January 2016 the Chrismont Cellar Door, Restaurant and Larder was opened. As well as its 7-day operation, the development can seat up to 300 guests, and is designed to host weddings, corporate events, business conferences and group celebrations. A feature is the 'floating' deck over the vineyard, which can seat up to 150 people and has floor-to-ceiling glass looking out over the Black Ranges and King Valley landscape. Exports to the Philippines, Malaysia and Singapore.

⟡⟡⟡⟡⟡ **La Zona King Valley Sangiovese 2016** Free-run only, 50% 7-day maceration, 50% 4-week maceration, matured for 15 months in French hogsheads (20% new). Nice, easy-access, juicy style, which nonetheless has good varietal expression with red and dark cherry fruit on a long palate. Bargain. Screwcap. 14% alc. **Rating** 94 To 2029 $26 ✪

⟡⟡⟡⟡⟡ **King Valley Chardonnay 2016 Rating** 92 To 2020 $24 ✪
La Zona King Valley Barbera 2016 Rating 92 To 2027 $26
King Valley Riesling 2017 Rating 90 To 2023 $17 ✪
King Valley Pinot Gris 2016 Rating 90 To 2020 $26
La Zona King Valley Fiano 2017 Rating 90 To 2020 $26
La Zona King Valley Marzemino 2016 Rating 90 To 2030 $30

Churchview Estate ★★★★
8 Gale Road, Metricup, WA 6280 **Region** Margaret River
T (08) 9755 7200 **www**.churchview.com.au **Open** Mon–Sat 10–5
Winemaker Greg Garnish **Est.** 1998 **Dozens** 40 000 **Vyds** 57.5ha
The Fokkema family, headed by Spike Fokkema, immigrated from the Netherlands in the 1950s. Business success in the following decades led to the acquisition of the 100ha Churchview Estate in '97, and to the progressive establishment of substantial vineyards (planted to 16 varieties), managed organically. Exports to all major markets.

⟡⟡⟡⟡⟡ **Estate Range Margaret River Sauvignon Blanc Semillon 2017** An 80/20% blend with textbook aromas and flavours of cut grass, kaffir lime and pea pods with passionfruit and guava. Bracingly fresh with lemony acidity screaming ahead to a decisive, crisp finish. Screwcap. 12.5% alc. **Rating** 90 To 2020 $20 JF ✪
St Johns Limited Release Margaret River Marsanne 2017 Mixes freshness with rich flavours and texture to great effect; white blossom, honeysuckle, ripe pears and stone fruit with plenty of ginger spice. A little phenolic grip and a lick of residual sugar ensuring the palate is just so. Screwcap. 12.2% alc. **Rating** 90 To 2022 $35 JF

⟡⟡⟡⟡ **St Johns Limited Release Margaret River Malbec 2016 Rating** 89 To 2023 $35 JF

Circe Wines

PO Box 22, Red Hill, Vic 3937 **Region** Mornington Peninsula
T 0417 328 142 **www**.circewines.com.au **Open** Not
Winemaker Dan Buckle **Est.** 2010 **Dozens** 800 **Vyds** 2.9ha

Circe was a seductress and minor goddess of intoxicants in Homer's Odyssey. Circe Wines is the partnership of winemaker Dan Buckle and marketer Aaron Drummond, very much a weekend and holiday venture, inspired by their mutual love of pinot noir. They have a long-term lease of a vineyard in Hillcrest Road, not far from Paringa Estate. 'Indeed,' says Dan, 'it is not far from the Lieu-dit "Buckle" Vineyard my dad planted in the 1980s.' Circe has 1.2ha of vines, half chardonnay and half MV6 pinot noir. They have also planted 1.7ha of pinot noir (MV6, Abel, 777, D2V5 and Best's Old Clone) at a vineyard in William Road, Red Hill. Dan Buckle's real job is chief winemaker at Chandon Australia. Exports to the UK.

☆☆☆☆☆ **Utopies Grampians Shiraz 2016** Dense, deep colour; resplendent with the power and depth of its dark/black fruit flavours, licorice and spice, oak and tannins wrapped in the folds of the fruit. Balance underwriting a wine with its future measured in decades, not years. Screwcap. 13.5% alc. **Rating** 97 **To** 2046 $50 **☉**

☆☆☆☆☆ **Hillcrest Road Vineyard Mornington Peninsula Pinot Noir 2016** The colour may be light, the bouquet and palate anything but. It is full of sweet satsuma and blood plum, instantaneously engaging all the senses. It has some puppy fat to shed, and will become even better than it is now. Screwcap. 12.5% alc. **Rating** 95 **To** 2027 $70

Red Hill Mornington Peninsula Chardonnay 2016 This is the variety at its mellifluous best. Stone fruit, custard apples, oak-spice and bran flavours all presented in juicy form, with flint and grapefruit notes then flourishing through the finish. Swallow, and the flavours linger appreciably. Screwcap. 12.5% alc. **Rating** 94 **To** 2021 $35 CM

Pinot Noir 2016 Reductive, tight and firm in its conviction. Sweet-savoury flavours of forest berries, beet and dried herbs turn quickly towards pepper, gun smoke and sulphur. You get the feeling its maker, Dan Buckle, could have played to the crowd but chose not to. Fruit volume is not in question but the wine's personality feels sinewy and uncompromised. It encourages contemplation. Screwcap. 13% alc. **Rating** 94 **To** 2024 $40 CM

☆☆☆☆☆ **Blanc de Blancs 2012 Rating** 91 $60 CM

Clairault | Streicker Wines

3277 Caves Road, Wilyabrup, WA 6280 **Region** Margaret River
T (08) 9755 6225 **www**.clairaultstreicker.com.au **Open** 7 days 10–5
Winemaker Bruce Dukes **Est.** 1976 **Dozens** 23 000 **Vyds** 113ha

This multifaceted business is owned by New York resident John Streicker. It began in 2002 when he purchased the Yallingup Protea Farm and Vineyards. This was followed by the purchase of the Ironstone Vineyard in '03, and finally the Bridgeland Vineyard, which has one of the largest dams in the region: 1km long and covering 18ha. The Ironstone Vineyard is one of the oldest vineyards in Wilyabrup. In April '12 Streicker acquired Clairault, with a further 40ha of estate vines, including 12ha now over 40 years old. The two brands are effectively run as one venture. A large part of the grape production is sold to winemakers in the region. Exports to the US, Canada, Dubai, Malaysia, Singapore, Hong Kong and China.

☆☆☆☆☆ **Clairault Margaret River Chardonnay 2016** This lovely chardonnay brings a striking display of complexity and purity to the table. It will sit happily next to a Grand Cru White Burgundy – two different wines with a shared link of extreme complexity. 40yo vines and the supreme skills of winemaker Bruce Dukes provide the magic. Screwcap. 13% alc. **Rating** 97 **To** 2029 $27 **☉**

☆☆☆☆☆ **Clairault Estate Margaret River Chardonnay 2016** A wine of rare purity, intensity and length. Grapefruit is the dominant flavour, white peach and Granny Smith apple adding to the complexity. French oak plays its all-important role in providing structure and texture, its flavour unimportant. Screwcap. 13.5% alc. Rating 96 To 2028 $38 ✪

Streicker Bridgeland Block Margaret River Sauvignon Semillon 2016 Meticulous vinification achieves the desired explosive flavours of lemon skin, zest and juice in a single mouthwatering stream of flavours. Natural acidity, preserved by preventing mlf, is a constant companion through to the extremely long finish and aftertaste. Screwcap. 13% alc. Rating 95 To 2021 $30 ✪

Streicker Bridgeland Block Margaret River Syrah 2015 The extreme complexity of the vinification has resulted in the power and weight of a wine with higher alcohol. Here the grapes were picked when ripe, no more, no less, the end result exceptional length to the jet black fruits. There are some of the savoury notes generally found with quality cabernets, not shiraz. The tannins, too, could come from cabernet, but in saying so, not to denigrate the positive role they (and the oak) play here. Screwcap. 14% alc. Rating 95 To 2035 $43

Clairault Margaret River Cabernet Sauvignon 2016 Another drop-dead bargain. The colour waves the starting flag, the aromas and flavours of cassis leading the way, the texture plush and evocative, yet with all the structure needed. A lovely Margaret River cabernet. Screwcap. 14% alc. Rating 95 To 2036 $27 ✪

Streicker Nysa 2015 67% cabernet franc, 33% cabernet sauvignon. As expected, the cabernet franc gives the wine a distinctive aroma, almost-but-not-quite pungent, its lighter structure also contributing much to the open face of the wine. The finish is at once spicy and juicy, driven by flavours, not tannins. The way the wine has soaked up the new French oak is exceptional. Screwcap. 13.5% alc. Rating 95 To 2035 $120

Clairault Margaret River Sauvignon Blanc Semillon 2017 Barrel fermentation makes its presence felt on the bouquet, but much less on the powerful fruit-and-acid-driven palate. Grapefruit and mineral hurl bolts of lightning at each other, paying no attention to bystanders, innocent or otherwise. Good now or in 5 years' time. Screwcap. 13% alc. Rating 94 To 2023 $22 ✪

Clairault Margaret River Cabernet Sauvignon Merlot 2016 77% cabernet sauvignon, 17% merlot and 6% petit verdot. Vivid colour and richly endowed with classic Margaret River cabernet characteristics; cassis and a touch of black olive joining in with the tannins to complete a wine at an unbelievably low price. And think of the care needed to blend in the small contribution of petit verdot. Screwcap. 14% alc. Rating 94 To 2031 $22 ✪

Clairault Estate Margaret River Cabernet Sauvignon 2014 Deep crimson-purple, exceptional for its age. A powerful, intense, introverted cabernet warning those who approach to back off, the tannins needing a number of years to resolve. They will, but you'll have to be patient. Screwcap. 14.5% alc. Rating 94 To 2039 $43

♀♀♀♀♀ **Streicker Ironstone Block Chardonnay 2015** Rating 93 To 2023 $41 DB
Streicker Bridgeland Block Rose 2017 Rating 93 To 2018 $28 DB

Clare Wine Co   ★★★☆

PO Box 852, Nuriootpa, SA 5355 **Region** Clare Valley
T (08) 8562 4488 **www**.clarewineco.com.au **Open** Not
Winemaker Reid Bosward, Stephen Dew **Est.** 2008 **Dozens** 5000 **Vyds** 36ha
An affiliate of Kaesler Wines, its primary focus is on exports. Its vines are predominantly given over to shiraz and cabernet sauvignon. It also has riesling and semillon, but no chardonnay, which is presumably purchased from other Clare Valley growers. Exports to Malaysia, Singapore, Hong Kong and China.

♀♀♀♀♀ **Watervale Riesling 2017** Lots to enjoy here starting with the heady aromas of lemon, ginger blossom and lemongrass. The palate has verve and there's some sweetness rounding out the finish, not quite tempering the searing acidity. Screwcap. 12% alc. Rating 90 To 2028 $16 JF ✪

Clarendon Hills

Brookmans Road, Blewitt Springs, SA 5171 **Region** McLaren Vale
T (08) 8363 6111 **www**.clarendonhills.com.au **Open** By appt
Winemaker Roman Bratasiuk **Est.** 1990 **Dozens** 15000 **Vyds** 63ha

Age and experience, it would seem, have mellowed Roman Bratasiuk – and the style of his wines. Once formidable and often rustic, they are now far more sculpted and smooth, at times bordering on downright elegant. Roman took another major step by purchasing a 160ha property high in the hill country of Clarendon at an altitude close to that of the Adelaide Hills. Here he has established a vineyard with single-stake trellising similar to that used on the steep slopes of Germany and Austria; it produces the Domaine Clarendon Syrah. He makes up to 20 different wines each year, all consistently very good, many a tribute to the old vines. Exports to the US and other major markets.

ŸŸŸŸŸ **Romas Grenache 2014** Remarkable wine. Distinctive aroma and flavour profile: iodine, wood smoke, redcurrant, licorice and bitumen, perhaps graphite, perhaps gun smoke. It's both dry and tannic but the wild display of assorted smoke and spice notes is what sets it so clearly apart. It does not go quietly, but takes a stand. Cork. 14.5% alc. **Rating** 97 **To** 2032 $100 CM ✪

ŸŸŸŸŸ **Astralis 2014** It takes richness and ripeness to extremes and yet it's elegant, controlled and long. It's precision engineering in wine form. The thrust of dark fruit, the sleek veneer of cedary, smoky oak, the attention to detail evident everywhere you look. Cork. 14.5% alc. **Rating** 96 **To** 2040 $450 CM

Brookman Cabernet Sauvignon 2014 It's an inky, full-bodied, muscular wine with blackcurrant, bay leaf, graphite and wood smoke powering through the palate. It acts as though it's the last authority on cabernet sauvignon; every step along the way it feels in total command. Cork. 14.5% alc. **Rating** 96 **To** 2042 $50 CM ✪

Hickinbotham Clarendon Cabernet Sauvignon 2014 Pure, glorious cabernet. Redcurrant and blackcurrant, violets, cedar wood, peppercorns, tobacco; there are many indicators of quality cabernet here, strong arms of tannin among them, but mostly it's about respect for the variety, for the position of the long-lived red, for the Clarendon district and for powerful red wine, full stop. Majestic. Cork. 14.5% alc. **Rating** 96 **To** 2040 $110 CM

Hickinbotham Syrah 2014 Overt choc-mint characters introduce a fruit-sweet wine of great intensity. Ozone, blackberry and boysenberry-like flavours fill the mouth and surge out through the finish. It's hard to get a word in edgewise; the wine dominates proceedings. The sustained finish ensures there's glory to go with the power. Cork. 14.5% alc. **Rating** 95 **To** 2036 CM

Onkaparinga Syrah 2014 Jammed with fruit but more characterised by the immense softness of the palate. The grapes for this wine must have grown silk for skin. Oak is a player but it's not the driver; fresh red and black berries pour through the palate in buoyant, sweet, succulent form. Cork. 14.5% alc. **Rating** 95 **To** 2036 CM

Domaine Clarendon Syrah 2014 Taut style with dark, brooding fruit, lifts of cocoa powder and whispers of fragrant herbs. The throttle here is well and truly open, though maybe it's been backed off fractionally; for all its depth it remains fresh and fragrant, the finish incredibly finely stitched. Cork. 14% alc. **Rating** 94 **To** 2032 CM

Blewitt Springs Grenache 2014 Perfumed, bright and expressive even in the face of both alcohol warmth and Cherry Ripe sweetness. Oak taps about the edges but this is essentially (and beautifully) a fruit/variety-driven wine. Fennel notes add bass; raspberry rips through the palate; tannin, as velvety as it is, offers spread and control. Cork. 14.5% alc. **Rating** 94 **To** 2026 CM

Onkaparinga Grenache 2014 Volume of fruit, volume of tannin. It's a simple display of flavours but it has might and power on its side. It tastes/smells of fresh leather and anise, florals and bright red berries, its prettiness a stark relief to its immensity. Cork. 14.5% alc. **Rating** 94 **To** 2032 $100 CM

ŶŶŶŶŶ Kangarilla Grenache 2014 Rating 93 To 2028 $75 CM
Hickinbotham Grenache 2014 Rating 92 To 2027 CM
Liandra Syrah 2014 Rating 91 To 2029 CM
Clarendon Grenache 2014 Rating 91 To 2024 CM

Clarnette & Ludvigsen Wines ★★★★☆

Westgate Road, Armstrong, Vic 3377 **Region** Grampians
T 0409 083 833 **www.**clarnette-ludvigsen.com.au **Open** By appt
Winemaker Leigh Clarnette **Est.** 2003 **Dozens** 500 **Vyds** 15.5ha

Winemaker Leigh Clarnette and viticulturist Kym Ludvigsen's career paths crossed in late 1993 when both were working for Seppelt. Kym had a 14ha vineyard in the heart of the Grampians region, mostly planted to rare clones of shiraz sourced from the Great Western area, plus some chardonnay, viognier and riesling. They met again in 2005 when both were employed by Taltarni. The premature death of Kym in '13 was widely reported, in no small measure due to his (unpaid) service to wine industry bodies. With next generations on both sides, the plans are to continue the business. Exports to China.

ŶŶŶŶŶ Grampians Shiraz 2016 Made from the St Ethel clone, a descendant of the mid-19th-century plantings in the Grampians region, and from what Leigh Clarnette classifies as one of their greatest vintages. It is indeed a lovely wine, its fruit intensity building as the flavours of red/dark cherries unroll along the medium-bodied palate. It has exceptional mouthfeel from its gentle extraction and moderate alcohol. Screwcap. 14% alc. **Rating** 95 **To** 2036 $35
Reserve Grampians Shiraz 2015 Bright hue; its focused palate has more red than black fruits, alcohol and tannins balanced but tightly wound. It is demanding time to soften and fill out, but will surprise with age. Screwcap. 14% alc. **Rating** 94 **To** 2040 $50

ŶŶŶŶ Limited Release Grampians Sangiovese Rose 2017 Rating 89 To 2019 $23

Claymore Wines ★★★★★

7145 Horrocks Way, Leasingham, SA 5452 **Region** Clare Valley
T (08) 8843 0200 **www.**claymorewines.com.au **Open** 7 days 10–5
Winemaker Marnie Roberts **Est.** 1998 **Dozens** 35 000 **Vyds** 50ha

Claymore Wines is the venture of Anura Nitchingham, a medical professional who imagined this would lead the way to early retirement (which, of course, it did not). The starting date depends on which event you take first: the 4ha vineyard at Leasingham purchased in 1991 (with 70-year-old grenache, riesling and shiraz); '96, when a 16ha block at Penwortham was purchased and planted to shiraz, merlot and grenache; '97, when the first wines were made; or '98, when the first releases came onto the market. The labels are inspired by U2, Pink Floyd, Prince and Lou Reed. Exports to the UK, Canada, Denmark, Malaysia, Singapore, Taiwan, Hong Kong and China.

ŶŶŶŶŶ Superstition Reserve Clare Valley Riesling 2016 Wastes no time in casting its spell over the bouquet and palate. It is packed with Clare Valley fruit: lime, lemon and Granny Smith apple, given structure, balance and length by perfectly balanced acidity. Typical high quality riesling. Good now, in 5 years, and who knows how long thereafter. Screwcap. 13% alc. **Rating** 95 **To** 2036 $28 ✪
Bittersweet Symphony Clare Valley Cabernet Sauvignon 2015 Includes 7% merlot. I'm not sure I agree with Claymore that generous cabernet is particularly well suited to the Clare Valley, but this has to be an exception if my general rule is correct. It is a lively, fresh, cassis-filled, medium-bodied cabernet, with merlot adding a touch of elegance. Its balance is faultless, and so is the price. Screwcap. 14% alc. **Rating** 95 **To** 2030 $25 ✪
Superstition Reserve Clare Valley Riesling 2017 Compact and bristling with intent, this is the most tightly coiled of the estate's riesling triumvirate, with notes of Granny Smith apple, pear gelato and citrus fruit etched along a balance

beam of crunchy mineral energy and high-toned, juicy acidity. Screwcap. 12% alc. Rating 94 To 2029 $32 NG

You'll Never Walk Alone Clare Valley Grenache Shiraz Mataro 2016
A 65/25/10% blend. Here is a major surprise packet even before you look at the price. Clare Valley GSM blends are often full of confection notes, yet also lack flavour. This is the opposite in every respect, full of juicy fruits ranging through red, purple and black, the richness with a neat trimming of tannins. Screwcap. 14% alc. Rating 94 To 2026 $20 **○**

The Miseducation of Carissa Major Clare Valley Tempranillo 2016
Tempranillo is theoretically a cool-climate variety unsuited to the Clare Valley, but is grown indiscriminately around Australia in all sorts of climates. Named in honour of Claymore's general manager, this wine offers a fragrant, flowery, red-fruit bouquet and a sprightly palate, with freshness its keyword. Seductive. Screwcap. 13.2% alc. Rating 94 To 2024 $25 **○**

🍷🍷🍷🍷🍷 Bittersweet Symphony Cabernet 2016 Rating 93 To 2024 $25 NG **○**
Black Magic Woman Reserve Cabernet Sauvignon 2015 Rating 93 To 2027 $45 NG
London Calling Cabernet Malbec 2016 Rating 93 To 2023 $22 NG **○**
God is a DJ Riesling 2017 Rating 92 To 2027 $20 NG **○**
Dark Side of the Moon Shiraz 2016 Rating 92 To 2024 $25 NG **○**
Skinny Love Summer White 2016 Rating 92 To 2020 $20 **○**
Signature Series Shiraz 2014 Rating 91 To 2030 $95 JF
Joshua Tree Riesling 2017 Rating 90 To 2023 $20 NG **○**

Clockwork Wines   ★★★☆

8990 West Swan Road, West Swan, WA 6056 (postal) **Region** Swan Valley
T 0401 033 840 **Open** Not
Winemaker Ragan Wood **Est.** 2008 **Dozens** 7000 **Vyds** 5ha
This is a separate business from Oakover Wines, although both are owned by the Yukich family. Grapes come from the Swan Valley vineyard and are also sourced from around WA, with the majority from Margaret River, and from Geographe and Frankland River. The 2007 Clockwork Cabernet Merlot, somewhat luckily perhaps, found itself in the line-up for the Jimmy Watson Trophy at its first show entry, part of a dominant contingent from Margaret River thanks to a great vintage.

🍷🍷🍷🍷 Sauvignon Blanc Semillon 2016 Sourced from the southern Margaret River – the cooler nature of this district comes through with its focus on grass/snow pea/ acidity, tropical fruits there in the background to fill out the mid-palate. Screwcap. 12.7% alc. Rating 89 To 2020 $19 **○**
Vermentino 2016 Has a touch of white pepper à la gruner veltliner, and a persistence of flavour that doesn't drop its gaze under close inspection. Interesting wine. Screwcap. 12.2% alc. Rating 89 To 2021 $19 **○**

Clonakilla   ★★★★★

Crisps Lane, Murrumbateman, NSW 2582 **Region** Canberra District
T (02) 6227 5877 **www**.clonakilla.com.au **Open** Mon–Fri 10–4, w'ends 10–5
Winemaker Tim Kirk, Bryan Martin **Est.** 1971 **Dozens** 20 000 **Vyds** 14ha
The indefatigable Tim Kirk, with an inexhaustible thirst for knowledge, is the winemaker and manager of this family winery founded by his father, scientist Dr John Kirk. It is not at all surprising that the quality of the wines is exceptional, especially the Shiraz Viognier, which has paved the way for numerous others but remains the icon. Demand for the wines outstrips supply, even with the 1998 acquisition of an adjoining 20ha property by Tim and wife Lara, planted to shiraz and viognier. The first Hilltops Shiraz was made in 2000 from the best vineyards. In '07 the Kirk family purchased another adjoining property, planting another 1.8ha of shiraz, plus 0.4ha of grenache, mourvedre and cinsaut; the same year they made their first O'Riada Shiraz. Exports to all major markets.

🍷🍷🍷🍷🍷 **Murrumbateman Syrah 2016** Is it the perfume? The structure? The detail? It's all that and so much more for this complex and exquisitely balanced wine. There's a purity to the fruit, a mix of florals, spice and herbs; while it's fuller-bodied with some depth, there's lightness, too, then the finely chiselled tannins take this to a resounding finish. A long future assured and rather stunning now. Screwcap. 14% alc. **Rating** 98 **To** 2040 $120 JF ✪

Shiraz Viognier 2016 The perfumed, spicy bouquet with red flowers and fruits doesn't prepare you for the intensity and piercing length of its beautifully balanced medium-bodied palate. This is a truly glorious wine that draws you back again and again to explore the wealth of red fruit flavours, and the majesty of its texture and structure. Screwcap. 14% alc. **Rating** 98 **To** 2041 $120 ✪

🍷🍷🍷🍷🍷 **O'Riada Canberra District Shiraz 2016** Full crimson-purple; there is a masterful and utterly harmonious blend of dark fruits, warm spices, ripe tannins and French oak. The very large X-factor is its freshness, which will underwrite its very long life. Bargain basement shelf. Screwcap. 14% alc. **Rating** 96 **To** 2041 $36 ✪

Canberra District Riesling 2017 Reinforces the truth that newly born riesling of high quality can speak as an adult, the grainy acidity of the palate being one mode of communication, the depth of the citrus fruit another, filling in the gaps where needed. But none of this is intended to suggest there is any premature ageing – there is none, and the wine has a sure 15-year future etched in stone. Screwcap. 12.5% alc. **Rating** 95 **To** 2032 $38

Tumbarumba Chardonnay 2017 A fine and flinty rendition that shows a lot of restraint, not a lot of fruit. A whisper of citrus, some white nectarines with a sprinkling of spice. The oak influence, totally integrated, adds another layer. Tightly coiled and needs more time to unfurl, but so compelling. Screwcap. 13% alc. **Rating** 95 **To** 2025 $55 JF

Canberra District Viognier 2017 A beautiful interpretation that stakes its claim first with aromatics and then a tightly woven palate. A touch of honeysuckle, melon with creamed honey, and a fleck of spice. The palate is textural but not weighty, with lemony freshness and terrific length. Screwcap. 13.5% alc. **Rating** 95 **To** 2024 $55 JF

Ceoltoiri 2017 A super blend of grenache 50%, mourvedre 28%, and splashes of shiraz, cinsaut, roussanne and counoise for added interest and flavour. It's so lively, aromas emanating from a baker's kitchen with cardamom, ginger and star anise; floral too. The palate is lighter-framed, juicy with supple tannins, but it's not simple, there's just a joyous ease to this with tangy acidity to close. Delicious. Screwcap. 14.5% alc. **Rating** 95 **To** 2025 $45 JF

🍷🍷🍷🍷🍷 **Hilltops Shiraz 2017** Rating 93 To 2030 $35 JF
Murrumbateman Pinot Noir 2017 Rating 90 To 2023 $55 JF

Clos Clare ★★★★★

45 Old Road, Watervale, SA 5452 **Region** Clare Valley
T (08) 8843 0161 **www**.closclare.com.au **Open** W'ends 11–5
Winemaker Sam Barry, Tom Barry **Est.** 1993 **Dozens** 1600 **Vyds** 2ha
Clos Clare was acquired by the Barry family in 2008. Riesling continues to be made from the 2ha unirrigated section of the original Florita Vineyard (the major part of that vineyard was already in Barry ownership), and newly introduced red wines are coming from a 49-year-old vineyard beside the Armagh site. Exports to the UK.

🍷🍷🍷🍷🍷 **The Hayes Boy Grenache 2016** Runner-up in the James Halliday Grenache Challenge '17; a wine I was smitten with during the deciding rounds of the top golds. It has superb colour, and I was astounded to find it was from the Clare Valley after the conclusion of judging when the region was disclosed. It has exceptional structure and mouthfeel to the array of raspberry, cherry and strawberry fruits. There isn't a hint of confection – just this line of fruit reminiscent of the Rhône Valley's Chateau Rayas. Screwcap. 14.1% alc. **Rating** 97 **To** 2030 $26 ✪

Cemetery Block Shiraz 2014 Very well balanced and structured, with a spicy/savoury underplay to its blackberry and blood plum fruit. The tannins are lithe and help build and sustain the length of a very good wine; the oak treatment subtle. Gold medal Clare Valley Wine Show '17. Screwcap. 14% alc. **Rating** 95 To 2034 $26 ❂

Watervale Riesling 2017 Pale straw-green; a scented bouquet of lemon and lime blossom sets the scene for a wine of great purity and balance. These fruits drive the long palate, sustained by minerally acidity. Lovely wine, longevity assured by quality and evidenced by gold medals for the '09 and '10 at the Clare Valley Wine Show '17. Screwcap. 12.5% alc. **Rating** 94 To 2030 $16 ❂

The Hayes Boy Grenache 2017 Bright crimson hue; a lively, bright and juicy grenache repaying the decision to pick at a point before the alcohol became an issue. Clearly varietal, and the length is convincing. A worthy successor to the '16. Screwcap. 14.1% alc. **Rating** 94 To 2025 $26 ❂

Cloudburst ★★★★★

PO Box 1294, Margaret River, WA 6285 **Region** Margaret River
T (08) 6323 2333 www.cloudburstwine.com **Open** Not
Winemaker Will Berliner **Est.** 2005 **Dozens** 450 **Vyds** 5ha

An extremely interesting young winery. Will Berliner and wife Alison Jobson spent several years searching for a place in Australia that resonated with them, and on their first visit to Margaret River were immediately smitten, drawn by its biodiversity, beaches, farms, vineyards, community and lifestyle. When they purchased their land in 2004 they hadn't the slightest connection with wine and no intention of ever getting involved. Within 12 months Will's perspective had entirely changed, and in '05 he began planting the vineyard and applying biodynamic preparations, seeking to build microbial life in the soil. They set about planting as if it were a garden, with short rows, initially putting in 0.2ha each of cabernet sauvignon and chardonnay, and 0.1ha of malbec. Cloudburst's packaging is truly striking and imaginative. The unseen hand is that of the Watson family, the wines being made by Will at Woodlands under the watchful eye of Stuart Watson. Exports to the US.

Margaret River Chardonnay 2016 Speaks with utmost clarity of its place. The bouquet has peach blossom as its first message, while the subtle barrel ferment inputs the second. The palate welcomes a wash of pink grapefruit coupled with carefully measured nutty oak. Screwcap. 13% alc. **Rating** 96 To 2036

Margaret River Cabernet Sauvignon 2015 Perhaps it's the alcohol at the lower limit of usual, but if so, it's reduced the weight, not the flavour or structure of this lovely medium-bodied cabernet, with that purity and attention to detail one expects from this label. Cassis and blackcurrant have recesses of dried herbs and a smear of olive tapenade; the tannins no more than a cobweb, the oak there to be heard but not seen. Screwcap. 12.5% alc. **Rating** 96 To 2040

Margaret River Malbec 2015 A deficiency of malbec can be a lack of structure, but (emphatically) not here. Cassis, bramble and plum rumble along and across the palate. The deep crimson-purple hue has set the antennae waving, and wasn't a false prophet as you try to decide whether the juicy fruit or the ripe tannins linger longest on the finish. Screwcap. 13.7% alc. **Rating** 96 To 2030

Clovely Estate ★★★★

Steinhardts Road, Moffatdale via Murgon, Qld 4605 **Region** South Burnett
T (07) 3876 3100 www.clovely.com.au **Open** W'ends & public hols 10–4
Winemaker Luke Fitzpatrick, Sarah Boyce, Greg Foster **Est.** 1997 **Dozens** 25000
Vyds 173.76ha

Clovely Estate has the largest vineyards in Queensland, with immaculately maintained vines at two locations in the Burnett Valley. There are 140ha of red grapes (including 60ha of shiraz) and 34ha of white grapes. The attractively packaged wines are sold in various styles at various price points. The estate also has a second cellar door at 210 Musgrave Road, Red Hill, Brisbane (open Tues–Sat 11–7). Exports to Denmark, Papua New Guinea, Taiwan and China.

ΥΥΥΥΥ **Double Pruned South Burnett Shiraz 2013** 18 months' oak maturation has imparted cedar, mocha, clove and turmeric, while the tannin and acid meld is one of ferrous authority. There is nothing sweet about this. Not an ounce of jam! Long and persuasive. Iconoclastic, sure, but a maverick to applaud. Screwcap. 14.5% alc. **Rating** 94 **To** 2026 $90 NG

South Burnett Terroir Saperavi 2014 The dense colour, opaque even, leaves little doubt as to what is in store. Cedar, thyme and violet scents kick-start the cavalry of pulpy plum and dark cherry. Anise, baking spice and varnish, too. Bolshie, leathery tannins bode well for the future, bolstered by well positioned oak. Screwcap. 14.9% alc. **Rating** 94 **To** 2029 $25 NG ✪

ΥΥΥΥΩ **South Burnett Terroir Semillon 2014 Rating** 93 **To** 2017 $20 NG ✪
Estate Reserve South Burnett Blanc de Blanc 2010 Rating 93 $35 NG
South Burnett Terroir Semillon 2017 Rating 91 **To** 2025 $20 NG ✪

Clover Hill

60 Clover Hill Road, Lebrina, Tas 7254 **Region** Northern Tasmania
T (03) 5459 7900 **www**.cloverhillwines.com.au **Open** 7 days 10–4.30
Winemaker Robert Heywood, Peter Warr **Est.** 1986 **Dozens** 12000 **Vyds** 23.9ha
Clover Hill was established by Taltarni in 1986 with the sole purpose of making a premium sparkling wine. It has 23.9ha of vineyards (chardonnay, pinot noir and pinot meunier) and its sparkling wine quality is excellent, combining finesse with power and length. The American owner and founder of Clos du Val (Napa Valley), Taltarni and Clover Hill has brought these businesses and Domaine de Nizas (Languedoc) under the one management roof, the group known as Goelet Wine Estates. Exports to the UK, the US and other major markets.

ΥΥΥΥΥ **Vintage Methode Traditionelle 2012** Excellent intensity, especially upfront. Lemon pie, steel, grapefruit, baked strawberries and lees flavours charge through the palate in confident style. There's a slight dip just before the finish but it recovers the situation well. Diam. 12.5% alc. **Rating** 94 $45 CM

Prestige Late Disgorged Vintage Brut 2006 Wild with flavour. Liquid brioche, honey, stewed peaches, grapefruit, Vegemite on toast. There's nowhere to hide; it lays it all on you. It's not exceptionally long but it has exceptional character. Cork. 12% alc. **Rating** 94 $150 CM

Clyde Park Vineyard

2490 Midland Highway, Bannockburn, Vic 3331 **Region** Geelong
T (03) 5281 7274 **www**.clydepark.com.au **Open** 7 days 11–5
Winemaker Ben Mullen, Terry Jongebloed **Est.** 1979 **Dozens** 6000 **Vyds** 10.1ha
Clyde Park Vineyard, established by Gary Farr but sold by him many years ago, has passed through several changes of ownership. Now owned by Terry Jongebloed and Sue Jongebloed–Dixon, it has significant mature plantings of pinot noir (3.4ha), chardonnay (3.1ha), sauvignon blanc (1.5ha), shiraz (1.2ha) and pinot gris (0.9ha), and the quality of its wines is consistently exemplary. Exports to the UK and Hong Kong.

ΥΥΥΥΥ **Single Block B3 Bannockburn Chardonnay 2017** P58 (Penfolds) clone planted in '95 on river flats. Whole-bunch pressed, full-solids ferment in French oak (30% new), matured for 8 months. As complex as it is classy, this could oh so easily be identified as Meursault (Burgundy) in a blind tasting. A layered, slightly funky, richness expands on the finish. Screwcap. 13% alc. **Rating** 97 **To** 2029 $75 ✪

Single Block D Bannockburn Pinot Noir 2017 Clone MV6 planted in '98; hand-picked, 8-day wild ferment with 20% whole bunches, matured for 8 months in French oak (20% new), 130 dozen made. Light, clear colour; the fragrant bouquet exudes red fruits and spices, the palate long, silky and delicious. Elegance and poise takes the day. Screwcap. 13.5% alc. **Rating** 97 **To** 2030 $75 ✪

ΨΨΨΨΨ **Geelong Pinot Noir 2017** This is the cat's whiskers, making you itch to taste the individual block wines. Deep, bright crimson-purple, its flavours are strung along a high-tensile wire of foresty notes ex whole bunches, dripping satsuma plum and strawberry, curtailed and balanced by savoury notes and fine tannins on the finish. Screwcap. 13% alc. **Rating** 96 **To** 2030 $40 ✪

Single Block F College Bannockburn Pinot Noir 2017 Clone MV6 planted in '88; 10-day wild ferment with 20% whole bunches, matured for 8 months in French oak (25% new). The bouquet has notes of rhubarb and blue fruits; the palate is very long and persistent, the balance underscoring the cellaring potential of a high class wine. Screwcap. 12% alc. **Rating** 96 **To** 2032 $75 ✪

Geelong Chardonnay 2017 Three clones planted on river flats, matured for 9 months on lees. Elegant, fresh and long, the mlf a positive influence. Bright straw-green; tangy pink/white grapefruit and nectarine. Vital freshness ex the '17 vintage shines through. Screwcap. 13% alc. **Rating** 95 **To** 2030 $40

Estate Geelong Rose 2017 Pinot noir and shiraz, 50% whole-bunch pressed, tank-fermented, 50% saignee fermented in used French oak. Perfect balance and mouthfeel; gently spicy red fruits fill the palate without any sense of sweetness. Instead a savoury wine of considerable complexity. Screwcap. 13% alc. **Rating** 95 **To** 2022 $30 ✪

Moranghurk Pinot Noir 2017 Jam-packed with flavour (no pun intended); dark plum and black cherry fruits flow even and deep across the palate; full-on ripeness, but bright and fresh in best silken-glove style. Really, seriously, good pinot. Screwcap. 12.5% alc. **Rating** 95 **To** 2029 $65

Single Block B2 Bannockburn Pinot Noir 2017 Clone F6V7 planted in '95; 9-day wild ferment with 35% whole bunches, matured for 8 months in French oak (33% new), 130 dozen made. The deep crimson-purple is the first obvious sign of difference between the Single Block pinots; a powerful wine with plum/ bramble/forest notes, part fruit, part whole bunch. A long, well balanced finish. Screwcap. 13% alc. **Rating** 95 **To** 2029 $75

Geelong Shiraz 2017 Lighter in colour and body than the '16, purely a reflection of a very different vintage. Mind you, the colour is very good, the bouquet and palate speaking volumes for the cool vintage with the length, complexity and intensity of the spicy red and black fruits. Spice, pepper and licorice are the usual flavours in cool-grown shiraz, and they're here. Screwcap. 13% alc. **Rating** 95 **To** 2037 $40

Geelong Sauvignon Blanc 2017 Rating 94 **To** 2020 $30 CM ✪
Locale Geelong Pinot Noir 2017 Rating 94 **To** 2027 $25 ✪

ΨΨΨΨῙ **Single Block E Bannockburn Shiraz 2017 Rating** 92 **To** 2027 $75
Geelong Fume Blanc 2017 Rating 91 **To** 2020 $40

Coates Wines   ★★★★★

185 Tynan Road, Kuitpo, SA 5172 **Region** Adelaide Hills
T 0417 882 557 **www.**coates-wines.com **Open** W'ends & public hols 11–5
Winemaker Duane Coates **Est.** 2003 **Dozens** 2500
Duane Coates has a Bachelor of Science, a Master of Business Administration and a Master of Oenology from Adelaide University; for good measure he completed the theory component of the Master of Wine in 2005. Having made wine in various parts of the world, and in SA, he is more than qualified to make (and market) Coates wines. Nonetheless, his original intention was to simply make a single barrel of wine employing various philosophies and practices outside the mainstream. The key is organically grown grapes. Exports to the UK and the US.

ΨΨΨΨΨ **The Garden of Perfume & Spice Syrah 2015** Matured for 12 months in French barriques (30% new). An elegant wine singing the same song from the first whiff of the bouquet through to the finish – blackberry and blueberry faithfully replaying on the immaculately balanced palate, likewise oak and gently savoury/ foresty tannins. Screwcap. 14% alc. **Rating** 95 **To** 2028 $30

The Chardonnay 2016 Melon and stone fruits mingle on the nose, but the soul of the wine is surely the kernel of nougatine, cashew and roasted hazelnut that defines the wine's midriff. This is a more generous chardonnay than the status quo, with impeccably handled oak and savvy lees work, reminiscent of a solid Meursault. Screwcap. 13% alc. **Rating** 95 **To** 2025 $30 NG

🍷🍷🍷🍷🍷 The LBV McLaren Vale 2007 Rating 90 $25
La Petite Blanc 2016 Rating 91 To 2020 $18
La Petite Rose 2016 Rating 92 To 2019 $18

Cobaw Ridge   ★★★★

31 Perc Boyers Lane, Pastoria, Vic 3444 **Region** Macedon Ranges
T (03) 5423 5227 **www**.cobawridge.com.au **Open** Thurs–Mon 12–5
Winemaker Alan Cooper **Est.** 1985 **Dozens** 1000 **Vyds** 5ha
When the Coopers started planting in the early 1980s there was scant knowledge of the best varieties for the region, let alone for the Cobaw Ridge site. They have now settled on four varieties, chardonnay and syrah always being part of the mix. Lagrein and close-planted, multi-clonal pinot noir are more recent arrivals to thrive. Cobaw Ridge is now fully certified biodynamic, and all winery operations are carried out according to the biodynamic calendar. Exports to the EU, Sweden and Hong Kong.

🍷🍷🍷🍷🍷 Syrah 2014 The vinification of Cobaw Ridge shiraz differs year by year, with nothing predetermined other than whole-berry fermentation followed by 2 years in oak, then 12–24 months in bottle. This has more flesh than the '13 l'altra, yet retains its cool-climate characteristics of dark fruits studded with pepper, spice and licorice. Diam. 12.7% alc. **Rating** 93 **To** 2024 $50
l'altra Syrah 2013 A very different vintage is the driving force, alcohol hitting the dizzy heights of 14%. It was matured in Mercurey puncheons (20% new) for 24 months, then bottle-aged until Jul '17. It's a mix of luscious black fruits, savoury tannins and some cedar from the oak. Will surely live for decades. Diam. **Rating** 93 **To** 2033 $36

Cockfighter's Ghost   ★★★★

576 De Beyers Road, Pokolbin, NSW 2320 **Region** Hunter Valley
T (02) 4993 3688 **www**.cockfightersghost.com.au **Open** 7 days 10–5
Winemaker Jeff Byrne, Xanthe Hatcher **Est.** 1988 **Dozens** 30 000 **Vyds** 38ha
Cockfighter's Ghost and Poole's Rock were founded in 1988 by the late David Clarke OAM, and acquired by the Agnew family in 2011 (they also own neighbouring Audrey Wilkinson). The brands retain separate identities but share the same winery. The wines of Cockfighter's Ghost are made by Xanthe Hatcher, with white grapes sourced from key growers in SA, and red grapes entirely from the Agnew family's Chairmans vineyard in Blewitt Springs, McLaren Vale. Jeff Byrne makes the Poole's Rock wines with chardonnay, semillon and shiraz from the Hunter Valley; there are also some small-batch wines including a pinot noir from Tasmania.

🍷🍷🍷🍷🍷 Poole's Rock Premiere Tasmania Pinot Noir 2014 Grown in the Tamar Valley in northern Tasmania but processed in the Hunter Valley. It's still finding its feet but the attributes are good. Foresty berries, dried spice, mint and a keen, cranberried acidity. Dry, spice-riddled tannin rears up through the back half of the wine but the fruit goes with it toe-to-toe. Screwcap. 13.5% alc. **Rating** 92 **To** 2024 $40 CM
Poole's Rock Post Office Hunter Valley Shiraz 2017 A substantial price hike from the vast majority of wines across the range, thankfully explained in the quality. Mulberry and blueberry fruits collude with anise, pepper and the Hunter's polished leather tannins. This should age well, despite the alcohol that impacts the wine's glide and detail across the long finish. Screwcap. 14.8% alc. **Rating** 92 **To** 2032 $65 NG
Poole's Rock Premiere Hunter Valley Semillon 2017 Brittle, sharp and chewy, this needs time to gel. Talc, lemon blossom and grassy notes engage the

drinker at this nascent stage, given a thorough chill. The ship will surely steady in about 5 years, with solid drinking to be had over the next 15. Screwcap. 12% alc. **Rating** 91 **To** 2032 $40 NG

Poole's Rock Premiere Hunter Valley Chardonnay 2017 A bright, highly flavourful chardonnay pulling punches of white peach, nectarine and pink grapefruit across a ring corralled by firm oak pillars and a core of mineral crunch. A bit paint-by-numbers, but there is plenty going on. Screwcap. 12.8% alc. **Rating** 91 **To** 2023 $40 NG

Cockfighter's Ghost Single Vineyard Adelaide Hills Pinot Gris 2017 A good, mid-weighted gris, transcending the usual slushy of nashi and ripe bosc pear, to offer scents of anise and raw almond, meandering along gentle phenolic rails to a long finish. Screwcap. 12.9% alc. **Rating** 91 **To** 2021 $25 NG

Cockfighter's Ghost Single Vineyard Adelaide Hills Chardonnay 2017 This offers good value, glimpsing the contemporary zeitgeist of tensile crunch, while smearing it with plenty of peachy goodness and a lick of creamy vanilla-pod oak. Screwcap. 13% alc. **Rating** 90 **To** 2020 $25 NG

Cockfighter's Ghost Sangiovese Rose 2017 This is pretty good. Palpably dry. Sour cherry and orange rind, pickled. Zesty, sassy, crunchy and thirst-slaking. Screwcap. 12.5% alc. **Rating** 90 **To** 2019 $25 NG

♟♟♟♟   **Cockfighter's Ghost Nebbiolo 2017** **Rating** 89 **To** 2022 $25 NG

Cofield Wines   ★★★★

Distillery Road, Wahgunyah, Vic 3687 **Region** Rutherglen
T (02) 6033 3798 **www**.cofieldwines.com.au **Open** Mon–Sat 9–5, Sun 10–5
Winemaker Damien Cofield, Brendan Heath **Est.** 1990 **Dozens** 13 000 **Vyds** 15.4ha
Sons Damien (winery) and Andrew (vineyard) have taken over responsibility for the business from parents Max and Karen Cofield. Collectively, they have developed an impressively broad range with a strong base of cellar door sales. The Pickled Sisters Cafe is open for lunch Wed–Mon; (02) 6033 2377. A 20ha property at Rutherglen, purchased in 2007, is planted to shiraz, durif and sangiovese.

♟♟♟♟♟   **Rutherglen Topaque NV** Dare you not to love it. A beautiful rendition of sweet tea and butterscotch, all fluid and lovely. 375ml. Screwcap. 17.5% alc. **Rating** 92 $25 CM ❂

Rutherglen Durif 2015 Sweet licorice, malt, toast and earth flavours march weightily through the palate. There's no let up; from start to finish it's all about volume of flavour. Truth is, it does the 'big' style of red pretty well. Screwcap. 14.6% alc. **Rating** 91 **To** 2030 $26 CM

♟♟♟♟   **King Valley Riesling 2017** **Rating** 89 **To** 2024 $18 CM ❂
King Valley Pinot Grigio 2017 **Rating** 89 **To** 2019 $20 CM
Sparkling Shiraz 2015 **Rating** 89 $28 CM

Coldstream Hills   ★★★★★

31 Maddens Lane, Coldstream, Vic 3770 **Region** Yarra Valley
T (03) 5960 7000 **www**.coldstreamhills.com.au **Open** 7 days 10–5
Winemaker Andrew Fleming, Greg Jarratt, James Halliday (Consultant) **Est.** 1985
Dozens 25 000 **Vyds** 100ha
Founded by the author, James Halliday, Coldstream Hills is now a small part of TWE, with 100ha of estate vineyards as its base, three in the Lower Yarra Valley and two in the Upper Yarra Valley. Chardonnay and pinot noir continue to be the principal focus; merlot and cabernet sauvignon came on-stream in 1997, sauvignon blanc around the same time, Reserve Shiraz later still. Vintage conditions permitting, chardonnay and pinot noir are made in Reserve, Single Vineyard and varietal forms. In addition, Amphitheatre Pinot Noir was made in tiny quantities in 2006 and '13. In '10 a multimillion-dollar winery was erected around the original winery buildings and facilities; it has a capacity of 1500t. A plaque in the fermentation

area commemorates the official opening on 12 October '10 and the naming of the facility the 'James Halliday Cellar'. Exports to the UK, the US and Singapore.

ŸŸŸŸŸ **Deer Farm Vineyard Pinot Noir 2017** Length is the order of the day. This is a wine of structural integrity first and foremost, though crackles of wood spice, smoke and leaf matter make sure that the sweet-sour nature of the cherried fruit is complex. Everywhere you look here you see absolute signs of quality. It's bright, brooding, savoury and sweet at once; it offers both tang and velvet. A glittering star of a wine. Screwcap. 13.5% alc. **Rating** 97 **To** 2028 $50 CM ✪

ŸŸŸŸŸ **Rising Vineyard Yarra Valley Chardonnay 2017** Bit of a wowee moment. The length of this wine is quite astonishing; so too the finesse. It's steely and pear-like, milky and dry. It has flavour but it slashes its way through the palate and out into tomorrow. Bottle age will make this yet more beautiful. Screwcap. 13% alc. **Rating** 96 **To** 2026 $45 CM ✪
Reserve Yarra Valley Chardonnay 2017 First you notice the power, then the poise, then the persistence. All the ducks are in a row here. White peach, flint, toast, fresh fennel and cedar-wood characters create a seductive weave from the start to the impressively long finish. Screwcap. 13% alc. **Rating** 96 **To** 2028 $60 CM ✪
Deer Farm Vineyard Chardonnay 2017 It's an elegant chardonnay with lactose, stone fruit and spice notes running effortlessly through the mouth, nashi pear flavours bursting through the finish. It's good now; it'll be better in a year or three. Screwcap. 13.5% alc. **Rating** 94 **To** 2026 $45 CM
Yarra Valley Chardonnay 2017 Hard to imagine anyone being disappointed with this. It's a cracking chardonnay, modern in style but full of flavour. It's fleshy, sunny, savoury and picked out with spice. The finish takes care of itself. Peaches, stone, meal and flint. Fabulous. Screwcap. 13.5% alc. **Rating** 94 **To** 2023 $35 CM
Yarra Valley Pinot Noir 2017 Generous, varietal, complex and persistent. This hits the bulls-eye for quality, not to mention impeccable winemaking. The sheets are pulled tight, the flowers arranged just so, the curtains pulled to allow the perfect amount of light – if this wine was a hotel room you'd immediately book again for next year. Macerated cherries, bright red berries, undergrowth, sweet spices; all here, all in good shape, polished to a higher level by a light kiss of cedary oak. Screwcap. 13.5% alc. **Rating** 94 **To** 2026 $35 CM
The Esplanade Yarra Valley Pinot Noir 2017 Surly at this early stage. Macerated (black) cherry and undergrowth; spice and woodsy spices; forest berries and cedar wood. It's not an eager pinot noir – it's a patient one, set to play the long game. The kick of both tannin and flavour through the finish makes it an easy wine to place a bet on. Screwcap. 14% alc. **Rating** 94 **To** 2028 $50 CM

ŸŸŸŸŸ **Pinot Noir Chardonnay 2014 Rating** 93 $35 CM

Collalto   ★★★★

Lot 99, Adelaide-Lobethal Road, Lobethal, SA 5241 **Region** Adelaide Hills
T 0429 611 290 **www**.collalto.com.au **Open** Not
Winemaker Revenir (Peter Leske) **Est.** 2006 **Dozens** 800 **Vyds** 8ha
To say this is a business with a difference is a masterly understatement. It has a real vineyard of 5.5ha of pinot noir and 2.5ha of chardonnay planted in 2001; a real viticulturist (Damon Koerner); and a real winemaker (Peter Leske). Its two owners (who grew up in the Adelaide Hills) are London-based QC James Drake, and Scott Drake, Professor of Architecture in the international program in design and architecture at Chulalongkorn University, Bangkok. Most of the grapes are sold to Petaluma, but they hold back enough to make 1200 dozen or so a year. The name 'Collalto' describes the high vineyard, and is also a tribute to James and Scott's mother Palimira Drake (née Tosolini) whose father came from the village of that name just north of Udine in northeastern Italy. Exports to the UK.

ŸŸŸŸŸ **Pinot Noir 2016** Quintessentially Adelaide Hills in its wood-smoky, varnished sort of way, this is a good pinot. Bing cherry and cedar, too, seep across the bows of gently astringent tannins, flecked with some whole-cluster briar and cardamom. This should expand nicely in the mid-term. Screwcap. 14% alc. **Rating** 92 **To** 2025 $30 NG

Chardonnay 2016 Tight, tangy and energetic, this chardonnay boasts serious intention. Hand-picked at night, the fruit is pristine. The oak, attractive. The wine, redolent of stone fruits and leesy, nutty pick-up. However, the finish is hard and a bit overworked. Screwcap. 13.5% alc. **Rating** 90 **To** 2022 $30 NG

Colmar Estate ★★★★★

790 Pinnacle Road, Orange, NSW 2800 **Region** Orange
T 0419 977 270 **www**.colmarestate.com.au **Open** W'ends & public hols 10.30–5
Winemaker Chris Derrez, Lucy Maddox **Est.** 2013 **Dozens** 2000 **Vyds** 5.9ha
The inspiration behind the name is clear when you find that owners Bill Shrapnel and his wife Jane have long loved the wines of Alsace: Colmar is the main town in that region. The Shrapnels realised a long-held ambition when they purchased the established, high-altitude (980m) vineyard in May 2013. Everything they have done has turned to gold, notably grafting cabernet sauvignon to pinot noir, merlot to chardonnay, and shiraz to pinot gris. The plantings are now 1.51ha of pinot noir (clones 777, 115 and MV6), 1.25ha of chardonnay (clones 95, 96 and P58), 1.24ha of riesling and lesser quantities of sauvignon blanc, pinot gris and traminer.

🍷🍷🍷🍷🍷 **Orange Sauvignon Blanc 2017** There's a pure, unforced quality about this wine. Less is more, in a way. The bouquet and palate offer the requisite gooseberry and citrus aromas and flavours with a touch of tropical fruit and subtle minerality adding dimension, and the acidity, although fine, is persistent and lingering. Beautifully poised all through and a pleasure to drink. Two trophies under its belt so far. Screwcap. 12% alc. **Rating** 95 **To** 2020 $28 SC ✪

Block 2 Orange Chardonnay 2016 This takes the style of the estate release and dials up the depth of fruit, with a bit more oak spiciness. It shares the defining characters of citrus and stone fruit, with the lemon-pith acidity a little more pronounced but completely in balance. Elegant but not underpowered. Gold medal National Cool Climate Wine Show '17. Screwcap. 13% alc. **Rating** 94 **To** 2022 $38 SC

Orange Pinot Rose 2017 Trophy for Best Rose at the Orange Wine Show '17. Continues in the good form shown by previous releases. While essentially dry and savoury in style, the subtle floral and sweet fruit characters soften the edges and add dimension to the bouquet and palate, and the finely tuned astringency adds a mouthwatering quality. Screwcap. 12.5% alc. **Rating** 94 **To** 2020 $28 SC ✪

Block 3 Orange Pinot Noir 2016 There's an extra degree of complexity here. Along with the cherry and other red fruits, there are attractive aromas of stewed rhubarb and sweet Asian spices, and 30% new oak adds a toasty dimension and some spice of its own. There's considerable depth and richness on the palate, although it doesn't sit heavily at all, and the both ripe and savoury flavours always feel restrained (in a positive sense) by quite persistent tannin, which then draws out the finish. Screwcap. 13.5% alc. **Rating** 94 **To** 2023 $45 SC

🍷🍷🍷🍷🍷 **Orange Chardonnay 2016 Rating** 92 **To** 2021 $30 SC
Orange Pinot Noir 2016 Rating 92 $35 SC

Colvin Wines ★★★★

19 Boyle Street, Mosman, NSW 2088 (postal) **Region** Hunter Valley
T (02) 9908 7886 **www**.colvinwines.com.au **Open** Not
Winemaker Andrew Spinaze, Mark Richardson **Est.** 1999 **Dozens** 500 **Vyds** 5.2ha
In 1990 Sydney lawyer John Colvin and wife Robyn purchased the De Beyers Vineyard, which has a history going back to the second half of the 19th century. By 1967, when a syndicate bought 35ha of the original vineyard site, no vines remained. The syndicate planted semillon on the alluvial soil of the creek flats and shiraz on the red clay hillsides. Up to '98 all the grapes were sold to Tyrrell's, but since '99 quantities have been made for the Colvin Wines

label. These include sangiovese, from a little over 1ha of vines planted by John in '96 because of his love of the wines of Tuscany.

ȲȲȲȲȲ **De Beyers Vineyard Semillon 2016** With all its varietal flavours of lime zest, lemon curd and lemongrass, and some bees wax too, this is bound to please. It will also reward the patient. Screwcap. 11% alc. **Rating** 92 **To** 2026 $35 JF
De Beyers Vineyard Chardonnay 2015 A mere 20 dozen produced and in a way, it's a chardonnay of yore – the rich stone fruit and buttery flavours, the sweet and spicy oak. Yet, it all works. There's tension and reviving acidity at play. Screwcap. 12.5% alc. **Rating** 92 **To** 2023 $65 JF

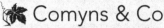 # Comyns & Co

Hermitage Road, Pokolbin, NSW 2320 **Region** Hunter Valley
T 0400 888 966 **www**.comynsandco.com.au **Open** Not
Winemaker Scott Comyns **Est.** 2015 **Dozens** 2000
The stars came into alignment for Scotty Comyns in 2018. Having left Pepper Tree Wines in a state of glory at the end of 2015, he went out on his own establishing Comyns & Co, with nothing other than his experience as a winemaker in the Hunter Valley to sustain him. Then Andrew Thomas found his first permanent home in the region, and Scotty joined him as a full-time winemaker, leaving Comyns & Co as a side activity. He says, 'With no cellar door, winery or vineyard, and a day job with Thommo, my nights and weekends are just about all tied up with wine festivals, pop-up tastings and knocking on doors.' A cellar door of his own is in planning; to get to his wines you have to go through the online cellar door and wine club.

ȲȲȲȲȲ **Single Vineyard Casuarina Hunter Valley Semillon 2017** Right in the heartland of Hunter Valley semillon style, with unsweetened lemon, lemongrass and sharp-edged acidity. Has all the makings if you wait 4–5 years before cracking the cap. Screwcap. 11% alc. **Rating** 94 **To** 2029 $28 ❂
Black Cluster Hunter Valley Shiraz 2016 Not the easiest of Hunter Valley vintages, but as Scott Comyns shows with this wine, if you kept in control of disease in the vineyard, shiraz with good varietal character could be made. And, as always, this speaks of its region. Screwcap. 13.5% alc. **Rating** 94 **To** 2031 $35

ȲȲȲȲȲ **Single Vineyard Hunter Valley Fiano 2017** **Rating** 93 **To** 2023 $28
Mr Red Hunter Valley Blend 2016 **Rating** 91 **To** 2029 $35
Mrs White Hunter Valley Blend 2017 **Rating** 90 **To** 2023 $28
Hunter Valley Rose 2017 **Rating** 90 **To** 2019 $28
Hunter Valley Tempranillo 2016 **Rating** 90 **To** 2021 $35

 # Contentious Character ★★★★

810 Norton Road, Wamboin, NSW 2620 **Region** Canberra District
T 0403 189 266 **www**.contentiouscharacter.com.au **Open** W'ends 10–5
Winemaker Jeremy Wilson **Est.** 2016 **Dozens** NFP **Vyds** 10ha
Contentious Character brings together Jeremy Wilson (chief winemaker), Ben Jarrett (sales and viticulture), Ross Appleton (operations, finance and viticulture) and Tony Mansfield (brand, marketing and sales). I'm not entirely clear who is the contentious character, but so be it. There are a number of other close friends/relatives who have fringe involvements in the business. It's based on 10ha of chardonnay, riesling, pinot noir, shiraz, pinot gris, merlot and cabernet sauvignon, all of which were planted in 1998, almost a decade before Contentious Character purchased the property (then known as Lambert Vineyards). They have tended the grounds, overhauled the kitchen, given the restaurant a facelift and fired up the pizza oven for the weekends when Contentious Character is open. Whether the name maybe too esoteric is something that only time will tell, but the quality of the wines is certainly not going to cause any problems: they are all very well made.

ȲȲȲȲȲ **Come the Raw Prawn Canberra District Riesling 2017** There's nothing contentious about this wine, with its regional imprint of Meyer lemon, lime, apple peel and crunchy acidity. Screwcap. 10.5% alc. **Rating** 94 **To** 2027

ŢŢŢŢŢ Empty Vessels Make the Most Noise Chardonnay 2016 Rating 93
To 2021 $35
Shiraz 2016 Rating 93 To 2025
Born to Make Taste Buds Bloom Pinot Gris 2016 Rating 90 To 2019 $35

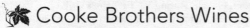 Cooke Brothers Wines ★★★★

PO Box 23, Verdun, SA 5242 **Region** Adelaide Hills
T 0409 170 684 **www.**cookebrotherswines.com.au **Open** Not
Winemaker Ben Cooke **Est.** 2016 **Dozens** 300
This is the venture of three brothers, eldest to youngest: Simon, Jason and Ben. Ben is the partner of Charlotte Hardy, winemaker/owner of Charlotte Dalton Wines, together parents of a 10-month-old daughter (as at March 2018). Ben has had a long career in wine – seven years' retail for Booze Brothers while at university the first time around; two vintages at Langhorne Creek '00–01; and full-time cellar hand/assistant winemaker at Shaw + Smith '03–12 while undertaking two degrees externally (wine science and viticulture) at CSU from '04–11. If this were not enough, he had three northern Californian vintages at the iconic Williams Selyem winery in '08, '12 and '13. He is now a full-time viticulturist with a vineyard management contracting company that he founded in '12. The elder brothers are not actively involved in the business.

ŢŢŢŢŢ Schoenthal Vineyard Adelaide Hills Chardonnay 2017 Altogether elegant,
its perfect balance evident through every facet of the wine. The fruit flavours are poised between citrus and stone fruit, alcohol pleasingly low, the acidity soft but sufficient (no mlf?), and the new oak absorbed by the fruit. Screwcap. 12.5% alc.
Rating 94 To 2025

ŢŢŢŢŢ Broderick Vineyard Adelaide Hills Cabernet Sauvignon 2016 Rating 90

Cooks Lot ★★★★★

Ferment, 87 Hill Street, Orange, NSW 2800 **Region** Orange
T (02) 9550 3228 **www.**cookslot.com.au **Open** Tues–Sat 11–5
Winemaker Duncan Cook **Est.** 2002 **Dozens** 4000
Duncan Cook began making wines for his eponymous brand in 2002 while undertaking his oenology degree at CSU. He completed this in '10 and now works with a number of small growers. Orange is unique in that it literally has multiple site climates at various altitudes, and fruit is sourced from vineyards at altitudes that are best suited for the varietal and wine styles. Exports to China.

ŢŢŢŢŢ Allotment 8 Handpicked Orange Shiraz 2015 This is one special shiraz.
It's exuberant with the fruit bursting onto the palate, all cherries and raspberries, plenty of spice and pepper, with just the right cedary oak notes. It maintains a medium-bodied structure matched to velvety tannins, some tension, and super bright acidity. Wow. Just wow. Screwcap. 13.5% alc. **Rating** 96 To 2027 $35 JF **✪**
Allotment 1010 Orange Shiraz 2016 Sometimes a wine just hits the spot, as this does. Heady aromas of dark fruits with a shelf of spices from licorice and pepper to cinnamon plus charry oak, not too much though. Medium-bodied (just), textured tannins with some grip on the finish, ultra-fresh and gorgeous to drink. And all that joy for $23. Screwcap. 14% alc. **Rating** 95 To 2023 JF **✪**

ŢŢŢŢŢ Allotment 666 Pinot Gris 2017 Rating 93 To 2019 $23 JF **✪**
Allotment 1111 Pinot Noir 2016 Rating 92 To 2021 $23 JF **✪**
Allotment 8989 Cabernet Merlot 2016 Rating 92 To 2025 $23 JF **✪**
Allotment 333 Riesling 2017 Rating 91 To 2023 $23 JF **✪**
Allotment 3 Chardonnay 2015 Rating 91 To 2022 $35 JF

Coola Road ★★★★

Private Mail Bag 14, Mount Gambier, SA 5291 **Region** Mount Gambier
T 0487 700 422 **www**.coolaroad.com **Open** Not
Winemaker John Innes, Peter Douglas, Sue Bell **Est.** 2013 **Dozens** 1000 **Vyds** 103.5ha
Thomas and Sally Ellis are the current generation of the Ellis family, who has owned the
Coola grazing property on which the vineyard is now established for over 160 years. They
began planting pinot noir in the late 1990s and have since extended to include sauvignon
blanc, chardonnay, riesling and pinot gris. As the largest vineyard owner in the region, they
decided they should have some of the grapes vinified to bring further recognition to the area.
If global warming should increase significantly, the very cool region will stand to gain.

PPPP **Single Vineyard Riesling 2017** A super intense riesling, fermented dry, but
only 11% alc. It's still quartz-white, the palate with a lemon–sherbet blast of power.
Whatever else, this wine needs a bare minimum of 5 years, more probably 10.
Given its price, finding room to lay down a dozen bottles and embark on a long
journey of discovery shouldn't be a problem. It could be the bargain of a lifetime.
Screwcap. **Rating** 91 **To** 2023 $20 ✪
Single Vineyard Sauvignon Blanc 2017 Intensely flavoured, although not as
assertive as the Riesling. That said, its cut grass and herb aromas and sour lemon
fruit flavours are very unusual, albeit not the least unpleasant, and perfect for fish
and chips. Screwcap. 11% alc. **Rating** 90 **To** 2022 $20 ✪
Single Vineyard Chardonnay 2015 There's a wealth of intensity and no
shortage of complexity here. Needless to say the very cool climate shapes the
flavours along an unsweetened citrus path marked by a strongly mineral mouthfeel.
Screwcap. 12.8% alc. **Rating** 90 **To** 2023 $22

Coolangatta Estate ★★★★★

1335 Bolong Road, Shoalhaven Heads, NSW 2535 **Region** Shoalhaven Coast
T (02) 4448 7131 **www**.coolangattaestate.com.au **Open** 7 days 10–5
Winemaker Tyrrell's **Est.** 1988 **Dozens** 5000 **Vyds** 10.5ha
Coolangatta Estate is part of a 150ha resort with accommodation, restaurants, golf course,
etc. Some of the oldest buildings were convict-built in 1822. The standard of viticulture is
exceptionally high (immaculate Scott Henry trellising), and the contract winemaking
is wholly professional. Coolangatta has a habit of bobbing up with medals at Sydney and
Canberra wine shows, including gold medals for its mature semillons. In its own backyard,
Coolangatta won the trophy for Best Wine of Show at the South Coast Wine Show for 17 out
of the show's 18 years.

PPPPP **Aged Release Estate Grown Semillon 2009** In remarkable form. Fully
mature and awash with developed character, but it remains talkative and indeed
vibrant. Toast, lanolin, lemongrass and citrus characters slip deliciously through the
palate. Screwcap. 11% alc. **Rating** 95 **To** 2020 $45 CM

PPPP **Estate Grown Semillon 2017** **Rating** 93 **To** 2023 $25 CM ✪
Wollstonecraft Semillon 2017 **Rating** 91 **To** 2022 $25 CM

Coombe Farm ★★★★

673–675 Maroondah Highway, Coldstream, Vic 3770 **Region** Yarra Valley
T (03) 9739 0173 **www**.coombeyarravalley.com.au **Open** 7 days 10–5
Winemaker Nicole Esdaile **Est.** 1999 **Dozens** 7000 **Vyds** 60ha
Once the Australian home of world-famous opera singer Dame Nellie Melba, the Melba
Estate is now also the home of Coombe Farm. The renovated motor house and stable block
of the estate now house the cellar door as well as a providore, gallery and restaurant that
overlooks the gardens. Tours of the gardens are also available. In the absence of a representative
range of wines, the 2018 winery rating has been retained. Exports to the UK and Japan.

ŶŶŶŶ **Blanc de Blancs NV** Aged on lees for 12 months. It serves apple, grapefruit and dry pear flavours in crisp, simple form, the emphasis more on refreshment than on power or 'seriousness'. A dry, lively wine with just enough dosage to make it appealing to all-comers. Diam. 12.5% alc. **Rating** 89 $30 CM

Cooper Burns   ★★★★

494 Research Road, Nuriootpa, SA 5355 **Region** Barossa Valley
T (08) 7513 7606 **www**.cooperburns.com.au **Open** By appt
Winemaker Russell Burns **Est.** 2004 **Dozens** 3000
Cooper Burns is the winemaking partnership of Mark Cooper and Russell Burns. It is a virtual winery focusing on small batch, handmade wine from the Eden Valley and the northern end of the Barossa Valley. Production has been increased to add a riesling and grenache to the shirazs. Exports to the US and Hong Kong.

ŶŶŶŶŶ **GSM Barossa Grenache Shiraz Mourvedre 2014** A rich, voluptuous blend aged for 18 months in seasoned French oak. A tsunami of flavour from plum, cherry cola, star anise and green walnuts to earth and ferrous notes. Full-bodied and with a smooth palate thanks to swathes of fleshy ripe tannins. Screwcap. 14% alc. **Rating** 94 To 2027 $25 JF

ŶŶŶŶŶ **Barossa Valley Shiraz 2014** Rating 93 To 2028 $40 JF

Cooter & Cooter   ★★★★

82 Almond Grove Road, Whites Valley, SA 5172 **Region** McLaren Vale
T 0438 766 178 **www**.cooter.com.au **Open** Not
Winemaker James Cooter, Kimberly Cooter **Est.** 2012 **Dozens** 1800 **Vyds** 23ha
The cursive script on the Cooter & Cooter wine labels was that of various Cooter family businesses operating in SA since 1847. James comes from a family with a modern history of more than 20 years in the wine industry. Kimberley is also a hands-on winemaker, having spent her early years with father Walter Clappis, a veteran McLaren Vale winemaker. Their vineyard is on the southern slopes of Whites Valley and has 18ha of shiraz and 3ha of cabernet sauvignon planted in 1996, and 2ha of old vine grenache planted in the '50s. They also buy Clare Valley grapes to make riesling.

ŶŶŶŶŶ **Watervale Riesling 2017** Quartz-green. Ripe lemon, wet stone and talc morphing into custard apple with yeasty complexity. There's both generosity of flavour and saline texture, and a citric acidity on the finish maintaining the line and length of the wine. Clare Valley all over, and very good value. Screwcap. 12% alc. **Rating** 94 To 2024 $22 DB ✪

ŶŶŶŶŶ **McLaren Vale Shiraz 2016** Rating 93 To 2025 $22 DB
Adelaide Hills Pinot Noir 2017 Rating 92 To 2023 $30 DB

Coppabella of Tumbarumba   ★★★★☆

424 Tumbarumba Road, Tumbarumba, NSW 2653 (postal) **Region** Tumbarumba
T (02) 6382 7997 **www**.coppabella.com.au **Open** Not
Winemaker Jason Brown **Est.** 2011 **Dozens** 4000 **Vyds** 71.9ha
Coppabella is owned by Jason and Alecia Brown, owners of the highly successful Moppity Vineyards in Hilltops. They became aware of the quality of Tumbarumba chardonnay and pinot noir, in particular the quality of the grapes from the 71ha Coppabella vineyard, when purchasing grapes for the Moppity business. This was the second vineyard established (in 1993) by the region's founder, Ian Cowell, but frost and other problems led him to lease the vineyard to Southcorp, an arrangement that continued until 2007. The reversion of the management of the vineyard coincided with several failed vintages, and this precipitated a decision by the owner to close the vineyard and remove the vines. In October '11, at the last moment, the Browns purchased the vineyard and have since invested heavily in it, rehabilitating the vines and grafting a number of blocks with earlier-ripening Dijon clones of pinot noir and chardonnay. Coppabella is run as an entirely separate venture from Moppity.

ΨΨΨΨΨ The Crest Single Vineyard Pinot Noir 2016 777, MV6 and D5V12 clones, matured for 12 months in French barriques. Light, clear colour, holding onto some crimson-purple tones; distinctly but pleasantly savoury, with the whole-bunch inclusion working well. The flavours span red, blue and purple fruits, neither tannins nor oak stepping out of line. In the mainstream, and none the worse for that. Screwcap. 13.5% alc. **Rating** 95 **To** 2024 $35 **۞**

ΨΨΨΨΨ Sirius Single Vineyard Pinot Noir 2016 **Rating** 93 **To** 2021 $60
Single Vineyard Pinot Rose 2017 **Rating** 92 **To** 2020 $26
Single Vineyard Chardonnay 2016 **Rating** 91 **To** 2024 $26
Cuvee Prestige 5 Years Pinot Noir Chardonnay NV **Rating** 90 $60

Corduroy ★★★★

15 Bridge Terrace, Victor Harbour, SA 5211 (postal) **Region** Adelaide Hills
T 0405 123 272 **www.**corduroywines.com.au **Open** Not
Winemaker Phillip LeMessurier **Est.** 2009 **Dozens** 320
Phillip and Eliza LeMessurier have moved to the Adelaide Hills, but are continuing the model they originally created in the Hunter under the tutelage of Andrew Thomas at Thomas Wines. In the new environment, they are matching place and variety to good effect.

ΨΨΨΨΨ Pedro's Paddock Adelaide Hills Pinot Noir 2017 Hand-picked, MV6, 70% whole berries, 30% whole-bunch pressed, open-fermented, 10 months in used French oak. Identical vinification to the Single Vineyard, but from that point on markedly different, having the intensity and drive missing from its sibling. It's distinctly savoury, and has tangy wild-strawberry flavours and ample spices that will increase as the wine ages. Screwcap. 12.5% alc. **Rating** 94 **To** 2027 $48
The Wale Adelaide Hills Shiraz 2016 Power and intensity are undiminished, but there is a distinct spike of brightness before the powerful savoury fruits seek (but don't succeed) to close it. I'm far from sure that I understand this wine. Screwcap. 13.7% alc. **Rating** 94 **To** 2039 $78

ΨΨΨΨΨ Single Vineyard Adelaide Hills Shiraz 2016 **Rating** 93 **To** 2036 $34
Single Vineyard Adelaide Hills Pinot Noir 2017 **Rating** 91 **To** 2025 $28

Coriole ★★★★★

Chaffeys Road, McLaren Vale, SA 5171 **Region** McLaren Vale
T (08) 8323 8305 **www.**coriole.com **Open** Mon–Fri 10–5, w'ends & public hols 11–5
Winemaker Alex Sherrah **Est.** 1967 **Dozens** 32 000 **Vyds** 48.5ha
While Coriole was not established until 1967, history here goes back to 1860, when the original farmhouses that now constitute the cellar door were built. The oldest shiraz forming part of the estate plantings dates back to 1917, and since '85, Coriole has been an Australian pioneer of sangiovese and the Italian white variety fiano. More recently it has planted picpoul, adding to grenache blanc, negro amaro, sagrantino, montepulciano and prosecco. Exports to all major markets.

ΨΨΨΨΨ Lloyd Reserve McLaren Vale Shiraz 2015 The swagger and the silk. This marries an exaggerated volume of inky, berried flavour with the surest, softest touch, the end result guaranteed to both seduce and satisfy. This is shiraz to the power of ten, and yet for all its sweetness and wealth it never really feels overdone. Such is class. Screwcap. 14.5% alc. **Rating** 96 **To** 2040 $100 CM
Mary Kathleen McLaren Vale Cabernet Merlot 2015 Much could be said about McLaren Vale and its ability or otherwise to get cabernet right, but when you taste a wine like this the babble quickly fades and the marvel settles in. Everything is in the right place here, its form high, its flavour and flow impressive in an effortless way. This will mature gracefully for pretty much as long as you choose. Screwcap. 14% alc. **Rating** 96 **To** 2035 $65 CM **۞**
McLaren Vale Picpoul 2017 Tight, searing and long. An enthusiast's wine if ever there was one. Red and green apples, seaspray and citrus. It darts through the

mouth like it's on a mission. Its acid-driven length comes laden with perfumed flavour. Phenolic grip to the finish almost rubs your nose in its individuality. Well worth hunting a bottle down just for the experience of it. Screwcap. 11.8% alc. Rating 95 To 2022 $25 CM ✪

Estate McLaren Vale Shiraz 2016 Most of the estate shiraz vines are now 50yo, with some 100yo vines also employed here. This is a silken release, fresh as a daisy too, with plum, cassis and redcurrant flavours lifted by notes of violet. A gentle creaminess to the texture doesn't hurt a jot. When you reach for a bottle of McLaren Vale shiraz, you're hoping it tastes like this. Screwcap. 14.5% alc. Rating 95 To 2032 $32 CM ✪

The Soloist McLaren Vale Shiraz 2016 If a wine's going to show a lot of oak, then make it gorgeous oak. That's the case here. This is a slinky-smooth shiraz, splashed with vanilla cream and smoked cedar wood but blessed with pure, ripe, plum-shot fruit flavour too. It's as polished as it is powerful. It will make many red wine drinkers swoon. Screwcap. 14.5% alc. Rating 95 To 2032 $45 CM

McLaren Vale Sangiovese 2016 Straight into excellent territory. Bright, powerful, juicy and structured. It serves up savoury-accented fruit at its drinkable best, but builds strong scaffolding around it. You have to marvel at the price. This is a compelling offering. Screwcap. 14.4% alc. Rating 95 To 2025 $27 CM ✪

Sparta McLaren Vale Shiraz 2016 It barely sees any new oak but it still feels polished and perfect, its flavours of blackberry, peppercorn and plum sweeping irresistibly through the palate. Tannin is deceptive; it's assertive but buried in the dark lusciousness of the fruit. This is a prime candidate to be bought in volume. Screwcap. 14.5% alc. Rating 94 To 2028 $25 CM ✪

Estate McLaren Vale Cabernet Sauvignon 2016 Strength of purpose, strength of character. Cabernet flexes its muscle here. It's brimful of blackcurrant, peppercorn and bay leaf–like flavour, but it's the combination of strong, ripe fruit and the tumbling surf of tannin that really makes you sit up and take notice. Screwcap. 14.5% alc. Rating 94 To 2032 $32 CM

🍷🍷🍷🍷🍷 **McLaren Vale Fiano 2017** Rating 93 To 2022 $27 CM ✪
Windmill Hill McLaren Vale Shiraz 2016 Rating 93 To 2036 $60 CM
Dancing Fig McLaren Vale Mourvedre Grenache Shiraz 2016 Rating 93 To 2026 $25 CM ✪
McLaren Vale Sangiovese Shiraz 2016 Rating 93 To 2023 $20 CM ✪
McLaren Vale Montepulciano 2016 Rating 93 To 2023 $27 CM ✪
Redstone McLaren Vale Shiraz 2016 Rating 92 To 2024 $20 CM ✪
McLaren Vale Nero 2017 Rating 92 To 2022 $25 CM ✪
Songbird McLaren Vale Cabernet Sauvignon 2016 Rating 91 To 2026 $20 CM ✪
McLaren Vale Barbera 2016 Rating 90 To 2021 $25 CM

Cosmo Wines   ★★★★

187 Victoria Road, Chirnside Park, Vic 3116 **Region** Yarra Valley
T 0408 519 461 **www**.cosmowines.com.au **Open** W'ends 11–5, Mon–Fri by appt
Winemaker Lindsay Corby **Est.** 2008 **Dozens** 3000 **Vyds** 2.25ha
Cosmo wines are made at Bianchet Winery, which was established many years ago, but Lou Bianchet passed away without leaving sufficient records, meaning that the planning and liquor licensing approval were required to re-establish the property detail. Three years' work resulted in the creation of a new business structure. Winemaker Lindsay Corby brings an impressive CV, including laboratory work, cellar door sales and vineyard management, leading in turn to teaching 'the art and science of the vine and wine' at La Trobe University and managing the small campus vineyard. An arrangement with the new owners of Bianchet has been finalised, with Lindsay leasing the winery and vineyard, and opening the Cosmo Wines cellar door. Bianchet Bistro (onsite) is a separate business that sells some of the Cosmo wines as part of their wine list. Exports to China.

ŸŸŸŸ♀ **Heathcote Shiraz 2014** A luscious wine with ripe blackberry fruitcake wrapped in dark chocolate ex new French oak. A striking wine with broad-based appeal. Screwcap. 13.5% alc. **Rating** 91 **To** 2034 $30

Estate Cabernet Sauvignon Merlot Cabernet Franc 2015 Lindsay Corby doesn't shrink from using the full doctor's bag of treatments during fermentation. The wine is still very youthful, and the purple and black fruits need time, notwithstanding the beneficial impact of crossflow filtration (used by Lindsay for all his wines), the best method of eliminating unwanted elements. Screwcap. 14% alc. **Rating** 91 **To** 2030 $30

Estate Verduzzo 2016 The vines were planted the day Bianchet was established in '76. I'm not sure about the retention of the pressings in the ferment given its baume of 13.9° and pH of 3.77 – it needed at least 1g/l of tartaric acid added during the ferment. Still, a very interesting wine. Screwcap. 14.4% alc. **Rating** 90 **To** 2021 $30

ŸŸŸŸ **Yarra Valley Cabernet Sauvignon 2014 Rating** 88 **To** 2029 $35

Costanzo & Sons

602 Tames Road, Strathbogie, Vic 3666 **Region** Strathbogie Ranges
T 0447 740 055 **www**.costanzo.com.au **Open** By appt
Winemaker Ray Nadeson (Contract) **Est.** 2011 **Dozens** 500 **Vyds** 6ha
This is the venture of Joe Costanzo and Cindy Heath, Joe with grapegrowing in his DNA. He was raised on his parents' 20ha vineyard on the Murray River in NSW, the family business selling grapes to Brown Brothers, Seppelt, Bullers and Miranda Wines. By the age of 17 he had decided to follow in their footsteps, working full-time in vineyards, and studying viticulture for five years. He and Cindy searched for the perfect vineyard, and in 2011 finally acquired one that had been planted between 1993 and '94 to 1.5ha each of sauvignon blanc and chardonnay and 3ha of pinot noir.

ŸŸŸŸŸ **Single Vineyard Reserve Strathbogie Ranges Pinot Noir 2015** Hand-picked, 21yo vines (MV6 and D5V12), destemmed, wild-fermented, matured in French oak (35% new) for 12 months. Good retention of crimson-purple hue; a very well made pinot taking full advantage of the excellent vintage. It combines dark cherry plum varietal fruit with a fresh, long, elegant mouthfeel and aftertaste. Surprise packet. Screwcap. 13.5% alc. **Rating** 95 **To** 2025 $50

ŸŸŸŸ♀ **Kinship Chardonnay 2016 Rating** 91 **To** 2020 $50

Coulter Wines

6 Third Avenue, Tanunda, SA 5352 (postal) **Region** Adelaide Hills
T 0448 741 773 **www**.coulterwines.com **Open** Not
Winemaker Chris Coulter **Est.** 2015 **Dozens** 450
Chris Coulter had a 22-year previous life as a chef, but fell in love with wine in the early 1990s, and managed to fit in a vintage at Coldstream Hills as a cellar rat. From 2007 he undertook a winemaking degree, and secured work with Australian Vintage Limited, gaining large-volume winemaking experience in Mildura and at the then Chateau Yaldara in the Barossa Valley. He remained at Yaldara through 2014 under Australian Vintage Limited, and thereafter as part of the 1847 winemaking team after its acquisition of the site. Coulter Wines was born in the 2015 vintage as a side project, making wines from another universe – adding nothing other than SO$_2$, movements by gravity, and the wine unfiltered where practicable. He purchases and hand-picks grapes from premium vineyards in the Adelaide Hills (chardonnay, sangiovese and barbera). Exports to Singapore.

ŸŸŸŸŸ **C2 Sangiovese 2017** Nails it. The flavours flow freely from the outset, but just when you think they're about to stop – they get a second wind. Their spread through the finish is really quite something. Cherries, plums, dry spice and earth. It takes complexity in its stride and makes (high) quality look easy. An outstanding wine. Screwcap. 13.5% alc. **Rating** 95 **To** 2024 $30 CM ✪

C1 Chardonnay 2017 Sure-bet chardonnay. As delicious as it is persistent. Pear, peach and grapefruit, a touch of smoky oak, a creaminess to the mouthfeel. It looks ready to drink now, but time won't be unkind. Screwcap. 12.5% alc. Rating 94 To 2023 $30 CM ❍

❦❦❦❦❦ C3 Pinot Noir 2017 Rating 93 To 2024 $30 CM
C4 Experimental Mourvedre 2017 Rating 93 To 2024 $30 CM
C5 Barbera 2017 Rating 90 To 2021 $30 CM

Coward & Black Vineyards ★★★★☆

448 Tom Cullity Drive, Wilyabrup, WA 6280 **Region** Margaret River
T (08) 9755 6355 **www**.cowardandblack.com.au **Open** 7 days 9–5
Winemaker Clive Otto (Contract) **Est.** 1998 **Dozens** 1325 **Vyds** 9.5ha
Patrick Coward and Martin Black have been friends since they were five years old. They acquired a property directly opposite Ashbrook and on the same road as Vasse Felix, and began the slow establishment of a dry-grown vineyard; a second block followed five years later. In all there are 2.5ha each of cabernet sauvignon and shiraz, and 1.5ha each of chardonnay, semillon and sauvignon blanc. The cellar door is integrated with another of their businesses, the Margaret River Providore, which sells produce from their organic garden and olive grove.

❦❦❦❦❦ The Black Prince Cabernet Sauvignon 2014 A distinguished medium-bodied cabernet that fully deserved its gold medal at the James Halliday Cabernet Challenge '16, its silver medal at the Decanter World Awards '17 and its gold medal at the Margaret River Wine Show '16. It is elegant and fresh and has pure cassis/blackcurrant fruit, with nigh-on perfect cabernet tannins – there but not obstreperous – and integrated oak. Screwcap. 14.1% alc. Rating 96 To 2034 $27 ❍
Chardonnay 2017 So fluid and accessible it's worthy of the word 'mellifluous'. Juicy pear and peach flavours draw you straight in, flashes of cedar wood and oak-spice helping to keep you there. Tasty, tangy and well finished; not a foot wrong here. Screwcap. 12.7% alc. Rating 94 To 2024 $35 CM

❦❦❦❦❦ The Black Prince Cabernet Sauvignon 2016 Rating 93 To 2034 $35 CM

Crabtree Watervale Wines ★★★★☆

North Terrace, Watervale, SA 5452 **Region** Clare Valley
T (08) 8843 0069 **www**.crabtreewines.com.au **Open** 7 days 10.30–4.30
Winemaker Kerri Thompson **Est.** 1984 **Dozens** 6000 **Vyds** 13.2ha
Crabtree is situated in the heart of the historic and iconic Watervale district, the tasting room and courtyard (set in the produce cellar of the original 1850s homestead) looking out over the estate vineyard. The winery was founded in 1984 by Robert Crabtree, who built a considerable reputation for medal-winning riesling, shiraz and cabernet sauvignon. In 2007 it was purchased by an independent group of wine enthusiasts, and the winery firmly continues in the tradition of estate-grown premium wines. Robert remains a shareholder.

❦❦❦❦❦ Riesling 2017 The floral bouquet of lime and apple blossom introduces a lively, expressive palate, the finish long, crisp and fresh. A long-term future is assured, but there is no reason to eschew cracking the cap right now. Screwcap. 12.4% alc. Rating 95 To 2030 $28 ❍
Hilltop Riesling 2017 A fragrant bouquet with fruit-spice nuances and a lively lemon-zest palate. Has the high quality acidity of the vintage, and all the parts hang together well. Screwcap. 12.8% alc. Rating 94 To 2027 $22 ❍

❦❦❦❦❦ Shiraz 2016 Rating 92 To 2031 $25 ❍

cradle of hills   ★★★★☆

76 Rogers Road, Sellicks Hill, SA 5174 **Region** McLaren Vale
T (08) 8557 4023 **www**.cradle-of-hills.com.au **Open** By appt
Winemaker Paul Smith **Est.** 2009 **Dozens** 800 **Vyds** 6.88ha

Paul Smith's introduction to wine was an unlikely one: the Royal Australian Navy, and in particular the wardroom cellar at the tender age of 19. A career change took Paul to the world of high-performance sports, and he met his horticulturist wife Tracy. From 2005 they travelled the world with their two children, spending a couple of years in Europe, working in and learning about the great wine regions, and about how fine wine is made. Paul secured a winemaking diploma, and they now have almost 7ha of cabernet sauvignon and shiraz (roughly 50% each), supplementing this with purchased grenache and mourvedre.

 Darkside McLaren Vale Shiraz Mourvedre 2014 Good colour; tells a tale of savoury dark fruits, blackberry and blood plum ex the shiraz, and moody/earthy/briary notes ex the mourvedre. Bitter dark chocolate (70% cacao) is the glue binding the flavours. This is an intriguing wine that may turn out to be something quite special down the track. P.S. the influence of 5% grenache is minimal. Screwcap. 14% alc. **Rating** 95 **To** 2029 $29 ○
Maritime McLaren Vale Cabernet Shiraz 2014 Excellent hue for age; an interesting wine, it has a racy, spicy freshness that could have led me to the Adelaide Hills if the wine was served blind. The 60% cabernet has left a very delicate tannin footprint, further food for thought. What to make of all this? A truly delicious wine to be enjoyed whenever you feel like it. Screwcap. 14% alc. **Rating** 94 **To** 2025 $29 ○

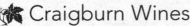 **Old Rogues Shiraz Grenache 2016 Rating** 93 **To** 2027 $25 ○
Route du Bonheur Grenache 2016 Rating 93 **To** 2026 $25 ○
Wild Child Adelaide Hills Chardonnay 2016 Rating 92 **To** 2022 $25 ○
Old Rogue Sellicks Hill Shiraz 2016 Rating 91 **To** 2029 $25

Cragg Cru Wines   ★★★★

Unit 4, 2 Whinnerah Avenue, Aldinga Beach, SA 5173 (postal) **Region** McLaren Vale
T 0432 734 574 **www**.craggcruwines.com.au **Open** Not
Winemaker Robert Cragg **Est.** 2015 **Dozens** 325

Robert Cragg was first involved in the periphery of the wine industry in 2005, when he had the task of pruning and grafting grapevines on his family property, making his first wine from those vines. He moved on to be a cellar hand at Southern Highlands Wines in Moss Vale, later appointed assistant winemaker, but almost immediately moving to the Hunter Valley in '12, where he became familiar with organic winemaking techniques. After two years he was offered a job in McLaren Vale, where he works full-time, but in spare hours and days established this business together with partner Jessica Ward. Exports to Hong Kong.

McLaren Vale Grenache Shiraz Touriga 2017 A 65/25/10% blend, whole berries, open-fermented separately, extended post-ferment maceration, matured for 6 months in used oak (66% French, 34% American), 88 dozen made. This has the goods. Red and blue fruit flavours have a fine savoury overcast, juicy berry sweetness at their hearts. Screwcap. 14.8% alc. **Rating** 95 **To** 2025 $25 ○

Single Vineyard McLaren Vale Grenache 2017 Rating 89 **To** 2022 $25

Craigburn Wines   ★★★

26 Coromandel Parade, Blackwood, SA 5051 **Region** McLaren Vale
T (08) 8125 5847 **www**.craigburnwines.com.au **Open** By appt
Winemaker Dean Compton, Tim Geddes **Est.** 2004 **Dozens** 40 000 **Vyds** 48ha

This business was founded in 2004 specifically for the purpose of developing exports to China and elsewhere in the Asia region. With Mandarin-speaking members of the business, it has enjoyed substantial success, building production to over 40 000 cases, and acquiring 48ha of vineyard. The style and quality of the wines is obviously acceptable to consumers in Asia. Exports to Thailand, Vietnam, Japan, Hong Kong and China.

Craiglee ★★★★★

Sunbury Road, Sunbury, Vic 3429 **Region** Sunbury
T (03) 9744 4489 **www**.craiglee.com.au **Open** Sun & public hols 10–5
Winemaker Patrick Carmody **Est.** 1976 **Dozens** 2500 **Vyds** 9.5ha
A winery with a proud 19th-century history, Craiglee recommenced winemaking in 1976 after a prolonged hiatus. It produces one of the finest cool-climate shirazs in Australia, redolent of cherry, licorice and spice in the better (warmer) vintages, lighter-bodied in the cooler ones. Mature vines and improved viticulture have generally made the wines more consistent over the past 10 years or so. Exports to the UK, the US, Italy, Hong Kong and China. No wines were received for this edition.

Craigow ★★★★

528 Richmond Road, Cambridge, Tas 7170 **Region** Southern Tasmania
T 0418 126 027 **www**.craigow.com.au **Open** 7 days Christmas–Easter
Winemaker Frogmore Creek (Alain Rousseau) **Est.** 1989 **Dozens** 800 **Vyds** 8.75ha
Hobart surgeon Barry Edwards and wife Cathy have moved from being grapegrowers with only one wine to having a portfolio of impressive wines, their long-lived Riesling of particular quality, closely attended by pinot noir. They continue to sell most of their grapes.

ＹＹＹＹＹ **Riesling 2017** Lime dressed with florals, slate etched with spice. It's exotic, it's tasty, it carries well through the finish and it simply makes you want to keep reaching for more. Screwcap. 13.4% alc. **Rating** 93 **To** 2026 $32 CM
Chardonnay 2017 Lit up with pink grapefruit, citrus and stone-fruit flavour. It's not out-and-out intense, but it's well powered and finished and should mature well over the medium term, too. Screwcap. 13% alc. **Rating** 93 **To** 2024 $34 CM
Sauvignon Blanc 2017 Simple tropical-fruit flavours come spruced with Turkish delight and musk. There's a smidgen of oak here and it's done the trick both to the wine's texture and to the interest-factor. Screwcap. 13.2% alc. **Rating** 91 **To** 2020 $26 CM
Pinot Noir 2016 It's a light, fluid, spicy, water-based rendition of the variety. Florals and woodsy spices are as important to the overall 'look' as overt ripe fruit. A touch more sunshine would have done wonders. Screwcap. 12.2% alc. **Rating** 90 **To** 2024 $40 CM

Crawford River Wines ★★★★★

741 Hotspur Upper Road, Condah, Vic 3303 **Region** Henty
T (03) 5578 2267 **www**.crawfordriverwines.com **Open** By appt
Winemaker John Thomson, Belinda Thomson **Est.** 1975 **Dozens** 3500 **Vyds** 10.5ha
Time flies, and it seems incredible that Crawford River celebrated its 40th birthday in 2015. Once a tiny outpost in a little-known wine region, Crawford River is a foremost producer of riesling (and other excellent wines) thanks to the unremitting attention to detail and skill of its founder and winemaker, John Thomson (and moral support from wife Catherine). Talented elder daughter Belinda has returned part-time after completing her winemaking degree and working along the way in Marlborough (NZ), Bordeaux, Rivera del Duress (Spain), Bolgheri and Tuscany, and the Nahe (Germany), Crawford River filling in the gaps. She continues working in Spain, effectively doing two vintages each year. Younger daughter Fiona is in charge of sales and marketing. Exports to the UK.

ＹＹＹＹＹ **Riesling 2017** Wow this is good. There's a lot of very good riesling around but the details here are so punchy and so vivid; it just has that extra something. Lime, slate and spice flavours, but it's the palate intensity and power through the finish that sets it apart. Screwcap. 13.5% alc. **Rating** 96 **To** 2032 $48 CM ✪
Rose 2017 Unusually (and for the first time at Crawford River), this is made with cabernet and semillon. It has flavour and punch, fleshed with dusty spice and bursting through the finish. Standout rose. May even live (and drink well) for a year or two beyond the norm. Screwcap. 12.5% alc. **Rating** 95 **To** 2020 $28 CM ✪

Young Vines Riesling 2017 Vines planted in '00, so they're only young in relative terms. This has a gorgeous, upfront, juicy appeal, its flavours on open display, its quality crystal clear. Lemon, mandarin, a splash of lime. It doesn't reinvent the wheel; it runs frictionless and free. Screwcap. 13.5% alc. **Rating** 94 To 2025 $35 CM

♟♟♟♟♀ **Cabernets Merlot 2015 Rating** 90 To 2024 $38 CM

Credaro Family Estate   ★★★★★

2175 Caves Road, Yallingup, WA 6282 **Region** Margaret River
T (08) 9756 6520 **www**.credarowines.com.au **Open** 7 days 10–5
Winemaker Dave Johnson **Est.** 1993 **Dozens** 10 000 **Vyds** 150ha
The Credaro family first settled in Margaret River in 1922, migrating from northern Italy. Initially a few small plots of vines were planted to provide the family with wine in the European tradition. However, things began to change significantly in the '80s and '90s, and changes have continued. The most recent has been the acquisition of a 40ha property, with 18ha of vineyard, in Wilyabrup (now called the Summus vineyard) and the expansion of winery capacity to 1200t with 300 000l of additional tank space. Credaro now has seven separate vineyards (150ha in production) spread throughout the Margaret River region: Credaro either owns or leases each property and grows/manages the vines with its own viticulture team. Exports to Thailand, Singapore and China.

♟♟♟♟♟ **1000 Crowns Shiraz 2016** Serious fruit, serious oak, serious tannin. It's not thick or overdone, but it's a substantial red wine, imposing almost; its clothes woven of rope rather than cotton. Plum and black cherry, coffee grounds, peppercorns and musk. It has both the balance and the texture to drink well soon-ish but clearly it's been made for, and is best suited to, the cellar. Screwcap. 14% alc. **Rating** 96 To 2036 $75 CM ✪
1000 Crowns Chardonnay 2016 Its quality is bell clear. It's almost rich, almost elegant, not especially complex but not simple either. It's long. Oak and fruit form a happy marriage before striding out to a refreshing, confident finish. A beautiful chardonnay. Screwcap. 12.5% alc. **Rating** 95 To 2026 $65 CM
Kinship Chardonnay 2016 Mouthwatering style with pear and custard apple flavours mingling with peach and cedar-spiced oak. Cohesion, deliciousness, balance, length: all are in this wine's favour. The finish has a steely resolve – a good thing – but in any case it's well and truly won you over by that stage. Screwcap. 12.5% alc. **Rating** 94 To 2023 $32 CM
Kinship Shiraz 2016 We get texture, we get flavour, we get a thoroughly successful red wine. Roasted plums, peppercorns, graphite-like notes, and just enough savouriness to give the fruit an offset. Tannin fingers its way through the back half of the palate in intricate fashion. It's an easy wine to recommend. Screwcap. 14% alc. **Rating** 94 To 2030 $32 CM
Kinship Cabernet Sauvignon 2016 The blackcurrant comes cloaked in toasty vanilla and mint. It's sweet and syrupy but it remains fresh, the finish both tannic and cleansing at once. It feels confident at every turn; it drinks well now but it's staring the future in the eye. Screwcap. 14% alc. **Rating** 94 To 2032 $32 CM

♟♟♟♟♀ **Kinship Chardonnay 2017 Rating** 93 To 2024 $32 CM
Kinship Cabernet Merlot 2016 Rating 93 To 2032 $32 CM
Kinship Sauvignon Blanc 2017 Rating 92 To 2021 $25 CM ✪
Five Tales Shiraz 2016 Rating 91 To 2023 $22 CM ✪
Five Tales Cabernet Sauvignon 2016 Rating 90 To 2023 $22 CM

CRFT Wines   ★★★★☆

45 Rangeview Drive, Carey Gully, SA 5144 **Region** Adelaide Hills
T 0413 475 485 **www**.helbigandrieswines.com **Open** W'ends 12–4
Winemaker Candice Helbig, Frewin Ries **Est.** 2012 **Dozens** 1200 **Vyds** 1.9ha

Life and business partners Frewin Ries (NZ-born) and Candice Helbig (Barossa-born) crammed multiple wine lives into a relatively short period before giving up secure jobs and establishing CRFT in time for their inaugural 2013 vintage. Frewin started with four years at Cloudy Bay before heading to Saint Emilion, France, then to Williams Selyem, the iconic pinot maker in Sonoma. Returning home, he spent four years with Kingston Estate, and a subsequent time as a contract winemaker. Candice is a sixth-generation Barossan and trained as a laboratory technician. She spent eight years with Hardys, gained her degree in oenology and viticulture from CSU, then moved to Boar's Rock and Mollydooker in '11. Exports to the UK, Luxembourg, Singapore and Hong Kong.

⚐⚐⚐⚐⚐ **K1 Vineyard Kuitpo Adelaide Hills Gruner Veltliner 2017** Wild-fermented, unfined, vegan friendly. Some honeysuckle, smoky aromas akin to marsanne, not usually to gruner veltliner. The palate unwinds and unfolds as the wine is tasted and retasted; it's full-bodied in white-wine terms, but isn't phenolic or coarse. Screwcap. 13% alc. **Rating** 90 **To** 2020 $29

Longview Vineyard Macclesfield Adelaide Hills Gruner Veltliner 2017 Wild-fermented, unfined, vegan friendly. The bouquet brings back childhood memories of smelling and tasting black wattle gum and wild honey. Significantly richer than its K1 sibling on the palate; then coats the mouth and refuses point-blank to allow things to return to normal for several minutes. Screwcap. 13.5% alc. **Rating** 90 **To** 2020 $29

Arranmore Vineyard Piccadilly Valley Adelaide Hills Pinot Noir 2016 Very pale, although bright, colour; the bouquet is spicy/foresty, the palate firm and as yet ungiving – it's highly unusual for a 14% alc. pinot noir to be thus. CRFT suggest it will improve with cellaring. Screwcap. **Rating** 90 **To** 2020 $39

Budenberg Vineyard Piccadilly Valley Adelaide Hills Pinot Noir 2016 This has a slight deeper colour than the other pinots in the individual vineyard range, the flavours and mouthfeel fractionally riper on the mid-palate, but with the same slight herbal/green finish. Screwcap. 14% alc. **Rating** 90 **To** 2020 $39

Whisson Lake Vineyard Piccadilly Valley Adelaide Hills Pinot Noir 2016 Fractionally more developed colour than its siblings, and unexpectedly there's slightly more developed fruit flavours. Screwcap. 14% alc. **Rating** 90 **To** 2020 $39

Broderick Vineyard Basket Range Adelaide Hills Pinot Noir 2016 All the CRFT pinot noirs have 14% alc., and all are made the same way with cold soak, wild yeast open ferment, 25% whole bunches, 75% whole berries, all matured in 15% new French oak, all bottled 17 Feb. This would be a classic comparative tasting trial evaluating the character of each vineyard. Screwcap. **Rating** 90 **To** 2020 $39

Chapel Valley Vineyard Piccadilly Valley Adelaide Hills Pinot Noir 2016 Shares exactly the same slight green finish. Screwcap. 14% alc. **Rating** 90 **To** 2020 $39

Crittenden Estate   ★★★★★

25 Harrisons Road, Dromana, Vic 3936 **Region** Mornington Peninsula
T (03) 5981 8322 **www.**crittendenwines.com.au **Open** 7 days 10.30–4.30
Winemaker Rollo Crittenden **Est.** 1984 **Dozens** 8000 **Vyds** 4.8ha
Garry Crittenden was one of the pioneers on the Mornington Peninsula, establishing the family vineyard over 30 years ago, and introducing a number of avant garde pruning and canopy management techniques. In the manner of things, much has changed – and continues to change – in cool-climate vineyard management. Pinot noir and chardonnay remain the principal focus, and in 2015 winemaking returned to the family vineyard on the Mornington Peninsula in a newly built facility, with son Rollo very much in charge. Exports to the UK and the US.

⚐⚐⚐⚐⚐ **Cri de Coeur Mornington Peninsula Savagnin 2013** In French, 'sous voile' means under a veil and in this instance, it is flor yeast keeping the wine protected and fresh while in barrel. Rollo Crittenden's inspiration came from France's famed Jura wine, vin jaune. This spent 4 years under flor in old French barriques and yes, it is an oxidative style. It has savoury complexity to the max with a hint of lemon thyme, preserved salty Meyer lemons and grilled almonds. The palate is textural and creamy with neat phenolics, then finishing dry with a twist of saline tang. One of the most remarkable wines crafted in Australia. Bravo. Diam. 14.5% alc. **Rating** 96 **To** 2023 $80 JF

Peninsula Chardonnay 2016 It's largely the wine's restraint that makes it appealing. Plus its savouriness, the swathe of stone fruit, ginger spice and lemon zest, the just-right creamy leesy flavours and texture. Well composed with the fine acidity pulling it all together, ensuring it flows smoothly across the fleshy palate. The fruit is purchased from a single vineyard at Main Ridge. Screwcap. 13.3% alc. **Rating** 95 **To** 2021 $34 JF ✪

Kangerong Mornington Peninsula Chardonnay 2016 This is a Goldilocks wine, everything just right. It has layers of flavour with stone fruit, a smidge of lemon and pith plus spice. It unfurls on the supple palate with some creamy-lees influence, again not too much. This has found its groove with detail and deliciousness in equal measure. Screwcap. 13.3% alc. **Rating** 95 **To** 2023 $45 JF

The Zumma Mornington Peninsula Chardonnay 2016 The trio of estate chardonnays aren't about an ascending order of quality, rather they're about difference. A balanced mix of stone fruit, ginger flower and spice, nougat and creamed honey; all those really satisfying and complex solidsy elements. Screwcap. 13.4% alc. **Rating** 95 **To** 2023 $57 JF

The Zumma Mornington Peninsula Pinot Noir 2016 A yin and yang wine as it has power and depth of flavour yet brightness and ease at the same time. There's a whirl of cherry, from sweet, dark and red to spiced. The 20% whole bunches in the ferment adds complexity, so too the judicious use of 11 months in French oak (30% new). A medium-bodied frame taking in fine, ripe tannins and delicious chalky acidity. Screwcap. 13.3% alc. **Rating** 95 **To** 2026 $57 JF

Cri de Coeur Mornington Peninsula Pinot Noir 2016 Initially made in two parts with a portion of fruit destemmed and the other remaining as whole-bunches, left for 2 weeks then foot-stomped; both parcels blended for maturing in French oak puncheons for 1 year (33% new). While obvious whole-bunch characters abound, such as in the spicy, smoky fragrance, herbal tones, and the certain vivacity, they are integrated into the fabric of the wine alongside precise textural tannins and excellent length. Diam. 13.3% alc. **Rating** 95 **To** 2027 $80 JF

Peninsula Sauvignon Blanc Fume 2016 Heady aromatics of baked quinces, lemon curd and nougat with lots of ginger and a hint of oak spice. It's textural as the style should be, with razor-sharp lemony acidity driving this to a resounding finish. Screwcap. 13.5% alc. **Rating** 94 **To** 2022 $30 JF ✪

Peninsula Pinot Gris 2016 Everything a pinot gris should be is on display here with its flurry of stone fruit, spiced pears topped with creamed honey, and the all-important texture on the palate. It's luscious but not heavy, with a savoury twist and enough refreshing acidity to keep buoyant. Screwcap. 13.7% alc. **Rating** 94 **To** 2021 $34 JF

Kangerong Mornington Peninsula Pinot Noir 2016 A charming pinot with heady aromas of spiced black cherries, warm earth and woodsy spices, immediately stating their regional appeal. A flurry of intensely sweet cherries dipped in kirsch unfold on the medium-bodied palate, supple tannins making this very satisfying. Screwcap. 13.5% alc. **Rating** 94 **To** 2023 $45 JF

♀♀♀♀♀ Peninsula Pinot Noir 2016 Rating 93 To 2023 $34 JF

Cullen Wines   ★★★★★

4323 Caves Road, Wilyabrup, WA 6280 **Region** Margaret River
T (08) 9755 5277 **www**.cullenwines.com.au **Open** 7 days 10–4.30
Winemaker Vanya Cullen, Trevor Kent **Est.** 1971 **Dozens** 20 000 **Vyds** 49ha
One of the pioneers of Margaret River, producing long-lived wines of highly individual style from the mature estate vineyards. The vineyard has progressed beyond organic to biodynamic certification and, subsequently, has become the first vineyard and winery in Australia to be

certified carbon neutral. This requires the calculation of all the carbon used and of the CO_2 emitted in the winery; the carbon is then offset by the planting of new trees. Winemaking is in the hands of Vanya Cullen, daughter of the founders; she is possessed of an extraordinarily good palate and generosity to the cause of fine wine. Exports to all major markets.

ŶŶŶŶŶ **Vanya Wilyabrup Margaret River Cabernet Sauvignon 2015** Stripping away all the obvious questions re price – and, in fact, it is cheap compared to Grange and Hill of Grace – this is a truly beautiful and graceful cabernet. Its purity of varietal fruit expression, its perfect fruit/oak/tannin balance and its length are exceptional, amply justifying Vanya Cullen's belief that the wine will age well for at least 50 years. Screwcap. 13.5% alc. **Rating** 99 **To** 2055 $500
Diana Madeline 2016 93% cabernet sauvignon, 5% merlot, 1% each of malbec and petit verdot, matured for 14 months in French barriques (67% new). Elegance personified, with no compromise, and racking up extraordinary attention to detail. The fluid grace of this beautiful wine might seem almost inevitable, but of course it's not – it's the distillation of two generations. Screwcap. 12.5% alc. **Rating** 98 **To** 2041 $130 **O**

ŶŶŶŶŶ **Cullen Vineyard Margaret River Sauvignon Blanc Semillon 2015** A 74/26% blend fermented and matured in new French oak for 5 months. The complex bouquet brings toasty oak, cut grass and hints of stone fruit (also lurking in the Mangan SBS) into play, the palate pulling out all the stops with its mix of tropical fruits and citrussy acidity. Screwcap. 13% alc. **Rating** 96 **To** 2025 $32 **O**
Kevin John 2016 Bright straw-green; in best Cullen style, a wine that balances richness and complexity with freshness. The flavours focus on white peach, nectarine and fig, with creamy notes offset by citrussy acidity, and the new French oak integrated. Screwcap. 13.5% alc. **Rating** 96 **To** 2026 $115
Mangan Vineyard Margaret River Sauvignon Blanc Semillon 2016 57% sauvignon blanc, 38% semillon, 5% verdelho. Gleaming straw-green; the bouquet is fragrant and expressive, bonding gooseberry, citrus and lemongrass tightly together on the very long palate. Early picking has preserved the natural acidity that will in turn give the wine longevity. Screwcap. 13% alc. **Rating** 95 **To** 2021 $29 **O**

Cumulus Wines ★★★★

892 Davys Plains Road, Cudal, NSW 3864 **Region** Orange
T (02) 6390 7900 **www**.cumuluswines.com.au **Open** Not
Winemaker Rod Hooper, Debbie Lauritz, David Richards **Est.** 2004 **Dozens** NFP
The wines are released under five brands: Rolling and Five Friends from the Central Ranges; Climbing and Six Hundred Above, solely from Orange fruit; and Cumulus, super-premium from the best of the estate vineyard blocks. Beelgara merged with Cumulus in 2015 and relocated to the Cumulus winery. Beelgara also owns Moss Brothers, The Habitat and Pepperton Estate. Exports to most major markets.

ŶŶŶŶŶ **Cumulus Luna Rosa Central Ranges Rosado 2017** 47% each of shiraz and merlot, 2% each of sangiovese, tempranillo and barbera. Early picking was one step in the plan, as was arresting the fermentation while some residual sugar remained, in turn balanced by acidity. Judging the amounts is no easy task, but this wine shows just what can be achieved with its perfumed and bright red fruits on full display. Screwcap. 11.5% alc. **Rating** 94 **To** 2022 $16 **O**

ŶŶŶŶŶ **JT, The Patriarch Clare Valley Shiraz 2015** Rating 93 **To** 2030 $30
Cumulus Climbing Orange Shiraz 2016 Rating 92 **To** 2036 $24 **O**
Moss Brothers Cabernet Merlot 2016 Rating 92 **To** 2031 $20 **O**
Cumulus Rolling Central Ranges Semillon Sauvignon Blanc 2017 Rating 91 **To** 2019 $19 **O**
Cumulus Climbing Orange Pinot Gris 2017 Rating 90 **To** 2019 $24
Beelgara Black Grenache Rose 2017 Rating 90 **To** 2020 $20 **O**
Cumulus Six Hundred Above Orange Merlot 2014 Rating 90 **To** 2021 $28

Cupitt's Winery

58 Washburton Road, Ulladulla, NSW 2539 **Region** Shoalhaven Coast
T (02) 4455 7888 **www**.cupittwines.com.au **Open** Wed–Sun 10–5
Winemaker Rosie Cupitt, Wally Cupitt, Tom Cupitt **Est.** 2007 **Dozens** 4000 **Vyds** 3ha
Griff and Rosie Cupitt run a combined winery and restaurant complex, taking full advantage
of the location on the south coast of NSW. Rosie studied oenology at CSU and has more
than a decade of vintage experience, taking in France and Italy; she also happens to be the
Shoalhaven representative for Slow Food International. The Cupitts have 3ha of vines centred
on sauvignon blanc and semillon, and also buy viognier and shiraz from Tumbarumba,
shiraz, chardonnay and sauvignon blanc from the Southern Highlands, and verdelho from
Canowindra (Cowra). Sons Wally and Tom have now joined the winery.

Hilltops Nebbiolo 2016 Nebbiolo is the ultimate red wine challenge, but
Hilltops has had a record of (relative) success. Rosie Cupitt has done it again,
holding her nerve and her palate during the long (2-week) primary ferment and
8-week post-ferment maceration, aligning herself with old Barolo practice, not the
new short style of maceration. This has every sort of cherry flavour you wish to
nominate, and lingering fine, savoury tannins. A terrific wine. Screwcap. 14% alc.
Rating 97 To 2031 $40 ✪

Dusty Dog Hilltops Shiraz 2015 Co-fermented with 2% viognier. A lovely
wine, with a complex, shifting array of aromas that are brought to heel on the
vital, fresh, medium-bodied palate with its Thai silk range of predominantly red
fruits criss-crossed by superfine tannins and bright acidity. Screwcap. 14% alc.
Rating 95 To 2029 $52
Hilltops Merlot 2016 The bright colour and aromatic bouquet are full of the
promise that is largely delivered by the medium to full-bodied palate. Cassis, bay
leaf and char are occupants of the mid-palate, a faint whisper of bitterness on the
aftertaste. The sheer quality of the makeup of the rest of the wine, and the inanity
of most merlots, drives me to nominate gold medal status. Screwcap. 14% alc.
Rating 95 To 2031 $35 ✪
Yarra Valley Chardonnay 2016 Bright straw-green; a wine made with
attention to detail, but not pushing the boundaries of accepted vinification. The
one partial lack is drive through to the finish, a carping criticism perhaps. If true,
it's the vineyard at fault, not the winemaking. Screwcap. 12.8% alc. Rating 94
To 2022 $35
Canberra Pinot Gris 2017 Salmon hue, some pink; the 25% portion fermented
on skins, i.e. crushed berries, has had a profound impact on the colour, bouquet
and palate. This is a pinot gris with a thoroughly rebellious attitude. The flavour
set reaches as far as tropical fruits, along with more conventional nashi pear; the
texture with more relevance than is the norm. Screwcap. 12.5% alc. Rating 94
To 2021 $30 ✪
Hilltops Viognier 2017 Viognier is meant to taste of apricot, but few do. This
is one of the exceptions – apricot the main event after a complex vinification.
It is opulent and rich, and a level of phenolics had to be part of the outcome.
A pea and thimble trick if ever there was one. Screwcap. 13.5% alc. Rating 94
To 2021 $35

Alphonse Shoalhaven Coast Sauvignon 2017 Rating 93 To 2021 $35
Mia Bella Orange Arneis 2017 Rating 91 To 2020 $28
Rosie's Rose 2017 Rating 91 To 2020 $30

Curator Wine Company

28 Jenke Road, Maranaga, SA 5355 **Region** Barossa Valley
T 0411 861 604 **www**.curatorwineco.com.au **Open** By appt
Winemaker Tom White **Est.** 2015 **Dozens** 5000 **Vyds** 8ha
This business is owned by Tom and Bridget White, who have made a number of changes
in direction over previous years, and have now decided to focus on shiraz and cabernet

sauvignon from the Barossa Valley, a decision that has been rewarded. The vineyard at Marananga is planted on ancient red soils rich in ironstone and quartzite, and the wines are naturally fermented. Exports to China.

ŶŶŶŶŶ Marananga Barossa Valley Shiraz 2015 Licorice strapped to an engine of blackberry. There's sweet, cedar wood–like oak here and hints of lavender, peppermint and blueberry, but those rich, dark berry flavours hold sway. Clearly it sits at the bigger end of town but it remains fresh, composed and well shaped. Diam. 15% alc. **Rating** 94 **To** 2035 $60 CM

ŶŶŶŶŶ Marananga Barossa Valley Shiraz 2016 Rating 93 **To** 2026 $38 CM
Marananga Barossa Valley Cabernet Sauvignon 2016 Rating 93 **To** 2028 $38 CM

Curly Flat   ★★★★★
263 Collivers Road, Lancefield, Vic 3435 **Region** Macedon Ranges
T (03) 5429 1956 **www**.curlyflat.com **Open** W'ends 12–5
Winemaker Matt Harrop, Ben Kimmorley **Est.** 1991 **Dozens** 6000 **Vyds** 13ha
In October 2017 founders Phillip Moraghan and Jenifer Kolkka parted ways. Not without anguish, Phillip relinquished his share of the business, leaving Jenifer with sole ownership of Curly Flat. Matt Harrop was headhunted for the position of senior winemaker, and will be able to continue his role at Silent Way, the Macedon vineyard he owns with wife Tamara Grischy. Exports to the UK, Japan and Hong Kong.

ŶŶŶŶŶ The Curly Pinot Noir 2015 From the oldest estate vines planted in '92. 100% whole bunches fermented with wild and cultured yeast, matured for 20 months in new French oak. This has had the whole shooting box thrown at it, but has responded in fine style. Yes, the whole bunches are obvious, as is the 100% new oak, but the fruit steps daintily around the road blocks that might have otherwise been too much, and in doing so underlines its excellent length and finish. Screwcap. 14.1% alc. **Rating** 96 **To** 2030 $64 ❂
Chardonnay 2016 Bright straw-green; a rich and complex wine with good balance between the fruit, oak (62% new or 1yo) and acidity (7.2g/l). The quality of the fruit in barrels selected for this wine (compared to those relegated to Williams Crossing) is clear. The warm vintage hasn't impacted on the high-elevation Macedon region. Screwcap. 13.6% alc. **Rating** 95 **To** 2024 $46
Pinot Noir 2015 10% whole bunches fermented with wild and cultured yeast, 30 days on skins, matured for 20 months in French oak (28% new). The bouquet is complex with gently spicy/forest floor/briar aromas that link with the wild strawberry, red cherry and pomegranate fruit flavours. It's a deceptive wine, with more wire in its muscles than appears at first (or second) sight. Screwcap. 14.2% alc. **Rating** 95 **To** 2025 $52

ŶŶŶŶŶ Williams Crossing Chardonnay 2016 Rating 91 **To** 2022 $26

Curtis Family Vineyards   ★★★★
514 Victor Harbor Road, McLaren Vale, SA 5171 **Region** McLaren Vale
T 0439 800 484 **www**.curtisfamilyvineyards.com **Open** Not
Winemaker Mark Curtis, Claudio Curtis **Est.** 1973 **Dozens** 10 000
The Curtis family traces its history back to 1499 when Paolo Curtis was appointed by Cardinal de Medici to administer papal lands in the area around Cervaro. (The name Curtis is believed to derive from Curtius, a noble and wealthy Roman Empire family.) Locally, the family has been growing grapes and making wine in McLaren Vale since 1973, having come to Australia some years previously. Exports to the US, Canada, Thailand and China.

ŶŶŶŶŶ Martins Vineyard McLaren Vale Shiraz 2016 60+yo vines, matured in 100% new American oak. Follows in the footsteps of the Limited Series Shiraz, but is arguably a little lighter and a little more complex. But it's still full-bodied-plus and if the price is no deterrent, this has decades of development ahead. These

two wines have been given the benefit of the doubt. Diam. 14% alc. **Rating** 95
To 2060 $100

Limited Series McLaren Vale Shiraz 2016 60+yo vines, matured in 100%
new American oak. The back label of this and its Martins Vineyard sibling describe
the fruit as red. Try as I might, I couldn't get past black fruits, licorice and a thick
vanillan coating of American oak. Like its sibling, this has a life that will ultimately
depend on the Diam cork. 14% alc. **Rating** 94 **To** 2056 $100

Limited Series McLaren Vale Grenache 2016 A thoroughly intimidating
wine, built in heroic style. The fruit is dialled up to maximum, tannins and oak
draped over its full body. It's a legitimate style, abounding with fresh fruits from
its 100yo vines. As long as the Diam closure works, the wine will live. **Rating** 94
To 2036 $100

ŸŸŸŸ̈ Heritage McLaren Vale Shiraz 2016 Rating 92 To 2026 $20

D'Angelo Estate ★★★★

41 Bayview Road, Officer, Vic 3809 **Region** Yarra Valley
T 0417 055 651 **www.**dangelowines.com.au **Open** Fri–Sat 6–11, Sun 12–5
Winemaker Benny D'Angelo, Corey Hamilton **Est.** 2001 **Dozens** 2500 **Vyds** 4ha
In 2001 Benny D'Angelo purchased and planted a 4ha vineyard on a north-facing hillside
in Officer, Victoria, and began making wines under the D'Angelo Estate Vineyard label.
A cellar door was established in '10 and with increasing popularity has progressed from a small
boutique set-up to a 300-seat tapas restaurant and venue with live music and wedding hosting.
D'Angelo Estate expanded in '16 by building a new state-of-the-art winery just down the
road from the vineyard. This allowed greater production. The vines include sauvignon blanc,
pinot grigio, chardonnay, viognier, pinot noir and shiraz. Wines are also produced from
Heathcote shiraz and Langhorne Creek shiraz and cabernet.

ŸŸŸŸ̈ **il Berardino Reserve Officer Pinot Noir 2015** Light in colour, but the
appealing fruit-driven aromatics and juicy palate give this a keen drinkability. You
wouldn't say no to a glass, or to a second. Ripe cherry and redcurrant, autumnal
hints and just a whisper of sourness. Structure isn't its strong point but varietal
character certainly is. Screwcap. 13.8% alc. **Rating** 91 **To** 2022 $40 CM

Sab's Langhorne Creek Shiraz 2015 It has a rich, truffle-accented sweetness
of berried fruit, all soft and ripe and round. It's generosity in a glass. Screwcap.
14% alc. **Rating** 91 **To** 2024 $20 CM

Officer Sauvignon Blanc 2016 Hit-up with tropical fruit flavour; soft as it
floats through the mouth. Complexed by lemongrass notes and picked out by
strawberry (yes, strawberry). Interesting wine, outside of the norm, offering texture
and flavour. Screwcap. 12.5% alc. **Rating** 90 **To** 2020 $26 CM

ŸŸŸŸ **Officer Pinot Grigio 2016** Rating 89 To 2019 $24 CM
Officer Madame Rose 2017 Rating 89 To 2020 $20 CM

d'Arenberg ★★★★★

Osborn Road, McLaren Vale, SA 5171 **Region** McLaren Vale
T (08) 8329 4888 **www.**darenberg.com.au **Open** 7 days 10–5
Winemaker Chester Osborn, Jack Walton **Est.** 1912 **Dozens** 270 000 **Vyds** 197.2ha
Nothing, they say, succeeds like success. Few operations in Australia fit this dictum better than
d'Arenberg, which has kept its 100-year-old heritage while moving into the 21st century with
flair and élan. At last count the d'Arenberg vineyards, at various locations, have 24 varieties
planted, as well as 120 growers in McLaren Vale. There is no question that its past, present and
future revolve around its considerable portfolio of richly robed red wines, shiraz, cabernet
sauvignon and grenache being the cornerstones. The quality of the wines is unimpeachable,
the prices logical and fair. d'Arenberg has a profile in both the UK and the US that far larger
companies would love to have. It celebrated 100 years of family grapegrowing in 2012 on the
property that houses the winery, cellar door and restaurant. A founding member of Australia's
First Families of Wine. Exports to all major markets.

ŸŸŸŸŸ **The Dead Arm McLaren Vale Shiraz 2015** This is a particularly good Dead Arm, its alcohol miraculously the same as the '14, but however that may be, it has an elegance to its mouthfeel and lingering finish. Screwcap. 14.4% alc. **Rating** 96 To 2045 $70 ✪

The Laughing Magpie McLaren Vale Shiraz Viognier 2013 94% shiraz and 6% viognier are co-fermented, which gives the expected result of a more ethereal bouquet and a spicy, lifted red-and-black-fruit palate, the tannin need diminished, all without robbing the wine of the generosity which in one way or another always marks the d'Arenberg reds. Screwcap. 14.6% alc. **Rating** 95 To 2038 $29 ✪

The Coppermine Road McLaren Vale Cabernet Sauvignon 2015 What a boon the '15 vintage was. My mind snapped to attention as I tasted this wine. It's so perfectly pitched, all the components from the bouquet to the aftertaste lining up on the parade ground, split-second timing à la Chinese marchers. Cassis is permeated with fine-grained tannins and framed by oak; McLaren Vale chocolate absent – with leave. Screwcap. 14.3% alc. **Rating** 95 To 2035 $70

The Ironstone Pressings McLaren Vale Grenache Shiraz Mourvedre 2015 Deep crimson; one of the pioneers of this now classic blend, it's a relatively full-bodied example, but is balanced and not extractive. Another few years will make a world of difference. Screwcap. 14.3% alc. **Rating** 94 To 2030 $70

The Conscious Biosphere McLaren Vale Aglianico Petit Sirah 2015 How much of the most attractive red fruits of this delicious wine is due to the wonderful vintage, and how much from the varieties, I don't know, but it barely matters. The tannin load is small, making the wine more accessible (and enjoyable). Screwcap. 13.9% alc. **Rating** 94 To 2030 $29 ✪

ŸŸŸŸŸ **The Footbolt McLaren Vale Shiraz 2015** Rating 93 To 2028 $18 CM ✪
The Derelict Vineyard Grenache 2015 Rating 93 To 2028 $29
The Bonsai Vine Genache Shiraz Mourvedre 2015 Rating 93 To 2027 $29 CM
The Sticks & Stones Tempranillo Grenache Shiraz 2014 Rating 93 To 2028 $29
The Noble Botryotinia Fuckeliana Adelaide Hills Semillon Sauvignon Blanc 2017 Rating 93 To 2029 $20 ✪
The Lucky Lizard Chardonnay 2016 Rating 92 To 2021 $25 CM ✪
The Anthropocene Epoch Mencia 2017 Rating 92 To 2022 $29 CM
The Broken Fishplate Sauvignon Blanc 2017 Rating 91 To 2018 $20 CM ✪
The Feral Fox Pinot Noir 2016 Rating 91 To 2020 $30
The Sticks & Stones Tempranillo Grenache Souzao Tinta Cao 2013 Rating 91 To 2023 $29
d'Arry's Original Shiraz Grenache 2015 Rating 90 To 2030 $18 ✪
The Stump Jump Genache Shiraz Mourvedre 2015 Rating 90 To 2021 $11 ✪
The Twenty Eight Road Mourvedre 2015 Rating 90 To 2030 $29

🍇 Dabblebrook Wines ★★★★

69 Dabblebrook Road, Sellicks Hill, SA 5174 **Region** McLaren Vale
T 0488 158 727 **www**.dabblebrookwines.com **Open** By appt
Winemaker Ian Adam **Est.** 2007 **Dozens** 1000 **Vyds** 10ha

This is the change-of-life occupation of Ian Adam and Libbi Langford, who left Port Douglas after running a waste management business for 20 years, moving south to find what the larger world offered. They had no thought of establishing a wine business, but came across a property with 5ha of shiraz and 2ha of grenache, planted in 1990. They took it on and in the early years they were content to grow grapes for d'Arenberg (both shiraz and grenache), an arrangement which ran for five years. Over the same period, Ian worked on the Battle of Bosworth vineyards, gaining experience from Joch Bosworth. In 2011 he took the decision to make wine; undeterred by the constant rain of that very difficult vintage, he decided there was no turning back, and a vintage in the Loire Valley has further cemented his role as a winemaker. The red wines are made with little or no machinery, typically hand-plunged and basket-pressed, with minimal additions. Ian Adam's current CV reads 'Vigneron, part-time flagpole painter, chandelier cleaner (seasonal) and Doer of Lunch'. Exports to Singapore.

🍷🍷🍷🍷🍷 **Long Lunch Rose 2017** Just as a grenache rose should be: a perfumed rose-petal bouquet and a crisp, dry finish. The filling of this sandwich is fresh-picked raspberry fruit, with the overall low-alcohol and light-bodied palate allowing more than a glass in good conscience. Screwcap. 12.5% alc. **Rating** 90 **To** 2019 $19 ○
Grenache 2016 The restrained alcohol has maximised the potential of this medium-bodied grenache with fragrant red berry aromas and spices. It is at or near to its best, its freshness an important part of its charm (and quality). Screwcap. 13.8% alc. **Rating** 90 **To** 2021 $28

Dal Zotto Wines

Main Road, Whitfield, Vic 3733 **Region** King Valley
T (03) 5729 8321 **www**.dalzotto.com.au **Open** 7 days 10–5
Winemaker Michael Dal Zotto **Est.** 1987 **Dozens** 30 000 **Vyds** 48ha
The Dal Zotto family is a King Valley institution; ex-tobacco growers, then contract grapegrowers, they are now primarily focused on their Dal Zotto wine range. Led by Otto and Elena, and with sons Michael and Christian handling winemaking and sales/marketing respectively, the family is producing increasing amounts of wine of consistent quality from its substantial estate vineyard. The cellar door is in the centre of Whitfield and is also home to their Trattoria (open weekends). Exports to the UK, the United Arab Emirates, the Philippines, Singapore and China, which all appear to be flying.

🍷🍷🍷🍷🍷 **King Valley Nebbiolo 2015** Open-fermented, matured in French barrels. Highly aromatic bouquet with a range of varietal characters on display and a decent measure of oak. Follows through with appropriate nebbiolo structure, quite silky through the palate, leading to a tangy finish with fine-grained but insistent tannin lingering in the aftertaste. Screwcap. 13.9% alc. **Rating** 94 **To** 2027 $40 SC

🍷🍷🍷🍷🍷 **Museum Release King Valley Riesling 2008** **Rating** 93 **To** 2020 $65 SC
King Valley Arneis 2017 **Rating** 93 **To** 2021 $27 SC ○
King Valley Nebbiolo 2014 **Rating** 93 **To** 2026 $85 CM
Pucino Col Fondo 2016 **Rating** 92 **To** 2020 $27 SC
Cuore del Re 2016 **Rating** 90 **To** 2021 $22 SC
Pucino King Valley Prosecco 2017 **Rating** 90 **To** 2019 $23 SC
Pucino King Valley Prosecco NV **Rating** 90 **To** 2019 $19 SC ○

Dalfarras

PO Box 123, Nagambie, Vic 3608 **Region** Nagambie Lakes
T (03) 5794 2637 **www**.tahbilk.com.au **Open** At Tahbilk
Winemaker Alister Purbrick, Alan George **Est.** 1991 **Dozens** 8750 **Vyds** 20.97ha
The project of Alister Purbrick and artist wife Rosa (née Dalfarra), whose paintings adorn the labels of the wines. Alister is best known as winemaker at Tahbilk, the family winery and home, but this range of wines is intended to (in Alister's words) 'allow me to expand my winemaking horizons and mould wines in styles different from Tahbilk'.

🍷🍷🍷🍷🍷 **Rosato 2017** Pale pink; red cherry and berry aromas are the starting flag, sangiovese the motor with its mouth-coating yet dry fruit flavours; a touch of savoury spice the finishing line. Screwcap. 12% alc. **Rating** 90 **To** 2020 $19 ○
Prosecco 2017 Nashi pear, lemon zest and apple provide flavour and length. A very good example of the style at a mouthwatering price. Screwcap. 11.5% alc. **Rating** 90 **To** 2019 $19 ○

🍷🍷🍷🍷 **Pinot Grigio 2017** **Rating** 89 **To** 2019 $19 ○

Dalrymple   ★★★★★

1337 Pipers Brook Road, Pipers Brook, Tas 7254 **Region** Northern Tasmania
T (03) 6382 7229 **www.**dalrymplevineyards.com.au **Open** By appt
Winemaker Peter Caldwell **Est.** 1987 **Dozens** 4000 **Vyds** 17ha
Dalrymple was established by the Mitchell and Sundstrup families, then acquired by Hill-Smith
Family Vineyards in late 2007. Plantings are split between pinot noir and sauvignon blanc,
and the wines are made at Jansz Tasmania. In '10 Peter Caldwell was appointed, responsible
for the vineyard, viticulture and winemaking. He brought with him 10 years' experience at
Te Kairanga Wines (NZ), and two years with Josef Chromy Wines. His knowledge of pinot
noir and chardonnay is comprehensive. In December '12 Hill-Smith acquired another 120ha
property on which the original Frogmore Creek vineyard was established; 10ha of that is pinot
noir specifically for Dalrymple.

🍷🍷🍷🍷🍷 **Cave Block Pipers River Chardonnay 2016** Finely tuned, its ultra-fresh
acidity holding tight in the driver's seat yet allowing some white stone fruit and
citrus to come along for the ride. Complex and fleshy on the palate with a hint
of creamed honey on toast, and tangy lemon with leesy nuances; quite precise in
outlook. Screwcap. 12.5% alc. **Rating** 95 **To** 2026 $38 JF
Single Site Swansea Pinot Noir 2015 A complex mix of stewed rhubarb,
wood smoke and beetroot-earthy-stemmy notes mingling with dark cherries, yet
savoury through and through. Cloves and cinnamon aplenty, full-bodied, muscular
with persuasive tannins. Still tightly coiled and needs another couple of years
before it's ready. Screwcap. 13.5% alc. **Rating** 95 **To** 2028 $64 JF
Single Site Coal River Pinot Noir 2015 Comparing all the Single Site pinot
noirs, the impression is Coal River is the most composed and complete and
slightly lighter on its feet. While it has plenty of depth and structure, there's an
earthy allure too, starting with its aromatics of wood smoke, woodsy spices, a
whole-bunch stemmy character, juniper berries and dark cherries. More medium-
bodied, sinewy tannins with some Campari-like bitterness on the finish making
this moreish and savoury. Screwcap. 13.5% alc. **Rating** 95 **To** 2028 $64 JF

🍷🍷🍷🍷🍷 **Cave Block Pipers River Chardonnay 2015** **Rating** 93 **To** 2025 $38 JF
Single Site Cottage Block Pinot Noir 2015 **Rating** 93 **To** 2028 $64 JF

Dalwhinnie   ★★★★★

448 Taltarni Road, Moonambel, Vic 3478 **Region** Pyrenees
T (03) 5467 2388 **www.**dalwhinnie.com.au **Open** 7 days 10–5
Winemaker David Jones **Est.** 1976 **Dozens** 3500 **Vyds** 25ha
David and Jenny Jones make wines with tremendous depth of flavour, reflecting the
relatively low-yielding but well maintained vineyards. The vines are dry-grown and managed
organically, hence the low yield, but the quality more than compensates. A 50t high-tech
winery allows the wines to be made onsite. Exports to the UK, the US and China.

🍷🍷🍷🍷🍷 **Moonambel Shiraz 2015** Dalwhinnie seldom misses the target, and certainly
didn't in '15. This has Rolls Royce power, with no need to flaunt it. Black fruits
of all descriptions have a (fruit) sweet edge that is quite delicious, the mouthfeel
supple, the palate of effortless length, French oak just a cog in the engine.
Screwcap. 14.5% alc. **Rating** 96 **To** 2040 $65 ✪
Moonambel Cabernet 2015 Clear, deep crimson-purple; just as you would
expect from the region, the fully mature vines, the winemaker and the judicious
use of French oak. The flavours are deep and deceptively powerful, tannins
plentiful, but submerged in the fruit, the overall balance and length faultless.
Screwcap. 14% alc. **Rating** 96 **To** 2040 $55 ✪

Dandelion Vineyards ★★★★★

PO Box 138, McLaren Vale, SA 5171 **Region** McLaren Vale
T (08) 8556 6099 **www**.dandelionvineyards.com.au **Open** Not
Winemaker Elena Brooks **Est.** 2007 **Dozens** NFP **Vyds** 124.2ha
Dandelion Vineyards brings together sites spread across the Adelaide Hills, Eden Valley,
Langhorne Creek, McLaren Vale, Barossa Valley and Fleurieu Peninsula. Elena Brooks is
not only the wife of industry dilettante Zar, but also a gifted winemaker. Exports to all
major markets.

ᵠᵠᵠᵠᵠ **Red Queen of the Eden Valley Shiraz 2015** Loaded with oak but the fruit
is so bright and floral – so pretty – that it's entirely up for the challenge. Sweet,
smoky, savoury and perfumed at once, this blue/red/black-berried wine comes
shot with woodsy spice and primed with fine-grained tannin. Screwcap. 14.5% alc.
Rating 95 **To** 2035 $100 CM
Wonderland of the Eden Valley Riesling 2017 A piercing, wincing,
uncompromising wine; drinking it is like falling over a waterfall of acidity. From
the first sip you lose all control; you're rushed along, you're on the canoe whether
you like it or not. You'd call it lemony, or steely, though it's not really a wine for
flavour descriptors. Screwcap. 11% alc. **Rating** 94 **To** 2050 $60 CM

ᵠᵠᵠᵠᵠ **Lioness of McLaren Vale Shiraz 2016** **Rating** 93 **To** 2027 $28 CM
Pride of the Fleurieu Cabernet 2016 **Rating** 93 **To** 2026 $27 CM ✪
Fairytale of the Barossa Rose 2017 **Rating** 92 **To** 2020 $28 CM
Lion's Tooth of McLaren Vale Shiraz Riesling 2015 **Rating** 92 **To** 2025
$27 CM
Twilight of the Adelaide Hills Chardonnay 2017 **Rating** 91 **To** 2022
$27 CM
Menagerie of the Barossa Grenache Shiraz Mataro 2016 **Rating** 91
To 2024 $27 CM

David Franz ★★★★☆

94 Stelzer Road, Stone Well, SA 5352 **Region** Barossa Valley
T 0419 807 468 **www**.david-franz.com **Open** Mon, Thurs, Fri 11–4, w'ends 11–5
Winemaker David Franz Lehmann **Est.** 1998 **Dozens** 5500 **Vyds** 33.92ha
David Franz Lehmann is one of Margaret and Peter Lehmann's sons, and took a very
circuitous path around the world before establishing his eponymous winery. Wife Nicki
accompanied him on his odyssey and they, together with three children, two dogs, a mess of
chickens and a surly shed cat, all happily live together in their house and winery. The utterly
unique labels stem from (incomplete) university studies in graphic design. An extended family
of five share the work in the vineyard and the shed. Exports to the UK, the US, Japan, Hong
Kong and China.

ᵠᵠᵠᵠᵠ **Long Gully Road Ancient Vine Semillon 2015** A textured, intense and
seductive wine. Lemon, stone fruit, cream and cedar spice combine to beautiful
effect. Screwcap. 12.2% alc. **Rating** 94 **To** 2025 $22 CM ✪
Moskos Vineyard Adelaide Hills Chardonnay 2015 Highly refined, racy and
blessed with succulent length. Chardonnay in full flight. It tastes of white peach
and juicy pear, lactose, honeysuckle and cream. Moreish is the word. Screwcap.
12.8% alc. **Rating** 94 **To** 2023 $45 CM

ᵠᵠᵠᵠᵠ **Eden Edge Riesling Semillon 2017** **Rating** 93 **To** 2024 $22 CM ✪
Benjamin's Promise Shiraz 2013 **Rating** 93 **To** 2024 $50 CM
Waxing Lyrical Bin E621 2015 **Rating** 92 **To** 2023 $25 CM ✪
Plane Turning Right 2014 **Rating** 92 **To** 2024 $25 CM ✪
Eden Valley Riesling 2017 **Rating** 91 **To** 2023 $27 CM
Ricca Terra Farms Vermentino 2015 **Rating** 91 **To** 2019 $25 CM
Georgie's Walk Cabernet Sauvignon 2012 **Rating** 91 **To** 2023 $50 CM
108 Varieties Red Rose 2016 **Rating** 90 **To** 2019 $22 CM

David Hook Wines   ★★★★

Cnr Broke Road/Ekerts Road, Pokolbin, NSW 2320 **Region** Hunter Valley
T (02) 4998 7121 **www**.davidhookwines.com.au **Open** 7 days 10–4.30
Winemaker David Hook **Est.** 1984 **Dozens** 10 000 **Vyds** 8ha
David Hook has over 25 years' experience as a winemaker for Tyrrell's and Lake's Folly, also
doing the full Flying Winemaker bit with jobs in Bordeaux, the Rhône Valley, Spain, the US
and Georgia. The Pothana vineyard has been in production for over 30 years, and the wines
made from it are given the 'Old Vines' banner. This vineyard is planted on the Belford Dome,
an ancient geological formation that provides red clay soils over limestone on the slopes, and
sandy loams along the creek flats; the former for red wines, the latter for white.

ΨΨΨΨΨ **Reserve Central Ranges De Novo Bianco 2014** Attractive blend of pinot
grigio, riesling, chardonnay and sauvignon blanc. It has body, perfume and
momentum and it slings well through the finish. Both floral and citrussy with a
rind-like kick. Use of oak has been judicious but complementary; the softness
of the palate aids the overall harmony of the wine. Drinking at its peak now.
Screwcap. 13% alc. **Rating** 91 **To** 2018 $30 CM

ΨΨΨΨ **Hunter Valley Pinot Grigio 2017 Rating** 89 **To** 2018 $18 CM ✪
Hunter Valley Shiraz 2016 Rating 89 **To** 2021 $18 CM ✪

Dawson & James   ★★★★★

1240B Brookman Road, Dingabledinga, SA 5172 **Region** Southern Tasmania
T 0419 816 335 **www**.dawsonjames.com.au **Open** Not
Winemaker Peter Dawson, Tim James **Est.** 2010 **Dozens** 1200 **Vyds** 3.3ha
Peter Dawson and Tim James both had long and highly successful careers as senior
winemakers for Hardys/Accolade Wines. Tim jumped ship first, becoming managing director
of Wirra Wirra for seven years until 2007, while Peter stayed on longer with the group. Now
both have multiple consulting roles. Their desire to grow and make wine in Tasmania came to
fruition in '10. Exports to the UK and Singapore.

ΨΨΨΨΨ **Chardonnay 2015** Trophy at the Tasmanian Wine Show '17, thanks to its super-
intense bouquet and super-long palate. Sometimes chardonnays can wear their
acidity on their sleeve, but here it couples with a complex display of citrus and
stone fruit with a garland of quality oak, finishing with bright (not excessive)
acidity. Screwcap. 12.2% alc. **Rating** 97 **To** 2027 $58 ✪
Pinot Noir 2016 Brooding dark garnet with red hues. Intense, bright and
unmistakably pinot. Black cherries, fragrant red berries, wet earth, flecks of herbs.
Almost opulent, but without losing its inherent freshness. Depth of flavour, texture,
persistence and sheer pleasure are all presented in spades. Screwcap. 13.3% alc.
Rating 97 **To** 2030 $68 DB ✪
Pinot Noir 2014 Still retains exceptional depth to its bright colour, and has the
immense structure and richness that you expect from the great wines of Vosne-
Romanée, Burgundy. There is a wealth of spices in the powerful dark fruits of the
bouquet and palate alike, yet the wine remains light on its feet. If you are a pinot
devotee, don't expect to be satisfied by one glass. Campbell Mattinson's 97-point
rating in Feb '16 was right on the money, although the wine is still on an upward
path. Screwcap. 13.5% alc. **Rating** 97 **To** 2029 $68 ✪

ΨΨΨΨΨ **Chardonnay 2016** Pale quartz-green and bright. Intentions clearly stated with
a complex array of white flowers, nectarine, melon skin and grapefruit bound
together with yeast, sulphide and judicious use of oak (40% new). The palate has
on-point acidity that enhances the flavours and draws the wine out to a satisfying
long finish. Nothing out of place, everything present. Very good. Screwcap.
12.5% alc. **Rating** 96 **To** 2026 $58 DB ✪

De Bortoli

De Bortoli Road, Bilbul, NSW 2680 **Region** Riverina
T (02) 6966 0100 **www**.debortoli.com.au **Open** Mon–Sat 9–5, Sun 9–4
Winemaker Darren De Bortoli, Julie Mortlock, John Coughlan **Est.** 1928
Dozens NFP **Vyds** 367ha

Famous among the cognoscenti for its superb Noble One, which in fact accounts for only a minute part of its total production, this winery turns out low-priced varietal and generic wines that are invariably competently made. They come in part from estate vineyards, but also from contract-grown grapes. In June 2012 De Bortoli received a $4.8 million grant from the Federal Government's Clean Technology Food and Foundries Investment Program. This grant supported an additional investment of $11 million by the De Bortoli family in their project called 'Re-engineering Our Future for a Carbon Economy'. De Bortoli is a founding member of Australia's First Families of Wine. Exports to all major markets.

ΨΨΨΨΨ **Noble One Botrytis Semillon 2015** This sets the benchmark for luscious, rich botrytised semillons anywhere in the world. It does so in an elegant, balanced fashion, with flashes of fresh citrus among the vibrant cumquat marmalade and juicy acidity. 375ml. Screwcap. 9.5% alc. **Rating** 96 **To** 2025 $33 **O**
Old Boys Show Reserve Release 21 Years Old Barrel Aged Tawny NV A very rich and luscious release: toffee, coffee grounds, chocolate, Christmas cake, spirit no issue. The extra age has brought an element of finesse with it. Screwcap. 19% alc. **Rating** 95 $58
Black Noble NV Full mahogany-brown colour; way out in left field all on its own. Super tangy, with dried and candied citrus peel notes. Full of its own rancio. Screwcap. 17.5% alc. **Rating** 94 $48

ΨΨΨΨΨ **Down the Lane Shiraz Tempranillo 2017 Rating** 93 **To** 2027 $13 **O**
Show Liqueur Oak Barrel Aged 8 Years Muscat NV Rating 92 $31
DB Winemaker Selection Cabernet Sauvignon 2015 Rating 90 **To** 2021 $11 CM **O**
Deen Vat Series No 5 Botrytis Semillon 2013 Rating 90 **To** 2020 $14 CM **O**

De Bortoli (Victoria)

Pinnacle Lane, Dixons Creek, Vic 3775 **Region** Yarra Valley
T (03) 5965 2271 **www**.debortoli.com.au **Open** 7 days 10–5
Winemaker Stephen Webber, Sarah Fagan, Andrew Bretherton **Est.** 1987
Dozens 350 000 **Vyds** 520ha

Arguably the most successful of all Yarra Valley wineries, not only in terms of the sheer volume of production, but also taking into account the quality of its wines. It is run by the husband and wife team of Leanne De Bortoli and Steve Webber, but owned by the De Bortoli family. The wines are released in three quality and price groups: Single Vineyard at the top, then Estate Grown, and Villages in third place. Small volume labels also increase the offer with Riorret Single Vineyard, Melba, La Boheme, an aromatic range of Yarra Valley wines, and Vinoque, enabling trials (at the commercial level) of new varieties and interesting blends in the Yarra. The BellaRiva Italian varietal wines are sourced from the King Valley, and Windy Peak from Victorian regions including the Yarra, King Valley and Heathcote. Finally, in mid-2016, De Bortoli purchased one of the most distinguished Upper Yarra vineyards, Lusatia Park. Exports to all major markets.

ΨΨΨΨΨ **Melba Vineyard Yarra Valley Cabernet Sauvignon 2015** From the oldest (circa 50yo) vines on the Melba vineyard. Its extreme power and concentration is balanced by the freshness achieved with the modest alcohol. Those who have long championed the cause of Yarra Valley cabernet will be very happy to welcome this into the fold. Cork. 13.8% alc. **Rating** 98 **To** 2050 $160 **O**
The Estate Vineyard Dixons Creek Yarra Valley Pinot Noir 2016 From five blocks of east and south-facing vines dating back to '71. A beautifully made wine that has soared above the challenge of a generally fast and furious vintage.

Attention to detail is a much used (soon to be overmuch) expression, but appropriate for the silky delicacy of this beautiful wine. P.S. It also has superb tannin structure. Screwcap. 13% alc. **Rating** 97 **To** 2031 $30 **✪**

Melba Vineyard Yarra Valley Cabernet Sauvignon 2012 Hand-picked from the A2 and D2 vineyards at Dixons Creek. An exceptional cabernet of supreme elegance, line, length and balance. It has a silky rustle to the palate, shot with flavours of black fruits, black olive and cedar. Startling purity. Cork. 13% alc. **Rating** 97 **To** 2037 $110 **✪**

🍷🍷🍷🍷🍷 **The Estate Vineyard Dixons Creek Yarra Valley Shiraz 2015** Archetypal cool-climate, medium-bodied shiraz. Its core of red and black cherry fruit has flecks of pepper, licorice and spice, the tannins smooth and supple, the oak totally integrated. Lovely style. Screwcap. 14% alc. **Rating** 96 **To** 2035 $30 **✪**

Section A8 Yarra Valley Syrah 2015 The vines are some of the oldest in the Yarra Valley (planted '71), and the wine has the particular structure that comes from the grapes such vines produce. While elegant, the wine has intensity and drive, its tannin backbone part fruit, part oak-derived, the whole-bunch component there from start to finish. A dazzler from a dazzling vintage. Screwcap. 14% alc. **Rating** 96 **To** 2040 $55 **✪**

Section A5 Yarra Valley Chardonnay 2017 The bouquet is complex and the varietal character is as clear as a spring day. The wine went through mlf and came out enhanced; it fills the mouth with white peach, almond kernel and grapefruit acidity, oak merely a means to an end. Screwcap. 12.7% alc. **Rating** 95 **To** 2027 $55

La Boheme Act Two Yarra Valley Dry Pinot Noir Rose 2017 (Very) pale salmon colour. Strawberried aromas blaze from the glass, and combine with apple and rosewater to drive through the palate in fine, dry style. This spends time in old oak, albeit briefly, though there are certainly no signs of oak flavour. It wouldn't be out of order to label this as 'benchmark'. Screwcap. 12.8% alc. **Rating** 95 **To** 2019 $20 CM **✪**

Riorret Lusatia Park Yarra Valley Pinot Noir 2017 Bright crimson-purple; it's dry, but sweet in its heart, with utterly perfect tannins dusted across the palate adding to the juicy cherry notes. A purity runs though this wine like a rivulet. Diam. 13.5% alc. **Rating** 95 **To** 2025 $45

Melba Reserve Yarra Valley Cabernet Sauvignon 2015 From estate blocks A2, B3 and D2; 28 days' maceration, matured for 12 months in French oak (35% new). By De Bortoli's standards, this has been made with vigorous attention to detail. In the final analysis, it is a wine of elegance and finesse, cassis the star of the show. Screwcap. **Rating** 95 **To** 2035 $50

The Estate Vineyard Dixons Creek Yarra Valley Pinot Noir 2017 Plenty of pinot packed into this offering. Crystal clear varietal expression moves from fragrant cherry through sweet spice to sappy, slightly stemmy whole-bunch character, with the texture and palate weight pitch perfect. Lively tannin sustains the finish with length and freshness. Screwcap. 13.5% alc. **Rating** 94 **To** 2027 $30 SC **✪**

La Boheme Act Four Yarra Valley Syrah Gamay 2017 Bright colour. The aim was a bright and crunchy style, and it hit the bullseye. Lovely warm, spicy elements are threaded through the red fruits – cherry and strawberry – and just enough oak and tannin support to complete the song. Screwcap. 14% alc. **Rating** 94 **To** 2025 $22 **✪**

The Estate Vineyard Dixons Creek Yarra Valley Cabernet Sauvignon 2015 Textbook Yarra cabernet, so the descriptors are a given: dusty blackcurrant, cedar and camphor wood, a touch of leafiness and a hint of earthy fungi. Slightly restrained and perfectly medium-bodied, endowed with lovely fine tannin. Screwcap. 13.8% alc. **Rating** 94 **To** 2030 $30 SC **✪**

Vinoque Novo Tinto King Valley Touriga Tempranillo Tinta Cao 2017 The bouquet is as attractive as it is complex, with dark fruits glinting bright every now and then, some charcuterie notes adding to the considerable appeal. Notwithstanding all its flavour and activity, best enjoyed soonish. Screwcap. 14.5% alc. **Rating** 94 **To** 2023 $22 **✪**

ŸŸŸŸŸ Vinoque Yarra Valley Vin Sauvignon 2017 Rating 93 To 2020 $25 SC **○**
The Estate Vineyard Dixons Creek Yarra Valley Pinot Blanc 2017
Rating 93 To 2022 $30 SC
Vinoque Same Same Yarra Valley Pinot Meunier Pinot Noir 2017
Rating 93 To 2025 $25 SC **○**
The Estate Vineyard Dixons Creek Yarra Valley Chardonnay 2016
Rating 92 To 2021 $30 SC
Woodfired Heathcote Shiraz 2016 Rating 92 To 2023 $20 CM **○**
Riorret Lusatia Park Chardonnay 2017 Rating 91 To 2023 $42
Villages Heathcote Grenache Rose 2017 Rating 91 To 2019 $20 CM **○**
Vinoque Yarra Valley Nebbiolo Rose 2017 Rating 91 To 2018 $25
Villages Heathcote Shiraz Grenache 2016 Rating 91 To 2021 $20 CM **○**
Vinoque Heathcote Ridge Grenache 2016 Rating 91 To 2021 $25 CM

Deep Woods Estate

889 Commonage Road, Yallingup, WA 6282 **Region** Margaret River
T (08) 9756 6066 **www**.deepwoods.com.au **Open** Wed–Sun 11–5 (7 days during hols)
Winemaker Julian Langworthy, Emma Gillespie **Est.** 1987 **Dozens** 30 000 **Vyds** 14ha
Owned by Perth businessman Peter Fogarty and family, who also own Lake's Folly in the
Hunter Valley and Millbrook in the Perth Hills. The 32ha property has 14ha of cabernet
sauvignon, shiraz, merlot, cabernet franc, chardonnay, sauvignon blanc, semillon and verdelho.
Named 'Winery of the Year' by Ray Jordan in his *West Australian Wine Guide* 2017. Winemaker
Julian Langworthy has distinguished himself as one of the foremost talents in Australia, his
2014 Reserve Cabernet Sauvignon also named 'Wine of the Year' and 'Red Wine of the Year'
in the book. Exports to Germany, Malaysia, Singapore, Japan and China.

ŸŸŸŸŸ Reserve Margaret River Chardonnay 2016 Mainly sourced from Wilyabrup,
this wine has a special type of phenolic grip (not limited to white wines), which
makes the taster incapable of doing anything other than swallow it (bad phenolics
have the opposite effect). Perfect fruit/oak balance. Screwcap. 13% alc. **Rating** 97
To 2030 $45

ŸŸŸŸŸ Margaret River Sauvignon Blanc 2017 Julian Langworthy's palate and
winemaking skills (essentially one and the same) are in full flight. Passionfruit is
the recurrent component of the bouquet and palate making this wine special,
surrounded by support from citrussy acidity. Screwcap. 12.5% alc. **Rating** 96
To 2020 $20
Hillside Margaret River Cabernet Sauvignon 2015 Good colour; the wine
has a compelling mouthfeel – supple and long – but remains in the medium-
bodied class. Its flavours are of dark berries, spice and cedar that link themselves
structurally to the oak. Screwcap. 14% alc. **Rating** 96 To 2035 $25
Margaret River Chardonnay 2017 Pale straw-green. Wow, this takes off like an
Exocet missile with the acidity of the vintage part-reduced by mlf; white flowers
on the bouquet seem to reappear, tantalising on the aftertaste. The main game is
played out between white-fleshed stone fruit and grapefruit. Screwcap. 13% alc.
Rating 95 To 2025 $20
Hillside Margaret River Chardonnay 2015 A decidedly complex bouquet
with some reduction and a hint of fermentation with cloudy juice. This feeds into
a palate of similar complexity, slatey minerality adding its contribution hand in
hand with oak. Screwcap. 13% alc. **Rating** 95 To 2025 $25 **○**
Harmony Margaret River Rose 2017 Light pink with a shimmer of salmon.
Produced from a blend of shiraz and tempranillo, this has a proud history of high
quality predecessors. The length of the wine is prodigious, offering strawberry,
red cherry and raspberry, cut and shaped by persistent acidity. Screwcap. 13% alc.
Rating 95 To 2019 $15 **○**
Margaret River Rose 2017 The pale but bright hue opens the door for this
blend of shiraz and tempranillo. Its fragrant bouquet is attractive enough, but
doesn't quite prepare you for the intensity and drive that spears through to the

finish and aftertaste. Wild strawberry and hints of forest make this a very special rose. Screwcap. 12.5% alc. **Rating** 95 **To** 2021 $30 ✪

Ivory Margaret River Semillon Sauvignon Blanc 2017 There's an almost savage overtone to this wine, and an unqualified purity as citrus and tropical fruits dance through the bouquet; the palate, the embers of the flavours. Lemony acidity sways through on the back-palate. Screwcap. 12% alc. **Rating** 94 **To** 2021 $15 ✪

Margaret River Cabernet Sauvignon Merlot 2016 Parcels of cabernet sauvignon and merlot were separately vinified and matured in new and used French oak, which is still to knit fully with the fruit. The fruit is of good quality and will prevail given time. Screwcap. 14.5% alc. **Rating** 94 **To** 2031 $35

DEGEN ★★★★

365 Deasys Road, Pokolbin, NSW 2320 **Region** Hunter Valley
T 0427 078 737 **www**.degenwines.com.au **Open** W'ends 10–5
Winemaker Various contract **Est.** 2001 **Dozens** 1880 **Vyds** 4.5ha
In June 1997 marine engineer Tom Degen, together with wife Jean, an IT project manager, took a weekend drive to the Hunter Valley with no particular plan in mind, but as a consequence became the owners of an 11ha bush block, wild, heavily wooded and dotted with boulders, with no fencing or water. So the weekend drive became an every weekend drive to mount their John Deere tractor and slowly but surely clear tonnes of timber, remove the boulders, build a dam and work the soil. In September 2001 they planted 1.8ha of shiraz, 1.7ha of chardonnay and 1ha of semillon, and by '13 opened the cellar door and Vine Stay (now accommodating 20 guests).

🍷🍷🍷🍷🍷 **Single Vineyard Hunter Valley Chardonnay 2016** The Hunter Valley has its own ripening engineering, so forget alcohol levels from other regions. This juicy, supple chardonnay shows no tart sauvignon blanc notes, which can affect chardonnays with an alcohol under 12.5%. Here white peach, melon and citrus acidity are briefly kissed by oak, the length and balance exemplary. Screwcap. 12.3% alc. **Rating** 94 **To** 2023 $25

🍷🍷🍷🍷 **Single Vineyard Hunter Valley Shiraz 2016 Rating** 89 **To** 2023 $35

Delamere Vineyards ★★★★★

Bridport Road, Pipers Brook, Tas 7254 **Region** Northern Tasmania
T (03) 6382 7190 **www**.delamerevineyards.com.au **Open** 7 days 10–5
Winemaker Shane Holloway, Fran Austin **Est.** 1982 **Dozens** 5000 **Vyds** 13.5ha
Delamere was one of the first vineyards planted in the Pipers Brook area, its history going back to 1982. It was purchased by Shane Holloway and wife Fran Austin and their families in 2007. Shane and Fran are in charge of viticulture and winemaking. The vineyard has been expanded with an additional 4ha of pinot noir and chardonnay. Exports to China.

🍷🍷🍷🍷🍷 **Chardonnay 2016** The oldest estate vines were hand-picked and whole-bunch pressed direct to French oak for wild fermentation; partial mlf and 10 months' maturation on lees. A notably complex bouquet with white flowers and wisps of oak, then a taut and long palate. White stone fruits and grapefruit are held together by silver beads of acidity. Screwcap. 13.5% alc. **Rating** 96 **To** 2025 $50 ✪

Block 3 Chardonnay 2015 A very classy wine, made to take full advantage of the Indian summer in April. A key decision was to keep the wine for 12 months after bottling before release. The result is a rich, layered white peach and nectarine-flavoured wine with captivating grapefruit and mineral acidity. Diam. 13.4% alc. **Rating** 96 **To** 2025 $110

Block 3 Chardonnay 2014 Hand-picked from the oldest estate vines, matured for 12 months in new oak with lees stirring, aged a further year in bottle. An exceedingly powerful, complex and intense chardonnay with layer upon layer of flavours orbiting around grapefruit, unfazed by the new oak, which is simply woven into the fruit. Diam. 13.7% alc. **Rating** 96 **To** 2029 $110

Hurlo's Rose 2016 Pale salmon-pink; the most striking attribute of the varietal character is the way it has soaked up French oak (50% new) and 10 months' maturation. Not for nothing is it the most expensive Australian rose, and you can see why it should be. The scented floral bouquet flows into the complex palate, with both texture and flavour immediately supporting Delamere's suggestion of a 10-year cellaring horizon. Screwcap. 14.6% alc. **Rating** 96 **To** 2026 $80

Naissante Riesling 2015 From three vineyard sites on the eastern and western sides of the Tamar Valley; free-run juice wild-fermented. The wine has great balance, filling the mouth with complex citrus, apple and stone-fruit flavours. Screwcap. 11.9% alc. **Rating** 95 **To** 2025 $27 **☺**

Rose 2017 The light, vivid magenta hue is the first attraction. This is an ultra-pure, crisp and bone-dry style that can be matched with virtually any dish you care to name. Its bevy of red fruits can dance around or slice through its food companion. Screwcap. 12.8% alc. **Rating** 95 **To** 2022 $25 **☺**

Block 8 Pinot Noir 2015 A compelling pinot currently with lots of latent spice and fruit perfume, and demonstrating the layers of dark fruits that will long be the foundation of this classy wine. Diam. 13.6% alc. **Rating** 95 **To** 2030 $110

Blanc de Blancs 2012 A gorgeous sparkling wine. Taut, long, powerful and distinctive. Seaspray, honeysuckle, lemon delicious pudding and the richness of stone fruit. It both seduces and slices its way along the palate. That seaspray/oyster-like character is quite a thing. A beauty. Diam. 12% alc. **Rating** 95 $65 CM

Pinot Noir 2016 Bright colour; complex spicy/savoury dark cherry notes; the palate opens with dark cherry and plum fruit before foresty/briary notes arrive on the back-palate and finish, adding to the complexity. Screwcap. 13.6% alc. **Rating** 94 **To** 2029 $50

ᵭᵭᵭᵭᵭ **Cuvee 2014 Rating** 93 $50 CM
Rose NV Rating 92 $35 CM
Cuvee NV Rating 90 $35 CM

Delatite ★★★★★

26 High Street, Mansfield, Vic 3722 **Region** Upper Goulburn
T (03) 5775 2922 **www**.delatitewinery.com.au **Open** 7 days 10–5
Winemaker Andy Browning **Est.** 1982 **Dozens** 16 000 **Vyds** 27ha
With its sweeping views across to the snow-clad alps, this is uncompromising cool-climate viticulture. Increasing vine age (the earlier plantings were spread between 1968–82, others between 1984–2011), and the adoption of organic (and partial biodynamic) viticulture, seem to have played a role in providing red wines with more depth and texture. The white wines are also as good as ever; all are wild-yeast fermented. In 2011 Vestey Holdings Limited, the international pastoral giant, acquired a majority holding in Delatite, stating that the property represents one of 'what we hope will be a number of agricultural businesses here'. Exports to Denmark, China, Japan and Malaysia.

ᵭᵭᵭᵭᵭ **Vivienne's Block Reserve Riesling 2017** Hand-picked ex 49yo vines, whole-bunch pressed, fermented with wild yeast. It's a delicious riesling, taking the best features of its 2017 sibling onto another level. Higher acidity and lower pH rein in the exuberance. Screwcap. 13.5% alc. **Rating** 95 **To** 2032 $45

ᵭᵭᵭᵭᵭ **Pinot Gris 2017 Rating** 92 **To** 2023 $27
David's Block Reserve Pinot Noir 2016 Rating 92 **To** 2026 $75
Donald's Block Reserve Cabernet Merlot 2015 Rating 91 **To** 2035 $75
Riesling 2017 Rating 90 **To** 2025 $27
Tempranillo Rose 2017 Rating 90 **To** 2021 $27
Dungeon Gully Malbec Merlot 2015 Rating 90 **To** 2023 $35

Delinquente Wine Co

36 Brooker Terrace, Richmond, SA 5033 **Region** Riverland
T 0437 876 407 **www.**delinquentewineco.com **Open** Not
Winemaker Various **Est.** 2013 **Dozens** 3500
A Hollywood actress was famous for saying, 'I don't care what they say about me as long as they spell my name right'. Con-Greg Grigoriou might say, 'I don't care how bad people think my wine labels are as long as they remember them'. Con-Greg grew up on a vineyard in the Riverland, and spent a lot of time in wineries with his father and grandfather. He has decided to concentrate on southern Italian grape varieties. It's a virtual winery operation, buying fruit from growers who share his vision and having the wine made wherever he is able to find a facility prepared to assist in the making of micro-quantities. Delinquente is getting a lot of airplay from the set, and it's no surprise to see production jump from 600 to 3500 dozen. Exports to the UK, the US, Singapore and Japan.

🍷🍷🍷🍷 **Pretty Boy Riverland Nero d'Avola Rosato 2017** Hard to argue with this. It's dry and juicy with redcurrant and musk-like characters tripping through the palate. Everything here feels well handled – it drinks well as a result. Screwcap. 11.5% alc. **Rating** 90 **To** 2018 $22 CM

🍷🍷🍷🍷 **The Bullet Dodger Riverland Montepulciano 2017 Rating** 89 **To** 2020 $22 CM

Della Fay Wines ★★★★☆

3276 Caves Road, Yallingup, WA 6284 **Region** Margaret River
T (08) 9755 2747 **www.**kellysvineyard.com.au **Open** By appt
Winemaker Michael Kelly **Est.** 1999 **Dozens** 2500 **Vyds** 6.6ha
This is the venture of the Kelly family, headed by district veteran Michael Kelly. He gained his degree in wine science from CSU before working at Seville Estate and Mount Mary in the Yarra Valley and Domaine Louis Chapuis in Burgundy, then coming back to WA and working for Leeuwin Estate and Sandalford. From there Michael became the long-term winemaker at Fermoy Estate, but he and his family laid the groundwork for their own brand, buying prime viticultural land in Caves Road, Yallingup, in 1999. They have planted cabernet sauvignon, sauvignon blanc, vermentino, nebbiolo, chardonnay, merlot, malbec and petit verdot. Shiraz from the Geographe region is also a focus. 'Della Fay' honours the eponymous Kelly family matriarch. Exports to the Netherlands, South Korea, Singapore, Hong Kong and China.

🍷🍷🍷🍷🍷 **Margaret River Chardonnay 2015** Gin Gin (aka Mendoza) clone, machine-harvested, fermented in French oak (70% new) with cultured yeast, 12 months on lees. A typical, rich Margaret River chardonnay, layered and complex. Close to its peak now, and a giveaway price with its waves of stone fruit, toasty oak and acidity. Screwcap. 13.5% alc. **Rating** 95 **To** 2021 $30 ✪
Reserve Geographe Shiraz 2015 Crushed and destemmed, open-fermented, 12 days on skins, 16 months in French oak (50% new). The vintage was of lesser quality than '14, and the wine reflected this because it is dominated by the oak. On previous experience it may break free, but paradoxically its elegance and medium body may prevent it from doing this. Screwcap. 14% alc. **Rating** 94 **To** 2030
Margaret River Cabernet Sauvignon 2015 Machine-harvested, no sorting, crushed and destemmed, 15 days on skins, matured in French oak (40% new) for 18 months. Good colour retention; minimalist winemaking hasn't detracted from a medium-bodied wine with clear cassis varietal character. Screwcap. 14% alc. **Rating** 94 **To** 2030 $30 ✪

🍷🍷🍷🍷 **Margaret River Semillon Sauvignon Blanc 2017 Rating** 90 **To** 2019 $20 ✪

Dell'uva Wines

194 Richards Road, Freeling, SA 5372 **Region** Barossa Valley
T (08) 8525 2245 **www**.delluvawines.com.au **Open** By appt
Winemaker Wayne Farquhar **Est.** 2014 **Dozens** 1500 **Vyds** 20ha

Owner and winemaker Wayne Farquhar moved from horticulture to viticulture, acquiring his first vineyard in 1979. His viticultural career was low-key for a number of years, but having tasted wines from all over the world during a decade of business travel, he decided to establish Dell'uva Wines off the back of his existing conventional vineyard on the western ridge of the Barossa Valley. In short order he established additional small plots of an A–Z of varieties: aglianico, albarino, ansonica, arinto, barbera, cabernet sauvignon, canaiolo nero, carmenere, carnelian, chardonnay, dolcetto, durif, fiano, freisca, garnacha, graciano, grillo, lagrein, marsanne, mencia, merlot, montepulciano, moscato bianco, mourvedre, negroamaro, nero d'Avola, pinot blanc, pinot grigio, pinot noir, primitivo, roussanne, sagrantino, sangiovese, saperavi, shiraz, tannat, tempranillo, touriga nacional, verdelho, verdicchio, vermentino, viognier! With only 20ha available, the production of each wine is necessarily limited, the vinification as unconventional as the vineyard mix, utilising barrels, ceramic eggs, demijohns and tanks. The winemaking techniques have been chosen to throw maximum attention onto the inherent quality of the varieties, and this story has a long way to run.

ΨΨΨΨΨ **Barossa Lagrein 2014** Hand-picked, 70% destemmed, 30% whole bunches, open-fermented with heading down board, 3 weeks on skins, matured for 3 years in used French oak. Deep crimson-purple, with a flavour of deep, rich chocolate and choc-mint; almost elegant, strikingly different. Screwcap. 14% alc. **Rating** 94 To 2025 $35

Barossa Nero d'Avola 2014 Hand-picked, destemmed, open-fermented with heading down board, 3 weeks on skins, matured for 3 years in used French oak. Very good texture with fine, ripe tannins and nice, vanillan oak. Screwcap. 14.5% alc. **Rating** 94 To 2029 $35

ΨΨΨΨΨ **Barossa Cabernet Sauvignon 2014 Rating** 93 To 2029 $35
Barossa Sangiovese 2014 Rating 93 To 2024 $35
Barossa Mencia 2014 Rating 92 To 2024 $35
Barossa Montepulciano 2014 Rating 91 To 2023 $35
Barossa Arinto 2017 Rating 90 To 2024 $24

De Iuliis

1616 Broke Road, Pokolbin, NSW 2320 **Region** Hunter Valley
T (02) 4993 8000 **www**.dewine.com.au **Open** 7 days 10–5
Winemaker Michael De Iuliis **Est.** 1990 **Dozens** 20000 **Vyds** 30ha

Three generations of the De Iuliis family have been involved in the establishment of the vineyard. The family acquired a property at Lovedale in 1986 and planted 18ha of vines in '90, selling the grapes from the first few vintages to Tyrrell's but retaining increasing amounts for release under the De Iuliis label. In '99 the land on Broke Road was purchased and a winery and cellar door were built prior to the 2000 vintage. In '11 De Iuliis purchased 12ha of the long-established Steven Vineyard in Pokolbin. Winemaker Michael De Iuliis completed postgraduate studies in oenology at the Roseworthy campus of Adelaide University and was a Len Evans Tutorial scholar. He has lifted the quality of the wines into the highest echelon.

ΨΨΨΨΨ **Lucy's Run Vineyard Shiraz 2016** Aromas of lilac and rosewater infer lighter soils than the typical loams. The skein of mineral-clad acidity and the detailed fibre of the tannins, too. This wine, almost weightless in the mouth, verges on incandescent before a push of black fruit allusions expand across the finish, growing in sweetness. Long of flavour and high on finesse. Great success for the vintage. Screwcap. 13.2% alc. **Rating** 96 To 2028 $40 NG ✪

Single Vineyard Semillon 2017 From what is known as The Garden Vineyard, which is situated on a sandy flat in central Pokolbin. The wine demonstrates how much ripe citrus/lemongrass/vanilla-bean flavour can come from a semillon at the dawn of its life. Gold medal Hunter Valley Wine Show '17. Screwcap. 10.3% alc. **Rating** 95 **To** 2029 $30 ⊙

Steven Vineyard Chardonnay 2017 This is plush of ripeness, but fine-boned and fibrous in its mineral-clad detail and oak supports. Mid-weighted but intense, this is long and brimming with flavour. Curd, cashew and truffle nourishment at its core. Fruit descriptives are a waste of time. This is all about texture. Screwcap. 13% alc. **Rating** 95 **To** 2031 $35 NG ⊙

Limited Release Shiraz 2016 250 dozen bottles from the best barrels of the vintage. It is fuller bodied than usual, and likewise it has higher alcohol, but the selection has worked to perfection. The flavours are in a cherry (red and black) and plum spectrum, tannins and oak managed with the usual De Iuliis skill. Screwcap. 14.6% alc. **Rating** 95 **To** 2036 $80

Ablington Vineyard Shiraz 2016 Hunter scents of satsuma plum, dark cherry, anise and leather polish waft across the nose, taking time to emerge from their reticence. Subtle, medium-bodied and classic of proportions, this augurs extremely well for a long life ahead. Threaded with fine-boned tannins and a flush of juicy acidity, this has propulsion and expansion. Screwcap. 13.8% alc. **Rating** 95 **To** 2031 $40 NG

LDR Vineyard Shiraz Touriga 2016 An 80/20% blend that has surmounted the challenges of the vintage to produce a vibrantly fresh medium-bodied blend that is so well balanced it is a classic each-way, drink-now-or-later proposition. The tannins are fine, and the purity of the fruit is exceptional. One from left field, but a galloper. Screwcap. 13.5% alc. **Rating** 95 **To** 2031 $40

Semillon 2017 The bouquet has a quiver of citrus, lemongrass and talc, the palate firing its arrows with prefect precision, filling the senses with Meyer lemon juice and crisp acidity. The wine is open for business but also has a great future. Screwcap. 10.9% alc. **Rating** 94 **To** 2037 $20 ⊙

ㅇㅇㅇㅇㅇ **Limited Release Chardonnay 2017 Rating** 92 **To** 2023 $35 NG
Chardonnay 2017 Rating 91 **To** 2022 $20 NG ⊙
Pinot Noir 2017 Rating 91 **To** 2021 $35 NG
Shiraz Pinot Noir 2017 Rating 91 **To** 2021 $35 NG

Denton Viewhill Vineyard ★★★★★

160 Old Healesville Road, Yarra Glen, Vic 3775 **Region** Yarra Valley
T (03) 9012 3600 **www**.dentonwine.com **Open** By appt
Winemaker Luke Lambert **Est.** 1996 **Dozens** 2000 **Vyds** 31.3ha
Leading Melbourne architect John Denton and son Simon began the establishment of their vineyard with a first-stage planting in 1997, completing the plantings in 2004. The name Viewhill derives from the granite plug 'created 370 million years ago, sitting above the surrounding softer sandstones and silt of the valley'. This granite base is most unusual in the Yarra Valley, and together with the natural amphitheatre that the plug created, has produced consistently exceptional grapes. The principal varieties planted are pinot noir, chardonnay and shiraz, with lesser quantities of nebbiolo, cabernet sauvignon, merlot, cabernet franc and petit verdot. Exports to Japan.

ㅇㅇㅇㅇㅇ **Yellow Chardonnay 2015** The flotilla tacks one way, this yacht tacks another. Packaged in a slender 500ml bottle and complete with sherry and brown bread notes aplenty, it's an assault as much on varietal expectations as it is on the senses, waging a serious war on the latter. Production was 2 barrels only, though only one has been bottled and released; the second will stay locked away for another 2 years. The key detail: it's chardonnay given 2 years under flor. The result is nutty and floral in the extreme, though it still kicks with grapefruit-like flavour. It boasts extreme length. The effect is little short of mesmerising. Diam. 12.5% alc. **Rating** 96 **To** 2020 $45 CM ⊙

Denton Shed Nebbiolo Rose 2017 Excellent rose. Lays out the fruit and imbeds it with spice. A nod to savouriness, to smokiness even, but the core value

is fruit. Salmon-coloured and totally delicious. Screwcap. 13% alc. **Rating** 94
To 2020 $27 CM ☉

ΥΥΥΥ♀ **Denton Shed Cabernet Franc 2016 Rating** 91 To 2024 $30 CM

Derwent Estate

329 Lyell Highway, Granton, Tas 7070 **Region** Southern Tasmania
T (03) 6263 5802 **www.**derwentestate.com.au **Open** 7 days 10–4
Winemaker John Schuts **Est.** 1992 **Dozens** 2500 **Vyds** 10.08ha
Three generations of the Hanigan family are involved in the management of their historic
Mt Nassau property, owned by them since 1913. Given that the property has at various times
been involved with sheep, cattle, vegetable production, quarrying and the production of lime,
the addition of viticulture in '92 was not surprising. The vineyard has grown in stages, some
of the grapes bound for Bay of Fires and Penfolds Yattarna. The grapes retained by Derwent
Estate have produced consistently exceptional wines.

ΥΥΥΥΥ **Late Harvest Riesling 2015** Hand-picked, cool-fermented, 60g/l residual sugar,
7.5g/l acidity. Top gold Tasmanian Wine Show. Beautifully balanced – blossom,
nectar and lime juice don't come better than in this exquisitely detailed wine. It is
even richer than when first tasted in Mar '16, coating every corner of the mouth.
Screwcap. 10% alc. **Rating** 97 To 2025 $27 ☉

ΥΥΥΥΥ **Calcaire Chardonnay 2015** Bright and fresh straw-green; the complex bouquet
of white peach, pink grapefruit, brioche and spice pours it on with a stream of
tightly knit fruit, acidity and oak on the long palate. Will flourish with yet more
age. Screwcap. 12.8% alc. **Rating** 95 To 2030
Rose 2017 Bright, clear magenta; fragrant and flowery, the palate has delicious
red berry flavours set within a crown of bright but balanced acidity, residual sugar
not apparent. Lovely rose. Screwcap. 12.8% alc. **Rating** 95 To 2020 $27
Pinot Noir 2015 Bright, full crimson-purple; a seriously complex pinot,
the bouquet still to fully open, the palate leaving no doubt it will do so given
time. It has layer upon layer of black cherry and plum fruit supported by ripe,
unapologetic tannins à la Burgundy. This will be superb in '25. Screwcap.
13.7% alc. **Rating** 95 To 2028 $39
Riesling 2016 Typical of Tasmanian riesling, never lacking a spine of natural
acidity, promising and delivering a long life. Has already started to build on the
depth and length of its pure, ripe citrus and Granny Smith apple. Screwcap.
13% alc. **Rating** 94 To 2026 $27

ΥΥΥΥ♀ **Lime Kiln Point Pinot Noir 2016 Rating** 93 To 2029 $27 ☉
Pinot Gris 2017 Rating 92 To 2020 $30

Deviation Road

207 Scott Creek Road, Longwood, SA 5153 **Region** Adelaide Hills
T (08) 8339 2633 **www.**deviationroad.com **Open** 7 days 10–5
Winemaker Kate Laurie, Hamish Laurie **Est.** 1999 **Dozens** 10 000 **Vyds** 11ha
Deviation Road was created in 1998 by Hamish Laurie, great-great-grandson of Mary Laurie,
SA's first female winemaker. He initially joined with father Chris Laurie in '92 to help build
the Hillstowe Wines business; the brand was sold in 2001, but the Laurie family retained the
vineyard, which now supplies Deviation Road with its grapes. Wife Kate joined the business
in '01, having studied winemaking and viticulture in Champagne, then spending four years
at her family's Stone Bridge Estate in Manjimup. Deviation Road also has 3ha of pinot noir
and shiraz at Longwood, where its cellar door is situated. Exports to the UK, the US and
Hong Kong.

ΥΥΥΥΥ **Adelaide Hills Gruner Veltliner 2017** This has a very distinctive display of the
varietal character of gruner, not so much the white pepper (it's there in a minor
key) as the dappled texture and the fantastic grip it exerts within your mouth.
It's not phenolic in the negative sense of the term, but is talking long and loud.
A fascinating wine. Screwcap. 13.5% alc. **Rating** 96 To 2027 $32 ☉

Mary's Reserve Adelaide Hills Shiraz 2015 Sophisticated winemaking has been its own reward in this striking medium-bodied shiraz that doesn't put a foot wrong at any stage. It is bright and fresh, with spicy red and black cherry fruit, the whole-bunch component punching above its weight. A seriously good Adelaide Hills shiraz. Screwcap. 14% alc. **Rating** 95 **To** 2035 $45

Loftia Adelaide Hills Vintage Brut 2015 It feels generous and soft, and invigorates via a dart of flavour through the finish. Red apple; crunchy, blossomy, perfumed and inviting. Citrus. Custard creme. Brioche. You get the idea. It blooms with flavour and aroma but it's relentless in its charge through to an extended finish. Diam. 12.5% alc. **Rating** 95 $45 CM

Beltana Adelaide Hills Blanc de Blancs 2012 Once again, this shows Kate Laurie's years of experience in Champagne and the Adelaide Hills. Some brioche/biscuit has been brought into play with 5 years on lees, but not as much as there might have been with mlf (this is not a criticism). The result is a brilliantly fresh and crisp wine, the dosage spot on. Diam. 12% alc. **Rating** 95 $100

Adelaide Hills Chardonnay 2016 Maybe it will develop well, but finding a good reason to wait is difficult. This is alive with both flavour and complexity. White peach and honeysuckle, flint and nutty oak come charging at you, candied citrus notes trailing behind like the vapour of a jet. Screwcap. 12.5% alc. **Rating** 94 **To** 2021 $45 CM

Adelaide Hills Pinot Gris 2017 Balance, power, intensity of fruit, texture. All make a strong impression. It tastes of nashi pear and crisp, crunchy apple, feathered with honeysuckle and sweet spice notes, and with an impressive citrussy drive to the finish. Oak adds confidence more than flavour; it's a wine with its chest puffed out. Screwcap. 12.5% alc. **Rating** 94 **To** 2020 $30 CM ✪

ŦŦŦŦŢ **Adelaide Hills Pinot Noir 2016 Rating** 91 **To** 2023 $45 CM
Southcote Adelaide Hills Blanc de Noirs 2016 Rating 91 $55
Altair Adelaide Hills Sparkling Rose NV Rating 91 $35 CM

Devil's Cave Vineyard   ★★★★

250 Forest Drive, Heathcote, Vic 3523 **Region** Heathcote
T 0438 110 183 **www**.devilscavevineyard.com **Open** By appt
Winemaker Luke Lomax, Steve Johnson **Est.** 2012 **Dozens** 550 **Vyds** 0.4ha
This is an acorn and oak story. After retiring from 40+ years of business in Heathcote, Steve and Gay Johnson purchased this property to enjoy their retirement. In 2010 they planted 0.4ha of shiraz, and in '12 Steve asked Luke Lomax (his niece's husband, and a winemaker at Yabby Lake and Heathcote Estate) to help with the first vintage of 33 dozen bottles. The camaraderie was such that the Johnsons formed a partnership with Luke and Jade Lomax, and it's been onwards and upwards since, with an impressive collection of gold and silver medals for the '13, '14 and '15 shirazs. The winery's name comes from an adjacent cave locally known as 'the Devil's Cave'.

ŦŦŦŦŢ **Heathcote Grenache Rose 2017** Pale crimson. Vibrant fruit and spice, all rose oil and fennel, the juice of red cherries making sure it moves swiftly along. A most appealing rose. Screwcap. 13.5% alc. **Rating** 91 **To** 2019 $25 CM
Heathcote Shiraz 2016 No-one will be complaining about the flavour. It's fresh, juicy and hearty at once, a black cherried centre infused with dry licorice and leather and coated in milk chocolate. Well balanced and well polished throughout, the finish just satisfying enough. Screwcap. 14% alc. **Rating** 91 **To** 2024 $33 CM

Devil's Corner   ★★★★★

The Hazards Vineyard, Sherbourne Road, Apslawn, Tas 7190 **Region** East Coast Tasmania
T (03) 6257 8881 **www**.devilscorner.com.au **Open** 7 days 10–5
Winemaker Tom Wallace **Est.** 1999 **Dozens** 70 000 **Vyds** 175ha
This is one of the separately managed Tasmanian operations of Brown Brothers, taking The Hazards Vineyard on the east coast as its chief source; it is planted to pinot noir, chardonnay, sauvignon blanc, pinot gris, riesling, gewurztraminer and savagnin. The avant-garde labels

mark a decided change from the past, and also distinguish Devil's Corner from the other Tasmanian activities of Brown Brothers. Exports to all major markets.

ΤΤΤΤΤ Resolution Chardonnay 2016 After an inspection of the straw-green colour, and taking in the bouquet of some complexity, the immediate power of this wine as it enters the palate comes as no surprise. It has layered white peach, grapefruit and cashew flavours and savoury acidity. Screwcap. 13% alc. **Rating** 95 **To** 2026 $34 **✪**

Resolution Pinot Gris 2017 No suggestion of barrel fermentation or skin contact, but the sheer volume of flavour suggests the tendency to high yields has been strictly controlled. Nashi pear, spice and apple and faintly citrussy acidity provide context and support. Screwcap. 14% alc. **Rating** 95 **To** 2021 $32 **✪**

Pinot Grigio 2017 Some nashi pear and, in particular, fresh ginger on the bouquet. Texture and structure provide another level of interest. The climate, of course, is right. Screwcap. 12.5% alc. **Rating** 94 **To** 2020 $20 **✪**

Resolution Pinot Noir 2016 The colour is star-bright red, but so light it's not much more than a rose. The bouquet reaches another level with its pure fragrance, and the palate opens the curtains with its red-berried elegance, and even more its intensity and length. Screwcap. 13% alc. **Rating** 94 **To** 2025 $34

ΤΤΤΤ Riesling 2017 Rating 89 **To** 2023 $20

Devil's Lair ★★★★★

Rocky Road, Forest Grove via Margaret River, WA 6285 **Region** Margaret River
T 1300 651 650 **www**.devils-lair.com **Open** Not
Winemaker Ben Miller **Est.** 1981 **Dozens** NFP
Having rapidly carved out a high reputation for itself through a combination of clever packaging and impressive wine quality, Devil's Lair was acquired by Southcorp in 1996. The estate vineyards have been substantially increased since then, now with sauvignon blanc, semillon, chardonnay, cabernet sauvignon, merlot, shiraz, cabernet franc and petit verdot, supplemented by grapes purchased from contract growers. Production has increased from 40 000 dozen to many times greater, largely due to its Fifth Leg and Dance with the Devil wines. Exports to the UK, the US and other major markets.

ΤΤΤΤΤ 9th Chamber Chardonnay 2015 Much of the striking power and complexity of the wine can be taken straight back to the vineyard. If there is a question about Margaret River terroir, it's regarding the picking window needed to keep natural acidity functioning on the one hand, and achieving true fruit ripeness and flavour on the other. Chardonnay must avoid any similarity to sauvignon blanc of any quality, and its new oak must be seamlessly welded to the fruit. Screwcap. 12.5% alc. **Rating** 98 **To** 2035 $100 **✪**

ΤΤΤΤΤ Cabernet Sauvignon 2016 The colour is nigh-on perfect, the bouquet and palate with cassis and just the odd twig or two of bay leaf and dried herb. The tannins have been handsomely polished during fermentation, maceration and maturation, but they left the fruit untouched. Screwcap. 14% alc. **Rating** 96 **To** 2036 $50 **✪**

9th Chamber Cabernet Sauvignon 2013 A single small batch, fermented in tank for extended maceration, matured in new French oak for 16 months. Mouth-puckeringly intense, its disposition akin to Bordeaux of yore, and at odds with 14.5% alc. However, it has outstanding length and balance, and has an almost limitless cellaring future. Screwcap. **Rating** 96 **To** 2043 $120

Chardonnay 2016 Trembles on the brink of heading to sauvignon blanc territory, but doesn't fall. It is finer and more elegant than the usual complex Margaret River model, and also has exceptional length and balance to its stone-fruit and citrus base. Screwcap. 12.5% alc. **Rating** 95 **To** 2026 $50

Dance with the Devil Cabernet Sauvignon 2016 Includes 5% shiraz. Bright, deep crimson; a perfect model of a medium-bodied, mid-priced Margaret River cabernet. The quality of the fruit is the key, not oak (or tannins) — what you save on the oak you spend on the fruit, perfectly ripened and handled. Screwcap. 14% alc. **Rating** 94 **To** 2031 $25 ♻

🍷🍷🍷🍷♀ Fifth Leg Sauvignon Blanc Semillon 2017 **Rating** 90 **To** 2023 $18 ♻

 # Dewey Station Wines

14 Jane Street, Smithfield, SA 5114 **Region** Barossa Valley
T 0476 100 245 **www**.deweystationwines.com.au **Open** Not
Winemaker Stefan Dewey **Est.** 2017 **Dozens** 135
This micro-business will grow, but by exactly how much and when, all depends on your vision of the glass of water. What I can say is it's half full, not the reverse. Winemaker Stefan Dewey has covered a lot of ground since 2007 – all within the Barossa Valley. He worked in retail, distribution and marketing (enrolling in the wine marketing course at the University of Adelaide) before taking the ultimate step of beginning to make wine. He and wife Eleanor share a conviction that wine should be shared with friends and lots of laughter. Boring it should not be. But there has to be a limit, and I'll declare my hand by saying the label designs and production names will only ever gain niche market shares. But, of course, if you establish that niche, demand drawing supply, the game changes, because Stefan has X-factor in his GSM, and I wait for the hogshead of top tier shiraz to be released July/August '18.

🍷🍷🍷🍷♀ Venus Express GSM Barossa 2017 The label is every bit as outlandish as that of its siblings, but this deliciously juicy, red-berried GSM deserves to be taken seriously, even enjoyed to the max. A brown paper bag might come into play. Screwcap. 14.5% alc. **Rating** 92 **To** 2024 $25 ♻

🍷🍷🍷🍷 The Mars Express Barossa Shiraz 2017 **Rating** 89 **To** 2047 $25

Dexter Wines

210 Foxeys Road, Tuerong, Vic 3915 (postal) **Region** Mornington Peninsula
T (03) 5989 7007 **www**.dexterwines.com.au **Open** Not
Winemaker Tod Dexter **Est.** 2006 **Dozens** 2100 **Vyds** 7.1ha
Tod Dexter travlled to the US with the intention of enjoying some skiing; having done that, he became an apprentice winemaker at Cakebread Cellars, a well-known Napa Valley establishment. After seven years he returned to Australia and the Mornington Peninsula, and began the establishment of his vineyard in 1987, planted to pinot noir (4ha) and chardonnay (3.1ha). To keep the wolves from the door he became winemaker at Stonier, and leased his vineyard to them. Having left Stonier to become the Yabby Lake winemaker, and spurred on by turning 50 in 2006 (and at the urging of friends), he and wife Debbie established the Dexter label. The quality of his wines has been impeccable, the Pinot Noir especially so. Exports to the UK, the United Arab Emirates and Japan.

🍷🍷🍷🍷🍷 Mornington Peninsula Chardonnay 2016 This is all about crafting elegance and balance, length a by-product of those two elements. It stakes its case without fanfare, just stone fruit and cashew with a garland of citrussy acidity, the finish fresh. Screwcap. 13.5% alc. **Rating** 95 **To** 2028 $40
Mornington Peninsula Pinot Noir 2016 Bright, clear crimson is a subterfuge for a pinot with well above average weight, intensity and length. It is spicy, savoury and complex, and has a range of berry and plum fruit, all of it a clear expression of pinot. Screwcap. 13.5% alc. **Rating** 95 **To** 2029 $55

Di Fabio Estate

5 Valleyview Drive, McLaren Vale, SA 5171 (postal) **Region** McLaren Vale
T (08) 8383 0188 **www**.difabioestatewines.com.au **Open** Not
Winemaker Goe Di Fabio **Est.** 1994 **Dozens** 5000 **Vyds** 38.91ha
Di Fabio Estate is the venture of brothers Goe and Tony Di Fabio. Their parents Giovanni and Maria purchased their first vineyard in McLaren Vale in 1966 (with a tradition stretching back further to Italy) and became long-term contract grapegrowers for other winemakers. The business carried on by their sons has a 56ha property at McLaren Vale and 8.5ha at Waikerie.

The plantings are dominated by 12.5ha of grenache, 10.5ha of shiraz and 3.6ha of mourvedre; petit verdot, merlot, chardonnay, cabernet franc, sauvignon blanc and semillon are also grown. Exports to Macau, Singapore and China.

ϙϙϙϙϙ **Bush Vine McLaren Vale Shiraz 2016** Fruit from old bushvines at Blewitt Springs has a very good shiraz pedigree. There's attractive fragrance around the solid blackberry and dark cherry aromas, and it's flavoursome but not heavy through the palate, the black and red fruits supplemented by hints of milky chocolate and sweet spice with just enough tannin to provide balance. Screwcap. 14.5% alc. **Rating** 93 **To** 2028 $37 SC
Marietta GSM McLaren Vale Grenache Shiraz Mataro 2015 This is a no-frills approach to a blend that has stood the test of time. Grenache provides the framework, with its aromatics on the bouquet and its sweet-fruited flavours. Shiraz is more of a structural contributor and mataro adds some savoury spice and tannin. It all works. Screwcap. 14.5% alc. **Rating** 92 **To** 2027 $41 SC
McLaren Vale Grenache Shiraz 2015 Ripe, rounded and spicy, the aromas and flavours show typical regional earthiness with the sweet and savoury characters of grenache to the fore in a generous and softly textured structure. It's the sort of amiable red you could take anywhere. Screwcap. 14.5% alc. **Rating** 90 **To** 2025 $23 SC

Di Sciascio Family Wines ★★★★☆

2 Pincott Street, Newtown, Vic 3220 **Region** Various Victoria
T 0417 384 272 **www** dsaswines.com.au **Open** Not
Winemaker Matthew Di Sciascio, Andrew Santarossa **Est.** 2012 **Dozens** 2000
Matthew Di Sciascio's journey through wine has been an odyssey of Homeric proportions. His working life began as an apprentice boilermaker in his father's business. In 1991 he accompanied his father on a trip to Italy, where a shared bottle of wine in the kitchen of his uncle sowed the seed that flowered back in Australia, taking the form of garage winemaking with his father and friends. In '97, the vinous pace increased with vineyard work in the Yarra Valley and enrolment in Dookie Agricultural College's viticultural course. It accelerated further with the establishment of Bellbrae Estate in Geelong, and enrolling (in 2002) in the new Deakin University wine and science degree, graduating in '05 as co-dux. In Dec '10 the responsibility for seriously ill parents and a young daughter led to the decision to sell his share of Bellbrae to his financial partners, and (in '12) to start this venture.

ϙϙϙϙϙ **D'Sas Heathcote Shiraz 2016** Plum into blackberry, cloves into spice, some floral notes too. This is a hearty red with a pretty face, its warmth backed up by its abundance of flavour. Supple tannin and texture never go astray. Screwcap. 14.4% alc. **Rating** 93 **To** 2030 $40 CM
D'Sas Heathcote Sangiovese 2016 You can't help but be impressed by the mouthfeel, the flavour, the ripple of ripe tannin. This is as polished as it is savoury, its heart of cherry and plum safely ensconced in nutty oak and dry spice. If it wasn't for alcohol warmth, it would really be pushing high points, but even so, there's much to recommend it. Screwcap. 14% alc. **Rating** 92 **To** 2023 $40 CM
D'Sas King Valley Pinot Grigio 2017 The bouquet has an Italianate quality to it, and the varietal pear and almond aromas are quite subdued. Dry but textural through the palate, the lemony acidity gives it life, although it's perhaps a little too tart on the finish. Feels like a wine made to enjoy with food rather than analyse. Screwcap. 12% alc. **Rating** 90 **To** 2020 $32 SC
D'Sas King Valley Rosato 2017 More fruity than you'd expect by the appearance, with strawberries-and-cream aromas, and slightly sweet pink confectionery flavours on the palate. It has freshness, decent length, and there's a lightness of touch to it which makes for easy drinking. Screwcap. 12.5% alc. **Rating** 90 **To** 2019 $32 SC

Dickinson Estate

2414 Cranbrook Road, Boyup Brook, WA 6244 **Region** Blackwood Valley
T (08) 9769 1080 **www**.dickinsonestate.com.au **Open** Not
Winemaker Coby Ladwig, Luke Eckersley **Est.** 1994 **Dozens** 6000 **Vyds** 8.52ha
Trevor and Mary Dickinson went from a 20-year life at sea with the Australian Navy to
becoming farmers at Boyup Brook in 1987. They learned on the job, initially cropping, and
breeding sheep for wool, then cattle and fat lambs. In '94 they diversified further, planting
shiraz, chardonnay, sauvignon blanc and cabernet sauvignon, and appointing the highly
experienced team of Coby Ladwig and Luke Eckersley to make the wines. Exports to China.

ΨΨΨΨΨ **Limited Release Cabernet Sauvignon 2016** 19yo vines, machine-harvested,
crushed and destemmed, 6 days' cold soak, 2 weeks' post-ferment maceration,
matured for 14 months in French oak (32% new). There are parallels with the
Shiraz – both beautiful wines with effortless power. Cork. 14.2% alc. **Rating** 96
To 2036 $40 ✪
Limited Release Shiraz 2016 11yo vines, machine-harvested, crushed and
destemmed, matured for 12 months in French oak (32% new). There's a world of
difference between this wine and its junior sibling. This is full-bodied and dense,
with spice, pepper and licorice twinned with deep-seated blackberry, black cherry
and a generous serve of French oak. The cork suggests some is headed for foreign
shores. 14.5% alc. **Rating** 95 To 2036 $40

ΨΨΨΨΨ **Blackwood Valley Cabernet Sauvignon 2016** Rating 92 To 2026 $23 ✪
Blackwood Valley Shiraz 2016 Rating 90 To 2020 $23

DiGiorgio Family Wines

14918 Riddoch Highway, Coonawarra, SA 5263 **Region** Coonawarra
T (08) 8736 3222 **www**.digiorgio.com.au **Open** 7 days 10–5
Winemaker Peter Douglas, Bryan Tonkin **Est.** 1998 **Dozens** 25000 **Vyds** 353.53ha
Stefano DiGiorgio emigrated from Abruzzo, Italy, in 1952. Over the years, he and his family
gradually expanded their holdings at Lucindale in the Limstone Coast to 126ha. In '89 he
began planting cabernet sauvignon, chardonnay, merlot, shiraz and pinot noir. In 2002 the
family purchased (from Southcorp) the historic Rouge Homme winery in Coonawarra
and its surrounding 13.5ha of vines. The plantings here have since been increased to almost
230ha, the lion's share to cabernet sauvignon. The enterprise offers full winemaking services
to vignerons in the Limestone Coast. Exports to all major markets.

ΨΨΨΨΨ **Kongorong Riesling 2017** From the cool Mount Gambier region, much
unexplored but potentially very good. This has riveting acidity and lime-sorbet
flavours, and exciting development potential. I have five bob each way. Screwcap.
11.5% alc. **Rating** 94 To 2029 $19 ✪

ΨΨΨΨ **Coonawarra Shiraz 2015** Rating 89 To 2025 $26

Dinny Goonan

880 Winchelsea-Deans Marsh Road, Bambra, Vic 3241 **Region** Geelong
T 0438 408 420 **www**.dinnygoonan.com.au **Open** 7 days (Jan), w'ends &
public hols (Nov–Jun)
Winemaker Dinny Goonan, Angus Goonan **Est.** 1990 **Dozens** 1500 **Vyds** 5.5ha
The establishment of Dinny Goonan dates back to 1988, when Dinny bought a 20ha property
near Bambra in the hinterland of the Otway coast. Dinny had recently completed a viticulture
diploma at CSU, and initially a wide range of varieties was planted in what is now known as
the Nursery Block, to establish those best suited to the area. As these came into production
Dinny headed back to CSU, where he completed a wine science degree. Production is now
focused on shiraz and riesling.

ΨΨΨΨΨ **Single Vineyard Riesling 2017** Estate-grown, hand-picked, whole-bunch
pressed, cool-fermented. Wow. Loaded to the gills with Rose's lime juice, and with

both persistence and length. Remarkable. Screwcap. 11.5% alc. **Rating** 95 **To** 2032 $25 ✪

🍷🍷🍷🍷 Single Vineyard Shiraz 2016 **Rating** 92 **To** 2021 $30
Cabernets 2016 **Rating** 92 **To** 2029 $30
Proserpina Sparkling Riesling 2017 **Rating** 90 $25

Dionysus Winery ★★★★☆

1 Patemans Lane, Murrumbateman, NSW 2582 **Region** Canberra District
T (02) 6227 0208 **www**.dionysus-winery.com.au **Open** W'ends & public hols 10–5
Winemaker Michael O'Dea **Est.** 1998 **Dozens** 1000 **Vyds** 4ha

Michael and Wendy O'Dea founded the winery while they had parallel lives as public servants in Canberra; they have now retired, and devote themselves full-time to Dionysus. They purchased their property in 1996, and planted chardonnay, sauvignon blanc, riesling, viognier, merlot, pinot noir, cabernet sauvignon and shiraz between '98 and 2001. Michael has completed an associate degree in winemaking at CSU, and is responsible for viticulture and winemaking; Wendy has completed various courses at Canberra TAFE and is responsible for wine marketing and (in their words) 'nagging Michael and being a general slushie'.

🍷🍷🍷🍷🍷 Riesling 2016 Absolutely flooded with Rose's lime juice; Granny Smith apple an afterthought. Ample acidity provides balance and underwrites the future, but it's of secondary importance for a wine that Dionysus himself would have consumed in large quantities. Screwcap. 11.2% alc. **Rating** 95 **To** 2025 $23 ✪

Riesling 2017 Generous, but not going to the point of losing its shape or line. An abundance of Rose's lime juice, plus a slice of Granny Smith apple, the acidity nicely balanced. Screwcap. 10.6% alc. **Rating** 94 **To** 2029 $23 ✪

Shiraz Viognier 2015 A powerful wine reflecting the vintage more than the unspecified amount of co-fermented viognier. Canberra is a two-horse race between riesling and shiraz, and is gaining in reputation, led by Clonakilla (a long way in front of the runners up). This wine demands 5 years for its intense black fruits to loosen their hold. Screwcap. 14.1% alc. **Rating** 94 **To** 2035 $28 ✪

🍷🍷🍷🍷 Canberra District Viognier 2017 **Rating** 93 **To** 2021 $23 ✪
Canberra District Gamay 2017 **Rating** 90 **To** 2022 $28
Canberra District May Riesling 2017 **Rating** 90 **To** 2025 $28

Doc Adams ★★★☆

2/41 High Street, Willunga, SA 5172 **Region** McLaren Vale
T (08) 8556 2111 **www**.docadamswines.com.au **Open** By appt
Winemaker Adam Jacobs **Est.** 2005 **Dozens** 10 000 **Vyds** 27ha

Doc Adams is a partnership between viticulturist Adam Jacobs and orthopaedic surgeon Dr Darren Waters, hence the combination of their names for the winery. Adam graduated from CSU with a degree in viticulture and has had over 25 years' experience as a consultant viticulturist and winemaker. Darren has grown low-yielding shiraz vines in McLaren Vale since 1998. Exports to China.

🍷🍷🍷🍷 Cabernet Sauvignon 2015 Part of the premium range, it's a compilation of savoury notes from new leather, dried berries, woody spices and eucalyptus. Full-bodied, the oak somewhat dominating and drying the finish, although there's some suppleness to the tannins. Screwcap. 14.4% alc. **Rating** 89 **To** 2024 $35 JF

Tempranillo 2015 Good colour; hint of raspberry and cinnamon with some red licorice; fresh with ripe furry tannins. It's uncomplicated, making it a perfect barbecue wine. Screwcap. 14.4% alc. **Rating** 89 **To** 2020 $25 JF

Dr Edge ★★★★★

5 Cato Avenue, West Hobart, Tas 7000 (postal) **Region** Southern Tasmania
T 0439 448 151 **www**.dr-edge.com **Open** Not
Winemaker Peter Dredge **Est.** 2015 **Dozens** 550 **Vyds** 1.5ha

Having worked as a winemaker for Petaluma, Peter Dredge moved to Tasmania in 2009, spending 7 years within the Accolade group, becoming chief winemaker at Bay of Fires. He then moved proactively to become a consultant and self-employed winemaker, short-circuiting the uncertainty that existed around Accolade and its future. In '15 he sourced a small amount of pinot noir from Joe Holyman of Stoney Rise and Gerald Ellis of Meadowbank to start his own label, making his wine at Moorilla. During vintage in '15, the Ellis family approached Pete to form a partnership to relaunch Meadowbank. As part of the deal, they gave Pete a sole lease arrangement on 1.5ha of pinot noir. Exports to the US.

🍷🍷🍷🍷🍷 **Pinot Noir 2017** MV6, 777 and 115 clones, 60% from the Derwent Valley, 30% East Coast and 10% Tamar Valley. The bouquet is multifaceted, with no clear message from the group of single vineyards. The palate moves onto another tier, but carries with it the higher-toned red fruits of clone 115 (compared to MV6 last year). It also achieves a lightness of touch without any sacrifice of line or length. This is for the serious business of enjoyment, not the science of dissecting small pieces of a large puzzle. Screwcap. 12.5% alc. **Rating** 97 **To** 2025 $50 ✪

🍷🍷🍷🍷🍷 **East Tasmania Pinot Noir 2017** The Dr Edge pinots are part of a voyage of discovery, so it is that the East, North and South are all clone 115 (the '16s were MV6), and all have identical vinification. Fragrant, with more red fruits, long and silky; reflects the clonal change, is driven by the very cool vintage, the tannin sotto voce. Screwcap. 12.5% alc. **Rating** 96 **To** 2025 $50 ✪
South Tasmania Pinot Noir 2017 From the Meadowbank vineyard. Unexpectedly one of the most loquacious of the single-vineyard pinots. A complex bouquet with hints of lamb's wool. The tannins have distinct shape, and the palate is very long and insistent. Screwcap. 12.5% alc. **Rating** 96 **To** 2025 $50 ✪
North Tasmania Pinot Noir 2017 From the Stoney Rise vineyard in the Tamar Valley. Extremely expressive, precise and detailed; dark glossy cherries and cherry pips; positive supple tannins. Screwcap. 12.5% alc. **Rating** 95 **To** 2024 $50

Dodgy Brothers   ★★★★★

PO Box 655, McLaren Vale, SA 5171 **Region** McLaren Vale
T 0450 000 373 www.dodgybrotherswines.com **Open** Not
Winemaker Wes Pearson **Est.** 2010 **Dozens** 2000
This is a partnership between Canadian-born Flying Winemaker Wes Pearson, viticulturist Peter Bolte and grapegrower Peter Sommerville. Wes graduated from the University of British Columbia's biochemistry program in 2008, along the way working at wineries including Chateau Leoville Las Cases in Bordeaux. In '08 he and his family moved to McLaren Vale, and after working at several wineries, he joined the Australian Wine Research Institute as a sensory analyst. Peter Bolte has over 35 vintages in McLaren Vale under his belt, and was the original 'Dodgy Brother'. Peter Sommerville's vineyard provides cabernet sauvignon, cabernet franc and petit verdot for the Dodgy Brothers Bordeaux blend. Exports to Canada.

🍷🍷🍷🍷🍷 **Juxtaposed Grenache 2016** The label is out there – a sketch of Mr T behind the wheel of a convertible: it'll appeal to a certain demographic. The wine has much broader appeal – it's a beauty. A splash of mataro (8%) and a drop of shiraz (1%) add another layer of complexity to what is a subtle blend of florals, red fruits and licorice, with fresh acidity and fine-grained tannins leading long onto the effortlessly smooth palate. Screwcap. 14.2% alc. **Rating** 96 **To** 2026 $29 JF ✪
Juxtaposed Shiraz 2016 12% mataro in the mix; gentle handling including ageing in French and American oak hogsheads (7% new). It's not a big red. It's full of red fruit though, buoyant and juicy with the right amount of spice, licorice with well knitted tannins providing a savoury twist on the finish. Screwcap. 14.2% alc. **Rating** 95 **To** 2030 $29 JF ✪
Juxtaposed Sangiovese 2016 While there's 12% cabernet franc adding a perfumed, peppery lift, this sings of sangio, which is picked early to retain freshness and vibrancy. Aromas of morello and red cherries, black tea and warm earth right

through to the palate. Medium-bodied with spritely acidity and Italianate tannins. Utterly delicious. Screwcap. 13% alc. **Rating** 95 **To** 2026 $29 JF ✪

🍷🍷🍷🍷🍷 **Juxtaposed Bigger Boat Fiano 2017 Rating** 93 **To** 2020 $25 JF ✪
Fiano 2016 Rating 93 **To** 2020 $25 JF ✪
Juxtaposed Mr Furley Pinot Meunier Rose 2017 Rating 93 **To** 2019 $25 JF ✪

DogRock Winery   ★★★★★
114 Degraves Road, Crowlands, Vic 3377 **Region** Pyrenees
T 0409 280 317 **www**.dogrock.com.au **Open** By appt
Winemaker Allen Hart **Est.** 1999 **Dozens** 800 **Vyds** 6.2ha
This is the micro-venture of Allen (now full-time winemaker) and Andrea (viticulturist) Hart. Having purchased the property in 1998, the planting of shiraz, riesling, tempranillo, grenache, chardonnay and marsanne began in 2000 (0.2ha of touriga nacional added in '16). Given Allen's former post as research scientist/winemaker with Foster's, the attitude taken to winemaking is unexpected. The estate-grown wines are made in a low-tech fashion, without gas cover or filtration, the Harts saying, 'All wine will be sealed with a screwcap and no DogRock wine will ever be released under natural cork bark'. DogRock installed the first solar-powered irrigation system in Australia, capable of supplying water 365 days a year, even at night or in cloudy conditions.

🍷🍷🍷🍷🍷 **Degraves Road Pyrenees Shiraz 2016** The glorious, deep crimson-purple colour, and the sheer intensity of the flavours, attest to a top quality vintage. Plum, blackberry and licorice fruit is punctuated by savoury, earthy, ripe tannins, all adding up to a full-bodied wine with a future stretching out for decades. Screwcap. 14% alc. **Rating** 96 **To** 2046 $35 ✪
Pyrenees Grenache 2016 Trophy for Best Other Red Varietal Victorian Wine Show '17. Although the wine was matured for 14 months, it hasn't seen oak, instead slowly developing in tank. It is ultra-juicy, with red fruits led by cherry flooding the mouth, and splashes of spice and pepper. Screwcap. 14.5% alc. **Rating** 95 **To** 2031 $30 ✪
Degraves Road Pyrenees Riesling 2017 Gleaming straw-green; the bouquet is presently reticent, the palate anything but. Granny Smith apple, citrus zest and pith, crunchy acidity and texture all add up to the 20–30-year future suggested by Allen Hart. It does need to show all that it presently conceals. Screwcap. 11% alc. **Rating** 94 **To** 2043 $25 ✪
Pyrenees Shiraz 2016 This and its Degraves Road sibling offer exceptional value for money. Part of the explanation is the contract-grown percentage of fruit used for this wine. The rest is attention to detail, and a lavish oak budget. Red berry/cherry fruit is supported by fine, supple tannins ex both the fruit and the oak. Screwcap. 14% alc. **Rating** 94 **To** 2036 $25 ✪

🍷🍷🍷🍷🍷 **Grampians Pyrenees Tempranillo 2016 Rating** 93 **To** 2026 $25 ✪
Pedro's Sparkling Red NV Rating 93 $30

Domaine A   ★★★★★
105 Tea Tree Road, Campania, Tas 7026 **Region** Southern Tasmania
T (03) 6260 4174 **www**.domaine-a.com.au **Open** Mon–Fri 10–4
Winemaker Peter Althaus **Est.** 1973 **Dozens** 5000 **Vyds** 11ha
The striking black label of the premium Domaine A wine, dominated by the single multicoloured 'A', signified the change of ownership from George Park to Peter Althaus many years ago. The wines are made without compromise, and reflect the low yields from the immaculately tended vineyards. They represent aspects of both Old World and New World philosophies, techniques and styles. Exports to the UK, Canada, Denmark, Switzerland, Taiwan, Hong Kong, Singapore, Japan and China.

ŶŶŶŶŶ **Cabernet Sauvignon 2009** There is no reason whatsoever to disparage this wine just because it's cabernet from Tasmania. The reason it's so good is its varietal makeup (including 4% each of cabernet franc/merlot and 2% petit verdot) and the time it's been given in bottle. The tannins have been vanquished, and the blackcurrant/bramble flavours are in fine fettle, with a touch of cedary oak the final touch. Length and balance are its trademarks. Cork. 13.5% alc. **Rating** 96 **To** 2039

Domaine Asmara

Gibb Road, Toolleen, Vic 3551 **Region** Heathcote
T (03) 5433 6133 **www**.domaineasmara.com **Open** 7 days 9–6.30
Winemaker Sanguine Estate **Est.** 2008 **Dozens** 2000 **Vyds** 12ha
Chemical engineer Andreas Greiving had a lifelong dream to own and operate a vineyard, and the opportunity came along with the global financial crisis. He was able to purchase a vineyard planted to shiraz, cabernet sauvignon, cabernet franc, durif and viognier, and have the wines contract-made. The venture is co-managed by dentist wife Hennijati. The red wines are made from controlled yields of 1–1.5t per acre, hence their concentration. Exports to the UK, Vietnam, Malaysia, Hong Kong and China.

ŶŶŶŶŶ **Heathcote Viognier 2017** This is viognier in full flight: rich and forceful, with layered fruits and the phenolic derriere that comes with such power. Love it or leave it. Screwcap. 14.5% alc. **Rating** 92 **To** 2021 $27
Reserve Heathcote Shiraz 2015 It's no shrinking violet, generous of fruit, oak, and alcohol. Characters of ripe plum and blackberry with a touch of Christmas pudding are prominent on the bouquet and run through the palate, with the breath of 15.1% alc., and sawdusty dry tannins dominant on the finish. It's well done in its particular style. Cork. **Rating** 91 **To** 2030 $49 SC
Infinity Heathcote Shiraz 2016 Impenetrable purple-red. Ripe black fruit and oak vie for attention across a grainy, high density sweet-fruited core. Full throttle, high octane stuff. Big fruit, tannin, oak and alcohol. Cork. 15.5% alc. **Rating** 90 **To** 2035 $85 DB
Private Collection Heathcote Shiraz 2016 Ripe, cooked blackberry and dark plum underpinned with big grainy tannins. The tannins need the ripeness; the ripe fruit, the tannins. If you like big wines, look no further. Screwcap. 15.3% alc. **Rating** 90 **To** 2030 $35 DB
The Lady Killer Heathcote Vine de Paille Viognier 2016 The label should read Vin, not Vine. Made by desiccating the grapes for a very long time on racks/ straw in the winery. It is apricot essence, the sort of wine that in bygone centuries was held for hundreds of years in Tokaji, Hungary. Given its cork, its life in Australian cellars will be much shorter. 375ml. 12.4% alc. **Rating** 90 **To** 2025 $35

ŶŶŶŶ **Reserve Heathcote Shiraz 2016 Rating** 89 **To** 2030 $49 DB

Domaine Carlei G2

1 Alber Road, Upper Beaconsfield, Vic 3808 **Region** Various Victoria
T (03) 5944 4599 **Open** By appt
Winemaker David Carlei **Est.** 2010 **Dozens** 2000
This is the venture of David Carlei, son of Sergio Carlei; the two have worked together for some years. David studied wine marketing at CSU, and his focus is on using organic and/ or biodynamic grapes, and macerating white wines on skins for up to 90 days, followed by prolonged lees contact with minimal fining. The reds see a similar process: whole clusters, wild yeast fermentation and prolonged maceration periods with ageing on lees. They are, in short, natural wines, the red wines with more intrinsic quality than most of their peers. Exports to the US, the UK and China.

ŶŶŶŶŶ **Yarra Valley Syrah 2015** Bright crimson-purple; this works off a savoury theme with wood smoke, iodine and tangy red/blue fruits. There's a balanced waft of pepper and whole-bunch stemmy flavours, though. Medium-bodied with ripe and sinewy tannins, just a little drying on the finish and that holds this back. Diam. 14% alc. **Rating** 93 **To** 2025 $40 JF

Viognier 2016 A rich but not over-the-top mix of yellow flowers, creamed honey and apricot kernel with a minerally thread holding everything together. Grippy phenolics but overall, a very savoury, moreish wine. Screwcap. 14% alc. **Rating** 92 **To** 2021 $40 JF

Domaine Dawnelle ★★★★☆

PO Box 89, Claremont, Tas 7011 **Region** Southern Tasmania
T 0447 484 181 **www**.domainedawnelle.com **Open** Not
Winemaker Michael O'Brien **Est.** 2013 **Dozens** 430 **Vyds** 1.2ha
Domaine Dawnelle is a partnership between Michael O'Brien and Kylie Harrison. The name of the venture honours Michael's great-grandmother (and farm) in rural NSW. He studied at CSU, and is a viticulturist and winemaker with 20 years' experience in mainland Australia, abroad and, more recently, Tasmania. As well as planting 1.2ha of vineyard overlooking the Derwent River, he manages the Tinderbox Vineyard, providing the partnership with grapes until the estate vineyard comes into full bearing.

🍷🍷🍷🍷🍷 **Gloria Chardonnay 2016** It didn't see any new oak but it did go through mlf. The result is a full vindication of the decisions made. It's textural and long, elegant and interesting. White peach, chalk, honeysuckle and powdered milk characters; a toasty, minerally rub to the finish. Time will be very kind. Cork. 13.4% alc. **Rating** 95 **To** 2025 $46 CM

🍷🍷🍷🍷🍷 **Pinot d'Or 2016 Rating** 91 **To** 2021 $60 CM

Domaine Naturaliste ★★★★★

Cnr Hairpin Road/Bussell Highway, Carbunup, WA 6280 **Region** Margaret River
T (08) 9755 1188 **www**.domainenaturaliste.com.au **Open** Not
Winemaker Bruce Dukes **Est.** 2012 **Dozens** 10 000
Bruce Dukes' career dates back over 25 years, its foundations built around a degree in agronomy from the University of WA, followed by a masters degree in viticulture and agronomy from the University of California (Davis). A four-year stint at Francis Ford Coppola's iconic Niebaum-Coppola winery in the Napa Valley followed. Back in WA Bruce worked with a consultancy and contract winemaking business in Margaret River in 2000. His winery was set up to handle small and large amounts of fruit, but it was not until '12 that he made his own wine under the Domaine Naturaliste label. The quality of all the wines is excellent. Exports to the UK, the US, Canada and China.

🍷🍷🍷🍷🍷 **Artus Margaret River Chardonnay 2016** Hand-picked, whole-bunch pressed, cloudy juice wild-fermented in French oak (40% new), matured for 12 months. It's exceptionally fresh and pure, white peach and nectarine at its core. Roasted cashew and citrussy acidity dance around this, creating a very long and crisp finish. Screwcap. 13% alc. **Rating** 97 **To** 2029 $45 **✪**

🍷🍷🍷🍷🍷 **Sauvage Margaret River Sauvignon Blanc Semillon 2015** The hauntingly complex bouquet has passionfruit, lemongrass and French oak aromas, the palate with unusual depth and classic length. Trophies at the Sydney International Wine Competition '16 and Margaret River Wine Show '16, both thoroughly deserved. Screwcap. 13% alc. **Rating** 96 **To** 2021 $30 **✪**

Morus Margaret River Cabernet Sauvignon 2015 Redcurrant, blackberry, violets and bay leaf on the bouquet; cedar and chocolate on the palate, oak-derived, but sitting seamlessly within the wine as well. The fruit and the tannin filling the mouth expansively. ProCork. 13.5% alc. **Rating** 96 **To** 2035 $85 SC

Sauvage Wallcliffe Margaret River Sauvignon Blanc 2016 Genuine complexity, with a suite of desirable varietal characters and spicy French oak. Most impressive though is the shape and feel in the mouth; taut, textured, persistent — it finds every tastebud on the tongue. Screwcap. 13% alc. **Rating** 95 **To** 2021 $30 SC **✪**

Rachis Margaret River Syrah 2016 A trophy and several gold medals to its credit. It opens peppery, gamey, herbal and cedary. Within that, there's lovely fruit purity as well. It's perfectly medium-bodied in weight, and the effect of the tannin and acid astringency lends a feeling of both structure and freshness. Screwcap. 13.8% alc. **Rating** 95 **To** 2026 $30 SC ☻

Floris Margaret River Chardonnay 2016 Aromas of white peach and lemon, with the distinctive feel of the Gin Gin clone in evidence as well as some creamy, spicy oak. Richly textured with sweet fruit flavours and juicy citrus-like acidity, which picks up towards the end of the palate and makes for a lip-smacking finish. Screwcap. 13% alc. **Rating** 94 **To** 2021 $30 SC ☻

🍷🍷🍷🍷🍷 Discovery Sauvignon Blanc Semillon 2017 **Rating** 93 **To** 2020 $24 SC ☻
Discovery Chardonnay 2016 **Rating** 93 **To** 2025 $24 ☻
Discovery Syrah 2015 **Rating** 93 **To** 2025 $24 SC ☻
Discovery Cabernet Sauvignon 2016 **Rating** 92 **To** 2026 $24 SC ☻

Dominique Portet   ★★★★★

870–872 Maroondah Highway, Coldstream, Vic 3770 **Region** Yarra Valley
T (03) 5962 5760 **www**.dominiqueportet.com **Open** 7 days 10–5
Winemaker Ben Portet **Est.** 2000 **Dozens** 15 000 **Vyds** 6.3ha
Dominique Portet was bred in the purple. He spent his early years at Chateau Lafite (where his father was régisseur), and was one of the first Flying Winemakers, commuting to Clos du Val in the Napa Valley, where his brother was also a winemaker. He then spent over 20 years as managing director of Taltarni and Clover Hill. After retiring from Taltarni, he moved to the Yarra Valley, a region he had been closely observing since the mid-1980s. In 2001 he found the site he had long looked for and built his winery and cellar door, planting a quixotic mix of viognier, sauvignon blanc and merlot. The newly installed sorting line eliminates all green stalks and unripe/overripe grapes. Son Ben is now executive winemaker, leaving Dominique with a roving role as de facto consultant and brand marketer. Ben himself has a winemaking CV of awesome scope, covering all parts of France, South Africa, California and four vintages at Petaluma. Exports to Canada, India, Dubai, Hong Kong, Singapore, Malaysia and Japan.

🍷🍷🍷🍷🍷 Heathcote Shiraz 2015 It's shiraz on a long lead, the flavours running free, the tannin there but low key, the finish full of energy. This wine manages depth of both fruit and spice, keeps a close watch on vibrancy even as it tips into richness, and throws blossomy notes atop clovey oak to make it all seem one and the same. A peak release. Cork. 14% alc. **Rating** 96 **To** 2035 $55 CM ☻

Yarra Valley Cabernet Sauvignon 2015 It's cabernet built on pure blackcurrant and boysenberry, infused with bay leaf and tobacco-like notes, kissed so lightly by cedary oak that the effect is little more than textural. It's a soft, free-flowing and yet exquisitely well shaped red with all the length you could ever hope for. Take a bow Ben Portet. Cork. 14% alc. **Rating** 96 **To** 2040 $60 CM ☻

Origine Yarra Valley Chardonnay 2016 This is what Yarra Valley chardonnay is all about, its exceptional length and freshness glinting like a sword in the early morning, the flavours of grapefruit and al dente white peach, plus crunchy acidity. Screwcap. 13.5% alc. **Rating** 95 **To** 2029 $45

Fontaine Yarra Valley Cabernet Sauvignon 2016 87% cabernet sauvignon, 10% merlot, 2% malbec and 1% petit verdot. This is fresh, lively and juicy, with as much cassis as tannins and oak, all three gliding through on the way to the finish and aftertaste. Its gold medal at the Sydney Wine Show '17 serves to emphasise the value offered. Screwcap. 13.5% alc. **Rating** 95 **To** 2026 $22 ☻

Andre Pierre Yarra Valley Pyrenees Cabernet Sauvignon 2014 Named after Ben's grandfather, Andre Pierre, and reminiscent of some of the features of Ben's father Dominique's best Taltarni cabernets. It is an autocratic style, with plentiful tannins to feed on, but with the balm of varietal blackcurrant fruit to provide balance, the role of vanillan oak ambivalent. My conservative drink-to date derives from wine stain on the sides of the cork. 14% alc. **Rating** 95 **To** 2039 $180

Fontaine Yarra Valley Rose 2017 60% shiraz, 25% cabernet sauvignon and 15% merlot. Gently spicy red berry aromas sing from the same page as the palate, with a savoury cast of considerable complexity, the finish elongated by perfectly pitched tannins. Screwcap. 13% alc. **Rating** 94 **To** 2020 $22 ✪

Dorrien Estate ★★★★★

Cnr Barossa Valley Way/Siegersdorf Road, Tanunda, SA 5352 **Region** Barossa Valley
T (08) 8561 2200 **www**.cellarmasters.com.au **Open** Not
Winemaker Julie Montgomery **Est.** 1982 **Dozens** 1 million
Dorrien Estate is the physical base of the vast Cellarmasters network – the largest direct-sale outlet in Australia. It also makes wine for many producers across Australia at its modern winery, which has a capacity of 14.5 million litres in tank and barrel; however, a typical make of each wine will be little more than 1000 dozen. Most of the wines made for others are exclusively distributed by Cellarmasters. Acquired by Woolworths in May 2011.

🍷🍷🍷🍷🍷 **Redemption Tumbarumba Chardonnay 2016** You'd take this any day of the week. It has power, there's no worries about that, but the elegance and length on offer here are what sets it apart. It drives both beautifully and harmoniously from start to finish and then just sails on from there. Screwcap. 13% alc. **Rating** 95 **To** 2024 $42 CM
Black Wattle Vineyards Mount Benson Shiraz 2015 The interesting thing is the level of spice. It's sweet spice, quite floral, with fennel and black cherry running through, but it gives the wine personality and a distinct savouriness. This is in the context of deli meat characters and indeed of a certain jellied aspect to the fruit. There are a lot of bases covered here. It's high quality. Screwcap. 14% alc. **Rating** 95 **To** 2030 $33 CM ✪
Mockingbird Hill Single Vineyard Hayshed Block Clare Valley Riesling 2017 It somehow manages to combine intensity with restraint. It's all there and yet it's cool, almost shy, the flavours of lemon, lime and talc rearing and then turning away, the finish shooting forward, nothing left to chance. Screwcap. 12.5% alc. **Rating** 94 **To** 2028 $30 CM ✪
Mockingbird Hill Single Vineyard Skilly Block Clare Valley Riesling 2017 It has a textural element and a keen intensity to the fruit, the finish then punching long. Slate, lime and bath salts are the order of the day. You can't help but admire its power, and note its elegance too. Screwcap. 12.5% alc. **Rating** 94 **To** 2027 $38 CM
Mockingbird Hill Single Vineyard MCR Block Clare Valley Shiraz 2016 It's a brutish red with dark-berried fruit, chocolate, molasses and mint flavours laid on, chunky tannin looking the goods in context. You can drink this now if you like 'em big, but this has many years up its sleeve. Screwcap. **Rating** 94 **To** 2034 $64 CM
Black Wattle Vineyards Icon Mount Benson Cabernet Sauvignon 2015 Power and impact are a given, perfume and balance are the icing. This is a well constructed wine. It tastes of blackcurrant, fresh mint, violets and creamy vanilla, some tobacco in there too, though it's essentially seamless, nothing really sticking out. The finish is rugged with tannin in a good way. It will mature well too. Screwcap. 14% alc. **Rating** 94 **To** 2030 $46 CM

🍷🍷🍷🍷🍷 **Avon Brae Riesling 2017** **Rating** 93 **To** 2026 $30 CM
Tolley Elite Adelaide Hills Chardonnay 2016 **Rating** 93 **To** 2023 $38 CM
Dorrien Estate Bin 1A Chardonnay 2016 **Rating** 93 **To** 2023 $31 CM
Wordsmith Upper Blocks Shiraz 2015 **Rating** 93 **To** 2030 $65 CM
Mockingbird Hill Slate Lane Clare Valley Cabernet Malbec 2016 **Rating** 93 **To** 2028 $30 CM
Avon Brae Moculta Eden Valley Shiraz 2016 **Rating** 91 **To** 2026 $30 CM
Krondorf Symmetry Barossa Shiraz 2014 **Rating** 91 **To** 2023 $45 JF
Stonyfell Bin 62 2015 **Rating** 91 **To** 2025 $25 CM
Krondorf Symmetry Barossa Shiraz 2015 **Rating** 90 **To** 2024 $45 CM
Dorrien Estate Bin 1 Barossa Shiraz 2015 **Rating** 90 **To** 2026 $44 CM

DOWIE DOOLE

598 Bayliss Road, McLaren Vale, SA 5171 **Region** McLaren Vale
T (08) 7325 6280 **www**.dowiedoole.com **Open** 7 days 10–5
Winemaker Chris Thomas **Est.** 1995 **Dozens** 25 000 **Vyds** 53ha
DOWIE DOOLE was founded in 1995 by Drew Dowie and Norm Doole, who were connected to the McLaren Vale community for many years as grapegrowers. Vineyard management is now led by champion of sustainable viticulture practices Dave Gartelmann, along with Drew. In May '16, DOWIE DOOLE winemaker and managing director Chris Thomas led a group of like-minded investors into acquiring 35ha of vines from the Conte Tatachilla Vineyard, book-ended by 50-year-old bushvine grenache plus some grafted vermentino, aglianico and lagrein. Exports to all major markets.

Estate McLaren Vale Cabernet Sauvignon 2015 This is a near-perfect, elegant cabernet, reflecting the Tintookie estate vineyard in Blewitt Springs. The balance of the fruit, oak and tannin is perfect, as is the contrast of cassis and black olive. Screwcap. 14% alc. **Rating** 96 **To** 2030 $25 ✪

The Banker Tatachilla McLaren Vale Cabernet Sauvignon 2015 High class cabernet by any standards, its varietal expression very good indeed. Blackcurrant, sage and black olive flavours are backed by fine, savoury tannins on the long palate. The oak choice was spot on, simply framing the fruit. Diam. 14.5% alc. **Rating** 96 **To** 2045 $80

C.T. McLaren Vale Shiraz 2015 24 months in French and American oak before a barrel selection. A full-bodied shiraz that ticks all the boxes without hesitation at any point. Its balance and structure give the wine a deceptive lightness of foot. Dark berry fruits are a juicy stream, the ripe tannins and French oak forming its banks. Screwcap. 14.3% alc. **Rating** 95 **To** 2030 $35 ✪

Reserve McLaren Vale Shiraz 2015 At the apex of the DOWIE DOOLE range of wines, it screams McLaren Vale at the top of its voice. The mix of dark chocolate and tannins combine to form a framework for the intense blackberry fruits of a full-bodied shiraz at the dawn of what will be a very long life. Diam. 14.5% alc. **Rating** 95 **To** 2045 $95

The Architect Tatachilla McLaren Vale Shiraz 2015 The dark, dense colour heralds the bouquet and palate with black cherry, blackberry and dark chocolate (70% cacao). The oak choice was brilliant – 24 months in 2yo French hogsheads, matching the dark fruits, softening the tannins and imparting a subtle taste. Diam. 14.5% alc. **Rating** 95 **To** 2035 $80

Cali Road McLaren Vale Shiraz 2015 Just when you expect another thumping McLaren Vale shiraz, you get this perfectly balanced, medium-bodied wine that leaves no box unticked. The mouthfeel is soft, the fruit flavours varietal (some regional chocolate sneaks in), with fine tannins and integrated oak. Diam. 14.5% alc. **Rating** 95 **To** 2035 $55

Estate McLaren Vale Cabernet Sauvignon 2016 Clear varietal character on both bouquet and palate is immediately established, cassis to the fore. The tannins have been polished, and oak was never going to be an issue. A medium-bodied cabernet offering each-way drinking – now or later. Screwcap. 14.2% alc. **Rating** 94 **To** 2031 $25 ✪

Mr G's C.S.M. 2015 58% cabernet sauvignon, 39% shiraz and 3% merlot. You don't need a corkscrew but a crowbar to extract the hard-as-nails cork. The blend is a throwback in style, accentuated by the choice of 50% American oak. It is rich, with place having a lot to say about the overall flavour, which is undeniably attractive. 14.5% alc. **Rating** 94 **To** 2030 $35

Mr G's C.S.M. 2014 41% cabernet sauvignon, 39% shiraz, 17% merlot and 3% mourvedre. The differences in the oak and the inclusion of mourvedre (not used in '15) made this wine even richer, with the get out of jail card being the lower alcohol here. Screwcap. 14% alc. **Rating** 94 **To** 2029 $35

McLaren Vale Rose 2017 Rating 93 **To** 2020 $20 ✪
B.F.G. McLaren Vale Grenache 2016 Rating 93 **To** 2031 $30

Moxie McLaren Vale Sparkling Shiraz NV **Rating** 92 $30
McLaren Vale Vermentino 2017 **Rating** 90 To 2021 $20 ⚙
G&T McLaren Vale Grenache & Tempranillo 2016 **Rating** 90 To 2029 $25

Drake ★★★★

PO Box 417, Hamilton, NSW 2303 **Region** Yarra Valley
T 0417 670 655 **www**.drakesamson.com.au **Open** Not
Winemaker Mac Forbes, Matt Dunne, Tim Shand **Est.** 2012 **Dozens** 2500
Drake is the handshake business of Nicholas Crampton, winemaker Matt Dunne, and friend of Nicholas, Andrew Dunn. Mac Forbes is the executive winemaker for the Drake wines made in the Yarra Valley, with the intention being to focus future activities on the valley. Quality is uniformly high.

♟♟♟♟♟ Single Vineyard Heathcote Shiraz 2016 Makes it look easy with its pure show of berried fruit. Boysenberry flavours add velocity to the palate, while a light kiss of French oak keeps the talk smooth. Stand back and admire Heathcote shiraz flavour on open display. Screwcap. 13.5% alc. **Rating** 92 To 2024 $20 CM ⚙

Drayton's Family Wines ★★★★★

555 Oakey Creek Road, Pokolbin, NSW 2321 **Region** Hunter Valley
T (02) 4998 7513 **www**.draytonswines.com.au **Open** Mon–Fri 8–5, w'ends 10–5
Winemaker Edgar Vales, Max Drayton, John Drayton **Est.** 1853 **Dozens** 30 000 **Vyds** 72ha
This substantial Hunter Valley producer has suffered more than its share of misfortune over its many years, but has risen to the challenges. Edgar Vales is now the chief winemaker after previous experience as assistant winemaker with David Hook and First Creek wines. His arrival coincided with the release of a range of high quality wines. Exports to Ireland, Bulgaria, Turkey, Vietnam, Malaysia, Indonesia, Singapore, Taiwan and China.

♟♟♟♟♟ Susanne Semillon 2012 The colour continues to be pale straw-green. The wine, while still very youthful, has heart-stopping power, drive and intensity on the palate, where all things lemon embed themselves in the sherbet/mineral acidity. This has decades rather than years in front of it. Screwcap. **Rating** 96 To 2037 $60 ⚙
Joseph Hunter Valley Shiraz 2011 Hand-picked from the dry-grown Bull Paddock vineyard. The colour is still primary, and the silky palate only just clicks into medium-bodied territory. Great quality wine from 50yo vines in a classic vintage. Screwcap. 14% alc. **Rating** 96 To 2041 $90
Vineyard Reserve Pokolbin Semillon 2013 From the estate vineyard planted in 1899, which are the oldest vines in the Hunter Valley. Still more in primary than secondary phase, but utterly delicious, with all things lemon – grass, curd and Meyer. It is as fresh as a daisy; terrific stuff. Screwcap. 11.5% alc. **Rating** 95 To 2028 $30 ⚙
William Shiraz 2013 The vintage was overshadowed by '14, but was a very good one in its own right. Still crimson-purple; perfectly ripe fruit seamlessly joined by fine, savoury tannins and integrated oak. It's a classic medium-bodied Hunter shiraz, eminently drinkable tonight, or many years after my ashes have been scattered. Screwcap. 14% alc. **Rating** 95 To 2043 $60
Heritage Vines Chardonnay 2014 It's amazing how the discussion of chardonnay in Australia has accepted '71 as the first vintage of modern times (Tyrrell's and Craigmoor), ignoring this planting of the Penfolds clone (ex HVD?) by Max Drayton in '64. The warm vintage seems to have blunted the usual edge that the wine has, but it's not lacking in flavour or attitude. Screwcap. **Rating** 94 To 2022 $60

♟♟♟♟♟ Hunter Valley Semillon 2017 **Rating** 90 To 2022 $20 SC ⚙
Vineyard Reserve Pokolbin Shiraz 2015 **Rating** 90 To 2025 $30

Driftwood Estate

3314 Caves Road, Wilyabrup, WA 6282 **Region** Margaret River
T (08) 9755 6323 **www**.driftwoodwines.com.au **Open** 7 days 10–5
Winemaker Eloise Jarvis, Paul Callaghan **Est.** 1989 **Dozens** 15 000
Driftwood Estate is a well established landmark on the Margaret River scene. Quite apart from offering a brasserie restaurant capable of seating 200 people (open 7 days for lunch and dinner) and a mock-Greek open-air theatre, its wines feature striking and stylish packaging and opulent flavours. They are released in three ranges: The Collection, Artifacts and Oceania. Exports to the UK, Canada, Singapore and China.

🍷🍷🍷🍷🍷 **Single Site Margaret River Chardonnay 2017** Complexity and power are the name of the game, power both in depth and length. Fresh acidity is woven like a thread of silver through a tapestry; orange blossom, lemon curd, white peach and nectarine, pink grapefruit and toasty oak notes come and go. Screwcap. 13% alc. **Rating** 97 **To** 2027 $60 ❂

🍷🍷🍷🍷🍷 **Artifacts Margaret River Chardonnay 2017** The energy and drive of this wine is exceptional, particularly given its finesse and freshness. Indeed, there's a delicacy to the precise way the components move across the palate and onto the finish and aftertaste. Screwcap. 13% alc. **Rating** 96 **To** 2025 $32 ❂
Artifacts Margaret River Sauvignon Blanc Semillon 2017 Intensely lively and energetic, with vibrant herb, lemon and crisp acid flavours. It is as much about texture as flavour, and can be enjoyed in 5 years or tonight. Length and balance make it seem easy, but it's not. Screwcap. 12.5% alc. **Rating** 95 **To** 2023 $28 ❂

🍷🍷🍷🍷🍷 **The Collection Chardonnay 2017** **Rating** 92 **To** 2023 $22 ❂
The Collection Shiraz Cabernet Sauvignon 2016 **Rating** 92 **To** 2036 $22 ❂
The Collection Classic White Semillon Sauvignon Blanc 2017 **Rating** 90 **To** 2019 $22
The Collection Cabernet Merlot 2016 **Rating** 90 **To** 2026 $22

Dudley Wines

1153 Willoughby Road, Penneshaw, Kangaroo Island, SA 5222 **Region** Kangaroo Island
T (08) 8553 1333 **www**.dudleywines.com.au **Open** 7 days 10–5
Winemaker Brodie Howard **Est.** 1994 **Dozens** 3500 **Vyds** 14ha
This is one of the most successful wineries on Kangaroo Island, owned by Jeff and Val Howard, with son Brodie as winemaker at the onsite winery. It has three vineyards on Dudley Peninsula: Porky Flat, Hog Bay River and Sawyers. Two daughters and a daughter-in-law manage the cellar door sales, marketing and accounts. Most of the wines are sold through licensed outlets on the island.

🍷🍷🍷🍷🍷 **The Stud Kangaroo Island Shiraz 2014** It has been some time since I've come across a red as richly endowed as this, with its ripe red and black berry aromas, bitter chocolate notes, heady alcohol and sweet, bourbon-vanillan oak. It all runs smoothly enough on cylinders oiled with sheer extract and a waft of balancing acidity. Screwcap. 14.5% alc. **Rating** 91 **To** 2029 $88 NG

🍷🍷🍷🍷 **Porky Flat Kangaroo Island Shiraz 2015** **Rating** 89 **To** 2023 $38 NG
13 Sparkling Shiraz NV **Rating** 89 $22 NG

Duke's Vineyard

Porongurup Road, Porongurup, WA 6324 **Region** Porongurup
T (08) 9853 1107 **www**.dukesvineyard.com **Open** 7 days 10–4.30
Winemaker Robert Diletti **Est.** 1998 **Dozens** 3500 **Vyds** 10ha
When Hilde and Ian (Duke) Ranson sold their clothing manufacturing business in 1998, they were able to fulfil a long-held dream of establishing a vineyard in the Porongurup subregion with the acquisition of a 65ha farm at the foot of the Porongurup Range. They planted shiraz and cabernet sauvignon (3ha each) and riesling (4ha). Hilde, a successful artist, designed the

beautiful scalloped, glass-walled cellar door sales area, with its mountain-blue cladding. Great wines at great prices.

ΨΨΨΨΨ **Magpie Hill Reserve Riesling 2017** Be prepared to kneel before the perfection of a supreme riesling, the bouquet's blossom floating in the air of a spring day, the palate a celebration of the purity, elegance, drive and length of a white wine that you absolutely know will outlive your patience. Screwcap. 11.6% alc. **Rating** 99 To 2047 $35 ✪
Single Vineyard Riesling 2017 Bright, light quartz-green; it's truly difficult to imagine a riesling with greater purity and effortless intensity than this wine, aside from its Reserve sibling. You don't even notice the fact the wine is bone-dry, yet has fruit to live and prosper for decades. Bargain++. Screwcap. 11.5% alc. **Rating** 97 To 2032 $26 ✪

ΨΨΨΨΨ **Magpie Hill Reserve Shiraz 2016** There's an energy and beauty to wines from the Great Southern generally, and Porongurup specifically. This shiraz is an example, restrained and well composed. It's a gentle, pretty wine with a delicate mix of florals, sweet red berries and plums, vanilla, musk and spice; the palate is medium-bodied at best with supple, soft tannins – it just feels effortless. Screwcap. 13.7% alc. **Rating** 95 To 2025 $35 JF ✪
Invitation Winemaker Shiraz 2016 A different local winemaker makes a wine from Duke's fruit each vintage, here styled by Andrew Hoadley of La Violetta fame. Dark garnet, it's super savoury and rich; a little reductive, which adds a meaty element to the structured body. The oak rules (it will settle) with toasty nuances alongside intriguing roasted peppers and smoked pimiento before leading to the sweet dark plums in the mix. Compelling and different. Screwcap. 14% alc. **Rating** 95 To 2028 $35 JF ✪

ΨΨΨΨΨ **Single Vineyard Rose 2017 Rating** 93 To 2019 $20 ✪
Magpie Hill Reserve Cabernet Sauvignon 2016 Rating 92 To 2026 $35 JF
Single Vineyard Off Dry Riesling 2017 Rating 90 To 2027 $26

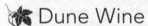

Dune Wine ★★★★★

PO Box 9, McLaren Vale, SA 5171 **Region** McLaren Vale
T 0403 584 845 **www.**dunewine.com **Open** Not
Winemaker Duncan Lloyd, Peter Lloyd **Est.** 2017 **Dozens** 650 **Vyds** 8ha
This is the project of Duncan and Peter Lloyd (of Coriole fame) using fruit sourced from a single vineyard in the Blewitt Springs district. The brothers grew up immersed in a world of wine, olive oil, illegal goat's cheese and great food. Both worked in kitchens from the age of 13 and continued to develop a love of good food and wine. Duncan studied winemaking before leaving McLaren Vale to work in Tasmania and Margaret River, and then in Chianti and the Rhône Valley. He returned to McLaren Vale as he couldn't understand why you would want to live anywhere else. Peter also left the area after university, with eclectic occupations in France and England. He shares Duncan's views on McLaren Vale, though for now he lives in Melbourne.

ΨΨΨΨΨ **Blewitt Springs McLaren Vale Shiraz 2016** A seriously good medium-bodied shiraz, with a foresty/earthy/twiggy bouquet, letting fly on the very long and complex palate with its sinuous mix of dark berry flavours on entry. A turbo charger lifts the finish and aftertaste with a whirl of red, purple and black fruit. Screwcap. 14.5% alc. **Rating** 95 To 2026 $25 ✪
The Empty Quarter 2016 A co-fermented blend of grenache, mourvedre, carignan and shiraz, a dash of montepulciano added post-ferment. Light, bright and clear hue; the bouquet is perfumed with meadow flowers and forest berries, precisely replayed on the intensely juicy, light to medium-bodied palate. The finish could be that of a white wine if you were blindfolded, thanks to its natural acidity. Screwcap. 14% alc. **Rating** 95 To 2025 $26 ✪
Pyla 2016 Nero d'Avola, mourvedre, carignan and shiraz. Light, clear crimson-purple; this has a super-fragrant bouquet, then a palate hosting a corps de ballet

of different red, purple and blue fruit flavours. Just beautiful. Screwcap. 13.5% alc. Rating 95 To 2024 $26 ⊙

Nosu Blewitt Springs McLaren Vale Shiraz 2017 No SO$_2$ added at all (hence its name). Fragrant spice and shoe-leather bouquet. You know before you taste it that it's going to be light-bodied, fresh and juicy, with red berry and cherry flavours, and a tweak of fresh fruit (as if unfermented) on the finish. Drink without a care in the world. Screwcap. 14% alc. **Rating** 94 **To** 2019 $28 ⊙

ЩЩЩЩ Bonaire McLaren Vale Rose 2017 Rating 93 To 2019 $25 ⊙

Dutschke Wines   ★★★★★

Lot 1 Gods Hill Road, Lyndoch, SA 5351 **Region** Barossa Valley
T (08) 8524 5485 **www**.dutschkewines.com **Open** By appt
Winemaker Wayne Dutschke **Est.** 1998 **Dozens** 6000 **Vyds** 15ha
Wayne Dutschke set up business with uncle and grapegrower Ken Semmler in 1990 to produce their first wine. Since then, Dutschke Wines has built its own small winery around the corner from Ken's vineyard, and the portfolio has increased. While Wayne has now been making small-batch wines for over 25 years, his use of whole-berry ferments, open fermenters, basket presses and a quality oak regime have all remained the same. He was crowned Barossa Winemaker of the Year in 2010 and inducted into the Barons of Barossa in '13; he's also the author of a children's book about growing up in a winery called *My Dad has Purple Hands*. Exports to the US, Canada, Denmark, Germany, the Netherlands and Taiwan.

ЩЩЩЩЩ Single Barrel 75 Block Barossa Valley Shiraz Pressings 2015 Not blended, not fined, not filtered, 1 barrel only (French, new). Rich, svelte, super-concentrated but super inviting. It's not at all hard to take; indeed it's moreish in a hedonistic way. Dark chocolate, pure blackberry, saltbush and sarsaparilla. Velvety texture is a keen feature. Stunning combination of concentration and mouthfeel. Screwcap. 14.5% alc. **Rating** 96 **To** 2035 $125 CM

GHR Neighbours Barossa Valley Shiraz 2016 Glorious mouthful of flavour. Oak and fruit in complete harmony. Coffee cream, blackberry, asphalt and tar, sweet, dry spices. It explodes from the outset and then croons its way to all corners of the mouth. Given its concentration and overall balance, it will surely develop or at least hold for many years, but fruit this luscious can be enjoyed fully even in its youth. Screwcap. 14.5% alc. **Rating** 95 **To** 2032 $35 CM ⊙

St Jakobi Single Vineyard Lyndoch Barossa Valley Shiraz 2016 Silky smooth and rich with sweet fruit flavour. Raspberry and blackberry jam, caramel, coal and earth. Hefty but remarkably fresh and energetic. It takes tannin and alcohol in its stride. Finishes with a creamy burst of flavour, oak pulling slightly ahead in the race. It's the Barossa writ large. Screwcap. 14.5% alc. **Rating** 94 **To** 2034 $45 CM

Oscar Semmler St Jakobi Vineyard Barossa Valley Shiraz 2015 Dense but not overwhelming, as freshness seems to have been a priority. Cedar-like oak is abundant but it's hand-in-glove with the fruit, at no point even threatening to overwhelm. This qualifies as an elegant red; it doesn't have the pound-for-pound impact of the '16 GHR, for instance, but it makes up for it in finesse. Captivating by its own design. Screwcap. 14.5% alc. **Rating** 94 **To** 2030 $75 CM

ЩЩЩЩЩ Uncle St Jakobi Vineyard 2016 Rating 91 To 2025 $27 CM

Eastern Peake   ★★★★★

67 Pickfords Road, Coghills Creek, Vic 3364 **Region** Ballarat
T (03) 5343 4245 **www**.easternpeake.com.au **Open** 7 days 11–5
Winemaker Owen Latta **Est.** 1983 **Dozens** 1200 **Vyds** 5.6ha
Norm Latta and Di Pym established Eastern Peake, 25km northeast of Ballarat on a high plateau overlooking the Creswick Valley, over 30 years ago. In the early years the grapes were sold, but the 5.6ha of vines are now dedicated to the production of Eastern Peake wines. Son Owen Latta has been responsible for the seismic increase in the quality of the wines.

🍷🍷🍷🍷🍷 **Walsh Block Syrah 2015** It's always made in a savoury style with spiciness laid on, but this year's release comes bursting with fresh fruit too; the end result is mesmerising. It tastes of boysenberry and fresh plum, anise and lavender, crushed black pepper and garden herbs. It feels as though the paints used (so to speak) were water-based – thanks to the lower alcohol – which is entirely positive. A wonderful shiraz/syrah. Screwcap. 13% alc. **Rating** 96 **To** 2026 $40 CM ✪

Intrinsic Pinot Noir 2015 A cascade of sweet, rose-like, extravagant florals unfolds through the wine, aided by the cool, succulent acidity, and undoubtedly connected to the sheer purity of the fruit. It's openly seductive but it's also taken some effort; it's built on acidity, twigs and tannin but the core of fruit, pips and florals is crucial. The tensions run high here. The perfume flies. Sparks. Screwcap. 13% alc. **Rating** 95 **To** 2026 $40 CM

Morillon Block 89 OBC Pinot Noir 2015 Fragrant, tangy, free-flowing wine with spice, deli meat and sweet berried flavours aplenty, a bed of decaying florals too. It's both juicy and seductive, the finish particularly impressive. Screwcap. 13% alc. **Rating** 95 **To** 2025 $65 CM

Block I10V5 Chardonnay 2015 Wildly expressive. Exaggerated florals and roasted nut characters come attached to nashi pear and apple flavours. The honeysuckle/musk/lavender qualities have to be experienced to be believed. It floats long, it floats free. It dares to be different. Screwcap. 12.5% alc. **Rating** 94 **To** 2023 $50 CM

OB Terroir Pinot Noir 2015 Complex in an easy-going way. It just seems to take life in its stride. Undergrowth, boysenberry, meaty spice and cranberry. Sweetness, savouriness, spiciness. There's tannin here, inbuilt, though it's more about juiciness and flow. It appeals from the outset but its quality creeps up on you, each mouthful showing something more. Screwcap. 13% alc. **Rating** 94 **To** 2024 $65 CM

Block 89 Tres Ancienne Pinot Noir 2015 Gorgeous flavours. Florals, blue and red berries, undergrowth, sweet spices, anise, beetroot and orange. It's tangy, sweet and savoury at once; it's almost kaleidoscopic, in a good way, without being wearying. Indeed it's so fluid, so freestyle, that it almost forgets to make a sprint for the finish; it just keeps sailing on. Screwcap. 13% alc. **Rating** 94 **To** 2026 $65 CM

🍷🍷🍷🍷🍷 **Intrinsic Chardonnay 2015** Rating 93 To 2022 $40 CM
Pinot Tache 2016 Rating 93 To 2020 $32 CM
Walsh Block Tres Ancienne Pinot Noir 2015 Rating 93 To 2026 $55 CM
Project Zero SO2 Syrah 2016 Rating 92 To 2021 $40 CM
Walsh Block Pinot Noir 2014 Rating 91 To 2021 $40 CM

Eclectic Wines   ★★★★

687 Hermitage Road, Pokolbin, NSW 2320 (postal) **Region** Hunter Valley
T 0410 587 207 **www.eclecticwines.com.au Open** Fri–Mon 10–4.30, or by appt
Winemaker First Creek Wines, David Hook, Paul Stuart **Est.** 2001 **Dozens** 3000
This is the venture of Paul and Kate Stuart, who are based in the Hunter Valley, where they live and have a vineyard planted to shiraz and mourvedre; 'nominally', because Paul's 30+ years in the wine industry have given him the marketing knowledge to sustain the purchase of grapes from various regions, including Canberra. Paul balances the production of his own wines with his role as an independent marketing and sales consultant to other producers, selling his clients' wine in different markets from those in which he sells his own. Exports to the Netherlands, Taiwan and China.

🍷🍷🍷🍷🍷 **Clare Valley Riesling 2017** Aromas of lemon blossom, candied peel, creamed honey and mango lead onto the palate. An off-dry style, neatly balanced to the fresh, zingy acidity. Screwcap. 11.5% alc. **Rating** 92 **To** 2026 $28 JF

Hunter Valley Semillon 2017 No question of its regional status with lemon and lime zest, lanolin and lemongrass streaking through some green notes of basil and cut grass. It's lively and very refreshing with bracing acidity. Great now, even better in a few years. Screwcap. 10.5% alc. **Rating** 92 **To** 2027 $28 JF

🍷🍷🍷🍷 **Pewter Hunter Valley Shiraz Mataro 2016** Rating 89 To 2022 $30 JF

Eddie McDougall Wines

PO Box 2012, Hawthorn, Vic 3122 **Region** King Valley
T 0413 960 102 **www.**eddiemcdougall.com **Open** Not
Winemaker Eddie McDougall **Est.** 2007 **Dozens** 6000
Eddie McDougall is an award-winning winemaker, wine judge, columnist and host of the 13-episode TV series *The Flying Winemaker* on Discovery network's TLC. In 2012 Eddie was named one of the Top 20 People Changing the Way We Eat and Drink by *Time Out Hong Kong*. Eddie's winemaking credentials extend over a decade of experience with some of the world's most influential wineries. He has made wines with the likes of Vietti (Barolo), Mas de Daumas Gassac (Languedoc), Deep Woods Estate (Margaret River), Giant Steps (Yarra Valley) and O'Leary Walker (Clare Valley). Eddie holds a Bachelor of International Business from Griffith University, and a post-graduate Diploma of Wine Technology and Viticulture from the University of Melbourne. In '13 he was one of 12 elite wine professionals selected for the annual Len Evans Tutorial, regarded as the world's most esteemed wine education program. Exports to Singapore, Thailand, Hong Kong, Macau, Taiwan and China.

ΨΨΨΨΨ **King Valley Rosato 2017** 52% shiraz, 25% barbera, 19% nebbiolo, 4% sangiovese. Sophisticated winemaking has led to a very lively and spicy rose that goes close to mouthwatering, the low level of residual sugar well below threshold. A multipurpose rose that is real wine. Screwcap. 12.8% alc. **Rating** 93 **To** 2019 $22 ✪
King Valley Sangiovese 2016 Clones M6 and M7, whole-berry fermented, pumped over 2–3 times daily, matured in French barriques (10% new). Bright, clear colour; a fragrant basket of small red fruits peppered by allspice flavours, and complexed by balanced tannins. Screwcap. 14% alc. **Rating** 93 **To** 2023 $26 ✪
Margaret River Cabernets 2016 Bright purple-red. Very much in the medium-bodied claret school – blackberry, briar and sauvage leafiness. Structural rather than fleshy. A line of acidity giving refreshment and sitting nicely with the fine savoury tannins. Screwcap. 14.5% alc. **Rating** 92 **To** 2027 DB
Margaret River Rose 2017 Lovely tea-rose pink and bright. Strawberry fruit, rose petals, light peach and citrus nuances. The combination of tempranillo, nebbiolo and syrah unimportant as it delivers a crunchy, chalky dry rose that is not without texture or length. Screwcap. 13.5% alc. **Rating** 90 **To** 2019 $35 DB

ΨΨΨΨ **King Valley Prosecco NV Rating** 89 **To** 2018 $23

Eden Hall

6 Washington Street, Angaston, SA 5353 **Region** Eden Valley
T 0400 991 968 **www.**edenhall.com.au **Open** 7 days 11–5
Winemaker Kym Teusner, Christa Deans **Est.** 2002 **Dozens** 4000 **Vyds** 32.3ha
David and Mardi Hall purchased the historic Avon Brae Estate in 1996. The 120ha property has been planted to cabernet sauvignon (13ha), riesling (9.25ha), shiraz (6ha) and smaller amounts of merlot, cabernet franc and viognier. The majority of the production is contracted to Yalumba, St Hallett and McGuigan Simeon, with 10% of the best grapes held back for the Eden Hall label. Exports to Canada and China.

ΨΨΨΨΨ **Reserve Riesling 2017** From the best block each vintage: this year, Block 10. Marries elegance and finesse with intensity and length; already has balance, with the citrus-driven varietal character augmented by fresh tingling natural acidity. Gold medal Adelaide Wine Show '17. Screwcap. 11.5% alc. **Rating** 95 **To** 2029 $35 ✪
Gruner Veltliner 2017 From the Avon Brae vineyard, made with only the free-run juice. A delicious gruner, closer to riesling than most, and deserving of its gold medal from the Wisewise Small Vignerons Awards '17. Meyer lemon and yellow peach lie behind the balancing acidity. Screwcap. 12.1% alc. **Rating** 95 **To** 2025 $35 ✪
Springton Shiraz 2016 A junior brother to the Block 4 Shiraz, but sharing all the characters within a slightly reduced frame. It's deeply coloured, rich and filled to the brim with black fruits, yet its finish is elegant, underlining its balance. Terrific value. Screwcap. 14.5% alc. **Rating** 95 **To** 2035 $25 ✪

Block 4 Shiraz 2016 Inky purple-black; super rich, voluptuous, arms open wide to welcome all who come here. Not over-extracted nor tannic. The balance is such that much will be consumed sooner rather than later, but that wouldn't be a crime. Screwcap. 14.5% alc. **Rating** 95 **To** 2041 $40

Riesling 2017 A highly aromatic bouquet with lime blossom to the fore; intensely flavoured and extremely long. A powerhouse riesling with fruit and acidity intertwined so tightly it's impossible to separate them. Gold medal Small Winemakers Show '17. Screwcap. 11.3% alc. **Rating** 94 **To** 2029 $22 ✪

ƳƳƳƳƳ **Block 3 Cabernet Sauvignon 2016 Rating** 93 **To** 2030 $40
Springton Cabernet Sauvignon 2015 Rating 92 **To** 2030 $25 ✪

Eden Road Wines   ★★★★★

3182 Barton Highway, Murrumbateman, NSW 2582 **Region** Canberra District
T (02) 6226 8800 **www.edenroadwines.com.au Open** Wed–Sun 11–4
Winemaker Celine Rousseau **Est.** 2006 **Dozens** 12 000 **Vyds** 5ha
The name of this business, now entirely based in the Canberra District, reflects an earlier stage of its development when it also had a property in the Eden Valley. That has now been separated, and since 2008 operations have focused on Hilltops, Canberra District and Tumbarumba wines. Eden Road has purchased the former Doonkuna winery and mature vineyard, and its marketing was greatly assisted by winning the Jimmy Watson Trophy in '09. Exports to the UK and the US.

ƳƳƳƳƳ **Canberra Riesling 2017** Filled with scents of white flowers and blossom on
the evocative bouquet that are parlayed onto a perfectly balanced, elegant palate. It pushes buttons the moment the wine enters the mouth and continues unabated onto the finish. A riesling with one message: drink me quick. Screwcap. 12.5% alc.
Rating 95 **To** 2027 $26 ✪
Tumbarumba Chardonnay 2017 A sumptuous chardonnay, it boasts aromas of toasted hazelnut, nougat, caramel and cashew segueing to a ripe, layered palate soused with white peach. The generosity of flavour belies the streamlined, mineral-clad finish and lowish alcohol (12.8%). Screwcap. **Rating** 95 **To** 2029 $45 NG

ƳƳƳƳƳ **Museum Release Tumbarumba Pinot Noir 2012 Rating** 93 **To** 2025 $45 NG
The Long Road Sangiovese 2017 Rating 93 **To** 2023 $28 NG
The Long Road Tumbarumba Chardonnay 2016 Rating 92 **To** 2025 $28 NG
The Long Road Pinot Noir 2017 Rating 92 **To** 2025 $28 NG
Tumbarumba Pinot Noir 2017 Rating 92 **To** 2029 $45 NG
The Long Road Sauvignon Blanc 2017 Rating 91 **To** 2021 $28 NG
The Long Road Pinot Gris 2017 Rating 91 **To** 2021 $28 NG

 # Edilillie   ★★★☆

PO Box 628, Clare, SA 5453 **Region** Clare Valley
T 0419 837 361 **Open** Not
Winemaker Michael Corbett **Est.** 2013 **Dozens** 1000 **Vyds** 8ha
David and Heather Cook have 8ha of vines (5ha of shiraz and 3ha of cabernet sauvignon) planted with a morning-sun aspect in the Skillogalee/Sevenhill area of the Clare Valley. The vines were established between 1980 and '89 and acquired by the Cooks in 2001. In '13 David started making small batches of wine, now done on a commercial scale by Michael Corbett. The Cook family lives on the property and are involved throughout the year in the care of the vineyards from picking to pruning. 'Edilillie' is an Aboriginal word meaning two hills and a water source, and 'sums up the vineyard'.

ƳƳƳƳƳ **Reserve Single Vineyard Sevenhill Clare Valley Shiraz 2016** Crammed
to the rafters with black fruits of every persuasion, spice and red licorice in the background. Authentic and durable; even better things in store. Screwcap. 13.9% alc. **Rating** 91 **To** 2031 $33

ƳƳƳƳ **Clare Valley Shiraz 2016 Rating** 89 **To** 2029 $28

1847 | Yaldara Wines

Chateau Yaldara, Hermann Thumm Drive, Lyndoch, SA 5351 **Region** Barossa Valley
T (08) 8524 5328 **www**.1847wines.com **Open** 7 days 9.30–5
Winemaker Alex Peel, Chris Coulter, **Est.** 1996 **Dozens** 50 000 **Vyds** 53.9ha
1847 Wines is wholly owned by Chinese group Treasure Valley Wines. The year is when
Barossa pioneer Johann Gramp planted his first vines in the region; there is in fact no other
connection between Gramp and the business he established and that of 1847 Wines, other than
the fact that the 80ha estate is in the general vicinity of Gramp's original plantings. A 1000t
winery was built in 2014, handling the core production together with new varieties and
blends. This was underpinned by the acquisition of Chateau Yaldara in '14, providing a major
retail outlet and massively enhanced production facilities. Exports to Canada, Germany,
Taiwan, Hong Kong and China.

ΨΨΨΨΨ **Chateau Yaldara 20 Year Old Special Aged Tawny NV** Long aged, serving
to soften the edges of oak and grape to a smooth, viscous elixir. A cornucopia of
spice, walnut, mahogany and chestnut notes mingle with a rancio lift, providing an
energetic thrust across the wine's dense midriff. The finish is endless. **Rating** 97 NG

ΨΨΨΨΨ **Yaldara Foundations Petit Verdot 2016** Boysenberry, molten cherry liqueur,
tar and a ferrous grind across the tannins, pulpy and palate-whetting. The oak
choice is made with aplomb: French and the more tannic Hungarian ably
harnessing the cascading fruit. This will age, but best to enjoy in the mid-term
while the fruit is primary and luscious. Screwcap. 14% alc. **Rating** 95 **To** 2028
$27 NG ✪

Chateau Yaldara 20 Year Old Special Aged Muscat NV Is there anything
quite as exotic and hedonistic as muscat? Grapey, spicy and brimming with scents
of rosewater, orange blossom and manuka honey. Nuts, too. Viscous to the point of
unctuous, this coats the mouth and never lets go. **Rating** 95 NG

Yaldara Chardonnay Pinot Noir 2015 This is very good fizz. An assemblage
of 92% chardonnay, the remainder pinot meunier, aged for 18 months on lees.
Creamy and toasty, this barrels along rails of lemonade acidity and crunchy
red fruits, hitting all the right notes. Most impressive is the dosage, perfectly
appropriated to the acidity, complexity and mineral crunch. Cork. 12.5% alc.
Rating 94 $50 NG

ΨΨΨΨΩ **Yaldara Reserve Chardonnay 2016** Rating 93 To 2024 $40 NG
Yaldara Retro Shiraz 2015 Rating 93 To 2027 $35 NG
Yaldara Reserve Shiraz 2015 Rating 93 To 2027 $40 NG
Yaldara Retro Merlot 2017 Rating 93 To 2025 $35 NG
Yaldara Foundations Cabernet 2016 Rating 93 To 2025 $27 NG ✪
Chateau Yaldara Classic Tawny NV Rating 93 $30 NG
Yaldara Foundations Grenache 2016 Rating 92 To 2022 $27 NG
Yaldara Reserve Grenache Shiraz Mourvedre 2015 Rating 92 To 2021
$40 NG
1847 Home Block Petit Verdot 2015 Rating 92 To 2030 $40 NG
Yaldara Foundations Sauvignon Blanc 2017 Rating 91 To 2019 $22 NG ✪
Yaldara Foundations Pinot Gris 2017 Rating 91 To 2021 $22 NG ✪
Yaldara Rose 2017 Rating 91 To 2019 $20 NG ✪
Yaldara CY Shiraz 2015 Rating 91 To 2023 $17 NG ✪
Yaldara Retro Cabernet Franc 2016 Rating 91 To 2024 $35 NG
Yaldara Moscato 2017 Rating 91 To 2020 $20 NG ✪

Ekhidna

67 Branson Road, McLaren Vale, SA 5171 **Region** McLaren Vale
T 0499 002 633 **www**.ekhidnawines.com.au **Open** 7 days 11–5
Winemaker Matthew Rechner **Est.** 2001 **Dozens** 2000
Matt Rechner entered the wine industry in 1988, spending most of his years since at Tatachilla
in McLaren Vale, starting as laboratory technician and finishing as operations manager.

Frustrated by the constraints of large winery practice, he decided to strike out on his own in 2001. The quality of his wines has enabled him to build a winery and cellar door, the winery facilitating the use of various cutting-edge techniques. Exports to China.

ΨΨΨΨΨ **Rarefied McLaren Vale Shiraz 2013** It takes richness and adds to it, and while it's super-ripe and carries the associated alcohol warmth, it's also well balanced and lengthy; in summary, it nails the style. Rich chocolate, a wealth of inky, berried fruit flavour, floral notes and a splash of saltbush. Minor signs of development have just entered the edge of the frame, as is appropriate given the wine's age. Screwcap. 14.5% alc. **Rating** 95 **To** 2033 $100 CM
Linchpin McLaren Vale Shiraz 2016 Full-throttle shiraz with porty blackcurrant and blackberry flavour, pure and straightforward, and commanding from the attack to the extended finish. Screwcap. 14.5% alc. **Rating** 94 **To** 2036 $45 CM
Rechner McLaren Vale Shiraz 2013 Full-bodied red with saturated plum and malted milk flavours laid on thick. It's big and robust with assertive tannin pulling through the back half. It does everything it can to make sure you're convinced. Screwcap. 14.5% alc. **Rating** 94 **To** 2034 $65 CM

ΨΨΨΨΨ **Adelaide Hills Fiano 2017** **Rating** 92 **To** 2019 $27 CM
McLaren Vale Grenache 2016 **Rating** 91 **To** 2023 $27 CM
She Viper McLaren Vale Grenache Shiraz Mourvedre 2016 **Rating** 91 **To** 2023 $23 CM ♥
McLaren Vale Mourvedre 2016 **Rating** 90 **To** 2024 $25 CM

Elbourne Wines

236 Marrowbone Road, Pokolbin, NSW 2320 **Region** Hunter Valley
T 0416 190 878 **www**.elbournewines.com.au **Open** By appt
Winemaker Nick Paterson **Est.** 2009 **Dozens** 500 **Vyds** 4ha
Adam and Alexys Elbourne have done what many thousands of young families have dreamt of doing: selling their house in Sydney and moving to the unpolluted environment of the Hunter Valley to bring up their family. They had already made many trips to the Hunter, simply to enjoy the wine and food scene – and Alexys was raised on an 80ha property on the banks of the Patterson River. So it seemed inevitable that they would find and buy the 22ha Marrowbone Road property, with 2ha each of rundown chardonnay and shiraz and enough land to have a boutique racehorse stud and a Noah's Ark of animals including rare Wessex Saddleback pigs. The last pieces of the puzzle were the two-year restoration of the vineyard under the direction of one of the great viticulturists of the valley, Neil Stevens (who continues to manage the vineyard), and the appointment of Nick Paterson as contract winemaker.

ΨΨΨΨΨ **Single Vineyard Hunter Valley Chardonnay 2016** The wine has been very well made, bravely picked early, but not at the expense of white peach, apple and citrus varietal fruits. The acidity, most likely adjusted, is spot on. Screwcap. 12.1% alc. **Rating** 94 **To** 2021 $30 ♥

ΨΨΨΨΨ **H.A.E Single Vineyard Hunter Valley Shiraz 2016** **Rating** 91 **To** 2036 $40

Elderton

3–5 Tanunda Road, Nuriootpa, SA 5355 **Region** Barossa Valley
T (08) 8568 7878 **www**.eldertonwines.com.au **Open** Mon–Fri 10–5, w'ends & hols 11–4
Winemaker Richard Langford **Est.** 1982 **Dozens** 45 000 **Vyds** 65ha
The founding Ashmead family, with mother Lorraine supported by sons Allister and Cameron, continues to impress with their wines. The original source was 30ha of fully mature shiraz, cabernet sauvignon and merlot on the Barossa floor; subsequently 16ha of Eden Valley vineyards (shiraz, cabernet sauvignon, chardonnay, zinfandel, merlot and roussanne) were incorporated into the business. Energetic promotion and marketing in Australia and overseas are paying dividends. Elegance and balance are the keys to these wines. Exports to all major markets.

🍷🍷🍷🍷🍷 **Ashmead Barossa Cabernet Sauvignon 2016** Cabernet's bursting swag of currant, dried sage and olive – at least its voice in warmer climes – is all here in spades. What makes this wine impressive is its sheer strut across the palate. Buxom and confident, yet dichotomously restrained (at least in the warm climatic context), it coats the inner sanctum with a smooth veneer of tannin and old vine glycerol. Screwcap. 14.5% alc. **Rating** 96 **To** 2036 $120 NG

Ode to Lorraine Barossa Valley Cabernet Shiraz Merlot 2015 Cabernet's voice rises above all else with its potpourri of herbal berry notes and sagacious tannins, compressing the warm-climate hedonism into a nourishing whole. A rich phalanx of fruit and glossy structural attributes. Screwcap. 14.9% alc. **Rating** 96 **To** 2037 $60 NG ✪

Command Barossa Shiraz 2015 The violet, pepper grind and meld of plummy fruit and Chinese five-spice remain this brooding, highly ageable wine's calling card. Vanillan oak serves as a welcome restraining device to the exuberance. Exaggerated? You be the judge. Screwcap. 14.7% alc. **Rating** 95 **To** 2042 $130 NG

Western Ridge Barossa Valley Grenache Carignan 2017 A rarity on these shores, this logical blend is archetypal Mediterranean, from the Languedoc to Spain. Why? Grenache's bumptious hedonism is ably tamed by carignan's bristling acidity and sinew. Barossan fruitcake spice and raspberry liqueur DNA is all there, but with a wiry bristle of carnal allure and a welcome rasp. Screwcap. 14.6% alc. **Rating** 95 **To** 2027 $60 NG

Neil Ashmead Grand Tourer Barossa Valley Shiraz 2016 The wine is rich and glossy; polished beautifully by massaged tannins, oak endowment and dutiful acidity. The flavours are strongly regional: dark plum, fruitcake spice and beef bouillon to coffee-marinated barbecue ribs, presumably coming from barrel fermentation and extended lees handling. Salacious, but delicious! Screwcap. 14.5% alc. **Rating** 94 **To** 2036 $60 NG

🍷🍷🍷🍷♀ **Eden Valley Riesling 2017 Rating** 92 **To** 2031 $30 NG
Barossa Shiraz 2015 Rating 92 **To** 2035 $34
Barossa Grenache Shiraz Mourvedre 2015 Rating 91 **To** 2027 $34
Barossa Merlot 2016 Rating 90 **To** 2024 $34 NG
Barossa Cabernet Sauvignon 2015 Rating 90 **To** 2030 $34

Eldorado Road ★★★★★

46–48 Ford Street, Beechworth, Vic 3747 **Region** North East Victoria
T (03) 5725 1698 **www.**eldoradoroad.com.au **Open** Fri–Sun 11–5
Winemaker Paul Dahlenburg, Ben Dahlenburg, Laurie Schulz **Est.** 2010
Dozens 1500 **Vyds** 4ha

Paul Dahlenburg (nicknamed Bear), Lauretta Schulz (Laurie) and their children have leased a 2ha block of shiraz planted in the 1890s with rootlings supplied from France (doubtless grafted) in the wake of phylloxera's devastation in Glenrowan and Rutherglen. The vineyard, was in a state of serious decline after years of neglect. Four years of tireless work reconstructing the old vines has resulted in tiny amounts of exceptionally good shiraz; a small area of nero d'Avola and durif has also been planted.

🍷🍷🍷🍷🍷 **Riserva Nero d'Avola 2016** Fantastic wine. It stops you in its tracks just a bit. It's wild with struck-match and deli meat complexity but the berried fruit is all finesse and insistence, the finish finely spun and long. Captivating. Screwcap. 13.9% alc. **Rating** 96 **To** 2028 $55 CM ✪

Quasimodo Nero d'Avola Shiraz Durif 2015 One of those wines giving you a 'come on' signal before you've had a chance to even smell it. It combines insouciant elegance with intensity, its balance already set in stone. You can tuck this under your arm and walk into any Italian BYO restaurant and walk out very happy. Bravo. Screwcap. 14% alc. **Rating** 95 **To** 2030 $29 ✪

Beechworth Chardonnay 2016 Delicious chardonnay with length to burn. Stone fruit, toast, toffee and fig flavours soar through the palate. Finishes long. No mlf; it bursts juicily out through the finish. All the flavour you could hope for. Screwcap. 13.2% alc. **Rating** 94 **To** 2022 $37 CM

Luminoso Rose 2017 It gets the mix of come-hither fruit sweetness and spice-led savouriness just right. If you like rose of any style, you will enjoy this. The texture is lovely, the flavour well set, the finish juicy, refreshing and satisfying. The copper tinge to the colour is a nice touch too. Screwcap. 13% alc. **Rating** 94 **To** 2020 $25 CM **O**

Onyx Durif 2016 A medium-weight red with a solid heart of dark-berried flavour and pretty aromatics – florals and spice – flying about. Modern, approachable red with fruit volume left intact. Spot on. Screwcap. 14.8% alc. **Rating** 94 **To** 2033 $37 CM

ŸŸŸŸŸ **Comrade Nero d'Avola 2016 Rating** 93 **To** 2024 $37 CM

Eldredge

Spring Gully Road, Clare, SA 5453 **Region** Clare Valley
T (08) 8842 3086 **www.**eldredge.com.au **Open** 7 days 11–5
Winemaker Leigh Eldredge **Est.** 1993 **Dozens** 7500 **Vyds** 20.9ha
Leigh and Karen Eldredge established their winery and cellar door in the Sevenhill Ranges at an altitude of 500m above Watervale. The mature estate vineyard is planted to shiraz, cabernet sauvignon, merlot, riesling, sangiovese and malbec. Exports to the UK, the US, Canada, Singapore and China.

ŸŸŸŸŸ **Clare Valley Riesling 2017** Light straw-green; the bouquet and palate driven by a juicy blend of lime and grapefruit, the balance good. Each way drinking: now or later. Screwcap. 12.5% alc. **Rating** 90 **To** 2023 $22

ŸŸŸŸ **Kitty Clare Valley Rose 2017 Rating** 89 **To** 2018 $20

Eldridge Estate of Red Hill ★★★★★

120 Arthurs Seat Road, Red Hill, Vic 3937 **Region** Mornington Peninsula
T 0414 758 960 **www.**eldridge-estate.com.au **Open** Mon–Fri 12–4, w'ends & hols 11–5
Winemaker David Lloyd **Est.** 1985 **Dozens** 1000 **Vyds** 2.8ha
The Eldridge Estate vineyard was purchased by David and the late Wendy Lloyd in 1995. Major retrellising work has been undertaken, changing to the Scott Henry system, and all the wines are estate-grown and made. David has also planted several Dijon pinot noir clones (114, 115 and 777) and Dijon chardonnay clones (95 and 96), which have been contributing since 2004. Attention to detail permeates all David does in the vineyard and winery. Exports to the US.

ŸŸŸŸŸ **Wendy Chardonnay 2016** 50/50% clones 95 and 96, whole-bunch pressed, fermented in French oak (25% new). These two most distinguished Dijon clones seem to shine wherever they are planted in Australia, and certainly do so here. The flavours are more precisely articulated, the mouthfeel in similar mode. The length, too, is greater. Screwcap. 13% alc. **Rating** 95 **To** 2028 $55

Gamay 2016 David Lloyd has done more work with gamay than any other maker. The plantings are mature, and he endowed this vintage with what I call glossy berry fruit (plus sweet spices). It is perfectly balanced. Screwcap. 13.5% alc. **Rating** 95 **To** 2026 $45

Mornington Peninsula Pinot Noir 2016 Poached strawberries, Turkish delight, red cherry and fistfuls of meaty spice. It has personality and difference within a taut, disciplined frame. It gives up plenty, even this young, but everything suggests there are more delights tucked up its flamboyant sleeves. Screwcap. 13.5% alc. **Rating** 95 **To** 2026 $65 CM

Fume Blanc 2017 100% fermented in French oak (37.5% new), partial mlf. The super-cool vintage has worked in tandem with the vinification to give the wine the attitude missing from most Mornington Peninsula sauvignon blancs. There is plenty of texture and structure to frame the tropical fruits that run from start to finish. Screwcap. 12% alc. **Rating** 94 **To** 2019 $33

Chardonnay 2016 A mix of six estate-grown clones, whole-bunch pressed, fermented in French oak (25% new). An elegant, well balanced wine with stone fruit (white peach, nectarine) and rockmelon gently cosseted by cashew and oak. Nothing omitted, nothing overworked. Screwcap. 13% alc. **Rating** 94 **To** 2026 $50

North Patch Chardonnay 2016 In the mainstream Eldridge style, elegant and unforced. The varietal fruit flavours cover white peach and hints of grapefruit. Oak is subservient to the fruit, building texture and structure rather than flavour. Screwcap. 13% alc. **Rating** 94 **To** 2026 $45

Single Clone Pinot Noir 2016 An elegant, spicy, savoury pinot with enough cherry (red, sour, morello) fruit flavours to provide balance and length. Just a fraction too light now. Screwcap. 13.5% alc. **Rating** 94 **To** 2025 $70

Eldridge Clone 1 Pinot Noir 2016 At the fuller end of the flavour palate and colour palette, darker plum fruit to the fore, Pommard-esque. '16 was a stern vintage in very different idiom to the seductive relaxation of the red fruits of '15, so patience is essential but will work. Screwcap. **Rating** 94 **To** 2027

Clonal Blend Pinot Noir 2016 Bright, clear crimson; a tangy, zesty wine that still sends out the purity message. Wild and cultivated berry aromas and flavours, but does need time to soften and open up. Screwcap. 13.5% alc. **Rating** 94 **To** 2026 $75

♥♥♥♥♡ **PTG 2017 Rating** 93 **To** 2023 $35

Elgee Park ★★★★★

24 Junction Road, Merricks North, Vic 3926 **Region** Mornington Peninsula
T (03) 5989 7338 **www**.elgeeparkwines.com.au **Open** At Merricks General Wine Store
Winemaker Geraldine McFaul (Contract) **Est.** 1972 **Dozens** 1600 **Vyds** 4.4ha
The pioneer of the Mornington Peninsula in its 20th-century rebirth, owned by Baillieu Myer and family. The vineyard is planted to riesling, chardonnay, viognier (some of the oldest vines in Australia), pinot gris, pinot noir, merlot and cabernet sauvignon, and is set in a picturesque natural amphitheatre with a northerly aspect, looking out across Port Phillip Bay towards the Melbourne skyline.

♥♥♥♥♥ **Pinot Noir 2016** A lot of subtlety with just-ripe red cherries, cranberries, florals, warm earth and spices. There's a prettiness, too; it's deceptive, because it's medium-bodied with detail and precision, soft acidity and fine tannins giving it drink-now status. Screwcap. 13.5% alc. **Rating** 95 **To** 2023 $60 JF

Family Reserve Pinot Noir 2015 Hand-picked, destemmed into small open fermenters, wild yeast, maceration for 16 days then pressed to French oak barrels (30% new) for 10 months. The result is representative of the gentle winemaking and the good vintage. It's a gorgeous pinot noir, lightly framed but with depth, starting with wild raspberries and spiced cherries then moving onto chalk-like acidity and lithe, fine tannins to close. Screwcap. 13% alc. **Rating** 95 **To** 2025 $50 JF

♥♥♥♥♡ **Pinot Gris 2017 Rating** 93 **To** 2019 $35 CM
Family Reserve Cabernet Merlot 2015 Rating 93 **To** 2024 $35 JF
Cuvee Brut 2012 Rating 93 $50 CM
Chardonnay 2016 Rating 91 **To** 2022 $60 JF
Riesling 2017 Rating 90 **To** 2021 $30 JF

Elgo Estate ★★★★

2020 Upton Road, Upton Hill, Vic 3664 **Region** Strathbogie Ranges
T (03) 5798 5563 **www**.elgoestate.com.au **Open** Not
Winemaker Grant Taresch **Est.** 1999 **Dozens** 5000 **Vyds** 100ha
Elgo Estate, owned by the Taresch family, is located high in the hills of the Strathbogie Ranges, 125km northeast of Melbourne and a stone's throw from the southern end of the Heathcote region. Elgo Estate is committed to sustainable viticulture reflecting and expressing

the characteristics of this cool-climate region. Two distinct wine portfolios via the Allira and Elgo Estate labels are produced. Wines are 100% estate-grown from three vineyards, with plantings dating back to the early 1970s. Elgo Estate was the first winery in Australia to be fully powered by self-generated renewable wind energy. The installation of a 30m tall 150kW wind turbine in 2007 enables Elgo to save around 400t of greenhouse gas emissions per year, while generating enough electricity to power the winery twice over (the excess green electricity is fed back into the grid). In '12 Elgo purchased the Mount Helen vineyard from Robert Kirby (previously used for Cooralook wines). Exports to China.

🍷🍷🍷🍷🍷 **Allira Chardonnay 2017** With very attractive and crystal clear varietal expression, pitched between pink grapefruit and white peach. There is a hint of oak, which needed the restraint it received. One of the best value chardonnays on the market. Screwcap. 13% alc. **Rating** 90 **To** 2021 $14
Cabernet Sauvignon 2006 Quite why it has been held back for so long prior to release, I don't know, but it's ready now or soonish; the tannins and oak are spicy, and mesh well with the blackcurrant fruit of the medium-bodied palate. Screwcap. 13.5% alc. **Rating** 90 **To** 2019 $25

🍷🍷🍷🍷 **Allira Pinot Noir 2017 Rating** 89 **To** 2021 $14
Shiraz 2014 Rating 89 **To** 2021 $25

Ellis Wines   ★★★★
3025 Heathcote-Rochester Road, Colbinabbin, Vic 3559 (postal) **Region** Heathcote
T 0401 290 315 **www.elliswines.com.au Open** Not
Winemaker Guy Rathjen **Est.** 1998 **Dozens** 700 **Vyds** 54.6ha
Bryan and Joy Ellis own this family business, while daughter Raylene Flanagan is the sales manager, and seven of the vineyard blocks are named after family members. For the first 10 years the family was content to sell the grapes to a range of distinguished producers. However, since then, a growing portion of the crop has been vinified.

🍷🍷🍷🍷🍷 **Signature Label Heathcote Shiraz 2015** Silken palate, no doubt helped along by oak. Pure plum, clove and cream flavours sweep through in uncomplicated fashion. The alcohol shows through slightly. Screwcap. 14.9% alc. **Rating** 91 **To** 2025 $34 CM

Elmswood Estate   ★★★★☆
75 Monbulk-Seville Road, Seville, Vic 3139 **Region** Yarra Valley
T (03) 5964 3015 **www.elmswoodestate.com.au Open** W'ends 12–5
Winemaker Han Tao Lau **Est.** 1981 **Dozens** 3000 **Vyds** 7.5ha
Planted to cabernet sauvignon, chardonnay, merlot, sauvignon blanc, pinot noir, shiraz and riesling on the red volcanic soils of the far southern Yarra Valley. The cellar door operates from 'The Pavilion', a fully enclosed glass room situated on a ridge above the vineyard, with 180-degree views of the Upper Yarra Valley. It seats up to 110 guests and is a popular wedding venue. Exports to Hong Kong and China.

🍷🍷🍷🍷🍷 **Yarra Valley Pinot Noir 2016** This wine opens with a burst of spices from Greece/Lebanon. It then moves on into deep red and black cherry; the (good) surprise is that the fruit is ripe, not overripe. Plenty more action from this yet to come. Screwcap. 14% alc. **Rating** 92 **To** 2026 $38
Yarra Valley Merlot 2016 Good colour, and perfumed fruit on the bouquet a promising start, but even though harvest was 2 weeks earlier than '15, it still left a hammer blow of alcohol and extract with damaged varietal DNA. Screwcap. 14.7% alc. **Rating** 90 **To** 2026 $35

🍷🍷🍷🍷 **Yarra Valley Syrah 2016 Rating** 89 **To** 2022 $35
Yarra Valley Cabernet Sauvignon 2016 Rating 89 **To** 2029 $35

Eloquesta   ★★★★★

10 Stroud Avenue, Dubbo, NSW 2830 (postal) **Region** Mudgee
T 0458 525 899 **www.eloquesta.com.au Open** Not
Winemaker Stuart Olsen **Est.** 2008 **Dozens** 1200 **Vyds** 6ha

The full name of the business is Eloquesta by Stuart Olsen, Stuart being the sole owner and winemaker. He is a trained scientist and teacher, gaining winemaking experience since 2000, variously working at Cirillo Estate, Lowe Wines and Torbreck, as well as at a German winery in the Rheinhessen. His aim is to make the two varieties that he believes grow consistently well year after year in the cooler foothills of Mudgee and Rylstone: shiraz and petit verdot, with an occasional bucket of viognier.

🍷🍷🍷🍷🍷 **by Stuart Olsen Mudgee Shiraz Petit Verdot 2014** A 85/15% blend aged in French, Hungarian and Russian oak for 32 months. Excellent dark crimson with an explosion of fruit, spice and florals, medium-bodied on the palate with the oak evenly placed, signing off with crunchy acidity and exacting tannins. Screwcap. 14% alc. **Rating** 95 **To** 2026 $35 JF ✪
by Stuart Olsen Mudgee Shiraz Petit Verdot 2015 This vintage is a 70/30% split, and while there's slightly riper fruit in the midst, it's another compelling wine. Ripe plums and red licorice saturate the full-bodied palate, followed by a puff of spices, warm earth and florals. Ripe succulent tannins and a freshness keep this in the moreish category. Screwcap. 14% alc. **Rating** 95 **To** 2025 $35 JF ✪
by Stuart Olsen Blush Black Muscat Viognier 2017 The colour of a dark cherry rose, and phenolic. If you dig those characters, you'll love this. Gorgeous fragrance of musk, mangosteen, dried peaches and fresh apricots plus potpourri. It has texture and while there's the phenolic grip to the tannins, it's like Campari on steroids. Screwcap. 13% alc. **Rating** 94 **To** 2021 $25 JF ✪

🍷🍷🍷🍷🍷 **by Stuart Olsen Mudgee Chardonnay 2016 Rating** 93 **To** 2023 $25 JF ✪
A Boy With Fruit Orange Chardonnay 2014 Rating 93 **To** 2023 $32 JF

Elsewhere Vineyard   ★★★★☆

584 Silver Hill Road, Glaziers Bay, Tas 7109 **Region** Southern Tasmania
T 0401 975 195 **www.elsewherevineyard.com.au Open** Sun 10–6 Oct–Apr, or by appt
Winemaker Glenn James **Est.** 1984 **Dozens** 4000 **Vyds** 10ha

Kylie and Andrew Cameron's evocatively named Elsewhere Vineyard used to jostle for space with a commercial flower farm. The estate-produced range comes from the 6ha of pinot noir, 3ha of chardonnay and 1ha of riesling which constitute the immaculately tended vineyard.

🍷🍷🍷🍷🍷 **Huon Valley Pinot Noir 2016** There's a fair amount to get excited about here. The satiny mouthfeel, the undergrowthy complexity, the brightness of the fruit, the way tannin flies under the radar but still manages to keep the palate neat and tidy. You'd swear you can detect a glint in this wine's eye. Screwcap. 12.8% alc. **Rating** 95 **To** 2026 $48 CM
Huon Valley Riesling 2017 A joyous riesling. There's a slip of sweetness and a wealth of fruit, with lime and pink grapefruit infused with rose petals and sweet apple. This wine has body, extravagance. It's effectively guaranteed to please. Screwcap. 12% alc. **Rating** 94 **To** 2024 $34 CM

🍷🍷🍷🍷 **Huon Valley Gewurztraminer 2017 Rating** 89 **To** 2021 $32 CM

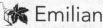 Emilian   ★★★★☆

1295 Mt Dandenong Tourist Road, Kalorama, Vic 3766 (postal) **Region** Yarra Valley
T 0421 100 648 **www.emilian.com.au Open** Not
Winemaker Robin Querre **Est.** 2015 **Dozens** 300

This is the venture of Robin Querre and wife Prue. Robin is the fourth generation of a family invloved in winemaking since 1897, variously in Saint Emilion and Pomerol, France. Robin commenced studies in medicine at the University of Bordeaux, but changed to oenology in 1990. He studied under some of the Bordeaux greats (such as Yves Glory, Denis

Dubourdieu and Aline Lonvaud), and worked vintages at Chateau Canon and Moueix (under Jean-Claude Berrouet, who was supervising Chateau Petrus), as well as at Rudd Estate in the Napa Valley. This led Robin to work in research, travelling to Australia, Germany, Austria, Switzerland, England, Japan and Israel. He currently works for Laffort Oenology, a private research company based in Bordeaux, developing, producing and selling oenological products to winemakers. He and Prue also make small quantities of very good wine at Allinda in the Yarra Valley.

ŤŤŤŤŤ **Yarra Valley Pinot Noir 2016** Not the easiest viticulture in the Yarra Valley, but Robin Querre's handling of the fruit (a single parcel from Dixons Creek) makes it seem easy. It is medium-bodied, with supple dark cherry flavour that will become more spicy with time in the bottle; the balance and length ensure it will repay cellaring. Screwcap. 13.5% alc. **Rating** 95 **To** 2026 $33 **○**

ŤŤŤŤŤ **Single Vineyard Dixons Creek Yarra Valley Cabernet Syrah Rose 2017** **Rating** 93 **To** 2021 $25 **○**
Single Vineyard Limestone Road Block Yea Valley Pinot Noir MV6 2017 **Rating** 90 **To** 2024 $25

Epsilon   ★★★★
43 Hempel Road, Daveyston, SA 5355 **Region** Barossa Valley
T 0417 871 951 **www**.epsilonwines.com.au **Open** By appt
Winemaker Aaron Southern **Est.** 2004 **Dozens** 3000 **Vyds** 7ha
Epsilon, named after the fifth star of the Southern Cross constellation, is a great example of how a background star can come to the fore. Content to follow in the footsteps of their forebears, fifth-generation grapegrowers Aaron and Julie (née Kalleske) Southern took ownership of the vineyard in 1994, when they were in their 20s. In 2004 friends Jaysen Collins and Dan Standish (both of Massena winery) helped them realise their dream of producing their own wine.

ŤŤŤŤŤ **Barossa Valley Shiraz 2016** A quiver of boysenberry fruit tamed by anise, clove and a gentle whir of pepper across the midriff. There is no doubting the wine's sheer richness, but it is sheathed in palpably smooth tannins, a burr of acidity conferring balance. A fully flared wine performing well beyond its price point. Screwcap. 14.5% alc. **Rating** 94 **To** 2024 $20 NG **○**
Nineteen Ninety Four Barossa Valley Shiraz 2015 Dark fruited, plum, blueberry, pulpy cherry. Intense. Licorice all-sorts, cardamom, charcuterie and an exotic souk of spice, thruming from nose to palate. Real thrust and parry here, with pepper-grind acidity and a bristle of tannin. Bitter chocolate oak, too, all giving poise. Screwcap. 14.8% alc. **Rating** 94 **To** 2028 $45 NG

Ernest Hill Wines   ★★★★★
307 Wine Country Drive, Nulkaba, NSW 2325 **Region** Hunter Valley
T (02) 4991 4418 **www**.ernesthillwines.com.au **Open** 7 days 10–5
Winemaker Mark Woods **Est.** 1999 **Dozens** 6000 **Vyds** 12ha
This is part of a vineyard originally planted in the early 1970s by Harry Tulloch for Seppelt; it was later renamed Pokolbin Creek Vineyard, and later still (in '99) the Wilson family purchased the upper (hill) section of the vineyard and renamed it Ernest Hill. It is now planted to semillon, shiraz, chardonnay, verdelho, traminer, merlot, tempranillo and chambourcin. Exports to the US and China.

ŤŤŤŤŤ **Cyril Premium Hunter Semillon 2011** From a small block on the estate planted over 35 years ago. A Peter Pan wine, still incredibly fresh at 8yo and with years to go, the changes only incremental. Screwcap. 11% alc. **Rating** 95 **To** 2031 $28 **○**
CEO Shiraz 2014 An elegant, medium-bodied shiraz from a great vintage, showing how Hunter Valley shiraz can give great satisfaction from an early stage, but live for decades like Burgundy. Cork. 14% alc. **Rating** 95 **To** 2034 $40

William Henry Premium Hunter Shiraz 2013 This was a very good wine in its youth, and remains so to this day. The bouquet and palate reflect maturation in French oak for 12 months, but it is still the fruit of the medium-bodied palate that gives the wine its special mouthfeel, an array of supple cherry, plum and blackberry flavours. Fresh earth and sweet leather give regional authenticity. Lovely wine, the modest price increase from $50 to $60 reasonable. Diam. 13.2% alc. **Rating** 95 To 2033

ŶŶŶŶŶ **Cyril Premium Hunter Semillon 2017 Rating** 92 To 2032 $26
Cyril Premium Hunter Semillon 2016 Rating 91 To 2021 $26
Alexander Reserve Chardonnay 2017 Rating 90 To 2020 $35
Shareholders Shiraz 2011 Rating 90 To 2024 $30

Ernest Schuetz Estate Wines   ★★★★☆

778 Castlereagh Highway, Mudgee, NSW 2850 **Region** Mudgee
T 0402 326 612 **www**.ernestschuetzestate.com.au **Open** W'ends 10.30–4.30
Winemaker Liam Heslop **Est.** 2003 **Dozens** 10 500 **Vyds** 4.1ha
Ernest Schuetz's involvement in the wine industry started in 1988 at the age of 21. Working in various liquor outlets and as a sales representative for Miranda Wines, McGuigan Simeon and Watershed gave him an in-depth understanding of all aspects of the wine market. In 2003 he and wife Joanna purchased the Arronvale vineyard (first planted in 1991), at an altitude of 530m. Originally with merlot, shiraz and cabernet sauvignon, the Schuetzs have since grafted 1ha to riesling, pinot blanc, pinot gris, zinfandel and nebbiolo. A new cellar door overlooking the vineyard was scheduled to open in August '18. Exports to Vietnam, Hong Kong and China.

ŶŶŶŶŶ **Epica Amarone Method Mudgee Shiraz Cabernet 2015** Air-dried on racks for about 28 days to concentrate the flavours, hence an Amarone-style. It spends 26 months in French and American oak hogsheads (33% new). As the back label says, the wine is an intensive labour of love. It's well done. There's no bitterness or too much ripeness; sure, it's full-bodied and rich, decadently so, but it all comes together well. Cork. 15.6% alc. **Rating** 95 To 2030 $80 JF

ŶŶŶŶŶ **Terra X Mudgee Dry Rose 2017 Rating** 90 To 2018 $18 JF❂

Espier Estate   ★★★☆

Room 1208, 401 Docklands Drive, Docklands, Vic 3008 **Region** Southeastern Australia
T (03) 9670 4317 **www**.jnrwine.com **Open** Mon–Fri 9–5
Winemaker Sam Brewer **Est.** 2007 **Dozens** 25 000
This is the venture of Robert Luo and Jacky Lin. Winemaker Sam Brewer has been closely linked with the business since its establishment. The principal focus is affordable, good value wines. The Espier Estate wines are made at the family-owned boutique winery of Yarran Wines, which is also partly owned by Robert and Jacky. Exports to Asia.

Estate 807   ★★★★

807 Scotsdale Road, Denmark, WA 6333 **Region** Denmark
T (08) 9840 9027 **www**.estate807.com.au **Open** Thurs–Sun 10–4
Winemaker Mike Garland **Est.** 1998 **Dozens** 1250 **Vyds** 4.2ha
Dr Stephen Junk and Ola Tylestam purchased Estate 807 in 2009. Stephen was a respected embryologist working in IVF, while Ola came from a financial background. They chose the property due to its range of pinot noir and chardonnay clones (there are also plantings of cabernet and sauvignon blanc). Farm animals are used in the vineyard: chickens and ducks eat the pests, and sheep and alpacas provide manure and keep the vineyard neat and tidy.

ŶŶŶŶŶ **Mount Barker Riesling 2017** Pure riesling fruit flavour; it's hard to beat. This is a floral example, musk and red apple notes mingling with lime and slate. It is, of course, quite delicious. Screwcap. 12% alc. **Rating** 93 To 2024 $24 CM❂

Sauvignon Blanc 2017 Sound delivery of varietal flavour, gooseberry and nettle to the fore. A hint of texture, decent intensity and noticeable freshness. Screwcap. 12.6% alc. **Rating** 91 **To** 2019 $20 CM ✪

Esto Wines ★★★☆

PO Box 1172, Balhannah, SA 5242 **Region** Adelaide Hills
T 0409 869 320 **www.estowines.com.au Open** Not
Winemaker Charlotte Hardy, Phil Christiansen **Est.** 1994 **Dozens** 500 **Vyds** 23.5ha
The Dean family have been grapegrowers in the Adelaide Hills since 1994, progressively establishing three vineyards: the largest is 13ha planted in '94 at Balhannah, with a clonal mix of shiraz, semillon, chardonnay, sauvignon blanc and pinot noir, from which Charlotte Hardy makes semillon and sauvignon blanc. Shiraz, made by Phil Christiansen, is also made from this block. The next block (mostly pinot noir and chardonnay, with a postage stamp-sized planting of sangiovese) nestles in the Piccadilly Valley, in the afternoon shadow of Mt Lofty. All of the grapes from this vineyard are purchased by a distinguished group of Adelaide Hills winemakers. The third block, of 6.5ha – The Farside – is mostly sauvignon blanc and pinot gris, purchased by Petaluma, Bird in Hand and Primo Estate.

🍷🍷🍷🍷🍷 **Adelaide Hills Semillon 2017** Very cleverly made, the use of some oak and sub-13% alcohol have resulted in a fresh, lively semillon, its varietal character on show for all to see. The usual attempts to add body and interest are more clumsy and less effective. Screwcap. 11.9% alc. **Rating** 91 **To** 2025 $29

🍷🍷🍷🍷 **Adelaide Hills Sauvignon Blanc 2017 Rating** 89 **To** 2019 $22

Evans & Tate ★★★★★

Cnr Metricup Road/Caves Road, Wilyabrup, WA 6280 **Region** Margaret River
T (08) 9755 6244 **www.evansandtate.com.au Open** 7 days 10.30–5
Winemaker Matthew Byrne, Lachlan McDonald **Est.** 1970 **Dozens** NFP **Vyds** 12.3ha
The 48-year history of Evans & Tate has a distinct wild-west feel to its ownership changes since 1970, when it started life as a small two-family-owned business centring on the Swan District. Suffice to say, it is part of a corporate chess game between McWilliam's (its most recent owner) and the Fogarty group. Vineyards, brands, a viticultural services business and existing operations extend as far as Lake's Folly in the Hunter Valley (an iconic odd-man-out georgraphically). Locally, Evans & Tate, Deep Woods, Smithbrook, Millbrook and Pemberton Estate, plus Selwyn Viticultural Services, will share the production facility and other assets of the Margaret River Vintners group, which in the wash up will be owned 70% by Fogarty and 30% by McWilliam's. This will double Fogarty's production to 600 000 dozen, cementing its place as the largest producer of WA wine. Exports to all major markets.

🍷🍷🍷🍷🍷 **Redbrook Reserve Chardonnay 2015** Outrageously delicious; it may not be as complex as some, but everything is as finely tuned as a grand piano prepared for a major concert. It soars on the finish with green apple, grapefruit and white peach. The new oak was only 18%, and that was all that was required. Screwcap. 13% alc. **Rating** 97 **To** 2025 $49 ✪
Redbrook Reserve Chardonnay 2014 Made in precisely the same way as the '15, one irrelevant difference being less new oak at 15%. Underlines just how slowly this wine develops, and how long it will take to reach its plateau of perfection. Screwcap. 12.5% alc. **Rating** 97 **To** 2024 $49 ✪

🍷🍷🍷🍷🍷 **Breathing Space Sauvignon Blanc 2017** The riotous, joyous burst of flavours takes your breath away. It opens with passionfruit, pineapple and guava, then swings decisively to fresh cut grass, asparagus and nettle. And there's no shortage of crunchy acidity to cleanse the finish and aftertaste. Screwcap. 12.5% alc. **Rating** 95 **To** 2020 $19 ✪
Broadway Chardonnay 2016 Oh boy, this is clever winemaking: 30% wild-fermented in French oak (48% new), the balance fermented in tank, all kept on yeast lees for 10 months. The texture is little short of amazing, tethered to the

complex array of varietal fruit flavours, the usual calling cards of high quality Margaret River chardonnay. Screwcap. 12.5% alc. **Rating** 95 **To** 2025 $29 ○

Redbrook Reserve Cabernet Sauvignon 2014 If you are looking for a Margaret River cabernet that is as classy as it is classic, with intensity of varietal cassis flavour springing from a medium-bodied palate at modest alcohol, go no further. Many vinification methods were used, and once in barrel, each was monitored for its development; thereafter, the wine spent 14 months in French hogsheads (20% new). Screwcap. 14% alc. **Rating** 95 **To** 2039 $49

Breathing Space Chardonnay 2017 It's amazing how a wine of this provenance and quality has a RRP of $19, which probably means $16–$17 from the larger retailers. Screwcap. 13.5% alc. **Rating** 94 **To** 2023 $19○

♀♀♀♀♀ **Broadway Cabernet Sauvignon 2016 Rating** 93 **To** 2029 $29
Breathing Space Cabernet Sauvignon 2016 Rating 90 **To** 2022 $19○

Evoi Wines

92 Dunsborough Lakes Drive, Dunsborough, WA 6281 **Region** Margaret River
T 0407 131 080 **www**.evoiwines.com **Open** By appt
Winemaker Nigel Ludlow **Est.** 2006 **Dozens** 12 000

Nigel Ludlow has a Bachelor of Science in human nutrition, but after a short career as a professional triathlete, he turned his attention to grapegrowing and winemaking, with a graduate diploma in oenology and viticulture from Lincoln University, NZ (where he was born). Time at Selaks Drylands (NZ) was a stepping stone to Flying Winemaker stints in Hungary, Spain and South Africa, before a return to NZ as senior winemaker at Nobilo. He thereafter moved to Victoria, and finally to Margaret River. It took time for Evoi to take shape, the first vintage of chardonnay being made in the lounge room of Nigel's house. By 2010 the barrels had been evicted to more conventional storage, and since '14 the wines have been made in leased space at a commercial winery. Quality has been exceptional. Exports to the UK, Norway and Hong Kong.

♀♀♀♀♀ **Reserve Chardonnay 2016** Except for the pale green colour, you might think this will be an armful and then some. Well, you'd be very wrong. It has power, but it's hidden by the finesse and balance of the fruits. White peach, nectarine, fig and grapefruit coalesce with the oak; gentle acidity is never far away, but never obvious. Screwcap. 13.5% alc. **Rating** 98 **To** 2031 $69 ○

The Satyr Reserve 2015 A 56/27/17% blend of cabernet sauvignon, petit verdot and malbec. Pressed to French barriques for the conclusion of fermentation and maturation. Evoi's trademark is the ability to walk the tight line between finesse and power with seeming ease, here resoundingly achieving both. Juicy cassis opens the batting, then the more savoury aspects of cabernet appear, tannins arriving on time and in perfect position. Screwcap. 14.5% alc. **Rating** 97 **To** 2040 $69 ○

Malbec 2016 When an owner or winemaker says the wine is made in very small volume, you'd better believe them. Stop and ask questions and the wine will be gone before you know it. Malbec is seldom difficult to enjoy, but this is on another plane altogether. Screwcap. 14.5% alc. **Rating** 97 **To** 2036 $32 ○

♀♀♀♀♀ **Sauvignon Blanc Semillon 2017** Very clever winemaking has added an extra level of flavour and texture. It fills the mouth with a complex stream of fruit, green pea, lemon zest and spice, crowned by a minerally/citrussy finish. Screwcap. 12.5% alc. **Rating** 96 **To** 2030 $24 ○

art by Evoi Blackwood Valley Shiraz 2016 Deep colour; spice, pepper, blackberry, black cherry and licorice flood the bouquet with aromas and the palate with flavours, augmented by ripe tannins and a splash of oak. Will age with distinction. Screwcap. 14.5% alc. **Rating** 95 **To** 2036 $27 ○

Petit Verdot 2016 A more than useful 100% petit verdot that has very good structure. Flesh and bone contribute to the balanced array of cassis, black cherry and chocolate notes that appear in other Evoi red wines. The classy, supple finish is another common family trademark. Screwcap. 14.5% alc. **Rating** 95 **To** 2036 $32 ⊙

art by Evoi Malbec 2016 Attractive, rich and dark-berried, with soft tannins and good oak wound around and into each other. Each time you retaste the wine, it becomes more difficult to go past the velvety richness and find anything new to say – it's simply magical. Screwcap. 14.5% alc. **Rating** 95 **To** 2033 $25 ⊙

ɣɣɣɣ♀ **art by Evoi Cabernet Sauvignon 2016 Rating** 90 **To** 2031 $25

Faber Vineyard ★★★★★

233 Haddrill Road, Baskerville, WA 6056 **Region** Swan Valley
T (08) 9296 0209 **www.**fabervineyard.com.au **Open** Fri–Sun 11–4
Winemaker John Griffiths **Est.** 1997 **Dozens** 4000 **Vyds** 4.5ha
John Griffiths, former Houghton winemaker, teamed with wife Jane Micallef to found Faber Vineyard. They have established shiraz, verdelho (1.5ha each), brown muscat, chardonnay and petit verdot (0.5ha each). Says John, 'It may be somewhat quixotic, but I'm a great fan of traditional warm-area Australian wine styles, wines made in a relatively simple manner that reflect the concentrated ripe flavours one expects in these regions. And when one searches, some of these gems can be found in the Swan Valley.' Exports to Hong Kong and China.

ɣɣɣɣɣ **Reserve Swan Valley Shiraz 2015** Hand-picked from selected estate rows planted in '98. The difference between this and its Millard label sibling lies entirely in the vineyard, with the selection of single rows giving this wine an extra layer. Opulence in the marriage of (French) oak and fruit. Cork. 14.5% alc. **Rating** 95 **To** 2035 $70
Frankland River Cabernet Sauvignon 2015 A gloriously rich and succulent cabernet, the cassis fruit having totally absorbed the oak, leaving the wine to strut its stuff from now through decades to come. Cork. 14% alc. **Rating** 95 **To** 2035 $50
Millard Vineyard Swan Valley Shiraz 2015 Matured for 22 months in new French hogsheads. The impact of this wine could leave you so short of breath you'd have no energy to argue about it. A retaste brings everything into perspective, and it's pretty good provided you realise the oak will soften with time and fall back into the wine. Cork. 14.5% alc. **Rating** 94 **To** 2030 $50

ɣɣɣɣ♀ **The Scarp 2017 Rating** 93 **To** 2027 $23 ⊙
Ferguson Valley Semillon 2017 Rating 91 **To** 2023 $34 CM
Ferguson Valley Chardonnay 2016 Rating 91 **To** 2023 $30
Swan Valley Petit Verdot 2016 Rating 91 **To** 2026 $30
Swan Verdelho 2017 Rating 90 **To** 2020 $20 CM ⊙
Pure Rose 2017 Rating 90 **To** 2018 $24
Swan Valley Petit Verdot 2015 Rating 90 **To** 2023 $30 CM

Fallen Giants ★★★★★

4113 Ararat-Halls Gap Road, Halls Gap, Vic 3381 **Region** Grampians
T (03) 5356 4252 **www.**fallengiants.com.au **Open** Wed–Mon 10–5
Winemaker Justin Purser **Est.** 1969 **Dozens** 2700 **Vyds** 10.5ha
I first visited this vineyard when it was known as Boroka Vineyard and marvelled at the location in the wild country of Halls Gap. It wasn't very successful; Mount Langi Ghiran acquired it in 1998 and it was a useful adjunct for a while, but by 2013 it had outlived its purpose. It was then that the opportunity arose for Aaron Drummond and family to purchase the somewhat rundown vineyard. They moved quickly; the '13 vintage was made at Mount Langi Ghiran, but thereafter it was controlled under contract by Circe Wines (Aaron's business with Dan Buckle).

ɣɣɣɣɣ **Halls Gap Estate Block 3 Grampians Shiraz 2016** It is fascinating that the vinification of this wine is identical to that of the lesser priced shiraz, with both wines picked on the same day and made in exactly the same way. Of course there has to be differences, and this wine came from vines solely at 220m (100 dozen made), the other from vines between 180–220m (1400 dozen made). This achieves even greater depth, power and length that its sibling. Screwcap. 14.5% alc. **Rating** 98 **To** 2050 $50 ✪

Shiraz 2016 This has classic Grampians shiraz flavours: all black fruits and a strongly structured palate with a rocky edge to the fruit on the mid-palate; spices, cracked pepper and licorice all at maximum levels. Indeed, you would never have believed it possible that an even bigger wine would exist a few metres up the hill. Let me say, however, that although this is super-full-bodied, it doesn't rely on tannins. Screwcap. 14.5% alc. **Rating** 98 **To** 2045 $30 ✪

Block 1 Riesling 2017 From 18yo vines at 200m. Exceptional quality; fine, elegant, an intense note of Rose's lime juice, all cornerstones of a great wine from a vineyard with a long (48yo) history. Only 90 dozen made. Screwcap. 11% alc. **Rating** 97 **To** 2037 $35 ✪

♟♟♟♟♟ **Riesling 2017** From vines 18–48yo at 180–200m. It seems that part lower altitude and part older vines (possibly lesser clone/clones) are the reasons for Block 1 having the edge. The price differential is justified. 400 dozen made. Screwcap. 11% alc. **Rating** 96 **To** 2032 $25 ✪

Farmer and The Scientist   ★★★☆

Jeffreys Road, Corop, Vic 3559 **Region** Heathcote
T 0400 141 985 **www.**farmerandthescientist.com **Open** Not
Winemaker Brian Dwyer, Jess Dwyer, Ron Snep **Est.** 2013 **Dozens** 1500 **Vyds** 8ha
The Farmer is Bryan Dwyer, the Scientist wife Jess. Bryan is a viticulturist who learnt his craft with Southcorp, while Jess has a degree in science and is also qualified in teaching. She worked in wineries and vineyards from a young age. Ron Snep plays an important and successful role in the winery.

Farr | Farr Rising   ★★★★★

27 Maddens Road, Bannockburn, Vic 3331 **Region** Geelong
T (03) 5281 1733 **www.**byfarr.com.au **Open** Not
Winemaker Nick Farr **Est.** 1994 **Dozens** 5500 **Vyds** 13.8ha
By Farr and Farr Rising continue to be separate brands from separate vineyards, the one major change being that Nick Farr has assumed total responsibility for both labels, leaving father Gary free to pursue the finer things in life without interruption. This has in no way resulted in any diminution in the quality of the pinot noir, chardonnay, shiraz and viognier made. The vineyards are based on ancient river deposits in the Moorabool Valley. There are six different soils spread across the Farr property, with the two main types being rich, friable red and black volcanic loam, and limestone. The other soils are sandstone, volcanic lava, quartz gravel through red volcanic soil and ironstone (called buckshot) in grey sandy loam with a heavy clay base. The soil's good drainage and low fertility are crucial in ensuring small yields of intensely flavoured fruit. Exports to the UK, Canada, Denmark, Sweden, Hong Kong, Singapore, Taiwan, the Maldives, China and Japan.

♟♟♟♟♟ **Tout Pres by Farr Pinot Noir 2015** From a 1ha vineyard in an amphitheatre with three different soil types, and with six clones mutated into a single Tout Pres clone planted at 7300 vines per ha (the densest planting on the estate, hence the name Tout Pres, translating to 'very cosy'). From 100% whole bunches, open-fermented, matured in new French (Allier) oak. This wine, from a brilliant vintage, has a depth to its silently throbbing power, from the moment it enters the mouth to the lingering aftertaste. It would be impossible to buy a Burgundy of this quality for less than $250. Bravo. Cork. 13.5% alc. **Rating** 99 **To** 2040 $110 ✪

GC Chardonnay by Farr 2015 The very close-planted vineyard adds an extra layer of power and complexity that one expects from the best Farr chardonnays. The vintage, too, has played a role. This stands tall in the pantheon of top-end Aus chardonnays, planting its own stake in the ground through sheer length. Diam. 13% alc. **Rating** 97 **To** 2030 $110 ✪

Sangreal by Farr Geelong Pinot Noir 2016 Always made with 50–70% whole bunches, and 60–70% new oak maturation for 18 months. While the power of the wine is typical Farr, this vintage bestows a measure of linearity – a sinuous line to the palate that links and loops around the complex flavours of forest floor/ spice and wild strawberry. Cork. **Rating** 97 **To** 2035 $80 ❂

By Farr Shiraz 2016 From the original vineyard planted in '94, open-fermented with 2–4% viognier, 20% whole bunches, matured for 18 months in French oak (20% new). Complex and rich? Of course, it's Farr. Skilfully sculptured? Ditto. The key to this compelling shiraz is its seismic power and endless length. Cork. **Rating** 97 **To** 2046 $65 ❂

▼▼▼▼▼ **Irrewarra Chardonnay 2016** Has the usual Farr stamp of complexity from go to whoa, yet also has great purity and precision. Grapefruit and green apple lead the band, oak simply a vehicle for the fruit to express itself. The potential extreme longevity of the wine under screwcap has been squandered by the Diam. 13.5% alc. **Rating** 96 **To** 2029 $62 ❂

Farrside by Farr Geelong Pinot Noir 2016 Here 40–50% of the grapes are destemmed, the remainder left as whole bunches, and this increases complexity with its foresty, gamey (in the good sense), spicy overlay to the black cherry and plum fruit. The outstanding feature of the wine is its weight, suspended by some magic just above the palate – you sense it rather than taste it. Cork. **Rating** 96 **To** 2031 $80

Three Oaks Vineyard by Farr Chardonnay 2016 Hand-picked, whole-bunch pressed, wild-fermented in French oak (30% new), matured for 11 months. A very complex, opulent wine with stone fruits and fig, then a shaft of citrussy acidity spearing through the middle of the palate, cleansing the finish. Diam. 13% alc. **Rating** 95 **To** 2023 $78

Farr Rising Geelong Saignee 2017 Farr is upfront about the process hidden by some others: the destemmed pinot is taken to tank and after 2–3 hours the juice is run off for the rose, leaving the must more concentrated than it would otherwise be (for the pinot). Wild fermentation in used oak is followed by 10 months' maturation. Farr also thumbs its nose to natural winemakers by filtering the wine pre-bottling. It's light, bright salmon-pink, and far more intense and 'winey' than most roses. Fruit-sweet, but bone dry. Terrific. Diam. **Rating** 95 **To** 2022 $28 ❂

Farr Rising Geelong Pinot Noir 2016 As ever a complex wine, a 50/50 split between place/vine husbandry and the hand of the winemaker. If you master the wile of Geelong, you'll see it produces some of Australia's best and most distinctive wines. Diam. 13.5% alc. **Rating** 95 **To** 2031 $48

Irrewarra Pinot Noir 2015 Supple and silky, flooded with dark cherry and satsuma plum, this has only just embarked on a journey that, over the next 5+ years, will reveal the spice and sous bois notes presently locked up in it, albeit already in perfect balance. Diam. 14% alc. **Rating** 95 **To** 2025 $62

Farr Rising Geelong Shiraz 2016 Entry point wine? Yes but consider its impeccable breeding. It's oh so juicy, so light on its quicksilver feet. Irresistible? Yes, but if your wine budget is seriously restricted, think about the '17s and you'll likely drool, saving this year to spend next. Diam. **Rating** 95 **To** 2031 $48

Farr Rising Geelong Chardonnay 2016 Fluid chardonnay with savouriness as its headline. Grapefruit, cedar spice, tinned pear and green pineapple flavours come draped in wood smoke and meal. There's a slight warmth,,but it's a wine of body, texture and length. Diam. 13% alc. **Rating** 94 **To** 2024 $45 CM

Fermoy Estate   ★★★★☆

838 Metricup Road, Wilyabrup, WA 6280 **Region** Margaret River
T (08) 9755 6285 **www.fermoy.com.au Open** 7 days 10–5
Winemaker Jeremy Hodgson **Est.** 1985 **Dozens** 16 000 **Vyds** 47ha
A long-established winery with 17ha of semillon, sauvignon blanc, chardonnay, cabernet sauvignon and merlot. The Young family acquired Fermoy Estate in 2010, and built a larger

cellar door which opened in '13, signalling the drive to increase domestic sales. It is happy to keep a relatively low profile, however difficult that may be given the quality of the wines. Jeremy Hodgson brings with him a first-class honours degree in oenology and viticulture, and a CV encompassing winemaking roles with Wise Wine, Cherubino Consultancy and, earlier, Plantagenet, Houghton and Goundrey Wines. Exports to Europe, Asia and China.

🍷🍷🍷🍷🍷 **Reserve Margaret River Chardonnay 2017** This has clear ambitions of being among the region's best. White fig, peach and vibrant notes of orchard fruits are beamed across the flavoursome mid-palate, toned by crystalline acidity and mineral crunch. Screwcap. 13% alc. **Rating** 94 **To** 2027 $60 NG
Reserve Margaret River Shiraz 2016 Oozing blue fruit along its sinuous veins of pepper grind, camphor and clove, the acidity perfectly positioned, the tannins nicely edgy, the finish long and juicy with a nod to reductive tension rather than a subservient bow. Screwcap. 14.5% alc. **Rating** 94 **To** 2024 $65 NG
Reserve Margaret River Cabernet Sauvignon 2015 Red and blackcurrant, bay leaf, licorice all-sorts and a spread of tapenade open the attack. This is a full-bodied wine, allied with high quality French oak (75% new, 19 months) and maritime acidity. Screwcap. 14.5% alc. **Rating** 94 **To** 2035 $95 NG

🍷🍷🍷🍷🍷 **Reserve Margaret River Semillon 2017** Rating 93 To 2029 $45 NG
Margaret River Cabernet Sauvignon 2015 Rating 93 To 2027 $45 NG
Margaret River Sauvignon Blanc 2017 Rating 92 To 2020 $25 NG ✪
Margaret River SSB 2017 Rating 92 To 2020 $25 NG ✪
Margaret River Shiraz 2015 Rating 92 To 2023 $30 NG
Margaret River Merlot 2016 Rating 92 To 2022 $30 NG
Margaret River Cabernet Merlot 2015 Rating 92 To 2027 $25 NG ✪

Ferngrove   ★★★★★

276 Ferngrove Road, Frankland River, WA 6396 **Region** Frankland River
T (08) 9363 1300 **www**.ferngrove.com.au **Open** Mon–Fri 10–4
Winemaker Craig Grafton, Marco Pinares, Marelize Russouw **Est.** 1998
Dozens NFP **Vyds** 340ha
Known for producing consistent examples of cool-climate wines across multiple price brackets, the Ferngrove stable includes the Stirlings, Orchid, Frankland River and Symbols ranges. Ferngrove Vineyards Pty Ltd enjoys the benefits of majority international ownership, but remains Australian-run. Exports to all major markets.

🍷🍷🍷🍷🍷 **Cossack Riesling 2017** Ferngrove has a long history of excellence with riesling, this vintage right in the slot. No reliance on props (residual sugar, etc) to make its mark, and nigh-on bone dry, which allows the purity of its fruit to express itself. Blossom-scented, with grapefruit, lemon and Granny Smith apple all playing roles that will underwrite a multi-decade future. Screwcap. 12% alc. **Rating** 96 **To** 2037 $23 ✪
King Malbec 2016 Matured in French and Hungarian oak for 14 months. Richer and deeper than its Black Label sibling, yet still with a degree of elegance and freshness to its medium-bodied palate. The purity of the varietal expression is striking, and you have to wonder where the oak went. A very smart wine at this price, good now and 10 years down the track. Screwcap. 13.5% alc. **Rating** 95 **To** 2031 $32 ✪

🍷🍷🍷🍷🍷 **Black Label Dry-Style Riesling 2017** Rating 92 To 2027 $20 ✪
Black Label Sauvignon Blanc 2017 Rating 92 To 2019 $20 ✪
Black Label Off-Dry Riesling 2017 Rating 91 To 2030 $20 ✪
Diamond Chardonnay 2016 Rating 90 To 2023 $25
Cabernet Sauvignon 2015 Rating 90 To 2027 $20 SC ✪
Black Label Malbec 2016 Rating 90 To 2023 $20 ✪

Fetherston Vintners ★★★★★

1/99A Maroondah Highway, Healesville, Vic 3777 **Region** Yarra Valley
T (03) 5962 6354 **www.**fetherstonwine.com.au **Open** Not
Winemaker Chris Lawrence **Est.** 2015 **Dozens** 1500
The establishment of Fetherston Vintners in 2015 by Chris Lawrence and Camille Koll was, in hindsight, the logical consequence of their respective careers in wine, food and hospitality. Chris began his career in the kitchen in establishments all over Australia. In '09 he enrolled in the science (oenology) degree with the University of Southern Queensland, graduating in '14 as valedictorian, receiving the Faculty Medal for Science. During his time at Yering Station ('10–14) he worked his way up from junior cellar hand to assistant winemaker. A vintage at Domaine Serene in Oregon's Willamette Valley in '12 gave him further insight into great chardonnay and pinot noir. In '14 he took on the role of winemaker at Sunshine Creek in the Yarra Valley. Camille is Yarra born and bred, growing up at Hoddles Creek. After finishing school she began a seven-year stint at Domaine Chandon, giving her invaluable insight into professional branding, marketing and customer service. She is now working in hospitality management as her day job. Chris's late grandfather was Tony Fetherston.

♟♟♟♟♟ **Pyrenees Nebbiolo 2016** Bright and brilliantly clear in colour; cherry blossom, rose petals, violets and spices whether you're taking in the bouquet or cradling the palate. This really is a nebbiolo to make you think of pinot noir. Gorgeous wine. Screwcap. 14% alc. **Rating** 96 **To** 2026 $30 ✪
Yarra Valley Chardonnay 2016 Sizzling follow-up to the excellent '15. Grapefruit, oak spice, white peach and bran-like flavours put on an impressive display. It somehow manages to feel creamy, mouthwatering, flinty and seamless at once. The carry of flavour through to the finish goes into the realms of the exquisite. Screwcap. 13% alc. **Rating** 95 **To** 2023 $25 CM ✪

♟♟♟♟♟ **King Valley Dolcetto Rose 2017 Rating** 93 **To** 2020 $22 CM ✪
Yarra Valley Pinot Noir 2016 Rating 93 **To** 2025 $28
Yarra Valley Shiraz 2016 Rating 92 **To** 2036 $25 ✪

Fighting Gully Road ★★★★★

Kurrajong Way, Mayday Hill, Beechworth, Vic 3747 **Region** Beechworth
T 0407 261 373 **www.**fightinggully.com.au **Open** By appt
Winemaker Mark Walpole, Adrian Rodda **Est.** 1997 **Dozens** 3500 **Vyds** 8.3ha
Mark Walpole (who began his viticultural career with Brown Brothers in the late 1980s) and partner Carolyn De Poi found their elevated north-facing site south of Beechworth in 1995. They commenced planting the Aquila Audax vineyard in '97 with cabernet sauvignon and pinot noir, subsequently expanding with significant areas of sangiovese, tempranillo, shiraz, petit manseng and chardonnay. In 2009 they were fortunate to lease the oldest vineyard in the region, planted by the Smith family in 1978 to chardonnay and cabernet sauvignon – in fact, Mark shares the lease with long-time friend Adrian Rodda (see A. Rodda Wines). Says Mark, 'We are now making wine in a building in the old and historic Mayday Hills Lunatic Asylum – a place that should be full of winemakers!' Exports to Hong Kong.

♟♟♟♟♟ **Beechworth Shiraz 2015** 35% whole bunches on the bottom of the fermenter, 2% viognier skins above, then 63% crushed/destemmed berries on top, left alone to ferment naturally until 2% baume left. Pigéaged, 3 weeks on skins in total, matured in new and used French oak for 18 months. This approach, coupled with 13.5% alcohol, results in a vibrantly fresh, fragrant and lively wine bursting with cherry fruit, spice and pepper. Now the journey in the bottle begins. Screwcap. **Rating** 96 **To** 2035 $40 ✪
Beechworth Tempranillo 2014 Matured in French oak (50% new) for 18 months, with a further 30 months in bottle. It's an expensive business holding the wine for 4 years, whether in oak or (even more so) in bottle as they do in Spain in Rioja and Ribera del Duero. The reward is the elegance of this tempranillo, coupled with varietal integrity – a superior wine in many ways. Screwcap. 13.5% alc. **Rating** 96 **To** 2034 $34 ✪

Beechworth Chardonnay 2016 Wild-fermented in Italian-coopered French oak and matured for 10 months. Has that distinctive Beechworth chardonnay flavour, pitched precisely in the midpoint between stone fruit and citrus, with the polished mouthfeel that follows. Screwcap. 13% alc. **Rating** 95 **To** 2030 $38

Beechworth Sangiovese 2016 A good sangiovese that has repaid complex vinification, first up with a fragrant rose petal/cherry blossom bouquet. The palate is in a state of flux as savoury notes come and go, sour and fresh cherries playing hide and seek. Screwcap. 14% alc. **Rating** 94 **To** 2026 $28 ✪

ΨΨΨΨΨ **Beechworth Pinot Noir 2016 Rating** 92 **To** 2023 $30

Finestra   ★★★★

PO Box 120, Coldstream, Vic 3770 **Region** Yarra Valley
T (03) 9739 1690 **Open** Not
Winemaker Alan Johns, Bruce Lang **Est.** 1989 **Dozens** 500 **Vyds** 2.9ha
Owners Bruce and Jo-Anne Lang have combined professional careers and small-scale winemaking for over 30 years. In the early 1970s they gained holiday employment at wineries in the Yarra Valley, and at the end of that decade they joined with friends in purchasing the old Brown Brothers' Everton Hills vineyard near Beechworth. In '87 they acquired their property adjacent to Yeringberg, overlooking Domaine Chandon, and planted the vineyard in '89, extending it in '96. With a total of 2.9ha of pinot noir, chardonnay, shiraz and cabernet sauvignon, it is small, and until 2002 all of the grapes were sold to two major Yarra Valley wineries. Since then, 50% of the grapes have been used for the Finestra label.

ΨΨΨΨΨ **Dalla Mia Yarra Valley Cabernet 2015** Plenty of density about this release, from the colour onwards. Dark-berried fruit takes a little time to reveal itself on the bouquet, but then it's followed by savoury and cedary notes with some influence from the (50% new) oak. A firm line of tannin runs through the palate, flanked by juicy but slightly tart flavours in the mulberry and just-ripe-blackberry spectrum, all the elements flowing seamlessly on to a long finish. Screwcap. 13.6% alc. **Rating** 94 **To** 2030 $28 SC ✪

ΨΨΨΨΨ **Dalla Mia Yarra Valley Shiraz Cabernet 2015 Rating** 93 **To** 2025 $28 SC
Dalla Mia Yarra Valley Cabernet 2014 Rating 93 **To** 2026 $28 SC
Dalla Mia Yarra Valley Pinot Noir 2016 Rating 92 **To** 2024 $25 SC ✪

Finniss River Vineyard   ★★★★

15 Beach Road, Christies Beach, SA 5165 **Region** Currency Creek
T (08) 8326 9894 **www.**finnissvineyard.com.au **Open** Mon–Wed 11–5, Thurs–Sun 11–8
Winemaker Adam Parkinson **Est.** 1999 **Dozens** 3000 **Vyds** 146ha
The Hickinbotham family established several great vineyards, the last of these being that of Finniss River in 1999. The planting mix was good, dominated by 31.3ha of shiraz and 20.9ha of cabernet sauvignon. Between then and February 2015, when Adam and Lauren Parkinson purchased the vineyard, all the grapes were sold. During Adam's time as general manager of a McLaren Vale winery, as well as general manager of one of Australia's largest vineyard management companies, he had come into contact with the family and its grapes, which led to the purchase. Exports to China, the US and Singapore have already been established.

ΨΨΨΨΨ **Shiraz 2016** Matured for 8 months in tank with new French oak staves. Deep colour; an intense medium to full-bodied shiraz that has flavours (and aromas) ranging from spice and licorice to plum and dark chocolate. The tannins are soft, the French oak doing the job nicely. Screwcap. 14.9% alc. **Rating** 91 **To** 2029 $25

Cabernet Sauvignon 2016 Matured in tank with new French oak staves for 8 months. Good colour; has an abundance of varietal character, and the staves have done their job. It has some reductive hardness ex tank maturation, raising the question of whether micro-oxygenation was used (seemingly not). That said, the wine will soften with time, and the glass is more than half full. Screwcap. 14.5% alc. **Rating** 90 **To** 2026 $25

Fire Gully ★★★★★

Metricup Road, Wilyabrup, WA 6280 **Region** Margaret River
T (08) 9755 6220 **www.firegully.com.au Open** By appt
Winemaker Dr Michael Peterkin **Est.** 1988 **Dozens** 5000 **Vyds** 13.4ha
A 6ha lake created in a gully ravaged by bushfires provided the name. In 1998 Mike Peterkin of Pierro purchased it. He manages the vineyard in conjunction with former owners Ellis and Margaret Butcher. He regards the Fire Gully wines as entirely separate from those of Pierro; the plantings are cabernet sauvignon, merlot, shiraz, semillon, sauvignon blanc, chardonnay, viognier and chenin blanc. Exports to all major markets.

ㅎㅎㅎㅎㅎ **Margaret River Sauvignon Blanc Semillon 2017** An ultra-refreshing drink with wafts of basil, lemon blossom, passionfruit, a touch of guava and while stone fruit. The semillon adds an invigorating lemon edge and spiciness, the palate full of verve and zest with citrus sorbet–like acidity. Screwcap. 12.5% alc. **Rating** 95 To 2022 $26 JF

Margaret River Chardonnay 2017 Kicks off with just the right amount of leesy, nutty notes wound around a core of very good fruit: mostly citrus with grapefruit pith, plus stone fruit. Zesty acidity keeps it tightly coiled. It's so well composed that before you know it, the bottle is empty. Screwcap. 13.5% alc. **Rating** 95 **To** 2025 $35.50 JF

ㅎㅎㅎㅎㅎ **Margaret River Rose 2017 Rating** 93 **To** 2020 $33 JF

Fireblock ★★★★☆

28 Kiewa Place, Coomba Park, NSW 2428 (postal) **Region** Clare Valley
T (02) 6554 2193 **Open** Not
Winemaker O'Leary Walker **Est.** 1926 **Dozens** 3000 **Vyds** 6ha
Fireblock (formerly Old Station Vineyard) is owned by Bill and Noel Ireland, who purchased the then almost-70-year-old Watervale vineyard in 1995. The vines planted in '26 (3ha of shiraz and 2ha of grenache) are dry-grown; the riesling (1ha) was replanted to the Geisenheim clone in 2008 when town water became available. The wines are skilfully contract-made, winning trophies and gold medals at capital city wine shows. Exports to Sweden and Malaysia.

ㅎㅎㅎㅎㅎ **1926 Old Vine Shiraz 2015** Following the acquisition of the vineyard by Noel and Bill Ireland, much work has been undertaken to rejuvenate the old vines, which makes the giveaway price of this shiraz all the more remarkable. It's full-bodied and dense, yet perfectly balanced, giving pride of place to blackberry fruit and licorice, the tannins tightly furled. A long life ahead. Screwcap. 15% alc. **Rating** 95 **To** 2045 $20 ○

ㅎㅎㅎㅎㅎ **1926 Old Bush Vine Grenache Shiraz Mourvedre 2015 Rating** 92 **To** 2035 $18 ○

Geisenheim Clone Watervale Riesling 2017 Rating 90 **To** 2027 $18 ○

Firetail ★★★★☆

21 Bessell Road, Rosa Glen, WA 6285 **Region** Margaret River
T (08) 9757 5156 **www.firetail.com.au Open** 7 days 11–5
Winemaker Bruce Dukes, Peter Stanlake **Est.** 2002 **Dozens** 1000 **Vyds** 5.3ha
Jessica Worrall and Rob Glass are fugitives from the oil and gas industry. In 2002 they purchased a 5.3ha vineyard in Margaret River that had been planted between 1979 and '81 to sauvignon blanc, semillon and cabernet sauvignon. Jessica has gained a Masters of Wine Technology and Viticulure from the University of Melbourne. The wine quality is exemplary and the prices almost old-fashioned.

ㅎㅎㅎㅎㅎ **Margaret River Cabernet Sauvignon 2016** Exceptional elegance and length, achieved without obvious effort, with a purity of varietal character seldom achieved. Diam. 13.1% alc. **Rating** 96 **To** 2031 $28 ○

ㅎㅎㅎㅎ **Margaret River Rose 2014 Rating** 89 **To** 2019 $16 CM

First Drop Wines

Beckwith Park, Barossa Valley Way, Nuriootpa, SA 5355 **Region** Barossa Valley
T (08) 8562 3324 **www**.firstdropwines.com **Open** Wed–Sat 10–4
Winemaker Matt Gant **Est.** 2005 **Dozens** 15 000

The First Drop Wines of today has been transformed since its establishment in 2005. It now has its own winery, part of the old Penfolds winery at Nuriootpa, shared with Tim Smith Wines. The group of buildings is called Beckwith Park in honour of the man who did so much groundbreaking work for Penfolds: Ray Beckwith OAM, recipient of the Maurice O'Shea Award, who died in 2012, but not before his 100th birthday. Exports to the UK, the US, Canada, Denmark, Japan, Hong Kong and NZ.

The Cream Barossa Valley Shiraz 2015 A dark well of flavour; one sip and you sink into its inky depths. It tastes of cocoa and coffee, licorice and blackberry, a lift of raspberry and violet-like like character showing through the finish. Clearly it's at the (very) big end of town, but the fruit is of monumental proportions and it somehow manages to feel tied down and neat. Cork. 15% alc. **Rating** 95 **To** 2035 $150 CM

Fat of the Land Ebenezer Single Vineyard Barossa Valley Shiraz 2015 Thoroughly seductive. It's saturated with dark-berried flavour but it melts in your mouth. It tastes of milk chocolate and blackberries, earth and sweet plums, a peppermint character hovering thereabouts. There's tannin here, and ground coffee notes, and alcohol warmth, but it all feels cuddly, drawing you in. Cork. 15% alc. **Rating** 95 **To** 2035 $100 CM

Two Percent Barossa Shiraz 2016 Yes there's size and warmth, but it has a smile on its dial and charm on its side. It's light and heavy at once, floral and fat with ripe berries, buzzy alcohol drenched in juicy, dark, energetic fruit flavour. It's a toothsome red wine. Screwcap. 15% alc. **Rating** 94 **To** 2030 $38 CM

Vivo Adelaide Hills Arneis 2017 Rating 93 **To** 2020 $25 CM ❂
Mother's Milk Barossa Shiraz 2016 Rating 93 **To** 2026 $25 CM ❂
Fat of the Land Single Vineyard Greenock Barossa Valley Shiraz 2015 Rating 93 **To** 2035 $100 CM
Mother's Ruin McLaren Vale Cabernet Sauvignon 2016 Rating 93 **To** 2024 $25 CM ❂
Minchia Adelaide Hills Montepulciano 2014 Rating 92 **To** 2024 $38 CM
Mere et Fils Adelaide Hills Chardonnay 2016 Rating 91 **To** 2021 $25 CM
Fat of the Land Seppeltsfield Single Vineyard Barossa Valley Shiraz 2015 Rating 91 **To** 2028 $100 CM
The Matador Barossa Garnacha 2016 Rating 91 **To** 2022 $25 CM

First Foot Forward

6 Maddens Lane, Coldstream, Vic 3770 **Region** Yarra Valley
T 0402 575 818 **www**.firstfootforward.com.au **Open** By appt
Winemaker Martin Siebert **Est.** 2013 **Dozens** 500

Owner and winemaker Martin Siebert's daytime job is at Tokar Estate, where he has been chief winemaker for a number of years. In 2013 he had the opportunity to purchase pinot noir and chardonnay from a mature vineyard in The Patch, high in the Dandenong Ranges on the southern edge of the Yarra Valley. It is cooler and wetter than the floor of the valley, and the fruit is consistently picked after Tokar's, reducing the stress that might otherwise have occurred. He says that so long as the fruit is available, he will be purchasing it. Tim added a sauvignon blanc from Steels Creek to slightly broaden the offer to quality-focused restaurants and specialty wine stores around Melbourne.

The Patch Vineyard Yarra Valley Chardonnay 2017 This would immediately be identified as an Upper Yarra Valley wine, but it's nowhere near all the other vineyards – it's higher and leans steeply into the morning sun. The wine is intensely focused, long and linear. All the right winemaking steps have been taken, but it's like polishing 24-carat gold. Screwcap. 13.5% alc. **Rating** 96 **To** 2030 $28 ❂

Yarra Valley Pinot Noir 2017 Takes a little time to wind up and get into gear, but having done so offers a very complex bouquet of plums and bakers' spices. The palate gained length and purpose each time I came back to it, although the flavour spectrum didn't crumble. Screwcap. 13.5% alc. **Rating** 95 **To** 2027 $30 ✪

First Ridge ★★★★

Cnr Castlereagh Highway/Burrundulla Road, Mudgee, NSW **Region** Mudgee
T 0407 701 014 **www**.firstridge.com.au **Open** 7 days 10–4
Winemaker James Manners **Est.** 1998 **Dozens** 5000 **Vyds** 20ha
Sydney architect John Nicholas and wife Helen began the establishment of what is now a 20ha vineyard on undulating hillsides above an open valley below in 1998. The soils vary from shallow topsoils of basalt and quartz on the highest ridges to deeper loams over neutral clays. Barbera, sangiovese and vermentino are planted in the ridges; fiano, pinot grigio, tempranillo, shiraz and merlot in the deeper soils. The vineyard manager, Colin Millot, began work in McLaren Vale 30 years ago, moving to Mudgee in 1995 to manage the Rosemount Hill of Gold and Mountain Blue vineyards. Winemaker James Manners (son of famed chef Ned Manners) plays his part in realising the desire of the Nicholases to 'enjoy tables of abundant food, friends and fiery conversation, not unlike a vibrant Italian table'.

♟♟♟♟♟ **Mudgee Rose 2017** Effort and ingenuity have combined with whole-bunch pressing and separate cuts (amounts in the press), keeping the free-run and light pressings separate, the latter fined more aggressively. This vintage prevented the normal fermenting to dryness, so the wine has low level residual sugar. I think many consumers wouldn't taste the sweetness, just the elegant, fresh strawberry flavours. Screwcap. 13% alc. **Rating** 90 **To** 2019 $20 ✪
Mudgee Barbera 2016 A well made wine following in the footsteps of the '15 with its plum and dark cherry fruits, the tannins playing a pure support role. Overall, fresh and well balanced. Screwcap. 14.5% alc. **Rating** 90 **To** 2026 $30

Five Geese ★★★★☆

389 Chapel Hill Road, Blewitt Springs, SA 5171 (postal) **Region** McLaren Vale
T (08) 8383 0576 **www**.fivegeese.com.au **Open** Not
Winemaker Mike Farmilo **Est.** 1999 **Dozens** 5000 **Vyds** 28ha
Sue Trott is devoted to her Five Geese wines, which come from vines planted in 1927 and '65 (shiraz, cabernet sauvignon, grenache and mataro), nero d'Avola a more recent arrival. She sold the grapes for many years, but in '99 decided to create her own label and make a strictly limited amount of wine from the pick of the vineyards, which are run on organic principles. Exports to the UK, South Korea and Singapore.

♟♟♟♟♟ **Indian File Old Vine Grenache 2016** This is grenache with its head held high. It's bright with both red and black cherry flavours, though saltbush, aniseed, assorted florals and dry spice notes are here in abundance. It's ribbed with tannin, feels velvety on the tongue, and pulses impressively through the finish. A delight of a wine. Screwcap. 14.5% alc. **Rating** 95 **To** 2026 $28 CM ✪
The Pippali Old Vine Shiraz 2015 Modest (French) oak is threaded through pure, fresh, boysenberried fruit. Plum, mint and even redcurrant flavours are here too, but this is old vine McLaren Vale shiraz in buoyant mode. It makes for joyous drinking. Screwcap. 14.5% alc. **Rating** 94 **To** 2030 $28 CM ✪
Jon's Block Reserve Blewitt Springs Shiraz 2015 It's a plum-shot, curranty shiraz running on rails of satin. Make hay, the sun's been shining and the grapes taste of pure blue sky. It's both vibrant and deep, smells of more than just fruit, has taken oak in its stride and feels fussed over in the best of ways. Screwcap. 14.5% alc. **Rating** 94 **To** 2030 $45 CM
Shiraz 2015 Rich with plum, mint and boysenberry-like flavour, carrying a gentle splash of hay-like, smoky oak. Finessed with tannin and drawing out juicily through the finish. Vibrant and delicious. Everything is in the drinker's favour. Screwcap. 14.5% alc. **Rating** 94 **To** 2028 $22 CM ✪

♟♟♟♟♟ **McLaren Vale Nero d'Avola 2016 Rating** 90 **To** 2021 $20 CM ✪

Five Oaks Vineyard   ★★★★☆

60 Aitken Road, Wandin East, Vic 3139 **Region** Yarra Valley
T (03) 5964 3704 **www**.fiveoaks.com.au **Open** W'ends & public hols 11–5
Winemaker Wally Zuk **Est.** 1995 **Dozens** 1000 **Vyds** 3ha
Wally Zuk and wife Judy run all aspects of Five Oaks – far removed from Wally's background
in nuclear physics. He has, however, completed the wine science degree at CSU, and is thus
more than qualified to make the wines. The lion's share of the vineyard is planted to cabernet
sauvignon (2.6ha), with 0.2ha each of riesling and merlot. Exports to Canada, Macau, Hong
Kong and China.

🍷🍷🍷🍷🍷 SGS Yarra Valley Cabernet Sauvignon 2016 The bright, clear crimson-
purple colour is tantalising, and doesn't deceive: this is a pure cabernet, with nigh-
on perfect line, length and balance, the flavours anchored on cassis. Really lovely
wine. Screwcap. 13.9% alc. **Rating** 96 **To** 2036 $95
Yarra Valley Merlot 2016 Bright, full, clear crimson; an elegant, juicy, medium-
bodied wine that has been well made, and entices you to drink it just through its
colour in the first place, thereafter by its pure cassis and spice. Old clone (3DV14),
difficult to do better. Screwcap. 12.9% alc. **Rating** 94 **To** 2031 $40

Flametree   ★★★★★

Cnr Caves Road/Chain Avenue, Dunsborough, WA 6281 **Region** Margaret River
T (08) 9756 8577 **www**.flametreewines.com **Open** 7 days 10–5
Winemaker Cliff Royle, Julian Scott **Est.** 2007 **Dozens** 20 000
Flametree, owned by the Towner family (John, Liz, Rob and Annie), has had extraordinary
success since its first vintage in 2007. The usual practice of planting a vineyard then finding
someone to make the wine was turned on its head: a state-of-the-art winery was built, and
grape-purchase agreements signed with growers in the region. Show success was topped
by winning the Jimmy Watson Trophy with the 2007 Cabernet Merlot. If all this were not
enough, Flametree secured the services of winemaker Cliff Royle. Exports to the UK, Canada,
Indonesia, Malaysia, Singapore, Papua New Guinea, Fiji and Hong Kong.

🍷🍷🍷🍷🍷 S.R.S. Wallcliffe Margaret River Chardonnay 2016 The freshness and
intensity of the palate led to the trophy for Best Chardonnay at the Sydney Wine
Show '17. Cliff Royle judged the amount of new oak, and the time the wine
spent in the oak, to perfection, placing maximum focus on the ripe flavours.
Screwcap. 13% alc. **Rating** 97 **To** 2029 $65 ✪

🍷🍷🍷🍷🍷 Margaret River Pinot Rose 2017 A stunning rose. Crisp and dry with flutters
of flavour – the right amount of red-berried fruit, spice, some texture too. It's
moreish and savoury. What are you waiting for? Screwcap. 13% alc. **Rating** 95
To 2019 $25 JF ✪
S.R.S. Wilyabrup Margaret River Cabernet Sauvignon 2015 Red and
black currant, anise, clove, bay leaf and the rest of the varietal cavalcade rumble
across a sheen of fine-tuned gravelly tannins. The oak is an adjunct, rather than a
yell, positioning itself as assistant to the slinky tannic mettle. This will age very well.
Screwcap. 14% alc. **Rating** 95 **To** 2030 $75 NG ✪
S.R.S. Karridale Margaret River Sauvignon Blanc 2017 A fine wine that
embodies the Aristotelean ideal of sass and sophistication across impeccably ripe
fruit, an attractive lick of oak, judicious lees handling for textural detail, and
flavours that run the gamut of herbal, tropical, and stone fruits, all careening
effortlessly along a rail of bright acidity infused with mineral crunch. Screwcap.
13% alc. **Rating** 94 **To** 2022 $33 NG

🍷🍷🍷🍷🍷 Margaret River Cabernet Merlot 2015 **Rating** 93 **To** 2030 $30 CM
Margaret River Sauvignon Blanc Semillon 2017 **Rating** 92 **To** 2020 $25
NG ✪
Frankland River Pinot Grigio 2017 **Rating** 92 **To** 2019 $25 JF ✪
Margaret River Shiraz 2016 **Rating** 91 **To** 2024 $29 NG

Flaxman Wines

662 Flaxmans Valley Road, Flaxmans Valley, SA 5253 **Region** Eden Valley
T 0411 668 949 **www.**flaxmanwines.com.au **Open** Thurs–Sun 11–5
Winemaker Colin Sheppard **Est.** 2005 **Dozens** 1500 **Vyds** 2ha
After visiting the Barossa Valley for over a decade, Melbourne residents Colin Sheppard and wife Fi decided on a tree-change, and in 2004 found a small, old vineyard overlooking Flaxmans Valley. It consists of 1ha of 60+ and 90-year-old riesling, 1ha of 65+ and 90-year-old shiraz, and 0.8ha of 60+ year-old semillon. The vines are dry-grown, hand-pruned and hand-picked, and treated – say the Sheppards – as their garden. Yields are restricted to under 4t/ha, and exceptional parcels of locally grown grapes are also purchased. Colin has worked at various Barossa wineries, and his attention to detail (and understanding of the process) is reflected in the consistent high quality of the wines.

Riesling 2017 A somewhat fleshy, ripe version pointing more to drinking in its youth, with lovely flavours of preserved lemon, melon and ginger blossom. There's a juiciness here and it feels smooth across the palate, with fresh acidity and a ripper spice kick on the finish. Screwcap. 12% alc. **Rating** 95 **To** 2025 $27 JF ✪
Semillon 2016 Heartbreakingly small quantities made (40 dozen), this being the first dry style, as it's usually a sweet cordon-cut wine. There's an incredible evenness with the flavours of honeysuckle, hay, lemon curd and poached quinces, then lemony acidity shoots right through the middle. Screwcap. 12.5% alc. **Rating** 95 **To** 2024 $22 JF ✪
Estate Shiraz 2015 Easy to drink, yet waves of complexity keep one's interest until the very last drop. The flavour profile is of dark fruits, a raft of spices and balanced oak (33% new French barrels, the wine aged 23 months), with an intriguing savoury note like ironstone, and minerally acidity to close. Merely 90 dozen made. Screwcap. 14% alc. **Rating** 95 **To** 2035 $60 JF
Reserve Eden Valley Cabernet 2015 Pulses with energy and drive. Cassis, black olive, dried herbs, ferrous, tobacco and oak spices all blend perfectly with the medium body, full of textural savoury tannins followed by a fine, long finish. Really impressive. Screwcap. 14% alc. **Rating** 95 **To** 2028 $50 JF
Barossa Valley Mataro 2015 It manages to fulfil a flavour profile of great complexity yet remain tight and linear. Mouthwatering prosciutto, pomegranate, licorice tea, earth and menthol, plus satsuma plums, cherries and pips. The medium-to-lighter frame is ultra-refreshing, the bright acidity seeing to that with fine tannins to close. Screwcap. 14% alc. **Rating** 95 **To** 2028 $37 JF
The Stranger Barossa Shiraz Cabernet 2015 A balanced blend of bright dark fruit – blood orange studded with cloves, pepper and baking spices – but savoury through and through. Medium-bodied with supple tannins. It's in a drinking sweet-spot now although will continue to age well. Screwcap. 13.5% alc. **Rating** 94 **To** 2030 $37 JF

Chardonnay 2016 Rating 91 **To** 2023 $27 JF
Barossa Sparkling Shiraz NV Rating 90 $60 JF

Flint's of Coonawarra

Flint Road, Coonawarra, SA 5263 **Region** Coonawarra
T (08) 8736 5046 **www.**flintsofcoonawarra.com.au **Open** By appt
Winemaker Contract **Est.** 2001 **Dozens** 2000 **Vyds** 84ha
Six generations of the Flint family have lived and worked in Coonawarra since 1840. Damian Flint and his family began the development of their 84ha of cabernet sauvignon, shiraz and merlot in 1989, but it was not until 2000 that they decided to have a small portion of cabernet sauvignon made. Damian and Sue oversee the day-to-day running of both the vineyard and farm, with Matthew, who studied viticulture in the Barossa, managing the vineyard.

Gammon's Crossing Cabernet Sauvignon 2015 23yo vines, machine-harvested, crushed and destemmed, fermented in tank with cultured yeast, 14 days on skins, matured for 22 months in oak (40% new). The wine is charged with cassis fruit that flirts at the border of being ripe or overripe, staying (just) on the right side. The upside is there's no need to wait for tannins for soften. Screwcap. 15% alc. **Rating** 90 **To** 2023 $25

Flowstone Wines ★★★★★

11 298 Bussell Highway, Forest Grove, WA 6286 **Region** Margaret River
T 0487 010 275 **www.**flowstonewines.com **Open** By appt
Winemaker Stuart Pym **Est.** 2013 **Dozens** 1500 **Vyds** 2.25ha
Flowstone is the venture of Stuart Pym and Phil Giglia. Stuart's involvement with wine commenced in 1983, when he moved to Margaret River to help his parents establish their vineyard and winery in Wilyabrup (since sold). Lengthy winemaking careers at Voyager Estate (1991–2000), Devil's Lair ('00–08) and Stella Bella ('08–13) were rounded out with concurrent vintage work overseas. Phil is a self-confessed wine tragic, his fascination starting at the University of WA's Wine Club. He met Phil at a Margaret River Great Estates lunch in the late 1990s, and they hatched the idea of starting a small business, which took shape in 2003 when the property was purchased. A small area of chardonnay was planted the following year, the remainder in '09. Estate grapes are augmented by contract-grown grapes. The attention to detail of the venture is typified by the appealing labels, made from 81% limestone and the remainder bonding resin (there is no wood fibre or pulp).

♟♟♟♟♟ **Margaret River Chardonnay 2015** I know of no other Australian maker of chardonnay who holds the wine for 30 months prior to sale. Gleaming straw-green; there are few chardonnays from '15 with the intensity and freshness of this one. Despite its power and concentration, it moves with athletic grace across the palate and aftertaste. A beautiful chardonnay. 320 dozen made. Screwcap. 13% alc. **Rating** 97 **To** 2030 $36 ✪
Queen of the Earth Margaret River Chardonnay 2015 The brilliant straw-green hue says there's something special here, for it's incredibly detailed, precise and balanced. The three spears of perfect varietal fruit, high quality oak and acidity are all unsheathed. Only 88 dozen made. Screwcap. 13.3% alc. **Rating** 97 **To** 2035 $55 ✪

♟♟♟♟♟ **Margaret River Gewurztraminer 2016** I truly have no idea how Stuart Pym conjures up so much varietal fruit flavour in the face of a theoretically unsuitable climate and almost baroque vinification. Heady spices soar out of the glass without coaxing, the palate layered and rich with hints of tropical fruits as well as orange/citrus. Screwcap. 14% alc. **Rating** 96 **To** 2023 $32 ✪
Margaret River Sauvignon Blanc 2016 Flowstone keeps its reputation for exceptionally complex wines riding high with this one – complexity, texture and longevity are its passwords. In its own oenological universe, fruit descriptors are superfluous, each consumer encouraged to put their opinion on the tasting bench. Screwcap. 13% alc. **Rating** 96 **To** 2026 $32 ✪
Margaret River Sauvignon Blanc 2015 Green-gold; a barrel-fermented sauvignon blanc that challenges normal beliefs and practices, made possible by the quality of the grapes. It marries honeyed richness with complexity, crystallised grapefruit skin with dancing acidity. Screwcap. 13% alc. **Rating** 96 **To** 2022 $32 ✪
Queen of the Earth Margaret River Cabernet Sauvignon 2014 Matured in French barriques for 3 years with a further 15 months in bottle before release. Stuart Pym makes light work of what is a complex exercise, and a patient one at that given the time in oak and bottle. It has a texture and structure all of its own, verging on velvety, yet reminding me that the cassis, black olive and dried bay leaf could only come from cabernet. Screwcap. 14.1% alc. **Rating** 96 **To** 2034 $74 ✪
Moonmilk 2017 64% savagnin, 18% viognier, 12% gewurztraminer and 6% sauvignon blanc. This is truly a tour de force by Stuart Pym. It should have ended up in a flavour dead-end, with phenolics everywhere, the varieties shading each other out, yet it is full of fruit, crisp and crunchy, the finish fresh. 235 dozen made. Screwcap. 13% alc. **Rating** 94 **To** 2022 $21✪

♟♟♟♟♟ **Moonmilk Shiraz Grenache 2016 Rating** 93 **To** 2025 $22✪
Margaret River Cabernet Sauvignon Touriga 2014 Rating 93 **To** 2030 $36

Flying Fish Cove

Caves Road, Wilyabrup, WA 6280 **Region** Margaret River
T (08) 9755 6600 **www**.flyingfishcove.com **Open** By appt
Winemaker Simon Ding, Damon Easthaugh **Est.** 2000 **Dozens** NFP **Vyds** 25ha
Flying Fish Cove has two strings to its bow: contract winemaking for others, and the development of its own brand. Long-serving winemaker Simon Ding had a circuitous journey before falling prey to the lure of wine. He finished an apprenticeship in metalwork in 1993. In '96 he obtained a Bachelor of Science, then joined the Flying Fish Cove team in 2000. Exports to the US, Canada and Malaysia.

🍷🍷🍷🍷🍷 **Wildberry Estate Reserve Margaret River Cabernet Sauvignon 2016**
The Wildberry vineyard is in Wilyabrup, the best address in Margaret River, and this wine is from select rows. Always Flying Fish Cove's best cabernet of the vintage, it is an opulent wine, so rich in cassis fruit you are tempted to call it voluptuous, hardly a description of high quality Margaret River cabernet. But there it is, seduction, with a capital S. Screwcap. 14.5% alc. **Rating** 96 **To** 2036
Margaret River Sauvignon Blanc Semillon 2016 An exceptionally complex bouquet with resounding surges of tropical fruits, the palate smoothly picking up the thread, threatening to go over-the-top, but pulled back into line by crackling acidity that both lengthens and refreshes the finish. Bargain basement. Screwcap. 12.5% alc. **Rating** 95 **To** 2021 $22 ✪
Wildberry Estate Reserve Margaret River Chardonnay 2016 This is the best chardonnay of the vintage. The flavours of grapefruit zest and juice come charging through the palate, largely masking the impact of the oak you know must be there, the aftertaste lingering long. Screwcap. 13.2% alc. **Rating** 95 **To** 2024
The Wildberry Reserve Margaret River Shiraz 2014 Deep crimson-purple; very focused, intense and spicy, this has many of the characteristics of very cool-climate shiraz. The style has great appeal for its freshness; how this came about with 14.5% alc. is quirky, which adds even more appeal. Screwcap. **Rating** 95 **To** 2034 $40

🍷🍷🍷🍷♀ **Wildberry Estate Two Passions Margaret River Chardonnay 2015**
Rating 90

Flynns Wines

29 Lewis Road, Heathcote, Vic 3523 **Region** Heathcote
T (03) 5433 6297 **www**.flynnswines.com **Open** First w'end each month 11.30–5
Winemaker Greg Flynn, Natala Flynn **Est.** 1999 **Dozens** 1500 **Vyds** 4.12ha
Greg and Natala Flynn spent 18 months searching for their property, which is 13km north of Heathcote on red Cambrian soil. They have established shiraz, sangiovese, verdelho, cabernet sauvignon and merlot. Greg is a Roseworthy marketing graduate, and has worked for over 25 years at the coal face of retail and wholesale businesses, interweaving 10 years of vineyard and winemaking experience, supplemented by the two-year Bendigo TAFE winemaking course. Natala has likewise completed the course.

🍷🍷🍷🍷♀ **MC Heathcote Shiraz 2015** A satisfying expression of buxom shiraz, for those who appreciate the style. Blueberry, floral lilacs and coffee grind to chocolate confectionery notes define the attack. Maturation for 14 months in French and American oak (40% new) parlays firm, toasty tannins that corset the wine's sheer mass. Anise, menthol and a spray of pepper complete the package. Screwcap. 14.8% alc. **Rating** 93 **To** 2030 $35 NG
Lewis Road Heathcote Shiraz 2015 Heathcote is an odd beast, displaying shiraz subtleties on one hand, molten warmer climatic attributes on the other. It is certainly far from 'cool climate'. This is a rich first cab off the rank, laden with black fruit notes, coffee bean, mocha and bitter chocolate. Anise and violet, too, with a twirl of eucalyptus across a gently astringent gait. Screwcap. 15% alc. **Rating** 92 **To** 2023 $26 NG

James Flynn Heathcote Shiraz 2014 Exaggerated, potent shiraz, this has been racked from one passage of oak to another: 12 months in a combination of French and American oak of varied age, to 100% new oak of the same origins for a further year. Phew! An additional year of bottle age follows, presumably to facilitate (at least the beginning) of a smoothing effect of polymerisation. Some must appreciate this style, but shiraz of this largesse is, for me at least, tiring. Menthol, soy, oak, desiccated black fruits ... on rewind. A hark back to the Parkerised era. Screwcap. 15% alc. **Rating** 90 **To** 2024 $70 NG

Forest Hill Vineyard ★★★★★

Cnr South Coast Highway/Myers Road, Denmark, WA 6333 **Region** Great Southern
T (08) 9848 2399 **www**.foresthillwines.com.au **Open** Thurs–Sun 10.30–4.30
Winemaker Liam Carmody, Guy Lyons **Est.** 1965 **Dozens** 12 000 **Vyds** 65ha
This family-owned business is one of the oldest 'new' winemaking operations in WA, and was the site of the first grape plantings in Great Southern in 1965. The Forest Hill brand became well known, aided by the fact that the '75 Riesling made by Sandalford from Forest Hill grapes won nine trophies. The quality of the wines made from the oldest vines (dry-grown) is awesome, released under numbered vineyard block labels. Exports to Taiwan, Hong Kong, Singapore and China.

🍷🍷🍷🍷🍷 **Block 1 Mount Barker Riesling 2017** A wine of great class, fully reflecting its distinguished place in WA winemaking history and the growing season of '17. Its titratable acidity of 9.13g/l is subsumed by the intensity of the citrus zest, grapefruit and Granny Smith apple. It lingers in the mouth long after it's been swallowed. Screwcap. 12.5% alc. **Rating** 97 **To** 2037 $38 ✪

Block 1 Mount Barker Riesling 2014 The bouquet is filled with citrus and apple blossom aromas, and the palate is still blissfully ignorant of the passage of time, tightly wound all the way through the finish and aftertaste where the strongly minerally mouthfeel is anchored by acidity. Screwcap. 12.5% alc. **Rating** 97 **To** 2030 $40 ✪

🍷🍷🍷🍷🍷 **Mount Barker Riesling 2017** The wine doesn't blush when it locks onto the mouth with lime and lemon zest running on rails of grippy acidity through to the finish. This is old-school severity of the highest calibre, good for 25 years. Screwcap. 12.5% alc. **Rating** 96 **To** 2020 $26 ✪

Mount Barker Chardonnay 2017 This is a sumptuously rich chardonnay that keeps its belt tight thanks to all-important natural acidity keeping off centrestage, allowing white peach and nectarine to joust with the grapefruit and melon flavours. Screwcap. 13% alc. **Rating** 96 **To** 2027 $30 ✪

Block 8 Mount Barker Chardonnay 2015 A beautifully crafted wine that seems even lighter than its 13.5% alc., and which has absorbed 10 months in French oak. It is one of those chardonnays that will develop slowly, and never disappoint along the way. Stone fruit, citrus of all kinds and green apple are all in the flavour mix. Screwcap. **Rating** 96 **To** 2027 $45 ✪

Block 9 Mount Barker Shiraz 2015 Growing season conditions of lower rainfall from winter through to picking led to poor fruit-set, the result very low yields. The tannins are still in play, but the red and black fruits are more than just a match; the only thing needed is patience. Screwcap. 14.1% alc. **Rating** 94 **To** 2035 $60

🍷🍷🍷🍷 **Highbury Fields Chardonnay 2017 Rating** 92 **To** 2025 $22 ✪
Estate Great Southern Gewurztraminer 2017 Rating 91 **To** 2030 $26
Estate Mount Barker Shiraz 2016 Rating 91 **To** 2031 $30

Forester Estate ★★★★★

1064 Wildwood Road, Yallingup, WA 6282 **Region** Margaret River
T (08) 9755 2788 **www**.foresterestate.com.au **Open** Not
Winemaker Kevin McKay, Todd Payne **Est.** 2001 **Dozens** 52 000 **Vyds** 33.5ha

Forester Estate is owned by Kevin and Jenny McKay, with a 500t winery that is half devoted to contract winemaking, the other half to the Forester label. Winemaker Todd Payne has had a distinguished career, starting in the Great Southern, thereafter the Napa Valley, back to Plantagenet, then Esk Valley in NZ, plus two vintages in the Northern Rhône Valley, one with esteemed producer Yves Cuillerón in 2008. His final move back to WA completed the circle. The estate vineyards are planted to sauvignon blanc, semillon, chardonnay, cabernet sauvignon, shiraz, merlot, petit verdot, malbec and alicante bouschet. Exports to Japan.

ȲȲȲȲȲ **Sauvignon Blanc 2017** Just the right amount of aroma, flavour and texture. Absolutely in the zone. Thistles, tropical fruits, cuts of green apple. Bursting with life. Screwcap. 13% alc. **Rating** 94 **To** 2020 $30 CM ◑

Semillon Sauvignon Blanc 2017 Highly expressive. Flavours of snow peas and assorted tropical fruits, a touch of wood smoke, herb notes. Drinking it is like a walk through the cool green woods. Core strength, balance, length, elegance. Screwcap. 12% alc. **Rating** 94 **To** 2021 $27 CM ◑

Cabernet Merlot 2015 It's fresh, lively and sturdy at once. Balance is a key feature in itself. It tastes of boysenberry, cassis and fragrant herbs, choc-coffee notes apparent as guiding hands only. An excellent drinking/cellaring bet-each-way style at a most attractive price. Screwcap. 13.5% alc. **Rating** 94 **To** 2030 $27 CM ◑

Cabernet Sauvignon 2015 Such a polished performer. Just the right amount of everything, and a real lustre to both the colour and texture. Pure blackcurrant, a kiss of cedar wood, fresh bay leaves. It's not complicated but nor is it simple. Screwcap. 13.5% alc. **Rating** 94 **To** 2032 $40 CM

ȲȲȲȲȲ **Chardonnay 2016 Rating** 93 **To** 2024 $40 CM

Jack out the Box Margaret River Fer 2015 Rating 92 **To** 2030 $50 CM

Shiraz 2015 Rating 91 **To** 2025 $27 CM

Foster e Rocco   ★★★★

PO Box 438, Heathcote, Vic 3523 **Region** Heathcote
T 0407 057 471 **www**.fostererocco.com.au **Open** Not
Winemaker Adam Foster **Est.** 2008 **Dozens** 2500
Foster e Rocco is a business that has a very clear vision: food-friendly wine based on the versatility of sangiovese. Adam Foster makes the wine at Syrahmi, building it from the ground up, with fermentation in both stainless steel and a mixture of used French oak. Exports to the US, Japan and China.

ȲȲȲȲȲ **Nuovo Sangiovese 2017** A juicy, easy-drinking sangiovese made with no oak influence. While it has upfront fruit, it also has a savoury twist and retains the variety's bright, talc-like acidity and tannins, thanks to the 20 days on skins during fermentation. Wafts of cherries, juniper berries and Mediterranean herbs. The lighter framed palate has a suppleness, a drive, and there's only thing to do: drink it now with glee. Screwcap. 13.5% alc. **Rating** 94 **To** 2020 $25 JF ◑

ȲȲȲȲȲ **Riserva Sangiovese 2012 Rating** 92 **To** 2019 $55 JF

Rose 2017 Rating 90 **To** 2019 $25 JF

Sangiovese 2015 Rating 90 **To** 2022 $37 JF

Four Sisters   ★★★☆

199 O'Dwyers Road, Tabilk, Vic 3608 **Region** Central Victoria
T (03) 5736 2400 **www**.foursisters.com.au **Open** Not
Winemaker Alan George, Jo Nash, Alister Purbrick **Est.** 1995 **Dozens** 40 000
The four sisters who inspired this venture were the daughters of the late Trevor Mast, a great winemaker who died before his time. The business is owned by the Purbrick family (the owner of Tahbilk). It orchestrates the purchase of the grapes for the brand, and also facilitates the winemaking. The production is wholly export, focused with limited sales in Australia. Four Sisters exports to 15 countries, including China; that number may well diminish if Chinese distribution fulfils all its potential.

🍷🍷🍷🍷🍷 Central Victoria Cabernet Sauvignon 2016 It is wonderful to taste wines fighting with valour at a friendly price point. Dark cherry, currant and a fleck of mint on the nose are guided by gently astringent tannins, to reverberate on the nourishing, juicy palate. Soft, approachable and carbon neutral, to boot. Screwcap. 15% alc. **Rating** 92 **To** 2020 $16 NG ✿

🍷🍷🍷🍷 Central Victoria Shiraz 2016 **Rating** 89 **To** 2021 $16 ✿

Four Winds Vineyard ★★★★☆

9 Patemans Lane, Murrumbateman, NSW 2582 **Region** Canberra District
T (02) 6227 0189 **www.**fourwindsvineyard.com.au **Open** Thurs–Mon 10–4
Winemaker Highside Winemaking **Est.** 1998 **Dozens** 3000 **Vyds** 11.9ha
Graeme and Suzanne Lunney conceived the idea for Four Winds in 1997, planting the first vines in '98, moving to the property full-time in '99, and making the first vintage in 2000. Daughter Sarah looks after marketing. Youngest daughter Jaime, complete with a degree in forensic biology, has joined in the winery, as has her husband Bill. She brings with her several years' experience at the former Kamberra winery, and three vintages in the Napa Valley.

🍷🍷🍷🍷🍷 Shiraz 2016 Instantly appealing, easy-drinking shiraz with an unmistakably cool-climate personality. Savoury and slightly earthy/gamey is the initial impression, but the underlying fruit isn't far behind. It's in the tangy to almost tart spectrum – cranberry, squishy raspberry and mulberry – but feels ripe, and buoyant with freshness and zippy acidity. Tannin keeps it all together. Good drinking now and for a while to come. Screwcap. 13.7% alc. **Rating** 92 **To** 2025 $30 SC

Fowles Wine ★★★★☆

Cnr Hume Freeway/Lambing Gully Road, Avenel, Vic 3664 **Region** Strathbogie Ranges
T (03) 5796 2150 **www.**fowleswine.com **Open** 7 days 9–5
Winemaker Victor Nash, Lindsay Brown **Est.** 1968 **Dozens** 80 000 **Vyds** 120ha
This family-owned winery is led by Matt Fowles, with Victor Nash as chief winemaker. The large vineyard is primarily focused on riesling, chardonnay, shiraz and cabernet sauvignon, but also includes arneis, vermentino, pinot gris, sauvignon blanc, pinot noir, mourvedre, sangiovese and merlot. Marketing is energetic, with the well known Ladies Who Shoot Their Lunch label available as large posters; the wines are even available in a six-bottle gun case. Exports to the UK, the US, Canada and China.

🍷🍷🍷🍷🍷 Ladies Who Shoot Their Lunch Wild Ferment Shiraz 2016 It's juicy and expressive and boasts good depth of flavour. It tastes of sweet black cherries, boysenberry, violet and anise, and carries a good lick of spicy/peppery flavour. Tannin is fine-grained, florals abound, and it makes you want to keep coming back for more. It's not a heavy shiraz, but a beautiful one. Screwcap. 14.4% alc. **Rating** 95 **To** 2026 $35 CM ✿

🍷🍷🍷🍷🍷 Ladies Who Shoot Their Lunch Riesling 2017 **Rating** 93 **To** 2025 $35 CM
Stone Dwellers Shiraz 2016 **Rating** 93 **To** 2026 $25 CM ✿
Stone Dwellers Arneis 2016 **Rating** 92 **To** 2020 $22 CM ✿
Ladies Who Shoot Their Lunch Wild Ferment Pinot Noir 2016 **Rating** 91 **To** 2024 $35 CM
Are You Game? Cabernet Sauvignon 2016 **Rating** 90 **To** 2023 $20 CM ✿

Fox Creek Wines ★★★★★

140 Malpas Road, McLaren Vale, SA 5171 **Region** McLaren Vale
T (08) 8557 0000 **www.**foxcreekwines.com **Open** 7 days 10–5
Winemaker Scott Zrna, Ben Tanzer **Est.** 1995 **Dozens** 40 000 **Vyds** 21ha
Fox Creek has a winemaking history that dates back to 1984, when Helen and Dr Jim Watts purchased a 32ha property in McLaren Vale. A portfolio of highly commended wines, many from vineyards dating back to the early 1900s, form the viticultural backbone. Minimal

intervention in the vineyard (no systemic chemicals used) and a $500000 winery expansion, designed in close collaboration with the winemaking team, underwrite the high quality of the portfolio. Exports to all major markets.

🍷🍷🍷🍷 **Limited Release McLaren Vale Grenache 2016** Fragrant and red fruited with cranberry, cooked strawberry and redcurrants, some brown spice, but clearly free from oak influence (only 2–8yo puncheons were used for maturation). Chalky, refreshing fruit tannins add positive grip and refreshment to its medium-bodied nature. More of this please. Screwcap. **Rating** 95 **To** 2026 $38 DB
Old Vine McLaren Vale Shiraz 2016 From vines planted in 1910. Opaque purple-red and concentrated looking. Big, ripe, black- and blue-fruited. Ribbons of vanilla, mocha and brown spice from barrel fermentation. There's a pleasing earthiness underpinning the wine that adds a savoury refreshment too. Bold and unashamed of its style. Screwcap. 14.5% alc. **Rating** 94 **To** 2030 $68 DB
Three Blocks McLaren Vale Cabernet Sauvignon 2015 A prime example of the synergy between McLaren Vale cabernet and a good vintage such as this. The bouquet starts the wine with fragrant cassis aromas before the going gets serious on the palate, where fruit, tannins and oak go into a cage fight, oak the only casualty. Screwcap. 14.5% alc. **Rating** 94 **To** 2040 $38

🍷🍷🍷🍷 **JSM McLaren Vale Shiraz Cabernet Sauvignon Cabernet Franc 2015** **Rating** 93 **To** 2026 $29 DB
Short Row McLaren Vale Shiraz 2016 Rating 92 **To** 2032 $38 DB
McLaren Vale Shiraz 2016 Rating 92 **To** 2036 $23
Postmaster McLaren Vale GSM 2016 Rating 92 **To** 2026 $29
McLaren Vale Cabernet Sauvignon 2016 Rating 92 **To** 2025 $23
Jim's Script McLaren Vale Cabernet Sauvignon Merlot Cabernet Franc Petit Verdot 2015 Rating 90 **To** 2026 $29 DB
Limited Release Nero d'Avola 2016 Rating 90 **To** 2018 $38 DB

Fox Gordon ★★★☆

44 King William Road, Goodwood, SA 5034 **Region** Barossa Valley/Adelaide Hills
T (08) 8377 7707 **www.**foxgordon.com.au **Open** Mon–Wed 9.30–2.30,
Thurs 9.30–4.30, Fri–Sat 12.30–5.30
Winemaker Marty O'Flaherty **Est.** 2000 **Dozens** 10000 **Vyds** 31ha
This is the venture of Rachel Atkins (nee Fox) and Jane Gordon. Established in 2000, Fox Gordon wines are made from family-owned and operated vineyards and select growers in the Adelaide Hills and Barossa Valley. Estate plantings comprise sauvignon blanc, chardonnay, fiano, shiraz, tempranillo and nero d'Avola. Classy packaging adds the final touch. Exports to the UK, China and other major markets.

🍷🍷🍷🍷 **Sassy Adelaide Hills Sauvignon Blanc 2017** At first, it smells and tastes of Sherbet Bombs and Fizzoes – the purple ones. Then more varietal nuances pop up such as guava, passionfruit and pith with some alpine herbs. Plenty of lemony acidity keeps it straight. Screwcap. 12.8% alc. **Rating** 90 **To** 2018 $19 JF ✪

🍷🍷🍷🍷 **Abby Adelaide Hills Fume Blanc 2017 Rating** 89 **To** 2019 $23 DB
The Empress Adelaide Hills Chardonnay 2016 Rating 89 **To** 2019 $25 SC
Eight Uncles Barossa Shiraz 2016 Rating 89 **To** 2027 $20 DB
The Dark Prince Nero d'Avola 2016 Rating 89 **To** 2021 $25 SC

Foxeys Hangout ★★★★★

795 White Hill Road, Red Hill, Vic 3937 **Region** Mornington Peninsula
T (03) 5989 2022 **www.**foxeys-hangout.com.au **Open** W'ends & public hols 11–5
Winemaker Tony Lee, Michael Lee **Est.** 1998 **Dozens** 5000 **Vyds** 3.4ha
This is the venture of Tony Lee and journalist wife Cathy Gowdie. Cathy explains where it all began: 'We were not obvious candidates for a seachange. When we talked of moving to the country, friends pointed out that Tony and I were hardly back-to-nature types. "Do you own a

single pair of shoes without heels?" asked a friend. At the end of a bleak winter, we bought an old farmhouse on 10 daffodil-dotted acres at Red Hill and planted a vineyard.' They planted pinot noir, chardonnay, pinot gris and shiraz on the north-facing slopes of the old farm.

ŢŢŢŢŢ **Scotsworth Farm Mornington Peninsula Pinot Noir 2016** Best Mornington Peninsula Red Wine Trophy at the International Cool Climate Wine Show '17. It's a wine of presence, power and charisma. It's both thoroughly convincing and exciting at once. Forest berries, slings of spice, violets and dried herbs, a fast-train of tannin shooting through. Each of the components is suggestive of size and volume, yet combined they tuck neatly together: Russian dolls of wine. Screwcap. 13.5% alc. **Rating** 97 **To** 2026 $65 CM ✪
Kentucky Road 777 Mornington Peninsula Pinot Noir 2015 Bright, clear colour; it has equal amounts of spicy red and purple fruits, superfine tannins and lipsmacking acidity coming together on the truly excellent and long finish. For the record, the block is planted to clone 777, grafted onto mature vines in '10. Screwcap. 13.5% alc. **Rating** 97 **To** 2025 $65 ✪

ŢŢŢŢŢ **Scotsworth Farm Mornington Peninsula Pinot Noir 2016** Made from the original vines planted in '98. Highly attractive red cherry and strawberry aromas are faithfully reproduced on the airy palate; fleecy tannins appearing as an afterthought as the wine leaves the mouth. Screwcap. 13.5% alc. **Rating** 96 **To** 2026 $65 ✪
Mornington Peninsula Pinot Noir 2016 Bright, clear crimson-purple; highly fragrant, with a cherry and plum-filled bouquet. The structure, texture and length are on another level, and the flavours more profound, intense to the point of drawing saliva from the mouth. Will harvest many gold medals, its first being from the International Cool Climate Wine Show '17. Screwcap. 13.5% alc. **Rating** 96 **To** 2029 $38 ✪
Red Lilac Vineyard Mornington Peninsula Chardonnay 2016 In stark contrast to its sibling, with a minerally fresh mouthfeel, flavours of stone fruit and melon, oak and mlf having given texture. If the Foxeys Hangout Chardonnays are entered in shows, it will be fascinating to see the judges' reactions to the two wines. Screwcap. 13% alc. **Rating** 95 **To** 2023 $45
Kentucky Road 777 Mornington Peninsula Pinot Noir 2016 It's sweetly perfumed with cherry blossom, a prologue to the elegant, fresh palate, itself in a mode that Foxeys has made its own. The fruit flavours have a gently savoury-spicy inflection, likewise the fine tannins. Screwcap. 13.5% alc. **Rating** 95 **To** 2026 $65
Mornington Peninsula Shiraz 2016 Very good colour; well made, with fragrant spicy berries on the bouquet flowing into the medium-bodied, complex palate. Here a juicy blackberry streak is accompanied by licorice and pepper, and fine-grained but persistent tannins. Screwcap. 13.5% alc. **Rating** 95 **To** 2031 $45
Scotsworth Farm Mornington Peninsula Pinot Noir 2015 Terrific vintage. Foxeys has cashed in with this single vineyard release. It packs dry spice, Italian herbs, spicy oak and floral aspects into a pure stream of cherried, almost boysenberried fruit. It works a treat, even at this early stage, and the pivot of acidity and anchor of tannin will serve it well as more time passes. Screwcap. 13.5% alc. **Rating** 94 **To** 2024 $65 CM
Mornington Peninsula Late Harvest Pinot Gris 2016 Made using the cordon cut method, and has worked a treat, amplifying the spiced pear flavours, the considerable sweetness balanced by acidity. 375ml. Screwcap. 11% alc. **Rating** 94 **To** 2023 $28 ✪

ŢŢŢŢŢ **Red Fox Mornington Peninsula Pinot Noir 2016 Rating** 92 **To** 2021 $28
Mornington Peninsula Chardonnay 2016 Rating 91 **To** 2021 $38
Mornington Peninsula Pinot Gris 2016 Rating 91 **To** 2019 $28

Frankland Estate

Frankland Road, Frankland, WA 6396 **Region** Frankland River
T (08) 9855 1544 www.franklandestate.com.au **Open** Mon–Fri 10–4,
public hols & w'ends by appt
Winemaker Hunter Smith, Brian Kent **Est.** 1988 **Dozens** 20000 **Vyds** 34.5ha
This significant operation is situated on a large sheep property owned by Barrie Smith and
Judi Cullam. The vineyard has been established progressively since 1988; the introduction of
an array of single vineyard rieslings has been a highlight, driven by Judi's conviction that terroir
is of utmost importance, and the soils are indeed different. The Isolation Ridge vineyard is
now organically grown. Frankland Estate has held important international riesling tastings and
seminars since 2001. Exports to all major markets.

ΨΨΨΨΨ **Poison Hill Vineyard Riesling 2017** Imbued with the distinctive minerally
personality of this estate's rieslings, and chock-full of classic varietal expression.
The aromas and flavours have an overarching citrus theme: grapefruit, lime juice,
the blossoms of Meyer lemon, the zest of a ripe mandarin. Tight and textured,
the tingly acidity holds the line along the palate and drives through the finish.
Screwcap. 13% alc. **Rating** 96 **To** 2035 $40 SC **☉**
Isolation Ridge Vineyard Riesling 2017 From one of the classic vineyards of
Frankland River. A heady, perfumed frangipani, honeysuckle and lime bouquet is
met with an equally dramatic suite of flavours thundering through to the finish.
Screwcap. 12.5% alc. **Rating** 96 **To** 2030 $40 **☉**
Smith Cullam Riesling 2017 Made in an off-dry style, and inevitably compared
with its counterparts from the Mosel and Rheingau. Risking repetition, it is one
of the few Australian rieslings that combines an intense, nervy minerality with
pure and delightful varietal character, a testament to the region, vineyard and
winemaker. A masterclass in poise and balance. Screwcap. 11.5% alc. **Rating** 96
To 2035 $60 SC **☉**
Riesling 2017 Some colour development, but not alarming. A wine of
impeccable bloodlines and breeding, not a hair out of place, nor a crease in its
clothing. The young rieslings from all parts of Great Southern are a pleasure to
do business with. Citrus, apple and silvery acidity are as refreshing as they are
cleansing. Screwcap. 12% alc. **Rating** 95 **To** 2029 $28 **☉**
Cabernet Sauvignon 2016 95% cabernet sauvignon and 5% malbec from
the organically grown Isolation Ridge vineyard. Purity and power stay within
a medium-bodied frame because everything is ergonomically measured and
delivered – blackcurrant, tapenade and dried herbs/leaves. Screwcap. 14% alc.
Rating 95 **To** 2036 $28 **☉**
Cabernet Sauvignon 2015 A delicious wine in every respect, its scented,
persistent cassis bouquet, its fresh, juicy palate and its fine tannins. Each component
plays a lead role somewhere along the way, all adding up to a cabernet made for
drinking or sipping – your call. Screwcap. 14% alc. **Rating** 95 **To** 2035 $28 **☉**
Olmo's Reward 2015 An estate-grown Bordeaux blend, throbbing with a
juicy kaleidoscope of red, purple, blue and black fruits. Fine tannins and carefully
managed French oak add up to a win-win scenario. Screwcap. 14% alc. **Rating** 95
To 2040 $85
Chardonnay 2016 A complex but understated style that will continue to build
in the bottle. Fruit characters are mainly in the citrus vein, with some spice and
savoury input from the seamlessly meshed oak. Fine and long, with a slinkiness
of texture held in a taut, convincing framework. Screwcap. 12.5% alc. **Rating** 94
To 2025 $28 SC **☉**

ΨΨΨΨΨ **Rocky Gully Riesling 2017 Rating** 90 **To** 2022 $20 CM **☉**

Fraser Gallop Estate

493 Metricup Road, Wilyabrup, WA 6280 **Region** Margaret River
T (08) 9755 7553 www.frasergallopestate.com.au **Open** 7 days 11–4
Winemaker Clive Otto **Est.** 1999 **Dozens** 11000 **Vyds** 20ha

Nigel Gallop began the development of the vineyard in 1999, planting cabernet sauvignon, semillon, petit verdot, cabernet franc, malbec, merlot, sauvignon blanc and multi-clone chardonnay. The dry-grown vines have modest yields, followed by kid-glove treatment in the winery. With Clive Otto (formerly of Vasse Felix) onboard, a 300t winery was built. The wines have had richly deserved success in wine shows and journalists' reviews. Exports to the UK, Sweden and Singapore.

ㅜㅜㅜㅜㅜ **Parterre Wilyabrup Margaret River Semillon Sauvignon Blanc 2017** This 50/50% blend strikes different notes than usual, tighter in some ways, looser in others. The two components spent 10 months in French oak and stainless steel, the oak obvious. It has more precision, drive and elegance, with juicy minerality. Screwcap. 12% alc. **Rating** 96 **To** 2025 $35 ✪

Parterre Wilyabrup Margaret River Chardonnay 2017 Hand-picked Gin Gin clone, wild-fermented in French oak (33% new), no mlf, matured for 9 months. This is a first class Margaret River chardonnay with a proven track record. White peach, grapefruit and a carefully managed French oak dressing form an immaculate wine. Screwcap. 13% alc. **Rating** 96 **To** 2028 $26 ✪

Margaret River Semillon Sauvignon Blanc 2017 The style and quality of this wine has been respected (and protected) for upwards of two decades. Partial barrel ferment is important in providing an extra degree of complexity and texture, but is also subtle, leaving the coast clear for the semillon to fly its lemon all-sorts flag, and the sauvignon blanc to float over the top with its tropical/green pea duo. Screwcap. 11.5% alc. **Rating** 95 **To** 2027 $24 ✪

Margaret River Cabernet Sauvignon 2016 Brilliant crimson glitters on the rim of the glass. Purity can't be slathered onto or into a wine, it has to be carefully built up like Chinese lacquer. It has to have the right nervosity, as the French say, and it has to have a soul, as we might say, and this more than meets both. Screwcap. 14% alc. **Rating** 95 **To** 2036 $33

Margaret River Cabernet Merlot 2016 55% cabernet sauvignon, 33% merlot, 5% petit verdot, 4% cabernet franc and 3% malbec, matured for 15 months in used French oak. A vibrantly fresh, light to medium-bodied blend, the blend itself mainstream Margaret River, but not often of this weight and shape; tannins and oak dialled down to keep in balance with the fruit. Screwcap. 14% alc. **Rating** 94 **To** 2026 $26 ✪

Misceo 2016 A blend of cabernet franc, malbec, petit verdot and merlot that until a few years ago, were only blended with cabernet sauvignon, but are now released on their own four feet. They really swell on the mid-palate, left to roam as they will, a win-win scenario. Screwcap. 14% alc. **Rating** 94 **To** 2036 $30

ㅜㅜㅜㅜㅗ **Margaret River Chardonnay 2017 Rating** 93 **To** 2025 $26 ✪

Freeman Vineyards   ★★★★★

101 Prunevale Road, Prunevale, NSW 2587 **Region** Hilltops
T (02) 6384 4299 **www**.freemanvineyards.com.au **Open** By appt
Winemaker Dr Brian Freeman **Est.** 2000 **Dozens** 5000 **Vyds** 173ha
Dr Brian Freeman spent much of his life in research and education, in the latter with a role as head of CSU's viticulture and oenology campus. The home block was established in 1999, and in 2004 he purchased the 30-year-old Demondrille vineyard, and has also established a vineyard next door. In all he has 22 varieties that range from staples such as shiraz, cabernet sauvignon, semillon and riesling, through to trendy varieties such as tempranillo, and onto the exotic with corvina, rondinella and harslevelu.

ㅜㅜㅜㅜㅜ **Rondo Rondinella Rose 2017** An enticing pastel-salmon pink; delicate aromas and flavours, a mix of watermelon, fresh herbs and redcurrants. It's tangy and spritely with a lick of sweetness to the finish, but mostly textural and very delicious. Screwcap. 13.5% alc. **Rating** 95 **To** 2019 $20 JF ✪

Dolcino 2017 70% viognier and 30% sauvignon blanc, heady with botrytis – a mix of saffron-infused apricots and pears, sweet lime and cumquat marmalade, honey and honeysuckle; the flavours plentiful and the palate silky and long. While certainly sweet, there's crisp acidity cutting right through, ensuring it remains fresh and lively. 500ml. Screwcap. 11% alc. **Rating** 95 **To** 2019 $25 JF **✪**

Corona Corvina Rondinella 2016 A 50/50% blend of two Italian reds, made in a Valpolicella style so it's juicy, fresh and lithe. This is a delightful, aromatic, barely medium-weighted wine laced with bright red fruits, menthol, florals, tangy raspberry-like acidity and savoury lighter-framed tannins. Screwcap. 13.5% alc. **Rating** 94 **To** 2022 $20 JF **✪**

Secco Rondinella Corvina 2013 Also a 50/50% split, picked late Apr into May with a portion dried for 10 days allowing the fruit to desiccate, concentrating the flavours. This was then added to the remaining fruit for fermentation, matured in seasoned French oak for 2 years, then aged in bottle for another 2 years. That's commitment to this Amarone-style. Complex and richly flavoured with layers of chocolate, spiced plum compote and morello and red cherries, yet savoury through and through. Screwcap. 15% alc. **Rating** 94 **To** 2022 $40 JF

🍷🍷🍷🍷🍷 **Altura Vineyard Sangiovese 2016** Rating 93 **To** 2022 $30 SC
Prosecco 2017 Rating 93 **To** 2018 $23 CM **✪**

Freycinet   ★★★★★

15919 Tasman Highway, via Bicheno, Tas 7215 **Region** East Coast Tasmania
T (03) 6257 8574 **www**.freycinetvineyard.com.au **Open** 7 days 10–5 (Oct–Apr),
10–4 (May–Sept)
Winemaker Claudio Radenti, Lindy Bull **Est.** 1979 **Dozens** 9000 **Vyds** 15.9ha
The Freycinet vineyards are situated on the sloping hillsides of a small valley. The soils are brown dermosol on top of Jurassic dolerite, and combined with aspect, slope and heat summation, produce red grapes with unusual depth of colour and ripe flavours. The winery is one of the foremost producers of pinot noir, with an enviable track record of consistency – rare in such a temperamental variety. The Radenti (sparkling), Riesling and Chardonnay are also wines of the highest quality. In 2012 Freycinet acquired part of the neighbouring Coombend property from Brown Brothers. This 42ha property extends to the Tasman Highway, and includes a 5.75ha mature vineyard and a 4.2ha olive grove. Exports to the UK and Singapore.

🍷🍷🍷🍷🍷 **Riesling 2017** Fills the senses with its perfume and floral blossom, which, however, doesn't prepare you for the purity and laser precision of the palate. The acidity is, of course, natural, but fits in discreetly behind the fruit, not seeking attention for its own sake, important though it is. Screwcap. 12.5% alc. **Rating** 96 **To** 2037 $30 **✪**

Chardonnay 2016 Barrel fermentation in French oak with some lees stirring is a conventional approach to chardonnay, and it's a case of not broken, don't fix. The fruit weight and depth is good, with creamy/nutty nuances behind the veil of white peach and pear. Its best days are still before it. Screwcap. 13% alc. **Rating** 94 **To** 2026 $42

Pinot Noir 2016 A wine that has always danced to the beat of its own drum, perhaps due in part to the relatively few vineyards on the east coast of Tasmania. Savoury tannins as fine as talcum powder provide a constant backdrop to the plum and cherry fruit. Lighter than the '15, but has compensating length. Screwcap. 13.5% alc. **Rating** 94 **To** 2023 $70

🍷🍷🍷🍷🍷 **Wineglass Bay Sauvignon Blanc 2017** Rating 93 **To** 2020 $27 **✪**
Louis Pinot Noir 2016 Rating 93 **To** 2025 $42 CM
Cabernet Merlot 2014 Rating 93 **To** 2030 $40 CM

Frog Choir Wines   ★★★★☆

PO Box 635, Margaret River, WA 6285 **Region** Margaret River
T 0427 777 787 **www**.frogchoir.com **Open** Not
Winemaker Naturaliste Vintners (Bruce Dukes) **Est.** 1997 **Dozens** 250 **Vyds** 1.2ha
Kate and Nigel Hunt have a micro-vineyard equally split between shiraz and cabernet sauvignon. It has top address credentials: adjacent to Leeuwin and Voyager estates, 6km from

the Margaret River township. The hand-tended vines are grown without the use of insecticides. The wines are only available at Redgate cellar door.

ŦŦŦŦŦ **Margaret River Cabernet Sauvignon Shiraz 2013** Each annual release is made in the same way, but the blend is entirely dependent on the vineyard yield of each variety. Here the cassis of the cabernet is the dominant player, not so much due to its percentage, but to its distinctive varietal expression. This is a lovely medium-bodied wine, its constituents in complete harmony. Screwcap. 13.8% alc. **Rating** 95 **To** 2028 $28 **✪**

Margaret River Shiraz Cabernet Sauvignon 2014 A super-elegant medium-bodied wine that is a relatively uncommon blend in Margaret River. The colour is bright, and the expressive, fragrant bouquet has red and black berry/cherry fruits, fine-grained tannins and gently cedary oak. Screwcap. 13.4% alc. **Rating** 94 **To** 2029 $28 **✪**

Margaret River Cabernet Sauvignon Shiraz 2008 Is still holding a youthful hue as it heads towards its 10th birthday. All its components are in harmony and symmetry, reflecting this remarkable little vineyard, so small it only sells direct from the cellar door. Red cherry and plum flavours are its G-spot. Screwcap. 14.5% alc. **Rating** 94 **To** 2023 $28 **✪**

ŦŦŦŦŦ **Margaret River Shiraz Cabernet Sauvignon 2011 Rating** 91 **To** 2019 $28

Frogmore Creek   ★★★★★

699 Richmond Road, Cambridge, Tas 7170 **Region** Southern Tasmania
T (03) 6248 4484 **www.frogmorecreek.com.au Open** 7 days 10–5
Winemaker Alain Rousseau, John Bown **Est.** 1997 **Dozens** 40 000 **Vyds** 55ha
Frogmore Creek is a joint venture between Tony Scherer of Tasmania and Jack Kidwiler of California. The business has grown very substantially, first establishing its own organically managed vineyard, and thereafter by a series of local acquisitions. First was the purchase of the Hood/Wellington Wines business; next the large Roslyn vineyard near Campania; and finally (in October 2010) Meadowbank Estate, where the cellar door is now located. In December '12 the original Frogmore Creek vineyard was sold to Hill-Smith Family Vineyards. Exports to the US, Japan, NZ and China.

ŦŦŦŦŦ **Riesling 2016** Has the focus, linearity and clarity of Tasmanian riesling that makes it such a great each-way proposition: now, tomorrow, or much later. The bouquet is scented and flowery, the palate with a wealth of citrus flavours flying on a magic carpet, the acidity fresh but far from painful. Lovely wine. Screwcap. 13% alc. **Rating** 95 **To** 2031 $29 **✪**

FGR Riesling 2016 This was the wine that started a style of riesling hitherto unknown – John Vickery had made it in the Clare and Eden valleys in the '60s and '70s, but the fruit base bore no resemblance to Tasmanian riesling. In the early '80s, winemaker Andrew Hood made the style his (and Tasmania's) own; gold medals eventually ensued and there was no turning back. FGR stands for 40g/l of residual sugar. Screwcap. 10% alc. **Rating** 95 **To** 2031 $29 **✪**

Pinot Noir 2016 Excellent colour as ever, ; a serious pinot noir, opening with a perfumed bouquet given an extra dimension with subtle French oak. The palate has striking length and persistence thanks to fine-grained tannins running from start to finish. Could well become spectacular over the next 5+ years – I'd be in no hurry to drink it. Screwcap. 14% alc. **Rating** 94 **To** 2029 $40

ŦŦŦŦŦ **Iced Riesling 2016 Rating** 93 **To** 2026 $29
42° S Sauvignon Blanc 2017 Rating 92 **To** 2019 $27
42° S Pinot Noir 2016 Rating 92 **To** 2024 $30

Gaelic Cemetery Wines   ★★★★★

PO Box 54, Sevenhill, SA 5453 **Region** Clare Valley
T (08) 8843 4370 **www.gaelic-cemeterywines.com Open** Not
Winemaker Neil Pike, Steve Baraglia **Est.** 2005 **Dozens** 1500 **Vyds** 6.5ha

Gaelic Cemetery is a joint venture between winemaker Neil Pike, viticulturist Andrew Pike and Adelaide retailers Mario and Ben Barletta. It hinges on a single vineyard owned by Grant Arnold, planted in 1996 adjacent to the historic cemetery of the region's Scottish pioneers. Situated in a secluded valley of the Clare hills, the low-cropping vineyard, say the partners, 'is always one of the earliest ripening shiraz vineyards in the region and mystifyingly produces fruit with both natural pH and acid analysis that can only be described as beautiful numbers'. The result is hands-off winemaking. Exports to the UK, the US, Canada, Germany, Singapore, Taiwan, Hong Kong and China.

♟♟♟♟♟ **Premium Cabernet Malbec 2014** Deep, complex, tannic and long. Cork (and storage) permitting, it will enjoy an extremely long and fruitful life. It tastes of earth, blackcurrant, cloves, milk chocolate and mint, perhaps even a slip of licorice. It jumps with flavour right upfront and holds the power throughout. A dry, ropey, sustained finish seals the deal. 13.5% alc. **Rating** 97 **To** 2040 $45 CM ✪

♟♟♟♟♟ **Premium Riesling 2017** A totally delicious riesling with succulent lime and lemon flavours floating on a raft of zesty acidity. It has coherent structure, texture and balance, and while its longer-term future is assured, patience isn't a prerequisite to cracking the screwcap. 11.5% alc. **Rating** 96 **To** 2037 $36 ✪
Celtic Farm Riesling 2017 The floral, fragrant bouquet is attractive, the palate more so. While made with an eye to early consumption, it has bracing unsweetened lemon-lime sherbet flavours coupled with Granny Smith apple skin. Screwcap. 11.5% alc. **Rating** 95 **To** 2029 $23 ✪

♟♟♟♟♟ **Premium Shiraz 2014** Rating 93 To 2030 $45 CM
Celtic Farm Shiraz Cabernet 2015 Rating 91 To 2025 $24 CM

Gala Estate   ★★★★☆

14891 Tasman Highway, Cranbrook, Tas 7190 **Region** East Coast Tasmania
T 0408 681 014 **www**.galaestate.com.au **Open** 7 days 10–4
Winemaker Glenn James, Pat Colombo **Est.** 2009 **Dozens** 5000 **Vyds** 11ha
This vineyard is situated on a 4000ha sheep station that is owned by Robert and Patricia (Amos) Greenhill, custodians of the land granted to Adam Amos in 1821; it is recognised as the second oldest family business in Tasmania. The 11ha vineyard is heavily skewed to pinot noir (7ha), the remainder planted (in descending order) to chardonnay, pinot gris, riesling, shiraz and sauvignon blanc. The main risk to grapegrowing here is spring frost, and overhead spray irrigation serves two purposes: it provides adequate moisture for early season growth, and frost protection at the end of the growing season.

♟♟♟♟♟ **Late Harvest Riesling 2017** Lime and lemon dance around the maypole, with sparklets of juicy sweet fruit bursting. Better put: don't think, just drink. Screwcap. 8.9% alc. **Rating** 94 **To** 2027 $65

♟♟♟♟♟ **Reserve Pinot Gris 2017** Rating 92 To 2019 $65
Pinot Gris 2017 Rating 91 To 2018 $30

Galafrey   ★★★★

Quangellup Road, Mount Barker, WA 6324 **Region** Mount Barker
T (08) 9851 2022 **www**.galafreywines.com.au **Open** 7 days 10–5
Winemaker Kim Tyrer **Est.** 1977 **Dozens** 3500 **Vyds** 13.1ha
The Galafrey story began when Ian and Linda Tyrer gave up high profile jobs in the emerging computer industry and arrived in Mount Barker to start growing grapes and making wine, the vine-change partially prompted by their desire to bring up their children-to-be in a country environment. They planted a dry-grown vineyard, and established a purpose-built winery in an ex-whaling building. The premature death of Ian at a time when the industry was buckling at the knees increased the already considerable stress on the family, but deal with it they did. Daughter Kim Tyrer is now winemaker and CEO of the business, with Linda still very much involved in the day-to-day management, and Galafrey now has over 40 years under its belt. Exports to China.

ㅇㅇㅇㅇㅇ **Dry Grown Reserve Riesling 2017** A floral riesling hinged to orange blossom, quince and a twist of lemon, grapefruit and lime. Slatey of texture, with a saliva-inducing pin-bone of sherbety acidity running from attack to punchy finish. A take-no-prisoners, acerbically dry style, which will be rewarded by ageing. Screwcap. 12% alc. **Rating** 92 **To** 2029 $25 NG ✪
Dry Grown Vineyard Cabernet Sauvignon 2015 Blackcurrant, cedar, tobacco and soy notes, all classic calling cards, are splayed across a medicinal undercarriage of root spice alluding to the vintage's ripening challenges. Nourishing and honest, nevertheless. Screwcap. 13.5% alc. **Rating** 90 **To** 2021 $30 NG

ㅇㅇㅇㅇ **Dry Grown Vineyard Mount Barker Shiraz 2015 Rating** 89 **To** 2022 $30 NG

Gallagher Wines ★★★★☆

2770 Dog Trap Road, Murrumbateman, NSW 2582 **Region** Canberra District
T (02) 6227 0555 **www**.gallagherwines.com.au **Open** W'ends & public hols 10–5
Winemaker Greg Gallagher **Est.** 1995 **Dozens** 2000 **Vyds** 2ha
Greg Gallagher was senior winemaker at Taltarni for 20 years, working with Dominique Portet. He began planning a change and, together with wife Libby, established a small vineyard at Murrumbateman in 1995, now with 1ha each of chardonnay and shiraz. Between '99 and 2004 Greg was winemaker at CSU, and now acts as both winemaker and consultant for a dozen or so wineries in and near the Canberra District.

ㅇㅇㅇㅇㅇ **Riesling 2017** Complex and demanding, it straddles a tightly coiled acid line, ensuring it will age well, while the texture, succulence and depth on the palate allow for more immediate drinking pleasure. Heady orange blossom, lemon verbena and bath salts, leading to a flinty, steely palate and a long, lingering finish. Its pedigree was assured with a four-trophy haul at the Canberra International Riesling Challenge '17. Screwcap. 11.4% alc. **Rating** 96 **To** 2030 $35 JF ✪

ㅇㅇㅇㅇㅇ **Shiraz 2016 Rating** 92 **To** 2024 $35 JF
Blanc de Blanc 2012 Rating 91 $55 JF

Galli Estate ★★★★★

1507 Melton Highway, Plumpton, Vic 3335 **Region** Sunbury
T (03) 9747 1444 **www**.galliestate.com.au **Open** 7 days 11–5
Winemaker Ben Ranken **Est.** 1997 **Dozens** 10 000 **Vyds** 160ha
Galli Estate has two vineyards: Heathcote, which produces the red wines (shiraz, sangiovese, nebbiolo, tempranillo, grenache and montepulciano), and the cooler climate vineyard at Plumpton, producing the whites (chardonnay, pinot grigio, sauvignon blanc and fiano). All wines are biodynamically grown and made on the estate. Exports to Canada, Singapore, China and Hong Kong.

ㅇㅇㅇㅇㅇ **Heathcote Lorenzo 2016** Wild-fermented with 75% whole bunches, 25+ days on skins, matured for 18 months in oak (40% new). Reading the background material before tasting the Galli '16 shirazs made me wonder whether I would enjoy this. Well, I shouldn't have worried – yes, it's full-bodied, but balanced, thus able to drink well 5, 10 or 20+ years down the track. Black, spicy, earthy flavours coat the walls of the mouth. Screwcap. 14.5% alc. **Rating** 95 **To** 2046 $60
Adele Nebbiolo 2015 Whole berries wild-fermented, 70+ days on skins, matured for 18 months in used French oak. The extreme skin time has done its job well. The colour is bright and clear, the flavour is of fresh and sour dark cherries and – best of all – the tannins are resolved. All up a major success. Screwcap. 14.5% alc. **Rating** 95 **To** 2045 $38
Adele Syrah 2016 Wild yeast–open fermented with 25% whole bunches, 50% kept on skins for 330 days in puncheons (25% new). Full biodynamic handling in the winery were used to make this luscious, rich and full-bodied syrah. It's entirely fruit-driven at this stage, but reasonable to expect that texture and structure will emerge with time. Screwcap. 13.5% alc. **Rating** 94 **To** 2041 $38

Camelback Heathcote Montepulciano 2016 This wine has attitude, lots and lots of it. The colour and bouquet are on song, but it's the palate that beats the drum. There's a firm grip of purple and black fruits that comes as much from the fruit as the tannins. Another bargain for alternative wine lovers. Screwcap. 13.8% alc. **Rating** 94 **To** 2031 $20 ✪

🍷🍷🍷🍷🍷 **Camelback Sangiovese Cabernet Merlot 2017 Rating** 93 **To** 2032 $20 ✪
Adele Tempranillo 2016 Rating 93 **To** 2026 $38
Adele Chardonnay 2016 Rating 92 **To** 2023 $38
Camelback Cabernet Merlot 2016 Rating 92 **To** 2026 $20 ✪
Tempranillo Grenache Mourvedre 2016 Rating 92 **To** 2031 $20 ✪
Camelback Shiraz 2016 Rating 91 **To** 2036 $20 ✪
Camelback Sangiovese 2016 Rating 91 **To** 2024 $20 ✪
Camelback Nebbiolo Rose 2017 Rating 90 **To** 2019 $20 ✪

Gallows Wine Co

Lennox Road, Carbunup River, WA 6280 **Region** Margaret River
T (08) 9755 1060 **www**.gallows.com.au **Open** 7 days 10–5
Winemaker Charlie Maiolo, Neil Doddridge **Est.** 2008 **Dozens** 11 000 **Vyds** 27ha
This is the venture of the Maiolo family, headed by winemaker Charlie. The macabre name is that of one of the most famous surf breaks on the Margaret River coast. The vineyard is planted to semillon, sauvignon blanc, chardonnay, pinot noir, shiraz, merlot and cabernet sauvignon. The site climate is strongly influenced by Geographe Bay, 5km to the north, and facilitates the production of wines with a large spectrum of flavours and characteristics.

🍷🍷🍷🍷🍷 **The Bommy Chardonnay 2016** A child of the sand, wind and ever-present surf – it's a rich cocktail played out in one form or another in Margaret River chardonnay. This is a confident, full-bodied version, aware of its allure for many (not all) who taste it. Screwcap. 13.5% alc. **Rating** 94 **To** 2026 $28 ✪
The Bommy Cabernet Sauvignon 2015 As ever, there's a lot of cabernet in the glass when you taste this. It's layered, rich and overflowing with cassis. Drink now or much later. Screwcap. 13.5% alc. **Rating** 94 **To** 2030 $31

Gapsted Wines

3897 Great Alpine Road, Gapsted, Vic 3737 **Region** Alpine Valleys
T (03) 5751 9100 **www**.gapstedwines.com.au **Open** 7 days 10–5
Winemaker Michael Cope-Williams, Toni Pla Bou, Matt Fawcett **Est.** 1997
Dozens 200 000 **Vyds** 256.1ha
Gapsted is the major brand of the Victorian Alps Winery, which started (and continues) as a large-scale contract winemaking facility. However, the quality of the wines made for its own brand has led to the expansion of production not only under this label, but also under a raft of cheaper, subsidiary labels. As well as the substantial estate plantings, Gapsted sources traditional and alternative grape varieties from the King and Alpine valleys. Exports to the UK, Canada, Sweden, Norway, the United Arab Emirates, India, Thailand, Hong Kong, Singapore, China and Japan.

🍷🍷🍷🍷🍷 **Ballerina Canopy Cabernet Sauvignon 2016** 86% cabernet with input from shiraz, dolcetto, merlot and durif. It has both density and freshness covered, its flavours of boysenberry, plum, milk chocolate and toasted spices combining to produce a substantial and smooth-textured red. It doesn't have enough sizzle through the finish for higher points, but boy does it have some stuffing. Screwcap. 14.5% alc. **Rating** 93 **To** 2029 $31 CM
Limited Release Heathcote Sangiovese 2017 Fresh anise, mint and jubey berry flavours present an immaculate case, tobacco-like aspects only aiding the cause. Impeccable. Screwcap. 14.5% alc. **Rating** 93 **To** 2023 $31 CM
Ballerina Canopy Alpine Valleys Durif 2016 Such a firm, steady hand. The oak is sawdusty and raw, and mars things a touch, but the firmness of the tannin, the glide of red-berried fruit, the touches of licorice; this wine's stuffing is

significant. Give it time and it will all come together. It has a long journey ahead. Screwcap. 14.5% alc. **Rating** 93 To 2032 $31 CM

Ballerina Canopy King Valley Chardonnay 2016 It mounts a persuasive case. Fig, ripe stone fruit, toasty oak and cashew flavours rumble powerfully through the palate and kick impressively on the finish. Reductive notes add rather than subtract. Arguably the best chardonnay release we've seen under this label. Screwcap. 13.5% alc. **Rating** 92 To 2022 $25 CM ✪

Ballerina Canopy Heathcote Shiraz 2016 The positive impression continues. As with many of the most recent releases from this workhorse winery, fruit freshness is to the fore, as indeed is flavour generosity. It tastes of plum, vanilla cream, gum nut and sweet red cherries. It's not half bad. Screwcap. 14.5% alc. **Rating** 92 To 2026 $31 CM

Ballerina Canopy Alpine Valleys Durif 2015 100% American oak. Intense colour and flavour; take a sip and you slide into its inky depths. It's like prunes and blackberries soaked in dark, liquid chocolate. Tannin has a commanding presence but not an overbearing one. Not a wine you'd want to argue with. Screwcap. 14.5% alc. **Rating** 92 To 2028 $31 CM

Tobacco Road Sangiovese Rose 2017 90/10% sangiovese/shiraz from the King Valley and Rutherglen. Vibrant cherry and spice aromatics before a juicy, engaging palate. Fruity, savoury and dry at once. Not a hair out of place. High value. Screwcap. 12.5% alc. **Rating** 91 To 2019 $16 CM ✪

High Country King Valley Shiraz 2016 Medium weight in a good way. Sweet, ripe, plum-like flavours pour deliciously through the mouth, offering pleasure at every turn. The simple things in life. This is fresh, clean and exceptionally easy to like. Screwcap. 14% alc. **Rating** 90 To 2023 $18 CM ✪

High Country Tempranillo 2017 King Valley. Purple colour and purple fruits. Gapsted wines seem to have picked things up a gear lately. This is fresh, jubey and moreish. It should definitely be on your shopping list. Screwcap. 13.5% alc. **Rating** 90 To 2021 $18 CM ✪

Limited Release Alpine Valleys Saperavi 2016 Wild. Truffles, heightened blackcurrant, herbs, spices, licorice, chocolate and blood orange. What doesn't it taste of? It has size but it's not an overly big wine, with the tannin kept lowish the key. Screwcap. 14% alc. **Rating** 90 To 2025 $31 CM

♟♟♟♟ Valley Selection Riesling 2017 **Rating** 89 To 2025 $18 CM ✪
Limited Release Sparkling Shiraz Rose 2017 **Rating** 89 $25 CM

Garagiste   ★★★★★

4 Lawrey Street, Frankston, Vic 3199 (postal) **Region** Mornington Peninsula
T 0439 370 530 **www.garagiste.com.au Open** Not
Winemaker Barnaby Flanders **Est.** 2006 **Dozens** 2200 **Vyds** 3ha

Barnaby Flanders was a co-founder of Allies Wines (see separate entry) in 2003, with some of their wines made under the Garagiste label. Garagiste and Barnaby have now gone their own way, and their focus is on the Mornington Peninsula. The grapes are hand-sorted in the vineyard and again in the winery. Chardonnay is whole-bunch pressed, and barrel-fermented with wild yeast in new and used French oak, with mlf variably used, and 8–9 months on lees. The wines are seldom fined or filtered. Exports to the UK, Singapore, Japan, Hong Kong and China.

♟♟♟♟♟ Tuerong Chardonnay 2015 Made identically to the Merricks wine, so another example of site (this being a slightly warmer one but you wouldn't know it). A thoroughbred. Racy acidity shoots through the palate of stone fruit, grapefruit and dried figs, savouriness galore with the restrained leesy/creamy characters doing their bit to tame the acidity. The finish line is a long way off. Screwcap. 13% alc. **Rating** 97 To 2025 $45 JF ✪

♟♟♟♟♟ Peninsula Chardonnay 2016 A cutting, quartz-like expression of chardonnay with mineral, flint and spice notes daring grapefruit and stone-fruit flavours to step out of line. Intensity, style, X-factor and length are all covered to brilliant effect. Screwcap. 13% alc. **Rating** 96 To 2024 $45 CM ✪

Tuerong Chardonnay 2016 Chardonnay in a happy place. Trim and taut but with flavour dripping from its every pore. Grapefruit and stone fruit, fig and spicy/toasty oak. It feels pure, complex, juicy, and it lingers appreciably. Quite terrific. Screwcap. 13% alc. **Rating** 95 **To** 2023 $45 CM

Balnarring Pinot Noir 2016 The whipcrack of quality. This has both depth and breadth though it never sways from its varietal home ground. Musk, cherry–plum, deli meats and cloves. There's velvet to the texture but a throatiness to the tannin; it both purrs and growls along the palate. Screwcap. 13% alc. **Rating** 95 **To** 2024 $45 CM

Merricks Pinot Noir 2016 The fruit is savoury and herbal, but musky oak helps build presence and the wine's dark cherry fruit maintains a solid hum. It's a moody wine, complex, with a sternness to its tannin and a chicory-like note to its aftertaste. It's on the way to a good place, just taking the back roads to get there. Screwcap. 13.5% alc. **Rating** 94 **To** 2026 $45 CM

🍇 Garden & Field   ★★★★☆

PO Box 52, Angaston, SA 5353 **Region** Eden Valley
T (08) 8564 2435 **www**.tasteedenvalley.com.au **Open** At Taste Eden Valley
Winemaker Jo Irvine, Peter Raymond **Est.** 2009 **Dozens** 450 **Vyds** 3.6ha
One of those stories that seems to be too good to be true. It is over 100 years since the Schilling family cleared the land of its granite boulders, built cottages from the rocks and planted a vineyard. In the late 1970s the stone-walled, south-facing block was sold, and when the Vine Pull Scheme was legislated, the new owners were quick to remove the vines. Another decade passed and the property was again on the market. Eventually viticulturist Peter Raymond and wife Melissa purchased it, and set about preparing 3.6ha for planting. As they arrived one Saturday morning to begin the long task, they found a group of octogenarian men armed with picks and shovels, there to help plant 3500 vines on what they regarded as holy viticultural land. Penfolds now buys most of the grapes for its RWT Shiraz at tip-top prices, but the Raymonds keep enough to make a small amount of wine each year.

🍷🍷🍷🍷🍷 **Gnadenberg Road Eden Valley Shiraz 2015** Packaged in a heavyweight dark bottle, the cork of good quality. Skates narrowly around its alcohol, but the intensity and depth of this black cherry, licorice and pepper shiraz, married with new French oak, carry the palate forward. The tannins are balanced, and the future is guaranteed. 14.9% alc. **Rating** 95 **To** 2040 $95

🍷🍷🍷🍷🍷 **Eden Valley Vermentino 2015 Rating** 90 **To** 2025 $20 ❂

Garners Heritage Wines   ★★★★

54 Longwood/Mansfield Road, Longwood East, Vic 3666 **Region** Strathbogie Ranges
T (03) 5798 5513 **www**.garnerswine.com.au **Open** W'ends 11–4
Winemaker Lindsay Brown **Est.** 2005 **Dozens** 700 **Vyds** 1.8ha
Leon and Rosie Garner established Garners Heritage Wines in 2005, celebrating their 10th anniversary in '15 (Leon passed away in August '16). The 1.8ha boutique vineyard may be small, and the newest in the Strathbogie Ranges, but it has produced high class shirazs. Although the region is classified as cool climate, the property is at the base of the mountain range where the warm summers are ideal for growing this variety. A very small amount is exported to Hong Kong.

🍷🍷🍷🍷🍷 **Leon's Strathbogie Ranges Shiraz 2016** The last vintage before Leon Garner's death. It is full-bodied, the style he preferred, with black fruits, oak and masculine tannins all refusing to take a backwards step. Sufficiently well balanced to justify long-term cellaring. Screwcap. 15.3% alc. **Rating** 93 **To** 2046
Strathbogie Ranges Bella Rose 2017 'Picked at 12° baume and made like a white wine', says a handwritten note on the bottle. Bright crimson, with maximum flavour of ripe cherries and some gas spritz – not visible in the glass but in the mouth. A very interesting, indeed downright challenging, shiraz rose. Screwcap. 12.5% alc. **Rating** 90 **To** 2020 $20

Gartelmann Wines

701 Lovedale Road, Lovedale, NSW 2321 **Region** Hunter Valley
T (02) 4930 7113 **www**.gartelmann.com.au **Open** Mon–Sat 10–5, Sun 10–4
Winemaker Jorg Gartelmann, Liz Silkman **Est.** 1996 **Dozens** 7600
In 1996 Jan and Jorg Gartelmann purchased what was previously the George Hunter Estate –
16ha of mature vineyards, most established by Oliver Shaul in '70. In a change of emphasis, the
vineyard was sold, and Gartelmann now sources its grapes from the Hunter Valley and other
NSW regions, including the cool Rylstone area in Mudgee. Exports to the US, Singapore
and China.

ɡɡɡɡɡ **Diedrich Orange Shiraz 2016** Don't let the alcohol reading turn you off.
This presents a pretty face to the world, is rich with red-berried fruit, uses oak to
seductive effect, and sings cleanly – and beautifully – through the finish, taking its
alcohol in its stride. It's not a particularly 'dark' wine in its fruit or colour, but it's
definitely a head turner. Screwcap. 15.2% alc. **Rating** 95 **To** 2034 $50 CM
Jesse Mudgee Shiraz 2015 Ripe and plush with generosity as its keystone.
Chocolate, plum, blueberry jam and cedar-wood characters result in a mouthfilling
red with plenty of strut. It pushes hard at both ripeness and sweetness but sure
makes it work. Screwcap. 14.9% alc. **Rating** 94 **To** 2030 $30 CM ⦿

ɡɡɡɡɡ **Benjamin Hunter Valley Semillon 2017** Rating 93 To 2025 $27 CM ⦿
Sarah Elizabeth Chardonnay 2017 Rating 93 To 2023 $30 CM
Lisa Chardonnay 2017 Rating 91 To 2024 $45 CM
Stephanie Orange Pinot Gris 2017 Rating 91 To 2018 $25 CM
Phillip Alexander Mudgee Cabernet Merlot 2016 Rating 91 To 2024
$27 CM
Jonathan Mudgee Cabernet Sauvignon 2016 Rating 91 To 2025 $35 CM
Georg Mudgee Petit Verdot 2016 Rating 91 To 2024 $35 CM

Gembrook Hill

Launching Place Road, Gembrook, Vic 3783 **Region** Yarra Valley
T (03) 5968 1622 **www**.gembrookhill.com.au **Open** By appt
Winemaker Andrew Marks **Est.** 1983 **Dozens** 1500 **Vyds** 5ha
Ian and June Marks established Gembrook Hill, one of the oldest vineyards in the coolest
part of the Upper Yarra Valley. The northeast-facing vineyard is in a natural amphitheatre,
and the low-yielding sauvignon blanc, chardonnay and pinot noir vines are not irrigated.
The minimal approach to winemaking produces wines of a consistent style with finesse and
elegance. The unexpected death of Ian in March 2017, and the decision of winemaker Timo
Mayer to concentrate on his own label, left son Andrew Marks in charge of winemaking (for
Gembrook Hill and for his own label, The Wanderer). Exports to the UK, the US, Denmark,
Japan and Malaysia.

ɡɡɡɡɡ **Yarra Valley Sauvignon Blanc 2017** Half of this wine is fermented in seasoned
French oak, the other in stainless steel, with both parcels on lees for 9 months. The
end result is a vibrant, fresh wine with complexity and as always, a whole lot of
restraint. Expect some lemon zest, bees wax and a smidge of pine needles. While
the palate is still tight, there are ripples of texture just below the surface. Delicious.
Screwcap. 12% alc. **Rating** 95 **To** 2024 $34 JF ⦿
Yarra Valley Chardonnay 2017 Everything slips into place with this restful
chardonnay. Stone fruit and citrus, creamy lees and an appealing savoury/umami
flavour of homemade chicken stock. Slippery and textural on the palate as it
glides to a most convincing conclusion. Terrific length and line. Diam. 13.3% alc.
Rating 95 **To** 2027 $40 JF
Yarra Valley Pinot Noir 2016 From its cherry-accented fruits, dusting of spices
and wood smoke to its savoury tannins, everything just snugly falls into place
in usual Gembrook Hill fashion: understated but detailed, complex yet subtle.
Medium-bodied with fresh acidity on the finish; a delight to drink now but will
continue to unfurl. Diam. 13.5% alc. **Rating** 95 **To** 2028 $50 JF

ŶŶŶŶȲ Village Yarra Valley Pinot Noir 2017 Rating 92 To 2023 $30 JF
Village Yarra Valley Pinot Noir 2017 Rating 91 To 2023 $28 CM

Gemtree Wines ★★★★★

167 Elliot Road, McLaren Flat, SA 5171 **Region** McLaren Vale
T (08) 8323 8199 **www.**gemtreewines.com **Open** 7 days 10–5
Winemaker Mike Brown, Joshua Waechter **Est.** 1998 **Dozens** 90 000 **Vyds** 123ha
Gemtree is a family-owned winery dedicated to growing better wine – naturally. Paul and Jill
Buttery established the Gemtree vineyards in McLaren Vale in 1980. Now their son Andrew
runs the business, their daughter Melissa Brown is the viticulturist and her husband Mike
is the chief winemaker. The vineyards are certified organic and farmed biodynamically, and
the wine portfolio is of high quality. Exports to the UK, the US, Canada, Sweden, Denmark,
Norway, Finland, Hong Kong, China and NZ.

ŶŶŶŶŶ **Ernest Allan Shiraz 2015** Deep, full crimson-purple; a sumptuously rich wine
that encapsulates everything that is best about McLaren Vale: a velvety mouthfeel; a
fusion of blackberry, black cherry and dark chocolate; and – best of all – princely
tannins that frame the fruit with a little bit of help from the oak. Screwcap.
14.5% alc. **Rating** 97 To 2035 $50 ✪
Obsidian Shiraz 2015 Everything about Ernest Allan is dialled up several
notches here. However, it needs more time; its tannins, in particular, need a few
more years to settle down. This points towards swapping the closures, because
this wine needs the security afforded by screwcaps more than Ernest Allan. Cork.
14% alc. **Rating** 97 To 2045 $80 ✪

ŶŶŶŶŶ **Subterra Shiraz 2016** One barrel of shiraz was coated in a thin layer of beeswax
and buried underground (hence the name), 2m deep, in the vineyard in which
the grapes were grown. It was kept there for 6 months, over the course of a wet
winter no less, then dug up, decanted off its lees straight into bottle, and hand-
sealed (with cork). It's a fascinating wine. It smells of hay, tastes of black berries
and earth, comes finished with a wall of lees-infused tannin, and carries meaty,
new leather characters throughout. It tastes different, fresh, free-range, mushroomy,
all manner of things, all at the same time. It's an experience. 13.8% alc. **Rating** 95
To 2035 $180 CM
Uncut Shiraz 2016 Deeply coloured crimson; a medium-bodied shiraz that sings
of its variety, place and vintage; the mouthfeel supple yet textured, the flavours
of black cherry/berry fruits, the finish long. Great value. Drink at your leisure.
Screwcap. 14.5% alc. **Rating** 94 To 2029 $25 ✪

ŶŶŶŶȲ **Luna de Fresa Tempranillo Rose 2017** Rating 93 To 2019 $20 ✪
The Phantom Red 2016 Rating 92 To 2030 $45

Geoff Merrill Wines ★★★★★

291 Pimpala Road, Woodcroft, SA 5162 **Region** McLaren Vale
T (08) 8381 6877 **www.**geoffmerrillwines.com.au **Open** Mon–Fri 10–4.30, Sat 12–4.30
Winemaker Geoff Merrill, Scott Heidrich **Est.** 1980 **Dozens** 55 000 **Vyds** 45ha
If Geoff Merrill ever loses his impish sense of humour or his zest for life, high and not-so-
high, we shall all be the poorer. The product range consists of three tiers: premium (varietal);
Reserve, being the older wines, reflecting the desire for elegance and subtlety in this otherwise
exuberant winemaker; and, at the top, Henley Shiraz. Exports to all major markets.

ŶŶŶŶŶ **Reserve McLaren Vale Shiraz 2010** The colour is remarkable for a high
quality 7yo McLaren Vale shiraz. The bouquet is nigh-on perfect, still fragrant, and
the wine has spicy/savoury blackcurrant fruit leading the pack on its medium-
bodied palate. 18 months in used French oak got it off to a flying start. Screwcap.
14.5% alc. **Rating** 96 To 2030 $60 ✪
Henley McLaren Vale Shiraz 2009 This is the zenith of the range, as reflected
by the price. A bit of a sledgehammer with its sheen of molten dark fruits,

pummelling degree of extract and heady oak veneer. The wine embodies a rich regional style that is poised between expressions of yore and the fresher styles of today. Its parts are, nevertheless, in harmony. It will age well. Cork. 14.5% alc. **Rating** 95 **To** 2031 $185 NG

Cilento McLaren Vale Sangiovese 2012 Frisky, edgy, precise grape-skin pucker – all are sangiovese. Bitter coffee American oak tannins, too. Thanks to their guidance, flavours of ripe cherry, tomato bush, anise and sassafras are chaperoned across a voluptuous palate and splayed into a long, bracing finish. Screwcap. 14.5% alc. **Rating** 95 **To** 2022 $28 NG ✪

Jacko's McLaren Vale Shiraz 2013 Reductive handling has worked well for this wine, which, despite 27 months of ageing in oak (20% American), maintains its freshness. Boysenberry, violet, star anise and a whiff of iodine bounce across the long finish line, with some vanilla tones as a mere echo. Screwcap. 14.5% alc. **Rating** 94 **To** 2025 $31 NG

Reserve Coonawarra McLaren Vale Cabernet Sauvignon 2010 One year after vintage every barrel is assessed for inclusion in the Reserve program, and after a further 20 months a final selection is made. This wine is still very much alive and kicking, with a cutting edge to the wealth of fruit 7 years on from its first release. Screwcap. 14.5% alc. **Rating** 94 **To** 2025 $48

🍷🍷🍷🍷♀ **Reserve McLaren Vale Shiraz 2012 Rating** 93 **To** 2028 $65 NG
Bush Vine Shiraz Grenache Mourvedre 2012 Rating 93 **To** 2025 $25 ✪
Reserve Cabernet Sauvignon 2012 Rating 92 **To** 2027 $51 NG
Fleurieu Cabernet Shiraz 2012 Rating 91 **To** 2022 $24 NG
Bush Vine McLaren Vale Grenache Rose 2017 Rating 90 **To** 2018 $20 ✪

Geoff Weaver   ★★★★★

2 Gilpin Lane, Mitcham, SA 5062 (postal) **Region** Adelaide Hills
T (08) 8272 2105 **www**.geoffweaver.com.au **Open** Not
Winemaker Geoff Weaver **Est.** 1982 **Dozens** 3000 **Vyds** 12.3ha
This is the business of one-time Hardys chief winemaker Geoff Weaver. The Lenswood vineyard was established between 1982 and '88, and invariably produces immaculate riesling and sauvignon blanc, and long-lived chardonnays. The beauty of the labels ranks supreme. Exports to the UK, Hong Kong and Singapore.

🍷🍷🍷🍷🍷 **Ferus Lenswood Sauvignon Blanc 2015** Estate-grown, wild-fermented in French barriques followed by 12 months' maturation, neither fined nor acidified. A fascinating comparison with Flowstone's barrel-fermented Sauvignon Blanc. Here the exercise is tighter and more restrained, the accent more on fruit purity than texture and structure. The fruits have as much citrus flavour as tropical, the finish bright and fresh. Screwcap. 13.5% alc. **Rating** 96 **To** 2022 $45 ✪

Single Vineyard Adelaide Hills Sauvignon Blanc 2017 The bouquet is precise and strongly varietal, but it's not until the palate that the wine sets sail, and does so in fine style with citrus and apple taking control on the long finish. It's the outcome of Geoff Weaver's long experience with the vineyard, and his undoubted skill as a winemaker. Screwcap. 12.5% alc. **Rating** 95 **To** 2021 $25 ✪

Lenswood Chardonnay 2015 A smoky/toasty edge to the white peach of the bouquet gives scant warning of the drive of the palate. Here grapefruit juice and zest take hold with a grip in the 'stop, stop I love it' genre. Impressive wine. Screwcap. 13.5% alc. **Rating** 95 **To** 2025 $45

Single Vineyard Adelaide Hills Pinot Noir 2016 Cherry-accented fruit on the bouquet and palate give a freshness that is a delight, and additional stalks haven't made the wine too stemmy, the oak likewise balanced. Screwcap. 14% alc. **Rating** 95 **To** 2029 $45

🍷🍷🍷🍷♀ **Single Vineyard Sauvignon Blanc 2016 Rating** 92 **To** 2019 $25 ✪

George Wyndham

167 Fullarton Road, Dulwich, SA 5065 **Region** South Eastern Australia
T (08) 8131 2400 **www**.georgewyndham.com **Open** Not
Winemaker Steve Meyer **Est.** 1828 **Dozens** 800 000 **Vyds** 75ha
Named in honour of George Wyndham, who planted Australia's first commercial shiraz
vineyard in 1830 at Dalwood in the Hunter Valley. Originally Dalwood Wines until 1970,
then Wyndham Estate (1970–2015), the wines were renamed George Wyndham in '15. The
Bin range, led by Bin 555 Shiraz, often represents good value for money, as do the 'George'
wines (I am George, George the Fixer). At the top is Black Cluster (shiraz) from the Hunter
Valley. The wines are made and bottled in the Barossa Valley.

 I Am George Langhorne Creek Shiraz 2016 A cuddly shiraz in the best of
ways. Rich berried fruit, smooth vanillan oak, a general toastiness and a warm-
but-satisfying finish. Right in the groove. Full-bodied red at its most accessible.
Screwcap. 14.8% alc. **Rating** 92 **To** 2026 $20 CM ❂
George The Fixer Margaret River Cabernet Sauvignon 2016 This is
Margaret River cabernet sauvignon in fine form, its curranty heart both shot
with plum and lifted by mint/peppercorn notes, its texture supple, its finish
satisfying. Black olive notes add to the show, as indeed does alcohol warmth.
Straight through the goals, no problems. Screwcap. 14.4% alc. **Rating** 92 **To** 2030
$25 CM ❂
George The Fixer Barossa McLaren Vale Shiraz 2016 The labels for 'I am
George' are psychedelic, utterly non-corporate big company stuff. This wine is
well made in full-bodied style, and all the components are in balance, with no sign
of over-extraction. Screwcap. 14.7% alc. **Rating** 91 **To** 2031 $25
I Am George Limestone Coast Cabernet Merlot 2015 Round-shouldered
red, but with a powerful mid-palate boasting ample blackcurrant, bay leaf and
ozone-like flavours. Fresh and hearty at once, the finish being its least impressive
feature. Extra time in the bottle won't hurt. Screwcap. 14.7% alc. **Rating** 90
To 2028 $20 CM ❂

Georges Wines ★★★☆

32 Halifax Street, Adelaide, SA 5000 (postal) **Region** Clare Valley
T (08) 8410 9111 **www**.georges-exile.com **Open** Not
Winemaker O'Leary Walker **Est.** 2004 **Dozens** 3500 **Vyds** 36ha
This venture began with Nick George's acquisition of the Springwood vineyard in the
Armagh Valley district of the Clare Valley. The 10ha vineyard was planted between 1996 and
2000, namely to shiraz. Nick understood its proud history, supplying Leasingham with all of its
grapes for a number of years. He appointed O'Leary Walker as contract winemaker, an astute
move. In '17 Georges Wines acquired Olssen's 26ha vineyard at Auburn, lifting it vineyards
to 36ha and allowing an expansion in the production of new and existing wines.

 Exile Clare Valley Shiraz 2014 Dark red-black; intensely flavoured with
blackberry essence, very ripe plum compote, licorice, cinnamon, eucalyptus and
lots of oak spice and wood notes. Full-bodied and voluptuous with expansive
tannins. Screwcap. 14.5% alc. **Rating** 90 **To** 2024 $20 JF ❂

Gestalt Wines ★★★★

PO Box 273, Uraidla, SA 5142 **Region** Adelaide Hills
T 0448 969 412 **www**.gestaltwines.com **Open** Not
Winemaker Anthony Pearce, Craig Turnbull **Est.** 2012 **Dozens** 1000
Gestalt Wines was founded in 2012 by Anthony Pearce, a graduate of the Adelaide University
viticulture and oenology program. He transferred from theory to reality, working with
Spinifex in the Barossa Valley and Deviation Road in the Adelaide Hills, focusing on pinot
noir, chardonnay and grenache. The two wineries in question were very well chosen, with
highly intelligent winemakers in charge. Anthony has been joined by Craig Turnbull as
co-owner. Craig moved from the Hunter Valley to Adelaide in '08, and four years later

graduated from the same university oenology program, receiving the SA Wine Industry Association Silver Medal. He gained practical experience in McLaren Vale working for Kangarilla Road and Gemtree before coming to Gestalt to help broaden the wine portfolio of the business. Anthony and Craig's different experiences mesh well. It is an example of the meaning of 'gestalt': an organised whole that is considered to be greater than the sum of its parts. Music, art, wine – they all are enhanced by the beauty of the composition. Exports to the US.

ΨΨΨΨΨ **Espalier Chardonnay 2015** A very interesting wine. Given its intensity, varietal expression, complexity and length, I would never have guessed that it was (particularly) early picked, 60% taken through mlf, and matured in very well used French barrels. I might have guessed 10 months' maturation, simply using poker odds. This tastes of perfectly ripened chardonnay, not a wannabe sauvignon blanc, and it has skipped along for 3 years without batting an eyelid. Screwcap. 12.5% alc. **Rating** 94 **To** 2023 $40

The Fugue Savagnin Traminer Petit Manseng 2016 A 55/35/10% blend, destemmed, crushed and wild-fermented separately, the savagnin and 90% of the traminer cool-fermented in tank, 10% of the traminer and the petit manseng fermented in old French hogsheads, matured for 8 months. A walk on the wild side from start to finish. It is fiercely intense, but technically without fault; indeed, the contortions of the very complex and micro-focused vinification have been played to perfection. Screwcap. 12.7% alc. **Rating** 94 **To** 2022 $25 **O**

ΨΨΨΨΨ **Rule of Thirds Barossa Valley GSM 2015** Rating 91 To 2025 $25
Blacklight Barossa Mataro Grenache 2016 Rating 90 To 2021 $30

Ghost Rock Vineyard ★★★★★

1055 Port Sorrell Road, Northdown, Tas 7307 **Region** Northern Tasmania
T (03) 6428 4005 **www**.ghostrock.com.au **Open** 7 days 11–5
Winemaker Justin Arnold **Est.** 2001 **Dozens** 14 000 **Vyds** 30ha
Cate and Colin Arnold purchased the former Patrick Creek vineyard (planted exclusively to pinot noir in 1989) in 2001. The vineyards, situated among the patchwork fields of Sassafras to the south and the white sands of the Port Sorell Peninsula to the north, now total 30ha: pinot noir (14 clones) remains the bedrock of the plantings, with other varieties including chardonnay, pinot gris, riesling and sauvignon blanc. Ownership has passed to son Justin, and wife Alicia (who runs the cooking school and cellar door). Justin's experience in the Yarra Valley (Coldstream Hills), Margaret River (Devil's Lair) and Napa Valley (Etude) has paid dividends – the business is going from strength to strength, and the capacity of the relatively new 100t winery may need to be expanded. Exports to Japan.

ΨΨΨΨΨ **The Pinots 2017** Rose made with pinot gris and pinot meunier, matured in both tank and neutral oak. There's a cuddliness to the texture, complexity aplenty, and a bit of sizzle to the finish. It's smoky, spicy, has an undercurrent of undergrowth, and splashes red cherry and cranberry flavours here and there. Both interesting and beautiful. Screwcap. 13% alc. **Rating** 95 **To** 2021 $30 CM **O**

Two Blocks Pinot Noir 2016 Light in profile, spicy in persona, smoky through the finish, sinewy too. The priorities here are (a) complexity and (b) length, and it's stellar at both. There isn't a lot of fruit flesh but there's just enough, with ample other intrigues. A wine for true pinot fetishists. Screwcap. 14% alc. **Rating** 95 **To** 2026 $38 CM

ΨΨΨΨΨ **Pinot Gris 2017** Rating 93 To 2019 $30 CM
Bonadale Pinot Noir 2016 Rating 93 To 2025 $60 CM
Zoe Brut Rose 2015 Rating 92 $38 CM
Fume Blanc 2017 Rating 91 To 2022 $34 CM

Giaconda

30 McClay Road, Beechworth, Vic 3747 **Region** Beechworth
T (03) 5727 0246 **www**.giaconda.com.au **Open** By appt
Winemaker Rick Kinzbrunner **Est.** 1982 **Dozens** 3000 **Vyds** 4.5ha
These wines have a super-cult status and, given the small production, are extremely difficult to find, sold chiefly through restaurants and via the website. All have a cosmopolitan edge befitting Rick Kinzbrunner's international winemaking experience. Their Chardonnay is one of Australia's greatest, and is made and matured in the underground wine cellar hewn out of granite. This permits gravity flow, and a year-round temperature range of 14–15°C. Exports to the UK and the US.

🍷🍷🍷🍷🍷 **Estate Vineyard Shiraz 2015** This is a constantly moving kaleidoscope of aromas and flavours, hard to pin down thanks to its deceptive complexity. Vignerons of the northern Rhône Valley receiving many hundreds of dollars a bottle for their wines might not like to be confronted by this. Cork. 13.5% alc. Rating 98 To 2040 $89 ✪

Giant Steps

336 Maroondah Highway, Healesville, Vic 3777 **Region** Yarra Valley
T (03) 5962 6111 **www**.giantstepswine.com.au **Open** Mon–Fri 11–late, w'ends 9–late
Winemaker Phil Sexton, Steve Flamsteed, Julian Grounds **Est.** 1997 **Dozens** 12 500 **Vyds** 45ha
In May 2016 the sale by Giant Steps of the Innocent Bystander brand and stock was completed. The former Innocent Bystander restaurant and shop has been substantially remodelled to put the focus on the high quality, single vineyard, single varietal wines in what is demonstrably a very distinguished portfolio. Its vineyard resources comprise the Sexton vineyard (32ha) in the Lower Yarra and Applejack vineyard (13ha) in the Upper Yarra; there is also the Primavera vineyard in the Upper Yarra under long-term supervised contract, and Tarraford vineyard in the Lower Yarra under long-term lease. Exports to the UK, the US and other major markets.

🍷🍷🍷🍷🍷 **Applejack Vineyard Yarra Valley Pinot Noir 2017** Bright crimson; the bouquet a perfumed mix of red-fruit blossom, symbiotically joined with the red-berry flavours of the palate. It is a wine of exquisite purity and detail in its texture and strength. As befits a pinot of this quality, the palate is very long, a peacock's tail opening on the finish and aftertaste. Screwcap. 13.5% alc. **Rating** 98 To 2027 $60
2017 Known Pleasures McLaren Vale Shiraz Wow. This is an extraordinary wine, handled with kid gloves from day one. Biodynamically grown, hand-picked, taken via refrigerated van to Giant Steps' Healesville winery, destemmed or whole-bunched, large format French oak, no fining or filtration. It's faintly turbid, the bouquet pretty red/purple fruits. Then comes the extraordinary power, pulse and drive of the palate, building intensity second-by-second, but equally building a dazzling freshness. It tastes like 12.5% alc, not 14.5%. The tannins are imbedded within the fruit flavours; you sense them, but can't isolate them. The finish is endless, ditto aftertaste. Screwcap. **Rating** 98 To 2037 $60 ✪
Lusatia Park Vineyard Yarra Valley Chardonnay 2016 Gleaming straw-green; first tasted in Mar '17. Unexpectedly, the freshness is even greater now, the Upper Yarra vibrancy more in focus, grapefruit just in front of peach. Almost inevitably, the natural acidity provides the wine with exceptional length. Screwcap. 13.5% alc. **Rating** 97 To 2028 $45 ✪
Yarra Valley Pinot Noir 2017 Very good colour; the intensity of the aromas and flavours unfolding with the first sip stop you in your tracks. The whole-bunch component (20%) is evident, but not dominant, simply one of many factors in shaping the flavour and texture of this lovely wine. Screwcap. 13.5% alc. **Rating** 97 To 2037 $35

🍷🍷🍷🍷🍷 **Applejack Vineyard Yarra Valley Chardonnay 2017** Sets the Giant Steps chardonnay winemaking pattern: minimal vineyard intervention, hand-picked, whole-bunch pressed, wild-fermented in French puncheons (20% new), no mlf, matured for 10 months. A lovely wine having opened its arms wide to this cool, high quality vintage, the notable Applejack vineyard adding to the purity of the grapefruit, Granny Smith apple and stone-fruit flavours. As cool as a snow-fed mountain stream. Screwcap. 13% alc. **Rating** 96 **To** 2027 $50

Wombat Creek Vineyard Yarra Valley Chardonnay 2017 Apple and peach-blossom aromas. A very long and intense palate with a most attractive contrast of white peach and grapefruit, and a cleansing finish. Screwcap. 13% alc. **Rating** 96 **To** 2028 $50

LDR Yarra Valley Pinot Noir Syrah 2017 The vintage conditions were ideal for this rapidly developing style pioneered by the pocket-rocket winemaker at Yarra Yering, Sarah Crowe (LDR stands for light dry red). The red cherry and plum flavours bond with each other with no sign of a dividing line – it's almost luminous in its vibrant taste and colour. Screwcap. 13% alc. **Rating** 96 **To** 2027 $35

Sexton Vineyard Yarra Valley Pinot Noir 2017 A powerful, expressive, dark berry and plum bouquet, the palate doubling up on the fruit and adding high quality pinot tannins. A quality wine for long ageing. Screwcap. 13.5% alc. **Rating** 96 **To** 2032 $60

Gruyere Farm Vineyard Ocarina Yarra Valley Chardonnay 2017 The bouquet shares aromas of Weet-Bix/toast nuances with Tasmanian chardonnay. The palate is slightly softer than Applejack, but retains complexity and stone-fruit flavours. Screwcap. 13% alc. **Rating** 95 **To** 2027 $60

Sexton Vineyard Yarra Valley Chardonnay 2017 One of the cornerstones of the estate-owned vineyards, the low yield obvious on the bouquet, shifting to purity and precision of the palate and lingering aftertaste. Screwcap. 13.5% alc. **Rating** 95 **To** 2027 $50

Tarraford Vineyard Yarra Valley Chardonnay 2017 Hints of chaff and wheat on the bouquet; intense grapefruit flavours lead the way on the palate, with complexity rocky acidity. Screwcap. 13.5% alc. **Rating** 95 **To** 2028 $50

Wombat Creek Vineyard Yarra Valley Pinot Noir 2017 Like all the Giant Steps pinots, this is not fined or filtered. Light, bright crimson-purple; red flowers and fruits with a continuous whole-bunch-shot text of savoury, earthy, foresty notes threaded through the red fruits. Screwcap. 13.5% alc. **Rating** 95 **To** 2025 $60

Tarraford Vineyard Yarra Valley Syrah 2016 Good hue and depth; it is notably powerful and complex, with fine-grained but persistent tannins threaded through the black fruits of the medium to full-bodied palate. Screwcap. 14% alc. **Rating** 95 **To** 2031 $50

Yarra Valley Merlot 2016 If you are going to grow merlot outside of Margaret River, the Yarra Valley is the next best thing. The cool climate brings out the fragrance of the variety, the mix of cassis and plum fruit driving the bouquet and (of course) the palate. Screwcap. 14% alc. **Rating** 94 **To** 2031 $35

ρρρρρ **Yarra Valley Chardonnay 2017** Rating 93 To 2023 $35
Yarra Valley Syrah 2016 Rating 93 To 2030 $35

Gibson   ★★★★★

190 Willows Road, Light Pass, SA 5355 **Region** Barossa Valley
T (08) 8562 3193 **www**.gibsonwines.com.au **Open** 7 days 11–5
Winemaker Rob Gibson **Est.** 1996 **Dozens** 11 000 **Vyds** 14.2ha
Rob Gibson spent much of his working life as a senior viticulturist for Penfolds, involved in research tracing the characters that particular parcels of grapes give to a wine, which left him with a passion for identifying and protecting original vineyard plantings in Australia. He has a vineyard in the Barossa Valley at Light Pass (merlot), and one in the Eden Valley (shiraz and riesling), and also purchases grapes from McLaren Vale and the Adelaide Hills. Exports to Germany, Thailand, Hong Kong and China.

ρρρρρ **Australian Old Vine Collection Eden Valley Shiraz 2012** The voice of the Eden Valley sings loud and clear, in contrast to the tones of its Barossa sibling. There is a burst of juicy plum and cherry as the wine is tasted, with a dark chocolate note as well, the tannins 'old money', as they say. Vines planted in the early 1900s are ultimately the key to this wine. Cork. 14.5% alc. **Rating** 97 **To** 2047 $106 **☺**

ⵟⵟⵟⵟⵟ **Australian Old Vine Collection Barossa Shiraz 2013** Hewn of fruit from mid-1800s to early 1900s vines, this is a legacy of their provisions, served up beautifully by Gibson's sensitive approach to oak and diplomatic extraction regime. This is rich, sure, but plush and eminently drinkable, while also boasting a prodigious capacity for age. Licorice, coffee grind, bitter chocolate and a molten lift of kirsch and violet are caressed by a spray of pepper grind. Forceful. Fresh. Cork. 14.5% alc. **Rating** 96 **To** 2033 $123 NG

Australian Old Vine Collection Barossa Shiraz 2012 Still youthful, as one might expect from the great '12 vintage and the seriously old vines (some over 100yo). The wine has what the French describe as nervosity: electrically powered live-lines to its black and purple fruits. The tannins are still very much in the game, but play a purely support role. Cork. 14.5% alc. **Rating** 96 **To** 2042 $120

The Dirtman Barossa Shiraz 2016 Violet, anise and bouncy blue fruits are tucked in neatly by a curl of western Barossan mineral and a seam of soft tannins, belying the hefty alcohol (14.8%). The ultimate impression is one of perfume, finesse, balance and juicy drinkability, stamped with regional generosity. Screwcap. **Rating** 95 **To** 2032 $33 NG **☺**

Reserve Barossa Shiraz 2015 This is serious gear in the inimitable Barossan way: dark fruit allusions meshed with fruitcake spice, hung meats, cherry liqueur, anise, sexy floral aromas and manicured bitter-coffee tannins. An avatar of warm-climate richness and balance, with the oak merely an echo of vanilla. Screwcap. 14.5% alc. **Rating** 95 **To** 2030 $49 NG

Discovery Road Barossa Tempranillo 2016 Tempranillo still needs work on these shores, but here is a delicious exception. Floral lilac, dark cherry and explosive raspberry bonbon aromas are guided to a long finish of considerable detail, by malt chocolate tannins sheathed with just the right measure of oak. Screwcap. 14.2% alc. **Rating** 95 **To** 2024 $24 NG **☺**

Eden Valley Riesling 2017 Gibson's work across their whites is on the ascendancy: the acidity juicy despite the dryness, the mineral thrust refreshing, and the pH work a platform for drinker-friendly wine. Kudos! Citrus spa salts, talc and grapefruit pulp team along seams of pumice. This is a special single vineyard wine stamped with limey Eden Valley DNA. Screwcap. 11.8% alc. **Rating** 94 **To** 2029 $33 NG

Reserve Barossa Merlot 2015 A grand merlot in a regional sense, with generous plummy fruit served by a waft of gentle balancing tannins, dried herb savour, bitter chocolate and high quality cinnamon oak nestled nicely into the fold. Like a warm leather armchair to which one returns time and time again. Plush and expansive. Screwcap. 14.2% alc. **Rating** 94 **To** 2025 $49 NG

Discovery Road Barossa Nero d'Avola 2016 A juicy mouthful of pickled cherries, baking spice and a dusty tannin weave across a wave of cranberry acidity. Nothing to dislike here! Mid-weighted, tactile and thoroughly delicious, the wine expands with hedonic sweet fruit flavours across the mouth. Screwcap. 13.2% alc. **Rating** 94 **To** 2021 $24 NG **☺**

ⵟⵟⵟⵟⵟ **The Smithy Barossa Shiraz Cabernet 2016** Rating 93 **To** 2029 $29 NG
Isabelle Cabernet Merlot 2016 Rating 93 **To** 2029 $29 NG
Discovery Road Montepulciano 2016 Rating 93 **To** 2028 $24 NG **☺**
Adelaide Hills Pinot Gris 2017 Rating 92 **To** 2020 $23 NG **☺**
Discovery Road IL Minestrone 2015 Rating 91 **To** 2020 $24 NG
Discovery Road Barossa Zinfandel 2016 Rating 90 **To** 2023 $24 NG

Gilbert Family Wines   ★★★★★

137 Ulan Road, Mudgee, NSW 2850 **Region** Orange/Mudgee
T (02) 6373 1371 **www**.gilbertfamilywines.com.au **Open** 7 days 10–6
Winemaker Simon Gilbert, Will Gilbert **Est.** 2010 **Dozens** 15 000 **Vyds** 25.81ha
For some time now, Simon Gilbert has devoted himself to his consultancy and wine brokering business, Wineworks of Australia. As that business has grown, Simon has returned to his family's winery, Gilbert Family Wines, wearing his Wineworks of Australia hat, overseeing the winemaking of the estate-grown grapes, with all wines exported. Fifth and sixth generations Simon, Will and Mark Gilbert have drawn on the family history (Joseph Gilbert was among the first to plant grapes in the Eden Valley, in 1842) to produce Gilbert + Gilbert Wines, sourced from the Eden Valley. Will has joined his father in the winery; still working his way through studies at CSU, he has worked in Baume with Benjamin Leroux (chardonnay and pinot noir), and was named Upcoming Winemaker at the International Riesling Challenge '17. Viticulturist Mark is based in SA (see Karrawatta). Simon has also established gilbert by Simon Gilbert, and makes the wines for this label at the same winery. Exports to Japan, Hong Kong and China.

🍷🍷🍷🍷🍷 **gilbert by Simon Gilbert Orange Sauvignon Blanc 2017** Bordeaux clone, small batches destemmed and chilled, pressed to a new 300l French barrel for wild fermentation, the remaining juice cold-settled and inoculated with yeast. 85% matured in oak, 15% in tank for 6 months. The barrel fermentation has been exemplary, introducing a tactile element and flavour level that does no more than provide a frame for the intense palate. This is in a grapefruit/citrus spectrum rather than tropical, giving the wine real prospects of even greater complexity over the short term. Screwcap. 13% alc. **Rating** 95 **To** 2020 $26 **✪**

gilbert by Simon Gilbert Barrel Select Orange Pinot Noir 2016 By some distance the best of the three Simon Gilbert pinots, with some left-field vinification, including wild fermentation in old open oak fermenters, draining to new French oak barrels and one 900l roll barrel filled with destemmed fruit. Once fermentation is complete the wine is delivered to new French puncheons. This weirdly has the highest pH of the three wines. It has whole-bunch/berry aromas, good cherry-accented fruit, and a long palate and finish. Screwcap. 13% alc. **Rating** 95 **To** 2026 $48

gilbert by Simon Gilbert Orange Riesling 2017 The retention of 5.8g/l residual sugar has worked well, balanced by a very low pH of 2.87 and 7.4g titratable acidity. Many – if not most – would simply see a crisp, dry lemon-and-lime palate with a minerally edge. Screwcap. 12.5% alc. **Rating** 94 **To** 2030 $26 **✪**

🍷🍷🍷🍷🍸 **gilbert by Simon Gilbert Orange Chardonnay 2016** Rating 93 **To** 2024 $30

gilbert by Simon Gilbert Mudgee Orange Saignee Rose 2017 Rating 90 **To** 2018 $24 CM

Gilberts   ★★★★☆

30 138 Albany Highway, Kendenup via Mount Barker, WA 6323 **Region** Mount Barker
T (08) 9851 4028 **www**.gilbertwines.com.au **Open** Fri–Mon 10–5
Winemaker West Cape Howe **Est.** 1985 **Dozens** 3000 **Vyds** 9ha
Once a part-time occupation for sheep and beef farmers Jim and Beverly Gilbert, now a successful full-time venture. The mature vineyard (shiraz, chardonnay, riesling and cabernet sauvignon), coupled with contract winemaking at West Cape Howe, has long produced high class riesling. The 3 Devils Shiraz is named after their sons.

🍷🍷🍷🍷🍷 **Mount Barker Riesling 2017** Meyer lemon, chalk, blossomy notes and spice. What a beautiful array of characters. It opens with aroma, is concentrated through the palate, and is both textural and satisfying to close. Standout wine. Screwcap. 11.5% alc. **Rating** 95 **To** 2028 $24 CM **✪**

ŸŸŸŸŸ Reserve Mount Barker Shiraz 2015 Rating 93 To 2030 $30 CM
　　　　 Alira Riesling 2017 Rating 91 To 2023 $24 CM
　　　　 3 Devils Mount Barker Shiraz 2016 Rating 91 To 2024 $20 CM ✪

Gioiello Estate ★★★★☆

350 Molesworth-Dropmore Road, Molesworth, Vic 3718 **Region** Upper Goulburn
T 0437 240 502 **www**.gioiello.com.au **Open** Not
Winemaker Scott McCarthy (Contract) **Est.** 1987 **Dozens** 3500 **Vyds** 8.97ha
The Gioiello Estate vineyard was established by a Japanese company and originally known as
Daiwa Nar Darak. Planted between 1987 and '96, it accounts for just under 9ha of a 400ha
property of rolling hills, pastures, bushland, river flats, natural water springs and billabongs.
Now owned by the Schiavello family, the vineyard continues to produce high quality wines.

ŸŸŸŸŸ Mt Concord Upper Goulburn Syrah 2015 An attractive, juicy, medium-
　　　　 bodied syrah, with fresh red and black cherries driving the fragrant bouquet and
　　　　 palate alike. Irresistible. Screwcap. 14.6% alc. **Rating** 95 To 2029 $45
　　　　 Old House Upper Goulburn Merlot 2015 Matured in French oak for
　　　　 18 months. This is what I term real merlot, thanks to its savoury mix of fruits,
　　　　 black olive and dried herbs. The handling of the oak and tannins are exemplary.
　　　　 Screwcap. 13.7% alc. **Rating** 94 To 2030 $45

ŸŸŸŸŸ Old Hill Upper Goulburn Chardonnay 2016 Rating 91 To 2023 $40

Gipsie Jack Wine Co ★★★★

1509 Langhorne Creek Road, Langhorne Creek, SA 5255 **Region** Langhorne Creek
T (08) 8537 3029 **www**.gipsiejack.com.au **Open** 7 days 10–5
Winemaker John Glaetzer, Ben Potts **Est.** 2004 **Dozens** 7000
The partners behind Gipsie Jack are John Glaetzer and Ben Potts, and they named their
business after John's Jack Russell dog Gipsie. Glaetzer and Potts say, 'We want to make this
label fun, like in the old days. No pretentiousness, no arrogance, not even a back label. A great
wine at a great price, with no discounting.' Exports to Switzerland and Singapore.

ŸŸŸŸŸ Langhorne Creek Cabernet Sauvignon 2016 This is prize-fighting
　　　　 cabernet with dukes raised! Despite its warmth, the Fleurieu bestows a maritime
　　　　 influence on its Bordeaux varieties, creating a regional DNA of herbal freshness
　　　　 complementing the wines' inherent richness. The result can be delicious. Here
　　　　 is an example, purportedly from old vines, many aged between 50 and 60 years.
　　　　 Screwcap. 14% alc. **Rating** 93 To 2022 $18 NG ✪
　　　　 Langhorne Creek Malbec 2016 Prime turf for malbec – Langhorne Creek
　　　　 is producing some beauties and this is no exception. Violet aromas segue to a
　　　　 juicy, fulsome palate of abundant blue and dark fruit, given tension and further
　　　　 complexity by a hint of reductive smokiness. Screwcap. 14.8% alc. **Rating** 93
　　　　 To 2024 $22 NG ✪
　　　　 Langhorne Creek Lagrein 2016 Delicious scents of blueberry, dried herb and
　　　　 red and black plum leap from the glass. The palate is firm and dutifully extracted,
　　　　 imparting a sinuous weave of tannin to complement the gentle oak and a spurt of
　　　　 obtuse acidity. Screwcap. 13.5% alc. **Rating** 92 To 2023 $22 NG ✪
　　　　 Langhorne Creek Dolcetto 2016 Meaning 'sweet little one' in Italian, this
　　　　 Dolcetto boasts an array of pulpy purple fruit allusions, moderate acidity and
　　　　 firm tannins, making for a gluggable, eminently enjoyable wine that holds plenty
　　　　 of food-pairing cards up its sleeve. Needs time for the oak tannins to integrate.
　　　　 Screwcap. 14% alc. **Rating** 91 To 2021 $22 NG ✪

GISA ★★★★☆

578 The Parade, Auldama, SA 5072 **Region** South Australia
T (08) 8338 2123 **www**.gisa.com.au **Open** Not
Winemaker Mat Henbest **Est.** 2006 **Dozens** 10 000

Mat and Lisa Henbest have chosen a clever name for their virtual winery – GISA stands for Geographic Indication South Australia – neatly covering the fact that their wines come variously from the Adelaide Hills (semillon, sauvignon blanc and chardonnay), Clare Valley (riesling), McLaren Vale (shiraz viognier) and Barossa Valley (Reserve shiraz). It in turn reflects Mat's long apprenticeship in the wine industry, working in retail while he pursued tertiary qualifications, thereafter wholesaling wine to the retail and restaurant trade. He then moved to Haselgrove, where he spent five years working closely with the small winemaking team, refining his style, and gaining experience on the other side of the fence. Exports to China.

🍷🍷🍷🍷🍷 **Ellipsis 2015** Smart to source 60+yo bushvine grenache from Blewitt Springs (75%), with added complexity from 13% Barossa Valley shiraz and 12% McLaren Vale mataro. Bright, full colour, the bouquet very fragrant and fruity, the medium-bodied palate supple and very long. Red and purple fruits hold sway throughout, the tannins are fine and soft, the oak barely perceptible. Lovely wine, now or in 20 years. Screwcap. 14.5% alc. **Rating** 96 **To** 2038 $30 ❂

🍷🍷🍷🍷🍷 **Single Vineyard Polish Hill River Riesling 2017 Rating** 92 **To** 2027 $25 ❂
Old School Barossa Valley Shiraz Mataro 2016 Rating 92 **To** 2031 $35
ARC Adelaide Hills Blanc de Noir 2K17 2017 Rating 90 $15 ❂

Gisborne Peak

69 Short Road, Gisborne South, Vic 3437 **Region** Macedon Ranges
T (03) 5428 2228 **www**.gisbornepeakwines.com.au **Open** 7 days 11–4
Winemaker Rob Ellis **Est.** 1978 **Dozens** 1800 **Vyds** 5.5ha
Bob Nixon began the development of Gisborne Peak way back in 1978, planting his dream vineyard row by row. It is planted to pinot noir, chardonnay, semillon, riesling and lagrein. The tasting room has wide shaded verandahs, plenty of windows and sweeping views.

🍷🍷🍷🍷🍷 **Macedon Ranges Riesling 2016** As it enters the first phase of development, lime juice flavours are unfurling their sails, braced by the usual acidity of very cool-grown grapes. Although there is further fruit to be explored, the wine already has the balance, length and flavour to justify what might otherwise be vinocide. Screwcap. 12.8% alc. **Rating** 95 **To** 2026 $39
Macedon Ranges Riesling 2017 A fragrant blossom-filled bouquet is followed by a tightly wound palate with lime and mineral acidity nipping at each other's heels. You know with certainty the game will change with more time in bottle, the certainty evidenced by the '16. Screwcap. **Rating** 94 **To** 2027 $39

🍷🍷🍷🍷🍷 **Macedon Ranges Chardonnay 2016 Rating** 92 **To** 2023 $32
Indian Summer Macedon Ranges Pinot Noir 2015 Rating 92 **To** 2025 $39
Limited Edition Macedon Ranges Pinot Noir 2014 Rating 91 **To** 2026 $39
Macedon Ranges Chardonnay 2015 Rating 90 **To** 2023 $29
Macedon Ranges Pinot Rose 2017 Rating 90 **To** 2020 $32

Glaetzer Wines   ★★★★★

PO Box 824, Tanunda, SA 5352 **Region** Barossa Valley
T (08) 8563 0947 **www**.glaetzer.com **Open** Not
Winemaker Ben Glaetzer **Est.** 1996 **Dozens** 15 000 **Vyds** 20ha
With a family history in the Barossa Valley dating back to 1888, and 30 years' winemaking experience himself, Colin Glaetzer established Colin Glaetzer Wines in 1996. Son Ben is now winemaker, having worked in the Hunter Valley and as a Flying Winemaker in many of the world's wine regions. The wines are made with great skill and abundant personality. Exports to all major markets.

🍷🍷🍷🍷🍷 **Bishop Barossa Valley Shiraz 2016** Matured for 15 months in hogsheads (90% French, 10% American; 40% new). A complex wine, both in terms of its savoury flavours and texture. Black fruits provide the core of the palate, with graphite, earth and tannins all on parade. It has absorbed and totally integrated the oak, which suits the wine to a T. Screwcap. 14.5% alc. **Rating** 95 **To** 2041 $33 ❂

Amon-Ra Unfiltered Barossa Valley Shiraz 2016 Deep, dense, inky hue; every step along the way (other than a wine-stained crease on the side of the cork) has been carefully scripted, starting and finishing with 15.5% alc. If you enjoy mammoth wines of enormous power and depth, go for it. Rating 95 To 2046 $100
Anaperenna 2016 84% shiraz, 16% cabernet sauvignon. The colour is typically deep, the bouquet complex, and likewise the palate (no surprise), but it doesn't hit you with its alcohol (most surprising of all). Black fruits (berry and currant) hold sway until the finish, when the alcohol does raise its head. I'm happy to accept that, but would choose my beef steak with care (5cm thick). Cork. 15.5% alc. Rating 94 To 2041 $52

♀♀♀♀ **Wallace Barossa Valley Shiraz Grenache 2016** Rating 89 To 2023 $23

Glaetzer-Dixon Family Winemakers ★★★★☆

93 Brooker Avenue, Hobart, Tas 7000 **Region** Southern Tasmania
T 0417 852 287 www.gdfwinemakers.com **Open** By appt
Winemaker Nick Glaetzer **Est.** 2008 **Dozens** 2500
History does not relate what Nick Glaetzer's high profile Barossa Valley winemaker relatives thought of his decision to move to Tasmania in 2005 to make cutting-edge cool-climate styles. Obviously wife Sally approves. While his winemaking career began in the Barossa Valley, he reached into scattered parts of the New and Old worlds alike, working successively in Languedoc, the Pfaltz, Margaret River, Riverland, Sunraysia, the Hunter Valley and Burgundy. Exports to the US, Canada, the Netherlands and Singapore.

♀♀♀♀♀ **Mon Pere Shiraz 2014** The full box and dice of cool-climate shiraz, all peppers and garden herbs, delivered here with ripe, smooth-skinned, red berries, mouth-watering acidity and impressive length. Immaculate. Screwcap. 13.4% alc. Rating 95 To 2028 $65 CM
Reveur Pinot Noir 2014 Fruit and oak combine to gorgeous effect. Cherry-plum, violet, blood orange and boysenberry flavours come swaddled in fresh cedar wood and assorted sweet, roasted spices. Tannin rumbles through the finish. Irresistible. Screwcap. 13.9% alc. Rating 94 To 2025 $56 CM
Mon Pere Shiraz 2015 Complex, tangy and seamless at once. Sweet-sour cherry, undergrowth, tomato leaf and spicy/smoky oak flavours are delivered on the smoothest ride imaginable. Essentially cool climate and yet utterly seductive from start to finish. Screwcap. 13.3% alc. Rating 94 To 2024 $65 CM

♀♀♀♀♀ **Avance Pinot Noir 2016** Rating 93 To 2023 $30 CM
Avance Pinot Noir 2015 Rating 93 To 2021 $30 CM
La Judith Pinot Noir 2013 Rating 93 To 2024 $220 CM

Glandore Estate ★★★★

1595 Broke Road, Pokolbin, NSW 2320 **Region** Hunter Valley
T (02) 4998 7140 www.glandorewines.com **Open** 7 days 10–5
Winemaker Duane Roy **Est.** 2004 **Dozens** 4000 **Vyds** 8ha
Glandore Estate is the reincarnation of the Brokenback vineyard established as part of The Rothbury Estate in the early 1970s, but it had an even longer history. It was purchased by legendary grapegrowers Mick and Jack Phillips in the '30s, and given the Glandore name. Owners David Madson, John Cambridge and Peter McBeath, who acquired the property in 2004 (with existing chardonnay vines), have extended the plantings with savagnin, semillon and viognier.

♀♀♀♀♀ **Elliott Reserve Semillon 2017** Whole-bunch pressed, cool-fermented. Its price may cause some to blink, but this is a very good young semillon with a virtually unlimited future. It is as fresh as a spring day, flowery and light-footed, the balance and length faultless. Screwcap. 10.5% alc. Rating 95 To 2037 $30 ✪

Glenguin Estate ★★★★★

Milbrodale Road, Broke, NSW 2330 **Region** Hunter Valley
T (02) 6579 1009 **www**.glenguinestate.com.au **Open** Thurs–Mon 10–5
Winemaker Robin Tedder MW, Rhys Eather **Est.** 1993 **Dozens** 2000 **Vyds** 6ha
Glenguin Estate was established by the Tedder family, headed by Robin Tedder. It is located close to the town of Broke and adjacent to Wollombi Brook. The backbone of the production comes from 25-year-old plantings of Busby clone semillon and shiraz (2ha each), plus a new planting of 2ha of shiraz. Andrew Tedder, who has considerable experience with organics and biodynamics, oversees the vineyard.

ᵀᵀᵀᵀᵀ **Classic Cellar Aged Schoolhouse Shiraz 2007** Given 95 points in Dec '09, and retaining all the positive qualities it had then, the medium-bodied palate showing how a mere 2% viognier can impact a wine. It is still fresh and vibrant, with a twist of spice to the dark fruits, and a long, even palate. The next 10 years won't trouble it one iota. I'm very tempted to lift the points to 96. Screwcap. 14% alc. **Rating** 95 **To** 2030 $60

ᵀᵀᵀᵀᵀ **Glenguin Vineyard Semillon 2017 Rating** 92 **To** 2024 $28 CM
Cellar Aged Schoolhouse Block Shiraz 2013 Rating 92 **To** 2033 $45

Glenlofty Wines ★★★★☆

123 Glenlofty-Warrenmang Road, Glenlofty, Vic 3469 (postal) **Region** Pyrenees
T (03) 5354 8228 **www**.glenloftywines.com.au **Open** Not
Winemaker Andrew Koerner, Chris Smales **Est.** 1995 **Dozens** 15 000 **Vyds** 132ha
The vineyard was established by Southcorp after exhaustive soil and climate research. In August 2010, TWE sold the vineyard to Canadian-based Roger Richmond-Smith and winemaking moved to Blue Pyrenees Estate. Glenlofty Wines also purchased the nearby 30ha Decameron Station, bringing the total vineyard holdings to over 130ha. Exports to Canada, Singapore and NZ.

ᵀᵀᵀᵀᵀ **Pyrenees Shiraz 2015** As sure-footed as they come. This is ripe and rich, its flavours of sweet plum, spearmint, blackberry and chocolate melting in your mouth as they roll impressively through. Seductive in a controlled way. Tannin has been set just right too. Terrific value. Screwcap. 14% alc. **Rating** 95 **To** 2030 $29 CM ●

ᵀᵀᵀᵀᵀ **Single Vineyard Pyrenees Shiraz 2014 Rating** 93 **To** 2030 $24 CM ●

Glenwillow Wines ★★★★

Bendigo Pottery, 146 Midland Highway, Epsom, Vic 3551 **Region** Bendigo
T 0428 461 076 **www**.glenwillow.com.au **Open** W'ends 11–5
Winemaker Greg Dedman, Adam Marks **Est.** 1999 **Dozens** 750 **Vyds** 2.8ha
Peter and Cherryl Fyffe began their vineyard at Yandoit Creek, 10km south of Newstead, in 1999, planting 1.8ha of shiraz and 0.3ha of cabernet sauvignon, later branching out with 0.6ha of nebbiolo and 0.1ha of barbera. Planted on a mixture of rich volcanic and clay loam interspersed with quartz and buckshot gravel, the vineyard has an elevated north-facing aspect, which minimises the risk of frost.

ᵀᵀᵀᵀᵀ **Reserve Bendigo Shiraz 2015** Fermented with 20% whole bunches, matured in French hogsheads (20% new). This ups its power compared to its sibling, fruit, oak and tannins rising in unison and proportion. It is worthy of extended cellaring, balance not in doubt. Screwcap. 14.4% alc. **Rating** 94 **To** 2035 $60

ᵀᵀᵀᵀᵀ **Bendigo Shiraz 2015 Rating** 90 **To** 2025 $28

Golden Ball ★★★★★

1175 Beechworth-Wangaratta Road, Beechworth, Vic 3747 **Region** Beechworth
T (03) 5727 0284 **www**.goldenball.com.au **Open** By appt
Winemaker James McLaurin **Est.** 1996 **Dozens** 1000 **Vyds** 3.2ha
The vineyard is on one of the region's original land grants, planted to grapes in recent times
by James and Janine McLaurin. The main varieties are chardonnay, shiraz (which was grafted
to chardonnay in 2013), cabernet sauvignon, merlot and malbec, with lesser plantings of
petit verdot, sagrantino and savagnin. The Lineage vineyard was planted in 2008 to shiraz, petit
verdot, sagrantino and savagnin. The wines are aged in one-third new French oak, the
remainder 2–4 years old. The low yields result in intensely flavoured wines, which are found
in a who's who of Melbourne's best restaurants and a handful of Beechworth and Melbourne
retailers. Exports to Singapore and China.

🍷🍷🍷🍷🍷 **Saxon Shiraz 2015** Blueberry and cream pie, dusted with cinnamon oak. Savvy
reductive handling imparts tension, and hints of olive, anise and smoked meat.
The finish is long and plush. Impressive in a salubrious sort of way. Diam. 14% alc.
Rating 95 **To** 2028 $55 NG

🍷🍷🍷🍷🍷 **là-bas Chardonnay 2016 Rating** 93 **To** 2026 $60 NG
Gallice Cabernet Merlot Malbec 2015 Rating 93 **To** 2024 $55 NG
bona fide Savagnin 2017 Rating 91 **To** 2022 $30 NG

Golden Grove Estate ★★★★★

Sundown Road, Ballandean, Qld 4382 **Region** Granite Belt
T (07) 4684 1291 **www**.goldengroveestate.com.au **Open** 7 days 9–4
Winemaker Raymond Costanzo **Est.** 1993 **Dozens** 4000 **Vyds** 12.4ha
Golden Grove Estate was established by Mario and Sebastian Costanzo in 1946, producing
stone fruits and table grapes. The first wine grapes (shiraz) were planted in '72, but it was not
until '85, when ownership passed to son Sam and his wife Grace, that the use of the property
began to change. In '93 chardonnay and merlot joined the shiraz, followed by cabernet
sauvignon, sauvignon blanc and semillon. The baton has now been passed down another
generation to Ray, who has lifted the quality of the wines remarkably, and has also planted
tempranillo, durif, barbera, malbec, mourvedre, vermentino and nero d'Avola. In recent years,
Golden Grove has had consistent wine show success with alternative varieties.

🍷🍷🍷🍷🍷 **The Little White Box Granite Belt G.S.M 2016** A 60/20/20% blend
matured for 12 months in used French oak, made (secretly) in honour of Ray
Costanzo's father Sam, the 'little white box' being Sam's grafting box made when
he was 17 and still in use today. Yet another triumph for Ray, this wine has great
balance: fleshy in the middle, spicy/savoury on the fringes. The components
were separately vinified, the picking decisions made with uncanny accuracy in
highlighting the varietal expression. Screwcap. 14% alc. **Rating** 95 **To** 2029 $50
Granite Belt Vermentino 2017 Made in six batches: free-run, pressings,
wild fermentation in barrel (2 months in new French oak), lees ferment, skin
maceration (4 days), and full-skin maceration (matured in French oak; 30% new).
All this achieved texture and structure rather than varietal character, but what is
remarkable is the power and length of the lemony fruit. Development potential++.
Screwcap. 11.6% alc. **Rating** 94 **To** 2023 $26 ✪
The Skins Vermentino 2017 Fermented on skins for 10 days, plunged twice
daily, basket-pressed, 300 bottles made. Some pinking to the hue. Reading the
vinification will draw natural wine lovers like moths to a flame, but they may be
disappointed by its success in building flavour without phenolics or yellow colour.
Screwcap. 12% alc. **Rating** 94 **To** 2021 $30 ✪
Granite Belt Malbec 2016 Malbec can be a contrary variety, but not here. This
has what I identify as one of the main varietal markers – plum jam, yet not sweet
or confected – plus spices, all of which come together as an elegant example of
the wine. Screwcap. 14.5% alc. **Rating** 94 **To** 2029 $28 ✪

Nero d'Avola 2016 A fresh and lively perfumed bouquet, then a light to medium-bodied palate with precision and length to its red cherry and raspberry fruits. Great on a summer day, especially if lightly chilled. Screwcap. 12.8% alc. **Rating** 94 **To** 2023 $26 ◗

🍷🍷🍷🍷🍷 **Granite Belt Durif 2016 Rating** 93 **To** 2029 $30
Granite Belt Mourvedre 2016 Rating 91 **To** 2026 $30
Granite Belt Rose Brose 2017 Rating 90 **To** 2019 $16 ◗

Golding Wines ★★★★

52 Western Branch Road, Lobethal, SA 5241 **Region** Adelaide Hills
T (08) 8389 5120 **www**.goldingwines.com.au **Open** 7 days 11–5
Winemaker Darren Golding, Brendon Keys **Est.** 2002 **Dozens** 6000 **Vyds** 26.12ha
The Golding family story began in the Adelaide Hills three generations ago through market gardening and horticulture. Viticulture became part of the picture in 1995 when their Western Branch Road vineyard was planted. Darren and Lucy Golding took the helm in 2002, launching the Golding Wines brand. Viticultural holdings have increased recently with the purchase of more vineyard and new plantings of gamay and dornfelder added to existing pinot noir, shiraz, chardonnay, savagnin, pinot gris and sauvignon blanc. The cellar door within a rustic sandstone barn has recently been refurbished. Exports to the UK, the US, Canada, Hong Kong, the Philippines, Malaysia, Singapore and China.

🍷🍷🍷🍷🍷 **Rocco Adelaide Hills Shiraz 2015** 20yo vines, 20 days on skins, French oak (20% new). A beautifully scented and flavoured wine with elegance on its side and ripe flavour too. Not to mention balance. This tastes, feels and smells good from many different angles. Screwcap. 14.5% alc. **Rating** 94 **To** 2030 $42 CM

🍷🍷🍷🍷🍷 **The East End Adelaide Hills Rose 2017 Rating** 93 **To** 2020 $25 CM ◗
The Handcart Adelaide Hills Shiraz 2015 Rating 93 **To** 2030 $25 ◗
Block 2 Adelaide Hills Chardonnay 2014 Rating 92 **To** 2023 $35 CM
The Handcart Adelaide Hills Shiraz 2016 Rating 92 **To** 2027 $25 CM ◗
Lil' Late Harvest Adelaide Hills Sauvignon Blanc 2013 Rating 92 **To** 2021 $25 JF ◗
Ombre Adelaide Hills Gamay 2017 Rating 91 **To** 2021 $35 CM
The Purveyor Adelaide Hills Pinot Noir 2016 Rating 91 **To** 2024 $25
Francis John Pinot Noir 2015 Rating 91 **To** 2024 $42 CM
The East End Adelaide Hills Rose 2016 Rating 90 **To** 2018 $25 JF

Goldman Wines ★★★★☆

11 Ercildoune Street, Cessnock, NSW 2325 (postal) **Region** Hunter Valley
T 0467 808 316 **www**.goldmanwines.com.au **Open** Not
Winemaker Various contract **Est.** 2014 **Dozens** 1500
Owner Callan Goldman grew up in the Hunter Valley, coming into contact with many of the people involved in growing grapes and making wine. His real job is working as a civil engineer in northwest WA, which funds his wine production. Jo Marsh of Billy Button Wines made the majority of the impressive portfolio in 2015, '16 and '17. The '17 wines were made at Jo's new winery in the Ovens Valley.

🍷🍷🍷🍷🍷 **Olivia Beechworth Chardonnay 2016** This is a very good example of Beechworth chardonnay, which has its own certain character. Indeed, one can argue it has the best characters of Margaret River chardonnay (depth) and Yarra Valley chardonnay (finesse and length). (I haven't compared it to Giaconda, which is in a space of its own.) Screwcap. 13% alc. **Rating** 95 **To** 2026 $38
Alpine Valleys Shiraz 2015 This is a pretty remarkable wine. Who would have imagined a relatively early-picked shiraz from the Alpine Valleys would be able to cope with 14 months in 100% new French oak? Well, it does so insouciantly, its black cherry and plum fruit supported by oak tannins and flavours. 'More full-bodied that the '14', says the back label, and it certainly is. Screwcap. 13.5% alc. **Rating** 94 **To** 2030 $35

Gomersal Wines ★★★★

203 Lyndoch Road, Gomersal, SA 5352 **Region** Barossa Valley
T (08) 8563 3611 **www**.gomersalwines.com.au **Open** 7 days 10–5
Winemaker Barry White, Peter Pollard **Est.** 1887 **Dozens** 8800 **Vyds** 20ha

The 1887 establishment date has a degree of poetic licence. That year, Friedrich W Fromm planted the Wonganella vineyards, following a few years later with a winery on the edge of Gomersal Creek; it remained in operation for 90 years, finally closing in 1983. In 2000 a group of friends 'with strong credentials in both the making and consumption ends of the wine industry' bought the winery and re-established the vineyard, planting 17ha of shiraz, 2ha of mourvedre and 1ha of grenache. Exports to Switzerland, Iceland, South Korea, Singapore and China.

ΨΨΨΨΨ **Eden Valley Riesling 2017** A very good example of the fusion of lime and lemon achieved in the Eden Valley, here with depth and length. Won a number of medals in '18. Screwcap. 11.5% alc. **Rating** 90 **To** 2027 $20 ✪
Reserve Barossa Valley Shiraz 2015 A good example of traditional Barossa Valley vinification, fully ripe grapes and immersion in American oak. Will totally please or displease those who taste it; the middle ground (on which I stand) is narrow. Screwcap. 15% alc. **Rating** 90 **To** 2030 $25

ΨΨΨΨ **Eden Valley Riesling 2016 Rating** 89 **To** 2021 $20 CM
Barossa Valley Grenache Shiraz Mataro 2015 Rating 89 **To** 2024 $20
Barossa Valley Cabernet Sauvignon 2014 Rating 89 **To** 2030 $20

Goodman Wines ★★★★★

PO Box 275, Healesville, Vic 3777 **Region** Yarra Valley
T 0447 030 011 **www**.goodmanwines.com **Open** Not
Winemaker Kate Goodman **Est.** 2012 **Dozens** 500

Kate Goodman started her winemaking career in McLaren Vale and the Clare Valley, thereafter spending seven years at Seppelt in the Grampians. In 2000 she became chief winemaker at Punt Road and remained there until '14, when she left to set up Goodman Wines, leasing a winery together with fellow winemaker Caroline Mooney (of Bird on a Wire). While still in the planning stages, and with the knowledge and approval of Punt Road's owners, she had made wines over the '12 and '13 vintages from mature Upper Yarra Valley vineyards. From '17 Kate is also winemaker for Penley and Zonzo estates.

ΨΨΨΨΨ **Yarra Valley Chardonnay 2016** Exhibit A, Yarra Valley chardonnay. Beautifully powered, poised and persistent. White peach and fig, nougat and flint. It drives straight down quality street without the slightest sign of deviation. Screwcap. 12.5% alc. **Rating** 96 **To** 2025 $40 CM ✪
Yarra Valley Chardonnay 2015 Layered and rich, with ripe citrus – Meyer lemon and a whisk of grapefruit – white peach and creamy cashew all coming to the party in the first stages of bottle development. Ready soonish but will, of course, hold. Screwcap. 12.5% alc. **Rating** 95 **To** 2023 $40
Yarra Valley Pinot Noir 2016 Ship-shape pinot noir. Light and shade, depth and length. It tastes of anise and red cherry, plum pie and spice, a light kiss of sweet oak making a positive contribution. You take a sip and immediately think 'yep, that's good'. Screwcap. 13% alc. **Rating** 94 **To** 2025 $40 CM
Yarra Valley Cabernet Sauvignon 2015 Strong with gum leaf and blackcurrant flavour; lightened with boysenberry and violet; tempered by a wash of supple tannin. Finding a hair out of place is effectively impossible. Screwcap. 13% alc. **Rating** 94 **To** 2032 $40 CM

ΨΨΨΨΨ **Nikkal Yarra Valley Chardonnay 2017 Rating** 92 **To** 2023 $28 CM
Nikkal Yarra Valley Rose 2017 Rating 91 **To** 2020 $25 CM
Nikkal Yarra Valley Pinot Noir 2017 Rating 91 **To** 2023 $28 CM

Gooree Park Wines

Gulgong Road, Mudgee, NSW 2850 **Region** Mudgee
T (02) 6378 1800 **www**.gooreepark.com.au **Open** Mon–Fri 10–5, w'ends 11–4
Winemaker Rueben Rodriguez **Est.** 2008 **Dozens** 3000 **Vyds** 546ha
Gooree Park Wines is part of a group of companies owned by Eduardo Cojuangco; his other
companies include a thoroughbred horse stud and a pastoral enterprise and in Mudgee and
Canowindra. Eduardo's interest in all forms of agriculture has resulted in the planting of over
500ha of vines, starting with the Tullamour vineyard in Mudgee in 1996, Fords Creek in
Mudgee in '97, and Mt Lewis Estate at Canowindra in '98.

Crowned Glory Mudgee Cabernet Sauvignon 2016 A cavalcade of currant
and strewn herbs flecked with mint is tightly wound around firmly detailed
tannins, the astringency setting a savoury pace. The oak is generous, but tucked in
nicely. This is polished and salubrious, the tannins well massaged in a Napa-esque
vein. Screwcap. 14% alc. **Rating** 93 **To** 2028 $35 NG

Mudgee Late Harvest Semillon NV This hits all the hedonic chimes: exotic,
whisper light, racy and a gentle waft of oaky complexity, tucking it in at the
seams. Expect candied orange rind, stewed stone fruits, lemon curd and pineapple.
Screwcap. 10% alc. **Rating** 91 **To** 2021 $22 NG ✪

Don Eduardo Mudgee Shiraz Cabernet 2016 Rating 89 **To** 2024 $38 NG

Gotham Wines

8 The Parade West, Kent Town, SA 5067 **Region** South Australia
T (08) 7324 3031 **www**.gothamwines.com.au **Open** Not
Winemaker Peter Pollard **Est.** 2004 **Dozens** 74 000
In 2014 a group of wine enthusiasts, including former BRL Hardy CEO Stephen Millar, came
together to purchase the Gotham Wines brands. The intention was (and is) to build on the
existing domestic and export distribution of the wines, which include Wine Men of Gotham,
Gotham, Stalking Horse and Step X Step labels, from Langhorne Creek, Clare Valley, Barossa
Valley and McLaren Vale. Exports to most major markets.

Stalking Horse McLaren Vale Shiraz 2016 Matured for 22 months in new
and used American oak. Dense purple-crimson; oak and fruit battle each other
without any tannins to complicate the issue. A lot of flavour, with a whisper of
sweetness. Screwcap. 14.5% alc. **Rating** 89 **To** 2023 $20

Stalking Horse Barossa Valley Shiraz 2014 Maturation in American oak
(40% new) stands out in lighthouse fashion for a $25 wine. If you like oak in full-
bodied reds, this is worth a look. Screwcap. 14.5% alc. **Rating** 89 **To** 2034 $25

Governor Robe Selection

Waterhouse Range Vineyards, Lot 11, Old Naracoorte Road, Robe, SA 5276
Region Limestone Coast
T (08) 8768 2083 **www**.governorrobe.com.au **Open** At The Attic House, Robe
Winemaker Cape Jaffa Wines (Nigel Westblade) **Est.** 1998 **Dozens** 1500 **Vyds** 57ha
Bill and Mick Quinlan-Watson, supported by a group of investors, began the development of
Waterhouse Range Vineyards in 1995, planting 15ha of vines, with further plantings over the
following few years lifting the total area to just under 60ha. The majority of the grapes are
sold. The new business name comes from the third Governor of SA, Frederick Holt Robe,
who in 1845 selected the Robe site for a port and personally put in the first survey peg.

Pinot Noir 2015 This has unequivocal varietal character, and equally good
balance, line and length. Dark cherry/berry flavours dance across the palate,
shedding notes of spice. Screwcap. 13% alc. **Rating** 93 **To** 2025 $20

Pinot Noir 2016 Rating 89 **To** 2028 $20

Grace Farm ★★★★★

741 Cowaramup Bay Road, Gracetown, WA 6285 **Region** Margaret River
T (08) 9384 4995 **www**.gracefarm.com.au **Open** By appt
Winemaker Jonathan Mettam **Est.** 2006 **Dozens** 3000 **Vyds** 8.17ha

Situated in the Wilyabrup district, Grace Farm is the small, family-owned vineyard of Elizabeth and John Mair, taking its name from the nearby coastal hamlet of Gracetown. Situated beside picturesque natural forest, the vineyard is planted to cabernet sauvignon, chardonnay, sauvignon blanc and semillon. Viticulturist Tim Quinlan conducts tastings (by appointment), explaining Grace Farm's sustainable viticultural practices.

ŸŸŸŸŸ **Margaret River Cabernet Sauvignon 2016** In fantastic form. This wine is beautifully fruited and deliciously smooth, its heart of blackcurrant wrapped in licorice, creamy vanilla and violets. Gum-leaf notes add lift while tannin adds a bit of scaffolding. Length is impressive. Everything here is in alignment. Screwcap. 14% alc. **Rating** 95 **To** 2036 $30 CM ✪
Reserve Margaret River Cabernet Sauvignon 2015 Closed and brooding but with ample fruit, tannin, texture and length. An archetype of the cellaring red. Balance is one of its main virtues, but so too is a weight of pure, ripe flavour. Time will be rewarded. Screwcap. 14% alc. **Rating** 95 **To** 2040 $60 CM

ŸŸŸŸŸ **Margaret River Chardonnay 2016 Rating** 93 **To** 2024 $35 CM

Grampians Estate ★★★★★

1477 Western Highway, Great Western, Vic 3377 **Region** Grampians
T (03) 5354 6245 **www**.grampiansestate.com.au **Open** 7 days 10–5
Winemaker Andrew Davey, Don Rowe **Est.** 1989 **Dozens** 2000 **Vyds** 8ha

Graziers Sarah and Tom Guthrie began their diversification into wine in 1989, but their core business continues to be fat lamb and wool production. They have acquired the Garden Gully winery at Great Western, giving them a cellar door and a vineyard with 140-year-old shiraz and 80-plus-year-old riesling. Grampians Estate was Champion Small Winery of Show at the Australian Small Winemakers Show '17, after collecting four gold and three silver medals. Exports to Singapore and China.

ŸŸŸŸŸ **Streeton Reserve Shiraz 2015** Bright fruit and spice come through loud and clear, while a savoury thread takes over on the palate to give this a little more complexity. Don't be fooled by its medium weight – it has a presence. Refreshing acidity in the mix, defined tannins and a promise of longevity, yet rather enticing now. Screwcap. 13.5% alc. **Rating** 95 **To** 2035 $75 JF
GST Grenache Shiraz Tempranillo 2016 A 57/27/16% blend. This manages to capture the brightness of fruit with grenache in the lead and yet keeps a savoury profile. Al dente tannins, plenty of spice, a medium-bodied palate and a lot to like. Screwcap. 14% alc. **Rating** 95 **To** 2023 $28 JF ✪

ŸŸŸŸŸ **Mafeking Shiraz 2016 Rating** 92 **To** 2028 $25 JF ✪
Rutherford Sparkling Shiraz 2014 Rating 92 $35 JF
Grenache 2016 Rating 91 **To** 2022 $25 JF

Granite Hills ★★★★★

1481 Burke and Wills Track, Baynton, Vic 3444 **Region** Macedon Ranges
T (03) 5423 7273 **www**.granitehills.com.au **Open** 7 days 11–6
Winemaker Llew Knight, Ian Gunter **Est.** 1970 **Dozens** 5000 **Vyds** 12.5ha

Granite Hills is one of the enduring classics, pioneering the successful growing of riesling and shiraz in an uncompromisingly cool climate. It is based on riesling, chardonnay, shiraz, cabernet sauvignon, cabernet franc, merlot and pinot noir (the last also used in its sparkling wine). The rieslings age superbly, and the Shiraz was the forerunner of the cool-climate school in Australia. Exports to Japan and China.

ΨΨΨΨΨ **Knight Macedon Ranges Riesling 2016** This wine and Crawford River are the only mainland rieslings to stand up to the best Tasmanian examples. The purity, drive and intensity when young isn't everyone's cup of tea (it is mine), but repays tenfold if held for 5–15 years, when hedonistic flavours and mouthfeel surge through to the finish. Screwcap. 13% alc. **Rating** 95 **To** 2031 $25
Knight Macedon Ranges Pinot Noir 2013 Remarkable deep but clear crimson-purple; amazing given its age. Dark cherry and plum varietal fruit pierces the bouquet with authority, repeating its message on the long palate. This is still developing, with years left before it reaches maturity, and even more years on a picture-perfect palate. Screwcap. 13.5% alc. **Rating** 95 **To** 2033 $30 ○
Knight Macedon Ranges Gruner Veltliner 2016 The first gruner veltliner from the estate, only 30 dozen made. Llew Knight says it is showing much promise, and he is right. It has character to burn, with spicy/white pepper aromas that carry through onto a palate with topnotch attitude and length. Definitely watch this space. Screwcap. 13% alc. **Rating** 94 **To** 2031 $35
Knight Macedon Ranges Shiraz 2012 The youthful colour earmarks a classic cool-climate shiraz with spice and black pepper sprinkled through the blackberry and black cherry fruits. Will coast serenely through the coming decades, its best yet to come. Screwcap. 14.5% alc. **Rating** 94 **To** 2037 $35

ΨΨΨΨΨ **Knight Macedon Ranges Chardonnay 2014** **Rating** 92 **To** 2023 $30

Grant Burge ★★★★★

279 Krondorf Road, Barossa Valley, SA 5352 **Region** Barossa Valley
T (08) 8563 7675 **www**.grantburgewines.com.au **Open** 7 days 10–5
Winemaker Craig Stansborough **Est.** 1988 **Dozens** 400 000
Grant and Helen Burge established their eponymous business in 1988. It grew into one of the largest family-owned wine operations in the valley. In February 2015, Accolade Wines announced it had acquired the brand and its historic Krondorf Winery. The 356ha of vineyards remain in family ownership, and will continue to supply premium grapes to the Accolade-owned business. Exports to all major markets.

ΨΨΨΨΨ **Meshach 2012** The 22nd release of Meshach coincides with the great Barossa Valley vintage of '12. A wine of the highest quality in the Olympian class of Barossan shiraz: seamless, calmly powerful and perfectly balanced. Black fruits dominate, but this is no one-dimensional power play, with hints of licorice, bitter chocolate and graphite. The tannins and oak contributions are perfectly placed and paced. Screwcap. 14% alc. **Rating** 98 **To** 2042 $175 ○

ΨΨΨΨΨ **Balthasar Eden Valley Shiraz 2015** Wow, the colour of Dior Sauvage nail polish – a deep inky red. The fruit profile is all wild berries and black plums dusted in cocoa. Velvety-smooth tannins glide across the full-bodied palate, and the oak (French, 44% new; wine aged 18 months) is superbly integrated. Great definition and poise. Diam. 14% alc. **Rating** 95 **To** 2030 $44 JF
Filsell Old Vine Barossa Shiraz 2016 A ball of concentration, from the black fruit flavours, chocolate, licorice and tar on the full-bodied palate to the integrated oak – 21 months in French and American (30% new). Ample tannins, too, so this will reward the patient, yet with a suppleness that makes it approachable in its youth. Screwcap. 14% alc. **Rating** 94 **To** 2036 $44 JF

ΨΨΨΨΨ **Summers Chardonnay 2017** **Rating** 93 **To** 2024 $27 JF ○
5th Generation Barossa Shiraz 2016 **Rating** 93 **To** 2023 $20 JF ○
The Holy Trinity Barossa Grenache Shiraz Mourvedre 2014 **Rating** 93 **To** 2024 $44 JF
Thorn Eden Valley Riesling 2017 **Rating** 91 **To** 2025 $27 JF
Miamba Barossa Shiraz 2016 **Rating** 91 **To** 2028 $27 JF
Cameron Vale Cabernet Sauvignon 2016 **Rating** 90 **To** 2026 $27 JF
Shadrach 2011 **Rating** 90 **To** 2021 $92 JF

Green Door Wines ★★★★☆

1112 Henty Road, Henty, WA 6236 **Region** Geographe
T 0439 511 652 **www**.greendoorwines.com.au **Open** Thurs–Sun 11–4.30
Winemaker Ashley Keeffe, Vanessa Carson **Est.** 2007 **Dozens** 1000 **Vyds** 4ha
Ashley and Kathryn Keeffe purchased what was a rundown vineyard in 2006. With a combination of new and existing vines, there are now 1ha of fiano and mourvedre, 0.75ha of grenache, 0.5ha of verdelho and tempranillo and 0.25ha of shiraz. The wines are made in a small onsite winery using a range of winemaking methods, including the use of amphora pots.

♀♀♀♀♀ **Amphora Geographe Grenache 2016** It's a triumph of a wine. It has impact, nuance and perfume, and scores high on the charm scale. It's bursting with redcurrants, but has keen savoury/spicy edges too. Firm, fruit-drenched tannin steps you through the finish. Screwcap. 14% alc. **Rating** 95 **To** 2024 $35 CM ✪
Amphora Geographe Tempranillo 2016 More bass than treble, in a good way. This tempranillo is not to be messed with. It's stern and tannic, minerally almost, with rust and licorice flavours mingling with the core of redcurrant. Black coffee notes add to the dark, broody impression. Impact without overt alcohol. Screwcap. 14% alc. **Rating** 94 **To** 2025 $35 CM

♀♀♀♀♀ **Geographe Fiano 2017 Rating** 92 **To** 2020 $25 CM ✪
Spanish Steps Geographe Grenache Shiraz Mourvedre 2016 Rating 91 **To** 2023 $20 CM ✪

Greenstone Vineyards ★★★★★

179 Glenview Road, Yarra Glen, Vic 3775 **Region** Yarra Valley/Heathcote
T (03) 9730 1022 **www**.greenstonevineyards.com.au **Open** Thurs–Mon 10–5
Winemaker Travis Bush, Sam Atherton **Est.** 2003 **Dozens** 7500 **Vyds** 45ha
Until 2014, Greenstone Vineyards was owned by three partners who resided in the UK, Italy and Australia respectively. After protracted (but unpublicised) discussions, the partners sold the property (a little over 20ha of vineyard and 20ha of bare land) to a private Chinese investor. It was, and is, a vineyard of very high quality, planted to shiraz (17ha), sangiovese (2.8ha), mataro (0.5ha) and colorino (0.1ha). Soon after the change of ownership, the investor also purchased the Sticks winery and its surrounding estate vineyards. Exports to China.

♀♀♀♀♀ **Estate Series Yarra Valley Sauvignon Blanc 2017** A pristine white wine with form, structure and length. The fruit looks out at the world with a cool, steely stare, full of intensity, searing impressively onwards. It's an incredibly particular wine; balance is its middle name. Screwcap. 12.7% alc. **Rating** 95 **To** 2021 $25 CM ✪
Estate Series Heathcote Shiraz 2015 The price is almost into double-take territory. You get volume and complexity, the finish then an example of finesse. It tastes of blue and black berries, uses reduction to its advantage, shows clove, leather and wood smoke, and pushes towards a sure-footed conclusion. There's no real reason to wait, the oak just integrated now, but it will certainly age well. Screwcap. 14.2% alc. **Rating** 95 **To** 2027 $28 CM ✪
Estate Series Yarra Valley Chardonnay 2016 This is quality with a blasé vibe to it. It's both deep-flavoured and (highly) textural, yet doesn't seem over-the-top; it feels as though it's not really trying at all. Nougat, white peach, hay, cedar wood and citrus – before you know it, it's charmed your socks off. Screwcap. 12.7% alc. **Rating** 94 **To** 2023 $27 CM ✪
Estate Series Yarra Valley Pinot Noir 2016 A pinot noir of depth, structure and class. Cherries macerated in dry spices, autumn leaves infused with fennel, orange blossom notes, a rake of chalky tannin. The value speaks for itself. Screwcap. 13% alc. **Rating** 94 **To** 2024 $30 CM ✪
Reserve Heathcote Shiraz 2015 This shiraz seems determined, on a scale from 1 to 10, to take things to 11. It's bold with fruit from the outset, all redcurrant and sweet plum, though almost as soon as it takes flight a crush of creamy, coffeed oak and associated spices rush in. It's a heady display, egged on by mint

and peppercorn, but the superfine tannin does a deft job tapping it all into line. Screwcap. 14.5% alc. **Rating** 94 **To** 2032 $50 CM

Estate Series Heathcote Sangiovese 2014 Balance and length: easy to say, hard to achieve. This wine nails it. Savoury to the gills, flowing, spicy, studded with saltbush and cloves, tannic but not in a halting way. Perfectly crafted red wine, lightish but lingering. Screwcap. 14% alc. **Rating** 94 **To** 2025 $28 CM ✪

♀♀♀♀♀ **Yarra Valley Methode Traditionnelle 2012** Rating 93 $40 CM

Greenway Wines ★★★★

350 Wollombi Road, Broke, NSW 2330 **Region** Hunter Valley
T 0418 164 382 **www**.greenwaywines.com.au **Open** W'ends 10–5 or by appt
Winemaker Michael McManus, Daniel Binet **Est.** 2009 **Dozens** 450 **Vyds** 6.5ha
John Marinovich and Anne Greenway purchased the vineyard in 2009 after many years of dreaming about becoming vignerons. It had been planted in 1999, with 2ha of merlot, the remainder shiraz and a little gewurztraminer. They said, 'We were not prepared for how beautiful our little vineyard would be. It's bordered by the foothills of the Brokenback mountains on one side, and skirted by Wollombi Brook on the other.'

♀♀♀♀♀ **Hunter Valley Pinot Grigio 2017** The pink colour attests to skin contact pre-pressing and fermentation. The scented, complex bouquet signals the mix of wild strawberries, Granny Smith apple, citrus zest and spice that all run through a long, fruity, yet dry, palate. Good stuff – pinot grigio from a warm climate such as this shouldn't be so good. Screwcap. 12% alc. **Rating** 92 **To** 2019 $26

Favoloso Hunter Valley Fiano 2016 Fresh-cut Granny Smith apple aromas lead into a clean, vibrantly fresh palate with tactile acidity that seems to be natural; white peach and lemon citrus join in for the chorus. A sensible price, too. The variety comes from southern Italy and Sicily, so it's a natural choice for the Hunter Valley. Screwcap. 12% alc. **Rating** 92 **To** 2022 $20 ✪

Grey-Smith Wines ★★★

8 Helen Road, Coonawarra, SA 5263 **Region** Coonawarra
T 0429 499 355 **www**.grey-smith.com.au **Open** By appt
Winemaker Ulrich Grey-Smith **Est.** 2012 **Dozens** 160
Ulrich Grey-Smith travelled wine roads near and far for decades before establishing his business. The original foundation for his career was the completion of the bachelor degree in oenology at Roseworthy Agricultural College (1987–90). His contibutions go well beyond the small amount of sparkling wine he makes – he works as a consultant and freelance winemaker, and for many years was executive officer and secretary of the Limestone Coast Grape & Wine Council. He also helped run the annual Limestone Coast Wine Show, crossing over to the other side of the fence as a judge.

♀♀♀♀ **Blanc de Blancs NV** 4 years on lees, no dosage. Straight-shooting style. Both honeyed and fresh with white peach and toast notes, contributing to a wine of surprising substance in flavour and texture. Crown seal. 12% alc. **Rating** 89 $45 CM

Groom ★★★★☆

28 Langmeil Road, Tanunda, SA 5352 (postal) **Region** Barossa Valley
T (08) 8563 1101 **www**.groomwines.com **Open** Not
Winemaker Daryl Groom **Est.** 1997 **Dozens** 1800 **Vyds** 27.8ha
The full name of the business is Marschall Groom Cellars, a venture owned by David and Jeanette Marschall and their six children, and Daryl and Lisa Groom and their four children. Daryl was a highly regarded winemaker at Penfolds before he moved to Geyser Peak in California. Years of discussion between the families resulted in the purchase of a 35ha block of bare land adjacent to Penfolds' 130-year-old Kalimna vineyard. Shiraz was planted in 1997, giving its first vintage in '99. The next acquisition was an 8ha vineyard at Lenswood in the

Adelaide Hills, planted to sauvignon blanc. In 2000, 3.2ha of zinfandel was also planted on the Kalimna bush block. Exports to the US, Canada, Hong Kong, Taiwan and China.

🍷🍷🍷🍷🍷 **Barossa Valley Shiraz 2016** Excellent dark purple-crimson; most appealing and easy to drink, thanks in part to its core of good fruit spiced with juniper, licorice and soy sauce with a whiff of bourbon and vanillan oak. A slinky, full-bodied palate with firm, sweet tannins and a persistent finish. This will easily age for a decade. Cork. 13.8% alc. **Rating** 95 **To** 2030 $50 JF

🍷🍷🍷🍷🍷 **Adelaide Hills Sauvignon Blanc 2017 Rating** 93 **To** 2019 $24 JF ✪

Grosset ★★★★★

King Street, Auburn, SA 5451 **Region** Clare Valley
T 1800 088 223 **www**.grosset.com.au **Open** 10–5 Wed–Sun (Spring)
Winemaker Jeffrey Grosset, Brent Treloar **Est.** 1981 **Dozens** 11 000 **Vyds** 22.2ha
Jeffrey Grosset wears the unchallenged mantle of Australia's foremost riesling maker. Grosset's pre-eminence is recognised both domestically and internationally; however, he merits equal recognition for the other wines in his portfolio: semillon sauvignon blanc from Clare Valley/Adelaide Hills, chardonnay and pinot noir from the Adelaide Hills, and Gaia, a Bordeaux blend from the Clare Valley. These are all benchmarks. His quietly spoken manner conceals a steely will. Trial plantings (2ha) of fiano, aglianico, nero d'Avola and petit verdot suggest some new wines may be gestating. Awarded Best value winery in the *Wine Companion* 2017. Exports to all major markets.

🍷🍷🍷🍷🍷 **Polish Hill Clare Valley Riesling 2017** This is a ravishing riesling of the highest order, X-factor multiplied. Throw up any part (flesh, juice, skin, pith) of lime or lemons of any kind, add ethereal acidity and marvel at the elegance and length of the palate. Jeffrey Grosset is the undisputed king of the Clare Valley. Screwcap. 12.7% alc. **Rating** 98 **To** 2042 $55 ✪
Alea Clare Valley Riesling 2017 So all you do is stop the fermentation, leaving a dialled-cup number of g/l of residual sugar? No, this is truly rocket science with all the measurable components of the fermenting juice, in turn of the highest quality. A divine nectar of not quite dry, not quite sweet wine. Its circle of pure riesling flavours run alongside mouthwatering acidity. In its style, it is perfection. Screwcap. 12% alc. **Rating** 97 **To** 2037 $36 ✪

🍷🍷🍷🍷🍷 **Nereus 2015** Made from estate-grown shiraz with a small amount of nero d'Avola. It has a bright crimson-purple hue, the fragrance a mix of exotic spices and perfumes, the palate a juicy mix of red and darker fruits, the tannins positive, the finish long and balanced. Screwcap. 13.7% alc. **Rating** 96 **To** 2030 $50 ✪
Gaia 2015 Classic cabernet (although 20% franc) with ripe black fruit flecked with herbs and hints of leaf. Tannins are fine and slightly chalky, acidity prominent but adding to the length and refreshment of this wine. 40% new oak was easily soaked up by the fruit and it's looking towards a long future. Screwcap. 13.5% alc. **Rating** 96 **To** 2032 $83 DB
Springvale Clare Valley Riesling 2017 Made by a winemaker who is never satisfied with the status quo and always seeks to look over the horizon. In a year such as this, and with all Grosset's other assets, the wine could hardly fail, and it doesn't. Screwcap. 12.7% alc. **Rating** 95 **To** 2032 $40
Semillon Sauvignon Blanc 2017 Lemony aromas and flavours plus texture and mouthfeel, from semillon, and the snappy snow pea and nettle thrust of sauvignon blanc. It glides along the palate without any dips or troughs and lingers beautifully with a minerally tang on the finish. Screwcap. 12.5% alc. **Rating** 94 **To** 2022 $35 SC
Apiana 2017 Grosset reveals his experiences with the two fiano clones he has worked with, first VCR3 from Chalmers (planted '07), the second the more recent Savio clone. 'Analytically,' he says, 'the two are chalk and cheese.' This wine has the tactile quality of fiano, and keeps citrus rind in the game. Screwcap. 12.5% alc. **Rating** 94 **To** 2021 $40

Grove Estate Wines

4100 Murringo Road, Young, NSW 2594 **Region** Hilltops
T (02) 6382 6999 www.groveestate.com.au **Open** 7 days 9–4.30
Winemaker Brian Mullany, Tim Kirk, Bryan Martin **Est.** 1989 **Dozens** 4000 **Vyds** 46ha
Grove Estate vineyard was re-established in 1989 by Brian and Suellen Mullany on the site
where grapes were first planted in Lambing Flat (Young) in 1861. One of the pickers' huts
has been refurbished as the cellar door. Further plantings were made in 1998 on their Bit O'
Heaven vineyard, the two sites with vastly different soils. The premium wines are made at
Clonakilla by Tim Kirk and Bryan Martin. Exports to China.

PPPPP The Cellar Block Hilltops Shiraz Viognier 2016 Co-fermentation of
2% viognier has added an aroma and flavour dimension to a wine that isn't more
than medium-bodied, but has excellent intensity and attitude. There is a spicy,
grainy texture to the black cherry/berry fruits of the palate, French oak adding
a neat touch. A very good vintage also helped. Screwcap. 13.5% alc. **Rating** 95
To 2036 $35 ✪

The Italian Hilltops Nebbiolo Sangiovese Barbera 2016 An elegant
medium-bodied wine that is an established leader of the Grove brand most years.
Extended maceration (50 days) has worked well, and maturation in used French
oak was on the money. The flavours are of spicy red berries, the tannins posing no
threat. Screwcap. 14% alc. **Rating** 94 To 2029 $25 ✪

Sommita Hilltops Nebbiolo 2016 Standing on its own, the power of nebbiolo
comes through strongly. Sour and black cherries, with taut tannins the referee, seek
dominance but neither has a clear-cut victory. This should cellar very well indeed.
Screwcap. 14.5% alc. **Rating** 94 To 2036 $45

Hilltops Late Harvest Viognier 2016 Extremely luscious and complex, with
dried apricots, coconut and buttered brioche with honey. A wine with genuine
style and interest. 375ml. Screwcap. 11% alc. **Rating** 94 To 2023 $20 ✪

PPPPP Single Vineyard Hilltops Semillon 2017 Rating 92 To 2027 $25 ✪
The Partners Cabernet Sauvignon 2015 Rating 92 To 2029 $25 ✪

Gundog Estate   ★★★★★

101 McDonalds Road, Pokolbin, NSW 2320 **Region** Hunter Valley
T (02) 4998 6873 www.gundogestate.com.au **Open** 7 days 10–5
Winemaker Matthew Burton **Est.** 2006 **Dozens** 8000 **Vyds** 5ha
Matt Burton makes four different Hunter semillons, and shiraz from the Hunter Valley,
Murrumbateman and Hilltops. He and wife Renee run the cellar door from the historic
Pokolbin schoolhouse, next to the old Rosemount/Hungerford Hill building on McDonalds
Road. The Burton McMahon wines are a collaboration between Matt Burton and Dylan
McMahon of Seville Estate and focus on the Yarra Valley. In 2016 Gundog opened a second
cellar door at 42 Cork Street, Gundaroo (Thurs–Sun 10–5). Exports to the UK.

PPPPP Canberra District Riesling 2017 The bouquet is having a sleep, the palate on
guard duty, but it needn't have bothered. This has fantastic energy, proportion and
length, finishing with a pH of 2.94 and titratable acidity of 7.3g/l. Its intensity and
varietal purity underline Canberra District's ability to grow riesling of the highest
possible quality. Screwcap. 12% alc. **Rating** 96 To 2037 $30 ✪

Burton McMahon D'Aloisio's Vineyard Chardonnay 2017 Pale, bright
straw-green; faintly nutty/toasty oak joins white peach and green apple on the
bouquet, the palate a reprise before expanding dramatically on the finish. A sorbet-
like aftertaste. Upper Yarra in fine voice. Screwcap. 13% alc. **Rating** 96 To 2028
$36 ✪

Hunter's Semillon 2017 Has an extra layer of ripe lemon and spicy talc on the
bouquet and palate, which is almost chewy it is so juicy. Despite this, it has a clear,
long and crisp finish. Screwcap. 11% alc. **Rating** 95 To 2032 $30 ✪

The Chase Hunter Valley Semillon 2017 Only 450–500l/t of juice is vinified
for this label. There is zest and drive on the palate and through to the finish, the

freshness possibly due to its low pH. Screwcap. 10.5% alc. **Rating** 95 **To** 2032 $30 ✪

Burton McMahon George's Vineyard Chardonnay 2017 The bouquet and palate sing from the same first page. While its Upper Yarra provenance is not in doubt, there is an air of confidence as it matches a touch of reduction against white peach fruit. Screwcap. 13% alc. **Rating** 95 **To** 2027 $36 ✪

Burton McMahon George's Vineyard Pinot Noir 2017 Bright colour; perfectly captures the freshness and brightness of the '17 vintage in the Yarra Valley. Juicy cherry plum up front, given context by the savoury whole-bunch finish. Screwcap. 13.6% alc. **Rating** 95 **To** 2025 $40

Burton McMahon Syme on Yarra Vineyard Pinot Noir 2017 Exuberantly flaunts the power and depth of the Syme vineyard fruit. I am very familiar with this vineyard in the Upper Yarra, and if you are fond of pinot noirs for the cellar, this is for you. Screwcap. 13.6% alc. **Rating** 95 **To** 2027 $40

Canberra District Shiraz 2016 A rich, medium to full-bodied shiraz with a supple mouthfeel, French oak contributes to the flavour of the black cherry core, tannins under commendably strict control. Screwcap. 14.5% alc. **Rating** 95 **To** 2031 $40

Marksman's Canberra District Shiraz 2016 The first vintage without viognier. Dark crimson, fragrant and elegant with bramble and spice. Tightly corseted oak tannins add structure and focus. It displays both varietal and regional integrity and improves noticeably as it sits in the glass. Screwcap. 14.5% alc. **Rating** 95 **To** 2031 $60 DB

Canberra District Rose 2017 While dry, it has a rose bowl of red, black and sour cherry flavours, with excellent length and focus. Screwcap. 13.5% alc. **Rating** 94 **To** 2022 $30 ✪

ᵀᵀᵀᵀᵀ **Hilltops Shiraz 2016** Rating 93 To 2031 $35 DB
Indomitus Rosa 2017 Rating 92 To 2022 $40 SC
Indomitus Albus Hunter Valley Semillon 2017 Rating 91 To 2027 $40 SC

Guthrie Wines   ★★★★★

661 Torrens Valley Road, Gumeracha, SA 5253 **Region** Adelaide Hills
T 0413 332 083 **www**.guthriewines.com.au **Open** By appt
Winemaker Hugh Guthrie **Est.** 2012 **Dozens** 2000
Growing up on his family's farm in the Adelaide Hills, Hugh Guthrie developed an early interest in the wines and vineyards of the region. He completed a Masters of Oenology at the University of Adelaide before working in wineries around Australia and abroad. Most recently he was a winemaker at The Lane Vineyard, winner of many awards for its wines. Wife Sarah works as an anaesthetist and mother, already a full-time job, though she looks after the business side of Guthrie Wines in her spare time. In 2014 Hugh held his breath, jumped, quit his day job, and became their full-time winemaker.

ᵀᵀᵀᵀᵀ **Clones Chardonnay 2017** Bernard (75, 76 and 95), Entav and I10V1 grapes hand-picked from neighbouring vineyards in Birdwood, whole-bunch pressed, wild-fermented in French oak (30% new), partial mlf, matured for 8 months. A pretty smart chardonnay is the outcome, the tension between the citrus components, stone fruit, oak and acidity maintained from start to finish. Born to rule for 20+ years. Screwcap. 13% alc. **Rating** 96 **To** 2037 $27 ✪

Sleepless Nights Pinot Rose 2017 50% fermented in tank, 50% in used puncheons, blended and bottled after 3 months. A scented, flowery bouquet points the way like a hound dog to the delicate, pure and totally delicious strawberry palate, the long finish just so. Screwcap. 12.5% alc. **Rating** 96 **To** 2020 $22 ✪

The Snare Syrah 2017 Wild-fermented with 40% whole bunches, left on skins for 60 days, matured for 8 months in used French hogsheads. The Guthrie vinification produces red wines that are distinctive, yet not extractive. There is a softness, a silky texture, and the tannins are already fully aged. The flavours reflect the cool Adelaide Hills and the whole-bunch stalky element. It's a strangely compelling wine. Screwcap. 13% alc. **Rating** 95 **To** 2032 $30 ✪

ŶŶŶŶ♀ Montepulciano 2015 Rating 91 To 2030 $25
Wild Gruner 2017 Rating 90 To 2027 $25
Ashton Pinot Noir 2017 Rating 90 To 2023 $30

Haan Wines   ★★★★

148 Siegersdorf Road, Tanunda, SA 5352 **Region** Barossa Valley
T (08) 8562 4590 www.haanwines.com.au **Open** Not
Winemaker Sarah Siddons (Contract) **Est.** 1993 **Dozens** 3500 **Vyds** 16.3ha
Hans and Fransien Haan established their business in 1993 when they acquired a vineyard
near Tanunda. The main plantings are shiraz (5.3ha), merlot (3.4ha), cabernet sauvignon (3ha),
viognier (2.4ha) and cabernet franc (1ha), with some malbec, petit verdot and semillon (0.4ha
each). Oak undoubtedly plays a role in the shaping of the wines, but it is perfectly integrated,
and the wines have the fruit weight to it. Exports to Switzerland, the Czech Republic, China
and other markets.

ŶŶŶŶ♀ **Merlot Prestige 2014** A cavalcade of ripe plum flavours, whisked with some
saltbush, tea, mint and tomato leaf, layer the cheeks. Long and pliant, the tannins
are detailed and briny, assuaging the rather high alcohol (15%) and folding it
beneath seams of classy French vanillan oak. Cork. **Rating** 93 **To** 2024 $65 NG
Wilhelmus 2014 A classic straitlaced Bordeaux blend, albeit with the sunny
disposition of the Barossa thrown into the mix. Plum, currant, spearmint and
bitter chocolate are all present, drawn across a bow of edgy acidity and French oak
tannins. Cork. 15% alc. **Rating** 91 **To** 2029 $65 NG
Barossa Valley Shiraz Cabernet Sauvignon 2015 Quintessentially Barossan,
with fruitcake spice milling about a dense palate of currant, bitter chocolate,
damson plum and mint. The tannins are terse and stiff-upper-lipped, helping to
mitigate the high alcohol. Screwcap. 15.5% alc. **Rating** 90 **To** 2023 $25 NG

ŶŶŶŶ **Barossa Valley Merlot Cabernet Franc 2015** Rating 89 To 2023 $25 NG

Hahndorf Hill Winery   ★★★★★

38 Pain Road, Hahndorf, SA 5245 **Region** Adelaide Hills
T (08) 8388 7512 www.hahndorfhillwinery.com.au **Open** 7 days 10–5
Winemaker Larry Jacobs **Est.** 2002 **Dozens** 6000 **Vyds** 6.5ha
Larry Jacobs and Marc Dobson, both originally from South Africa, purchased Hahndorf Hill
Winery in 2002. Before migrating, Larry had given up a career in intensive care medicine in
1988 when he bought an abandoned property in Stellenbosch, and established the near-iconic
Mulderbosch Wines. It was purchased at the end of '96, and the pair eventually found their
way to Australia and Hahndorf Hill. In 2006, their investment in the winery and cellar door
was rewarded by induction into the South Australian Great Tourism Hall of Fame. In '07 they
began converting the vineyard to biodynamic status, and they were among the first movers
in implementing a carbon offset program. They imported three clones of gruner veltliner
from Austria, and another variety, St Laurent. In '16 the winery was awarded Best Producer
of Show <100t at the Adelaide Hills Wine Show, and their wines, too, have had trophy and
medal success. Exports to the UK, Singapore, Japan and China.

ŶŶŶŶ♀ **GRU Adelaide Hills Gruner Veltliner 2017** Gold medal at the Australian
Alternative Varieties Wine Show '17. The wine places as much emphasis on texture
and structure as flavour, albeit there is no shortage of citrus, wild herb, apple
and white pepper here. The finish emphasises all that has gone before. Screwcap.
13% alc. **Rating** 96 **To** 2026 $29 ✪
GRU 2 Adelaide Hills Gruner Veltliner 2015 Rich, seductive, textural and
persistent. It's one of those rare white wines that makes you lean back in your
chair and marvel. Shaking your head, but smiling. It's flinty, candied, smoky and
floral. White pepper; that as well. Bring out the white linen, reach for the best
glassware, tell the chef the pressure's on, or off, depending on how you want to
play it. Screwcap. 13% alc. **Rating** 96 **To** 2023 $45 CM ✪

Adelaide Hills Pinot Grigio 2017 Trophy at the Australian Cool Climate Wine Show '17. Larry Jacobs treats all his wines seriously, and this is a prime example. It is pure and precise, with flavour and mouthfeel from a bone-dry foundation, green apple, pear and cleansing acidity doing the heavy lifting. Will accompany anything from the sea, especially if raw or served cold. Screwcap. 12.5% alc. **Rating** 95 To 2020 $25 ✪

White Mischief Adelaide Hills Gruner Veltliner 2017 Gold medals at the Australian Small Winemakers and Rutherglen Wine shows '17. A higher toned bouquet (with a sprinkle of white pepper) is followed by a tightly focused fruit line on the palate, with some savoury nuances, but more lemon and green apple than GRU. Screwcap. 13% alc. **Rating** 95 To 2025 $24 ✪

Adelaide Hills Shiraz 2015 This is a super-elegant wine, sailing with red cherry, spice, polished tannins and a rudder of French oak. Blue-gold Sydney International Wine Competition '18. Screwcap. 14% alc. **Rating** 95 To 2035 $40

Adelaide Hills Rose 2017 45% pinot noir, 28% merlot and 27% trollinger. A wildflower and spice bouquet is followed by a palate with wonderful drive and persistence through the bone-dry finish and aftertaste. A sophisticated rose reflecting assured winemaking, and an uncompromising quest for an unusual style. Screwcap. 12.5% alc. **Rating** 94 To 2020 $24 ✪

Blueblood Adelaide Hills Blaufrankisch 2015 On the one hand it's slatey and dry, on the other it's perfumed and fruit-expressive. It carries notes of anise, cedar wood and Italian herbs, and certainly has dry spice notes in abundance. It's not rich, indeed it's lightish, but it has presence. In short, it has a great deal to recommend it. Screwcap. 14% alc. **Rating** 94 To 2023 $45 CM

Green Angel Late Harvest Gruner Veltliner 2016 The vintage didn't produce botrytis, but did allow prolonged desiccation on the vine, increasing concentration and varietal character. It is very sweet (170g/l), but has an explosive build-up of white pepper and fresh ginger on the aftertaste. Screwcap. 10.5% alc. **Rating** 94 To 2026 $33

🍷🍷🍷🍷 **Adelaide Hills Sauvignon Blanc 2017** Rating 89 To 2018 $24
Zsa Zsa Zweigelt Nouveau 2017 Rating 89 $33
Compatriots 2015 Rating 89 To 2022 $35

Hamelin Bay   ★★★★★

McDonald Road, Karridale, WA 6288 **Region** Margaret River
T (08) 9758 6779 **www**.hbwines.com.au **Open** 7 days 10–5
Winemaker Richard Drake-Brockman **Est.** 1992 **Dozens** 8000 **Vyds** 23.5ha
Hamelin Bay was established by the Drake-Brockman family. Richard Drake-Brockman's great-grandmother, Grace Bussell, was famous for her courage when, in 1876, aged 16, she rescued survivors of a shipwreck not far from the mouth of the Margaret River. Richard's great-grandfather Frederick read about Grace's feat in Perth's press and rode 300km on horseback to meet her – they married in 1882. Frederick was known for his exploration of the Kimberley. The vineyard and winery are located close to the intersection of the Brockman and Bussell highways, named in honour of these pioneers. Exports to the UK, Canada, Malaysia, Singapore and China.

🍷🍷🍷🍷🍷 **Five Ashes Vineyard Margaret River Semillon Sauvignon Blanc 2017** Employs the standard Hamelin Bay unoaked protocol in the winery, the 51/49% blend delivering a wine with considerable drive and intensity, with semillon in the driver's seat. Each retaste simply adds to the intensity of the grassy/citrussy/gooseberry mix. The magic comes straight from the vineyard and the specific yeast selection. Screwcap. 12% alc. **Rating** 95 To 2024 $25 ✪

Five Ashes Vineyard Margaret River Chardonnay 2016 Hand-picked, 18.5% whole bunches, the balance destemmed and crushed, 70% wild yeast, 30% cultured, 10 months in French oak (22% new). A chardonnay that melds elegance with insistent power, purity with complexity. The approach to winemaking reflects a significant degree of reliance on the quality of the fruit, but not to the extent of leaving things to the will of Allah. Screwcap. 12.8% alc. Rating 95 To 2031 $30 ✪

Five Ashes Reserve Margaret River Cabernet Sauvignon 2013
85% cabernet sauvignon, 15% malbec. There is an attractive freshness to this otherwise rather dense and brooding style. Cherry liqueur, cassis, cedar and dark chocolate all throw their hats into the ring on the bouquet, and then continue to provide the flavour spectrum through the palate. At this stage it's impenetrable, but the quality is there; what's required is time for it all to unfold and show its best. Screwcap. 14% alc. Rating 94 To 2030 $49 SC

🍷🍷🍷🍷🍷 **Five Ashes Reserve Shiraz 2013** Rating 93 To 2025 $49 SC
Five Ashes Vineyard Cabernet Sauvignon 2013 Rating 92 To 2025 $32 SC

Hancock & Hancock ★★★★

210 Chalk Hill Road, McLaren Vale, SA 5171 **Region** McLaren Vale
T (02) 9433 3255 **Open** Not
Winemaker Larry Cherubino, Mike Brown **Est.** 2007 **Dozens** NFP **Vyds** 8.09ha
Industry doyen Chris Hancock and brother John returned to their family roots when they purchased the La Colline vineyard in 2007 and began Hancock & Hancock. Chris graduated as dux of the oenology degree at Roseworthy Agricultural College in 1963, taking up immediate employment with the Penfold family. In '76 he joined Rosemount Estate, and after the late Bob Oatley sold it to Southcorp, he stayed on with the business in the upper echelon of management. Bob went on to establish Robert Oatley Vineyards, of which Chris is today the deputy executive chairman. Unsurprisingly, Hancock & Hancock wines are distributed by Oatley Family Wine Merchants. Exports to the UK, Hong Kong and China.

🍷🍷🍷🍷🍷 **Home Vineyard Shiraz 2016** No doubting its provenance with all the dark plums, blackberries, chocolate and herbs the Vale can muster, placing it all on a full-bodied palate. Sweet oak and spice, the persimmon-like tannins need time to settle, although a juicy steak would help. Screwcap. 14% alc. Rating 91 To 2025 $23 JF✪

Home Vineyard Grenache Rose 2017 Enticing pale pastel orange-pink; smells of musk lollies, bubblegum, strawberries and crushed rosehips. Slippery texture and a sweet sensation with some warmth, almost a peppery note, on the finish. Screwcap. 13% alc. Rating 90 To 2018 $23 JF

Home Vineyard Cabernet Touriga 2015 Currants and cassis, lavender and freshly brewed lapsang souchong tea, a touch of bitter herbs and eucalyptus, even warm gravel. Medium-bodied, with depth, decent tannin structure and a freshness keeping it buoyant. Screwcap. 14% alc. Rating 90 To 2022 $23 JF

Handpicked Wines ★★★★★

50 Kensington Street, Chippendale, NSW 2008 **Region** Various
T (02) 9475 7888 **www.**handpickedwines.com.au **Open** Mon–Fri 11–10, w'ends 10–10
Winemaker Gary Baldwin, Peter Dillon **Est.** 2001 **Dozens** 100000 **Vyds** 83ha
Handpicked is part of DMG Fine Wines, a global operation with its head office in Australia. Its roots go back over 50 years to China and the vision of Ming Guang Dong, who built a successful broad-based business. His four children were educated in the UK, Australia and Singapore, and today they are all involved in DMG, with William Dong at the helm. Having worked with what became Handpicked Wines, William bought the business with the aim of creating great wines from great regions under one label. Today it makes wines in Italy, Chile, France and Spain, but the main arm is Australia, where Handpicked has vineyards in the Yarra Valley, the Mornington Peninsula and the Barossa Valley. It secured the services of Gary Baldwin as executive chief winemaker, and constructed a winery at the company's flagship Capella vineyard at Bittern on the Mornington Peninsula. In November 2014, Peter Dillon was successfully headhunted to assist Gary; Dillon has established his credentials as a winemaker of the highest quality. Exports to the US, Italy, the Philippines, South Korea, Cambodia, Vietnam, Japan, Hong Kong and China.

🍷🍷🍷🍷🍷 **Wombat Creek Vineyard Yarra Valley Chardonnay 2016** Wombat Creek vineyard is the highest in the Yarra Valley at 450m. This wine is whole-bunch pressed and fermented in French barriques (50% new), with partial mlf 12 months' maturation. The bouquet is very different from that of its siblings, possibility due to the greater use of oak. The palate is intense and long – lively grapefruit and white peach joining hands to propel the flavours through every corner of the mouth and through to the aftertaste. Screwcap. 13.5% alc. **Rating** 96 **To** 2026 $60 ✪

Capella Vineyard Mornington Peninsula Pinot Noir 2016 Hand-picked, open-fermented with twice-daily plunging, matured for 10 months in French barriques (40% new). Bright, clear purple-crimson; this is the outcome of infinite attention to detail, a great vintage and perfectly managed vinification. The bouquet is very expressive, with gently spiced red-fleshed plum fruit flowing through the long palate. Screwcap. 13% alc. **Rating** 96 **To** 2030 $80

No. 1 Shiraz 2013 A blend of small parcels of exceptional shiraz from the Pyrenees, Beechworth and Geelong. Black fruits (blackberry uppermost) are supported by fine-grained tannins and invest the palate with considerable drive. Cork. 14.3% alc. **Rating** 96 **To** 2033 $388

Capella Vineyard Mornington Peninsula Chardonnay 2016 Skilfully made in a vintage that ripened very quickly – not all succeeded as well as this. The flavours are dispensed smoothly and in an unhurried manner, allowing white peach and nectarine to lead the palate through to a long, supple and well balanced finish. Screwcap. 13% alc. **Rating** 95 **To** 2025 $60

Wombat Creek Vineyard Yarra Valley Pinot Noir 2016 Brilliant clear colour. 100% MV6 clone provides the structure underpinning the red berry and plum fruit of the elegant, long and intense palate. An exceptional outcome for the challenging vintage, helped by the altitude of this Upper Yarra vineyard. Screwcap. 13% alc. **Rating** 95 **To** 2026 $80

Collection Barossa Valley Grenache 2016 Mostly destemmed and open-fermented, a small portion with whole bunches, matured for 10 months in mostly used French oak. The fruit flavours are pure grenache, with the full expression of red fruits of all kinds joining together to sing in harmonic union. Lovely fresh grenache, best enjoyed now. Screwcap. 14.4% alc. **Rating** 95 **To** 2021 $70

Regional Selections Yarra Valley Chardonnay 2016 The early vintage in the Yarra Valley challenged everyone, and the decision to limit the amount of fermentation in oak to 9 months may have been dictated by the season, but has worked well here. The result is a juicy, fresh palate with a mix of grapefruit and stone fruit, citrussy acidity cleansing the finish. Screwcap. 12.5% alc. **Rating** 94 **To** 2023 $25 ✪

Collection Barossa Valley Shiraz 2016 Densely coloured and full-bodied. The regime in the winery doesn't point to over-extraction; the power of the blackberry, black cherry and licorice flavours comes from the vineyard. Will live for decades. Screwcap. 14.7% alc. **Rating** 94 **To** 2041 $70

🍷🍷🍷🍷🍷 **Regional Selections Coonawarra Cabernet Sauvignon 2015** **Rating** 93 **To** 2030 $25 ✪

Romance Was Born Yarra Valley Rose 2017 **Rating** 92 **To** 2020 $29

Regional Selections Yarra Valley Pinot Noir 2016 **Rating** 92 **To** 2022 $29

Hanging Rock Winery ★★★★★

88 Jim Road, Newham, Vic 3442 **Region** Macedon Ranges
T (03) 5427 0542 **www**.hangingrock.com.au **Open** 7 days 10–5
Winemaker Robert Ellis **Est.** 1983 **Dozens** 20 000 **Vyds** 14.5ha

The Macedon area has proved marginal in spots, and the Hanging Rock vineyards, with their lovely vista towards the Rock, are no exception. John Ellis thus elected to source additional grapes from various parts of Victoria to produce an interesting and diverse range of varietals at different price points. In 2011 John's children Ruth and Robert returned to the fold: Robert has an oenology degree from the University of Adelaide, since then working as a Flying Winemaker in Champagne, Burgundy, Oregon and Stellenbosch. Ruth has a degree in wine marketing from the University of Adelaide. Exports to the UK, the US and other major markets.

ŶŶŶŶŶ **Jim Jim Sauvignon Blanc 2017** It's varietal, intense, exudes style and finishes long. It's a brilliant sauvignon blanc. Passionfruit; the sweetness of fresh grass; wood smoke in the distance; slate-like notes as vapour trails. Screwcap. 12.9% alc. **Rating** 95 **To** 2022 $30 CM ✪

Jim Jim Pinot Noir 2014 Bright, light crimson, with clear varietal character from the opening whiff through to the finish. Vibrant red and purple fruits rise to expand on the back palate and aftertaste. Lovely pinot with years in front of it. Screwcap. 13.4% alc. **Rating** 95 **To** 2021 $50

Heathcote Shiraz 2015 A warm, concentrated red with blackberry, sandalwood, bitumen and roasted plum characters laid on the line. Oak (creamy vanillan) is at a high pitch, as is alcohol warmth, and there's no denying the impact of this wine. We're talking brutish intensity here. Screwcap. 15.3% alc. **Rating** 95 **To** 2040 $75 CM

Jim Jim Chardonnay 2016 In very good form. It slings confidently from start to finish, its steely flavours fleshed with white peach, ginger and pear, its sweet oak sitting absolutely hand-in-glove. The flinty finish is a nice parting touch. Screwcap. 13% alc. **Rating** 94 **To** 2026 $40 CM

Cuvee Ten Disgorged NV 60/40% pinot noir chardonnay. 15 years on lees in bottle. Complex, impactful and fresh all at once. Alive with fig, wholemeal croissants brushed with Vegemite, biscuits and toast; peach and pineapple or versions thereof sizzling throughout. It gives you everything it's got, but it's not without refinement. Diam. 12% alc. **Rating** 94 $50 CM

ŶŶŶŶŶ **The Jim Jim Three Riesling 2017 Rating** 93 **To** 2022 $30 CM
Cambrian Rise Heathcote Shiraz 2016 Rating 93 **To** 2032 $35 CM
Macedon Ranges Pinot Noir 2016 Rating 92 **To** 2026 $35 CM
Macedon Rose Brut NV Rating 91 $35 CM

Happs   ★★★★★

575 Commonage Road, Dunsborough, WA 6281 **Region** Margaret River
T (08) 9755 3300 **www**.happs.com.au **Open** 7 days 10–5
Winemaker Erl Happ, Mark Warren **Est.** 1978 **Dozens** 15 000 **Vyds** 35.2ha
One-time schoolteacher, potter and winemaker Erl Happ is the patriarch of a three-generation family. More than anything, Erl has been a creator and experimenter, building the self-designed winery from mudbrick, concrete form and timber, and making the first crusher. In 1994 he planted a new 30ha vineyard at Karridale to no less than 28 varieties, including some of the earliest plantings of tempranillo in Australia. The Three Hills label is made from varieties grown at this vineyard. Erl passed on to his son Myles his love of pottery, and Happs Pottery (onsite) now has four potters, including Myles. Exports to the US, Denmark, the Netherlands, Malaysia, the Philippines, Vietnam, Hong Kong, China and Japan.

ŶŶŶŶŶ **Three Hills Eva Marie 2016** The white Bordeaux blend of 56% semillon, 38% sauvignon blanc and 6% muscadelle is enriched by both the mouthfeel and flavour of barrel fermentation and maturation, although no details of vinification were supplied. Screwcap. 12.8% alc. **Rating** 95 **To** 2024 $30 ✪

Margaret River Chardonnay 2016 It's a combination of the climate and the decision to pick early that gives this wine its flinty Chablisesque flavours and mouthfeel. The flavours are in the grapefruit/bruised herb spectrum, the acidity seeming relatively high, although I'll bet it's not. Screwcap. 13% alc. **Rating** 95 **To** 2030 $24 ✪

Three Hills Margaret River Grenache Shiraz Mataro 2016 Bright, clear crimson-purple, and crisp, fresh and wonderfully juicy. I'm going to drink some of this tonight. Screwcap. 14.8% alc. **Rating** 95 **To** 2023 $30 ✪

Margaret River Cabernet Petit Verdot 2016 Brilliant crimson-purple, the wine has impeccable balance and focus, the flavours and textures of each variety permanently fused into each other. Blackcurrant, bay leaf and a touch of cedar run through to the smooth finish with fine-grained tannins. Screwcap. 14.2% alc. Rating 95 To 2036 $30 ✪

Three Hills Margaret River Chardonnay 2016 Light straw-green; fresh, elegant and long, with a fragrant bouquet and a light touch to the fruit. There's a gentle fusion of white-fleshed stone fruits, melon and citrus, French oak relegated to the back bench. Screwcap. 12.9% alc. Rating 94 To 2026 $45

ŶŶŶŶŶ **Margaret River Bone Dry Rose 2017** Rating 93 To 2020 $22 ✪
Margaret River Sauvignon Blanc Semillon 2017 Rating 92 To 2021 $24 ✪
East of Alice 2016 Rating 90 To 2020 $17 ✪
Margaret River Pinot Noir 2017 Rating 90 To 2022 $17 ✪
Three Hills Margaret River Malbec 2016 Rating 90 To 2029 $38

Harcourt Valley Vineyards ★★★★☆

3339 Calder Highway, Harcourt, Vic 3453 **Region** Bendigo
T (03) 5474 2223 **www**.harcourtvalley.com.au **Open** 7 days 11–5
Winemaker Quinn Livingstone **Est.** 1975 **Dozens** 2500 **Vyds** 4ha
Harcourt Valley Vineyards (planted 1975) has the oldest planting of vines in the Harcourt Valley. Using 100% estate-grown fruit, Quinn Livingstone (second-generation winemaker) makes a number of small-batch wines. Minimal fruit handling is used in the winemaking process. The tasting area overlooks the vines, with a large window that allows visitors to see the activity in the winery. Exports to China.

ŶŶŶŶŶ **Heathcote Rose 2017** Rose made with grenache from the Camelback vineyard in Heathcote. The quality is clear. It's strong with licorice and rose petal–like aromas and flavours, and while it's a dry style there's plenty of meat on the bones. Screwcap. 12.8% alc. Rating 94 To 2018 $20 CM ✪

Single Vineyard Old Vine Bendigo Shiraz 2016 An elegant red with herb, spice and mint notes having as much to say as the array of red and black berry flavours. Mouthfeel is creamy and soft; tannin has melted straight into the fruit; it feels juicy and energetic throughout. Not a hefty wine but an entirely satisfying one. Screwcap. 13.8% alc. Rating 94 To 2028 $60 CM

ŶŶŶŶŶ **Mt Camel Range Heathcote Shiraz 2016** Rating 93 To 2026 $25 CM ✪
Heathcote Bendigo GSM 2016 Rating 93 To 2024 $25 CM ✪
Old Vine Bendigo Cabernet Sauvignon 2016 Rating 93 To 2028 $60 CM
Barbara's Bendigo Shiraz 2016 Rating 92 To 2028 $25 CM ✪
Bendigo Cabernet Sauvignon 2016 Rating 90 To 2024 $25 CM

Hardys ★★★★★

202 Main Road, McLaren Vale, SA 5171 **Region** McLaren Vale
T (08) 8329 4124 **www**.hardyswine.com.au **Open** Mon–Fri 11–4, w'ends 10–4
Winemaker Paul Lapsley (Chief) **Est.** 1853 **Dozens** NFP
The 1992 merger of Thomas Hardy and the Berri Renmano group may have had some elements of a forced marriage, but the group prospered over the next 10 years. So successful was it that a further marriage followed in early 2003, with Constellation Wines of the US acting as the groom, and BRL Hardy the bride, creating the largest wine group in the world. It is now part of the Accolade Wines group. The Hardys wine brands are headed by Thomas Hardy Cabernet Sauvignon and Eileen Hardy Chardonnay, Pinot Noir and Shiraz, and also include the Sir James range of sparkling wines, the HRB wines, the Oomoo range and the Nottage Hill wines. The 'big company' slur is ill deserved – these are some of Australia's greatest wines. Exports to all major markets.

ŶŶŶŶŶ **165th Anniversary Edition Cabernet Shiraz 2014** From the best cabernet sauvignon from Frankland River, Margaret River and Coonawarra fused with 100yo shiraz from McLaren Vale's Upper Tintara district, the varieties evenly split. A vibrant crimson hue with a core of pristine fruit, although this remains in the savoury spectrum, leading onto a complex palate full of energy, the tannins as fine and strong as silk. An outlandishly long finish. A heart-skipping wine, exquisitely detailed and elegant. Screwcap. 14% alc. **Rating** 99 **To** 2044 $250 JF ✪

Eileen Hardy Chardonnay 2016 Tasmanian and Yarra Valley fruit bursting with flavour and complexity in equal measure, yet linear in profile. An amalgam of excellent fruit, mouthwatering sulphides, seamless oak integration and zest appeal, with everything reined-in by superfine acidity. Chardonnay nirvana well and truly thriving in Australia. Screwcap. 13.5% alc. **Rating** 97 **To** 2028 $95 JF ✪

Tintara Sub Regional Upper Tintara Shiraz 2016 Stakes its claim with its subregional expression and a beating heart from its 100+yo vines. There's an extraordinary depth of flavour and yet utter restraint. With its perfume, layers of red and black fruits, a dusting of spice and warm iron shavings, this is most definitely savoury in outlook. Fine tannins and mouthwatering freshness to the acidity dance across the palate. Screwcap. 14.5% alc. **Rating** 97 **To** 2040 $80 JF ✪

Barrel Selected Rare Muscat NV Blend A01. This is so glorious, it can cause one to swoon. Barrel-aged for at least 20 years. Espresso-coffee hue; pours like molten treacle, and smells of molasses, cold lapsang souchong tea, dried apricots, and the rum and raisin dark chocolate that Dad loved so much. The epitome of complexity with its silky palate of richness and deep flavours, yet a freshness on the finish and brilliant balance. 500ml. Vino-Lok. 17% alc. **Rating** 97 $100 JF ✪

Barrel Selected Rare Liqueur Sauvignon Blanc NV Blend A03. Mid-amber with a pink-red tinge; heady with wood smoke, preserved ginger, lavender and potpourri. The palate is complex, rich and very fresh; excellent blending. The flavours change – char-grilled pineapple drizzled with honey one minute, then toffee apple the next. Barrel aged 17 years. 500ml. Vino-Lok. 18% alc. **Rating** 97 $100 JF ✪

🍷🍷🍷🍷🍷 **HRB Riesling 2017** Bin D674. A harmonious blend from the Clare Valley and Tasmania. It steals the best from each – the lime-lemon juice and zest of the Clare matched with the mineral thread of acidity and depth of flavour from Tasmania – and rolls them into a synergistic whole. Pure, precise and pristine, with great length. Screwcap. 12.5% alc. **Rating** 96 **To** 2028 $35 JF ✪

HRB Pinot Gris 2015 Bin D665. From Adelaide Hills and Tasmania. The price isn't a marketeer's fancy, nor a pinot-gris lover's nightmare. It's real with a citrus and apple blossom bouquet setting the stage for a medium-bodied, layered wine that achieves intensity and mouthfeel through the quality of the fruit, not phenolics; the finish clean and clear. Screwcap. 13.5% alc. **Rating** 96 **To** 2022 $35 ✪

Eileen Hardy Shiraz 2014 Grown on 112yo vines. A meticulous shiraz of power and class. It's packed with dark, concentrated, dark-berried fruit – it's essentially kirsch-like – but discipline is its middle name. It pours on the flavour but its systems of tannin and acid ensure that nothing goes astray. Blackberry, earth, saltbush and dark chocolate all play key roles. Long haul written all over it. Screwcap. 14% alc. **Rating** 96 **To** 2040 $125 CM

Tintara Reserve McLaren Vale Grenache 2016 Has exceptional colour, and the wine is a vin de garde, needing – and deserving – at least 5 years (preferably 10) to trim down. It's not a question of balance or extract, simply of size. If Dr Who could locate me in 20 years and present a bottle (better still a case), I would be mightily obliged. Screwcap. 14.5% alc. **Rating** 96 **To** 2035 $70 ✪

Barrel Selected Rare Tawny NV Blend A01. Amber hue with a rim of garnet; complex and richly flavoured, the spirit with its brandy notes integrated. The hallmarks of quality aged material are in abundance (it is barrel-aged around 25 years), but the key to the impressive stature is freshness. Molasses, toffee, the aroma of cumquat marmalade on the stove bubbling away, spices wafting in and out; superbly balanced. 500ml. Vino-Lok. 20% alc. **Rating** 96 $100 JF

Bastard Hill Single Vineyard Chardonnay 2016 A steep single vineyard that has long produced excellent chardonnay. Linear, yet no shortage of flavour, starting with lemon and grapefruit, then white stone fruit; judiciously handled oak and lees influence just add the merest padding. It's pristine and savoury with mouthwatering acidity to close. Screwcap. 13.5% alc. **Rating** 95 **To** 2027 $80 JF

HRB Chardonnay 2016 Bin D668. A ripper of a blend. Heady with ginger fluff cake, lemon curd, oak spices, figs and stone fruit; unfurling further with nutty leesy flavours and creamed honey; the very good oak adding another layer. There's a lot going on, yet it's balanced and not heavy, the acidity and some smoking match-strike sulphides keeping everything reined in. Screwcap. 13% alc. **Rating** 95 **To** 2027 $35 JF ✪

HRB Pinot Noir 2016 Bin D672. The colour is positive and bright, the palate perfectly structured and balanced – fresh, strongly varietal, red and black cherries sitting forward. How much will be cellared is anyone's guess, but patient people should be happy with themselves. Screwcap. 13.5% alc. **Rating** 95 **To** 2033 $35 ✪

HRB Shiraz 2016 Bin D676. Excellent dark purple-black; just the right amount of spice, dark fruits, perfume and flavour. Surprisingly medium-bodied, although still with plenty of depth and complexity, plus finely chiseled tannins and a persistent finish. Best of all, savoury rather than purely fruit driven. Screwcap. 14.5% alc. **Rating** 95 **To** 2030 $35 ✪

Tintara Single Vineyard Yeenunga McLaren Vale Shiraz 2016 This is the very essence of McLaren Vale shiraz. The brilliant dark purple hue leads onto a mound of dark plums and red berries dipped in dark mint chocolate. Warm earth and oak aromas and flavours are also at play, but they'll recede in time. Full-bodied with velvety tannins, the palate cruises along for quite some distance. Screwcap. 14% alc. **Rating** 95 **To** 2034 $80 JF

HRB Cabernet Sauvignon 2016 Bin D673. Dark garnet; a flurry of dark fruit from blackberries to very ripe plums and spiced compote turns to oak flavours of cedar wood, licorice and soy sauce along the way. Full-bodied, fleshy and ripe with still-firm tannins and a savoury core. Screwcap. 14% alc. **Rating** 95 **To** 2030 $35 JF ✪

Tintara McLaren Vale Cabernet Sauvignon 2016 The inclusion of 6% merlot, 5% cabernet franc and 3% shiraz all contribute, starting with the outlandishly deep purple hue. While there's certainly ripe fruit with cassis and mulberries lurking, this is savoury through and through with gun smoke, dried gum leaves, Chinese five-spice, licorice and tamarind. Screwcap. 14% alc. **Rating** 95 **To** 2028 $28 JF ✪

♟♟♟♟♟ **Tintara McLaren Vale Cabernet Sauvignon 2015** **Rating** 93 **To** 2040 $28
The Chronicles Twice Lost Limestone Coast Langhorne Creek Pinot Grigio 2016 **Rating** 92 **To** 2019 $15 ✪
Tintara Geology McLaren Vale Shiraz 2016 **Rating** 92 **To** 2023 $30 JF
Tintara Geology McLaren Vale Cabernet Sauvignon 2015 **Rating** 90 **To** 2029 $19 ✪
Insignia Cabernet Sauvignon 2015 **Rating** 90 **To** 2025 $18 JF ✪

Harewood Estate ★★★★★

Scotsdale Road, Denmark, WA 6333 **Region** Denmark
T (08) 9840 9078 **www.**harewood.com.au **Open** 7 days 10–5
Winemaker James Kellie **Est.** 1988 **Dozens** 15 000 **Vyds** 19.2ha
In 2003 James Kellie, responsible for the contract making of Harewood's wines since 1998, purchased the estate with his father and sister as partners. A 300t winery was constructed, offering both contract winemaking services for the Great Southern region and the ability to expand the Harewood range to include subregional wines. In January '10 James and wife Careena purchased his father's and sister's shares to become 100% owners. Exports to the UK, the US, Denmark, Sweden, Switzerland, Indonesia, Hong Kong, Malaysia, Macau, Singapore, China and Japan.

♟♟♟♟♟ **Denmark Riesling 2017** An outstanding riesling from start to end. The bouquet is expressive, with citrus blossom to the fore, and a hint of passionfruit. The intensity of the palate is mouthwatering, with flavours of lemon sherbet and grapefruit running through to a brilliantly fresh finish and aftertaste. Screwcap. 12% alc. **Rating** 96 **To** 2032 $23

Porongurup Riesling 2017 The bouquet is classic Great Southern riesling, leaving it up to the palate to build on this, which it does so with elan. Its mouthwatering flavours span citrus, Granny Smith apple and slatey acidity, all soaring on the finish and aftertaste. Screwcap. 11.5% alc. **Rating** 96 **To** 2032 $27

Mount Barker Riesling 2017 A floral bouquet, citrus enhanced by nuances of talc, then a palate that progressively builds its flavour spectrum, taking in lime, mandarin and passionfruit. A riesling of distinction. Screwcap. 11.5% alc. **Rating** 95 **To** 2031 $23

Great Southern Chardonnay 2016 The bright straw-green hue announces a chardonnay with complexity as its second name. There's the first whiff of white peach, grapefruit zest and supportive oak, then the transition from bouquet to palate is seamless. Creamy notes ex 50% mlf are intertwined with gently toasted nuts and oak, finishing decisively with grapefruity acidity. Screwcap. 14% alc. **Rating** 95 **To** 2027 $27

Reserve Denmark Chardonnay 2016 Straw-coloured and alive to the day. Ripped with fig, pineapple and grapefruit before a fine etching of flint, smoke and cedar wood. It feels seductive, tastes sophisticated, and finishes with a satisfying kick. Screwcap. 13.5% alc. **Rating** 95 **To** 2023 $34 CM ❂

Frankland River Riesling 2017 Pale straw-green; a wine of purity, harmony and balance, no single part of the aroma or bouquet standing out from its counterparts. Will evolve into something special in 5 years' time, and flourish thereafter. Screwcap. 12% alc. **Rating** 94 **To** 2030 $23

Great Southern Sauvignon Blanc Semillon 2017 A 63/37% blend made with free-run juice cool-fermented in stainless steel. The wine has clearly benefited from this pristine juice. The fragrant bouquet has punchy cut grass/green pea ahead of passionfruit/tropical aromas. The palate neatly reverses the play, putting the tropical fruits in pride of place. Screwcap. 12% alc. **Rating** 94 **To** 2022 $21 ❂

Reserve Denmark Semillon Sauvignon Blanc 2017 All the thistles and burs, and snow pea and passionfruit flavours, you could ever hope for. This doesn't go quietly. It's a rage of scent and flavour – freshness and juiciness a given, texture an added bonus. Screwcap. 12.5% alc. **Rating** 94 **To** 2020 CM $27

♟♟♟♟♟ **Great Southern Cabernet Sauvignon 2015** Rating 93 To 2028 $21 CM ❂
Great Southern Chardonnay 2017 Rating 92 To 2024 $28 CM
Flux-III Great Southern Chardonnay 2016 Rating 92 To 2021 $29
Denmark Pinot Noir 2017 Rating 92 To 2025 $21
Flux-II Great Southern Pinot Gris 2016 Rating 91 To 2019 $29
Reserve Shiraz 2015 Rating 91 To 2024 $34 CM
Flux-I Great Southern Shiraz Tempranillo 2015 Rating 91 To 2030 $29
Reserve Great Southern Shiraz Cabernet 2015 Rating 91 To 2028 $27 CM
Flux-II Great Southern Pinot Gris 2017 Rating 90 To 2019 $28 CM

Hart & Hunter ★★★★★

Gabriel's Paddock, 463 Deasys Road, Pokolbin, NSW 2325 **Region** Hunter Valley
T 0401 605 219 **www**.hartandhunter.com.au **Open** Thurs–Sun 10–4
Winemaker Damien Stevens, Jodie Belleville **Est.** 2009 **Dozens** 2500
This is the venture of winemaking couple Damien Stevens and Jodie Belleville, with partners Daniel and Elle Hart. The grapes are purchased from highly regarded growers within the Hunter, with the emphasis on single vineyard wines and small-batch processing. Continuing success led to the opening of a cellar door in late 2015, offering not only the best-known Hunter varieties, but also experimental and alternative wines.

♟♟♟♟♟ **Single Vineyard Series Oakey Creek Semillon 2017** The sandy soils of the Oakey Creek district have long produced great semillon. Add the impact of the (relatively) cool vintage and you have a beautifully detailed wine, with balance from acidity that isn't raucous, just there to provide freshness and to protect the future longevity of a pure Hunter semillon. But yes, by all means drink it tonight if you wish. Screwcap. 10.5% alc. **Rating** 95 **To** 2032 $30 ✪

Single Vineyard Series The Remparts Semillon 2017 Has more immediate fruit than its Oakey Creek sibling, although I have to admit I had forgotten tasting The Remparts previously. Lemon zest, pith and juice flavours ride on a framework of slippery, rubbery (in tension, not flavour) acidity. Screwcap. 10.5% alc. **Rating** 95 **To** 2030 $30 ✪

75 Days Chardonnay 2016 This is a very good Hunter Valley chardonnay, with the grapefruit/white peach/lemony acidity of cool-grown vines. Having had no background for any of the Hart & Hunter wines at the time of tasting, I had no clue the 75 days denoted fermentation and maceration on skins for that period. Screwcap. 12.5% alc. **Rating** 94 **To** 2026 $42

🍷🍷🍷🍷 **Single Vineyard Series Syrah 2016** **Rating** 92 **To** 2023 $40
Dr B's Fiano 2017 **Rating** 91 **To** 2022 $28

Haselgrove Wines ★★★★★

187 Sand Road, McLaren Vale, SA 5171 **Region** McLaren Vale
T (08) 8323 8706 **www**.haselgrove.com.au **Open** By appt
Winemaker Alex Sherrah **Est.** 1981 **Dozens** 45 000 **Vyds** 9.7ha

Italian-Australian industry veterans Don Totino, Don Luca, Tony Carrocci and Steve Maglieri decided to purchase Haselgrove 'over a game of cards and couple of hearty reds' in 2008. They have completely changed the product range, its price and presentation: the Legend Series at $85–$150, the Origin Series at $30–$40, the Alternative Series at $24–$26 and First Cut at $22. A very large custom-crush facility provides all-important cash flow. Exports to Canada, Germany, Malaysia, South Korea, Hong Kong, China and NZ.

🍷🍷🍷🍷🍷 **The Lear McLaren Vale Shiraz 2016** A warm-climate shiraz with a welcome astringency embedded with clove, anise, cardamom, olive and a hint of mint, corralling plum and dark currant notes across a generous pillar of vanilla pod/mocha oak. Screwcap. 14.5% alc. **Rating** 95 **To** 2035 $90 NG

Vine-Sean Grenache 2016 This is exceptional: platforming grenache's eager showboat across a myriad of rosewater, scrub and molten kirsch aromas, while ably displaying its capacity for finessed tannins and cranberry acidity. Silken. Heady. Rakish. Haselgrove knows how to extract, with 40 days on skins. Others take note! Screwcap. 14.5% alc. **Rating** 95 **To** 2024 $30 NG ✪

Protector McLaren Vale Cabernet Sauvignon 2016 Tactile and vibrant, with currant and bay leaf flavours etched across pillars of well handled oak, pebbly acidity and lead tannins. A rich wine, but there is not an ounce of jam as it expands across the mouth. Screwcap. 14.5% alc. **Rating** 95 **To** 2029 $40 NG

Twist McLaren Vale Primitivo 2015 The build of structural focus across this estate's reds is exceptional. The tannins – dusty, pliant and expansive – are impeccably hewn. Plum, cherry ... the usual stuff, melded to a lift of orange rind and dried herb amaro. The bitter pucker on the finish is appetising and raffishly southern Italian. Screwcap. 15% alc. **Rating** 95 **To** 2021 $30 NG ✪

Catkin McLaren Vale Shiraz 2016 A smooth sheath of chiffon tannins, vibrant acidity and floral aromatics interplaying with black fruit flavours and anise as it glides across the mouth. A blend of select vineyard parcels proving a sum is far greater than its individual parts. Screwcap. 14.5% alc. **Rating** 94 **To** 2028 $40 NG

Il Padrone McLaren Vale Shiraz 2016 This is a lesson in how to make shiraz structured, savoury and appetising in a warm zone, by virtue of Old World extraction techniques: extended and not shy. Tapenade, violet, thyme and lavender; blueberry and mulberry, too. This is sinuous and very long. Screwcap. 14.5% alc. **Rating** 94 **To** 2031 $45 NG

Col Cross Single Vineyard McLaren Vale Shiraz 2016 A large-framed wine of dark fruit allusions melded to lavish oak. Saturated in plum, five-spice

and licorice with suggestions of cedar, coffee grind and vanilla. Cork. 14.5% alc.
Rating 94 **To** 2036 $90 NG
Cul-Stor Shiraz Cabernet Sauvignon Cabernet Franc 2016 Tannin
management is among Haselgrove's calling cards and this cuvee proves it in spades!
Florals, currant, mint and strewn herb, with tannins that are at once assertive yet
impeccably massaged, towing the flavours long. Screwcap. 14.5% alc. **Rating** 94
To 2030 $40 NG

♥♥♥♥♀ **Staff Adelaide Hills Chardonnay 2017** Rating 92 To 2022 $30 NG
The Ambassador Shiraz 2016 Rating 92 To 2025 $85 NG
Switch Grenache Shiraz Mourvedre 2016 Rating 92 To 2023 $40 NG
First Cut Shiraz 2016 Rating 91 To 2021 $22 NG ✪
First Cut Cabernet Sauvignon 2016 Rating 91 To 2028 $22 NG ✪

Hastwell & Lightfoot ★★★★

301 Foggos Road, McLaren Vale, SA 5171 **Region** McLaren Vale
T (08) 8323 8692 www.hastwellandlightfoot.com.au **Open** Fri–Sun 11–5
Winemaker James Hastwell **Est.** 1988 **Dozens** 4500 **Vyds** 16ha
Established in 1988 by Mark and Wendy Hastwell and Martin and Jill Lightfoot. Having
initially sold much of the production, they have made a significant commitment to the brand,
producing wines from the estate-grown varieties. The vines are grafted onto devigorating
rootstocks that restrain the development of dead fruit characters in warmer seasons. James
Hastwell, son of Mark and Wendy, has his winery just 2km from the vineyard. Exports to the
UK, the US, Canada, Malaysia, Taiwan, Singapore and China.

♥♥♥♥♀ **McLaren Vale Shiraz 2016** Cherry-plum flavours just edging into darker
territory of malt and asphalt. Toasty oak and a good deal of it. Chocolate too –
almost like chocolate milk. For all its might and old-school power it maintains a
fresh face. Tannin, melted into the fruit, has been handled well. It's big, sweet and
warm but it has the stuffing where it needs it. Screwcap. 14.5% alc. **Rating** 92
To 2026 $25 CM ✪
Sands of Time Single Vineyard McLaren Vale Shiraz 2015 From 28yo
vines. Ripe plum-soaked fruit, with bready, cedary nuances, a smear of vanilla
cream. Unusual aromatic profile, but many will find the rich, smooth palate
seductive. Screwcap. 14% alc. **Rating** 91 **To** 2028 $30 CM
McLaren Vale Cabernet Sauvignon 2015 Includes 7% cabernet franc. It feels
fractionally over-baked but the volume of flavours is impressive. Tar, blackberry,
saltbush and leather come wrapped in a coat of toasty oak. The pedal is pushed to
the floor; there's no room for subtlety. Screwcap. 14.5% alc. **Rating** 91 **To** 2027
$25 CM
McLaren Vale Vermentino 2017 Aroma lights up the glass; flavour swings
amiably through. This is all tropical fruit and citrus, but it feels/tastes buoyant and
bright and is a pleasure to spend time with. Screwcap. 13% alc. **Rating** 90 **To** 2019
$23 CM

Hay Shed Hill Wines ★★★★★

511 Harmans Mill Road, Wilyabrup, WA 6280 **Region** Margaret River
T (08) 9755 6046 www.hayshedhill.com.au **Open** 7 days 10–5
Winemaker Michael Kerrigan **Est.** 1987 **Dozens** 24000 **Vyds** 18.55ha
Mike Kerrigan, former winemaker at Howard Park, acquired the business in late 2006 (with
co-ownership by the West Cape Howe syndicate) and is now the full-time winemaker. He
had every confidence that he could dramatically lift the quality of the wines, and has done
precisely that. Their wines made from estate-grown grapes come under the Vineyard, White
Label and Block series. The Block series showcases the ultimate site-specific wines, made
from separate blocks within the vineyard. The Pitchfork wines are made from contract-grown
grapes in the region. Exports to the UK, the US, Denmark, Singapore, Malaysia, Japan, Hong
Kong and China.

ŶŶŶŶŶ **Block 2 Margaret River Cabernet Sauvignon 2014** Lays it all out there
from the first sip – a wine of uncompromising power and style, owing as much
to viticulture as winemaking. It does, however, do something unusual, with juicy
cassis fruit becoming more obvious on continued retastings, tannins less so –
normally it's vice versa. Screwcap. 14% alc. **Rating** 96 **To** 2039 $60 ✪
Pitchfork Margaret River Semillon Sauvignon Blanc 2017 Margaret River
does so well with these varieties, and offers them at such tempting prices, they
might as well have a monopoly on them. Judging a dozen or so becomes very
difficult as they impart their message so clearly, their flavours so similar to each
other. This wine, with its beautiful green colour, fits into all of the above. Screwcap.
11.5% alc. **Rating** 94 **To** 2021 $17 ✪
Block 6 Margaret River Chardonnay 2016 More new oak, more alcohol
and riper fruit distinguish this from its standard sibling. There are creamy nutty
notes running parallel with nectarine, peach and citrus fruits. Screwcap. 12.5% alc.
Rating 94 **To** 2026 $40
Margaret River Pinot Noir Rose 2017 Estate-grown and (unusually) whole-
bunch pressed. The fragrant bouquet offers spiced red fruits picked up with alacrity
by the seamless, intense and long palate, with a juicy lemony twist. The finish is
dry and bell clear. A lot of wine for the price. Screwcap. 12.5% alc. **Rating** 94
To 2019 $22 ✪
Pitchfork Margaret River Shiraz 2015 Margaret River shiraz is often
overlooked in discussions of the best regions for the variety. This medium-bodied
wine throws down the challenge. Its spicy bouquet has an overlay of violets, and
the palate is positively alive with the rainbow of flavours it offers: black fruits,
licorice, satsuma plum and a savoury raft of tannins. Screwcap. 14% alc. **Rating** 94
To 2029 $17 ✪

ŶŶŶŶŶ **Margaret River Cabernet Merlot 2016** Rating 92 **To** 2031 $22 ✪
Margaret River Sauvignon Blanc Semillon 2017 Rating 91 **To** 2021 $22 ✪
Margaret River Chardonnay 2016 Rating 91 **To** 2024 $28
Pitchfork Margaret River Shiraz 2015 Rating 91 **To** 2021 $16 CM ✪
Margaret River Cabernet Sauvignon 2015 Rating 91 **To** 2030 $28
Pitchfork Margaret River Semillon Sauvignon Blanc 2017 Rating 90
To 2018 $16 CM ✪

Hayes Family Wines   ★★★★★
102 Mattiske Road, Stone Well, SA 5352 **Region** Barossa Valley
T 0499 096 812 **www.**hayesfamilywines.com **Open** Fri–Sun & public hols 11–5, or by appt
Winemaker Andrew Seppelt **Est.** 2014 **Dozens** 1000 **Vyds** 5ha
Hayes Family Wines brings together the Hayes, Seppelt and Schulz families, each making
a different contribution. Andrew Seppelt has 20+ years of winemaking experience in the
Barossa, Marcus Schulz has more than 50 years of grapegrowing experience in the northern
Barossa, and Brett Hayes and family have 25+ years of agriculture and business experience. In
late 2016 the group purchased a 5ha old vineyard in the Stone Well district on the western
ridge of the Barossa Valley. The business is off to a flying start with its '15 vintage wines.

ŶŶŶŶŶ **Reserve Barossa Valley Shiraz 2016** Spent 20 months in a single French
barrique, yielding 300 bottles only. It not only has depth, it has spread. We're
looking at boysenberry and blackberry, plum and toast, with wood smoke and
clove characters wafting through. It's both pretty and profound, but the way both
tannin and flavour unfurl through the back half of the wine is the real cause for
excitement. Screwcap. 14.5% alc. **Rating** 96 **To** 2040 $100 CM
Winemaker's Selection Barossa Valley Rose 2017 Old vine grenache, hand-
picked, destemmed, open-fermented in a used French hogshead, 28 days on skins,
matured for 3 months, just 25 dozen made. Fragrant rose-petal aromas, backed
by spice, introduce a high quality rose. Bone dry, bright and fresh, with red berry
flavours and a lingering aftertaste. Impossible to find any chink in the armour of
perfection. Screwcap. 13.5% alc. **Rating** 95 **To** 2020 $26 ✪

Vineyard Series Ebenezer Barossa Valley Shiraz 2016 Single vineyard, 100% new French oak, 50 dozen made. The oak is clear and obvious but the fruit is right up to the task. Smoked cedar wood and meaty spice notes ripple through pure, ripe plum, clove and blackberry. For all its richness it feels manicured and controlled. It exudes class. Screwcap. 14.5% alc. **Rating** 95 **To** 2032 $60 CM

Carol & Ivan's Pick Barossa Valley Grenache Shiraz Mataro 2017 Old vine grenache, shiraz and mataro from Stone Well. Only 300 bottles produced. It's a gorgeous mid-weight wine, svelte, ripe, flowing and fine, weight here, finesse there, length to seal the deal. Screwcap. 13.8% alc. **Rating** 95 **To** 2028 $40 CM

Vineyard Series Greenock Shiraz 2016 Resiny vanilla characters open the batting but a sure-footed burst of purple-berried flavour soon takes the strike. This is very young and needs time to settle, but the underlying quality is certain. It's fresh, intense, perfumed and slipped with superfine tannin. There's no shortage of length either. Screwcap. 14% alc. **Rating** 94 **To** 2034 $60 CM

🍷🍷🍷🍷🍷 **Barossa Valley Shiraz 2016** Rating 92 To 2028 $35 CM
Winemaker's Selection Grenache 2017 Rating 92 To 2021 $40
Coonawarra Shiraz 2016 Rating 91 To 2028 $35 CM
Regional Series Barossa Valley Mataro 2017 Rating 90 To 2023 $26 CM

Head Wines   ★★★★★

Lot 1, Stonewell Road, Stone Well, SA 5352 **Region** Barossa Valley
T 0413 114 233 **www.**headwines.com.au **Open** By appt Feb–Apr
Winemaker Alex Head **Est.** 2006 **Dozens** 5000 **Vyds** 7.5ha

Head Wines is the venture of Alex Head, who came into the wine industry in 1997 with a degree in biochemistry from Sydney University. Experience at fine wine stores, importers and an auction house was followed by vintage work at wineries he admired: Tyrrell's, Torbreck, Laughing Jack and Cirillo Estate. The names of his wines reflects his fascination with Côte-Rôtie in the Northern Rhône Valley. The two facing slopes in Côte-Rôtie are known as Côte Blonde and Côte Brune. Head's The Blonde comes from an east-facing slope in the Stone Well area, while The Brunette comes from a very low-yielding vineyard in the Moppa area. In each case, open fermentation (with whole bunches) and basket pressing precedes maturation in French oak. Exports to Denmark, the Netherlands and Japan.

🍷🍷🍷🍷🍷 **The Brunette Moppa Barossa Valley Shiraz 2016** Rich and deep, with an abundance of flavours, yet never dipping into overripe territory. Perfect balance in every respect, the vortex of fruit, spice and integrated oak leading onto the full-bodied palate, greeted by velvety tannins and an overwhelming desire for another glass. Screwcap. 14.5% alc. **Rating** 97 **To** 2040 $60 JF ✪

Ancestor Vine Springton Eden Valley Grenache 2016 Sourced from the 158yo Stonegarden vineyard to produce a lone 600l barrel, this vintage given new oak for the first time. With the addition of mataro, the new oak component ended up around 85%, seamlessly integrated. This dips into more savoury, earthy tones, darkening the fruit and spice without ever losing its line. A complex and compelling wine with excellent length, detail and charm. Screwcap. 14.5% alc. **Rating** 97 **To** 2036 $100 JF ✪

🍷🍷🍷🍷🍷 **Old Vine Barossa Valley Grenache 2016** From the same vineyard as Ancestor Vine, but no new oak. 5% mataro inclusion; 20% whole bunches, wild yeast, plunged daily for 2 weeks, 17 months in seasoned 600l barrels. A glorious grenache that effortlessly stays in the savoury spectrum without losing its heart of excellent raspberry/red plum. Heady aromatics of Middle Eastern spices, especially sumac, plus Sichuan pepper, rosehips and warm earth. The pristine flavours sashay across the medium-bodied palate, taking the spongy tannins and talc-like acidity all in their stride. Screwcap. 14.5% alc. **Rating** 96 **To** 2031 $35 JF ✪

The Contrarian Greenock Barossa Valley Shiraz 2016 From a 54yo biodynamic site. Includes 10% mataro. Excellent bright crimson; charred red peppers, blue and red fruit, an array of spices. The medium-bodied palate, the finely detailed tannins and the fresh acidity all deliver a very satisfying shiraz. Screwcap. 14% alc. **Rating** 95 **To** 2030 $35 JF ○

The Blonde Stone Well Barossa Valley Shiraz 2016 There's a definite Stone Well intensity going on in this richly flavoured and compelling wine. Awash with sour cherries and plump sweet black plums, seasoned with pepper, mocha and earth. Ribbons of plush tannins wrap around the fuller bodied yet silky palate, with a flourish of fresh acidity on the finish. Screwcap. 14.5% alc. **Rating** 95 **To** 2036 $50 JF

The Redhead Flaxman Valley Barossa Shiraz 2016 The Redhead makes its return after a 4-year hiatus. The initial note of strong clove alongside green walnuts unfurls to a flood of flavour with sweet red and black plums, licorice, dark chocolate and some Mediterranean herbs. The compact palate is so detailed – ripped with energy and persimmon-like tannins – but it needs more time in bottle. With only 100 dozen made, get in quick. Diam. 14.5% alc. **Rating** 95 **To** 2036 $120 JF

🍷🍷🍷🍷🍷 **Head Red Barossa Valley Shiraz 2016** Rating 92 To 2029 $25 ○

Heartland Wines

The Winehouse, Wellington Road, Langhorne Creek, SA 5255 **Region** Langhorne Creek
T (08) 8333 1363 **www**.heartlandwines.com.au **Open** 7 days 10–5
Winemaker Ben Glaetzer **Est.** 2001 **Dozens** 50 000 **Vyds** 200ha
A joint venture of industry veterans: winemakers Ben Glaetzer and Scott Collett, and wine industry management specialist Grant Tilbrook. Heartland focuses on cabernet sauvignon and shiraz from Langhorne Creek, with John Glaetzer (Ben's uncle, and head winemaker at Wolf Blass for over 30 years) liaising with his network of growers and vineyards. The wines are made by Ben at Barossa Vintners. Exports to all major markets.

🍷🍷🍷🍷🍷 **First Release Malbec 2016** It's more about freshness and character than it is about depth or any great intensity, which is fine in itself, but might make the price a bridge too far. It tastes of leather and assorted fresh berries and has an easy-going, juicy appeal. Screwcap. 14% alc. **Rating** 92 **To** 2025 $50 CM

Spice Trader Shiraz 2014 The region and the winemaking skills of Ben Glaetzer join together to produce a sumptuously rich and complex wine at a bargain basement price. In this bracket, the oak is likely to have been contributed by planks or chips, but hasn't been overdone. Screwcap. 14.5% alc. **Rating** 90 **To** 2029 $17 ○

Heathcote Estate

Drummonds Lane, Heathcote, Vic 3523 (postal) **Region** Heathcote
T (03) 5974 3729 **www**.yabbylake.com **Open** Not
Winemaker Tom Carson, Chris Forge **Est.** 1999 **Dozens** 5000 **Vyds** 34ha
Heathcote Estate and Yabby Lake Vineyard are owned by the Kirby family of Village Roadshow Ltd. They purchased a prime piece of Heathcote red Cambrian soil in 1999, planting shiraz (30ha) and grenache (4ha). The wines are matured exclusively in French oak. The arrival of the hugely talented Tom Carson as group winemaker has added lustre to the winery and its wines. Exports to the US, the UK, Canada, Sweden, Singapore, Hong Kong and China.

🍷🍷🍷🍷🍷 **Single Block Release Block C Shiraz 2016** Mostly destemmed, part fermented with whole bunches, 11 months in French oak puncheons (20% new). Stunning dark purple hue; laden with savouriness, spice and detail with dark fruit, pencil shavings, graphite and iron shavings. The palate is just full-bodied with powdery-fine yet compact tannins, and exceptional length. Screwcap. 13.5% alc. **Rating** 96 **To** 2031 $60 JF ○

Single Block Release Block F Shiraz 2016 Fruit from the five estate blocks ended up creating 11 disparate batches of wine, all spending 11 months in French oak hogsheads and puncheons (20% new). The final blend is a beauty. While savoury-driven, it's awash with Heathcote's trademark dark black and blue fruits, flecked with bay leaves, pepper and spice leading onto the full-bodied palate. The tannin structure is at once powerful and plush, yet reined in. Screwcap. 14% alc. Rating 95 To 2032 $45 JF

ΥΥΥΥΥ Pressings Shiraz 2016 Rating 93 To 2028 $52 JF

Heathcote II

290 Cornella-Toolleen Road, Toolleen, Vic 3551 **Region** Heathcote
T (03) 5433 6292 www.heathcote2.com **Open** W'ends 11–5, or by appt
Winemaker Peder Rosdal **Est.** 1995 **Dozens** 500 **Vyds** 6.5ha
This is the venture of Danish-born, French-trained Peder Rosdal (a Flying Winemaker in California, Spain and Chablis) and viticulturist Lionel Flutto. The vineyard dates back to 1995, with further plantings since of shiraz (2.7ha) and smaller amounts of cabernet sauvignon, cabernet franc, merlot, tempranillo and grenache. The vines are dry-grown on the famed red Cambrian soil, and the wines are made onsite using hand-plunging, basket pressing and (since 2004) French oak maturation. Exports to Denmark, Japan and Singapore.

ΥΥΥΥΥ H.D. Shiraz 2013 Quite a heady bouquet with an amalgam of ultra ripe blackberries, dried fruit, sweet oak and a slightly volatile spirit-like lift, although the alcohol is moderate. Rich and mouthfilling, the flavours flood the palate with all those ripe, full-on fruit characters again to the fore and the new oak persisting in the aftertaste. The tannin is well balanced: firm but not aggressive and in keeping with the stature of the wine. Cork. 14% alc. Rating 94 To 2025 $89 SC

ΥΥΥΥΥ Myola 2013 Rating 90 To 2021 $55 SC

Heathcote Winery

Drummonds Lane, Heathcote, Vic 3523 **Region** Heathcote
T (03) 5974 3729 www.heathcotewinery.com.au **Open** Not
Winemaker Brendan Pudney **Est.** 1978 **Dozens** 5000 **Vyds** 14ha
The cellar door is situated in the main street of Heathcote, housed in a restored miner's cottage built by Thomas Craven in 1854 to help cater for the huge influx of goldminers. The winery is immediately behind the cellar door, having processed its first vintage in 1983. Shiraz and shiraz viognier account for 90% of the production.

ΥΥΥΥΥ The Origin Single Vineyard Shiraz 2016 36yo vines, whole berries open-fermented, 7 days on skins, matured for 14 months in French oak (30% new). It is difficult to avoid over-extraction with drought/heat leading to very small berries, and the French oak was a key decision here. The colour is deep, the flavours very intense, but without dead fruit characters. A full-bodied red that will be at its best post '30. Screwcap. 14.5% alc. Rating 95 To 2044 $49
Slaughterhouse Paddock Single Vineyard Shiraz 2016 47yo vines, open-fermented with 20% whole bunches, the balance crushed and destemmed, 9 days on skins, matured for 16 months in American oak (30% new). While full-bodied, the bouquet and palate tell an identical tale of generosity of blackberry, spice and licorice fruit flavours wrapped in choc-mint, American oak and soft tannins. Low yield was the driver. Screwcap. 14.5% alc. Rating 94 To 2036 $49

ΥΥΥΥΥ Cravens Place Shiraz 2017 Rating 91 To 2032 $20
Mail Coach Shiraz 2016 Rating 91 To 2029 $31

Heathvale

300 Saw Pit Gully Road, via Keyneton, SA 5353 **Region** Eden Valley
T (08) 8564 8248 www.heathvale.com **Open** At Taste Eden Valley, or by appt
Winemaker Trevor March, Chris Taylor **Est.** 1987 **Dozens** 1500 **Vyds** 10ha
The origins of Heathvale go back to 1865, when William Heath purchased the property, building the homestead and establishing a vineyard. The wine was initially made in the cellar

of the house that is now occupied by owners Trevor and Faye March. The vineyards were re-established in 1987, and consist of shiraz, cabernet sauvignon, riesling, sagrantino and tempranillo. Between 2011 and '12, fundamental changes for the better took place. Stylish new labels are but an outward sign of the far more important changes to wine style, with winemaking now under the control of consultant Chris Taylor (Quattro Mano). Exports to China.

⟡⟡⟡⟡⟡ **The Witness Eden Valley Riesling 2017** An extra lick of intensity and enough kick to the finish make this a tasty prospect. Lime rind, mandarin juice, talc and spice notes. There's body here but it's racy too. Screwcap. 12% alc. **Rating** 92 To 2023 $25 CM ✪

Hedonist Wines

Rifle Range Road, McLaren Vale, SA 5171 **Region** McLaren Vale
T (08) 8323 8818 **www.**hedonistwines.com.au **Open** Not
Winemaker Walter Clappis, Kimberley & James Cooter **Est.** 1982
Dozens 18 000 **Vyds** 35ha
Walter Clappis has been making wine in McLaren Vale for well over 30 years, and over that time has won innumerable trophies and gold medals, including the prestigious George Mackey Memorial Trophy with his 2009 The Hedonist Shiraz, chosen as the best wine exported from Australia that year. He now has daughter Kimberley and son-in-law James Cooter (both with impressive CVs) supporting him on the winery floor. The estate plantings of shiraz (14ha), cabernet sauvignon (10ha), merlot (9ha) and tempranillo (2ha) are the cornerstone of the business. Exports to the UK, the US, Canada and China.

⟡⟡⟡⟡⟡ **The Hedonist McLaren Vale Shiraz 2016** Deeply coloured; sophisticated winemaking has resulted in a full-bodied shiraz that will be very long lived. It has balance and length, and firm yet ripe tannins are one of its many building blocks. Gold medal International Shiraz Challenge '18 (no surprise). Great value. Screwcap. 14% alc. **Rating** 94 To 2041 $23 ✪
The Hedonist McLaren Vale Cabernet Sauvignon 2016 A medium-bodied, savoury wine with just a hint of mint/wintergreen, outweighed by the freshness and cassis flavours of the long palate – all in all, cool-climate references. Screwcap. 13.5% alc. **Rating** 94 To 2030 $23 ✪

⟡⟡⟡⟡⟡ **The Hedonist Reserve McLaren Vale Shiraz 2015 Rating** 91 To 2030 $65

Heemskerk

660 Blessington Road, White Hills, Tas 7258 (postal) **Region** Southern Tasmania
T 1300 651 650 **www.**heemskerk.com.au **Open** Not
Winemaker Peter Munro **Est.** 1975 **Dozens** NFP
The Heemskerk brand, established by Graham Wiltshire when he planted the first vines in 1965 (in the Pipers River region), is a very different business today. It is part of TWE, and sources its grapes from vineyards including the Riversdale vineyard in the Coal River Valley for riesling; the Lowestoft vineyard in the Derwent Valley for pinot noir; and the Tolpuddle vineyard in the Coal River Valley for chardonnay.

⟡⟡⟡⟡⟡ **Southern Tasmanian Pinot Noir 2016** Matured in new and used French oak of various sizes. An impressive example of Tasmanian pinot noir, with star-bright crimson colour, and cherry/berry fruits populating most of the bouquet and palate. Happily, there is space for fine, ripe tannins and well integrated oak. Screwcap. 13% alc. **Rating** 96 To 2033 $60 ✪
Coal River Valley Chardonnay 2016 Matured in French barriques and hogsheads, but otherwise made with minimal intervention in the winery (it had plenty of depth and complexity, so no elaboration was required). Gold medal Melbourne Wine Awards '17. Screwcap. 12.5% alc. **Rating** 95 To 2026 $50
Southern Tasmania Chardonnay Pinot Noir 2012 This terrific sparkling is packaged in a super-elegant bottle rising continuously from a broad base to a

narrow neck. The grapes are from southern Tasmanian vineyards. Tasmanian fruit intensity comes at you with a Roaring 40s force, a tangy, zesty array of all the citrus family flavours in an unending stream. Cork. 12% alc. **Rating** 95 $60
Abel's Tempest Pinot Noir 2016 Typical Tasmanian pinot noir with abundant colour and varietal character, yet not the least heavy, let alone heading into dry-red characters. Dark cherry fruit and a generous splash of plum team up with superfine tannins to get the job done. Screwcap. 13.5% alc. **Rating** 94 **To** 2026 $32

ŸŸŸŸŸ **Abel's Tempest Chardonnay 2016** Rating 93 To 2025 $25 ✪
Abel's Tempest Chardonnay Pinot Noir NV Rating 91 $32 TS

Heggies Vineyard ★★★★★
Heggies Range Road, Eden Valley, SA 5235 **Region** Eden Valley
T (08) 8561 3200 **www**.heggiesvineyard.com **Open** By appt
Winemaker Teresa Heuzenroeder **Est.** 1971 **Dozens** 15 000 **Vyds** 62ha
Heggies was one of the high-altitude vineyards established in the Eden Valley by the Hill-Smith family. Plantings on the 120ha former grazing property found at 570m altitude began in 1971. The principal varieties are riesling, chardonnay, viognier and merlot. There is also a 1.1ha reserve chardonnay block, and 27ha of various clonal trials. Exports to all major markets.

ŸŸŸŸŸ **Valley Riesling 2016** A tightly woven fabric from particular parcels of the vineyard, backed by natural acidity. One of those wines that takes several tastings to see its quality. Screwcap. 11% alc. **Rating** 95 **To** 2036 $26 ✪
Botrytis Riesling 2017 The balance between sweetness, acidity and varietal fruit is far harder to achieve than you might expect. This nails it. It is all about lime tinged with cumquat, fresh mouthfeel and a peacock's tail finish revealing a flash of exotic spice. Screwcap. 10% alc. **Rating** 95 **To** 2027 $27 ✪
Eden Valley Chardonnay 2015 This is a well made wine, at or near the apex of Eden Valley chardonnay in the shifting sands of modern style. The colour is still light and bright, the fruit with the best of both worlds (freshness and clear, ripe varietal character), oak kept under control. Screwcap. 13% alc. **Rating** 94 **To** 2025 $31

ŸŸŸŸŸ **Estate Eden Valley Chardonnay 2016** Rating 90 To 2026 $31

Heirloom Vineyards ★★★★★
Salopian Inn, Cnr Main Road/McMurtrie Road, McLaren Vale, SA 5171 **Region** Adelaide
T (08) 8556 6099 **www**.heirloomvineyards.com.au **Open** 7 days 10–5
Winemaker Elena Brooks **Est.** 2004 **Dozens** NFP
This is (yet another) venture for Zar Brooks and wife Elena. They met during the 2000 vintage, and one thing led to another, as they say. Dandelion Vineyards and Zonte's Footstep came along first, but other partners are involved in those ventures. Zar and Elena also co-own the Salopian Inn, which has the cellar door of Heirloom Vineyards in the restaurant. The lofty aims of Heirloom are 'to preserve the best of tradition, the unique old vineyards of SA, and to champion the best clones of each variety, embracing organic and biodynamic farming'. I don't doubt the sincerity of the sentiments, but there's a fair degree of Brooksian marketing spin involved. Exports to all major markets.

ŸŸŸŸŸ **A'Lambra Eden Valley Shiraz 2015** A wine of beauty and substance. From the first sip to the final swallow this has you wrapped around its finger. It tastes of fresh boysenberry and pure plum, mint and violets, wood smoke from oak, and five-spice notes adding some extra flash. Firm but ultra-fine tannin plays tugboat to the power of fruit, guiding it through the finish. It's a standout. Screwcap. 14.5% alc. **Rating** 97 **To** 2040 $80 CM ✪

ŸŸŸŸŸ **Eden Valley Riesling 2017** Textbook in a gorgeous way. All hail Eden Valley riesling. Taste it and find flavours of lemon, lime, bath salts and talc, sure – but it's also about the elegance, the length, the impression of extreme purity. Screwcap. 11.5% alc. **Rating** 95 **To** 2032 $30 CM ✪

Adelaide Hills Chardonnay 2016 Tasty and textural. Energetic too. A terrific style of chardonnay. Pear drops and barley, cooked apple and stone fruit. Toasty/cedary oak adds a layer. It delivers on every promise and then some. Screwcap. 12.5% alc. **Rating** 95 **To** 2023 $30 CM ✪

Anevo Fortress McLaren Vale Grenache Touriga Tempranillo 2016 A velvety red with pure (mostly red) berried fruit and classic inlays of cedar wood and spice. Smoky oak loosens the safety catch and lets the wine have it. Tannin here, both al dente and firm, is just so beautifully handled. Indeed the wine as a whole is a treat. Screwcap. 14.5% alc. **Rating** 95 **To** 2026 $80 CM

Alcala McLaren Vale Grenache 2016 Substance, satiny texture, style; this has the trifecta. It's not the brightest grenache on the catwalk, but its woody anise notes and fragrant herb and earth characters help make up for it in personality. Sweet-fruited but not to an excessive degree; the same judgement can be made of the alcohol. Clearly the quality of the grenache fruit itself is high. Screwcap. 14.5% alc. **Rating** 94 **To** 2025 $80 CM

Adelaide Hills Tempranillo 2016 It's a big wine for a tempranillo. Big on cola and herbs, raspberry and smoky/cedary oak. It fills the mouth to all corners; one sip and you know that you're in aspirational territory. Tannin places a firm hand on the reins but remains inconspicuous about it. Very good. Screwcap. 14% alc. **Rating** 94 **To** 2026 $40 CM

🍷🍷🍷🍷🍷 **Adelaide Hills Pinot Grigio 2017 Rating** 93 **To** 2019 $30 CM
Barossa Valley Shiraz 2016 Rating 93 **To** 2030 $40 CM
Adelaide Hills Pinot Noir 2016 Rating 92 **To** 2025 $40 CM
McLaren Vale Shiraz 2016 Rating 92 **To** 2028 $40 CM
Adelaide Hills Sauvignon Blanc 2017 Rating 91 **To** 2019 $30 CM
McLaren Vale Touriga 2016 Rating 90 **To** 2024 $40 CM

Helen & Joey Estate   ★★★★☆

12–14 Spring Lane, Gruyere, Vic 3770 **Region** Yarra Valley
T 1800 989 463 **www.**helenandjoeyestate.com.au **Open** 7 days 10–5
Winemaker Meg Brodtmann MW **Est.** 2011 **Dozens** 28 000 **Vyds** 35ha
This is the venture of Helen Xu, who purchased the large Fernando vineyard on Spring Lane in 2010. It is planted to pinot noir, cabernet sauvignon, merlot, chardonnay, pinot gris, shiraz and sauvignon blanc. Helen's background is quite varied. She has a masters degree in analytical chemistry, and was a QA manager for Nestlé for several years. She now owns a business in Shanghai, working in textile ink development together with husband Joey, and they currently split their time between China and Australia. Exports to the US, Singapore, Japan and China.

🍷🍷🍷🍷🍷 **Alena Single Vineyard Yarra Valley Chardonnay 2016** This is Helen & Joey's flagship chardonnay, and has been made to age with grace thanks to its natural acidity, restrained use of new oak and (bravely) low alcohol. Unless you have had the luck to be able to taste new vintages of a good wine and then watch them develop over 5–10 years, you might well think the wine is too thin. It's not. Screwcap. 12.5% alc. **Rating** 95 **To** 2026 $50

Layla Single Vineyard Yarra Valley Chardonnay 2017 Partial maturation in French oak emphasises the ability of the Yarra Valley to achieve high quality chardonnay with minimal winery inputs, and with the grapes picked to retain maximum freshness and flavour. Grapefruit, melon and apple are all in play, oak less so. Screwcap. 12.8% alc. **Rating** 94 **To** 2024 $35

Layla Single Vineyard Yarra Valley Pinot Noir 2017 Well made, with a multiple cherries (red, black, morello) on both the bouquet and medium-bodied palate. Has the requisite balance to mature gracefully, and has made the most of the excellent cool vintage. Screwcap. 13.6% alc. **Rating** 94 **To** 2027 $35

Alena Single Vineyard Yarra Valley Pinot Noir 2016 This is part of the flagship range, produced from identified vineyard blocks given special treatment during the growing season. The wine is a barrel selection. An elegant, well balanced pinot with considerable length. Screwcap. 13% alc. **Rating** 94 **To** 2026 $50

Alena Single Vineyard Yarra Valley Cabernet Merlot 2016 A most attractive example of this blend, the two varieties locked together so tightly they have become one. Cassis, spice and herbal nuances provide a medium-bodied, well balanced and long wine that was picked at exactly the right time. Screwcap. 13.9% alc. **Rating** 94 **To** 2031 $50

ŢŢŢŢŢ **Inara Single Vineyard Yarra Valley Rose 2017** **Rating** 93 **To** 2020 $25
Inara Single Vineyard Yarra Valley Chardonnay 2017 **Rating** 91
To 2022 $25
Inara Single Vineyard Yarra Valley Pinot Noir 2016 **Rating** 90 **To** 2022 $25
Alena Single Vineyard Yarra Valley Cabernet Sauvignon 2016 **Rating** 90
To 2022 $50

Helen's Hill Estate ★★★★★

16 Ingram Road, Lilydale, Vic 3140 **Region** Yarra Valley
T (03) 9739 1573 **www**.helenshill.com.au **Open** 7 days 10–5
Winemaker Scott McCarthy **Est.** 1984 **Dozens** 15 000 **Vyds** 53ha
Helen's Hill Estate is named after the previous owner of the property, Helen Fraser. Partners Andrew and Robyn McIntosh and Roma and Allan Nalder combine childhood farming experience with more recent careers in medicine and finance to manage the day-to-day operations of the estate. It produces two labels: Helen's Hill Estate and Ingram Road, both made onsite. Winemaker Scott McCarthy started his career early by working vintages during school holidays, later gaining diverse and extensive experience in the Barossa and Yarra valleys, Napa Valley, Languedoc, the Loire Valley and Marlborough. The winery, cellar door complex and elegant 140-seat restaurant command some of the best views in the valley. Exports to Hong Kong, the Maldives and China.

ŢŢŢŢŢ **Hill Top Single Vineyard Yarra Valley Syrah 2015** Co-fermented with 2% viognier, matured for 18 months in French puncheons (35% new). Revels in the exceptional quality of the vintage and the unrelenting attention to detail in the estate vineyards. The bouquet draws you back again and again to its rainbow of aromas of spices, forest floor, leaf, briar and dark chocolate, with most morphing into the very complex palate that adds licorice and oak to the equation. Screwcap. 14.5% alc. **Rating** 96 **To** 2035 $35 **۞**
Winemakers Reserve Single Vineyard Yarra Valley Shiraz 2013 The best 5 barrels of the Hill Top Syrah were selected for their capacity for extended time in bottle. This wine is only released in the best vintages. 2013 was a year notable for the small size of the berries and high tannin profiles, and the power and intensity of the palate fully lives up to expectations with its dark forest berry flavours and long finish. Diam. 14.5% alc. **Rating** 96 **To** 2043 $120
Lana's Single Vineyard Yarra Valley Rose 2017 Has a particularly fragrant bouquet of red flowers and fruits, which are also there on the glistening palate. X-factor? Yes, in spades, as the crushed strawberry fruits stream through to the finish and aftertaste. Screwcap. 12.8% alc. **Rating** 95 **To** 2021 $28 **۞**
Long Walk Single Vineyard Yarra Valley Pinot Noir 2016 This is a very good wine from a challenging vintage that ripened grapes of all varieties quickly. There is crystal-clear varietal expression of cherries and spices, the palate going further with a freshness and intensity of red fruit flavours, silky tannins, and integrated quality oak the ribbon to wrap it all up. Screwcap. 12.8% alc. **Rating** 95 **To** 2029 $35 **۞**
Breachley Block Single Vineyard Yarra Valley Chardonnay 2017
Taking the wine direct to barrel for 10 months on full lees with only occasional batonnage probably reduced the mouthfeel due to reduction. However, the wine had only just made its way to bottle when tasted, so 6–12 months may see growth in complexity. Screwcap. 12.8% alc. **Rating** 94 **To** 2025 $35

ŢŢŢŢŢ **Evolution Single Vineyard Yarra Valley Fume Blanc 2015** **Rating** 92
To 2020 $30

Ingram Road Single Vineyard Yarra Valley Cabernets 2015 Rating 92
To 2030 $22 ✪
Ingram Road Single Vineyard Yarra Valley Pinot Noir 2016 Rating 90
To 2024 $22

Helm ★★★★★

19 Butt's Road, Murrumbateman, NSW 2582 **Region** Canberra District
T (02) 6227 5953 **www.**helmwines.com.au **Open** Thurs–Mon 10–5
Winemaker Ken Helm, Stephanie Helm **Est.** 1973 **Dozens** 5000 **Vyds** 17ha
Ken Helm celebrated his 40th vintage in 2016. Over the years he has achieved many things, through dogged persistence on the one hand, vision on the other. Riesling has been an all-consuming interest, evidenced by his rieslings of consistently high quality. He has also given much to the wine community, extending from the narrow focus of the Canberra District to the broad canvas of the world of riesling: in '00 he established the Canberra International Riesling Challenge. He retired as chairman in '16 but keeps an active eye on the Challenge. In '14 his youngest child Stephanie (and husband Ben Osborne, Helm's vineyard manager) purchased Yass Valley Wines, rebranding it as 'The Vintner's Daughter', and but Ken has persuaded Stephanie to join him as winemaker at Helm. In '17 Helm completed construction of a separate 40000l insulated winery with a double-refrigeration system dedicated to the production of riesling. The old winery is now dedicated to cabernet sauvignon. Exports to the UK.

🍷🍷🍷🍷🍷 **Premium Riesling 2017** Akin to a litany of high citrus octaves, spicy undertones and a stone-fruit melody yet to unravel across scales of juicy acidity and muscular personality. Palate-staining intensity, here. Lay it down! Screwcap. 11.8% alc. **Rating** 95 **To** 2035 $58 NG
Classic Dry Riesling 2017 Despite its youth, this expression feels downright relaxed and juicy – a counterpoint to the rigidity of Helm's riesling from Orange. Cumquat, nectarine and apricot stream up the nostrils. Talc and citrus, too. Dry and tactile, this is a pleasure to drink. Full of pulsating juiciness pulled long and wide across the senses. Screwcap. 11.5% alc. **Rating** 94 **To** 2031 $38 NG

🍷🍷🍷🍷🍷 **Central Ranges Orange Riesling 2017** Rating 93 To 2029 $30 NG
Tumbarumba Canberra Riesling 2017 Rating 92 To 2025 $30 NG
Half Dry Riesling 2017 Rating 92 To 2025 $30 NG
Premium Cabernet Sauvignon 2015 Rating 90 To 2025 $58 NG

Henry's Drive Vignerons ★★★★

41 Hodgson Road, Padthaway, SA 5271 **Region** Padthaway
T (08) 8132 1048 **www.**henrysdrive.com **Open** 7 days 10–4
Winemaker Andrew Miller **Est.** 1998 **Dozens** 65000 **Vyds** 94.9ha
Named after the proprietor of the 19th-century mail coach service that once ran through Kim Longbottom and her late husband Mark's property. Kim is continuing to build on the winemaking with brands such as Henry's Drive, Pillar Box, The Scarlet Letter and The Postmistress. Exports to the UK, the US, Canada, Denmark, Singapore, Hong Kong, China and NZ.

🍷🍷🍷🍷🍷 **Padthaway Shiraz 2014** Excellent depth of dark-berried flavour with oak/texture to match. This is a 'big red' in winning form. The coating of choc-cream, the inherent density, the melt of tannin and the rise of spearmint to close; it's all positive; it all works. Screwcap. 14.5% alc. **Rating** 93 **To** 2030 $35 CM
Magnus Padthaway Shiraz 2014 A very full-bodied flagship shiraz coming from a rare slope protected by trees on the family property. It is made on the principle that more flavour is good, most flavour is best. This has the best fruit smothered in new oak, looking for a way out that it may or may not discover. Screwcap. 14.7% alc. **Rating** 90 **To** 2034 $60

🍷🍷🍷🍷 **H Padthaway Chardonnay 2016** Rating 89 To 2019 $25 CM
Padthaway Shiraz Cabernet 2014 Rating 89 To 2029 $35

Henschke   ★★★★★

1428 Keyneton Road, Keyneton, SA 5353 **Region** Eden Valley
T (08) 8564 8223 www.henschke.com.au **Open** Mon–Fri 9–4.30, Sat 9–12
Winemaker Stephen Henschke **Est.** 1868 **Dozens** 30 000 **Vyds** 121.72ha
Regarded as the best medium-sized red wine producer in Australia, Henschke has gone from strength to strength over the past three decades under the guidance of winemaker Stephen Henschke and viticulturist Prue Henschke. The red wines fully capitalise on the very old, low-yielding, high quality vines, and are superbly made with sensitive but positive use of new small oak: Hill of Grace is second only to Penfolds Grange as Australia's red wine icon. The 2012 Hill of Grace was Wine of the Year in the *Wine Companion* 2018. Henschke is a founding member of Australia's First Families of Wine. Exports to all major markets.

ŸŸŸŸŸ **Hill of Roses 2012** Made from a small patch of 25yo vines on the Hill of Grace that are considered too young for inclusion in Hill of Grace. Matured in French hogsheads (71% new) for 18 months. This has missile power and drive on an exact course stretching out far into the distance. Blackberry, blackcurrant, licorice (I won't use the word 'tar'), leather and earth flavours are wrapped by bonds of implacable tannins on a palate of prodigious length. Too good for Hill of Grace? A heretical question that in any event has no answer. Vino-Lok. 14.5% alc. **Rating** 98 **To** 2052 $390
Tappa Pass Vineyard Selection Barossa Shiraz 2016 From vines up to 70yo in the Eden and Barossa valleys. This has quite extraordinary depth to its dense crimson-purple hue, a clue to the palate of the wine, which first hit the headlines in '10 and has continued to do so every year since. It is awash with voluminous black fruits of every description, tannins and oak folded within. The magic of the wine is that it is neither heavy nor extractive, just very, very long. Vino-Lok. 14.5% alc. **Rating** 97 **To** 2046 $115 ✪
Mount Edelstone 2013 The 61st vintage, from 101yo ungrafted dry-grown vines. The decision to hold back the release until after the '14 was correct – this is a densely packed shiraz destined for a long life, as vertical tastings have proved again and again. Intensity and focus achieved without apparent effort. Medium-bodied, but with compelling black fruits riding on the back of tannins and carefully measured oak. Screwcap. 14.5% alc. **Rating** 97 **To** 2043 $225
Hill Of Grace 2013 The patchwork quilt of Hill of Grace was picked in small parcels between 21 Feb and 7 Mar. It's a rock-solid wine (to use a Henschke expression), matured in 86% French and 14% American oak (56% new). There are no dead fruits, but this is full-bodied with blackberry, licorice and anise fruit, the tannins exceptionally well managed, the oak likewise. Screwcap. 14.5% alc. **Rating** 97 **To** 2048 $825

ŸŸŸŸŸ **Green's Hill Adelaide Hills Riesling 2017** The vintage had its challenges with well above average rainfall. Ultra-pale colour, the wine explodes in the mouth with the intensity of its citrussy, minerally flavours. The finish leaves a sorbet-like aftertaste. Screwcap. 12.5% alc. **Rating** 95 **To** 2037 $35 ✪
Julius Eden Valley Riesling 2017 Rich and layered, with a mix of Rose's lime and Meyer lemon fruit flavours. The balance of flavours and length are excellent, which is no surprise given the alcohol, pH and titratable acidity are all textbook. Hard work in the vineyard has paid off handsomely. Screwcap. 11.5% alc. **Rating** 95 **To** 2037 $45
Giles Adelaide Hills Pinot Noir 2016 No vinification info gleaned from a 300+ word backgrounder (other than 10 months' maturation in French hogsheads). An extremely fragrant bouquet of red and blue fruits points the way for a long, loose-limbed and elegant palate, the tannins silky, the finish clean. Screwcap. 13.5% alc. **Rating** 95 **To** 2026 $55
Abbotts Prayer Vineyard 2015 57% cabernet sauvignon, 43% merlot from the Lenswood vineyard, matured in French hogsheads (30% new) for 18 months. Henschke was one of the early movers with this blend in the Adelaide Hills, and learned quickly. It is a super-elegant, medium-bodied style with cassis the

cornerstone, well trained tannins doing the job as expected, the finish fine. Vino-Lok. 14.5% alc. **Rating** 95 **To** 2035 $100

Johanne Ida Selma Lenswood Blanc de Noir MD NV A striking 100% pinot noir aged for up to 18 years on lees; the last blend in Nov '17. A striking feature is its gin-clear colour, but so are the remnants of pinot noir flavour, and its exceptional length. Be aware, however, the dosage may be zero or very low. Bottle development could be fascinating. Crown seal. 12% alc. **Rating** 95 $62

Peggy's Hill Eden Valley Riesling 2017 The grapes were delivered between 14 Mar and 1 Apr, and this spread has given the wine excellent mouthfeel and balance, only a touch behind its two siblings. Screwcap. 12% alc. **Rating** 94 **To** 2037 $25 **○**

The Rose Grower Eden Valley Nebbiolo 2014 This is a truly remarkable wine to arise from a vintage ravaged by rain (the wettest Feb in 44 years), and a record number of hot days over 40°C in Feb. Silky, mouthwatering tannins run through cherry/watermelon/spice fruit on the delicious palate. I would drink it tonight. Vino-Lok. 13% alc. **Rating** 94 **To** 2023 $60

Stone Jar Eden Valley Tempranillo 2016 Well above normal colour, body, flavour, length and tannins, resulting in a wine that will live for many years and always give pleasure as it moves through the changes of age. Screwcap. 14.5% alc. **Rating** 94 **To** 2036 $50

ΥΥΥΥΥ **Joseph Hill Gewurztraminer 2017** **Rating** 93 **To** 2037 $36
Croft Adelaide Hills Chardonnay 2016 **Rating** 93 **To** 2023 $50
Henry's Seven 2016 **Rating** 93 **To** 2036 $37
Louis 2016 **Rating** 90 **To** 2026 $33
Coralinga Adelaide Hills Sauvignon Blanc 2017 **Rating** 90 **To** 2020 $27

Henskens Rankin of Tasmania   ★★★★

PO Box 67, Sandy Bay, Tas 7005 **Region** Southern Tasmania
T (03) 6288 8508 **www**.henskensrankin.com **Open** Not
Winemaker Greer Carland, Frieda Henskens, Glenn James **Est.** 2010 **Dozens** 130
Choice and consequence began its complicated course in 1999 when Frieda Henskens and David Rankin independently came to Tasmania. His contribution to the business they eventually formed has been peripheral: designated driver (was and is a non-drinker) and father of their growing family. Frieda's original occupation was in agriculture, diverting to viniculture in 2006. By '09 she was working at Julian Alcorso's Winemaking Tasmania during vintage, performing cellar duties at other times. In '10 Frieda and David purchased a small quantity of fruit to make a traditional-method, chardonnay-dominant sparkling wine that they envisaged would be long-lived. While David and Frieda have moved on to other employment, their partnership with Winemaking Tasmania has as its ultimate aim the production of 600 dozen bottles per year.

ΥΥΥΥΥ **Vintage Brut 2011** 70% chardonnay, 30% pinot noir, 7 years on lees. Striking pale colour; notably elegant and fresh, the decision to keep the reserve wine (12%) in a 5500l foudre precisely correct. Excellent conception and execution. Cork. 11.9% alc. **Rating** 94 **To** 2022 $90

ΥΥΥΥΥ **Vintage Brut 2010** **Rating** 90 **To** 2021 $90

Hentley Farm Wines   ★★★★★

Cnr Jenke Road/Gerald Roberts Road, Seppeltsfield, SA 5355 **Region** Barossa Valley
T (08) 8562 8427 **www**.hentleyfarm.com.au **Open** 7 days 11–5
Winemaker Andrew Quin **Est.** 1999 **Dozens** 20 000 **Vyds** 44.7ha
Keith and Alison Hentschke purchased Hentley Farm in 1997, as an old vineyard and mixed farming property. Keith has thoroughly impressive credentials, having studied agricultural science at Roseworthy, graduating with distinction, later adding an MBA. During the '90s he had a senior production role with Orlando, before moving on to manage Fabal, one of

Australia's largest vineyard management companies. Establishing Hentley Farm might have seemed all too easy, but it required all his knowledge to create such a great vineyard. A total of 38.2ha were planted between '99 and 2005 with shiraz dominating the plantings. Situated on the banks of Greenock Creek, the vineyard has red clay loam soils overlaying shattered limestone, and lightly rocked slopes. In '04 an adjoining 6.5ha vineyard, christened Clos Otto, was acquired. Hentley Farm was Winery of the Year in the *Wine Companion* 2015. Exports to the US and other major markets.

♀♀♀♀♀ Museum Release The Creation Barossa Valley Shiraz 2013 As ever, the wine balances its formidable power so perfectly you don't notice it unless someone asks the question. Dark/black fruits are given precisely calibrated texture by the oak, and structure by the tannins. Attention to detail is the secret. Hentley Farm's success reflects the abnormally short time to reach museum status. The corks are perfectly inserted and of high quality. 14.8% alc. **Rating** 98 **To** 2043 $250
Museum Release Clos Otto Barossa Valley Shiraz 2012 This is a remarkable wine, reflecting a rare piece of earth on which the vines are planted, along with the '12 vintage and the skill of winemaker Andrew Quin. There is an intensity to the palate that soars almost above all others from this vintage, mouthwatering in its drive and length, its dark fruits in total harmony with the oak and tannins. Cork. 14.5% alc. **Rating** 98 **To** 2050 $290
The Creation Barossa Valley Shiraz 2016 Essentially the same vinification for the best wines of the portfolio, except here with 8 days on skins, and 50% new French oak. The colour of these wines is likewise identical. The move from American oak has been for the better, giving this wine a mouthwatering burst of fruit (and oak) from the first sip. It's full-bodied, but is the lightest of these top wines. The attention to detail at every step along the way has to be the crux of the achievement. Cork. 14.5% alc. **Rating** 96 **To** 2046 $170
Museum Release H-Block Barossa Valley Shiraz Cabernet 2013 22 months in two-thirds new French oak is frequently used with these ultra-premium Hentley Farm wines, but each has its own personality. Here the slightly firmer tannins and aromatic blackcurrant of the 35% cabernet generate the differences. Cork. 14.8% alc. **Rating** 97 **To** 2038 $250

♀♀♀♀♀ Clos Otto Barossa Valley Shiraz 2016 Destemmed estate fruit, open-fermented with cultured yeast, 6–12 days on skins, 22 months in French oak (65% new). Deep, dark crimson-purple; a wine of immense power matched by elegance achieved in the vinification. High quality cedary oak provides a platform for the succulent black berry fruits and velvety tannins on the finish. Cork. 14.8% alc. **Rating** 96 **To** 2046 $180
Rapscallion Barossa Valley Shiraz 2017 Very, very interesting style for Hentley Farm. It's estate fruit, but that's about all that's similar. Open-fermented with 70% whole bunches, 25 days on skins, 8 months in used oak. Rich purple-crimson hue and layered richness, then the complex palate in furious conversation about its spicy flavours and crosshatch texture from the whole-bunch fermentation. Screwcap. 13.5% alc. **Rating** 95 **To** 2037 $45
The Beast Barossa Valley Shiraz 2016 Identical vinification to Clos Otto, but a very different mouthfeel and structure. There is an urgency to the wine as it rushes forward to the finish, making sure it leaves its footprints along the way. While full-bodied, there is intensity and focus, leaving space for finely ground tannins (and, of course, French oak) to make their mark. Cork. 15% alc. **Rating** 95 **To** 2041 $89
H Block Shiraz Cabernet 2016 A 62/38% blend, 22 months in French oak (60% new). Full-bodied blackberry, plum and blackcurrant fruit in the typical glossy, supple Hentley Farm style, which more often than not makes the tannins become invisible; new oak just part of the furniture. Cork. 15% alc. **Rating** 95 **To** 2041 $170
The Quintessential Barossa Valley Shiraz Cabernet 2016 A 51/49% blend, matured for 22 months in French oak (35% new). Well named – this is indeed quintessential Barossa Valley flavour and weight, blocking the way for anyone

hoping to slip past without being noticed. The very long maceration of up to 65 days for some (unspecified) part of the blend has doubtless played a role, so too the new French oak on the bouquet and palate alike. A query is the slightly turbid colour. Screwcap. 14.5% alc. **Rating** 95 **To** 2031 $62

von Kasper Barossa Valley Cabernet Sauvignon 2016 The colour is a deep crimson-purple, and the wine packs lethal power given its mid-range alcohol. The long, high quality cork should help the wine reach its plateau 15 years or so hence, as its blackcurrant fruit and autocratic tannins join with cedary French oak to bring it all home. 14.5% alc. **Rating** 95 **To** 2041 $89

Eden Valley Riesling 2017 This is a pure expression of vineyard, vintage and variety. It has Meyer lemon and lesser lime aromas and flavours, the constant being the minerally acidity. A great future. Screwcap. 11.8% alc. **Rating** 94 **To** 2030 $24 ✪

Villain & Vixen Barossa Valley Shiraz 2016 Has a striking two-way bottle label, except I would reverse the assigned portraits of Villain and Vixen. The label illustrates Hentley Farm's preference for elegance over extraction, for soft, silky tannins and bright fruit; for new school over traditional school. The problem is that this wine borrows some of the best aspects of traditional winemaking. Screwcap. 14.2% alc. **Rating** 94 **To** 2036 $25 ✪

Villain & Vixen Barossa Valley Grenache 2017 This is much more to my liking; all the freshness and fruit coming from gentle extraction over a short period, alcohol of 14% not 14.5%, and little or no confection make this a Vixen style. Screwcap. **Rating** 94 **To** 2022 $25 ✪

🍷🍷🍷🍷♀ **Barossa Valley Shiraz 2017** **Rating** 93 **To** 2037 $28
Black Beauty Sparkling Shiraz NV **Rating** 93 $62 TS
Barossa Valley Viognier 2017 **Rating** 92 **To** 2019 $45
The Stray Mongrel 2017 **Rating** 92 **To** 2025 $28
Poppy Barossa Field Blend 2017 **Rating** 91 **To** 2019 $21 ✪
Barossa Valley Cabernet Sauvignon 2017 **Rating** 91 **To** 2027 $28
Barossa Valley Rose 2017 **Rating** 90 **To** 2020 $21 ✪
The Beauty Barossa Valley Shiraz 2016 **Rating** 90 **To** 2027 $62 DB

Henty Estate ★★★★★

657 Hensley Park Road, Hamilton, Vic 3300 (postal) **Region** Henty
T (03) 5572 4446 **www.**henty-estate.com.au **Open** Not
Winemaker Peter Dixon **Est.** 1991 **Dozens** 1400 **Vyds** 7ha
Peter and Glenys Dixon have hastened slowly with Henty Estate. In 1991 they began the planting of 4.5ha of shiraz, 1ha each of cabernet sauvignon and chardonnay, and 0.5ha of riesling. In their words, 'We avoided the temptation to make wine until the vineyard was mature', establishing the winery in 2003. Encouraged by neighbour John Thomson, they have limited the yield to 3–4t per ha on the VSP-trained, dry-grown vineyard.

🍷🍷🍷🍷🍷 **Riesling 2017** It's racy, fresh and undeniably pleasing, with a raft of citrus flavours – lemon and lime juice, zest, and mandarin too. The snag is an underlying yeasty/estery note; not unpleasant, just in the way of the fruit purity. Won't stop anyone enjoying this, as the super-dry finish ensures another glass is poured quickly. Screwcap. 12.2% alc. **Rating** 95 **To** 2028 $22 JF ✪

Hamilton Shiraz 2016 From the earliest vintage on record (and hot), yet retaining its cool-climate stamp. Charming and poised, fragrant with spice, pepper, florals and fruits in the blue-black spectrum, but it's the seamless palate that works its magic: medium-bodied and lithe, very fine tannins mingling with fresh acidity, everything sashaying to a lingering finish. Screwcap. 13.3% alc. **Rating** 95 **To** 2025 $26 JF ✪

Hamilton Cabernet Sauvignon 2016 A neat mix of currants, mulberries, tar and black licorice and some leafy freshness; ripe yet retaining elegance. Savoury notes abound, the oak integrated, the medium-bodied palate filled with tannins and drive. There's a little dryness on the finish, but overall, excellent value for a cool cabernet. Just like its Shiraz sibling, this is balanced and feels effortless – well, effortless to drink. Screwcap. 13.9% alc. **Rating** 94 **To** 2027 $26 JF ❍

🍷🍷🍷🍷♀ **Wannon Run Shiraz 2016 Rating** 93 **To** 2024 $22 JF ❍
Chardonnay 2016 Rating 92 **To** 2022 $24 JF ❍

Hentyfarm Wines   ★★★★☆

250 Wattletree Road, Holgate, NSW 2250 (postal) **Region** Henty
T 0423 029 200 **www.**hentyfarm.com.au **Open** Not
Winemaker Ray Nadeson, Jono Mogg **Est.** 2009 **Dozens** 1500
Dr John Gladstones names the Henty GI of Victoria the coolest climate in Australia, cooler than Tasmania and the Macedon Ranges. This is both bane and blessing, for when it's cold, it's bitterly so. The other fact of life it has to contend with is its remoteness, lurking just along the SA border. The rest is all good news, for this region is capable of producing riesling, chardonnay and pinot noir of the highest quality, with Seppelt's Drumborg vineyard and Crawford River adding lustre to the location. In 2009 Jonathan (Jono) Mogg and partner Belinda Low made several weekend trips in the company of (then) Best's winemaker Adam Wadewitz and his partner Nikki. They were able to buy grapes from renowned Henty grower Alastair Taylor, and the first vintage of chardonnay was made. The portfolio now also includes riesling, gewurztraminer, pinot gris, pinot noir, pinot meunier and The Farm Barossa Shiraz. The wines are made by Ray Nadeson at Lethbridge Wines. Exports to China.

🍷🍷🍷🍷🍷 **Riesling 2017** As different as it is driven. Textural and intense: grapefruit and Meyer lemon, a hint of wood smoke, almost a sweet musk-like note. A cracking wine, in short. Screwcap. 11.8% alc. **Rating** 94 **To** 2028 $25 CM ❍
Pinot Meunier 2016 Energy. This wine is bursting with it. It's perfumed too, almost floral, with sweet red/black cherry and musk-like notes bringing cranberry and twiggy spice along for the ride. Tannin sweeps through the finish. It's a light-on-its-feet style but there's more depth than you might expect. Screwcap. 13.5% alc. **Rating** 94 **To** 2026 $35 CM
The Farm Barossa Valley Shiraz 2016 30yo vines. Dark and sweet but it feels fresh, lively. Christmas cake, licorice, ripe plum and a gentle slide of sweet sawdusty oak. An exercise in pure, mouthfilling seduction. Screwcap. 14.5% alc. **Rating** 94 **To** 2032 $30 CM

🍷🍷🍷🍷♀ **Pinot Gris 2017 Rating** 93 **To** 2020 $25 CM ❍
Pinot Noir 2016 Rating 93 **To** 2025 $35 CM
Chardonnay 2009 Rating 92 **To** 2021 CM

Herbert Vineyard   ★★★★☆

Bishop Road, Mount Gambier, SA 5290 **Region** Mount Gambier
T 0408 849 080 **www.**herbertvineyard.com.au **Open** By appt
Winemaker David Herbert **Est.** 1996 **Dozens** 550 **Vyds** 2.4ha
David and Trudy Herbert have planted 1.9ha of pinot noir, and a total of 0.5ha of cabernet sauvignon, merlot, cabernet franc, shiraz and pinot gris. They have also built a two-level (mini) winery overlooking a 1300-square metre maze, which is reflected in the label logo.

🍷🍷🍷🍷🍷 **Mount Gambier Cabernet Plus 2016** 75% cabernet sauvignon, 20% merlot, 5% cabernet franc, co-fermented, matured for 15 months in French oak (40% new). Superb colour; this is as surprising as any wine tasted this year given the very cool climate. The adventurous vinification has paid dividends 10 times over, producing a fluid, medium-bodied Bordeaux blend with an abundance of cassis and just the right amount of tannin and bay leaf to complete the picture. Bravo. Screwcap. 13% alc. **Rating** 95 **To** 2031 $22 ❍
Barrel #7 Mount Gambier Pinot Noir 2015 D5V12 clone, wild-fermented with 50% whole bunches, matured for 18 months in a 1yo French hogshead. Good retention of hue; proves the point (by a slender margin) about greater richness from higher alcohol, grapes with greater texture and sweetness to the fruit than its Barrel #1 sibling. Screwcap. 13% alc. **Rating** 94 **To** 2027 $40

ΨΨΨΨ♀ **Mount Gambier Rose 2017** Rating 91 To 2020 $18 ✪
Barrel Number 1 **Mount Gambier Pinot Noir 2016** Rating 91 To 2023 $37
Mount Gambier Pinot Gris 2016 Rating 90 To 2021 $21 ✪
Mount Gambier Pinot Noir 2016 Rating 90 To 2022 $25

Heritage Estate   ★★★★★

Granite Belt Drive, Cottonvale, Qld 4375 **Region** Granite Belt
T (07) 4685 2197 **www.**heritagewines.com.au **Open** 7 days 9–5
Winemaker John Handy **Est.** 1992 **Dozens** 5000 **Vyds** 10ha
Heritage Estate (owned by Bryce and Paddy Kassulke) has two estate vineyards in the Granite
Belt, one at Cottonvale (north) at an altitude of 960m, where it grows white varieties, and
the other at Ballandean, a slightly warmer site, where red varieties and marsanne are planted.
Heritage Estate has been a prolific award-winner in various Queensland wine shows and it
has invested in a new bottling line, enabling it to use screwcaps. The weather gyrations since
2012 are reminiscent of the run of Burgundy with its up and down frost, hail and rain issues.
Nice to have some comparison, I suppose, but doesn't put money in the bank. Thus '13, '15
and '17 have all suffered, leaving only '14 and '16 to show what can be achieved. In these
circumstances, the 5-star rating from the *Wine Companion* 2018 has been retained.

Heritage Wines   ★★★★

399 Seppeltsfield Road, Marananga, SA 5355 **Region** Barossa Valley
T (08) 8562 2880 **www.**heritagewinery.com.au **Open** Mon–Fri 10–5, w'ends 11–5
Winemaker Stephen Hoff **Est.** 1984 **Dozens** 4500 **Vyds** 8.3ha
A little-known winery that deserves a wider audience, for veteran owner/winemaker Stephen
Hoff is apt to produce some startlingly good wines. At various times the Riesling (from old
Clare Valley vines), Cabernet Sauvignon and Shiraz (now the flag-bearer) have all excelled.
The vineyard is planted to shiraz (5.5ha), cabernet sauvignon (2.5ha) and malbec (0.3ha).
Exports to the UK, Thailand, Hong Kong, Malaysia and Singapore.

ΨΨΨΨΨ **Rossco's Shiraz 2015** Caramel and iced-coffee flavours blend beautifully into
dark berry and bitumen fruit. The alcohol reading is high but the wine takes it in
its stride. It's a powerful display topped by rapids of tannin through the back half.
By the finish, no prisoners have been taken. Cork. 15% alc. **Rating** 94 **To** 2030
$55 CM

ΨΨΨΨ♀ **Steve Hoff Cabernet Sauvignon 2016** Rating 93 To 2030 $25 CM ✪
Barossa Semillon 2017 Rating 91 To 2022 $15 CM ✪

"Heroes" Vineyard   ★★★★☆

14 Deal Avenue, Jan Juc, Vic 3228 (postal) **Region** Geelong
T 0490 345 149 **www.**heroesvineyard.com **Open** Not
Winemaker James Thomas **Est.** 2016 **Dozens** 950 **Vyds** 3.9ha
James Thomas was 16 when his parents planted a vineyard in the UK in 1996. He came
to Australia in 2004, and after achieving a postgraduate degree in oenology from La Trobe
University, he spent four years as assistant winemaker at Bannockburn Vineyards, followed
by three years as head winemaker back in England, making sparkling wine. Returning
to Australia he became head winemaker at Clyde Park for the '14–16 vintages. Wanting to
establish his own winery, he looked at many possible sites in Geelong, but didn't imagine he
would be able to find one as good as he did – a 3.4ha vineyard planted to pinot noir, shiraz,
riesling and sauvignon blanc. He is deeply wedded to organic vineyard practices and moving
towards certification. He has also increased the plantings with 0.5ha chardonnay. I was much
taken by the sophistication of the labels, even more by the quality of the wines.

ΨΨΨΨΨ **Otway Hinterland Geelong Rose 2017** Picked on 1 May, the shiraz grapes
were not sufficiently ripe to make a varietal wine. Wild-fermented in used French
oak; the bouquet a perfumed mix of rose petals and spice, the palate of unexpected
intensity and length. The finish yields a teasing mix of wild berries and zesty
acidity. First class winemaking. Screwcap. 12.1% alc. **Rating** 95 **To** 2021 $25 ✪

Otway Hinterland Geelong Sauvignon Blanc 2017 Hand-picked, whole-bunch pressed, 40% wild-fermented in tank, 60% in French oak (50% new), 5 months on lees. As ever, right on the money, building maximum texture and structure without obliterating varietal fruit. Screwcap. 12.4% alc. **Rating** 94 To 2020 $28 ✪

Otway Hinterland Geelong Riesling 2017 Obviously picked early given there is only 45g/l of residual sugar and alcohol of 7.6%. Delicious lemon/lime flavours, the acid, alcohol, pH and residual sugar all howling at the same moon – and having a ball. Screwcap. **Rating** 94 To 2027 $32

♀♀♀♀♀ **Otway Hinterland Geelong Pinot Noir 2017** Rating 91 To 2027 $40

Hersey Vineyard ★★★★☆
1003 Main Street, Hahndorf, SA 5245 (postal) **Region** Adelaide Hills
T 0401 321 770 **Open** Not
Winemaker Damon Koerner **Est.** 2014 **Dozens** 2000 **Vyds** 10ha
The Hersey Vineyard was established by Ursula Pridham, Australia's first female qualified winemaker, and was run organically and biodynamically long before that became fashionable. However, years passed, and it was largely abandoned before the Hersey family (led by Jono Hersey) purchased it in early 2013 – but had to spend a year rescuscitating the vines. Even then the yields for '15 and '16 were pathetically low, with only 1.2t from 3.5ha of chardonnay. The 10ha vineyard is separated into five parcels sprawling across 52ha of forest, scrub and paddocks, all with different aspects. Pinot gris, syrah and merlot are purchased from Adelaide Hills vineyards while soil preparation is underway to plant gamay and syrah in the near future.

♀♀♀♀♀ **Clos Kuitpo Single Vineyard Chardonnay 2016** From an east-facing (worth its weight in gold) slope, matured for 12 months in French oak (5% new). There's much discussion these days about chardonnays that are 'wannabe sauvignon blancs', having been picked too early. I'll stand up for this wine, which to me has a thrilling drive of complex fruit. Yes, citrus of most kinds are there, but its energy more than makes up for that. Cork. 12% alc. **Rating** 95 To 2026 $55

Tunnel Vision Adelaide Hills Syrah 2016 Hand-picked, crushed and destemmed, open fermented with wild yeast, 14 days on skins, matured for 18 months in used oak. Light but bright crimson; a delicious light to medium-bodied syrah with small red fruit flavours and no burdensome tannins, but keeping excellent length and shape. I'd be looking at putting it in the fridge for half an hour if it's a hot day. Cork. 12.5% alc. **Rating** 94 To 2030 $55

♀♀♀♀♀ **Hills Alive Chardonnay 2016** Rating 90 To 2022 $30

Hesketh Wine Company ★★★★★
28 The Parade, Norwood, SA 5067 **Region** South Australia
T (08) 8362 8622 **www.**heskethwinecompany.com.au **Open** Not
Winemaker Phil Lehmann, Charlie Ormsby, James Lienert **Est.** 2006 **Dozens** 40 000
Headed by Jonathon Hesketh, this is part of WD Wines Pty Ltd, which also owns Parker Coonawarra Estate and St John's Road in the Barossa Valley. Jonathon spent seven years as the global sales and marketing manager of Wirra Wirra, and two and a half years as general manager of Distinguished Vineyards in NZ. He also happens to be the son of Robert Hesketh, one of the key players in the development of many facets of the SA wine industry. Jonathon says, 'After realising long ago that working for the man (Greg Trott) was never going to feed two dogs, four children, two cats, four chickens and an ever-so-patient wife, the family returned to Adelaide in early 2006 to establish Hesketh Wine Company'. The closely related venture of Lehmann | Hesketh is a partnership between the Lehmann and Hesketh families stretching back to the '70s. Exports to all major markets.

♀♀♀♀♀ **Lehmann | Hesketh Mk. 02 Coonawarra Barossa Cabernet Sauvignon Shiraz 2015** 60% Reynell Selection cabernet sauvignon from Parker Coonawarra Estate's Abbey vineyard, 40% shiraz from the Eden Valley, fermented separately, matured for 18 months in French oak before blending. Given the grape resources and the vinification, it would be surprising if this wasn't a top-flight wine – and there's no surprise. It marries intensity with elegance, currants and cherries held in a filmy veil of high quality oak and ripe tannins. Great stuff. Screwcap. 14.5% alc. **Rating** 96 **To** 2040 $50 ✪

Ebenezer Barossa Shiraz 2016 Three clones, blended after fermentation in French oak (50% new), matured for 18 months. This is a seriously good Barossa shiraz that brings out the best modern style – generous and conscious of the generations that have gone before it. The colour is great, plum and blackberry at the epicentre of the fruit spectrum, oak tannins precisely positioned. Screwcap. 14.5% alc. **Rating** 95 **To** 2036 $33 ✪

Lehmann | Hesketh Mk. 03 Coonawarra Barossa Cabernet Sauvignon Shiraz 2016 A 60/40% blend, matured for 18 months in French oak (25% new). The powerful, full-bodied wine pulls no punches along the journey, black fruits dominant. Balance is already a key note, cabernet defending its place without obvious handling bias, shiraz following suit, sustaining the wine over its long life. Screwcap. 14.5% alc. **Rating** 95 **To** 2036 $50

ㅜㅜㅜㅜㅜ **Small Parcels Barossa Valley Negroamaro 2016 Rating** 92 **To** 2026 $25 ✪
Small Parcels Barossa Valley Bonvedro 2016 Rating 90 **To** 2023 $25

Heslop Wines   ★★★☆

PO Box 93, Mudgee, NSW 2850 **Region** Mudgee
T (02) 6372 3903 **www.**heslopwines.com.au **Open** Not
Winemaker Robert Heslop **Est.** 2011 **Dozens** 300 **Vyds** 4ha
This is the venture of Bob and Julie Heslop, who returned to Mudgee (where Julie was born) in 1984, purchasing a property across the road from Julie's father's vineyard. The vendor was Ferdie Roth, a member of the famous Mudgee wine family, who had planted the muscat Hamburg vines still on the property. Bob's winemaking career began at Kay Bros in McLaren Vale while undertaking oenology studies at CSU. Using sustainable viticulture practices, they have planted 4ha to a Joseph's coat of varieties.

Hewitson   ★★★★★

66 Seppeltsfield Road, Nuriootpa, SA 5355 **Region** Adelaide
T (08) 8212 6233 **www.**hewitson.com.au **Open** 7 days 9–5
Winemaker Dean Hewitson **Est.** 1996 **Dozens** 35000 **Vyds** 4.5ha
Dean Hewitson was a winemaker at Petaluma for 10 years, during which time he managed to do three vintages in France and one in Oregon as well as undertaking his masters at the University of California (Davis). It is hardly surprising that the wines are immaculately made from a technical viewpoint. Dean sources 30-year-old riesling from the Eden Valley and 70-year-old shiraz from McLaren Vale; he also makes a Barossa Valley Mourvedre from vines planted in 1853 at Rowland Flat, and Barossa Valley Shiraz and Grenache from 60-year-old vines at Tanunda. Exports to the UK, the US and other major markets.

ㅜㅜㅜㅜㅜ **Monopole Mother Vine Barossa Valley Shiraz 2015** Dean Hewitson took cuttings from one ancient vine planted in 1853 and laboriously increased the number of rootlings year by year. Freakishly good given the youth of the vines at this stage. The structure and texture are perfect, a mix of plum, blackberry and savoury notes, the length and balance faultless. Cork. 14% alc. **Rating** 97 **To** 2035 $150 ✪

Old Garden Vineyard Barossa Valley Mourvedre 2014 The 2-acre Old Garden vineyard was planted in 1853 and is recognised as the world's oldest mourvedre vineyard. Super intense, super juicy; the quality and character take hold immediately after you take the first sip, the bouquet a deceptively serene introduction. It is one of the most seductively savoury (or vice versa) wines of this medium-bodied style I can remember. Cork. 14% alc. **Rating** 97 **To** 2040 $88 ✪

ŸŸŸŸŸ **Gun Metal Eden Valley Riesling 2017** Pale, bright straw-green; a single vineyard riesling with a highly floral bouquet, then a palate brim-full of attitude courtesy of the precisely delineated fruit. Here lime, lime zest and Granny Smith apple shake hands with steely, minerally, zesty acidity, leaving the mouth thirsting for more. Screwcap. 12.5% alc. **Rating** 96 **To** 2032 $25 ✪

Belle Ville Barossa Valley Rose 2017 Grenache, cinsaut and mourvedre. The complexity of the fragrant bouquet with its exotic spice, dried rose petals and talcum powder segues to the palate with its Byzantine mosaic of juicy red fruits. It is so highly flavoured you might expect some sweetness on the finish, but it's dry. Screwcap. 12.5% alc. **Rating** 95 **To** 2018 $25 ✪

Miss Harry Barossa Valley Harriet's Blend 2015 A light, brilliantly coloured blend of grenache, shiraz, mourvedre, cinsaut and carignan. A finely wrought and balanced wine with just about every spice and every red berry you can imagine from this Southern Rhône blend. A truly wonderful trattoria wine that soars on the gently savoury finish. Screwcap. 14% alc. **Rating** 95 **To** 2030 $25 ✪

Baby Bush Barossa Valley Mourvedre 2015 Grown from cuttings from selected vines of the 1835 plantings via the 'selection massale' process, looking for clonal diversity, but also ensuring all clones have desirable growth and yield patterns. Unsurprisingly, the wine bows to its father with its complex blend of dark purple fruits and savoury/spicy/earthy structure. Screwcap. 14% alc. **Rating** 94 **To** 2034 $28 ✪

ŸŸŸŸŶ **LuLu Adelaide Hills Sauvignon Blanc 2017 Rating** 91 **To** 2019 $25

Heydon Estate   ★★★★★

325 Tom Cullity Drive, Wilyabrup, WA 6280 **Region** Margaret River
T (08) 9755 6995 **www.**heydonestate.com.au **Open** 7 days 10–5
Winemaker Mark Messenger **Est.** 1988 **Dozens** 1800 **Vyds** 10ha
Margaret River dentist and cricket tragic George Heydon and wife Mary have been involved in the region's wine industry since 1995. They became 50% partners in Arlewood, and when that partnership was dissolved in 2004 they retained this property and the precious 2ha of cabernet sauvignon and 2.5ha of Gin Gin clone chardonnay planted in 1988. Additional plantings from '95 include Dijon chardonnay clones, sauvignon blanc, semillon, shiraz and petit verdot. The estate is now biodynamic, close neighbour Vanya Cullen having inspired the decision. Exports to the UK, Singapore and Hong Kong.

ŸŸŸŸŸ **The Willow Single Vineyard Margaret River Chardonnay 2014** Hand-picked 100% Gin Gin clone, whole-bunch pressed, cloudy juice to French oak (40% new), wild fermentation. This is true elegance, the straightest of straight bats. Margaret River isn't given to producing Chablis style, but this has a go, with many years (and runs) ahead. Screwcap. 13.5% alc. **Rating** 97 **To** 2026 $60 ✪

ŸŸŸŸŸ **W.G. Grace Single Vineyard Margaret River Cabernet Sauvignon 2013** Vines planted '98, hand-picked, crushed, destemmed, 4 weeks on skins, matured for 18 months in French oak (60% new). A very powerful wine, cabernet at its Viv Richards haughtiest best. The tannins are a firm but balanced part of the long, structured blackcurrant and black olive finish. Screwcap. 14% alc. **Rating** 96 **To** 2038 $85

Chin Music Single Vineyard Margaret River Sauvignon Blanc 2017 Selectiv'-harvested, crushed and pressed with selected yeast, stirred for 2 months, settled and bottled soon thereafter. The fruit is exceptionally intense, with snow pea, pink grapefruit and guava encircled by acidity. Screwcap. 12.8% alc. **Rating** 95 **To** 2019 $25 ✪

Hallowed Turf Single Vineyard Margaret River Chardonnay 2016 Clonal mix of 50% 95 and 227, 50% Gin Gin. Selectiv'-harvested, 50% fermented in used French oak, 50% in stainless steel barrels. Extraordinarily intense chardonnay, the oak has disappeared, leaving a pure unadorned varietal mix of stone fruit and citrus. Screwcap. 12.5% alc. **Rating** 95 **To** 2024 $30 ✪

The Doc Single Vineyard Margaret River Petit Verdot 2015 Includes 15% cabernet sauvignon, hand-picked, matured for 18 months in French oak

(40% new). Bright crimson-purple; opens with a juicy flourish, then petit verdot tannins wake up and join the band, providing both balance and length. Screwcap. 14% alc. **Rating** 94 **To** 2035 $55

Hickinbotham Clarendon Vineyard   ★★★★★

92 Brooks Road, Clarendon, SA 5157 **Region** McLaren Vale
T (08) 8383 7504 **www**.hickinbothamwines.com.au **Open** By appt
Winemaker Charlie Seppelt, Chris Carpenter **Est.** 2012 **Dozens** 3500 **Vyds** 87ha
Alan Hickinbotham, a very successful builder, established the vineyard in 1971 when he planted dry-grown cabernet sauvignon and shiraz in contoured rows on the sloping site. This was his first venture into wine, but his father, Alan Robb Hickinbotham, had a long and distinguished career, co-founding the oenology diploma at Roseworthy in '36. In 2012 the property named Clarendon, and its stately sandstone house, was purchased by Jackson Family Wines, who also own Yangarra Estate Vineyard. Exports to all major markets.

ΨΨΨΨΨ **Brooks Road McLaren Vale Shiraz 2016** A shiraz that's full-bodied and complex yet charming and swoon-worthy all at once. Excellent colour; the generosity of flavour comes through with red and black fruits, some licorice, cinnamon and a dusting of mocha. Freshness, bright acidity, length and beautiful, fine tannins seal the deal. Screwcap. 14% alc. **Rating** 96 **To** 2033 $75 JF ✪
Trueman Cabernet Sauvignon 2016 Hand-picked, destemmed but whole berries, open-fermented on skins 18 days, basket-pressed, only free-run juice, new and 1yo Bordeaux barrels, aged 15 months. It's tempting to pour a glass immediately and savour it, for everything from the fruit, cedary oak and tannins to its acidity are in total balance. Screwcap. 14% alc. **Rating** 96 **To** 2032 $75 JF ✪
The Peake Cabernet Shiraz 2016 As always, it's about choosing the best parcels of fruit and barrels for this high end wine. It's seamless. The pristine fruit absorbing the oak, the filigreed tannins, the chalky acidity, everything doing its bit to create a complete picture. While incredibly fresh, its best days are ahead of it. 460 dozen. Screwcap. 14% alc. **Rating** 96 **To** 2036 $175 JF
The Elder Hill Grenache 2016 From a single block of bushvines planted in '62, aged in seasoned barrels for 7 months. Heady aromas of raspberries, star anise and a dash of Mediterranean herbs. Lovely balance and a succulence on the medium-bodied palate, where ripe, sandy tannins kick in. Pitch-perfect now. Screwcap. 14% alc. **Rating** 95 **To** 2026 $75 JF
The Revivalist Merlot 2016 It's an impressive merlot from its heady fragrance – a hint of cassis, florals, dried herbs and cedary oak – to its exceptionally silky, fuller-bodied palate. It builds flavour, the tannins sitting pretty and the finish as long as tomorrow. Makes you fall for merlot big time. Screwcap. 13.5% alc. **Rating** 95 **To** 2026 $75 JF

Hidden Creek   ★★★☆

Eukey Road, Ballandean, Qld 4382 **Region** Granite Belt
T (07) 4684 1383 **www**.hiddencreek.com.au **Open** Mon & Fri 11–3, w'ends 10–4
Winemaker Andy Williams **Est.** 1997 **Dozens** 1000 **Vyds** 2ha
A beautifully located vineyard and winery on a ridge at 1000m overlooking the Ballandean township and the Severn River valley. The granite, boulder-strewn hills mean that the 70ha property only provides 2ha of vineyard, in turn divided into three blocks planted to shiraz and merlot. Other varieties are sourced from local growers. The business is owned by a group of Brisbane wine enthusiasts.

ΨΨΨΨΨ **Granite Belt Pinot Gris 2017** Sophisticated gris, with gentle barrel work and batonnage imparting textural intrigue to a flood of nashi pear, ripe apple and jasmine notes. This has flow, crunch and ample mouthfeel. Kudos! Screwcap. 13% alc. **Rating** 93 **To** 2020 $30 NG

ΨΨΨΨ **Granite Belt Chardonnay 2017 Rating** 89 **To** 2022 $30 NG
Granite Belt Rare Tawny 2001 Rating 89 $45 NG

Higher Plane ★★★★★

98 Tom Cullity Drive, Cowaramup, WA 6284 **Region** Margaret River
T (08) 9755 9000 **www**.higherplanewines.com.au **Open** At Juniper Estate, 7 days 10–5
Winemaker Mark Messenger **Est.** 1996 **Dozens** 2000 **Vyds** 14.55ha
In 2006 Higher Plane was purchased by the late Roger Hill and Gillian Anderson (of Juniper Estate), but kept as a stand-alone brand. The Higher Plane vineyards are planted to all the key varieties: chardonnay and sauvignon blanc are foremost, with cabernet sauvignon, merlot, tempranillo, fiano, semillon, cabernet franc, malbec and petit verdot making up the rest. Exports to Hong Kong.

🍷🍷🍷🍷🍷 **Margaret River Semillon Sauvignon Blanc 2017** Whatever the percentage of semillon is unimportant, simply because it is the crunchy acidity, herbs, lemongrass and minerality that drives the wine. This in turn means it will change profoundly over the next 5+ years, gold creeping in to the colour, and a citrus/honey cadence to the flavours. Screwcap. 12.5% alc. **Rating** 95 **To** 2022 $23 ✪
Reserve Margaret River Chardonnay 2016 Single vineyard, hand-picked, whole-bunch pressed, wild yeast, 10% mlf, aged 10 months in French barriques (40% new). All the right stuff for a classy wine and it doesn't disappoint. A mix of nougat, grapefruit, lemon zest and curd, lees notes adding complexity. Despite that, it's very tight on the palate, with some nervy energy to burn. Either match this with food or leave it to settle. Screwcap. 12.5% alc. **Rating** 95 **To** 2026 $37 JF
Margaret River Cabernet Merlot 2015 Estate-grown, fermented in small batches, with small amounts of cabernet franc and merlot included in some, maturation in French oak for up to 18 months. This is only just medium-bodied, but everything in the wine is precisely proportioned and balanced. The blackcurrant/cassis fruit has trimmings of olive and bay leaf, and a whisper of French oak. Screwcap. 13.5% alc. **Rating** 95 **To** 2035 $25 ✪
Reserve Margaret River Cabernet Sauvignon 2014 Elegant Margaret River cabernet sauvignon? Here it is, with the full display of flavours on show from mulberries, red and blackcurrants, a sprinkling of spice, and cedary oak lingering, but not obtrusively. There's a juiciness on the supple medium-bodied palate, the lingering finish aided by fine-sculpted tannins. Screwcap. 14% alc. **Rating** 95 **To** 2032 $45 JF

🍷🍷🍷🍷🍷 **Forest Grove Chardonnay 2017 Rating** 93 **To** 2026 $25 JF ✪
Margaret River Fiano 2017 Rating 93 **To** 2020 $25 ✪
Margaret River Fume Blanc 2017 Rating 92 **To** 2023 $23 JF ✪

Hill-Smith Estate ★★★★

Flaxmans Valley Road, Eden Valley, SA 5235 **Region** Eden Valley
T (08) 8561 3200 **www**.hillsmithestate.com **Open** By appt
Winemaker Teresa Heuzenroeder **Est.** 1979 **Dozens** 5000 **Vyds** 12ha
The Eden Valley vineyard sits at an altitude of 510m, providing a cool climate that extends the growing season. Rocky, acidic soil, coupled with winter rainfall and dry summers, results in modest crops. The Parish vineyard in the Coal River Valley, Tasmania was purchased from Frogmore Creek in 2012; other white wines otherwise lacking a home have been put under the Hill-Smith Estate umbrella.

🍷🍷🍷🍷🍷 **Parish Vineyard Single Estate Coal River Valley Riesling 2017** Quartz-green. An exercise in raw power, it has length, intensity and elemental purity, but I'd be inclined to leave it for 5 years to soften its stance a little. Screwcap. 12.5% alc. **Rating** 94 **To** 2030 $30 ✪

Hillcrest Vineyard ★★★★★

31 Phillip Road, Woori Yallock, Vic 3139 **Region** Yarra Valley
T (03) 5964 6689 **www**.hillcrestvineyard.com.au **Open** By appt
Winemaker David Bryant, Tanya Bryant **Est.** 1970 **Dozens** 800 **Vyds** 8.1ha
The small, effectively dry-grown vineyard was established by Graeme and Joy Sweet, who sold it to David and Tanya Bryant. The pinot noir, chardonnay, merlot and cabernet sauvignon

grown on the property were of the highest quality and, when Coldstream Hills was in its infancy, were particularly important resources for it. For some years the wines were made by Phillip Jones (Bass Phillip), but the winemaking is now carried out onsite by David and Tanya. Exports to Singapore.

ȲȲȲȲȲ **Village Yarra Valley Chardonnay 2015** The Diam closure worked with this wine, whereas the cork in the Premium Chardonnay caused oxidation (both colour and flavour telling the same story). The glimpse of the bright straw-green of this wine established its bona fides, and neither the bouquet or palate let it down. It is generous, but not excessively so, the bouquet of white peach, the oak subtle, the palate long and perfectly balanced. 12.9% alc. **Rating** 95 **To** 2023 $30 ❂

Premium Yarra Valley Cabernet Sauvignon Merlot 2016 A rich and compelling wine of the quality and style of earlier years, and no oak issues. The vineyard is off the Warburton Highway and not easy to see or find, but its 30+yo vines produce grapes of high quality. Cork. 13.4% alc. **Rating** 95 **To** 2036 $75

Premium Yarra Valley Chardonnay 2016 There's a fair bit of French oak here, but there's also a lot of varietal fruit, and the acidity is fresh. How it will fare in the future is up to the cork gods. 13.1% alc. **Rating** 94 **To** 2026 $75

Village Yarra Valley Cabernet Sauvignon 2016 The cabernet varietal flavours are good, just on the cusp of full ripeness. Some concerns about the oak dissipated on retasting. Watch this space. Diam. 13.4% alc. **Rating** 94 **To** 2036 $30 ❂

ȲȲȲȲȲ **Village Yarra Valley Chardonnay 2016** **Rating** 91 **To** 2020 $30

Hirsch Hill Estate   ★★★★☆

2088 Melba Highway, Dixons Creek, Vic 3775 **Region** Yarra Valley
T 1300 877 781 **www**.hirschhill.com **Open** Not
Winemaker Rob Dolan Wines **Est.** 1998 **Dozens** 3500 **Vyds** 12ha

The Hirsch family has planted a vineyard to predominantly pinot noir plus cabernet sauvignon, chardonnay, merlot and cabernet franc. (New plantings of 2.5ha of sauvignon blanc, shiraz and viognier were lost in the Black Saturday bushfires.) The vineyard is part of a larger racehorse stud, situated in a mini-valley at the northern end of the Yarra Valley.

ȲȲȲȲȲ **Yarra Valley Chardonnay 2015** From a single vineyard block, matured on lees for 9 months. A standout bargain Yarra Valley chardonnay. It's supremely elegant and perfectly balanced, and it unhesitatingly asserts its sense of place. The flowery, aromatic bouquet, very long palate, freshness, and purity of grapefruit acidity are faultless. Screwcap. 13% alc. **Rating** 95 **To** 2028 $20 ❂

ȲȲȲȲȲ **Yarra Valley Shiraz 2015** **Rating** 93 **To** 2035 $20 ❂
Yarra Valley Cabernet Sauvignon 2015 **Rating** 90 **To** 2030 $20 ❂

Hither & Yon   ★★★★★

17 High Street, Willunga, SA 5172 **Region** McLaren Vale
T (08) 8556 2082 **www**.hitherandyon.com.au **Open** 7 days 11–4
Winemaker Richard Leask **Est.** 2012 **Dozens** 12000 **Vyds** 88ha

Brothers Richard and Malcolm Leask started Hither & Yon in 2012, the Old Jarvie label added in '16. The grapes are sourced from 88ha of family vineyards at seven sites scattered around McLaren Vale. Currently there are 14 varieties, with more to come. Richard manages the vineyards and makes the wine, while Malcolm runs the historic cellar door in Willunga, along with production, sales and marketing. The Hither & Yon labels feature the brands' ampersand, created by a different artist for each wine, and having won many domestic and international design awards. Old Jarvie (www.oldjarvie.com.au) focuses on varietal blends.

ȲȲȲȲȲ **McLaren Vale Grenache 2016** The first 100% varietal grenache by Hither & Yon. Bright, clear colour; a perfumed rose petal, spice and red-fruit bouquet, the palate 100% delicious. A beautiful, effortless achievement, the red fruits and satin-smooth tannins showing none of the hot alcohol and dead fruit characters that

I'm sure other makers might have achieved. I'm marching off with this to drink tonight. Cork. 14.2% alc. **Rating** 97 **To** 2026 $80 ◎

❡❡❡❡❡ **McLaren Vale Nero d'Avola 2017** Bright crimson-purple hue; juicy blood plums are the driver of the wine, but with good tannin structure and an attractive savoury nip to the fruit. Three trophies, including Best Wine of Show at the Australian Alternative Varieties Wine Show '17. Screwcap. 14.5% alc. **Rating** 95 **To** 2025 $27 ◎

Leask McLaren Vale Shiraz 2016 26yo vines, hand-picked, open-fermented, matured in used French puncheons for 18 months. It is medium to full-bodied with exceptional mouthfeel – velvety but not the least heavy, the role of oak limited (no new oak). It all works well. The cork is good quality, perfectly inserted. 14.5% alc. **Rating** 94 **To** 2036 $80

McLaren Vale Grenache Mataro 2017 Superb colour; at maximum turbo-charged revolutions, but the power is smoothly delivered across the palate. Because the balance is very good, this richly endowed wine will repay cellaring particularly well. Screwcap. 14.5% alc. **Rating** 94 **To** 2032 $27 ◎

❡❡❡❡❡ **Old Jarvie The Enforcer McLaren Vale Shiraz Mataro Malbec 2016** **Rating** 91 **To** 2030 $30

Old Jarvie The Charitable McLaren Vale Nero d'Avola Aglianico Rose 2017 **Rating** 90 **To** 2020 $25

Old Jarvie The Saviour McLaren Vale Tempranillo Monastrell Garnacha 2016 **Rating** 90 **To** 2025 $30

Hobbs of Barossa Ranges   ★★★★☆

550 Flaxman Valley Road, Angaston, SA 5353 **Region** Barossa Valley
T 0427 177 740 **www**.hobbsvintners.com.au **Open** At Artisans of Barossa
Winemaker Pete Schell, Chris Ringland (Consultant), Allison Hobbs, Greg Hobbs
Est. 1998 **Dozens** 1500 **Vyds** 6.2ha

Hobbs of Barossa Ranges is the high profile, if somewhat challenging, venture of Greg and Allison Hobbs. The estate vineyards revolve around 1ha of shiraz planted in 1905, 1ha planted in '88, 1ha planted in '97 and 1.82ha planted in 2004. In '09 0.4ha of old white frontignac was removed, giving space for another small planting of shiraz. The viticultural portfolio is completed with 0.6ha of semillon planted in the 1960s, and an inspired 0.4ha of viognier ('88). All the wines, made by Peter Schell (at Spinifex), push the envelope. The only conventionally made wine is the Shiraz Viognier, with a production of 130 dozen. Gregor, an Amarone-style shiraz in full-blooded table-wine mode, and a quartet of dessert wines, are produced by cane cutting, followed by further desiccation on racks. The Grenache comes from a Barossa floor vineyard, the Semillon, Viognier and White Frontignac from estate-grown grapes. Exports to the US, Denmark, Singapore, Taiwan and China.

❡❡❡❡❡ **1905 Shiraz 2015** Vines planted in 1905. French oak (100% new) for 24 months. Luxurious is the word that describes this wine. The fruit is deep, rich and soft, and the generous sweet and cedary oak exudes unmistakable quality. That the aromas and flavours veer towards brandy-soaked cherry and rum and raisin seems quite natural and appropriate here: it's a drinking experience like riding in a plush limousine, and that slightly hedonistic feel is part of the appeal. The underlying depth from the old vines will ensure that it continues to deliver for years to come. Diam. 14.8% alc. **Rating** 95 **To** 2035 $140 SC

Tango Shiraz Viognier 2015 Characteristic aromas of this blend much in evidence here, with a combination of gamey, spicy characters and more fragrant, almost floral notes. Lower in alcohol than some previous releases, and that's noticeable in the suppleness of texture and seamless finish. It's an even flow of soft, dark fruit through the palate with velvety tannins in support: 'smooth' can be a pejorative wine term, but it's a positive here. Diam. 14.3% alc. **Rating** 94 **To** 2030 $120 SC

♟♟♟♟♀ Tin Lids Aria Secca Shiraz 2016 Rating 93 To 2031 $50 SC
Gregor Shiraz 2015 Rating 93 To 2032 $140 SC
Tin Lids Shiraz Cabernet Sauvignon 2016 Rating 93 To 2031 $50 SC
Tin Lids Viognier 2016 Rating 90 To 2022 $39 SC

Hoddles Creek Estate ★★★★★

505 Gembrook Road, Hoddles Creek, Vic 3139 **Region** Yarra Valley
T (03) 5967 4692 **www**.hoddlescreekestate.com.au **Open** By appt
Winemaker Franco D'Anna, Chris Bendle **Est.** 1997 **Dozens** 30 000 **Vyds** 33.3ha
The D'Anna family established their vineyard on a property that had been in the family since
1960. The vines (chardonnay, pinot noir, sauvignon blanc, cabernet sauvignon, pinot gris,
merlot and pinot blanc) are hand-pruned and hand-harvested, and a 300t, split-level winery
was built in 2003. Son Franco is the viticulturist and inspired winemaker; he started to work
in the family liquor store at age 13, graduating to chief wine buyer by the time he was 21.
He completed a Bachelor of Commerce at Melbourne University before studying viticulture
at CSU. A vintage at Coldstream Hills, then two years' vintage experience with Peter Dredge
at Witchmount, and with Mario Marson (ex Mount Mary) as mentor in '03, has put an old
head on young shoulders. The Wickhams Road label uses grapes from an estate vineyard
in Gippsland as well as purchased grapes from the Yarra Valley and Mornington Peninsula.
Exports to the Netherlands, Denmark, Brazil, Dubai, Japan and China.

♟♟♟♟♟ Syberia Chardonnay 2016 A dramatic new take with a spartan black label, in
full-on minimalist mode providing only the bare information required by law,
and its price is almost 50% more than the previous top 1ᶜʳ Chardonnay. What is
not different is the impeccable handling of fruit and oak to produce a wine of
exceptional quality, with white peach, melon and a dash of grapefruit. Screwcap.
12.8% alc. Rating 97 To 2026 $60 ✪

♟♟♟♟♟ Road Block Chardonnay 2016 A wine wholly focusing on a single block with
the perfect row orientation facing east, so steep that it has been terraced. It only
sees the morning sun, and ripening is slow. It results in exceptional depth, more
significant than length (usually vice versa in the Yarra Valley). Screwcap. 12.5% alc.
Rating 96 To 2026 $60 ✪
Yarra Valley Chardonnay 2016 The bouquet and palate are at the midpoint
between white peach and pink grapefruit. When you consider the mix of the very
best clones, hand-picking, the use of the who's who of French coopers, the price is
a year-in, year-out bargain. Screwcap. 13.2% alc. Rating 95 To 2031 $21 ✪
Yarra Valley Pinot Noir 2016 Don't be deceived by the relatively light colour,
this is a pinot that has the trappings you would expect from a $30 wine, not $21.
It has a large core of red fruits wrapped in foresty/spicy/earthy tannins. Its future
is gold-plated, and will richly repay cellaring. Screwcap. 13.2% alc. Rating 95
To 2026 $21 ✪

♟♟♟♟♀ Wickhams Road Yarra Valley Pinot 2017 Rating 92 To 2024 $19 CM ✪
Wickhams Road Gippsland Pinot 2017 Rating 92 To 2024 $19 CM ✪
Yarra Valley Blanc de Blancs Brut 2015 Rating 92 $36
Yarra Valley Pinot Blanc 2017 Rating 91 To 2019 $22 CM ✪
Yarra Valley Pinot Gris 2017 Rating 90 To 2020 $21 ✪

Hoggies Estate Wines ★★★☆

Stentiford Vineyard, 26 Gaffney Road, Coonawarra, SA 5263 **Region** Coonawarra
T (08) 8736 3268 **www**.hoggieswine.com **Open** By appt
Winemaker Gavin Hogg **Est.** 1996 **Dozens** 16 000 **Vyds** 27.5ha
A complicated story. Founded by Gavin Hogg and Mike Press in 1996 and based on an 80ha
vineyard in the Wrattonbully region, which gave rise to the Kopparossa label in 2000. The
vineyard (not the brand) was sold in '02, and Mike set about building his eponymous winery
and vineyard in the Adelaide Hills (see Mike Press Wines). Various twists and turns followed
between then and '09, when Gavin purchased a 24ha vineyard on the Murray River adjacent

to his parents' vineyard; the majority of the fruit from this vineyard is used for the Hoggies Estate brand, and for various private labels. The Kopparossa wines come from the 3.5ha estate vineyard in Coonawarra. Exports to the US, Canada, Morocco, Vietnam, Japan, Hong Kong and China.

ŶŶŶŶŶ **Limestone Coast Riesling 2016** I strongly disapprove of the round gold sticker on the front label stating 'gold medal and trophy winning winemaker' – this wine has not won a gold medal or a trophy. That aside, it is very good value at its price, with the particular flavour that the Limestone Coast imparts to its rieslings, including notes of orange and citrus blossom. Screwcap. 12% alc. **Rating** 90 To 2026 $15 ✪

ŶŶŶŶ **Coonawarra Sauvignon Blanc 2017 Rating** 89 To 2021 $15 ✪

Hollick   ★★★★

Riddoch Highway, Coonawarra, SA 5263 **Region** Coonawarra
T (08) 8737 2318 www.hollick.com **Open** Mon–Fri 9–5, w'ends & public hols 10–5
Winemaker Trent Nankivell **Est.** 1983 **Dozens** 40 000 **Vyds** 87ha
In April 2014 the Hollick family announced that a major investment had been made in their business by the large Hong Kong Yingda Investment Co. Ltd. Involved in hospitality and tourism in China, part of its business involves vineyard and winery operations. The Hollick family continues to own a part of the business, and manages it in the same way as usual. Major benefits to Hollick are working capital and access to the Chinese market, while Hong Kong Yingda Investment Co. will gain expertise from the Hollick family. Exports to most major markets.

ŶŶŶŶŶ **Wrattonbully Shiraz 2016** An attractive bouquet with dark berry, plum and ripe tannins, oak merely an observer of the medium-bodied wine that will drink well sooner rather than later. Screwcap. 14.5% alc. **Rating** 92 To 2026 $25
Ravenswood Coonawarra Cabernet Sauvignon 2016 A young and boisterous wine with great colour, arms and legs all over the place. While the individual components are fair enough, the oak and tannins are the most obvious contributors, but past experience suggests they will soften and give more space to the cassis fruit. Screwcap. 14.5% alc. **Rating** 91 To 2030 $79

ŶŶŶŶ **Wilgha Coonawarra Shiraz 2016 Rating** 89 To 2023 $59
Old Vines Coonawarra Cabernet Sauvignon 2016 Rating 89 To 2026

Hollydene Estate   ★★★★

3483 Golden Highway, Jerrys Plains, NSW 2330 **Region** Hunter Valley
T (02) 6576 4021 www.hollydeneestate.com **Open** 7 days 9–5
Winemaker Matt Burton **Est.** 1965 **Dozens** 2000 **Vyds** 40ha
Karen Williams has three vineyards and associated properties, all established in the 1960s. They are Hollydene, Wybong and Arrowfield estates, the latter one of the original vinous landmarks in the Upper Hunter. The three vineyards produce grapes for the Juul and Hollydene Estate labels. Hollydene also makes sparkling wines from the Mornington Peninsula. Exports to Indonesia and China.

ŶŶŶŶŶ **Estate Upper Hunter Valley Semillon 2017** Generous palate, though the finish hones it tighter. Beautiful drink as a young wine. Lemon juice, wet slate and honeysuckle. The wine whispers, chatters and darts. Factor in the price and we have an attractive proposition here. Screwcap. 11% alc. **Rating** 92 To 2024 $22 CM ✪
Museum Release Estate Upper Hunter Valley Semillon 2007 Glowing yellow colour. Fully developed with honeysuckle, apricot, toast and lanolin flavours strung across the palate. The wine doesn't build much intensity, but it maintains a remarkably straight line from start to finish. Screwcap. 11% alc. **Rating** 91 To 2022 $28 CM

Hunter Valley Cabernet Sauvignon 2016 Warm around the edges, but powerful. Tar, earth, black cherry and sweet/dark soy-like flavours build to high revs through the palate, ripe saltbush-inflected tannin then helping to pull it all through the finish. A successful red. Screwcap. 14.5% alc. **Rating** 91 **To** 2028 $39 CM

Holm Oak

11 West Bay Road, Rowella, Tas 7270 **Region** Northern Tasmania
T (03) 6394 7577 www.holmoakvineyards.com.au **Open** 7 days 11–5
Winemaker Rebecca Duffy **Est.** 1983 **Dozens** 10000 **Vyds** 11.62ha
Holm Oak takes its name from its grove of oak trees, planted around the beginning of the 20th century and originally intended for the making of tennis racquets. Winemaker Rebecca Duffy, daughter of owners Ian and Robyn Wilson, has extensive winemaking experience in Australia and California, and husband Tim, a viticultural agronomist, manages the vineyard (pinot noir, cabernet sauvignon, chardonnay, riesling, sauvignon blanc and pinot gris, with small amounts of merlot, cabernet franc and arneis). Exports to the US, Canada, Norway and Japan.

🍷🍷🍷🍷🍷 **Riesling 2017** The highly fragrant bouquet and juicy palate are a celebration of all things lime: blossom, crushed leaf, fruit flavour, pith and zest. Granny Smith apple and scything acidity play significant support roles for a lovely, vibrant wine. Screwcap. 12% alc. **Rating** 95 **To** 2032 $28 ✪
Chardonnay 2016 The deliberate approach of early picking has worked, because there is substantial white peach to accompany the grapefruit/citrus. The intensity of the flavours is such that it has completely absorbed the French oak (30% new). Seriously good value for a Tasmanian chardonnay made this way. Screwcap. 12.5% alc. **Rating** 95 **To** 2024 $30 ✪
Pinot Gris 2017 Very faint blush hue; pear blossom and pear fruit hold centrestage on the bouquet, but do make room for other notes there and on the palate. It builds on re-evaluation, and there's no question the cool climate plus the very cool vintage have come up trumps. Screwcap. 13% alc. **Rating** 95 **To** 2022 $28 ✪
Pinot Noir 2016 Complex spicy, foresty notes intermingle with wild strawberry and red cherry aromatics across the bouquet and palate alike. Fine savoury tannins, red fruits and spices are in an articulate debate with no single winner. A lovely pinot. Screwcap. 13% alc. **Rating** 95 **To** 2029 $32 ✪

🍷🍷🍷🍷 **Sauvignon Blanc 2017 Rating** 89 **To** 2021 $28

Home Hill

38 Nairn Street, Ranelagh, Tas 7109 **Region** Southern Tasmania
T (03) 6264 1200 www.homehillwines.com.au **Open** 7 days 10–5
Winemaker Gilli Lipscombe, Paul Lipscombe **Est.** 1994 **Dozens** 2000 **Vyds** 5ha
Terry and Rosemary Bennett planted their first 0.5ha of vines in 1994 on gentle slopes in the beautiful Huon Valley. Between '94 and '99 the plantings were increased to 3ha of pinot noir, 1.5ha of chardonnay and 0.5ha of sylvaner. Home Hill has had great success with its exemplary pinot noirs, consistent trophy and gold medal winners in the ultra-competitive Tasmanian Wine Show. Impressive enough, but this paled into insignificance in the wake of winning the Jimmy Watson Trophy at the Melbourne Wine Awards 2015.

🍷🍷🍷🍷🍷 **Kelly's Reserve Pinot Noir 2016** The colour is little, if any, different from its Estate sibling, but the bouquet has more fragrant and varietally pure fruit. The palate unexpectedly reverses the plot, being more complex, more foresty and less fruity. There is presumably more whole-bunch use, but the wine's intensity draws saliva from the mouth. Screwcap. 13.8% alc. **Rating** 97 **To** 2030 $75 ✪

🍷🍷🍷🍷🍷 **Estate Pinot Noir 2016** Full crimson hue; the bouquet is suitably complex, and the palate takes off like a Tesla, accelerating with mind-snapping yet elegant speed. Blood plum and black cherry fruit flavours have savoury/spicy foresty tannins to provide complexity but not challenge the primacy of the fruit. Screwcap. 13.8% alc. **Rating** 96 **To** 2026 $45 ✪

Honey Moon Vineyard

135 Church Hill Road, Echunga, SA 5153 **Region** Adelaide Hills
T 0438 727 079 **www**.honeymoonvineyard.com.au **Open** By appt
Winemaker Jane Bromley, Hylton McLean **Est.** 2004 **Dozens** 800 **Vyds** 1.2ha
Jane Bromley and Hylton McLean planted 0.7ha of pinot noir (clones 777, 114 and 115) and
0.5ha of shiraz (selected from two old vineyards known for their spicy fruit flavours). A full
moon often strikes around harvest time, appearing as a dollop of rich honey in the sky –
hence the name. The first vintage was 2005, but Jane has been making wine since '01, with
a particular interest in champagne; Hylton is a winemaker, wine-science researcher and wine
educator with over 20 years' experience.

♀♀♀♀♀ **Adelaide Hills Shiraz 2013** This reminds me of a warm vintage, high quality
wine from the northern Rhône: mace, white pepper grind, blueberry, cardamom,
anise and iodine, all wafting over a delicatessen counter of smoked dried meats.
Mid-weighted despite the alcohol, with an energetic carriage of acidity. This could
use a little less oak and a little more lightness. Screwcap. 14.5% alc. **Rating** 94
To 2025 $55 NG

♀♀♀♀♀ **Adelaide Hills Chardonnay 2017 Rating** 92 **To** 2025 $40 NG
Adelaide Hills Shiraz 2014 Rating 92 **To** 2024 $55 NG
Adelaide Hills Fancy Rose 2017 Rating 91 **To** 2019 $26 NG

Horner Wines

12 Shedden Street, Cessnock, NSW 2325 **Region** Hunter Valley
T 0477 222 121 **www**.nakedwines.com.au **Open** Not
Winemaker Ashley Horner **Est.** 2013 **Dozens** 14 500 **Vyds** 12ha
Horner Wines is the family venture of Ashley and Lauren Horner, who have a certified
organic vineyard planted to chardonnay, viognier and shiraz. Grapes are also sourced from
organic vineyards in Orange and Cowra. Ashley had a 14-year career working at Rosemount
Estate, Penfolds, Kamberra Estate, Saint Clair (NZ) and Mount Pleasant, ultimately becoming
winemaker at Tamburlaine and completing a Diploma in Wine Technology at Dookie
College. Lauren has a degree in hospitality/tourism. The move from grapegrowing to
winemaking was precipitated by the fall in demand for grapes, and they sell their wines
through www.nakedwines.com.au.

♀♀♀♀♀ **Family Reserve Chardonnay 2017** From a 0.6ha estate block in the Upper
Hunter. Every effort was made to invest the wine with complexity, fermenting and
maturing in combinations of oak and stainless steel. It came together convincingly
with grapefruit, nectarine and apple, lightly brushed with oak. Screwcap. 12.5% alc.
Rating 90 **To** 2023 $25

Horseshoe Vineyard

Horseshoe Road, Horseshoe Valley via Denman, NSW 2328 **Region** Hunter Valley
T (02) 6547 3528 **Open** By appt
Winemaker John Hordern **Est.** 1969 **Dozens** 1500 **Vyds** 3.5ha
Horseshoe Vineyard, owned and operated by John and Wendy Hordern and family, was
established by Bob Hordern with cuttings of semillon and shiraz from Penfolds Wybong Park
vineyard, and further plantings of chardonnay, semillon and shiraz. A Roseworthy graduate,
John gained experience at Wybong and Arrowfield estates (now part of Hollydene) before
founding Hunter Wine Services with Rex D'Aquino in 2001. Riesling and sauvignon blanc
are made from purchased grapes from Orange. Exports to the UK and China.

♀♀♀♀♀ **Premium Reserve Hunter Valley Semillon 2016** Deserves the use of
Premium Reserve as part of its name. While still in the early stages of its journey,
its flavours are mouthwatering, and the low alcohol isn't threatened by the chalky/
minerally acidity. Give it a few more years to gain even more points. Screwcap.
10% alc. **Rating** 94 **To** 2026 $25 ✪

🍷🍷🍷🍷 Chardonnay 2016 Rating 89 To 2021 $30
Hunter Valley Rose 2017 Rating 89 To 2018 $20

Houghton ★★★★★

148 Dale Road, Middle Swan, WA 6065 **Region** Swan Valley
T (08) 9274 9540 **www.houghton-wines.com.au Open** 7 days 10–5
Winemaker Ross Pamment **Est.** 1836 **Dozens** NFP
Houghton's reputation was once largely dependent on its (then) White Burgundy, equally good when young or five years old. In the last 20 years its portfolio has changed out of all recognition, with a kaleidoscopic range of high quality wines from the Margaret River, Great Southern, Frankland River and Pemberton regions to the fore. The Jack Mann and Gladstones red wines stand at the forefront, but to borrow a saying from the late Jack Mann, 'There are no bad wines here'. With a history of 180 years, its future now lies in the hands of Accolade Wines. Exports to the UK and Asia.

🍷🍷🍷🍷🍷 **Thomas Yule Frankland River Shiraz 2014** Awash with creamy, toasty oak, but the power of fruit laying behind is quite magnificent. This is a full-bodied red wine of high style and quality. Black cherry, plum, licorice, lavender and leather notes. It's like dark suede, thick and rich. How long have you got? This wine is destined to mature, given appropriate storage, over an exceptionally long period. Screwcap. 14% alc. **Rating** 96 To 2045 $75 CM ✪
Jack Mann Cabernet Sauvignon 2015 If you're after bankable quality in your cellar then look no further. This is a mighty wine, the complete package. It's dark with berried flavour, coated in smoky vanillan oak, alive with spice and earth, and shooting ripples of flavour and tannin out through the finish. Topnotch in all respects. Screwcap. 14% alc. **Rating** 96 To 2040 $137 CM
CW Ferguson Great Southern Cabernet Malbec 2014 Strength of character. This is one of those red wines you almost feel as though you can lean on, its bold black fruit, planks of wood and waves of tannin all suggestive of power and size. Mint, lavender, bay and anise flavours make contributions but blackcurrants wrapped in cream is the main force here. It's a monty for the cellar. Screwcap. 14% alc. **Rating** 95 To 2034 $70 CM

🍷🍷🍷🍷🍷 **The Bandit Frankland River Shiraz 2015** Rating 93 To 2025 $20 CM ✪
Crofters Frankland River Shiraz 2015 Rating 92 To 2026 $19 CM ✪
Shiraz 2016 Rating 90 To 2023 $13 ✪

House of Arras ★★★★★

Bay of Fires, 40 Baxters Road, Pipers River, Tas 7252 **Region** Northern Tasmania
T (03) 6362 7622 **www.houseofarras.com.au Open** Mon–Fri 11–4, w'ends 10–4
Winemaker Ed Carr **Est.** 1995 **Dozens** NFP
The rise and rise of the fortunes of the House of Arras has been due to two things: first, the exceptional skills of winemaker Ed Carr, and second, its access to high quality Tasmanian chardonnay and pinot noir. While there have been distinguished sparkling wines made in Tasmania for many years, none has so consistently scaled the heights as Arras. The complexity, texture and structure of the wines are akin to that of Bollinger RD and Krug; the connection stems from the 7–15+ years the wines spend on lees prior to disgorgement.

🍷🍷🍷🍷🍷 **Blanc de Blancs 2008** 100% chardonnay made in the traditional method, with 8 years on lees prior to disgorgement. It has exceptional purity, power and complexity, the dosage hidden in all the other flavours and biscuity complexity of the wine. Cork. 12.5% alc. **Rating** 97 $87 ✪
Grand Vintage 2007 When previously tasted in Sept '16, I suggested a drink-to date of '18 – in retrospect that was too short for a 750ml bottle, and now there are also a limited number of magnums available. One of my few abiding regrets is that I purchased bottles of champagne and top-end Australian sparklings rather than magnums – I urge you to grab one or two bottles/magnums of Arras at its

towering best, with layer upon layer of complexity ex brioche, toast, flint, white peach and apple. Cork. 12.5% alc. **Rating** 97 $249

EJ Carr Late Disgorged 2003 The self-effacing Ed Carr is the unquestioned genius behind the success of the Arras wines, and must have squirmed about the use of his name. The 14 years this wine spent on lees would have suffocated a lesser wine; here it has added terrific drive and balance to a cornucopia of flavours. Cork. 12.5% alc. **Rating** 97 $190

Museum Release Blanc de Blancs 2001 An immediately striking feature of the wine is its light, bright straw-green colour. The bouquet and palate are in a class of their own, with a structure coming from the complete autolysis of the yeast lees (the sparkling wine equivalent of rancio in old Rutherglen fortified wines), and flavours of biscuit, honey and grapefruit rind. Cork. 12.5% alc. **Rating** 97 $350

Rose 2006 Trophy winner at the Tasmanian Wine Show '17. Two-thirds pinot noir, 7 years on yeast lees. Like all Arras wines, it has an extra level of texture and flavour complexity derived partly from the fruit and partly from extended time on lees, balanced by tangy acidity. Cork. 12.5% alc. **Rating** 97 $87 ✪

🍷🍷🍷🍷🍷 **A by Arras Premium Cuvee NV** A juicy, spicy, vibrant sparkling wine made from aged parcels of pinot noir, chardonnay and pinot meunier, its lightness of foot derived from the balance and carefully calibrated dosage. Drink any time. Screwcap. 12.5% alc. **Rating** 94 $30 ✪

House of Cards   ★★★★★

3220 Caves Road, Yallingup, WA 6282 **Region** Margaret River
T (08) 9755 2583 **www**.houseofcardswine.com.au **Open** 7 days 10–5
Winemaker Travis Wray **Est.** 2011 **Dozens** 5000 **Vyds** 12ha

House of Cards is owned and operated by Elizabeth and Travis Wray; Travis managing the vineyard and making the wines, Elizabeth managing sales and marketing. The name of the winery is a reflection of the gamble that all viticulturists and winemakers face every vintage: 'You have to play the hand you are dealt by Mother Nature.' They only use estate-grown grapes, open-top fermentation, hand-plunging and manual basket pressing. It's certainly doing it the hard way, but it must seem all worthwhile when they produce wines of such quality.

🍷🍷🍷🍷🍷 **The Royals Single Vineyard Margaret River Chardonnay 2017** Gin Gin clone, matured for 11 months in French hogsheads (65% new). The oak is perfectly integrated, and the wine was already in balance before it was bottled in Dec '17. White peach and grapefruit dispute sovereignty, but neither prevails, the process simply extending the length of the palate of a wine with a great future. Screwcap. 13% alc. **Rating** 97 **To** 2030 $40 ✪

🍷🍷🍷🍷🍷 **Three Card Monte Margaret River Sauvignon Blanc 2017** Machine-harvested, 7 days on skins, free-run juice wild-fermented and matured in oak (20% new) for 12 months. The full-on approach might have been a disaster, but was in fact a triumph. While creating layered complexity, the wine is long and fresh with a vibrant mouthfeel; lemon curd, citrus and integrated, faintly toasty oak. Screwcap. 11.9% alc. **Rating** 95 **To** 2023 $25 ✪

The Joker Margaret River Shiraz 2016 Open-fermented with 50% whole bunches, 20% carbonic maceration, 12 months in used French oak. Stacked with blackberry, plum and spice, the tannins smooth as marbles. A wine with soul, sold for a mere bagatelle. Screwcap. 14.2% alc. **Rating** 95 **To** 2036 $24 ✪

The Joker Margaret River Cabernet Merlot 2016 A 64/36% blend, 12 months in used French oak. For me the 'joker' is the way this (and other House of Cards wines) is made on a low-cost budget, yet you'd never guess by tasting the wine. Livewire purple and black fruits have the tannin structure that makes the absence of any new oak irrelevant; the used French oak providing all the texture and structure needed. Screwcap. 14.3% alc. **Rating** 94 **To** 2031 $24 ✪

Black Jack Single Vineyard Margaret River Malbec 2016 The dense purple colour offers an early insight. Deep, intense red and black fruit is the order of the day here. High quality French oak makes its spicy and savoury presence felt, as does the unrelenting tannin. It's all about the future for this wine, and it should be interesting. Cork. 14% alc. **Rating** 94 **To** 2031 $48 SC

♀♀♀♀♀ **Single Vineyard The Ace 2016 Rating** 93 **To** 2028 $65 SC
Lady Luck Single Vineyard Margaret River Petit Verdot 2016 Rating 93 **To** 2031 $48 SC

Howard Park ★★★★★

Miamup Road, Cowaramup, WA 6284 **Region** Margaret River
T (08) 9756 5200 **www**.burchfamilywines.com.au **Open** 7 days 10–5
Winemaker Janice McDonald, Mark Bailey **Est.** 1986 **Dozens** NFP **Vyds** 183ha
Burch Family Wines acts as an umbrella name for the Howard Park and MadFish brands. The Burch family has vineyards in Margaret River and Great Southern. The Margaret River vineyards range from Leston in Wilyabrup to Allingham in southern Karridale; Great Southern includes Mount Barrow and Abercrombie, both in Mount Barker, the latter acquired in 2014 and featuring Houghton cabernet clones planted in 1975. At the top of the portfolio are Abercrombie Cabernet Sauvignon and Allingham Chardonnay, followed by the rieslings, chardonnay and sauvignon blanc; next come pairs of shiraz and cabernet sauvignon under the Leston and Scotsdale labels. The Miamup and Flint Rock regional ranges were established in '12. MadFish produces the full range of varietal wines, Gold Turtle its second tier. The feng shui–designed cellar door is a must-see. A founding member of the Australian First Families of Wines. Exports to Thailand, Vietnam, Japan, Hong Kong and China.

♀♀♀♀♀ **Howard Park Leston Margaret River Cabernet Sauvignon 2015** Small parcels hand-picked and sorted, some parcels remaining on skins post-ferment, each batch matured separately for 18 months in French oak (40% new). Its varietal expression, balance and length are all perfect, the oak and tannin handling no less impressive. Screwcap. 14.5% alc. **Rating** 96 **To** 2035 $46 ✪
Howard Park Porongurup Riesling 2017 It has the future in its sights, but the intensity of citrus fruit flavour makes for scintillating drinking right now. It's a bit like putting a fire out with gasoline; the cool, leaf-infused, flavour-drenched acidity here places a salivating emphasis on a mouthwatering style. Screwcap. 12% alc. **Rating** 95 **To** 2030 $34 CM ✪
Howard Park Allingham Margaret River Chardonnay 2016 Harmony is a beautiful thing. This chardonnay boasts many different flavours and feels, but their forces are so well joined that it's hard to pick one from the other. The end result is that you just go with it. Spicy oak, white peach, grapefruit and sweet pear, sure, but they all flow in one delicious, long-lasting stream. Screwcap. 13% alc. **Rating** 95 **To** 2024 $89 CM
Howard Park Cellar Collection Cabernet Sauvignon Shiraz 2015 A neat 60/40% regional and varietal blend, the cabernet from Margaret River, the shiraz from Frankland River. Cabernet wins the discussion, although the shiraz plays into cabernet's hand with a spicy, black cherry profile. This is the second vintage released (the first in '13) and one I strongly support. Screwcap. 14% alc. **Rating** 95 **To** 2030 $35 ✪

♀♀♀♀♀ **Howard Park Miamup Sauvignon Blanc 2017 Rating** 93 **To** 2020 $28
Howard Park Scotsdale Cabernet 2015 Rating 93 **To** 2025 $46
Howard Park Cellar Collection Petit Verdot 2016 Rating 93 **To** 2026 $35
Howard Park Sauvignon Blanc 2017 Rating 92 **To** 2019 $31
Howard Park Miamup Rose 2017 Rating 92 **To** 2020 $28
Howard Park Flint Rock Great Southern Shiraz 2015 Rating 92 **To** 2030 $28
Howard Park Miamup Cabernet 2015 Rating 92 **To** 2030 $28
Howard Park Mount Barker Riesling 2017 Rating 91 **To** 2023 $33

Howard Park Miamup Sauvignon Blanc Semillon 2017 Rating 91
To 2021 $28
MadFish Sauvignon Blanc Semillon 2017 Rating 91 To 2019 $18 CM ✪
MadFish Shiraz Rose 2017 Rating 91 To 2018 $18 ✪
MadFish Vera's Cuvee Methode Traditionnelle NV Rating 91 $25

Howard Vineyard   ★★★★☆

53 Bald Hills Road, Nairne, SA 5252 **Region** Adelaide Hills
T (08) 8188 0203 **www**.howardvineyard.com **Open** Tues–Sun 10–5
Winemaker Tom Northcott **Est.** 2005 **Dozens** 6000 **Vyds** 60ha
Howard Vineyard is a family-owned Adelaide Hills winery set among towering gum trees
and terraced lawns. Pinot noir, chardonnay, pinot gris and sauvignon blanc are sourced from
Schoenthal 'Beautiful Valley' vineyard, at 470m altitude near Lobethal, while Howard's Nairne
vineyard in the warmer Mount Barker district is home to shiraz, cabernet sauvignon and
cabernet franc. All the wines are estate-grown. Winemaker Tom Northcott has a Bachelor in
Viticulture and Oenology from the University of Adelaide, and has worked vintages in the
south of France, Barossa Valley, WA and Tasmania. Exports to Hong Kong and China.

🍷🍷🍷🍷🍷 **Clover Adelaide Hills Cabernet Franc Rose 2017** This is a find. It's savoury,
juicy, spicy and inviting at once, its cherried bursts complemented beautifully by
sprays of herbs and dried flowers. Encore performance on the finish. Spot on.
Screwcap. 12.5% alc. **Rating** 95 To 2018 $28 CM ✪

🍷🍷🍷🍷🍷 **Adelaide Hills Sauvignon Blanc 2017** Rating 91 To 2018 $20 CM ✪
Clover Adelaide Hills Sauvignon Blanc 2017 Rating 91 To 2019 $25 CM
Clover Adelaide Hills Shiraz 2016 Rating 91 To 2026 $24 CM
Clover Adelaide Hills Cabernet Franc 2016 Rating 91 To 2021 $24 CM
Adelaide Hills Rose 2017 Rating 90 To 2018 $20 CM ✪
Clover Adelaide Hills Pinot Noir Chardonnay 2017 Rating 90 $28 CM

Hugh Hamilton Wines   ★★★★★

94 McMurtrie Road, McLaren Vale, SA 5171 **Region** McLaren Vale
T (08) 8323 8689 **www**.hughhamiltonwines.com.au **Open** 7 days 11–5
Winemaker Nic Bourke **Est.** 1991 **Dozens** 20 000 **Vyds** 21.4ha
In 2014, fifth-generation family member Hugh Hamilton handed over the reins to daughter
Mary, the sixth generation of the family. It was she who developed the irreverent black sheep
packaging. But it's more than simply marketing: the business will continue to embrace its
85-year-old shiraz and 65-year-old cabernet sauvignon from its Blewitt Springs vineyard,
along with mainstream and alternative varieties. There have been changes in the way the vines
are trellised, and the winery style is fermenting in small open fermenters, using gravity for
wine movements, and maturating in high quality French oak. The cellar door is lined with the
original jarrah from Vat 15 of Hamilton's historic Ewell winery – it was the largest wooden vat
ever built in the southern hemisphere. Exports to the UK, the US, Canada, Sweden, Finland,
Malaysia and China.

🍷🍷🍷🍷🍷 **Black Blood III Black Sheep Vineyard McLaren Vale Shiraz 2016** Mary
Hamilton says the Black Blood shirazs 'smell and taste like the characteristics of
the three distinct soil types and subregions they hail from'. This comes from 81yo
vines, but the colour is a touch lighter. The bouquet and palate are more spicy and
savoury, but the mouthfeel is gloriously supple and balanced. Screwcap. 14.5% alc.
Rating 95 To 2036 $79
Black Blood I Cellar Vineyard McLaren Vale Shiraz 2016 Effectively the
only differences in the Black Blood shirazs (other than vineyard) are the harvest
dates, a slight difference in the time on skins, and the vine age (this from 20yo
vines). All three are labelled 14.5% alc., but the alcohol as per detailed spreadsheets
supplied by the winery is 15.3% or 15.4% (nothing illegal in this – a variance of
1.5% alcohol is allowed for wine sold in Australia). Pronounced dark-chocolate

aromas have a hint of cigar box, and the palate has the best texture of the three wines. Screwcap. 14.5% alc. **Rating** 95 **To** 2036 $79

Black Blood II Church Vineyard McLaren Vale Shiraz 2016 23yo vines, 10 days on skins, matured for 17 months in used French oak. Rich black fruits, dark chocolate and licorice on the bouquet, then a sumptuously rich, layered palate, its balance and length exemplary. There is far more that builds the Black Blood wines than pushes them apart. Screwcap. 14.5% alc. **Rating** 95 **To** 2036 $79

Tonnellerie Damy Single Barrel Cellar Vineyard McLaren Vale Shiraz 2015 The Tonnellerie wines are single barrel wines (24 dozen each) from an identical vineyard source picked on the same day (17 Feb) and fermented identically, the only difference the cooper of each barrel. All bottled on the same day (16 Nov). Powerful fruit meets powerful oak. The problems are the lack of any forest characters, the degree of toast and the length of time in new oak, although there is very good varietal expression framed by the oak. Screwcap. 14.5% alc. **Rating** 95 **To** 2035 $50

Pure Black Shiraz 2014 Destemmed, open-fermented, 14 days on skins, matured for 20 months in French oak (30% new). Black fruits ride the bouquet, gaining another leg with the tannin; earth and graphite notes strung around its neck. There's nothing remarkable about the vinification, other than the balance that was ultimately achieved. Vino-Lok. 15.4% alc. **Rating** 95 **To** 2039 $180

Bloodline Hamilton 1837 McLaren Vale Grenache 2016 This is a gung-ho beast of McLaren Vale grenache, all of it very good, with layers of red fruits and just a hint of purple. The mouthfeel is particularly convincing, rich and supple, yet not heavy. Cork. 14.5% alc. **Rating** 95 **To** 2031

Tonnellerie Remond Single Barrel Cellar Vineyard McLaren Vale Shiraz 2015 This has the firmest oak impact, with a veiled suggestion of higher toast. Screwcap. 14.5% alc. **Rating** 95 **To** 2035 $50

Tonnellerie Francois Freres Single Barrel Cellar Vineyard McLaren Vale Shiraz 2015 The net outcome here is a vanillan oak nuance, slightly unexpected given the normal power of new François Frères oak. Screwcap. 14.5% alc. **Rating** 94 **To** 2035 $50

ΨΨΨΨΨ **The Floozie McLaren Vale Sangiovese Rose 2017** **Rating** 93 **To** 2019 $24 ✪

Black Ops McLaren Vale Shiraz Saperavi 2016 **Rating** 93 **To** 2031 $33
Bloodline Hamilton 1837 McLaren Vale Shiraz 2016 **Rating** 92 **To** 2030
Members Only Shearer's Cut Black Sheep Block McLaren Vale Shiraz 2016 **Rating** 92 **To** 2031 $31
The Mongrel McLaren Vale 2016 **Rating** 91 **To** 2020 $24
Oddball the Great Saperavi 2014 **Rating** 91 **To** 2024 $150
Bloodline Hamilton 1837 Pedro Ximenez NV **Rating** 91

Hugo ★★★★★

246 Elliott Road, McLaren Flat, SA 5171 **Region** McLaren Vale
T (08) 8383 0098 **www.**hugowines.com.au **Open** Mon–Fri 10–5, Sat–Sun 10.30–5
Winemaker Renae Hirsch, Brian Light **Est.** 1982 **Dozens** 8000 **Vyds** 20ha
Came from relative obscurity to prominence in the late 1980s with some ripe, sweet reds, which, while strongly American oak–influenced, were outstanding. It picked up the pace again after a dull period in the mid-'90s, and has made the most of the recent run of good vintages. The estate plantings include shiraz, cabernet sauvignon, chardonnay, grenache and sauvignon blanc, with part of the grape production sold. Exports to Canada.

ΨΨΨΨΨ **McLaren Vale Shiraz Cabernet 2016** Top gold medals at the Adelaide and National wine shows '17. The seamless 75/25% blend has resulted in a palate that overflows with red and black fruits yet is elegant and textured. Indeed there are some notes encountered in cool regions (spice and pepper and a juicy mouthfeel). Screwcap. 14% alc. **Rating** 96 **To** 2036 $28 ✪

Reserve McLaren Vale Shiraz 2015 The 46yo vines were planted by John Hugo in '69, matured in 65% French and 35% American hogsheads (40% new). The basics for the Reserve appellation are easy to see. The colour is deep and bright, and the bouquet and medium to full-bodied palate have a large range of aromas and flavours from red, purple and black fruits, the oak also joining in. Screwcap. 14.5% alc. **Rating** 95 **To** 2035 $55

McLaren Vale Grenache 2017 66yo bushvines, whole-bunch fermented, matured for 7 months in 5yo French hogsheads, 108 dozen made. Vibrant crimson-purple; has all the trademarks of McLaren Vale grenache, yet with a twist, notably the lower alcohol and used French (not American) oak. The bouquet is scented with red cherry and rose-petal notes, the palate wondrously and effortlessly full of vibrant, fresh red fruits. The finish is as fresh as a daisy (reflecting the low alcohol). Screwcap. 13.5% alc. **Rating** 95 **To** 2023 $45

McLaren Vale Grenache Shiraz Rose 2017 A highly fragrant bouquet and juicy (but bone dry) palate adds to the appeal of a lovely rose, full of small red fruits led by strawberry and raspberry. Top stuff, as is the suggested food match of Vietnamese cuisine or chilli crab. Screwcap. 13% alc. **Rating** 94 **To** 2020 $25 ✪

ㅇㅇㅇㅇ오 **McLaren Vale Cabernet Sauvignon 2015 Rating** 93 **To** 2030 $25 ✪
McLaren Vale Shiraz 2015 Rating 90 **To** 2023 $25

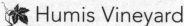

Humis Vineyard ★★★★

3730 Heathcote-Rochester Road, Corop, Vic 3559 **Region** Heathcote
T 0419 588 044 **www.**humisvineyard.com **Open** By appt
Winemaker Cathy Branson **Est.** 2011 **Dozens** 1200 **Vyds** 9.5ha
Both the wine labels and the letter from Hugh Jones to me giving the background to his and wife Michelle's venture share a battered, old-fashioned typeface. The letter was as interesting for what it didn't say as for what it did, although there was a connection in an improbable way because my mother Muriel's house name was Missy, also Michelle's nickname. The snapshot approach of the website's 'About Us' explains that in 2010, with the wine industry on its knees and a drought in full swing in Heathcote, Hugh saw a dusty paddock running down to a dry Lake Cooper with a 'for sale' sign up. The decision was obvious: buy, and promise that then very young twins, son Tex and daughter Mallee, wouldn't be too neglected. The ace in the hole was the irrigation water available to the property. 'The largest planting of carmenere in Australia'?

ㅇㅇㅇㅇ오 **Shiraz 2015** The Joneses decided to use the old Tahbilk clone (1860 origin), not the Barossa clones that dominate plantings, looking for a more savoury and substantial style, and have succeeded. The flavours are black fruited, with a briary/earthy note in the background. Plenty to chew on here. Screwcap. 14.6% alc. **Rating** 90 **To** 2029 $25

Carmenere 2015 Good colour, both in depth and hue. Light to medium-bodied, but with elegance and rich fruit; red berries, notes of leaf and spice, and fine tannins all providing balance and length. Not a powerhouse, but the presumably young vines promise more. Screwcap. 13.9% alc. **Rating** 90 **To** 2023 $25

ㅇㅇㅇㅇ **Heathcote Grenache Rose 2016 Rating** 89 **To** 2019 $20

Hungerford Hill ★★★★☆

2450 Broke Road, Pokolbin, NSW 2320 **Region** Hunter Valley
T (02) 4998 0710 **www.**hungerfordhill.com.au **Open** Sun–Thurs 10–5, Fri–Sat 10–7
Winemaker Bryan Currie **Est.** 1967 **Dozens** 17 000 **Vyds** 28ha
Sam and Christie Arnaout purchased Hungerford Hill in December 2016, planning to refocus the 50-year-old label on its Hunter Valley origin, also adding significant new Lower Hunter vineyards at Sweetwater (see separate entry) and Dalwood (the oldest continuously operating vineyard in Australia). Hungerford Hill will use these vineyards to bolster its Hunter Valley

wines while continuing its 20+ year association with the cool-climate Tumbarumba and Hilltops regions. Exports to all major markets.

♥♥♥♥♥ **Block 8 Dalwood Vineyard Chardonnay 2017** Cut and thrust. Straw-yellow in colour and a powerful release. Lime, peach, sawdusty oak and lemongrass. A waxy creaminess to the texture. Excellent length. Many ducks in a row here. Screwcap. 12.5% alc. **Rating** 95 **To** 2023 CM

♥♥♥♥♀ **Block 7B Dalwood Vineyard Semillon 2017** **Rating** 93 **To** 2026 CM
Hunter Valley Semillon 2017 **Rating** 93 **To** 2025 $27 CM ❂
Tumbarumba Pinot Meunier 2017 **Rating** 93 **To** 2024 CM
Epic McLaren Vale Shiraz 2015 **Rating** 93 **To** 2035 $120 CM
Tumbarumba Chardonnay 2016 **Rating** 92 **To** 2024 $40 CM
Heavy Metal 2015 **Rating** 92 **To** 2025 $55 CM
Tumbarumba Pinot Noir 2017 **Rating** 91 **To** 2024 $40 CM
Preservative Free Hunter Valley Shiraz 2017 **Rating** 91 **To** 2021 $28 CM
Tumbarumba Tempranillo 2017 **Rating** 91 **To** 2024 CM
Tumbarumba Sauvignon Blanc 2017 **Rating** 90 **To** 2019 $27 CM
Hunter Valley Fiano 2017 **Rating** 90 **To** 2020 CM
Hilltops Cabernet Sauvignon 2016 **Rating** 90 **To** 2026 CM
Hilltops Tempranillo Graciano 2017 **Rating** 90 **To** 2022 CM

Hunter-Gatherer Vintners ★★★★

362 Pipers Creek-Pastoria Road, Pipers Creek, Vic 3444 **Region** Macedon Ranges
T 0407 821 049 **www**.hgwines.com.au **Open** W'ends 12–5
Winemaker Brian Martin **Est.** 2015 **Dozens** 1000 **Vyds** 5ha
In late 2015 winemaker Brian Martin purchased a vineyard that had passed through a number of owners since its beginnings in 1999. It was first known as Loxley Vineyard, and later Harmony Row. It has a long-established cellar door, and offers shiraz, pinot noir, riesling and chardonnay (and a couple of sparkling wines) under the Hunter-Gatherer label. Alternative varieties are marketed under the Marvio label.

♥♥♥♥♀ **Heathcote Sangiovese 2016** It's an excellent example of the joy of sangiovese. Fresh and fruit-driven with ample spice/savouriness and a firm but refreshing finish. It places everything in its rightful place and does so with a little flair. Screwcap. 14% alc. **Rating** 93 **To** 2022 $30 CM
Macedon Riesling 2017 Still at the start of a long life, the bouquet subdued, the palate more lively, with an overt minerally shaft running through the middle of the lime and lemon zest flavours. Screwcap. 11% alc. **Rating** 91 **To** 2023 $25
Macedon Chardonnay 2016 Well put together; towards the lower end of ripeness, but it all works. Green apple, melon, white peach and a savoury finish. Screwcap. 12.5% alc. **Rating** 90 **To** 2023 $30

Huntington Estate ★★★★☆

Ulan Road, Mudgee, NSW 2850 **Region** Mudgee
T 1800 995 931 **www**.huntingtonestate.com.au **Open** Mon–Sat 10–5, Sun 10–4
Winemaker Tim Stevens **Est.** 1969 **Dozens** 13 000 **Vyds** 43.8ha
Since taking ownership of Huntington Estate from the founding Roberts family, Tim Stevens has sensibly refrained from making major changes. The policy of having older vintage wines available is continuing, making the cellar door a first port of call for visitors to Mudgee. The estate's music festival suffers only one problem: there are not enough tickets to satisfy the demand. Huntington Estate really has a well deserved life of its own, and will have so for years to come. Exports to China.

♥♥♥♥♥ **Special Reserve Cabernet Sauvignon 2014** A beacon of high quality regional cabernet, with earthy, leathery tannins; dark fruit allusions aplenty, star anise and dried tobacco too, corseted by a well applied frame of cedar oak. A

complex wine pushing the envelope of moderate restraint, but not unsealing it. Screwcap. 13.8% alc. **Rating** 95 **To** 2030 $34 NG ✪
Semillon 2017 Textbook semillon, though youthfully creamier than most. This is loaded with scents of lemon butter, quince marmalade and candied citrus peel, pushed effortlessly along a line of caressing acidity. Already delicious, this will prove a long-distance runner to boot. Screwcap. 12% alc. **Rating** 94 **To** 2029 $23 NG ✪
Cabernet Sauvignon Shiraz 2016 This fires on all cylinders thanks to the varietal synergy: shiraz's gushing exuberance and cabernet's line of detailed tannins and brighter acidity. The oak is judiciously applied as an adjunct rather than gloss. Coffee bean, currant, bitter chocolate and dried sage glide across the long finish. Screwcap. 14.1% alc. **Rating** 94 **To** 2028 $34 NG

🍷🍷🍷🍷🍷 **Basket Dried Shiraz 2016** Rating 93 To 2031 $65 NG
Special Reserve Merlot 2016 Rating 93 To 2024 $34 NG
Vintage Fortified Shiraz 2012 Rating 93 $25 NG ✪
Special Reserve Shiraz 2015 Rating 92 To 2030 $34 NG
Block 3 Cabernet Sauvignon 2014 Rating 92 To 2026 $65 NG
Late Harvest Semillon 2016 Rating 92 To 2022 $28 NG
Barrel Fermented Chardonnay 2017 Rating 91 To 2022 $24 NG
Special Reserve Shiraz 2014 Rating 91 To 2029 $34 NG
Grenache 2016 Rating 91 To 2021 $25 NG
Grenache 2015 Rating 91 To 2024 $26 CM
Methode Traditionelle Chardonnay Pinot Noir NV Rating 91 $29 NG
Tim Stevens Signature Shiraz 2016 Rating 90 To 2026 $65 NG

Hurley Vineyard ★★★★★

101 Balnarring Road, Balnarring, Vic 3926 **Region** Mornington Peninsula
T (03) 5931 3000 **www**.hurleyvineyard.com.au **Open** 1st w'end each month 11–5
Winemaker Kevin Bell **Est.** 1998 **Dozens** 1100 **Vyds** 3.5ha
It's never as easy as it seems. Despite leading busy city lives, Kevin Bell and wife Tricia Byrnes have done most of the hard work in establishing Hurley Vineyard themselves, with some help from family and friends. Kevin has completed the applied science (wine science) degree at CSU, drawing on Nat White of Main Ridge Estate for consultancy advice, and occasionally Phillip Jones of Bass Phillip and another winemaker in Gevrey-Chambertin, France. He has not allowed a significant heart issue to prevent him continuing.

🍷🍷🍷🍷🍷 **Garamond Pinot Noir 2016** It exudes power and concentration without losing focus or drive. Heady aromas of warm earth, spice and florals, with a core of sweet, plump dark cherries with charcuterie-like complexity; decisive tannins and freshness. A complete wine with exceptional length. Diam. 13.9% alc. **Rating** 96 **To** 2028 $85 JF
Lodestone Pinot Noir 2016 The key differences are the clones and site – Lodestone being north-sloping and warmest. Dark sweet cherries, earthy rhubarb, loads of spice with Mediterranean herbs. This is the most structured pinot noir. Textured tannins hold a certain sway on the full-bodied palate, and while there's a concentration, it's far from heavy. Diam. 13.5% alc. **Rating** 95 **To** 2026 $70 JF
Estate Pinot Noir 2016 A plush and approachable wine with a certain refinement ex supple tannins and fine acidity. Requisite sweet cherry–accented fruit, pips, woodsy spices, a waft of eucalyptus, and a promise of happy drinking in its youth. Diam. 13.5% alc. **Rating** 94 **To** 2024 $45 JF
Hommage Pinot Noir 2016 The most approachable pinot noir in its youth thanks to supple tannins and its overall plushness. Loaded with woodsy spices and spiced red berries and cherries, the fruit sweetness sashaying across the palate to a refreshing finish. It doesn't have the presence and depth on the palate as Lodestone and Garamond, but is lovely nonetheless. Diam. 13.2% alc. **Rating** 94 **To** 2024 $70 JF

Hutton Vale Farm

Stone Jar Road, Angaston, SA 5353 **Region** Eden Valley
T (08) 8564 8270 **www**.huttonvale.com **Open** By appt
Winemaker Kym Teusner **Est.** 1960 **Dozens** 1500 **Vyds** 27ha

John Howard Angas arrived in SA in 1843, purchasing and developing significant farming property close to the still embryonic town that would eventually be named after him. He named part of his property Hutton Vale, and it is this that is now owned and occupied by his great-great-grandson John and wife Jan Angas. In 2012, the Angas family and Teusner Wines shook hands on a partnership arrangement, under which the Angases grow the grapes, and Kym Teusner is responsible for the winemaking, sales and marketing. The vineyards first caught Kym's attention when he was at Torbreck. Just when the future seemed assured, the vineyards were badly affected by a grass fire in August '14. While much of the vineyard will ultimately be regenerated, some of the oldest grenache vines were completely destroyed, as were 55 of the magnificent 500yo gum trees that are part of the striking landscape of Hutton Vale. Small quantities are exported to China.

¶¶¶¶¶ Eden Valley Riesling 2017 If you ever want to show someone just how glorious the riesling grape can be, serve them a glass of this. It's agenda-free, fundamentally delicious, intense with flavour but not cutting, gorgeous at every turn, cellar-worthy if you so desire, but in no way is patience a prerequisite. Lime, orange blossom, a gently candied aspect, a slip of pure lemon. It's bold and it's beautiful. Screwcap. 13% alc. **Rating** 95 **To** 2027 $35 CM

Idavue Estate

470 Northern Highway, Heathcote, Vic 3523 **Region** Heathcote
T 0429 617 287 **www**.idavueestate.com **Open** W'ends 10.30–5
Winemaker Andrew Whytcross, Sandra Whytcross **Est.** 2000 **Dozens** 600 **Vyds** 5.7ha

Owners and winemakers Andrew and Sandra Whytcross both undertook a two-year winemaking course through Bendigo TAFE. With assistance from son Marty, they look after the vineyard, which is planted to shiraz (3ha), cabernet sauvignon (1.9ha), and semillon and chardonnay (0.4ha each). The red wines are made in typical small-batch fashion with hand-picked fruit, hand-plunged fermenters and a basket press.

¶¶¶¶¶ Blue Note Heathcote Shiraz 2016 Of the '16 Idavue shirazs, this is the most balanced in its structured, full-bodied style. Dark purple-black; laden with plum compote, black cherries and pips. Iron filings, roast beef and fresh coffee grounds lead the surge of savouriness, with the oak and firm tannins integrated. Screwcap. 14% alc. **Rating** 92 **To** 2026 $40 JF

¶¶¶¶ Heathcote Shiraz 2016 Rating 89 **To** 2025 $30 JF

In Dreams

179 Glenview Road, Yarra Glen, Vic 3775 **Region** Yarra Valley
T (03) 8413 8379 **www**.indreams.com.au **Open** Not
Winemaker Nina Stocker **Est.** 2013 **Dozens** 3000

In Dreams produces two wines: Chardonnay and Pinot Noir, with fruit sourced from the Upper Yarra Valley. The cooler microclimate of the area lends itself to traditional winemaking techniques, such as small-batch fermentation and delicate use of French oak, which allow the fruit to express itself.

¶¶¶¶¶ In Dreams Yarra Valley Pinot Noir 2016 Bright and brooding at once. Strawberries and cherries, a stewy character, integrated spice, lipstick, an all-round firmness. It's light in colour but there's real power here. Everything is in excellent order. Screwcap. 13% alc. **Rating** 94 **To** 2026 $30 CM ❂

¶¶¶¶ In Dreams Yarra Valley Chardonnay 2016 Rating 93 **To** 2023 $25 CM ❂

Indigo Vineyard

1221 Beechworth-Wangaratta Road, Everton Upper, Vic 3678 **Region** Beechworth
T (03) 5727 0233 **www**.indigovineyard.com.au **Open** Wed–Sun 11–4
Winemaker Stuart Hordern, Marc Scalzo **Est.** 1999 **Dozens** 5000 **Vyds** 46.15ha
Indigo Vineyard has a little over 46ha of vineyards planted to 11 varieties, including the top
French and Italian grapes. The business was and is primarily focused on growing grapes for sale
to Brokenwood, but since 2004 increasing amounts have been vinified for the Indigo label.
The somewhat incestuous nature of the whole wine business sees the Indigo wines being
made at Brokenwood (although Marc Scalzo makes the Pinot Grigio).

🍷🍷🍷🍷🍷 **Alpine Valleys Beechworth Pinot Grigio 2017** From the estate vineyard and
also Walpole vineyard in Whorouly. The result is a textural wine with nashi pear,
lemon curd and grapefruit pith, yet it's super tight, almost linear. Keeps a crunch
with the zesty acidity, refreshing to the last drop and impressive all the way to the
long finish. Screwcap. 13.5% alc. **Rating** 95 **To** 2021 $25 JF ❂

🍷🍷🍷🍷🍷 **Secret Village Beechworth Viognier 2016 Rating** 93 **To** 2022 $30 JF
Beechworth Shiraz 2016 Rating 93 **To** 2023 $35 JF
Secret Village Beechworth Shiraz 2016 Rating 92 **To** 2026 $45 JF
Beechworth Sangiovese 2016 Rating 92 **To** 2019 $30 JF
Secret Village Beechworth Roussanne 2016 Rating 91 **To** 2023 $45 JF
Beechworth Rose of Pinot Noir 2017 Rating 90 **To** 2019 $25 JF

Inkwell ★★★★

PO Box 33, Sellicks Beach, SA 5174 **Region** McLaren Vale
T 0430 050 115 **www**.inkwellwines.com **Open** By appt
Winemaker Dudley Brown **Est.** 2003 **Dozens** 800 **Vyds** 12ha
Inkwell was born in 2003 when Dudley Brown returned to Australia from California and
bought a rundown vineyard on the serendipitously named California Road. He inherited
5ha of neglected shiraz and planted an additional 7ha, including viognier (2.5ha), zinfandel
(2.5ha) and heritage shiraz clones (2ha). The five-year restoration of the old vines and the
establishment of the new reads like the ultimate handbook for aspiring vignerons, particularly
those who are prepared to work non-stop. The reward has been rich. Dudley is adamant that
the production will be capped at 1000 dozen; almost all the grapes are sold. Exports to the
US and Canada.

🍷🍷🍷🍷🍷 **Deeper Well McLaren Vale Shiraz 2012** Matured in French oak for
21 months and given 3 years in bottle prior to release. It's a dusty, curranty,
leathery wine with a gentle overlay of toasty oak and all the mellow-but-powerful
charm you could hope for. Floral highlights add a prettiness to an impressive show.
Screwcap. 14.9% alc. **Rating** 94 **To** 2024 $80 CM
McLaren Vale Primitivo 2016 An unusually well mannered expression of this
variety. It manages it without any loss of fruit power either. This is both neat and
intense, its berried flavours shot with spice, infused with orange rind, and carved
with rusty, savoury tannin. Freshness is another of its numerous positives. Screwcap.
14.1% alc. **Rating** 94 **To** 2024 $30 CM ❂

🍷🍷🍷🍷🍷 **Black and Blue Late Harvest Fortified Zinfandel 2015 Rating** 93 $40 CM
Dark Star Late Harvest Fortified Zinfandel NV Rating 93 $50 CM

Innocent Bystander

314 Maroondah Highway, Healesville, Vic 3777 **Region** Yarra Valley
T (03) 5720 5500 **www**.innocentbystander.com.au **Open** By appt
Winemaker Joel Tilbrook, Cate Looney, Geoff Alexander, Katherine Brown,
Tom Canning **Est.** 1997 **Dozens** 49 000 **Vyds** 45ha
On 5 April 2016 Brown Brothers and Giant Steps announced that the Innocent Bystander
brand (including Mea Culpa) and stock had been sold to Brown Brothers. As part of the

acquisition, Brown Brothers purchased the White Rabbit Brewery site adjacent to Giant Steps, and this has become the cellar door home of Innocent Bystander. Its business is in two completely different wine categories, both fitting neatly together. On the one hand is the big volume (a confidential amount) of vintage moscato, the grapes coming from the King Valley, plus non-vintage prosecco, similarly sourced. The other side of the business is the premium Yarra Valley single varietal wines, with substantial brand value. Exports to the UK, the US and other major markets.

ΥΥΥΥΥ **Rose 2017** A pinot noir rose with abundant juicy red fruits, its intensity something to stop you in your tracks. It's the '17 effect, of course, and it's remarkable. Rose can't get much better than this, nor be longer lived. Screwcap. 13% alc. **Rating** 95 **To** 2021 $20

Yarra Valley Syrah 2016 The colour and name makes it clear this isn't a full-bodied shiraz, but its distinctly fragrant and spicy red and black cherry fruits speak clearly of the cool climate of the Yarra Valley. The syrah name is appropriate, the juicy mouthfeel a major plus. Screwcap. 14% alc. **Rating** 94 **To** 2030 $25 ○

ΥΥΥΥΥ **Yarra Valley Arneis 2017 Rating** 91 **To** 2020 $25
Yarra Valley Pinot Noir 2017 Rating 91 **To** 2022 $25

Ipso Facto Wines ★★★★

PO Box 1886, Margaret River, WA 6285 **Region** Margaret River
T 0402 321 572 **Open** Not
Winemaker Kate Morgan **Est.** 2010 **Dozens** 300
This is the realisation of owner/winemaker Kate Morgan's dream of making her own wine with her own label. After graduating from Curtin University with a degree in viticulture and oenology, she worked vintages in Australia and overseas before returning to WA. There she worked at Houghton, Stella Bella and for the last three years as assistant winemaker at Fraser Gallop Estate. The wines are made with minimal additions (only SO_2 added).

ΥΥΥΥΥ **Margaret River Chenin 2014** Hand-picked, chilled overnight, whole-bunch pressed, wild-fermented in used French oak, matured for 9 months. 200 dozen released with 3 years bottle age. Stone fruit driven, and looking certain to fulfil Kate Morgan's 8-year drinking span. Screwcap. 13% alc. **Rating** 90 **To** 2023 $32

Margaret River Cabernet Sauvignon 2016 Bright but relatively light colour; a very lively wine, the bouquet with cassis fruit to the fore, the light to medium-bodied palate not forcing the issue at any point. The tannins are fine-spun and less imperious than cabernet tannins often are, oak a means to an end. Screwcap. 13.5% alc. **Rating** 90 **To** 2031 $35

Iron Cloud Wines ★★★★★

Suite 16, 18 Stirling Highway, Nedlands, WA 6009 (postal) **Region** Geographe
T 0401 860 891 www.ironcloudwines.com.au **Open** Not
Winemaker Michael Ng **Est.** 1999 **Dozens** 2500 **Vyds** 11ha
In 2003 owners Warwick Lavis and Geoff and Karyn Cross purchased the then-named Pepperilly Estate, which had been planted in 1999 on red gravelly loam soils. Peppermint trees line the Henty Brook, the natural water source for the vineyard. In '17 Michael Ng, chief winemaker for Rockcliffe, succeeded Coby Ladwig (who made the '15 and '16 wines). Exports to China.

ΥΥΥΥΥ **The Alliance Ferguson Valley Chardonnay 2016** An interesting array of contrasting characters; power on one hand, finesse and elegance on the other. There is a precision in the way the wine travels along the mouth, having made its opening statement. The complex, slightly funky (in the best sense) bouquet has an alliance with the power of the opening statement. Screwcap. 13.5% alc. **Rating** 95 **To** 2026 $45

Pepperilly Single Vineyard Ferguson Valley Rose 2017 This blend of 70% grenache and 15% each of shiraz and mourvedre is jumping out of its skin with vibrant red berry fruits and natural acidity. The fact that there is no obvious trace of fermentation and maturation in new and used French oak is doubly surprising – and admirable. Screwcap. 13% alc. **Rating** 95 **To** 2020 $25 ○

Rock of Solitude Purple Patch Single Vineyard Ferguson Valley GSM 2016 Bright, clear crimson-purple; as you would expect, largely shaped by its grenache component. A lithe and lacy wine driven by red fruits, cherry, raspberry, strawberry and rhubarb, all presenting to a lesser or greater degree on the fresh, medium-bodied palate, given further context by a pinch of spice and silky tannins. Screwcap. 14.5% alc. **Rating** 95 **To** 2032 $32 ○

Pepperilly Single Vineyard Ferguson Valley Cabernet Shiraz 2016 The attractive and unusual labels on the Pepperilly range will grasp the imagination and be easily remembered, and nor will the wine let you down. Blackcurrant ex the cabernet and blackberry/plum ex the shiraz are equal partners in the wrestling ring, supported by ripe tannins and appropriate new oak. Screwcap. 14.5% alc. **Rating** 94 **To** 2036 $25 ○

 The Alliance Cabernet Malbec 2014 Rating 93 To 2029 $45
Pepperilly Sauvignon Blanc Semillon 2017 Rating 90 To 2021 $25

Ironwood Estate ★★★★

2191 Porongurup Road, Porongurup, WA 6234 **Region** Porongurup
T (08) 9853 1126 **www.**ironwoodestatewines.com.au **Open** Wed–Mon 11–5
Winemaker Wignalls Wines (Michael Perkins) **Est.** 1996 **Dozens** 2500 **Vyds** 5ha
Ironwood Estate was established in 1996 by Mary and Eugene Harma. An estate vineyard of riesling, sauvignon blanc, chardonnay, shiraz, merlot and cabernet sauvignon (in more or less equal amounts) was planted on a northern slope of the Porongurup Range. Exports to Japan and Singapore.

 Reserve Chardonnay 2017 An amiable chardonnay with pear, peach and ginger flavours happily holding hands with spicy/toasty oak. Flesh, juice, flow; all are in good working order. Screwcap. 14.2% alc. **Rating** 91 **To** 2023 $26 CM

Porongurup Shiraz 2016 A lightish style with cherry and a touch of plum as the mainstays, dabs of sweet spice helping round it out. It feels soft in the mouth and shows little sign of oak, other than a gentle creaminess. Good now but it may well surprise in the medium term. Screwcap. 14% alc. **Rating** 90 **To** 2025 $22 CM

Sauvignon Blanc 2017 Rating 89 To 2019 $19 CM ○

Irvine ★★★★☆

PO Box 308, Angaston, SA 5353 **Region** Eden Valley
T (08) 8564 1046 **www.**irvinewines.com.au **Open** At Taste Eden Valley
Winemaker Kirk Lambert **Est.** 1983 **Dozens** 10 000 **Vyds** 80ha
When James (Jim) Irvine established his eponymous winery, he chose a singularly difficult focus for the business: the production of great merlot from the Eden Valley. Throughout the years of establishment, and indeed thereafter, he was a much-in-demand consultant, bobbing up in all sorts of places. Yet when he decided to sell the business in 2014, its potential was increased with the dowry provided by the buyers, the Wade and Miles families. The Miles family's involvement in wine goes back to 1867, when Henry Winter Miles planted 0.8ha of shiraz. Successive generations of the family added to the vineyard portfolio from 1967. Henry's great-grandson Peter Miles and Peter's business partner John Wade collectively own 160ha spread through the Barossa and Eden valleys (although only 80ha fall within the new Irvine partnership). Exports to the UK, Switzerland, the United Arab Emirates, Singapore, Malaysia, Japan, Taiwan, Hong Kong and China.

Special Release Eden Valley Grand Merlot 2013 Deeply coloured, this is a very full-bodied merlot that, within the constraints of its style, ticks all the boxes. It has length and depth, its blackcurrant/cassis fruit backed by firm tannins, the oak drawn into the heart of the wine. A double gold medal at the China Wine & Spirit Awards would mean more if it showed the year. Cork. 14.6% alc. **Rating** 95 To 2038 $130

The Estate Barossa Shiraz 2016 From the Ebenezer district. A deep but vivid crimson-purple signals the luxuriantly rich wine. Luscious black fruits and pillow-soft tannins; vanillan oak buried somewhere in the sybaritic display. Screwcap. 14.6% alc. **Rating** 94 To 2031 $28 ☺

ŢŢŢŢŢ **The Estate Eden Valley Shiraz 2016** Rating 93 To 2026 $28
Spring Hill Eden Valley Riesling 2017 Rating 92 To 2030 $22 SC ☺
Spring Hill Eden Valley Rose 2017 Rating 92 To 2019 $22 SC ☺
Eden Valley Primitivo Noir 2017 Rating 92 To 2019 $35
The Estate Merlot Cabernet Franc 2016 Rating 91 To 2029 $28
Spring Hill Merlot 2016 Rating 90 To 2026 $22
The Estate Eden Valley Merlot 2015 Rating 90 To 2028 $28

🍇 Ivybrook Farm ★★★★

34 Thomas Road, Maslin Beach, SA 5170 **Region** McLaren Vale
T 0427 809 580 **www**.ivybrook.com.au **Open** W'ends & public hols 11–5
Winemaker Nick Hunt, David Hunt **Est.** 2008 **Dozens** 400 **Vyds** 6.2ha
Ivybrook Farm is a family owned vineyard and winery in McLaren Vale. The farming property is rich in history with old stone buildings, and has belonged to the Hunt family for five generations. David Hunt and his wife Cheryl, the current custodians, first planted vineyards to shiraz in 1997 and sold their grapes to prominent wineries in the area. In 2010 they planted tempranillo followed by touriga nacional. In '14, son Nick, after completing his oenology studies and working in wineries locally, interstate and in the US, took over winemaking. Ivybrook Farm recently opened a cellar door in its renovated 1898 stone barn.

ŢŢŢŢŢ **McLaren Vale Shiraz 2016** Deep colour; McLaren Vale dark chocolate is tattooed on the liquid chest of this rich, supple shiraz and its waves of black fruits, plum and vanilla. Ultra-typical of the best fruit of the region, and a long life ahead. Screwcap. 14.5% alc. **Rating** 94 To 2031 $30 ☺
Reserve McLaren Vale Shiraz 2014 No details here, but all the dials (happily bar the alcohol) are turned up: more depth to the fruit, more new oak, more powerful tannins. It is still only medium to full-bodied, not a behemoth, and its best years are in front of it. Screwcap. 14.5% alc. **Rating** 94 To 2034 $45

ŢŢŢŢŢ **McLaren Vale Tempranillo 2017** Rating 93 To 2024 $25 ☺
Adelaide Hills Riesling 2017 Rating 92 To 2027 $22 ☺
McLaren Vale Shiraz 2014 Rating 90 To 2024 $30
McLaren Vale GSM 2014 Rating 90 To 2024 $25

J&J Wines ★★★★

39–45 Rivers Lane, McLaren Vale, SA 5172 **Region** McLaren Vale
T (08) 8323 9098 **www**.jjwines.com.au **Open** By appt
Winemaker Scott Rawlinson, Joe DiFabio **Est.** 1998 **Dozens** 4000 **Vyds** 5.5ha
J&J is owned and operated by three generations of the Mason family. The estate vineyards are organically managed, but are significantly supplemented by contract-grown grapes. It has come a long way since 2004, the first year when some of the estate grapes were vinified to make wine for the private use of the family. Exports to Canada, Hong Kong and China.

ŢŢŢŢŢ **Rivers Lane Organic Shiraz 2015** McLaren Vale is writ large on the face of this brilliantly coloured wine. It's so juicy you have to be careful not to dribble. Matured in French and American oak, it will coast along, bending to every whim. Screwcap. 14.5% alc. **Rating** 94 To 2029 $22 ☺

ŢŢŢŢŢ **Boots Hill McLaren Vale Shiraz 2016** Rating 90 To 2029 $18 ☺
Langhorne Creek McLaren Vale Shiraz 2015 Rating 90 To 2025 $15 ☺

Jack Estate   ★★★★

15025 Riddoch Highway, Coonawarra, SA 5263 **Region** Coonawarra
T (08) 8736 3130 **www**.jackestate.com **Open** By appt
Winemaker Shannon Sutherland, Conrad Slabber **Est.** 2011 **Dozens** 10000 **Vyds** 221ha
Jack Estate was founded in 2011 by a group of grapegrowers who acquired the large Mildara
Blass winery in Coonawarra. Wines are sourced from the estate vineyards in Coonawarra
(1ha of cabernet sauvignon) and the Murray Darling (200ha), and also from neighbouring
grapegrowers in Coonawarra and Wrattonbully to complete their three-tiered range. Exports
to Malaysia, Singapore, the Philippines, Thailand and China.

ＰＰＰＰＰ **Coonawarra Cabernet Sauvignon 2015** Inimitably Coonawarra with its
sinewy tannins, mint-flecked currant, tomato bush and cedar-toned oak, parading
across the medium to fullish palate, before the telltale lift of after-dinner mint. This
is of strong regional pedigree and priced astoundingly well. Screwcap. 14.5% alc.
Rating 93 **To** 2025 $25 NG ✪
Coonawarra Wrattonbully Shiraz 2015 This delivers a coterie of black
cherry and plum flavours flecked with mint and Australian scrub. Oak imparts a
cedar edge to the wine, reining in the flavours while demanding a few years to
settle. This is distinctly regional, poised; a decent drink at a keen price. Screwcap.
14.5% alc. **Rating** 91 **To** 2022 $22 NG ✪

Jack Rabbit Vineyard   ★★★★

85 McAdams Lane, Bellarine, Vic 3221 **Region** Geelong
T (03) 5251 2223 **www**.jackrabbitvineyard.com.au **Open** 7 days 10–5
Winemaker Nyall Condon **Est.** 1989 **Dozens** 8000 **Vyds** 2ha
Jack Rabbit Vineyard is owned by David and Lyndsay Sharp of Leura Park Estate. Nestled
next to the acclaimed Jack Rabbit Restaurant are 2ha of vineyards (planted equally to pinot
noir and cabernet sauvignon), plus 48ha of vines planted across the Bellarine Peninsula.

ＰＰＰＰＰ **Geelong Chardonnay 2016** A chardonnay with ample stone-fruit flavours as
its calling card, expanding across the mid-weighted palate and its vanillan French
oak supports. Full and convincing, lingering with toffee apple, butterscotch and
white fig. This fits a desirable niche for many drinkers, in an age of edgier styles.
Screwcap. 13.5% alc. **Rating** 91 **To** 2020 $35 NG
Geelong Pinot Grigio 2017 Straightforward, gentler gris, with a juicy beam of
acidity taking over the role held by the variety's usual phenolic pick-up. Orchard
fruit flavours and lemon drop notes barrel along effortlessly. This is poised, easy to
drink and thoroughly convincing. Screwcap. 12% alc. **Rating** 91 **To** 2020 $35 NG
Geelong Rose 2017 Dry, mid-weighted rose made from pinot noir, pushing
plenty of red-berried fruit flavours along a textural balancing beam of phenolics,
over acidity. Despite the variety at play, it reminds me of a southern Rhône rose,
with plenty of warmth and grip. Screwcap. 13% alc. **Rating** 91 **To** 2019 $35 NG
Bellarine Peninsula Merlot 2016 The structural attributes across the better
wines at this address are applied sensitively, facilitating fruit-forward, easy-drinking
styles. This is no exception, with plummy tones doused with cinnamon spice, anise
and a whiff of verdant herb. The tannins are firm but measured, the palate sweet
and just grippy enough. Screwcap. 13% alc. **Rating** 90 **To** 2021 $42 NG

ＰＰＰＰ **Bellarine Peninsula Pinot Noir 2016** Rating 89 To 2023 $40 NG

Jackson Brooke   ★★★★

126 Beaconsfield Parade, Northcote, Vic 3070 (postal) **Region** Henty
T 0466 652 485 **www**.jacksonbrookewine.com.au **Open** Not
Winemaker Jackson Brooke **Est.** 2013 **Dozens** 120
Jackson Brooke graduated from the University of Melbourne in 2004 with a science degree,
and having spent a summer working at Tarrington Vineyards, went to study oenology at
Lincoln University in NZ. A vintage at Wedgetail Estate in the Yarra Valley was followed

by stints in Japan, southern California and then three years as assistant winemaker to Ben Portet, accumulating his knowledge of boutique winemaking. Some reverse swing from creating his own wine label led to a full-time teaching career. He had already married and his first daughter, Olivia, was born in March '14. Jackson has abandoned any idea of building a winery for the foreseeable future, renting space in the little winery at Tarrington Vineyards. Annual production has edged up from 1t in '13 to 3t in '15, and 6t in '16 (15–20t is the ultimate plateau).

ΨΨΨΨΨ **Abbey Syrah 2016** It takes time to rise in the glass, but once unfurled this is an excellent shiraz – personality laden, riddled with clovey spice, florals and cured meat but served well by boysenberry and black cherry. Tannin is ultrafine too. A few more years under its belt and this should be a beauty. Cork. 13.5% alc. **Rating** 93 **To** 2028 $28 CM

Henty Chardonnay 2016 Don't let the straw-yellow colour fool you, and thank heavens full mlf was employed. This is a laser-like expression, its flavours of nectarine, apple, green pineapple and wood spice rushing through the palate at speed. But it doesn't all fly past unremarked; the turbulence created leaves an impression. Exactly how good this wine really is will take patience to properly determine. Cork. 12.5% alc. **Rating** 92 **To** 2025 $24 CM ✪

Cobboboonee Vineyard Cabernet Shiraz 2016 It's everything except dense – it's light, perfumed, structural and complex, with choc mint, florals, meaty spice, redcurrant and boysenberry flavours leaping this way and that. Not standard fare for this varietal blend, but there's plenty to pique your interest. Cork. 13% alc. **Rating** 92 **To** 2026 $24 CM ✪

Jacob's Creek   ★★★★★
2129 Barossa Valley Way, Rowland Flat, SA 5352 **Region** Barossa Valley
T (08) 8521 3000 www.jacobscreek.com **Open** 7 days 10–5
Winemaker Ben Bryant **Est.** 1973 **Dozens** NFP **Vyds** 740ha
Jacob's Creek (owned by Pernod Ricard) is one of the largest-selling brands in the world, and the global success of the base range has had the perverse effect of prejudicing many critics and wine writers who fail (so it seems) to objectively look behind the label and taste what is in fact in the glass. Exports to the UK, the US, Canada and China, and other major markets.

ΨΨΨΨΨ **Steingarten Barossa Riesling 2017** Notwithstanding its heritage and history, Steingarten has morphed into a crystalline riesling appreciated for its purity and exceptional drive. Pale straw; tightly coiled revealing only a little of its lemon blossom, zest and juice that'll increase in time. Screwcap. 10.9% alc. **Rating** 96 **To** 2030 $50 JF ✪

Lyndale Adelaide Hills Chardonnay 2017 An impressive wine and while no details were forthcoming, it sings of its region. Still tightly wound and almost linear, but it will unfurl in time. A mix of lemon and grapefruit, juice, zest and pith; there's texture, integrated oak and plenty of bright acidity to close. Savoury and moreish. Screwcap. 12.8% alc. **Rating** 95 **To** 2027 $50 JF

Centenary Hill Barossa Shiraz 2013 Excellent crimson–black hue for a 5yo wine; it's rich, smoky and toasty with freshly ground coffee and dark chocolate, plenty of dark plums too, with a waft of green walnut. Full-bodied, and while the flavours are concentrated, everything from the oak to the giving tannins are in their place. Well played. Screwcap. 14.5% alc. **Rating** 95 **To** 2033 $82 JF

ΨΨΨΨΨ **Reserve Limestone Coast Shiraz 2016 Rating** 93 **To** 2029 $18 ✪
Barossa Signature Shiraz Tempranillo 2016 Rating 93 **To** 2025 $20 JF ✪
Expedition Coonawarra Cabernet 2015 Rating 93 **To** 2035 $90 JF
Organic McLaren Vale Shiraz 2015 Rating 92 **To** 2028 $65 JF
Reserve Limestone Coast Cabernet Sauvignon 2016 Rating 92 **To** 2024 $18 CM ✪
Expedition Barossa Cabernet Shiraz 2015 Rating 91 **To** 2035 $90 JF
Barossa Signature Riesling 2017 Rating 90 **To** 2023 $20 CM ✪

Reserve Adelaide Hills Sauvignon Blanc 2017 Rating 90 To 2019 $18 JF ✪
Reserve Adelaide Hills Chardonnay 2017 Rating 90 To 2022 $18 JF ✪
Double Barrel Barossa Shiraz 2016 Rating 90 To 2022 $25 JF
Bungalow Lane Barossa Cabernet 2014 Rating 90 To 2032 $82 JF

James & Co Wines ★★★★☆

136 Main Street, Rutherglen, Vic 3685 **Region** Beechworth
T 0447 341 373 **www.**jamesandcowines.com.au **Open** Thurs–Mon 11–6
Winemaker Ricky James **Est.** 2011 **Dozens** 750
Ricky and Georgie James intended to buy land in Beechworth and establish a vineyard planted primarily to sangiovese. 'Serendipity led us to Mark Walpole, and we were given the chance to purchase fruit from his Fighting Gully Road vineyard,' they said. They have set up their home and cellar door in Rutherglen, and intend to float between the two regions.

🍷🍷🍷🍷🍷 **Alpine Valleys Pinot Grigio 2017** Super impressive. It sees some oak but there are no apparent oak flavours. This is briny and intense with a burst of nashi pear, a rip of honeysuckle and a crunch of apple. Few grigios prompt the word mouthfilling; this one does. It deserves to be a smash hit. Screwcap. 13% alc. **Rating** 95 **To** 2019 $24 CM ✪
Beechworth Sangiovese Rose 2017 Ricky James now grows sangiovese specifically for rose, a portion spending time in French oak. It's a pale crimson-copper colour, spicy and savoury, blooming with cherried, almost blackcurrant-like flavour. It's so juicy and delicious it should 100% be on your drinking radar. Screwcap. 13% alc. **Rating** 94 **To** 2019 $24 CM ✪

🍷🍷🍷🍷🍸 **Beechworth Sparkling Rose 2017** Rating 91 $38 CM

Jansz Tasmania ★★★★★

1216B Pipers Brook Road, Pipers Brook, Tas 7254 **Region** Northern Tasmania
T (03) 6382 7066 **www.**jansztas.com **Open** 7 days 10–4
Winemaker Louisa Rose **Est.** 1985 **Dozens** 38 000 **Vyds** 30ha
Jansz is part of Hill-Smith Family Vineyards, and was one of the early sparkling wine labels in Tasmania, stemming from a short-lived relationship between Heemskerk and Louis Roederer. Its 15ha of chardonnay, 12ha of pinot noir and 3ha of pinot meunier correspond almost exactly to the blend composition of the Jansz wines. Part of the former Frogmore Creek vineyard purchased by Hill-Smith in Dec 2012 is now dedicated to the needs of Jansz Tasmania. Exports to all major markets.

🍷🍷🍷🍷🍷 **Single Vineyard Vintage Chardonnay 2011** Stunning. Arresting. It puts on a powerful display and yet it has character; indeed it has elegance. It tastes of peach, custard, crisp green apples, butter, lemon. It pours beautifully through the palate and explodes on the finish. Diam. 12% alc. **Rating** 97 $65 CM ✪

🍷🍷🍷🍷🍷 **Vintage Rose 2013** 100% pinot noir, and 100% barrel-fermented, reflected in the blush-salmon hue. It combines power with elegance, replete with red cherry and wild strawberry flavours sprinkled with spice. Length and finesse are the marks of a classy Tasmanian sparkling. Diam. 13% alc. **Rating** 95 $53

🍷🍷🍷🍷🍸 **Vintage Cuvee 2013** Rating 93 $47 CM
Premium Cuvee NV Rating 91 $32 CM

Jarrah Ridge Winery ★★★☆

651 Great Northern Highway, Herne Hill, WA 6056 **Region** Swan Valley
T (08) 9296 6337 **www.**jarrahridge.com **Open** W'ends 10–5
Winemaker Mark Morton, Michael Ng **Est.** 1998 **Dozens** 10 000 **Vyds** 20.5ha
Following the death of founder Syd Pond, Mark Morton and Jimmy Wong have acquired Jarrah Ridge Winery, with their principal focus the development of the brand in China (where the pair has worked since 2008). The employment of a number of contract winemakers gives

them the flexibility to increase the volume and range of the portfolio in response to rapidly changing market dynamics. Exports to Malaysia, Singapore, Japan, Hong Kong and China.

🍷🍷🍷🍷🍷 **Zin Golden Era NV** 95% botrytis viognier, 5% botrytis riesling. Silver medals at the Interwine and Swan Valley wine shows '17. Luscious and well balanced; what's more there's some fresh ginger ex the viognier. Screwcap. 11.5% alc. **Rating** 90 To 2020 $25

Jasper Hill ★★★★★
Drummonds Lane, Heathcote, Vic 3523 **Region** Heathcote
T (03) 5433 2528 **www**.jasperhill.com.au **Open** By appt
Winemaker Ron Laughton, Emily McNally **Est.** 1979 **Dozens** 2500 **Vyds** 26.5ha
The red wines of Jasper Hill are highly regarded and much sought after. As long as vintage conditions allow, these are wonderfully rich and full-flavoured wines. The vineyards are dry-grown and managed organically. Exports to the UK, the US, Canada, France, Denmark, Hong Kong and Singapore.

🍷🍷🍷🍷🍷 **Georgia's Paddock Heathcote Nebbiolo 2016** Hand-picked from unirrigated vines planted '75. Berry sorted, wild-fermented, matured in French oak for 12 months. How strange that this should be Jasper Hill's premier red wine, but it certainly was this vintage. The colour is good, the cherry/berry fruits ripe, and the tannins do not seek to throttle, but instead sustain. Classy wine. Cork. 13.5% alc. **Rating** 95 **To** 2030 $64

Jeanneret Wines ★★★★☆
Jeanneret Road, Sevenhill, SA 5453 **Region** Clare Valley
T (08) 8843 4308 **www**.jeanneretwines.com **Open** Mon–Fri 9–5, w'ends 10–5
Winemaker Ben Jeanneret, Harry Dickinson **Est.** 1992 **Dozens** 18 000 **Vyds** 6ha
Ben Jeanneret has progressively built the range and quantity of wines he makes at the onsite winery. In addition to the estate vineyards, Jeanneret has grape purchase contracts with owners of an additional 20ha of hand-pruned, hand-picked, dry-grown vines spread throughout the Clare Valley. The rieslings are very good indeed, the red wines often extractive and difficult to enjoy. Exports to Sweden, Malaysia, Japan.

🍷🍷🍷🍷🍷 **Single Vineyard Watervale Riesling 2017** This is the standout wine of the three Jeanneret rieslings from '17. The sparkling acidity of the vintage is there, and so is the lime juice, apple and mineral fusion that – together with the acidity – gives the wine stature now, and the capacity to build into a high class mature riesling. Screwcap. 12.5% alc. **Rating** 95 **To** 2032 $30 ✪

🍷🍷🍷🍷🍷 **Single Vineyard Sevenhill Riesling 2017 Rating** 92 **To** 2027 $30
Big Fine Girl Clare Valley Riesling 2016 Rating 91 **To** 2026 $22 ✪
Clare Valley GSM 2016 Rating 90 **To** 2030 $22

Jericho Wines ★★★★☆
13 Seacombe Crescent, Seacombe Heights, SA 5047 (postal) **Region** Adelaide Hills/McLaren Vale
T 0499 013 554 **www**.jerichowines.com.au **Open** Not
Winemaker Neil Jericho, Andrew Jericho **Est.** 2012 **Dozens** 3000
Neil Jericho made wine for over 35 years in Victoria, mainly in the Rutherglen and King Valley regions. In this venture the whole family is in play, with wife Kaye, a 'vintage widow'; eldest daughter Sally, who worked for Wine Australia for 10 years then obtained marketing and accounting degrees from the University of Adelaide; and son Andrew, who obtained his Bachelor of Oenology from the University of Adelaide in 2003. Andrew worked for 10 years in McLaren Vale, but then moved outside the square for experience at the highly regarded Grace Vineyard in the Shanxi province of China. Son Kim was torn between oenology, hospitality and graphic design, and opted for the latter, providing help with label design. Exports to China.

ŸŸŸŸŸ **McLaren Vale GSM 2016** An 86/11/3% blend, the grenache from 40yo dry-grown bushvines. The restriction of the shiraz component to 11% was exactly correct. This has excellent colour, a red blossom and spice bouquet, and a quietly spoken but pure evocation of grenache. So easy to drink now or in a decade or more. Screwcap. 14.2% alc. **Rating** 95 **To** 2031 $26 ✪

ŸŸŸŸŸ **Adelaide Hills Fiano 2017 Rating** 93 **To** 2022 $26 ✪
Adelaide Hills Rose 2017 Rating 93 **To** 2020 $26 CM ✪
Adelaide Hills Tempranillo 2017 Rating 91 **To** 2024 $26
Single Vineyard McLaren Vale Shiraz 2015 Rating 90 **To** 2025 $38 DB

Jim Barry Wines   ★★★★★

33 Craigs Hill Road, Clare, SA 5453 **Region** Clare Valley
T (08) 8842 2261 **www**.jimbarry.com **Open** Mon–Fri 9–5, w'ends & hols 9–4
Winemaker Peter Barry, Tom Barry, Derrick Quinton, Jack Scholz **Est.** 1959
Dozens 80 000 **Vyds** 300ha
The patriarch of this highly successful wine business, Jim Barry, died in 2004, but the business continues under the active management of several of his many children, led by the irrepressible Peter Barry. The ultra-premium release is The Armagh Shiraz, with the McRae Wood red wines not far behind. Jim Barry Wines is able to draw upon mature Clare Valley vineyards, plus a small holding in Coonawarra. After studying and travelling, third-generation winemaker Tom Barry and commercial manager Sam Barry have joined the business, launching The Barry Bros label. In November 2016, Jim Barry Wines released the first commercial assyrtiko in Australia. A founding member of Australia's First Families of Wine. Exports to all major markets.

ŸŸŸŸŸ **The Florita Clare Valley Riesling 2017** Superlative Clare! Grapefruit pulp, lemon zest, jasmine, bath salts and Thai herbs stream across a bow of limestone-derived minerality and palate-whetting acidity. This is long, penetrative across a multitude of layers, and yet, despite the razor-sharp definition, it's relaxed. There is nothing hard or abrasive about this. It flows long with alacrity in its step. This will reward patience in the cellar. Screwcap. 12.5% alc. **Rating** 97 **To** 2032 $50 NG ✪

ŸŸŸŸŸ **Single Vineyard Tamar Valley Riesling 2017** I tasted this last across the swag of Barry rieslings and boy, talk about a distinctive regional voice! This is reticent and herbal of aroma. Little Clare Valley lime here. More pumice, pink grapefruit, a sash of Thai herbs and a subtle dash of marjoram. Impressionable. Compelling length and intensity with astute phenolic edges. This is fine. Screwcap. 11.6% alc. **Rating** 96 **To** 2029 $35 NG ✪
Spring Farm Block 114 Clare Valley Riesling 2017 Riesling, transparent and balletic across rails of acid crunch and mineral fibre – it can be challenging in its youth. It's all about texture, persistence and an effortless drive across the palate; nothing too abrasive, no edges too brittle. This is jangly and tightly coiled, but with a whiff of air it transforms into a giddy twirl of grapefruit pulp, Thai herbs, tonic and lemon zest. Pumice, too. Relaxed and delicious. Screwcap. 12.2% alc. **Rating** 95 **To** 2026 $50 NG
Spring Farm Block 18 Clare Valley Riesling 2013 This block is clearly the long-distance runner. Fully packed with lime to cumquat scents, far from nascent in their progression to a nourishing whiff of petroleum, but less in that direction than the 114. The acid line is juicy, filigreed, and like a show pony prancing about the mouth. Long and precise. The end point not quite visible yet. Screwcap. 12% alc. **Rating** 95 **To** 2025 $50 NG
The Armagh Clare Valley Shiraz 2015 Strong barrel-ferment aromas lead off, endowing this fully flared wine with a bouquet deli meats and smoke. Then the fruit: blue and black. Anise, clove, cardamom and vanilla-cased oak. Lots, yet it nestles in the ensemble of fruit and warmth rather than smothering it. The tannin management is creamy and luxuriant yet authoritative. Screwcap. 14% alc. **Rating** 95 **To** 2045 $320 NG

Watervale Riesling 2017 Answers the challenge from WA's Great Southern region in fine style. Lime, lemon and apple blossom aromas feed the long, intense palate in a high quality demonstration of place and variety, coupled with the firm acid finish providing the framework. No half glasses here – they are full to the brim. Screwcap. 12% alc. **Rating** 94 **To** 2030 $19 ○

Spring Farm Block 18 Clare Valley Riesling 2017 A fascinating comparison across two separate blocks in the same vintage: 18 is more intense, rapier-like, while 114 is looser, crunchy and mellifluous. My bets are on the 18, a more lime-scented wine of chiselled intent, to go the longer distance. The acidity is juicy, moreish and impeccably managed. Screwcap. 12% alc. **Rating** 94 **To** 2029 $50 NG

Clare Valley Assyrtiko 2017 Grows character with each vintage, especially its linearity and power on the finish. A crystalline, minerally and fresh aftertaste. Screwcap. 12.5% alc. **Rating** 94 **To** 2023 $35

The McRae Wood Clare Valley Shiraz 2015 The inaugural vintage was '92, serving this cuvee up as the younger sibling of the Armagh, though with its own very different skin. Less barrel ferment influence. Less smokiness. Molten raspberry bonbon, iodine, licorice and briar. Good energy. Impressive length. Some reductive chains, needs time to unravel. Screwcap. 14% alc. **Rating** 94 **To** 2036 $60 NG

St Clare Cabernet Malbec 2016 As persuasive as its hip, retro label. Reticent on the nose with violet, anise and menthol scrub; expansive across the palate with bitter chocolate, wine gums and dark fruit. The tannins are pulpy and honed nicely without their edge taken off, sashaying the fruit into a nourishing, persistent whole. Screwcap. 14.3% alc. **Rating** 94 **To** 2026 $60 NG

ŶŶŶŶ♀ **McKay's Clare Valley Riesling 2017** Rating 93 To 2027 $35 NG
Cellar Release The Lodge Hill Clare Valley Riesling 2012 Rating 93 To 2022 $25 NG ○
Eastern Ranges Clare Valley Shiraz 2016 Rating 93 To 2022 $35 NG
Single Vineyard Watervale Shiraz 2016 Rating 93 To 2024 $35 NG
Pb Shiraz Cabernet Sauvignon 2015 Rating 93 To 2027 $60 NG
Kirribilli Coonawarra Cabernet Sauvignon 2016 Rating 93 To 2026 $35 NG
First Eleven Coonawarra Cabernet Sauvignon 2015 Rating 93 To 2030 $60 NG
Single Vineyard Eastern Ranges Clare Valley Cabernet Malbec 2016 Rating 93 To 2026 $35 NG
Jim's Garden Clare Valley Riesling 2017 Rating 92 To 2025 $28 NG
Cellar Release The Florita Clare Valley Riesling 2012 Rating 92 To 2024 $60 NG
The Forger Clare Valley Shiraz 2016 Rating 92 To 2028 $35 NG
Single Vineyard Eastern Ranges Cabernet 2016 Rating 92 To 2024 NG
St Clare Malbec 2016 Rating 92 To 2024 $60 NG
The Benbournie Clare Valley Cabernet Sauvignon 2014 Rating 91 To 2040 $80 NG

Jim Brand Wines ★★★★

PO Box 18, Coonawarra, SA 5263 **Region** Coonawarra
T (08) 8736 3252 **www**.jimbrandwines.com.au **Open** Not
Winemaker Brand family **Est.** 2000 **Dozens** 2000 **Vyds** 39ha
The Brand family story starts with the arrival of Eric Brand in Coonawarra in 1950. He married Nancy Redman and purchased a 24ha block from the Redman family, relinquishing his job as a baker and becoming a grapegrower. It was not until '66 that the first Brand's Laira wine was made. The family sold 50% of the Brand's Laira winery in '94 to McWilliam's, Jim Brand staying on as chief winemaker until he died in 2005. Sam Brand is the son of Jim, and is the man behind Jim Brand Wines. Exports to Fiji, Hong Kong and China.

🍷🍷🍷🍷🍷 **Silent Partner Coonawarra Cabernet Sauvignon 2015** A touch above mid-weight. It's juicy and free-flowing for the most part before stern cabernet tannins impart their authority on the finish, or a version of authority at least. It's a ripe, well fruited, balanced and ultimately satisfying red wine. Screwcap. 14.5% alc. **Rating** 93 **To** 2028 $36 CM

Jim's Vineyard Coonawarra Shiraz 2015 Smooth and well flavoured. Bay leaves, blackcurrant, briar and a modest clip of creamy/resiny oak make for pretty attractive drinking. It responds well to air; a quick decant works wonders. Screwcap. 14.5% alc. **Rating** 91 **To** 2026 $36 CM

John Duval Wines ★★★★★

PO Box 622, Tanunda, SA 5352 **Region** Barossa Valley
T (08) 8562 2266 **www**.johnduvalwines.com **Open** At Artisans of Barossa
Winemaker John Duval **Est.** 2003 **Dozens** 7000
John Duval is an internationally recognised winemaker, having been the custodian of Penfolds Grange for almost 30 years as part of his role as chief red winemaker there. In 2003 he established his eponymous brand (and continues to provide consultancy services to clients all over the world). While his main focus is on old vine shiraz, he has extended his portfolio with other Rhône varieties. Exports to all major markets.

🍷🍷🍷🍷🍷 **Entity Barossa Shiraz 2016** Deeply coloured; this is at once full-bodied and elegant, not a common marriage in young red wines with decades in front of them. The flavours are all black: blackberry, blackcurrant, black cherry, earth and licorice. The old vines have also provided ripe tannins, the whole theme resonating with oak à la Grange. Screwcap. 14.5% alc. **Rating** 97 **To** 2056 $50 **☉**

Eligo The Barossa Shiraz 2015 The power and intensity of this wine takes your breath away. Its dark and brooding black fruits are woven together by firm tannins that are an essential part of the wine. It's certain that 20 months in French hogsheads (55% new) has also imprinted itself on the bouquet and palate, but its presence is (relatively) subtle. I would give an even longer drink-to date if it were under screwcap, but the cork used is high quality and should see out 25 years. 14.5% alc. **Rating** 97 **To** 2040 $120 **☉**

Annexus Barossa Grenache 2016 The marriage of ancient vines and modern skills in the winery has produced a remarkable grenache at the forefront of the revitalisation of the style. It is powerful and intense, yet the flavours are in the fresh red spectrum with a savoury crosscurrent of fine, dusty tannins. There is no confection, no Turkish delight anywhere to be seen. Screwcap. 13.5% alc. **Rating** 97 **To** 2031 $70 **☉**

Annexus Barossa Valley Mataro 2016 It's a fool's errand to nominate a drink-to date for this wine! Mataro is already a notable age-worthy variety, but this one is made from low-yielding, 100+yo vines, by a red-wine master who held responsibility for Grange for many years. The colour is beautiful – a deep, vibrant crimson. The bouquet is complex and rich, the palate with layer upon layer of mainly black fruits that keep their feet on the throat of any tannins daring to take centrestage. Screwcap. 14% alc. **Rating** 97 **To** 2056 $70 **☉**

🍷🍷🍷🍷🍷 **Plexus Barossa Shiraz Grenache Mourvedre 2016** A 52/30/18% blend. This is a very good Barossa Valley GSM (or SGM), looking to the future rather than the past. While the flavours are complex, there is a lightness of touch ex the winery after careful monitoring of ripeness in the vineyards. This should please everyone with its mix of cherry, plum and blackberry couched in savoury tannins on the finish. Screwcap. 14.5% alc. **Rating** 95 **To** 2026 $40

🍷🍷🍷🍷🍷 **Plexus Marsanne Roussanne Viognier 2017 Rating** 92 **To** 2020 $30

John's Blend ★★★★★

18 Neil Avenue, Nuriootpa, SA 5355 (postal) **Region** Langhorne Creek
T (08) 8562 1820 **www.**johnsblend.com.au **Open** At The Winehouse, Langhorne Creek
Winemaker John Glaetzer **Est.** 1974 **Dozens** 2000 **Vyds** 23ha
John Glaetzer was Wolf Blass's right-hand man almost from the word go; the power behind the throne of the three Jimmy Watson trophies awarded to their wines ('74, '75, '76) and the small matter of 11 Montgomery trophies for Best Red Wine at the Adelaide Wine Show. This has always been a personal venture on the side, as it were, of John and wife Margarete, officially sanctioned, of course, and needing little marketing effort. Exports to Canada, Switzerland, Indonesia, Singapore and Japan.

ϘϘϘϘϘ **Margarete's Langhorne Creek Shiraz 2015** From 3 vineyards, fermented and matured in new French (75%) and American (25%) oak, spending 29 months in barrel. This is not just FB (full-bodied), it is 2FB. How much more flavour can you get in a bottle? The points are given within the context of its style. Cork. 14.5% alc. **Rating** 95 **To** 2045 $35 ✪
Individual Selection Langhorne Creek Cabernet Sauvignon 2014 From 2 highly regarded vineyards. Completed primary fermentation and mlf in new French hogsheads, and spent 40 months in those barrels. It's worth remembering most of the oak flavour will be absorbed in the first 12 months of maturation, and that the cellar work has kept the wine fresh. If you accept the oak flavour, this will flourish with a decade in bottle. Cork. 14.5% alc. **Rating** 95 **To** 2030 $35 ✪

Jones Road ★★★★★

2 Godings Road, Moorooduc, Vic 3933 **Region** Mornington Peninsula
T (03) 5978 8080 **www.**jonesroad.com.au **Open** W'ends 11–5
Winemaker Travis Bush **Est.** 1998 **Dozens** 6000 **Vyds** 26.5ha
It's a long story, but after establishing a very large and very successful herb-growing business in the UK, Rob Frewer and family migrated to Australia in 1997. By a circuitous route they ended up with a property on the Mornington Peninsula, planting pinot noir and chardonnay, then pinot gris, sauvignon blanc and merlot; they have since leased another vineyard at Mount Eliza, and purchased Ermes Estate in 2007.

ϘϘϘϘϘ **Mornington Peninsula Shiraz 2015** The brilliant crimson–purple colour introduces a medium-bodied, cool-grown shiraz that shines with quality across every facet of its makeup. The evocative spicy/peppery black fruits of the bouquet flow into the intense palate with blackberry and black cherry carried on a finely wrought framework of integrated French oak and superfine tannins. Oh yeah. Screwcap. 13.3% alc. **Rating** 97 **To** 2040 $32 ✪

ϘϘϘϘϘ **Nepean Mornington Peninsula Chardonnay 2016** Although nothing is said about it, the percentage of new oak in this bottling of 200 dozen seems significantly higher than that of its sibling. The flavours also take in white peach and nectarine to further broaden the spectrum. Screwcap. 12.5% alc. **Rating** 95 **To** 2024 $60

ϘϘϘϘϘ **Mornington Peninsula Chardonnay 2016 Rating** 93 **To** 2022 $38
Nepean Mornington Peninsula Pinot Noir 2015 Rating 93 **To** 2025 $60
Mornington Peninsula Pinot Noir 2015 Rating 90 **To** 2023 $40

Jones Winery & Vineyard ★★★★

Jones Road, Rutherglen, Vic 3685 **Region** Rutherglen
T (02) 6032 8496 **www.**joneswinery.com **Open** Mon, Thurs, Fri 10–4, w'ends 10–5
Winemaker Mandy Jones **Est.** 1860 **Dozens** 3000 **Vyds** 9.8ha
Jones Winery & Vineyard stands as testament to a rich winemaking tradition. Established in 1860, the winery has been owned and operated by the Jones family since 1927. Two blocks of old vines have been preserved (including 1.69ha of shiraz), supported by further

blocks progressively planted between '75 and 2008. Today, Jones Winery & Vineyard is jointly operated by winemaker Mandy Jones, who brings years of experience working in Bordeaux, and her brother Arthur Jones. Together they produce a small range of boutique wines.

🍷🍷🍷🍷🍷 **Fiano 2017** Buoyant with flavour, textural through the finish, and with decent length too. This is clearly the result of an excellent season. Lemon blossom, honeysuckle, vanilla pod and stone-fruit flavours burst through the palate. A joyous white wine. Screwcap. 13.1% alc. **Rating** 93 **To** 2020 $25 CM ✪

Durif 2016 Freshness, tannin and dark-berried flavour happily coexist. This is a hearty but delicious red wine. Momentum, slipperiness to the texture and juiciness all round. Screwcap. 15% alc. **Rating** 93 **To** 2028 $35 CM

Rutherglen Marsanne Roussanne 2017 85/15% blend. Crunchy, textural, ripped with spice, alive with honeysuckle. There's a lot of cloth to work with here. Preserved lemon, musky vanilla and stone-fruit characters lift the volume higher. Pretty impressive. Screwcap. 12.5% alc. **Rating** 92 **To** 2021 $26 CM

LJ 2016 Vines planted in 1905. French oak (75% new). Strong aromas/flavours of toast, cola and caramel with a kicker of sweet, saturated plum. This shiraz is weighty, warm and un-reconstructed; it's not fresh or modern, just bold with inky flavour served in volume. Screwcap. 15% alc. **Rating** 91 **To** 2035 $70 CM

Rutherglen Malbec 2016 Fruit rumbles and grumbles; oak tells it to shhh. Rugged tannin, deep, dark-berried fruit, tar-like notes and earth. All this is covered in a silken sheet of vanillan oak, the marriage not seamless but still in working order. Best consumed alongside thick, juicy steak. Screwcap. 13.8% alc. **Rating** 91 **To** 2028 $35 CM

Rutherglen Ugni Blanc 2017 Flavour darts through the palate in direct fashion, but along the way there's quite a bit to it: lemon, spice, wood smoke, crushed fennel even. Just enough to pique your interest. Screwcap. 13.3% alc. **Rating** 90 **To** 2020 $25 CM

Apero NV Fortified trebbiano and pedro ximenez. It tastes mostly of idiosyncrasy. Sweet, nutty aromatics introduce an intense, honeyed, toffeed palate. Bursts firstly with scent and flavour and then with hot spirit. It's not without interest though it kicks like a mule. Screwcap. 19% alc. **Rating** 90 $28 CM

🍷🍷🍷🍷 **Rutherglen Shiraz 2016 Rating** 89 **To** 2027 $35 CM

Josef Chromy Wines   ★★★★★

370 Relbia Road, Relbia, Tas 7258 **Region** Northern Tasmania
T (03) 6335 8700 **www**.josefchromy.com.au **Open** 7 days 10–5
Winemaker Jeremy Dineen **Est.** 2004 **Dozens** 30 000 **Vyds** 60ha
Joe is at it again. After escaping from Czechoslovakia in 1950, he established Blue Ribbon Meats, used the proceeds of that sale to buy Rochecombe and Heemskerk vineyards, then sold those and established Tamar Ridge before it, too, was sold. This time Joe's invested $40 million in another wine-based business. If this were not remarkable enough, Joe is in his 80s and has recovered from a major stroke. The foundation of the new business is the Old Stornoway vineyard, with 60ha of mature vines, the lion's share to pinot noir and chardonnay. Joe's grandson, Dean Cocker, is business manager of the restaurant, cellar door, function and wine centre within the homestead; it offers WSET (Wine & Spirit Education Trust) courses. Exports to all major markets.

🍷🍷🍷🍷🍷 **Block 17 Pinot Noir 2014** Deeply coloured in Chromy style, 4 years has barely touched the wine. Luscious and velvety black-cherry fruit with exotic spices spun throughout, providing a complex flavour base, expanding into a persistent finish. Screwcap. 13.8% alc. **Rating** 96 **To** 2034 $150

Botrytis Riesling 2017 This is a superbly rich and luscious Auslese style with 125g/l of residual sugar and 8g/l of titratable acidity. It coats the mouth with a tingling sherbet blast of blood orange and spiced lemon, the acidity seeming higher than it in fact is. The price is absurdly low for a wine that resolutely holds to its varietal character, yet is so luscious. Screwcap. 10% alc. **Rating** 96 **To** 2027 $28 ✪

Riesling 2017 Processed quickly on the way to bottle. The titratable acidity of 8.4g/l and pH of 2.86 catch immediate attention, the residual sugar of 6.5g/l drowned by the suggestion of Rose's lime juice and green apple. German winemakers of dry riesling would immediately understand the chemistry involved. Screwcap. 11.7% alc. **Rating** 95 **To** 2029 $28 **✪**

Chardonnay 2016 Hand-picked, whole-bunch pressed, wild-fermented in French oak (33% new), a small percentage of mlf, matured for 12 months. Now in cruise mode and enjoying it, future development to be slow – a definite plus. As of now, all the components are in synergistic balance. Screwcap. 13.5% alc. **Rating** 95 **To** 2026 $38

Pinot Noir 2016 Bright yet light, clear crimson; the expressive bouquet is full of wild strawberry and spice aromas that flow into the perfectly balanced palate, which adds some discrete foresty nuances, promising yet more in the future. As it is, pretty smart. Screwcap. 13.9% alc. **Rating** 95 **To** 2030 $38

Vintage 2011 A chardonnay/pinot noir blend. The primary fermentation employed a neutral yeast, and the wine then spent 5 years on lees in bottle. Offers a rich array of white peach and creamy/nutty nuances balanced by natural acidity. Diam. 12.5% alc. **Rating** 95 $42

Vintage Late Disgorged 2008 54% chardonnay, 46% pinot noir. 6g/l dosage, 9 years on lees, disgorged Jul '17. A 'don't mess with me' sparkling, still with a remarkable quartz-green hue. The dosage is lowish, standing the wine in good form, fresh and vibrant. Diam. 12.1% alc. **Rating** 95 $105

2017 DELIKAT SGR Riesling This really does cut the mustard, built in Kabinett style, SGR standing for up to 60g/l of residual sugar (this wine has 58g/l residual sugar and 9.9g/l of titratable acidity). The grapes are hand-picked when ripe, but fermentation is stopped at 6.5% alcohol, a wine treated as illegal in Australia until a few years ago. It is intense and very long, Rose's lime juice balanced by crisp acidity. Screwcap. 6.5% alc. **Rating** 95 **To** 2025 $28

ΥΥΥΥΦ **Rose 2017 Rating** 92 **To** 2021 $28
Tasmanian Cuvee Methode Traditionelle NV Rating 92 $32
Fume Blanc 2017 Rating 90 **To** 2022 $28
Vintage 2013 Rating 90 $45

Journey Wines ★★★★★

2/26 Hunter Road, Healesville, Vic 3777 (postal) **Region** Yarra Valley
T 0427 298 098 **www**.journeywines.com.au **Open** Not
Winemaker Damian North **Est.** 2011 **Dozens** 3000
The name chosen by Damian North for his brand is particularly appropriate given the winding path he has taken before starting his own label. Originally a sommelier at Tetsuya's, he was inspired to enrol in the oenology course at CSU, gaining his first practical winemaking experience as assistant winemaker at TarraWarra Estate in the Yarra Valley. Then, with family in tow, he moved to Oregon's Benton-Lane Winery to make pinot noir, before returning to become winemaker at Leeuwin Estate for five years. The wheel has turned full circle as the family has returned to the Yarra Valley, securing 2ha of chardonnay, 2.5ha of pinot noir and 2ha of shiraz under contract arrangements, and making the wines at Medhurst. Exports to the UK, Singapore and Thailand.

ΥΥΥΥΥ **Heathcote Shiraz 2016** If you tasted this wine blind you might think 'that's a very nice wine' and move on, simply because it raised no challenges nor asked any questions. In fact, it's made by someone whose knowledge about every facet of wine makes it seem easy, but of course it's not. The wine is supple, juicy and silky, its fruit spanning plum to blackberry, and the very expensive, quality French oak (30% new) has been absorbed into the backdrop. Screwcap. 14% alc. **Rating** 95 **To** 2036 $40

Heathcote Fiano 2017 A wine of cut and thrust, it sits bright in the glass, flinging grapefruit and lemon rind, spice and dried pear. It has a gently textural, tongue-hugging quality. A delight. Screwcap. 13% alc. **Rating** 94 **To** 2019 $26 CM ✪

ŢŢŢŢŢ **Yarra Valley Pinot Noir 2016 Rating** 93 **To** 2023 $38 CM
Yarra Valley Chardonnay 2016 Rating 92 **To** 2023 $38

Juniper Estate   ★★★★★

98 Tom Cullity Drive, Cowaramup, WA 6284 **Region** Margaret River
T (08) 9755 9000 **www.**juniperestate.com.au **Open** 7 days 10–5
Winemaker Mark Messenger **Est.** 1973 **Dozens** 12 000 **Vyds** 19.5ha
When Roger Hill and Gillian Anderson purchased the Wrights' 10ha vineyard in 1998, the vines were already 25 years old, but in need of retrellising and a certain amount of nursing to bring them back to health. All of that has happened, along with the planting of additional shiraz and cabernet sauvignon. The Juniper Crossing wines use a mix of estate-grown grapes and grapes from other Margaret River vineyards, while the Juniper Estate releases are made only from the estate plantings. Since Roger's death in 2013, Gillian has continued running Juniper Estate (and Higher Plane). Exports to the UK, the US, Ireland, Canada, Hong Kong, the Philippines, Singapore and NZ.

ŢŢŢŢŢ **The Tribute 2013** The black, charcoal and ash of the label – and the name – reflect the tragic death of Roger Hill, founder of Juniper Estate, shortly after the '13 vintage. A single batch of cabernet picked on 4 Mar had been recognised for its potential even before it was picked. One could write reams about this wine but still not do it justice – sheer perfection as an ultimate Australian cabernet will have to do. No score is adequate or appropriate. Screwcap. 14.5% alc. **Rating** 98 **To** 2043 $150 ✪

ŢŢŢŢŢ **Margaret River Aquitaine Blanc 2016** Estate-grown sauvignon blanc and semillon, hand-picked, whole-bunch pressed direct to French oak for wild fermentation and 10 months' maturation. A very complex wine, initially oaky on the bouquet, but hauled into line by the layered palate, which rolls out to a thunder clap on the finish. Screwcap. 13% alc. **Rating** 96 **To** 2022 $33 ✪
Margaret River Chardonnay 2015 Hand-picked in small parcels from the Wilyabrup and Forest Grove estate vineyards, fermented and matured in French oak for 10 months before a barrel selection. Just when you think this is a silky picture of Margaret River chardonnay, it takes off with awesome power on the finish and aftertaste. Screwcap. 13% alc. **Rating** 96 **To** 2027 $40 ✪
Single Vineyard Margaret River Cabernet Sauvignon 2014 Cabernet forms 88% of the blend with petit verdot, malbec and merlot doing their bit for more complexity. Regional flavours of mulberries, currants, cassis, florals and eucalyptus are perfectly pitched to the integrated cedary oak, flowing through to the medium to full-bodied palate where the poised tannins await. Screwcap. 14% alc. **Rating** 96 **To** 2034 $70 JF ✪
Margaret River Cabernet Sauvignon 2013 This is an exceptionally good cabernet by whatever standards you choose. It is extremely intense, yet its impact only catches you in a silken web. The tannins, while very much present, are so soft, the aromas and flavours from another realm. Cedar, violets, spices, bay leaf and – of course – blackcurrant. Screwcap. 14% alc. **Rating** 96 **To** 2033 $70 ✪
Aquitaine Rouge 2014 A blend of cabernet sauvignon, merlot, malbec, cabernet franc and petit verdot, nodding to Bordeaux, part of the Aquitaine region. This oozes class, every inch along the palate having something to contribute to this lovely wine. Blackcurrant/cassis, ripe and full tannins, sophisticated oak (and integration) are all cause for joy. Screwcap. 14% alc. **Rating** 96 **To** 2039 $38 ✪
Margaret River Chardonnay 2016 10 months in French oak barriques (40% new), the best barrels selected. A classy wine with grapefruit, lemon and a hint of melon, laser-like acidity cutting through an already linear palate. There's substance and depth of flavour partly from the lees and oak – beautifully shaped. Screwcap. 12.5% alc. **Rating** 95 **To** 2026 $40 JF

Single Vineyard Margaret River Shiraz 2015 A slinky and ultimately savoury shiraz. Complex yet composed flavours of dark fruits, an array of spices, graphite and tamarind, with cedary oak that's well integrated. The structure and texture work in unison with the fine tannin profile. Screwcap. 14% alc. **Rating** 95 To 2030 $40 JF

Single Vineyard Margaret River Shiraz 2014 Matured for 18 months in French hogsheads (35% new). The bouquet is very fragrant, and the palate exceedingly intense. Its epicentre is spicy red fruits, sour cherries also part of the picture of a very juicy, elegant wine. Screwcap. 14% alc. **Rating** 95 To 2030 $38

Juniper Crossing Margaret River Cabernet Merlot 2016 According to winemaker Mark Messenger, 'We aim for a bright fruit-driven style that is juicy and structured'. The mission has been completed in fine style. This is perfectly balanced and fruited, and drinks well now, but there's a seriousness to the finish that will ensure it performs beautifully over the medium term, if not longer. Terrific value. Screwcap. 14% alc. **Rating** 95 To 2028 $22 CM ✪

Aquitaine Rouge 2015 A finer, leaner execution of the Bordeaux blend in this vintage, but no less impressive. Heady with mulberries and cassis, pepper and woodsy spices, the tannins textural and surprisingly sandy. 18 months in French barriques (33% new). While the oak is integrated, a cedary fragrance lingers lightly. Long and pure on the finish. Screwcap. 14% alc. **Rating** 95 To 2035 $38 JF

Single Vineyard Margaret River Malbec 2015 Stands tall as a prime example of top malbec. The colour is fabulous – bright mid-ruby-purple. It's restrained in both flavour and palate weight, with an array of plums from black to satsuma, damson, pips, skins and all. Layers of spice and tangy acidity with persimmon-like tannins. Impressive. Screwcap. 14% alc. **Rating** 95 To 2028 $40 JF

Single Vineyard Margaret River Semillon 2015 Barrel fermentation and bottle development have given the wine a superb colour and mouthwatering complexity. Distinct honey-on-toast richness, with attention-grabbing acidity on the finish, allied with positive phenolics. Screwcap. 13% alc. **Rating** 94 To 2035 $33

Small Batch Margaret River Fiano 2017 The back label says 'light, bright, juicy melon, peach, citrus, textural and juicy finish'. I'm not going to argue against a single word of that – especially not the citrussy and tangy textural finish descriptor. Screwcap. 12.5% alc. **Rating** 94 To 2022 $25 ✪

Juniper Crossing Margaret River Shiraz 2016 There's a powder keg of activity happening with this wine, with spice and pepper notes providing the backdrop to the predominantly red-berried fruits of the fragrant bouquet and medium-bodied palate. This is an elegant, cool-grown shiraz; oak and tannins of minor importance. Screwcap. 14% alc. **Rating** 94 To 2031 $23 ✪

Small Batch Margaret River Tempranillo 2016 Red, black and sour cherries form a fruit threesome, fine-grained tannins providing the path for the fruit to follow. Screwcap. 14% alc. **Rating** 94 To 2031 $27 ✪

ŸŸŸŸŸ **Juniper Crossing Sauvignon Blanc 2017** Rating 92 To 2020 $22 ✪
Juniper Crossing Chardonnay 2017 Rating 92 To 2024 $25 CM ✪
Juniper Crossing Semillon Sauvignon Blanc 2017 Rating 91 To 2021 $23 ✪
Margaret River Chardonnay 2017 Rating 91 To 2021 $25 JF
Margaret River Cane Cut Riesling 2016 Rating 90 To 2021 $27

Kaesler Wines   ★★★★★

Barossa Valley Way, Nuriootpa, SA 5355 **Region** Barossa Valley
T (08) 8562 4488 **www**.kaesler.com.au **Open** 7 days 11–5
Winemaker Reid Bosward **Est.** 1990 **Dozens** 20 000 **Vyds** 36ha

The first members of the Kaesler family settled in the Barossa Valley in 1845. The vineyards date back to 1893, but the Kaesler family ownership ended in 1968. Kaesler Wines was eventually acquired by a small group of investment bankers (who have since purchased Yarra Yering), in conjunction with former Flying Winemaker Reid Bosward and wife Bindy. Reid's experience shows through in the wines, which come from estate vineyards adjacent to the winery, and from 10ha in the Marananga area that includes shiraz planted in 1899. The Small Valley Vineyard wines, made by Stephen Dew, are produced from 49ha in the Adelaide Hills. Exports to all major markets.

TTTTT Alte Reben Barossa Valley Shiraz 2015 Fruit from the Marananga vineyard planted in 1899. The wine is matured in French oak (35% new) and aged 16 months. It's full-bodied, bold and rich with densely packed tannins and all manner of dark fruit, spice and gravelly/ironstone notes. Retains purity, even a brightness. Cork. 14.5% alc. **Rating** 96 **To** 2035 $150 JF
Old Vine Barossa Valley Semillon 2017 A fairly soft rendition of that lovely floral, beeswax-flavoured semillon from the valley. A touch of candied peel, grapefruit pith, white pepper and dried herbs. A savoury twist, and tangy lime sherbet–like acidity with some phenolic grip on the finish. All up, a lovely wine. Screwcap. 12.5% alc. **Rating** 95 **To** 2026 $22 JF ○
Reach For The Sky Barossa Valley Shiraz 2016 In the previous vintage, the wine was under screwcap, now cork. A bit odd given the wine is a more juicy, upfront style for immediate drinking pleasure. Still, this has lightly spiced plums and cherries with supple, giving tannins. 14% alc. **Rating** 95 **To** 2021 $38 JF
Reach For The Sky Barossa Valley Shiraz 2015 The elder sibling of the '16, sharing the same freshness, buoyancy and juiciness – all directed to drinking pleasure. There are florals, bright red fruits and the acidity of fresh raspberries. Screwcap. 14% alc. **Rating** 95 **To** 2022 $38 JF
Old Bastard 2015 The unbecoming label detracts, given the fruit is from a single vineyard planted in 1893. Still, this is a powerful rendition of shiraz that pulls no punches. Full-bodied, surly with a fist-full of tannins that are partly oak derived (French barrels; 40% new), but opening up to eventually allow the quality of fruit to speak. Needs time, naturally. Cork. 14.5% alc. **Rating** 95 **To** 2030 $220 JF

TTTTP Avignon Grenache Mourvedre Shiraz 2015 Rating 93 To 2023 $35 JF
The Fave Barossa Valley Grenache 2017 Rating 92 To 2020 $35 JF
Odd One Out Cabernet 2016 Rating 92 To 2026 $50 JF
Old Vine Barossa Valley Shiraz 2015 Rating 91 To 2030 $80 JF
Stonehorse Grenache Shiraz Mourvedre 2015 Rating 91 To 2022 $22 JF ○

Kakaba Wines   ★★★☆

PO Box 348, Hahndorf, SA 5245 **Region** Adelaide Hills
T 0438 987 010 **www.**kakaba.com.au **Open** Not
Winemaker Greg Clack **Est.** 2006 **Dozens** 2000
When I send an email to a new winery for the *Wine Companion*, I ask what inspired the vigneron to entertain the folly. Chris Milner, with wife Jill in tow, responded by saying, 'It has been an enjoyable journey and, incredible as it may seem, moderately profitable, which I attribute to having zero overheads (no vineyards and no winery), zero employees (Jill and I don't get paid) and zero bank debt (too much debt will kill you every time!)'. Chris had the great advantage of having worked in the wine business since the late 1990s, mainly in the finance and commercial operations of various businesses. In 2006 there was an opportunity to source premium wine from the Adelaide Hills, and sell it to other wineries as bulk either during vintage or shortly thereafter. This worked very well in '06 and '07, but then came the super-abundant vintage of '08, with supply exceeding demand. Kakaba was born.

TTTT Reserve Adelaide Hills Sauvignon Blanc 2017 Machine-harvested, destemmed, 2 days' cold soak, open-fermented, mlf completed in used French oak, matured for 9 months. The impact of the used oak is not obvious on the bouquet, but does impart texture on the palate. This gives the wine room to move when food choices come into play. Screwcap. 12% alc. **Rating** 89 **To** 2020 $24
Cat's Eyes Langhorne Creek Shiraz 2016 One way or another, you get a large bang for your buck from quality Langhorne Creek grapes. Glistening plum and spicy blackberry fruit with echoes of French oak and firm tannins adding

complexity to the bargain of the week. Screwcap. 14.5% alc. **Rating** 90 **To** 2031 $15

Reserve Adelaide Hills Pinot Noir 2016 Questions arise at various points along the way, to which there are no easy answers. In a few words, it should be brighter and tighter; it's at odds with Greg Clack's considerable skills. Screwcap. 13.5% alc. **Rating** 89 **To** 2024 $39

Cat's Eyes Langhorne Creek Shiraz 2015 A deep crimson-red. There are dark fruits and a little earth on the bouquet, while the palate, which is very ripe, manages to finish dry due to the balanced, gently grippy and persistent tannins. Screwcap. 15% alc. **Rating** 89 **To** 2022 $15

Kalleske ★★★★★

6 Murray Street, Greenock, SA 5360 **Region** Barossa Valley
T (08) 8563 4000 **www**.kalleske.com **Open** 7 days 10–5
Winemaker Troy Kalleske **Est.** 1999 **Dozens** 15 000 **Vyds** 50ha
The Kalleske family has been growing and selling grapes on a mixed farming property at Greenock for over 140 years. Sixth-generation Troy Kalleske, with brother Tony, established the winery and created the Kalleske label in 1999. The vineyard is planted to shiraz (27ha), grenache (7ha), mataro, cabernet sauvignon and durif (2ha each), chenin blanc, viognier, zinfandel, petit verdot, semillon and tempranillo (1ha each). The vines vary in age, with the oldest dating back to 1875. All are grown biodynamically. Exports to all major markets.

ΨΨΨΨΨ **Eduard Old Vine Barossa Valley Shiraz 2015** From 3 dry-grown estate blocks planted between 1905 and '60, matured in new and used French and American hogsheads for 2 years. The attractive bouquet leads serenely into a medium-bodied palate of predominantly black fruits, taking ripe, soft tannins and oak along for the journey without ever feeling threatened. Screwcap. 14.5% alc. **Rating** 96 **To** 2050 $85

Johann Georg Old Vine Single Vineyard Barossa Valley Shiraz 2015 A very good example of ancestor vine shiraz (planted 1875). It has a full-bodied palate – augmented, it's true, by abundant ripe tannins, but they will settle down quickly, leaving the blackberry and plum fruit free room to play in. Screwcap. 14.5% alc. **Rating** 96 **To** 2050 $150

Old Vine Single Vineyard Barossa Valley Grenache 2016 Fruit, tannin, lakes of savoury spice and a flourish of flavour through the finish. Kicks goals from every angle. Raspberry and red cherry, anise, spearmint, cloves and more. Beautiful grenache. Screwcap. 14.5% alc. **Rating** 96 **To** 2025 $45 CM

Nietschke Barossa Valley Shiraz 2016 Dense crimson-purple hue; rises above the odd challenge from the vintage. This is a quintessential Barossa Valley shiraz, with its red, purple and black fruits calmly supported by ripe tannins and enough oak to satisfy the hardest critic. Bargain. Screwcap. 14.5% alc. **Rating** 94 **To** 2036 $19

ΨΨΨΨΩ **Moppa Barossa Valley Shiraz 2016** Rating 93 To 2031 $28
Fordson Barossa Valley Zinfandel 2016 Rating 93 To 2024 $25 CM
Greenock Barossa Valley Shiraz 2016 Rating 92 To 2036 $40
Clarry's Barossa Valley GSM 2017 Rating 92 To 2024 $21
Merchant Barossa Valley Cabernet 2016 Rating 91 To 2026 $28 CM
Buckboard Barossa Valley Durif 2016 Rating 91 To 2025 $25 CM
Zeitgeist Barossa Valley Shiraz 2017 Rating 90 To 2020 $26 CM

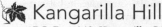 # Kangarilla Hill ★★★★

PO Box 143, Kangarilla, SA 5157 **Region** Adelaide Hills
T 0418 816 123 **www**.kangarillahill.com.au **Open** Not
Winemaker Phil Christiansen, Simon Parker **Est.** 2004 **Dozens** 550 **Vyds** 10ha
This is the business of retired veterinary surgeon Philip Christiansen and real estate agent Jan Boyd Turner, founded 30 years after their first wine venture when they purchased a property

in the Clare Valley with 18ha of very old vines. Work commitments and the travel time between their Adelaide activities led to a rethink, and to the sale of that property. But the ambition to make wine was never far from their minds. In 2004 they purchased Glengrove in the high country of Kangarilla, 45km from the Adelaide CBD. The 48ha of rolling hills includes a circa 1860 homestead and 10ha of roughly equal amounts of shiraz, cabernet sauvignon, pinot noir and merlot planted in 1998. Phil has been the winemaker since the first vintage in '04, with Simon Parker producing the first rose in '17. Around 550 dozen bottles are made each year, leaving 50t of grapes for annual sale.

ΨΨΨΨΩ **Adelaide Hills Pinot Noir 2013** Back on track with the '15, and benefiting from the extra few years in bottle, providing a supple elegance and brightness of finish. Although it has the same one-size-fits-all alcohol of 13.9% as its siblings, it has length (and balance) to its red fruit palate. Good wine by any measure. Screwcap. **Rating** 92 **To** 2023 $28

McLaren Vale Cabernet Sauvignon 2012 The back label is identical to that of their wines made from the Adelaide Hills, and is, quite simply, totally wrong. This to one side, the wine reflects the superb vintage with its pure cassis fruit, polished tannins and very long finish. Screwcap. 14% alc. **Rating** 92 **To** 2032 $22 ✪

Adelaide Hills Pinot Noir 2015 Borders on outright lusciousness, with layered plum and dark cherry fruit coupled with a sprinkle of cinnamon. Screwcap. 13.9% alc. **Rating** 90 **To** 2023 $28

ΨΨΨΨ **Adelaide Hills Shiraz 2014** **Rating** 89 **To** 2024 $22

Kangarilla Road Vineyard ★★★★★

Kangarilla Road, McLaren Vale, SA 5171 **Region** McLaren Vale
T (08) 8383 0533 **www**.kangarillaroad.com.au **Open** Mon–Fri 9–5, w'ends 11–5
Winemaker Kevin O'Brien **Est.** 1997 **Dozens** 65 000 **Vyds** 14ha
In January 2013 Kangarilla Road founders Kevin O'Brien and wife Helen succeeded in breaking the mould for a winery sale, crafting a remarkable win–win outcome. They sold their winery and surrounding vineyard to Gemtree Wines, which has had its wine made at Kangarilla Road since '01 under the watchful eye of Kevin. But the O'Briens have retained their adjacent JOBS vineyard and the Kangarilla Road wines continue to be made by Kevin at the winery. Luck of the Irish, perhaps. Exports to the UK, the US and other major markets.

ΨΨΨΨΨ **Alluvial Fans McLaren Vale Shiraz 2017** Bright, clear crimson-purple; a perfumed bouquet and fresh, medium-bodied palate. Rich in fruit and low in tannins meeting the objective of focusing on place, and doing so with delicious flavours and mouthfeel. 10 years may see further improvement. Screwcap. 14.5% alc. **Rating** 95 **To** 2027 $45

Blanche Point Formation McLaren Vale Shiraz 2017 Deep crimson-purple; a perfect example of terroir at work, the vinification identical to that of its Alluvial Fans sibling. Everything here is dialled up: the colour, the black fruits, the tannins and a savoury finish. Needs time. Screwcap. 14.5% alc. **Rating** 94 **To** 2037 $45

Blanche Point Formation McLaren Vale Shiraz 2016 A fascinating wine, with untold layers of black fruits, a dash of licorice and a lick of oak. It's full-bodied, but the tannins (which have to be there) are currently AWOL, texture and structure likewise. These will come with time, but in what shape and when, I don't know, but it will be good. Screwcap. 14.5% alc. **Rating** 94 **To** 2036 $45

The Devil's Whiskers McLaren Vale Shiraz 2016 Good colour; a very attractive medium-bodied regional shiraz with varietal black fruits, ripe tannins and integrated oak all singing harmoniously from the same page. Its balance is such that it will drink well at every point along the way. Screwcap. 14.5% alc. **Rating** 94 **To** 2030 $40

ΨΨΨΨΩ **McLaren Vale Primitivo 2016** **Rating** 93 **To** 2029 $30
McLaren Vale Shiraz 2016 **Rating** 92 **To** 2029 $25
McLaren Vale Cabernet Sauvignon 2016 **Rating** 90 **To** 2024 $25
Black St Peters McLaren Vale Zinfandel 2016 **Rating** 90 **To** 2026 $50

Karatta Wines

232 Clay Wells Road, Robe, SA 5276 **Region** Robe
T (08) 8735 7255 **www**.karattawines.com.au **Open** W'ends 11–4 (7 days Jan)
Winemaker Richard Bate, Chris Gray **Est.** 1994 **Dozens** 4000 **Vyds** 39.6ha
David and Peg Woods named Karatta Wines after the heritage-listed Karatta House at Robe,
built in 1858. In 2016 it was discovered that Peg's family were part owners of the steamer
SS *Karatta*, which plied the Southern Ocean between Robe, Kangaroo Island and Adelaide
up to the mid-20th century. The original life buoy of the *Karatta* adorns the tasting room and
is the inspiration for new branding, reflecting the maritime influence on the vines and wines.
Karatta has two vineyards: 12 Mile and Tenison; 12 Mile is less than 10km from the Southern
Ocean, the temperature 10–15°C cooler than Coonawarra. Winery and vineyard tours can be
arranged by contacting Charles Lawrence 0487 357 254.

ТТТТТ **Ibrida Malbec Cabernet Sauvignon 50/50% 2016** An impressive, brooding
wine that is more reminiscent of the Californian idiom than, perhaps, of the
Australian. That is to say: polished and well massaged tannins plying their sleek
veneer across oodles of mulberry, blueberry and anise. The richness is lifted by
bright lilac florals and shaped by abundant vanillan to coffee-bean oak tannins.
Buxom. The winemaking hand far from shy. Cork. 14.5% alc. **Rating** 94 To 2028
$70 NG

ТТТТ **Lost Ram Syrah 2017** Rating 93 To 2020 $20 NG **☉**
Frog Island Sauvignon Blanc 2017 Rating 91 To 2021 $20 NG **☉**
Brush Heath Cabernet Sauvignon 2016 Rating 91 To 2025 $25 NG
Geologist Cabernet Sauvignon 2017 Rating 90 To 2021 $20 NG **☉**
The Great Cabsy Cabernet Sauvignon Syrah 2017 Rating 90 To 2023
$23 NG
Pincushion Malbec 2016 Rating 90 To 2021 $35 NG

Karrawatta

164 Greenhills Road, Meadows, SA 5201 **Region** Adelaide Hills/Langhorne Creek
T (08) 8537 0511 **www**.karrawatta.com.au **Open** Fri–Mon 11–4
Winemaker Mark Gilbert **Est.** 1996 **Dozens** 5300 **Vyds** 46.6ha
Mark Gilbert is the great-great-great-grandson of Joseph Gilbert, who established the Pewsey
Vale vineyard (and winery) in 1847. What is not generally known is that Joseph Gilbert had
named the property Karrawatta, then found the name already in use for another property. The
right to use the name was decided on the toss of a coin in a local pub, forcing Gilbert (who
lost) to relinquish and adopt Pewsey Vale instead. The Karrawatta of today is not in the Barossa
Ranges, but the Adelaide Hills; there is a neat coincidence here, because in 1847 Pewsey Vale
was the highest vineyard planting in SA, and Mark Gilbert's Karrawatta is one of the highest
plantings in the Adelaide Hills. It is true that he only has 13.8ha of vines here, and 32.8ha in
Langhorne Creek, but never let the facts get in the way of a good story.

ТТТТТ **The Meddler Langhorne Creek Malbec 2016** This is an impressive first
release of a straight malbec, boasting a more silken, almost chiffon-like tannin
profile compared to the heftier reds in the stable. This is mid-ruby at best and
medium-bodied, with no heavy bones. A chassis of purple florals, blueberry and
a potpourri of dried herbs define the palate. The acidic cylinders are bright and
crunchy, 'meddling' effortlessly with a carburettor of slick oak, while driving the
flavours long and broad. Cork. 14.8% alc. **Rating** 96 To 2031 $54 NG **☉**
Dairy Block Adelaide Hills Shiraz 2016 This draws from the more moderate
climate of Meadows in the Adelaide Hills. Still, the propensity for ripe fruit, often
pushing the envelope, threads its way from the floral attack to the bitter chocolate
scents and cherry compote spread across the mid-palate. Relying as much on a
reductive tension for grip, as it does on the region's acidity, this has a cooler aura
mingling with potent ripeness. Screwcap. 14.9% alc. **Rating** 95 To 2028 $38 NG
Spartacus Langhorne Creek Cabernet Sauvignon Shiraz Malbec 2016
The very best barrels across each variety and boy, does it strut. In a flashy way,

mind you, employing impeccable management of the alloyed grape tannins and classy wood, with optimally ripe fruit and plenty of varietal chutzpah including a whiff of salinity and herb. While far from subtle, this is an exercise in a warm-climate blend that works very well, never straying into caricature. Cork. 14.9% alc. **Rating** 95 **To** 2039 $92 NG

Anna's Adelaide Hills Sauvignon Blanc 2017 An intriguing Hills' sauvignon blanc that bucks the unfortunate trend of 'bang-'em-in-bang-'em-out' cool-fermented styles. This has texture, with time spent in neutral French oak and partial mlf paying dividends. Detailed length and a confident poise are the welcome results, showcasing white fig, citrus, greengage and sugar-snap peas. Screwcap. 12.3% alc. **Rating** 94 **To** 2020 $26 NG ✪

Sophie's Hill Adelaide Hills Pinot Grigio 2017 This bridles the pop of the brighter grigio expressions, siding with a more ample and layered style. A product of considerable love across hand-harvesting, whole-bunch pressing and some handy barrel work to confer grip and texture to the teeming flavours of nashi pear, lime and apple gelato. There is an attractive pucker on the finish for refreshment. About as good as it gets. Screwcap. 12% alc. **Rating** 94 **To** 2020 $26 NG ✪

Joseph Langhorne Creek Shiraz 2016 An impressive rendition of warm-climate shiraz with violet, star anise and dark fruit barrelling along pillars of cedary oak. Following 18 months of ageing in French barriques, the oak nuances need time to resolve themselves with the gushing fruit. The wine's sheer extract and poise, however, leave little doubt that this will happen in good time. Screwcap. 14.9% alc. **Rating** 94 **To** 2036 $54 NG

Christo's Paddock Langhorne Creek Cabernet Sauvignon 2016 Picked across two windows, a week apart, this is another powerful wine in the stable, ably displaying Langhorne Creek's capacity for molten, albeit strongly varietal cabernet. Blackcurrant, notes of dried sage and pencil lead too, all mesh nicely with the ambitious oak and a perk of sea spray acidity. Screwcap. 14.8% alc. **Rating** 94 **To** 2036 $54 NG

🍷🍷🍷🍷♀ **Anth's Garden Chardonnay 2017** Rating 92 To 2026 $46 NG

KarriBindi   ★★★☆

111 Scott Road, Karridale, WA 6288 (postal) **Region** Margaret River
T (08) 9758 5570 **www**.karribindi.com.au **Open** Not
Winemaker Kris Wealand **Est.** 1997 **Dozens** 2000 **Vyds** 32.05ha
KarriBindi is owned by Kevin, Yvonne and Kris Wealand. The name is derived from Karridale and the surrounding karri forests, and from Bindi, the home town of one of the members of the Wealand family. In Nyoongar, 'karri' means strong, special, spiritual, tall tree, and 'bindi' means butterfly. The Wealands have established sauvignon blanc (15ha), chardonnay (6.25ha) and cabernet sauvignon (4ha), plus smaller plantings of semillon, shiraz and merlot. KarriBindi supplies grapes to a number of high profile Margaret River wineries, reserving approximately 20% for its own label. Exports to Singapore and China.

🍷🍷🍷🍷♀ **Margaret River Shiraz 2013** While it seems a long time between the making and releasing of this shiraz, it's looking good. A melange of savoury spices, dark fruits and woodsy notes that follow onto the medium-bodied palate, which is layered with plump tannins and a certain vivacity. And it's keenly priced. Screwcap. 13.4% alc. **Rating** 92 **To** 2023 $20 JF ✪

Kate Hill Wines   ★★★★★

21 Dowlings Road, Huonville, Tas 7109 **Region** Southern Tasmania
T 0448 842 696 **www**.katehillwines.com.au **Open** Fri–Mon 11–4
Winemaker Kate Hill **Est.** 2008 **Dozens** 2000 **Vyds** 4ha
When Kate Hill (and husband Charles) came to Tasmania in 2006, Kate had worked as a winemaker in Australia and overseas for 10 years. Kate's wines are made with grapes from a number of vineyards across southern Tasmania, the aim being to produce approachable, delicate wines. Exports to Singapore.

ŦŦŦŦŦ **Riesling 2016** A remarkable wine. Beg, borrow or steal territory. Such pure lime flavour, such exuberant florals, such exhilarating length. There's a sweetness here, but there's also searing acidity and length. Stunning riesling. Screwcap. 11% alc. **Rating** 97 **To** 2028 $30 CM ✪

ŦŦŦŦŦ **Huon Valley Pinot Noir 2014** This has the balance and inherent complexity to cause a bit of excitement. It's gently reductive, firm but fleshy, velvety to the touch and satisfying. It somehow manages to combine sweetness, savouriness and sourness as if they are all one and the same. Great potential here. Screwcap. 13% alc. **Rating** 95 **To** 2026 $42 CM
Pinot Noir 2014 It takes giant strides in a quality direction. Depth of flavour, formation of tannin, length and complexity are all resoundingly positive. It tastes of undergrowth, black cherry, wood spice and cedar wood and while it's good now, it looks good for mid-term development too. There is a riot of spice notes like glints in its eye. Screwcap. 13.2% alc. **Rating** 94 **To** 2024 $36 CM

Katnook Coonawarra

Riddoch Highway, Coonawarra, SA 5263 **Region** Coonawarra
T (08) 8737 0300 **www**.katnookestate.com.au **Open** Mon–Fri 10–4, w'ends 12–5
Winemaker Tim Heath **Est.** 1979 **Dozens** 90 000 **Vyds** 198ha
Second in size in the region to Wynns Coonawarra Estate, Katnook has taken significant strides since acquisition by Freixenet, the Spanish cava producer. Once Katnook sold most of its grapes, but it now sells only 10%. The historic stone woolshed in which the second vintage in Coonawarra (1896) was made, and which has served Katnook since 1980, has been restored. Likewise, the former office of John Riddoch has been restored and is now the cellar door, and the former stables serve as a function area. Well over half of the total estate plantings are cabernet sauvignon and shiraz, with the Odyssey Cabernet Sauvignon and Prodigy Shiraz the duo at the top of a multi-tiered production. In March 2018 Freixenet announced that Henkell, the Oetker Group's sparkling wine branch, had acquired 50.67% of Freixenet's shares, creating the world's leading sparkling wine group. In the same month, and by coincidence, Katnook announced that Tim Heath, Cloudy Bay's chief winemaker for the previous 14 years, had taken up the role at Katnook following the death of long-term incumbent Wayne Stehbens. Exports to all major markets.

ŦŦŦŦŦ **Odyssey Cabernet Sauvignon 2014** This has always been an iconic wine, and the bright crimson colour is a great start, quickly followed by beautifully pitched cassis/blackcurrant fruit and finely shaped tannins. There's not much to say about this wine, so perfect is the balance and mouthfeel. Screwcap. 14% alc. **Rating** 97 **To** 2044 $100 ✪

ŦŦŦŦŦ **Prodigy Shiraz 2014** Although the only obvious difference between this and its Estate sibling is 20% more new oak, there has to be some fruit and barrel selection. This is in the opulent style consistently made by Katnook for many years, with some gradual changes for the better being less new oak, compared to previous vintages, and less time in barrel. Screwcap. 14% alc. **Rating** 95 **To** 2039 $100
Estate Shiraz 2015 Matured in French and American oak (27% new) for 14 months. A very well made, medium-bodied wine, supple and long with high quality fruit its foundation, although oak had a hand in its elevage. It points the way for Prodigy in coming years. Screwcap. 13.5% alc. **Rating** 94 **To** 2035 $40
The Caledonian Cabernet Shiraz 2016 Clever winemaking. The influence of the American oak was absorbed into the synergy created by the two varieties, their flavours and the tannins. A full-bodied wine made to feel deceptively light. Screwcap. 14% alc. **Rating** 94 **To** 2036 $55

ŦŦŦŦ♀ **Estate Cabernet Sauvignon 2015** **Rating** 93 **To** 2030 $40
Amara Vineyard Cabernet Sauvignon 2016 **Rating** 90 **To** 2030 $55

Kay Brothers Amery Vineyards ★★★★★

57 Kays Road, McLaren Vale, SA 5171 **Region** McLaren Vale
T (08) 8323 8211 **www**.kaybrothersamerywines.com **Open** Mon–Fri 9–5, w'ends 11–5
Winemaker Duncan Kennedy, Colin Kay **Est.** 1890 **Dozens** 11 000 **Vyds** 22ha
A traditional winery with a rich history of more than 125 years, and just over 20ha of priceless old vines. While the white wines have been variable, the red and fortified wines can be very good. Of particular interest is Block 6 Shiraz, made from 120+ year-old vines; both vines and wines are going from strength to strength. Exports to the US, Canada, Switzerland, Germany, Malaysia, Hong Kong, Singapore, South Korea, Thailand and China.

ΨΨΨΨΨ **Griffon's Key Reserve Grenache 2016** Winner of the James Halliday Grenache Challenge '17. The second release, it is a full-bodied, concentrated grenache that takes no prisoners. It ripples with red and purple fruits held in a framework of tannins, oak providing the screws to keep the balance under control. Its finish asserts the grace and greatness of the wine, as the stream of pure fruit breaks free to express its beauty. Screwcap. 14.5% alc. **Rating** 97 **To** 2033 $45

ΨΨΨΨΨ **Block 6 Shiraz 2015** Mesmerising for its complexity and balance of flavours, everything in its place with the oak seamlessly integrated (23 months in French and American puncheons, 40% new). Defining velvety tannins are glorious on the long finish. Screwcap. 14.5% alc. **Rating** 96 **To** 2035 $95 JF
Hillside Shiraz 2015 Boysenberry dipped in dark chocolate, plus a side of black plums, licorice and spicy clove/cedar (21 months in American and French oak, 26% new). Full-bodied and densely layered, yet there's a vivacity, too, thanks to its refreshing acidity and oh-so-supple, spongy tannins. Screwcap. 14.5% alc. **Rating** 95 **To** 2035 $45 JF
Basket Pressed Shiraz 2016 Excellent dark garnet-purple; a jumble of black cherries, dark chocolate, licorice root and cinnamon lead the way to the full-bodied palate. While there's a drying touch of wood varnish on the finish, this is ultimately deep and luscious, with velvety tannins adding a glossy feel. Screwcap. 14% alc. **Rating** 94 **To** 2026 $28 JF ✪
Cuthbert Cabernet Sauvignon 2015 A sneaky 13% component of merlot adds a floral note to the blackberry, licorice, soy sauce and earthy tones, with a side of sweet oak spice (French barriques for 22 months, 23% new). It has restraint while still remaining fuller bodied, finishing with slightly drying, raspy tannins, which will probably be resolved in time. Screwcap. 13.5% alc. **Rating** 94 **To** 2030 $45 JF
Rare Muscat NV Mid-dark amber with a glint of red; luscious and laden with toffee brittle, brandy-soaked fruit and baking spices ready to be added to the fruit cake, just a hint of green walnuts. Sweet yet balanced, fresh yet complex. 375ml. Screwcap. 18.5% alc. **Rating** 94 $70 JF

ΨΨΨΨΨ **McLaren Vale Grenache Rose 2017 Rating** 92 **To** 2019 $25 JF ✪

Keith Tulloch Wine ★★★★★

Hermitage Road, Pokolbin, NSW 2320 **Region** Hunter Valley
T (02) 4998 7500 **www**.keithtullochwine.com.au **Open** 7 days 10–5
Winemaker Keith Tulloch **Est.** 1997 **Dozens** 12 000 **Vyds** 9.1ha
The Tulloch family has played a leading role in the Hunter Valley for over a century. Keith Tulloch was formerly a winemaker at Lindeman's and Rothbury Estate, and developed his own label in 1997. He has the same almost obsessive attention to detail, the same ascetic intellectual approach, the same refusal to accept anything but the best, as that of Jeffrey Grosset. Exports to the UK, Ireland, the United Arab Emirates, Indonesia and Japan.

ΨΨΨΨΨ **Museum Release Hunter Valley Semillon 2011** Pale quartz-green; a lovely wine from a very good vintage, now on a plateau that it should ride on for another 8 years or so without any discomfort. Tyrrell's is the pace – and price – setter these days. Screwcap. 11% alc. **Rating** 96 **To** 2026 $60 ✪

Hunter Valley Semillon 2017 Hand-picked, chilled overnight, crushed and destemmed, pressed and cold-fermented, 3 months on lees in tank. Has the typical layered style of Keith Tulloch, hence each-way young/old enjoyment. Length is the key. Screwcap. 10.5% alc. **Rating** 95 **To** 2027 $30 **○**

Vanguard Winemakers Selection Shiraz 2016 From a single block of 42yo vines in Fordwich. 6 weeks on skins, matured for 12 months in French oak (30% new). Light colour compared to its siblings, but the red fruits are juicy, and it will come around first. Screwcap. 14% alc. **Rating** 95 **To** 2036 $55

Winemakers Selection Marsanne 2017 From rogue vines interplanted in the Hunter Valley family vineyard. Has all the signs that it will develop very well, but it is left field. Those who buy it will find a rich source of honeysuckle on the back-palate. Screwcap. 12.2% alc. **Rating** 94 **To** 2027 $75

Tawarri Vineyard Hunter Valley Shiraz 2016 The Tawarri vineyard is in the upper reaches of the Hunter Valley at 450m. Matured for 18 months in French oak (30% new). Powerful black cherry and blackberry fruit, firm yet paradoxically juicy. More time please. Screwcap. 14.5% alc. **Rating** 94 **To** 2041 $48

🍷🍷🍷🍷🍷 **The Kester Hunter Valley Shiraz 2016** Rating 93 To 2041 $75
Museum Release The Kester Hunter Valley Shiraz 2010 Rating 92
To 2040 $100
Hunter Valley Chardonnay 2017 Rating 90 To 2022 $35
Epogee Marsanne Viognier Roussanne 2017 Rating 90 To 2019 $40
Hunter Valley Shiraz Viognier 2016 Rating 90 To 2031 $36
Forres Blend 2016 Rating 90 To 2026 $42

Kellermeister

Barossa Valley Highway, Lyndoch, SA 5351 **Region** Barossa Valley
T (08) 8524 4303 www.kellermeister.com.au **Open** 7 days 9.30–5.30
Winemaker Mark Pearce **Est.** 1976 **Dozens** 30 000 **Vyds** 20ha
Since joining Kellermeister from Wirra Wirra in 2009, Mark Pearce has successfully worked through challenging times to ensure the survival of the winery and its brands; and upon the retirement of founders Ralph and Val Jones in late '12, the Pearce family acquired the business. Surrounded by a young, close-knit team, Mark is committed to continuing to build on the legacy that the founders began more than 40 years ago. His winemaking focus is on continuing to preserve Kellermeister's best wines, while introducing new wines, made with the intention of expressing with purity the provenance of the Barossa. Exports to the US, Canada, Switzerland, Denmark, Israel, Taiwan, China and Japan.

🍷🍷🍷🍷🍷 **Rocamora Ancestor Vine Stonegarden Vineyard Eden Valley Grenache 2015** A field blend of grenache planted in 1858 and an estimated 10% of shiraz and mataro. Hand-picked, crushed and destemmed, fermented in an open oak vat, 12 days on skins, 24 months in used French oak. Nigh-on perfect winemaking; supple, fresh, all the expected plum and cherry flavours and superfine tannins. Priceless wine. Cork. 14% alc. **Rating** 98 **To** 2040 $175 **○**

Wild Witch Barossa Shiraz 2014 From the northern and eastern Barossa Valley, and Eden Valley, matured in French oak (40% new) for 36 months, bench trials determining the blend. An expressive shiraz of very high quality, achieving intensity, balance and length; black fruits, tempered oak and firm tannins all on song. Screwcap. 14.5% alc. **Rating** 97 **To** 2044 $85 **○**

🍷🍷🍷🍷🍷 **The Wombat General Hand Picked Eden Valley Riesling 2017** From a celebrated grower (Fechner); only the first 450l/t used for this wine. Tastes sweet on entry, but this is just the fruit, as the wine is dry. Flavours of stone fruit along with the dominant citrus. Totally delivers at any price, but this … Screwcap. 12.5% alc. **Rating** 96 **To** 2029 $23 **○**

🍷🍷🍷🍷🍷 **Threefold Farm The Firstborn Barossa Valley Shiraz 2015** Rating 92
To 2030 $45
The Curtain Raiser Barossa Tempranillo 2016 Rating 92 To 2031 $28
Threefold Farm Missy Moo Mataro 2015 Rating 92 To 2030 $45

Kellybrook
★★★★

Fulford Road, Wonga Park, Vic 3115 **Region** Yarra Valley
T (03) 9722 1304 **www**.kellybrookwinery.com.au **Open** Thurs–Mon 10–5
Winemaker Philip Kelly, Darren Kelly **Est.** 1962 **Dozens** 3000 **Vyds** 8.4ha
The vineyard is at Wonga Park, one of the outer-Melbourne gateways to the Yarra Valley. A very competent producer of both cider and apple brandy (in calvados style), as well as table wine. When it received its winery licence in 1970, it became the first winery in the Yarra Valley to open its doors in the 20th century, a distinction often ignored or forgotten (by this author as well as others).

🍷🍷🍷🍷🍷 **Yarra Valley Rose 2017** Mostly made with cabernet sauvignon, though there's cabernet franc, shiraz and pinot noir in the mix. The details fly out the window on tasting: it's simply delicious. It gets the mix of refreshment and flavour exactly right, its salmon colour in tune with its dry, fruit-driven-but-savoury-accented palate. Lovely. Screwcap. 12.6% alc. **Rating** 94 To 2019 $22 CM ✪
Yarra Valley Cabernet Merlot 2016 It's built more on acidity and the brightness of its fruit than on tannin or fruit depth/weight, but it's blessed with alluring perfume and boasts both elegance and persistence. Light to medium-weight, adorned with fresh mint, boysenberry, lead pencil and Ribena blackcurrant. You wouldn't consider it a big wine, but you would call it a considered one. Screwcap. 13% alc. **Rating** 94 To 2028 $28 CM ✪

🍷🍷🍷🍷🍷 **Yarra Valley Chardonnay 2016** Rating 93 To 2022 $25 CM ✪
Yarra Valley Chardonnay 2017 Rating 92 To 2022 $25 CM ✪
Yarra Valley Pinot Noir 2017 Rating 92 To 2024 $30 CM
Willowlake Vineyard Pinot Noir 2017 Rating 91 To 2025 $38 CM
Yarra Valley Shiraz 2016 Rating 91 To 2025 $28 CM
Yarra Valley Sauvignon Blanc 2017 Rating 90 To 2020 $222 CM

Kelman Vineyard
★★★★☆

2 Oakey Creek Road, Pokolbin, NSW 2320 **Region** Hunter Valley
T (02) 4991 5456 **www**.kelmanvineyard.com.au **Open** 7 days 10–4
Winemaker Jeff Byrne **Est.** 1999 **Dozens** 2000 **Vyds** 9ha
Kelman Vineyard is a community development spread over 40ha, with 9ha under vine. The estate is scattered with traditional country cottages and homesteads; vines and olive and lemon groves meander between the dwellings. Named in honour of William Kelman who travelled to Australia with John Busby (father of James Busby) in 1824, marrying John's daughter Katherine on the ship.

🍷🍷🍷🍷🍷 **Semillon 2016** There is something inherently poised and delicious about this estate's wines. They are easy to drink with gusto, to pair with food, and to love. This is fleshier than most Hunter semillon in all its Meyer lemon–clad, oyster-shelled, grassy glory. Juicy rather than abrasive. It is almost Chablisienne. It drinks well now, as it will for a decade or more. Screwcap. 11.5% alc. **Rating** 95 To 2028 $25 NG ✪

🍷🍷🍷🍷🍷 **Shiraz 2016** Rating 93 To 2028 $22 NG ✪
Chardonnay 2016 Rating 92 To 2023 $25 NG ✪
Hunter Valley Adelaide Hills Semillon Sauvignon Blanc 2017 Rating 91 To 2020 $24 NG
Sparkling Chardonnay 2013 Rating 91 $33 NG
Serendipity Vin de Vie Muscat NV Rating 91 $40 NG
Chairman's Reserve Chardonnay 2017 Rating 90 To 2024 $29 NG

Kennedy
★★★★☆

Maple Park, 224 Wallenjoe Road, Corop, Vic 3559 (postal) **Region** Heathcote
T (03) 5484 8293 **www**.kennedyvintners.com.au **Open** Not
Winemaker Glen Hayley (Contract) **Est.** 2002 **Dozens** 2000 **Vyds** 29.2ha

Having been farmers in the Colbinabbin area of Heathcote for 27 years, John and Patricia Kennedy were on the spot when a prime piece of red Cambrian soil on the east-facing slope of Mt Camel Range became available for purchase. They planted 20ha of shiraz in 2002. As they gained knowledge of the intricate differences within the site, further plantings of shiraz, tempranillo and mourvedre followed in '07.

ŸŸŸŸŸ **Cambria Heathcote Shiraz 2015** A best-barrel selection matured for 18 months in French oak (20% new). Flies the flag with justified price. Spices and cracked pepper notes infuse the bouquet and palate alike, and illuminate the dark berry flavours of the medium-bodied palate. Velvety tannins provide the structure, aided by integrated oak. Diam. 14% alc. **Rating** 95 **To** 2035 $32 **۞**
Pink Hills Heathcote Rose 2017 Made with mourvedre, hand-picked, whole-bunch pressed to neutral French oak for wild fermentation. A striking bouquet with rose petals and sweet spices; the palate is fresh and lively, yet also savoury. Almost feminine in its lightness of touch. Well above average. Screwcap. 13% alc. **Rating** 94 **To** 2021 $20 **۞**

ŸŸŸŸŸ **Heathcote Shiraz 2015 Rating** 92 **To** 2025 $25 **۞**
Henrietta Heathcote Shiraz 2017 Rating 91 **To** 2023 $20 **۞**

Kensington Wines   ★★★★

1590 Highlands Road, Whiteheads Creek, Vic 3660 **Region** Upper Goulburn
T (03) 5796 9155 **www.**kensingtonwines.com.au **Open** Sun 11–5
Winemaker Nina Stocker, Frank Bonic **Est.** 2010 **Dozens** 20 000 **Vyds** 4ha
This is the venture of husband and wife Anddy and Kandy Xu, born and raised in China, but now residents in Australia. They have built up Kensington Wines over the past seven years, creating a broad portfolio of wines by sourcing grapes and wines mostly from regions across Victoria, but also SA. While the primary market is China (and other Asian countries), the wines have not been made with residual sugar sweetness, and are also sold in Australia. Kandy and Anddy's purchase of the Rocky Passes vineyard (and cellar door) in the Upper Goulburn region in 2015 was a significant development in terms of their commitment to quality Australian wine, as was securing the services of winemaker Nina Stocker. Kandy has broadened her own experience and wine qualifications by completing the WSET diploma and undertaking a vintage at Brown Brothers. She was co-founder of the Chinese Wine Association of Australia and continues as the chair. She has translated wine books into Mandarin, including my *Top 100 Wineries of Australia*.

ŸŸŸŸŸ **King Valley Shiraz 2015** Good dark garnet–purple hue; there's a flurry of flavours from mulberry, spiced plums and cassis to dried herbs, soy sauce and hoisin, flowing through to the fuller bodied yet lithe palate. Supple, giving tannins, a smoothness to the finish all adding up to an approachable wine that will evolve well. Screwcap. 14.5% alc. **Rating** 93 **To** 2026 $45 JF
Selected Edition Cabernet Sauvignon 2015 Fresh and fragrant with blackcurrants, cassis and mulberries and just the right amount of woodsy spices and lift. The palate is surprisingly malleable and medium-weighted, tannins almost soft for a cabernet, although there's enough grip to allow this to age in the short to mid-term. Screwcap. 14.5% alc. **Rating** 93 **To** 2024 $35 JF
Rocky Passes Vineyard Goulburn Valley Shiraz 2016 Very good colour. A neat mix of satsuma plums and currants with a squirt of raspberry freshness, then dipping into the eucalyptus/mint zone, offset with some cedary oak and spices. A refreshing style; medium-bodied with a supple palate and ripe tannins. Screwcap. 14.5% alc. **Rating** 90 **To** 2025 $45 JF
Mundarlo Vineyard Gundagai Shiraz 2015 Mid-garnet and bright; restraint on the nose with a whisper of pepper, green olive, black and red fruits and woodsy spices. The palate is just shy of full-bodied, with a slight green–walnut note to the raspy tannins and some warmth on the finish. Pulpy fruit and spices go some way to tempering all that. Screwcap. 14.5% alc. **Rating** 90 **To** 2025 $28 JF

Kerrigan + Berry   ★★★★★

PO Box 221, Cowaramup, WA 6284 **Region** South West Australia
T (08) 9755 6046 **www**.kerriganandberry.com.au **Open** At Hay Shed Hill Wines
Winemaker Michael Kerrigan, Gavin Berry **Est.** 2007 **Dozens** 1200
Owners Michael Kerrigan and Gavin Berry have been making wine in WA for a combined
period of over 40 years, most closely associated with the two varieties that in their opinion
define WA: riesling and cabernet sauvignon. This is strictly a weekend and after-hours venture,
separate from their roles as chief winemakers at Hay Shed Hill (Michael) and West Cape
Howe (Gavin). They have focused on what is important, and explain, 'We have spent a total
of zero hours on marketing research, and no consultants have been injured in the making of
these wines'. Exports to the UK, the US, Denmark, Singapore and China.

♀♀♀♀♀ **Mt Barker Great Southern Riesling 2017** The back label discriminates
against those with prescription reading glasses. The grapes come from the Langton
vineyard planted in the early '70s (curious labelling for a single vineyard wine).
It has a richly scented bouquet with tropical and citrus aromas in abundance,
then a palate of awesome power and length, focusing on the citrus and minerally
components of a 'grand vin'. Screwcap. 12% alc. **Rating** 97 **To** 2037 $30 **❖**
Frankland River Shiraz 2015 The wine's colour is top stuff: bright yet deep.
The bouquet offers so much, you know for certain the palate will deliver. Black
cherry, blackberry, licorice, spice, pepper, cedar and superb tannins all underwrite
its ever-so-long future. Screwcap. 14.5% alc. **Rating** 97 **To** 2050 $40 **❖**

♀♀♀♀♀ **Mt Barker Margaret River Cabernet Sauvignon 2013** The path of its
varietal expression remains clear, reflecting Margaret River with its gently fleshy
cassis mid-palate, and a firm, no-compromise back-palate and finish courtesy of
high quality fruit from Mount Barker. It is the tannins on which the long-term
future of the wine has been built. Screwcap. 14.5% alc. **Rating** 96 **To** 2043 $60 **❖**
Frankland River Great Southern Shiraz 2016 Frankland River produces
shiraz of extraordinary depth and flavour and this is no exception. Leads with
exuberant sweet fruit; a mix of spiced plums and black cherries bolstered by
cherry wood and lead-pencil fragrance, yet this is also savoury. Full-bodied, the
integrated oak adding a layer, the tannins firm yet ripe. This is still unfurling and
has a way to go yet. 14.5S% alc. **Rating** 95 **To** 2030 $30 JF **❖**

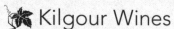 # Kilgour Wines   ★★★★

25 McAdams Lane, Bellarine, Vic 3223 **Region** Geelong
T 0448 785 744 **www**.kilgourwines.com **Open** Public hols & by appt
Winemaker Alister Timms **Est.** 2017 **Dozens** 750 **Vyds** 8ha
While this business has roots in the Bellarine Peninsula dating back to 1989, its reappearance
in 2017 is of a different venture altogether. Anne Timms planted the original vineyard in '89,
opening Kilgour Estate. In 2010 she sold the 3.2ha title with the winery, plus a separate 2ha
of vines, to David and Lyndsay Sharp, who renamed the business Jack Rabbit. Anne Timms
retained 8ha of grapes surrounding the Jack Rabbit property, and for the next five years sold
the grapes to other wineries. In '17 she retained part of the crop, and Alister Timms (chief
winemaker at Shadowfax) made the first Kilgour Wines under contract at Shadowfax.

♀♀♀♀♀ **Bellarine Rose 2017** Estate pinot noir, run off (saignee) from the previous day's
crush, fermented in used French oak, and held in barrel on light yeast lees for
6 months. Pale pink hue; the winemaker knows his trade, as this is a complex rose,
fermented dry, with a savoury/spicy overlay to light strawberry fruits. Screwcap.
13% alc. **Rating** 93 **To** 2020 $30
Bellarine Pinot Gris 2017 Pale straw-green; a well made gris with plenty of
attitude and grip to its pear and notes of nougat. Screwcap. 13% alc. **Rating** 90
To 2020 $30
Bellarine Pinot Noir 2017 Deeply coloured; an Aunty Jack (I'll rip your bloody
arms off) style with equivalent character. Full-bodied, just staying within accepted
pinot parameters. Black cherry, and (as Alister Timms says) 'complexed by game

meats and briary spice'. Needs either time or the accompaniment of no-holds-barred, charcoal-roasted venison/duck. Difficult to evaluate. Screwcap. **Rating** 90 **To** 2030 $40

Kilikanoon Wines

Penna Lane, Penwortham, SA 5453 **Region** Clare Valley
T (08) 8843 4206 **www**.kilikanoon.com.au **Open** 7 days 11–5
Winemaker Kevin Mitchell, Barry Kooij **Est.** 1997 **Dozens** 90 000 **Vyds** 117.14ha
Kilikanoon has travelled in the fast lane since winemaker Kevin Mitchell established it in 1997 on the foundation of 6ha of vines he owned with father Mort. With the aid of investors, its 90 000-dozen production now comes from over 100ha of estate-owned vineyards. Between 2013 and early '14, all links between Kilikanoon and Seppeltsfield were ended; the sale of Kilikanoon's share in Seppeltsfield, together with the sale of Kilikanoon's Crowhurst vineyard in the Barossa Valley, led to the Kilikanoon's purchase of the winery which it had previously leased, and the purchase of the Mt Surmon vineyard. The small-batch Mr Hyde wines are produced from individual vineyards/blocks in the Clare Valley. Exports to most major markets.

♥♥♥♥♥ **Mort's Block Watervale Riesling 2017** The floral bouquet wastes no time in establishing the region, variety and quality of this single vineyard, multi-block riesling. It leads into a palate of striking intensity, texture and structure, lime and lemon both claiming ascendancy, neither winning. More focus than Golden Hillside, but not richer. Screwcap. 12.5% alc. **Rating** 96 **To** 2029 $25 ✪

Mort's Reserve Watervale Riesling 2016 You can see the selection process giving rise to this wine and, I'm sure, the very small quantities made. It has X-factor, particularly in the unbridled power and complexity of the texture and structure. The concomitant varietal fruit flavours are likewise textbook, gold-plating the future of the wine. Screwcap. 12.5% alc. **Rating** 96 **To** 2031 $44 ✪

Prophecy McLaren Vale Shiraz 2015 McLaren Vale shiraz matured in all French oak for 18 months. It's seamless and smooth, the oak and fruit integration as textbook as you could possibly hope for. Blackberry, saltbush, charry oak and a drench of sweet, succulent plum. A generous red wine, managed and presented immaculately. Screwcap. 14.5% alc. **Rating** 95 **To** 2032 $44 CM

Covenant Clare Valley Shiraz 2015 A dash of viognier in the blend. Pushes ripeness of fruit and prominent oak to the edge without tipping over. Dark cherry, plum and licorice characters sit cheek-by-jowl with savoury, cedary elements and suede-like tannin, in a full-bodied but easily accessible package. Will age well too. Screwcap. 14.5% alc. **Rating** 95 **To** 2030 $44 SC

Crowhurst Reserve Barossa Valley Shiraz 2014 If you immerse yourself in the munificent bouquet you'll find just about every character imaginable for Barossa shiraz: ripe black fruit, tarry earth, dark chocolate, mocha and sweet spice are in the thick of it, with cedary French oak in tow. The palate is rich and full flavoured, but not impenetrable. Screwcap. 14.5% alc. **Rating** 95 **To** 2030 $120 SC

Blocks Road Clare Valley Cabernet Sauvignon 2014 It's unusually richly endowed with juicy blackcurrant fruit from the often reticent Clare Valley, giving cabernet permission to speak. Moreover, it doesn't front-end load the wine with tannins. Screwcap. 14% alc. **Rating** 95 **To** 2040 $33 ✪

Killerman's Run Clare Valley Riesling 2017 The flowery come-hither bouquet doesn't deceive, the palate pure joy. Lime, lemon and Granny Smith apples cascade through, the keynote squeaky acidity held in place by an invisible film. It's the mouthfeel quality most often encountered with young riesling, and sustains the very long finish. Screwcap. 12.5% alc. **Rating** 94 **To** 2027 $20 ✪

Golden Hillside Watervale Riesling 2017 Tasted alongside rieslings from very cool regions, emphasising just how far apart the Clare and Eden valley rieslings are. This isn't a quality comment, simply style. Here there are layers of rich lime/lemon fruit flavours, the acidity providing both balance and length. Screwcap. 12.5% alc. **Rating** 94 **To** 2027 $25 ✪

Miracle Hill McLaren Vale Shiraz 2014 One sniff of this wine takes you straight to its place of origin. The earthiness and white chocolate is unmistakable.

In the mouth it's rich and flavoursome, ripe blackberry and plum calling the tune, the tannin firm but in balance and therefore unobtrusive. Echoes of old-fashioned McLaren Vale shiraz in a most positive way. Screwcap. 14.5% alc. **Rating** 94 **To** 2034 $80 SC

Baudinet Blend Clare Valley Grenache Shiraz Mataro 2015 Manages to expertly walk the fine line between sweet fruit and savoury character, which is not always easy to achieve with this blend. The red fruit aromas and flavours of grenache are the foundation, the more structural and subtle elements of the other varieties just as important in the scheme of things, and the oak maturation skilfully employed as the finishing touch. Screwcap. 14.5% alc. **Rating** 94 **To** 2030 $55 SC

Mort's Cut Watervale Riesling 2017 Cane-cut riesling in the Clare Valley has long been made by Mount Horrocks. Opens with juicy lime fruit and moves through balancing acidity on the mid-palate, the aftertaste providing a flash of fresh ginger. Works very well. Screwcap. 11% alc. **Rating** 94 **To** 2023 $30 ❂

ŢŢŢŢŢ **Parable McLaren Vale Shiraz 2015** Rating 93 To 2025 $44 SC
Oracle Clare Valley Shiraz 2014 Rating 93 To 2030 $80 SC
Pearce Road Clare Valley Semillon 2016 Rating 92 To 2026 $25 ❂
Mr Hyde Bliss Clare Valley Riesling 2017 Rating 91 To 2027 $22 ❂
Killerman's Run Grenache Shiraz Mataro 2015 Rating 91 To 2029 $20 ❂
Killerman's Run Shiraz 2016 Rating 90 To 2026 $20 ❂
Killerman's Run Cabernet Sauvignon 2016 Rating 90 To 2024 $20 ❂

Killara Estate   ★★★★

773 Warburton Highway, Seville East, Vic 3139 **Region** Yarra Valley
T (03) 5961 5877 **www.**killaraestate.com.au **Open** Wed–Sun 11–5
Winemaker Travis Bush, Mac Forbes **Est.** 1997 **Dozens** 7000 **Vyds** 29.5ha
Owned by Leo and Gina Palazzo, the Sunnyside vineyard is the new home of Killara Estate. It features the Racers and Rascals Cafe and cellar door, enjoying sweeping views of the valley and nearby mountain ranges. The vineyard is planted to pinot noir (10ha), chardonnay (6.5ha), pinot gris (3.8ha), nebbiolo (2.3ha), and lesser amounts of shiraz and sangiovese. Exports to China.

ŢŢŢŢŢ **Palazzo Yarra Valley Nebbiolo 2015** Hand-picked, foot-stomped for 3–4 hours, 14 days on skins, hand-plunged twice daily, matured in old large-format French oak for 24 months. If you were to set yourself the task of making nebbiolo in the Yarra Valley, you couldn't have had a better vintage than '15 – nor, it must be said, could you hope to make it better. Red and dark cherries create the base for tannins that are fine, the mouthfeel rounded (an oxymoron). Screwcap. 13.5% alc. **Rating** 94 **To** 2030 $50

ŢŢŢŢŢ **Yarra Valley Pinot Noir 2016** Rating 92 To 2028 $35
Palazzo Yarra Valley Sangiovese 2016 Rating 90 To 2026 $25

Killerby   ★★★★

4259 Caves Road, Wilyabrup, WA 6280 **Region** Margaret River
T (08) 9755 5983 **www.**killerby.com.au **Open** 7 days 10–5
Winemaker Marco Pinares, Marelize Russouw **Est.** 1973 **Dozens** NFP **Vyds** 4ha
Owned by Ferngrove since 2008, Killerby has relaunched, opening its architect-designed 'Cellar Store' (with one of the longest tasting benches in Australia) in '13. With a variety of local produce available, it pays homage to the history of the Killerby family (in the late 1930s, Benjamin George Lee Killerby established a general store to supply the region, while grandson Benjamin Barry Killerby planted one of the first vineyards in Geographe in '73). Exports to the UK.

ŢŢŢŢŢ **Margaret River Semillon 2017** Stacked with depth and intensity, right in the heart of the citrus, grass, lemongrass trifecta. The fermentation of clear juice in used oak means patience will be needed for the wine to fully show its best – far

more than the 3 years suggested by Killerby. Screwcap. 12.5% alc. **Rating** 93
To 2027 $26 ✪

Margaret River Sauvignon Blanc 2017 This is made with grapes from a
single vineyard in Wilyabrup, which provides the quality of a pretty good wine
in a hot field of tropical/guava/passionfruit notes. Screwcap. 12% alc. **Rating** 92
To 2018 $26

Foundations Margaret River Chardonnay 2016 Partial wild fermentation in
barrel has worked well, the overall oak input subtle, giving free rein for the tangy
fruit (part stone fruit, part grapefruit) to express itself. The acidity, too, has been
well managed. Screwcap. 13.5% alc. **Rating** 91 To 2022 $30

Great Southern Pinot Noir 2016 Part whole-bunch fermented, part
destemmed and crushed, 'minimal oak contact'. The whole-bunch influence is
very obvious, with a savoury/forest floor platform for the potent red berry/cherry
fruits. It's arguably a little too savoury, but still outperforms expectations, and has a
promising future. Screwcap. 13.5% alc. **Rating** 91 To 2022 $26

Foundations Margaret River Shiraz 2015 Matured for 18 months in new and
used French oak. The colour doesn't give an indication that the wine is as good as
it is, the burden shared between the oak and the positive varietal fruit expression
(blackberry and plum), the tannins also assisting. Screwcap. 14% alc. **Rating** 91
To 2025 $32

Margaret River Great Southern Cabernet Merlot 2015 Gold medal at
the Sydney Wine Show '17. It's attractive drinking. Bay leaf, fragrant and savoury
red berry fruit, and a gently herbal quality carry through the bouquet and palate,
finishing with light tannin. Soft and approachable, it's ready to go now. Screwcap.
14% alc. **Rating** 91 To 2021 $16 SC ✪

Great Southern Margaret River Shiraz 2015 It's clearly made in a fresh,
ready-to-drink style. Spicy, cool-climate varietal character prevails, with red berries,
plums and a touch of pepper coming through on the bouquet. It has a bright,
buoyant feel in the mouth, with the gentle astringency barely noticeable but doing
its job. Screwcap. 14% alc. **Rating** 90 To 2021 $20 SC ✪

ŢŢŢŢ   **Semillon Sauvignon Blanc 2016** Rating 89 To 2019 $20 SC
Chardonnay 2016 Rating 89 To 2021 $20 SC

Killibinbin ★★★★

PO Box 10, Langhorne Creek, SA 5255 **Region** Langhorne Creek
T (08) 8537 3382 **www.killibinbin.com.au Open** Not
Winemaker Jim Urlwin **Est.** 1997 **Dozens** 3500 **Vyds** 10ha
In late 2010 Guy and Liz Adams (of Metala fame) acquired the Killibinbin brand. The wines
continue to be sourced solely from the Metala vineyards (10ha are dedicated to Killibinbin,
comprising 5ha each of shiraz and cabernet sauvignon). Exports to the UK, the US, Canada,
Sweden, Denmark, Ukraine, South Korea and Taiwan.

ŢŢŢŢŢ   **Scream Langhorne Creek Shiraz 2016** Dark colour and black berries creating
a deep pool of soft-hearted flavour. It's not complex but it's satisfying and rich, the
fruit pushed to the edge of overripeness but (just) managing to stay on the positive
side of the ledger. Choc-mint notes add to the pleasure dome. Screwcap. 14.5% alc.
Rating 91 To 2025 $27 CM

Scaredy Cat Langhorne Creek Cabernet Sauvignon Shiraz 2016 Ripe
and sweet, but the flow feels effortless, and the balance is spot on. Factor in the
price and we have some pretty keen buying here for lovers of fruit-filled reds on
the 'bigger' side of things. Screwcap. 14.5% alc. Rating 90 To 2023 $19 CM ✪

Killiecrankie Wines ★★★★

103 Soldier Road, Ravenswood, Vic 3453 **Region** Bendigo
T (03) 5435 3155 **www.killiecrankiewines.com Open** W'ends 11–6
Winemaker John Monteath **Est.** 2000 **Dozens** 400 **Vyds** 1ha

John Monteath moved to the Bendigo region in 1999 to pursue his interest in viticulture and winemaking, and while helping to establish this vineyard he gained experience at Water Wheel, Heathcote Estate, Balgownie and BlackJack. The vineyard is planted to four shiraz clones, and is the backbone of the label's Bendigo wine. The small crop is hand-picked, with the resultant wines made in true garagiste style. Small parcels of premium fruit are also sourced from meticulously tended vineyards in Bendigo and Heathcote.

ŸŸŸŸŸ **Crankie Pearl 2017** Two Rhône rangers (75% viognier and 25% marsanne) are fermented in seasoned French barriques. The wine ends up with lemon blossom and fennel flowers, lemon curd and quince paste, apricot kernel and baking spices; neat phenolics make it even more textural, yet it's as light as a ginger fluff cake. Screwcap. 13% alc. **Rating** 93 **To** 2020 $23 JF ❂
Crankie Ruby 2015 60% shiraz, 30% merlot and 10% cabernet sauvignon. Just the wine you can enjoy without thinking about it. Fresh, full of vibrant fruit, wafts of earth, eucalyptus and fresh blackberry leaves. Supple tannins on a leaner frame; very gluggable. Screwcap. 14% alc. **Rating** 90 **To** 2020 $23 JF

Kimbarra Wines ★★★★

422 Barkly Street, Ararat, Vic 3377 **Region** Grampians
T (03) 5352 2238 **www**.kimbarrawines.com.au **Open** By appt
Winemaker Peter Leeke, Ian MacKenzie **Est.** 1990 **Dozens** 200 **Vyds** 11ha
Peter Leeke has 9ha of shiraz and 2ha of riesling, the varieties that have proven best suited to the Grampians region. The particularly well made, estate-grown wines deserve a wider audience.

ŸŸŸŸŸ **Great Western Riesling 2017** A deceptive wine, for it starts out demure, offering a little floral here, a touch of spice there and some citrussy flavours. Then, whoa! The energy and drive of the acidity across the palate kicks in. There's texture, a depth of flavour, and a promise of a delicious drink. It doesn't disappoint. Screwcap. 11% alc. **Rating** 95 **To** 2027 $30 JF ❂

Kimbolton Wines ★★★★

The Winehouse Cellar Door, 1509 Langhorne Creek Road, Langhorne Creek, SA 5255
Region Langhorne Creek
T (08) 8537 3002 **www**.kimboltonwines.com.au **Open** 7 days 10–5
Winemaker Contract **Est.** 1998 **Dozens** 1200 **Vyds** 55.4ha
The Kimbolton property originally formed part of the Potts Bleasdale estate; in 1946 it was acquired by Henry and Thelma Case, parents of current owner Len Case. The grapes from the vineyard plantings (cabernet sauvignon, shiraz, chardonnay, carignan and montepulciano) are sold to leading wineries, with small amounts retained for the Kimbolton label. The name comes from a medieval town in Bedfordshire, UK, from which some of Len's wife Judy's ancestors emigrated.

ŸŸŸŸŸ **Montepulciano 2016** They've done a lovely job with this. It gets the pitch of light to medium-bodied fruit right – the acidity feels cleansing and balanced, and the tannin is strict but at one with the fruit and overall style of the wine. At every turn it's engaging. Different in a good way. Screwcap. 13% alc. **Rating** 93 **To** 2024 $30 CM
The Rifleman Shiraz 2016 Full-on choc-spearmint and vanilla cream flavours meet ripe, sweet, velvety plum and cassis. Smooth, intense, fresh, over-oaked, seductive; all these descriptions apply. Screwcap. 14.5% alc. **Rating** 92 **To** 2032 $50 CM
The Rifleman Cabernet Sauvignon 2016 It's blue in the face with resin, cream, and cedar-sawdust characters, though there's certainly a decent push of boysenberry, mint and blackcurrant-like flavour sitting beneath. Tannin is soft and supple. The oak will need to settle down and integrate for it to really hit its straps. Screwcap. 14% alc. **Rating** 92 **To** 2035 $50 CM
Chardonnay 2017 It's on the slim side of the chardonnay spectrum but only just; there's still a reasonable amount of flavour here, fruit and oak combined.

Tinned pears, stone fruit, citrus and toast. It doesn't just work, it works well. Screwcap. 12.5% alc. **Rating** 91 **To** 2022 $25 CM

Montepulciano Rose 2017 Not a lot of depth but plenty of spark. Super pale copper in colour, citrussy, kissed by red cherry and cranberry flavour, and ever-so-slightly touched by cedar wood. It has a bit to say and it sets about it energetically. Screwcap. 12.5% alc. **Rating** 91 **To** 2019 $22 CM ✪

Cabernet Sauvignon 2015 Clean and fruit-driven with only modest (flavour) input from creamy vanillan oak. Blackcurrant, gum leaf and chocolate notes put a fair number of runs on the board. This will drink well over the next handful of years, and likely longer. Screwcap. 13.5% alc. **Rating** 90 **To** 2026 $25 CM

Kings Landing

9 Collins Place, Denmark, WA 6333 (postal) **Region** Great Southern
T 0432 312 918 **www.**kingslandingwines.com.au **Open** Not
Winemaker Coby Ladwig, Luke Eckersley **Est.** 2015 **Dozens** 6000 **Vyds** 9ha
Winemakers Coby Ladwig and Luke Eckersley have accumulated many combined years making wines for others, so this is in some ways a busman's holiday. But it's also a serious business, with 9ha of vineyard plantings (3ha of chardonnay and 2ha each of shiraz, riesling and cabernet sauvignon) making this much more than a virtual winery. I feel it would be a good idea to watch this space.

🍷🍷🍷🍷🍷 **Frankland River Shiraz 2016** Good colour; all the pepper and spice one expects enriching the black and red cherry fruits of Frankland River. These are tempered on the palate by integrated French oak and fine but persistent tannins coming full circle to the pepper and spice of the bouquet. Screwcap. 14.4% alc. **Rating** 95 **To** 2029 $32 ✪

Mount Barker Riesling 2017 Rieslings from the Great Southern are typically very shy in their youth, but capable of dramatic change over the next 5+ years. What you look for is balance, length and the first notes of varietal character, as often as not a bound mix of citrus and acidity. This will make the grade, delicate though it is. Screwcap. 12.1% alc. **Rating** 94 **To** 2027 $32

Pemberton Chardonnay 2017 The near-identical vinification of this and the Rosenthal Wines' Chardonnay isn't surprising given the common ownership and winemaking team. There isn't a hair out of place with a delicate and refined mix of white stone fruit and grapefruit, the toasty oak integrated and the balance and length likewise. Screwcap. 13.2% alc. **Rating** 94 **To** 2027 $32

Mount Barker Cabernet Sauvignon 2016 Bright crimson-purple; an iconoclastic style beating the drum loud and clear. The cassis comes out immediately, followed by foresty/earthy aromas and cedary oak, the finish a crisp crescendo of tannins. This needs to go back to bed for a few years and stop frightening the children. Unlimited future. Screwcap. 14.2% alc. **Rating** 94 **To** 2034 $32

Kings of Kangaroo Ground

15 Graham Road, Kangaroo Ground, Vic 3097 **Region** Yarra Valley
T (03) 9712 0666 **www.**kkg.com.au **Open** Mon–Sat 10–5, Sun 12–5
Winemaker Ken King, Chris Ramsay **Est.** 1990 **Dozens** 500 **Vyds** 2.6ha
Kangaroo Ground, on Melbourne's northeast fringe, is home to Australia's only post office winery. Winemaker Ken King integrated the local post office into his small winery complex in 2004. As well as sorting the district's mail, Ken nurtures a number of local vineyards and makes all wines onsite. Ken's involvement in winemaking began in 1984 as a member of the Eltham and District Amateur Winemakers Guild. In '88 Ken purchased the 3ha site prized for its rich black volcanic soils that he refers to as 'chocolate cake'. Chardonnay and pinot noir vines were planted in '90 and grapes sold to Diamond Valley until 2000. The vines have not been irrigated since 1996 and are thriving in the deep soil. Cabernet sauvignon and riesling are sourced from other nearby black-soil vineyards. Pesticides are not used and the traditional winemaking process means that the wines are vegan compliant.

ΨΨΨΨΩ Heathcote Shiraz 2014 It's one of those strange things that this and its '15 sibling should have reversed vintage style ('15 normally generous but balanced, '14 tougher ex low yields). Plum, dark cherry and blackberry fruit glide seamlessly along the medium-bodied palate, oak and tannins in balanced support. Screwcap. 14% alc. **Rating** 93 **To** 2029 $50

Hilda May Chardonnay 2016 A good chardonnay, attesting to the reputation the region has for this variety, but also with depth to its nectarine and white peach fruit. Notes of creamy cashew ex long-term maturation in oak. Screwcap. 13.5% alc. **Rating** 90 **To** 2023 $27

Yarra Valley Pinot Noir 2015 Very good colour; there is no shortage of fruit, largely in the red spectrum, and pinot to its foundations. The length is good, the finish slippery. Screwcap. 13.5% alc. **Rating** 90 **To** 2023 $25

Heathcote Shiraz Cabernet 2015 This is a medium to full-bodied blend happy in its own skin, with layers of blackcurrant and blackberry fruit built on a base of firm tannins, oak incidental. Screwcap. 14.3% alc. **Rating** 90 **To** 2030 $27

Pedersen Cabernet Sauvignon 2015 An attractive cassis-centred cabernet, finishing with the firm tannins of the variety. Should come together well with 3+ years in the cellar. Diam. 14% alc. **Rating** 90 **To** 2029

ΨΨΨΨ Avondale Shiraz 2015 Rating 89 **To** 2035

Kingston Estate Wines ★★★★☆

Sturt Highway, Kingston-on-Murray, SA 5331 **Region** South Australia
T (08) 8243 3700 **www.**kingstonestatewines.com **Open** Not
Winemaker Bill Moularadellis, Brett Duffin, Steve Warne **Est.** 1979 **Dozens** 100000
Vyds 3100ha
Kingston Estate, under the direction of Bill Moularadellis, has its production roots in the Riverland region, but also has long-term purchase contracts with growers in the Clare Valley, Adelaide Hills, Coonawarra, Langhorne Creek and Mount Benson. It has been very active in purchasing vineyards, trebling the holdings from 1000ha to 3100ha. Kingston Estate has also spread its net wide to take in a range of varietals, mainstream and exotic, under a number of brands at various price points. Exports to all major markets.

ΨΨΨΨΨ Echelon Riverland Petit Verdot 2015 An opaque wine, powerful and loaded with saturated dark fruit and coffee flavours. Also brooding, finishing with dried tobacco and forceful, ferruginous tannins. There is nothing jammy about this. Palate-staining and brimming with personality. Screwcap. 14% alc. **Rating** 95 **To** 2030 $29 NG ✪

Limestone Coast Clare Valley Merlot 2015 The Limestone Coast confers tannic freshness, the Clare a mid-palate warmth. This is exceptional merlot and no, that is not an oxymoron! Plum, blackberry, gentle vanilla and dried herb expand across a weave of moderate tannin, given authority by the fine, pebbly thread. Screwcap. 14% alc. **Rating** 94 **To** 2025 $20 NG ✪

ΨΨΨΨΩ Padthaway Chardonnay 2017 Rating 93 **To** 2021 $20 NG ✪
Echelon Shiraz 2015 Rating 93 **To** 2027 $29 NG
Riverland Petit Verdot 2016 Rating 93 **To** 2025 $20 NG ✪
Adelaide Hills Pinot Gris 2017 Rating 91 **To** 2019 $20 NG ✪
Clare Valley Shiraz 2016 Rating 91 **To** 2021 $20 NG ✪

Kirrihill Wines ★★★★

12 Main North Road, Clare, SA 5453 **Region** Clare Valley
T (08) 8842 4087 **www.**kirrihillwines.com.au **Open** 7 days 10–4
Winemaker Will Shields **Est.** 1998 **Dozens** 35000 **Vyds** 600ha
Kirrihill was founded in 1998 in the picturesque Clare Valley. Grapes are sourced from specially selected parcels of Kirrihill's sizeable managed vineyards, as well as the Edwards and Stanway families' properties in the region. Kirrihill produces cool-climate wines that represent the unique characters of the valley. Exports to all major markets.

♟♟♟♟♟ **E.B.'s The Settler Clare Valley Riesling 2017** From the WSS vineyard planted in the '70s. Citrus blossom aromas, then a palate that positively bounces with limes. Low pH gives the wine its minerally mouthfeel and length. Screwcap. 11.5% alc. Rating 94 To 2027 $35

♟♟♟♟♀ **Vineyard Selection Clare Valley Shiraz 2015** Rating 93 To 2027 $20 CM ○
Vineyard Selection Clare Valley Cabernet Sauvignon 2015 Rating 93
To 2028 $20 CM ○
Gleeson & Co Clare Valley Riesling 2017 Rating 91 To 2023 $25
Piccoli Lotti Montepulciano 2016 Rating 91 To 2022 $27
Regional Selection Clare Valley Cabernet Sauvignon 2016 Rating 90
To 2023 $18 ○

Knee Deep Wines

160 Johnson Road, Wilyabrup, WA 6280 **Region** Margaret River
T (08) 9755 6776 www.kneedeepwines.com.au **Open** 7 days 10–5
Winemaker Bruce Dukes **Est.** 2000 **Dozens** 7500 **Vyds** 20.26ha
Perth surgeon and veteran yachtsman Phil Childs and wife Sue have planted their property in Wilyabrup to chardonnay (3.2ha), sauvignon blanc (4ha), semillon (1.48ha), chenin blanc (4ha), cabernet sauvignon (6.34ha) and shiraz (1.24ha). The name, Knee Deep Wines, was inspired by the passion and commitment needed to produce premium wine, and as a tongue-in-cheek acknowledgement of jumping in 'boots and all' during a testing time in the wine industry, the grape glut building more or less with the venture. Exports to Germany.

♟♟♟♟♟ **Kim's Limited Release Chardonnay 2016** More delicate wine than the Premium cuvee, this was whole-bunch pressed to deliver a wine that shimmers rather than sashays. White fig and cashew notes reverberate along a spine of chalky mineral and firm oak bulwarks. This needs time to flesh out, although it should deliver the goods based on its tenacious finish. Screwcap. 13.5% alc. Rating 94 To 2028 $45 NG

♟♟♟♟♀ **Premium Chardonnay 2016** Rating 93 To 2022 $28 NG
Kelsea's Limited Release Cabernet Sauvignon 2014 Rating 93 To 2029
$65 NG
Hayley's Limited Release Shiraz 2015 Rating 92 To 2028 $65 NG
Cabernet Merlot 2016 Rating 92 To 2024 $24 NG ○

Knotting Hill Estate Vineyard

247 Carter Road, Wilyabrup WA 6280 **Region** Margaret River
T (08) 9755 7733 www.knottinghill.com.au **Open** 7 days 11–5
Winemaker Flying Fish Cove (Simon Ding) **Est.** 1997 **Dozens** 4000 **Vyds** 37.5ha
The Gould family has been farming in WA since 1907, and still owns the land grant taken up on their arrival from Scotland. In '97 two generations of the family decided to diversify, and acquired Knotting Hill, their Wilyabrup property. In '98, using their extensive farming background, they propagated 56 000 cuttings in an onsite nursery, then supervised plantings, created a 5.5ha lake, and built the 45m bridge entry to the cellar door (made of local limestone). In 2002 they leased their wheat farm and have since devoted all their time to Knotting Hill. The spectacular vineyard is set within a natural amphitheatre, with the lake at the bottom.

♟♟♟♟♟ **Jack Gordon Margaret River Cabernet Sauvignon 2016** Sits neatly in its regional makeup with all manner of flavours, from mulberries and currants to florals, a hint of eucalyptus, chocolate and spice. Just shy of full-bodied, there's plenty of detail with its poised tannins, and a vitality as it confidently moves across the palate. Screwcap. 13.5% alc. Rating 95 To 2030 $48 JF
Jack Gordon Margaret River Cabernet Sauvignon 2015 Laden with cassis, currants, mulberries and leafy freshness. At first there's softness on the palate, then layers of fruit and spice roll through, brought to a halt by furry yet persuasive

tannins. More time to unfurl but a very stylish wine. Screwcap. 13.5% alc.
Rating 94 To 2028 $48 JF

🍷🍷🍷🍷🍷 Margaret River Cabernet Malbec 2015 Rating 93 To 2025 $38 JF
Margaret River Cabernet Merlot 2016 Rating 92 To 2026 $38 JF
Jack Gordon Margaret River Cabernet Sauvignon 2014 Rating 92
To 2027 $48 JF
Margaret River Shiraz 2014 Rating 91 To 2022 $28 JF

Koerner Wine   ★★★★★

935 Mintaro Road, Leasingham, SA 5452 **Region** Clare Valley
T 0408 895 341 **www**.koernerwine.com.au **Open** By appt
Winemaker Damon Koerner **Est.** 2014 **Dozens** 2000 **Vyds** 60ha
Brothers Damon and Jonathan (Jono) Koerner grew up in the Clare Valley, but flew the coop
to work and study in other parts of Australia and abroad. The substantial vineyards owned
and managed by their parents, Anthony and Christine Koerner, for 35 years, have now passed
to them. While the major part of the crop is sold to other wineries, in 2016 Damon made
11 wines, a major point of difference being the use of synonyms for well known varieties, as
well as adopting Australian name usage; and also turning the world upside down with left-field
winemaking practices exemplified by the '16 Watervale Riesling.

🍷🍷🍷🍷🍷 GV1 Riesling 2017 From 46yo vines on the Gullyview vineyard. Fantastic
concentration of flavour and all the texture – and length – you could ever hope
for. It's an excellent wine: characterful, buoyant, captivating. Diam. 12.1% alc.
Rating 95 To 2024 $27 CM ✪
Rolle Vermentino 2017 Lees, spice, stone fruit, nashi pear and honeysuckle. It's
rich in flavour, high in personality and long through the finish. Magical drinking.
Diam. 11.9% alc. Rating 95 To 2021 $35 CM ✪
Watervale Riesling 2017 Its two calling cards are texture and length, though
the interplay between lime and floral notes has an extra dimension to it, and the
way the wine 'flows' through the mouth feels a bit special too. Screwcap. 12% alc.
Rating 94 To 2024 $27 CM ✪
Classico 2016 Cabernet malbec. Highly expressive on the nose, but then stern
on the palate. A red wine of gravity and presence, despite its low alcohol reading.
Boysenberry into black cherry, graphite into fragrant herbs. Nuts and pencils.
Complex in both its aroma and flavour, but the authority of the tannin really sets
the tone. Will be very interesting to see this as a mature wine. Cork. 12.5% alc.
Rating 94 To 2029 $60 CM

🍷🍷🍷🍷🍷 Tiver Rose 2017 Rating 92 To 2019 $27 CM
The Clare 2017 Rating 92 To 2022 $27 CM
La Corse 2017 Rating 91 To 2020 $30 CM
Cannanou Grenache 2017 Rating 90 To 2020 $35 CM

Koonara   ★★★★★

44 Main Street, Penola, SA 5277 **Region** Coonawarra
T (08) 8737 3222 **www**.koonara.com **Open** Mon–Thurs 10–5, Fri–Sat 10–6, Sun 10–4
Winemaker Peter Douglas **Est.** 1988 **Dozens** 10 000 **Vyds** 9ha
Koonara is a sister, or, more appropriately, a brother company to Reschke Wines. The latter is
run by Burke Reschke, Koonara by his brother Dru. Both are sons of Trevor Reschke, who
planted the first vines on the Koonara property in 1988. Peter Douglas, formerly Wynns' chief
winemaker before moving overseas for some years, has returned and is consultant winemaker.
Since 2013 Koonara have leased and managed the Kongorong Partnership Vineyard in
Mount Gambier, which had previously sold its grapes to Koonara. Having not used pesticides
or herbicides for over a decade, Koonara's Coonawarra vineyard became the first certified
organic vineyard in the region, in January '18. Exports to the US, Canada, Europe, Singapore
and China.

🍷🍷🍷🍷🍷 **The Big Guns Coonawarra Shiraz 2015** A tribute to Burke and Dru's father Trevor Reschke, who represented Australia in clay target shooting. In the elite group of red wines selling for $100 or more, the striking label is likely to appeal to Chinese wine lovers looking for expensive (and special) wines. The wine is deep crimson-purple, and manages to combine full-bodied weight with balance, length and a supple, black fruit mouthfeel. Diam. 15.5% alc. **Rating** 96 **To** 2045 $100
Emily May Mount Gambier Pinot Noir Rose 2017 Gold medals at the Cool Climate, Melbourne and Sydney wine shows '17 are impressive enough, but two trophies at Sydney is another thing. The appeal of the wine is its purity and delicacy, with wild strawberry flavours that caress the mouth with no hint of sweetness. Screwcap. 11.5% alc. **Rating** 95 **To** 2019 $20 ☻

🍷🍷🍷🍷🍷 **Angel's Peak Coonawarra Shiraz 2015** Rating 92 To 2037 $25 ☻
Cape Banks Mount Gambier Chardonnay 2016 Rating 90 To 2023 $25
Lucy and Alice Mount Gambier Pinot Gris 2016 Rating 90 To 2019 $20 ☻
Wanderlust Coonawarra Cabernet Sauvignon 2015 Rating 90
To 2029 $25

Koonowla Wines   ★★★☆

18 Koonowla Road, Auburn, SA 5451 **Region** Clare Valley
T (08) 8849 2270 **www**.koonowla.com **Open** W'ends & public hols 10–5
Winemaker O'Leary Walker Wines **Est.** 1997 **Dozens** 6000 **Vyds** 48.77ha
Koonowla is a historic Clare Valley property. Situated just east of Auburn, it was first planted with vines in the 1890s, and by the early 1900s was producing 60000l of wine annually. A disastrous fire in '26 destroyed the winery and wine stocks, and the property was converted to grain and wool production. Replanting of vines began in '85, and accelerated after Andrew and Booie Michael purchased the property in '91; there are now almost 50ha of cabernet sauvignon, riesling, shiraz, merlot and semillon. In an all-too-familiar story, the grapes were sold until falling prices forced a change in strategy; now a major part of the grapes is vinified by the infinitely experienced David O'Leary and Nick Walker. Exports to the UK, the US, Scandinavia, Malaysia, China and NZ.

🍷🍷🍷🍷🍷 **Clare Valley Riesling 2017** Pale but bright straw-green; the wine is particularly intense, but its mix of lime and crisp acidity makes for a ready-to-rumble riesling ideal for seafood, whether cooked in a Chinese or Western fashion. Screwcap. 12.3% alc. **Rating** 90 **To** 2023 $20 ☻

Kooyong   ★★★★★

PO Box 153, Red Hill South, Vic 3937 **Region** Mornington Peninsula
T (03) 5989 4444 **www**.kooyongwines.com.au **Open** At Port Phillip Estate
Winemaker Glen Hayley **Est.** 1996 **Dozens** 13000 **Vyds** 40ha
Kooyong, owned by Giorgio and Dianne Gjergja, released its first wines in 2001. The vineyard is planted to pinot noir, chardonnay and, more recently, pinot gris. In July '15, following the departure of Sandro Mosele, his assistant of six years, Glen Hayley, was appointed to take his place. The Kooyong wines are made at the state-of-the-art winery of Port Phillip Estate, also owned by the Gjergjas. Exports to the UK, the US, Canada, Sweden, Norway, Singapore, Hong Kong, Japan and China.

🍷🍷🍷🍷🍷 **Faultline Single Vineyard Mornington Peninsula Chardonnay 2016** Jittery. Nervous. Chalky. Subtle. The most reticent wine of the swag. Apricot and faint stone-fruit allusions jangle across a beam of vanilla/cedar oak, a skein of mineral tension and a core of mealy nourishment. This will age beautifully, attested to by the pulse of flavour, thrilling complexity and exhilarating length. Buy and wait. Screwcap. 13% alc. **Rating** 97 **To** 2029 $61 NG ☻

🍷🍷🍷🍷🍷 **Farrago Single Vineyard Mornington Peninsula Chardonnay 2016** The Farrago is furled across a mineral beam that opens more readily, exposing the fruit

and joy of the wine with a little air. Tangerine, peach and nectarine segue to a lime-inflected flintiness, filling out across the palate with notes of hay, oatmeal and leesy curd. The oak is perfectly positioned as a signpost to guide this beauty across the next decade. Screwcap. 13.5% alc. **Rating** 96 **To** 2028 $61 NG ✪
Ferrous Single Vineyard Mornington Peninsula Pinot Noir 2016 Always my favourite pinot of the stable for structural reasons alone: the tannins are earthy and ferric, as the name implies. Nothing gritty, though. A magical carpet to carry and obviate the sweetness of the fruit: bing cherry, blood plum and root spice. Long, highly complex and flush. Screwcap. 13.5% alc. **Rating** 96 **To** 2028 $76 NG
Meres Single Vineyard Mornington Peninsula Pinot Noir 2016 The most refined pinot, perhaps. You might align Ferrous with a Gevrey pinot and this with a Chambolle. Sappy, crunchy and finessed across a red-fruited mineral thread. This lovely wine offers a long caress on the palate with nothing out of place. Screwcap. 13.5% alc. **Rating** 96 **To** 2026 $76 NG
Estate Mornington Peninsula Chardonnay 2016 Ample stone fruit and toasted hazelnut flavours are wrapped around a coil of mineral, underlain by the cinnamon oak that shimmies across the palate. Not as tense as the site-specific wines, this has more of a sleek glide. Screwcap. 13.5% alc. **Rating** 95 **To** 2022 $44 NG
Haven Single Vineyard Mornington Peninsula Pinot Noir 2016 Bright. Zinging. Delicate red fruit gives this third site-specific pinot more of a transparent quality, and it is yet to absorb the oak. A bit shins-and-elbows, this will greatly reward those with patience. Screwcap. 13.5% alc. **Rating** 95 **To** 2026 $76 NG
Beurrot Mornington Peninsula Pinot Gris 2017 This wine was once chardonnay-like with oak-derived vanillans and a lees-inflected midriff; mealy and creamy. Now a swan, exhibiting more gris-centric genetics and all the better for it. Slippery. Viscous. Nashi pear and ripe apple–gelato flavours teem, directed by a sash of almond-soused phenolics and mineral tension. About as good as gris gets. Screwcap. 13.5% alc. **Rating** 94 **To** 2024 $32 NG

ΨΨΨΨΨ **Estate Pinot Noir 2016** Rating 93 To 2024 $54 NG
Clonale Chardonnay 2017 Rating 92 To 2023 $34 NG
Massale Pinot Noir 2016 Rating 90 To 2021 $32 NG

Kooyonga Creek   ★★★☆

2369 Samaria Road, Moorngag, Vic 3673 **Region** North East Victoria
T (03) 9629 5853 **www.**kooyongacreek.com.au **Open** Fri–Sun & public hols 11–5
Winemaker Barry Saunders, Luis Simian **Est.** 2011 **Dozens** 5000 **Vyds** 8ha
When you read the name of this winery, you expect to find it somewhere on or near the Mornington Peninsula. In fact it's a very long way to the northeast of Victoria, where Barry and Pam Saunders planted vineyards on their farm and released the first wines under the name Kooyonga Chapel in 2003. They planted a sensibly focused range of 1.6ha each of shiraz, cabernet sauvignon, merlot, chardonnay and sauvignon blanc, and what started as a hobby has now become a business. Family and friends help in the peak seasons (picking and pruning). The name is now Kooyonga Creek and distribution into the Melbourne market has begun.

ΨΨΨΨΨ **Heathcote Shiraz 2014** Luscious and rich, with blackberries dipped in chocolate providing the flavour base. It is savoury and spicy at the same time, and treads lightly, giving it freshness and length. The cellaring recommendation on a supporting document says 'the wine will have no problem making it to 2014'. Or '24, perhaps. Screwcap. 14.6% alc. **Rating** 91 **To** 2024 $30

Krinklewood Biodynamic Vineyard   ★★★★

712 Wollombi Road, Broke, NSW 2330 **Region** Hunter Valley
T (02) 6579 1322 **www.**krinklewood.com **Open** Fri–Sun 10–5
Winemaker Rod Windrim, Peter Windrim **Est.** 1981 **Dozens** 8000 **Vyds** 19.9ha

Every aspect of this family owned property is managed in a holistic and sustainable way. Rod Windrim's extensive herb crops, native grasses and farm animals all contribute to biodynamically maintaining healthy soil biology. The small winery is home to a Vaslin Bucher basket press and two Nomblot French fermentation eggs, underpinning the natural approach to winemaking.

🍷🍷🍷🍷🍷 **Basket Press Shiraz 2017** This is exceptional Hunter shiraz in a contemporary mould. Boysenberry, black olive and dried seaweed notes meld with the Hunter's leather-varnished tannins, all complying with violet-scented, gushing fruit. Long, sappy and pliant. Screwcap. 13.5% alc. **Rating** 94 **To** 2029 $50 NG

🍷🍷🍷🍷🍷 **Basket Press Chardonnay 2017 Rating** 93 **To** 2023 $38 NG
Francesca Rose 2017 Rating 93 **To** 2020 $25 NG ✪
Shiraz 2017 Rating 93 **To** 2022 $40 NG
Semillon 2017 Rating 92 **To** 2027 $24 NG ✪
Vat 48 Orange Cabernet Merlot 2016 Rating 92 **To** 2023 $45 NG
Chardonnay 2017 Rating 91 **To** 2022 $28 NG
Verdelho 2017 Rating 91 **To** 2020 $24 NG
Spider Run White 2017 Rating 91 **To** 2021 $40 NG

Kurtz Family Vineyards ★★★★

731 Light Pass Road, Angaston, SA, 5353 **Region** Barossa Valley
T 0418 810 982 **www**.kurtzfamilyvineyards.com.au **Open** By appt
Winemaker Steve Kurtz **Est.** 1996 **Dozens** 2500 **Vyds** 15ha
The Kurtz family vineyard is at Light Pass, with 9ha of shiraz and the remainder planted to chardonnay, cabernet sauvignon, semillon, sauvignon blanc, petit verdot, grenache, mataro and malbec. Steve Kurtz has followed in the footsteps of his great-grandfather Ben Kurtz, who first grew grapes at Light Pass in the 1930s. During a career working first at Saltram, and then at Foster's until 2006, Steve gained invaluable experience from Nigel Dolan, Caroline Dunn and John Glaetzer, among others. Exports to the US and China.

🍷🍷🍷🍷🍷 **Schmick Barossa Shiraz 2013** Replete with the generous alcohol that is a hallmark of the Kurtz Family wines, it's got the fruit and oak to match it here. Aromas have an almost plum pudding–like richness, and there's a flood of ripe, sweet flavour with a hefty lick of tannin to finish. Screwcap. 15.5% alc. **Rating** 93 **To** 2030 $85 SC
Boundary Row Barossa Valley Shiraz 2015 Lower in alcohol this vintage, which makes for a more supple style. Shows the familiar elements of ripe plum, blackberry and chocolate with an overlay of cedary oak. Fresh and juicy, the velvety tannin is a good foil for the generous fruit. Screwcap. 14.5% alc. **Rating** 92 **To** 2023 $28 SC
Uncle Tony's Barossa Valley Mataro 2015 Likely to come from old vines. High alcohol and slightly subdued bouquet, not really flush with ripe, full-on Barossa generosity, but there's a feeling of depth with a savoury edge. Has some weight and density on the palate, texture as well, but there isn't complexity at this stage. Screwcap. 15% alc. **Rating** 92 **To** 2025 $35 SC

🍷🍷🍷🍷 **Seven Sleepers Barossa Valley Shiraz 2016 Rating** 89 **To** 2022 $18 SC ✪
Boundary Row Barossa Valley Grenache Shiraz Mataro 2015 Rating 89 **To** 2022 $28 SC

 # Kyara ★★★★

307 Sawpit Gully Road, Keyneton, SA 5353 **Region** Barossa Valley
T 0408 887 300 **www**.kyara.com.au **Open** Not
Winemaker Jo Irvine **Est.** 2012 **Dozens** 1200 **Vyds** 4.53ha
Kylie and Leon Pendergast are among the descendants of Eden Valley founder Heinrich Fiebiger. Their former careers in the fashion accessories industry in Melbourne, which involved travelling the world promoting products, has left its mark, such as in the slick

presentation of the material explaining their arrival in the Eden Valley, and their business plan. A cellar door was scheduled for late 2018. It's clear from the wines that the vineyard was mature when they purchased the property in 2012. Experienced contract winemaker Jo Irvine will ensure the vineyard's potential will be fully exploited. Exports to Hong Kong.

🍷🍷🍷🍷🍷 **Thistle & Burr Eden Valley Riesling 2014** The simultaneous release of three vintages ('15, '14 and '13) of this wine at the same price is unusual, as is the superior quality of this vintage (compared to the '15). It is intensely flavoured, lime juice to the fore, Granny Smith apple chiming in on the back-palate and finish. Screwcap. 12% alc. **Rating** 94 **To** 2029 $24 ✪

🍷🍷🍷🍷 **Thistle & Burr Eden Valley Riesling 2013** **Rating** 93 **To** 2025 $24 ✪
Justice of the Peace Single Vineyard Eden Valley Cabernet Sauvignon 2013 **Rating** 92 **To** 2033 $69
Thistle & Burr Eden Valley Riesling 2015 **Rating** 91 **To** 2023 $24

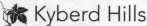

Kyberd Hills ★★★★☆

PO Box 208, Red Hill, Vic 3937 **Region** Mornington Peninsula
T 0417 556 836 **www**.kyberdhillswines.com.au **Open** Not
Winemaker Michael Kyberd **Est.** 2017 **Dozens** 600 **Vyds** 2ha

After making wine on the Mornington Peninsula for other people for 20 years, Michael Kyberd has finally got around to starting a brand with his wife Nicolette and friends Kim and David Wilson as partners. Starting with a combination of leased vineyard and purchased grapes and focussing on pinot noir and chardonnay, the plan is to plant a vineyard on their property in Red Hill. The winemaking style is gentle, with minimal extraction and intervention, purity the desired outcome. Hopefully such words as folly and regret will disappear from their conversation in less than a decade.

🍷🍷🍷🍷🍷 **Mornington Peninsula Pinot Noir 2016** Kyberd Hills is a new venture, but Michael has had many years of experience in making pinot noir, and it shows in this wine. Its fragrant red berry varietal expression on the bouquet is clear, but it's the insistence and length of the flavours and tannins of the palate that make the wine as good as it is. '16 wasn't as easy as '15 on the peninsula, so this portends very well. Screwcap. 13.5% alc. **Rating** 95 **To** 2025 $50

🍷🍷🍷🍷 **Mornington Peninsula Chardonnay 2014** **Rating** 92 **To** 2020 $50

Kyneton Ridge Estate ★★★★☆

90 Blackhill School Road, Kyneton, Vic 3444 **Region** Macedon Ranges
T (03) 5422 7377 **www**.kynetonridge.com.au **Open** W'ends & public hols 10.30–5.30
Winemaker John Boucher, Luke Boucher **Est.** 1997 **Dozens** 1200 **Vyds** 4ha

Established by John Boucher and partner Pauline Russell in the shadow of Black Mountain, an ideal environment for pinot noir and chardonnay vines. They maintain traditional processes, but new facilities have recently been introduced to enhance the production of the sparkling wines. The increased capacity also gives the opportunity to source additional quality parcels of shiraz and cabernet sauvignon from Macedon and Heathcote. A small amount is exported to Taiwan.

🍷🍷🍷🍷🍷 **The John Boucher 7 Years on Lees Macedon Ranges Pinot Noir Chardonnay 2009** The complexity and richness of this wine is obvious. It has great texture, and a flavour wheel taking in white peach and citrus at one point, biscuit and bread at the other, fig somewhere in the middle. Diam. 12.8% alc. **Rating** 95 $40
Premium Macedon Ranges Pinot Noir 2015 A medium to full-bodied pinot that has retained varietal expression in a plum/black cherry framework. The leisurely development of its '12 sibling reinforces the idea that this wine has excellent potential, as it is better than the '12 was when first tasted. Screwcap. 13.5% alc. **Rating** 94 **To** 2023 $45

Aged Release Premium Macedon Ranges Pinot Noir 2012 This is the third time this wine has been tasted, and each time it has asserted its longevity. There is a degree of mintiness not previously noted. A close eye should watch continued build-up of this character. Screwcap. 13% alc. **Rating** 94 **To** 2022 $42

Heathcote Shiraz 2015 Hand-plunging, a long cold soak and long maturation in French oak gave this wine a flying start. It is full of red and black cherry fruit, the tannins silky, the oak skilfully used. Achieves elegance without obvious effort. Screwcap. 13.8% alc. **Rating** 94 **To** 2030 $35

Macedon Pinot Noir Chardonnay 2011 A wine of considerable complexity, length and savoury/citrussy grip, yet paradoxically with a pure line of acidity that draws all the components into a coherent whole. Diam. 13.2% alc. **Rating** 94 $32

ooooo **Macedon Pinot Noir Chardonnay 2012 Rating** 91 $32

L.A.S. Vino   ★★★★

PO Box 361 Cowaramup, WA 6284 **Region** Margaret River
www.lasvino.com **Open** Not
Winemaker Nic Peterkin **Est.** 2013 **Dozens** 800
Nic Peterkin is the grandson of the late Diana Cullen (Cullen Wines) and the son of Mike Peterkin (Pierro). After graduating from the University of Adelaide with a masters degree in oenology, and travelling the world as a Flying Winemaker, he came back to roost in Margaret River with the ambition of making wines that are a little bit different, but also within the bounds of conventional oenological science. The intention is to keep the project small, and thus make only 200 dozen each of chardonnay, chenin blanc, pinot noir (Albino Pinot) and touriga nacional (Pirate Blend). Exports to the UK, Singapore and Japan.

ooooo **Jerusalem's Grace Margaret River Chardonnay 2016** Cut and thrust, eat your heart out. Speed and endurance aren't natural bedfellows but this attacks with flavour from the start, yet manages to rip through to an extended finish. Grapefruit, melon, shortbread, vanilla-cream and sweeter, peachier characters. Voluminous is the word. Diam. 13.5% alc. **Rating** 94 **To** 2023 $66 CM

ooooo **Chenin Blanc Dynamic Blend 2016 Rating** 92 **To** 2022 $55 CM

La Bise   ★★★★

PO Box 918, Williamstown, SA 5351 **Region** Adelaide Hills/Southern Flinders Ranges
T 0439 823 251 **www.**labisewines.com.au **Open** Not
Winemaker Natasha Mooney **Est.** 2006 **Dozens** 1500
This is a reasonably significant busman's holiday for Natasha Mooney, a well known and highly regarded winemaker whose 'day job' (her term) is to provide winemaking consultancy services for some of SA's larger wineries. This allows her to find small, unique parcels of grapes that might otherwise be blended into large-volume brands, which she manages to access without conflict of interest. Natasha's wines are about fruit and vineyard expression. She aims for mouthfeel and drinkability without high alcohol, and for that she should be loudly applauded.

ooooo **Adelaide Hills Chardonnay 2017** Despite its low alcohol, the flavours are absolutely ripe, with white peach and a hint of nougat filling the fore-palate, continuing on the long path to the finish. The choice of used 500l puncheons for 8 months' maturation helps keep the focus on the fruit, and gives gently creamy notes. Screwcap. 12.5% alc. **Rating** 93 **To** 2021 $25 ✪

Adelaide Hills Tempranillo 2017 Made to reflect the early ripening nature of tempranillo in a fruit-forward style without alcohol ripeness. Excellent colour, well made, ample red and black cherry fruit, attractive tannins and a fine-spun savoury finish. No need for excuses or qualifications here. Screwcap. 13.9% alc. **Rating** 92 **To** 2027 $25 ✪

Adelaide Hills Nero d'Avola 2017 Bright, clear crimson; a delicious, juicy wine that tastes of creaming soda and cherry, all joy and no off-notes at any point. Nothing to be gained from cellaring it, everything from drinking it – if not tonight, then tomorrow night. Screwcap. 13% alc. **Rating** 92 **To** 2018 $29

Adelaide Hills Pinot Gris 2017 Tash Mooney's strategy of 'trying to make a more intense style with texture and phenolics being an integral part of the wine' works for this very different wine compared to most of her others. It is rich and layered, and unexpectedly with only a bare hint of pink colour. Screwcap. 13% alc. **Rating** 90 **To** 2020 $22

Le Petite Frais Adelaide Hills Rose 2017 Pale salmon, made from 35yo vines. Fresh, dry and savoury, with texture more important than the echoes of fruits; spice and dried rose petals carry a second wave. Serve with any and every thing. Screwcap. 13% alc. **Rating** 90 **To** 2019 $22

♟♟♟♟ **Adelaide Hills Sangiovese 2016** Rating 89 To 2021 $25

La Curio

Cnr Foggo Road/Kangarilla Road, McLaren Vale, SA 5171 **Region** McLaren Vale
T (08) 8323 7999 **www**.lacuriowines.com **Open** By appt
Winemaker Adam Hooper **Est.** 2003 **Dozens** 1500
At 17, winemaker and owner Adam Hooper enrolled in the oenology course at Roseworthy College, and got off to a flying start. Following that, he worked as a winemaker with some of the best known wineries in McLaren Vale for 20 years, interspersed with Flying Winemaker trips to Italy and France. The wines have always had a certain frisson, largely as a result of extreme cold soak prior to the fermentation of uncrushed whole berries. Exports to the UK, Canada, Sweden and Hong Kong.

♟♟♟♟♟ **The Nubile Grenache Shiraz Mataro 2016** Recently bottled when tasted. The spiciness of grenache leads the way, with the depth and structure imparted by the other varieties more subtle. It's generous and full-fruited but fresh and light on its feet. Just needs time for complexity to build. Screwcap. 14.5% alc. **Rating** 92 **To** 2038 $25 SC ✪

The Original Zin Primitivo 2016 A juicy and jubey little wine, showing distinctive primitivo (aka zinfandel) varietal character which is reminiscent of coconut. The flavours are fairly simple, generally red fruited, soft through the mid-palate but pleasantly astringent to finish. Screwcap. 14.5% alc. **Rating** 91 **To** 2021 $25 SC

♟♟♟♟ **New World Order Sangiovese 2016** Rating 89 To 2021 $25 SC

La Linea

36 Shipsters Road, Kensington Park, SA 5068 (postal) **Region** Adelaide Hills
T (08) 8431 3556 **www**.lalinea.com.au **Open** Not
Winemaker Peter Leske **Est.** 2007 **Dozens** 3500 **Vyds** 9.5ha
La Linea is a partnership of several experienced wine industry professionals, including Peter Leske and David LeMire MW. Peter was among the first to recognise the potential of tempranillo in Australia, and his knowledge of it is reflected in the three wine styles he makes from the variety: Tempranillo Rose, tempranillo blended from several Adelaide Hills vineyards, and Norteno, from a single vineyard at the northern end of the Hills. Two rieslings are produced under the Vertigo label: TRKN (short for trocken), and the off-dry 25GR (25g/l residual sugar). Exports to the UK.

♟♟♟♟♟ **Adelaide Hills Mencia Rose 2017** It's dry and structural with a hit of rapsberried flavour at its centre; as a result, it's a quite beautiful rose to both drink and appreciate. It glows with colour, flavour and style. It should keep singing in tune for a bit longer than your average rose, too. Screwcap. 13% alc. **Rating** 94 **To** 2020 $25 CM ✪

♟♟♟♟♟ **Adelaide Hills Tempranillo 2016** Rating 92 To 2024 $27 CM
Adelaide Hills Mencia 2017 Rating 92 To 2022 $29 CM
Vertigo 25GR Adelaide Hills Riesling 2017 Rating 91 To 2024 $24 CM
Adelaide Hills Tempranillo Rose 2017 Rating 91 To 2019 $22 CM ✪

La Pleiade ★★★★☆

c/- Jasper Hill, Drummonds Lane, Heathcote, Vic 3523 **Region** Heathcote
T (03) 5433 2528 **www**.jasperhill.com.au **Open** By appt
Winemaker Ron Laughton, Michel Chapoutier **Est.** 1998 **Dozens** 500 **Vyds** 9ha
A joint venture of Michel and Corinne Chapoutier and Ron and Elva Laughton. In spring 1998, a vineyard of Australian and imported French shiraz clones was planted. It is run biodynamically, and the winemaking is deliberately designed to place maximum emphasis on the fruit quality. Exports to the UK, the US, France, Singapore and Hong Kong.

♀♀♀♀ Heathcote Shiraz 2014 Has retained excellent colour. A wine with much to offer, but the dominance of French oak won't be denied at this stage. The future? I don't know. Cork. 14.5% alc. **Rating** 89 **To** 2034 $68

Lake Breeze Wines ★★★★★

Step Road, Langhorne Creek, SA 5255 **Region** Langhorne Creek
T (08) 8537 3017 **www**.lakebreeze.com.au **Open** 7 days 10–5
Winemaker Greg Follett **Est.** 1987 **Dozens** 20000 **Vyds** 90ha
The Folletts have been farmers at Langhorne Creek since 1880, and grapegrowers since the 1930s. Part of the grape production is sold, but the quality of Lake Breeze's own wines is exemplary, with the reds particularly appealing. Lake Breeze also owns and makes the False Cape wines from Kangaroo Island. Exports to the UK, the US, Switzerland, Denmark, Germany, Peru, Vietnam, Singapore, Hong Kong, Japan and China.

♀♀♀♀♀ Section 54 Shiraz 2016 While there's complexity and depth in both structure and flavour, Section 54 never loses its deft touch. A balanced combination of juicy spiced plums, dark chocolate and a savoury stamp. Fresh and lively acidity with ribbons of tannin layering across the supple palate, making it rewarding now, but it will last some distance. Screwcap. 14.5% alc. **Rating** 95 **To** 2028 $26 JF ✪
Old Vine Grenache 2016 A wine that offers composure, depth and delight all at once. Subtle flavours of red fruits, the tang of pomegranate, and red licorice, yet also with a savoury note. Everything glides across a palate that is lighter than mid-weight, with lithe tannins and plenty of freshness. Screwcap. 14.5% alc. **Rating** 95 **To** 2024 $26 JF ✪
The Drake 2013 A barrel selection, the blend 75% cabernet sauvignon and 25% shiraz. Richly flavoured with black fruits, all spicy and earthy, with some tamarind-like acidity and much savouriness as it moves onto a full-bodied palate. Ripe and substantial tannins; the oak needs to recede, and it will. Screwcap. 14.2% alc. **Rating** 95 **To** 2028 $90 JF
False Cape Unknown Sailor Kangaroo Island Cabernet Sauvignon 2015 Alluring red-purple; always a compelling and intriguing wine, quite different from any other Australian cabernet, reflecting its place. Heady aromas of blackcurrants, black tea, olives, iodine, saltbush and a crush of dried herbs. Savoury through and through with a restrained, more medium-bodied, palate. Screwcap. 14% alc. **Rating** 94 **To** 2025 $32 JF

♀♀♀♀♀ Rosato 2017 Rating 93 **To** 2019 $19 JF ✪
Cabernet Sauvignon 2016 Rating 93 **To** 2025 $26 JF ✪
Reserve Chardonnay 2017 Rating 92 **To** 2022 $26 JF
Bernoota Shiraz Cabernet 2016 Rating 92 **To** 2025 $23 JF ✪

Lake's Folly ★★★★★

2416 Broke Road, Pokolbin, NSW 2320 **Region** Hunter Valley
T (02) 4998 7507 **www**.lakesfolly.com.au **Open** 7 days 10–4 (while wine available)
Winemaker Rodney Kempe **Est.** 1963 **Dozens** 4000 **Vyds** 12.2ha
The first of the weekend wineries to produce wines for commercial sale; long revered for its cabernet sauvignon and nowadays its chardonnay. Just as they should, terroir and climate produce a distinctive wine style. Lake's Folly no longer has any connection with the

Lake family, having been acquired some years ago by Perth businessman Peter Fogarty, who previously established Millbrook Winery in the Perth Hills and has since acquired Deep Woods Estate in Margaret River and Smithbrook Wines in Pemberton. Peter is no stranger to the joys and agonies of running a small winery and has been an exemplary owner of all the brands, providing support where needed but otherwise not interfering.

ŸŸŸŸŸ Hunter Valley Chardonnay 2017 A richly flavoured, mid-weighted chardonnay from an exceptional vintage, with crunch and energy more synonymous with wine from a cooler zone. A chorus of orchard and stone fruits is flecked with a mineral pungency playing soprano to a bass of truffle, toasted hazelnut and lees. The track record of this wine is exemplary, auguring a great future ahead. Screwcap. 13% alc. **Rating** 95 **To** 2029 $80 NG

Hunter Valley Cabernets 2016 Despite the challenges of '16, this is a sublimely elegant, crunchy wine, mid-weighted with herbs aplenty, brimming with the urgent drinkability of a Loire red. That said, there is not an iota of cabernet franc in the blend. This is a Super Second rather than a Premier Cru, but boy is it a delightful meld of currant, sap and finely tuned, svelte tannins. Screwcap. 13.5% alc. **Rating** 95 **To** 2032 $80 NG

Lambrook Wines   ★★★★☆

PO Box 3640, Norwood, SA 5067 **Region** Adelaide Hills
T 0437 672 651 **www**.lambrook.com.au **Open** By appt
Winemaker Adam Lampit **Est.** 2008 **Dozens** 5000
This is a virtual winery created by husband and wife team Adam and Brooke Lampit. With almost two decades of industry experience between them, they began purchasing sauvignon blanc, shiraz and pinot noir (for sparkling) in 2008. Adam's experience working with Stonehaven, Norfolk Rise and Bird in Hand comes through.

ŸŸŸŸŸ Emerson 2012 This spent a hefty 4 years on lees following a second fermentation in bottle. The variety's red-fruited tang is joined by lees-derived truffle, buttered toast and iodine tones, sweeping the fruit into a zone of savouriness. Impressively detailed and very long, this has pulse, crunch and creaminess. The dosage is a measured 4g/l, but I reckon it could go lower in the future. Cork. 12% alc. **Rating** 95 $50 NG

ŸŸŸŸŸ Adelaide Hills Chardonnay 2016 **Rating** 93 **To** 2022 $30 NG
Amelia Reserve Adelaide Hills Shiraz 2015 **Rating** 93 **To** 2024 $45 NG
Adelaide Hills Pinot Noir 2016 **Rating** 92 **To** 2023 $30 NG
Adelaide Hills Shiraz 2016 **Rating** 92 **To** 2024 $25 NG ✪
Adelaide Hills Sauvignon Blanc 2017 **Rating** 91 **To** 2019 $20 NG ✪
Adelaide Hills Rose 2017 **Rating** 91 **To** 2019 $20 NG ✪
ALOFT Adelaide Hills Shiraz 2016 **Rating** 91 **To** 2022 $15 NG ✪

Landaire   ★★★★

PO Box 14, Padthaway, SA 5271 **Region** Padthaway
T 0417 408 147 **www**.landaire.com.au **Open** Not
Winemaker Pete Bissell **Est.** 2012 **Dozens** 2000 **Vyds** 200ha
David and Carolyn Brown have been major grapegrowers in Padthaway over the past 18 years, David with a vineyard and farming background, Carolyn with a background in science. Landaire has evolved from a desire to select small quantities of their best grapes from Glendon vineyard and have them vinified by Pete Bissell, chief winemaker at Balnaves. It has proved a sure-fire recipe for success. A cellar door and accommodation are planned. Exports to the UK, Hong Kong and China.

ŸŸŸŸŸ Single Vineyard Shiraz 2016 It's a luscious shiraz with deep plum, asphalt and blackberry flavours surging through the palate, roasted coffee and cedar wood hitched along for the ride. Everything here feels plush; it's one smooth operator. Screwcap. 14.3% alc. **Rating** 93 **To** 2030 $40 CM

Cabernet Sauvignon 2016 A distinctly chocolatey expression of cabernet, its cassis-filled heart rendered smooth and satiny. There is tannin throughout, but with fruit and oak well out in front. You could argue that this is fractionally overripe, but freshness has not been curtailed; indeed it mounts a pretty seductive case. Screwcap. 14% alc. **Rating** 92 **To** 2032 $40 CM

Block 22 Shiraz 2016 Spirituous, jammed with fruit and oak, soft and free-flowing. This is well into 'gobfuls of fruit' territory. If more is never enough, this will be right up your alley. Cork. 14.5% alc. **Rating** 90 **To** 2028 CM

Landhaus Estate ★★★★★

102 Main Street, Hahndorf, SA 5245 **Region** Barossa Valley
T (08) 8353 8442 **Open** Thurs–Mon 11–5
Winemaker Kane Jaunutis, Shane Harris **Est.** 2002 **Dozens** 15 000
John, Barbara and son Kane Jaunutis purchased Landhaus Estate in 2002, followed by 'The Landhaus' cottage and 1ha vineyard at Bethany. Bethany is the oldest German-established town in the Barossa (1842) and the cottage was one of the first to be built. Kane has worked vintages for Mitolo and Kellermeister, as well as managing East End Cellars, one of Australia's leading fine wine retailers, while John brings decades of owner/management experience and Barbara 20 years in sales and marketing. Rehabilitation of the estate plantings and establishing a grower network have paid handsome dividends. Exports to Canada, Singapore and China.

🍷🍷🍷🍷🍷 **Rare Barossa Valley Shiraz 2013** 'Rare' represents the best parcels of fruit from outstanding vintages, this from the Hoffman vineyard in Ebenezer. A single new French puncheon, 3 years on lees. It is so fresh, with a terrific dark garnet–purple colour; full-bodied with swathes of velvety yet strong tannins. Densely packed fruit, layers of spice and an overall savoury outlook. Demands to be noticed, all in good time. Screwcap. 14.3% alc. **Rating** 97 **To** 2045 $140 JF

🍷🍷🍷🍷🍷 **Classics Barossa Valley Shiraz Mourvedre 2015** 50/50% blend 20 months in French oak (50% new). While there's more grunt to the tannin structure via the integrated oak, shiraz and mourvedre unite their flavours and shapes into a harmonious whole. Vibrant red plums, cherries and blueberries sprinkled with chocolate shavings, cinnamon and crushed juniper berries. Full-bodied with beautiful detail from start to finish. Screwcap. 14% alc. **Rating** 96 **To** 2030 $30 JF

Classics Barossa Valley Mourvedre Grenache Shiraz 2015 There's exceptional quality right across the '15 Landhaus range, with the blends the most thrilling. And here's another at 44/42/14%, adopting low-yielding 70–100yo vines and 16 months in French oak (20% new). Savoury-toned, earthy and spicy, with deep fruit flavours, lithe tannins and excellent length, and so fresh. This is classy stuff. Screwcap. 14% alc. **Rating** 96 **To** 2027 $30 JF

Classics Barossa Valley Shiraz 2015 Dark purple-black; 18 months in French oak (100% new). Every skerrick of rawness has been obliterated; instead woodsy spices and rich vanillan notes. Dark fruits abound, overlaid with cinnamon, cloves and licorice. Full-bodied, fleshy round tannins and chalky acidity, and overall a powerhouse that is not over-the-top and built for the long haul. Screwcap. 14.1% alc. **Rating** 95 **To** 2040 $50 JF

Lane's End Vineyard ★★★★★

885 Mount William Road, Lancefield, Vic 3435 **Region** Macedon Ranges
T (03) 5429 1760 www.lanesend.com.au **Open** By appt
Winemaker Howard Matthews, Kilchurn Wines **Est.** 1985 **Dozens** 500 **Vyds** 2ha
Pharmacist Howard Matthews and family purchased the former Woodend Winery in 2000, with 1.8ha of chardonnay and pinot noir (and a small amount of cabernet franc) dating back to the mid-1980s. The cabernet franc has been grafted over to pinot noir, and the vineyard is now made up of 1ha each of chardonnay and pinot noir. Howard has been making the wines for over a decade.

ΥΥΥΥΥ **Macedon Ranges Pinot Noir 2016** 32yo vines, 4 clones, matured for 19 months in extra-tight-grain French oak (66% new). Classy presentation (especially the label) appropriate for a seriously good pinot with supple cherry and plum fruit. The complex texture reflects the quality of the winemaking. The finish, too, is long and balanced. Screwcap. 13.2% alc. **Rating** 97 **To** 2031 $45 ✪

ΥΥΥΥΥ **Macedon Ranges Chardonnay 2016** The wine pauses fractionally on the finish, but you can't point to anything done or omitted to cause it – repeated visits to the glass giving no further clues. It's flawless when you take the presumption of innocence, and is almost certainly just having a day off. Screwcap. 13% alc. **Rating** 95 **To** 2024 $35 ✪

L'autre Macedon Ranges Pinot Noir 2017 Excellent crimson-purple colour and clarity; Lane's End is establishing a constant style that throws the quality of the fruit onto centrestage. This is a great example, with no whole bunches and no new oak. There's a depth to the red and black cherry fruit that is remarkable, and will underwrite the development of spicy floral notes over the next 3–5 years. Screwcap. 13% alc. **Rating** 95 **To** 2029 $28 ✪

Museum Release Isanda Macedon Ranges Chardonnay 2013 I first tasted this wine 38 months ago in Jan '15, and commented, 'It is bracingly complex, and will have a fascinating future', with a drink-to date of '25 and 94 points. Nothing much has changed, the journey is ongoing. Screwcap. 12.5% alc. **Rating** 94 **To** 2025 $30 ✪

ΥΥΥΥΩ **L'autre Macedon Ranges Pinot Noir 2016** **Rating** 90 **To** 2031 $28

Lange's Frankland Wines ★★★★☆

633 Frankland-Cranbrook Road, Frankland River, WA 6396 **Region** Frankland River
T 0438 511 828 **www**.langesfranklandwines.com.au **Open** Not
Winemaker James Kellie **Est.** 1997 **Dozens** 4000 **Vyds** 13.5ha
This venture involves three generations of the Lange family, with Don and Maxine the grandparents, son Kim and wife Chelsea the second generation, and their children Jack, Ella and Dylan the third generation. The first vines were planted in 1997 and the vineyard now consists of 8ha of shiraz, 3ha of sauvignon blanc and 2.5ha of semillon.

ΥΥΥΥΥ **Old Growth Vines Riesling 2017** These vines are over 50yo, and are doubtless responsible for the intensity and drive of the wine, which is still water-white. Its length is extreme, carried by citrus pith and minerally flavours. Will cruise through the next 20 years. Screwcap. 12% alc. **Rating** 95 **To** 2033 $26 ✪

Shiraz 2013 While the vinification of this wine was identical to the '15, the two wines are a world apart. The colour is deep, the wine pulsating with elegant power that effortlessly unfurls on the palate. The fruits are dark, but not excessively savoury, and the tannins and overall extract are attractive. Screwcap. 14.5% alc. **Rating** 94 **To** 2028 $35

Langmeil Winery ★★★★★

Cnr Para Road/Langmeil Road, Tanunda, SA 5352 **Region** Barossa Valley
T (08) 8563 2595 **www**.langmeilwinery.com.au **Open** 7 days 10.30–4.30
Winemaker Paul Lindner, Tyson Bitter **Est.** 1996 **Dozens** 35 000 **Vyds** 31.4ha
Vines were first planted at Langmeil in the 1840s (it possesses the oldest block of shiraz in Australia), and the first winery on the site, known as Paradale Wines, opened in 1932. In '96, cousins Carl and Richard Lindner with brother-in-law Chris Bitter formed a partnership to acquire and refurbish the winery and its 5ha shiraz vineyard. Another vineyard was acquired in '98, which included cabernet sauvignon and grenache. In late 2012 the Lindner family put a succession plan into action: Richard and Shirley Lindner, and sons Paul and James, have acquired 100% ownership of the business. In terms of management, little changes: Paul has been chief winemaker and James sales and marketing manager since the winery began in '96. Exports to all major markets.

ŶŶŶŶŶ **The Freedom 1843 Barossa Shiraz 2015** It feels lightish at first but it's not. As it breathes it builds and builds. Before long, the full size and extent is apparent. This is a monumental red wine, as seamless as it is solid, its folds of sweet coffee and black-berried flavour sweeping through the palate with quite irresistible force. Tannin is brilliantly well handled; it's the axis around which the density revolves. This wine doesn't tilt at or hope for quality, it declares it. Screwcap. 14.5% alc. **Rating** 97 **To** 2040 $130 CM ✪

ŶŶŶŶŶ **Hallowed Ground Barossa Shiraz 2014** This wine is 4yo and just settling into itself. It's like a soft leather chair near the start of a long life. Coffee cream, blackberry, some floral notes, a rusty kind of earthiness. Texture, power, tannin and length; this has it all dialled in. Diam. 14.5% alc. **Rating** 95 **To** 2034 $50 CM
Pure Eden Barossa Shiraz 2015 High in oak, fruit and quality. This is warm but fresh, its raspberry, boysenberry and violet-like drivers layered with cedar wood and sweet smoke, fine-grained tannin pulling everything into a neat, powerful package. Screwcap. 15% alc. **Rating** 94 **To** 2032 $130 CM

ŶŶŶŶŶ **Wattle Brae Eden Valley Riesling 2017** **Rating** 93 **To** 2026 $30 CM
Della Mina Sangiovese Barbera 2016 **Rating** 93 **To** 2023 $25 CM ✪
Black Beauty Malbec 2016 **Rating** 93 **To** 2026 $25 CM ✪
Prime Cut Barossa Shiraz 2016 **Rating** 92 **To** 2025 $25 CM ✪
Kernel Barossa Cabernet Sauvignon 2014 **Rating** 92 **To** 2027 $50 CM
Blockbuster Barossa Shiraz 2016 **Rating** 91 **To** 2024 $25 CM
Jackaman's Barossa Cabernet 2015 **Rating** 91 **To** 2025 $55 CM
Blacksmith Barossa Cabernet 2015 **Rating** 91 **To** 2026 $30 CM
Hangin' Snakes Barossa Shiraz 2016 **Rating** 90 **To** 2024 $20 CM ✪
Resurrection Barossa Mataro 2015 **Rating** 90 **To** 2023 $20 CM ✪

Lansdowne Vineyard ★★★★

180 Forreston Road, Forreston, SA 5233 **Region** Adelaide Hills
T 0402 505 763 **www**.lansdownevineyard.com **Open** Not
Winemaker Tim Smith, Simon Greenleaf **Est.** 2003 **Dozens** 500 **Vyds** 18.6ha
The vineyard was planted between 1996 and 2004, and takes its name from the late-Victorian house built at Forreston in 1896. Since the 1940s, a 3m hedge has been trimmed with 'Lansdowne' written into it, creating a local landmark. Janet and Brendan Cameron purchased the house and existing vineyard in 2002, and have since retrained or replanted the current mix of viognier, chardonnay, semillon, pinot gris, pinot noir and sauvignon blanc. Most of the grapes are sold, but since '05 small quantities have been held for the Lansdowne Vineyard label. The Camerons are moving to an organic regime.

ŶŶŶŶŶ **Adelaide Hills Pinot Grigio 2017** 40% of the juice fermented in used French barriques, the balance cool-fermented in stainless steel. Matured on lees, blended and bottled in Aug. This is a very useful pinot grigio. It has intensity and complexity to its array of pear, apple and citrus flavours, with texture also in the bargain. Screwcap. 12% alc. **Rating** 93 **To** 2023 $22 ✪
Peloton Adelaide Hills Syrah 2016 From the Talunga Ridge vineyard, matured in new and used French oak. A medium-bodied wine offering lots to think about, and to taste. Unless it was sterile-filtered, the most unusual use of partial mlf could cause it to blow up without warning. Casting this question aside, it is vibrantly fresh and spicy, part savoury, part dark-berry fruits. Screwcap. 14% alc. **Rating** 92 **To** 2026 $24 ✪
Adelaide Hills Chardonnay 2016 Estate-grown, matured for 8 months in French barriques. It's not until the second sip that the intensity buried in the wine comes to the surface. It is led by pink grapefruit, nectarine in tow; slippery acidity adding to the length (and appeal). Screwcap. 12.5% alc. **Rating** 91 **To** 2026 $28

Lanz Vineyards

296 Scenic Road, Lyndoch, SA 5351 **Region** Barossa Valley
T 0417 858 967 **www.**lanzvineyards.com **Open** By appt
Winemaker Richard Freebairn **Est.** 1998 **Dozens** 500 **Vyds** 16ha
The major part of the grape production is sold to premium producers in the Barossa Valley. However, Marianne and Thomas Lanz retain enough to make some wines of their own, including shiraz and grenache shiraz mourvedre. Their choice of David Paxton as their vineyard manager is no accident: he is a committed biodynamic grower and all Lanz Vineyards fields are being transformed to biodynamics, focusing on sustainability, soil health, low intervention and a lower carbon footprint. Exports to Switzerland, Denmark and Singapore.

ⓎⓎⓎⓎⓎ **The Soloist Limited Edition Mourvedre 2016** Whole berries, open-fermented, matured for 15 months in used French barriques. No particular magic in the vinification, unless it be preserving the beautiful crimson-purple hue and allowing the varietal fruit free play – red and black cherry, blackberry and a splash of wild herbs. It's inviting from the time you first see its colour through to its aftertaste. Screwcap. 14% alc. **Rating** 93 **To** 2027 $29
Scenic Road Single Vineyard Shiraz 2016 Matured for 15 months in used French barriques. Shows that Barossa Valley shiraz doesn't need to have 14% or above alcohol; here the analysis is 13.8% rounded down to 13.5% to meet EU label requirements. Nor does it need to be embalmed in American oak. The wine's gently spiced black fruits do the talking, and the tannins are ripe. Ready when you are. Screwcap. **Rating** 91 **To** 2026 $25

ⓎⓎⓎⓎ **The Club Grenache Shiraz Mourvedre 2016** **Rating** 89 **To** 2026 $20

Lark Hill

521 Bungendore Road, Bungendore, NSW 2621 **Region** Canberra District
T (02) 6238 1393 **www.**larkhillwine.com.au **Open** Wed–Mon 10–5
Winemaker Dr David Carpenter, Sue Carpenter, Chris Carpenter **Est.** 1978
Dozens 6000 **Vyds** 10.5ha
The Lark Hill vineyard is situated at an altitude of 860m, offering splendid views of the Lake George escarpment. The Carpenters have made wines of real quality, style and elegance from the start, but have defied all the odds (and conventional thinking) with the quality of their pinot noirs in favourable vintages. Significant changes have come in the wake of son Christopher gaining three degrees, including a double in wine science and viticulture through CSU, and also with the biodynamic certification of the vineyard. In 2011 Lark Hill purchased one of the two Ravensworth vineyards from Michael Kirk, with plantings of sangiovese, shiraz, viognier, roussanne and marsanne; they have renamed it Dark Horse and manage it biodynamically.

ⓎⓎⓎⓎⓎ **Canberra District Riesling 2017** Reliably compelling, especially for those schooled in the joys of dry Germanic styles. Pulpy citrus fruits careen along rails of juicy, natural acidity, before a long, crunchy finish with an element of white pepper (a trait I increasingly note as a regional voice). This has a distinctive energy and pulse, with just the right amount of fruit sweetness in the tank. Screwcap. 11.5% alc. **Rating** 96 **To** 2029 $39 NG ❂

ⓎⓎⓎⓎⓎ **Canberra District Gruner Veltliner 2017** **Rating** 93 **To** 2023 $49 NG
Canberra District Chardonnay 2016 **Rating** 91 **To** 2024 $49 NG
Mr.V 2015 **Rating** 91 **To** 2020 $25 NG

Larry Cherubino Wines
★★★★★

3462 Caves Road, Wilyabrup, WA 6280 **Region** Various Western Australia
T (08) 9382 2379 **www.**larrycherubino.com **Open** 7 days 10–5
Winemaker Larry Cherubino, Andrew Siddell **Est.** 2005 **Dozens** 8000 **Vyds** 120ha

Larry Cherubino has had a particularly distinguished winemaking career, first at Hardys Tintara, then Houghton, and thereafter as consultant/Flying Winemaker in Australia, NZ, South Africa, the US and Italy. He has developed three ranges of his own wines: at the top is Cherubino; next The Yard, single vineyard wines from WA; and at last the Ad Hoc label, all regional wines. The range and quality is extraordinary, the prices irresistible. The runaway success of the business has seen the accumulation of 120ha of vineyards, the appointment of additional winemakers, and Larry's own appointment to Robert Oatley Vineyards as director of winemaking. Exports to the UK, the US, Canada, Ireland, Switzerland, Hong Kong, South Korea, Singapore, China and NZ.

Cherubino Pemberton Sauvignon Blanc 2017 Wow. This is as strident, yet enjoyable, as any sauvignon blanc in Australia, fermented and matured in French oak for 4 months. It is a supple, rich and mouthfilling wine with almost freakish balance and mouthfeel, picking up custard apple, peach, banana and a jolt of cleansing acidity to conclude. Screwcap. 13% alc. **Rating** 97 **To** 2021 $35 ✪

Cherubino Beautiful South White Wine 2017 90% sauvignon blanc and 10% semillon, wild yeast, barrel-fermented, matured for 6 months in used French oak. It has intense flavours, but it is the texture and structure of the wine that immediately capture the attention. It is grippy in the best possible way, and there's a mouthwatering reception to it, all in all resulting in a very long palate and a long life ahead. Screwcap. 12% alc. **Rating** 96 **To** 2024 $35 ✪

The Yard Acacia South Frankland River Shiraz 2016 You could hardly ask for a more pitch-perfect Frankland River shiraz. It blends ripeness and impact with savouriness bordering on earthiness. It offers peppercorn and sweet black cherry/plum flavours and comes with an intricate latticework of tannin. It extends through the finish without any problem at all. Smoky oak looks as though it was born to be there. Voila, just like that. Screwcap. 13.9% alc. **Rating** 96 **To** 2034 $35 CM ✪

Cherubino Laissez Faire Riesling 2017 Hand-picked and sorted, wild-fermented, with little added during the vinification, possibly just a sensible amount of SO_2. This is a riesling with the smarts: fruit, alcohol and titratable acidity all read from the same page, crying out for seafood, preferably raw. Screwcap. 11.1% alc. **Rating** 95 **To** 2027 $29 ✪

The Yard Channybearup Pemberton Sauvignon Blanc 2017 This spends a brief period in oak but the fruit bursts through brilliantly. The fruit flavours here are bell clear: apples, tropical fruit, gravel and wood smoke. Excellent intensity and finish. Excellent release. Screwcap. 12.5% alc. **Rating** 95 **To** 2020 $25 CM ✪

Cherubino Laissez Faire Syrah 2016 More restrained than you might expect, but it maintains a slinky smoothness and the finish is long. Peppercorn and black cherry with sweet herb/mint notes and a woodsy undergrowth character. There's a ground-coffee note here too, but a particularly earthen version. Everything here suggests that this wine will develop beautifully over the medium term and beyond. Screwcap. 14% alc. **Rating** 95 **To** 2033 $39 CM

The Yard Riversdale Frankland River Shiraz 2016 Walk up the ramp of flavours and it just seems to keep going. It starts as a frolic of cherries (red and black) but as it progresses it turns deeper and darker; boards of cedar laid straight and tight as an array of fruit, licorice, spice and smoke-like notes strut their way along. It's as commanding as it is compelling. Screwcap. 13.8% alc. **Rating** 95 **To** 2036 $35 CM ✪

Ad Hoc Wallflower Great Southern Riesling 2017 The apple blossom bouquet is as yet a little reticent, but the palate is well and truly open for business. It is bursting with lime, lemon and Granny Smith apple flavours riding on a surge of crispy, crunchy acidity. Screwcap. 12% alc. **Rating** 94 **To** 2032 $19 ✪

Cherubino Porongurup Riesling 2017 Purity meets persistence. There isn't the slightest semblance of a misstep here. It's fine, elegant, powerful where it needs to be, and simply beautiful to drink. Screwcap. 11% alc. **Rating** 94 **To** 2032 $39 CM

Mount Barker Riesling 2017 You could call it juicy and generous, but it would be equally accurate to call it slatey and long. This zesty, mouthwatering, do-it-all riesling engages you with its crunchy apple and lime sorbet characters. Screwcap. 11% alc. **Rating** 94 **To** 2026 $35 CM

Ad Hoc Straw Man Margaret River Sauvignon Blanc Semillon 2017 The bouquet has a distinct crosscut of herbs and grass, the juicy palate with a mix of tropical fruits and a reprise of lemony acidity squeezed over guava. Grade A bargain. **Rating** 94 **To** 2022 $21 ○

Cherubino Laissez Faire Fiano 2017 Larry Cherubino talks about natural winemaking, but gives no taste descriptors. No matter, the textural, slightly savoury, wine walks the walk very nicely. Screwcap. 13.6% alc. **Rating** 94 **To** 2022 $29 ○

Cherubino Frankland River Shiraz 2016 So firm it's almost crunchy. It's all graphite and dark earth, blackberry and crushed cloves. Asphalt too. And peppercorns. It has brood, it has depth, it smokes its way through your mouth, but there are also redcurrant notes; it's not all shade, there's light too. Herb-strewn tannin takes the general theme here and runs with it. Screwcap. 14.3% alc. **Rating** 94 **To** 2036 $55 CM

The Yard Justin Frankland River Shiraz 2016 It presents black cherry, herb flower, campfire and sweet spice notes in elegant form, tannin then rippling over smooth stones through the finish. It never gives up on either fruitiness or savouriness, and adds a gentle, well-integrated creaminess to the texture. Every egg a bird. Screwcap. 14.3% alc. **Rating** 94 **To** 2031 $35 CM

ⴺⴺⴺⴺⴺ **Cherubino Great Southern Riesling 2017 Rating** 93 **To** 2025 $35 CM
Margaret River Semillon 2017 Rating 93 **To** 2024 $35 CM
Ad Hoc Avant Gardening Frankland Cabernet Sauvignon Malbec 2016 **Rating** 93 **To** 2030 $21 CM ○
Pedestal Margaret River Semillon Sauvignon Blanc 2017 Rating 92 **To** 2023 $25 ○
Cherubino Laissez Faire Field Blend 2017 Rating 92 **To** 2023 $29
Ad Hoc Pip Margaret River Rose 2017 Rating 92 **To** 2019 $21 ○
Pedestal Cabernet Merlot 2016 Rating 92 **To** 2028 $25 CM ○

Latitude 34 Wine Co   ★★★★★

St Johns Brook, 283 Yelverton North Road, Yelverton, WA 6281 **Region** Margaret River
T (08) 9417 5633 www.latitude34wineco.com **Open** By appt
Winemaker Mark Thompson, Giulio Corbellani **Est.** 1997 **Dozens** 70 000 **Vyds** 120ha
Family-owned and -operated Latitude 34 Wine Co was established in 1997 – with their first vineyards in the Blackwood Valley (83ha), followed by the St Johns Brook vineyard in Yallingup (37ha) in '98. A 1200t winery with temperature-controlled wine storage was built in 2004. The wines are released under the St Johns Brook, Optimus, The Blackwood, and Crush labels.

ⴺⴺⴺⴺⴺ **St Johns Brook Reserve Margaret River Cabernet Sauvignon 2016** There is more new wood on this cuvee, bridling greater intensity of flavours and age-worthiness. Hand-plunged before spending 9 months in French barriques, this is a pointed cabernet of well alloyed, ball-bearing tannins melding with the cedar oak spice to coat the mouth. Behind lies currant, pastille, olive and bay leaf, to be liberated further with time in the cellar. This is excellent. Screwcap. 14.5% alc. **Rating** 96 **To** 2028 $50 NG ○

Optimus Blackwood Valley Cabernet Sauvignon 2016 From a vineyard that operates to a sustainable creed. The '16 seems to provide a shift in the cabernet paradigm at this estate. Considerably lower in alcohol (13.4%). Substantially more relaxed in the mouth. Less reliant on the oak pillars to impress, this is at once a joy to drink already, as it is prodigiously age-worthy. There is more bite and frisk to the tannins, too, conferring savour to the teeming notes

of blackcurrant, bouquet garni, black olive and violet. Some may think this a bit herbal. I think it more claret-like. Screwcap. **Rating** 95 To 2032 $100 NG
Optimus Blackwood Valley Cabernet Sauvignon 2015 The name alludes to greater ambition and it is evident in spades here, from the denser character of the fruit, the application of oak and the dutifully massaged tannins that are coated with creamy vanilla mocha. In need of time to unravel; patience will be rewarded. Screwcap. 13.9% alc. **Rating** 94 To 2031 $100 NG

ŸŸŸŸŸ St Johns Brook Chardonnay 2015 Rating 93 To 2023 $28 NG
St Johns Brook Shiraz 2015 Rating 93 To 2024 $28 NG
St Johns Brook Cabernet 2015 Rating 93 To 2025 $28 NG
Optimus Blackwood Valley Shiraz 2016 Rating 92 To 2027 $100 NG
St Johns Brook Semillon Sauvignon Blanc 2016 Rating 91 To 2021 $28 NG
St Johns Brook Reserve Shiraz 2016 Rating 91 To 2027 $65 NG
St Johns Brook Cabernet Merlot 2015 Rating 91 To 2024 $28 NG
St Johns Brook Recolte Margaret River Cabernet Sauvignon 2015
Rating 91 To 2021 $24 NG
St Johns Brook Semillon 2017 Rating 90 To 2024 $35 NG
St Johns Brook Recolte Margaret River Chardonnay 2017 Rating 90
To 2021 $24 NG
The Blackwood The Far Side Shiraz Cabernet 2013 Rating 90 To 2025
$45 NG

Laughing Jack   ★★★★★

194 Stonewell Road, Marananga, SA 5355 **Region** Barossa Valley
T (08) 8562 3878 **www.**laughingjackwines.com.au **Open** By appt
Winemaker Shawn Kalleske **Est.** 1999 **Dozens** 5000 **Vyds** 38.88ha
The Kalleske family has many branches in the Barossa Valley. Laughing Jack is owned by Shawn, Nathan, Ian and Carol Kalleske, and Linda Schroeter. The lion's share of the vineyard is planted to shiraz, with lesser amounts of semillon and grenache. Vine age varies considerably, with old dry-grown shiraz the jewel in the crown. In the past the kookaburra was called the laughing jackass, and there is a resident flock of kookaburras in the blue and red gums surrounding the vineyards. Exports to Malaysia, Hong Kong and China.

ŸŸŸŸŸ Moppa Hill Block 6 Barossa Valley Shiraz 2016 Whole berries, open-fermented, 14 days on skins, 20 months in 80% French (12% new) and 20% American hogsheads. This is very full-bodied, the power and concentration deriving from the high quality vineyard, not excessive extraction in the winery, nor even the new oak. It has a spring in its step, with spice and dark licorice threaded through blackberry. Screwcap. 14.5% alc. Rating 95 To 2031 $35 ✪
Jack's Barossa Valley Grenache Shiraz Mourvedre 2016 A 53/25/22% blend from dry-grown estate vineyards, matured for 18 months in used French puncheons. Medium-bodied; a rich mix of red and black fruits, totally avoiding confection. Instead there is a faintly spicy touch to the fresh, supple fruits, balance one of many virtues. This should age very well. Screwcap. 14.5% alc. Rating 95 To 2036 $25 ✪

ŸŸŸŸŸ Jack's Barossa Valley Shiraz 2016 Rating 93 To 2031 $25 ✪
Jack's Barossa Valley Semillon 2017 Rating 91 To 2027 $20 ✪

Laurel Bank   ★★★★★

130 Black Snake Lane, Granton, Tas 7030 **Region** Southern Tasmania
T (03) 6263 5977 **www.**laurelbankwines.com.au **Open** By appt
Winemaker Greer Carland **Est.** 1986 **Dozens** 1500 **Vyds** 3.5ha
Laurel Bank was established by Kerry Carland in 1986, but deliberately kept a low profile by Kerry withholding release of most of its early wines. When the time came, she entered the Royal Hobart Wine Show in '95, and won the Trophy for Most Successful Tasmanian Exhibitor. The moderate slope of the north-facing vineyard overlooking the Derwent River has two radically different soil types, one high vigour, the other low. Intelligent matching of

variety to soil has led to a natural balance and (relative) ease of canopy management – and to balanced wines.

ŶŶŶŶŶ Riesling 2016 Gold medal at Winewise '17; elite gold in the Tasmanian class at Canberra Riesling Challenge '17. The fragrant, flowery bouquet has wafts of lime, lemon and fresh-cut apple, the palate with superb balance and length, the finish with the type of acidity that only Tasmania achieves, and then only by winemakers with an unerring eye for detail. Screwcap. 12.8% alc. **Rating** 95 **To** 2029 $22 **☉**
Pinot Noir 2016 10–25yo vines, 82% whole berries/18% whole bunches, 6 days cold soak, wild-fermented, 15 days on skins, matured for 10 months in French oak (20% new). The bright and lively crimson-purple is an appropriate colour for this elegant yet intense pinot. There is a gentle savoury underplay throughout that supports the deceptively long palate, spices already building, none of this threatening the varietal fruit core or aftertaste of cherry and plum. Screwcap. 13.4% alc. **Rating** 95 **To** 2029 $33 **☉**

ŶŶŶŶŶ Sauvignon Blanc 2017 Rating 90 To 2020 $22
Cabernet Merlot 2016 Rating 90 To 2023 $29

Leasingham ★★★★★

PO Box 57, Clare, SA 5453 **Region** Clare Valley
T 1800 088 711 **www**.leasingham-wines.com.au **Open** Not
Winemaker Paul Lapsley **Est.** 1893 **Dozens** NFP
Leasingham has experienced death by a thousand cuts. First, then owner CWA sold its Rogers vineyard to Tim Adams in 2009, and unsuccessfully endeavoured to separately sell the winemaking equipment and cellar door while retaining the winery. In January '11 Tim purchased the winery, cellar door and equipment, making once proud Leasingham into a virtual winery (or brand). The quality of the wines has not suffered, however. Exports to the UK and Canada.

ŶŶŶŶŶ Classic Clare Riesling 2012 A special cellar release. Luminous green-gold, the bouquet and palate an exercise in harmony. Meyer lemon and lime flavours lead the journey, hints of lightly browned toast in the background. The acidity is essential, but it is likewise simply part of the team. Screwcap. 12.5% alc. **Rating** 98 **To** 2027 $53 **☉**

ŶŶŶŶŶ Classic Clare Vintage Release Riesling 2017 A striking riesling, as much for its 'classic' Clare DNA of tangy acidity doused in lime cordial, as for its herbal complexity. Orange blossom, honeysuckle and sherbet are nicely offset by an undercarriage of wild fennel that is reminiscent of the Mediterranean in the best sense. Long. A strong pulse bodes well for the future. Screwcap. 12.5% alc. **Rating** 94 **To** 2029 $35 NG

ŶŶŶŶŶ Bin 56 Clare Valley Cabernet Malbec 2015 Rating 93 To 2031 $20 **☉**
Classic Clare Cabernet Sauvignon 2016 Rating 92 To 2028 $72 NG
Classic Clare Shiraz 2016 Rating 90 To 2031 $72 NG

Leconfield ★★★★☆

Riddoch Highway, Coonawarra, SA 5263 **Region** Coonawarra
T (08) 8737 2326 **www**.leconfieldwines.com **Open** Mon–Fri 11–4.30, w'ends 11–4
Winemaker Paul Gordon, Tim Bailey **Est.** 1974 **Dozens** 25 000 **Vyds** 43.7ha
Sydney Hamilton purchased the property that was to become Leconfield in 1974, having worked in the family wine business for over 30 years until his retirement in the mid-'50s. When he acquired the property and set about planting it he was 76, and reluctantly bowed to family pressure to sell Leconfield to nephew Richard in '81. Richard has progressively increased the vineyards to their present level, over 75% dedicated to cabernet sauvignon, the winery's specialty. Exports to most major markets.

♥♥♥♥♥ **The Sydney Reserve Coonawarra Cabernet Sauvignon 2014** A one-off celebration of the 40th anniversary of Leconfield, established by Sydney Hamilton when he planted the first vines in '74 and famously advertised for 'experienced women' to work in the vineyards. This is a suitably rich cabernet, blackcurrant and bay leaf flavours nestled in a bed of new French oak. Screwcap. 14% alc. **Rating** 95 To 2039

McLaren Vale Shiraz 2016 From estate vines planted by branches of the Hamilton family over the past five decades, matured in French and American oak. It is only medium-bodied, but flooded with dark fruits, and given texture, structure and balance by fine but persistent tannins on the finish. Screwcap. 14.5% alc. **Rating** 94 **To** 2036 $26

Coonawarra Merlot 2016 I enjoy this style of medium to full-bodied merlot, with savoury sage, earth and black olive running alongside purple and black fruits, structure provided by fine tannins that are partly ex oak, partly ex fruit. The excellent balance will stand the wine in good stead for many years. Screwcap. 14.5% alc. **Rating** 94 **To** 2036 $26 ✪

Coonawarra Cabernet Franc 2016 Released as a single varietal only in outstanding vintages, matured in used hogsheads for 15 months. This certainly meets the Leconfield criteria for release. It has fragrance verging on perfume, the medium-bodied palate with juicy red and purple berries, the tannins positively silky. All the right decisions were made in vinification. Screwcap. 14% alc. **Rating** 94 **To** 2026 $29 ✪

♥♥♥♥♡ **Coonawarra Cabernet Sauvignon 2016** Rating 91 To 2036 $35
Syn Rouge Sparkling Shiraz NV Rating 90 $18

Leeuwin Estate   ★★★★★

Stevens Road, Margaret River, WA 6285 **Region** Margaret River
T (08) 9759 0000 **www.leeuwinestate.com.au Open** 7 days 10–5
Winemaker Tim Lovett, Phil Hutchison **Est.** 1973 **Dozens** 50 000 **Vyds** 121ha
This outstanding winery and vineyard is owned by the Horgan family, founded by Denis and Tricia, who continue their involvement with son Justin Horgan and daughter Simone Furlong now joint chief executives. The Art Series Chardonnay is, in my opinion, Australia's finest example, based on the wines of the last 30 vintages. The move to screwcap brought a large smile to the faces of those who understand just how superbly the wine ages. The large estate plantings, coupled with strategic purchases of grapes from other growers, provide the base for high quality Art Series Cabernet Sauvignon and Shiraz; the hugely successful, quick-selling Art Series Riesling and Sauvignon Blanc; and lower priced Prelude and Siblings wines. Exports to all major markets.

♥♥♥♥♥ **Art Series Margaret River Chardonnay 2015** Generous of flavour and texture, imparted by Leeuwin's stamp of extended skin contact, an approach that demands impeccably ripe fruit. White peach and nectarine notes are strung pitch-perfect across scales of clotted-cream oak and juicy acidity. Long and pliant. Each piece of the jigsaw is in perfect synchronicity. A pedigreed wine boasting an impressive track record. I have had older vintages reminiscent of top Meursault. Screwcap. 14% alc. **Rating** 96 **To** 2027 $102 NG

Art Series Margaret River Sauvignon Blanc Semillon 2013 Barrel-fermented and aged in French oak for 9 months, this relies on vanilla/cedar pillars to sashay aged semillon's lemon curd and spring meadow scents along the zest and gentle herbaceous waft of the sauvignon. This is delicious. Complex, persistent and compelling of intensity and length, this is not at the finish line yet. Screwcap. 13.5% alc. **Rating** 95 **To** 2023 $37 NG

Prelude Vineyards Margaret River Chardonnay 2016 Death, taxes and Leeuwin Estate chardonnay. This may 'only' be the Prelude version, but its quality is as clear as a bright blue sky. Pure stone fruit, sweet oak, pear and a cleansing flush of citrus through the finish. It builds, satisfies and refreshes. Elegance and power in one. Screwcap. 13.5% alc. **Rating** 94 **To** 2023 $34 CM

ŸŸŸŸŸ Art Series Sauvignon Blanc 2017 Rating 93 To 2022 $30 NG
Art Series Cabernet Sauvignon 2014 Rating 93 To 2026 $70 NG
Art Series Sauvignon Blanc 2016 Rating 92 To 2020 $30 CM
Siblings Shiraz 2016 Rating 92 To 2022 $23 NG ✪
Prelude Vineyards Cabernet 2014 Rating 92 To 2023 $28 NG
Siblings Sauvignon Blanc 2017 Rating 91 To 2019 $22 NG ✪
Pinot Noir Chardonnay Brut 2014 Rating 91 $35 NG
Art Series Shiraz 2015 Rating 90 To 2021 $36 NG

Lenton Brae Wines   ★★★★★

3887 Caves Road, Margaret River, WA 6285 **Region** Margaret River
T (08) 9755 6255 **www.**lentonbrae.com **Open** 7 days 10–5
Winemaker Edward Tomlinson **Est.** 1982 **Dozens** NFP **Vyds** 9ha
The late architect Bruce Tomlinson built a strikingly beautiful winery (heritage listed by
the Shire of Busselton), now in the hands of winemaker son Edward. Ed consistently makes
elegant wines in classic Margaret River style. A trip to Pomerol in Bordeaux to research
merlot was an indication of his commitment. Exports to the UK, Indonesia and Singapore.

ŸŸŸŸŸ **Wilyabrup Margaret River Cabernet Sauvignon 2013** Includes 6% merlot.
Estate-grown, hand-picked, matured for 20 months in French barriques
(40% new). The oldest and the best of the Lenton Brae cabernets in this tasting,
the texture superfine, the fruit with gently sweet cassis flavours, and all-round
purity and balance. Screwcap. 14% alc. **Rating** 96 To 2043 $70 ✪
Wilyabrup Margaret River Semillon Sauvignon Blanc 2015 Still as fresh
as a daisy, proving beyond doubt that this blend can handle – indeed be improved
by – cellaring for 5+ years, for it's got a way to go yet. It is tilted towards the green
capsicum/snow pea end of the spectrum, citrus and oak taking it across the bridge
to gooseberry and guava nuances. Screwcap. 12.5% alc. **Rating** 95 To 2022 $60
Wilyabrup Margaret River Chardonnay 2015 Archetypal Margaret River
chardonnay, generous and rich, yet not flabby. Stone-fruit flavours are foremost,
with a hint of nougat, citrus-tinged acidity picking up the pace on the finish.
Screwcap. 13.5% alc. **Rating** 95 To 2023 $60
Margaret River Cabernet Merlot 2016 46% cabernet sauvignon, 45% merlot,
9% petit verdot. Very well assembled. Fragrant, supple and smooth, complexity
coming from the fruit rather than from oak and/or tannins. It's far from a simple
fruit-bomb style, with cassis/blackcurrant, spice and a hint of bay leaf all woven
together on the long, medium-bodied palate. Screwcap. 14% alc. **Rating** 94
To 2031 $28 ✪
Lady Douglas Margaret River Cabernet Sauvignon 2016 Includes 5%
malbec and 3% merlot. Unsurprisingly, cabernet rules the roost, along with the
firm tannins expected of the variety. Fragrant cassis and cedar aromas lead into a
pure palate with a linear profile that is most impressive and satisfying. Screwcap.
14% alc. **Rating** 94 To 2031 $30 ✪
Wilyabrup Margaret River Cabernet Sauvignon 2014 The colour is
fractionally advanced for its age, but the fruit, tannins and oak are in the process
of becoming welded to each other, and in another 3–4 years the union will be
complete. Its future stretches out for a further decade or so. Screwcap. 14% alc.
Rating 94 To 2035 $70

ŸŸŸŸŸ Margaret River Shiraz 2016 Rating 91 To 2029 $30
Margaret River Semillon Sauvignon Blanc 2017 Rating 90 To 2020 $22

Leo Buring   ★★★★★

Sturt Highway, Nuriootpa, SA 5355 **Region** Eden Valley/Clare Valley
T 1300 651 650 **Open** Not
Winemaker Peter Munro **Est.** 1934 **Dozens** NFP

Between 1965 and 2000, Leo Buring was Australia's foremost producer of rieslings, with a rich legacy left by former winemaker John Vickery. After veering away from its core business into other varietal wines, it has now refocused on riesling. Top of the range are the Leonay and Leopold Tasmania rieslings, supported by Clare Valley and Eden Valley rieslings at significantly lower prices.

ŸŸŸŸŸ **Leopold Tasmania Riesling 2017** DW U20. As usual the fruit for this release is grown on the highly regarded White Hills vineyard. The aromas run the gamut from scented herbs through just-squeezed citrus to sweeter blossom-like notes. The palate shows the soft but pinpointed intensity that Tasmanian riesling can achieve, brimming with juicy flavours, but taut and precise, the acidity fine yet unwavering. Screwcap. 12.5% alc. **Rating** 96 **To** 2027 $40 SC ✪

Leonay Riesling 2017 DW U15 Polish Hill River. One of the best Leonays for some years. Not every maker got the acidity right in this vintage, and there is wonderful quality awaiting those who did, as you'll find here. Its lime leaf aromas and tinkling acidity are the marks of a wine with a great future. Screwcap. 12.5% alc. **Rating** 95 **To** 2037 $40

ŸŸŸŸŸ **Clare Valley Riesling Dry 2017 Rating** 92 **To** 2027 $20 SC ✪

Leogate Estate Wines ★★★★★

1693 Broke Road, Pokolbin, NSW 2320 **Region** Hunter Valley
T (02) 4998 7499 **www.**leogate.com.au **Open** 7 days 10–5
Winemaker Mark Woods **Est.** 2009 **Dozens** 30 000 **Vyds** 127.5ha
Since purchasing the substantial Brokenback Vineyard in 2009 (a key part of the original Rothbury Estate, with vines over 40 years old), Bill and Vicki Widin have wasted no time. Initially the Widins leased the Tempus Two winery, but prior to the '13 vintage they completed the construction of their own winery and cellar door. They have also expanded the range of varieties, supplementing the long-established 30ha of shiraz, 25ha of chardonnay and 3ha of semillon with between 0.5 and 2ha of each of verdelho, viognier, gewurztraminer, pinot gris and tempranillo. They have had a string of wine-show successes for their very impressive portfolio. In '16 Leogate purchased a 61ha certified organic vineyard at Gulgong (Mudgee) planted to shiraz, cabernet sauvignon and merlot. Exports to the US, Malaysia, Hong Kong and China.

ŸŸŸŸŸ **The Basin Reserve Hunter Valley Shiraz 2013** An imperious wine from a region that, at its best, is defined by the savoury, firm, polished-leather tannins embedded in a highly complex expression. Here lilac florals, smoked deli meats, black olives and an umami thread of bouillon are all tamed by the regional genetics, assisted by well applied oak (15% new, all French, 14 months) and by tempered acidity. Screwcap. 14% alc. **Rating** 97 **To** 2025 $150 NG ✪

ŸŸŸŸŸ **Creek Bed Reserve Hunter Valley Semillon 2014** This is beginning to exert authority on the cusp of aged complexity: a plume of lemon oil, freshly lain tatami mat, grapefruit pulp and quince with a gentle smear of buttered toast, all shimmying along a juicy finish of persuasive length. This will continue to age supremely well. Screwcap. 11% alc. **Rating** 96 **To** 2034 $30 NG ✪

Western Slopes Reserve Hunter Valley Shiraz 2013 Made in an identical manner to the lauded Basin, this is more about fruit, teeming and exuberant across its mulberry, currant and iodine tones from the outset. Sweet, plush and hedonistic, at least as far as the Hunter goes. The regional tannic restraint is palpable, yet looser and more joyous. For the medium term. Screwcap. 14% alc. **Rating** 96 **To** 2023 $150 NG

Museum Release Creek Bed Reserve Hunter Valley Semillon 2011 A wonderful vintage in the Hunter that miraculously – despite the bottle age – is still of talc, citric twine and compelling energy. Featherweight and glimpsing ever-so-slightly the toast and lanolin of age, this will proceed into a long future. All the parts are impeccably bound. Just be patient! Not as mellifluous as the '14, but likely a longer keeper. Screwcap. 11% alc. **Rating** 95 **To** 2035 $70 NG

Creek Bed Reserve Hunter Valley Chardonnay 2013 There is good chardonnay springing from the Hunter despite climatic challenges. Moreover, the soft, peachy fruit makes for a refreshing change to the taut, more linear expression that defines cool-climate styles. A meld of a spontaneous ferment in barrel and a tank-fermented component, with partial mlf across the former, this is plush and juicy. The oak and mineral thread serve as restraining orders across the flush stone-fruit allusions and core of nougat and raw cashew. Screwcap. 13% alc. **Rating** 94 To 2023 $40 NG

ɁɁɁɁɁ **Brokenback Vineyard Shiraz 2013** Rating 93 To 2021 $60 NG
Museum Release Brokenback Vineyard Semillon 2011 Rating 92 To 2023 $22 NG ❂
Museum Release Creek Bed Reserve Chardonnay 2011 Rating 92 To 2020 $50 NG
Brokenback Vineyard Shiraz 2015 Rating 92 To 2024 $40 NG
Brokenback Vineyard Chardonnay 2011 Rating 91 To 2022 $26 NG

Lerida Estate   ★★★★★

The Vineyards, Old Federal Highway, Lake George, NSW 2581 **Region** Canberra District
T (02) 6295 6640 www.leridaestate.com.au **Open** 7 days 10–5
Winemaker Malcolm Burdett **Est.** 1997 **Dozens** 6000 **Vyds** 7.93ha
Lerida Estate, owned by Jim Lumbers and Anne Caine, owes a great deal to the inspiration of Dr Edgar Riek. It is planted immediately to the south of Edger's former Lake George vineyard, and likewise planted mainly to pinot noir (Lerida also has smaller plantings of pinot gris, chardonnay, shiraz, merlot, cabernet franc and viognier). The Glenn Murcutt–designed winery, barrel room, cellar door and cafe complex has spectacular views over Lake George. In May 2017 Jim and Anne decided to retire, and Lerida was purchased by Michael McRoberts. Exports to China.

ɁɁɁɁɁ **Cullerin Canberra District Chardonnay 2017** This makes it all look so easy: hand-picked, wild-fermented, 40% mlf, matured for 8 months in French oak (40% new), the best barrels selected for this wine. It tastes every bit as ripe as it should – interesting given that the vinification of each Lerida parcel is identical. Management of the new oak is the key to the wine, so well integrated and balanced that it's easy to walk past it. Screwcap. 13.5% alc. **Rating** 95 To 2029 $38
Canberra District Shiraz Viognier 2016 Consistently one of the best of its portfolio. The bright crimson colour reflects the co-fermentation, as does the silky palate and its profusion of berry fruits. Tannins and French oak play supporting roles in a very well made wine from a top vintage. Screwcap. 14.3% alc. **Rating** 95 To 2031 $75

ɁɁɁɁɁ **Canberra District Chardonnay 2017** Rating 93 To 2027 $24 ❂
Canberra District Chardonnay 2016 Rating 93 To 2022 $24
Lake George Canberra District Pinot Noir 2017 Rating 92 To 2027 $26
Canberra District Botrytis Pinot Gris 2017 Rating 92 To 2024 $39
Cullerin Saignee 2017 Rating 91 To 2021 $28
Canberra District Shiraz 2016 Rating 91 To 2023 $26
Orange Tempranillo 2017 Rating 90 To 2023 $26
Orange Tempranillo 2016 Rating 90 To 2026

Lethbridge Wines   ★★★★★

74 Burrows Road, Lethbridge, Vic 3222 **Region** Geelong
T (03) 5281 7279 www.lethbridgewines.com **Open** Mon–Fri 11–3, w'ends 11–5
Winemaker Ray Nadeson, Maree Collis **Est.** 1996 **Dozens** 6000 **Vyds** 10ha
Lethbridge was founded by scientists Ray Nadeson, Maree Collis and Adrian Thomas. In Ray's words, 'Our belief is that the best wines express the unique character of special places'. As well as understanding the importance of terroir, the partners have built a unique straw-bale winery, designed to recreate the controlled environment of cellars and caves in Europe.

Winemaking is no less ecological: hand-picking, indigenous yeast fermentation, small open fermenters, pigeage (foot-stomping) and minimal handling throughout the maturation process are all part and parcel of the highly successful Lethbridge approach. Ray also has a distinctive full-blown style with chardonnay and pinot noir. There is a contract-winemaking limb to the business. Exports to the UK, Denmark, Singapore, Thailand and China.

ΨΨΨΨΨ **Dr Nadeson Riesling 2017** Ripe quince, nashi pear and red apple are punctuated by apricot and pith, sluicing across the palate on cylinders of juicy natural acidity and a bit of pucker. Long. Emphatic. Textural. This is a complex riesling of an effortless intensity, seldom experienced on these shores. Palpably dry, with just a lick of sweetness to tame the acidic DNA of the variety. Screwcap. 12% alc. **Rating** 96 **To** 2032 $32 NG **☉**

The Bartl Geelong Chardonnay 2016 A homage to Stefan Bartl, a meticulous vineyard worker. This is a richly flavoured chardonnay corseted by pillars of judiciously appointed cedar oak, a crunchy mineral core and palate-whetting acidity, making one crave for another glass. The finish flows long without pucker or rasp. Stone fruits, ginger, toasted hazelnuts and cashew flavours abound. Screwcap. 13.5% alc. **Rating** 95 **To** 2026 $45 NG

Allegra Geelong Chardonnay 2014 Vineyard outbreaks of millerandage caused low yields for an already meagre-yielding plot. Ripe stone fruit, toasted nuts, marzipan and violet crumble all run along seams of vanillan oak, which is tucked in for focus and further complexity. Pungent mineral and tangy acidity keep it from OTT territory. Screwcap. 13.5% alc. **Rating** 95 **To** 2022 $85 NG

Pyrenees Nebbiolo 2014 Nebbiolo shows great promise in the Pyreness, and this wine attests to that bright future. The cliches ring true with scents of dried flowers, orange rind, sour cherry, wood smoke, twig and sandalwood, segueing to a brisk, mid-weighted palate etched with nebbiolo's mosaic of spider-web tannins and febrile acidity. This is very good. Screwcap. 13.5% alc. **Rating** 95 **To** 2024 $50 NG

Geelong Shiraz 2016 This is immaculately poised, beaming violet, wakame and licorice scents over a bow of bouncy blue fruits. It holds its alcohol effortlessly and strikes a pose between peppery cool-climate compactness and right-on-the-money ripeness. Highly aromatic and finely wrought, this impressive wine unravels across a detailed weave of tannin, with effusive acidity towing it all long. Screwcap. 14.5% alc. **Rating** 94 **To** 2024 $45 NG

Il regalo di compleanno Pyrenees Nebbiolo 2015 Sweeter and easier to approach in its youth than the '14, this is still prime nebbiolo. Red cherries and darker berries, violets, autumnal forest floor. The spine of tannins is not to be taken lightly, but the exuberance of fruit makes them easier to breach. Sappy and energetic. Enjoy this now and across the next decade. Screwcap. 14% alc. **Rating** 94 **To** 2025 $50 NG

ΨΨΨΨΨ **Geelong Chardonnay 2016** Rating 93 To 2023 $45 NG
Pinot Gris 2017 Rating 93 To 2021 $32 NG
Malakoff Vineyard Shiraz 2016 Rating 92 To 2023 $45 NG
Geelong Pinot Noir 2016 Rating 90 To 2022 $45 NG

Leura Park Estate   ★★★★☆

1400 Portarlington Road, Curlewis, Vic 3222 **Region** Geelong
T (03) 5253 3180 **www.**leuraparkestate.com.au **Open** W'ends 10.30–5 (7 days Jan)
Winemaker Darren Burke **Est.** 1995 **Dozens** 5000 **Vyds** 15.94ha
Leura Park Estate's vineyard is planted to chardonnay (50%), pinot noir, pinot gris, sauvignon blanc, riesling and shiraz. Owners David and Lyndsay Sharp are committed to minimal interference in the vineyard, and have expanded the estate-grown wine range to include Vintage Grande Cuvee. The onsite winery has been in operation since 2010, and has led to increased production and ongoing wine-show success. Exports to South Korea and Singapore.

ΨΨΨΨΨ **Bellarine Peninsula Shiraz 2016** Cool-climate shiraz to its back teeth, but ripe and generously proportioned. This is in fine voice. Black cherries, plums, black pepper, cloves, wood smoke. A wide gamut of flavours. Roasted nut and garden herb characters too, though ripe fruit is in charge. Cracking wine. Screwcap. 14% alc. **Rating** 95 **To** 2030 $35 CM ✪

Limited Release Block 1 Reserve Chardonnay 2016 Glowing straw-yellow in colour, but fresh, lively and powerful in the mouth. This is a wine of drive and reach. White and yellow peach, nashi pear, lemon curd, flint and fresh-roasted nuts. It puts on a classy show. Screwcap. 13.5% alc. **Rating** 94 **To** 2023 $45 CM

🍷🍷🍷🍷🍷 **25 d'Gris Bellarine Peninsula Pinot Gris 2017** Rating 91 To 2020 $28 CM
Bellarine Peninsula Rose 2017 Rating 91 To 2020 $25 CM
Bellarine Peninsula Pinot Noir 2016 Rating 91 To 2024 $33 CM
Geelong Sauvignon Blanc 2017 Rating 90 To 2020 $25 CM
Blanc de Blanc 2017 Rating 90 $30 CM

 # Levrier by Jo Irvine

PO Box 838, Lyndoch, SA 5355 **Region** South Australia
T (08) 8562 3888 **www.**levrierwines.com.au **Open** Not
Winemaker Joanne Irvine **Est.** 2017 **Dozens** 3000

What do I and Jo Irvine have in common? The only person in the world able to answer that question is myself, not – as you might guess – Jo. Because I'm sure she doesn't know that in my younger days I was a part-owner of two greyhounds, neither of which were as fast as those they raced against. Levrier is French for greyhound, and Jo has looked after retired racing greyhounds for 20 years, currently Maggie (12 years) and Georgia (4 years), who hang out at her winery. The wines she now makes are given the names of famous racing greyhounds. All of which has precious little to do with Jo's second career as a skilled contract winemaker. Aged 35, she gave up her occupation as a theatre nurse and joined her father, Jim Irvine in the winemaking game. Jo had enjoyed gap years travelling internationally and doing vintages in the US. She made wines at Irvine, her father's winery, notably his Grand Merlot, before he sold the business. Jo was in no hurry to hang her own shingle up until all the pieces were in place: grape supply, winemaking, maturation and packaging. The old saying 'slow boat to China' fits well with Jo's wines.

🍷🍷🍷🍷🍷 **Argos Single Vineyard Eden Valley Shiraz 2014** Selectiv'-harvested, whole-berry fermentation, 66% on skins 7–10 days, then to French oak (30% new) 33% on skins 2–3 months, and finally maturation in new French oak for 18–24 months. Overall 40% new oak after a best barrels selection, and it all shows – it will need 5+ years in bottle to allow the fruit to gain primacy. Screwcap. 14.5% alc. **Rating** 95 **To** 2039 $50

Anubis Single Vineyard Eden Valley Cabernet Sauvignon 2014 An exceedingly complex vinification, with portions going in and out of tank and in and out of new French hogsheads. The wine is so full-bodied it takes all the moves in its stride, with blackcurrant fruit and expansive tannins helping provide balance and length. Screwcap. 14% alc. **Rating** 95 **To** 2044 $50

🍷🍷🍷🍷🍷 **Meslier Brut Rose NV** Rating 91 $45

Liebich Wein

151 Steingarten Road, Rowland Flat, SA 5352 **Region** Barossa Valley
T (08) 8524 4543 **www.**liebichwein.com.au **Open** Wed–Mon 11–5
Winemaker Ron Liebich **Est.** 1992 **Dozens** 900 **Vyds** 11.93ha

The Liebich family have been grapegrowers and winemakers at Rowland Flat since 1919, with CW 'Darkie' Liebich one of the great local characters. His nephew Ron began making wine in '69, but it was not until '92 that he and wife Janet began selling wine under the Liebich Wein label. The business has grown surely but steadily, a new warehouse commissioned in 2008 vastly improving storage and handling capacity. Exports to the UK, Denmark, Germany, Switzerland and China.

ŸŸŸŸŸ **Rare Semillon NV** Just 3 barrels of this 20yo fortified semillon released in '17 to celebrate the 25th anniversary of the winery. Mid-amber with a lighter rim; heady aromas and flavours of sultanas soaked in brandy, light fruitcake, panforte, spices, glace lemon and plenty of savoury umami notes. It's balanced and slinky with the spirit beautifully integrated and the refreshing acidity giving it terrific drive. 375ml. Cork. 20% alc. **Rating** 95 $70 JF

Lillypilly Estate

47 Lillypilly Road, Leeton, NSW 2705 **Region** Riverina
T (02) 6953 4069 **www.**lillypilly.com **Open** Mon–Sat 10–5.30, Sun by appt
Winemaker Robert Fiumara **Est.** 1982 **Dozens** 12000 **Vyds** 27.9ha
Botrytised white wines are by far the best offering from Lillypilly, with the Noble Muscat of Alexandria unique to the winery. These wines have both style and intensity of flavour and can age well. Their table wine quality is always steady – a prime example of not fixing what is not broken. Exports to the UK, the US, Canada and China.

ŸŸŸŸŸ **Family Reserve Noble Blend 2016** Made with sauvignon blanc, semillon and vermentino. It's a full-on style with honey and apricot jam flavours pouring through the palate. The finish, importantly, is cut with fresh lime and cumquat, thus lending the ultra sweetness some zip. There's certainly no shortage of flavour. 375ml. Screwcap. 12% alc. **Rating** 92 **To** 2023 $27 CM

Lindeman's (Coonawarra) ★★★★★

58 Queensbridge Street, Southbank, Vic 3006 (postal) **Region** Coonawarra
T 1300 651 650 **www.**lindemans.com **Open** Not
Winemaker Brett Sharpe **Est.** 1965 **Dozens** NFP
The Lindeman's Coonawarra vineyards have assumed greater importance than ever thanks to the move towards single region wines. The Coonawarra Trio of Limestone Ridge Vineyard Shiraz Cabernet, St George Vineyard Cabernet Sauvignon and Pyrus Cabernet Sauvignon Merlot Malbec are all of exemplary consistency and quality.

ŸŸŸŸŸ **Coonawarra Trio Limestone Ridge Vineyard Shiraz Cabernet 2016** Rarely, if ever, misses a beat. Entirely characteristic of the vineyard on the bouquet, with blackberry and raspberry showing through, and elements of mint, chocolate and licorice in attendance. A beautifully elegant palate, fine and lively and silky in texture. Melting tannins carry the flavours effortlessly through the long finish. Screwcap. 14% alc. **Rating** 96 **To** 2041 $70 SC ✪
Coonawarra Trio St George Vineyard Cabernet Sauvignon 2016 Shows the plush, sweet-fruited side of Coonawarra cabernet, but the structure is impeccable. Aromas of blackcurrant and blackberry are supported by vanillan oak and tinged with a hint of leafiness, and the flavours, generous but undoubtedly elegant, flow smoothly through the length of the palate, the tannin building quietly without distracting or dominating. Screwcap. 14.5% alc. **Rating** 95 **To** 2040 $70 SC
Coonawarra Trio Pyrus Cabernet Sauvignon Merlot Malbec 2016 The most 'fruit-driven' of the trio, with each component of the blend eager to express itself. Blackcurrant, mulberry and raspberry dominate the aroma and flavour spectrum, with savoury, cedary oak sitting in the background. There's a fresh, sappy feel about the tannin, and of the three it seems the least evolved. Time will remedy that of course. Screwcap. 14% alc. **Rating** 94 **To** 2040 $70 SC

Lindeman's (Karadoc)

44 Johns Way, Karadoc, Vic 3496 **Region** South East Australia
T 1300 651 650 **www.**lindemans.com **Open** Not
Winemaker Wayne Falkenberg **Est.** 1974 **Dozens** NFP

This is the production centre for many of the TWE premium (an elastic term) wines, variously making and/or bottling them. The very large winery also allows all-important economies of scale and is the major processing centre for TWE's beverage wine sector (casks, flagons and low-priced bottles).

ŸŸŸŸŸ **Bin 45 Cabernet Sauvignon 2017** The best of the red wines from '17 under this label. It has remarkable texture and structure, and good length and balance. Screwcap. 13.5% alc. **Rating** 90 **To** 2021 $10 ✪

Lindenderry at Red Hill   ★★★★★

142 Arthurs Seat Road, Red Hill, Vic 3937 **Region** Mornington Peninsula
T (03) 5989 2933 **www**.lindenderry.com.au **Open** W'ends 11–5
Winemaker Barney Flanders **Est.** 1999 **Dozens** 1000 **Vyds** 3.35ha
Lindenderry at Red Hill is a sister operation to Lancemore Hill in the Macedon Ranges and Lindenwarrah at Milawa. It has a five-star country-house hotel, conference facilities, a function area, day spa and restaurant on 16ha of gardens, and also has a little over 3ha of vineyards, planted equally to pinot noir and chardonnay over 15 years ago. Notwithstanding the reputation of the previous winemakers for Lindenderry, the wines being made by Barney Flanders are excellent. He has made the most of the estate-grown grapes, adding cream to the cake by sourcing some excellent Grampians shiraz.

ŸŸŸŸŸ **Reserve Grampians Shiraz 2016** Comparing Australian wine to French benchmarks is, in a way, a vainglorious waste of time. Perversely, though, it is fascinating and I am writing this note, so you will simply have to accept that Côte-Rôtie is a paragon of syrah to which this noble wine rightly aspires. It is tightly wound across a beam of perfectly tuned oak, smoked meats, an arc of mineral, and pulpy, palate-whetting tannins. Gorgeous scents of violet, vanilla, blueberry and iodine, too. Long, and defined by an extraction regime and taste of the highest order. Screwcap. 13.5% alc. **Rating** 97 **To** 2026 $50 NG ✪

ŸŸŸŸŸ **Grampians Shiraz 2016** This kicks off an exceptional shiraz duo, or is that syrah? Stylistically, perhaps more attuned to the latter. A smear of tapenade across blue to black fruits, dried seaweed, camphor and floral-lilac aromas, sewn by a thread of bright, peppery, clove acidity in parry to the fruit's thrust. This is incredibly refreshing without the reductive bane of contemporary Aussie cool-climate shiraz ... or is that syrah? Will hold, but why wait? Screwcap. 13.5% alc. **Rating** 94 **To** 2024 $35 NG

ŸŸŸŸŸ **Mornington Peninsula Pinot Noir 2016** Rating 93 To 2024 $45 NG
Macedon Ranges Pinot Noir 2016 Rating 93 To 2024 $40 NG
Mornington Peninsula Chardonnay 2016 Rating 92 To 2025 $40 NG
Mornington Peninsula Sparkling Chardonnay 2011 Rating 91 $50 NG

Lino Ramble   ★★★★☆

2 Hall St, McLaren Vale, SA 5171 (postal) **Region** McLaren Vale
T 0409 553 448 **www**.linoramble.com.au **Open** Not
Winemaker Andy Coppard **Est.** 2012 **Dozens** 700
After 20 years of working for other wine companies big and small, both interstate and international, Andy Coppard and Angela Townsend said, 'We've climbed on top of the dog kennel, tied a cape around our necks, held our breaths, and jumped'. And if you are curious about the name (as I was), the story has overtones of James Joyce's stream-of-consciousness mental rambles.

ŸŸŸŸŸ **Ludo McLaren Vale Fiano 2017** From the Lacey vineyard, 30% fermented in French oak, 70% fermented on skins for 60 days. Wow. The faint straw colour and the notes of hay and white blossoms on the bouquet are simply a warm-up for the main event that follows: amazingly fresh and vibrant citrus and oyster shell notes carried on the long palate to the finish and aftertaste. This is oh so fresh. Screwcap. 12.8% alc. **Rating** 95 **To** 2023 $25 ✪

Vinyl Adelaide Hills Pinot Grigio 2017 From the Meingunya vineyard in
Kuitpo; destemmed, pressed, only the free-run juice used. The wine is bright, crisp
and fresh, all the things it should be, no baggage to contend with. Apple, Meyer
lemon and acidity cleanse the mouth. Excellent example. Screwcap. 12.4% alc.
Rating 94 To 2020 $20 ❍

Red Rover Adelaide Hills Pinot Noir 2016 Rating 92 To 2022 $45 CM
Knuckle Bones Adelaide Hills Nebbiolo 2016 Rating 92 To 2023 $40
Blind Man's Bluff McLaren Vale Bastardo 2017 Rating 92 To 2021 $30
Tom Bowler McLaren Vale Nero d'Avola 2016 Rating 90 To 2019 $30

Little River Estate   ★★★☆

20 Sharrock Court, Taggerty, Vic 3714 **Region** Upper Goulburn
T (03) 5774 7644 **www.**littleriverwines.com.au **Open** By appt
Winemaker Philip Challen, plus various contract **Est.** 1986 **Dozens** 1200 **Vyds** 2.5ha
Philip (a chef and hotelier) and Christine Challen began the establishment of their vineyard in
1986 with the planting of 0.5ha of cabernet sauvignon. Several years later, 2ha of chardonnay
(and a few vines of pinot noir) followed. Vineyard practice and soil management are based on
organic principles, and there are low yields despite the age of the vines.

Sparkling Shiraz NV Traditional method, made by fizz expert David Cowburn.
Power-packed with spice and a cascade of dark fruits. The critical disgorgement
and dosage have been expertly handled. Time in bottle will be rewarded. Crown
seal. 12.5% alc. Rating 90 $30

Livewire Wines   ★★★★

PO Box 369, Portarlington, Vic 3223 **Region** Geelong
T 0439 024 007 **www.**livewirewines.com.au **Open** Not
Winemaker Anthony Brain **Est.** 2011 **Dozens** 1000
Anthony Brain started working life as a chef, but in the late 1990s 'took a slight bend into the
wine industry'. He started gathering experience in the Yarra Valley, and simultaneously started
oenology studies at CSU. Margaret River followed, as did time in SA before a return to the
Yarra, working at De Bortoli from 2003 to '07 (undertaking vintages in the Hunter, King and
Yarra valleys). Five vintages as winemaker at Bellarine Estate came next, giving him 'a platform
and understanding of the Geelong region and the opportunity to learn more about sites,
viticulture and winemaking decisions'. It hasn't prevented him from foraging far and wide.

Grampians Shiraz 2017 It's dangerously easy to drink this lighter bodied red
with lofty aromas of roses and violets, red fruits to the fore, and a decent dose of
cinnamon and ginger. The palate is perfectly poised with supple tannins and ferric
and savoury flavours, and everything glides effortlessly. More please. Screwcap.
13.4% alc. Rating 94 To 2023 $30 JF ❍

Valley of the Moon Pinot Noir 2017 Rating 92 To 2023 $32 JF
Chardonnay 2017 Rating 90 To 2021 $28 JF
Summer 2017 Rating 90 To 2020 $24 JF

Lloyd Brothers   ★★★☆

34 Warners Road, McLaren Vale, SA 5171 **Region** McLaren Vale
T (08) 8323 8792 **www.**lloydbrothers.com.au **Open** 7 days 11–5
Winemaker Ross Durbidge **Est.** 2002 **Dozens** 10 000 **Vyds** 42.4ha
Lloyd Brothers Wine and Olive Company is owned and operated by David and Matthew
Lloyd, third-generation McLaren Vale vignerons. Their 25ha estate overlooks the township,
and is planted to 20ha of shiraz, 2.5ha of bushvine grenache and 1ha of bushvine mataro (plus
18.9ha of sauvignon blanc, chardonnay, pinot gris and shiraz in the Adelaide Hills). The shiraz
planting allows the creation of a range of styles including rose, sparkling shiraz and fortified
shiraz. The White Chalk Shiraz is so named because of the white chalk used to mark each
barrel during the classification process. Exports to the UK.

🍷🍷🍷🍷♀ **McLaren Vale Grenache Rose 2017** From estate bushvines. A highly aromatic bouquet with spice, rose petal and musk starts the music, carrying the wine through to a talkative palate with its red fruits fresh, long and dry. A very attractive grenache rose. Screwcap. 12.5% alc. **Rating** 92 **To** 2020 $20 ✪

🍷🍷🍷🍷 **McLaren Vale Shiraz 2016** Rating 89 To 2040 $30
McLaren Vale Shiraz 2015 Rating 89 To 2025 $30
McLaren Vale Grenache 2016 Rating 89 To 2023 $30

Lobethal Road Wines   ★★★★☆

2254 Onkaparinga Valley Road, Mount Torrens, SA 5244 **Region** Adelaide Hills
T (08) 8389 4595 www.lobethalroad.com **Open** W'ends & public hols 11–5
Winemaker David Neyle, Michael Sykes **Est.** 1998 **Dozens** 6000 **Vyds** 10.5ha
Dave Neyle and Inga Lidums bring diverse but very relevant experience to the Lobethal Road vineyard, which is planted to shiraz and smaller amounts of chardonnay, tempranillo, sauvignon blanc and graciano. Dave has been in vineyard development and management in SA and Tasmania since 1990. Inga has 25+ years' experience in marketing and graphic design in Australia and overseas, with a focus on the wine and food industries. The property is managed with minimal chemical input. Exports to the UK.

🍷🍷🍷🍷🍷 **Adelaide Hills Pinot Gris 2017** This is exceptional gris. When picked within an optimal ripening window, with crunch, a phenolic pucker and oodles of nashi pear and red apple, then tamed by gentle oak, this often anaemic variety can be versatile at the table and highly enjoyable. Here lies the proof. Screwcap. 12.8% alc. **Rating** 95 **To** 2021 $25 NG ✪

🍷🍷🍷🍷♀ **Adelaide Hills Sauvignon Blanc 2017** Rating 93 To 2019 $22 NG ✪
Bacchant Adelaide Hills Shiraz 2015 Rating 92 To 2023 $45 NG
Adelaide Hills Tempranillo Graciano 2016 Rating 92 To 2021 $25 NG ✪
Bacchant Adelaide Hills Chardonnay 2016 Rating 91 To 2024 $45 NG
Adelaide Hills Roussanne 2016 Rating 90 To 2021 $25 NG
Adelaide Hills Shiraz 2016 Rating 90 To 2024 $25 NG

Lofty Valley Wines   ★★★★

100 Collins Road, Summertown, SA 5141 **Region** Adelaide Hills
T 0400 930 818 www.loftyvalleywines.com.au **Open** Sat by appt
Winemaker Various **Est.** 2004 **Dozens** 400 **Vyds** 3ha
Medical practitioner Brian Gilbert began collecting wine when he was 19, flirting with the idea of becoming a winemaker before being firmly directed towards medicine by his parents. Thirty or so years later he purchased a blackberry and gorse-infested 12ha property in the Adelaide Hills. Chardonnay (2ha) was planted in 2004, and 1ha of pinot noir in '07, both on steep slopes.

🍷🍷🍷🍷🍷 **Steeper Single Vineyard Adelaide Hills Pinot Noir 2016** Noticeably pale, pinot-esque colour in the glass. Toasty vanillan oak, sour cherry, small red berries, and a touch of whole-bunch stemminess (25% employed here). Lightly framed and gentle through the palate, the flavour builds quietly but finishes strongly, the finely etched tannin and acidity lingering in the aftertaste. A very attractive expression of Hills pinot. Of 10 barrels made, four made it to this bottling. Screwcap. 13% alc. **Rating** 94 **To** 2023 $50 SC

🍷🍷🍷🍷♀ **Ascent Single Vineyard Adelaide Hills Chardonnay 2016** Rating 93 **To** 2022 $40 SC

Logan Wines   ★★★★☆

Castlereagh Highway, Apple Tree Flat, Mudgee, NSW 2850 **Region** Mudgee
T (02) 6373 1333 www.loganwines.com.au **Open** 7 days 10–5
Winemaker Peter Logan **Est.** 1997 **Dozens** 50 000

Logan is a family owned and operated business with an emphasis on cool-climate wines from Orange and Mudgee. The business is run by husband and wife team Peter (winemaker) and Hannah (sales and marketing). Peter majored in biology and chemistry at Macquarie University, moving into the pharmaceutical world working as a process chemist. In a reversal of the usual roles, his father encouraged him to change careers, and Peter obtained a Graduate Diploma of Oenology from the University of Adelaide in 1996. The winery and tasting room are situated on the Mudgee vineyard, but the best wines are all made from grapes grown in the Orange region. Exports to the EU, Japan and other major markets.

ŸŸŸŸŸ **Ridge of Tears Orange Shiraz 2015** Sourced from a vineyard at an eye-popping 970m, the cool climate shows itself here with notes of black pepper and herbs laced through blackcurrant and bramble fruit. It's pretty, fragrant and spicy and it compels you to come back for more with its tangy and refreshing finish. Screwcap. 14% alc. **Rating** 94 **To** 2027 $45 DB

ŸŸŸŸŸ **Weemala Orange Riesling 2017 Rating** 93 **To** 2027 $20 DB **✿**
Hannah Orange Rose 2017 Rating 93 **To** 2019 $23 DB **✿**
Ridge of Tears Mudgee Shiraz 2015 Rating 93 **To** 2027 $45 DB
Orange Sauvignon Blanc 2017 Rating 91 **To** 2019 $23 **✿**
Weemala Orange Pinot Gris 2017 Rating 90 **To** 2020 $20 **✿**
Apple Tree Flat Rose 2016 Rating 90 **To** 2018 $13 CM **✿**
Vintage M Orange Cuvee 2015 Rating 90 $35

Lome ★★★★

83 Franklings Road, Harcourt North, Vic 3453 **Region** Bendigo
T 0438 544 317 **Open** Not
Winemaker Tony Winspear **Est.** 2004 **Dozens** 800 **Vyds** 5ha
Tim and Diane Robertson lived and worked for 23 years in the Bendigo region, and happened to be in the right place at the right time in 2008, purchasing a newly established vineyard at Harcourt North. They have since expanded the vineyard to 5ha of shiraz, marsanne, viognier and roussanne. Their interest grew from dabbling in backyard viticulture and garage-based winemaking when they lived in Burgundy.

ŸŸŸŸŸ **Bendigo Shiraz 2015** Sweet-fruited for sure and easy-going as a result, though it also boasts ample savoury inputs and gives off a general impression of elegance. It's a best-of-both-worlds style destined to have widespread appeal. Nutty oak, served in a modest but important measure, helps seal the deal. Screwcap. 13.8% alc. **Rating** 93 **To** 2027 $38 CM

ŸŸŸŸ **Bendigo Viognier Marsanne Roussanne 2016 Rating** 89 **To** 2022 $27 CM

Lonely Vineyard ★★★★★

16C Debneys Road, Norton Summit, SA 5136 (postal) **Region** Eden Valley
T 0413 481 163 **www**.lonelyvineyard.com.au **Open** Not
Winemaker Michael Schreurs **Est.** 2008 **Dozens** 500 **Vyds** 1.5ha
This is the venture of winemaker Michael Schreurs, a commercial lawyer from Adelaide, and wife Karina Ouwnes. Daughter Amalia can 'hoover a box of sultanas in record time' while Meesh, the family cat, 'treats Amalia well, and Michael with the contempt he deserves. As cats do'. Someone has a great sense of humour. Michael's winemaking career began at Seppelt's Great Western winery, where he spent three years, followed by six years at Henschke and, more recently, a stint at The Lane Vineyard in the Adelaide Hills, backed up by time in Burgundy, the Rhône Valley, the US and Spain. Exports to the UK.

ŸŸŸŸŸ **Riesling 2017** A gorgeous riesling with ginger flower, lime and lemon zest leading onto a racy palate. Bracingly fresh acidity; spicy with a savoury twist on the finish, making it really moreish to the last drop. Screwcap. 12.5% alc. **Rating** 95 **To** 2027 $26 JF **✿**
Rosato 2017 A new addition to the range, and rightly labelled rosato given the variety used is the Italian montepulciano. A delightfully refreshing drop. The palest

pastel pink with hints of cranberries and watermelon, and lemon-zesty acidity, then a crisp, dry finish that snaps, crackles and pops. Screwcap. 13% alc. **Rating** 95 To 2019 $26 JF ○

Shiraz 2016 This has all the allure and charm of the Eden Valley. Inky; smelling of crushed gravel with flecks of spice and licorice, yet at its heart excellent fruit. Full-bodied and richly flavoured with neatly enmeshed fine-grained tannins and oak (aged in French puncheons, 33% new, 16 months). Screwcap. 13.5% alc. **Rating** 95 To 2028 $36 JF

Arneis 2017 Inaugural release; tinglingly fresh with light aromatics, a waft of white blossom, thyme and citrus. The palate is pure arneis and has a dash of texture, but the lemon sorbet–like acidity and a minerally thread take the lead. Such pleasure in this. Screwcap. 12.5% alc. **Rating** 94 To 2020 $26 JF ○

♟♟♟♟♀ Montepulciano 2016 **Rating** 93 To 2021 $36 JF

Longline Wines   ★★★★☆

PO Box 28, Old Noarlunga, SA 5168 **Region** McLaren Vale/Adelaide Hills
T 0415 244 124 **www.**longlinewines.com.au **Open** Not
Winemaker Paul Carpenter **Est.** 2013 **Dozens** 830
Over 40 years ago Bob Carpenter gave up his job as a bank manager, becoming a longline fisherman at Goolwa; he then moved to McLaren Vale and became a farmer. Son Paul graduated from the University of Adelaide and began his professional life as a cereal researcher for the university, but a vintage job at Geoff Merrill Wines led to the decision to switch to winemaking. Over the next 20 years he worked both locally and internationally, in the Rhône Valley and Beaujolais, and at Archery Summit in Oregon. Back in Australia he worked for Hardys and Wirra Wirra and is currently senior winemaker at Hardys Tintara. Together with partner Martine, Paul secures small parcels of outstanding grenache and shiraz from four growers (three vineyards in McLaren Vale, the fourth in the Adelaide Hills).

♟♟♟♟♟ GSM McLaren Vale Grenache Shiraz Mourvedre 2017 This is a lovely, richly tapestried wine covering the full array of aromas and flavours of the blend. It coats the mouth without ever stopping the flow of flavour through to the finish, new oak correctly dispensed. Screwcap. 14.5% alc. **Rating** 95 To 2032 $22 ○

Blood Knot McLaren Vale Shiraz 2016 The grapes are from McLaren Vale's greatest district: Blewitt Springs. The vineyard is dry-grown, the grapes crushed and destemmed, open-fermented for 12 days on skins, pressed to demi-muid French fermenters (33% new) for 15 months' maturation It is generous in flavour, medium to full-bodied with black fruits to the fore, tannins superfine. Screwcap. 14.5% alc. **Rating** 94 To 2030 $26 ○

♟♟♟♟♀ Bimini Twist McLaren Vale Rose 2017 **Rating** 90 To 2019 $20 ○

Longview Vineyard   ★★★★★

Pound Road, Macclesfield, SA 5153 **Region** Adelaide Hills
T (08) 8388 9694 **www.**longviewvineyard.com.au **Open** 7 days 11–5
Winemaker Ben Glaetzer **Est.** 1995 **Dozens** 25000 **Vyds** 61.4ha
With a lifelong involvement in wine and hospitality, the Saturno family are now approaching their 10th vintage at the helm of Longview. Recent plantings of barbera, gruner veltliner and new clones of chardonnay and pinot grigio add to significant holdings of 20-year-old shiraz, cabernet sauvignon, nebbiolo and sauvignon blanc. Winemaking is overseen by Ben Glaetzer, in close consultation with Peter and Mark Saturno. A new cellar door and kitchen was unveiled in 2017, adding to 12 accommodation suites, a popular function room and unique food and wine events in the vineyard. In 10 years, this 100% family-owned, estate-grown producer has gone from two markets to selling in more than 14 countries.

♟♟♟♟♟ The Piece Shiraz 2015 Powerhouse red. Rich, meaty, perfumed, lashed with oak, dashed with sweet spice. Adelaide Hills shiraz with the lot. Tannin is fine, infused with coffee, and in control. It's going to mature – quite gloriously – over a long period. Diam. 14.5% alc. **Rating** 96 To 2035 $80 CM

Kuhl Adelaide Hills Gruner Veltliner 2017 Crunchy, spicy, aromatic, even grainy; this wine can be appreciated from a number of different angles, but it's the body, the flow and the sheer confidence it exudes that really sets it apart. This is a white wine of real presence. All things considered, the price is a steal. Screwcap. 13% alc. **Rating** 95 **To** 2021 $25 CM ◐

Yakka Adelaide Hills Shiraz 2016 You can't help but admire the integration of sweet, sawdusty French oak with black-cherried fruit, assorted spices and woody herbs. Plum flavours add yet more flesh to sink into; smoke notes a bit of fantasy. A velvety texture is the cushion upon which it's all propped. It's a wonderful red to settle in with. Screwcap. 14.5% alc. **Rating** 95 **To** 2033 $30 CM ◐

Adelaide Hills Nebbiolo Riserva 2015 As serious as it is impressive. There's plenty of strut to this release, its flavours of black cherry, rose petals, orange peel, leather and anise raked firmly with dry, herb-flecked tannin. It throws aroma, flavour and dry length aplenty. This is a nebbiolo to be reckoned with. Diam. 14% alc. **Rating** 95 **To** 2032 $50 CM

♟♟♟♟♟ **Nebbiolo Rosato 2017 Rating** 92 **To** 2020 $25 CM ◐
Vista Shiraz Barbera 2016 Rating 92 **To** 2023 $24 CM ◐
Iron Knob Riesling 2017 Rating 91 **To** 2024 $21 CM ◐
Whippet Sauvignon Blanc 2017 Rating 91 **To** 2018 $21 CM ◐
Fresco Nebbiolo 2017 Rating 91 **To** 2021 $36 CM
Fresco Nebbiolo 2016 Rating 91 **To** 2020 $36 CM
Queenie Pinot Grigio 2017 Rating 90 **To** 2018 $21 CM ◐

Lou Miranda Estate ★★★★☆

1876 Barossa Valley Way, Rowland Flat, SA 5352 **Region** Barossa Valley
T (08) 8524 4537 **www**.loumirandaestate.com.au **Open** Mon–Fri 10–4, w'ends 11–4
Winemaker Lou Miranda, Janelle Zerk **Est.** 2005 **Dozens** 20000 **Vyds** 23.29ha
Lou Miranda's daughters Lisa and Victoria are the driving forces behind the estate, albeit with continuing hands-on involvement from Lou. The jewels in the crown of the estate plantings are 0.5ha of mourvedre planted in 1897 and 1.5ha of shiraz planted in 1907. The remaining vines have been planted gradually since '95, expanding the varieties to cabernet sauvignon, merlot, chardonnay and pinot grigio. Exports to the UK, the US and other major markets.

♟♟♟♟♟ **Old Vine Angel's Vineyard Barossa Valley Shiraz Mourvedre 2013** Whatever percentage of mourvedre was used (we aren't told), it has added an X-factor in the subtle interplay between fine tannins and juicy red and black fruit. Screwcap. 14.5% alc. **Rating** 95 **To** 2038 $53

Old Vine Individual Vineyard Barossa Valley Shiraz 2013 Matured for 34 months in American oak (50% new). Within its terms of reference – American oak and 15% alc. – this wine still manages to reflect the concentration of the 106yo vines. The colour is still good, the tannins rounded, the black fruits hinged on those tannins. Screwcap. 15% alc. **Rating** 94 **To** 2038 $43

♟♟♟♟♟ **Individual Vineyard Sagrantino 2015 Rating** 92 **To** 2029 $33
Single Vineyard Shiraz 2012 Rating 90 **To** 2022 $90 SC
Old Vine Shiraz Mataro 2014 Rating 90 **To** 2030 $90 SC

Lowe Wines ★★★★★

Tinja Lane, Mudgee, NSW 2850 **Region** Mudgee
T (02) 6372 0800 **www**.lowewine.com.au **Open** 7 days 10–5
Winemaker David Lowe, Paul Martung **Est.** 1987 **Dozens** 15000 **Vyds** 41.3ha
Lowe Wines has undergone a number of changes in recent years, including the acquisition of the two Louee vineyards. The first is at Rylstone, led by shiraz, cabernet sauvignon, petit verdot and merlot, with chardonnay, cabernet franc, verdelho and viognier making up the balance. The second is on Nullo Mountain, bordered by Wollemi National Park at an altitude of 1100m, high by any standard, and one of the coolest sites in Australia. Lowe Wines

continues with its organic profile. The Tinja property has been owned by the Lowe family for five generations.

🍷🍷🍷🍷🍷 **Block 5 Mudgee Shiraz 2014** High quality shiraz with depth and brood and plenty of spread through the finish. It's a standout wine. Black cherries, roasted plums, chestnuts, sweet spices and earth-like notes. A creaminess, too. It's up there from the outset, but the finish is quite something, taking you to a place and then propelling you further. One out of the box. Cork. 14.6% alc. **Rating** 97 **To** 2040 $50 CM ✪

🍷🍷🍷🍷🍷 **Nullo Mountain Sauvignon Blanc 2017** It scores points for complexity, adds to them via texture, and then really wins the day with what's best described as 'elegant control'. It's not flamboyant or try-hard with flavour, but feels and tastes classy from start to finish. Screwcap. 13.4% alc. **Rating** 94 **To** 2020 $30 CM ✪

🍷🍷🍷🍷🍷 **Nullo Mountain Riesling 2015 Rating** 93 **To** 2024 $50 CM
Organic Block 8 Mudgee Shiraz 2014 Rating 93 **To** 2034 $35 CM
Louee Organic Cabernet Franc 2015 Rating 92 **To** 2024 $35 CM
PF 500 Shiraz 2017 Rating 91 **To** 2020 $18 CM ✪
Mudgee Blue Shiraz Cabernet 2015 Rating 91 **To** 2027 $30 CM
Organic Mudgee Zinfandel 2014 Rating 91 **To** 2024 $75 CM
Nullo Mountain Pinot Gris 2017 Rating 90 **To** 2019 $30 CM
Headstone Mudgee Rose 2017 Rating 90 **To** 2020 $28 CM

Lyons Will Estate   ★★★★★

60 Whalans Track, Lancefield, Vic 3435 **Region** Macedon Ranges
T 0412 681 940 www.lyonswillestate.com.au **Open** 4th w'end of each month 11–5
Winemaker Oliver Rapson, Renata Morello, Shaun Crinion (Consultant) **Est.** 1996
Dozens 750 **Vyds** 4.2ha
Oliver Rapson (with a background in digital advertising) and Renata Morello (a physiotherapist with a PhD in public health) believe the Macedon Ranges has the best of both worlds: less than an hour's drive to Melbourne, ideal for pinot and chardonnay, and still sparsely settled. The property had 2ha of vines planted in 1996 (pinot noir clones D5V12, D4V2 and 115, and chardonnay), and they have extended the pinot noir to 1.2ha (increasing the 115 and introducing MV6) and planted 1ha each of riesling and gamay. A winery was completed for the 2016 vintage, with additional plantings of chardonnay, pinot noir and riesling planned for '18. The wines are made under the guidance of friend Shaun Crinion of Dappled Wines. *Wine Companion* 2018 Best New Winery.

🍷🍷🍷🍷🍷 **Macedon Ranges Riesling 2017** Young vines planted '13, destemmed, short skin contact, basket-pressed, fermented in old oak, matured for 3 months in oak then 2 months in tank. The long, most slender bottle sends a message. The vinification has worked very well indeed, the clarity of fruit expression and overall balance impressive. Lime and Granny Smith apple flavours have a fine backbone of acidity. Diam. 12.5% alc. **Rating** 96 **To** 2027 $33 ✪
Macedon Ranges Chardonnay 2016 20yo vines, hand-picked, destemmed, basket-pressed, fermented in French oak (30% new), matured for 12 months. Oliver Rapson has calmly taken all of the steps needed to bring the best out of what is clearly high quality fruit. The fruit/oak balance and integration are top class, as is the wine. Diam. 13.5% alc. **Rating** 95 **To** 2024 $35 ✪

M. Chapoutier Australia   ★★★★

141–143 High Street, Heathcote, Vic 3523 **Region** Pyrenees/Heathcote
T (03) 5433 2411 www.mchapoutieraustralia.com **Open** 7 days 10–5
Winemaker Michel Chapoutier **Est.** 1998 **Dozens** 10 000 **Vyds** 50ha
M. Chapoutier Australia is the offshoot of the famous Rhône Valley producer. The business focuses on vineyards in the Pyrenees, Heathcote and Beechworth, with collaboration from Ron Laughton of Jasper Hill and Rick Kinzbrunner of Giaconda. After first establishing a

vineyard in Heathcote adjacent to Jasper Hill (see La Pleiade), Michel Chapoutier purchased the Malakoff vineyard in the Pyrenees in 2000 to create Domaine Terlato & Chapoutier, a joint venture. In '09 Michel purchased two neighbouring vineyards, Landsborough Valley and Shays Flat, which now come under the name Domaine Tournon (as does Lady's Lane Estate in Heathcote). Exports to all major markets.

ΨΨΨΨΨ **Domaine Terlato and Chapoutier L-Block Pyrenees Shiraz 2014** Has retained excellent hue, albeit of moderate depth; an energetic medium-bodied shiraz with intensity and drive to its mouthfeel. While blackberry and black cherry are the mainstays, I'm attracted to the Chapoutier description of 'slightly acid wild strawberries' on the finish. Plenty of graphite tannins, too. Cork. 14.5% alc. **Rating** 91 **To** 2029 $80

Tournon Shays Flat Vineyard Pyrenees Cabernet Sauvignon 2014 Good crimson-purple hue. This wine does show polymerised (softened) tannins. It is medium-bodied, and the discrete use of oak (a portion was matured in French puncheons, 40% new, for 10 months) has likewise been well judged. All up, has good varietal character. Screwcap. 13.5% alc. **Rating** 91 **To** 2024 $30

Tournon Landsborough Vineyard Pyrenees Chardonnay 2016 Whole-bunch pressed, wild-fermented in French oak (20% new), matured for 6 months with light batonnage. Both the bouquet and palate reflect the new oak to a surprising, though not unpleasant, degree. It has a complex array of ripe flavours of stone fruits and brioche, plus the oak, of course. Needs a touch more acidity, but otherwise good to go. Screwcap. 13.5% alc. **Rating** 90 **To** 2023 $40

Tournon Landsborough Vineyard Pyrenees Grenache Shiraz Touriga 2015 A powerful, rich and intense 48/32/20% blend, trembling on the brink of overripeness, but this is part of the journey to produce the wine. It will polarise opinions, and those who support it will say patience will be rewarded. I'm not so sure, my points a compromise. Screwcap. 15% alc. **Rating** 90 **To** 2025 $50

Tournon Shays Flat Vineyard Pyrenees Sangiovese 2016 Typical light colour of sangiovese. Here the tannins have been very well handled, allowing the sour cherry fruit of the variety free play. Attractive partner for Italian pasta. Screwcap. 13.5% alc. **Rating** 90 **To** 2022 $30

Mac Forbes ★★★★★

Graceburn Wine Room, 11A Green Street, Healesville, Vic 3777 **Region** Yarra Valley
T (03) 9005 5822 **www.**macforbes.com **Open** Thurs–Sat 11–9, Sun–Tues 11–5
Winemaker Mac Forbes, Austin Black **Est.** 2004 **Dozens** 6000
Mac Forbes cut his vinous teeth at Mount Mary, where he was winemaker for several years before heading overseas in 2002. He spent two years in London working for Southcorp in a marketing liaison role, then travelled to Portugal and Austria to gain further winemaking experience. He returned to the Yarra Valley prior to the '05 vintage, purchasing grapes to make his own wines. He has a two-tier portfolio: first, the Victorian range, employing unusual varieties or unusual winemaking techniques; and second, the Yarra Valley range of multiple terroir-based offerings of chardonnay and pinot noir. Exports to the UK, the US, Canada, Spain, Sweden, Norway, Hong Kong and Thailand.

ΨΨΨΨΨ **Hoddles Creek Chardonnay 2016** From 0.8ha planted on volcanic loam in '97. Matured for 9 months in used oak. A very attractive wine with the tension and life typical of the Upper Yarra. A light to medium-bodied blend of 50% white peach, 40% grapefruit and 10% Granny Smith apple. The decision to use cork almost certainly means the wine will be sabotaged before the end of its natural life. 12.5% alc. **Rating** 95 **To** 2021 $60

Healesville Syrah 2016 150 dozen made with the standard vinification: wild yeast–open fermented, matured for 11 months in used oak, neither fined nor filtered. Aromatic blackberry, sauteed plum and pepper aromas and flavours. Might have benefited from fining, and the tannins are magnified by the low pH of 3.28. Points for the glass half full. Cork. 13% alc. **Rating** 95 **To** 2037 $50

Hugh Merlot 2015 From a 0.32ha vineyard in Gruyere, planted in '95; wild-fermented, matured for 14 months in used oak. A medium-bodied wine with clear varietal expression and no green/unripe characters at all. Cassis and black olive flavours with fine tannins. Creased and stained cork a worry. 12.5% alc. **Rating** 94 **To** 2025 $70

ŸŸŸŸŸ **Yarra Valley Pinot Noir 2016** **Rating** 92 **To** 2024 $30
Yarra Junction Pinot Noir 2016 **Rating** 91 **To** 2023 $50
Wesburn Pinot Noir 2016 **Rating** 91 **To** 2025 $75
Yarra Valley Chardonnay 2016 **Rating** 90 **To** 2023 $30
Woori Yallock Chardonnay 2016 **Rating** 90 **To** 2021 $60

Macaw Creek Wines   ★★★★

Macaw Creek Road, Riverton, SA 5412 **Region** Mount Lofty Ranges
T (08) 8847 2657 **www**.macawcreekwines.com.au **Open** By appt
Winemaker Rodney Hooper **Est.** 1992 **Dozens** 8000 **Vyds** 10ha
The property on which Macaw Creek Wines is established has been owned by the Hooper family since the 1850s, but development of the vineyards did not begin until 1995. The Macaw Creek brand was established in '92 with wines made from grapes from other regions. Rodney Hooper is a highly qualified and skilled winemaker with experience in many parts of Australia, and in Germany, France and the US. Exports to Canada, Sweden, Norway, the Netherlands, Finland and China.

ŸŸŸŸŸ **Em's Table Premium Organic Clare Valley Riesling 2016** Has had SO_2 added in the normal way. Gleaming straw-green; it has length and depth to its display of citrus aromas and flavours of all kinds, from blossom to skin to pith. It is very well balanced, and actively suggests a second glass should be enjoyed pronto. Screwcap. 12.5% alc. **Rating** 94 **To** 2031 $18
Reserve Mt Lofty Ranges Shiraz Cabernet 2014 A 53/47% blend, matured for 12 months in new and used American hogsheads. Full crimson-purple; blackberry and blackcurrant flavours march, arms interlocked, with vanillan oak and tannins that are now well and truly integrated. The tannins are balanced and ripe, providing the framework for the fruit. Screwcap. 14.5% alc. **Rating** 94 **To** 2030 $28

ŸŸŸŸ **Mt Lofty Ranges Semillon Viognier 2016** **Rating** 89 **To** 2023
Mt Lofty Ranges Shiraz 2015 **Rating** 89 **To** 2029
Mt Lofty Ranges Cabernet Shiraz 2015 **Rating** 89 **To** 2025 $17

McGuigan Wines   ★★★★☆

Cnr Broke Road/McDonalds Road, Pokolbin, NSW 2321 **Region** Hunter Valley
T (02) 4998 7400 **www**.mcguiganwines.com.au **Open** 7 days 9.30–5
Winemaker Peter Hall, James Evers **Est.** 1992 **Dozens** 1.5 million
McGuigan Wines is an Australian brand operating under parent company Australian Vintage Ltd. The McGuigan family has winemaking roots going back to 1880 in the Hunter Valley. Today McGuigan's vine holdings extend across SA, from the Barossa Valley to the Eden and Clare valleys and the Adelaide Hills, into Victoria and NSW. McGuigan's processing facilities operate out of three core regions: the Hunter Valley, Sunraysia and the Barossa Valley. Exports to all major markets.

ŸŸŸŸŸ **The Philosophy Cabernet Shiraz 2013** SA is the only region mentioned on the label. In any case the weight of the bottle and the weight of the wine itself will shout down the minor details. This is an explosive red, all blood-rich berries and thunderous tannin, the sizeable hit of chocolate and toast entirely appropriate given the concentration of the fruit and the extractive claw of the tannin. If you've already started planning for New Year's Eve 2050, this should just about have settled down by then, Diam permitting. 14.5% alc. **Rating** 95 **To** 2050 $150 CM

♀♀♀♀♀ The Shortlist Hunter Valley Semillon 2014 Rating 92 To 2029 $30 NG
The Shortlist Adelaide Hills Chardonnay 2016 Rating 92 To 2025 $28 NG
The Shortlist Eden Valley Riesling 2017 Rating 91 To 2025 $28 NG
The Shortlist Barossa Valley Montepulciano 2016 Rating 91 To 2024
$28 NG

McHenry Hohnen Vintners ★★★★★

5962 Caves Road, Margaret River, WA 6285 **Region** Margaret River
T (08) 9757 7600 **www**.mchenryhohnen.com.au **Open** 7 days 10.30–4.30
Winemaker Julian Grounds **Est.** 2004 **Dozens** 7500 **Vyds** 105ha
McHenry Hohnen is owned by the McHenry and Hohnen families, sourcing grapes from
three vineyards owned by various members of the families. Vines established on the McHenry,
Calgardup Brook and Rocky Road properties are all farmed biodynamically. The family
members with direct executive responsibilities are Murray McHenry, a leading Perth retailer,
and David Hohnen, Cape Mentelle founder and former long-term winemaker. The arrival of
Julian Grounds, Len Evans Tutorial '17 dux, has underwritten the status of the brand. Exports
to the UK, Ireland, Indonesia, Japan, Singapore, Hong Kong and China.

♀♀♀♀♀ **Margaret River BDX 2016** Still has good depth of colour, and the
components – fruit, oak and tannins – have come together convincingly. The
mouthfeel is totally delicious, seeming to create a line of juicy flavour that grows
as it travels through the mouth, peaking as it reaches the back-palate. Screwcap.
14.6% alc. **Rating** 96 **To** 2036 $40 ✪
Burnside Vineyard Margaret River Sauvignon Blanc 2017 Hand-picked,
whole-bunch pressed direct with full solids to barriques, a small percentage
fermented on skins for extra phenolics and weight, no mlf, frequent stirring; later
in the year taken with solids to tank for 3 months. Certainly succeeded in building
texture and structure without diminution or corruption of fruit flavour. Screwcap.
13% alc. **Rating** 95 **To** 2019 $28 ✪
Burnside Vineyard Margaret River Chardonnay 2016 A big, rich, generous
Margaret River chardonnay, white clingstone peach plus nectarine. Impossible not
to like this amiable wine. Screwcap. 13.5% alc. **Rating** 95 **To** 2023 $60
Hazel's Vineyard Margaret River Chardonnay 2016 A different expression
of funk that backs off somewhat having made its point, and moves into elegant
mode. Nice wine. Screwcap. 13.5% alc. **Rating** 95 $60
Rocky Road Margaret River Semillon Sauvignon Blanc 2017 A 55/45%
blend, part fermented in new 2800l French casks, part in tank on full lees to build
texture. The oak is perceptible on the bouquet, less so on the lively, fresh and
supple palate. Screwcap. 12.5% alc. **Rating** 94 **To** 2023 $20✪
Laterite Hills Margaret River Chardonnay 2017 A new line for McHenry
Hohnen from three estate vineyards (Burnside, Calgardup and Hazel's). The
same vinification as for the single vineyard chardonnays, blended in October
into tank on full lees. Reflects the southern Margaret River: bright and almost
savoury juiciness, zesty phenolic grip to the finish. Screwcap. 13.5% alc. **Rating** 94
To 2026 $40
Calgardup Brook Vineyard Margaret River Chardonnay 2016 Particularly
complex, slightly funky bouquet with hints of hessian. The palate largely dismisses
the bouquet with a stream of lively/zesty citrus skin, oak merely a vehicle.
Screwcap. 13.5% alc. **Rating** 94 **To** 2024 $60
Amigos Margaret River Marsanne Roussanne 2017 A 65/35% blend.
Richly layered and textured, yet doesn't trip over itself (unlike the ladies on the
label). Clever play by Julian Grounds, treading a delicate path through fields of
plenty. Screwcap. 13.5% alc. **Rating** 94 **To** 2021 $28✪
Hazel's Vineyard Margaret River Syrah 2017 From a single block, hand-
picked, wild-fermented with 100% whole bunches, 14 days on skins, pressed to
one 2800l French cask for mlf and extended skin contact and maturation. Deep
crimson-purple; it has unexpected but welcome savoury tannins that give texture

and structure to the blackberry/black cherry fruit. A long future for this wine. Screwcap. 12.9% alc. **Rating** 94 **To** 2037 $35

Hazel's Vineyard Margaret River Zinfandel 2016 Two clones imported from California, destemmed, cool-fermented, matured in hogsheads. David Hohnen's experience in making zinfandel in Australia is unmatched, and it shows in this deeply coloured, deeply flavoured wine. A few tannins wander around, but hey, it's zinfandel – and a pretty good one. Screwcap. 14.6% alc. **Rating** 94 **To** 2029 $50

Hazel's Vineyard Cabernet Sauvignon 2015 Rating 93 To 2030 $60
Amigos Shiraz Grenache Mataro 2016 Rating 92 To 2021 $29

McKellar Ridge Wines

2 Euroka Avenue, Murrumbateman, NSW 2582 **Region** Canberra District
T 0409 780 861 **www**.mckellarridgewines.com.au **Open** Sun 12–5 (Sept–Jun)
Winemaker Dr Brian Johnston **Est.** 2005 **Dozens** 600 **Vyds** 5.5ha
Dr Brian Johnston established McKellar Ridge in 2005, then decided to retire after 10 years. John and Marina Sekoranja worked with Brian for 12 months before purchasing the winery in July '17. Brian continues to provide support as winemaking consultant during vintage, and John and Marina are completing wine science degrees at CSU. The change has seen an increase in the number of wines available, including from Tumbarumba.

Canberra District Shiraz 2017 From the Point of View vineyard at Murrumbateman; hand-picked, 5 days' cold soak, open-fermented with 15% whole bunches, matured for 9 months in French oak (33% new). A very good wine that says there's likely to be a seamless transition to the new owners. Underlines just how good Canberra District can be (and usually is), with luminous dark cherry fruits, fine tannins and a built-in medium-bodied complexity that can express so much. Screwcap. 13.6% alc. **Rating** 95 **To** 2032 $34 ✪

Canberra District Pinot Noir 2017 Hand-picked from two vineyards, 7 days' cold soak, open-fermented with 15% whole bunches, matured for 9 months in French oak (33% new). Bright, deep colour; a very neat and intense pinot with faultless vinification, simply needing 2–3 years for complexity to build on the base of dark cherry and plum fruits. Screwcap. 13.1% alc. **Rating** 94 **To** 2032 $30 ✪

Tumbarumba Pinot Noir 2017 Identical vinification to the Canberra District Pinot down to the last detail. However, the taste and mouthfeel are different – here the fruit flavours and structure are lighter, fresher and brighter, yet less complex both now and in the future. Screwcap. 13.4% alc. **Rating** 94 **To** 2031 $30 ✪

Canberra District Riesling 2017 Rating 93 To 2025 $22 ✪

McLaren Vale III Associates

309 Foggo Road, McLaren Vale, SA 5171 **Region** McLaren Vale
T 1800 501 513 **www**.mclarenvaleiiiassociates.com.au **Open** Mon–Fri 9–5, w'ends 11–5
Winemaker Campbell Greer **Est.** 1999 **Dozens** 12 000 **Vyds** 34ha
McLaren Vale III Associates is a quality boutique winery owned by Mary and John Greer and Reg Wymond. The impressive and consistent portfolio of estate-grown wines has had deserved success in Australian and international wine shows. The signature wine is the Squid Ink Shiraz. Exports to the US, Canada, Indonesia, Hong Kong, Singapore, South Korea, Japan and China.

French Oak Shiraz 2015 A full-bodied shiraz that has plenty of activity in the mouth without needing to worry about the oak. Retasting it in the wake of the American oak shiraz leaves no doubt in my mind that this is the most attractive, with more spicy, cedary, savoury notes picking up the earthy varietal fruits of the region. 14.5% alc. **Rating** 95 **To** 2035 $80

Squid Ink Reserve Shiraz 2016 From the estate vineyard. It spends 18 months in new American oak, but as with the previous release in '14, it's far less obvious than you might expect. The wine is full-bodied, but with a certain lightness of touch to its amalgam of black berries and cherries, savoury tannins, and a farewell kiss of regional dark chocolate. For the record, it is described as 'Reserve' on the back label. Screwcap. 14.5% alc. **Rating** 95 **To** 2036 $65

American Oak Shiraz 2015 Has the roundness and richness of American oak, which can suffocate varietal and regional markers of wine. But here region, variety and oak come together without animus – a meld of black fruits, dark chocolate, supple tannins and vanilla notes. 14.5% alc. **Rating** 94 **To** 2030 $80

The Descendant of Squid Ink Shiraz 2017 Matured for 9 months in 4yo oak previously used for Squid Ink, which acts as a framework for this full-bodied rendition of McLaren Vale shiraz. It has layers of black fruits, licorice and upright tannins – all with a coat of bitter dark chocolate on the finish. Screwcap. 14.5% alc. **Rating** 94 **To** 2032 $43

McLean's Farm ★★★★☆

barr-Eden Vineyard, Menglers Hill Road, Tanunda, SA 5352 **Region** Eden Valley
T (08) 8564 3340 **Open** Not
Winemaker Contract **Est.** 2001 **Dozens** 6000 **Vyds** 5.3ha
The ever-convivial, larger-than-life Bob McLean covered a lot of wine turf until his death in April 2015. Many people, myself included, were good friends with Bob, and all of us were immensely saddened by his death. The wines continue to be made, although the 45ha barr-Eden Vineyard has been purchased by Two Hands Wines. Exports to the UK.

🍷🍷🍷🍷🍷 **Master Barossa Shiraz 2014** Heft, fruit, oak and acid, a little too much of the latter but mountains of all of the former. It tastes of leather and dark chocolate, roasted plum, red licorice and asphalt, the texture smooth, and all the dials set to rich. It will hold for some years but its best drinking is soonish. Screwcap. 14.5% alc. **Rating** 91 **To** 2024 $52 CM

McLeish Estate ★★★★★

462 De Beyers Road, Pokolbin, NSW 2320 **Region** Hunter Valley
T (02) 4998 7754 **www**.mcleishestatewines.com.au **Open** 7 days 10–5
Winemaker Andrew Thomas (Contract) **Est.** 1985 **Dozens** 8000 **Vyds** 17.3ha
Bob and Maryanne McLeish have established a particularly successful business based on estate plantings. The wines are consistently high quality, and more than a few have accumulated show records leading to gold medal–encrusted labels. (Over the years there have been 37 trophies, and 86 gold and 80 silver medals, the majority won in the Hunter Valley and Sydney wine shows). The quality of the grapes is part of the equation, another the skills of winemaker Andrew Thomas. Exports to the UK, the US and Asia.

🍷🍷🍷🍷🍷 **Cellar Reserve Hunter Valley Semillon 2013** When I first tasted this wine in Mar '14 I wrote, 'Trust me, buy as much of this wine as you possibly can. Paying $20 today is a whole lot more attractive than paying $85 in 6 years' time.' The only correction is the price – now $50. The palate is still incredibly youthful, the lime alongside lemon every bit as powerful. This has a minimum of 5 more years of positive development. Screwcap. 10.5% alc. **Rating** 96 **To** 2023 $50 ○

Hunter Valley Semillon 2017 The bouquet has nuances of herb, lanolin and lemon zest, the palate is very expressive 15 months post vintage, with a faint tickle of CO_2 coupled with delicious Meyer lemon. The acidity is there, but not obvious. A lovely wine now, will be superb in '22. Screwcap. 11.3% alc. **Rating** 95 **To** 2022 $25 ○

🍷🍷🍷🍷🍷 **Semillon Sauvignon Blanc 2017 Rating** 92 **To** 2021 $18 ○
Hunter Valley Adelaide Hills Semillon Sauvignon Blanc 2017 Rating 92 **To** 2021 $18 ○

McPherson Wines

6 Expo Court, Mount Waverley, Vic 3149 (postal) **Region** Nagambie Lakes
T (03) 9263 0200 **www**.mcphersonwines.com.au **Open** Not
Winemaker Jo Nash **Est.** 1968 **Dozens** 500 000 **Vyds** 262ha
McPherson Wines is, by any standards, a substantial business. Its wines are largely produced for
the export market, with enough sales in Australia to gain some measure of local recognition.
Made from the estate vineyards and contract-grown grapes at various locations, their wines
represent very good value. McPherson Wines is a joint venture between Andrew McPherson
and Alister Purbrick, both of whom have had a lifetime of experience in the industry (Alister
is a winemaker at Tahbilk). Exports to all major markets.

🍷🍷🍷🍷🍷 **Don't tell Gary. 2016** From the Grampians, matured in new and used French
oak. The cool climate comes through strongly, giving the black fruits focus and
length, coupled with overall balance; the finish is fresh and vibrant. Screwcap.
14.5% alc. **Rating** 95 **To** 2031 $24 ✪

🍷🍷🍷🍷🍷 **MWC Shiraz Mourvedre 2016** Rating 92 To 2024 $22 CM ✪
Laneway Chardonnay 2016 Rating 90 To 2019 $19 ✪
La Vue Shiraz 2015 Rating 90 To 2023 $19 ✪
Andrew McPherson's The Full Fifteen Reserve Shiraz Cabernet 2017
Rating 90 To 2024 $29 CM
MWC Cabernet Sauvignon 2016 Rating 90 To 2024 $22 CM

McWilliam's

Jack McWilliam Road, Hanwood, NSW 2680 **Region** Riverina
T (02) 6963 3400 **www**.mcwilliams.com.au **Open** Wed–Sat 10–4
Winemaker Russell Cody, Andrew Higgins **Est.** 1916 **Dozens** NFP **Vyds** 455.7ha
The best wines to come from this Riverina winery are from other regions (either in whole
or in part), notably Hilltops, Coonawarra, Yarra Valley, Tumbarumba, Margaret River and
Eden Valley. As McWilliam's viticultural resources have expanded, it has been able to produce
regional blends from across Australia of startlingly good value. The winery rating is strongly
reliant on the exceptional value for money of the Hanwood Estate and Inheritance labels.
McWilliam's is the owner of Mount Pleasant (Hunter Valley), Barwang (Hilltops) and Evans
& Tate (Margaret River), the value of which will become ever more apparent as the ability
of these brands to deliver world-class wines at appropriate prices is leveraged by group chief
winemaker Jim Chatto (see separate entries for each of these wineries). McWilliam's is a
founding member of Australia's First Families of Wine, and 100% owned by the McWilliam
family. Exports to all major markets.

🍷🍷🍷🍷🍷 **842 Tumbarumba Chardonnay 2015** Fermented and matured in French oak.
A rich and powerful mix of grapefruit, white peach and roasted-nut nuances, with
excellent length and balance. A big chardonnay, but light on its feet. Screwcap.
13% alc. **Rating** 95 **To** 2027 $70
1877 Canberra Shiraz 2016 The quality largely speaks for itself, the colour
deep but bright. The bouquet is expressive, pointing to the cool-grown, medium-
bodied palate. It has dark cherry, satsuma plum, spice and pepper flavours in a
luscious flow across the palate into a long finish. It's certain some quality oak is
also on board. Screwcap. 13.5% alc. **Rating** 95 **To** 2036 $80
Show Reserve Limited Release Aged 25 Years Muscat NV The most
striking of the three McWilliam's fortified wines in this group. Brandy snaps, a
spice showcase, rum and raisin liqueur with rancio the key to a very good wine.
Bottled '15, batch 002. Screwcap. 18.5% alc. **Rating** 95 $80
McW Reserve 660 Canberra Syrah 2016 Bright crimson-purple; a slickly
made wine featuring fruit first and foremost. It establishes its sense of place with
its spicy medium-bodied berry and currant fruits before the fine-grained tannins
and integrated oak click in. High quality wine at the price. Screwcap. 14% alc.
Rating 94 **To** 2029 $25 ✪

McW Reserve 660 Hilltops Cabernet Sauvignon 2015 Very good crimson-purple hue; Hilltops is equally at home with its cabernet as its shiraz. The wines have a gravitas that subtly commands respect, here with pure cassis/blackcurrant and black olive to the fore. Great value. Screwcap. 14% alc. **Rating** 94 **To** 2040 $25 ✪

Show Reserve Limited Release Aged 25 Years Tawny NV Tawny hue, as appropriate. Striking taste, a mix of dried and crystallised fruit – raisins, apricot, plus chocolate and Christmas pudding. Has retained freshness despite some components 50+yo. Bottled '15, batch 002. Screwcap. 19.5% alc. **Rating** 94 $80

Show Reserve Limited Release Aged 25 Years Topaque NV A highly aromatic bouquet merges with the vibrant malt and butterscotch/toffee flavours of the palate. The display of varietal character is most impressive. Screwcap. 18.5% alc. **Rating** 94 $80

ΨΨΨΨႺ **McW Reserve 660 Chardonnay 2016** Rating 93 To 2026 $25 ✪
McW Reserve 660 Pinot Noir 2016 Rating 91 To 2021 $25
McW Reserve 660 Shiraz 2015 Rating 91 To 2030 $25
Parkes Chardonnay 2016 Rating 90 To 2021 $40

Magpie Estate ★★★★

PO Box 126, Tanunda, SA 5352 **Region** Barossa Valley
T (08) 8562 3300 **www.**magpieestate.com **Open** At Rolf Binder
Winemaker Rolf Binder, Noel Young **Est.** 1993 **Dozens** 10 000 **Vyds** 16ha
A partnership between two Rhône-philes, Barossa winemaker Rolf Binder and UK wine impresario Noel Young. Fruit is sourced from a group of select growers, with the recent acquisition of the Smalltown vineyard in Ebenezer providing estate-grown fruit from the 2017 vintage. Each fruit batch is kept separate, giving the winemakers more blending options. The intent is to make wines that have a sense of place and show true Barossa characters; wines that are complex with a degree of elegance. The style is very much focused on minimal intervention, with an aversion to massive extract and over-oaked wines. Rolf and Noel say they have a lot of fun making these wines, but they are also very serious about quality. Exports to the UK, Canada, Denmark, Poland, Finland and Singapore.

ΨΨΨΨႺ **Songlines Barossa Valley Grenache 2016** 40yo vines. Fermented wild with 30% whole bunches. No oak at all. We live in a heyday of Australian grenache and this is the result. The fruit is sweet but there's a savouriness about the edges; it feels completely unforced, not wearying, and is fragrant, expressive and lively. Drinking it is like plucking the berries from the vine and simply savouring their goodness. The appeal is obvious. Screwcap. 14% alc. **Rating** 93 **To** 2024 $25 CM ✪

Rag & Bones Eden Valley Riesling 2017 We get flesh and body but we also get sizzling acidity. A modest but attractive sweetness marries it together while lime, musk, spice and nectarine characters romp through the palate. Screwcap. 12.5% alc. **Rating** 92 **To** 2025 $25 CM ✪

The Sack Barossa Valley Shiraz 2016 Barossa blackberry and toast with inflections of dried fruits, orange peel included, to the point where the famed 'Christmas cake' descriptor is apt. It's not a huge release but there's ample flavour here and the balance of all components is good. A wine you can rely on. Screwcap. 14% alc. **Rating** 92 **To** 2026 $30 CM

The Black Sock Barossa Valley Mourvedre 2015 Mostly mourvedre but with ripe, old vine shiraz in the mix. Aged in used American and French oak, though it isn't a major player. This is sweet and raspberried with leather, earth and floral inputs. It's mid-weight but still manages to reach to all corners of your mouth; there's plenty of fruit to suckle on. Both generosity and neatness reign. Screwcap. 14% alc. **Rating** 92 **To** 2023 $30 CM

The Black Craft Barossa Valley Shiraz 2016 Shiraz with the afterburners on. Blackberry jam and asphalt flavours come tipped with toasty, bourbon-like oak. You wouldn't call it sophisticated but you would call it tasty – and then some. Screwcap. 14% alc. **Rating** 91 **To** 2025 $25 CM

The Wit & Shanker Barossa Valley Cabernet Sauvignon 2015 Sawdusty oak splashes through the volume of sweet, ripe, curranty fruit. It's soft, easy-going and smooth. Dust and tobacco-like flavours give the clearest indication of the variety, but in truth this is full-bodied red wine first and foremost, cabernet second. Harmony of oak and fruit isn't spot on, but regardless few will be complaining. Screwcap. 13.5% alc. **Rating** 91 **To** 2025 $30 CM

Main & Cherry   ★★★★☆

Main Road, Cherry Gardens, SA 5157 **Region** Adelaide Hills
T 0431 692 791 **www.**mainandcherry.com.au **Open** By appt
Winemaker Michael Sexton **Est.** 2010 **Dozens** 2500 **Vyds** 4.5ha
Michael Sexton grew up on this property, and graduated in oenology at the University of Adelaide in 2003. Grapes from the existing shiraz plantings were once sold to other wineries, but in '10 the first single vineyard shiraz was made and the Main & Cherry brand was born. Since then, some bushvine grenache and mataro have been planted. The business continues to grow with the purchase of an established vineyard in Clarendon planted to shiraz and grenache. Exports to Vietnam and China.

🍷🍷🍷🍷🍷 **Adelaide Hills Tempranillo 2016** Hand-picked, open-fermented with 10% whole bunches, 16 days on skins, matured for 12 months in used French oak. The bouquet is aromatic, but it is the caressing mouthfeel that makes the first and last impression. Both the viticulturist and winemaker, the vines and grapes, have contributed to a light to medium-bodied and juicy tempranillo that will give pleasure wherever and whenever it's tasted. Screwcap. 14.2% alc. **Rating** 95 **To** 2026 $25 ❂
Adelaide Hills Rose 2017 Pale pink; tangy, savoury and spicy, and the mouthfeel very good indeed, reflecting maturation in used French oak for 6 months, gently softening the edges of a bone-dry wine. Refreshing. More please. Screwcap. 12.5% alc. **Rating** 94 **To** 2020 $20 ❂
Adelaide Hills Sangiovese 2016 Part fermented and matured for 90 days on skins in ceramic eggs, the balance open-fermented and basket-pressed into used oak. There's plenty to like about the wine, starting with the positive clear colour and the multi-cherry varietal fruit expression. It is medium-bodied, has good balance, and I fancy the shorter time on skins in the eggs was well judged. Screwcap. 14.2% alc. **Rating** 94 **To** 2031 $25 ❂

🍷🍷🍷🍷🍷 **Single Vineyard Adelaide Hills Shiraz 2016** **Rating** 93 **To** 2031 $30
Adelaide Hills Fiano 2017 **Rating** 92 **To** 2023 $24 ❂
McLaren Vale GSM 2016 **Rating** 92 **To** 2026 $25 ❂

Main Ridge Estate   ★★★★★

80 William Road, Red Hill, Vic 3937 **Region** Mornington Peninsula
T (03) 5989 2686 **www.**mre.com.au **Open** Mon–Fri 12–4, w'ends 12–5
Winemaker James Sexton, Linda Hodges, Nat White (Consultant) **Est.** 1975
Dozens 1200 **Vyds** 2.8ha
Quietly spoken and charming Nat and Rosalie White founded the first commercial winery on the Mornington Peninsula. It has an immaculately maintained vineyard and equally meticulously run winery. In December 2015, ownership of Main Ridge Estate passed to the Sexton family, following the retirement of Nat and Rosalie after 40 years. Tim and Libby Sexton have an extensive background in large-scale hospitality, first in the UK, then with Zinc at Federation Square, Melbourne, and at the MCG. Son James Sexton completed the Bachelor of Wine Science at CSU in '15. Nat will continue as a consultant to Main Ridge.

Majella   ★★★★★

Lynn Road, Coonawarra, SA 5263 **Region** Coonawarra
T (08) 8736 3055 **www.**majellawines.com.au **Open** 7 days 10–4.30
Winemaker Bruce Gregory, Michael Marcus **Est.** 1969 **Dozens** 26 000 **Vyds** 60ha

The Lynn family has been in residence in Coonawarra for over four generations, starting as storekeepers. The Majella property was originally owned by Frank Lynn, then purchased in 1960 by nephew George, who ran merinos for wool production and prime lambs. In '68 Anthony and Brian (the Prof) Lynn established the vineyards, since joined by Peter, Stephen, Nerys and Gerard. Bruce Gregory has been at the helm for every wine made at Majella. The Malleea is one of Coonawarra's classics; The Musician one of Australia's most outstanding red wines selling for less than $20 (having won many trophies and medals). The largely mature vineyards are principally shiraz and cabernet sauvignon, with a little riesling and merlot. Exports to the UK, Canada and Asia.

ŸŸŸŸŸ **Coonawarra Cabernet Sauvignon 2015** This hits the bullseye, a great example of the synergy between place and variety. Its colour is good, as is the bouquet, and that arrow arrives the moment the wine enters the mouth. It has waves of luscious and juicy red and black fruits that fill every corner of the palate, tannins and oak doing the job expected of them. Screwcap. 14.5% alc. **Rating** 96 To 2040 $35 ✪

GPL68 Coonawarra Cabernet Sauvignon 2014 Made to commemorate 25 years of winemaking. GPL refers to George Patrick Lynn, a patriarch of the Lynn family who passed away (at 50) in '76. It's a hulking cabernet, as tannic as it is intense, with blackcurrant and boysenberry flavours charging into dusty, tobacco-strewn tannin. Creamy oak plays a clear role, as do eucalyptus flavours, but this wine's power, glory and age-worthiness cannot be disputed. Screwcap. 14.5% alc. **Rating** 96 To 2035 $120 CM

Coonawarra Shiraz 2015 A very elegant wine, almost-but-not-quite shy and retiring, with bright red and black cherry fruit and attendant spices (and pepper) coming through on the precisely balanced palate. Oak and tannins observe their duties on the finish and aftertaste. Screwcap. 14.5% alc. **Rating** 95 To 2030 $30 ✪

Coonawarra Merlot 2016 Fermented in 300l French hogsheads, matured for 15 months. Trophy for Best Merlot, Limestone Coast Wine Show '17. Bright crimson-purple, and distinctly fragrant; the palate no less expressive with its mix of red berry and cassis fruits. Shows the benefit of partial barrel fermentation with the texture and integration of the oak. A major success. Screwcap. 14.5% alc. **Rating** 95 To 2030 $30 ✪

The Musician Coonawarra Cabernet Shiraz 2016 A 70/30% blend, fermented in stainless steel and oak, matured for 6 months before blending. Great colour; one of life's sweet mysteries is Majella keeping the price identical to that of the first release in '04. It is a joyous wine, revelling in its blend of blackcurrant, blackberry and plum fruit. Made with minimal oak contact, retaining maximum fruit freshness. Screwcap. 14.5% alc. **Rating** 94 To 2026 $18 ✪

ŸŸŸŸŸ **Coonawarra Riesling 2017 Rating** 90 To 2027 $17 ✪

Malcolm Creek Vineyard ★★★★

33 Bonython Road, Kersbrook, SA 5231 **Region** Adelaide Hills
T (08) 8389 3619 **www**.malcolmcreekwines.com.au **Open** By appt
Winemaker Peter Leske, Michael Sykes **Est.** 1982 **Dozens** 800 **Vyds** 2ha
Malcolm Creek was the retirement venture of Reg Tolley, who decided to upgrade his retirement by selling the venture to Bitten and Karsten Pedersen in 2007. The wines are invariably well made and develop gracefully; they are worth seeking out, and are usually available with some extra bottle age at a very modest price. Unfortunately, a series of natural disasters have decimated Malcolm Creek's production in recent years: '11 cabernet sauvignon not harvested due to continuous rain; '14 chardonnay not produced because of a microscopic yield following rain and wind at flowering; and the '15 vintage tainted by bushfire smoke. Exports to the UK, the US, Denmark, Malaysia and China.

ŸŸŸŸŸ **Adelaide Hills Sauvignon Blanc 2017** Another string to the bow of Adelaide Hills sauvignon blanc. There's the immediacy of the varietal pull, the wines born with a graceful suite of gently tropical fruits and balancing acidity. Screwcap. 13% alc. **Rating** 91 To 2020 $25

Ashwood Estate Adelaide Hills Cabernet Sauvignon 2013 Matured for 24 months in French oak. It is very youthful for a 5yo wine, especially cabernet. There's good balance between all the usual elements (most boxes ticked), and this still has time on its side. Cork. 13.5% alc. **Rating** 91 **To** 2027 $30

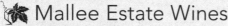 # Mallee Estate Wines ★★★

20 055 Renmark Avenue, Renmark, SA 5341 **Region** Riverland
T (08) 8595 1088 www.malleeestatewines.com.au **Open** 7 days 10.30–5
Winemaker Jim Markeas **Est.** 1998 **Dozens** 60 000 **Vyds** 53ha
This is the venture of the Markeas family. Parents Peter and Eleni migrated to Australia in the early 1960s. In '68 they purchased their first mixed-fruit block in Renmark, and they were looking at retirement in '94, a time when many family blocks were for sale. Their son Arthur, who was living in Adelaide at the time, encouraged Peter to take the opposite course, and purchase the neighbour's 8ha block giving room for expansion and specialisation. The crux of the deal was that their youngest son Jim, then in year 11 at high school, should abandon his career aspirations as a cabinetmaker and instead enrol into the wine science degree at CSU. The plan was realised, production grew, but then drought and oversupply issues led them to investigate the US market. In the wake of the GFC, they abandoned the US and went instead to China, where their wines proved popular at their price. Today Mallee Estate is successful in selling into the US market, and they have also seen the Chinese market grow substantially. The sales in Australia are of negligible importance.

Mandala ★★★★☆

1568 Melba Highway, Dixons Creek, Vic 3775 **Region** Yarra Valley
T (03) 5965 2016 www.mandalawines.com.au **Open** Mon–Fri 10–4, w'ends 10–5
Winemaker Charles Smedley, Scott McCarthy **Est.** 2007 **Dozens** 8500 **Vyds** 29ha
Mandala is owned by Charles Smedley, who acquired the established vineyard in 2007. It has vines up to 25 years old; the spectacular restaurant and cellar door complex is a more recent addition. As well as the Dixons Creek vineyard (chardonnay, pinot noir, cabernet sauvignon, sauvignon blanc, shiraz and merlot), there is a separate vineyard at Yarra Junction planted entirely to pinot noir with an impressive clonal mix. Exports to China.

♥♥♥♥♥ **The Mandala Butterfly Yarra Valley Cabernet Sauvignon 2015** March it straight to the cellar. This is a substantial red with flames of tannin running all along its sides. Cassis, mint, violet, blueberry and foresty notes. Size, shape, freshness and length. A big-picture wine for the long haul. Screwcap. 14.3% alc. **Rating** 96 **To** 2045 $50 CM ✪

♥♥♥♥♡ **Yarra Valley Chardonnay 2016** Rating 93 To 2023 $30 CM
Yarra Valley Pinot Noir 2016 Rating 92 To 2023 $30 CM
The Rock Yarra Valley Shiraz 2015 Rating 91 To 2028 $50 CM

Mandoon Estate ★★★★★

10 Harris Road, Caversham, WA 6055 **Region** Swan District
T (08) 6279 0500 www.mandoonestate.com.au **Open** 7 days 10–5
Winemaker Ryan Sudano **Est.** 2009 **Dozens** 10 000 **Vyds** 15ha
Mandoon Estate, headed by Allan Erceg, made a considerable impression with its wines in a very short time. In 2008 the family purchased a 13.2ha site in Caversham in the Swan Valley. Construction of the winery was completed in time for the first vintage, in '10. Winemaker Ryan Sudano has metaphorically laid waste to Australian wine shows with the quality of the wines he has made from the Swan Valley, Frankland River and Margaret River.

♥♥♥♥♥ **Reserve Margaret River Chardonnay 2015** A beautifully elegant chardonnay, picked at exactly the right time, and not stage-managed at any point. It is on a stage of its own, full of grace and charm, and has pure white peach/pink grapefruit aromas and flavours doing all that's needed, oak off stage. Screwcap. 12.5% alc. **Rating** 97 **To** 2027 $39 ✪

Reserve Frankland River Shiraz 2014 Bright, deep crimson; its quality and character hit the second you taste the wine, the flavours, texture and structure are still imprinted in my mouth as I write this tasting note. Black cherry fruit stands tall while fine, savoury tannins scurry about, but they don't make any impression on the fruit. A wine of considerable stature worthy of a back label that can be read. Screwcap. 14.5% alc. **Rating** 97 **To** 2044 $49 ✪

Reserve Research Station Margaret River Cabernet Sauvignon 2014 Small quantity made from vines that were planted in '76 for the government-owned Bramley Research Station. A very elegant and balanced wine, made with reverence and great skill since Mandoon acquired and rejuvenated the very run-down vineyard. This will have cassis dribbling down your chin if you don't pay attention. Screwcap. 14% alc. **Rating** 97 **To** 2044 $79 ✪

🍷🍷🍷🍷🍷 **Swan Valley Verdelho 2017** A verdelho that has a fanfare of flavour – and relies on fruit not residual sugar – is as uncommon as the unicorn. WA has always made it into the running with theirs, particularly in the hands of the late Jack Mann. These wines are 120+yo. The way the wine soars and then swoops on the finish is remarkable. Screwcap. 13% alc. **Rating** 96 **To** 2027 $23 ✪

Reserve Frankland River Riesling 2017 Pale straw with a bright green hue. Orange blossom, slate, kaffir lime leaf and grapefruit. It has the sense of being ripe and rich, but the palate defies that notion with its tensile mineral line and length. With 12% alc. and suitably low pH, this is one for the cellar. Screwcap. **Rating** 95 **To** 2023 $29 DB ✪

Old Vine Shiraz 2016 Beautiful, deep and vibrant purple-red. Ripe concentrated blackberry, hints of raspberry and cassis sweetness, vanilla and cedar. Aromas are mirrored on the palate, tannins fine and fruit-based with the 40% new French oak largely absorbed by the concentration and youthful exuberance of the fruit. Very good value and quality. Screwcap. 14.5% alc. **Rating** 95 **To** 2028 $29 DB ✪

Old Vine Grenache 2016 Medium purple-red and bright. It's all about the fruit, and as it was sourced from vineyards planted in '55 and '46, so it should be. Macerated black cherries, redcurrants and blueberry. Concentrated fruit, not the tutti-frutti that characterises many a grenache. Tannins are tight and chalky adding real structure and shape to the wine, which finishes with a curl of savoury tannin. More of this. Screwcap. 14.5% alc. **Rating** 95 **To** 2028 $29 DB ✪

Margaret River Sauvignon Blanc 2017 A small percentage is barrel-fermented, but the majority is fermented in stainless steel. The complex bouquet, with an elusive citrus rind note, is followed by an elegant, detailed palate; the barrel ferment having as much impact on texture as flavour. Screwcap. 12.5% alc. **Rating** 94 **To** 2020 $23 ✪

🍷🍷🍷🍷🍸 **Reserve Frankland River Shiraz 2015 Rating** 93 **To** 2028 $49 DB
Surveyors Red 2016 Rating 93 **To** 2028 $24 DB ✪
Reserve Margaret River Chardonnay 2016 Rating 90 **To** 2025 $39 DB

🍇 Manser Wines ★★★★

c/- 3 Riviera Court, Pasadena, SA 5042 (postal) **Region** Adelaide Hills
T 0400 251 168 **www**.manserwines.com.au **Open** Not
Winemaker Phil Christiansen **Est.** 2015 **Dozens** 1000 **Vyds** 6ha
Phil Manser has a long history of involvement in the wine industry in various parts of the world, and has now teamed up with brother Kevin and father Bernie to run a family vineyard. It was established in 1997 by Tim James, a skilled winemaker with senior winemaking and management roles at Hardys and Wirra Wirra. He planted four clones of shiraz randomly mixed throughout the vineyard, a common practice in France. The Mansers acquired the property in '15, Tim remaining an enthusiastic spectator during vintage. The Mansers also source fruit from a 65-year-old vineyard in Blewitt Springs, and a third vineyard on the McMurtrie Mile that feeds their One Mad Moment range. Winemaker Phil Christiansen looks after the destinies of a considerable number of vineyards throughout McLaren Vale.

ㅜㅜㅜㅜㅜ One Mad Moment McLaren Vale Shiraz 2016 It has good depth to the colour, and the full panoply of McLaren Vale shiraz aromas and flavours ranging across black cherry, plum and blackberry, with a waistband of dark chocolate and soft tannins. Screwcap. 14.6% alc. **Rating** 93 **To** 2031 $30

One Mad Moment McLaren Vale Shiraz 2013 Excellent colour gets the wine away to a flying start, and it's onwards and upwards. It has depth and is a lovely example of McLaren Vale shiraz, with luscious fruits, choc-mint, plum and blackberry all contributing. Screwcap. 14.6% alc. **Rating** 93 **To** 2033

Barely Dressed Adelaide Hills Shiraz 2016 The potent bouquet is matched to a full-bodied palate, with red, black and sour cherries driving the fruit profile through to a firm finish. The half-suggestion (on the front label) of short oak ageing seems to fit. Needs time to soften. Screwcap. 14.3% alc. **Rating** 90 **To** 2030 $30

ㅜㅜㅜㅜ One Mad Moment McLaren Vale Shiraz 2015 **Rating** 89 **To** 2025

Mansfield Wines   ★★★★

201 Eurunderee Lane, Mudgee, NSW 2850 **Region** Mudgee
T (02) 6373 3871 **www**.mansfieldwines.com.au **Open** Thurs–Tues & public hols 10–5
Winemaker Bob Heslop, Ian McLellan **Est.** 1975 **Dozens** 1500 **Vyds** 5.5ha
Ian McLellan and family purchased Mansfield Wines from his cousin Peter Mansfield in 1997. The original plantings, which included chardonnay, frontignac, sauvignon blanc, cabernet sauvignon, merlot and shiraz, were removed, to be replaced by a Joseph's coat of varieties including savagnin, vermentino, petit manseng, parellada, tempranillo, touriga, zinfandel and tinta cao, supported by grenache, mourvedre and pedro ximenez. Souzao and carignan are more recent arrivals.

ㅜㅜㅜㅜㅜ Shiraz Cabernet 2014 Currant, plum, mint and a combination of leaf and leather-like characters combine with supple texture to create a satisfying red. The finish kicks with tannin, but the fruit flavours more or less go with it. Drinking well now; no need to cellar it further. Screwcap. 13.5% alc. **Rating** 91 **To** 2023 $23 CM ○

Firetail 2015 A 40/30/23/7% blend of garnacha, shiraz, monastrel and tempranillo. Sweet plum–shot fruit, coffeed oak and various earth and spice notes. It's fluid and ripe but has enough going on around the edges to keep you coming back for more. Screwcap. 13.5% alc. **Rating** 90 **To** 2023 $19 CM ○

Mourvedre 2016 Coffeed oak helps fill it out, but the fruit ripeness and weight here is decent, especially in a varietal context. This is neat, tidy and warm, and offers a good flow of fruit flavour. Screwcap. 14% alc. **Rating** 90 **To** 2022 $19 CM ○

🍇 Marble Hill Winemakers   ★★★★

314 Marble Hill Road, Marble Hill, SA 5137 **Region** Adelaide Hills
T 0455 844 323 **www**.marblehill.com.au **Open** Not
Winemaker Brendon Keys **Est.** 2012 **Dozens** 1295 **Vyds** 3.9ha
The pages of history paint a vivid picture of the swings of fortune in the Adelaide Hills over the past 140 years. The climate and the rich red soils remain as they were in 1878 when SA's Governor Jervois chose Marble Hill for his summer residence. But in January 1955, the Black Sunday bushfires destroyed much of the magnificent multistorey mansion, the governor vowed never to return after he and his family almost lost their lives. The governor's stables were also destroyed, but in '73 the National Trust restored them (converting them into a tea room), along with a caretakers cottage. Again, these buildings fell into disuse, but now there is a full-fledged renaissance taking place. The tea room complex has been restored, and the extensive gardens meticulously brought back to full glory, assisted by the purchase of an adjoining property that had a water licence (and coincidentally almost 4ha of vineyards). Restoration work has begun on the governor's residence, and there is constant demand on the venue for weddings and similar events. The Marble Hill wine lable has now been added into the mix.

ΥΥΥΥΥ **Sunset Adelaide Hills Rose 2017** Made from estate-grown pinot noir. The highly fragrant bouquet has flowery, strawberry, red-fruit aromas, and brisk acidity highlighting the fruity nature of what is a deliciously dry style. Great bargain. Screwcap. 12.5% alc. **Rating** 94 **To** 2020 $20 ✪

ΥΥΥΥΥ **Adelaide Hills Black Sunday 2016 Rating** 90 **To** 2023 $45

Marchand & Burch   ★★★★☆

PO Box 180, North Fremantle, WA 5159 **Region** Great Southern
T (08) 9336 9600 **www.**burchfamilywines.com.au **Open** Not
Winemaker Janice McDonald, Pascal Marchand **Est.** 2007 **Dozens** 1100 **Vyds** 8.46ha
A joint venture between Canadian-born, Burgundian-trained Pascal Marchand and Burch Family Wines. Grapes are sourced from single vineyards, and in most cases from single blocks within those vineyards (the estate vineyards comprise 4.51ha of chardonnay and 3.95ha of pinot noir in Mount Barker and Porongurup). Biodynamic practices underpin the viticulture, and Burgundian techniques have been adopted (e.g. narrow rows and high density plantings, Guyot pruning, vertical shoot positioning, and leaf and lateral shoot removal). Exports to the UK, the US and other major markets.

ΥΥΥΥΥ **Villages Rose 2017** 50/50% shiraz and pinot noir; 89% Great Southern, 11% Margaret River. Enticing bouquet with a savoury, earthy accent to the red-berry aromas. Has immediate impact in the mouth, where juicy, slightly tangy flavours fill the palate from start to finish. Textural and long, it shows real energy and liveliness. Screwcap. 13% alc. **Rating** 94 **To** 2019 $26 SC ✪

Marcus Hill Vineyard   ★★★★

560 Banks Road, Marcus Hill, Vic 3222 (postal) **Region** Geelong
T (03) 5251 3797 **www.**marcushillvineyard.com.au **Open** Not
Winemaker Chip Harrison **Est.** 2000 **Dozens** 1000 **Vyds** 3ha
In 2000, Richard and Margot Harrison, together with 'gang pressed friends', planted 2ha of pinot noir overlooking Port Lonsdale, Queenscliff and Ocean Grove, a few kilometres from Bass Strait and Port Phillip Bay. Since then, chardonnay, shiraz, more pinot noir, and three rows of pinot meunier have been added. The vineyard is run with minimal sprays, and the aim is to produce elegant wines that truly express the maritime site.

ΥΥΥΥΥ **Bellarine Peninsula Shiraz 2015** Shows gamey, cool-climate spiciness but an underlying ripeness of fruit as well. Bright, tangy cherry flavours run through the medium-bodied palate with a buoyancy and energy that carry it confidently along, and the tannins provide a tight and well balanced finish. Screwcap. 13.8% alc. **Rating** 92 **To** 2035 $24 SC ✪
Bellarine Peninsula Pinot Gris 2017 Certainly seems to have picked up some desirable texture from 6 months in French oak, complementing the very clear varietal character. Nashi pear is at the forefront on the bouquet and palate, the flavours ripe, veering towards sweetness but staying just short of that. Screwcap. 12.5% alc. **Rating** 91 **To** 2020 $24 SC
People Madly Stomping Bellarine Peninsula Pinot Noir 2017 Predominantly MV6 clone, a portion crushed and destemmed, the balance wild-fermented with whole bunches and extended time on skins. The whole-bunch component is evident with its mulchy, gamey character, but it is ripe cherry-like fruit that fills the palate. The flavour isn't particularly complex, but it's an attractive style. Screwcap. 13.2% alc. **Rating** 90 **To** 2025 $21 SC ✪

ΥΥΥΥ **Bellarine Peninsula Chardonnay 2016 Rating** 89 **To** 2021 $30 SC
Bellarine Peninsula Pinot Meunier 2017 Rating 89 **To** 2022 $30 SC

Margan Family

1238 Milbrodale Road, Broke, NSW 2330 **Region** Hunter Valley
T (02) 6579 1317 **www**.margan.com.au **Open** 7 days 10–5
Winemaker Andrew Margan **Est.** 1997 **Dozens** 30 000 **Vyds** 98ha
Andrew Margan, following in his late father's footsteps, entered the wine industry over 20 years ago, working as a Flying Winemaker in Europe, then for Tyrrell's. The growth of the Margan Family business over the following years has been the result of unremitting hard work and a keen understanding of the opportunities Australia's most visited wine region provides. They have won innumerable awards in the tourism sector, against competition in the Hunter Valley, across NSW and Australia-wide. The next generation looks similarly set to cover all bases when their parents retire: eldest son Ollie is finishing a double degree in winemaking and viticultural science at the University of Adelaide; daughter Alessa is studying communications at UTS while working in wine and food PR; and younger son James is enrolled in economics at Sydney University. Andrew has continued to push the envelope in the range of wines made, without losing focus on the varieties that have made the Hunter famous. He planted barbera in 1998, and since then has progressively added mourvedre, albarino, tempranillo and graciano. Exports to the UK, Germany, Norway, Indonesia, Malaysia, Vietnam, Hong Kong and China.

Aged Release Semillon 2012 A classic 6yo Hunter semillon, now making the transition from youth to maturity. Lemon zest and juice ride in the carriage of the acidity that is so much part and parcel of this style. Another 5 years will show all its vinous treasures. Screwcap. 11% alc. **Rating** 95 **To** 2032 $50

Albarino 2017 Rating 93 **To** 2019 $30 CM
Semillon 2017 Rating 92 **To** 2030 $20 SC ✪
Breaking Ground Shiraz Mourvedre 2016 Rating 92 **To** 2026 $40
Breaking Ground Barbera 2016 Rating 91 **To** 2029 $40
Breaking Ground Tempranillo Graciano Shiraz 2016 Rating 90 **To** 2029 $40

Margaret Hill Vineyard

18 Northcote Avenue, Balwyn, Vic 3103 (postal) **Region** Heathcote
T (03) 9836 2168 **www**.guangtiangroup.com.au **Open** Not
Winemaker Ben Portet **Est.** 1996 **Dozens** 1100 **Vyds** 12.5ha
Formerly known as Toolleen Vineyard, the name Margaret Hill Vineyard was chosen by owner Linchun Bao (and wife Chunye Qiu) after they acquired the Heathcote business from the Huang family in 2010. They have upgraded the vineyard equipment and irrigation system, and are restoring full health and vigour to the vineyard, which is equally split between cabernet sauvignon and shiraz. Wines are released under the Margaret Hill and Kudo labels. The quality of the vineyard, and the skill of contract winemaker Ben Portet, have together been responsible for the high quality of the wines. Exports to China.

Kudo Shiraz 2016 Ripe and raisiny but savoury too, with the real decider a surge of ripe, smoky tannin – the carpet on which the fruit rides. You could dismiss this wine for its sweet exuberance, but the truth is there are many tricks to this pony. Sandalwood, clove and dark earth notes add features to the landscape of fruit. Robust in nature, svelte by design. Cork. 14.5% alc. **Rating** 94 **To** 2034 CM

Marjico

Wine Wise Winery, 928 Research Road, Nuriootpa, SA 5355 **Region** Barossa Valley
T 0411 721 633 **www**.marjicowines.com.au **Open** Not
Winemaker Joanne Irvine **Est.** 2014 **Dozens** 300
The irrepressible Jim Irvine comes up once again, this time in conjunction with wife Marjorie (and daughter Joanne as winemaker), and with cabernet franc rather than merlot being the main attraction. Cabernet franc is a variety that has never achieved prominence in Australia; it is planted to the greatest extent in Margaret River. Thus it's no surprise that Marjico's annual crush will produce a low 300 dozen bottles of wine. Because of the small size of the business, selling online will be the most likely distribution method. Exports to China.

♟♟♟♟♀ The Harvesters Barossa Valley Cabernet Franc Merlot 2014 'A tiny touch of deluxe merlot was added, just to add a little plummy softness on the mid-palate.' Well, it does just that, but you end up looking for tannins to give structure. It's sybaritic, though. Screwcap. 14.5% alc. **Rating** 90 **To** 2030 $40
The Harvesters Barossa Valley Cabernet Franc 2015 The class of the '15 vintage shows through. Both generations of the Irvine family are devotees of merlot and cabernet franc, loving the latter for the violet aromatics they fervently believe can be captured from the two valleys (Eden and Barossa). Their wines are strictly on style. Screwcap. 14.5% alc. **Rating** 90 **To** 2030 $40

♟♟♟♟ The Harvesters Barossa Valley Rose 2017 **Rating** 89 **To** 2020 $20

Mark's Vineyard   ★★★☆

143 Onkaparinga Valley Road, Woodside, SA 5224 **Region** Adelaide Hills
T 0488 997 200 **www**.marksvineyard.com.au **Open** At Ekhidna
Winemaker Darryl Catlin, Matt Rechner **Est.** 2014 **Dozens** 21 000 **Vyds** 41.5ha
The current vineyard in Mark's Vineyard was the Shaw + Smith M3 Vineyard, which was established in 1994 by Mark, Margie, Matthew and Michael Hill Smith. They, collectively, owned 70% of the property, with Shaw + Smith owning the remaining 30%. In September 2014, Matthew and daughter Christobel came into full ownership of the property, and the former M3 Vineyard (a registered trademark of Shaw + Smith) has now undergone a name change. What does not change, though, is the 27ha plantings of sauvignon blanc, chardonnay and shiraz.

♟♟♟♟♀ Adelaide Hills Sauvignon Blanc 2017 Fresh and lively, tropical fruits to the fore, backed up by minerally acidity. From a distinguished vineyard, and well made. Screwcap. 12% alc. **Rating** 90 **To** 2020 $25

Massena Vineyards   ★★★★★

PO Box 643, Angaston, SA 5353 **Region** Barossa Valley
T 0408 821 737 **www**.massena.com.au **Open** At Artisans of Barossa
Winemaker Jaysen Collins **Est.** 2000 **Dozens** 5000 **Vyds** 4ha
Massena Vineyards draws upon 1ha each of mataro, saperavi, petite syrah and tannat at Nuriootpa, also purchasing grapes from other growers. It is an export-oriented business, although the wines can also be purchased by mail order, which, given their quality and innovative nature, seems more than ordinarily worthwhile. Exports to the US, Switzerland, Denmark, South Korea, NZ, Hong Kong and China.

♟♟♟♟♀ Stonegarden Eden Valley Riesling 2017 1940s vines. Textural, powerful, persistent. Lime juice and crystals, talc, spice, mineral and a hint of orange blossom. A trace of fruit sweetness. It's pretty and it's purposeful, and it feels soft as it extends along your tongue. A treat of a wine. Screwcap. 12.5% alc. **Rating** 95 **To** 2028 $30 CM ✪
The Moonlight Run 2016 Constructed from 34% estate mataro fermented with partial stalk inclusion, 33% early-harvested 150yo bushvine grenache, and 33% Tanunda shiraz. The secret ingredient that invests the wine with savoury spices and freshness is the slightly lower alcohol, usually 14.5% and above in the Barossa Valley. The length and finish have zest and texture. Screwcap. 14% alc. **Rating** 95 **To** 2029 $30 ✪
The Eleventh Hour Barossa Valley Shiraz 2016 100% destemmed, open-fermented, basket-pressed, matured in used oak. The inky crimson–purple colour holds court all the way to the rim, and tells of the sheer (black) fruit power of the palate, licorice and pepper adding complexity. The mouthfeel is super velvety, which adds to the density of the fruit. It will be 10 years before it opens the doors for inspection. Screwcap. 14% alc. **Rating** 94 **To** 2046 $43

♟♟♟♟♀ The Howling Dog Saperavi 2016 **Rating** 93 **To** 2024 $35 CM
Dadds Block Primitivo 2016 **Rating** 90 **To** 2026 $28

Matriarch & Rogue ★★★★

PO Box 6752, Clare, SA 5453 **Region** Clare Valley
T 0419 901 892 **www.**matriarchandrogue.com.au **Open** Not
Winemaker Marnie Roberts **Est.** 2014 **Dozens** 2500
The catchy name is based on five sisters who are the third generation of the Byrne family,
with a history going back to Ireland. The sisters are known as the Patrick Byrne girls, and
the name is a tribute to the strong women of the family, and the rogues they married.
Winemaker/proprietor Marnie Roberts (also Claymore winemaker) is, one assumes, one of
the strong women.

ΨΨΨΨΨ **Alice Clare Valley Shiraz 2016** Intense deep purple-black. Plums and cherries
mixed with cinnamon, earth, dried herbs and enough charry French oak
(20% new) to make its presence felt. It should settle with time, as there's plenty of
fruit concentration. Screwcap. 14.5% alc. **Rating** 91 **To** 2028 $28 JF
Mary Clare Valley Tempranillo 2016 Good purple-red hue; a juicy, buoyant
wine and so spicy with pine needle/mint freshness, working off a lighter frame. In
hipster wine bars this would be called smashable. Screwcap. 13.8% alc. **Rating** 90
To 2022 $28 JF

Maverick Wines ★★★★★

981 Light Pass Road, Vine Vale, Moorooroo, SA 5352 **Region** Barossa Valley
T (08) 8563 3551 **www.**maverickwines.com.au **Open** Mon–Tues 1.30–4.30 or by appt
Winemaker Ronald Brown, Leon Deans **Est.** 2004 **Dozens** 10000 **Vyds** 61.7ha
This is the business established by highly experienced vigneron Ronald Brown. It has
evolved, now with seven vineyards across the Barossa and Eden valleys, all transitioned into
biodynamic grape production. The vines range from 40 to almost 150 years old, underpinning
the consistency and quality of the wines. Exports to the UK, France, Russia, Thailand, Japan
and China.

ΨΨΨΨΨ **Old Ben Eden Valley Shiraz 2016** Eden Valley's floral scents are plied with
anise and pepper-clad acidity, towing a sublimely elegant manifest of warm-climate
shiraz. It is long and plush, with dried seaweed, blueberry and cardamom crush.
There is plenty of vanillan oak here, too, buried amid the cornucopia of fruit.
Complex stuff. Cork. 14.9% alc. **Rating** 96 **To** 2031 $120 NG
The Maverick Barossa Shiraz 2016 A meld of select Eden Valley terroirs, this
has a largesse built to last. The fruit is supported by a lavish wall of oak. There is
plenty of spice, flesh and florals, a reductive clench of tension and a vivid mineral
skein. The oak will dissolve. Just be patient! Cork. 14.9% alc. **Rating** 96 **To** 2036
$300 NG
Trial Hill Eden Valley Shiraz 2016 This has thrust and edge: warm plummy
fruit moving into cooler blue fruits, Eden Valley's signature lilac lift, and plenty of
toasty oak smeared with tapenade to chaperone it across a very long finish line.
Cork. 14.7% alc. **Rating** 95 **To** 2031 $120 NG
Greenock Rise Barossa Valley Shiraz 2016 Thick, vinous fruit; Turkish
delight exotica! Violet and blueberry underlain by a heady carpet of oak tannins
and a charge of volatility, lifting the concentration across the scented length. This
has a fierce pulse, charging out of the gates from the nose and bouncing across
the mid-palate. Pulpier than the other wines in the upper rank. It should age very
well. Cork. 15.1% alc. **Rating** 95 **To** 2031 $120 NG
Trial Hill Eden Valley Riesling 2017 Jasmine, green apple, spa salts and a twirl
of citrus rind meld effortlessly with a ricochet of juicy acidity and a phenolic
rail. With great appeal, given the palpably natural feel to it. Screwcap. 12.2% alc.
Rating 94 **To** 2029 $32 NG

ΨΨΨΨΨ **Twins Barossa Cabernet Sauvignon 2017 Rating** 93 **To** 2026 $29 NG
Twins Barossa Grenache Shiraz Mourvedre 2017 Rating 92 **To** 2025
$29 NG

Twins Barrel Select Barossa Valley Cabernet Sauvignon Merlot Petit
Verdot Cabernet Franc 2017 Rating 92 To 2025 $29 NG
Twins Barrel Select The Barossa Shiraz 2017 Rating 91 To 2025 $29 NG
Trial Hill Eden Valley Chardonnay 2017 Rating 90 To 2025 $45 NG
Breechens Barossa Shiraz 2017 Rating 90 To 2025 $22 NG

Maxwell Wines ★★★★☆

Olivers Road, McLaren Vale, SA 5171 **Region** McLaren Vale
T (08) 8323 8200 **www**.maxwellwines.com.au **Open** 7 days 10–5
Winemaker Andrew Jericho, Mark Maxwell **Est.** 1979 **Dozens** 30 000 **Vyds** 40ha
Maxwell Wines has carved out a reputation as a premium producer in McLaren Vale, making
some excellent red wines in recent years. The majority of the vines on the estate were planted
in 1972, and include 19 rows of the highly regarded Reynella clone of cabernet sauvignon.
The Ellen Street shiraz block in front of the winery was planted in '53. Owned and operated
by Mark Maxwell. Exports to all major markets.

🍷🍷🍷🍷🍷 Eight Bells Reserve McLaren Vale Shiraz 2015 A best-barrels selection.
25 months in oak (mostly American, some French, 20% new). For all its might it
remains mannered. Blueberry, blackberry, violet and saltbush flavours are given a
gentle tickle by the nutty, smoky oak. Tannin is an exercise in intricacy and there's
a decent push of flavour through the finish. It's a voluptuous wine; the quality is
up there. Cork. 14.8% alc. **Rating** 95 To 2033 $45 CM
Eocene Ancient Earth McLaren Vale Shiraz 2015 It makes you want to
stand back and admire it. It's a full-on red, big and smooth, the fruit rich and
raisiny, the oak (100% French, 20% new) poured liberally on top. Cedar wood
and cream, sweet and soft. Flashes of choc-mint too. Beneath is a wave of rich,
ripe plum, and sweet, suede-like leather. For all that, it persists well through the
finish; it seals the deal. At no point does the alcohol intrude. Screwcap. 14.8% alc.
Rating 94 To 2030 $55 CM

🍷🍷🍷🍷🍸 Minotaur Reserve Shiraz 2014 Rating 93 To 2040 $75 CM
Four Roads Old Vine Grenache 2016 Rating 93 To 2024 $28 CM
Silver Hammer Shiraz 2016 Rating 92 To 2025 $22 CM ○
Fresca McLaren 2017 Rating 92 To 2021 $25 CM ○
Lime Cave Cabernet Sauvignon 2015 Rating 92 To 2026 $40 CM
Ellen Street Shiraz 2015 Rating 91 To 2027 $40 CM

Mayer ★★★★★

66 Miller Road, Healesville, Vic 3777 **Region** Yarra Valley
T (03) 5967 3779 **www**.timomayer.com.au **Open** By appt
Winemaker Timo Mayer **Est.** 1999 **Dozens** 1500 **Vyds** 2.4ha
Timo Mayer, also winemaker at Gembrook Hill, teamed with partner Rhonda Ferguson to
establish Mayer on the slopes of Mt Toolebewong, 8km south of Healesville. The steepness of
those slopes is presumably 'celebrated' in the name given to the wines (Bloody Hill). Pinot
noir is the main variety in the high density vineyard, with smaller amounts of shiraz and
chardonnay. Mayer's winemaking credo is minimal interference and handling, and no filtration.
Exports to the UK, France, Germany, Denmark, Sweden, Singapore and Japan.

🍷🍷🍷🍷🍷 Dr Mayer Pinot Noir 2016 100% whole bunches in the ferment but not an
overt or extreme rendition; the wine finely tuned with a thirst-quenching quality.
There are fine, supple, slightly powdery tannins, some stemmy pomegranate
flavours, spices, crunchy daikon radish and a pleasing bitter radicchio note, with a
lemony tang to the acidity. Everything contained and balanced on a lighter frame,
but still with intensity to the fruit. Diam. 13.5% alc. **Rating** 96 To 2026 $60 JF ○
Pinot Noir 2016 A surprisingly lighter hue of pale-mid ruby. It's ethereal with
a certain elegance, and feels as unforced as the cherry-accented fruit with forest-
floor aromas and florals. Not quite medium-bodied with filigreed tannins; sweet,
savoury and moreish. Lovely wine. Diam. 13.5% alc. **Rating** 95 To 2025 $60 JF

Syrah 2016 A striking wine: balanced and restrained, yet with layers of depth and flavour. Hints of blue fruits and black plums, earthy, stemmy and pulpy with a roll-call of spices. One of the signature traits of the Mayer wines is succulence, and it's here aplenty. Diam. 14% alc. **Rating** 95 **To** 2027 $60 JF

Cabernet 2016 Timo Mayer doesn't shy away from using 100% whole bunches in his cabernet. Yes, cabernet. Incorporating them with fruit that is plump and ripe has worked a treat. This is juicy and vibrant, with a mix of blackcurrants and plums, juniper and woodsy spices, crunchy acidity and finely tuned tannins. Dangerously drinkable now. Diam. 14% alc. **Rating** 95 **To** 2026 $60 JF

♥♥♥♥♡ **Bloody Hill Yarra Valley Pinot Noir 2016** Rating 93 To 2023 $30 JF

Mayford Wines   ★★★★★

6815 Great Alpine Road, Porepunkah, Vic 3740 **Region** Alpine Valleys
T (03) 5756 2528 **www.**mayfordwines.com **Open** By appt
Winemaker Eleana Anderson **Est.** 1995 **Dozens** 800 **Vyds** 3.9ha

The roots of Mayford go back to 1995, when Brian Nicholson planted a small amount of shiraz, chardonnay and tempranillo. Further plantings of shiraz, tempranillo, cabernet sauvignon and malbec have increased the total vineyard to 3.9ha, with more plantings planned. In their words, 'In-house winemaking commenced shortly after Brian selected his seasoned winemaker bride in 2002'. Wife and co-owner Eleana Anderson was a Flying Winemaker, working four vintages in Germany while completing her wine science degree at CSU (having much earlier obtained an arts degree). Vintages in Australia included one at Feathertop (also at Porepunkah), where she met her husband-to-be. Initially, she was unenthusiastic about tempranillo, which Brian had planted after consultation with Mark Walpole, Brown Brothers' viticulturist. But since making the first vintage in '06, she has been thoroughly enamoured of the variety. Eleana practises minimalist winemaking, declining to use enzymes, cultured yeasts, tannins and/or copper. Exports to Singapore.

♥♥♥♥♥ **Porepunkah Shiraz 2015** Dramatically different from the '16, as it should be. 13 clones of shiraz made in small batches, variously spending 3–8 weeks on skins, matured for 22 months in French barriques (36% new). It's luscious, filling the mouth and then some with its multifaceted purple and black fruits, rounded tannins and high quality oak judged to perfection. One of those wines tempting you to have a mouthful or so. Screwcap. 13.9% alc. **Rating** 96 **To** 2035 $40 ✪

Porepunkah Chardonnay 2016 If there is a heavier Burgundy-style bottle, I haven't encountered it, and have no wish to do so. Happily for those who have lugged a 6-bottle case into their cellar, the wine is full of character. If they've picked up 12 bottles they are either Olympic weightlifters or in hospital after cardiac arrest. The wine has a ramrod-straight link through the length of the palate, and will soften slowly as it ages. It will be worth the weight and the wait. Screwcap. 13% alc. **Rating** 95 **To** 2029 $38

Grapes of Wrath Shiraz 2016 In contrast to the perfect weather of '15, a wall of hail in the lead-up to vintage destroyed over half the crop. Unexpected offers of help from friends resulted in this regional blend from Heathcote, Beechworth and the Alpine Valleys. It ripples with flavour and texture patterns – red, purple and black fruits with a collage of tannins. Still to settle down, which it will surely do over the next few years. Screwcap. 13.9% alc. **Rating** 94 **To** 2031 $32

Ovens Crossing 2015 A blend of tempranillo and cabernet sauvignon. Deep colour; a powerful, savoury, dark fruited, sombre wine that momentarily looks like derailing itself, recovers quickly, and moves confidently on thereafter. Spicy cherry fruit ex the tempranillo staring down the autocratic cabernet blackcurrant. Screwcap. 13.9% alc. **Rating** 94 **To** 2029 $55

Maygars Hill Winery ★★★★★

53 Longwood-Mansfield Road, Longwood, Vic 3665 **Region** Strathbogie Ranges
T 0402 136 448 **www**.maygarshill.com.au **Open** By appt
Winemaker Contract **Est.** 1997 **Dozens** 900 **Vyds** 3.2ha
Jenny Houghton purchased this 8ha property in 1994, planting shiraz (1.9ha) and cabernet sauvignon (1.3ha). The name comes from Lieutenant Colonel Maygar, who fought with outstanding bravery in the Boer War in South Africa in 1901, and was awarded the Victoria Cross. In World War I he rose to command the 8th Light Horse Regiment, winning further medals for bravery. The Shiraz and Cabernet Sauvignon, both in Reserve and standard guise, have been consistently excellent for a number of years. Exports to China.

♜♜♜♜♜ **Reserve Shiraz 2016** This is the best Reserve Shiraz Maygars Hill has made to date. There is an urgency, a freshness to the expression, the new oak easily absorbed on the long palate. This isolated vineyard is one of the jewels of the Strathbogie Ranges. Screwcap. 13.5% alc. **Rating** 96 **To** 2036 $42 ✪
Shiraz 2016 Generosity is the keyword, with soft, pillowy plum and blackberry fruits in a typically well made wine. The balance of fruit, tannins and oak can't be faulted. Screwcap. 15% alc. **Rating** 94 **To** 2031 $30 ✪

♜♜♜♜♀ **Reserve Cabernet Sauvignon 2016 Rating** 90 **To** 2029 $42

Mayhem & Co

49 Collingrove Avenue, Broadview, SA 5083 **Region** Adelaide Hills
T 0468 384 817 **www**.mayhemandcowine.com.au **Open** Not
Winemaker Andrew Hill **Est.** 2009 **Dozens** 1400
Mayhem & Co is owned by Andrew Hill, who worked vintages at Wirra Wirra and Chapel Hill before taking on senior sales and marketing roles with Koonara, Tomich Wines and Reschke Wines. The wines are made from grapes purchased from various growers in the Adelaide Hills, Eden Valley and McLaren Vale. Andrew is also the Australian/NZ manager for the cooper Nadalie, and is scaling down his winemaking to just two offerings – Small Berries Syrah and the Keg Old Vines Shiraz – aimed at the Chinese market with some direct sales locally. Exports to Hong Kong and China.

♜♜♜♜♜ **Small Berries Blewitt Springs Syrah 2016** 40yo vines, whole berries, inoculated, aged 14 months in French barriques (20% new). A pitch-perfect rendition with everything balanced and in its place, from the succulent fruit and plush, velvety tannins to the long palate and the sheer deliciousness of it. Screwcap. 13.8% alc. **Rating** 95 **To** 2028 $36 JF

♜♜♜♜♀ **Keg Old Vines Barossa Valley Shiraz 2016 Rating** 93 **To** 2024 $40 JF

Meadowbank Wines ★★★★★

652 Meadowbank Road, Meadowbank, Tas 7140 **Region** Southern Tasmania
T 0439 448 151 **www**.meadowbank.com.au **Open** Not
Winemaker Peter Dredge **Est.** 1976 **Dozens** 1200 **Vyds** 52ha
In 1976 Gerald and Sue Ellis picked the first grapes from their large Glenora property at the top end of the Derwent River, having planted the vines in 1974. There have been four major expansions since, most recently a 10ha planting of pinot noir, chardonnay, syrah and gamay in 2016, lifting the total to 52ha, the major part as fully mature vines. Meadowbank Wines opened its cellar door and restaurant in July '00 at Cambridge in the Coal River Valley. The wines were made next door at what is now Frogmore Creek. Eventually Frogmore Creek purchased Meadowbank's cellar door and restaurant (since they didn't previously have either), leaving Meadowbank to concentrate on further developing its vineyards. Meadowbank supplies grapes to six or so small wineries, and also leases 32ha to Accolade. Peter Dredge, having been intimately associated with the vineyard for six years, formed a partnership with the Ellis family (Gerald, Sue, daughter Mardi and her husband, Alex Dean) to relaunch

Meadowbank. From '16 the wines were made by Peter at Moorilla Estate from the potion of vineyard set aside for the Meadowbank wines.

ŸŸŸŸŸ **Pinot Noir 2017** Exceptionally powerful on the bouquet and all the way to the finish and aftertaste. Has that tension between savoury fruits on the one hand, and gleaming red and purple fruits on the other. The result is a wine with almost painful length, keeping the tastebuds working flat out keeping up to progress along and across the palate. Screwcap. 13% alc. **Rating** 97 **To** 2030 $55 ✪

ŸŸŸŸŸ **Riesling 2017** Quite simply a beautiful riesling, tracking the German idea that the g/l of residual sugar and titratable acidity should be roughly the same; here 10g/l residual sugar and 9.1g/l ta. The wine swoops and soars with its flavours, never pausing for a break. Screwcap. 11.5% alc. **Rating** 96 **To** 2035 $32 ✪

Chardonnay 2017 Three clones, hand-picked, whole bunches, wild-fermented in French barriques (14% new), matured for 9 months. While Tasmania has at times faltered with chardonnay, both small and large producers are coming to understand it better, and this is a good example. It is intense and precise, acidity simply part of a much larger whole, the fruit spectrum balanced to include apple and pear. Screwcap. 12.5% alc. **Rating** 95 **To** 2025 $50

Gamay 2017 This comes seriously close to the real deal, as it's made in France. Delicious, dark plum fruit offset by lively acidity and multi-spices. Now at its best as a young wine, but its juicy acidity will stand it in good stead for those who cellar it. Fun stuff. Screwcap. 12.5% alc. **Rating** 94 **To** 2020 $45

Medhurst ★★★★★

24–26 Medhurst Road, Gruyere, Vic 3770 **Region** Yarra Valley
T (03) 5964 9022 **www**.medhurstwines.com.au **Open** Thurs–Mon & public hols 11–5
Winemaker Simon Steele **Est.** 2000 **Dozens** 4500 **Vyds** 12.21ha
The wheel has come full circle for Ross and Robyn Wilson. In the course of a very distinguished corporate career, Ross was CEO of Southcorp when it brought the Penfolds, Lindemans and Wynns businesses under its banner. Robyn spent her childhood in the Yarra Valley, her parents living less than a kilometre away from Medhurst. The vineyard is planted to sauvignon blanc, chardonnay, pinot noir, cabernet sauvignon and shiraz, all running on a low-yield basis. The winery focuses on small-batch production, and also provides contract winemaking services. The visual impact of the winery has been minimised by recessing the building into the slope of land and locating the barrel room underground. The building was recognised for its architectural excellence at the Victorian Architecture Awards. The arrival of Simon Steele (his loss much mourned by Brokenwood) has enhanced the already considerable reputation of Medhurst.

ŸŸŸŸŸ **Estate Vineyard Chardonnay 2016** What makes this wine special is the perfect balance of the fruit flavours: white peach and pink grapefruit locked in a symbiotic embrace, with a near-invisible net of creamy/nutty flavours ex the oak and use of lees in full-solids fermentation. Regional winner of the James Halliday Chardonnay Challenge '17. Screwcap. 13% alc. **Rating** 96 **To** 2026 $40 ✪

Estate Vineyard Rose 2017 Salmon tinged with a copper hue. A blend of 61% cabernet sauvignon and 39% shiraz, this is a rose built from the ground up with a burst of creamy fruit flavours ricocheting around the mouth before acidity and savoury notes enter the fray on the back-palate and super-long finish. A serious rose. Screwcap. 13% alc. **Rating** 95 **To** 2020 $26 ✪

YRB 2017 A co-fermented blend (whole berries, no stems) of 50% pinot noir and 50% shiraz that spent 12 days on skins before maturation in used French puncheons. It's no namby-pamby with its wealth of red apple fruits allied with deceptively fine tannins, which are the beams and joists of the long palate. Seductive now, but nowhere near the joyous complexity it will have in 5 years' time. Screwcap. 13% alc. **Rating** 95 **To** 2027 $38

Estate Vineyard Pinot Noir 2016 The brilliant crimson colour is underlined by the perfumed bouquet of cherry blossom and spice, the palate picking up the bouquet then precisely delivering a pinot of excellent length, line and balance. Very good in the context of a challenging vintage. Screwcap. 13% alc. **Rating** 94 To 2028 $38

♚♚♚♚ Estate Vineyard Sauvignon Blanc 2017 Rating 89 To 2020 $27

Meerea Park ★★★★★

Cnr Broke Road/McDonalds Road, Pokolbin, NSW 2320 **Region** Hunter Valley
T (02) 4998 7474 **www**.meereapark.com.au **Open** 7 days 10–5
Winemaker Rhys Eather **Est.** 1991 **Dozens** 11 000
This is the project of Rhys and Garth Eather, whose great-great-grandfather, Alexander Munro, established a famous vineyard at Singleton in the 19th century, known as Bebeah. While the range of wines chiefly focuses on semillon and shiraz, it extends to other varieties (including chardonnay), and also into other regions. Meerea Park's cellar door is located at the striking Tempus Two winery, owned by the Roche family. It hardly need be said that the quality of the wines, especially with 5 years' cellaring, is outstanding. Exports to the US, Canada, Singapore and China.

♚♚♚♚♚ **Aged Release Alexander Munro Individual Vineyard Hunter Valley Shiraz 2009** High quality Hunter Valley shiraz such as this has an amazing ability, when tasted alongside full-bodied shiraz from any other region, be it warm or cool, to glide past them all without even needing to acknowledge their quality or style. Spicy, earthy, great texture and length; this is reminiscent of Maurice O'Shea's wines (though those were without the benefit of a screwcap). 13% alc. **Rating** 97 To 2049 $120 ✪

♚♚♚♚♚ **Alexander Munro Individual Vineyard Hunter Valley Semillon 2013** Alexander Munro is made from the best 'individual vineyard' parcel of fruit each year. This was released when 5yo and has terrific intensity and drive; its structure and balance encapsulates Hunter semillon at its best. Screwcap. 10.5% alc. **Rating** 96 To 2033 $45 ✪

Terracotta Individual Vineyard Hunter Valley Syrah 2016 Shiraz with 2% viognier, co-fermented; the shiraz component with 40% whole bunches; matured in French puncheons (33% new) for 17 months. The deep, bright colour is seemingly due to the co-fermentation of the viognier, the richer dark fruits, the old vines, and the whole-bunch fermentation. This soars above the limitations of the vintage, and can be enjoyed now or 30+ years hence. Screwcap. 13.5% alc. **Rating** 96 To 2051 $70 ✪

Cellar Release BLACK Hunter Valley Shiraz 2011 A best-barrels selection made in Meerea Park's 20th vintage. Don't pay any attention to the light colour, because the wine is elegant, finely structured and with the infinitely complex and unique aromas and flavours of shiraz entering what will be a long plateau of perfection. It is earthy, spicy, and has purple (plum) and black (blackberry) fruits and savoury tannins. If you decant the wine 2 hours before serving, you won't have to work hard to find them; they will immediately find every corner of your mouth. Screwcap. 13.5% alc. **Rating** 96 To 2031 $250

Terracotta Individual Vineyard Hunter Valley Semillon 2013 Held back for extended cellaring, and it is easy to see why. Brilliantly coloured, it has a delicious collage of lime, honey and mineral flavours. Its purity and mouthfeel are striking. Drinking the wine now is not a sin if you have some more in the further recesses of your cellar. Screwcap. 11.5% alc. **Rating** 95 To 2033 $35 ✪

Aged Release Alexander Munro Individual Vineyard Hunter Valley Semillon 2009 Gleaming quartz-green; an unusually complex but most attractive bouquet with an orange blossom cast to the more usual citrus spectrum. The palate zeros in on the minerally, lemon-accented suite of flavours, leaving the mouth as fresh as a spring day. This is only now getting close to its best, with a long future ahead. Screwcap. 10.5% alc. **Rating** 95 To 2029 $80

Terracotta Individual Vineyard Hunter Valley Semillon 2014 Garth Eather says that the wines from the elevated loam vineyard are quicker to develop flavour than those from the sandy flats, and I agree. Citrus flavours join with lemongrass and a hint of toast, the length and balance exemplary. 200 dozen made. Screwcap. 10.5% alc. **Rating** 94 **To** 2024 $35

♀♀♀♀♀ **Alexander Munro Individual Vineyard Chardonnay 2016** Rating 93 To 2023 $45 CM
Hell Hole Individual Vineyard Shiraz 2016 Rating 91 To 2031 $60
Hell Hole Individual Vineyard Semillon 2016 Rating 90 To 2031 $28

Mercuri Estate   ★★★☆

9484 Horrocks Highway, Clare, SA 5453 **Region** Clare Valley
T (08) 8842 3081 **www**.mercuriestate.com **Open** By appt
Winemaker Hamish Seabrook **Est.** 2015 **Dozens** 5000
This is the venture of Ennio Mercuri, whose family has had a 50-year history in the manufacturing industry. The business has been a staged development, which gained massively with the acquisition of the 52.6ha Cardinham Estate vineyard. This will give rise to a number of ranges of wines in the future, along with the planned opening of a cellar door. Exports to China

♀♀♀♀♀ **Ryder Watervale Riesling 2017** From the St Clare vineyard. Only 50% of the free-run juice used for this wine. What more could you ask for at this price? A single vineyard, a yield of only 5t/ha, free-run juice, and titratable acidity and residual sugar neatly balanced on a long and satisfying palate. Screwcap. 12% alc. **Rating** 90 **To** 2029 $15

Merindoc Vintners   ★★★★

Merindoc Vineyard, 2905 Lancefield–Tooborac Road, Tooborac, Vic 3522
Region Heathcote
T (03) 5433 5188 **www**.merindoc.com.au **Open** W'ends 10–4
Winemaker Steve Webber, Sergio Carlei, Bryan Martin **Est.** 1994 **Dozens** 2500 **Vyds** 60ha
Stephen Shelmerdine has been a major figure in the wine industry for over 25 years, like his family (who founded Mitchelton winery) before him. He has been honoured for his many services to the industry. Substantial quantities of the grapes produced are sold to others; a small amount of high quality wine is contract-made. The Merindoc and Willoughby Bridge wines are produced from the two eponymous estate vineyards in Heathcote. Exports to China.

♀♀♀♀♀ **Willoughby Bridge Heathcote Rose 2017** Very pale pastel pink; barrel-fermented so there's lovely texture among the watermelon, toffee apple and wild strawberries. A sensation of sweetness, mixing it up with grenache spices (the variety used in this), a whisper of tannin, and a flourish on the finish in preparation for the next sip. Screwcap. 13.6% alc. **Rating** 93 **To** 2019 $27 JF
Willoughby Bridge Heathcote Shiraz 2016 By Heathcote standards, this is light. An attractive mix of ripe red fruits, a sprinkling of spice, and soft, fine-grained tannins. As there's no new oak influence, there's an evenness across the palate. A really slurpable style. Screwcap. 13.8% alc. **Rating** 92 **To** 2022 $33 JF
Merindoc Heathcote Viognier 2017 Almost a pared-back style, as there's the right amount of ginger spice, apricot kernel and stone fruit. It's glossy across the palate with some creamy curd notes and a gentle finish. 13.5% alc. **Rating** 90 **To** 2021 $27 JF

Mérite Wines   ★★★★☆

PO Box 167, Penola, SA 5277 **Region** Wrattonbully
T 0437 190 244 **www**.meritewines.com **Open** Not
Winemaker Mike Kloak **Est.** 2000 **Dozens** 2000 **Vyds** 40ha
Mérite Wines was established in 2000 after Mike Kloak and Colleen Miller's protracted search for high quality viticultural land. Their particular focus was on merlot, specifically some recently released clones, holding the promise of producing merlot of a quality not previously

seen. However, it's not a case of all eggs in the same basket, for malbec, cabernet sauvignon and shiraz have also been planted. Finally, in '13, the first small amount of wine was made (until then most of the grapes were, and will continue to be, sold to other winemakers). Their merlot is indeed very high quality, and the plan to increase total production to 2000 dozen should be achieved with ease.

🍷🍷🍷🍷🍷 **Ultra Single Vineyard Wrattonbully Merlot 2015** Five clones (8R, Q45, 181, 343 and D3V14) fermented and matured in French oak separately before a barrel selection and blending. Fastidious winemaking is evident all along the way, but at this stage, the French oak is very obvious in the context of a pure, medium-bodied wine with the finest possible fruit tannins increasing the oak's influence. With only 62 dozen made, not much will remain to tell the tale 15 years from vintage – balanced or not. Cork. 14% alc. **Rating** 94 **To** 2030 $130
Wrattonbully Malbec 2016 Fine domestic malbec of boysenberry, violet and minty scents, sophisticated in its swathe of moreish, middle-weight tannins and the integration of oak from a United Nations of origins (30% new). Vanilla, cedar and bitter chocolate find a welcome companion in malbec's generous girth. The tannins are this estate's calling card: finely tuned and on just the right side of grit. Screwcap. 14% alc. **Rating** 94 **To** 2028 $60 NG

🍷🍷🍷🍷🍷 **Wrattonbully Merlot Rose 2017 Rating** 93 **To** 2019 $22 NG **◐**
Wrattonbully Shiraz Malbec 2016 Rating 93 **To** 2026 $32 NG

Mermerus Vineyard ★★★★

60 Soho Road, Drysdale, Vic 3222 **Region** Geelong
T (03) 5253 2718 **www.**mermerus.com.au **Open** Sun 11–4
Winemaker Paul Champion **Est.** 2000 **Dozens** 600 **Vyds** 2.5ha
Paul Champion has established pinot noir, chardonnay and riesling at Mermerus. The wines are made from the small but very neat winery on the property, with small-batch handling and wild yeast fermentation playing a major part in the winemaking, oak taking a back seat. Paul also acts as a contract winemaker for small growers in the region.

🍷🍷🍷🍷🍷 **Bellarine Peninsula Pinot Noir 2016** As complex as it is engaging, as open and accessible as it is firm and ready for the cellar. We have a very good release here. Spicy, stewy and flushed with tannin. It exudes confidence. Price looks sharp in the context of the wine's quality. Screwcap. 13.5% alc. **Rating** 94 **To** 2027 $32 CM

Merricks Estate ★★★★

Thompsons Lane, Merricks, Vic 3916 **Region** Mornington Peninsula
T (03) 5989 8416 **www.**merricksestate.com.au **Open** 1st w'end of month
Winemaker Simon Black (Contract) **Est.** 1977 **Dozens** 2500 **Vyds** 4ha
Melbourne solicitor George Kefford and wife Jacky run Merricks Estate as a weekend and holiday enterprise. It produces distinctive, spicy, cool-climate shiraz, which has accumulated an impressive array of show trophies and gold medals. As the tasting notes demonstrate, the fully mature vineyard and skilled contract winemaking by Simon Black are producing top class wines. Exports to Hong Kong.

🍷🍷🍷🍷🍷 **Thompson's Lane Rose 2017** An enticing pale pastel pink; brimming with bright red berries, watermelon (plus its rind), and just the right amount of spice. A lick of sweetness rounds out the palate, but it is essentially tangy and refreshing right down to the last drop. Screwcap. 13.5% alc. **Rating** 93 **To** 2019 $25 JF **◐**
Mornington Peninsula Pinot Noir 2015 Bright, pale-mid ruby; a lovely perfume to this with raspberries and musk, rhubarb and bitter herbs plus a dash of woodsy spices. A lighter framed pinot, not wimpy though, as the supple tannins give some shape, as does the integrated French oak (30% new; wine aged 11 months). It has a core of sweet yet tangy fruit, with crunchy acidity and a breezy freshness. To be enjoyed in its youth. Screwcap. 13.7% alc. **Rating** 93 **To** 2023 $40 JF

Mornington Peninsula Shiraz 2013 Rich flavours abound with spiced plums and hoisin sauce, charred radicchio and a smattering of bitter herbs and licorice. The medium-bodied palate is reined in, and there's a vibrancy with tangy fruit and peppery notes, but the sinewy tannins are a little drying on the finish. Screwcap. 13.5% alc. **Rating** 91 **To** 2023 $35 JF

Mornington Peninsula Chardonnay 2016 Mid straw–gold; a luscious style with ripe stone fruit and baked pears drizzled with spiced honey and cinnamon, and sweet French oak in the mix (25% new; wine aged 11 months). Creamy and full-bodied with some warmth and a bit of a kick on the finish, but overall a pleasant drink. Screwcap. 13.7% alc. **Rating** 90 **To** 2021 $35 JF

Merum Estate

PO Box 840, Denmark, WA 6333 **Region** Great Southern
T (08) 9848 3443 **www**.merumestate.com.au **Open** Not
Winemaker Harewood Estate (James Kellie) **Est.** 1996 **Dozens** 4000
Merum Estate stirred from slumber after morphing from grower and winemaker to pure grapegrowing after the 2006 vintage, though producing wine again from the '16 vintage. Viticulturist Mike Melsom is the link with the past, for it was he and partner Julie Roberts who were responsible for the extremely good wines made in '05 and '06. The wines are released under the Merum and Curious Nature labels.

Chardonnay 2016 From Denmark, although the back label's only claim is South West Australia. Bright straw-green; it's a richly flavoured peaches-and-cream style that spent 3 months in French oak (25% new). Screwcap. 13.5% alc. **Rating** 89 **To** 2022 $20

Mewstone Wines

11 Flowerpot Jetty Road, Flowerpot, Tas 7163 **Region** Southern Tasmania
T 0425 253 218 **www**.mewstonewines.com.au **Open** Not
Winemaker Jonathan Hughes **Est.** 2011 **Dozens** 2250 **Vyds** 2.65ha
Brothers Matthew and Jonathan (Jonny) Hughes established Mewstone vineyard on the banks of the D'Entrecasteaux Channel in the tiny hamlet of Flowerpot in 2011, making single site wines with a minimum of intervention in the winery. The vineyard is a former cherry orchard, and new plantings in '18–19 are set to expand it to a final size of 3.5ha. (The original 2ha planting consists mainly of pinot noir, with small amounts of chardonnay, syrah, riesling and sauvignon blanc.) Jonny is the winemaker in this family venture; he studied winemaking in NZ before working in Langhorne Creek, Central Otago (NZ), Mornington Peninsula, Barolo (Italy), Hunter Valley and Okanagan Valley (Canada). Heading home to Tasmania, Jonny worked in various roles in the local industry before settling in as the assistant winemaker at Moorilla Estate for seven years. With the vineyard now established to produce the Mewstone wines, the brothers have embarked on a second label, Hughes & Hughes, encompassing winemaking in Tasmania as a whole. Purchasing quality grapes, this label uses some slightly unconventional techniques that Jonny encountered on his world travels. Small-batch production means he can put maximum effort in. The focus of Hughes & Hughes is pinot noir, chardonnay and riesling. Exports to Singapore and Hong Kong. Best New Winery *Wine Companion* 2019.

Hughes & Hughes Co-Ferment Pinot Noir 2017 From the D'Entrecasteaux Channel. The colour has a little more purple than its 15% Whole Bunch sibling, probably ex the co-ferment components of the blend (one with 5% chardonnay, the other 4% pinot gris). The wine has a profoundly complex bouquet, with spices woven through dark cherry and plum fruit, the palate seamlessly building and expanding the baroque splendour of a very, very good pinot noir. Screwcap. 13.8% alc. **Rating** 96 **To** 2032 $40 ✪

Hughes & Hughes Riesling 2017 From two districts, 209 dozen made and, like all the Mewstone wines, not fined. A flowery citrus and honeysuckle bouquet paves the way for a riesling of authority, resting easy on its laurels thanks to

inherent length and clarity of varietal expression. Screwcap. 12.9% alc. **Rating** 95
To 2032 $27 **○**

Hughes & Hughes Chardonnay 2017 From the Derwent and Huon valleys,
this is 100% barrel-fermented in new and used oak, then matured for 4 months on
lees. The aromas and flavours are in the grapefruit/citrus corner of the ring with a
minerally acidity in tandem. Screwcap. 12.9% alc. **Rating** 95 **To** 2027 $32 **○**

D'Entrecasteaux Channel Chardonnay 2016 Hand-picked; whole-bunch
pressed direct to French oak for wild fermentation and ageing on lees; 96 dozen
made. Here new French oak and a rich, supple, yet intense palate with white
peach and nectarine all sing in perfect harmony from the same page. The lingering
aftertaste reaffirms everything you have encountered on the bouquet and palate.
Screwcap. 13.6% alc. **Rating** 95 **To** 2026 $55

Hughes & Hughes 15% Whole Bunch Pinot Noir 2017 From the Derwent
Valley. The avant-garde winemaking is an unqualified success: barrel-fermented
with 15% whole bunches, left strictly alone with no plunging (nigh-on impossible)
or pumpovers. Elegance is the key descriptor of a wine with potent pinot berry
and plum fruit within a garland of savoury notes, coupled with very good tannins.
Screwcap. 13.5% alc. **Rating** 95 **To** 2029 $40

Hughes & Hughes Barrel Ferment Riesling 2017 More avant-garde
winemaking: fermented with solids in old oak and matured on lees. There is a
nearly invisible touch of sweetness deliberately retained to provide the balance
(and length). 91 dozen made. Screwcap. 13.1% alc. **Rating** 94 **To** 2032 $32

Hughes & Hughes Sauvignon Blanc 2017 Tasmania hasn't been a happy
hunting ground for sauvignon blanc, but there are some positive signs, especially
from wines such as this where the tropical fruits are lively, ranging through guava
and passionfruit with a dressing of lemon juice. Screwcap. 12.8% alc. **Rating** 94
To 2020 $27 **○**

Hughes & Hughes Pinot Noir 2017 Light, bright, clear crimson; the most
attractive, fresh, relatively light-bodied pinot, left to express itself without forcing,
purity its essence. The palate is filled with red and purple fruits, and given texture
by superfine, savoury tannins. Screwcap. 13.5% alc. **Rating** 94 **To** 2027 $32

🍷🍷🍷🍷♀ **Hughes & Hughes Skin Ferment Pinot Gris 2017** Rating 93 To 2022 $32
D'Entrecasteaux Channel Riesling 2016 Rating 91 To 2026 $45
D'Entrecasteaux Channel Pinot Noir 2016 Rating 90 To 2022 $55

Mia Valley Estate   ★★★☆

203 Daniels Lane, Mia Mia, Vic 3444 **Region** Heathcote
T (03) 5425 5515 **www.miavalleyestate.com.au** **Open** 7 days 10–5
Winemaker Norbert & Pamela Baumgartner **Est.** 1999 **Dozens** 1000 **Vyds** 3.2ha
Norbert and Pamela Baumgartner both had indirect connections with wine, plus a direct
interest in drinking it. In the early 1980s, based in Melbourne, they began a search for suitable
vineyard land. However, it proved too difficult to find what they wanted, and the plans were
put on hold. It took until '98 for them to discover their property: 40ha of softly undulating
land with the Mia Mia (pronounced mya-mya) Creek running through it. They planted
1.6ha of shiraz and in 2002 produced their first vintage. It encouraged them to plant another
1.6ha. Along the way Norbert completed winemaking and viticulture courses, and worked
with David Anderson of Wild Duck Creek, and Peter Beckingham. They made the wines of
'02–05 in their air-conditioned garage in Melbourne. In '05 they converted the vineyard shed
into a mini winery, expanding it in '06 to a winery with temporary accommodation so they
had somewhere to stay on their weekend commutes from Melbourne. They ran into the '09
bushfires, the '11 rains, floods and disease, a '12 vintage more than they could handle, the '14
frosts, and the '15 and '16 severe drought. Are they giving up? No sign of it so far. Exports to
the UK, the US and China.

🍷🍷🍷🍷♀ **Reserve Heathcote Shiraz 2015** Matured in both French and American oak.
It puts on a warm, powerful display, all ripe plum and sweet mint, milk chocolate
and peppercorns. Tannin nudges it into order on the finish. Well done within the
bigger style. Diam. 14.8% alc. **Rating** 92 **To** 2028 $35 CM

Miceli ★★★★☆

60 Main Creek Road, Arthurs Seat, Vic 3936 **Region** Mornington Peninsula
T (03) 5989 2755 **www**.miceli.com.au **Open** W'ends 12–5, public hols by appt
Winemaker Anthony Miceli **Est.** 1991 **Dozens** 3500 **Vyds** 5.5ha
This may be a part-time labour of love for general practitioner Dr Anthony Miceli, but that
hasn't prevented him from taking the venture very seriously. He acquired the property in 1989
specifically to establish a vineyard, planting 1.8ha in '91. Subsequent plantings have brought it
to its present size, with pinot gris, chardonnay and pinot noir. Between '91 and '97 Anthony
completed the wine science course at CSU; he now manages both vineyard and winery. One
of the top producers of sparkling wine on the peninsula.

🍷🍷🍷🍷🍷 **Lucy's Choice Mornington Peninsula Pinot Noir 2015** Bright, clear colour;
red fruits and flowers on the bouquet reflect the great vintage Mornington
Peninsula enjoyed in '15. The light-bodied palate provides a mirror image of
the bouquet with notes of spice and forest framing the pure fruits and flowers.
Screwcap. 14% alc. **Rating** 95 **To** 2021 $40
Olivia's Mornington Peninsula Chardonnay 2015 Barrel-fermented,
100% mlf and 12 months on lees in time-honoured Mornington Peninsula
fashion. This has the drive and precision you seldom find in warmer regions.
Screwcap. 13.5% alc. **Rating** 94 **To** 2025 $35
Michael Mornington Peninsula Brut 2008 Based on pinot noir with
chardonnay and pinot grigio in support. It's crisp, fine and zesty. Made in the
traditional method, with 8 years on tirage/lees, continuing a legacy of fine
sparkling wines from Miceli. Diam. 11% alc. **Rating** 94 $40

🍷🍷🍷🍷🍷 **Olivia's Mornington Peninsula Chardonnay 2014** **Rating** 90 **To** 2023
Iolanda Mornington Peninsula Pinot Grigio 2016 **Rating** 90 **To** 2019 $25

Michael Hall Wines ★★★★★

103 Langmeil Road, Tanunda, SA 5352 **Region** Mount Lofty Ranges
T 0419 126 290 **www**.michaelhallwines.com **Open** Fri–Sat 11–5, or by appt
Winemaker Michael Hall **Est.** 2008 **Dozens** 3000
Though no longer relevant (however interesting), Michael Hall was once a jewellery valuer
for Sotheby's in Switzerland. He came to Australia in 2001 to pursue winemaking, a lifelong
interest, and undertook the wine science degree at CSU, graduating as dux in '05. His CV of
vintage work in Australia and France is a veritable who's who of producers: in Australia with
Cullen, Giaconda, Henschke, Shaw + Smith, Coldstream Hills and Veritas; in France with
Domaine Leflaive, Meo-Camuzet, Vieux Telegraphe and Trevallon. He is now involved full-
time with his eponymous brand, and does some teaching at the Nuriootpa TAFE. The wines
are as impressive as his experience suggests they should be. Exports to the UK and the US.

🍷🍷🍷🍷🍷 **Piccadilly Adelaide Hills Sauvignon Blanc 2017** A sauvignon of compelling
exactitude, persistence and textural intrigue, layering herbaceous varietal DNA
across the signature purr of Damy oak. There is ample breadth and mineral tension,
wild fermentation in barrel and significant time on lees, conferring authority to a
wine that will convince nay-sayers, while astonishing those accustomed to mass-
market savvy. Screwcap. 12.8% alc. **Rating** 97 **To** 2025 $35 NG ✪

🍷🍷🍷🍷🍷 **Mount Torrens Adelaide Hills Syrah 2016** A velour of blue and black fruits
glide across a carapace of pepper-grind acidity and a sheen of perfectly integrated
oak. Fully destemmed, and it shows. Smooth. Luxurious. The emphasis is on a
detailed textural patina with violet scents reverberating from fore to aft. This is a
cool-climate expression with the gloss of somewhere warmer. Screwcap. 14.2% alc.
Rating 96 **To** 2031 $50 NG ✪
Greenock Barossa Valley Roussanne 2017 This brims with stone-fruit notes,
jasmine, roasted nuts and assorted herbs, defined by a creamy kernel imparted
by partial mlf, barrel fermentation and maturation (9 months), and wild-yeast
nourishment. A powerful wine of compelling texture and a precision that belies its
heft. Screwcap. 13.5% alc. **Rating** 95 **To** 2025 $38 NG

Lenswood Adelaide Hills Pinot Noir 2016 Production runs to a mere 1550 bottles. This mid-weight, sappy pinot is a chiaroscuro of forest floor and root spice, mingling with brighter notes of crushed red berries and bing cherry. The flavours, sinuous and fleshy, expand nicely across structural support of oak (11 months in Francois Freres barrels, 25% new). Tactile grape tannins and a cardamom-soused whole-bunch element add to the picture. Firmer than most pinot from the Hills, this will age nicely. Screwcap. 13.5% alc. **Rating** 95 **To** 2025 $50 NG

Lenswood Adelaide Hills Chardonnay 2016 A bumptious peachy chardonnay, heavily worked across an ambient barrel ferment, with 60% mlf and an exclamatory 11 months in the cinnamon-scented barrels of famed French cooper, Damy (36% new). This is better at cellar temperature (13–14°C) than chilled, allowing the welcome skein of pungent minerality and febrile acidity to calm the intensity of flavour. Nougat, gingerbread and toasted nuts at the core. Plenty to chew on! Screwcap. 13.2% alc. **Rating** 94 **To** 2025 $50 NG

Flaxman's Valley Eden Valley Syrah 2016 Labelled 'syrah' as opposed to the Barossan 'shiraz', this draws stylistic differentiation across a mid-weighted bow, comparatively taut and equipped with a quiver of peppery acidity, floral scents and smoked meat notes, nestled amid blueberry fruit and well applied vanilla oak. Screwcap. 13.5% alc. **Rating** 94 **To** 2031 $50 NG

🍷🍷🍷🍷🍷 **Sang de Pigeon Pinot Noir 2016** Rating 93 To 2023 $30 NG
Stone Well Barossa Valley Shiraz 2016 Rating 93 To 2030 $50 NG
Sang de Pigeon Barossa Valley Shiraz 2016 Rating 93 To 2026 $30 NG

Michelini Wines   ★★★☆

Great Alpine Road, Myrtleford, Vic 3737 **Region** Alpine Valleys
T (03) 5751 1990 **www.**micheliniwines.com.au **Open** 7 days 10–5
Winemaker Federico Zagami **Est.** 1982 **Dozens** 10 000 **Vyds** 60ha
The Michelini family are among the best-known grapegrowers of the Buckland Valley in northeast Victoria. Having migrated from Italy in 1949, they originally grew tobacco, diversifying into vineyards in '82. The main vineyard, on terra rossa soil, is at an altitude of 300m, mostly with frontage to the Buckland River. The Devils Creek vineyard was planted in '91 on grafted rootstocks, with merlot and chardonnay taking the lion's share. A vineyard expansion program has seen the vineyards reach 60ha. Exports to China.

🍷🍷🍷🍷🍷 **Alpine Valleys Chardonnay 2017** The labelling here is starkly traditional in an Italianate sense, evocative of the family's Alto Adige heritage. Apt, then, that they are based in the Alpine Valleys, like the mountainous region of Italy. This is a mid-weighted and sleek chardonnay with orchard fruits, a hint of apricot and just enough leesy nourishment to provide generosity across rails of cool-climate acidity. Tensile and compact for a chardonnay at this price. Screwcap. 12.5% alc. **Rating** 90 **To** 2022 $20 NG ✪

Mike Press Wines   ★★★★★

PO Box 224, Lobethal, SA 5241 **Region** Adelaide Hills
T (08) 8389 5546 **www.**mikepresswines.com.au **Open** Not
Winemaker Mike Press **Est.** 1998 **Dozens** 12 000 **Vyds** 22.7ha
Mike and Judy Press established their Kenton Valley vineyards in 1998 when they purchased 34ha of land in the Adelaide Hills at an elevation of 500m. They planted mainstream cool-climate varieties, intending to sell the grapes to other producers. Even a 43-year career in the wine industry did not prepare Mike for the downturn in grape prices that followed, which led to the development of the Mike Press wine label. They produce high quality sauvignon blanc, chardonnay, pinot noir, merlot, shiraz, cabernet merlot and cabernet sauvignon, which are sold at mouthwateringly low prices. I've decided to give this winery/maker five stars because there is no other producer offering estate-grown and made wines at prices to compete with these.

ŸŸŸŸŸ **Single Vineyard Adelaide Hills Pinot Noir 2016** The vines were thinned three times, a very expensive process for an $18 pinot noir, but it was repaid by the sheer power and depth of this savoury, complex wine. Spices, plum and dark cherry fruit point to a prosperous future, but at this price you can afford to cellar some, drink some. Screwcap. 14% alc. **Rating** 94 **To** 2024 $18 ✪

ŸŸŸŸŸ **Single Vineyard Adelaide Hills Merlot 2016 Rating** 92 **To** 2023 $14 CM ✪
Adelaide Hills Sauvignon Blanc 2017 Rating 90 **To** 2018 $13 ✪
Single Vineyard Adelaide Hills Merlot 2016 Rating 90 **To** 2026 $15 ✪

Miles from Nowhere   ★★★★

PO Box 197, Belmont, WA 6984 **Region** Margaret River
T (08) 9267 8555 **www**.milesfromnowhere.com.au **Open** Not
Winemaker Rory Clifton-Parks, Gary Stokes **Est.** 2007 **Dozens** 18 000 **Vyds** 46.9ha
Miles from Nowhere is one of the two wineries owned by Franklin and Heather Tate (the other is Franklin Tate Estates). Franklin worked with his parents in establishing Evans & Tate from 1987 until 2005. The Miles from Nowhere name for Franklin's own venture comes from the journey his ancestors made over 100 years ago from Eastern Europe to Australia. The plantings include petit verdot, chardonnay, shiraz, sauvignon blanc, semillon, viognier, cabernet sauvignon and merlot, spread over two vineyards that were established over 20 years ago. Exports to the UK, Canada, Asia and NZ.

ŸŸŸŸŸ **Best Blocks Margaret River Chardonnay 2016** It has richness dripping from its pores. Ripe stone fruit, creamy oak, the lingering finish shot with citrus and pine needles. There's a whole lot of flavour here and a whole lot of length. Fennel-like notes add yet more spark. Big chardonnay, done well. Screwcap. 13.2% alc. **Rating** 93 **To** 2022 $32 CM
Best Blocks Margaret River Shiraz 2016 There's too much (resiny) oak, but at least there's a corresponding richness to the fruit. There's an approximation of balance. Blue and black berries, peppercorns, vanilla cream and wood smoke. It's a hefty shiraz, particularly in a Margaret River context, but it's well structured, persistent and has ample grunt. There's plenty in the tank here; its life won't be short. Screwcap. 14.8% alc. **Rating** 93 **To** 2034 $32 CM
Margaret River Shiraz 2016 You get a lot for your money. Bold berried flavours, flashes of cloves and violets, a slim line of creamy oak. It's pretty decent structurally, too. This has picked up a couple of gold medals on the show circuit and it's not hard to see why; it would easily outshine many other wines at multiples of the price. Screwcap. 14.5% alc. **Rating** 93 **To** 2026 $18 CM ✪
Best Blocks Margaret River Semillon Sauvignon Blanc 2017 A 51/49% blend. 10% fermented in second-use oak. It's a gravelly, grassy expression with velvet to the texture and just enough oomph to the fruit. Electrifying aromatics, and while the palate isn't quite so exciting, it does put on a good show. Screwcap. 12.3% alc. **Rating** 91 **To** 2019 $32 CM
Margaret River Cabernet Merlot 2016 72% cabernet sauvignon, 22% merlot, 6% petit verdot. The fruit comes fresh and unadorned, all blackcurrant and gum nuts, redcurrant and violets. There's more than enough substance here to satisfy, and a pretty aspect too. Value is very good. Screwcap. 14.5% alc. **Rating** 91 **To** 2024 $18 CM ✪

Milhinch Wines   ★★★★

27 Gerald Roberts Road, Seppeltsfield, SA 5355 **Region** Barossa Valley
T 0412 455 553 **www**.seizetheday.net.au **Open** By appt
Winemaker Contract **Est.** 2003 **Dozens** 1200 **Vyds** 4ha
In 1999 Peter Milhinch and Sharyn Rogers established 2ha of each of shiraz and cabernet sauvignon on the banks of Greenock Creek. At the foot of their vineyard is their award-winning Seppeltsfield Vineyard Cottage, a restored 1860s German settlers cottage offering luxury accommodation for couples. The cottage restoration, and Peter and Sharyn's wine

production, began in 2003, when Peter was recovering from a serious illness. The Seize the Day phrase on their wine labels acknowledges their journey through adversity; as Peter notes, 'Carpe diem – we never know what tomorrow may bring!'

🍷🍷🍷🍷🍷 **Seize The Day Barossa Valley Shiraz 2014** 165 dozen made. It's a big wine but not a bruiser. Intense plum and blackberry flavours slide seamlessly into spearmint, milk chocolate and licorice. Tannin is ultrafine and meshed beautifully with the fruit. Acidity is fresh, top notes are floral, texture is silken. Everything is in place to see this mature over a long period. Oak makes a key appearance, but the end result is seductive. Screwcap. 14.7% alc. **Rating** 94 **To** 2034 $120 CM

Millbrook Winery

Old Chestnut Lane, Jarrahdale, WA 6124 **Region** Perth Hills
T (08) 9525 5796 **www**.millbrookwinery.com.au **Open** Wed–Mon 10–5
Winemaker Damian Hutton, Adair Davies **Est.** 1996 **Dozens** 10 000 **Vyds** 8ha
Millbrook is situated in the historic town of Jarrahdale, southeast of Perth. Located at the picturesque Chestnut Farm, the property backs onto the Serpentine River and is nestled among jarrah forests. The farm dates back to 1865, when the original owner planted an orchard and grapevines, providing fruit to the local timber millers. In 1996, Chestnut Farm was bought by Peter and Lee Fogarty, and together with their children John, Mark and Anna, they planted the vineyard of today. In 2001 a state-of-the-art winery was completed, also home to a restaurant. In addition to the 8ha estate, Millbrook sources sauvignon blanc, vermentino, chardonnay, tempranillo, grenache, mourvedre and pedro ximenez from prime locations across WA. Exports to Germany, Malaysia, Hong Kong, Singapore, China and Japan.

🍷🍷🍷🍷🍷 **Single Vineyard Chardonnay 2017** Hand-picked, whole-bunch pressed, wild-fermented in French barriques (50% new), matured on lees for 6 months. A striking chardonnay with 8g/l of acidity driving the palate at breakneck speed before it settles down. But the theme continues with citrus of all sorts (lemon, grapefruit and lime), which should by rights make you think of sauvignon blanc or riesling. But you don't – for the chardonnay birthmark is burnt into the heart of the wine. Screwcap. 13.5% alc. **Rating** 94 **To** 2027
Estate Shiraz Viognier 2015 Hand-picked, destemmed, fermented with 3% whole-bunch viognier, 10 days on skins, matured in French barriques (40% new) for 16 months. Has retained good hue; the Perth Hills is a warm region, so the amount of spice and licorice woven through the black fruits and plum are doubly surprising, and appealing. Screwcap. 14.5% alc. **Rating** 94 **To** 2025 $40
LR Liqueur Muscat NV 80+yo vines, picked at 20° baume with some raisined fruit; fortification after 5 days on skins halting fermentation and allowing retention of a high level of natural sweetness. Matured in small used barrels for 20 years. Highly sophisticated making. It is super luscious, the rancio needed for gold medal status yet to take shape. Screwcap. 17.5% alc. **Rating** 94

🍷🍷🍷🍷🍷 **Viognier 2017** Rating 93 **To** 2022 $20 DB ✪
Grenache Shiraz Mourvedre 2017 Rating 93 **To** 2027 $25
LR Chardonnay 2016 Rating 92 **To** 2023 $50
Vermentino 2017 Rating 90 **To** 2022 $20 DB ✪
PX Pedro Ximenes NV Rating 90 $60 DB

Milton Vineyard

14 635 Tasman Highway, Swansea, Tas 7190 **Region** East Coast Tasmania
T (03) 6257 8298 **www**.miltonvineyard.com.au **Open** 7 days 10–5
Winemaker Derwent Estate, Pooley Wines **Est.** 1992 **Dozens** 11 000 **Vyds** 19.6ha
Michael and Kerry Dunbabin have one of the most historic properties in Tasmania, dating back to 1826. It encompasses 1800ha, so the vineyard (9ha of pinot noir, 6ha of pinot gris, 1.5ha of chardonnay, 1ha each of gewurztraminer and riesling, plus 10 rows of shiraz) still has plenty of room for expansion.

ŸŸŸŸŸ **Reserve Riesling 2017** An intense, well balanced and very long palate; vibrant, crisp acidity provides excellent structure without threatening the citrus flavours. Screwcap. **Rating** 95 **To** 2030

Shiraz 2015 Another stake in the Tasmanian ground for shiraz. Yes, it's cool-grown (obviously it has to be), but the fruit is perfectly ripe, with red cherry to the fore, and elegance written all over it. Attention to detail in the vineyard and winery has brought maximum reward. Screwcap. 14.2% alc. **Rating** 95 **To** 2025 $65

Iced Riesling 2015 Bottle development complexity is starting to kick in: luscious fruit with a crosscut of acidity. Balance is difficult to achieve, but has crossed the bridge here. Drink over the next few years. Screwcap. 8.5% alc. **Rating** 95 **To** 2020 $33 ✪

Pinot Gris 2017 Typical coppery gris colour, and then a suite of correct varietal characters on the bouquet, with poached pear, ginger and sweet spice in the mix. Full and soft on the palate, there's ripeness to the fruit and viscosity of texture although the wine doesn't feel heavy. Seemingly low in acidity, there's a gentle (perhaps skins-derived) astringency balancing the finish. **Rating** 94 **To** 2020 $28 SC

ŸŸŸŸŸ **Freycinet Coast Pinot Noir Rose 2017** Rating 93 To 2019 $28 SC
Dunbabin Family Reserve Pinot Noir 2015 Rating 93 To 2024 $65
Gewurztraminer 2017 Rating 92 To 2022 $28 SC
Dunbabin Family Reserve Pinot Noir 2014 Rating 92 To 2023 $65
Riesling 2017 Rating 91 To 2022 $28
Pinot Noir 2016 Rating 91 To 2023 $38

Ministry of Clouds   ★★★★★

39A Wakefield Street, Kent Town, SA 5067 **Region** Various
T 0417 864 615 **www.**ministryofclouds.com.au **Open** By appt
Winemaker Julian Forwood, Bernice Ong, Tim Geddes **Est.** 2012 **Dozens** 3500 **Vyds** 9ha
Bernice Ong and Julian Forwood say, 'The name Ministry of Clouds symbolises the relinquishing of our past security and structure (ministry) for the beguiling freedom, independence and adventure (clouds) inherent in our own venture'. I doubt whether there are two partners in a young wine business with such extraordinary experience in sales and marketing of wine, stretching back well over 20 years. At first they bypassed owning vineyards or building wineries, instead headhunting key winemakers in the Clare Valley and Tasmania for riesling and chardonnay respectively, and the assistance of Tim Geddes at his winery in McLaren Vale, where they make the red wines. In 2016 they took the plunge and purchased part of the elevated Seaview block adjacent to some of the McLaren Vale greats including Chapel Hill, Coriole and Hardys (Yeenunga vineyard). The block has 7ha of shiraz and 2ha of cabernet sauvignon, and they have enlisted the very experienced Richard Leaske to help manage it. Exports to the UK, Sweden, Malaysia, Singapore and Hong Kong.

ŸŸŸŸŸ **Tasmania Chardonnay 2016** High quality grapes, high quality wine. Fine, very long and elegant, yet also intense and flying the varietal flag at full mast. In the upper echelon of Tasmanian chardonnay. Screwcap. 12.5% alc. **Rating** 96 **To** 2029 $48 ✪

Single Vineyard Blewitt Springs Shiraz 2015 A modest colour, such purple as it may have had now turned to red, but don't judge a book by its cover, for the wine is in fact swarming with all things Blewitt Springs. Its mid-palate is cashmere-rich and welcoming, but doesn't let you simply relax; superfine tannins contribute to both flavour and texture, with a hint of dark chocolate on the finish. A classy wine. Screwcap. 14% alc. **Rating** 96 **To** 2030 $58 ✪

McLaren Vale Grenache 2016 The bright, clear colour is on the light side, as grenache so often is. The fragrant, spicy bouquet is hugely appealing, as is the palate. It engages you in conversation with armfuls of roses, rosehips, and of small baskets of whatever red fruits you choose. Screwcap. 13.8% alc. **Rating** 96 **To** 2031 $38 ✪

Minnow Creek

42 Frontenac Avenue, Panorama, SA 5041 (postal) **Region** McLaren Vale
T 0404 288 108 **www.**minnowcreekwines.com.au **Open** Not
Winemaker Tony Walker **Est.** 2005 **Dozens** 1800

Tony Walker spent six years as winemaker at Fox Creek Wines, after two vintages in Beaujolais and Languedoc. He founded Minnow Creek in 2005, not with any fanfare of (marketing) trumpets, but simply to make very good wines that reflected their place and their variety. The Lopresti family provides many of the grapes for the best red wines.

McLaren Vale Shiraz 2016 Thoroughly full-bodied, fruit tannins and oak all contributing, crucially in balance, encouraging consumers to keep their hands off it for at least 5 years (even though the balance means earlier consumption with a hunk of venison would do no harm). Screwcap. 14.5% alc. **Rating** 93 To 2036 $30

The Silver Minnow Adelaide Hills Sauvignon Blanc 2017 This is no vinous minnow, more like a bone fish fabled for its weight and power. The 40% barrel ferment component is perfectly balanced, and totally integrated with the stainless steel portion. It's a rare sauvignon blanc that will develop excellently over the next 3–4 years, held together by its vibrant acidity. No tropical gardens here. Screwcap. 12.5% alc. **Rating** 92 To 2021 $21 ✪

Chardonnay 2017 An altogether superior chardonnay compared to most coming from McLaren Vale, and not by early picking. It has excellent mouthfeel, and pear, white peach and apple flavours – not oak – fill the palate. Screwcap. 13% alc. **Rating** 92 To 2021 $24 ✪

The Black Minnow Sangiovese Cabernet Sauvignon 2016 Typical light crimson colour. The blend (75/25%) was sanctified in Tuscany many years ago, the cabernet providing firm fruit structure. The tannins of both varieties have been kept under control, leaving a savoury mix of red and black fruits. Screwcap. 13.5% alc. **Rating** 91 To 2024 $21 ✪

Mino & Co

113 Hanwood Avenue, Hanwood, NSW 2680 **Region** Riverina
T (02) 6963 0200 **www.**minoandco.com.au **Open** Mon–Fri 8–5
Winemaker Greg Bennett **Est.** 1997 **Dozens** NFP

The Guglielmino family, specifically father Domenic and sons Nick and Alain, founded Mino & Co in 1997. From the outset they realised that their surname could cause problems of pronunciation, so they simply took the last four letters of their name for the business. Mino & Co has created two brands, the first Signor Vino, the second A Growers Touch. Signor Vino covers wines made from Italian varieties sourced from the Adelaide Hills, Riverina and Riverland. A Growers Touch covers traditional varieties, often drawing on local growers who have been working with the family for two decades. The wines are made at their Hanwood winery (established on what was once a drive-in cinema). Winemaker Greg Bennett has previously worked in the Mornington Peninsula, Central Victoria and the Riverina, and brings a broad understanding of the markets in which the wines are to be sold, and prices that are sustainable. Exports to China are a significant part of the business.

Mr Barval Fine Wines

7087 Caves Road, Margaret River, WA 6285 **Region** Margaret River
T 0481 453 038 **www.**mrbarval.com **Open** 7 days 11–5
Winemaker Robert Gherardi **Est.** 2015 **Dozens** 825

Robert Gherardi was born with wine in his blood, going to Margaret River as a small boy to pick grapes with three generations of his extended Italian family. The grapes were taken to his grandmother's suburban backyard to begin the fermentation, followed by a big lunch or dinner to celebrate the arrival of the new vintage-to-be. Nonetheless, his first university degree was in marine science and biotechnology; while completing the course he worked in an independent wine store in Perth. Having tasted his way around the world in the bottle, at age 25, he enrolled in an oenology and viticulture degree. This led to employment at Moss Wood for four years, then Brown Hill Estate as assistant winemaker, and finally to Cullen for three years. Vanya Cullen encouraged him to travel to Barolo, Italy, and work with Elio Altare, which he did for three harvests over a five-year period. This included moving with his wife and children to experience the full four seasons of viticulture and winemaking. He returns to Italy each year for his boutique travel business that offers customised tours of Barolo, Valtellina and further north. The name Mr Barval comes from (M)argaret (R)iver, (Bar)olo and (Val)tellina. Exports to Singapore and Hong Kong.

🍷🍷🍷🍷🍷 **Margaret River Cabernet Merlot 2016** A finely tuned interpretation of a blend that excels in Margaret River. 80% cabernet sauvignon, 15% merlot and 5% petit verdot; 21 months in French oak barriques (22% new). Nothing forced here, just a gentle wave of fragrance and flavour, filigreed tannins and refreshing acidity. Very classy. Screwcap. 13.9% alc. **Rating** 96 **To** 2030 $40 JF ✪

Margaret River Chardonnay 2017 The range of Mr Barval wines reveals a respect to the sites and an attuned, thoughtful winemaking style, resulting in such beautifully balanced wines. This is a finely tuned chardonnay with stone fruit, a splash of citrus and texture galore; creamy, leesy nuances with oak spices adding another layer of flavour. Persistent, detailed and most importantly, such good drinking. Screwcap. 13.7% alc. **Rating** 95 **To** 2027 $38 JF

Margaret River Rose 2017 A stunning rose made from syrah. Hand-picked, destemmed direct to basket press, wild yeast, barrel-fermented, aged 5 months in seasoned French barriques. This is everything the style should be: pale pastel, a bouquet of florals, spiced red fruits but not too much, the palate textural and with plenty of crunchy acidity. And a perfectly dry finish. Screwcap. 11.8% alc. **Rating** 95 **To** 2020 $27 JF ✪

Vino Rosso 2016 When vino rosso is on a label, I'm expecting Italian grape varieties, not 58% petit verdot and 42% merlot. Regardless, this is a beauty. Bright crimson-garnet; so juicy and vibrant with plums and cherries, and spicy as all get-out with supple tannins and bright acidity. These two varieties coming together and morphing into a balanced, super-drinkable red is worth rewarding. Screwcap. 14.5% alc. **Rating** 95 **To** 2022 $29 JF ✪

🍷🍷🍷🍷🍷 **Mistral 2017 Rating** 93 **To** 2023 $29 JF

Mr Mick ★★★★

7 Dominic Street, Clare, SA 5453 **Region** Clare Valley
T (08) 8842 2555 www.mrmick.com.au **Open** 7 days 10–5
Winemaker Tim Adams, Brett Schutz **Est.** 2011 **Dozens** 30 000 **Vyds** 145ha
This is the venture of Tim Adams and wife Pam Goldsack, with the name chosen to honour KH (Mick) Knappstein, a legend in the Clare Valley and the broader Australian wine community. Tim worked at Leasingham Wines with Mick between 1975 and '86, and knew him well. When Tim and Pam acquired the Leasingham winery in January 2011, together with its historic buildings, it brought the wheel full circle. Various commentators (including myself) have used Mick's great one-liner: 'There are only two types of people in the world: those who were born in Clare, and those who wish they had been'. Exports to China and NZ.

🍷🍷🍷🍷🍷 **Tempranillo 2015** A delicious tempranillo at an incredibly sharp price. It tastes of redcurrant, cola, chocolate and vanilla, the flavour profile ripe and sweetish but the finish roasted, spicy and dry. It doesn't look dark or deep but there's impressive volume to the flavours. It's ready now. Mad not to seek this out. Screwcap. 13.5% alc. **Rating** 93 **To** 2022 $17 CM ✪

Vermentino 2017 As fresh, fruit-driven and frisky as you could hope for. Citrus flavours with a gentle run of passionfruit, the finish full. No question of its value. Screwcap. 11% alc. **Rating** 90 **To** 2020 $17 CM ✪

Shiraz 2013 Clare Valley shiraz aged in American oak. Coffee and cola flavours with blackberry and saltbush tossed through. Talks a pretty big game, especially

given the asking price. Toffeed/toasty aftertaste. Will be widely enjoyed. Screwcap.
14.5% alc. **Rating** 90 **To** 2022 $17 CM ✪

Novo Sangiovese Malbec 2016 It's incredibly light, both in colour and
flavour, but there's a seriousness to the tannin and it has plenty of well defined
length. It's chewy, refreshing, savoury. It's Clare Valley Chianti of its own design.
Screwcap. 12.5% alc. **Rating** 90 **To** 2021 $17 CM ✪

ꪶꪶꪶꪶ **Riesling 2017 Rating** 89 **To** 2022 $17 CM ✪
Limestone Coast Pinot Grigio 2017 Rating 89 **To** 2018 $17 CM ✪

Mr Riggs Wine Company   ★★★★★

55A Main Road, McLaren Flat, SA 5171 **Region** McLaren Vale
T (08) 8383 2050 **www.**mrriggs.com.au **Open** Sat–Thurs 10–5, Fri 10–late
Winemaker Ben Riggs **Est.** 2001 **Dozens** 20 000 **Vyds** 7.5ha
With over a quarter of a century of winemaking experience, Ben Riggs is well established
under his own banner. Ben sources the best fruit from individual vineyards in McLaren
Vale, Clare Valley, Adelaide Hills, Langhorne Creek and Coonawarra, and from his own
Piebald Gully vineyard (shiraz and viognier). Each wine expresses the essence of not only
the vineyard's, but also the region's, terroir. The vision of the brand is unpretentious and
personal: 'to make the wines I love to drink'. He drinks very well. Exports to the US, Canada,
Denmark, Sweden, Germany, the Netherlands, Switzerland, China, Hong Kong, Singapore,
Japan and NZ.

ꪶꪶꪶꪶꪶ **Piebald Adelaide Hills Syrah 2015** This has its nose well in front of its '14
predecessor with its exhilarating display of red and black fruits from opposite ends
of the Adelaide Hills. I cannot remember enjoying a Mr Riggs Shiraz more than
this; Ben Riggs has taken to the Adelaide Hills as if it was his ancestral birthplace.
Screwcap. 14.5% alc. **Rating** 96 **To** 2035 $30 ✪

Watervale Riesling 2017 Finds a good gear and sticks with it through to an
extended finish. Lemon, lime and bath salts. It could hardly be more regional, or
more varietal. There's (ripe) fruit to the mid-palate but the finish is gorgeously dry.
Screwcap. 12.5% alc. **Rating** 95 **To** 2030 CM $25

Piebald McLaren Vale Syrah 2016 Beautifully balanced, perfumed and
flavoured. There's an array of spices, a flush of fruit, the tannin helping to tease
the floral and spice notes out through the finish. Only just into medium-weight
territory, but good for it. Dry licorice characters in the background. Delicious.
Screwcap. 14.5% alc. **Rating** 95 **To** 2026 $30 CM ✪

Scarce Earth McLaren Vale Shiraz 2015 A strong, commanding wine with
bulging muscles of tannin, and cherry-berry and (dark) chocolate flavours in
abundance. Diam-permitting, this will mature positively over a long period of
time. 14.5% alc. **Rating** 95 **To** 2042 $50 CM

McLaren Vale Shiraz 2015 Ripeness is pushed to its boundaries, and introduces
bitumen notes to this bold and generally well balanced shiraz. Indeed there's a
lot that seems measured about this. The deft application of coffee-cream oak. The
finesse of the tannin. The run of brighter rapsberry/redcurrant flavours. In short,
there's a whole lot to like here, so long as the bigger end of town is your fancy.
Diam. 15% alc. **Rating** 94 **To** 2040 CM

ꪶꪶꪶꪶꪷ **Montepulciano d'Adelaide 2016 Rating** 93 **To** 2029 $30
Outpost Coonawarra Cabernet 2016 Rating 92 **To** 2028 $25 CM ✪
Yacca Paddock Tempranillo 2016 Rating 92 **To** 2025 $30 CM
Mrs McLaren Vale Viognier 2016 Rating 91 **To** 2019 $25 CM
Cold Chalk Adelaide Hills Chardonnay 2016 Rating 90 **To** 2022 $30 CM
The Gaffer McLaren Vale Shiraz 2016 Rating 90 **To** 2025 $24 CM
The Delinquent McLaren Vale Shiraz 2016 Rating 90 **To** 2024 $20 CM ✪

Mistletoe Wines ★★★★★

771 Hermitage Road, Pokolbin, NSW 2320 **Region** Hunter Valley
T (02) 4998 7770 **www**.mistletoewines.com.au **Open** 7 days 10–6
Winemaker Scott Stephens **Est.** 1989 **Dozens** 4000 **Vyds** 5.5ha

Mistletoe Wines, owned by Ken and Gwen Sloan, can trace its history back to 1909, when a vineyard was planted on what was then Mistletoe Farm, before disappearing. The Sloans have long since created a winery business here to stay. Ken and Gwen still live at the winery, Ken working seven days a week with no intention of retiring. Son Robert is the viticulturist and assistant winemaker; daughter Cassandra runs the cellar door with Gwen; granddaughter Jessica is studying wine science at CSU and assists in the cellar door and winery; and youngest granddaughter Natane, who says she's nearly 15, assists in the cellar by cleaning glasses and packing boxes, and runs a weekend child-minding service for parents wishing to enjoy a tasting without being hassled by their kids. The quality and consistency of these wines is irreproachable, as is their price.

🍷🍷🍷🍷🍷 **Museum Release Reserve Hunter Valley Semillon 2007** Straw-green. 11yo, and still with time up its sleeve. The original back label advice is to drink to '14, but the taste of the wine today underlines the longevity, and the magic, of these aged semillons' ability to build from a slender foundation. Here the flavours have moved confidently into the honey-on-toast phase, the acidity as precise as it was on day one. Screwcap. 10% alc. **Rating** 96 **To** 2022 $40 ✪

Reserve Hunter Valley Semillon 2017 Whole-bunch pressed, extended lees contact. Has abundant citrus/lemon/mineral notes. This was an excellent vintage (as was '07), so taste the '07 if you want to see the magic of 10 years in the bottle. Screwcap. 11% alc. **Rating** 95 **To** 2027 $27 ✪

🍷🍷🍷🍷 **Reserve Hunter Valley Chardonnay 2017** **Rating** 93 **To** 2024 $32 SC
Hunter Shiraz 2016 **Rating** 93 **To** 2028 $27 SC ✪
Home Vineyard Hunter Valley Shiraz 2016 **Rating** 93 **To** 2030 $40 SC
Home Vineyard Hunter Valley Semillon 2017 **Rating** 92 **To** 2025 $24 ✪
Hilltops Sangiovese 2016 **Rating** 91 **To** 2023 $26 SC
LHS Hilltops Fortified Shiraz 2016 **Rating** 90 $25

Mitchell ★★★★★

Hughes Park Road, Sevenhill via Clare, SA 5453 **Region** Clare Valley
T (08) 8843 4258 **www**.mitchellwines.com **Open** 7 days 10–4
Winemaker Andrew Mitchell **Est.** 1975 **Dozens** 30 000 **Vyds** 75ha

One of the stalwarts of the Clare Valley, established by Jane and Andrew Mitchell and producing long-lived rieslings and cabernet sauvignons in classic regional style. The range now includes very creditable semillon, grenache and shiraz. A lovely old apple shed made of stone provides the cellar door and upper section of the upgraded winery. Children Angus and Edwina are now working in the business, heralding generational changes. Over the years the Mitchells have established or acquired 75ha of vineyards on four excellent sites, some vines over 50 years old; all are managed organically, with the use of biodynamic composts for over a decade. Exports to the UK, the US, Canada, Singapore, Hong Kong, China and NZ.

🍷🍷🍷🍷🍷 **Watervale Riesling 2017** Lovely estate-grown riesling. Crisp and vibrant with classic running intertwined lemon, lime and acidity in a stream from start to finish. The reflection of a great vintage and mature vines. Screwcap. 13% alc. **Rating** 95 **To** 2027 $24 ✪

McNicol Clare Valley Riesling 2010 The stages of honey and toast in mature riesling are now on full display, with a sustaining acidity still running through. To drink over the next few years. Screwcap. 13.5% alc. **Rating** 95 **To** 2022 $40

McNicol Clare Valley Shiraz 2010 Still retains most of its colour, power, depth and youth; dark fruits, spice, oak and tannins are now all on the same page. Its thoroughly traditional makeup can be regarded as a strength or a weakness, but either way its resilience has to be admired. Screwcap. 14.5% alc. **Rating** 94 **To** 2025 $45

ΨΨΨΨ♀ Sevenhill Vineyard Cabernet Sauvignon 2014 Rating 93 To 2029 $28
Auburn Hills Clare Valley Rose 2016 Rating 92 To 2018 $27 CM

Mitchell Harris Wines ★★★★★

38 Doveton Street North, Ballarat, Vic 3350 **Region** Ballarat
T (03) 5331 8931 **www**.mitchellharris.com.au **Open** Sun–Tues 11–6, Wed 11–9,
Thurs–Sat 11–11
Winemaker John Harris **Est.** 2008 **Dozens** 1750
Mitchell Harris Wines is a partnership between Alicia and Craig Mitchell and Shannyn and
John Harris. John, the winemaker, began his career at Mount Avoca, then spent eight years
as winemaker at Domaine Chandon in the Yarra Valley, cramming in northern hemisphere
vintages in California and Oregon. The Mitchells grew up in the Ballarat area, and have
an affinity for the Macedon and Pyrenees districts. While the total make is not large, a lot
of thought has gone into the creation of each of the wines, which John makes at Taltarni
(using their own fermenters, tanks and barrels). In 2012 a multipurpose space was created
in an 1880s brick workshop and warehouse providing a cellar door and education facility.
Exports to China.

ΨΨΨΨΨ Pinot Noir Rose 2017 Whole-bunch pressed, wild-fermented, 4 months in
used French hogsheads: that's why there's texture and depth on the palate. A pale
cherry-pink hue with a splash of copper; a delicate mix of watermelon, cherry
pips and cranberries with plenty of crisp acidity. A rose with integrity and intent –
bloody delicious. Screwcap. 12% alc. **Rating** 95 **To** 2019 $25 JF ✪
Peerick Vineyard Pyrenees Shiraz 2016 Excellent colour; has a core of juicy,
tangy, blue and red fruit, and liberal amounts of spice, tar and scorched earth.
Medium-bodied with finely tuned tannins making this moreish to the last drop.
Screwcap. 13.5% alc. **Rating** 95 **To** 2030 $35 JF ✪
Peerick Vineyard Pyrenees Cabernet Sauvignon 2016 Excellent dark
crimson; smells of the Aussie bush with gum leaves, wood smoke, warm earth,
ferric nuances and buckshot, with a decent dose of blackberries and boysenberries.
A structured yet buoyant palate – ribbons of tannin and a certain elegance seals the
deal. Screwcap. 13.5% alc. **Rating** 95 **To** 2030 $30 JF ✪
Sabre Vintage Rose 2013 60% chardonnay and 40% pinot noir and given its
copper-pink blush from 5% pinot noir wine. 4 years on lees. Very fresh, with loads
of fine bead, a bouquet of flowers and plush red fruits. Neat tension between the
acidity and the impression of softness on the palate. There's texture, verve and a
long finish. Diam. 12% alc. **Rating** 95 $55 JF
Sabre 2014 Chardonnay dominant with 15% pinot noir; 3 years on lees. Finely
tuned with white blossom and citrus notes, and fine bead. While there's a smidge
of complex autolysis, this is racy with the perky acidity balanced by the dosage of
4g/l of residual sugar. Diam. 11.5% alc. **Rating** 94 $45 JF

ΨΨΨΨ♀ Sabre 2013 Rating 92 $42 CM
Curio Syrah Pyrenees Shiraz 2016 Rating 90 To 2030

Mitchelton ★★★★

Mitchellstown via Nagambie, Vic 3608 **Region** Nagambie Lakes
T (03) 5736 2222 **www**.mitchelton.com.au **Open** 7 days 10–5
Winemaker Travis Clydesdale **Est.** 1969 **Dozens** 12 000 **Vyds** 148ha
Mitchelton was founded by Ross Shelmerdine, who had a vision splendid for the striking
winery, restaurant, observation tower and surrounding vineyards. The expected volume of
tourism did not eventuate, and the business became embroiled in a long-running dispute.
In 1994 it was acquired by Petaluma but, once again, did not deliver the expected financial
return, notwithstanding the long and faithful service of chief winemaker Don Lewis, or
the quality of its best wines. In August 2012 a new chapter opened for Mitchelton, with
the completion of an acquisition agreement by Gerry Ryan OAM, and son Andrew. Gerry
founded caravan company Jayco in 1975, and as a consequence of its success has a virtually

unlimited budget to take Mitchelton to the next level. Winemaker Travis Clydesdale has had a long association with Mitchelton, dating back to when he was a small boy and his father was cellar manager. In December 2017 a $16 million, 58-room, hotel and spa was opened. Exports to all major markets.

ΥΥΥΥΥ **Preece Nagambie Shiraz 2016** Deep crimson, and punching well above its price category. It is medium to full-bodied, with an amalgam of blackberry fruit and savoury tannins, the only question being whether it will grind to a stop. This was answered with a resounding no – the finish is well structured and balanced. Screwcap. 14% alc. **Rating** 92 **To** 2031 $20 ○

Preece Nagambie Cabernet Sauvignon 2016 Also punching well above its weight in every respect. The blackcurrant/dried bay leaf bouquet and palate have a side-play of cedar, and the management of tannins is first class. Won't be intimidated by 10 years in the cellar. Screwcap. 14% alc. **Rating** 92 **To** 2026 $20 ○

ΥΥΥΥ **Preece Nagambie Chardonnay 2016 Rating** 89 **To** 2021 $20

Mitolo Wines   ★★★★★

141 McMurtrie Road, McLaren Vale, SA 5171 **Region** McLaren Vale
T 1300 571 233 **www.**mitolowines.com.au **Open** 7 days 10–5
Winemaker Ben Glaetzer **Est.** 1999 **Dozens** 40 000

Mitolo had a meteoric rise once Frank Mitolo decided to turn a winemaking hobby into a business. In 2000 he took the plunge, inviting Ben Glaetzer to make the wines. Split between the Jester range and single vineyard wines, Mitolo began life as a red wine–dominant brand, but now also produces rose and vermentino. In November '17 Mitolo opened their $3 million tasting room, restaurant and event space with a flourish. Exports to all major markets.

ΥΥΥΥΥ **Savitar McLaren Vale Shiraz 2015** The full, bright and deep colour isn't a false prophet. Ben Glaetzer's skill as a winemaker is writ large across the face of this beautifully shaped and balanced wine. Its purity and line of wild blackberry fruits comes into full focus on the back-palate and finish. An altogether exceptional wine from a very good vintage. Screwcap. 14.5% alc. **Rating** 97 **To** 2045 $80 ○

ΥΥΥΥΥ **Cantiniere McLaren Vale Shiraz 2015** Cantiniere (Italian for cellar master) comes from two vineyards with differing soils, matured in French oak for 14 months, then a best-barrels selection. Proclaims its regional origin from the first sip, and simply builds on it from there, yet does so with a degree of elegance. Blackberry, black cherry and plum have a dark chocolate note buried in their hearts, the tannins fine and supple. Screwcap. 14.5% alc. **Rating** 95 **To** 2035 $68

G.A.M. McLaren Vale Shiraz 2015 A lavish and luxuriant wine effortlessly presenting a ripe, soft tannin basket of red and black fruits of every description. Oak also plays a role, but of lesser moment than the fruit, tannins and bitter dark chocolate. Screwcap. 14.5% alc. **Rating** 95 **To** 2035 $58

Jester McLaren Vale Sangiovese Rose 2017 Pale pink; a fragrant, flowery and warmly spiced bouquet grabs attention, but is smartly replaced by intense, dry acidity as the wine enters the mouth. Wild strawberries and crab-apple flavours add to a wine with far more attitude than most roses. Screwcap. 13% alc. **Rating** 94 **To** 2020 $22 ○

Small Batch Series McLaren Vale Grenache Rose 2017 All the action is on the palate, initiated by a flood of red cherry and strawberry fruit flavours that don't rely on residual sugar in any way, shape or form. A purist's rose with attention to detail from start to finish. Vino-Lok. 13% alc. **Rating** 94 **To** 2020 $28 ○

Jester McLaren Vale Shiraz 2016 Estate-grown at the southern end of McLaren Vale near Aldinga, cooled by sea breezes. The crimson–purple colour leads the way for a wine of considerable intensity and length. This nimbly steps around any sledgehammer blows of full-bodied shiraz. Elegance? Yes, but modesty might be a better one-word description, value another. Screwcap. 14.5% alc. **Rating** 94 **To** 2031 $25 ○

Angela McLaren Vale Shiraz 2015 From the Lopresti family's Sandra's Block vineyard at the southern end of McLaren Vale near Willunga. The free-draining soils here are considered to produce bright, lifted shiraz. 18 months in oak, predominantly older French puncheons. A very composed and polished wine, with generous blackberry, chocolate and typically regional earthy characters seamlessly woven together. The oak and tannin subtly play their part. A high quality crowd-pleaser. Screwcap. 14.5% alc. **Rating** 94 To 2030 $35 SC

ŶŶŶŶŶ **The Nessus McLaren Vale Shiraz 2016** Rating 91 To 2023
7th Son 2015 Rating 90 To 2025 $35 SC
Jester McLaren Vale Cabernet Sauvignon 2015 Rating 90 To 2027 $25 SC
Ourea McLaren Vale Sagrantino 2015 Rating 90 To 2025 $35

Molly's Cradle

17/1 Jubilee Avenue, Warriewood, NSW 2102 **Region** Hunter Valley
T (02) 9979 1212 **www**.mollyscradle.com.au **Open** By appt
Winemaker Liz Jackson **Est.** 2002 **Dozens** 20 000 **Vyds** 15ha
Steve Skidmore and Deidre Broad created the Molly's Cradle brand concept in 1997, moving to reality with the first planting of estate vines in 2000, the first vintage following in '02. They have verdelho, chardonnay, merlot, shiraz and petit verdot in the Hunter Valley, but also look to other regions to supplement the estate-grown grapes. Exports to India, Indonesia and China

ŶŶŶŶŶ **Cradle Vignerons Selection Premium Hunter Valley Shiraz 2016** Sits squarely in the time-honoured, medium-bodied Hunter shiraz category. The fruit characters are ripe and forward but not overpowering, with blackberry, blackcurrant and plum combining with the spicy regional influence and a decent measure of toasty oak. Smooth and supple along the palate, there's a gentle rasp of astringency providing a moderate firmness of finish. Screwcap. 13.5% alc. Rating 92 To 2026 $25 SC ✪

ŶŶŶŶ **Orange Sauvignon Blanc 2017** Rating 89 To 2019 $19 SC ✪
Hunter Valley Shiraz Rose 2017 Rating 89 To 2019 $19 SC ✪
Cradle Vignerons Selection McLaren Vale Cabernet Sauvignon 2014 Rating 89 To 2022 $25 SC

🍇 Momentum Wines

161 Wakefield Street, Adelaide, SA 5000 **Region** Kangaroo Island/Clare Valley
T 0438 314 040 **www**.momentumfoodandwine.com.au **Open** Not
Winemaker O'Leary Walker Wines **Est.** 2006 **Dozens** 2000
Momentum Wines was originally established as PB1 wines in 2006. Their first vineyard was located in Padthaway, and the name 'PB1' referenced its location: Padthaway Block 1. As the business grew in momentum, the name of the venture was changed. Momentum Wines is owned by John Hood, who has had a distinguished career as an accountant and business advisor to organisations ranging from privately owned to multinational. The general manager of Momentum is Sandra North, who has also had an impressive career spanning 25 years in export, including seven years for Yalumba between the late 1990s and early 2000s. This is a virtual operation, owning neither vineyards nor winery. They source grapes from Kangaroo Island and Clare Valley. O'Leary Walker makes all the wines, with Nick Walker handling the whites and David O'Leary the reds. Exports to the UK, the US and Canada.

ŶŶŶŶŶ **Kangaroo Island Shiraz 2015** A delicious medium-bodied shiraz from the strongly maritime and moderately cool climate of Kangaroo Island, which faces the Southern Ocean. It has spicy/cedary fruits ranging from red cherry through to purple plum. The finish has a slightly citric touch, in no way a fault. Screwcap. 14.5% alc. Rating 94 To 2030 $22 ✪

ŶŶŶŶ **Kangaroo Island Sauvignon Blanc 2016** Rating 89 To 2018 $30

Mon Tout ★★★★

PO Box 283, Cowaramup, WA 6284 **Region** Margaret River
T (08) 9336 9600 **www**.montout.com.au **Open** Not
Winemaker Janice McDonald, Mark Bailey **Est.** 2014 **Dozens** NFP **Vyds** 28ha
Mon Tout is the venture of second-generation vintner Richard Burch, son of Jeff and Amy. Richard spent two years at Curtin University studying viticulture and oenology, before deciding this wasn't his thing. But after a gap year, travelling through Europe and Asia with friends, he returned like a homing pigeon to Perth and enrolled in a three-degree wine marketing course at Edith Cowan University. Mon Tout is a small side venture from his position with Burch Family Wines as brand manager for the east coast of Australia. The wines reflect Janice McDonald's exceptional experience and skill.

🍷🍷🍷🍷🍷 **Margaret River Chardonnay 2016** Hand-picked from a single vineyard in southern Margaret River, wild-fermented, matured in new French oak. It has the grapefruit-dominant aroma and flavour of its cooler terroir, and good intensity and length, the impact of the new oak controlled. Screwcap. 13% alc. **Rating** 94 **To** 2025 $29 ✪
Great Southern Shiraz 2016 From Frankland River and Mount Barker, wild-fermented, matured in new French oak. Bright crimson-purple, this intense, medium to full-bodied shiraz has a great deal going for it. Frankland River is seemingly the dominant player with its black, not-quite-savoury fruit flavours that have soaked up the new oak and made the tannins (which are evident) redundant. Screwcap. 14.5% alc. **Rating** 94 **To** 2036 $29 ✪

🍷🍷🍷🍷🍷 **Margaret River Rose 2016 Rating** 93 **To** 2019 $25 ✪
Margaret River Rose 2017 Rating 92 **To** 2019 $25 SC ✪
Margaret River Sauvignon Blanc 2017 Rating 91 **To** 2019 $25 CM
Margaret River Sauvignon Blanc 2016 Rating 91 **To** 2020 $23 ✪

Monkey Business ★★★★

2 Headingly Street, Hope Valley, SA 5090 (postal) **Region** Adelaide Hills/Clare Valley
T 0400 406 290 **www**.monkeybiz.net.au **Open** Not
Winemaker Jo Irvine **Est.** 2012 **Dozens** 2000
Tom Maxwell has a 30+ year track record in sales and management. His initial plan with Monkey Business was to provide a conduit between growers, makers and the retail market. Tom developed brands for external clients, and ultimately decided to develop Monkey Business's own brand, establishing the Eccentric Wines label and purchasing Leabrook Estate in the Adelaide Hills.

🍷🍷🍷🍷🍷 **Eccentric Wines Great Little Grooner Adelaide Hills Gruner Veltliner 2017** From the Longview vineyard, made by Jo Irvine using standard white wine tank fermentation, seeking – and achieving – maximum varietal expression. This is yet further evidence of the moderate-climate regions doing well with this variety. Screwcap. 12.5% alc. **Rating** 91 **To** 2022 $25
Leabrook Estate Adelaide Hills Cabernet Franc 2017 Wonderful ruby-purple colour; a fresh, fruit-driven style with no new oak influence thankfully (8 months in used French barrels), as this is full-bodied and loaded with tannin anyway. A mix of ripe black cherries and pips, freshly roasted coffee beans, violets, chicory, and an astringent finish. Screwcap. 14% alc. **Rating** 90 **To** 2026 $32 JF

Mont Rouge Estate ★★★★

232 Red Hill Road, Red Hill, Vic 3937 **Region** Mornington Peninsula
T (03) 5931 0234 **www**.montrougeestate.com.au **Open** Fri–Mon 11–5
Winemaker Michael Kyberd **Est.** 1989 **Dozens** 400 **Vyds** 3.23ha
Mont Rouge Estate was purchased in late 2016 by Jennifer Smith, Thea Salter and Jeffrey Smith, with Michael Kyberd (winemaker) and Geoff Clarke (vineyard manager) onboard. Both are veterans of the Mornington Peninsula, able to pick up the reins of the two vineyards

(1.6ha each) in Red Hill and Main Ridge. The aim of the partners is disarmingly simple: to produce fine wine and fine food.

🍷🍷🍷🍷🍷 **Single Vineyard Main Ridge Mornington Peninsula Chardonnay 2016**
Long and linear but not underdone. This has a future ahead of it. Wood spice, lemon curd, white peach, lactose and oyster shell notes. It flings itself through the back half of the wine, and on out through the finish. Pure chardonnay. Screwcap. 13.5% alc. **Rating** 94 **To** 2025 $40 CM

🍷🍷🍷🍷🍷 **Single Vineyard Main Ridge Mornington Peninsula Shiraz 2016**
Rating 92 **To** 2026 $45 CM
Single Vineyard Red Hill Vineyard Mornington Peninsula Pinot Noir 2016 Rating 91 **To** 2024 $50 CM

Montalto ★★★★★

33 Shoreham Road, Red Hill South, Vic 3937 **Region** Mornington Peninsula
T (03) 5989 8412 **www**.montalto.com.au **Open** 7 days 11–5
Winemaker Simon Black **Est.** 1998 **Dozens** 12 000 **Vyds** 46.9ha
John Mitchell and family established Montalto in 1998, but the core of the vineyard goes back to '86. It is planted to pinot noir, chardonnay, pinot gris, riesling, shiraz, tempranillo and sauvignon blanc. Intensive vineyard work opens up the canopy, with yields of 3.7–6.1t/ha. Wines are released in three ranges: the flagship Single Vineyard, Montalto and Pennon Hill. Montalto leases several external vineyards that span the peninsula, giving vastly greater diversity of pinot noir sources, and greater insurance against weather extremes. There is also a broad range of clones adding to that diversity. Montalto has hit new heights with its wines from these blocks. Exports to the Philippines and China.

🍷🍷🍷🍷🍷 **Estate Mornington Peninsula Chardonnay 2016** Once the complex bouquet has sent its message, the palate takes it onto another level with a compelling range of funky characters, the sort you might find from some makers in Burgundy. Flavour and texture play an equal role in this impressive wine. Screwcap. 13.2% alc. **Rating** 96 **To** 2029 $42 ✪
Estate Mornington Peninsula Pinot Noir 2016 Very good colour; full, bright and clear. There is no shortage of complexity on the bouquet, and absolutely none on the supple, perfectly balanced, medium-bodied palate. Cherries and plums have decided on a truce from the word go, each contributing an equal share. Exotic winemaking practices developed by Simon Black are used, although not especially obvious here. Screwcap. 13.5% alc. **Rating** 96 **To** 2031 $50 ✪
Estate Mornington Peninsula Shiraz 2016 This is both clean as a whistle and chocked with savoury character. Coffee grounds, black cherries, black pepper and wood spice mount an enthusiastic campaign through the entirety of the palate. Tannin is fine-grained and spice-shot. The clovey aftertaste works a treat in context. Pure excellence. Screwcap. 14.5% alc. **Rating** 96 **To** 2032 $50 CM ✪
Pennon Hill Mornington Peninsula Chardonnay 2017 Scintillating quality, and value. This crackles with flinty, minerally character and pops with white peach flavour. It's balanced, stylish and elegant, and drives long through the finish. You can ask for little more. Screwcap. 13.2% alc. **Rating** 95 **To** 2024 $28 CM ✪
Pennon Hill Mornington Peninsula Chardonnay 2016 Clear varietal expression à la Montalto, with subtle interplay between the fruit and its bandmaster, Simon Black. The grapefruit component to the palate isn't overblown, but is an important part of a wine that has as much complexity as drive. Screwcap. 13.2% alc. **Rating** 95 **To** 2027 $28 ✪
Single Vineyard Tuerong Block Mornington Peninsula Chardonnay 2016 Grapefruit pulp, lemon, white peach and pear. This chardonnay rockets straight for the stars. Add oatmeal and nougat-like oak influences and you have a thoroughly convincing wine; it powers around every corner, and finishes strong. Screwcap. 12.9% alc. **Rating** 95 **To** 2024 $60 CM

Pennon Hill Mornington Peninsula Pinot Grigio 2017 Flushed with pear, barley and lemon flavours, bushed with musk and spice, juicy with acidity. Tip-top pinot gris. Screwcap. 13.3% alc. **Rating** 94 **To** 2020 $25 CM ○

Pennon Hill Mornington Peninsula Pinot Noir 2017 It's clearly from an excellent season. This is perfumed, juicy, varietal and incredibly drinkable. It begs the word moreish. Sweet-sour cherries, fresh strawberries, an infusion of woodsy spice and foresty notes. It all works beautifully. Screwcap. 13.5% alc. **Rating** 94 **To** 2024 $32 CM

Single Vineyard Red Hill Block Mornington Peninsula Pinot Noir 2016 Sweet fruit, lively acidity, mandarin notes, toffee, redcurrant, cranberry: there's more colour and movement here than at a '70s swingers party. It feels light on its feet throughout, flitting through spice, wood smoke and fennel-like nuances. Screwcap. 13.8% alc. **Rating** 94 **To** 2025 $70 CM

♀♀♀♀♀ **Pennon Hill Pinot Noir 2016** Rating 93 To 2023 $32 CM
Pennon Hill Shiraz 2016 Rating 93 To 2025 $32 CM

Montara

76 Chalambar Road, Ararat, Vic 3377 **Region** Grampians
T (03) 5352 3868 **www**.montarawines.com.au **Open** Fri–Sun 11–4
Winemaker Leigh Clarnette **Est.** 1970 **Dozens** 3000 **Vyds** 19.2ha
Montara gained considerable attention for its pinot noirs during the 1980s, and continues to produce wines of distinctive style under the ownership of no less than six siblings of the Stapleton family. As I can attest from several visits over the years, the view from the cellar door is one of the best in the Grampians region. Leigh Clarnette was appointed chief winemaker at Montara in 2006, having had an exceptionally intense and varied career since 1984. He worked at Chateau Yarrinya (now De Bortoli) and TarraWarra Estate, and helped produce base wine for Domaine Chandon's first venture in the Yarra Valley. He moved to Padthaway Estate in '90 and installed the first traditional wooden champagne press in Australia; returned to Victoria and Seppelt Great Western to produce sparkling wines and top-class shirazs; joined McPherson Wines in Nagambie Lakes in '99 as chief winemaker; thence to the Pyrenees in '03 as chief winemaker at Taltarni. Exports to the US, Canada, Indonesia, Hong Kong and China.

♀♀♀♀♀ **Grampians Shiraz 2016** Shiraz is clearly a standout among red varieties in the region and this vibrant, mid-weighted wine showcases the reasons. Violet scents segue to a sash of anise, menthol, iodine and cardamom-soused tannins, encasing giddy flavours of blueberry, satsuma plum and bing cherry. Each element slots mellifluously into the jigsaw of balance. Screwcap. 14.5% alc. **Rating** 95 **To** 2026 $30 NG ○

Old Vines Single Vineyard Grampians Riesling 2017 This is a very good riesling of textural cladding rather than mono-dimensional acid bones. The variety's lively DNA is well intact, but 7 months' lees ageing has conferred authority, comfort across the cheeks and real detail. Rose's lime, a splash of tonic and orange blossom hit soprano pitch then meander long. Screwcap. 12% alc. Rating 94 To 2025 $35 NG

♀♀♀♀♀ **Grampians Riesling 2017** Rating 91 To 2023 $27 NG
Grampians Pinot Noir 2016 Rating 91 To 2022 $30 NG

🍇 Monterra Wines

RSD1436 Meadows Road, Willunga, SA 5172 **Region** McLaren Vale
T 0428 581 177 **www**.monterrawines.com.au **Open** Not
Winemaker Mike Farmilo **Est.** 2014 **Dozens** 10 000 **Vyds** 15ha
Yet another venture by Canadian-born and raised (but long-term McLaren Vale resident) Norm Doole. A grapegrower for decades, Norm also had his fingers in financial services, and founded DOWIE DOOLE with Drew Dowie in 1995. For the past two years, his new Monterra has been a centre of activity in McLaren Vale, though it flew under the radar as it

was establishing itself with barrel finance and logistics (and Norm's mind-spinning roles with the Willunga Basin Water Company, Southern Adelaide Economic Development Board and Boar's Rock Winery, not to mention DOWIE DOOLE). Monterra's estate vineyards are in the Adelaide Hills with 5ha each of sauvignon blanc, pinot gris and pinot noir. Its sole export focus is not China but Norm's native Canada.

ŶŶŶŶŶ **Adelaide Hills Pinot Noir 2015** Open-fermented with 10% whole bunches, and twice-daily punch downs; matured in French oak for 10 months. The miserable yield of 1.9t/ha has given unusual depth to the bright colour, and the extremely expressive plum and cherry aromas of the bouquet continue the story. The palate opens expansively, and it's only on the finish and aftertaste that the vinosity falters a touch. Time in bottle may cure this imperfection. Terrific value. Screwcap. 13.5% alc. **Rating** 94 **To** 2030 $22 ✪
McLaren Vale Cabernet Tempranillo 2015 An 80/20% blend, matured in 90% French and 10% American oak for 10 months. Yet another very well made wine punching above its weight. The cassis and sour cherry duo are supported by fine, savoury tannins, the finish mouthwatering and balanced. Screwcap. 14% alc. **Rating** 94 **To** 2022 $22 ✪

ŶŶŶŶŶ **McLaren Vale Shiraz 2015 Rating** 93 **To** 2030 $22 ✪
McLaren Vale Shiraz 2016 Rating 92 **To** 2025 $22 ✪
Fleurieu Peninsula Rose 2016 Rating 91 **To** 2020 $22 ✪
Adelaide Hills Sauvignon Blanc 2016 Rating 90 **To** 2020 $22
Adelaide Hills Pinot Gris 2015 Rating 90 **To** 2020 $22
McLaren Vale Merlot 2015 Rating 90 **To** 2032 $22
Fleurieu Nero d'Avola 2016 Rating 90 **To** 2020 $22

Montgomery's Hill   ★★★★☆

45 821 South Coast Highway, Kalgan, WA 6330 **Region** Albany
T (08) 9844 3715 **www**.montgomeryshill.com.au **Open** 7 days 11–5 (Jun–Aug 12–4)
Winemaker Plantagenet, Castle Rock **Est.** 1996 **Dozens** 6000
Montgomery's Hill is 16km northeast of Albany on a north-facing slope on the banks of the Kalgan River. Previously an apple orchard, it has chardonnay, cabernet sauvignon, cabernet franc, sauvignon blanc, shiraz and merlot, planted in 1996–97 by founders Pamela and Murray Montgomery. Michelle and Phil Shilcock purchased the property in 2017; with experience in hospitality and the wine industry in their younger years, and 20 years in IT, it had always been their dream to own their own vineyard and restaurant.

ŶŶŶŶŶ **Albany Chardonnay 2012** Three clones, machine-harvested, fermented and matured for 10 months on full lees in French oak (20% new). Still as fresh as a daisy, its length leaving its message well beyond expectation, acidity playing a prime role. Its varietal fruit is tailored with precision, the oak merely a murmur in the background. Surely has to be the best 6yo chardonnay on the market today. Screwcap. 14% alc. **Rating** 95 **To** 2025 $28 ✪
Albany Shiraz 2014 The screwcap has kept the wine very fresh, and there is little left to say or add to my original tasting note made in Jan '16 (other than the fact I have increased the points from 92 to 94). Good colour; a medium-bodied shiraz that speaks clearly about its cool-grown origins. Spice, pepper and a whisper of dark chocolate on the bouquet, building focus and power on the palate thanks to a fine web of tannin and French oak that help provide convincing length. 14% alc. **Rating** 94 **To** 2029 $34
Albany Merlot 2014 A merlot of rare power and conviction, full of blackcurrant fruit, spice and a splash of plum; the tannins are there but sheathed, and oak is likewise consigned to a support role. Its balance is excellent, guaranteeing future development. Screwcap. 13.5% alc. **Rating** 94 **To** 2030 $20 ✪

ŶŶŶŶŶ **Albany Chardonnay 2013 Rating** 91 **To** 2023 $28

Montvalley   ★★★★☆

150 Mitchells Road, Mount View, NSW 2325 (postal) **Region** Hunter Valley
T (02) 4991 7993 **www**.montvalley.com.au **Open** Not
Winemaker Daniel Binet **Est.** 1998 **Dozens** 2000 **Vyds** 5.7ha
Having looked at dozens of properties over the previous decade, John and Deirdre Colvin
purchased their 80ha in 1998. They chose the name Montvalley in part because it reflects
the beautiful valley in the Brokenback Ranges of which their property forms part, and also
because the name Colvin originates from France with 'col' meaning valley and 'vin' meaning
vines. They have planted almost 6ha of vines, the lion's share to shiraz, with lesser amounts of
chardonnay and semillon.

🍷🍷🍷🍷🍷 **Reserve Hunter Valley Shiraz 2014** From an outstanding vintage, the growing
season weather having been perfect for shiraz. The colour is bright crimson-purple,
the bouquet a spray of red and black fruits with touches of spice and earth, the
palate only just into medium-bodied territory but all the better for that, the finish
exuberantly juicy. Screwcap. 12.5% alc. **Rating** 95 **To** 2034 $30 ❂
Hunter Valley Chardonnay 2016 Still with the colour of a 1yo chardonnay,
the palate in particular sending the same message. This has a trifecta of green apple,
white peach and Meyer lemon flavours, acidity the glue gently binding them in a
single, satisfying stream. Screwcap. 13% alc. **Rating** 94 **To** 2024 $26 ❂

🍷🍷🍷🍷🍷 **Hunter Valley Chardonnay 2017 Rating** 93 **To** 2025 $26 ❂
Reserve Hunter Valley Semillon 2016 Rating 91 **To** 2026 $26
Hunter Valley Semillon 2017 Rating 90 **To** 2027 $26

Moores Hill Estate   ★★★★

3343 West Tamar Highway, Sidmouth, Tas 7270 **Region** Northern Tasmania
T (03) 6394 7649 **www**.mooreshill.com.au **Open** 7 days 10–5
Winemaker Julian Allport **Est.** 1997 **Dozens** 5000 **Vyds** 7ha
The Moores Hill Estate vineyard (jointly owned by winemaker Julian Allport with Fiona
Weller and Tim and Sheena High) consists of pinot noir, riesling, pinot gris and chardonnay,
with a very small amount of cabernet sauvignon and merlot. The vines are located on a
northeast-facing hillside, 5km from the Tamar River and 30km from Bass Strait.

🍷🍷🍷🍷🍷 **Pinot Noir 2016** Neither the light, clear crimson colour, nor the perfumed,
flowery bouquet, give any warning of the intense palate, with its small red fruits
and a savoury/foresty underlay. I wonder where this wine is headed. Screwcap.
13.2% alc. **Rating** 93 **To** 2026 $40

Moorilla Estate   ★★★★★

655 Main Road, Berriedale, Tas 7011 **Region** Southern Tasmania
T (03) 6277 9900 **www**.moorilla.com.au **Open** Wed–Mon 9.30–5
Winemaker Conor van der Reest **Est.** 1958 **Dozens** 10 500 **Vyds** 15.36ha
Moorilla Estate was the second winery to be established in Tasmania in the 20th century, with
Jean Miguet's La Provence beating it to the punch by two years. However, through much
of its history, it was the most important winery in the state, if not in size but as the icon.
Magnificently situated on a mini isthmus reaching into the Derwent River, it has always been
a must-visit for wine lovers and tourists. Production is around 90t per year, sourced entirely
from its estate vineyards and St Matthias vineyard (Tamar Valley). The winery is part of an
overall development said by observers (not Moorilla) to have cost upwards of $150 million.
Its raison d'être is the establishment of the MONA art gallery, housing extraordinary ancient
and contemporary collections assembled by Moorilla's owner, David Walsh, along with visiting
exhibitions from major art museums around the world. Exports to the UK, South Korea,
Japan, Hong Kong and China.

🍷🍷🍷🍷🍷 **Muse St Matthias Vineyard Sauvignon 2016** Quite unusual in the sense that
the typically pervasive varietal character of sauvignon blanc is not dominant, but

more of a backdrop to the wine overall. The bouquet offers white flowers, alpine herbs, redcurrant and a suggestion of tropical fruit. It's waxy in texture, the flavours more subtle than the aromas, with tannins providing length and drive on the finish. Very good indeed. Screwcap. 13.4% alc. **Rating** 95 **To** 2022 $32 SC ○

♥♥♥♥♡ **Cloth Label White 2014** Rating 93 To 2025 $110 SC
Cloth Label Red 2014 Rating 93 To 2025 $110
Muse Extra Brut Methode Traditionelle 2012 Rating 93 $54
Praxis Sauvignon Blanc 2017 Rating 91 To 2020 $24

Moorooduc Estate ★★★★★

501 Derril Road, Moorooduc, Vic 3936 **Region** Mornington Peninsula
T (03) 5971 8506 **www**.moorooducestate.com.au **Open** 7 days 11–5
Winemaker Dr Richard McIntyre, Jeremy Magyar **Est.** 1983 **Dozens** 5000 **Vyds** 6.5ha
Richard McIntyre has taken Moorooduc Estate to new heights, having completely mastered the difficult art of gaining maximum results from wild yeast fermentation. Starting with the 2010 vintage, there was a complete revamp of grape sources, and hence changes to the tiered structure of releases. These changes were driven by the simple fact that the estate vineyards had no possibility of providing the 5000–6000 dozen bottles of wine desired to be sold each year. The entry-point wines under the Devil Bend Creek label remain, as before, principally sourced from the Osborn vineyard. The mid-priced Chardonnay and Pinot Noir are no longer single estate wines, and are now simply labelled by vintage and variety. Next come the Robinson Vineyard Pinot Noir and Chardonnay, elevated to reserve wine status, priced a little below the ultimate 'Ducs' (The Moorooduc McIntyre wines). Exports to the UK, the US and Hong Kong.

♥♥♥♥♥ **The Moorooduc McIntyre Chardonnay 2016** From the oldest vines on McIntyre vineyard. The bouquet is significantly more complex than its siblings, although the vinification remains the same. The palate dutifully follows suit, with more power and a fruit range including Granny Smith apple as an additional, but not dominant, component. Screwcap. 12.5% alc. **Rating** 96 $70 ○
Robinson Vineyard Chardonnay 2016 Produced from the two best Dijon/ Bernard clones 95 and 96; otherwise standard winemaking protocols. Here precision and urgency take over, grapefruit entering the fray, generating extra length as it does so. Screwcap. 12.5% alc. **Rating** 96 **To** 2025 $60 ○
The Moorooduc McIntyre Pinot Noir 2016 The most subtle and finely honed of the Moorooduc Pinots from this vintage – with an X-factor. At the risk of annoying those who don't like such comparisons, it's hard to not see a Burgundian connection here: the quality of the fruit character, the interplay of oak, the beautifully integrated tannin and acid, the minerally, elemental undertone. It seems superfluous to pick it all apart, suffice to say that it's pinot of high quality by any measure. Screwcap. 13.5% alc. **Rating** 96 **To** 2028 $70 SC ○
Robinson Vineyard Pinot Noir 2016 Really quite exotic – hedonistic even – on the bouquet, with a panoply of intriguing aromas, cinnamon, cedar wood, satsuma plum, white flowers and minty herbs among them. The luscious palate is flooded with all sorts of berry flavours, the savoury and earthy nuances of the bouquet buried within them. Despite these riches, the astringency of acid and tannins keeps things tight, making its presence felt right through and defining the finish emphatically. Screwcap. 14% alc. **Rating** 95 **To** 2028 $60 SC
McIntyre Vineyard Shiraz 2016 A veritable spice cabinet and herb garden of a wine, with cool-climate shiraz written all over it. Aromas of star anise, licorice root, rosemary and thyme all play a part, seasoned with a whiff of white pepper. Red-fleshed plum and rose petal are in the mix as well. Silky and slinky on the palate, there's a tangy sweetness of just-ripe red and black fruit with the spice again in evidence, and pliable tannins that guide it along firmly but gently. Screwcap. 14% alc. **Rating** 95 **To** 2030 $60 SC
Chardonnay 2016 'Simple natural winemaking (with a pinch of quality control) including wild yeast fermentation of unsettled juice in French oak barrels.'

Smooth and relaxed, supple and unhurried. The wine generates such comments. Practice makes perfect? Yes, something in that. Screwcap. 12.5% alc. **Rating** 94 **To** 2024 $40

Pinot Noir 2016 Plenty of attractive cool-climate pinot character on the bouquet here, with aromas of sappy cherry, woody spice, earth and game. High quality oak adds cedar and char, perhaps even a little too generously. Silky texture, spice and cherry are again prominent in the flavour spectrum, with tangy acidity and gently firm tannin providing the structure. In the manner of quality pinot, it fans out expansively along the palate and lingers engagingly on the finish. Screwcap. 14% alc. **Rating** 94 **To** 2026 $40 SC

ΨΨΨΨΨ **Garden Vineyard Pinot Noir 2016** Rating 93 To 2026 $60 SC
Pinot Gris On Skins 2016 Rating 92 To 2022 $38 SC
Pinot Gris 2016 Rating 90 To 2021 $38

Moortangi Estate   ★★★

120 Wills Road, Dixons Creek, Vic 3775 **Region** Yarra Valley
T (03) 9600 4001 **www**.moortangiestate.com.au **Open** Not
Winemaker Sergio Carlei **Est.** 2002 **Dozens** 300 **Vyds** 5.75ha

Paul and Pamela Hyland purchased a beautiful grazing property at Dixons Creek that was already christened 'Moortangi'. They planted the north-facing paddocks with shiraz (4ha), cabernet sauvignon (0.9ha), merlot (0.5ha) and viognier (0.35ha), and while waiting for the vines to mature purchased shiraz from Heathcote for their first vintage. They have continued to make Old Vine Heathcote Shiraz from vines planted in the 1950s in grey loam soils, and Cambrian Shiraz from red soils. By 2009 their own vines were flourishing and they anticipated their first vintage, but the Black Saturday bushfires devastated the property, destroying the majority of vines. In '10 they saw shoots on their main planting of shiraz, and they have since laboriously resurrected the vineyard on a vine-by-vine basis, now overseeing what they regard as an exceptional vineyard. They say their love of wine brought them to this place, and has been sorely tested, but ultimately fulfilled.

ΨΨΨΨ **Cambrian Shiraz 2011** Hand-picked from vines grown in Cambrian soil just to the north of Heathcote. Wild-fermented in large wooden vats, matured in new and used French oak for 18 months. A light coloured survivor from the rain-sodden '11 vintage with a curious bouquet. Diam. 13.5% alc. **Rating** 89 **To** 2020 $35

Moppity Vineyards   ★★★★★

Moppity Road, Young, NSW 2594 (postal) **Region** Hilltops
T (02) 6382 6222 **www**.moppity.com.au **Open** Not
Winemaker Jason Brown **Est.** 1973 **Dozens** 30 000 **Vyds** 73ha

Jason Brown and wife Alecia, with backgrounds in fine-wine retail and accounting, purchased Moppity Vineyards in 2004 when it was already 31 years old. Initially they were content to sell the grapes to other makers, but that changed with the release of the '06 Shiraz, which won top gold in its class at the London International Wine & Spirit Competition. In November '09 the '08 Eden Road Long Road Hilltops Shiraz, made from Moppity Vineyards' grapes, won the Jimmy Watson Trophy. These awards are among a cascade of golds for its shiraz, riesling, chardonnay and cabernet sauvignon. Production (and sales) have soared, and all the grapes from the estate are now used for the Moppity Vineyards brand. The Lock & Key range provides exceptional value for money. Jason and Alecia have also established Coppabella of Tumbarumba, a separate venture. Exports to the UK and China.

ΨΨΨΨΨ **Lock & Key Reserve Hilltops Shiraz 2016** 5 days' cold soak, open-fermented for 12 days, matured in French oak (25% new) for 12 months. Deep crimson-purple, this is a genuine step above its non-Reserve sibling, deeper and darker in flavour with its black fruits, firm tannins and new French oak. Right in the Moppity slot, its trophy for Best NSW Shiraz at the Great Australian Shiraz Challenge '17 was richly deserved. Screwcap. 14% alc. **Rating** 96 **To** 2036 $30 ✪

Estate Hilltops Shiraz 2016 Co-fermented with 2% viognier, matured in new and used French barriques for 12 months; the usual shower of gold medals. The Lock & Key wines have a remarkable consistency in their supple, fresh mouthfeel and varietal purity. Shortly put, they are beautifully made wines from a high quality region. Screwcap. 14% alc. **Rating** 96 **To** 2036 $35 ○

Escalier Hilltops Shiraz 2014 The second release of Moppity's flagship wine; from a single block, co-fermented with 2% viognier, matured in new and used French puncheons for 36 months. There's no room for argument about a wine that's received six gold medals, the most recent from the Great Australian Shiraz Challenge '17, and earlier from Melbourne and NSW wine awards. The viognier has disappeared into the voluminous folds of black fruits. Screwcap. 14% alc. **Rating** 96 **To** 2034 $130

Cato Pepe Bianco Tumbarumba Gruner 2017 From 1ha of gruner grafted onto 23yo pinot meunier vines, hand-picked, whole-bunch pressed, free-run juice cool-fermented. This has the white pepper components of the bouquet loud and clear, with no previous tasting so marked. Very exciting to taste, not only for the white pepper as for the delicate yet laser pinpointed palate of citrussy acidity. Screwcap. 12.5% alc. **Rating** 95 **To** 2027 $35 ○

Lock & Key Hilltops Shiraz 2016 Cold-soaked pre-ferment, 12 days' fermentation, matured in used French hogsheads and stainless steel. Gold medal Melbourne Wine Awards '17. It is a wine built around its texture and structure, the dark berry and earthy flavours held within mouthwatering tannins. Screwcap. 14% alc. **Rating** 95 **To** 2031 $25 ○

Reserve Hilltops Cabernet Sauvignon 2016 Hand-picked from the best two parcels of estate fruit. A 16-day cool fermentation on skins, matured in French oak for 14 months. The usual care in the vineyards and winery is on display – you can't find any shortcoming. Here intense cabernet fruit will appeal to all, even pinot devotees. Screwcap. 13.9% alc. **Rating** 95 **To** 2036 $80

Lock & Key Reserve Hilltops Tempranillo 2016 Matured in used French oak for 9 months. Gold medal from the Melbourne Wine Awards '17. The quality of the wine is excellent, the decision to not use any new oak spot on. It focuses attention on the red and dark cherry aromas and palate. Screwcap. 14% alc. **Rating** 95 **To** 2031 $30 ○

Estate Hilltops Riesling 2017 Trophy for Best Riesling at the Canberra and Region Wine Show. The depth, length and intensity of the flavours put the quality of the wine beyond question. Great now, but will be greater still later. Screwcap. 12% alc. **Rating** 94 **To** 2032 $35

Estate Hilltops Merlot 2015 This has more richness and structure than the vast majority of Australian merlots. The new French clones should lead to a major improvement at all levels. Screwcap. 13.9% alc. **Rating** 94 **To** 2030 $35

ҼҼҼҼҼ **Lock & Key Hilltops Rose 2017** Rating 93 To 2021 $25 ○
Estate Hilltops Cabernet Sauvignon 2016 Rating 92 To 2029 $35
Lock & Key Hilltops Riesling 2017 Rating 90 To 2027 $25
Lock & Key Hilltops Cabernet Sauvignon 2016 Rating 90 To 2029 $25

Morambro Creek Wines   ★★★★☆

Riddoch Highway, Padthaway, SA 5271 **Region** Padthaway
T (08) 8723 1065 www.morambrocreek.com.au **Open** Not
Winemaker Ben Riggs **Est.** 1994 **Dozens** 30 000 **Vyds** 178.5ha
The Bryson family has been involved in agriculture for more than a century, moving to Padthaway in 1955 as farmers and graziers. From the '90s they have progressively established large plantings of shiraz (88.5ha), cabernet sauvignon (47.5ha), chardonnay (34.5ha) and sauvignon blanc (8ha). The Morambro Creek and Mt Monster wines have been consistent winners of medal. Exports to the UK, the US and other major markets.

ҼҼҼҼҼ **Padthaway Cabernet Sauvignon 2015** There's heft, tannin, general prettiness and plenty of length. We have ourselves a prime target here. Violets and mint,

boysenberry and blackcurrant, smoky/cedary oak. Chains of tannin pull through
a volume of satiny fruit. In for the long haul. Screwcap. 14.5% alc. **Rating** 95
To 2035 $35 CM ✪

Padthaway Chardonnay 2016 Essence of chardonnay. Golden flavours come
cut and polished. Peach and pear, apple and ginger. Oak is present, but managed to
a tee. The Morambro Creek wines are in such excellent shape, and this is as good
an example as any. Screwcap. 13% alc. **Rating** 94 **To** 2023 $35 CM

🍷🍷🍷🍷🍷 **Padthaway Shiraz 2015** Rating 93 To 2028 $35 CM
The Bryson Barrel Select 2015 Rating 93 To 2030 $55 CM
Jip Jip Rocks Shiraz 2016 Rating 92 To 2025 $21 CM ✪
Jip Jip Rocks Shiraz Cabernet 2016 Rating 91 To 2026 $21 CM ✪

Morgan Simpson   ★★★☆

PO Box 39, Kensington Park, SA 5068 **Region** McLaren Vale
T 0417 843 118 **www**.morgansimpson.com.au **Open** Not
Winemaker Richard Simpson **Est.** 1998 **Dozens** 1200 **Vyds** 17.1ha
Morgan Simpson was founded by SA businessman George Morgan (since retired) and
winemaker Richard Simpson, who is a graduate of CSU. The grapes are sourced from the
Clos Robert vineyard, planted to shiraz (9ha), cabernet sauvignon (3.5ha), mourvedre (2.5ha)
and chardonnay (2.1ha), established by Robert Allen Simpson in 1972. Most of the grapes are
sold, the remainder used to make the reasonably priced, drinkable wines for which Morgan
Simpson has become well known; they are available through their website.

🍷🍷🍷🍷🍷 **Reprieve Shiraz 2016** 18 months in American oak hogsheads (30% new), which
adds enormously to the wine's concentration, with ripe flavours of blackstrap
licorice, plums soaked in kirsch, blackberry essence and sweet-sour notes, too. The
reasonable alcohol level and freshness on the palate are saving graces. Screwcap.
14.1% alc. **Rating** 90 **To** 2026 $45 JF

Morningside Vineyard   ★★★★☆

711 Middle Tea Tree Road, Tea Tree, Tas 7017 **Region** Southern Tasmania
T (03) 6268 1748 **Open** By appt
Winemaker Peter Bosworth **Est.** 1980 **Dozens** 600 **Vyds** 2.8ha
The name Morningside was given to the old property because it gets the morning sun
first; the property on the other side of the valley was known as Eveningside. Consistent
with this observation of the early settlers, the Morningside grapes achieve full maturity with
good colour and varietal flavour. Production will increase as the vineyard matures; recent
additions of clonally selected pinot noir (including 8104, 115 and 777) are now bearing. The
Bosworth family, headed by Peter and wife Brenda, do all the vineyard and winery work, with
conspicuous attention to detail.

🍷🍷🍷🍷🍷 **Tasmanian Riesling 2017** Mid-straw and bright; an off-dry style, yet a backbone
of racy natural acidity cuts right through, leaving barely a ripple in its wake.
Flavours of lemon barley water, lemon and lime juice, and sherbet; super zesty and
delicious. Screwcap. 12% alc. **Rating** 95 **To** 2027 $25 JF ✪

🍷🍷🍷🍷🍷 **Pinot Noir 2015** Rating 93 To 2026 $37 JF
Six Long Rows Pinot Noir 2015 Rating 93 To 2022 $27 JF ✪

Morris   ★★★★★

Mia Mia Road, Rutherglen, Vic 3685 **Region** Rutherglen
T (02) 6026 7303 **www**.morriswines.com **Open** Mon–Sat 9–5, Sun 10–5
Winemaker David Morris **Est.** 1859 **Dozens** 100 000 **Vyds** 96ha
One of the greatest of the fortified winemakers, ranking with Chambers Rosewood. Morris
has changed the labelling system for its sublime fortified wines, with a higher-than-average
entry point for the (Classic) Liqueur Muscat; Tokay and the ultra-premium wines are being
released under the Old Premium Liqueur (Rare) label. The art of these wines lies in the

blending of very old and much younger material. These Rutherglen fortified wines have no equivalent in any other part of the world (with the honourable exception of Seppeltsfield in the Barossa Valley). In July 2016, Casella Family Brands acquired Morris after decades of disinterested ownership by Pernod Ricard.

🍷🍷🍷🍷🍷 **Old Premium Rare Liqueur Muscat NV** The juxtaposition of extreme complexity and concentration with unusually smooth mouthfeel will undoubtedly add to the speed with which the glass is emptied – if consumed outside home, a designated driver is essential. Possibly from a batch with a little more young(ish) wine included. Screwcap. 17.5% alc. **Rating** 97 $90 ❂

🍷🍷🍷🍷🍷 **Cellar Reserve Grand Liqueur Rutherglen Topaque NV** Wow this is dense. You might question the freshness, but for sheer opulent impact look no further. Fruitcake, toffee, crushed dried spices, a kind of old, rich cedar-wood character. It's quite incredible that you can snare this quality at this price. Sanity and the wine world aren't always aligned. 500ml. Screwcap. 17% alc. **Rating** 96 $50 CM ❂
Classic Liqueur Rutherglen Topaque NV Mid-amber with a ruby shimmer; luscious with the flavours of raisins soaked in aged brandy and drizzled with malt, lapsang souchong tea, fruitcake and molasses. Good acidity keeps this fresh, with the spirit neatly integrated. 500ml. Screwcap. 17.5% alc. **Rating** 94 $22 JF ❂
Classic Liqueur Muscat NV The colour is burnished cedar with a garnet glow; plump raisins dipped in toffee, fruitcake straight from the oven, orange peel and fresh muscat notes. The acidity cuts through the sweetness and the spirit is balanced. 500ml. Screwcap. 18% alc. **Rating** 94 $24 JF ❂

🍷🍷🍷🍷🍷 Mia Pale Flor Rutherglen Apera NV **Rating** 91 $20 CM ❂

Mosquito Hill Wines ★★★

18 Trinity Street, College Park, SA 5069 (postal) **Region** Southern Fleurieu
T 0411 661 149 **www.**mosquitohillwines.com.au **Open** Not
Winemaker Glyn Jamieson **Est.** 2004 **Dozens** 1800 **Vyds** 4.2ha
This is the venture of Glyn Jamieson, who happened to be the prestigious Dorothy Mortlock Professor of Surgery at the University of Adelaide. His interest in wine dates back decades, and in 1994 he commenced the part-time (distance) degree at CSU; he says that while he never failed an exam, it did take him 11 years to complete the course. A year in France led him to Burgundy rather than Bordeaux, hence the planting of chardonnay, pinot blanc and savagnin on the slopes of Mt Jagged in the Magpies Song vineyard, and pinot noir (clones 114 and MV6) in the Hawthorns vineyard. Glyn built a small winery for the first vintage in 2011.

🍷🍷🍷🍷 **Pinot Noir 2016** Stylistically, this really shows up its whole-bunch influence – 60% used, making the wine stalky, like poached rhubarb without sugar, and bitter with an amaro-like edge. It's savoury, yet ripe with a lot of sweetness, and also influenced by the French oak barriques and hogsheads (40% new). This needs savoury food to show it at its best. Screwcap. 13.4% alc. **Rating** 89 **To** 2023 $32 JF

Moss Wood ★★★★★

926 Metricup Road, Wilyabrup, WA 6284 **Region** Margaret River
T (08) 9755 6266 **www.**mosswood.com.au **Open** By appt
Winemaker Clare Mugford, Keith Mugford **Est.** 1969 **Dozens** 12000 **Vyds** 18.14ha
Widely regarded as one of the best wineries in the region, producing glorious chardonnay, power-laden semillon and elegant cabernet sauvignon that live for decades. Moss Wood also owns the Ribbon Vale Estate, the wines treated as vineyard-designated within the Moss Wood umbrella. Exports to all major markets.

🍷🍷🍷🍷🍷 **Wilyabrup Margaret River Semillon 2017** Imposing bright straw-green; the complexity of the bouquet is immediately obvious with crushed citrus leaves, wood smoke and spice, not bad for an unwooded semillon. Its raw power on the palate is formidable, as is the acidity. Will always dance to the beat of its own drum – like it or leave it. Screwcap. 13.5% alc. **Rating** 95 **To** 2027 $38

Wilyabrup Margaret River Chardonnay 2016 Is always the richest and fullest bodied of the top end of the Moss Wood portfolio of chardonnay, with its multi-tiered stone fruit and creamy cashew flavours. It is largely about the site and the age of the vines, so fiddling with the style wouldn't be to the advantage of the wine. Screwcap. 13.5% alc. **Rating** 95 **To** 2030 $65

Amy's 2016 A blend of cabernet sauvignon, petit verdot, malbec and merlot. Bright crimson-purple, and the fruit, oak and tannins have been dialled up to maximum, the oak in particular throwing its weight around. It's a glass almost full, and Moss Wood devotees will decide to rely on its breeding. Be prepared to wait. Screwcap. 14.5% alc. **Rating** 94 **To** 2036 $39

ŶŶŶŶŶ **Ribbon Vale Sauvignon Blanc Semillon 2017** Rating 93 To 2027 $32
Ribbon Vale Merlot 2015 Rating 93 To 2030 $65 DB
Wilyabrup Margaret River Pinot Noir 2015 Rating 90 To 2025 $60
Ribbon Vale Cabernet Sauvignon 2015 Rating 90 To 2037 $65 DB

Mountadam

High Eden Road, Eden Valley, SA 5235 **Region** Eden Valley
T (08) 8564 1900 **www**.mountadam.com.au **Open** By appt
Winemaker Helen McCarthy **Est.** 1972 **Dozens** 15 000 **Vyds** 80ha
Founded by the late David Wynn for the benefit of winemaker son Adam, Mountadam was (somewhat surprisingly) purchased by Cape Mentelle (doubtless under the direction of Möet Hennessy Wine Estates) in 2000. Rather less surprising was its part sale in '05 to Adelaide businessman David Brown, who has extensive interests in the Padthaway region. This acquisition was of the vineyard on the western side of the High Eden Road. In '07 David purchased the unplanted parcel of land on the opposite (eastern) side of the road, and in '15 he acquired from TWE the large vineyard on the eastern side of the road, thus reassembling all the land originally purchased by David Wynn in the late 1960s. The Brown family named the vineyards 'Mountadam West' and 'Mountadam East'. Exports to the UK, France, Switzerland, Poland and Hong Kong.

ŶŶŶŶŶ **High Eden Estate Chardonnay 2016** From the oldest plantings on the estate, fermented in French oak, matured for 12–14 months before a barrel selection for this wine, which is one of the best produced ex the Eden Valley as a whole. It has fluid grace and effortless power, the fruit flavours at the midpoint of the white peach/grapefruit spectrum. Lovely wine. Screwcap. 14% alc. **Rating** 97 To 2026 $40

ŶŶŶŶŶ **Patriarch High Eden Shiraz 2015** Selected parcels of grapes from the best sites of the vineyard are individually fermented and matured separately for 20–24 months in French barriques, the best barrels blended and held in bottle for another year before release. This is a compelling wine, its quality coming through both the bouquet and the perfectly balanced and long medium-bodied palate. Dark berry fruits, cedary oak and supple tannins all contribute, but fruit is by some distance the most important. Screwcap. 14.8% alc. **Rating** 96 To 2040

Eden Valley Riesling 2017 The natural acidity of most rieslings from the Eden Valley and Clare Valley is excellent. This wine stands a little apart with its supple mouthfeel on the mid-palate tightening up when it needs to on the finish and aftertaste. Screwcap. 12% alc. **Rating** 95 To 2029 $27

Eden Valley Shiraz 2016 The higher alcohol of this wine than that of its Five-Fifty sibling rounds the palate and delivers its message in a more considered fashion. There are layers of sombre black fruits, with licorice, cracked pepper, tannins and oak following its trail. Screwcap. 14.8% alc. **Rating** 95 To 2036 $27

High Eden The Red 2015 An estate-grown blend of cabernet sauvignon and merlot separately fermented and matured in French barriques for 20–24 months, a barrel selection blended and bottle-aged for 12 months before release. The extra elevation of High Eden makes the difference for an attractive, supple and well balanced wine that glides on titanium castors, cassis fruit and black olive a background whisper. Screwcap. 14.5% alc. **Rating** 95 To 2036

Eden Valley Chardonnay 2017 A very well executed Eden Valley chardonnay with bell-clear varietal character. Its cornerstones are white peach and nectarine fruit, the mid-palate with gentle grapefruit and oak. It's in Brideshead Revisited style: elegant and refined, under- rather than overstated. Screwcap. 12.5% alc. **Rating** 94 **To** 2025
Eden Valley Pinot Gris 2017 Pale quartz-green; stands high in the pinot gris stakes with unexpected but very enjoyable citrus and apple flavours, pear also in the game. Has good length and focus. Screwcap. 13% alc. **Rating** 94 **To** 2020 $27

ƭƭƭƭƭ **Five-Fifty Eden Valley Chardonnay 2017** Rating 92 To 2024 $20
Eden Valley Cabernet Sauvignon 2016 Rating 92 To 2026 $27
Eden Valley Gewurztraminer 2017 Rating 91 To 2023 $27
Five-Fifty Barossa Shiraz 2016 Rating 91 To 2029 $20

Mount Avoca ★★★★★

Moates Lane, Avoca, Vic 3467 **Region** Pyrenees
T (03) 5465 3282 **www.**mountavoca.com **Open** 7 days 10–5
Winemaker David Darlow **Est.** 1970 **Dozens** 10000 **Vyds** 23.46ha
This winery has long been one of the stalwarts of the Pyrenees region, owned by Matthew and Lisa Barry. The estate vineyards include shiraz, sauvignon blanc, cabernet sauvignon, chardonnay, merlot, cabernet franc, tempranillo, lagrein, viognier, sangiovese, nebbiolo and semillon. The Moates Lane wines are partly or wholly made from contract-grown grapes, but other releases are estate-grown. Mount Avoca's vineyards and winery achieved full organic certification in 2016. Exports to China.

ƭƭƭƭƭ **Old Vine Pyrenees Shiraz 2015** Displays the sort of all-round unforced intensity that old vines can impart. Multi-faceted bouquet, with ripe dark fruit, chocolate, earth, pepper and licorice framed by well judged French oak. Ample weight on the palate, though it's really more medium than full-bodied, with a quietly saturating depth of flavour. The slightly assertive astringency on the finish should soften with time. Screwcap. 14% alc. **Rating** 95 **To** 2030 $46 SC
Estate Range Pyrenees Cabernet Sauvignon 2015 Under various incarnations, Mount Avoca has provided excellent cabernet sauvignon over the years, and this is a very good release. Lovely varietal bouquet; blackcurrant with leaves, dust and cedar. Well matched French oak is right on the money. Perfect medium-to-full cabernet weight on the palate, with depth and length of flavour and elegance of form. Screwcap. 14% alc. **Rating** 95 **To** 2030 $38 SC

ƭƭƭƭƭ **Estate Range Pyrenees Shiraz 2015** Rating 93 To 2030 $38 SC
Malakoff Pyrenees Shiraz 2015 Rating 93 To 2030 $46 SC
Limited Release Pyrenees Sangiovese 2016 Rating 93 To 2025 $46 SC
Jack Barry Pyrenees Sparkling Shiraz NV Rating 92 To 2025 $47
Limited Release Tempranillo 2016 Rating 91 To 2025 $46 SC

Mount Burrumboot Estate

3332 Heathcote-Rochester Road, Colbinabbin, Vic 3559 **Region** Heathcote
T 0438 329 238 **www.**burrumboot.com **Open** W'ends & public hols 11–5
Winemaker Cathy Branson **Est.** 1999 **Dozens** 500 **Vyds** 16.5ha
To quote: 'Mount Burrumboot Estate was born in 1999, when Andrew and Cathy Branson planted vines on the Home Block of the Branson family farm, Donore, on the slopes of Mt Burrumboot, on the Mt Camel Range, above Colbinabbin. Originally the vineyard was just another diversification of an already diverse farming enterprise. However, the wine bug soon bit, and a winery was established. The first wine was contract-made in 2001 – however, '02 saw the first wine made by Cathy in the machinery shed, surrounded by headers and tractors. Very primitive, and the appearance of the new 50t winery in '02 was greeted with great enthusiasm!' The original plantings of a little over 11ha of shiraz and merlot have since been expanded with lesser amounts of petit verdot, sangiovese, tempranillo, gamay, marsanne and viognier.

ΨΨΨΨ In Vino Veritas Grenache Rose 2016 Plenty to like about this rose, its red cherry and plum fruit glistening as it is tasted, held in place by natural acidity. Screwcap. 12.5% alc. **Rating** 91 **To** 2020 $20 🔾

Mount Cathedral Vineyards   ★★★☆

125 Knafl Road, Taggerty, Vic 3714 **Region** Upper Goulburn
T 0409 354 069 **www**.mtcathedralvineyards.com **Open** By appt
Winemaker Oscar Rosa, Nick Arena **Est.** 1995 **Dozens** 950 **Vyds** 5ha
The Rosa and Arena families established Mount Cathedral Vineyards in 1995, at an elevation of 300m on the north face of Mt Cathedral. The first plantings were 1.2ha of merlot and 0.8ha of chardonnay, followed by 2.5ha of cabernet sauvignon and 0.5ha of cabernet franc in '96. No pesticides or systemic chemicals are used in the vineyard. Oscar Rosa, chief winemaker, has a Bachelor of Wine Science from CSU, and gained practical experience working at Yering Station in the late '90s. Exports to Singapore.

ΨΨΨΨ **Cabernet Merlot 2015** You can't argue with the fruit freshness of the '15 Mount Cathedral reds. They all rush up to greet you. This is plummy and boysenberried and feels generous from the outset, the flow free and the feet light. There's a drift of herb-like flavour in the background and a gentle sawdust-like character, nothing to worry about and complexing in any case. Screwcap. 14% alc. **Rating** 89 **To** 2023 $25 CM
Cabernet Sauvignon 2015 Exaggerated boysenberry, red cherry and plum flavours, perhaps just tipping into redcurrant. Exceptionally fresh and lively, both aromatically and in the mouth. It all works well until the finish, which is ripe but slightly pinched. Screwcap. 14% alc. **Rating** 89 **To** 2023 $26 CM

Mount Charlie Winery   ★★★★

228 Mount Charlie Road, Riddells Creek, Vic 3431 **Region** Macedon Ranges
T (03) 5428 6946 **www**.mountcharlie.com.au **Open** Thurs–Sun 10–5
Winemaker Trefor Morgan **Est.** 1991 **Dozens** 600 **Vyds** 3ha
Mount Charlie's wines are sold principally by mail order and through selected restaurants. A futures program encourages mailing-list sales, with a substantial discount to the eventual release price. Owner/winemaker Trefor Morgan is perhaps better known as Professor of Physiology at the University of Melbourne. The vineyard is planted to 0.5ha each of chardonnay, sauvignon blanc, tempranillo, merlot, malbec and shiraz.

ΨΨΨΨΨ **Sauvignon Blanc 2017** Made in a non-NZ style, says Trefor Morgan, and he's right. It's the antithesis of Marlborough's fruit bowl of aromas and flavours – textured in a big canvas way. It's curious how the cold climates of Macedon and Tasmania shut the gate to sauvignon blanc even before winemaking starts. So it's an act of God as much as man. Screwcap. 12.5% alc. **Rating** 90 **To** 2020 $20 🔾
Bordeaux Quartet 2015 A co-fermented blend of 45% merlot, 40% malbec, 12% cabernet sauvignon and 3% cabernet franc, matured in French oak (15% new) for 27 months. Shows what can be achieved in a vintage as good as '15, and with appropriate responses in the vinification. The wine is light-bodied but the flavours are ripe, and there's been nothing left in the vineyard or winery. My only query is 27 months in barrel. Since there has been no surfeit of tannins, why not bottle at 18 months and retain that little extra fruit depth? Screwcap. 14% alc. **Rating** 90 **To** 2023 $25

Mount Coghill Vineyard   ★★★☆

Cnr Pickfords Road/Coghills Creek Road, Coghills Creek, Vic 3364 **Region** Ballarat
T (03) 5343 4329 **www**.ballaratwineries.com/mtcoghill.htm **Open** W'ends 10–5
Winemaker Owen Latta **Est.** 1993 **Dozens** 350 **Vyds** 0.7ha
Ian and Margaret Pym began planting their tiny vineyard in 1995 with 1280 pinot noir rootlings, adding 450 chardonnay rootlings the next year. Wine has been made and released

under the Mount Coghill Vineyard label since 2001. Ian is an award-winning photographer and his photographs are on display at the cellar door.

🍷🍷🍷🍷🍷 **Ballarat Chardonnay 2016** There can be no question about the ripeness of the fruit, with stone fruit to the fore, backed by citrussy acidity. A little one-dimensional perhaps, but will be a pleasant dinner companion. Screwcap. 12.5% alc. **Rating** 90 **To** 2026 $25

Mount Eyre Vineyards

173 Gillards Road, Pokolbin, NSW 2320 **Region** Hunter Valley
T 0438 683 973 **www**.mounteyre.com **Open** At Garden Cellars, Hunter Valley Gardens
Winemaker Andrew Spinaze, Mark Richardson, Michael McManus **Est.** 1970
Dozens 1000 **Vyds** 45.5ha
This is the venture of two families whose involvement in wine extends back several centuries in an unbroken line: the Tsironis family back to Peleponnese, Greece, and the Iannuzzi family to Vallo della Lucania, Italy. Their largest vineyard is at Broke, with a smaller vineyard at Pokolbin. The three principal varieties planted are chardonnay, shiraz and semillon, with small amounts of merlot, viognier, chambourcin, verdelho, negro amaro, fiano and nero d'Avola. Exports to Canada, Vanuatu, Hong Kong and China.

🍷🍷🍷🍷🍷 **Three Ponds Grosser Semillon 2017** A top-drawer selection across parcels, this cuvee is only made in superlative years, as was the case in '17. Tatami, wet stone, flint, lemon drop and lanolin form the cavalcade of aromas. Slatey and briny, the wine is also judiciously phenolic, adding additional textural armour to the pitched acidity. Screwcap. 11.8% alc. **Rating** 94 **To** 2033 $25 NG ✪

🍷🍷🍷🍷🍷 **Three Ponds Hunter Valley Semillon 2017 Rating** 92 **To** 2030 $20 NG ✪

Mount Horrocks

The Old Railway Station, Curling Street, Auburn, SA 5451 **Region** Clare Valley
T (08) 8849 2243 **www**.mounthorrocks.com **Open** W'ends & public hols 10–5
Winemaker Stephanie Toole **Est.** 1982 **Dozens** 3500 **Vyds** 9.4ha
Owner/winemaker Stephanie Toole has never deviated from the pursuit of excellence in the vineyard and winery. She has three vineyard sites in the Clare Valley, each managed using natural farming and organic practices. The attention to detail and refusal to cut corners is obvious in all her wines. The cellar door is in the renovated old Auburn railway station. Exports to the UK, China and other major markets.

🍷🍷🍷🍷🍷 **Alexander Vineyard Clare Valley Shiraz 2015** Remarkable consistency of alcohol year on year. This is even more remarkable in the mouth with a near magical combination of complexity, power and perfect balance. Oh, and the bouquet keeps beeping too. Plum, blackberry, black cherry – they're all there, all happy to share the limelight. A wonderful wine. Screwcap. 13.8% alc. **Rating** 96 **To** 2040 $43 ✪
Watervale Riesling 2017 A riesling of the kind John Vickery might have made, with the benefit of screwcaps. It has depth and attitude (like its maker), but doesn't run the risk of blowing out/softening with age. Its balance and storehouse of limes, lemons and green apples make it a sure-fire each-way bet, now or later. Screwcap. 12.5% alc. **Rating** 95 **To** 2032 $33 ✪
Clare Valley Semillon 2017 Crisp and textural at once. The focus is acute. Lemon curd, citrus, cedar spice and a whisper of herbs. Beautiful wine, for now or for later. Screwcap. 12.5% alc. **Rating** 95 **To** 2026 $33 CM ✪
Clare Valley Cabernet Sauvignon 2016 Two of the most beautiful words in the English language, when used in tandem, are 'medium-bodied'. Or that's what a wine like this makes you think. It's cabernet sauvignon in effortless mode, its curranty, brambly, toasty flavours travelling through the palate in calm, confident style. Something of a masterclass. Screwcap. 14% alc. **Rating** 95 **To** 2035 $45 CM

Clare Valley Nero d'Avola 2016 Bright with red-berried flavour, though blessed with flashes of savoury spice. Needless to say, it's a pleasure to spend time with. Tannin adds texture and chew as much as anything. Not especially deep but perfectly formed. Screwcap. 14% alc. **Rating** 94 **To** 2024 $39 CM

♥♥♥♥♀ Alexander Vineyard Clare Valley Shiraz 2016 **Rating** 93 **To** 2028 $43 CM

Mount Langi Ghiran Vineyards ★★★★★

80 Vine Road, Buangor, Vic 3375 **Region** Grampians
T (03) 5354 3207 www.langi.com.au **Open** 7 days 10–5
Winemaker Ben Haines, Jessica Robertson **Est.** 1963 **Dozens** 60 000 **Vyds** 86ha
A maker of outstanding peppery cool-climate shiraz, crammed with flavour and vinosity – long pointing the way for others – and also very good cabernet sauvignon. The business was acquired by the Rathbone family in 2002, with the marketing integrated with Yering Station and Xanadu Wines, a synergistic mix with no overlap. Exports to all major markets.

♥♥♥♥♥ Hollows Grampians Shiraz 2015 The Hollows vineyard was planted in '96, and forms the core component of this wine. Open-fermented, hand-plunged, matured in French oak (30% new). Full crimson-purple hue; a fragrant, spicy bouquet leads into a very intense and impeccably tailored palate, fine and textured with black pepper woven through black fruits. It ticks all the boxes of balance, length and clarity of finish. Screwcap. 13.7% alc. **Rating** 95 **To** 2035
Langi Grampians Riesling 2016 Scents of lemon curd, lime, Thai herbs, ripe brown pear and bitter almond kick off the dialogue. The palate, lightweight but brimming with intensity akin to a richer wine, is soused with marzipan. Again, this estate is not afraid of exploiting grape-skin phenolics for their grip, texture and capacity to balance a wine. Very Old World in its composure; Australian in its joyousness. An ode to a challenging year. Screwcap. 11.5% alc. **Rating** 94 **To** 2026 $35 NG
Langi Grampians Riesling 2015 Expected colour development, but the bouquet, and in particular the palate, are as fresh as they are detailed. This is as much about structure and complexity as it is about fruit – there's a Rheingau austerity. It's in between youth and (moderate) maturity, with time needed to complete the transition. Screwcap. 13% alc. **Rating** 94 **To** 2030 $35
Cliff Edge Grampians Pinot Gris 2016 Barrel fermentation of fruit with well above average flavour creates a true gris style. Spices and lemongrass embedded in nashi pear. Time to go. Screwcap. 11.5% alc. **Rating** 94 **To** 2021 $24 ✪
Cliff Edge Grampians Shiraz 2016 This wine benefited handsomely from the egregious weather that beset vintage '16. Hail saw to it that the fruit usually assigned to the Mount Langi Ghiran Shiraz and the special Mast cuvee was declassified, landing in this. Medium-bodied; an effusion of cherry, anise, black plum, menthol and five-spice with some cool-climate reticence. Finishes with a smear of black olive tannins and a whirr of peppery acidity, this can be enjoyed now or aged in the medium term. Screwcap. 13.8% alc. **Rating** 94 **To** 2025 $33 NG
Hollows Grampians Sangiovese 2015 The colour is bright and clear, with the first stages of development. Intensely spicy on the bouquet, and more savoury on the palate – but without sandpaper tannins. This wine would make a brilliant partner to Italian, Spanish or other Mediterranean food. Screwcap. 13.2% alc. **Rating** 94 **To** 2025 $25 ✪

♥♥♥♥♀ Billi Billi Pinot Gris 2016 **Rating** 92 **To** 2019 $18 ✪
Cliff Edge Grampians Riesling 2016 **Rating** 91 **To** 2024 $24 NG
Billi Billi Shiraz 2015 **Rating** 91 **To** 2038 $18 ✪
Spinoff Grampians Sangiovese Barbera 2016 **Rating** 91 **To** 2022 $45 NG

Mt Lofty Ranges Vineyard ★★★★★

Harris Road, Lenswood, SA 5240 **Region** Adelaide Hills
T (08) 8389 8339 **www.**mtloftyrangesvineyard.com.au **Open** Fri–Sun & public hols 11–5
Winemaker Peter Leske, Taras Ochota **Est.** 1992 **Dozens** 3000 **Vyds** 4.6ha
Mt Lofty Ranges Vineyard is owned and operated by Sharon Pearson and Garry Sweeney.
Nestled high in the Lenswood subregion of the Adelaide Hills at an altitude of 500m, the
very steep north-facing vineyard (pinot noir, sauvignon blanc, chardonnay and riesling)
is hand-pruned and hand-picked. The soil is sandy clay loam with a rock base of white
quartz and ironstone, and irrigation is kept to a minimum to allow the wines to display
pure characteristics.

🍷🍷🍷🍷🍷 **S&G Adelaide Hills Shiraz 2016** This is defined by a buttress of slinky, pulpy
grape tannins, masterfully extracted. The wine's structure is even more applaudable
given the quaffable, carbonic-centric wines that have come to define the
region. An outlier? Perhaps, but, this is serious gear towing notes of charcuterie,
blackberry, tapenade and a souk of spice along a finely tuned bow of nestled oak
and lively acidity. Superb. Screwcap. 13.2% alc. **Rating** 96 **To** 2028 $85 NG
Home Block Lenswood Riesling 2017 Five clones, hand-picked. Still crystal-
white 12 months on from vintage; a top flight example of the clarity and purity of
Adelaide Hills riesling from this vintage. The steely acidity at the core of the lime
fruit flavours is mouthwatering, the finish correspondingly long. Screwcap. 12% alc.
Rating 95 **To** 2030 $29 ✪
Old Apple Block Lenswood Chardonnay 2016 This is, as with the other
second-tier wines (for lack of a much better word), very fine. Mid-weighted
and comparatively dry, with pointed reductive handling and lees work imparting
Street's lime Splice and a creamy heart of oatmeal to a framework of gentle oak.
Burgundian, deceptively so. Screwcap. 13% alc. **Rating** 94 **To** 2024 $30 NG ✪
S&G Lenswood Pinot Noir 2016 Satsuma plum, lacquered duck and crunchy
red berry notes are corralled by abundant French oak and exotic Indian clove and
cardamom spice. This is fine. It took me a while to acclimatise to the oak, but it
bridges the gap between sweetness and savour and should settle in time. Screwcap.
13.2% alc. **Rating** 94 **To** 2025 $85 NG

🍷🍷🍷🍷🍷 **Old Pump Shed Pinot Noir 2016** Rating 93 **To** 2022 $34 NG
Methode Traditionelle 2015 Rating 93 $40 NG
Old Cherry Block Sauvignon Blanc 2017 Rating 92 **To** 2020 $22 NG ✪
S&G Chardonnay 2016 Rating 92 **To** 2024 $85 NG
Adelaide Hills Shiraz 2016 Rating 92 **To** 2022 $32 NG
Methode Traditionelle 2014 Rating 92 $40 NG
Late Harvest Riesling 2016 Rating 92 **To** 2024 $24 NG ✪

Mount Majura Vineyard ★★★★★

88 Lime Kiln Road, Majura, ACT 2609 **Region** Canberra District
T (02) 6262 3070 **www.**mountmajura.com.au **Open** 7 days 10–5
Winemaker Dr Frank van de Loo **Est.** 1988 **Dozens** 4000 **Vyds** 9.3ha
Vines were first planted in 1988 by Dinny Killen at a site on her family property that had
been especially recommended by Dr Edgar Riek; its attractions were red volcanic soil over
limestone, with reasonably steep east and northeast slopes providing an element of frost
protection. The tiny vineyard has been significantly expanded since it was purchased in '99.
The blocks of pinot noir and chardonnay have been joined by pinot gris, shiraz, tempranillo,
riesling, graciano, mondeuse, cabernet franc and touriga nacional. In addition, there has been
an active planting program for the pinot noir, introducing Dijon clones 114, 155 and 777. All
the wines come from these estate plantings. A star performer in the Canberra District.

🍷🍷🍷🍷🍷 **Canberra District Riesling 2017** Canberra riesling, when as good as this,
transcends its armour of citrus flavours to take on a complex whirr of pepper,
jasmine and fennel, meshing with the juicy spout of crunchy acidity and minerals.
This hits all the right notes and the end sensation is one of a thrumming

joyousness, bounce and compelling length. Palpably dry despite a balancing dash of residual sugar. Screwcap. 11.5% alc. **Rating** 96 To 2032 $29 NG ✪

Little Dam Canberra District Tempranillo 2016 More brooding, structured and ferruginous than its Rock Block brethren, this is a densely packed ball of black fruits, chocolate and anise, coiled around a spring of fibrous, herb-soused tannin. Similarly extracted following fermentation under the aegis of ambient yeast, the overall impression is of latent power. To make the inevitable comparison, this is more akin to a modern Rioja. Screwcap. 14% alc. **Rating** 95 To 2031 $45 NG

Canberra District Mondeuse 2017 This has to be among my finds of the year. The varietal personality is spot on in that quasi-alpine white pepper/violet/iodine sort of way. A little riper and more chocolatey than examples from the Savoie, with less astringency than those called Refosco in Italy's Friuli. Refreshment, poise, mettle, grace and sheer deliciousness. Far from prosaic, it is a wine to drink with a large grin. Screwcap. 13.5% alc. **Rating** 95 To 2025 $29 NG ✪

🍷🍷🍷🍷🍷 **Shiraz 2016 Rating** 93 To 2031 $34 NG
Rock Block Tempranillo 2016 Rating 93 To 2029 $45 NG
Graciano 2017 Rating 93 To 2021 $29 NG
Lime Kiln Red 2017 Rating 91 To 2022 $25 NG
TSG Tempranillo Shiraz Graciano 2016 Rating 91 To 2024 $34 NG

Mount Mary ★★★★★

Coldstream West Road, Lilydale, Vic 3140 **Region** Yarra Valley
T (03) 9739 1761 **www**.mountmary.com.au **Open** Not
Winemaker Sam Middleton **Est.** 1971 **Dozens** 4000 **Vyds** 12ha
Mount Mary was one of the pioneers of the rebirth of the Yarra Valley after 50 years without viticultural activity, and right from the outset produced wines of rare finesse and purity. Today its star shines brighter than that of any of the 174 wineries in the valley. The late founder, Dr John Middleton, practised near-obsessive 'attention to detail' long before that phrase slid into oenological vernacular. He relentlessly strove for perfection, and all four of the wines in the original Mount Mary portfolio achieved just that (within the context of each vintage). Charming grandson Sam Middleton is equally dedicated. An all-encompassing tasting of every vintage of these four wines left me in no doubt that somehow he is making even better wines since assuming the winemaker mantle in June 2011. Moreover, after protracted trials, two Rhône Valley–inspired wines have been released, looking to the future yet also honouring John's late wife, Marli Russell. Winery of the Year in the *Wine Companion* 2018. Exports to the UK, the US, Denmark, Hong Kong, Singapore, South Korea and China.

🍷🍷🍷🍷🍷 **Yarra Valley Triolet 2016** 65% sauvignon blanc, 25% semillon, 10% muscadelle. Gleaming straw-green; the combination of finesse and intensity is on the highest scale, as is the purity of fruit expression. This is the vineyard speaking, shaping a blend of sauvignon blanc and semillon (leaving the muscadelle to one side) into a wine like no other. This is all about doing less, the hardest task for a winemaker. Screwcap. 13.5% alc. **Rating** 97 To 2029 $95 ✪

Yarra Valley Pinot Noir 2016 Hand-picked, sorted via vibrating sorting tables, part crushed, part whole berries, 10–14 days on skins, matured for 11 months in French oak (27% new). The Upper Yarra Valley giving its typical complex texture, flavour and structure. Dark berries/plums with pinot tannins woven through the fabric of the palate, length and balance up to the usual standards. A great achievement for the vintage. Cork. 13.3% alc. **Rating** 97 To 2031 $135 ✪

Yarra Valley Quintet 2016 45% cabernet sauvignon, 25% merlot, 20% cabernet franc, 6% malbec, 4% petit verdot, separately vinified and matured in French oak (35% new) for 18–22 months. The ultimate Bordeaux blend, both in theory and reality. Almost butterfly-wing transparency, yet compelling intensity and length, the flavours spanning cassis to blueberry to plum and blackcurrant, all with a textured backing. Cork. 13.2% alc. **Rating** 97 To 2041 $150 ✪

ΥΥΥΥΥ **Yarra Valley Chardonnay 2016** Clones P58, Mendoza, I10V1, 76 and 277, hand-picked, destemmed and crushed, barrel-fermented with a wide range of cultured yeasts, 11 months in French oak (27% new). Pale straw-green; very youthful in every respect. Attention to detail has led to a sophisticated wine destined for a long life. Screwcap. 13.5% alc. **Rating** 96 **To** 2031 $110

Marli Russell by Mount Mary RP2 2016 50% grenache, 20% each of mourvedre and shiraz, 10% cinsaut, each separately vinified and matured in large French oak vats (1575–2500l) for 15–18 months. A totally delicious medium-bodied wine, the cascade of spicy red fruits as one, the tannins silky smooth, the finish clean and fresh. Another frontier passed. Screwcap. 13.5% alc. **Rating** 96 **To** 2026 $75 ⊙

Marli Russell by Mount Mary RP1 2016 40% marsanne, 40% roussanne and 20% clairette, hand-picked, destemmed and crushed, barrel-fermented (5% new oak), 11 months' maturation. The vines are much younger than those of Triolet, making the hands-off approach even harder. Its time will come, but it will take longer. Screwcap. 13% alc. **Rating** 94 **To** 2024 $55

Mount Monument Vineyard ★★★★

1399 Romsey Road, Romsey, Vic 3434 **Region** Macedon Ranges
T 0410 545 646 **www**.mountmonumentwines.com **Open** Not
Winemaker Ben Rankin **Est.** 2008 **Dozens** 800 **Vyds** 2.3ha
Mount Monument nestles into the shoulder of Mount Macedon, one of Australia's coolest wine regions. The vineyard lies at 600m with chardonnay, pinot noir and riesling growing in volcanic silica soils, planted many years ago by Nonda Katsalidis. Under viticulturist John Heitmann, the vineyard is managed with minimal chemical intervention and utilises organic and biodynamic inputs.

ΥΥΥΥΥ **Riesling 2017** Estate-grown, whole-bunch pressed, wild-fermented in stainless steel, bottled Jun. This is a no-compromise, power-laden riesling, steely and dry, but with intense unsweetened lime and lemon juice flavours. Will richly reward cellaring. Screwcap. 11.5% alc. **Rating** 94 **To** 2027 $35

Chardonnay 2016 Whole-bunch pressed, settled, fermented in barrel with light lees, matured in French oak (25% new). Straw-green hue; a very complex chardonnay with rich grapefruit-accented fruit joined by white peach and a long, juicy and focused palate. The oak is balanced and positive. Screwcap. 12.3% alc. **Rating** 94 **To** 2026 $35

ΥΥΥΥΨ **Pinot Noir 2015 Rating** 90 **To** 2022 $40
Pinot Noir 2014 Rating 90 **To** 2021 $40

Mt Moriac Estate/Waurn Ponds Estate ★★★

580 Hendy Main Road, Mount Moriac, Vic 3240 **Region** Geelong
T (03) 5266 1116 **Open** Not
Winemaker Kelly Pearson **Est.** 1987 **Dozens** 9600 **Vyds** 35.3ha
The development of the quite extensive Kurabana vineyard west of Geelong in the foothills of Mt Moriac, began in 1987. Pinot noir (7.8ha) is the largest portion, followed by (in descending order) shiraz, chardonnay, sauvignon blanc, pinot gris and viognier. In 2009 there were a number of major changes: the name became Mt Moriac Estate, and the business purchased the Waurn Ponds Estate label and all current wine from Deakin University. It also leased the Waurn Ponds vineyard from Deakin, lifting the aggregate area to over 35ha. The two brands continue, and have a common headquarters and ownership.

ΥΥΥΥ **Mt Moriac Geelong Pinot Noir 2015** This steps up to the plate with mint, meat and wood smoke flavours before pouring on a solid serve of stewed black/red cherries. Wimpy it is not. Chewy tannin adds to the impression of substance though it's all within a varietal context. The asking price is more than fair. Screwcap. 13.5% alc. **Rating** 89 **To** 2021 $19 CM ⊙

Mt Pilot Estate ★★★☆

208 Shannons Road, Byawatha, Vic 3678 **Region** North East Victoria
T 0419 243 225 **www.**mtpilotestatewines.com.au **Open** By appt
Winemaker Marc Scalzo **Est.** 1996 **Dozens** 550 **Vyds** 11ha
Lachlan and Penny Campbell have planted shiraz (6ha), cabernet sauvignon (2.5ha) and
viognier (2.5ha) in deep, well drained granitic soils at an altitude of 250m near Eldorado.

ŸŸŸŸŸ **Viognier Chardonnay 2016** Estate viognier (66%) is combined with
Beechworth chardonnay, both fermented and matured in old French oak. Pure,
fresh apricot flavour (emphasis on the word fresh) meets spice and toast notes.
The important fact is that it remains fluid and supple without turning oily. If you
throw this into a wide-bowled glass it fills the space nicely. Screwcap. 13.5% alc.
Rating 91 **To** 2019 $25 CM

Mount Pleasant ★★★★★

401 Marrowbone Road, Pokolbin, NSW 2320 **Region** Hunter Valley
T (02) 4998 7505 **www.**mountpleasantwines.com.au **Open** 7 days 10–4
Winemaker Adrian Sparks **Est.** 1921 **Dozens** NFP **Vyds** 88.2ha
The glorious Elizabeth and Lovedale semillons are generally commercially available with four
to five years of bottle age; they are treasures with a consistently superb show record. Mount
Pleasant's individual vineyard wines, together with the Maurice O'Shea memorial wines, add
to the lustre of this proud name. The appointment of Jim Chatto as group chief winemaker in
2013, and the '14 vintage – the best since 1965 – has lifted the range and quality of the red
wines back to the glory days of Maurice O'Shea, who founded Mount Pleasant and proved
himself one of Australia's great winemakers. Winery of the Year in the *Wine Companion* 2017.
Exports to all major markets.

ŸŸŸŸŸ **1946 Vines Lovedale Vineyard Hunter Valley Semillon 2017** Hunter Valley
semillon is one of the most chameleon-like styles: it can age gracefully and yet be
utterly delicious and vibrant in youth. Then there's this wine that adds depth and
complexity too. The requisite linear profile with a line of pure, strong, talc-like
acidity glides right through the palate, as do flavours of lemongrass, lemon and
mandarin. Screwcap. 11.5% alc. **Rating** 96 **To** 2037 $75 JF ✪
Lovedale Hunter Valley Semillon 2013 As if by alchemy, aged semillon slips
into a waxy realm of toast, buttery brioche and lime marmalade without its acidity
wavering. This certainly has freshness and plenty of years ahead of it. Screwcap.
10.5% alc. **Rating** 96 **To** 2028 $90 JF
Elizabeth Hunter Valley Semillon 2010 The gleaming straw-green with the
light bulb inside the glass is the only sign of its age. This really is something special,
and a gold medal at the Sydney Wine Show barely does it justice. It has a lightness,
a spring in its step, that can be suppressed by the Hunter Valley acidity code, but
not here. Screwcap. 11.5% alc. **Rating** 96 **To** 2030 $35 ✪
Maurice O'Shea Hunter Valley Shiraz 2016 Of the '16 Mount Pleasant reds,
some of which didn't pass muster, this flagship deserves its pole position. Savoury
to the max smelling of wood smoke, coal briquettes, orange peel and tar. The fruit
hasn't come through, it's there just buried among the earthy notes and charry oak.
Best to revisit in few years. Screwcap. 13% alc. **Rating** 95 **To** 2040 $250 JF
Mountain C Light Bodied Dry Red 2016 Hand-picked, destemmed, open-
top fermenters, 6 days on skins then pressed to French oak (20% new), aged
15 months. At first, this shiraz didn't want to budge it was so tightly coiled. After
a decent airing, it started to unfurl. Red cherries, pips and satsuma plums, pepper
and dried herbs all subtly brought together. A lighter frame but more medium-
bodied, savoury with a suppleness. Screwcap. 12.5% alc. **Rating** 95 **To** 2030 $75 JF

Mount Stapylton Wines ★★★★

14 Cleeve Court, Toorak, Vic 3142 (postal) **Region** Grampians
T 0425 713 044 **www**.mts-wines.com **Open** Not
Winemaker Don McRae **Est.** 2002 **Dozens** 200 **Vyds** 1ha
Mount Stapylton's vineyard is planted on the historic Goonwinnow Homestead farming property at Laharum, on the northwest side of the Grampians in front of Mt Stapylton. In 2010 founders Howard and Samantha Staehr sold the homestead property, but leased back their vineyard. The wines are listed with several iconic restaurants in Sydney and Melbourne. Exports to the UK.

ⓎⓎⓎⓎ **Grampians Shiraz 2016** Dense crimson-purple hue; has the full suite of power ex the Grampians terroir with spicy black fruits on the fore-palate, but it inexplicably looses drive and finishes very short. Strange, particularly when compared to the '15. Screwcap. 14.5% alc. **Rating** 89 **To** 2023

Mount Terrible ★★★★★

289 Licola Road, Jamieson, Vic 3723 **Region** Central Victoria
T (03) 5777 0703 **www**.mountterriblewines.com.au **Open** By appt
Winemaker John Eason **Est.** 2001 **Dozens** 350 **Vyds** 2ha
John Eason and wife Janene Ridley began the long, slow (and at times very painful) business of establishing their vineyard just north of Mt Terrible in 1992. In 2001 they planted 2ha of pinot noir (MV6, 115, 114 and 777 clones) on a gently sloping, north-facing river terrace adjacent to the Jamieson River. DIY trials persuaded John to have the first commercial vintage contract-made in '06, but he has since made the wines himself in a fireproof winery built on top of an underground wine cellar. John has a sense of humour second to none, but must wonder what he has done to provoke the weather gods, alternating in their provision of fire, storm and tempest. Subsequent vintages have provided some well earned relief. Exports to the UK.

ⓎⓎⓎⓎⓎ **Jamieson Pinot Noir 2015** Estate-grown, hand-picked, clones 114, 115, 777 and MV6. 3 days' cold soak in an open fermenter with 10% whole bunches, post-ferment maceration, matured for 18 months in French oak. The full crimson-purple colour introduces a very high quality, ultra-fragrant pinot with the depth, complexity and length reminiscent of high quality Burgundies. Made with a sure touch. Screwcap. 13.5% alc. **Rating** 97 **To** 2030 $42 ✪

Mount Trio Vineyard ★★★★

2534 Porongurup Road, Mount Barker WA 6324 **Region** Porongurup
T (08) 9853 1136 **www**.mounttriowines.com.au **Open** By appt
Winemaker Gavin Berry, Andrew Vesey, Caitlin Gazey **Est.** 1989 **Dozens** 3000
Vyds 8.5ha
Mount Trio was established by Gavin Berry and wife Gill Graham (plus business partners) shortly after they moved to the Mount Barker area in late 1988. Gavin took up the position of chief winemaker at Plantagenet, which he held until 2004, then he and partners acquired West Cape Howe, now very successful and much larger. They have slowly built up Mount Trio, increasing estate plantings with riesling (3.5ha), shiraz (2.4ha) and pinot noir (2.6ha). Exports to the UK, Denmark and China.

ⓎⓎⓎⓎⓎ **Porongurup Riesling 2017** There is an enticing and certain future for this lovely riesling, as yet to fully emerge from its swaddling clothes. The bouquet is clean but muted, the palate providing the gold medal quality with its bright and juicy Granny Smith apple, lime and lemon flavours clasped by brisk acidity. Screwcap. 12% alc. **Rating** 94 **To** 2032 $22 ✪
Great Southern Chardonnay 2017 65% Mount Barker, 35% Frankland River. 50% fermented in mostly new French oak, 50% in tank with French oak staves; 33% of the barrel-fermented portion undergoing mlf. Adroit winemaking courtesy of vast experience and a cool vintage has produced a high quality chardonnay at a

bargain price. It is an elegant wine with stone fruit, melon and citrus flavours, the oak a match for the fruit. Screwcap. 13% alc. **Rating** 94 **To** 2023 $17 ○
Great Southern Cabernet Merlot 2015 With 99% cabernet sauvignon, there is no way this can legally be labelled as it is – a minimum of 5% is required to name the second variety. It's of academic interest only, because this is an exceptional cabernet at a giveaway price, with a lovely tension between cassis and savoury, dried herb flavours (plus cabernet tannins). Screwcap. 14.5% alc. **Rating** 94 **To** 2029 $17 ○

♀♀♀♀♀ **Porongurup Pinot Noir 2016 Rating** 92 **To** 2026 $22 ○
Geographe Sangiovese Rose 2017 Rating 91 **To** 2020 $17 ○

Mount View Estate   ★★★★★

Mount View Road, Mount View, NSW 2325 **Region** Hunter Valley
T (02) 4990 3307 **www**.mtviewestate.com.au **Open** Mon–Sat 10–5, Sun 10–4
Winemaker Scott Stephens **Est.** 1971 **Dozens** 4000 **Vyds** 16ha
Mount View Estate's vineyard was planted by the very knowledgeable Harry Tulloch 45 years ago; he recognised the quality of the red basalt volcanic soils of the very attractive hillside site. Prior owners John and Polly Burgess also purchased the adjoining Limestone Creek vineyard in 2004 (planted in 1982), fitting it seamlessly into Mount View Estate's production. The quality of the wines is outstanding. The business changed hands in '16, now owned by a Chinese national with no further details available. Exports to China.

♀♀♀♀♀ **Museum Release Flagship Hunter Valley Semillon 2010** A beautiful wine, 8 years young. Deliciously juicy yet finely structured; length, finesse, a basket of citrus fruits waiting to be peeled and eaten, quarter by quarter. Third release, third tasting. Screwcap. 11% alc. **Rating** 97 **To** 2025 $70 ○

♀♀♀♀♀ **Museum Release Reserve Hunter Valley Semillon 2006** Lime, lemon and honey get a rapturous reception from the palate; the balance between fruit and acidity is perfect. When released as a yearling, Mount View suggested cellaring for 4–5 years to see it develop into a classic toasty semillon. They got that one wrong, didn't they? Screwcap. 10.3% alc. **Rating** 96 **To** 2021 $50 ○
Reserve Hunter Valley Shiraz 2014 The sheer power and length of the palate is intimidating, as is its complexity, picking at will characters from cool climates as well as from the (very) warm Hunter Valley. The fruits are predominantly black, but there are also red flashes, and the tannins intertwine with the earthy nuances and the oak. Screwcap. 13.5% alc. **Rating** 95 **To** 2044 $40
Reserve Hunter Valley Semillon 2017 Hand-picked, crushed and destemmed, must chilled, air bag-pressed, fermented at 14–16°C, 4 months on lees. You can easily see the richness that will develop with time in bottle, juicy/grassy notes already on display. Screwcap. 12% alc. **Rating** 94 **To** 2027 $35
Reserve Hunter Valley Chardonnay 2017 Hand-picked, crushed and destemmed, 33% wild-fermented in barrel, the balance cold-fermented in tank with cultured yeast, transferred to barrel at 4° baume to finish fermentation, 7 months in oak (40% new). Only the faintest catch on the finish to betray its climate. Screwcap. 13.5% alc. **Rating** 94 **To** 2027 $40
Reserve Hilltops Cabernet Sauvignon 2016 Similar vinification to the Reserve Shiraz: 2 days' cold soak, 4–6 days on skins, 8 months in French oak (30% new). Good colour; a medium to full-bodied cabernet with potent blackcurrant fruit and ample tannins running through to the long finish. A good future awaits. Screwcap. 14% alc. **Rating** 94 **To** 2031 $40

♀♀♀♀♀ **Reserve Hilltops Shiraz Viognier 2016 Rating** 93 **To** 2026 $40
Liqueur Shiraz NV Rating 92 $55 JF
Hunter Valley Shiraz 2016 Rating 90 **To** 2029 $25

Munari Wines

Ladys Creek vineyard, 1129 Northern Highway, Heathcote, Vic 3523 **Region** Heathcote
T (03) 5433 3366 **www**.munariwines.com **Open** Tues–Sun 11–5
Winemaker Adrian Munari **Est.** 1993 **Dozens** 3000 **Vyds** 6.9ha
Established on one of the original Heathcote farming properties, Ladys Creek vineyard
occupies some of the narrow Cambrian soil strip, 11km north of town. Adrian Munari has
harnessed traditional winemaking practices to New World innovation to produce complex,
fruit-driven wines that marry concentration and elegance. They are produced from estate
plantings of shiraz, cabernet sauvignon, merlot, cabernet franc and malbec. Exports to France,
Denmark, Taiwan and China.

Ladys Pass Heathcote Shiraz 2015 Oak and fruit sit slightly separate, but it's a
quibble. This is seductively fruited (and oaked), its flavours of rich plum, black cherry,
peppercorn and sweet sawdust pouring lusciously through the palate. A cold night,
a bottle of this; you're sorted. Screwcap. 14% alc. **Rating** 93 **To** 2028 $30 CM
The Gun Picker Shiraz Cabernet 2014 61% shiraz from the Upper Goulburn,
39% cabernet sauvignon from the estate vineyard. Asphalt, ozone, peppermint and
licorice. It's a different, if not exotic, flavour profile, and while there's a graininess
to the texture, a soft heart lies beneath. Rustic in a good way. Screwcap. 14% alc.
Rating 91 **To** 2024 CM
Schoolhouse Red 2015 Made with merlot, malbec, cabernet and shiraz. It tastes
of ripe plum, leather, liquid toast and vanilla, and while it's both firm and minty
to finish, it's smooth sailing for the most part. Good colour and decent impact too.
Screwcap. 14% alc. **Rating** 91 **To** 2024 $30 CM
India Red Heathcote Cabernet Sauvignon 2015 The bouquet is both minty
and floral, the first impression one of elegance. But the palate is all boysenberry
and port-wine jelly with leather and blackcurrant in the background. It feels as
though it's still growing into itself; nothing to be alarmed about. The fruit here is
sweet, ripe and tasty. Screwcap. 14% alc. **Rating** 90 **To** 2026 $30 CM

Heathcote Rose 2016 Rating 89 **To** 2018 $20 CM

Murdoch Hill ★★★★★

260 Mappinga Road, Woodside, SA 5244 **Region** Adelaide Hills
T (08) 8389 7081 **www**.murdochhill.com.au **Open** By appt
Winemaker Michael Downer **Est.** 1998 **Dozens** 4000 **Vyds** 20.48ha
A little over 20ha of vines have been established on the undulating, gum-studded countryside
of Charlie and Julie Downer's 60-year-old Erika property, 4km east of Oakbank. In descending
order of importance, the varieties planted are sauvignon blanc, shiraz, cabernet sauvignon and
chardonnay. Son Michael, with a Bachelor of Oenology from the University of Adelaide, is
winemaker. Exports to the UK and China.

The Tilbury Adelaide Hills Chardonnay 2017 Clones 76 and 95,
whole-berry pressed, French barriques (20% new) and 1500l foudre (40% new).
The substantial oak inputs work well to invest the wine with structure as well as
toasty oak flavour. Screwcap. 12.5% alc. **Rating** 95 **To** 2024 $50
The Landau Single Vineyard Oakbank Adelaide Hills Syrah 2017
Hand-picked from a single block, 15% whole bunches, some new French oak.
Bright crimson-purple hue; intense black and red berries on the palate have a
spicy/savoury/earthy nuance that is very likely ex the whole bunches. Striking
wine. Screwcap. 13% alc. **Rating** 95 **To** 2032 $50

Adelaide Hills Sauvignon Blanc 2017 Rating 93 **To** 2019 $22
Adelaide Hills Chardonnay 2017 Rating 93 **To** 2022 $30
Ridley Adelaide Hills Pinot X Three 2017 Rating 91 **To** 2022 $35
Adelaide Hills Sulky Rouge 2017 Rating 91 **To** 2027 $35
The Phaeton Pinot Noir 2017 Rating 90 **To** 2021 $50
Adelaide Hills Pinot Noir 2017 Rating 90 **To** 2020 $30

Murray Street Vineyards   ★★★★★

Murray Street, Greenock, SA 5360 **Region** Barossa Valley
T (08) 8562 8373 **www**.murraystreet.com.au **Open** 7 days 10–6
Winemaker Craig Viney **Est.** 2001 **Dozens** 20 000 **Vyds** 50ha
Andrew Seppelt and business partner Bill Jahnke (the latter a successful investment banker)
established Murray Street Vineyards in 2001. It very quickly established itself as a producer
of exceptionally good wines. In '15 Bill assumed total ownership, appointing Craig Viney
as winemaker, and intending to upscale the production capability and distribution network.
Exports to Denmark, Laos, Macau, Singapore and NZ.

🍷🍷🍷🍷🍷 **Greenock Estate Barossa Valley Shiraz 2016** There are no flourishes to the
vinification, and the outcome from the 20yo block is a medium-bodied wine with
typical flavours of predominantly black fruits and gently persistent tannins. There
is no kickback from the alcohol, and the wine will develop slowly but surely
through to the early '30s. Diam. 15% alc. **Rating** 93 **To** 2031 $50

Murrumbateman Winery

Cnr Barton Highway/McIntosh Circuit, Murrumbateman, NSW 2582
Region Canberra District
T (02) 6227 5584 **www**.murrumbatemanwinery.com.au **Open** Fri–Sun & public hols 10–5
Winemaker Bobbie Makin **Est.** 1972 **Dozens** 1000 **Vyds** 4ha
Draws upon 4ha of estate-grown sauvignon blanc and shiraz. It also incorporates an à la carte
restaurant and function room, together with picnic and barbecue areas.

🍷🍷🍷🍷🍷 **The Dual Citizen Shiraz 2016** From Canberra District and Hilltops, the back
label with a very funny description of the possibility that this wine may become
prime minister in 12 years' time. It is by some distance the best of the winery's
'16 shirazs. The black fruit flavours are intense, the medium-bodied palate long
and harmonious with its cross-weave of fine-spun tannins. Screwcap. 14.5% alc.
Rating 95 **To** 2036 $45

🍷🍷🍷🍷🍷 **Shiraz 2016** Rating 92 To 2031 $30
Old Block Shiraz Rose 2017 Rating 91 To 2021 $25
Cabernet Sauvignon 2016 Rating 91 To 2026 $40
Old Block Shiraz 2016 Rating 90 To 2020 $45
Tempranillo 2016 Rating 90 To 2020 $30
Malbec 2016 Rating 90 To 2024 $50

Muster Wine Co

c/- 60 Sheffield Street, Malvern, SA 5061 **Region** Barossa Valley
T 0430 360 350 **www**.musterwineco.com.au **Open** By appt
Winemaker David Muster **Est.** 2007 **Dozens** 2500
Gottfried Muster arrived from Europe with his young family in 1859, settling in the Barossa
Valley. Direct descendent David Muster was born and bred in the purple (though of wine,
not horses). This is a virtual winery business; David has been buying and selling wine since
2007. He forages for small batches in the Barossa and Clare valleys, and clearly has developed
some very useful contacts, allowing the release of relatively small amounts under each label,
sometimes offering very good value. Exports to the US.

🍷🍷🍷🍷🍷 **Polish Hill River Riesling 2017** Textbook lime and orange blossom notes careen
across dry acid lines. Glimpses of stone fruit. Pumice stone. Acerbically dry, yet
long and persistent. Needs time to flesh out and gain traction, generosity and a bit
of love. Screwcap. 11.9% alc. **Rating** 92 **To** 2029 $25 NG ✪

MyattsField Vineyards

Union Road, Carmel Valley, WA 6076 **Region** Perth Hills
T (08) 9293 5567 **www**.myattsfield.com.au **Open** Fri–Sun and public hols 11–5
Winemaker Josh Davenport, Rachael Davenport, Josh Uren **Est.** 1997 **Dozens** 3000
Vyds 4.5ha

MyattsFieldVineyards is owned by Josh and Rachael Davenport. Both have oenology degrees, and domestic and Flying Winemaker experience, especially Rachael. In 2006 they decided they would prefer to work for themselves. They left their employment, building a winery in time for the '07 vintage. Their vineyards include cabernet sauvignon, merlot, petit verdot, shiraz and chardonnay, and they also purchase small parcels of grapes from as far away as Manjimup. Exports to Singapore and Taiwan.

ꕤꕤꕤꕤꕤ **Kenneth Green Vintage Fortified 2015** Touriga nacional with some durif and shiraz form the core of this incredibly youthful wine, fortified with neutral spirit (70%) and brandy spirit (30%) and integrated exceptionally well. There's plenty to like from the excellent dark purple hue to the layers of flavour with notes of dried citrus peel, pomander and baking spices. There are some raisin notes, too, but the brightness of the touriga shines through. The sweetness is tempered by the raw silk tannins and depth of flavour. 500ml. Diam. 18% alc. **Rating** 95 $38 JF

ꕤꕤꕤꕤꕤ **Vermentino 2017 Rating** 93 **To** 2019 $20 JF ✪
Rose 2017 Rating 93 **To** 2019 $20 JF ✪
Joseph Myatt Reserve 2015 Rating 93 **To** 2025 $45 JF
Left Field Club Touriga 2016 Rating 92 **To** 2022 $26 JF
Shiraz Mourvedre Viognier 2016 Rating 91 **To** 2025 $26 JF
Cabernet Sauvignon Merlot Franc 2016 Rating 91 **To** 2024 $26 JF
Left Field Club John Francis Reserve 2016 Rating 90 **To** 2025 $35 JF
Durif 2016 Rating 90 **To** 2021 $30 JF

Myrtaceae

53 Main Creek Road, Main Ridge, Vic 3928 **Region** Mornington Peninsula
T (03) 5989 2045 **www**.myrtaceae.com.au **Open** W'ends & public hols 12–5
Winemaker Julie Trueman **Est.** 1985 **Dozens** 300 **Vyds** 1ha

John Trueman (viticulturist) and wife Julie (winemaker) purchased their Mornington Peninsula property near Arthurs Seat in 1984. Chardonnay (0.6ha) and pinot noir (0.4ha) were planted in '98–99. Just one Chardonnay and one Pinot Noir are made each year from the estate grapes; a Rose made from pinot is a more recent addition. Meticulous viticulture using Scott Henry trellising is used to maximise sunlight and airflow at this cool, elevated site. Extensive gardens surround the winery.

Naked Run Wines

36 Parawae Road, Salisbury Plain, SA 5109 (postal) **Region** Clare Valley/Barossa Valley
T 0408 807 655 **www**.nakedrunwines.com.au **Open** Not
Winemaker Steven Baraglia **Est.** 2005 **Dozens** 1200

Naked Run Wines (not to be confused with Naked Wines) is the virtual winery of Jayme Wood, Bradley Currie and Steven Baraglia, their skills ranging from viticulture through to production, and also to the all-important sales and marketing. Riesling is sourced from Clare Valley, grenache from the Williamstown area of the Barossa Valley, and shiraz from Greenock.

ꕤꕤꕤꕤꕤ **The First Clare Valley Riesling 2017** This really is a cut above, with gold medals from the Adelaide and Melbourne wine shows. Its lime, lemon and sherbet flavours have exceptional line, drive and length. Great now, and in 20 years hence. Screwcap. 12% alc. **Rating** 97 **To** 2037 $22 ✪

ꕤꕤꕤꕤꕤ **Place in Time Sevenhill Clare Valley Riesling 2012** An aged release, having won gold medals at the Clare Valley Wine Show '13, Canberra International

Riesling Challenge '14, Winewise '16, Small Winemakers Wine Show '16, and again the Canberra International Riesling Challenge and Boutique Wine Show '17. You know a great wine when it wins as this has done. It's exceptionally fine and elegant in the the manner of great German dry rieslings, and its future stretches out beyond the horizon. Screwcap. 12% alc. **Rating** 95 **To** 2032 $40

🍷🍷🍷🍷🍷 BWC Barossa Valley Shiraz 2015 **Rating** 93 **To** 2028
The Aldo Old Vine Barossa Valley Grenache Shiraz 2016 **Rating** 92 **To** 2026 $22 ○
Place in Time Sevenhill Clare Valley Shiraz 2013 **Rating** 91 **To** 2028 $40
Hill 5 Clare Valley Shiraz Cabernet 2016 **Rating** 90 **To** 2026

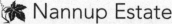 Nannup Estate ★★★★★

Lot 25 Perks Road, Nannup, WA 6275 **Region** Blackwood Valley
T (08) 9756 2005 **www.**nannupestate.com.au **Open** Not
Winemaker Michael Ng **Est.** 2017 **Dozens** 3500 **Vyds** 14.43ha
Nannup Estate (with the vineyard held under this title) is owned by Mark Blizzard and family, and the adjacent Nannup Ridge Estate under another title owned by Ray Fitzgerald and family. Until recently, these two properties were both farmed together as a single property, although the grapes went to the respective families once harvested. The vineyard sits high on the granite ridges of the Blackwood River escarpment. During the growing season the vines enjoy long hours of sunshine followed by moderate coastal breezes in the afternoons and cool evenings – idyllic growing conditions. Abundant water, granite loam soils, and low frost and disease pressure all contribute to reliable quality and consistent vintages. The first 6ha of vines were planted in 1998, with subsequent plantings in 2000 and '06. The vineyard now comprises 14.5ha of cabernet sauvignon, merlot, chardonnay, tempranillo and malbec. Exports to China.

🍷🍷🍷🍷🍷 Reserve Chardonnay 2016 9 months in French oak (60% new). This is the big brother of Rolling Hills, all the components, except the oak, scaled up to the same degree; the oak just a bit assertive, but likely to stand back in the future. High quality, well made wine. Screwcap. **Rating** 95 **To** 2029 $40
Rolling Hills Chardonnay 2016 Fermented in tank and barrel (30% new French), matured for 9 months. An attractive and expressive wine with white peach dominant, pink grapefruit and apple following the lead. The oak handling has worked precisely as intended, leaving freshness and complexity, and not sitting on top of the fruit. Screwcap. 13.2% alc. **Rating** 95 **To** 2025 $32 ○
Reserve Chardonnay 2015 Identical vinification to the '16. Tasted after the '16, and indeed the oak has now been absorbed into this lovely, perfectly balanced wine. Screwcap. **Rating** 95 **To** 2030 $40
Rolling Hills Shiraz 2016 A full-bodied shiraz that hits you between the eyes with a clinically delivered blow – there's nothing accidental about this wine. The bouquet is full of spicy black fruits, which are also the backbone of the palate. The winemaking has been resolutely normal, so this is terroir speaking loud and clear. Screwcap. 14.5% alc. **Rating** 95 **To** 2036 $32 ○
Rolling Hills Cabernet Sauvignon 2016 A medium-bodied cabernet that achieves all it needs to and then some. The opening stanzas of the bouquet and fore-palate throw the accent onto blackcurrant fruit, which then shifts to more savoury notes, and finally to impeccably behaved tannins on the finish. Screwcap. 14.5% alc. **Rating** 95 **To** 2030 $32 ○
Rolling Hills Merlot 2016 Very good hue; not all merlot addicts will self-administer doses of this wine, simply because it's too good, too correct, in its varietal expression. There's cassis/blackcurrant first up, then a herbal cut on the finish that counterintuitively underlines the finish. Screwcap. 14.5% alc. **Rating** 94 **To** 2029 $32
Rolling Hills Malbec 2016 20yo vines, matured in French oak (30% new) for 12 months. Deep, bright, clear crimson-purple; effortless delivery of varietal aroma and fruit, satsuma plum to the fore. Ripe tannins, good French oak and very good balance. Screwcap. 14.5% alc. **Rating** 94 **To** 2031 $32

ㅜㅜㅜㅜㅜ Rolling Hills Tempranillo 2016 Rating 93 To 2022 $32
Firetower Tempranillo Rose 2017 Rating 91 To 2020 $23 ⦿
Firetower Sauvignon Blanc 2017 Rating 90 To 2020 $23
Firetower Shiraz Malbec Tempranillo 2016 Rating 90 To 2031 $25

Narkoojee ★★★★★

170 Francis Road, Glengarry, Vic 3854 **Region** Gippsland
T (03) 5192 4257 **www**.narkoojee.com **Open** 7 days 10.30–4.30
Winemaker Axel Friend **Est.** 1981 **Dozens** 5000 **Vyds** 13.6ha
Narkoojee, originally a dairy farm owned by the Friend family, is near the old goldmining
town of Walhalla and looks out over the Strzelecki Ranges. The wines are produced from
the estate vineyards, with chardonnay accounting for half the total. Former lecturer in civil
engineering and extremely successful amateur winemaker, Harry Friend, changed horses in
1994 to take joint control of the vineyard and winery with son Axel, and they haven't missed
a beat since; their skills show through in all the wines. Exports to China.

ㅜㅜㅜㅜㅜ Valerie Gippsland Shiraz 2015 Named in honour of Valerie Friend, a lifetime
contributor to Narkoojee. Estate-grown, wild-fermented, matured in French oak
(33% new). This is indeed a quite beautiful shiraz from a great vintage, with an
orchestra of red and black fruits, spice and supple tannins. Screwcap. 14.5% alc.
Rating 96 To 2035 $60 ⦿
Valerie Gippsland Shiraz 2016 A full-bodied sibling to the Francis Road
Shiraz. Here everything is dialled up a notch, the black fruits, licorice and tar, the
oak and web of tannins. All add up to a wine of great length and power. Screwcap.
14.5% alc. **Rating** 95 To 2036 $60
Valerie Gippsland Pinot Noir 2016 A delicious pinot with grace and a fluid
line to all the senses. Here the fruit flavours are in the red spectrum, spices already
starting to develop and pointing to the future. The tannin and oak support is finer,
and thus balanced. Screwcap. 14.5% alc. **Rating** 94 To 2032 $60
Reserve Maxwell Gippsland Cabernet 2016 The colour is full and bright,
the mouthfeel smooth and supple, the palate with juicy cassis and French oak
entwined throughout, providing textural and structural support. Screwcap. 14% alc.
Rating 94 To 2036 $40
Reserve Maxwell Gippsland Cabernet 2015 The benison of the vintage led
to the use of one-third new French oak, and it is a little assertive as yet. That said,
there's no doubt another 5 years will see it assume its due place. Screwcap. 14% alc.
Rating 94 To 2030 $40

ㅜㅜㅜㅜㅜ Gippsland Pinot Noir 2016 Rating 92 To 2029 $29
Reserve Gippsland Pinot Noir 2016 Rating 90 To 2024 $43
Francis Road Gippsland Shiraz 2016 Rating 90 To 2029 $29

Nashwauk ★★★☆

PO Box 852, Nuriootpa, SA 5355 **Region** McLaren Vale
T (08) 8562 4488 **www**.nashwaukvineyards.com.au **Open** Not
Winemaker Stephen Dew **Est.** 2005 **Dozens** 5000 **Vyds** 20ha
This is an estate-based venture, with 17ha of shiraz, 2ha of cabernet sauvignon and 1ha of
tempranillo – all except the tempranillo are between 15 and 40+ years old. It is a stand-alone
business of the Kaesler family, and the first time they have extended this far beyond the Barossa
Valley. The striking label comes from satellite photos of the vineyard, showing the contour
planting; the name Nashwauk comes from Canada's Algonquin language, meaning 'land
between'. The property is situated in the (unofficial) Seaview subregion of McLaren Vale, with
Kay Brothers, Chapel Hill and Coriole as neighbours; they all benefit from sea breezes and
cooler nights. Exports to the US, Singapore, Malaysia, Hong Kong and China.

ㅜㅜㅜㅜㅜ Wrecked McLaren Vale Shiraz 2014 At full-throttle with its ripeness and
savouriness. Awash with dark fruit, smoky spices, meaty aromas and a touch
of eucalyptus. Expansive yet supple tannins with little room to move. For the
dedicated. Cork. 14.5% alc. **Rating** 90 To 2030 $70 JF

Nepenthe ★★★★

Jones Road, Balhannah, SA 5242 **Region** Adelaide Hills
T (08) 8398 8888 **www**.nepenthe.com.au **Open** 7 days 10–4
Winemaker Alex Trescowthick **Est.** 1994 **Dozens** 40 000 **Vyds** 108.68ha
Nepenthe quickly established its reputation as a producer of high quality wines, but founder
Ed Tweddell died unexpectedly in 2006, and the business was purchased by Australian Vintage
Limited the following year. The winery was closed in '09, and winemaking operations
transferred to McGuigan Wines (Barossa Valley). The winery has since been purchased
by Peter Leske and Mark Kozned, who use it for contract winemaking services via their
Revenir venture. Nepenthe has over 100ha of close-planted vines spread over four vineyards
in the Adelaide Hills, with an exotic array of varieties. Exports to the UK, the US and other
major markets.

ΨΨΨΨΨ **Pinnacle Ithaca Adelaide Hills Chardonnay 2016** Sure-footed chardonnay,
its quality obvious, its wilder/funkier notes tucked neatly into a pure stream of
yellow stone fruit and grapefruit. The words 'this is how you do it' spring to mind.
Richness isn't its shtick; it's all about an elegant presentation of complex flavours.
Toasty/smoky oak characters are the icing. Screwcap. 12.5% alc. **Rating** 94
To 2024 $35 CM
Altitude Adelaide Hills Pinot Gris 2017 This nabbed a gold medal and trophy
for the best pinot gris at the Adelaide Hills Wine Show '17. It's a fresh, lively
wine with some texture; flavours of ginger-poached pears and white nectarines,
with a blossom breeze. It's quite crisp for a gris-style – and goes down a treat –
but beyond the region, not quite trophy territory. Screwcap. 13°alc. **Rating** 94
To 2019 $22 JF ✪

ΨΨΨΨ **Pinnacle Gate Block Adelaide Hills Shiraz 2016 Rating** 93 **To** 2024 $35 JF
Winemaker's Selection Gewurztraminer 2017 Rating 92 **To** 2019 $30 JF
Pinnacle Petraea Adelaide Hills Sauvignon Blanc 2017 Rating 92 **To** 2020
$35 JF

New Era Vineyards ★★★★☆

PO Box 391, Woodside SA 5244 **Region** Adelaide Hills
T 0413 544 246 **www**.neweravineyards.com.au **Open** Not
Winemaker Robert Baxter, Iain Baxter **Est.** 1988 **Dozens** 1000 **Vyds** 13ha
The New Era vineyard is situated over a gold reef that was mined for 60 years until 1940,
when all recoverable gold had been extracted. The vineyard was originally planted to
chardonnay, shiraz, cabernet sauvignon, merlot and sauvignon, mostly contracted to Foster's.
Recently 2ha of cabernet sauvignon and 1.1ha of merlot have been grafted over to sauvignon
blanc. Much of the production is sold to other winemakers in the region. The small amount
of wine made has been the subject of favourable reviews.

ΨΨΨΨΨ **Barrel Select Adelaide Hills Shiraz 2016** The longer maceration period
(21 days), rather than the common extended time in oak when stepping up
the range, has served this wine very well. The alloyed tannins, as precise as ball
bearings, passage this shiraz to a long, layered finish. The reductive card is played
ever so gently, yet the resounding impression is one of lilac florals and generous
blue fruits, skirting across peppery acidity. Screwcap. 14% alc. **Rating** 95 **To** 2028
$50 NG

ΨΨΨΨ **Adelaide Hills Shiraz 2015 Rating** 93 **To** 2025 $25 NG ✪
Langhorne Creek Touriga Nacional 2016 Rating 93 **To** 2024 $25 NG ✪
Adelaide Hills Pinot Rose 2017 Rating 91 **To** 2019 $20 NG ✪

Ngeringa ★★★★☆

119 Williams Road, Mount Barker, SA 5251 **Region** Adelaide Hills
T (08) 8398 2867 **www**.ngeringa.com **Open** By appt
Winemaker Erinn Klein **Est.** 2001 **Dozens** 2500 **Vyds** 5.5ha

Erinn and Janet Klein say, 'As fervent practitioners of biodynamic winegrowing, we respect biodynamics as a sensitivity to the rhythms of nature, the health of the soil and the connection between plant, animal and cosmos. It is a pragmatic solution to farming without the use of chemicals, and a necessary acknowledgement that the farm unit is part of a great whole'. It is not an easy solution, and the Kleins have increased the immensity of the challenge by using ultra-close vine spacing of 1.5 × 1m, necessitating a large amount of hand-training plus the use of a tiny crawler tractor. Lest it be thought that they stumbled onto biodynamic growing without understanding wine science, it should be stated that they teamed up while studying at the University of Adelaide in 2000 (Erinn – oenology, Janet – viticulture/wine marketing), and then spent time looking at the great viticultural regions of the Old World, with a particular emphasis on biodynamics. Their JE label is used for the basic wines, Ngeringa only for the very best (NASAA Certified Biodynamic). Exports to the US, Canada, Austria, Belgium, Norway, Japan, Hong Kong and China.

🍷🍷🍷🍷🍷 **Single Vineyard Adelaide Hills Chardonnay 2015** Has developed well with additional bottle age, the angles gently rounded, adding a hint of vanilla, but leaving the essence of the fruit unchanged. This is still moving to full maturity, but will arrive at that point soon. Screwcap. 13.5% alc. **Rating** 95 **To** 2023 $40
Elliptic Single Vineyard Adelaide Hills Chardonnay 2016 Gleaming green colour; a complex, intense, long and very well made chardonnay, pretty much as good as they come from the Adelaide Hills. Stone fruits are soused in a citrus sorbet, barrel fermentation driving texture and mouthfeel. Vino–Lok. 13.5% alc. **Rating** 94 **To** 2026 $40
Single Vineyard Adelaide Hills Syrah 2015 There's a lot of wine in the bottle, opening with blackberry fruit, then a whisk of licorice and finely wrought tannins towards the finish. In transition from adolescence to maturity, and handling it well. Great value. Screwcap. 13.5% alc. **Rating** 94 **To** 2033 $50

🍷🍷🍷🍷♀ **Single Vineyard Adelaide Hills Sangiovese 2016 Rating** 90 **To** 2023 $35

Nick Haselgrove Wines ★★★★

281 Tatachilla Road, McLaren Vale, SA 5171 **Region** Adelaide
T (08) 8383 0886 **www**.nhwines.com.au **Open** By appt
Winemaker Nick Haselgrove, Marcus Hofer **Est.** 1981 **Dozens** 10 000
After various sales, amalgamations and disposals of particular brands, Nick Haselgrove now owns The Old Faithful (the flagship brand, see separate entry), Blackbilly, Clarence Hill, James Haselgrove and The Wishing Tree brands. Exports to the US and other major markets including Canada, Hong Kong and China.

🍷🍷🍷🍷♀ **Clarence Hill Reserve McLaren Vale Shiraz 2014** If it was a book it would have the word 'oak' in large letters on the cover. Oak presents as the star of the show here, its resiny, coffeed, honeyed character exerting clear influence over the plum-drenched nature of the fruit. Orange-like acidity plays a role too. Tannin is fine-grained and in the end the wine pulls itself into some kind of shape, though it lumbers its way there. It needs to spend a few years in a cool, dark place at a minimum. Cork. 14.5% alc. **Rating** 93 **To** 2028 $35 CM
Blackbilly McLaren Vale Grenache Shiraz Mourvedre 2015 It sure can't be criticised on volume grounds. This is a hefty red, soft to the touch, with both red and black berry flavours running at high revs through the palate. Oak is a minor player at most; anise notes hover; the finish is warm but convincing. Super ripe but very good. Screwcap. 14.5% alc. **Rating** 93 **To** 2026 $24 CM ✪
Old Vine McLaren Vale Grenache 2013 From 80yo grenache vines at Blewitt Springs. Depth of fruit and modest oak combine to create a supple, satisfying wine complete with blueberry, prune and black cherry flavours, floral aromas and a mere whisper of creamy oak. The flavour spectrum is at the riper end, but importantly it feels and tastes harmonious. Diam. 14% alc. **Rating** 92 **To** 2024 $24 CM ✪
Blackbilly Adelaide Sauvignon Blanc 2017 Works up a good head of steam via gooseberry, citrus and lime-like flavours and, indeed, does so cleanly and well.

Pretty much bang on as a fruit-driven example of the variety. Screwcap. 13% alc.
Rating 90 **To** 2018 $24 CM

Blackbilly McLaren Vale Shiraz 2016 You get what you come for –
blackberried fruit coated in dark chocolate – with the added benefit that it's
all soundly balanced. Certainly there are toast and saltbush characters here, but
they're mere window dressings to the main show. Screwcap. 14.5% alc. **Rating** 90
To 2024 $24 CM

Nick O'Leary Wines   ★★★★★

149 Brooklands Road, Wallaroo, NSW 2618 **Region** Canberra District
T (02) 6230 2745 **www.**nickolearywines.com.au **Open** By appt
Winemaker Nick O'Leary **Est.** 2007 **Dozens** 9000 **Vyds** 5ha

At the ripe old age of 28, Nick O'Leary had been involved in the wine industry for over a
decade, working variously in retail, wholesale, viticulture and winemaking. He had laid the
foundation for Nick O'Leary Wines, purchasing shiraz from local vignerons (commencing in
2006); riesling following in '08. His wines have had extraordinarily consistent success in local
wine shows and competitions since the first vintages, which built in spectacular fashion when
the Shiraz was awarded the NSW Wine of the Year trophy in '14 and '15 – the first time any
winery had won the award in consecutive years. In late '16, Nick purchased a 60ha property
in Hall with a 19-year-old vineyard planted to shiraz, riesling and tempranillo, adding 2.8ha of
riesling and shiraz in late '17 (and Nick continues to buy fruit from many vineyards across the
Canberra District). A state-of-the-art 500t winery has been built on the property, and a cellar
door, restaurant and bar were expected to be open for business in late 2018.

ΨΨΨΨΨ **White Rocks Riesling 2017** From the Westering vineyard, one of the oldest in
the Canberra District (45yo), and bottled in brown glass. This gives you a frosty,
reserved welcome with its green citrus flavours, but opens up on repeated tastings,
notably the mouthfeel. It will develop more slowly than its siblings, and outlive
them. Screwcap. 12% alc. **Rating** 96 **To** 2037 $38 ❂

Tumbarumba Riesling 2017 The vinification of all Nick O'Leary rieslings are
the same: whole-bunch pressed on a slow champagne cycle for 3 hours, cool-
fermented with neutral yeast. These grapes were from the Cribbin vineyard. The
bouquet of this wine is full of white flowers, the palate gloriously intense and juicy,
very different from the Canberra rieslings. Screwcap. 12% alc. **Rating** 96 **To** 2035
$35 ❂

Bolaro Shiraz 2016 From a single vineyard in the Canberra District, 70% whole
berries, 30% whole bunches, open-fermented, matured for 10 months in French
oak, (25% new). Has a lot in common with its cheaper sibling, except that all
the bouquet and flavour inputs are scaled up. The fruit is in the blackberry and
blood plum quarter, and both intensity and length are significantly increased, the
impact and quality of the oak more evident, although still in impeccable balance.
Screwcap. 13.5% alc. **Rating** 96 **To** 2036 $55 ❂

Riesling 2017 From seven vineyards in the Canberra District. A more than useful
entry point for the Nick O'Leary '17 rieslings, its flowery and fragrant bouquet
dictating terms for the palate to follow. The varietal mix of pink grapefruit and
Meyer lemon fills the mouth. Screwcap. 12% alc. **Rating** 95 **To** 2032 $25 ❂

Shiraz 2016 From five vineyards in the Canberra District. 65% whole berries,
35% whole bunches, 7 days' cold soak, open-fermented, part with extended post-
ferment maceration, matured for 12 months in French oak (35% new). Good
colour, clarity and depth; an attractive medium-bodied shiraz that starts ticking
all the boxes from the first whiff and sip. The flavours are tilted towards plum and
dark cherry, the mouthfeel provided by the freshness of moderate alcohol and
supple tannins. Screwcap. 13.5% alc. **Rating** 95 **To** 2031 $30 ❂

Heywood Riesling 2017 From the home block. A tight and bright wine with
blossom aromas and a framework of minerally acidity that captures the citrussy
flavours of zest and pith. Screwcap. 12% alc. **Rating** 94 **To** 2032 $30 ❂

Seven Gates Tempranillo 2016 This is a seriously good tempranillo if you
want a long-lived red wine and don't mind that tannin might be included as part

of the ticket. It has depth and length, and all the things you find in Rioja when
tasting wines from barrel. Patience will be richly rewarded. Screwcap. 13.5% alc.
Rating 94 **To** 2036 $30 **❂**

🍷🍷🍷🍷♀ **Rose 2017 Rating** 90 **To** 2019 $21 **❂**

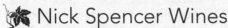 # Nick Spencer Wines

11 Loch St, Yarralumla, ACT 2600 (postal) **Region** Gundagai
T 0419 810 274 **www**.nickspencerwines.com.au **Open** Not
Winemaker Nick Spencer **Est.** 2017 **Dozens** 2500

No winemaker's career starts with receiving a degree in oenology at the University of
Adelaide. The desire to make wine comes well before the inception to the studies. Some string
the process out, others don't even undertake it. Nick Spencer didn't procrastinate. In the early
years he worked for Rosemount Estate, Coldstream Hills, Madew Wines and Tertini. He won
the biggest wine show trophy in 2009: the Jimmy Watson. In '11 he was a Len Evans Tutorial
scholar, and in '14 a finalist in the Young Gun of Wine awards, as well as in the *Gourmet
Traveller* Winemaker of the Year award. Over the years he's travelled extensively through
France, NZ and California, and in '14 made wine in Khakheti in Georgia. Having led the
team at Eden Road for seven years, he finally moved to establish his own business in '17. His
two main regions of interest are Tumbarumba and Gundagai – adjoining but very different.
The quality of his wines from Gundagai make him the captain of that ship.

🍷🍷🍷🍷🍷 **Gundagai Dry Red Blend 2017** This is an exceptional blend – 58% shiraz and
31% touriga, with splashes of tempranillo and cabernet sauvignon. Excellent dark
crimson; heady aromatics of dark fruit, Middle Eastern spices, warm earth and flint.
The just-medium-bodied palate is an exercise in restraint with fine tannins and
fresh acidity, and it leaves such an impression. Beautifully modulated and delicious.
Screwcap. 13.5% alc. **Rating** 95 **To** 2027 $33 JF **❂**
Gundagai Tempranillo 2017 The new home of tempranillo? Mid crimson-red;
dark cherries and pips, and really earthy and savoury with flecks of pepper and
exotic spices. Lighter-framed with superfine tannins, some texture though. A wine
that makes no apology for immediate drinking pleasure. A delightful surprise.
Screwcap. 13.5% alc. **Rating** 95 **To** 2023 $33 JF **❂**

🍷🍷🍷🍷♀ **Gundagai Cabernet Sauvignon 2017 Rating** 93 **To** 2025 $33 JF

Night Harvest

PO Box 921, Busselton, WA 6280 **Region** Margaret River
T (08) 9755 1521 **www**.nightharvest.com.au **Open** Not
Winemaker Bruce Dukes **Est.** 2005 **Dozens** 4000 **Vyds** 300ha

Andy and Mandy Ferreira arrived in Margaret River in 1986 as newly married young
migrants. They soon became involved in the wine industry, as well as in growing vegetables for
the local and export markets. Their vineyard-contracting business expanded quickly when the
region experienced its rapid growth in the late '90s, so their vegetable business was closed and
they put all their focus into wine. They were involved in the establishment of many Margaret
River vineyards, 16 of which they continue to manage today (Woodside Valley Estate and
Chapman Grove among them). As their fortunes grew, they purchased their own property and
produced their first wines in 2005. Exports to the US.

🍷🍷🍷🍷♀ **John George Margaret River Chardonnay 2015** Luscious style with cedar
wood, popcorn and cream characters running neck and neck with sweet, ripe
peach. It brings a keen freshness to the table through the back half of the wine, but
it's big and generous to that point. It's a bet each way, done pretty well. Screwcap.
12.3% alc. **Rating** 92 **To** 2023 $35 CM

Nillahcootie Estate

3630 Midland Highway, Lima South, Vic 3673 **Region** Upper Goulburn
T (03) 5768 2685 **www.**nillahcootieestate.com.au **Open** Not
Winemaker Various contract **Est.** 1988 **Dozens** 1200
In 2009 Jim and Maria Kakridas purchased Nillahcootie Estate, with big plans for their family's future. Jim and Maria's children, grandchildren, nephews and nieces all contribute, with daughter Christina running the business. The grapes are hand-picked, and the wines are made by well known local winemakers including Ros Ritchie, Sam Plunkett and David Ritchie. Exports to the US and China.

♀♀♀♀♀ **Upper Goulburn Semillon 2016** An artisanal semillon picked fully ripe and all the better for it. This is medium-bodied and highly complex, loaded with textural attributes from a billow of chewy, sudsy phenolics, a leesy tang and vanillan oak, offset by flavours of quince, lemon curd, lanolin and tangerine. This has plush fruit and real pulse. A delicious maverick in an era of skinny semillon. Screwcap. 14% alc. **Rating** 95 **To** 2022 $28 NG ✪

♀♀♀♀♀ **Upper Goulburn Shiraz 2012 Rating** 91 **To** 2022 $35 NG

Nillumbik Estate

195 Clintons Road, Smiths Gully, Vic 3760 **Region** Yarra Valley
T 0408 337 326 **www.**nillumbikestate.com.au **Open** Fri 12–5, w'ends 11–6
Winemaker John Tregambe **Est.** 2001 **Dozens** 1250 **Vyds** 1.6ha
John and Chanmali Tregambe established Nillumbik Estate, drawing on the winemaking experience of John's parents, Italian immigrants who arrived in Australia in the 1950s. The estate plantings of pinot noir are supplemented by cabernet sauvignon, chardonnay, shiraz and nebbiolo purchased from Sunbury, Heathcote and the King Valley.

♀♀♀♀♀ **Old Earth Heathcote Shiraz 2015** While there's all the power of Heathcote in the dark plum fruit flecked with bay leaves, pepper and blood orange, and in the full-bodied palate and ripe firm tannins, this also has a brightness. It's juicy. It has completely absorbed the French oak (50% new; wine aged 2 years). Well played. Screwcap. 14% alc. **Rating** 95 **To** 2028 $38 JF

♀♀♀♀♀ **Northern Hills Yarra Valley Chardonnay 2016 Rating** 90 **To** 2021 $36 JF

916

916 Steels Creek Road, Steels Creek, Vic 3775 (postal) **Region** Yarra Valley
T (03) 5965 2124 **www.**916.com.au **Open** Not
Winemaker Ben Haines **Est.** 2008 **Dozens** 260 **Vyds** 2ha
A year after John Brand and Erin-Marie O'Neill acquired their 8ha property, bushfires destroyed their home and all their possessions. But they rebuilt their lives and home, and reinvested in the vineyard. Viticulturist John Evans, formerly at Yering Station and now at Rochford Wines, became involved in 1996. They chose their viticulturist well, and they also have a highly gifted winemaker in the form of Ben Haines. Exports to the US, China and Singapore.

♀♀♀♀♀ **South Yarra Valley Pinot Noir 2016** Meaty and wild. This is pinot noir to make your head spin. Cranberry, musk, sour cherry, sweet herbs, tang and silk. If you get the chance you must try this. It's captivating. Diam. 13.6% alc. **Rating** 96 **To** 2025 $90 CM

♀♀♀♀♀ **West Yarra Valley Pinot Noir 2016 Rating** 93 **To** 2025 $90 CM

919 Wines

39 Hodges Road, Berri, SA 5343 **Region** Riverland
T 0408 855 272 **www.**919wines.com.au **Open** Wed–Sun & public hols 10–5
Winemaker Eric Semmler, Jenny Semmler **Est.** 2002 **Dozens** 2000 **Vyds** 17ha

Eric and Jenny Semmler have a special interest in fortified wines. Eric previously made fortified wines for Hardys and worked at Brown Brothers. Jenny has worked for Strathbogie Vineyards, Pennyweight Wines and St Huberts. They have planted micro-quantities of fortified wine varieties: palomino, durif, tempranillo, muscat à petits grains, tinta cao, shiraz, tokay and touriga nacional. They use minimal water application, deliberately reducing the crop levels, and practise organic and biodynamic techniques. In 2011 they purchased the 12.3ha property at Loxton that they now call Ella Semmler's vineyard.

🍷🍷🍷🍷 **Classic Muscat NV** Muscat is at its zenith when fortified and long-aged. This is in full plume. Rancio's whisper of varnish and walnuts sew savour to rosewater, ginger candy and grape spice. As gum-staining-sweet as this is, any treacle is curtailed by the bright acidity. Highly impressive. Screwcap. 18.5% alc. **Rating** 95 $42 NG

Reserve Sangiovese 2017 A swigging sangiovese made in a light, sensitive fashion: dutiful extraction, randy tannins and red berry fruits that pop across the mouth, laced with anise, clove and assuaging oak. This is good. Fresh. Dangerous, even. Screwcap. 14% alc. **Rating** 94 To 2020 $35 NG

Classic Topaque NV Burnt maple to caramel, coffee, caramelised ginger and a cornucopia of russet, toasted notes. This is very good. The spirit is of integrity, well nestled in. Viscous but not unctuous, with some volatile fibre toning the back end. The food suggestion on the back label is wondrous: bacon! Screwcap. 19% alc. **Rating** 94 $42 NG

🍷🍷🍷🍷🍸 **Reserve Petit Manseng 2017** **Rating** 93 To 2020 $26 NG ✪
Reserve Vermentino 2017 **Rating** 92 To 2021 $30 NG
Sparkling Durif NV **Rating** 91 $45 NG

Nintingbool ★★★★

56 Wongerer Lane, Smythes Creek, Vic 3351 (postal) **Region** Ballarat
T 0429 424 399 **www**.nintingbool.com.au **Open** Not
Winemaker Peter Bothe **Est.** 1998 **Dozens** 600 **Vyds** 2ha
Peter and Jill Bothe purchased the Nintingbool property in 1982 and built their home in '84, using bluestone dating back to the goldrush period. They established an extensive Australian native garden and home orchard, but in '98 diversified by planting pinot noir, plus a further planting the following year lifting the total to 2ha. Ballarat is one of the coolest mainland regions, and demands absolute attention to detail (and a warm growing season) for success.

🍷🍷🍷🍷 **Smythes Creek Pinot Noir 2015** Estate-grown and 390 dozen made. Creamy oak adds velvet to the texture but the fruit sizzles through, all red cherry and sweet-sour plum, spice notes studded throughout. It's of impeccable form and shape, its lines of tannin helping to usher it all along and keep things neat without interrupting the momentum. Maybe there's some warmth, but the fan of flavours doesn't really give it space to show. It's a lovely pinot, for now or later. Screwcap. 14% alc. **Rating** 95 To 2025 $35 CM ✪

🍷🍷🍷🍷🍸 **Smythes Creek Rose 2017** **Rating** 92 To 2019 $23 CM ✪
Smythes Creek Chardonnay 2017 **Rating** 91 To 2022 $27 CM

Noble Red ★★★☆

18 Brennan Avenue, Upper Beaconsfield, Vic 3808 (postal) **Region** Heathcote
T 0400 594 440 **www**.nobleredwines.com **Open** Not
Winemaker Roman Sobiesiak, Osicka Wines **Est.** 2002 **Dozens** 700 **Vyds** 6ha
Roman and Margaret Sobiesiak acquired their property in 2002. There was 0.25ha of shiraz planted in the 1970s, and a progressive planting program has seen this increase to 6ha, shiraz (3.6ha) accounting for the lion's share, the remainder equally split to tempranillo, mourvedre, merlot and cabernet sauvignon. They adopted a dry-grown approach, which meant slow development during the prolonged drought, but their commitment remains undimmed. Indeed, visiting many wine regions around the world and working within the industry locally has increased their determination. Exports to China.

ŸŸŸŸŸ **BST Heathcote Shiraz 2015** 'Blood, Sweat and Tears' shiraz. Hefty, blackberried fruit comes at you in sweet, ripe fashion, a raspberried note adding a smidgen of brightness. Cocoa and gum leaf play along too before warming alcohol takes over the finish. It's been pushed a little too far but it still tells a hearty tale. Screwcap. 15% alc. **Rating** 90 **To** 2028 $45 CM

Noble Road Wines ★★★★

33–37 Wright Street, Adelaide, SA 5000 **Region** Clare Valley
T (08) 8212 6959 **www**.nobleroad.com.au **Open** 7 days 11–4
Winemaker Scott Curtis **Est.** 2007 **Dozens** 150 000 **Vyds** 80ha
Owner and winemaker Scott Curtis has three other occupations: first, to manage/advise grapegrowers over three regions, dealing in quantites of 9000t per year; second, to continue work with grape varieties bred by the CSIRO; third, to make and sell small amounts of Clare Valley shiraz and cabernet sauvignon. In this, his own business, he makes varieties such as vermentino, montepulciano, fiano, lagrein and saperavi. Exports to Singapore, Hong Kong, Taiwan and China.

ŸŸŸŸŸ **Cellar Project Blewitt Springs Grenache 2015** A full-bodied grenache full of plums and a hint of raspberry, some jubes too, a dash of spice and dried herbs. The palate fleshes out with plump tannins and plenty of refreshing acidity. The cork was not in good shape; be wary of cellaring. 14.5% alc. **Rating** 92 **To** 2024 $45 JF
Cellar Project Montepulciano 2016 The cork was dodgy – creviced with seeped wine, so beware. A dense, richly flavoured wine awash with juicy dark fruits, Chinese spices, boot polish and licorice. Expansive tannins across the full-bodied palate. 14% alc. **Rating** 91 **To** 2022 $28 JF
Cellar Project Vermentino 2017 Juicy and clean with lemon flavours, from squeezed juice and pith to zest. Refreshing saline note with a touch of basil and a savouriness. Simple yet appealing. Screwcap. 12.5% alc. **Rating** 90 **To** 2018 $25 JF
Cellar Project PF Shiraz 2017 Not sure where the fruit comes from; the label just says a blend of grapes from SA (PF stands for preservative free). Drink now as it offers bright purple fruit laced with spice, and supple, slightly grippy tannins and zesty acidity. Prickly across the palate and looking vibrant. Screwcap. 14% alc. **Rating** 90 **To** 2018 $25 JF

Norfolk Rise Vineyard ★★★★

Limestone Coast Road, Mount Benson, SA 5265 **Region** Mount Benson
T (08) 8768 5080 **www**.norfolkrise.com.au **Open** Not
Winemaker Daniel Berrigan **Est.** 2000 **Dozens** 20 000 **Vyds** 130ha
Norfolk Rise Vineyard is by far the largest and most important development in the Mount Benson region. It is owned by privately held Belgian company G and C Kreglinger, which was established in 1797. In early 2002 Kreglinger acquired Pipers Brook Vineyard, and has since maintained the separate brands of Pipers Brook and Norfolk Rise. There are 46 blocks of sauvignon blanc, pinot gris, pinot noir, shiraz, merlot and cabernet sauvignon, allowing a range of options in making the six single-variety wines in the portfolio. The business has moved from the export of bulk wine to bottled wine, which gives significantly better returns to the winery. Exports to Europe and Asia.

ŸŸŸŸŸ **Mount Benson Shiraz 2017** Machine-harvested, crushed, destemmed, fermented, pressed to stainless steel and 10% French oak barriques for 10 months. Highly perfumed, inexpensive and totally enjoyable, punching well above its weight. All florals, black pepper and spice, with juicy red fruits and a savoury overlay. It's medium-bodied, buoyant with supple tannins, ultra-refreshing, and frighteningly easy to drink. Screwcap. 14.5% alc. **Rating** 95 **To** 2022 $18 JF ✪

ŸŸŸŸŸ **Reserve Mount Benson Shiraz 2015 Rating** 93 **To** 2024 $25 JF ✪

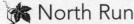 North Run

Harvest Food & Wine, 55 View Street, Bendigo, Vic 3550 **Region** Bendigo
T 0434 365 504 **www**.northrunwine.com.au **Open** Tues–Sat 8–4
Winemaker Lincoln Riley **Est.** 2014 **Dozens** 650 **Vyds** 1ha
This is the venture of Lincoln Riley and Marsha Busse. Lincoln has had a very active and successful career as a sommelier and winemaker, starting in 2008 in the winemaking sphere with Foster e Rocco. This was the same year that he received the Judy Hirst Award – Sommelier of the Year, one of several major awards under his belt. He finished as a sommelier in '14, moving back to central Victoria and, with Marsha, purchasing their Harcourt property. They have planted it to equal quantities of shiraz and nebbiolo with close spacing, and currently run their cellar door from their eatery Harvest Food & Wine in Bendigo, which offers a seasonal menu. They are renovating an old apple cool-store at the vineyard where they will also offer regional food and wine.

♀♀♀♀♀ **Shiraz 2016** The vineyard source (Lome) is the same as that of its sibling, and you can see the same DNA, but earlier picking, far less whole bunches (30%), and 20% new French oak have all contributed to a wine that is supple, elegant and refreshing, with a tight set of juicy and savoury counterparts. Screwcap. 13.5% alc. **Rating** 95 **To** 2036 $35 **○**

♀♀♀♀♀ **Harvest Shiraz 2016 Rating** 91 **To** 2031 $29

Norton Estate

758 Plush Hannans Road, Lower Norton, Vic 3401 **Region** Western Victoria
T (03) 5384 8235 **www**.nortonestate.com.au **Open** Fri–Sun & public hols 11–4
Winemaker Best's Wines **Est.** 1997 **Dozens** 1200 **Vyds** 4.66ha
In 1996 the Spence family purchased a rundown farm at Lower Norton and, rather than looking to the traditional wool, meat and wheat markets, trusted their instincts and planted vines on the elevated, frost-free, buckshot rises. The surprising vigour of the initial planting of shiraz prompted further plantings of shiraz, cabernet sauvignon and sauvignon blanc, plus a small planting of the American variety 'Norton'. The vineyard is halfway between the Grampians and Mt Arapiles, 6km northwest of the Grampians wine region, having to be content with the Western Victoria zone, even though the wines show Grampians regional character and style.

♀♀♀♀♀ **Wendy's Block Shiraz 2016** While all three Norton shiraz siblings have deep colour, this one has the edge. It is immediately and strikingly full-bodied, both fruit and oak dialled up to maximum, yet retaining shape, proportion and balance. The intensity of this wine is amazing: it's more Grampians-esque than many wines that are able to claim the Grampians as their GI. Screwcap. 14.3% alc. **Rating** 97 **To** 2041 $65 **○**

♀♀♀♀♀ **Arapiles Run Shiraz 2016** A very complex, rich and compelling medium to full-bodied shiraz. Multiple layers of succulent black fruits, a pantry of spices and dry peppers, evident French oak. Great length and balance. Screwcap. 14% alc. **Rating** 96 **To** 2041 $38 **○**
Rockface Shiraz 2016 Deep colour, and a lively, complex display of blackberry/cherry fruits studded with black pepper, spice and licorice, a strong style statement of its Grampians association. While its power is obvious, the finish has a most attractive, supple lick of fruit one minute, savoury the next. Screwcap. 14% alc. **Rating** 95 **To** 2036 $25 **○**
Cabernet Sauvignon 2016 Deep colour runs in its blood, so it seems. The palate is medium to full-bodied, but elegant and very well balanced. It is the excellent varietal blackcurrant, not oak or artifice, that drives yet another top wine from Norton Estate. Screwcap. 13.5% alc. **Rating** 94 **To** 2036 $25 **○**

Nova Vita Wines

11 Woodlands Road, Kenton Valley, SA 5235 **Region** Adelaide Hills
T (08) 8356 0454 **www**.novavitawines.com.au **Open** Not
Winemaker Mark Kozned **Est.** 2005 **Dozens** 20 000 **Vyds** 49ha
Mark and Jo Kozned's 30ha Woodlands Ridge vineyard is planted to chardonnay, sauvignon blanc, pinot gris and shiraz. They have subsequently established the Tunnel Hill vineyard, with 19ha planted to pinot noir, shiraz, cabernet sauvignon, sauvignon blanc, semillon, verdelho, merlot and sangiovese. The name Nova Vita reflects the beginning of the Kozneds' new life, the firebird on the label coming from their Russian ancestry. It is a Russian myth that only a happy or lucky person may see the bird or hear its song. The Kozneds have joined forces with Peter Leske to form Revenir, a contract winemaking business that has purchased the former Nepenthe winery. Exports to the US, Thailand, Singapore and China.

🍷🍷🍷🍷🍷 **Reserve Adelaide Hills Chardonnay 2015** Nova Vita shows a hand of considerable expertise across all of its chardonnay tiers. This is the zenith. Toasted hazelnut, nougatine, truffle and oatmeal set the tone. Richly flavoured and expansive of stone fruit, the oak is seamless, the mineral pungency on the good side of flint, the finish scintillating. Screwcap. 13.5% alc. **Rating** 96 **To** 2027 $100 NG
Firebird Adelaide Hills Chardonnay 2015 This is a richly flavoured and highly detailed chardonnay. Mid-weighted and flecked with a crystalline mineral crunch, the emphasis is on white peach, apricot, toasted nuts and nectarine. The colour is a luminescent yellow tinged with green – always a good sign. Strident across the mouth, long of flavour and emphatic of quality. Screwcap. 13.5% alc. **Rating** 95 **To** 2024 $30 NG ⬤

🍷🍷🍷🍷🍷 **Firebird Chardonnay 2016 Rating** 93 **To** 2025 $30 NG
Reserve Cabernet Sauvignon 2013 Rating 93 **To** 2028 $100 NG
Woodlands Ridge Vineyard Shiraz 2016 Rating 92 **To** 2021 $17 NG ⬤
Firebird Shiraz 2015 Rating 92 **To** 2026 $35 NG
Firebird Sauvignon Blanc 2016 Rating 91 **To** 2021 $20 NG ⬤
Firebird Sangiovese Rose 2016 Rating 91 **To** 2020 $20 NG ⬤
Firebird Pinot Noir 2014 Rating 91 **To** 2024 $35 NG
Firebird Cabernet Sauvignon 2014 Rating 91 **To** 2023 $35 NG
Firebird Gruner Veltliner 2016 Rating 90 **To** 2021 $25 NG

Nugan Estate ★★★★

Kidman Way, Wilbriggie, NSW 2680 **Region** Riverina
T (02) 9362 9993 **www**.nuganestate.com.au **Open** Mon–Fri 9–5
Winemaker Daren Owers **Est.** 1999 **Dozens** 500 000 **Vyds** 606ha
Nugan Estate arrived on the scene like a whirlwind. It is an offshoot of the Nugan Group headed by Michelle Nugan (until her retirement in February 2013), inter alia the recipient of an Export Hero Award in '00. In the mid-1990s the company began developing vineyards, and it is now a veritable giant, with five: Cookoothama (335ha), Talinga Park (115ha) and Manuka Grove (46ha) in the Riverina, Frasca's Lane (100ha) in the King Valley, and McLaren Parish (10ha) in McLaren Vale. Nugan Estate is now in the energetic hands of Matthew and Tiffany Nugan, Michelle's children. Exports to the UK, the US and other major markets.

🍷🍷🍷🍷🍷 **Alcira Vineyard Coonawarra Cabernet Sauvignon 2016** An intriguing combination of deli meat and spearmint aromas introduce a wine that dares, in an accessible way, to be different. It's all backed by a substantial serve of cassis fruit, and includes both a handy tether of tannin and sound length. Now or later, this will rise to the occasion. Screwcap. 14.5% alc. **Rating** 94 **To** 2028 $23 CM ⬤

🍷🍷🍷🍷🍷 **Cookoothama Limited Release Darlington Point Botrytis Semillon 2014 Rating** 93 **To** 2022 $23 CM ⬤
Frasca's Lane Vineyard King Valley Sauvignon Blanc 2017 Rating 91 **To** 2020 $20 CM ⬤

Alfredo Dried Grape Shiraz 2015 Rating 91 To 2025 $23 CM ✪
Manuka Grove Vineyard Riverina Durif 2012 Rating 91 To 2022 $23 ✪
Alfredo Frasca's Lane Vineyard King Valley Sangiovese 2015 Rating 90
To 2023 $23 CM

🍇 Nuova Scuola Wines   ★★★

681 Barambah Road, Moffatdale, Qld 4605 **Region** South Burnett
T 0408 850 595 **www.**nuovascuola.com.au **Open** Not
Winemaker Sarah Boyce, Stefano Radici **Est.** 2017 **Dozens** 250
Winemakers Sarah Boyce and Stefano Radici met each other in NZ in 2009, fell in love, and
haven't looked back since. They have been working side by side in many different wineries
in many parts of the world, including Italy, France, Canada, the US, NZ, Mexico and – of
course – Australia. Working in Queensland's South Burnett has its limitations, but they believe
the climate is ideal for Iberian and Italian varieties such as barbera, nebbiolo, tempranillo,
sangiovese and viognier. The demand for these varieties is increasing rapidly, and while
currently purchasing grapes, they are planning to establish their own vineyard by the end
of '18. Another way forward is to produce these varieties via a highly motivated local winery
and vineyard operator.

O'Leary Walker Wines   ★★★★★

Horrocks Highway, Leasingham, SA 5452 **Region** Clare Valley
T (08) 8843 0022 **www.**olearywalkerwines.com **Open** Mon–Sat 10–4, Sun 11–4
Winemaker David O'Leary, Nick Walker, Keeda Zilm **Est.** 2001 **Dozens** 16 000
Vyds 35ha
David O'Leary and Nick Walker together had more than 30 years' winemaking experience
working for some of the biggest Australian names when they took the plunge in 2001 and
backed themselves to establish their own winery and brand. Initially the principal focus was
on the Clare Valley, with 10ha of mainly riesling, shiraz and cabernet sauvignon; thereafter
attention swung to the Adelaide Hills, where they now have 25ha of chardonnay, cabernet
sauvignon, pinot noir, shiraz, sauvignon blanc and merlot. The vineyards were certified organic
in '13. Exports to the UK, Ireland, Canada, the United Arab Emirates, Asia and Japan.

🍷🍷🍷🍷🍷 **Polish Hill River Riesling 2017** Combines finesse with power, varietal fruit with
elegance – this is Polish Hill River calling the tune with that edge of clarity that
takes it out of the ruck. Screwcap. 12.5% alc. **Rating** 95 To 2029 $25 ✪
Clare Valley Gruner Veltliner 2017 So intense, fruit-filled and refreshing that
it seems flashy. This races through the mouth and bursts out through the finish,
imparting flavour at every step. Super white wine. Sizzling. Screwcap. 12.5% alc.
Rating 95 To 2023 $20 CM ✪
Watervale Riesling 2017 The first reaction to the wine is 'where's the catch?'
It has drive and intensity to its clearly defined varietal fruit, citrus leading the
obedient acidity with a firm hand. Screwcap. 12% alc. **Rating** 94 To 2027 $19 ✪
Clare Valley Shiraz 2016 Spot on for flavour, texture and length. If you're
looking for a full-bodied red then here is your target. It basically delivers plum, bay
leaf and coffee-cream flavours but all in such balanced measure and all so velvety
smooth. Acidity here could do with a little fine tuning but it won't stop this wine
from pleasing a lot of folks. Screwcap. 14.5% alc. **Rating** 94 To 2032 $25 CM ✪

🍷🍷🍷🍷🍷 **The Lucky Punter Adelaide Hills Sauvignon Blanc 2017** Rating 93
To 2019 $20 CM ✪
Poppy Rouge Chardonnay 2017 Rating 93 To 2022 $22 CM ✪
Cabernet Sauvignon 2015 Rating 93 To 2028 $25 CM ✪
Hurtle Adelaide Hills Pinot Noir Chardonnay 2013 Rating 92 $28 CM
Poppy Rouge 2017 Rating 91 To 2019 $20 CM ✪
Blue Cutting Road Cabernet Merlot 2014 Rating 91 To 2025 $20 CM ✪
Malbec 2014 Rating 91 To 2024 $25 CM

Oakdene ★★★★★

255 Grubb Road, Wallington, Vic 3221 **Region** Geelong
T (03) 5256 3886 **www**.oakdene.com.au **Open** 7 days 10–4
Winemaker Robin Brockett, Marcus Holt **Est.** 2001 **Dozens** 8000 **Vyds** 32ha

Bernard and Elizabeth Hooley purchased Oakdene in 2001. Bernard focused on planting the vineyard (shiraz, pinot gris, sauvignon blanc, pinot noir, chardonnay, merlot, cabernet franc and cabernet sauvignon) while Elizabeth worked to restore the 1920s homestead. Much of the wine is sold through the award-winning Oakdene Restaurant and cellar door. The quality is exemplary, as is the consistency; Robin Brockett's skills are on full display. A new vineyard 11km from Oakdene and planted in '17 (to shiraz, pinot noir, pinot gris, chardonnay, sauvignon blanc, merlot, riesling, cabernet franc and cabernet sauvignon) has increased the total vineyards to 32ha.

♟♟♟♟♟ **Bernard's Single Vineyard Bellarine Peninsula Cabernets 2016**
63% cabernet franc, 23% cabernet sauvignon, 14% merlot. A co-fermented blend of these three varieties is unusual, with their different ripening patterns, but is made to look easy here. It is full of juicy fruit, the new clones of merlot Q45-14 and 8R making a disproportionate contribution to the intense flavours. The tannin structure is immaculate, the oak contribution likewise. Something special, with the cabernet franc happily accepting the support of the other varieties. Screwcap. 13.4% alc. **Rating** 96 **To** 2036 $30 ✪

Bellarine Peninsula Sauvignon Blanc 2017 No-frills winemaking throws all the focus onto the fragrant bouquet and highly expressive palate. Has thrived in the cool vintage, with tropical/lemongrass notes – unusual bedfellows – clearly well satisfied by their union. Screwcap. 12.6% alc. **Rating** 95 **To** 2021 $23 ✪

Jessica Single Vineyard Bellarine Peninsula Sauvignon 2017 The use of 'sauvignon' (dropping 'blanc') is European (particularly French, more particularly Loire Valley). Barrel fermentation and maturation reflect Robin Brockett's experience on the Bellarine Peninsula, just as the wine reflects the quality of the vineyard's terroir. Screwcap. 12.8% alc. **Rating** 95 **To** 2025 $28 ✪

Liz's Single Vineyard Bellarine Peninsula Chardonnay 2016 Green-gold, it stops well short of going over the top with its compendium of stone-fruit flavours of all kinds, balanced and lengthened by firm acidity. Screwcap. 13.4% alc. **Rating** 95 **To** 2026 $30 ✪

Ly Ly Single Vineyard Bellarine Peninsula Pinot Gris 2017 Entirely fermented and matured (for 18 months) in French barriques (15% new). Pinot gris doesn't get much more complex or serious than this. It's a wine-drinker's wine, not for amateurs. Screwcap. 13.5% alc. **Rating** 95 **To** 2019 $28 ✪

Peta's Single Vineyard Bellarine Peninsula Pinot Noir 2016 Matured for 12 months in new and used French barriques. The pure cherry/plum bouquet leads into the same fruits on the palate with added spicy savoury notes. The overall fruit/oak/tannin balance can't be faulted. Screwcap. 13.6% alc. **Rating** 95 **To** 2029 $43

William Single Vineyard Bellarine Peninsula Shiraz 2016 This is a cool-climate shiraz that manages to be full-bodied, rich and complex. The black and red fruits are upholstered with licorice, spice and pepper, not allowing you to drop your eyes for a moment. Ripe tannins and quality French oak complete a grand picture. Screwcap. 14.3% alc. **Rating** 95 **To** 2036 $43

Bellarine Peninsula Chardonnay 2016 An unexpectedly complex bouquet, doubtless reflecting fermentation in barrel on solids. The fruit flavours span citrus to stone fruit, meeting seamlessly in the middle, and giving rise to a juicy character that has as much to do with mouthfeel as flavour. Screwcap. 13.4% alc. **Rating** 94 **To** 2025 $24 ✪

Bellarine Peninsula Pinot Grigio 2017 The yield isn't shown, but must have surely been low to produce such a concentrated wine. It has unexpected texture, and a precocious display of pear-accented flavours. Screwcap. 13.2% alc. **Rating** 94 **To** 2021 $23 ✪

ŸŸŸŸŸ Bellarine Peninsula Pinot Noir 2016 Rating 93 To 2026 $24 ✪
Matilda Macedon Ranges Blanc de Noirs 2014 Rating 93 $35
Bellarine Peninsula Rose 2017 Rating 91 To 2019 $28
Yvette Bellarine Peninsula Pinot Noir Chardonnay 2015 Rating 91 $35
Bellarine Peninsula Shiraz 2016 Rating 90 To 2026 $24

Oakover Wines   ★★★

14 Yukich Close, Middle Swan, WA 6056 **Region** Swan Valley
T (08) 9374 8000 **www**.oakoverwines.com.au **Open** 7 days 11–4
Winemaker Ragan Wood **Est.** 1990 **Dozens** 50 000 **Vyds** 100ha
Oakover Wines is a family-operated winery located in the Swan Valley. Formerly part of
Houghton, in 1990 it came into the Yukich family's ownership as Oakover Estate. Prominent
Perth funds manager Graeme Yukich and his family have been involved in the region since
Nicholas Yukich purchased his first block of land in 1929. Today Oakover Wines is the third
largest winery in the Swan Valley. The White Label brand is currently sold in over 500
independent liquor outlets in WA and Victoria, with expansion into NSW and Queensland
planned. Exports to China, Indonesia, Malaysia and Singapore.

ŸŸŸŸ **White Label Margaret River Sauvignon Blanc Semillon 2017** Even at
this price, the quality of the wine is enough to cause eastern states' producers to
shiver. There's possibly some unfermented sugar, but the depth and complexity of
the fruits ranging from grassy/herbal to passionfruit is, to say the least, impressive.
Screwcap. 12.7% alc. **Rating** 89 To 2020 $13 ✪

Oakridge Wines   ★★★★★

864 Maroondah Highway, Coldstream, Vic 3770 **Region** Yarra Valley
T (03) 9738 9900 **www**.oakridgewines.com.au **Open** 7 days 10–5
Winemaker David Bicknell **Est.** 1978 **Dozens** 30 000 **Vyds** 32ha
David Bicknell has proved his worth time and again as an extremely talented winemaker.
At the top of the Oakridge brand tier is 864, all Yarra Valley vineyard selections and only
released in the best years (chardonnay, pinot noir, shiraz, cabernet sauvignon, riesling); next is
the Local Vineyard Series (chardonnay, pinot noir and sauvignon blanc come from the cooler
Upper Yarra Valley; shiraz, cabernet sauvignon and viognier from the Lower Yarra); and the
Over the Shoulder range, drawn from all of the sources available (sauvignon blanc, pinot
grigio, pinot noir, shiraz viognier, cabernet sauvignon). The estate vineyards are Oakridge
vineyard (10ha), Hazeldene vineyard (10ha) and Henk vineyard (12ha). Exports to the US,
Canada, the UK, Sweden, the Netherlands, Norway, Fiji, Papua New Guinea, Singapore, Hong
Kong and China.

ŸŸŸŸŸ **Local Vineyard Series Willowlake Vineyard Yarra Valley Chardonnay
2016** Willow Lake vineyard is the oldest in the Upper Yarra, and one of the oldest
in the entire valley. This wine has a vibrancy, an edge, giving it a mouthfeel and set
of flavours firmly anchored on grapefruit. Great success for the vintage. Screwcap.
13.2% alc. **Rating** 97 To 2026 $38 ✪

ŸŸŸŸŸ **Local Vineyard Series Hazeldene Vineyard Yarra Valley Chardonnay
2016** From the Upper Yarra. This is a chardonnay of exceptional power, drive
and intensity, the flavours in a tightly furled umbrella that opens on the finish
and particularly on the aftertaste. Great outcome in a challenging year. Screwcap.
13.6% alc. **Rating** 96 To 2028 $38 ✪
**864 Single Block Release Drive Block Funder & Diamond Vineyard
Yarra Valley Chardonnay 2016** Very interesting wine. Both its 6-month
sojourn in tank after 10 months in barrel, and its alcohol of 14.2%, should have
given a pronounced shift in mouthfeel versus other Oakridge chardonnays.
Counterintuitively, the finesse ex the vineyard at the outset and the winemaking
leave it until the last gasp and aftertaste to magically produce it. Screwcap.
Rating 96 To 2031 $78

Meunier 2017 It's not deep or terribly intense, but as lighter bodied reds go, this offers sensational drinking. Cranberry, strawberry and sweet red cherry flavours flow into woody anise, aromatic herbs and peppercorns. But it's not the flavours themselves, it's the ultrafine tannin, the liveliness, the downright succulence. Irresistible is the word. Screwcap. 13.7% alc. **Rating** 96 **To** 2024 $28 CM ✪

Local Vineyard Series Henk's Vineyard Yarra Valley Pinot Noir 2016 From a north-facing slope of red volcanic soil in Woori Yallock. 100% whole-berry open fermentation for 3 weeks, matured for 10 months in French oak. It all comes together very well, its red fruits peppered by studs of fruit spice and bramble. Good length and balance. Screwcap. 14% alc. **Rating** 96 **To** 2031 $38 ✪

Local Vineyard Series Hazeldene Vineyard Yarra Valley Pinot Noir 2016 From the Upper Yarra's red volcanic soils. The scented bouquet is filled with red fruits and flowers, the palate taking the wine onto another level with its elaborate tapestry of red and blue fruits offset by a spicy/savoury cross-stitch. Great outcome for '16. Screwcap. 14.5% alc. **Rating** 96 **To** 2031 $38 ✪

864 Single Block Release Close Planted Block Oakridge Vineyard Yarra Valley Syrah 2016 Deeply coloured; has tremendous tenacity and length, and equally juicy dark fruits. Tannin and oak whisper in the background, but this is about fruit purity and harmony in its beating heart. Screwcap. 14.5% alc. **Rating** 96 **To** 2036 $78

864 Single Block Release Winery Block Oakridge Vineyard Yarra Valley Cabernet Sauvignon 2015 Yarra Valley cabernet is typically elegant, this no exception. But this is cabernet in regal mode, hosting firm tannins along with blackcurrant and dried herb/bay leaf nuances on the long finish. Screwcap. 14% alc. **Rating** 96 **To** 2040 $78

Local Vineyard Series Barkala Ridge Vineyard Yarra Valley Chardonnay 2016 There is a very deliberate touch of funky complexity to the bouquet and the finish of the palate, stemming from the barrel fermentation on 100% solids juice. It's accepted, indeed welcomed, by most judges and consumers. Screwcap. 13.8% alc. **Rating** 95 **To** 2023 $38

Over the Shoulder Yarra Valley Rose 2017 The innovative blend of 75% pinot noir, 16% pinot meunier and 9% pinot gris has proved to be a brilliant success thanks to attention to detail in the vinification. Wild strawberry flavours are on intimate terms with the spicy, tangy acidity. Rose doesn't come better than this. Screwcap. 13.2% alc. **Rating** 95 **To** 2018 $19 ✪

Over the Shoulder Yarra Valley Pinot Noir 2017 Bright crimson-purple; a sign of great things to come from the '17 vintage in the Yarra Valley. A beautiful pinot for drinking now or later. Long, pure cherry-plum fruit; fine tannins. Great value. Screwcap. 13.3% alc. **Rating** 95 **To** 2029 $23 ✪

864 Single Block Release Block 1 Hazeldene Vineyard Yarra Valley Pinot Noir 2016 The spicy, savoury bouquet and palate have resulted from perfectly balanced fruit, oak and tannin support. There is no chest-beating here, simply encouraging the Upper Yarra to express itself. Screwcap. 14% alc. **Rating** 95 **To** 2024 $78

Local Vineyard Series Oakridge Vineyard Yarra Valley Cabernet Sauvignon 2015 The vintage was a very good one, and David Bicknell's approach was minimal interference and maximum patience, resulting in this perfect expression of Yarra Valley cabernet, cassis/blackcurrant fruit with a hint of dried bay leaf and fine tannins. Screwcap. 14.5% alc. **Rating** 95 **To** 2035 $38

Skelete Riesling 2017 You can't do much more with Yarra Valley Riesling; here its back-palate and finish have a seductive roll of Rose's lime juice and Meyer lemon. Screwcap. 10.4% alc. **Rating** 94 **To** 2023 $25 ✪

Local Vineyard Series Oakridge Vineyard Yarra Valley Shiraz 2016 A wine of unbridled richness and power showing how much flavour can be extracted for those seeking wines for long-term cellaring. While full-bodied, the wine has balance and ticks the boxes. Screwcap. 14.5% alc. **Rating** 94 **To** 2040 $38

864 Single Block Release Winery Block Oakridge Vineyard Yarra Valley Cabernet Sauvignon 2016 The 864 releases are always small-volume wines, but this year the yields (and the release) were miniscule. Vinification options were damned if you do, damned if you don't when it came to extraction. I'm far from convinced about the choice adopted by David Bicknell, but his long track record of success can't be ignored. Screwcap. 14.2% alc. **Rating** 94 **To** 2046 $78

🍷🍷🍷🍷🍷 **Local Vineyard Series Willowlake Vineyard Yarra Valley Sauvignon 2016** Rating 93 To 2023 $28
Over the Shoulder Chardonnay 2016 Rating 93 To 2022 $19 **○**
Meunier 2017 Rating 91 To 2025 $28

🍇 Oates Ends ★★★★☆

22 Carpenter Road, Wilyabrup, WA 6280 **Region** Margaret River
T 0401 303 144 **www.**oatesends.com.au **Open** By appt
Winemaker Cath Oates **Est.** 1998 **Dozens** 1000 **Vyds** 10ha
Cath Oates grew up in Margaret River with her school teacher and farmer parents Stu and Sue Oates, spending the endless summers 'shearing sheep, picking up lots of sticks and rocks, and trying to slip away to hitch a ride to the beach to avoid the tedium of work'. As vineyards started to appear, so did picking grapes on holidays and weekends, leading to a career in wine (originally studying viticulture but moving to winemaking after her first vintage in 1998). Then followed winemaking in Italy, NZ, the US and Margaret River, heading the team at Plantagenet. Brother Russ followed the viticultural path and was a key player in planting the Wilagri vineyard in '99. The name Oates Ends comes from Cath hand-picking the bunches left by the harvester at the ends of the rows.

🍷🍷🍷🍷🍷 **Margaret River Cabernet Sauvignon 2014** The colour isn't deep, but the hue is excellent; there's a lot to please in this wine, notably its freshness and varietal expression. The tannins are fine and persistent, as they should be. A stylish medium-bodied cabernet that takes you by grace, not storm. Screwcap. 13.5% alc. **Rating** 95 **To** 2029 $45
Margaret River Semillon Sauvignon Blanc 2016 Sophisticated packaging, and beneath it a very experienced winemaker. The wine has been barrel-fermented to add texture to the intense citrus, green pea and lemongrass flavours. Length and balance tick the boxes. Screwcap. 12.5% alc. **Rating** 94 **To** 2022 $24 **○**

🍷🍷🍷🍷 **Margaret River Tempranillo 2015** Rating 89 To 2023 $28

Occam's Razor | Lo Stesso ★★★★

c/- Jasper Hill, Drummonds Lane, Heathcote, Vic 3523 **Region** Heathcote
T (03) 5433 2528 **www.**jasperhill.com.au **Open** By appt
Winemaker Emily McNally **Est.** 2001 **Dozens** 300 **Vyds** 2.5ha
Emily McNally (née Laughton) decided to follow in her parents' footsteps after first seeing the world and having a range of casual jobs. Growing up at Jasper Hill, winemaking was far from strange, but she decided to find her own way with it, buying the grapes from a small vineyard owned by Jasper Hill employee Andrew Conforti and his wife Melissa. She then made the wine 'with guidance and inspiration from my father'. The name comes from William of Ockham (1285–1349), also spelt Occam, a theologian and philosopher responsible for many sayings, including that appearing on the back label of the wine: 'what can be done with fewer is done in vain with more'. Lo Stesso is made by Emily and friend Georgia Roberts, who purchase 2.5t of fiano from a vineyard in Heathcote, making the wine at Jasper Hill. Exports to the UK, the US, Canada and Singapore.

🍷🍷🍷🍷🍷 **Lo Stesso Heathcote Fiano 2017** Mid-straw and bright; closed and reductive at first, opening up to reveal lemon myrtle, honeysuckle, creamed honey, nougat, almond, a touch of marzipan and smoke. Well handled phenolics add to the overall texture with a long thread of acidity giving it plenty of drive. It's luscious but not heavy. Screwcap. 13% alc. **Rating** 93 **To** 2022 $30 JF
Occam's Razor Heathcote Shiraz 2016 Dark black–red hue, with fully ripe fruit – a ball of boysenberry, plum and currants uploaded onto the full-bodied

palate. In the mix is soy sauce and licorice; it's tarry, smells of scorched earth and sumac, with savoury, fleshy tannins. Among the richness, there's give; a suppleness. The alcohol heat detracts, but the wine stops just short of being too ripe and big. Cork. 15.5% alc. **Rating** 92 **To** 2024 $46 JF

Ocean Eight Vineyard & Winery   ★★★★★

271 Tucks Road, Shoreham, Vic 3916 **Region** Mornington Peninsula
T (03) 5989 6471 **www**.oceaneight.com **Open** Thurs–Sat 11–5, Sun 11–3
Winemaker Michael Aylward **Est.** 2004 **Dozens** 6000 **Vyds** 16ha
Chris, Gail and Michael Aylward were involved in the establishment of the Kooyong vineyard and winery, and after selling it in 2003, retained a 6ha pinot gris vineyard at Shoreham. After careful investigation they purchased another property, where they have now planted 7ha of pinot noir and 3ha of chardonnay. A small winery has been set up, and the focus is on estate-grown grapes. Exports to the UK, the US, Germany and Japan.

🍷🍷🍷🍷🍷 **Grande Mornington Peninsula Chardonnay 2014** Straw-gold in colour. Matchstick aromatics introduce an intense palate, all richness and swagger. It's chardonnay in full flight. We see sweet spice, yellow stone fruit, honey and citrus. It's bold but it soars through the finish. Killer quality. Screwcap. 13.2% alc. **Rating** 96 **To** 2022 $70 CM ✪
Aylward Reserve Mornington Peninsula Pinot Noir 2013 It's an autumnal pinot noir with a power of fruit; a classic combination. Macerated cherry and raspberry, fennel, dry spice, fallen leaves. It feels intense, taut and long at once. The quality is right up there. Screwcap. 13.2% alc. **Rating** 96 **To** 2026 $80 CM
Verve Mornington Peninsula Chardonnay 2015 From a single vineyard at the northern end of the peninsula, picked 2 weeks earlier than anywhere else in the region. Wild yeast ferment. Straw-coloured but fresh and lively. It sizzles through the palate, tasting of citrus, white peach, wet stones and honeysuckle, oak essentially nowhere to be seen, at least in flavour terms. There's a subtle, sweet, lactose character to the aftertaste; an attractive parting gesture. Screwcap. 12.5% alc. **Rating** 94 **To** 2023 CM

🍷🍷🍷🍷🍷 **Mornington Peninsula Pinot Gris 2017 Rating** 92 **To** 2020 $36 CM
Mornington Peninsula Pinot Noir 2015 Rating 92 **To** 2024 $55 CM

Ochota Barrels   ★★★★★

Merchants Road, Basket Range, SA 5138 **Region** Adelaide Hills
T 0400 798 818 **www**.ochotabarrels.com **Open** Not
Winemaker Taras Ochota **Est.** 2008 **Dozens** 900 **Vyds** 0.5ha
Taras Ochota has had an incredibly varied career as a winemaker since completing his oenology degree at the University of Adelaide. He's made wine for top Australian producers and had a Flying Winemaker role in many parts of the world, most recently as consultant winemaker for one of Sweden's largest wine-importing companies, Oenoforos, working on Italian wines from Puglia and Sicily. Wife Amber has accompanied him to many places, working in a multiplicity of technical and marketing roles. Exports to the UK, the US, Canada, Denmark, Norway and Japan.

🍷🍷🍷🍷🍷 **Kids of the Black Hole Riesling 2017** Transcendental. A nose of clarity, purity and an ineffable subtlety. No lime in these parts. Think rock, florals, mineral, slate. Ironstone, too (the label says so). Immaculate farming and sensitive winemaking meld effortlessly. This thirst-quencher boasts the dangerous drinkability of Spanish Txakoli. It's long, too, across a laser beam of energy. Cork. 12.2% alc. **Rating** 97 **To** 2023 $40 NG ✪

🍷🍷🍷🍷🍷 **The Slint Vineyard Chardonnay 2017** Nougatine and cashew. Toasted almond. This billows across the mouth, cushioning the cheeks with a phenolic pillow. Mid-weighted and juicy with stone fruit and minerals, generosity threaded through a needle of tension. Cork. 12.2% alc. **Rating** 95 **To** 2025 $40 NG

5VOV Chardonnay 2017 Sort of cuddly in a light to mid-weighted way, but with a skein of mineral-clad cheesy pungency, a chutney-inflected bite, stony, and nutty acidity, driving it all long. There are few fruit-derived reference points to cling to. Conversely, the textural ride is thrilling and the length compelling. Cork. 12.4% alc. **Rating** 95 **To** 2022 $60 NG

Heckler Pinot Meunier 2017 A gorgeous wine: gently scented red berry fruit against a tapestry of whole-bunch spike and gently hewn tannins. The wine's lacy delicacy – balletic and strident – will sate those seeking textural intrigue alongside hedonic pleasure. Cork. 12.2% alc. **Rating** 95 **To** 2022 $80 NG

Impeccable Disorder Pinot Noir 2017 This wine coaxes the drinker to reach for the next glass with a twine of textural persuasion woven across gentle oak, deft extraction and some root-spicy whole-bunch fabric. Pale colour, yet expansive and intense in flavour. Think amaro, five-spice, satsuma plum and orange rind. Cork. 11.8% alc. **Rating** 94 **To** 2022 $80 NG

I am the Owl Syrah 2017 There's a cool-climate air to this syrah of precision, tension and mouthwatering peppery acidity. The light to barely mid-weighted wine is defined by a lowish alcohol and deft use of whole bunches, conferring an edginess and spike, sans a wisp of greenness. Poised, measured, crunchy and energetic. Sapid Rhône-inspired scents of iodine, violet, olive and blueberry are curled around cloves. A joy to drink. Cork. 11.2% alc. **Rating** 94 **To** 2022 $40 NG

♟♟♟♟♟ **Weird Berries in the Woods Gewurztraminer 2017** Rating 93 To 2021 $35 NG

A Sense of Compression Grenache 2017 Rating 93 To 2025 $80 NG

The Fugazi Grenache 2017 Rating 93 To 2021 $40 NG

Hello Morning Rose Grenache 2017 Rating 92 To 2020 $40 NG

A Forest Pinot Noir 2017 Rating 92 To 2023 $40 NG

The Green Room Grenache Syrah 2017 Rating 92 To 2020 $35 NG

Texture Like Sun 2017 Rating 92 To 2021 $35 NG

Surfer Rosa Grenache 2017 Rating 91 To 2019 $25 NG

From the North Mourvedre 2017 Rating 91 To 2022 $40 NG

The Price of Silence Gamay 2017 Rating 90 To 2021 $45 NG

Oddfellows Wines   ★★★

523 Chapel Road, Langhorne Creek, SA 5255 **Region** Langhorne Creek
T (08) 8537 3326 **www**.oddfellowswines.com.au **Open** Not
Winemaker David Knight **Est.** 1997 **Dozens** 2500 **Vyds** 46.1ha
Oddfellows began in 1997 with a charter to produce premium quality wines that exemplify the character of Langhorne Creek. The circular fingerpint logo is representative of the six founders coming together to work in unity. Winemaker David Knight was one of the founders, and in 2007 took over the ownership and operation of the business. The wines are now all estate-grown. Exports to the UK, the US, Canada, Singapore, Indonesia, Hong Kong and China.

♟♟♟♟ **Langhorne Creek Cabernet Sauvignon 2015** This would shine more brightly if there had been less oak, and less time spent in it (aged 18 months in French barrels that were 25% new). Some fresh currant and cassis popping through, drizzled with molten chocolate. Screwcap. 14.5% alc. **Rating** 89 **To** 2024 $25 JF

Old Kent River Wines

687 Ellen Brook Road, Cowaramup, WA 6284 **Region** Frankland River
T (08) 9755 5999 **www**.oldkentriverwines.com.au **Open** Thurs–Mon 10–5
Winemaker Marius Mencel **Est.** 1985 **Dozens** 800 **Vyds** 17ha
The Rocky Gully sheep-farming property was established in the early 1950s by the Noack family. They planted the first vines (pinot noir) in '85, and the subsequent wines made from their cool-climate site in the Frankland River region gained much respect. In 2015 there were

many changes throughout the business, including a new owner, a new winemaker, a brand refresh and a new cellar door in Margaret River.

ŸŸŸŸŸ Frankland River Sauvignon Blanc 2017 Well and truly into passionfruit, guava and kiwi fruit tropical flavours. Intensity married with an unexpected delicacy and a refreshing citrussy finish. Screwcap. 12.5% alc. **Rating** 94 **To** 2019 $24
Frankland River Pinot Noir 2016 The very light, bright, clear colour and the rose-petal aromas introduce a fresh, elegant palate solely focused on red fruits, ranging from wild strawberry to red cherry. The winemaking was astute, avoiding the trap of over-extraction. Screwcap. 13.7% alc. **Rating** 94 **To** 2025 $35
Frankland River Pinot Noir 2015 Old Kent River has always had the potential to produce good pinot noir weather permitting. This wine shows what can be achieved, with very good texture, structure, balance and length. The bouquet is fragrantly spicy, the palate showcasing dark cherry fruit in a lattice of fine tannins and French oak. Screwcap. 14.5% alc. **Rating** 94 **To** 2025 $35
Frankland River Shiraz 2015 Meaty shiraz with peppercorn and violet-like notes playing off one another. It's ribald at first but settles down as it breathes, the pour of blackberry and plum flavours gradually taking over the show. Spice-infused but with ample ripe fruit. Plenty to like. Screwcap. 14.5% alc. **Rating** 94 **To** 2028 $35 CM
Frankland River Shiraz 2014 A very lively, medium-bodied shiraz with an onrush of flavours and textures – red and black cherry/berry fruits, fine but persistent tannins, and a swish of French oak. The more it is retasted, the more it sings its message. Screwcap. 14.5% alc. **Rating** 94 **To** 2029 $30 ✪

ŸŸŸŸŸ Frankland River Sauvignon Blanc 2016 Rating 93 To 2019 $24 CM ✪
Frankland River Sauvignon Blanc 2015 Rating 93 To 2019 $24 ✪
Frankland River Chardonnay 2016 Rating 93 To 2023 $29 CM
Margaret River Semillon Sauvignon Blanc 2017 Rating 90 To 2019 $22 CM

Old Oval Estate   ★★★☆

18 Sand Road, McLaren Vale, SA 5171 **Region** McLaren Vale
T (08) 8323 9100 **www**.oldovalestate.com.au **Open** Fri–Sun 11–5
Winemaker Phil Christiansen, Matt Wenk **Est.** 1998 **Dozens** 1000 **Vyds** 6ha
Joan Rowley purchased an 8ha allotment in the heart of McLaren Vale, where she built a new home for herself and her three children. Ben Paxton was working at Hardys at the time, and arranged a 10-year grape supply contract if she were to plant vines on the property. When the contract came to an end in 2007, Joan recruited local winemaker Phil Christiensen to make the wines. She had established the gardens and grounds of the Old Oval Estate for weddings/functions, and for cellar door sales. Daughter Patrisse Caddle (with a bed & breakfast in McLaren Vale) assists with the marketing and strategy of Old Oval. Son Cameron has purchased a vineyard in Whitings Road to contribute to the supply of grapes, and daughter Amanda works in the cellar door on weekends and does the bookkeeping. Grandchildren are all already in Joan's sights to work at the cellar door while they undertake their university studies.

ŸŸŸŸŸ Fork in the Road Reserve McLaren Vale Shiraz 2016 It reaches straight into warm asphalt, saltbush and blackberry flavour, its intent clear, its style as simple as it is uncompromised. Rich and hearty, served straight up. Smoothness of texture won't displease anyone either. Screwcap. 14.5% alc. **Rating** 92 **To** 2028 CM

ŸŸŸŸ Fork in the Road McLaren Vale Shiraz 2016 Rating 89 To 2025 $25 CM

Old Plains   ★★★★

71 High Street, Grange, SA 5023 (postal) **Region** Adelaide Plains
T 0407 605 601 **www**.oldplains.com **Open** Not
Winemaker Domenic Torzi, Tim Freeland **Est.** 2003 **Dozens** 4000 **Vyds** 14ha

Old Plains is a partnership between Tim Freeland and Domenic Torzi, who have acquired small parcels of old vine shiraz, grenache and cabernet sauvignon in the Adelaide Plains region. A portion of the wines is exported to the US, Denmark, Hong Kong, Singapore and China.

🍷🍷🍷🍷🍷 **Power of One Old Vine Adelaide Plains Shiraz 2015** Vines planted in the '50's on the Adelaide Plains, a region sadly all but swallowed up by development. Shows the 'twang' you typically see in wines from here, with a home-cooked jam top-note prevailing on the bouquet and continuing on the palate. Ripe, sweet fruit all the way, but it's fresh and juicy with just enough tannin and acidity to maintain good form. Screwcap. 14.5% alc. **Rating** 93 **To** 2025 $30 SC

Terreno Old Vine Adelaide Plains Grenache 2016 From a vineyard planted in the '50's and now surrounded up to the fence line on all sides by suburban housing. Living on borrowed time, one would think. Sweet raspberry fruit is the theme running through the wine, with a suggestion of Asian spice and a gently earthy character. The light astringency provides freshness, and there's a feeling of buoyancy on the palate. Screwcap. 14.5% alc. **Rating** 92 **To** 2026 $30 SC

Oliver's Taranga Vineyards ★★★★★

246 Seaview Road, McLaren Vale, SA 5171 **Region** McLaren Vale
T (08) 8323 8498 **www**.oliverstaranga.com **Open** 7 days 10–4
Winemaker Corrina Wright **Est.** 1841 **Dozens** 8000 **Vyds** 85.42ha
William and Elizabeth Oliver arrived from Scotland in 1839 to settle at McLaren Vale. Six generations later, members of the family are still living on the Whitehill and Taranga farms. The Taranga vineyard has 15 varieties planted (the lion's share to shiraz and cabernet sauvignon, with lesser quantities of chardonnay, chenin blanc, durif, fiano, grenache, mataro, merlot, petit verdot, sagrantino, semillon, tempranillo, viognier and white frontignac). Corrina Wright is the Oliver family's first winemaker, and in 2011 the family celebrated 170 years of grapegrowing. Exports to Canada, Hong Kong and China.

🍷🍷🍷🍷🍷 **HJ McLaren Vale Shiraz 2015** The quality of the 70yo estate vineyard is immediately obvious. The wine has a rare multiplicity of aromas and flavours spanning the earth and sky: old polished leather and dark chocolate in a silken web of rich purple and black fruits, with ultra-soft but persistent tannins. Screwcap. 14.5% alc. **Rating** 97 **To** 2050 $60 ✪

M53 McLaren Vale Shiraz 2014 Only made in exceptional years, this is the third release following '10 and '14. Pre-fermentation maceration is one of the keys to a beautifully cadenced wine, so supple and polished is the fruit and tannin profile. There's no sense of alcohol intrusion, seemingly less than the 14.5%. The French oak has paid its way many times over. Screwcap. **Rating** 97 **To** 2049 $180

🍷🍷🍷🍷🍷 **McLaren Vale Shiraz 2016** Destemmed, crushed, open-fermented, matured in used French oak. It's impossible to find any issue, nitpicking or otherwise, with this medium to full-bodied wine, so perfectly balanced, so clearly reflecting its regional origin. Black cherry, ripe blackberry, earth and dark chocolate flavours rest on a bed of ripe, plush tannins and integrated oak. Great value. Screwcap. 14.5% alc. **Rating** 96 **To** 2046 $30 ✪

HJ McLaren Vale Shiraz 2014 Hand-picked from the Old Block, lightly crushed, 3 days' cold soak, wild yeast, open-fermented, matured in French hogsheads (35% new). Remarkable retention of hue. Expressive black fruits drive the bouquet, with bits 'n' pieces of licorice, dark chocolate and briar. The full-bodied palate is positively juicy and luscious until the fine but firm, tannins take hold on the finish. The oak has that integration that only comes from finishing fermentation in barrel (especially new). Screwcap. 14.5% alc. **Rating** 95 **To** 2039 $55

DJ McLaren Vale Cabernet Sauvignon 2015 Rich McLaren Vale cabernet; it's full-bodied but carries its weight easily. The tannins were never going to be a problem, and the oak was well judged, leaving the great Reynell clone free to speak in its effortlessly pure fashion. Screwcap. 14.5% alc. **Rating** 95 **To** 2035 $55

DJ McLaren Vale Cabernet Sauvignon 2014 A thoroughly unusual – and very good – McLaren Vale cabernet that has a degree of elegance seldom found in the region. It has a notable yet fine tannin structure providing the stage for the dance of blackcurrant fruit, oak a whisper from the wings. Bottle no. 1813. Screwcap. 14.5% alc. **Rating** 95 **To** 2034 $55

Small Batch McLaren Vale Grenache 2016 Bright and clear in colour, this is McLaren Vale grenache at its sternest best: red fruits and a dusting of savoury, superfine tannins. No oak flavour, just texture. Screwcap. 14.5% alc. **Rating** 94 **To** 2026 $30 ✪

ᵀᵀᵀᵀᵀ **Corrina's McLaren Vale Shiraz Cabernet 2016** **Rating** 93 **To** 2031 $32
Small Batch McLaren Vale Grenache 2016 **Rating** 92 **To** 2023 $30 CM
Chica McLaren Vale Mencia Rose 2017 **Rating** 91 **To** 2018 $25 CM
Small Batch McLaren Vale Tempranillo 2015 **Rating** 91 **To** 2029 $32

One Block   ★★★★★

Nyora Road, Mount Toolebewong, Vic 3777 **Region** Yarra Valley
T 0419 186 888 **www**.oneblock.com.au **Open** By appt
Winemaker Jayden Ong **Est.** 2010 **Dozens** 1200 **Vyds** 5ha

Jayden Ong, a first-generation Eurasian-Australian, was infected by the wine virus working at the Melbourne Wine Room from 2000–06, and has moved with bewildering speed across many facets of the industry since then. Wedging in vintages at Curly Flat ('06), Moorooduc Estate ('07) and Allies/Garagiste ('08–09) while completing the CSU oenology course, he also opened Cumulus Inc, a restaurant and bar in Melbourne, with superstar chef Andrew McConnell and business partners; he continues to mentor the Cumulus wine team. Apart from an annual pilgrimage to France to further his grapegrowing and winemaking experience, he went to Italy in '06 and '12, Germany in '10, Spain in '11 and '13, and California in '14. He founded One Block in '10 with the philosophy of making single vineyard wines 'from quality individual vineyard sites where the variety grown suits the site', making 100 dozen of his first love, chardonnay, in '10. In '15 he and partner Morgan Ong purchased a small property and home at Mount Toolebewong, 700m above sea level in the Yarra Valley. They immediately began biological site preparation for a close-planted vineyard with three new clones of chardonnay. He also leases the dry-grown Chestnut Hill vineyard and winery at Mount Burnett, and has begun conversion of the vineyard to organic and biological farming methods. He doesn't intend to slow down, with all sorts of projects in mind for the coming years. A star in the making. Exports to the US.

ᵀᵀᵀᵀᵀ **Yellingbo Yarra Valley Shiraz 2015** This has the overall style and elegance of the wines made by Jayden Ong as he plays the whole-bunch game as hard as he can in some of the cooler/coolest sites of the Yarra Valley. Here dark fruits come out on top, but that foresty underlay is still there tugging at your tastebuds. Screwcap. 13% alc. **Rating** 95 **To** 2032 $38

Glory Yarra Valley Shiraz 2015 From Seville East. The wine has a lot of French oak pushing the flavour barrow, but it's classy, and the fruit fully reflects the quality of the '15 Yarra Valley vintage. The aromas and flavours fill the spectrum from spicy to foresty, from whole-bunchy to dark forest berry fruits, the last winning the game. Its finesse manages to outpoint the hint of green that appears intermittently. Screwcap. 13% alc. **Rating** 95 **To** 2030 $38

Granite Yarra Valley Chardonnay 2015 Its youthful colour and freshness of flavour are what you might expect from a 1yo chardonnay, not 3yo. It's not a Peter Pan wine, frozen in time; it has fine texture, with stone fruit kissed by grapefruit acidity, the finish long and well balanced. Screwcap. 13% alc. **Rating** 94 **To** 2028 $33

Yarra Valley Shiraz 2015 Snakes, centipedes, wasps, beetles, grubs – they're all there monstering a person with a dislocated head. All a bit off-putting, but the wine has many things in common with the style of Glory. 375ml. Screwcap. 13% alc. **Rating** 94 **To** 2027 $20 ✪

ᵀᵀᵀᵀᵀ **La Maison de Ong The Hermit Yarra Valley Syrah 2014** **Rating** 92 **To** 2029 $48

Orange Mountain Wines ★★★★

10 Radnedge Lane, Orange, NSW 2800 **Region** Orange
T (02) 6365 2626 **www**.orangemountain.com.au **Open** Wed–Fri 9–3, w'ends 9–5
Winemaker Terry Dolle **Est.** 1997 **Dozens** 2000 **Vyds** 1ha
Having established the business back in 1997, Terry Dolle made the decision to sell the vineyard in 2009. He now makes wine from small parcels of hand-picked fruit, using an old basket press and barrel maturation. These are in principle all single vineyard wines reflecting the terroir of Orange. Exports to China.

ɥɥɥɥɥ **Limited Release Viognier 2016** A well framed viognier balancing its rich flavours of apricots, grated ginger, lemon cream and vanillan oak (aged for 1 year in French puncheons; 50% new). Certainly, the palate has a richness, with pleasing phenolics adding grip but not bitterness to the finish while maintaining elegance throughout. Screwcap. 14% alc. **Rating** 93 **To** 2019 $35 JF
Limited Release Riesling 2017 Really floral aromatics from lavender to orange blossom with a hint of fennel, ginger and spice. The palate is bracingly fresh and dry with green apple, lemon zest and a tart acidity. Screwcap. 12% alc. **Rating** 91 **To** 2025 $25 JF
1397 Shiraz Viognier 2015 Co-fermented with 7% viognier, 14 days on skins, aged 18 months in French barrels (80% new). The oak is in sync and frames the fuller bodied wine while adding cedary spice, tar and sweet vanillan flavours to the ripe fruit. Screwcap. 14.5% alc. **Rating** 91 **To** 2024 $42 JF

Oranje Tractor ★★★★☆

198 Link Road, Albany, WA 6330 **Region** Albany
T (08) 9842 5175 **www**.oranjetractor.com **Open** Sun 11–5 or by appt
Winemaker Rob Diletti **Est.** 1998 **Dozens** 1000 **Vyds** 2.9ha
The name celebrates the 1964 orange Fiat tractor acquired when Murray Gomm and Pamela Lincoln began the establishment of their vineyard. Murray was born next door, but moved to Perth to work in physical education and health promotion. Here he met nutritionist Pamela, who completed the wine science degree at CSU in 2000 before being awarded a Churchill Fellowship to study organic grape and wine production in the US and Europe. Murray and Pamela's vineyards are managed organically, and their wines are natural.

ɥɥɥɥɥ **Riesling 2017** Has echoes of Crawford River, another very cool maritime climate. Here delicate lime and passionfruit aromas and flavours make their mark from the word go, and with the aid of crisp acidity, carry the wine on its long journey to the finish. Screwcap. 11.5% alc. **Rating** 95 **To** 2027 $33
Albany Sauvignon Blanc 2016 You don't have to use your imagination to find passionfruit at the head of the tropical fruit chain, nor breezy crisp acidity on the finish. Easy to enjoy, but don't ignore the fact that this is a well grown, well made sauvignon blanc of distinctive character. Screwcap. 12.5% alc. **Rating** 94 **To** 2018 $34

ɥɥɥɥ **Sparkling Riesling 2016** Rating 90 $43

Orlando ★★★★☆

Barossa Valley Way, Rowland Flat, SA 5352 **Region** Barossa Valley
T (08) 8521 3111 **www**.pernod-ricard-winemakers.com **Open** Not
Winemaker Ben Bryant **Est.** 1847 **Dozens** NFP
Orlando is the parent who has been separated from its child, Jacob's Creek (see separate entry). While Orlando is 170 years old, Jacob's Creek is little more than 45 years old. For what are doubtless sound marketing reasons, Orlando aided and abetted the separation, but the average consumer is unlikely to understand the logic, and – if truth be known – is unlikely to care.

ɥɥɥɥɥ **Jacaranda Ridge Coonawarra Cabernet Sauvignon 2015** It always comes laden with oak and this release is no different, though it's been artfully applied here; of bigger importance is this wine is flooded with quality fruit flavour.

This is a Jacaranda Ridge cabernet to really sink into. It's plush with blackcurrant, brightened by mint, slipped with cedar wood and drilled with ripe, integrated tannin. Screwcap. 14.5% alc. **Rating** 95 **To** 2040 $110 CM
Lawson's Padthaway Shiraz 2013 This takes boysenberry, sweet plum and blackcurrant flavours and injects them with both choc/cedar oak and an incredible burst of trademark peppermint. It's distinctive, charming, seductive. Ripe tannin is largely consumed by the wealth of delicious, full-bodied flavour. Screwcap. 14.6% alc. **Rating** 94 **To** 2033 $65 CM

🍷🍷🍷🍷 **Gramp's Barossa Valley Shiraz 2016** **Rating** 89 **To** 2024 $22 CM

Ottelia ★★★★☆

2280 V&A Lane, Coonawarra, SA 5263 **Region** Coonawarra
T 0409 836 298 **www**.ottelia.com.au **Open** Thurs–Mon 10–4
Winemaker John Innes **Est.** 2001 **Dozens** 5000 **Vyds** 9ha
John and Melissa Innes moved to Coonawarra intending, in John's words, to 'stay a little while'. The first sign of a change of heart was the purchase of a property ringed by red gums, and with a natural wetland dotted with *Ottelia ovalifolia*, a native water lily. They still live in the house they built there. John worked as winemaker at Rymill Coonawarra while Melissa established a restaurant. After 20 years, John left Rymill to focus on consultancy work throughout the Limestone Coast, and to establish and run Ottelia.

🍷🍷🍷🍷🍷 **Mount Gambier Riesling 2017** Wow. This is positively breathtaking, the complex spray of citrus flavours impacting the second the wine enters the mouth, and lingering long after the finish. The citrus element leans towards unsweetened green grapefruit juice and zest, acidity a given and playing an important role. Trophy for Best White Wine, Limestone Coast Wine Show '17, not the least surprising. For the record: pH 2.83, titratable acidity 9.36g/l, residual sugar 6g/l. Screwcap. 11% alc. **Rating** 98 **To** 2037 $22 ✪

🍷🍷🍷🍷🍷 **Mount Gambier Sauvignon Blanc 2017** **Rating** 93 **To** 2020 $22 SC ✪
Limestone Coast Sangiovese 2016 **Rating** 93 **To** 2025 $26 SC ✪

Ouse River Wines ★★★★

PO Box 40, Ouse, Tas 7140 **Region** Southern Tasmania
T (03) 6287 1309 **www**.ouseriverwines.com **Open** Not
Winemaker Peter Caldwell, Anna Pooley (Contract) **Est.** 2002 **Dozens** 250 **Vyds** 17.8ha
Ouse River Wines is one of the most interesting developments in Tasmania. Bernard and Margaret Brain own a 1000ha property north of Ouse at the top end of the Derwent Valley, on the edge of the central highlands. They run nine enterprises on the property, including the vineyard that is the furthest inland in Tasmania, with a continental climate and a diurnal temperature range during ripening of 7°C more than the areas surrounding Hobart. In the early 1990s Bernard and Margaret attended wine-tasting classes run by Phil Laing, which prompted the planting of a trial area of six varieties to see whether they would ripen. In 2002 they approached Ray Guerin to see what he thought: the answer was a contract with Hardys for 10 years. The first planting of 1ha in late '02 was followed by an extra ha planted each year until '06; further plantings over the years resulted in a total of 6.55ha of pinot noir, 10.25ha of chardonnay and 1ha of riesling. The pinot has been used by House of Arras from the second vintage, and in every vintage since. Ouse River's grapes continue to be sought after, which is driving substantial new plantings on their ample land.

🍷🍷🍷🍷🍷 **Pinot Noir 2016** A sure-footed release with fresh ripe fruit, hints of reduction and an attractive curl of tannin through the back half. Nothing out of place from start to finish. Orange rind, cherry plum and twiggy spice. In a good place. Screwcap. 13.5% alc. **Rating** 92 **To** 2024 $50 CM
Chardonnay 2016 Elegant, balanced and lengthy. Nicely put together. Tinned pear, apple, cedar spice and citrus flavours. Not a lot of depth, but it feels fluid and extends beautifully through the finish. We're seeing it very young here; it has a way to go. Screwcap. 13.3% alc. **Rating** 91 **To** 2024 $50 CM

Out of Step

6 McKenzie Avenue, Healesville, Vic 3777 (postal) **Region** Yarra Valley
T 0419 681 577 **www.**outofstepwineco.com **Open** Not
Winemaker David Chatfield, Nathan Reeves **Est.** 2012 **Dozens** 2100
Out of Step is the micro virtual winery of David Chatfield and Nathan Reeves. Nathan is currently in Tasmania on a sabbatical from the business, while David continues to work on the label as well as helping to look after the vineyards at Oakridge. Along the way they have variously chalked up experience at Stella Bella (Margaret River), Lusatia Park (now owned by De Bortoli), Sticks Yarra Valley and Vinify (California). Their initial foray with a sauvignon blanc sourced from Lusatia Park was spectacular. Among other wines, they also now make chardonnay, pinot noir, nebbiolo and shiraz from various acclaimed vineyards in the Yarra Valley and Pyrenees. Exports to Singapore and Hong Kong.

Willowlake Vineyard Yarra Valley Sauvignon Blanc 2017 It's certainly not an exercise in overbearing varietal expression. Savoury, grassy, tropical fruit characters are there, woven into an overall impression on the bouquet and palate of minerally, flinty vinosity as the wine's real personality. Silky texture and superfine natural acidity help persuade you to go back for another taste, or another glass. Screwcap. 12.5% alc. **Rating** 95 To 2022 $30 SC ✪
Lone Star Creek Vineyard Yarra Valley Sauvignon Blanc 2017 Gunflint, slate and fresh herbal aromas upfront, with a touch of reduction. More obvious varietal characters emerge as it sits in the glass, but stay mainly at the leaner, greener end of the spectrum. On tasting the wine it feels more accessible, with a riper, quite juicy feel to the fruit, although the texture and taut, almost grippy acidity are the definitive elements. Screwcap. 12.5% alc. **Rating** 94 To 2022 $30 SC ✪

Willowlake Yarra Valley Pinot Noir 2016 Rating 93 To 2023 $33 CM
Malakoff Estate Pyrenees Shiraz 2016 Rating 93 To 2026 $32 CM

Paisley Wines

PO Box 648, Tanunda, SA 5352 **Region** Barossa Valley
T 0491 377 737 **www.**paisleywines.com.au **Open** Not
Winemaker Derek Fitzgerald **Est.** 2017 **Dozens** 650
Derek Fitzgerald had made wines for nearly 20 years in WA, Langhorne Creek and the Barossa Valley, before gentle persuasion by wife Kirsten led to the decision to make wine on their own account. The three varieties produced are classic Barossa – grenache, mataro and shiraz – made in three ranges: Mixed by DJ Deadly, Paisley Fabric and top-of-the-ticket Paisley Celtic. Derek has winkled out some small parcels of grapes from long-proven vineyards up to 70 years old.

Mixed by DJ Deadly Turntable Grenache Shiraz Mataro 2016 This is a livewire blend (65/27/8%), the colour an immediate come-on. Then there are mountain rivulets of red fruits coursing along and down the palate, the freshness and vibrancy on the finish utterly exceptional. It would be a crying shame not to drink this wine before the end of '18. Screwcap. 14.5% alc. **Rating** 96 To 2018 $22 ✪
Silk Shiraz 2016 Whole bunches, pre- and post-fermentation maceration, wild yeast, matured for 12 months in French oak. Deep crimson-purple; the wine delivers maximum complexity with a juicy, spicy intensity, yet remains light on its feet. It has great length, and you sense the fresh acidity and low pH. Screwcap. 14% alc. **Rating** 94 To 2046 $27 ✪

Maeve Single Vineyard Shiraz 2016 Rating 93 To 2046 $60
Velvet Grenache 2016 Rating 92 To 2024 $27
Clurichaun Single Vineyard Mataro 2016 Rating 91 To 2026 $45

Palmer Wines

1271 Caves Road, Dunsborough, WA 6281 **Region** Margaret River
T (08) 9756 7024 **www**.palmerwines.com.au **Open** 7 days 10–5
Winemaker Mark Warren, Bruce Dukes, Clive Otto **Est.** 1977 **Dozens** 10 000
Vyds 51.39ha

Steve and Helen Palmer have mature plantings of cabernet sauvignon, sauvignon blanc, shiraz, merlot, chardonnay and semillon, with smaller amounts of malbec and cabernet franc. Recent vintages have had major success in WA and national wine shows. Exports to Indonesia, Hong Kong and China.

🍷🍷🍷🍷🍷 **Merlot 2016** A fine merlot indeed. Volume, mouthfeel, character and length. It sets you back on your heels a bit. Gravel, blackcurrant, mulberry, peppercorn and cedar-wood oak. A spot of aniseed too. A spread of fine but assertive tannin. Draws you in and keeps you there. Screwcap. 14.5% alc. **Rating** 95 **To** 2031 $30 CM ✪
Cabernet Sauvignon 2016 In excellent shape. Milk chocolate, gravel and gum-leaf notes team impressively with blackcurrant and licorice flavours, tannin roping it all neatly together. It's firm, sizeable, persistent and utterly convincing. Screwcap. 14.5% alc. **Rating** 95 **To** 2034 $30 CM ✪
Reserve Chardonnay 2016 Full-bodied and flavoured Margaret River chardonnay. There's nothing quite like it. Peach-driven fruit, bursts of grapefruit, lashings of creamy oak, and the sweet, spicy, toasty character of cedar wood. Ready to roll now but will hold. Screwcap. 12.9% alc. **Rating** 94 **To** 2024 $35 CM
Shiraz 2016 Suede-like softness, plum-like flavour, highlights of choc-spearmint and a smooth, even finish. We're in the pleasure business here. Add leather and raspberry notes and you have yourself a plump-bodied red with no kinks whatsoever and enough tannin to see it age well over the medium term. It's already drinking well. Screwcap. 14.4% alc. **Rating** 94 **To** 2030 $30 CM ✪
Krackerjack Shiraz Cabernet 2016 Hefty red with all the fruit flavour you could want, the oak to match, and the tannin and overall finish strapping quality firmly to the mast. Krackerjack name, crackerjack value. Screwcap. 14.5% alc. **Rating** 94 **To** 2030 $25 CM ✪
Cabernet Franc Merlot 2016 In some ways it's light and grassy, and in other ways that gives entirely the wrong impression. There's bold fruit here, and strong tannin, its redcurrant and gum-leaf flavours doused with smoky oak. There's little doubt this will cellar well. Screwcap. 14.5% alc. **Rating** 94 **To** 2032 $30 CM ✪

🍷🍷🍷🍷🍸 **Reserve Chardonnay 2017 Rating** 93 **To** 2024 $35 CM
The Grandee Reserve Margaret River Cabernets 2016 Rating 93 **To** 2034 $38 CM
Krackerjack Chardonnay 2017 Rating 92 **To** 2022 $25 CM ✪
Malbec 2016 Rating 92 **To** 2030 $30 CM
Purebred by Mark Warren Malbec 2014 Rating 92 **To** 2025 CM
Purebred by Clive Otto Malbec 2016 Rating 91 **To** 2028 $39 CM
Sauvignon Blanc Semillon 2017 Rating 90 **To** 2020 $20 CM ✪
Reserve Shiraz 2016 Rating 90 **To** 2025 $38 CM

Paracombe Wines

294B Paracombe Road, Paracombe, SA 5132 **Region** Adelaide Hills
T (08) 8380 5058 **www**.paracombewines.com **Open** By appt
Winemaker Paul Drogemuller **Est.** 1983 **Dozens** 15 000 **Vyds** 22.1ha

Paul and Kathy Drogemuller established Paracombe Wines in 1983 in the wake of the devastating Ash Wednesday bushfires. The winery is located high on a plateau at Paracombe, looking out over the Mount Lofty Ranges, and the vineyard is run with minimal irrigation and hand-pruning to keep yields low. The wines are made onsite. Exports to the US, Canada, Denmark, Sweden, Indonesia, Singapore, Taiwan and China.

🍷🍷🍷🍷🍸 **Adelaide Hills Cabernet Franc 2013** Terrific colour and flavours too with a cheery mix of plums, cassis, freshly rolled tobacco, violets and bouquet garni.

Tannins are assertive and raspy but the palate is buoyant and the acidity bright. All up, satisfying. Screwcap. 14% alc. **Rating** 93 **To** 2025 $27 JF ✪
Holland Creek Adelaide Hills Riesling 2017 Pale-straw and bright; a delicate style with white blossom, citrus, preserved lemon and some white stone fruit. While it's lively, the acidity is restrained and there's texture rounding out the palate. Screwcap. 12% alc. **Rating** 92 **To** 2025 $20 JF ✪
Adelaide Hills Pinot Blanc 2017 Exuberant with flavour. Cooked apple and stone fruit, pear and citrus. Clean and fresh in its presentation of flavour, but with real grip to the texture. Arguably a 'food style' but pretty good from any angle. Screwcap. 12% alc. **Rating** 91 **To** 2019 $22 CM ✪
Adelaide Hills Malbec 2015 Another beefy release, but it rounds things out through the finish fairly well. Blueberry, mint and black cherry flavours with subtexts of game and fresh leather. It gets down and dirty, but there's a prettiness to both the fruit and (vanillan) oak. Plenty of years ahead of it. Screwcap. 14.2% alc. **Rating** 90 **To** 2029 $30 CM

🍷🍷🍷🍷 Adelaide Hills Pinot Gris 2017 Rating 89 To 2019 $20 CM
Adelaide Hills Cabernet Sauvignon 2013 Rating 89 To 2023 $23 JF

Paradigm Hill   ★★★★★

26 Merricks Road, Merricks, Vic 3916 **Region** Mornington Peninsula
T (03) 5989 9000 **www.**paradigmhill.com.au **Open** W'ends 12–5
Winemaker Dr George Mihaly **Est.** 1999 **Dozens** 1400 **Vyds** 4.2ha
George Mihaly (with a background in medical research, biotechnology and pharmaceutical industries) and wife Ruth (a former chef and caterer) realised a 30-year dream of establishing their own vineyard and winery, abandoning previous careers to do so. George made the 2001 Merricks Creek wines before Paradigm Hill became home base in '02, all along receiving guidance and advice from Nat White of Main Ridge Estate. The vineyard, under Ruth's control with advice from Shane Strange, is planted to 2.1ha of pinot noir, 0.9ha of shiraz, 0.82ha of riesling and 0.38ha of pinot gris. Exports to the US, Germany, Denmark, Sweden and China.

🍷🍷🍷🍷🍷 Mornington Peninsula Riesling 2017 Hand-picked 19yo vines, matured on lees for 6 months. It's very difficult to find rieslings that enjoy a maritime climate, but this comes close, sustained by George Mihaly's relentless attention to detail. Here lime essence is heightened by intense mineral acidity that runs through to the finish and aftertaste. Screwcap. 11.9% alc. **Rating** 95 **To** 2037 $39
Mornington Peninsula Pinot Gris 2017 Paradigm Hill has for many years treated pinot gris with respect, here using French oak for barrel fermentation (33% of it new). The varietal expression is right on the money with nashi pear and apple skin flavours on the long palate. The $60 price will stop many would-be experimenters in their tracks. Screwcap. 12.9% alc. **Rating** 95 **To** 2023 $60
Adesso Mornington Peninsula Pinot Noir 2016 Made along the same lines as L'ami Sage but without new oak and all MV6. Dark crimson with purple hues. Brooding ripe plum, and while no new oak, there is an underlying ribbon of vanilla woven through the fruit, adding dimension to the wine but letting the fruit speak. It's wonderfully persistent, with a 'just right' refreshing acidity. Screwcap. 13% alc. **Rating** 95 **To** 2027 $72 DB
L'ami Sage Mornington Peninsula Pinot Noir 2016 A 50/50% blend of MV6 and 115. Whole berries fermented for 3 weeks before maturing in oak (34% new) for 18 months. Ripe mulberry and poached plum over redcurrants and brown spice. Quite bold with the oak apparent, however it sits within the fruit not on it. Screwcap. 13.6% alc. **Rating** 94 **To** 2027 $72 DB

🍷🍷🍷🍷🍷 Les Cinq Pinot Noir 2016 Rating 93 To 2032 $85 DB
Col's Block Shiraz 2016 Rating 92 To 2027 $49 DB

Paradise IV ★★★★★

45 Dog Rocks Road, Batesford, Vic 3213 (postal) **Region** Geelong
T (03) 5276 1536 www.paradiseivwines.com.au **Open** Not
Winemaker Douglas Neal **Est.** 1988 **Dozens** 800 **Vyds** 3.1ha
The former Moorabool Estate has been renamed Paradise IV for the very good reason that it is the site of the original Paradise IV vineyard, planted in 1848 by Swiss vigneron Jean-Henri Dardel. It is owned by Ruth and Graham Bonney. The winery has an underground barrel room, and the winemaking turns around wild yeast fermentation, natural mlf, gravity movement and so forth. Exports to China.

🍷🍷🍷🍷🍷 **Chaumont 2016** A blend of cabernet sauvignon, shiraz and cabernet franc. While a little more assertive than the '15, the wine is well balanced and juicy, the tannins fine and in tune with the fruit. A really nice wine (better than its winemaker gives it credit for). Screwcap. 14% alc. **Rating** 95 **To** 2036 $60
Geelong Chardonnay 2016 Strong straw-green, this is as elegant as it is complex (or vice versa). It has a juicy, soft, stone-fruit motor, and citrussy acidity brightening up the finish. Screwcap. 13% alc. **Rating** 94 **To** 2025 $55
J.H. Dardel 2016 Matured for 12 months, bottled without fining or filtration. This shiraz is in the lap of the gods: will the structure and black fruits hold sway, or the bitter edge of the tannins? Screwcap. 14% alc. **Rating** 94 **To** 2031 $75

Paringa Estate ★★★★★

44 Paringa Road, Red Hill South, Vic 3937 **Region** Mornington Peninsula
T (03) 5989 2669 www.paringaestate.com.au **Open** 7 days 11–5
Winemaker Lindsay McCall, Jamie McCall **Est.** 1985 **Dozens** 15 000 **Vyds** 24.7ha
Schoolteacher-turned-winemaker Lindsay McCall became known for an absolutely exceptional gift for winemaking across a range of styles, but with his immensely complex pinot noir and shiraz leading the way. The wines have had an unmatched level of success in the wine shows and competitions that Paringa Estate has been able to enter, its limitation being the relatively small production of the top wines in the portfolio. Lindsay's skills are no less evident in contract winemaking for others. But time has passed and son Jamie, joined the winemaking team in 2012, after completing a winemaking and viticulture course at the University of Adelaide. He was put in charge of winemaking at Paringa in '17 following five home vintages, and one in Oregon, focusing on pinot noir. Exports to the UK, Canada, Denmark, Ukraine, Singapore, Hong Kong, China and Japan.

🍷🍷🍷🍷🍷 **The Paringa Single Vineyard Pinot Noir 2015** The Prince of Paringa, and off on a voyage of its own, finer and more savoury than any of the '16 Paringa pinots. Red cherry, wild strawberry and spice form irresistible waves of flavour and texture. Elegance at a stratospheric level. Screwcap. 14% alc. **Rating** 97 **To** 2035 $95 ❂
Peninsula Shiraz 2016 Absolutely classic Paringa, one of the best – if not *the* best – of the early starters, with full-on cool-climate shiraz thrust. Classic blackberry, blood plum and licorice flavours are supported by fine tannins and subtle oak. Screwcap. 14% alc. **Rating** 97 **To** 2046 $29 ❂

🍷🍷🍷🍷🍷 **Robinson Vineyard Pinot Noir 2016** Highly aromatic, with dark cherry and plum fruit supported by a textured weave of oak and fine tannins. The richest of the '16 Paringa pinots, with a succulent finish and aftertaste. Screwcap. 13.5% alc. **Rating** 96 **To** 2031 $65 ❂
The Paringa Single Vineyard Shiraz 2015 Matured for 18 months in French barriques (40% new). Striking clear, fresh red hue; flavours of juicy cherry and plum fruits. A particularly elegant and balanced example of a top class vintage. Screwcap. 14% alc. **Rating** 96 **To** 2045 $80
The Paringa Single Vineyard Chardonnay 2016 Whole-bunch pressed, unclarified juice wild-fermented in new and 1yo French puncheons, 100% mlf, matured for 11 months. A no-holds-barred style that still has a strong following,

and a very good example of the style. Screwcap. 13.5% alc. **Rating** 95
To 2023 $60

Estate Pinot Noir 2016 Good depth to the colour; shares the distinctive power
and drive of all the top-tier Mornington Peninsula pinots from '16, with red and
black cherry fruits contesting front place. Spices evident and will increase with
time. Screwcap. 14% alc. **Rating** 95 To 2027 $60

Estate Shiraz 2015 Matured for 18 months in French barriques (20% new).
Very complex, powerful and savoury: blackberry, licorice and pepper all to the fore.
The tannins are ripe, and demand you give them their due. Screwcap. 14% alc.
Rating 95 To 2045 $50

Peninsula Pinot Noir 2016 Total of 16 batches picked between 16 Feb and
22 Mar from vineyards across the Peninsula, destemmed, open-fermented, 21 days
on skins, matured for 11 months in French oak. Reflects the decision to invest in
this wine with more fruit and more attention in the winery. The bargain of the
'16 Paringa Pinots. Screwcap. 13.5% alc. **Rating** 94 To 2025 $29 ✪

🍷🍷🍷🍷♀ **Peninsula Chardonnay 2017** Rating 93 To 2025 $29
Estate Pinot Gris 2017 Rating 93 $25 ✪
Estate Chardonnay 2016 Rating 92 To 2022 $45
Peninsula Pinot Noir 2017 Rating 92 To 2025 $29

Parker Coonawarra Estate ★★★★★
15 688 Riddoch Highway, Penola, SA 5263 **Region** Coonawarra
T (08) 8737 3525 **www**.parkercoonawarraestate.com.au **Open** 7 days 10 4
Winemaker Phil Lehmann, Charlie Ormsby, James Lienert **Est.** 1985 **Dozens** 30 000
Vyds 20ha
Parker Coonawarra Estate is at the southern end of Coonawarra, on rich terra rossa soil
over limestone. Cabernet sauvignon is the dominant variety (17.45ha), with minor plantings
of merlot and petit verdot. It is now part of WD Wines, which also owns Hesketh Wine
Company and St John's Road in the Barossa Valley. Production has risen substantially since the
change of ownership. Exports to all major markets.

🍷🍷🍷🍷🍷 **Terra Rossa Cabernet Sauvignon 2016** This is a welcome return to form: a
beacon of light for a region that has begun to lag behind those on western shores.
The tannin management here, recently lacking in Coonawarra, is exemplary. The
mid-weighted wine has pure varietal clarity with cassis, bay leaf, cedar, olive and
bouquet garni. Nothing is excessive and the oak is well appointed. Screwcap.
14.5% alc. **Rating** 96 To 2035 $34 NG ✪

95 Block 2015 80.5% cabernet meshed with 19.5% petit verdot, the latter giving
colour and a ferruginous, structural core. This is a brooding wine built to be the
anvil of your cellar. All gristle of oak and sinuous, refined tannins corralling anise,
eucalyptus, clove, black olive and the ooze of blackcurrant. This augurs well for
a bright future with the emphasis on patience. Tough going right now, though.
Screwcap. 14.5% alc. **Rating** 94 To 2038 $65 NG

🍷🍷🍷🍷♀ **Terra Rossa Shiraz 2016** Rating 93 To 2025 $34 NG
Terra Rossa Merlot 2016 Rating 93 To 2028 $34 NG
Pinot Noir Rose 2017 Rating 91 To 2018 $20 ✪
Cabernet Sauvignon 2016 Rating 91 To 2031 $24
Shiraz 2016 Rating 90 To 2029 $24

Pasadera Wines ★★★★☆
3880 Frankston–Flinders Road, Shoreham, Vic 3916 **Region** Mornington Peninsula
T 0413 602 023 **www**.pasadera.com.au **Open** Not
Winemaker Michael Kyberd **Est.** 2014 **Dozens** 600 **Vyds** 5.2ha
The vineyard was planted in 1990, and for a number of years (and through different owners)
the property was called The Pines, hence the stylised pine cone on the label. The grapes were
sold, and at various times the vineyard was leased. Then in early 2014, owners Rusty and

Nancy French decided to retain the grapes of the mature, low-cropping vines and engage the services of contract winemaker Michael Kyberd. Pasadera is also a horse stud with a number of Arabian thoroughbreds.

ΨΨΨΨΨ **Chardonnay 2015** While there's an intensity of fruit flavour and a certain level of complexity, this somehow manages to rein everything in to a fairly tight frame. Expect a blossoming of fruit flavours, from white nectarines to citrus, with layers of lemon curd and zest with lots of savoury inputs. The oak imparts sweetness and spice, and as the wine builds to a crescendo, the acidity ensures this doesn't go overboard. Screwcap. 13.5% alc. **Rating** 95 **To** 2024 JF

ΨΨΨΨΨ **Pinot Noir 2015 Rating** 90 **To** 2023 JF

Passel Estate

655 Ellen Brook Road, Cowaramup, WA 6284 **Region** Margaret River
T (08) 9717 6241 **www**.passelestate.com **Open** 7 days 10.30–5
Winemaker Bruce Dukes **Est.** 1994 **Dozens** 1500 **Vyds** 6.7ha
Wendy and Barry Stimpson were born in England and South Africa respectively, and during numerous visits to Margaret River over the years, they fell in love with the region's environment. They made Margaret River home in 2005, and in '11 purchased the vineyard planted to 2.6ha of shiraz, 1.5ha of cabernet sauvignon and 2.6ha of chardonnay. Viticulturist Andy Ferreira manages the vineyard with sustainable practices, keeping yields restricted to 6.5–7t/ha. The very talented and highly experienced contract winemaker Bruce Dukes is responsible for the wines. Exports to Singapore.

ΨΨΨΨΨ **Lot 71 Reserve Cabernet Sauvignon 2015** There is an inevitability to its progression from bouquet to palate, waves of fruit advancing and retreating before the high tension of fine-grained cabernet tannins take control. Gold medals Margaret River Wine Show '17, James Halliday Cabernet Challenge '17. Screwcap. 14% alc. **Rating** 96 **To** 2037 $95
Sauvignon Blanc 2017 This makes you reach for the bottle to pour yourself another glass (or so). It is intense and racy, but relies on fruit, not just acidity, to provide its energy. Each taste reveals more, with white fruits, sugar-snap peas and lemon. Screwcap. 12.5% alc. **Rating** 95 **To** 2026 $30 ❂
Chardonnay 2016 A particularly bright and fresh chardonnay with excellent varietal character, length and balance. It cleared the bar for minimum alcohol; any lower and there might have been issues (but it wasn't and there weren't). Screwcap. 12.5% alc. **Rating** 95 **To** 2026 $32 ❂
Shiraz 2015 Bright crimson-purple; there's a lot of high quality French oak stamped on the bouquet and medium-bodied palate, creating both flavour and texture for the plum and savoury black cherry fruit. The finish is long and convincing, and gets it over the oak line. Screwcap. 14.5% alc. **Rating** 95 **To** 2030 $35 ❂

ΨΨΨΨΨ **Margaret River Cabernet Sauvignon 2016 Rating** 90 **To** 2025 $45

Passing Clouds

30 Roddas Lane, Musk, Vic 3461 **Region** Macedon Ranges
T (03) 5348 5550 **www**.passingclouds.com.au **Open** 7 days 10–5
Winemaker Cameron Leith **Est.** 1974 **Dozens** 4600 **Vyds** 9.8ha
Graeme Leith and son Cameron undertook a monumental change when they moved the entire operation that started way back in 1974 in Bendigo to its new location at Musk, near Daylesford. The vines at Bendigo had been disabled by ongoing drought and all manner of pestilence, and it was no longer feasible to continue the business there. However, they still have a foot in Bendigo courtesy of their friends, the Adams at Rheola. Graeme has now left the winemaking in the hands of Cameron, instead using his formidable skills as a writer. Exports to all major markets.

ŢŢŢŢŢ **The Angel Cabernet Sauvignon 2016** Passing Clouds' acumen lies with robust red wines that hold their heft within binds of gum-staining tannins and well handled oak. The best examples are firmly of place. This is no exception, and the pinnacle of the range. An apotheosis of power and strutting ripe fruit flavours soused with herb, never straying into sweetness. Very good old-school cabernet. Screwcap. 14% alc. **Rating** 96 **To** 2040 $53 NG ✪
Graeme's Shiraz Cabernet 2016 In many ways this is the quintessential Aussie table wine: a blend of shiraz and cabernet that is as sturdy as it is inimitable. Yet while many examples of the idiom can be sweet and soft, this has firm cocoa tannins serving as a tactile bow for an avalanche of dark fruit, anise and bay leaf notes. Personality over gloss. Screwcap. 14.7% alc. **Rating** 94 **To** 2031 $34 NG

ŢŢŢŢŢ **Fools on the Hill Chardonnay 2016** Rating 92 **To** 2024 $47 NG
Kilmore Pinot Noir 2016 Rating 92 **To** 2023 $29 CM
Fools on the Hill Pinot Noir 2016 Rating 92 **To** 2025 $47 NG

Patina ★★★★

109 Summerhill Lane, Orange, NSW 2800 **Region** Orange
T (02) 6362 8336 **www**.patinawines.com.au **Open** W'ends 11–5
Winemaker Gerald Naef **Est.** 1999 **Dozens** 1600 **Vyds** 3ha
Gerald Naef's home in Woodbridge, California, was surrounded by the vast vineyard and winery operations of Gallo and Robert Mondavi. It would be hard to imagine a more different viticultural environment than that provided by Orange. Gerald and wife Angie left California in 1981, initially establishing a farm in northwest NSW; 20 years later they moved to Orange, and Gerald enrolled in wine science at CSU. He set up a micro-winery at the Orange Cool Stores and his first wine was the trophy-winning '03 Chardonnay.

ŢŢŢŢŢ **Reserve Orange Chardonnay 2015** Glowing yellow with a green tinge. Rich at heart but long of finish. Nectarine and peach, fig and nashi pear. A bran-like character, edging into cedar spice, creamy cashew and vanilla. Plenty of flavour to hang onto here, both fruit and oak derived, but sizzling and fresh to close. Screwcap. 12.8% alc. **Rating** 94 **To** 2023 $45 CM

ŢŢŢŢŢ **Orange Chardonnay 2015** Rating 92 **To** 2021 $35 CM
Reserve Orange Chardonnay 2014 Rating 92 **To** 2022 $45 CM
Scandalous Orange Riesling 2016 Rating 90 **To** 2023 $25 CM
Orange Riesling 2016 Rating 90 **To** 2022 $25 CM

Patrick of Coonawarra ★★★★★

Cnr Ravenswood Lane/Riddoch Highway, Coonawarra, SA 5263 **Region** Coonawarra
T (08) 8737 3687 **www**.patrickofcoonawarra.com.au **Open** 7 days 10–5
Winemaker Luke Tocaciu **Est.** 2004 **Dozens** 5000 **Vyds** 93.5ha
Patrick Tocaciu (who died in 2013) was a district veteran, having worked at Tollana, Penfolds, Hollick, Heathfield Ridge and DiGiorgio Family Wines. There are almost 55ha of shiraz, riesling and sauvignon blanc at Wrattonbully, and 38.5ha of cabernet sauvignon, riesling, chardonnay and sauvignon blanc at Coonawarra (the Grande Reserve and Home Block cabernets are produced from the low yielding Home Block vineyard). Son Luke, with a degree in oenology from the University of Adelaide and vintage experience in Australia and the US, now runs the business.

ŢŢŢŢŢ **Home Block Cabernet Sauvignon 2013** Matured in new French and American oak for 28 months – a powerful start in life. Both during its time in barrel and since being bottled, the oak has been integrated to a surprising degree, making space for blackcurrant. This is a wine of exceptional quality, with a now-to-whenever drinking platform. Screwcap. 13.8% alc. **Rating** 96 **To** 2038 $45 ✪
Limited Cellar Release Home Block Cabernet Sauvignon 2008 Has retained exceptional colour, and is still strikingly youthful in its flavours of cassis and mulberry, and in its structure. Like its '13 sibling, this spent 28 months in new

French and American oak, which in Australian slang, it ate for breakfast. The two wines are a great pair. Cork. 13.8% alc. **Rating** 96 **To** 2033 $75 ⚫

Estate Grown Mount Gambier Pinot Noir 2016 Provides further evidence of the potential of Mount Gambier to produce elegant pinot noirs with impeccable varietal expression. Very well made. The red and black cherry fruits have a gentle but persistent savoury twist that refreshes and complexes the wine. Screwcap. 12.8% alc. **Rating** 95 **To** 2023 $29 ⚫

🍷🍷🍷🍷🍷 **Estate Grown Riesling 2017** **Rating** 90 **To** 2023 $25

Patritti Wines   ★★★★★

13–23 Clacton Road, Dover Gardens, SA 5048 **Region** Adelaide
T (08) 8296 8261 **www.**patritti.com.au **Open** Mon–Sat 9–5 (7 days Dec)
Winemaker James Mungall, Ben Heide **Est.** 1926 **Dozens** 190 000 **Vyds** 16ha
A family-owned business with impressive vineyard holdings of 10ha of shiraz in Blewitt Springs and 6ha of grenache at Aldinga North. The surging production points to success in export and also to the utilisation of contract-grown as well as estate-grown grapes. Patritti is currently releasing wines of very high quality at enticing prices, and a range of lesser quality wines at unfathomably low prices. The JPB Single Vineyard celebrates Giovanni Patritti, who arrived in Australia in 1925; he sold his wines under the 'John Patritti Brighton' label. Exports to the UK and other major markets, including China.

🍷🍷🍷🍷🍷 **JPB Single Vineyard Shiraz 2016** Concentration is the order of the day. This has immense flavour, both fruit and oak-derived, and a raging churn of tannin to match. It tastes of roasted plums, sweet blackberry, resin and toast, saltbush too. It's full-on and neat at once. It needs a great deal of time for everything to knit together and soften, but it's all here. Cork. 14.5% alc. **Rating** 96 **To** 2045 $60 CM ⚫

Lot Three Single Vineyard McLaren Vale Shiraz 2016 French oak, 5% whole bunches, grapes from Blewitt Springs. It's packed with fruit and spread with tannin, and while $35 might not sound like a bargain, if it had $100 written on it you wouldn't blink. It's saturated with fruit and oak flavour and is incredibly well structured and finished. Cork. 14% alc. **Rating** 96 **To** 2040 $35 CM ⚫

Adelaide Hills Sauvignon Blanc 2017 The one-time conservative, low profile Patritti has gone to the other extreme with some of its labels, including for this. A distraction perhaps, as this is a seriously good Adelaide Hills sauvignon blanc, full of luscious fruit that doesn't go over the top. Citrus, stone fruit, red apple and tropical fruits all contribute, acidity embedded. Screwcap. 12.5% alc. **Rating** 95 **To** 2020 $25 ⚫

Section 181 Single Vineyard McLaren Vale Grenache 2016 15% whole bunches, large format French oak. It starts with fresh, succulent raspberry before diving into deeper, darker pools of flavour. Classy (cedary) oak hovers with whispers of fragrant herbs and woody spices, anise chief among them. In short, it's a beautiful wine to spend time with, firm tannin completing a most impressive picture. Cork. 14.5% alc. **Rating** 95 **To** 2027 $35 CM ⚫

McLaren Vale Cabernet Sauvignon 2016 Patritti does it again – a perfectly weighted medium-bodied cabernet that has elegance and persistence. Cassis fruit with tannins lying at its feet, sufficient to establish the bona fides of the wine without raising its voice. Perfect balance and length, oak a bystander. Screwcap. 13.5% alc. **Rating** 95 **To** 2031 $25 ⚫

Adelaide Hills Pinot Grigio 2017 Straw-green, with as much flavour as grigio can be expected to have. Spiced pear and apple blossom. A real wine with intensity and length. Screwcap. 12.5% alc. **Rating** 94 **To** 2020 $25 ⚫

Merchant McLaren Vale Shiraz 2016 Hand-picked, small amount of whole bunches, American and French oak for 16 months. It's not easy to get these wines right in terms of balance, but this one is spot on. American oak exerts a coffeed influence but doesn't intrude; spice ripples through the tannin without ever begging for the front seat; the fruit is rich and tar-like but not hot or overdone. Value is very high. Screwcap. 13.5% alc. **Rating** 94 **To** 2034 $25 CM ⚫

Old Gate McLaren Vale Shire Shiraz 2016 80% American and the remainder French oak (20% new). 95% of the grapes were from a single vineyard at Blewitt Springs, 5% coming in from the Barossa. It's robust with red and black berries teaming admirably with toasty vanillan oak, and chocolate notes hovering throughout. It has firm, muscular tannins and a sound, satisfying finish. If rich reds are your preferred style, you can't go wrong here. Cork. 14.5% alc. **Rating** 94 To 2030 $20 CM ✪

Merchant McLaren Vale Grenache Shiraz Mourvedre 2016 50/40/10% blend (the latter component from the Barossa). 95% French oak, 5% American, and only 10% of the overall oak was new. Raspberry and redcurrant with subtle notes of fennel, violets and oak spice. Fresh and well formed. Ripper drinking. Screwcap. 13.5% alc. **Rating** 94 To 2025 $25 CM ✪

🍷🍷🍷🍷🍷 **Barossa Valley Saperavi 2014** Rating 93 To 2029 $24 ✪
Merchant Adelaide Hills Chardonnay 2017 Rating 92 To 2023 $25 CM ✪
Barossa Valley Saperavi 2015 Rating 91 To 2024 $24

Paul Conti Wines

529 Wanneroo Road, Woodvale, WA 6026 **Region** Greater Perth
T (08) 9409 9160 **www**.paulcontiwines.com.au **Open** Mon–Sat 10–5, Sun by appt
Winemaker Paul Conti, Jason Conti **Est.** 1948 **Dozens** 4000 **Vyds** 14ha
Third-generation winemaker Jason Conti has assumed control, although father Paul (who succeeded his own father in 1968) remains involved in the business. Over the years Paul challenged and redefined industry perceptions and standards; the challenge for Jason is to achieve the same degree of success in an increasingly and relentlessly competitive market, and he is doing just that. Plantings at the Carabooda vineyard have been expanded with tempranillo, petit verdot and viognier, and pinot noir and chardonnay are purchased from Pemberton. In a further extension, a property at Cowaramup in Margaret River (with sauvignon blanc, shiraz, cabernet sauvignon, semillon, muscat and malbec) has been acquired. The original 2ha Mariginiup vineyard (shiraz) remains the cornerstone. Exports to Japan.

🍷🍷🍷🍷🍷 **Mariginiup Shiraz 2016** Carries its 15% alc. quite comfortably, although there is a feeling of warmth about it. The fruit characters are ripe, with just a hint of cherry liqueur and currant, and the palate is soft, rich and surprisingly supple. The tannin firms up as it rolls along, but sits in balance with the wine overall. Screwcap. **Rating** 92 To 2028 $28 SC

Margaret River Cabernet Sauvignon 2016 Redcurrant and forest fruit aromas lead the way, with black olive, savoury oak and a touch of lanolin in support. Essentially quite soft in style, but gently firm tannins provide the structure filled out by the fleshy berry flavours. Screwcap. 14.5% alc. **Rating** 92 To 2026 $25 SC ✪

Margaret River Chardonnay 2017 Clearly displays green apple and stone-fruit characters, French oak adding some nutty complexity to the bouquet and palate. Shows the freshness of a non-mlf style with lively acidity running through the finish. Screwcap. 13% alc. **Rating** 91 To 2022 $25 SC

Roccella Grenache Shiraz 2016 Grenache grown in sandy soils at the foot of the Perth Hills, and shiraz from limestone-based soils of The Tuarts vineyard, Carabooda. The bright, aromatic red fruits of grenache take the lead in terms of bouquet and flavour, with shiraz providing structure and a touch of spice. Screwcap. 14.5% alc. **Rating** 90 To 2020 $18 SC ✪

Nero d'Avola 2016 Definitely has a warm–climate Italianate feel about it. Aromas of ripe cherry, fruitcake, baked-dry earth and a touch of vanillan oak. Just medium-bodied, but generous enough, the elements of the bouquet are reprised on the palate, with the texture supple, the tannins fine. It's juicy and enjoyable. Screwcap. 14% alc. **Rating** 90 To 2023 $20 SC ✪

🍷🍷🍷🍷 **Tuart Block Chenin Blanc 2017** Rating 89 To 2022 $18 SC ✪

Paul Nelson Wines ★★★★☆

14 Roberts Road, Denmark, WA 6333 (postal) **Region** Great Southern
T 0406 495 066 **www.**paulnelsonwines.com.au **Open** School hols 11–5
Winemaker Paul Nelson **Est.** 2009 **Dozens** 1500 **Vyds** 2ha
Paul Nelson started making wine with one foot in the Swan Valley, the other in the Great Southern, while completing a degree in viticulture and oenology at Curtin University. He then worked at Houghton in the Swan Valley, Goundrey in Mount Barker, Santa Ynez in California, and in South Africa for four vintages, before hemisphere-hopping to the Rheinhessen, and Cyprus for three vintages. Following that he moved to a large Indian winemaker in Mumbai before returning to work for Houghton. Now, in partnership with wife Bianca, Paul makes small quantities of table wines.

🍷🍷🍷🍷🍷 **Karriview Vineyard Denmark Chardonnay 2016** Aromas and flavours evocative of precision: lime curd flecked with a reductive flint, nestled oak, and juicy acidity melded with nectarine and white peach. This is smart. A core of oatmeal and nougatine funk imparts a winning generosity that stains the cheeks. A domestic Meursault with a restraining order. Screwcap. 13% alc. **Rating** 96 To 2027 $58 NG ○

🍷🍷🍷🍷🍷 **Mount Barker Fume Blanc 2017 Rating** 93 To 2025 $30 NG
Army of Grapes Fiano 2017 Rating 93 To 2022 $25 NG ○
Nodus Tollens Field Blend White 2017 Rating 93 To 2020 $28 NG
Army of Grapes Riesling 2017 Rating 92 To 2027 $20 NG ○
PN Ferguson Valley Arneis 2017 Rating 92 To 2020 $28 NG
Army of Grapes Chardonnay 2017 Rating 91 To 2022 $25 NG

Paul Osicka ★★★★★

Majors Creek Vineyard at Graytown, Vic 3608 **Region** Heathcote
T (03) 5794 9235 **Open** By appt
Winemaker Paul Osicka, Simon Osicka **Est.** 1955 **Dozens** NFP **Vyds** 13ha
The Osicka family arrived from Czechoslovakia in the early 1950s. Vignerons in their own country, their vineyard in Australia was the first new venture in central and southern Victoria for over half a century. With the return of Simon Osicka to the family business, there have been substantial changes. Simon held senior winemaking positions at Houghton, Leasingham, and as group red winemaker for Constellation Wines Australia, interleaved with vintages in Italy, Canada, Germany and France, working at the prestigious Domaine Jean-Louis Chave for the '10 vintage. The fermentation of the red wines has been changed from static to open fermenters, and French oak has replaced American. The year 2015 marked the 60th anniversary of the planting of the vineyard. Exports to Denmark.

🍷🍷🍷🍷🍷 **Cabernet Sauvignon 2016** From 30yo vines, and some older material from the '50s. This was fermented in a single open-top fermenter across a 25 day maceration. Thereafter aged for 16 months in Bordeaux oak (25% new). The result is seamless, a rich wine stamped with bitter chocolate and a terracotta regional DNA, with underlying dried herbs and currant. The modus operandi, though, is the precisely chiselled graphite tannins that will see a long future. Screwcap. 14.5% alc. **Rating** 94 To 2031 $35 NG

🍷🍷🍷🍷🍷 **Riesling 2017 Rating** 92 To 2025 $24 NG ○
Shiraz 2016 Rating 92 To 2028 $35 NG
Riesling 2016 Rating 90 To 2022 $24 CM

Paulett Wines ★★★★★

752 Jolly Way, Polish Hill River, SA 5453 **Region** Clare Valley
T (08) 8843 4328 **www.**paulettwines.com.au **Open** 7 days 10–5
Winemaker Neil Paulett, Kirk McDonald **Est.** 1983 **Dozens** 16000 **Vyds** 61ha
The Paulett story is a saga of Australian perseverance, commencing with the 1982 purchase of a property with 1ha of vines and a house, promptly destroyed by the Ash Wednesday bushfires

the following year. Son Matthew joined Neil and Alison as a partner in the business some years ago; he is responsible for viticulture, which has been much expanded following the purchase of a large vineyard at Watervale. The winery and cellar door have wonderful views over the Polish Hill River region, the evidence of the bushfires long gone. Exports to the US, the UK, Denmark, Germany, Singapore, Malaysia, China and NZ.

ΨΨΨΨΨ **Polish Hill River Riesling 2017** From a winery with a great track record, reflecting the ability of the Polish Hill River to produce wines with more focus, length and intensity than much of the Clare Valley proper. This is one such Polish Hill to stand tall, with its intense unsweetened lime and grapefruit flavours, the best still to come. Screwcap. 12.8% alc. **Rating** 95 **To** 2027 $24 ✪

Andreas Polish Hill River Shiraz 2014 As mouthfilling and mouth-coating as ever. Thick with sweet fruit, its concentrated plum, chocolate, cream and sweet mint flavours exploding upfront and roaring all the way through to a warm, resounding finish. Tannin crashes through, sweeping the fruit with it. It can be cellared with confidence. Screwcap. 14.4% alc. **Rating** 95 **To** 2034 $60 CM

Polish Hill River Aged Release Riesling 2011 It is well known that '11 was a cold, wet summer, but time has a produced a honeyed, blossomy, toasty riesling; what a wonder the maturation process can be. This has body, charm and length, a gentle waxiness to the texture simply adding another element. Screwcap. 11% alc. **Rating** 94 **To** 2023 $60 CM

Polish Hill River Cabernet Merlot 2014 It's not a common blend in the Clare Valley, but this elegant, medium-bodied wine pays no attention to any preconceptions. Cassis and a touch of black olive are provided by the cabernet, black fruit and plum by the merlot; the tannins are supple, the oak integrated. Seriously good wine at this price. Screwcap. 14.4% alc. **Rating** 94 **To** 2034 $26 ✪

Alison Botrytis Riesling 2017 A very good wine with rich lime fruit gliding along rails of residual sugar and the largely unseen engine of acidity. The more you taste the wine, the more it captures your palate and lingers in the aftertaste. 500ml. Screwcap. 10% alc. **Rating** 94 **To** 2032 $28 ✪

ΨΨΨΨΨ **Polish Hill River Shiraz 2015** Rating 93 To 2029 $25 ✪
47/74 Hand Crafted Malbec Cabernet 2013 Rating 92 To 2026 $110 CM
Polish Hill River Late Harvest Riesling 2017 Rating 91 To 2023 $24 CM
Watervale Semillon 2017 Rating 90 To 2021 $24 CM
Watervale Grenache Rose 2017 Rating 90 To 2019 $24 CM

Payne's Rise   ★★★★☆

10 Paynes Road, Seville, Vic 3139 **Region** Yarra Valley
T (03) 5964 2504 **www**.paynesrise.com.au **Open** Thurs–Sun 11–5
Winemaker Franco D'Anna (Contract) **Est.** 1998 **Dozens** 1200 **Vyds** 5ha
Tim and Narelle Cullen have progressively established 5ha of cabernet sauvignon, shiraz, pinot noir, chardonnay and sauvignon blanc since 1998, with new plantings continuing on a small scale, including several clones of chardonnay in 2014. They carry out all the vineyard work; Tim is also a viticulturist for a local agribusiness, and Narelle is responsible for sales and marketing. The contract-made wines have won gold medals and trophies at the Yarra Valley Wine Show since '10.

ΨΨΨΨΨ **Yarra Valley Chardonnay 2017** Has all the intensity, and then some, from '17 in the Yarra Valley, especially the Upper Yarra. It has gobbled up the oak, and my advice would be to leave it strictly alone for as long as your patience allows. It's not easy to prognosticate how long is long, but the '11 Coldstream Hills Chardonnays are still in the prime of their extraordinary life. Screwcap. 12.4% alc. **Rating** 95 **To** 2032 $30 ✪

Redlands Yarra Valley Shiraz 2016 A modern visage of Yarra shiraz, well structured but too often reliant on stemmy bristle for savour. This one is mid-weighted and cool climate–confident across scents of violet, pepper grind and iodine; the mace, cardamom and clove of whole-bunch work evident but not obtuse. The fruit: an unfailing flow of blue to dark allusions spliced by anise. Very good. Screwcap. 13.5% alc. **Rating** 94 **To** 2024 $35 NG

Yarra Valley Cabernet Sauvignon 2016 A gorgeously scented cabernet, slung across a chassis of ball-bearing tannins and alloyed acidity. Red and blackcurrant, cedar, pencil lead, bay leaf and the Yarra's green-bean zip code are on display. Yet it is the pulpy structure, harnessing the fruit into a coy mould of reticence, that makes this wine. Enjoyable now, but I want to see what lies ahead in the mid-term. Screwcap. 13% alc. **Rating** 94 **To** 2024 $35 NG

Peccavi Wines   ★★★★★

1121 Wildwood Road, Yallingup Siding, WA 6282 **Region** Margaret River
T 0423 958 255 **www**.peccavi-wines.com **Open** By appt
Winemaker Brian Fletcher **Est.** 1996 **Dozens** 2500 **Vyds** 16ha
Jeremy Muller was introduced to the great wines of the world by his father when he was young, and says he spent years searching New and Old World wine regions (even looking at the sites of ancient Roman vineyards in England), but did not find what he was looking for until one holiday in Margaret River. He found a vineyard in Yallingup for sale, and did not hesitate, quickly putting together an impressive contract winemaking team, and appointing Colin Bell as viticulturist. The wines are released under two labels: Peccavi, for 100% estate-grown fruit (all hand-picked), and No Regrets, for wines with a combination of contract-grown grapes and estate material. The quality of the wines is very good, reflecting the skills and experience of Brian Fletcher. Exports to the United Arab Emirates, Singapore, Hong Kong and China.

🍷🍷🍷🍷🍷 **Margaret River Chardonnay 2015** A mid-weighted chardonnay, without the buxom feel of others from the region. Stone-fruit flavours are positioned across the palate, and there's a fiery streak of mineral-infused energy, well poised oak pillars and leesy crunch and funk, leaving a hint of cashew and nougat. Elegant but intense, and impressively long across the senses. Screwcap. 13% alc. **Rating** 95 **To** 2023 $58 NG

Margaret River Shiraz 2014 A rich wine endorsed by its structural components as much as its gushing black fruit flavours. Reductive tension is played well with the cedary oak and the coffee-grind tannins, svelte yet grippy. Iodine and anise provide a savoury underbelly to the hedonism. About as good as it gets from the region. Screwcap. 14% alc. **Rating** 95 **To** 2025 $52 NG

Margaret River Cabernet Sauvignon 2014 A superb Margaret River cabernet set to a plush mould of massaged tannins, which are chewy and clad in bitter chocolate, reflective of the oak that is so well handled it is buried beneath the morass of flavour. Of a riper idiom, yet far from over the top, each mechanism of the wine is reliant on the other for precision, intensity and length. Cassis, black olive and bay leaf linger. Screwcap. 14% alc. **Rating** 95 **To** 2027 $68 NG

Margaret River Cabernet Sauvignon 2015 This mid-weighted, herbal-scented cabernet clocks in at a suave 12.5% alc. Redolent of high class Bordeaux – think cedar, pencil lead and graphite. Initially I rated this higher than the more robust '14 by virtue of its precise tannins, an apotheosis of structure and elegance. Yet as delicious as it is, this is a little shorter, a bit ropier, and overall, slightly less complete. A wonderful wine, nevertheless. Screwcap. **Rating** 94 **To** 2024 $68 NG

Penfolds

30 Tanunda Road, Nuriootpa, SA 5355 **Region** Barossa Valley
T (08) 8568 8408 **www**.penfolds.com **Open** 7 days 10–5
Winemaker Peter Gago **Est.** 1844 **Dozens** NFP
Penfolds is the star in the crown of Treasury Wine Estates (TWE), but its history predates the formation of the group by close to 170 years. Its shape has changed in terms of its vineyards, its management, its passing parade of great winemakers, and its wines. There is no other single winery brand in the New or Old World with the depth and breadth of Penfolds. Retail prices range from less than $20 to $850 for Grange, which is the cornerstone produced every year,

albeit with the volume determined by the quality of the vintage, not by cash flow. There is now a range of regional wines of single varieties, and the Bin range of wines that include both regional blends and (in some instances) varietal blends. Despite the very successful Yattarna and Reserve Bin A chardonnays, and some impressive rieslings, this remains a red wine producer at heart. Exports to all major markets.

TTTTT **Bin 95 Grange 2013** 96% shiraz, 4% cabernet sauvignon from the Barossa Valley, McLaren Vale, Coonawarra and Magill Estate, matured for 20 months in new American hogsheads. Gloriously, splendiferously complex. There are so many layers of flavour it's labyrinthine, yet you never lose the thread, the path, of the wine. Austerity is not a term often used with Grange, but it's here, and to the benefit of the wine. Cork. 14.5% alc. **Rating** 99 **To** 2053 $850

Bin 144 Yattarna Chardonnay 2015 From Tasmania and the Adelaide Hills, matured for 8 months in French barriques (65% new). A perfect example of the original aim of finding a white wine partner to Grange. Power and stealth are an unlikely combination, but endeavouring to unpick the multitude of flavours isn't useful. The heart of this great chardonnay is its balance, and the extreme length built on its bracing acidity. 13% alc. **Rating** 97 **To** 2025 $150 ✪

Reserve Bin A Adelaide Hills Chardonnay 2016 Matured for 9 months in French barriques (40% new). Towers over Bin 311; gloriously complex and expressive with fruit and high quality French oak both on song. Grapefruit/nectarine flavours are tightly wound together, and ride high, wide and handsome on the back of perfectly pitched acidity. Screwcap. 13.5% alc. **Rating** 97 **To** 2026 $125 ✪

Bin 798 RWT Barossa Valley Shiraz 2015 All the power and glory of full-bodied Barossa Valley shiraz achieved at (relatively) modest alcohol. French oak is another plus for a wine stacked – with extreme care – full of dark fruits and ripe, rounded tannins. Makes winemaking look easy, which of course it isn't. Length is the key to a great wine. Screwcap. 14.5% alc. **Rating** 97 **To** 2040 $200

Bin 389 Cabernet Shiraz 2015 Unapologetically made with the don't-fix-if-it-isn't-broken aphorism. It is tightly structured, with faultless attention to detail – wheels within wheels stuff – but it's inexorable in sending its black fruits (blackberry, blackcurrant) flavour message. Despite its full body, and its far-reaching longevity, it's tailor-made for the saltbush lamb shoulder of tonight's dinner. 14.5% alc. **Rating** 97 **To** 2045 $95 ✪

TTTTT **Bin 28 Kalimna Shiraz 2015** McLaren Vale instantly makes its mark with the seductive lick of dark chocolate on the bouquet, and even more so on the palate. But it's not the make-up, least of all heavy, for there are many voices of red, purple and black fruits in the choir. The wine is medium to full-bodied, and perfectly balanced both in terms of flavour and structure. 14.5% alc. **Rating** 96 **To** 2035 $45 ✪

Bin 138 Shiraz Mataro Grenache 2015 Salt of the Barossa earth, with no airs or graces, but calmly asserting its lineage from the word go through to the aftertaste. I particularly like the licorice and edgy/smoky charcuterie nuances that flow easily across the palate. 14.5% alc. **Rating** 96 **To** 2030 $45 ✪

Bin 407 Cabernet Sauvignon 2015 A testament to the formidable skills and experience of the Penfolds winemaking team: a blend of five very different regions (Wrattonbully, Coonawarra, Padthaway, McLaren Vale and Barossa Valley) with an assembly of oak treatments. The bouquet is utterly convincing, as is the genetic expression of cabernet sauvignon on the long, powerful, medium-bodied palate – which brings with it a silver platter of cabernet tannins. 14.5% alc. **Rating** 96 **To** 2035 $95

Bin 51 Eden Valley Riesling 2017 Super-fragrant and flowery. Exceptional depth and intensity, but even greater balance and length. It makes you itch to drink it – not spit it out. Flawless. Screwcap. 12.5% alc. **Rating** 95 **To** 2031 $30 ✪

Bin 128 Coonawarra Shiraz 2015 The bouquet immediately bursts into vinous song from the first whiff, with fragrant red fruits to the fore. The palate wastes no time in adding darker fruits and substantial tannins to the mix. This demands time

and will be very long lived, as it has the balance to richly repay patience. 14.5% alc.
Rating 95 **To** 2040 $45

St Henri Shiraz 2014 Matured for 12 months in 50+yo large oak vats. No
barrel fermentation, no oak flavours of any description; none needed. This is all
about fruit purity – shiraz with the faintest damask of blackcurrant wrapped
around it. More than any other member of the top range of Penfolds red wines,
this will repay patience. 14.5% alc. **Rating** 95 **To** 2044 $125

Bin 707 Cabernet Sauvignon 2015 From Coonawarra, Barossa Valley,
McLaren Vale and Padthaway, matured for 20 months in new American hogsheads.
No-one could seriously suggest that 707 should be matured in French oak, any
more than they could suggest it of Grange. It is a product of its time, and has
to be honoured for what it is: a very, very good, full-bodied Australian dry red.
14.5% alc. **Rating** 95 **To** 2040 $500

Bin 2 Shiraz Mataro 2015 The bouquet is harmonious, the oak and tannin
contributions second to that of the purple and black fruits. The components come
through the medium-bodied palate with intent, and the wine has a very long
future. 14.5% alc. **Rating** 94 **To** 2029 $35

ȲȲȲȲȲ **Bin 150 Marananga Shiraz 2015 Rating** 92 **To** 2030 $100
Bin 311 Tumbarumba Chardonnay 2016 Rating 91 **To** 2023 $45

Penfolds Magill Estate   ★★★★★

78 Penfold Road, Magill, SA 5072 **Region** Adelaide
T (08) 8301 5569 www.penfolds.com **Open** 7 days 9–6
Winemaker Peter Gago **Est.** 1844 **Dozens** NFP **Vyds** 5.2ha
This is the birthplace of Penfolds, established by Dr Christopher Rawson Penfold in 1844;
his house is still part of the immaculately maintained property. It includes 5.2ha of precious
shiraz vines used to make Magill Estate Shiraz, along with the original and subsequent winery
buildings, most still in operation or in museum condition. In May 2015, Penfolds unveiled
the redevelopment of Magill Estate with the opening of a new cellar door (where visitors can
taste Grange by the glass) and the Magill Estate Kitchen, a casual dining environment with a
grazing menu built on local and fresh ingredients and meant for sharing. The much-awarded
Magill Estate Restaurant, with its panoramic views of the city, remains a temple for sublime
food and wine matching. Exports to all major markets.

ȲȲȲȲȲ **Magill Estate Shiraz 2015** Matured for 18 months, 70% in new French oak,
30% in new American hogsheads. There is so much complexity, power, depth and
structure, it steps confidently outside the usually graceful but faintly apologetic
Magill Estate. In so doing, it also brings an utterly harmonious trifecta of fruit,
oak and tannins (in that order), all integral parts of a quite wonderful wine. Cork.
14.5% alc. **Rating** 97 **To** 2035 $130 ✪

Penley Estate   ★★★★★

McLeans Road, Coonawarra, SA 5263 **Region** Coonawarra
T (08) 8736 3211 www.penley.com.au **Open** 7 days 10–4
Winemaker Kate Goodman, Matt Tilby **Est.** 1988 **Dozens** 35 000 **Vyds** 111ha
In 1988, Kym, Ang and Bec Tolley joined forces to buy a block of land in Coonawarra.
'Penley' is an amalgamation of family names Penfold and Tolley, for the founders' mother was a
Penfold and their father a Tolley, both well known families in wine. In 2015 Ang and Bec took
full ownership of the company. They have made a number of changes, including installing
general manager Michael Armstrong and, even more importantly, appointing Kate Goodman
as winemaker. Behind the scenes, Ang's husband David Paxton, one of Australia's foremost
viticulturists, has been working as a consultant, with improvements in vineyard performance
already evident. In December '17, Penley opened another cellar door in the main street of
McLaren Vale. Exports to all major markets.

ȲȲȲȲȲ **Helios Coonawarra Cabernet Sauvignon 2015** The high-shouldered brown
glass bottle, with the far extreme of minimalist labelling (the statutory requirements

of vintage and alcohol on a detachable neck label), is doubtless calculated to attract discussion. So should the ravishing cabernet inside made by Yarra Valley winemaker Kate Goodman. It's only medium-bodied, but its intensity is on a scale seldom encountered. The cassis fruit is the ruby set within a necklace of bay leaf and superbly honed tannins. A vineyard bursting into song after 30 years of silence. Cork. 14.5% alc. **Rating** 98 **To** 2045 $100 ✪

Helios Coonawarra Cabernet Sauvignon 2016 All French oak, 60% new. 200 dozen made. Pure cabernet. Bold of fruit, assertive of tannin, laced with spice, muscular, commanding. Balanced, and with finish that extends into tomorrow. This will age and impress for as long as you want it to. Cork. 14.5% alc. **Rating** 97 **To** 2040 $100 CM ✪

ɣɣɣɣɣ **Steyning Coonawarra Cabernet Sauvignon 2015** It carries a sweet, toffeed warmth which, in the context of the wine's flamboyant display of dark chocolate and ground coffee flavours, doesn't seem out of place. Both balance and freshness have been tweaked in quality's favour, and tannin has a sweet, ripe sense of control to it. But you're still left wondering why the alcohol has been allowed to run so high. Screwcap. 15% alc. **Rating** 94 **To** 2034 $45 CM

Chertsey 2015 70% cabernet sauvignon, 20% cabernet franc, 10% merlot. French oak (40% new). It's not the deepest wine in the range, but chains of tannin pull it long. Tobacco, mint, tar and blackcurrant flavours – in that order of priority – create a wine of both substance and warmth. Screwcap. 15% alc. **Rating** 94 **To** 2030 $45 CM

ɣɣɣɣɣ **Argus Shiraz Cabernet Sauvignon Merlot Cabernet Franc 2016** Rating 93 To 2028 $20 CM ✪
Scottsburn Cabernet Shiraz 2015 Rating 93 To 2030 $45 CM
Atlas Shiraz 2016 Rating 92 To 2026 $20 CM ✪
Tolmer Cabernet Sauvignon 2016 Rating 92 To 2026 $30 CM
11 Barrels Shiraz 2016 Rating 91 To 2025 $35 CM
Timbrell Cabernet Shiraz Merlot 2016 Rating 91 To 2025 $30 CM
Phoenix Cabernet Sauvignon 2016 Rating 91 To 2027 $20 CM ✪
Gryphon Merlot 2016 Rating 90 To 2024 $20 CM ✪

Penna Lane Wines ★★★★

Lot 51 Penna Lane, Penwortham via Clare, SA 5453 **Region** Clare Valley
T 0403 462 431 **www**.pennalanewines.com.au **Open** Fri–Sun 11–5
Winemaker Peter Treloar, Chris Proud **Est.** 1998 **Dozens** 4500 **Vyds** 4.37ha
Penna Lane is located in the beautiful Skilly Valley, 10km south of Clare. The estate vineyard (shiraz, cabernet sauvignon and semillon) is at an elevation of 450m, which allows a long, slow ripening period, usually resulting in wines with intense varietal fruit flavours.

ɣɣɣɣɣ **Skilly Valley Riesling 2017** A neat mix of florals, hay and lime marmalade. It's taut; there's tension with the acidity across the palate. It will reward even more after a few years in bottle. Screwcap. 12% alc. **Rating** 92 **To** 2026 JF

Clare Valley Shiraz 2016 Attractive mid purple-red; really savoury and earthy with plenty of eucalyptus in the mix. It's medium-bodied with quite firm tannins and appealing intensity of flavours. Better in a few years' time. Screwcap. 14% alc. **Rating** 90 **To** 2028 JF

ɣɣɣɣ **Clare Valley Cabernet Sauvignon 2016** Rating 89 To 2028 JF

Penny's Hill ★★★★☆

281 Main Road, McLaren Vale, SA 5171 **Region** McLaren Vale
T (08) 8557 0800 **www**.pennyshill.com.au **Open** 7 days 10–5
Winemaker Alexia Roberts **Est.** 1988 **Dozens** 72 000 **Vyds** 44ha
Founded in 1988 by Tony and Susie Parkinson, Penny's Hill produces high quality shiraz (Footprint and Skeleton Key) from its close-planted McLaren Vale estate, which is also the

source of the Edwards Road Cabernet Sauvignon and The Experiment Grenache. Malpas Road and Goss Corner vineyards complete the estate holdings, providing fruit for Cracking Black Shiraz and Malpas Road Merlot. White wines (The Agreement Sauvignon Blanc and The Minimalist Chardonnay) are sourced from 'estates of mates' in the Adelaide Hills. Also produces the Black Chook and Thomas Goss brands. Penny's Hills cellars are located at the historic Ingleburne Farm, which also houses the award-winning The Kitchen Door restaurant and Red Dot Gallery. The wines are noted for their distinctive red dots on the bottles. Exports to all major markets.

🍷🍷🍷🍷🍷 **Footprint McLaren Vale Shiraz 2016** Matured in French barriques (50% new) for 18 months. The bouquet and palate are in total agreement about the message this wine sends: black fruits, dark chocolate, firm tannins and, above all else, its complex savoury cast that runs from the first whiff through to the last sip. Screwcap. 14.5% alc. **Rating** 95 **To** 2031

The Agreement Single Vineyard Adelaide Hills Sauvignon Blanc 2017 A voluminous bouquet, bordering pungent, with lychee in the lead, then guava, and citrus pith following; then a palate with well above average intensity. A pretty smart sauvignon blanc, the acidity of the vintage putting the icing on the cake. Screwcap. 12.5% alc. **Rating** 94 **To** 2018 $22 ✪

The Minimalist Single Vineyard Adelaide Hills Chardonnay 2016 Bright straw-green; has significant bottle-developed flavour, but not at the expense of finesse. The fruit flavours are neatly balanced between citrus and stone fruit; white peach and grapefruit have dealt with the new oak in fine fashion. Screwcap. 13% alc. **Rating** 94 **To** 2021 $35

Skeleton Key McLaren Vale Shiraz 2016 This is classic McLaren Vale. Opaque garnet-red. Big, ripe and brooding – full of black fruit, tapenade, tar and cedar. The prominence of oak (40% new; 18 months) looms large. What it may lack in detail it makes up for in volume. Screwcap. 14.5% alc. **Rating** 94 **To** 2030 $40 DB

The Experiment McLaren Vale Grenache 2016 Pure grenache flavour, sweet and spicy at once, and at no point overdone, over-oaked or ever threatening. Delivered along the palate in svelte form and as a result, tremendously delicious. Screwcap. 14.5% alc. **Rating** 94 **To** 2025 $35 CM

🍷🍷🍷🍷🍷 **The Black Chook Shiraz 2016 Rating** 93 **To** 2031 $18 ✪
The Specialized McLaren Vale Shiraz Cabernet Merlot 2016 Rating 90 **To** 2030 $25 DB

Peos Estate ★★★★★

Graphite Road, Manjimup, WA 6258 **Region** Manjimup
T (08) 9772 1378 **www.**peosestate.com.au **Open** Not
Winemaker Coby Ladwig, Michael Ng **Est.** 1996 **Dozens** 12 000 **Vyds** 36.8ha
The Peos family has farmed in the west Manjimup district for over 50 years, with the third generation of four brothers developing the vineyard from 1996. There is a little over 35ha of vines including shiraz, merlot, chardonnay, cabernet sauvignon, sauvignon blanc, pinot noir and verdelho. Exports to China.

🍷🍷🍷🍷🍷 **Four Kings Manjimup Chardonnay 2017** The wine is positively vibrant, every part living up to the promise of that which has gone before. A fragrant bouquet with citrus blossom and white flowers, then a focused and long palate with grapefruit, Granny Smith apple and white peach, wafts of oak floating past, the acidity evident but not grippy. Screwcap. 13% alc. **Rating** 95 **To** 2029 $28 ✪

Four Kings Manjimup Pinot Noir 2017 21yo vines, whole berries, wild-fermented, 14–20 days on skins, matured for 10 months in French oak (30% new). Nigh-on perfect colour, deep but brilliantly clear. The straightforward approach to the vinification has given maximum results for this delicious cherry-filled pinot. Screwcap. 14% alc. **Rating** 95 **To** 2029 $28 ✪

Four Aces Manjimup Shiraz 2015 Excellent depth and clarity to the crimson-purple hue. Cool-grown shiraz in best style, with structure and texture to sustain it for many years. Sombre black fruits with notes of bramble, pepper and licorice run through to a long finish. Screwcap. 14.5% alc. **Rating** 95 **To** 2040 $35 ♦

♀♀♀♀♀ **Four Aces Manjimup Cabernet Sauvignon 2015 Rating** 93 **To** 2035 $35

Pepper Tree Wines   ★★★★★
86 Halls Road, Pokolbin, NSW 2320 **Region** Hunter Valley
T (02) 4909 7100 **www**.peppertreewines.com.au **Open** Mon–Fri 9–5, w'ends 9.30–5
Winemaker Gwyn Olsen **Est.** 1991 **Dozens** 50000 **Vyds** 172.1ha
Pepper Tree is part of a complex that contains The Convent guesthouse and Circa 1876 restaurant. It is owned by a company controlled by Dr John Davis, who also owns 50% of Briar Ridge. It sources the majority of its Hunter Valley fruit from its Tallavera Grove vineyard at Mt View, but also has premium vineyards at Orange, Coonawarra and Wrattonbully. The wines are exceptional value for money. The highly credentialled Gwyn Olsen (2012 dux, Advanced Wine Assessment course, AWRI; '14 Young Winemaker medal, *Gourmet Traveller WINE*; '15 Rising Star of the Year, Hunter Valley Legends Awards; '15 Len Evans Tutorial scholar) was appointed winemaker in '15. Exports to the UK, Canada, Denmark, Finland, Singapore and China.

♀♀♀♀♀ **Museum Release Single Vineyard Reserve Coquun Hunter Valley Shiraz 2007** Good colour; there is so much potential here it would be a pity not to keep a few bottles hidden for a special celebration. This wine was, is and will be a Hunter Valley classic. Its length is exceptional, but isn't driven by any one flavour, with spice in abundance, French oak playing a support role. Screwcap. 14.5% alc. **Rating** 98 **To** 2057 $90 ♦

♀♀♀♀♀ **Single Vineyard Premium Reserve Alluvius Hunter Valley Semillon 2017** From the famous Travena vineyard planted in 1920 on alluvial sandy soils. The freshness and sherbet-like zest of the lemon/lime flavours of the long palate put this into the big boys league of Hunter semillon. All it needs now is a minimum of 5 years' hands-off patience. Screwcap. 10.8% alc. **Rating** 95 **To** 2037 $35 ♦
Single Vineyard Premium Reserve The Gravels Wrattonbully Shiraz 2016 Supple, rich and juicy, with a flowing stream of black fruits studded with sparks of spice. The oak is integrated, the tannins fine, the finish long. Screwcap. 14.2% alc. **Rating** 95 **To** 2036 $44
Premium Reserve Single Vineyard 8R Wrattonbully Merlot 2016 8R is a newly imported clone from Bordeaux, and is likely to give the variety a good name once the public gets over the jujube flavours and wobbly tannins commonly found in merlot. This stands upright and proud with a delicious savoury swirl through the cassis and plum fruit, classy tannins giving it the certainty of a long, prosperous life. Screwcap. 14.1% alc. **Rating** 95 **To** 2033 $65
Premium Reserve Single Vineyard Block 21A Wrattonbully Cabernet Sauvignon 2016 Good colour. Has that particular mouthfeel of good Wrattonbully cabernet – it's not soft in the sense of weakness, but is plush and rich with fruit at well controlled alcohol levels. Here that plush fruit also has support from integrated oak and balanced, fine-grained tannins. Screwcap. 14.4% alc. **Rating** 95 **To** 2036 $65
Museum Release Single Vineyard Reserve Elderslee Road Wrattonbully Cabernet Sauvignon 2007 This is amiably moving out of adolescence towards maturity, where it will find a home for several decades. As it is now, blackcurrant, plum, cedar and spice make up the players in the band, fine-grained tannins beating a respectful drum. Screwcap. 14.8% alc. **Rating** 95 **To** 2042 $65
Limited Release Coonawarra Rose 2017 Produced from estate-grown merlot. Pale yet bright pink; the highly fragrant/perfumed bouquet flirts with spices, then stands aside for the crisp, lively palate to take centrestage, throwing in strawberry coulis as an afterthought. Snappy wine. Screwcap. 13.5% alc. **Rating** 94 **To** 2018 $24 ♦

Members Reserve Orange Pinot Shiraz 2015 A thoroughly attractive blend with very good colour and a seamless fusion of dark cherry fruit, hints of spice (with yet more to come), silky but persistent tannins, and an integrated touch of oak. Screwcap. 13.8% alc. **Rating** 94 **To** 2027 $25 ✪

Premium Reserve Calcare Single Vineyard Coonawarra Cabernet Sauvignon 2016 This is a wine that really expresses the synergy of the variety and the region. The cassis, green leaf and cedar on the bouquet are pure varietal aromas, with the underlying mint and limestone characters typical of Coonawarra. Full to medium-bodied, there's a fruit sweetness to the dark flavours rolling smoothly along the palate. The tannin is firm and dry. Screwcap. 14.4% alc. **Rating** 94 **To** 2030 $44 SC

ҭҭҭҭҭ **Stone Mountain Single Vineyard Premium Reserve Orange Riesling 2017 Rating** 93 **To** 2027 $38

Semillon Sauvignon Blanc 2017 Rating 93 **To** 2022 $19 ✪

Limited Release Orange Pinot Noir Rose 2017 Rating 93 **To** 2018 $24 ✪

Limited Release Orange Shiraz 2016 Rating 93 **To** 2026 $35 SC

Premium Reserve Single Vineyard Elderslee Road Wrattonbully Cabernet Sauvignon 2016 Rating 93 **To** 2031 $44

Museum Release Grand Reserve Strandlines Single Vineyard Wrattonbully Cabernet Shiraz 2007 Rating 93 **To** 2032 $65

Limited Release Semillon 2017 Rating 92 **To** 2030 $24 SC ✪

Limited Release Vermentino 2017 Rating 91 **To** 2022 $24

Wrattonbully Coonawarra Merlot 2015 Rating 91 **To** 2025 $19 ✪

Silenus Orange Chardonnay Pinot Noir 2014 Rating 91 $42

Limited Release Wrattonbully Chardonnay 2016 Rating 90 **To** 2020 $24

Petaluma   ★★★★★

254 Pfeiffer Road, Woodside, SA 5244 **Region** Adelaide Hills
T (08) 8339 9300 **www.**petaluma.com.au **Open** 7 days 10–5
Winemaker Andrew Hardy, Mike Mudge **Est.** 1976 **Dozens** 100 000 **Vyds** 240ha
The Petaluma range has been expanded beyond the core group of Croser sparkling, Clare Valley Riesling, Piccadilly Valley Chardonnay and Coonawarra Merlot. Newer arrivals of note include Adelaide Hills Viognier and Shiraz. The plantings in the Clare Valley, Coonawarra and Adelaide Hills provide a more than sufficient source of estate-grown grapes for the wines. A new winery and cellar door opened in 2015 on a greenfield site with views of Mt Lofty. In '17 Petaluma (along with all wine brands owned by Lion Nathan) was acquired by Accolade. Exports to all major markets.

ҭҭҭҭҭ **Tiers Piccadilly Valley Chardonnay 2016** The wine lives up to its reputation as one of Australia's greatest chardonnays, and you wonder why it isn't more frequently mentioned. The answer is at least partly due to the very small amounts judged by Petaluma to be up to its strict standards. Grapefruit leads the superb flavours of the palate, white peach in close attendance. The acidity is precise, the oak merely a means to an end. Screwcap. 14% alc. **Rating** 97 **To** 2031 $115 ✪

ҭҭҭҭҭ **B & V Vineyard Adelaide Hills Shiraz 2015** Good depth to the colour; a powerful, medium to full-bodied shiraz expressing place, variety and vinification to maximum benefit. The black cherry and satsuma plum fruit has the usual cool-grown exotic spices, and the tannins do their job to perfection. Screwcap. 14% alc. **Rating** 96 **To** 2035 $40 ✪

Hanlin Hill Clare Valley Riesling 2017 A very interesting and compelling riesling. Here the acidity of the vintage is contained within highly attractive fruit that is supple and mouthfilling – not words I use often in the context of riesling, especially when young. Screwcap. 12.5% alc. **Rating** 95 **To** 2029 $25 ✪

Piccadilly Valley Chardonnay 2016 The palate is straining on the leash with its choir of nectarine, white peach and lemony acidity. This more than compensates for the bouquet, which dissipates over time in the glass. Screwcap. 14% alc. **Rating** 95 **To** 2027 $46

Coonawarra Merlot 2015 Matured for 20 months in new Dargaud & Jaegle French oak. Undoubtedly one of the best merlots going around, but I do wonder at the lavish use of new oak. There is so much going for the wine I'll stick my neck out on the basis of the flood of cassis and plum fruit. Screwcap. 13.5% alc. **Rating** 95 $50

Croser Adelaide Hills Blanc de Blancs NV 100% chardonnay, made in the traditional method. A wine of purity and finesse, its low dosage a feature that allows grapefruit and Granny Smith apple full freedom of expression. No information was provided on the length of time on lees, nor the vintages used, but the quality of the wine makes these questions largely irrelevant. Diam. 13% alc. **Rating** 94 $28 ○

Croser Rose NV Pale pink. The strawberry-accented flavours are totally delicious, and the dosage is relatively low. On a hedonic scale, this is the best of the three Croser releases. Diam. 13% alc. **Rating** 94 $28

♀♀♀♀♀ **Evans Vineyard Coonawarra 2014** Rating 93 To 2032 SC
Croser Piccadilly Valley Pinot Noir Chardonnay 2013 Rating 93 $37
Croser Late Disgorged 2004 Rating 92 $55 TS
Croser NV Rating 92 $28
White Label Coonawarra Cabernet 2015 Rating 90 To 2035 $27

Peter Lehmann

Para Road, Tanunda, SA 5352 **Region** Barossa Valley
T (08) 8565 9555 **www**.peterlehmannwines.com **Open** Mon–Fri 9.30–5, w'ends & public hols 10.30–4.30
Winemaker Nigel Westblade **Est.** 1979 **Dozens** 750 000
The seemingly indestructible Peter Lehmann (the person) died in June 2013, which led to the end of the Lehmann family's minor ownership in the company. The Hess Group of California had acquired control in '03 (leaving part of the capital with the Lehmann family), but a decade later it became apparent that Hess wished to quit its holding. Various suitors put their case forward, but Margaret Lehmann (Peter's widow) wanted ongoing family – not corporate – ownership. Casella was thus able to make the successful bid in November '14, followed by them also aquiring Brand's Laira in December '15. Exports to the UK, the US and Canada.

♀♀♀♀♀ **THE Barossan Shiraz 2015** Curious marketing. Comes in a deluxe heavy bottle with a challenging foil label and a theme suggesting this is the peak of Barossa Valley shiraz. It's not that, but it's an impressive wine at the price, full-bodied but not porty or extractive. Blackberry and blood plum fruits, balanced oak and massaged tannins tick all the boxes. Screwcap. 14.5% alc. **Rating** 95 To 2035 $24 ○
H&V Barossa Valley Shiraz 2016 A glorious purple-black hue – as dark as the fruits you can taste in the wine. They're mixed with chocolate and licorice, and all manner of spices, especially oak-derived ones. Fleshy and ripe on the fuller bodied palate, yet quite buoyant with powerful velvety tannins. In the zone, on form and a ripper price. Screwcap. 14.5% alc. **Rating** 94 To 2026 $25 JF ○

♀♀♀♀♀ **Portrait Eden Valley Riesling 2017** Rating 93 To 2027 $18 JF ○
Wigan Eden Valley Riesling 2013 Rating 93 To 2022 $35 JF
Margaret Barossa Semillon 2012 Rating 93 To 2019 $26 JF ○
8 Songs Barossa Shiraz 2014 Rating 93 To 2032 $45 JF
Stonewell Barossa Shiraz 2014 Rating 93 To 2030 $100 JF
Portrait Barossa Shiraz 2016 Rating 91 To 2025 $18 JF ○
Mentor Barossa Cabernet 2014 Rating 91 To 2024 $45 JF
Portrait Barossa Shiraz 2015 Rating 90 To 2022 $19 CM ○
Futures Barossa Shiraz 2015 Rating 90 To 2026 $26 JF

Petersons

Mount View Road, Mount View, NSW 2325 **Region** Hunter Valley
T (02) 4990 1704 **www**.petersonswines.com.au **Open** Mon–Sat 9–5, Sun 10–5
Winemaker Colin Peterson, Gary Reed **Est.** 1971 **Dozens** 15 000 **Vyds** 66ha
Ian and Shirley Peterson were among the early followers in the footsteps of Max Lake,
contributing to the Hunter Valley renaissance that has continued to this day. Grapegrowers
since 1971 and winemakers since '81, the second generation of their family, headed by Colin
Peterson, now manages the business. It has been significantly expanded to 16ha at Mount
View, with an additional 42ha vineyard in Mudgee (Glenesk) and an 8ha vineyard near
Armidale (Palmerston). Each site has its own cellar door.

Jamie's Mudgee Quatro 2015 Zinfandel, chambourcin, petit verdot and durif.
Trophy for Best Red Wine Not Cabernet or Shiraz at the Mudgee Wine Show
'17. It's a soft, somewhat gloopy wine with tar, licorice and raspberry jam flavours
surging through the palate. Alcohol thins and interrupts the finish. Cork. 16% alc.
Rating 90 **To** 2026 $60 CM

Pettavel

159 Muhlebach Road, Sutherlands Creek, Vic 3331 **Region** Geelong
T (03) 9988 7678 **www**.pettavel.net **Open** By appt
Winemaker Rob Dolan, Ray Nadeson **Est.** 1990 **Dozens** 17 200 **Vyds** 120ha
Platina Wines is owned by Pettavel Pty Ltd, which is in turn owned by the husband and
wife team of Lily Wang and William Hou. Their journey into wine commenced in the
1980s when they were in the US studying for MBA degrees. The Napa Valley caught
their imagination, leading to the long-term aim of having their own fully fledged wine
business. The next step was their decision to leave their successful careers in the US, and
in 2009 they worked with European winemakers to set up a winery in China. Around
the same time they started to look at purchasing premium vineyards in Australia. Their
first acquisition was the 55ha Pettavel vineyard in '11, followed by the 60ha Yarra Glen
vineyards in '13, and finally the 5ha Staughton Vale vineyard in '15. The wines from
Pettavel and Staughton Vale are made by the highly experienced Ray Nadeson, the Yarra
Valley wines made by Rob Dolan. Exports to Hong Kong and China.

Platina Yarra Valley Chardonnay 2016 Bight straw-green; a very interesting
chardonnay, planned from the ground up to provide an extra layer of varietal fruit
flavour from the vine. It has hallmark Yarra Valley white peach and grapefruit flesh
and zest, gaining power as the wine travels along the palate; grilled cashew and
cream appear as the very last burst of flavour on the finish and aftertaste. Screwcap.
13% alc. **Rating** 96 **To** 2031 $39 ◯
Platina Reserve Geelong Syrah 2016 Impressive from go to whoa. Bright
crimson-purple; spicy, peppery red fruits are the engine room for this energetic
and intense wine. It has captured all the needed flavour at modest alcohol, adding
another level to its appeal. Screwcap. 13% alc. **Rating** 95 **To** 2029 $39

Platina Yarra Valley Pinot Noir 2016 Rating 93 **To** 2025 $39
Platina Reserve Yarra Valley Cabernet 2016 Rating 92 **To** 2031 $39
Platina Geelong Riesling 2017 Rating 90 **To** 2023 $36

Pewsey Vale

Eden Valley Road, Eden Valley, SA 5353 **Region** Eden Valley
T (08) 8561 3200 **www**.pewseyvale.com **Open** By appt
Winemaker Louisa Rose **Est.** 1847 **Dozens** 20 000 **Vyds** 65ha
Pewsey Vale was a famous vineyard established in 1847 by Joseph Gilbert, located at high
altitude in the Eden Valley. It was appropriate that when the Hill-Smith family began the
renaissance of the Eden Valley plantings in 1961, it should do so by purchasing Pewsey Vale
and establishing 50ha of riesling. The riesling also benefited from being the first wine to be
bottled with a Stelvin screwcap, in '77. While public reaction forced the abandonment of

the initiative for almost 20 years, Pewsey Vale never lost faith in the technical advantages of the closure. Exports to all major markets.

🍷🍷🍷🍷🍷 **Prima Single Vineyard Estate Eden Valley Riesling 2017** Extensive trials preceded the first vintage in '07. Super-intense lime juice flavours reflect this vintage and the brilliant balance between 22g/l residual sugar and 8.4g/l titratable acidity. Screwcap. 9.5% alc. **Rating** 96 **To** 2032 $28 ❍

1961 Block Riesling 2017 The first release from the 56yo vines. It has the precision, length and balance of the best of the Contours; crisp acidity lifts the finish and aftertaste. The drink-to date 20 years hence is not fanciful. Screwcap. 12.5% alc. **Rating** 95 **To** 2037 $32 ❍

Pewsey Vale Vineyard Riesling 2017 Louisa Rose's description of soft acidity is apt, as it is buried in the palate, the fruit more lemon than lime, the wine already dangerously delicious. History is likely to make my points appear miserly. **Rating** 94 **To** 2037

The Contours Museum Reserve Single Vineyard Estate Eden Valley Riesling 2013 Out of childhood and into adolescence with confidence built on the balance the wine has achieved. The aromas and flavours are all citrus-related, acidity neatly aligned with its allies. Screwcap. 12% alc. **Rating** 94 **To** 2028 $38

Pfeiffer Wines

167 Distillery Road, Wahgunyah, Vic 3687 **Region** Rutherglen
T (02) 6033 2805 **www.**pfeifferwines.com.au **Open** Mon–Sat 9–5, Sun 10–5
Winemaker Chris Pfeiffer, Jen Pfeiffer **Est.** 1984 **Dozens** 20 000 **Vyds** 32ha
Family-owned and run, Pfeiffer Wines occupies one of the historic wineries (built in 1880) that abound in northeast Victoria, and which is worth a visit on this score alone. Both hitherto and into the future, Pfeiffer's muscats, topaques and other fortified wines are a key part of the business. In 2012 Chris Pfeiffer was awarded an Order of Australia Medal for his services to the wine industry. He celebrated his 45th vintage in '18, well and truly setting the scene for his supremely gifted daughter Jen to assume the chief winemaking role. Her arrival has dramatically lifted the quality of the table wines, led by the reds. Exports to the UK, the US, Canada, Belgium, Malaysia, Singapore and China.

🍷🍷🍷🍷🍷 **Rare Rutherglen Muscat NV** Sheer quality, hands down. Intense, fluid and seductive, and noteworthy for its exquisite balance too. A parade of flavours and textures, a perfect mix of bass and treble notes, and soaring length. 500ml. Screwcap. 17.5% alc. **Rating** 97 CM

🍷🍷🍷🍷🍷 **Rare Rutherglen Topaque NV** It has a great deal to say and it says it with erudition. Fruit bread, toasted and slathered with fresh honey; glace cherries studded through tea leaves and cinnamon tea cake; leatherwood and raisins. Fresh. Stunning. 500ml. Screwcap. 17.5% alc. **Rating** 96 $125 CM

Grand Rutherglen Topaque NV A perfect example of rancio characters being put to good use. This has intensity, length, light and shade, colour and dramatic movement. Fresh, candied notes are the perfect complement to the wine's roasted, leathery, malty depths. And then those rancio notes help to lift and lengthen. 500ml. Screwcap. 17.5% alc. **Rating** 96 CM

Grand Rutherglen Muscat NV Strong flavour but impeccably well balanced. It's a wine of calm intensity: chocolate, spice, rosewater, leather and malt. Intensely sweet but it keeps moving; it keeps refreshing itself, and so too your palate. A belter of a wine. 500ml. Screwcap. 17.5% alc. **Rating** 96 CM

Rare Rutherglen Tawny NV Fresh with fruit, slippery with vanilla, complex, layered, exuberant; all that and more. Overt cherry notes lend it a distinctive persona. It smells exotic; it tastes like a delicacy. 500ml. Screwcap. 20% alc. **Rating** 95 CM

Classic Rutherglen Topaque NV Remarkable how different this is to the base 'Rutherglen' release. It's like moving over to a different flavour chart. This is malty, honeyed in a leatherwood way, volatile, and as much of green tea as black. Overall

intensity kicks up a level too. Elegance takes a back seat to personality. 500ml.
Screwcap. 17.5% alc. **Rating** 94 $30 CM ✪
Classic Rutherglen Muscat NV Again the colour is stunning.Vividly inviting.
It tastes of cherry syrup and raisins, sweet spices and malt. It's as fluid as it is
delicious. And it's long. 500ml. Screwcap. 17.5% alc. **Rating** 94 $30 CM ✪

ℙℙℙℙℙ **Shiraz 2016 Rating** 93 To 2026 $25 CM ✪
Rutherglen Topaque NV Rating 93 CM
Riesling 2017 Rating 92 To 2024 $20 CM ✪
Gamay 2017 Rating 92 To 2021 $18 CM ✪
Cabernet Sauvignon 2016 Rating 92 To 2028 CM
Tempranillo 2016 Rating 92 To 2027 $25 CM ✪
Durif 2015 Rating 92 To 2035 $33 CM

Phaedrus Estate   ★★★★☆

220 Mornington-Tyabb Road, Moorooduc,Vic 3933 **Region** Mornington Peninsula
T (03) 5978 8134 **www**.phaedrus.com.au **Open** W'ends & public hols 11–5
Winemaker Ewan Campbell, Maitena Zantvoort **Est.** 1997 **Dozens** 3000 **Vyds** 2.5ha
Since Maitena Zantvoort and Ewan Campbell established Phaedrus Estate, they have gained a
reputation for producing premium cool-climate wines. Their winemaking philosophy brings
art and science together to make wines showing regional and varietal character with minimal
winemaking interference. The vineyard includes 1ha of pinot noir and 0.5ha each of pinot
gris, chardonnay and shiraz. Exports to Hong Kong.

ℙℙℙℙℙ **Single Vineyard Reserve Mornington Peninsula Pinot Noir 2016**
Following a wild-yeast ferment, extraction was carried out by foot and pigeage.
Thereafter, an extended post-fermentation maceration to attenuate the tannins,
and boy, does it work! Sarsaparilla, dark cherry and orange-rind amaro; the tannins
like chiffon. Still forceful and in the mould of Pommard and possibly Corton, this
is beguiling, soulful gear. Screwcap. 13.9% alc. **Rating** 95 To 2028 $45 NG

ℙℙℙℙℙ **Mornington Peninsula Chardonnay 2017 Rating** 93 To 2023 $26 NG ✪
Mornington Peninsula Pinot Noir 2016 Rating 93 To 2024 $26 NG ✪
Single Vineyard Reserve Mornington Peninsula Shiraz 2016 Rating 93
To 2024 $45 NG
Mornington Peninsula Fiano 2017 Rating 92 To 2022 $26 NG
Mornington Peninsula Shiraz 2016 Rating 91 To 2022 $26 NG

Philip Shaw Wines   ★★★★★

100 Shiralee Road, Orange, NSW 2800 **Region** Orange
T (02) 6362 0710 **www**.philipshaw.com.au **Open** 7 days 11–5
Winemaker Daniel Shaw **Est.** 1989 **Dozens** 25 000 **Vyds** 47ha
Philip Shaw, former chief winemaker of Rosemount Estate and then Southcorp, became
interested in the Orange region in 1985. In '88 he purchased the Koomooloo vineyard and
began extensive plantings, the varieties including shiraz, merlot, pinot noir, sauvignon blanc,
cabernet franc, cabernet sauvignon and viognier. Son Daniel has joined in the winery, at a
time when the quality of the portfolio is going from strength to strength. Exports to the UK,
Norway, Finland, the Philippines, Indonesia, Hong Kong, China and NZ.

ℙℙℙℙℙ **No. 5 Orange Cabernet Sauvignon 2015** Both the palate and bouquet show
beautifully pure varietal character, with blackcurrant, black olive and green herbs
to the fore, and savoury notes of cedar, lanolin and tobacco in support. No doubt
oak plays a big part in all this, but it's cabernet that steals the show. Screwcap.
13.8% alc. **Rating** 95 To 2027 $75 SC
No. 11 Orange Chardonnay 2016 The elements of citrus and stone fruit
within the aromas and flavours are typically regional and varietal, with the oak
contributing spiciness and a nutty, savoury complexity. Creamy mouthfeel and
texture are a feature, with grapefruit-like acidity and fruit sweetness lingering

in the aftertaste. A polished style with the Philip Shaw thumbprint clear to see. Screwcap. 12.8% alc. **Rating** 94 **To** 2021 $35 SC

No. 89 Orange Shiraz 2016 Shows quite upfront whole-bunch influence with savoury, gamey notes and a liberal dose of cool-climate white pepper. Medium-bodied, but plenty of flesh in the flavours of ripe red and black fruits. Tannins are velvety and well judged. Good wine. Screwcap. 13.8% alc. **Rating** 94 **To** 2028 $50 SC

ТТТТ♀ **Experimenting Orange Chardonnay Block 12 2015** Rating 93 **To** 2022 $25 SC ○
No. 8 Orange Pinot Noir 2016 Rating 93 **To** 2025 $40 SC
Experimenting Orange Shiraz Whole Bunch 2015 Rating 93 **To** 2025 $60 SC
The Idiot Orange Shiraz 2016 Rating 92 **To** 2025 $22 SC ○
The Gardener Orange Pinot Gris 2017 Rating 90 **To** 2019 $22 SC
Pink Billy Orange Saignee 2017 Rating 90 **To** 2020 $25 SC

Piano Piano

852 Beechworth-Wangaratta Road, Everton Upper, Vic 3678 **Region** Beechworth
T (03) 5727 0382 **www**.pianopiano.com.au **Open** By appt
Winemaker Marc Scalzo **Est.** 2001 **Dozens** 1500 **Vyds** 4.6ha
'Piano piano' means 'slowly slowly' in Italian, and this is how Marc Scalzo and wife Lisa Hernan have approached the development of their business. Marc has a degree in oenology from CSU, many years' practical experience as a winemaker with Brown Brothers, and vintage experience with Giaconda and John Gehrig, and in NZ with Seresin Estate and Delegat's. In 1997 they planted 2.6ha of merlot, cabernet sauvignon, tempranillo and touriga nacional on their Brangie vineyard in the King Valley; they followed up with 1.2ha of chardonnay (2006) and 0.8ha of shiraz ('08) on their Beechworth property.

ТТТТТ **Sophie's Block Beechworth Chardonnay 2016** There's no denying the glorious power of Beechworth chardonnay. Plenty of citrus and some white peach, but merely incidental here as this is playing a savoury tune. Creamy lees, roasted nuts, flint, and super oak flavours and integration (French barriques/hogsheads; 30% new). Eschewing mlf has kept this riper style compact and tight. Screwcap. 13.8% alc. **Rating** 95 **To** 2025 $42 JF
Henry's Block Beechworth Shiraz 2015 Its regional expression makes this a delicious wine that feels effortless. It starts with sweet red plums flecked with licorice, woodsy spices, pepper, and the fragrance of violets wafting in and out. There's a succulence, a brightness to the acidity, and some grip as the oak continues to settle. Screwcap. 13.5% alc. **Rating** 95 **To** 2026 $42 JF

Pier 10   ★★★★

10 Shoreham Road, Shoreham, Vic 3916 **Region** Mornington Peninsula
T (03) 5989 8849 **www**.pier10.com.au **Open** Wed–Sun 11–5, 7 days Dec–Jan
Winemaker Andrew Thomson **Est.** 1996 **Dozens** 2500 **Vyds** 3.8ha
Eric Baker and Sue McKenzie began the development of Pier 10 in 1996 while still working in Melbourne, with the aim of creating first a lifestyle, then perhaps a retirement business. Their vineyard is planted to pinot noir, chardonnay and pinot gris.

ТТТТТ **Mornington Peninsula Pinot Noir 2016** Good colour; the fragrant bouquet of spicy red fruits is picked up in a millisecond by the palate that expands to the same flavour bandwidth. It's lively and fresh, with purity an important signpost of a very good pinot. Screwcap. 14% alc. **Rating** 94 **To** 2029 $50
Heathcote Cabernet Sauvignon 2017 Both front and back labels specifically (but erroneously) state Mornington Peninsula as the region. It's a well made wine, with juicy cabernet varietal expression, firm but fine tannins, and a balanced palate. Screwcap. 13.5% alc. **Rating** 94 **To** 2032 $40

ТТТТ♀ **Barelli Mornington Peninsula Pinot Grigio 2017** Rating 93 **To** 2020 $25 ○

Pierrepoint Wines   ★★★★☆

271 Pierrepoint Road, Tarrington, Vic 3300 **Region** Henty
T 0439 476 198 **www**.pierrepointwines.com.au **Open** Most days 11–6
Winemaker Scott Ireland (Contract) **Est.** 1998 **Dozens** 450 **Vyds** 5ha
Pierrepoint was established by Andrew and Jennifer Lacey at 200m altitude on the foothills
of Mt Pierrepoint, between Hamilton and Tarrington. The predominantly red buckshot soils
of the vineyard are derived from ancient volcanic basalt, rich in minerals, and free-draining.
In all, 2ha each of pinot noir and pinot gris, and 1ha of chardonnay are planted on an ideal
north-facing slope.

♀♀♀♀♀ **Alexandra Chardonnay 2016** A richly flavoured, seamless chardonnay,
effortlessly melding melon, honeysuckle and stone-fruit flavours to cinnamon oak,
a welcome phenolic rail, and a nougat-nutty nourishment, derived from handy lees
work. This will grow in stature in the cellar mid-term, but is absolutely delicious
already. **Rating** 95 **To** 2024 NG

♀♀♀♀♀ **Nicks Pick Pinot Gris 2016** Rating 92 **To** 2026 NG
Pinot Noir 2016 Rating 91 **To** 2024 NG
Lacey Dessert Pinot Gris 2016 Rating 91 **To** 2022 NG

Pierro   ★★★★★

Caves Road, Wilyabrup via Cowaramup, WA 6284 **Region** Margaret River
T (08) 9755 6220 **www**.pierro.com.au **Open** 7 days 10–5
Winemaker Dr Michael Peterkin **Est.** 1979 **Dozens** 10 000 **Vyds** 7.85ha
Dr Michael Peterkin is one of the legion of Margaret River medical practitioner vignerons;
he married into the Cullen family for good measure. Pierro is renowned for its stylish white
wines, which often exhibit tremendous complexity; the Chardonnay can be monumental
in its weight and texture. That said, its red wines from favourable vintages can be every bit
as good. Exports to the UK, Denmark, Belgium, Russia, Malaysia, Indonesia, Hong Kong,
Singapore and Japan.

♀♀♀♀♀ **Reserve Margaret River Cabernet Sauvignon Merlot 2014** The extraction
levels on this set of Pierro wines are exemplary. The alcohols more balanced, too.
None is more suggestive of the savoury idyll for which they strive, than this. Red
and blackcurrant notes are brushed with sage ever so gently. The milk-chocolate
oak pillars are a mere adjunct. Persistent of flavour, long of finish, graceful.
Screwcap. 13.5% alc. **Rating** 95 **To** 2026 $81 NG
Margaret River Chardonnay 2016 An iconic wine in its shameless embrace of
flavour and ample texture. Ripe stone-fruit flavours billow across a core of toasted
hazelnut, nougat and cashew. Butterscotch, too, imparted by a combination of mlf,
partial wild yeast fermentation and well appointed oak. The acidity is just fresh
enough to taper the wine long. Screwcap. 13.5% alc. **Rating** 94 **To** 2022 $86 NG

♀♀♀♀♀ **Margaret River Cabernet Sauvignon VR 2013** Rating 93 **To** 2023 $120 NG
L.T.C. 2017 Rating 92 **To** 2025 $34 NG

Pig in the House   ★★★★

Balcombe Road, Billimari, NSW 2804 **Region** Cowra
T 0427 443 598 **www**.piginthehouse.com.au **Open** Fri–Sun 11–5 by appt
Winemaker Antonio D'Onise **Est.** 2002 **Dozens** 3000 **Vyds** 25ha
Jason and Rebecca O'Dea established their vineyard (7ha of shiraz, 6ha of cabernet
sauvignon, 5ha of merlot, 4.5ha of chardonnay and 2.5ha of sauvignon blanc) on a block
of land formerly used as a home for 20 free-range pigs. Given its prior use, one would
imagine the vines would grow lustily, and it is no surprise that organic certification has been
attained. The O'Deas have in fact taken the process several steps further, using biodynamic
preparations and significantly reducing all sprays. The wines made are good advertisements
for organic/biodynamic farming. Exports to Japan and China.

ŢŢŢŢ♀ **Organic Chardonnay 2016** Most of this wine was fermented/matured in stainless steel, only 15% seeing oak. It presents bright, fresh, lemon sorbet characters, gradually adding breadth via notes of rose oil and talc. It's a mouthwatering style to say the least, but the wine's elegance and length are its real quality markers. Screwcap. 13.5% alc. **Rating** 91 **To** 2021 $25 CM
Organic Rose 2017 Pale copper. The wine saw the inside of old oak and the effect has been positive. It tastes of raspberry, strawberry and citrus and has plenty of zip. Fresh, aromatic and just a little exotic. There's a gentle texture element too; almost a touch of grip. Nice style. Nice wine. Screwcap. 12.5% alc. **Rating** 91 **To** 2019 $25 CM
Organic Chardonnay 2017 Fresh citrus, pear and white peach flavours are given a light touch of spicy/toasty oak. It's clean, crisp, light in colour and lively in the mouth, a kind of 'sun and steel' style with versatility written all over it. Screwcap. 13% alc. **Rating** 90 **To** 2021 $25 CM
Organic Cabernet Sauvignon 2016 Inviting cabernet. Sweet-fruited and lively, all redcurrant, licorice, wood spice and tobacco. All the flavours flow here in easy-going fashion, the aim to please, and the best time to enjoy it right now. Screwcap. 14.5% alc. **Rating** 90 **To** 2023 $20 CM ✪

Pike & Joyce   ★★★★☆

730 Mawson Road, Lenswood, SA 5240 **Region** Adelaide Hills
T (08) 8389 8102 **www**.pikeandjoyce.com.au **Open** Not
Winemaker Neil Pike, Steve Baraglia **Est.** 1998 **Dozens** 5000 **Vyds** 18.5ha
This is a partnership between the Pike family, of Clare Valley fame, and the Joyce family, who have been orchardists at Lenswood for over 100 years, and also have extensive operations in the Riverland. Andrew Pike together with wife Cathy and their family have established a vineyard planted to sauvignon blanc (5.9ha), pinot noir (5.73ha), pinot gris (3.22ha), chardonnay (3.18ha) and semillon (0.47ha). The wines are made at Pikes (see separate entry). Exports to the UK, China and other major markets.

ŢŢŢŢŢ **The Kay Reserve Adelaide Hills Chardonnay 2016** There is an extra dimension of flinty intensity to this, imparting a Meyer lemon–peel soprano pitch to the apricot and nectarine notes. Mineral. Pungent. Superb reductive handling. The oak is an accent, imparting complexity and bass, nestled amid the goings-on. This is very long and not an ounce of it is out of place. Screwcap. 13% alc. **Rating** 96 **To** 2026 $55 NG ✪
Sirocco Adelaide Hills Chardonnay 2016 This is very smart chardonnay, moulded in the crunchy, mineral-clad, contemporary Australian mould. Plenty of oatmeal and roasted nuts toned by lees handling, too, conferring breadth and detail to the stone-fruit swing. Screwcap. 13.5% alc. **Rating** 94 **To** 2022 $36 NG

ŢŢŢŢ♀ **W.J.J. Reserve Adelaide Hills Pinot Noir 2016** Rating 93 To 2025 $55 NG
L'Optimiste Shiraz 2016 Rating 93 To 2024 NG
Beurre Bosc Adelaide Hills Pinot Gris 2017 Rating 92 To 2020 $28 NG
Vue du Nord Adelaide Hills Pinot Noir 2016 Rating 92 To 2022 $36 NG
Descente Sauvignon Blanc 2017 Rating 91 To 2019 $26 NG
Methode Cuve Adelaide Hills Sparkling Rose NV Rating 91 $28 NG

Pikes   ★★★★★

Polish Hill River Road, Sevenhill, SA 5453 **Region** Clare Valley
T (08) 8843 4370 **www**.pikeswines.com.au **Open** 7 days 10–4
Winemaker Neil Pike, Steve Baraglia **Est.** 1984 **Dozens** 35000 **Vyds** 73ha
Owned by the Pike brothers (Andrew was for many years the senior viticulturist with Southcorp, and Neil was a winemaker at Mitchell). Pikes now has its own winery, with Neil presiding. In most vintages its white wines, led by riesling, are the most impressive. Planting of the vineyards has been an ongoing affair, with a panoply of varietals, new and traditional. The Merle is Pikes' limited-production flagship riesling. Exports to the UK, the US, China and other major markets.

ΨΨΨΨΨ The Merle Clare Valley Riesling 2017 Bright quartz and glowing. 'Classic' written large. Fresh, fragrant with citrus blossom, slatey and enticing. Pure, long, mouthwatering and effortless. It is doubtless that years under its belt will improve it even further. Lovely purist stuff. Screwcap. 12% alc. **Rating** 97 **To** 2032 $45 DB ◯

ΨΨΨΨΨ Traditionale Clare Valley Riesling 2017 Both estate and contract-grown, this is the 33rd consecutive release, and also from one of the great Clare Valley vintages (joining '02, '05, '09 and '12). Crisp acidity and the faintest hint of spritz lift the palate from the word go; the freshness of lime and lemon fruit is underwritten by minerally notes ex the acidity. Screwcap. 11.5% alc. **Rating** 96 **To** 2032 $28 ◯
Premio 2017 Pale glowing green. Not your classic white blend, but with waxy fiano notes sitting astride fragrant gris florals; it all seems to work, because it is crafted carefully and balanced. Just enough texture, line and judged citrus acidity to make it quite delicious. Screwcap. 12.5% alc. **Rating** 94 **To** 2022 $34 DB
Eastside Clare Valley Shiraz 2015 From Pikes' Polish Hill River vineyard, hence 'Eastside'. The texture of the palate is a highlight, with spicy/savoury notes thatched with blackberry and satsuma fruit. It is like a pair of long-worn and very comfortable slippers. Screwcap. 14% alc. **Rating** 94 **To** 2035 $28 ◯
The E.W.P. Clare Valley Shiraz 2015 Spearmint, plum, coffee cream and earth are served up in impressive volume. There's a real meatiness to this full-bodied red. It's braced with tannin but for all its heft, it feels well balanced. We're in very good territory here. Screwcap. 14% alc. **Rating** 94 **To** 2034 $65 CM
The Hill Block Clare Valley Cabernet 2015 It has a certain command. This is a sturdy, upstanding wine with rich blackcurrant, tar and peppercorn flavours booming through the palate, and ample, muscular tannin roping it all in. A long life awaits. Screwcap. 14% alc. **Rating** 94 **To** 2035 $65 CM

ΨΨΨΨΨ Clare Hills Riesling 2017 **Rating** 93 **To** 2025 $17 CM ◯
Impostores Clare Valley Savignan 2017 **Rating** 93 **To** 2021 $21 CM ◯
Luccio Clare Valley Fiano 2017 **Rating** 92 **To** 2018 $20 CM ◯
Eastside Clare Valley Shiraz 2015 **Rating** 92 **To** 2025 $28 CM
Los Companeros Shiraz Tempranillo 2015 **Rating** 92 **To** 2023 $20 CM ◯
Valley's End Clare Valley Sauvignon Blanc Semillon 2017 **Rating** 91 **To** 2021 $20 CM ◯
The Assemblage Clare Valley Shiraz Grenache Mourvedre 2015 **Rating** 91 **To** 2024 $23 CM ◯
Olga Emmie Clare Valley Riesling 2017 **Rating** 91 **To** 2025 $22 ◯
Luccio Clare Valley Sangiovese Rose 2017 **Rating** 90 **To** 2018 $20 CM ◯
Premio Clare Valley Sangiovese 2016 **Rating** 90 **To** 2025 $38 CM

Pimpernel Vineyards   ★★★★★

6 Hill Road, Coldstream, Vic 3770 **Region** Yarra Valley
T 0457 326 436 **www.**pimpernelvineyards.com.au **Open** Fri–Sat & public hols 11–5
Winemaker Damien Archibald, Mark Horrigan **Est.** 2001 **Dozens** 3000 **Vyds** 6ha
Lilydale-based cardiologist Mark Horrigan's love affair with wine started long before he had heard about either the Yarra Valley or his family's links, centuries ago, to Condrieu, France. He is a descendant of the Chapuis family, his ultimate ancestors buried in the Church of St Etienne in 1377. In a cosmopolitan twist, his father came from a Welsh mining village, but made his way to university and found many things to enjoy, not the least wine. When the family moved to Australia in 1959, wine remained part of everyday life and, as Mark grew up in the '70s, the obsession passed from father to son. In 2001 he and wife Fiona purchased a property in the Yarra Valley on which they have built a (second) house, planted a vineyard, and erected a capacious winery designed by WA architect Peter Moran. In the course of doing so, they became good friends of near neighbour, the late Dr Bailey Carrodus; some of the delphic labelling of Pimpernel's wines is pure Carrodus. Exports to the UK and Singapore.

ΨΨΨΨΨ Grouch 2016 Estate-grown shiraz co-fermented with 6% marsanne. The bright colour comes as no surprise, nor does the spicy complexity of the bouquet. The intensity is ratcheted up further on the imposing palate with its mouthwatering fusion of black fruits, herbs and admirable tannins drawing out a long, lingering finish. The surprise? 14.8% alcohol. Diam. **Rating** 97 **To** 2046 $80 ❍

🍷🍷🍷🍷 **Yarra Valley Pinot Noir One 2016** Clones 114, 115 and 777 (especially 777) are early ripening, and the north-facing slope receives maximum sun. Into the bargain, the vintage was very warm and early, all leading to the success of the Pimpernel team in producing a wine of this quality. It is mouthfilling and juicy, very much in a now-or-later consumption pattern. Diam. 14.3% alc. **Rating** 95 **To** 2031 $50
Yarra Valley Rose 2017 The Rhône Valley comes to the Yarra Valley with this 50% grenache, 28% shiraz and 22% mourvedre blend. The floral bouquet brings mandarin into play, an unusual citrus scent for table wine, but it's there in force before yielding to pink grapefruit – unusual again – on the brisk palate, acidity also on parade. Diam. 13% alc. **Rating** 94 **To** 2020 $25 ❍
Yarra Valley Shiraz 2016 Co-fermented with 2% viognier and some ripe stalks added back to the must; 18 months in French oak (30% new). Here the palate does show its alcohol, ameliorated by the lingering dark cherry fruit flavours that continue into the aftertaste. Diam. 15% alc. **Rating** 94 **To** 2031 $50

🍷🍷🍷🍷🍸 **Yarra Valley Chardonnay 2016 Rating** 91 **To** 2021 $50

Pindarie

946 Rosedale Road, Gomersal, SA 5352 **Region** Barossa Valley
T (08) 8524 9019 **www**.pindarie.com.au **Open** Mon–Fri 11–4, w'ends 11–5
Winemaker Peter Leske **Est.** 2005 **Dozens** 8000 **Vyds** 32.4ha
Owners Tony Brooks and Wendy Allan met at Roseworthy College in 1985. Tony was the sixth generation of farmers in SA and WA, and was studying agriculture; NZ-born Wendy was studying viticulture. On graduation Tony worked overseas managing sheep feedlots in Saudi Arabia, Turkey and Jordan, while Wendy worked for the next 12 years with Penfolds, commencing as a grower liaison officer and working her way up to become a senior viticulturist. She also found time to study viticulture in California, Israel, Italy, Germany, France, Portugal, Spain and Chile, working vintages and assessing vineyards for wine projects. In 2001 she completed a graduate diploma in wine business. The cellar door and Grain Store cafe (winner of Australian tourism awards in '13 and '14 as well as entering the SA Tourism Hall of Fame) has panoramic views. Exports to Taiwan and China.

🍷🍷🍷🍷🍷 **Schoff's Hill Barossa Valley Cabernet Sauvignon 2016** From the Schoff's Hill block on the Western Ridge. Shows crystal-clear varietal character, not always the case with Barossa cabernet. Dusty, herbal elements lead the way, but riper notes of blackcurrant build on the bouquet and juicy palate as the wine opens up. The tannins work well, with good integration of the fruit. Gold medal Adelaide Wine Show '17. Screwcap. 14% alc. **Rating** 95 **To** 2031 $35 ❍
Black Hinge Reserve Barossa Valley Shiraz 2016 Estate-grown, hand-picked/sorted, whole berries open-fermented, 13 days on skins, matured in French oak (25% new) for 16 months, 250 dozen made. Bright hue, although faintly turbid; the black fruits neatly structured and textured, the finish long and devoid of heavy extract and alcohol heat. Will cruise along for 15+ years. Cork. 15% alc. **Rating** 94 **To** 2033 $75
Black Hinge Reserve Barossa Valley Tempranillo 2016 If you are looking for an ultra-full-bodied tempranillo, go no further. This could kill a Spanish bull and provide the perfect wine and food match. Tempranillos as powerful as this can be kept in oak for 4+ years with repeated rackings, then blended with garnacha to make a topflight Rioja red wine with a 100-year life. Drinking this now is a challenge. Gold medal Alternative Varieties Australian Wine Show '17. Screwcap. 14.5% alc. **Rating** 94 **To** 2046 $50

🍷🍷🍷🍷🍸 **Western Ridge Shiraz 2016 Rating** 93 **To** 2031 $28 SC
Black Hinge Reserve Shiraz Cabernet 2016 Rating 92 **To** 2030 $75
The Risk Taker Tempranillo 2016 Rating 92 **To** 2026 $26

Pinelli Wines ★★★★

30 Bennett Street, Caversham, WA 6055 **Region** Swan District
T (08) 9279 6818 **www**.pinelliwines.com.au **Open** Mon–Sat 9–5, Sun & public hols 10–5
Winemaker Robert Pinelli, Daniel Pinelli **Est.** 1980 **Dozens** 17 000 **Vyds** 9.78ha
Domenic and Iolanda Pinelli emigrated from Italy in the mid-1950s, and it was not long
before Domenic was employed by Waldeck Wines, then one of the Swan Valley's more
important wineries. With the benefit of 20 years' experience gained at Waldeck, in '80 he
purchased a 2.8ha vineyard that had been established many years previously. It became
the site of the Pinelli family winery, cellar door and significantly expanded vineyard, with
cabernet sauvignon, colombard, merlot and shiraz. Son Robert graduated with a degree in
ocnology from Roseworthy in '87, and has been the winemaker at Pinelli for over 20 years.
His brother Daniel obtained a degree in civil engineering from the University of WA in '94,
but eventually the lure of the family winery became too strong, so he joined his brother in
2002 and obtained his oenology degree from CSU in '07. He graduated with distinction,
and was awarded the Domaine Chandon Sparkling Wine Award for best sparkling wine
production student.

ɷɷɷɷɷ **Reserve Vermentino 2017** Fresh as a daisy, the flavours led by citrus, and
impressively persistent. There's isn't a lot of volume here but it's more than
compensated for by the energy and drive of the palate. Screwcap. 12% alc.
Rating 90 **To** 2020 $18 CM ✪
Grand Tawny NV Average age of 20 years. Toffee, coffee, Christmas cake and
buttered toast. No issue with the volume of flavour and it's certainly well sustained
throughout, if never quite reaching the heights of Australia's best tawnies. Top gold
Swan Valley Wine Show '17. 375ml. Cork. 18.5% alc. **Rating** 90 $55 CM

Pipers Brook Vineyard ★★★★★

1216 Pipers Brook Road, Pipers Brook, Tas 7254 **Region** Northern Tasmania
T (03) 6382 7527 **www**.pipersbrook.com.au **Open** 7 days 10–5
Winemaker Brian Widstrand **Est.** 1974 **Dozens** 70 000 **Vyds** 194ha
The Pipers Brook empire has almost 200ha of vineyard supporting the Pipers Brook and
Ninth Island labels. Fastidious viticulture and winemaking, immaculate packaging and
enterprising marketing are a potent and effective blend. Pipers Brook operates two cellar
door outlets, one at the headquarters, the other at Strathlyn. It is owned by Belgian company
Kreglinger, which has also established the large Norfolk Rise winery and vineyard at Mount
Benson in SA. Exports to the UK, the US and other major markets.

ɷɷɷɷɷ **Riesling 2017** The floral bouquet of white flowers (lilies/hibiscus) and blossom
(apple/citrus) charts the path for the palate to follow. And don't think you've
discovered all that the wine has to offer until you've swallowed and licked your
lips. Screwcap. 13% alc. **Rating** 95 **To** 2029 $35 ✪
Rose 2017 No colour change – pure pink. The wine was 100% barrel-
fermented, followed by lees contact, and this has built texture and an upsurge in
both mouthfeel and fruit flavour. The magic baton of chief winemaker Jim Chatto
at work. Screwcap. 13.5% alc. **Rating** 95 **To** 2021
Kreglinger Vintage Brut 2007 Hand-picked in the early morning, whole-
bunch pressed, cool-fermented in tank and barrel, then with traditional method
in bottle. It is cruising along peacefully, its crisp acidity underpinning the richness
developed during 9 years on yeast lees prior to disgorgement. Spice and dried and
fresh fruits provide texture and flavour. Cork. 12.5% alc. **Rating** 95 $55
The Lyre Pinot Noir 2015 Has the feel of a flagship style. Plenty of impact
in the bouquet, with aromas of liqueur cherry, toasty oak, and gamey, herbal
characters. Rich and full-bodied on the palate (in the varietal context), the flavours
run through dark cherry to chocolatey oak to earthy spice, with firm acid/tannin
astringency taking over on the finish. Screwcap. 13.5% alc. **Rating** 94 **To** 2027 SC
Vintage Sparkling 2010 Still a pale, bright green (no pink or straw) that is very
welcoming, and it's not a blanc de blanc. It is long and crisp, with enough flesh on

the bone to satisfy you now or for years to come if properly cellared. Traditional method. Cork. 12.5% alc. **Rating** 94

♀♀♀♀♀ Sauvignon Blanc 2017 **Rating** 93 To 2021
Pinot Gris 2017 **Rating** 92 To 2020
Ninth Island Pinot Noir 2017 **Rating** 92 To 2024
New Certan Pinot Noir 2016 **Rating** 92 To 2023 $120
Ninth Island Sparkling NV **Rating** 92
Ninth Island Sparkling Rose NV **Rating** 91
Chardonnay 2017 **Rating** 90 To 2017
Ninth Island Rose 2017 **Rating** 90 To 2019

Pirathon

Suite 163, 79 Longueville Road, Lane Cove, NSW 2066 (postal) **Region** Barossa Valley
T (02) 8006 6987 **www**.pirathon.com **Open** Not
Winemaker Contract **Est.** 2005 **Dozens** 9000
Pirathon was formerly a brand owned by a group of tech-savvy entrepreneurs, with Troy Kalleske having a share of the business. He has now sold his share to the other partners. Pirathon is currently a one-variety wine company, focusing on full-bodied Barossa Valley shiraz grown in the north-western Barossa, encompassing the districts of Greenock, Moppa, Belvedere, Koonunga and Ebenezer. Each district contributes to the complexity of the wine. Ben Li heads the group, and it seems a fair assumption that future sales will be largely directed to China. Exports to all major markets.

♀♀♀♀♀ Barossa Valley Shiraz 2016 A densely packed and powerful wine, each parcel of grapes separately open-fermented then taken to new and used puncheons (from four countries). Deeply coloured and complex, the oak is presently flexing its muscles, with the ripe tannins, black fruits, dark chocolate and spices keeping a respectful distance. Screwcap. 14.5% alc. **Rating** 94 To 2030

Pirramimma

Johnston Road, McLaren Vale, SA 5171 **Region** McLaren Vale
T (08) 8323 8205 **www**.pirramimma.com.au **Open** Mon–Fri 10–4.30, w'ends & public hols 10.30–5
Winemaker Geoff Johnston **Est.** 1892 **Dozens** 50000 **Vyds** 91.5ha
A long-established family-owned company with outstanding vineyard resources, which it is using to full effect. A series of intense old vine varietals includes semillon, sauvignon blanc, chardonnay, shiraz, grenache, cabernet sauvignon and petit verdot, all fashioned without over-embellishment. Wines are released under several ranges: Pirramimma, Stock's Hill, White Label, ACJ, Katunga, Eight Carat and Gilded Lilly. Exports to all major markets.

♀♀♀♀♀ Ironstone McLaren Vale Shiraz 2015 A thick soup of plum-drenched flavour, toasty vanillan oak and choc-mint sprinkled over the top, nips of kirsch for good measure. A full-on red wine; dense, inky, mouthfilling. Ripe tannin steps in on the finish and pulls the load of flavour forward. Cork. 14.8% alc. **Rating** 95 To 2039 $50 CM
War Horse Shiraz 2015 A sweet, exaggerated style, but an undeniably powerful one. This has blackberry jam and fresh, cedary oak laid on, violet-like notes ramping the headiness yet more. Tannin struts through the wine; acid buzzes. It's a whopper with a bit of wow factor. Cork. 14.8% alc. **Rating** 95 To 2040 $80 CM

♀♀♀♀♀ Ironstone McLaren Vale GSM 2016 **Rating** 93 To 2026 $50 CM
McLaren Vale Cabernet Sauvignon 2015 **Rating** 91 To 2025 $30 CM
McLaren Vale Shiraz 2015 **Rating** 90 To 2025 $30 CM

Pizzini ★★★★☆

175 King Valley Road, Whitfield, Vic 3768 **Region** King Valley
T (03) 5729 8278 www.pizzini.com.au **Open** 7 days 10–5
Winemaker Joel Pizzini **Est.** 1980 **Dozens** 45 000 **Vyds** 88.3ha
Fred and Katrina Pizzini have been grapegrowers in the King Valley for over 30 years. Originally much of the grape production was sold, but today it is retained for the Pizzini brand. Pizzini's winemaking success has resulted in an increase in its vineyard holdings to almost 90ha, and an increase in production (with more to come). The hectareage of its alternative varieties speaks for itself: 13.3ha of prosecco, 3.22ha of brachetto, 2ha of colorino, 2ha of arneis, 1.5ha of piccolit, 1.3ha of verdicchio, 1.3ha of verduzzo and 0.43ha of trebbiano. Exports to the UK and Japan.

🍷🍷🍷🍷🍷 **Il Barone 2016** 53% cabernet sauvignon, 22% shiraz, 18% sangiovese, 7% nebbiolo, fermented separately and matured for 12 months in French oak before blending. The immense amount of work that went into this wine has been repaid. The colour is bright, as is the rainbow of red, purple and black aromas and flavours. This is not tannin or oak-driven; its heart beats vividly with fresh flavours to the very end. Screwcap. 13.8% alc. **Rating** 95 **To** 2026 $45
Forza di Ferro King Valley Sangiovese 2015 Matured for 14–18 months in French oak (15% new), plus a further 12 months in bottle before release. This is a rich and complex wine first and foremost, a varietal sangiovese second. Cloves, nutmeg, rosemary and Chinese five-spice; also some delicious and pure red fruits, and fine tannins completing the story. It grows and grows on you. Screwcap. 13.8% alc. **Rating** 94 **To** 2025 $55

🍷🍷🍷🍷🍷 **King Valley Riesling 2017 Rating** 93 **To** 2027 $18 ❂
King Valley Pinot Grigio 2017 Rating 90 **To** 2021 $21 ❂
King Valley Shiraz 2016 Rating 90 **To** 2023 $25
Pietra Rossa King Valley Sangiovese 2015 Rating 90 **To** 2020 $28
King Valley Prosecco 2017 Rating 90 **To** 2018 $21 ❂

Plan B Wines ★★★★

Freshwater Drive, Margaret River, WA 6285 (postal) **Region** Great Southern/Margaret River/Geographe
T 0413 759 030 www.planbwines.com **Open** Not
Winemaker Bill Crappsley, Vanessa Carson **Est.** 2005 **Dozens** 40 000 **Vyds** 20ha
Plan B is a joint venture between Terry Chellappah, wine consultant, Bill Crappsley, a veteran winemaker/consultant, and Andrew Blythe. The shiraz is sourced from Bill's Calgardup vineyard, and the remaining wines from Arlewood; all are single vineyard releases. Recently Plan B has been notably successful under Terry's management, with significant increases in production. In 2014 Bill was awarded the Jack Mann Memorial Medal for significant services to the WA wine industry, coinciding with his 50 years of winemaking in WA. He has also won the Di Cullen Award (in '07), and the George Mulgrue Award (in 1999), both recognising his services to the industry. Exports to all major markets.

🍷🍷🍷🍷🍷 **DR Frankland River Riesling 2017** Light straw-green; a brilliantly fresh and dry riesling that skips across the palate in a flash, yet imprints the aftertaste with lingering flavours of citrus and green apple. The 2.2g/l of residual sugar is more than balanced by the fruit and acidity. Drink whenever the mood takes you. Screwcap. 12.9% alc. **Rating** 94 **To** 2025 $26 ❂

🍷🍷🍷🍷🍷 **OD Frankland River Riesling 2017 Rating** 93 **To** 2027 $23 ❂
ST Frankland River Shiraz 2014 Rating 92 **To** 2024 $23 ❂
MR Frankland River Modern Red 2017 Rating 90 **To** 2020 $26
GT Cabernet Sauvignon Sangiovese 2016 Rating 90 **To** 2023 $23

Plantagenet   ★★★★★

Albany Highway, Mount Barker, WA 6324 **Region** Mount Barker
T (08) 9851 3111 **www**.plantagenetwines.com **Open** 7 days 10–4.30
Winemaker Luke Eckerseley **Est.** 1974 **Dozens** 30000 **Vyds** 130ha
Plantagenet was established by Tony Smith, who continues to be involved in its management over 40 years later, notwithstanding that the business has been owned by Lionel Samson & Son for many years. He planted five vineyards: Bouverie in 1968 (sold in 2017), Wyjup in '71, Rocky Horror 1 in '88, Rocky Horror 2 in '97 and Rosetta in '99. These are the cornerstones of the substantial production of consistently high quality wines, which have always been the mark of Plantagenet: highly aromatic riesling, tangy citrus-tinged chardonnay, glorious Rhône-style shiraz and ultra-stylish cabernet sauvignon. Exports to the UK, the US, Canada, China and Japan.

🍷🍷🍷🍷🍷 **Aged Release Great Southern Riesling 2013** The wine looks 5 years young, not old. It speaks volumes about the development potential of the Plantagenet rieslings. The interplay between fruit and acidity is much the same as before, although there is actually an increase in both acidity and body. This will enter the plateau of perfection around '23 and go on from there. Screwcap. 12.3% alc. **Rating** 96 **To** 2033 $30 ❁
The House of Plantagenet 'Angevin' Mount Barker Riesling 2017 Takes a little time to get into its stride, but there's no stopping it once it gets going. The palate has mouthwatering lemon citrus fruit embraced by minerally acidity, the finish long and convincing. Screwcap. 12% alc. **Rating** 95 **To** 2029 $28 ❁
Great Southern Shiraz 2013 An infusion of ultra-fragrant spice, pepper and licorice opens proceedings, the vibrant red cherry and blood plum fruit unfazed and in no way threatened by tannins or French oak, either. Classic cool-climate style. Screwcap. 13.5% alc. **Rating** 95 **To** 2033 $45
Three Lions Great Southern Riesling 2017 Out of the blocks fractionally quicker than its Angevin sibling, the floral bouquet first up, the round palate letting its waist expand with lemon and lime fruit. Screwcap. 12% alc. **Rating** 94 **To** 2027 $25 ❁
The House of Plantagenet 'York' Mount Barker Chardonnay 2017 Fermented and matured for 8 months in French oak (30% new). An altogether elegant wine, employing just the right amount of new oak. Pink grapefruit and white peach occupy the same amount of ground, with no sign of one yielding to the other. The oak is well handled, the length good. Screwcap. 13% alc. **Rating** 94 **To** 2024 $35
The House of Plantagenet 'Lancaster' Mount Barker Shiraz 2015 45+yo vines, whole berries fermented in open and Potter fermenters, 14 days on skins, matured for 18 months in French oak (40% new). In very different style to its Three Lions sibling, this is slightly lighter in colour, lower in alcohol, lighter bodied, more elegant, more aromatic. It also carries its new French oak well, with total integration just around the corner. Screwcap. 13.5% alc. **Rating** 94 **To** 2032 $35

🍷🍷🍷🍷🍷 **The House of Plantagenet 'Normand' Mount Barker Pinot Noir 2017** **Rating** 92 **To** 2027 $35
Three Lions Great Southern Sauvignon Blanc 2017 **Rating** 91 **To** 2021
Three Lions Great Southern Shiraz 2015 **Rating** 90 **To** 2030 $25

Poacher's Ridge Vineyard   ★★★★★

1630 Spencer Road, Narrikup, WA 6326 **Region** Mount Barker
T (08) 9857 6066 **www**.poachersridge.com.au **Open** Fri–Sun 10–4
Winemaker Robert Diletti (Contract) **Est.** 2000 **Dozens** 100 **Vyds** 6.9ha
Alex and Janet Taylor purchased the Poacher's Ridge property in 1999. It had previously been used for cattle grazing. The vineyard includes shiraz, cabernet sauvignon, merlot, riesling, marsanne and viognier. In 2007 its '05 Louis' Block Great Southern Merlot won the

Tri Nations (merlot class) against the might of Australia, NZ and South Africa. A dream come true. It wasn't a one-time success either: Poacher's Ridge Merlot is another always at, or near, the top of the tree. Exports to Malaysia and Singapore.

ŶŶŶŶŶ **Aged Release Louis' Block Great Southern Riesling 2007** A marvellous marriage of delicacy and intensity: lime juice, lime zest and crystalline acidity skipping around the palate of a Peter Pan wine with another decade up its sleeve. It won a gold medal at Perth in '08, and the judges got it right. Screwcap. 12.5% alc. **Rating** 96 **To** 2027 $35 **○**

Great Southern Riesling 2017 This tightly wound wine is all about the future, and its place of origin. Yes it can be enjoyed now, but in 5 years' time it will be singing from the rooftops as the lime juice flavours will have deepened and the length increased. Its future is underwritten by the simultaneous release of its '07 sibling. Screwcap. 12.2% alc. **Rating** 95 **To** 2027 $26 **○**

Great Southern Shiraz 2015 Very good crimson-purple hue; a high quality wine, with both the vineyard and skilled winemaking sending the message of shiraz grown in a cool to temperate climate. The peppery, spicy black fruits have a ripe and fleshy mid-palate, the finish long and perfectly balanced. Screwcap. 14% alc. **Rating** 95 **To** 2035 $30 **○**

ŶŶŶŶŶ **Great Southern Marsanne 2017** **Rating** 93 **To** 2025 $26 **○**

Pt. Leo Estate   ★★★★☆

3649 Frankston-Flinders Road, Merricks, Vic 3916 **Region** Mornington Peninsula
T (03) 5989 9011 **www.**ptleoestate.com.au **Open** 7 days 11–5
Winemaker Tod Dexter (Consultant) **Est.** 2006 **Dozens** 600 **Vyds** 20ha
Pt. Leo Estate is owned by one of Australia's wealthiest families, headed by octogenarian John Gandel and wife Pauline. They have donated countless millions of dollars to charity, and 30 years ago they purchased 20ha of land on the wild side of the Mornington Peninsula, building several houses for the exclusive use of family. Over the ensuing years they added parcels of land, created a lake at the entrance of the property, and in 2006 planted a 20ha vineyard. It is now also the site of a major sculpture park, populated by some very large pieces, and many smaller. A cellar door and restaurant opened in October '17. A second fine dining restaurant, Laura, opened in March '18. Both restaurants are managed by Ainslie Lubbock (ex Attica and The Royal Mail Hotel), with chef Phil Wood (ex Rockpool) and head sommelier Andrew Murch (ex Rockpool and Stokehouse).

ŶŶŶŶŶ **Mornington Peninsula Chardonnay 2015** '15 was such a wonderful vintage. The higher alcohol is no problem for this nigh-on perfect chardonnay. The fruit flavours are at the midpoint between stone fruit and citrus, the mouthfeel is excellent, the subtle use of oak and the length are all part of the story. Screwcap. 14% alc. **Rating** 95 **To** 2023 $46

ŶŶŶŶŶ **Mornington Peninsula Pinot Noir 2016** **Rating** 93 **To** 2026 $46
Mornington Peninsula Pinot Noir 2015 **Rating** 92 **To** 2020 $46

Pokolbin Estate   ★★★★★

McDonalds Road, Pokolbin, NSW 2321 **Region** Hunter Valley
T (02) 4998 7524 **www.**pokolbinestate.com.au **Open** 7 days 9–5
Winemaker Jeff Byrne (Contract) **Est.** 1980 **Dozens** 290 **Vyds** 15.7ha
Pokolbin Estate always has a very unusual, but very good, multi-varietal, multi-vintage array of wines available for sale. The Riesling is true riesling, not misnamed semillon; the latter is in turn one of their best wines. Wines under screwcap go back six or seven vintages, and there are single vineyard offerings to boot.

ŶŶŶŶŶ **Phil Swannell Hunter Valley Semillon 2009** First tasted Dec '09, then Sept '14, and now for the third time. Its colour is still light (and bright, but not yet gleaming); the richness and depth of the palate has increased significantly, with an overt juicy quality akin to riesling. Glorious stuff, unique in the world of wine. Screwcap. 11% alc. **Rating** 96 **To** 2024

Phil Swannell Hunter Valley Semillon 2014 Calmly on the journey to the first stage of maturity, the emphasis still on purity and tingling acidity with its mix of mineral and citrus flavours. When first tasted in Sept '14, my drink-to date was '29, and that still stands, as do the points. Screwcap. 10.8% alc. **Rating** 95 **To** 2029

Aged Release Hunter Valley Semillon 2004 An iridescent gold flecked with green, this is a delicious, aged semillon. Lemon drop, cumquat and marmalade toast jitterbug across the mouth with an intensity of flavour and scented length, belying the alcohol. The acidity is soft for the category, the wine poised and effusive in its attestation to regionality. At its optimal drinking window, but will hold. Screwcap. 11.7% alc. **Rating** 95 **To** 2022 $60 NG

Limited Release Reserve Hunter Valley Shiraz 2011 Behaving precisely as a first class Hunter Valley shiraz from a very good vintage should, slowly gaining a patina of spice without losing its cherry and plum fruit. Indeed, the fruit has gained a little extra punch, leaving the tannins and French oak intact. Balance is the key to a wine with a very long life ahead. Screwcap. 13.6% alc. **Rating** 95 **To** 2036 $60

ŸŸŸŸŸ **Belebula Limited Release Hunter Valley Sangiovese 2014** Rating 93 To 2024

Hunter Valley Riesling 2014 Rating 92 To 2024 $25 ✪
Belebula Hunter Valley Nebbiolo Rose 2016 Rating 92 To 2019 $25 ✪
Limited Release Reserve Hunter Valley Shiraz 2014 Rating 92 To 2026 $60 NG
Belebula Limited Release Hunter Valley Nebbiolo 2009 Rating 92 To 2024
North South Hunter Valley Shiraz 2016 Rating 91 To 2024 $30 NG

Polperro | Even Keel ★★★★

150 Red Hill Road, Red Hill, Vic 3937 **Region** Mornington Peninsula
T 0405 155 882 **www.**polperrowines.com.au **Open** Thurs–Mon 11–2
Winemaker Samuel Coverdale **Est.** 2006 **Dozens** 3000 **Vyds** 13ha
Sam Coverdale lives on the Mornington Peninsula, making wine full-time and surfing part-time. Before taking up residence on the peninsula, he obtained his degree in oenology from CSU, and accumulated 10 years of winemaking experience in Australia, France, Spain and Italy. Polperro is his single vineyard Mornington Peninsula range, and includes pinot noir, chardonnay and pinot gris. The Even Keel label uses grape varieties that best represent their region. Exports to Hong Kong.

ŸŸŸŸŸ **Even Keel Mornington Peninsula Chardonnay 2016** It's a 'just enough' wine. Just enough flint, just enough stone fruit, just enough oak. It makes for balanced, enjoyable drinking – no real fireworks but excellent swing, flow, whatever you want to call it, while avoiding the tag of 'simple'. It's nicely done. Screwcap. 13% alc. **Rating** 92 **To** 2022 $35 CM

Polperro Mornington Peninsula Pinot Gris 2017 Friendly gris with texture and flavour well on its side. Pear and fresh cream with spice and sea-spray characters. Not too simple, not too complex; balanced. Drinks like a charm as a result. Screwcap. 13.2% alc. **Rating** 92 **To** 2019 $29 CM

Even Keel Mornington Peninsula Pinot Noir 2016 Brilliant with varietal aroma, and eager to please on the palate. An excellent result from a season that tested many. Sweet and sour cherries, beetroot, herbs and spices. Both tangy and satiny at once. Smoky oak as seasoning. It all sings in harmony. Screwcap. 13.5% alc. **Rating** 92 **To** 2022 $35 CM

Even Keel Rose 2017 Heathcote and Canberra, pinot noir and sangiovese. Pale crimson. It walks to the beat of its own drum. It's yeasty and savoury with beer-like aromas and fresh garden herb characters on the palate. It gets you salivating but it also gets you thinking. Cranberry and strawberry flavours stroll in but stick

to the back row seats. Food will be its best friend. Screwcap. 13% alc. **Rating** 90
To 2019 $28 CM

ŸŸŸŸ   **Even Keel Canberra District Syrah 2016** Rating 89 To 2024 $35 CM

Pondalowie Vineyards

55 Bambra School Road, Bambra, Vic 3241 **Region** Bendigo
T 0439 373 366 **www.**pondalowie.com.au **Open** Not
Winemaker Dominic Morris, Krystina Morris **Est.** 1997 **Dozens** 3000 **Vyds** 10ha
Dominic and Krystina Morris both have strong winemaking backgrounds gained in Australia,
France and Portugal, where Dominic worked alternate vintages from 1995 to 2012. They
have established 5.5ha of shiraz, 2ha each of tempranillo and cabernet sauvignon, and a little
malbec at Bridgewater on Loddon in central Victoria. They are also establishing a cool-
climate vineyard at Bambra in the Otways (primarily MV6 pinot noir, with some 667 and
115 clones). Incidentally, the illustration on the Pondalowie label is not a piece of barbed wire,
but a very abstract representation of the winery kelpie dog. Exports to Hong Kong and Japan.

ŸŸŸŸŸ   **Vineyard Blend 2016** 55% shiraz, 39% cabernet sauvignon and 6% malbec.
Matured in both French and American oak, 25% new. Creme caramel and toast
flavours help bring dense, ferric, red and black-berried fruit flavours to life. It
all feels a little scorched but there's a good deal of heft here; the tannin is nicely
dusted with herbs, and it's hard to deny its robust drinking appeal. All things
considered the value is pretty high. Screwcap. 14% alc. **Rating** 92 **To** 2026
$20 CM ✪

 # Pontifex Wines

PO Box 161, Tanunda, SA 5352 **Region** Barossa Valley
T 0418 811 066 **www.**pontifexwines.com.au **Open** Not
Winemaker Peter Kelly **Est.** 2011 **Dozens** 2000 **Vyds** 7ha
Sam Clarke is the son of David and Cheryl Clarke, founders of Thorn-Clarke Wines, a
leading Barossa Valley winery (see separate entry). Thus it was easy for the family to meet Sam
and wife Helen's wish to buy a 6ha slice of shiraz planted in 1991. For good measure, Peter
Kelly (Thorn-Clarke's winemaker) is the winemaker for the venture. After six years, Pontifex
planted an additional ha of mourvedre on the rich Bay of Biscay soils of the Krondorf district.
They also puchase old vine grenache. China a major sales focus.

ŸŸŸŸŸ   **Barossa Valley Grenache Shiraz Mourvedre 2016** 57% 80yo grenache,
33% 28yo shiraz, 10% 4yo mourvedre, blended after fermentation, matured for
15 months in French oak (15% new). Each of the three varieties contributes to
this medium-bodied, well balanced wine. Shiraz is likely responsible for the tannins
that provide both texture and structure, mourvedre adding a savoury flourish.
Convincing wine. Screwcap. 14.5% alc. **Rating** 93 **To** 2030 $35

ŸŸŸŸ   **Barossa Valley Shiraz 2016** Rating 89 To 2023 $35

Pooley Wines

Butcher's Hill vineyard, 1431 Richmond Road, Richmond, Tas 7025
Region Southern Tasmania
T (03) 6260 2895 **www.**pooleywines.com.au **Open** 7 days 10–5
Winemaker Anna Pooley **Est.** 1985 **Dozens** 5000 **Vyds** 16ha
Three generations of the Pooley family have been involved in the development of Pooley
Wines, although the winery was previously known as Cooinda Vale. Plantings have now
reached 16ha in a region that is warmer and drier than most people realise. In 2003 the family
planted pinot noir and pinot grigio (with more recent plantings of pinot noir and chardonnay)
at Belmont vineyard, which is part of a heritage property with an 1830s Georgian home and
a (second) cellar door in the old sandstone barn and stables.

ΨΨΨΨΨ **Cooinda Vale Single Vineyard Pinot Noir 2016** The gloriously fragrant bouquet is mesmerising, the flavour spectrum more spicy/savoury than its siblings', and its finely spun tannins more frequently found in Burgundies. The overall balance and elegance are first class. Screwcap. 13.5% alc. **Rating** 97 **To** 2030 $58 ◯

Butcher's Hill Single Vineyard Pinot Noir 2016 Clear and bright colour; fragrance is a given with the Pooley pinot noirs, the product of climate and vinification that gently but efficiently bring all the wine's qualities to the table. Here the accent is on plummy fruit flavours allied with lacey acidity and silky tannins. Screwcap. 13.3% alc. **Rating** 97 **To** 2030 $58 ◯

Clarence House Vineyard Single Vineyard Pinot Noir 2015 One year older than the other pinots, which, along with the great '15 vintage, gives this wine great depth and unalloyed richness, with blood plum and luscious dark cherries held together by decorous acidity and silky tannins. Screwcap. 13.9% alc. **Rating** 97 **To** 2029 $50 ◯

ΨΨΨΨΨ **Margaret Pooley Tribute Riesling 2017** A good example of the reasons why I have always rated Tasmanian riesling above Tasmanian chardonnay. They age slowly and gracefully, never losing their shape or balance – particularly when they are of the quality of this polished wine with its floral bouquet building presence, its palate with the grip achieved from the time on skins. Screwcap. 13% alc. **Rating** 96 **To** 2030 $65 ◯

Cooinda Vale Single Vineyard Chardonnay 2016 Slightly deeper colour than Butcher's Hill; significantly richer, in part reflecting the 45% new oak, and some puncheons. Like a Chassagne-Montrachet. Screwcap. 12.5% alc. **Rating** 96 $58 ◯

Butcher's Hill Single Vineyard Chardonnay 2016 Fermented in French puncheons (30% new) on full solids, matured for 10 months. Very elegant, but not the least skinny. Every aspect is finely weighed and balanced. Looks to Chablis. Screwcap. 12.5% alc. **Rating** 96 $58 ◯

Riesling 2017 Still quartz-white; I'm tempted to say 'made in the vineyard'. Fine citrus flavours are given dimension and length by bracing acidity. Received the Consistency of Excellence Award at the Melbourne Wine Awards '17 for the '15, '16 and '17 vintages. Screwcap. 13% alc. **Rating** 95 **To** 2029 $38

Pinot Noir 2016 It's too easy to say this is a delicious pinot noir and walk on by to the single vineyard wines, as this is so much more than that when you register the continuing waves of red berry flavours rolling back and forth in the mouth on the finish and aftertaste. Then you go back and breathe in the purity of the fruit on the bouquet. Screwcap. 13.5% alc. **Rating** 95 **To** 2026 $46

J.R.D. Single Vineyard Syrah 2016 Bless the designer and printer of the black bottle labels that can be read in any light. This is an elegant light to medium-bodied wine made in similar fashion to Pooley's pinot noirs. It is fragrant, juicy, finely detailed and balanced. The fruits are of plum and forest berry, supported by gentle oak nuances. Screwcap. 13.5% alc. **Rating** 94 **To** 2029 $90

Poonawatta   ★★★★★

1227 Eden Valley Road, Flaxman Valley, SA 5235 **Region** Eden Valley
T (08) 8565 3248 **www.**poonawatta.com **Open** By appt
Winemaker Reid Bosward, Andrew Holt **Est.** 1880 **Dozens** 1800 **Vyds** 4ha
The Poonawatta story is complex, stemming from 0.8ha of shiraz planted in 1880. When Andrew Holt's parents purchased the Poonawatta property, the vineyard had suffered decades of neglect, and the slow process of restoration began. While that was underway, the strongest canes available from the winter pruning of the block were slowly and progressively dug into the stony soil, establishing the 0.8ha Cuttings Block over the course of seven years; the yield is even lower than that of the 1880 Block. The Riesling is produced from a separate vineyard of 2ha planted by the Holts in the 1970s. Exports to Canada, France, Denmark and Taiwan.

ΨΨΨΨΨ **The 1880 Eden Valley Shiraz 2015** Rich, sweet, perfumed and voluptuous. The end result: delicious. Blue and black berries, coffee-cream oak, mint and florals. It's deep, it's soft, it invites you in and keeps you there. In short it's a wine you're happy to disappear into. Cork. 14.5% alc. **Rating** 96 **To** 2035 $90 CM

The Eden Riesling 2017 Pure, crunchy, intense young riesling. It has lemons and limes turning their insides out, it unloads bursts of talc and bath salts, and has a gentle grippiness to the finish; it's quite stunning. Screwcap. 11.5% alc. **Rating** 95 **To** 2032 $28 CM ✪

The Cuttings Eden Valley Shiraz 2014 Bold and beautiful. Plums, violets, mint and darker blackberried characters on all fronts. It's a floral wine with impact; it's pure Eden Valley shiraz. Sawdusty oak plays a minor role, as indeed does a melt of tannin. It offers a world of freshness and life over the '13 release. Screwcap. 14.5% alc. **Rating** 95 **To** 2035 $54 CM

Regional Series The Four Corners of Eden Valley Shiraz 2013 An intense shiraz, strapped with licorice and sweet blackberried flavour, infusions of saltbush, cloves and wood smoke taking it a notch further. This is grunty in both flavour and tannin, but the texture remains creamy and the finish, while warm, avoids any overt heat. Long life ahead. Screwcap. 14.7% alc. **Rating** 94 **To** 2035 $39 CM

The Centenarian Single Barrel Reserve Eden Valley Shiraz 2009 There's no doubting this wine's incredible intensity of flavour, even as it nears 10 years of age, and there's also no doubting its high alcohol, which shows itself keenly. It's a sweet, porty shiraz with a fair kick on it. It tastes of blackberry jam, toffee, dried herbs and baked earth, dark chocolate studded liberally throughout. Immense is the word. Cork. 15% alc. **Rating** 94 **To** 2034 $180 CM

🍷🍷🍷🍷🍷 **The Cuttings Eden Valley Shiraz 2013** Rating 93 To 2030 $54 CM
Regional Series The Four Corners of Eden Valley Cabernet Shiraz 2015 Rating 93 To 2032 $39 CM
Regional Series The Four Corners of Eden Valley Shiraz 2015 Rating 92 To 2029 $39 CM
BS Barossa Shiraz 2015 Rating 92 To 2025 $23 CM ✪

Port Phillip Estate   ★★★★★

263 Red Hill Road, Red Hill, Vic 3937 **Region** Mornington Peninsula
T (03) 5989 4444 **www**.portphillipestate.com.au **Open** 7 days 11–5
Winemaker Glen Hayley **Est.** 1987 **Dozens** 7000 **Vyds** 9.3ha
Port Phillip Estate has been owned by Giorgio and Dianne Gjergja since 2000. The site produces outstanding syrah, pinot noir and chardonnay, and very good sauvignon blanc. In July '15, following the departure of Sandro Mosele, his assistant of six years, Glen Hayley, was appointed to take his place. The futuristic, multimillion-dollar restaurant, cellar door and winery complex, designed by award-winning Wood/Marsh Architecture, overlooks the vineyards and Westernport Bay. Exports to the UK, Canada, Singapore and China.

🍷🍷🍷🍷🍷 **Single Site Red Hill Chardonnay 2016** Hand-picked, whole-bunch pressed direct to French barriques (15% new) for wild fermentation and 11 months' maturation on lees without batonnage. The intensity of the wine is remarkable, imprinting its message of citrus, spice and white peach girdled by mineral acidity in a split second. Screwcap. 13.5% alc. **Rating** 96 **To** 2030 $35 ✪

Balnarring Mornington Peninsula Pinot Noir 2016 This is a live one. It's a brooding pinot noir, but it throws glorious scents and pushes assertively through the finish; in between all this it is also an ode to joy. Dark, macerated cherries, undergrowth, sweet herbs and chicory smoke. Both bass and treble are emphasised. In excellent shape from every angle. Screwcap. 13.5% alc. **Rating** 95 **To** 2023 $39 CM

Mornington Peninsula Sauvignon 2017 It slides seductively along the tongue but it's zippy too. Another excellent release under this label. Pink grapefruit, lemongrass and citrus flavours give it plenty of impact, but it's also the resounding finish and the mouthfeel that elevate it. Screwcap. 13% alc. **Rating** 94 **To** 2019 $27 CM ✪

Salasso Mornington Peninsula Rose 2017 Alive with scent, fruit and spice, and then perfectly pitched on the palate. Rose oil, redcurrant, struck match and dry spice notes give this both a juicy drinkability and a sophisticated edge. Class act all round. Screwcap. 12.5% alc. **Rating** 94 **To** 2019 $26 CM ❂

Single Site Red Hill Pinot Noir 2016 Wild-fermented in a combination of large foudre oak vats and tank, 18 days on skins, matured for 11 months in French barriques (20% new). Has the robust style of Port Phillip Estate, with red and dark fruits contesting possession. Screwcap. 13.5% alc. **Rating** 94 **To** 2026 $39

Mornington Peninsula Shiraz 2016 From a 0.53ha section of estate vineyard. The effect of a small amount of whole bunches is clear but, the satiny softness of the fruit makes this a pleasure to drink. Boysenberry and black cherry flavours with judiciously applied smoky/creamy/nutty oak. Herb and pepper-infused tannin. In fine shape. Screwcap. 14% alc. **Rating** 94 **To** 2028 $39 CM

Portsea Estate

7 Pembroke Place, Portsea, Vic 3944 **Region** Mornington Peninsula
T (03) 5984 3774 **www**.portseaestate.com **Open** By appt
Winemaker Tim Elphick **Est.** 2000 **Dozens** 2750 **Vyds** 4ha
Noted filmmaker Warwick Ross and sister (silent partner) Caron Wilson-Hawley have moved fast and successfully since the first vintage in 2004. Starting out with the luxury of having the first seven vintages made at Paringa Estate by Lindsay McCall and team, Portsea Estate has now built an onsite winery and hired Tim Elphick, who has a wealth of cool-climate winemaking experience. Warwick's film *Red Obsession* was given high ratings by film critics around the world. It takes an inside look at the Chinese fascination for the greatest wines of Bordeaux.

🍷🍷🍷🍷🍷 **Estate Pinot Noir 2016** This is a great success in a slightly difficult year. It has the depth, texture and structure of what will be a long-lived pinot, its dark plum and black cherry fruit shot through with spices and high quality tannins. I wouldn't quarrel with anyone arguing that it's good to go right now; it's simply going to get even better. Screwcap. 12.9% alc. **Rating** 97 **To** 2031 $42 ❂

🍷🍷🍷🍷🍷 **Estate Chardonnay 2016** Estate-grown, fermented and matured in French oak (30% new). Deeper colour than Back Beach. It's powerful, complex and compelling, with rich white peach, apricot and grapefruit flavours neatly tucked into its trousers, plus firm acidity. Screwcap. 13.1% alc. **Rating** 96 **To** 2036 $36 ❂

Back Beach Chardonnay 2016 Grapes sourced from local growers. What it lacks in depth it makes up in length and elegance. Fresh citrus/stone-fruit flavours are augmented by barrel-ferment inputs, although these two Portsea chardonnays are about subtlety not power. The mlf used isn't obvious. Screwcap. 12.7% alc. **Rating** 94 **To** 2026 $25 ❂

Estate Pinot Gris 2017 Fermented in tank, then aged on light lees in barrel. Shares with its chardonnay and pinot noir sisters a greater than average complexity and power of its variety. Of course, it isn't in the class of its sisters, but it's as good as gris gets. Screwcap. 13.2% alc. **Rating** 94 **To** 2023 $27 ❂

Back Beach Pinot Noir 2016 Grapes sourced from local growers. Bright, clear crimson-purple; razor-sharp delineation of both variety and place. It is perfectly balanced and structured, putting its hand out to you for a gentle stroll over the next 5 or so years as the latent rose petals and spices assume their place alongside the firm red fruits of today. Screwcap. 13.2% alc. **Rating** 94 **To** 2025 $29 ❂

🍷🍷🍷🍷🍷 **Estate Pinot Noir Rose 2017 Rating** 91 **To** 2020 $27

Prancing Horse Estate

39 Paringa Road, Red Hill South, Vic 3937 **Region** Mornington Peninsula
T (03) 5989 2602 **www**.prancinghorseestate.com **Open** W'ends 12–5
Winemaker Richard McIntyre, Jeremy Magyar **Est.** 1990 **Dozens** 1600 **Vyds** 6.5ha

Anthony and Catherine Hancy acquired the Lavender Bay vineyard in early 2002, renaming it Prancing Horse Estate and embarking on increasing the hectarage. The vineyard has chardonnay, pinot noir and pinot gris, and moved to organic farming in '03, progressing to biodynamic in '07. An additional property 150m west of the existing vineyard was purchased, and 2ha of vines planted. Prancing Horse has become one of a small group of Australian wineries having wines made for them in Burgundy. Pascal Marchand makes an annual release of Morey-St-Denis Clos des Ormes Premier Cru and Meursault Premier Cru Blagny, while Patrick Piuze makes four Chablis appellation wines. Exports to the UK, the US and France.

ΨΨΨΨΨ **The Pony Mornington Peninsula Chardonnay 2017** Described as a chardonnay for everyday drinking; well, that is up for debate. Quite a bit of colour – straw-yellow yet bright. Not too complicated or complex, yet with a host of flavours from stone fruit, ginger spice, creamy lees influences, and oak both spicy and sweet. Falls short on the finish but overall, a pleasant juiciness on the palate should make you pour a second glass. Screwcap. 13.3% alc. **Rating** 90 **To** 2021 JF

Mornington Peninsula Pinot Gris 2017 Heady aromas of blossom and poached pears spiced with ginger and some creamed honey and lemon curd, but the flavours are more restrained. The oak spices and leesy influence add another layer, and thankfully the wine never appears too big. Screwcap. 14% alc. **Rating** 90 **To** 2021 JF

The Pony Mornington Peninsula Pinot Noir 2017 It's bright and juicy, not overly complex but pleasing with its cherry-accented flavours, stewed rhubarb and lots of earthy overtones. Lighter framed, supple tannins and ready now. Screwcap. 13% alc. **Rating** 90 **To** 2022 JF

Precipice Wines   ★★★★☆

25 Maddens Lane, Gruyere, Vic 3770 (postal) **Region** Yarra Valley
T 0403 665 980 **www**.precipicewines.com.au **Open** Not
Winemaker Marty Singh **Est.** 2011 **Dozens** 1000
Marty Singh says that after 20 years of selling, tasting, drinking and making wine, the temptation to start his own brand was just too strong, although the scale of production means it is still very much a part-time job. His practical skills were learned over a decade of working alongside winemakers such as David Bicknell and Adrian Rodda. Precipice focuses on single vineyard wines (chardonnay, pinot noir and syrah) from the Yarra Valley, exploring the geographical diversities of the region. Production is steadily rising.

ΨΨΨΨΨ **Willow Lake Vineyard Chardonnay 2017** Precipice has nailed the '17 vintage, not picking too early. It's elegant and hand-tailored, fruit, oak and acidity are all in sync. The fruit spectrum in particular is perfectly balanced, becoming a seamless whole. Screwcap. 12.9% alc. **Rating** 95 **To** 2025 $38

ΨΨΨΨΨ **Willow Lake Vineyard Pinot Noir 2017 Rating** 92 **To** 2024 $38
Stewart's Vineyard Pinot Noir 2017 Rating 90 **To** 2021 $38

Pressing Matters   ★★★★★

665 Middle Tea Tree Road, Tea Tree, Tas 7017 **Region** Southern Tasmania
T (03) 6268 1947 **www**.pressingmatters.com.au **Open** By appt (0408 126 668)
Winemaker Winemaking Tasmania, Paul Smart **Est.** 2002 **Dozens** 2300 **Vyds** 7.2ha
Greg Melick simultaneously wears more hats than most people manage in a lifetime. He is a major general (the highest rank in the Australian Army Reserve), a top level barrister (senior counsel), and has presided over a number of headline special commissions and enquiries into subjects as diverse as cricket match–fixing and the Beaconsfield mine collapse. More recently he became deputy president of the Administrative Appeals Tribunal and chief commissioner of the Tasmanian Integrity Commission. Yet, if asked, he would probably nominate wine as his major focus in life. Having built up an exceptional cellar of the great wines of Europe, he has turned his attention to grapegrowing and winemaking, planting 2.9ha of riesling at his vineyard in the Coal River Valley. It is on a perfect north-facing slope, and the Mosel-style

rieslings are making their mark. His multi-clone 4.2ha pinot noir block is also striking gold. Exports to the US and Singapore.

ŢŢŢŢŢ **R0 Riesling 2017** It's spine-tinglingly fresh with a burst of lemon zest and lime juice across the palate. Crisp and dry, linear and long with sprightly acidity and an almost nervous energy. Yet there's a succulence too. Super now, better in a few years. Screwcap. 12.8% alc. **Rating** 95 **To** 2031 $36 JF

R69 Riesling 2017 The pristine, fresh acidity is a given, and rather than mere sweetness from the 69g/l residual sugar, it has morphed this wine altogether, adding layers of flavour. Preserved ginger and oranges, lemon balm infused tea, and cardamom rally together on the long finish. Beautiful balance. Screwcap. 8.1% alc. **Rating** 95 **To** 2028 $36 JF

R139 Riesling 2017 A wine of great delicacy yet with a certain verve too, the latter driven by the acidity, the former by the subtle fruit flavours. A mix of lime juice, cardamom and ginger infused poached pears, glace lemon dusted with sugar, and a gentle flinty/chalky nuance to the finish. 375ml. Screwcap. 9.4% alc. **Rating** 95 **To** 2025 $33 JF ✪

ŢŢŢŢŢ **R9 Riesling 2017 Rating** 93 **To** 2025 $36 JF
Coal River Valley Pinot Noir 2015 Rating 93 **To** 2027 $56 JF

Preveli Wines

Prevelly Liquor Store, 99 Mitchell Drive, Prevelly, WA 6285 **Region** Margaret River
T (08) 9757 2374 **www.**preveliwines.com.au **Open** Mon–Fri 8.30–7, w'ends 10–7
Winemaker Fraser Gallop Estate (Clive Otto, Kate Morgan) **Est.** 1995 **Dozens** 4500
Vyds 5.5ha
While Preveli Wines is a relative newcomer, its owners, the Home family, have lived on the property for three generations. Vince and Greg Home also operate the Prevelly Park Beach Resort and Prevelly Liquor Store, where the wines are available for tasting. Fruit from the vineyard at Rosa Brook (semillon, sauvignon blanc, cabernet sauvignon, pinot noir and merlot) is supplemented by contracts with local growers.

ŢŢŢŢŢ **Wild Thing Margaret River Pinot Rose 2017** Fragrant cherry/berry aromas and a fresh, perfect black-cherry palate show what can be achieved with a simple fermentation and maturation regime. The additions of pinot gris (1%) and chardonnay (0.5%) shouldn't have had much impact, but there's a hint of salmon to the pink colour, and there's definitely some complexity to the mouthfeel. All this earned the wine the trophy for Best Rose at the Margaret River Wine Show '17. Screwcap. 13% alc. **Rating** 96 **To** 2019 $24 ✪

Wild Thing Margaret River Sauvignon Blanc 2017 This sure is a wild thing, but for all the right reasons, surging and surfing with super-lively lime and Meyer lemon, then guava and green pineapple, citrus pith and zest. Then there's the electrifying acid envelope in which the fruit is delivered. Screwcap. 12.5% alc. **Rating** 95 **To** 2022 $24 ✪

Margaret River Cabernet Sauvignon Malbec 2014 This is the first vintage to include malbec (6%). An altogether elegant blend with counterpoints of red, purple and black fruits; the tannins are supple, the finish long and composed. Trophy Australian Cool Climate Wine Show '16, gold medal Boutique Wine Awards '16. Screwcap. 14% alc. **Rating** 94 **To** 2034 $35

Primo Estate

McMurtrie Road, McLaren Vale, SA 5171 **Region** McLaren Vale
T (08) 8323 6800 **www.**primoestate.com.au **Open** 7 days 11–4
Winemaker Joseph Grilli, Daniel Zuzolo **Est.** 1979 **Dozens** 30 000 **Vyds** 34ha
Joe Grilli has always produced innovative and excellent wines. The biennial release of the Joseph Sparkling Red (in its tall Italian glass bottle) is eagerly awaited, the wine immediately selling out. The core wines include the La Biondina Colombard, the Il Briccone Shiraz Sangiovese and the Joseph Moda Cabernet Merlot. The business has expanded to take in

both McLaren Vale and Clarendon, with plantings of colombard, shiraz, cabernet sauvignon, riesling, merlot, sauvignon blanc, chardonnay, pinot gris, sangiovese, nebbiolo and merlot. Also highly regarded are Primo Estate's vintage-dated extra virgin olive oils. Exports to all major markets.

ŸŸŸŸŸ Joseph Sparkling Red NV Sells out very quickly after release, the disgorgement taking place every 18–24 months, this in Aug '16. The base wine includes some of Primo's cabernet merlot from every vintage since the '80s, and a small amount of shiraz from the '60s and '70s. The oak input is negligible, and the dosage is less than many of its peers, the wine ending up very rich and velvety, but not too sweet or oaky. One of Australia's treasures. Cork. 13.5% alc. **Rating** 96 $90

Shale Stone McLaren Vale Shiraz 2016 Primarily sourced from the estate's Clarendon vineyard, imparting the perfume and gravelly nuances, and from the McMurtrie Road vineyard, giving the wine its deep-set black fruits, licorice and dark chocolate flavours. There's plenty here to ponder on – and enjoy – with each big sip. Screwcap. 14.5% alc. **Rating** 94 To 2031 $35

ŸŸŸŸŸ La Biondina Colombard 2017 Rating 93 To 2022 $20 ✪
Joseph d'Elena Clarendon Pinot Grigio 2017 Rating 93 To 2021 $35
Il Briccone McLaren Vale Shiraz Sangiovese 2016 Rating 90 To 2026 $25
Merlesco McLaren Vale Merlot 2017 Rating 90 To 2021 $20 ✪
Zamberlan McLaren Vale Cabernet Sauvignon Sangiovese 2016 Rating 90 To 2023 $40

Principia   ★★★★★

139 Main Creek Road, Red Hill, Vic 3937 (postal) **Region** Mornington Peninsula
T (03) 5931 0010 **www**.principiawines.com.au **Open** By appt
Winemaker Darrin Gaffy **Est.** 1995 **Dozens** 600 **Vyds** 3.5ha
Darrin Gaffy's guiding philosophy for Principia is minimal interference, thus the vines (2.7ha of pinot noir and 0.8ha of chardonnay) are not irrigated and yields are restricted to 3.75t/ha or less. All wine movements are by gravity or by gas pressure, which in turn means there is no filtration, and both primary and secondary fermentation are by wild yeast. 'Principia' comes from the word 'beginnings' in Latin.

ŸŸŸŸŸ Kindred Hill Mornington Peninsula Pinot Noir 2016 Excellent colour and clarity; the bouquet is very expressive with perfectly ripened pinot noir notes to the fore, warm spices in the background. A tantalisingly seductive palate, with the flavours washing across and along the mouth, leaving an imprint that takes a seeming eternity to diminish. Screwcap. 13.3% alc. **Rating** 96 To 2031 $55 ✪

Mornington Peninsula Chardonnay 2016 A beguiling bouquet, initially showing creamy, nutty, nougat-like characters, but opening up to reveal a complexity of stone fruit and citrus. The flavours share a similar richness, but the cool-climate origins come into play with a tautness of structure and a long, lemony finish, which has a stamp of high quality. Screwcap. 13.3% alc. **Rating** 95 To 2023 $40 SC

Altior Mornington Peninsula Pinot Noir 2016 The colour is star-bright light crimson; red blossom and spice aromas are attractive, but don't strike as decisively as the intense, long and beautifully proportioned palate, with its sparkling red fruits, spices and bramble in total harmony with oak and acidity, and tannins that bow to the fruit. Screwcap. 13.5% alc. **Rating** 95 To 2029 $55

Mornington Peninsula Pinot Noir 2016 All the indications are of high quality grapes left to do their own thing in the winery. The crimson-purple colour is excellent, and is a sure pointer to a very good Mornington Peninsula pinot noir. The flavours are of dark cherry and satsuma plum, and the finish has great drive, energy and length. Screwcap. 13.3% alc. **Rating** 95 To 2029 $40

Printhie Wines

489 Yuranigh Road, Molong, NSW 2866 **Region** Orange
T (02) 6366 8422 **www.**printhiewines.com.au **Open** Mon–Sat 10–4
Winemaker Drew Tuckwell **Est.** 1996 **Dozens** 20 000 **Vyds** 30ha
Owned by the Swift family, with the next generation Edward and David having taken over
the reins to guide the business into its next era. In 2016 Printhie clocked up 10 years of
commercial wine production, and the vineyards are now reaching a good level of maturity
at 20 years. They are planted at lower elevations and supply all the red varieties and the pinot
gris; other varieties are purchased from growers in the region. Winemaker Drew Tuckwell has
been at Printhie for a decade, and has over 20 years of winemaking experience in Australia
and Europe. Exports to Canada and China.

ㅇㅇㅇㅇㅇ **Mountain Range Orange Shiraz 2016** Perfumed and peppery with supple
black cherry flavours washing through the palate. It's a recipe for success. There
are floral notes here, ripe berried flavours, a suggestion of nutty oak and plenty
of spunky spice notes. The result is 100% delicious. Buy. Screwcap. 14.5% alc.
Rating 94 To 2026 $20 CM ✪

ㅇㅇㅇㅇㅇ **Mountain Range Sauvignon Blanc 2017** Rating 93 To 2019 $20 CM ✪
MCC Orange Chardonnay 2016 Rating 93 To 2023 $35 CM
Super Duper Orange Chardonnay 2016 Rating 93 To 2022 $85 CM
MCC Orange Riesling 2017 Rating 92 To 2025 $25 CM ✪
Mountain Range Cabernet 2016 Rating 92 To 2024 $20 CM ✪
Swift Blanc de Blancs 2010 Rating 92 $40 CM
Swift Cuvee Brut NV Rating 92 $40 CM
Mountain Range Orange Merlot 2017 Rating 91 To 2024 $20 CM ✪
Swift Rose Brut 2011 Rating 90 $40 CM

Project Wine

83 Pioneer Road, Angas Plains, SA 5255 **Region** South Australia
T (08) 8537 0600 **www.**projectwine.com.au **Open** Not
Winemaker Peter Pollard **Est.** 2001 **Dozens** 150 000
Originally designed as a contract winemaking facility, Project Wine has a sales and distribution
arm that has rapidly developed markets both domestically and overseas. Located in Langhorne
Creek, it sources fruit from most key SA wine regions, including McLaren Vale, Barossa Valley
and Adelaide Hills. The diversity of grapes allows the winery to produce a wide range of
products under the Tail Spin, Pioneer Road, Parson's Paddock, Bird's Eye View and Angas &
Bremer labels. Exports to the UK, Canada, Japan and China.

ㅇㅇㅇㅇㅇ **Angas & Bremer Langhorne Creek Shiraz Cabernet 2016** 60% cabernet
sauvignon, 40% shiraz, blended after fermentation, matured for 12 months in
American oak (10% new). Good depth to the colour; this is full-bodied and there's
a lot on offer at this price, black fruits in super-abundance. Screwcap. 14.8% alc.
Rating 90 To 2026 $15 ✪
Angas & Bremer Langhorne Creek Cabernet Sauvignon 2015 Crushed
and destemmed, 3 days' cold soak, 7 days' fermentation, matured in French and
American oak for 15 months. Langhorne Creek at its compliant best: medium-
bodied with soft mouthfilling cassis fruit, oak well judged, the tannins ditto.
Screwcap. 14.5% alc. Rating 90 To 2025 $20 ✪
Angas & Bremer Langhorne Creek Malbec 2016 Machine-harvested,
crushed and destemmed, 10 days on skins including 3 days' cold soak, matured
for 16 months in American oak (20% new). Deep, dense crimson-purple;
unequivocally full-bodied, blackberry and plum fruit slugging it out with oak. Best
leave them to continue the battle for 5 years, and approach then to see how the
fruit fared. Screwcap. 14% alc. Rating 90 To 2036 $40

Provenance Wines

100 Lower Paper Mills Road, Fyansford, Vic 3221 **Region** Geelong
T (03) 5222 3422 **www**.provenancewines.com.au **Open** By appt
Winemaker Scott Ireland, Sam Vogel **Est.** 1997 **Dozens** 6000 **Vyds** 14.2ha
In 1997 when Scott Ireland and partner Jan Lilburn established Provenance Wines, they knew it wouldn't be easy starting a winery with limited capital and no fixed abode. The one thing the business had was Scott's over 36 years' experience operating contract wine filtration and bottling services, moving from winery to winery in the Hunter Valley, Barossa, Coonawarra, Mudgee, Clare Valley, Yarra Valley and Tasmania regions. Looking back, he says he met so many dedicated small winemakers – and he was hooked for life. In 2004 he moved to Austins & Co, the largest winery in Geelong. Scott was Austins' winemaker, but with their knowledge and consent he continued to grow the much smaller Provenance business, developing key relations with growers in Geelong, the ultra-cool Macedon, Ballarat and Henty. Scott took a long-term lease of 25% of the Fyansford Paper Mill, and serious refurbishment has been happening over the last 15 months on the heritage-listed buildings. Built out of local bluestone on the banks of the Barwon River on the outskirts of Geelong, this 1870s industrial complex provides excellent wine cellar conditions. The cellar door opened in March 2017, and their vintage '18 took place onsite in the new 150t winery.

ＹＹＹＹＹ **Regional Selection Geelong Chardonnay 2015** From the Strathmore vineyard in the Moorabool Valley, hand-picked, whole-bunch pressed, wild-fermented in French barriques (40% new), matured for 10 months on lees, then a barrel selection. The vinification is identical to its Regional Selection siblings' apart from the percentage of new oak (the others at 33%). The reason is quite possibly the ultra-close 1 × 1m vineyard spacing. While the oak is a little more obvious, it is easily carried by the flow of perfectly ripened fruit, white peach to the fore. Screwcap. 13.2% alc. **Rating** 97 To 2030 $47 ❂
Regional Selection Henty Chardonnay 2015 This is the most finely built of the three Regional Selection chardonnays, which is the impact of the ultra-cool climate of Henty – the coolest region in Australia according to Dr John Gladstones, who is the ultimate source in such matters. Its flavours bring more Granny Smith apple into play than white peach. Screwcap. 13% alc. **Rating** 97 To 2030 $47 ❂
Regional Selection Henty Pinot Noir 2015 Another Provenance wine from the coolest region in Victoria, with wondrously fragrant aromas of red flowers and spices. The common themes across Provenance's '15 pinots are their elegance, attention to detail, length, balance and distillation of pinot noir varietal character from vineyards painstakingly selected in the first place. Screwcap. 13.2% alc. **Rating** 97 To 2030 $47 ❂

ＹＹＹＹＹ **Regional Selection Ballarat Pinot Noir 2015** The bouquet is expressive and fragrant to the point of perfume; violets, spice and wood smoke ex the whole-bunch component. The palate is super-elegant, becoming more juicy each time you return to it, but not throwing off the savoury complex architecture of the wine, nor the intensity of varietal character. Screwcap. 13% alc. **Rating** 96 To 2030 $47 ❂
Regional Selection Geelong Pinot Noir 2015 Notably deep in colour, aromas and flavours. Rich and velvety, but not heavy, its persona of red and purple fruits, the tannins fine, the finish long. You can see its future spelt out in capital letters – particularly complexities/florals – but there's every reason you should be drinking some right now. Screwcap. 13.2% alc. **Rating** 96 To 2035 $47 ❂
Geelong Shiraz 2016 Australian shiraz has 100 faces reflecting vine age, clone, vine site, climate, soil, canopy management, organic/biodynamic or traditionally grown, the list goes on. This vividly and deeply coloured wine is very cool-grown, but its flavour overflows the fermenter, the barrel, the glass and the mouth. The predominantly black fruits are so juicy they move past or through the tannins and oak. This is grossly underpriced. Screwcap. 13.5% alc. **Rating** 96 To 2041 $32 ❂
Golden Plains Chardonnay 2016 Makes one itch to taste the '17s. A very well made wine of great quality, light to medium-bodied palate singing like a bird

in flight without an avian care in the world. White stone fruit, citrus and toasted almonds running through to a carefree finish. Screwcap. 13.5% alc. **Rating** 95 To 2023 $29 **○**

Regional Selection Ballarat Chardonnay 2015 Attention to detail, with a carefully constructed pathway to achieve the best regional influence on the best balanced wine. The vinification is essentially identical to the other Regional Selection chardonnays. Zesty and tingling but not over the top, because there is nothing hidden in the elegant grapefruit-accented aftertaste. Screwcap. 13.2% alc. **Rating** 95 To 2029 $47

Tarrington Pinot Gris 2016 Another easy demonstration of Scott Ireland's skill. He has created a wine that transcends variety, needing nothing more. Its balance is perfect, the texture likewise. Nashi pear and apple join hands. Screwcap. 13.5% alc. **Rating** 95 To 2021 $26 **○**

Golden Plains Pinot Noir 2016 A beautifully balanced pinot, which shows the influence of the relatively small Ballarat component. There is a tantalising brushstroke of smoky spice before the complex array of red and black cherries, oak and tannins spot on. Screwcap. 13.2% alc. **Rating** 95 To 2026 $30 **○**

Long Night Rose 2017 From 100% pinot noir. Crisp and crunchy, with a delightful mid-palate of wild strawberry and crab apple on the dry, but compelling, palate. Serious rose. Screwcap. 12.9% alc. **Rating** 94 To 2021 $25 **○**

Punch ★★★★★

10 Scott Street, St Andrews, Vic 3761 **Region** Yarra Valley
T 0424 074 234 **www.**punched.com.au **Open** W'ends 12–5
Winemaker James Lance **Est.** 2004 **Dozens** 1800 **Vyds** 3.45ha
In the wake of Graeme Rathbone taking over the brand (but not the real estate) from previous owners David and Catherine Lance, the Lances' son James and his wife Claire became the new lessees of this vineyard and winery. Punch has 2.25ha of pinot noir (including a small close-planted block), 0.8ha of chardonnay and 0.4ha of cabernet sauvignon. Exports to China.

ΨΨΨΨΨ Lance's Vineyard Yarra Valley Pinot Noir 2015 Bright, full colour; a very complex, spicy wine, the bouquet and palate singing the same song. It gives the impression of more than 5% whole bunches, but regardless, it has utterly exceptional length and drive. The flavours are an Aladdin's cave of endless delights; red, purple and blue fruits bouncing off each other. Screwcap. 13.5% alc. **Rating** 97 To 2030 $55 **○**

ΨΨΨΨΨ Lance's Vineyard Yarra Valley Chardonnay 2015 Gleaming, pale straw-green; it is the complexity, integrity and length of Yarra Valley chardonnays as good as this that show the limitations of warmer regions' wines. Here white peach/nectarine flavours lead the way, albeit with complex texture and structure built on the back-palate by citrussy acidity and the positive influence of seriously good Burgundian oak. Screwcap. 13.5% alc. **Rating** 96 To 2025 $45 **○**

Lance's Vineyard Close Planted Yarra Valley Pinot Noir 2015 Deep, clear colour; a pocket rocket, built to travel far and live long. Black cherry, plum and spice all come through strongly after the lengthy elevage. Its tiny production (69 dozen, sold in 6-packs) is a shame, but it enabled James Lance to calculate an average 91g bunch weight! Its best is years away. Screwcap. 13.5% alc. **Rating** 96 To 2035 $90

Lance's Vineyard Yarra Valley Cabernet Sauvignon 2015 Making micro-quantities (65 dozen) like this isn't easy; James Lance just makes it look that way. Cassis and bay leaf run the flavour line perfectly, with the usual balance of quality oak and fine tannins. Screwcap. 13.5% alc. **Rating** 95 To 2035 $45

Punt Road ★★★★★

10 St Huberts Road, Coldstream, Vic 3770 **Region** Yarra Valley
T (03) 9739 0666 **www.**puntroadwines.com.au **Open** 7 days 10–5
Winemaker Tim Shand, Angus Ridley **Est.** 2000 **Dozens** 20 000 **Vyds** 65.61ha

Punt Road is owned by the Napoleone family, third-generation fruit growers in the Yarra Valley. Their vineyard in Coldstream is one of the most historic sites in Victoria, first planted to vines by Swiss immigrant Hubert De Castella in 1860. The Napoleone vineyard was established on the property in 1987. Winemaker Tim Shand joined the winery in 2014, and it has been a successful move for all concerned, highlighted by Punt Road's three trophies at the Melbourne Wine Awards '16. The two main ranges are Punt Road and Airlie Bank, plus a small production, single vineyard 'Block' selection, only available at the cellar door and made only in the best vintages. Exports to the US, the UK, Denmark, Singapore, Taiwan, China and Sri Lanka.

????? **Napoleone Vineyard Block 8 Yarra Valley Shiraz 2015** Grown on vines planted in '91. 4% viognier, co-fermented. 30% whole bunches. Intensity of flavour and the personality to match – we have ourselves a beautiful wine here. Set deep with black cherry and gun smoke, studded with cloves, blessed with black pepper, a rumble-tumble of savoury spice through the extended finish. Tannin is ultrafine, quality is ultra-good. Screwcap. **Rating** 97 **To** 2035 $70 CM **✪**

????? **Napoleone Vineyard Yarra Valley Pinot Gris 2017** Pear, citrus and grapefruit flavours burst onto the palate in confident style. It's both amiable and impressive; you can ask for little more. Partial oak maturation has softened the edges but there's still plenty of drive here. Screwcap. 12.5% alc. **Rating** 94 **To** 2020 $23 CM **✪**

Yarra Valley Pinot Noir 2017 If this is what the '17 vintage has in store, then happy days. It's just so gorgeously varietal. Savouriness all the way up, herbal in a sweet and ripe way, flushed with cherry and wood smoke, and lengthy through the finish. It's summer and autumn in one, though with a slight emphasis on the latter. In pinot noir terms the value here is right up there. Screwcap. 13% alc. **Rating** 94 **To** 2016 $29 CM **✪**

Napoleone Vineyard Yarra Valley Shiraz 2016 Wild with spice, herbs and peppers but alive with berried fruit too; it's cool climate in style but warm-hearted by nature. Indeed it's hard not to marvel at the polish and poise on show here; winemaker Tim Shand is a dab hand at getting things exactly so. It doesn't have a lot of heft, but it has enough, and it makes up for it anyway with the array of different flavours and the way they linger appreciably. Screwcap. 14% alc. **Rating** 94 **To** 2028 $32 CM

????? **Napoleone Vineyard Block 2 Yarra Valley Chardonnay 2017** Rating 93 To 2027 $50 CM

Napoleone Vineyard Block 18 Yarra Valley Gamay 2017 Rating 93 To 2023 $29 CM

Napoleone Vineyard Block 3 Yarra Valley Cabernet Sauvignon 2016 Rating 93 To 2032 $32 CM

Airlie Bank Yarra Valley Franc 2017 Rating 93 To 2022 $22 CM **✪**

Napoleone Vineyard Yarra Valley Chardonnay 2017 Rating 92 To 2024 $23 CM **✪**

Napoleone Vineyard Chardonnay Pinot Noir 2014 Rating 91 $38 CM

Pure Vision | Nature's Step   ★★★☆

PO Box 258, Virginia, SA 5120 **Region** Adelaide Plains
T 0412 800 875 **www.lightsviewgroup.com.au** **Open** Not
Winemaker Joanne Irvine, Ken Carypidis **Est.** 2001 **Dozens** 13 000 **Vyds** 55ha

The Carypidis family runs two brands: Pure Vision (15ha of organically grown wine grapes) and Nature's Step (56ha over three vineyards, with the oldest planted in 1975; organic conversion began in 2009). Growing grapes under a certified organic regime is much easier if the region is warm to hot and dry, conditions unsuitable for botrytis and downy mildew. You are still left with weed growth (no herbicides are allowed) and powdery mildew (sulphur sprays are permitted), but the overall task is much simpler. The Adelaide Plains, where Pure Vision's vineyard is situated, is such a region. Ken Carypidis has been clever enough to secure the services of Joanne Irvine as co-winemaker. Exports to the US, Canada, Taiwan, Hong Kong and China.

🍷🍷🍷🍷🍷 **Pure Vision Shiraz 2016** Matured in used oak for 9 months. The SA region might not do the wine justice, for there's complexity in the fruit flavours giving rise to a most attractive juicy/savoury palate, and fine, ripe tannins thrown in for good measure. A bargain for everyone. Screwcap. 14.5% alc. **Rating** 92 **To** 2026 $15 ✪

Purple Hands Wines

32 Brandreth Street, Tusmore, SA 5065 (postal) **Region** Barossa Valley
T 0401 988 185 **www.purplehandswines.com.au Open** Not
Winemaker Craig Stansborough **Est.** 2006 **Dozens** 3000 **Vyds** 14ha
This is a partnership between Craig Stansborough, who provides the winemaking know-how and an 8ha vineyard of shiraz (northwest of Williamstown in a cooler corner of the southern Barossa), and Mark Slade, who provides the passion. Don't ask me how this works – I don't know – but I do know they are producing outstanding single vineyard wines (the grenache is contract-grown) of quite remarkable elegance. The wines are made at Grant Burge, where Craig is chief winemaker. Exports to the Philippines.

🍷🍷🍷🍷🍷 **After Five Wine Co. Serata 2016** 51/39/10% blend of shiraz, montepulciano and aglianico. Depth of fruit is striking, but more so is the wine's balance. This feels fussed over in the best of ways. Red and black cherries, earth, asphalt, licorice and a mere caress of creamy oak. Tannin casts a web from the mid-palate on. It's high class; high quality. Screwcap. 13.5% alc. **Rating** 96 **To** 2031 $45 CM ✪
After Five Wine Co. Grenache 2016 Velvety smooth, brilliantly perfumed and fruited, structured just so, and totally convincing to close. These 'After Five' wines have arrived on the marketplace in emphatic fashion. This wine adds yet more revs to the modern day grenache revolution. Screwcap. 14% alc. **Rating** 96 **To** 2028 $45 CM ✪
Planta Circa Barossa Valley Cabernet Sauvignon 2016 PF Zimmermann planted 468 cabernet sauvignon vines on his family property on the outskirts of Lyndoch in 1880. It's humbling, if not inspiring, to think that we still get to enjoy the fruits of that long-ago labour. This is a thick, intense, mouth-coating wine, its flavours of asphalt, blackberry, licorice and dark chocolate exploding through the palate and out through the finish. Concentrated fruit sits on the throne, its rule both firm and decisive. Safe to say this is a long-term cellaring proposition. Diam. 14% alc. **Rating** 96 **To** 2042 $70 CM ✪
After Five Wine Co. Shiraz 2016 Shots of licorice and pure blackberry melt slowly into liquid milk chocolate. It's as seductive as it sounds. It's a great pleasure to sink into this wine's inky depths, its folds of tannin drenched in fruit, its finish resounding. Screwcap. 14% alc. **Rating** 95 **To** 2036 $45 CM

🍷🍷🍷🍷🍷 **Barossa Valley Shiraz 2016 Rating** 93 **To** 2032 $30 CM
Barossa Valley Montepulciano 2016 Rating 91 **To** 2024 $30 CM

Pyramid Hill Wines

194 Martindale Road, Denman, NSW 2328 **Region** Hunter Valley
T (02) 6547 2755 **www.pyramidhillwines.com Open** By appt
Winemaker First Creek Winemaking Services **Est.** 2002 **Dozens** 5000 **Vyds** 72ha
Pyramid Hill is a partnership between the Adler and Hilder families. Richard Hilder is a veteran viticulturist who oversaw the establishment of many of the Rosemount vineyards. Nicholas Adler and Caroline Sherwood made their mark in the international film industry before moving to Pyramid Hill in 1997. The vineyard (chardonnay, semillon, shiraz, verdelho and merlot) has a computer-controlled irrigation system connected to a network of radio-linked weather and soil moisture sensors that constantly relay data detailing the amount of available moisture at different soil depths, thus avoiding excess irrigation and preventing stress.

Most of the grapes are sold, but part has been vinified, with cautious expansion planned. Exports to the UK, Canada, Japan and Singapore.

🍷🍷🍷🍷🍷 **Hunter Valley Semillon 2017** A classic regional expression of semillon, with lemon, lanolin and mineral acidity all in the mix. It has good length and balance, and 5 years in bottle will see radical changes in the weight of the wine. Screwcap. 10.5% alc. **Rating** 93 **To** 2027 $20 ❂

Quarisa Wines

743 Slopes Road, Tharbogang, NSW 2680 (postal) **Region** South Australia
T (02) 6963 6222 **www**.quarisa.com.au **Open** Not
Winemaker John Quarisa **Est.** 2005 **Dozens** NFP
John Quarisa has had a distinguished career as a winemaker spanning over 20 years, working for some of Australia's largest wineries, including McWilliam's, Casella and Nugan Estate. He was also chiefly responsible in 2004 for winning the Jimmy Watson Trophy (Melbourne) and the Stodart Trophy (Adelaide) for Casella. John and wife Josephine have set up a very successful family business using grapes from various parts of SA and NSW, making the wines in leased space. Production has risen in leaps and bounds, doubtless sustained by the exceptional value for money provided by the wines. Exports include the UK, Canada, Denmark, Sweden, Malaysia, Indonesia, Hong Kong and NZ.

🍷🍷🍷🍷🍷 **Treasures McLaren Vale Shiraz 2016** By far the best Quarisa red from '16, though remaining thunderous in its delivery onto the palate. Screwcap. 14.5% alc. **Rating** 90 **To** 2030 $19 ❂

🍷🍷🍷🍷 **The Great Bonza Reserve Shiraz Cabernet 2017 Rating** 89 **To** 2022 $17 ❂
Caravan Petite Sirah 2017 Rating 89 **To** 2026 $17 ❂

R. Paulazzo

852 Oakes Road, Yoogali, NSW 2680 **Region** Riverina
T 0412 696 002 **www**.rpaulazzo.com.au **Open** By appt
Winemaker Rob Paulazzo **Est.** 2013 **Dozens** NFP **Vyds** 12ha
Rob Paulazzo began winemaking in 2000, and covered a lot of ground before establishing his eponymous Riverina business. In Australia he worked for McWilliam's and Orlando, and in NZ for Giesen, also completing four vintages in Burgundy, plus vintages in Tuscany, the Napa Valley and Niagara Peninsula (Canada). In addition to the family's vineyard, established over 80 years ago, Rob also sources fruit from Hilltops, Tumbarumba, Orange and Canberra District.

🍷🍷🍷🍷🍷 **G-0501 Hilltops Shiraz 2015** The perfumed bouquet runs along twin roads of spice/pepper and red fruits. The intensity and length increase on retasting, and insist on the extra half-point initially not awarded. Screwcap. 14% alc. **Rating** 95 **To** 2029 $30 ❂
F-1366 Riverina Botrytis Semillon 2014 Has the classic mix of cumquat, apricot and orange marmalade on the bouquet and mid-palate, then pauses to change gear just when you think it may be too sweet. Here the botrytis inserts its cutting edge of acidity, which almost heads the wine back to dryness. Screwcap. 12% alc. **Rating** 95 **To** 2024 $28 ❂

🍷🍷🍷🍷🍷 **K-1707 Tumbarumba Pinot Noir 2016 Rating** 93 **To** 2029 $30
M-2305 Tumbarumba Chardonnay 2016 Rating 92 **To** 2023 $30

Rahona Valley Vineyard

6 Ocean View Avenue, Red Hill South, Vic 3937 **Region** Mornington Peninsula
T (03) 5989 2924 **www**.rahonavalley.com.au **Open** By appt
Winemaker John Salmons **Est.** 1991 **Dozens** 300 **Vyds** 1.6ha
John and Leonie Salmons have one of the older and more interesting small vineyards on the Mornington Peninsula, on a steep north-facing slope of a small valley in the Red Hill area.

Red Hill takes its name from the ancient red basalt soils. Five clones of pinot noir are planted (MV6, D5V12, G5V15, 115 and D2V5) totalling 1.2ha, plus a few hundred vines each of pinot meunier and pinot gris.

🍷🍷🍷🍷🍷 **Mornington Peninsula Pinot Noir 2015** The colour is light, but with a remarkably bright crimson hue; the bouquet and palate are faultless, with fragrance and purity the watchwords. The flavours are largely in the red fruit group, effortlessly floating past the fine, supple tannins and oak. Super delicious from an exceptional vintage. Screwcap. 13.5% alc. **Rating** 96 **To** 2025 $35 ✪

🍷🍷🍷🍷🍷 **Mary's Block Gewurztraminer 2016** **Rating** 92 **To** 2026 $30
Pinot Gris 2015 **Rating** 92 **To** 2020 $25 ✪
Pinot Noir Rose 2016 **Rating** 92 **To** 2021 $28

Ravensworth ★★★★★

312 Patemans Lane, Murrumbateman, ACT 2582 **Region** Canberra District
T (02) 6226 8368 **www**.ravensworthwines.com.au **Open** Not
Winemaker Bryan Martin **Est.** 2000 **Dozens** 2000
Winemaker, vineyard manager and partner Bryan Martin (with dual wine science and winegrowing degrees from CSU) has a background in wine retail, food and beverage experience in the hospitality industry, and teaches part-time. He is also assistant winemaker to Tim Kirk at Clonakilla, after seven years at Jeir Creek. Judging at wine shows is another string to his bow. Ravensworth's organically managed vineyard is mainly planted to shiraz (four clones, including Best's and Tahbilk), riesling (three Geisenheim clones) and sangiovese (three clones), with lesser amounts of white varieties.

🍷🍷🍷🍷🍷 **Riesling 2017** Bright straw-green; the bouquet is fragrant, charged with flowers and blossoms, the generous palate built around the lead of the bouquet, with both flavour and textural complexity ex citrus and Granny Smith apple at its core. Punchy acidity is another plus. Screwcap. 12% alc. **Rating** 95 **To** 2029 $26 ✪
The Grainery 2017 A multi-variety blend led by viognier, followed by marsanne, roussanne, chardonnay and riesling. This is a flavoursome, unctuous wine. Beautifully composed with florals, candied peel and stone fruit, and creamy with nougat-like leesy characters. Juicy and succulent. A joy to drink. 13% alc. **Rating** 95 **To** 2025 $35 JF ✪
The Tinderry 2017 DNA research shows that cabernet franc and sauvignon blanc spawned cabernet sauvignon, here as a 75/25% blend. This has created an utterly convincing whole, that is refreshing and vibrant with its mix of cassis, woodsy spices, black pepper and bouquet garni, with crunchy acidity and ever-so-supple tannins. Screwcap. 13.5% alc. **Rating** 95 **To** 2022 $35 JF ✪
Estate Murrumbateman Sangiovese 2016 A pure expression of the variety and site. Heady aromatics with red cherries and pips, cinnamon, with a sprinkling of basil that follows through on the medium-bodied palate. There's considerable depth of flavour but it's not overwhelming, its ribbons of tannin and bright acidity holding everything in place. Screwcap. 13% alc. **Rating** 95 **To** 2026 $40 JF
Estate Shiraz Viognier 2016 Pay no attention to the slightly vapid colour; the bouquet is highly fragrant, red and sour cherries to the fore. The medium-bodied palate has a complex array of savoury/spicy fruit flavours, joined by dried herbs on the elegant palate. Screwcap. 13.5% alc. **Rating** 94 **To** 2029 $38
Zin-Zin Baby Murrumbateman Primitivo 2017 If you think primitivo is a big red, think again. Here it's medium-weighted, full of bright red fruit, pepper and orange zest, with supple tannins and a mouth-watering amaro-like finish. Has a real Italianate feel to it. Screwcap. 14% alc. **Rating** 94 **To** 2022 $28 JF ✪

🍷🍷🍷🍷🍷 **Murrumbateman Sangiovese 2017** **Rating** 93 **To** 2021 $28 JF
Hilltops Barbera 2017 **Rating** 93 **To** 2021 $28 JF
Charlie-Foxtrot Gamay Noir 2017 **Rating** 92 **To** 2023 $32
Hilltops Nebbiolo 2016 **Rating** 92 **To** 2022 $45 JF
Pinot Gris 2017 **Rating** 90 **To** 2020 $28

Red Art | Rojomoma

16 Sturt Road, Nuriootpa, SA 5355 **Region** Barossa Valley
T 0421 272 336 **www**.rojomoma.com.au **Open** By appt
Winemaker Bernadette Kaeding, Sam Kurtz **Est.** 2004 **Dozens** 400 **Vyds** 5.4ha
Winemaker and life partner of Bernadette Kaeding, Sam Kurtz, left his position as chief winemaker within the Orlando group in 2015, where he had worked for over 20 years. He had in fact helped Bernadette with the care of Red Art since 1996, when Bernadette purchased the nucleus of the vineyard. It had 1.49ha of 80-year-old dry-grown grenache; the remaining 3.95ha were planted over several years to shiraz, cabernet sauvignon, petit verdot and tempranillo. Until 2004 the grapes from the old and new plantings were sold to Rockford, Chateau Tanunda, Spinifex and David Franz. In that year Bernadette decided to make a small batch of wine (with advice from Sam) and continued to accumulate wine until '11, when she began selling wines under the Red Art label. With Sam onboard full-time it seems likely that all the grapes will be henceforth used in making the Red Art wines.

Red Art Single Vineyard Barossa Valley Grenache 2016 It's in a lighter spectrum: fresh, pleasing and restrained, with a bouquet of pretty florals, tar and rose hips. Sweet strawberries and raspberries filter through the savouriness of the palate with supple tannins on the elegant finish. Screwcap. 14.1% alc. **Rating** 93 **To** 2024 $35 JF
Red Art Single Vineyard Barossa Valley Tempranillo 2016 Harvested at various stages from 28 Jan to 2 Mar. Dried on racks for 12 days, matured in French oak for 12 months. It's come together very well, retaining its savoury, sandy tannins while staying fresh and bright, with plenty of florals, red licorice, warm earth and wood spices draped over the sour/ripe cherry fruit. 60 dozen produced. Screwcap. 13.9% alc. **Rating** 93 **To** 2023 $35 JF
Red Art Single Vineyard Barossa Valley Shiraz 2015 A sway of dark fruit comes encased in sweet oak, roasted coffee, soy sauce and all manner of spices. Richly flavoured, with plenty of muscle to the dense structure, and a radicchio bitter finish. Screwcap. 14.3% alc. **Rating** 92 **To** 2027 $35 JF

Red Feet Wines

49 Cemetery Lane, King Valley, Vic 3678 **Region** King Valley
T (03) 5729 3535 **www**.redfeet.com.au **Open** Thurs–Mon 10–5
Winemaker Damien Star **Est.** 2010 **Dozens** 450 **Vyds** 1.8ha
Red Feet is the venture of Damien and sister Megan Star, he the winemaker and viticulturist, she the business manager. Damien graduated with a wine science degree from CSU in 2001, and worked in the Riverina and Riverland, then in Germany, to Fingerlakes in the US, and finally Kamberra in the ACT, for three valuable years with Alex McKay. Megan grew up on a farm with Damien, and understands the importance of quality and value-adding, obtaining a Bachelor of Agricultural Economics and a PhD in Natural Resource Management. Damien found his way to the King Valley, working for several local wineries before he and Megan purchased their 33ha property in the King Valley which had a house, a dilapidated vineyard and a farm shed. They replanted the 1.8ha vineyard split between sangiovese, nebbiolo, tempranillo and zinfandel. The shed, with its earth floor, became a de facto winery, its pride and joy a 300kg hand-operated basket press. Brother Vincent, with a degree in commerce, has joined the business, his wood-crafting skills put to good use in the building of the new cellar door.

King Valley Gewurztraminer 2016 Has spicy lychee rose petal flavours that are strongly varietal, and avoids the heavy/phenolic/flat finish that often spoils the start. Screwcap. 12.6% alc. **Rating** 91 **To** 2023 $25
King Valley Syrah 2014 Machine-harvested, open-fermented with 10% whole bunches, matured for 15 months in French oak. A substantial wine by any standards, particularly the King Valley. Ample blackberry, plum and cherry fruits are given context and structure by well judged extraction of tannins and oak. Screwcap. 14% alc. **Rating** 91 **To** 2029 $35

King Valley Riesling 2016 This is a pretty good King Valley riesling, developing nicely and with more to come. The same price as Henschke Peggy's Hill Riesling, by chance tasted next to each other, but this is what can happen out in the market place. Screwcap. 12.3% alc. **Rating** 90 **To** 2026 $25

King Valley Pinot Gris 2016 Hand-picked, crushed and destemmed, fermented with cultured yeast. Has more pear – fresh, poached, dried – than many pinot gris. Screwcap. 13.5% alc. **Rating** 90 **To** 2019 $25

King Valley Rose 2017 Wow. 15% gewurztraminer pressings (skins) and saignee of 50% sangiovese and 35% shiraz. This is innovation in a glass: the aromas and flavours like quicksilver, dancing across the palate – citrus, spice and red fruits – first you see it, next it's gone. Well worth a bottle with friends. Screwcap. 12.8% alc. **Rating** 90 **To** 2018 $20 ✪

Red Hill Estate

53 Shoreham Road, Red Hill South, Vic 3937 **Region** Mornington Peninsula
T (03) 5989 2838 **www**.redhillestate.com.au **Open** 7 days 11–5
Winemaker Donna Stephens **Est.** 1989 **Dozens** 25 000 **Vyds** 9.7ha
Red Hill Estate was established in 1989 by the Derham family. It is now owned and run by the Fabrizio family. Fruit is sourced from two estate vineyards: the main property and the Merricks Grove vineyard. The cellar door and Max's Restaurant have spectacular views across the Red Hill vineyard and Westernport Bay. Exports to the US, Canada, Ireland, Poland, Sweden, Singapore, Japan and Hong Kong.

🍷🍷🍷🍷🍷 Single Vineyard Chardonnay 2015 Saucy oak and a slash of ripe fruit makes a statement upfront and continues its fine form all the way to the finish line. Nougat, grapefruit, stone fruit, an all-round creaminess and excellent persistence. Top notch. Screwcap. 13.5% alc. **Rating** 95 **To** 2023 $60 CM

Single Vineyard Shiraz 2015 White pepper and peppercorn characters establish the landscape from the outset. This wears its cool-climate origin as a badge of honour. Red and black cherry flavours provide ample support, as do stringy herb notes and a push of smoky oak. Tannin has a slightly bunchy, drying aspect; the only moment of pause. There's a lot to love about this. A little extra time in bottle and it will sing. Screwcap. 13.5% alc. **Rating** 94 **To** 2028 $70 CM

🍷🍷🍷🍷🍷 Merricks Grove Chardonnay 2016 Rating 93 To 2027 $37 CM
Pinot Gris 2017 Rating 91 To 2021 CM
Merricks Grove Pinot Noir 2016 Rating 90 To 2024 CM

Redbank

Whitfield Road, King Valley, Vic 3678 **Region** King Valley
T (08) 8561 3200 **www**.redbankwines.com **Open** Not
Winemaker Marc Van Haldren **Est.** 2005 **Dozens** 33 000 **Vyds** 15ha
The Redbank brand was for decades the umbrella for Neill and Sally Robb's Sally's Paddock. In 2005 Hill-Smith Family Vineyards acquired the Redbank brand from the Robbs, leaving them with the winery, surrounding vineyard and the Sally's Paddock label. Redbank purchases grapes from the King Valley, Whitlands, Beechworth and the Ovens Valley (among other vineyard sources). Exports to all major markets.

🍷🍷🍷🍷🍷 Sunday Morning King Valley Pinot Gris 2017 The balance of acidity and low-level residual sugar lies behind the juicy, spiced pear flavours. A gold medal Melbourne Wine Awards '17 for a simply made wine may seem generous, but is understandable. Screwcap. 13% alc. **Rating** 94 **To** 2021 $22 ✪

🍷🍷🍷🍷 King Valley Prosecco 2017 Rating 89 To 2019 $22
Ellora King Valley Vintage Chardonnay Pinot Noir Brut Cuvee 2013 Rating 89 $25 TS

Redgate ★★★★☆

659 Boodjidup Road, Margaret River, WA 6285 **Region** Margaret River
T (08) 9757 6488 **www**.redgatewines.com.au **Open** 7 days 10–4.30
Winemaker Joel Page **Est.** 1977 **Dozens** 6000 **Vyds** 18ha
Founder and owner of Redgate, the late Bill Ullinger, chose the name not simply because of the nearby eponymous beach, but also because – so it is said – a local farmer (with a prominent red gate at his property) had run an illegal spirit-still 100 or so years ago, and its patrons would come to the property and ask whether there was any 'red gate' available. True or not, Redgate was one of the early movers in the region, and now has close to 20ha of mature estate plantings (the majority to sauvignon blanc, semillon, cabernet sauvignon, cabernet franc, shiraz and chardonnay, with smaller plantings of chenin blanc and merlot). Exports to Denmark, Switzerland, Singapore, Japan and China.

TTTTT **Reserve Margaret River Chardonnay 2016** A fully flavoured chardonnay to swoon over. Mid-weighted and vibrant, yet confidently flooding the drinker with scents of peaches and cream; vanilla pod oak, nougat, cashew and caramelised apple tart with a wisp of cinnamon. Exuberant, yet welcome mineral energy and pungent acidity guide the long finish. Screwcap. 13.2% alc. **Rating** 95 To 2025 $60 NG

TTTTY **Margaret River Cabernet Sauvignon 2016** Rating 93 To 2024 $38 NG
Reserve Margaret River Cabernet Sauvignon 2016 Rating 93 To 2035 $65 NG
Margaret River Cabernet Franc 2016 Rating 92 To 2033 $40 NG
Margaret River Shiraz 2016 Rating 90 To 2026 $33 NG

RedHeads Studios ★★★★☆

258 Angaston Road, Nuriootpa, SA 5353 **Region** South Australia
T 0457 073 347 **www**.redheadswine.com **Open** By appt
Winemaker Dan Graham **Est.** 2003 **Dozens** 10 000
RedHeads was established by Tony Laithwaite in McLaren Vale, and has since moved to the Barossa Valley. The aim was to allow winemakers working under corporate banners to produce small batch wines. The team 'liberates' premium parcels of grapes from large companies, 'a few rows at a time, to give them the special treatment they deserve and to form wines of true individuality and character. It's all about creating wines with personality, that are made to be enjoyed'.

TTTTT **Night of the Living Red Durif Cabernet Sauvignon Touriga 2016** It's akin to the front row of a rugby union scrum: cabernet the hooker, durif and touriga the props. It's seemingly impossible to suggest this wine could possibly be serious and worth $40, but it is. It is richly endowed with all the black fruits and tannins, yet its balance is so good; the flavours melt in the mouth like dark Belgian chocolate. Screwcap. 14.5% alc. **Rating** 95 To 2036 $40
Whip Hand Barossa Cabernet Sauvignon 2015 This is a good Barossa cabernet – it could be part Eden Valley or Clare Valley, but RedHeads doesn't even think of giving a sucker an even break. It is medium-bodied, with plenty of blackcurrant to go around, tannins and oak outriders observing the action. Cork. 14.5% alc. **Rating** 94 To 2035 $55

TTTTY **Princess of Thieves Barossa Mourvedre Grenache Shiraz 2016** Rating 92 To 2023 $35
R'dotto Royale 2016 Rating 91 To 2023 $28

Redman ★★★★★

Main Road, Coonawarra, SA 5263 **Region** Coonawarra
T (08) 8736 3331 **www**.redman.com.au **Open** Mon–Fri 9–5, w'ends 10–4
Winemaker Bruce, Malcolm and Daniel Redman **Est.** 1966 **Dozens** 18 000 **Vyds** 34ha

In March 2008 the Redman family celebrated 100 years of winemaking in Coonawarra. The '08 vintage also marked the arrival to the business of Daniel, fourth-generation Redman winemaker. Daniel gained winemaking experience in Central Victoria, the Barossa Valley and the US before taking up his new position. It was felicitous timing, for although the '04 Cabernet Sauvignon and '04 Cabernet Merlot were each awarded a gold medal from the national wine show circuit in '07, they were the first such accolades for a considerable time. A major vineyard rejuvenation program is underway, but there will be no change to the portfolio of wines. The quality has stabilised at a level in keeping with the long history of the winery and its mature vines.

ΨΨΨΨΨ **Coonawarra Cabernet Sauvignon 2015** 40yo vines, crushed, open-fermented, 7 days on skins, matured in French oak (25% new) for 12 months. Six gold medals, four trophies. A great example of hands-off winemaking, and of the very best of the Redman medium-bodied style. Cassis fruit, modest oak and ripe but fine tannins are seamlessly woven together. The X-factor? Picked at perfect ripeness, down to the very day. If the wine had a screwcap it would be a 40-year proposition. Cork. 14.2% alc. **Rating** 96 **To** 2035 $33 ✪

The Last Row Limited Release Coonawarra Shiraz 2015 From the last remaining row of shiraz over 100yo, the remainder from 80yo vines; wild yeast–open fermented, matured for 18 months in French hogsheads. A shiraz of great distinction, its 300 dozen made available only at cellar door. It's elegant, medium-bodied, and has perfect balance and length. The first screwcap from Redman. Hurrah. 14.9% alc. **Rating** 95 **To** 2035 $30 ✪

ΨΨΨΨΨ **Coonawarra Cabernet Sauvignon Merlot 2014 Rating** 90 **To** 2029 $36

Reillys Wines   ★★★★

Cnr Leasingham Road/Hill Street, Mintaro, SA 5415 **Region** Clare Valley
T (08) 8843 9013 **www.**reillyswines.com.au **Open** 7 days 10–4
Winemaker Justin Ardill **Est.** 1994 **Dozens** 25 000 **Vyds** 115ha
This has been a very successful venture for Adelaide cardiologist Justin Ardill and wife Julie, beginning as a hobby in 1994, but growing significantly over the intervening years. They now have vineyards at Watervale, Leasingham and Mintaro, growing riesling, cabernet sauvignon, shiraz, grenache, tempranillo and merlot. The cellar door and restaurant were built between 1856 and 1866 by Irish immigrant Hugh Reilly; 140 years later they were restored by the Ardills, distant relatives of Reilly. Exports to Canada, Malaysia, Singapore, NZ, Hong Kong and China.

ΨΨΨΨΨ **Watervale Riesling 2017** Gleaming straw-green; the bouquet gives little hint of what is to come on the palate. It's driven and magnified by crunchy natural acidity, which provides the framework for lime, lemon and Granny Smith apple flavours. Gold medal Canberra International Riesling Challenge '17. Screwcap. 12% alc. **Rating** 94 **To** 2027 $25 ✪

ΨΨΨΨΨ **Epitaph Clare Valley Shiraz 2014 Rating** 93 **To** 2029 $80 SC
Dry Land Clare Valley Shiraz 2015 Rating 91 **To** 2030 $32 SC
Clare Valley Shiraz 2015 Rating 90 **To** 2029 $25
Stoneflower Limited Release Clare Valley Merlot Cabernet Sauvignon 2014 Rating 90 **To** 2024 $30
The Dancer Limited Release Clare Valley Cabernet Sauvignon 2014 Rating 90 **To** 2044 $45
Dry Land Clare Valley Tempranillo 2016 Rating 90 **To** 2025 $29 SC

Renzaglia Wines   ★★★★

38 Bosworth Falls Road, O'Connell, NSW 2795 **Region** Central Ranges
T (02) 6337 5756 **www.**renzagliawines.com.au **Open** By appt
Winemaker Mark Renzaglia **Est.** 2011 **Dozens** 2000 **Vyds** 5ha

Mark Renzaglia is a second-generation vigneron, his father growing vines in southern Illinois, US. Mark and wife Sandy planted their first vineyard in 1997 (1ha of chardonnay, cabernet sauvignon and merlot), Mark making wine in small quantities while working as a grapegrower/winemaker at Winburndale Wines. In 2011 he and Sandy started their own business. Mark also manages a vineyard in the middle of the famous Mount Panorama race circuit, and has access to the grapes from the 4ha Mount Panorama Estate (another vineyard, from which Brokenwood purchased chardonnay for some years). This gives him access to shiraz, semillon, cabernet sauvignon and chardonnay. He also purchases grapes from other local growers. Exports to the US.

♥♥♥♥♀ **Mount Panorama Estate Shiraz 2016** A firm, dry, stylish red, with black cherry, satsuma plum and red licorice flavours running impressively through the palate. It's well cut, well polished and well presented, the finish yet another tick in its favour. Screwcap. 13.8% alc. **Rating** 93 **To** 2026 $35 CM
Bella Luna Chardonnay 2017 Clearly varietal and served fresh, the flavours run in uncomplicated fashion through the palate before exiting cleanly on the finish. White peach, green pineapple, citrus and a dash of grapefruit; it puts on a juicy display. Screwcap. 12.5% alc. **Rating** 90 **To** 2024 $35 CM

♥♥♥♥ **Dog's Day Chardonnay 2017 Rating** 89 **To** 2022 $22 CM
Stone Wall Sangiovese 2016 Rating 89 **To** 2022 $28 CM

Reschke Wines

Level 1, 183 Melbourne Street, North Adelaide, SA 5006 (postal) **Region** Coonawarra
T (08) 8239 0500 **www**.reschke.com.au **Open** Not
Winemaker Peter Douglas (Contract) **Est.** 1998 **Dozens** 25 000 **Vyds** 155ha
The Reschke family has been a landowner in Coonawarra for 100 years, with a large holding that is part terra rossa, part woodland. Cabernet sauvignon (with 120ha) takes the lion's share of the plantings, with merlot, shiraz and petit verdot making up the balance. Exports to the UK, Canada, Germany, Malaysia, Japan, Hong Kong and China.

Reynella

Reynell Road, Reynella, SA 5161 **Region** McLaren Vale/Fleurieu Peninsula
T 1800 088 711 **www**.reynellawines.ocm.au **Open** Fri 11–4
Winemaker Paul Carpenter **Est.** 1838 **Dozens** NFP
John Reynell laid the foundations for Chateau Reynella in 1838; over the next 100 years the stone buildings, winery and underground cellars, and attractive gardens, were constructed. Thomas Hardy's first job in SA was with Reynella; he noted in his diary that he would be able to better himself soon. He did just that, becoming by far the largest producer in that state by the end of the 19th century; 150 or so years after Chateau Reynella's foundation, CWA (now Accolade Wines) completed the circle by making it its corporate headquarters, while preserving the integrity of the Reynella brand in no uncertain fashion. Exports to all major markets.

♥♥♥♥♥ **Basket Pressed McLaren Vale Grenache 2016** Vivid crimson-purple hue; grenache can hardly be more complex than this, yet it is immaculately balanced. Its flavours are in a dark cherry, raspberry spectrum; tannins are like silk, the finish fresh. Above all else, not a scintilla of confection. Screwcap. 14.5% alc. **Rating** 97 **To** 2036 $69 ✪

♥♥♥♥♥ **Basket Pressed McLaren Vale Shiraz 2016** If you are looking for a full-bodied shiraz with real class, it's hard to go past this. It offers regional bitter chocolate, blackberry and plum fruit, oak and tannins lined up in disciplined support. A super-long future ahead. Screwcap. 14.5% alc. **Rating** 95 **To** 2041 $69
Basket Pressed McLaren Vale Cabernet Sauvignon 2016 The wine is a richly textured and structured carpet of blackcurrant fruit, cabernet tannins dancing a jig at every point along the way to the finish. Oak makes a contribution, but it is the least of the three pillars. Screwcap. 14% alc. **Rating** 95 **To** 2041 $69

Richard Hamilton

Cnr Main Road/Johnston Road, McLaren Vale, SA 5171 **Region** McLaren Vale
T (08) 8323 8830 **www**.leconfieldwines.com **Open** Mon–Fri 10–5, w'ends hols 11–5
Winemaker Paul Gordon, Tim Bailey **Est.** 1972 **Dozens** 25 000 **Vyds** 71.6ha
Richard Hamilton has outstanding estate vineyards, some of great age, all fully mature. An experienced and skilled winemaking team has allowed the full potential of those vineyards to be realised. The quality, style and consistency of both red and white wines has reached a new level; being able to keep only the best parcels for the Richard Hamilton brand is an enormous advantage. For reasons outside the *Wine Companion*'s control, not all the current releases were available for tasting for the 2019 edition. Exports to the UK, the US, Canada, Denmark, Sweden, Germany, Belgium, Malaysia, Vietnam, Hong Kong, Singapore, Japan, China and NZ.

Centurion Shiraz 2016 From 124yo vines, part fermented in a new French oak vat, the balance in small static fermenters with 4 pumpovers daily and 600kg open fermenters with whole bunches/whole berries and hand-plunged, the free-run and pressings matured separately in new and used French hogsheads. The extremely complex processes, plus new (22%) and used oak, have given rise to a very attractive full-bodied wine. This is a great wine, with its storehouse of black fruits, round but plentiful tannins and high quality oak, all perfectly balanced against each other. Screwcap. 14.5% alc. **Rating** 97 **To** 2046 $80 ❂

Little Road Shiraz 2016 This wine was tasted immediately after the Centurion, and rose to the challenge without blinking once. The colour is good, the wine with resounding fruit flavours of black cherry and Cherry Ripe, which are carried by fine, persistent tannins through the length of the palate. Fantastic value. Screwcap. 14.5% alc. **Rating** 94 **To** 2036 $21 ❂
Burton's Vineyard Old Bush Vine Grenache 2016 From vines planted in 1947. Bright crimson colour; the varietal character is undeniable, but, as Burton's Vineyard is wont, at the upper end of the ripeness scale, with raspberry and plum in a fairly warm embrace. Screwcap. 15% alc. **Rating** 94 **To** 2026

Colton's GSM 2016 Rating 93 **To** 2030 DB
Hut Block Cabernet Sauvignon 2016 Rating 91 **To** 2026
The Smuggler Shiraz 2016 Rating 90 **To** 2028 DB

Ridgemill Estate

218 Donges Road, Severnlea, Qld 4352 **Region** Granite Belt
T (07) 4683 5211 **www**.ridgemillestate.com **Open** Fri–Mon 10–5, Sun 10–3
Winemaker Martin Cooper, Peter McGlashan **Est.** 1998 **Dozens** 900 **Vyds** 2.1ha
Martin Cooper and Dianne Maddison acquired what was then known as Emerald Hill Winery in 2004. In '05 they reshaped the vineyards, which now have plantings of chardonnay, tempranillo, shiraz, merlot, cabernet sauvignon, saperavi, verdelho and viognier, setting a course down the alternative variety road. There is a quite spectacular winery and cellar door facility, and self-contained cabins in the vineyard.

The Czar Granite Belt Saperavi 2015 Dense, deep crimson-purple; I was concerned that this would be a monster given its extended maceration – in fact it's a particularly good saperavi, with almost succulent fruit, an expression I never imagined I would use with this variety. Its tannins are ripe and balanced, the black cherry and plum fruits in perfect harmony. Screwcap. 14% alc. **Rating** 95 **To** 2030 $45
WYP Granite Belt Chardonnay 2016 Hand-picked, destemmed, a portion fermented and matured for 9 months in French oak, the remainder in stainless steel with regular stirring. The winemaking plan achieved all of its aims, protecting the varietal fruit and framing it with precisely worked oak; the finish is long and clean, with crisp acidity to close. Screwcap. 13% alc. **Rating** 94 **To** 2022 $35

Joshua's Pup Granite Belt Shiraz Grenache 2016 Rating 91 **To** 2031 $45
Granite Belt Viognier 2017 Rating 90 **To** 2018 $35
The Spaniard Granite Belt Tempranillo 2015 Rating 90 **To** 2025 $28

RidgeView Wines

273 Sweetwater Road, Pokolbin, NSW 2320 **Region** Hunter Valley
T (02) 6574 7332 **www**.ridgeview.com.au **Open** Wed–Sun 10–5
Winemaker Darren Scott, Gary MacLea **Est.** 2000 **Dozens** 2500 **Vyds** 9ha
Darren and Tracey Scott have transformed a 40ha timbered farm into a vineyard, together with self-contained accommodation and a cellar door. The greater part of the plantings are 4.5ha of shiraz, with cabernet sauvignon, chambourcin, merlot, pinot gris, viognier and traminer making up a somewhat eclectic selection of other varieties.

ŸŸŸŸŸ **Impressions Hunter Valley Shiraz 2016** Made by Mark Woods (Leogate).
A deep, lustrous crimson, with notes of blueberry and blackberry pressing a gentle throttle of fruit from nose to palate. This accelerates across relaxed cylinders of anise, leather cream and bracken. The tannic pistons are well oiled, but firm – attractively so. A dutifully built chassis of drinkability. A fine effort from a challenging year, trophy for Best Named Vineyard Red at the Hunter Valley Wine Show '17. Screwcap. 14% alc. **Rating** 95 **To** 2028 $40 NG

Museum Release Hunter Valley Semillon 2005 Transformed with age; the lightness and transparency of youth morphing with a rich, textural core of butter, lemon curd and truffle. The thread of acidity is juicy, no longer shins and elbows, keeping the festivities lively. Delicious. I would be drinking this now, but it shan't drop from its balletic graces any time soon. Screwcap. 11.5% alc. **Rating** 94 **To** 2021 $50 NG

ŸŸŸŸŸ **Generations Reserve Semillon 2017** **Rating** 93 **To** 2027 $25 NG ✪
Impressions Hunter Valley Shiraz 2015 **Rating** 93 **To** 2030 $35 NG
Museum Release Generations Reserve Semillon 2013 **Rating** 92 **To** 2023 $35 NG
Museum Release Impressions Hunter Valley Chardonnay 2012 **Rating** 92 **To** 2020 $40 NG
Museum Release Impressions Hunter Valley Shiraz 2011 **Rating** 92 **To** 2022 $50 NG
Generations Reserve Shiraz 2014 **Rating** 91 **To** 2026 $40 NG
Museum Release Generations Reserve Hunter Valley Semillon 2008 **Rating** 90 **To** 2022 $35 NG

Rieslingfreak ★★★★★

8 Roenfeldt Drive, Tanunda, SA 5352 **Region** Clare Valley
T (08) 8563 3963 **www**.rieslingfreak.com **Open** By appt
Winemaker John Hughes **Est.** 2009 **Dozens** 5000 **Vyds** 35ha
The name of John Hughes' winery leaves no doubt about his long-term ambition: to explore every avenue of riesling, whether bone dry or sweet, coming from regions across the wine world, albeit with a strong focus on Australia. The wines made from his Clare Valley vineyard offer dry (No. 2, No. 3 and No. 4), off-dry (No. 5 and No. 8), sparkling (No. 9) and fortified (No. 7) styles. Exports to Canada, Norway, Hong Kong and NZ.

ŸŸŸŸŸ **No. 2 Riesling 2017** If this wine doesn't stop you in your tracks, nothing will. It's the very essence of Polish Hill River – superfine acid line, pristine and defined. A whisper of white florals, white pepper, wet pebbles and requisite lemon peel and pith. And, of course, it is dry, crisp, the length going on and on. There is such drive to this; arguably the most commanding of Rieslingfreak's '17s. Screwcap. 11.5% alc. **Rating** 97 **To** 2032 $35 JF ✪

ŸŸŸŸŸ **No. 10 Zenit Riesling 2017** Zenit is German for zenith and thus represents the pinnacle for winemaker John Hughes, the wine created with partner Belinda Sinclair to celebrate their wedding in Oct '17. Thankfully there was enough made to share with Rieslingfreak's fans. Made from 50% Clare Valley, 40% Eden Valley and 10% Polish Hill River grapes and very much the sum of its parts: fine lemon-sorbet acidity mingling with lemon blossom, lithe, long and pure. Screwcap. 11.5% alc. **Rating** 96 **To** 2027 $45 JF ✪

No. 4 Riesling 2017 Eden Valley riesling is in a class of its own with such a unique stamp, from its heady fragrance to how it feels on the palate. While this has a touch more weight from well handled phenolics, it also has precision. Juicy, with a core of very good fruit, a fusion of lemon-lime freshness and mandarin peel and no shortage of invigorating acidity. Screwcap. 11.5% alc. **Rating** 96 **To** 2030 $25 JF ○

No. 3 Riesling 2017 From the family White Hutt vineyard. While there's a hint of savouriness, it starts with cottage garden aromas of white blossom and ginger spice, and lemon juice freshness and the fragrance of wet stones. It's a giving wine with very fine, soft acidity, which means it's drinking beautifully now yet will reward the patient. Oh, and it snaffled five awards at the Sydney Wine Show '17 including Best Wine Of Show. Screwcap. 11.5% alc. **Rating** 95 **To** 2027 $25 JF ○

♟♟♟♟♟ No. 6 Riesling 2013 **Rating** 93 **To** 2022 $40 JF
No. 5 Riesling 2017 **Rating** 93 **To** 2028 $25 JF ○
No. 8 Riesling 2017 **Rating** 92 **To** 2024 $35 JF

 # Rikard Wines

140 McLachlan Street, Orange, NSW 2800 (postal) **Region** Orange
T 0428 633 320 **www**.rikardwines.com.au **Open** Not
Winemaker William Rikard-Bell **Est.** 2015 **Dozens** 600
This is a remarkable 17-year story of a freewheeling youth that seemed to accidentally lead William Rikard-Bell into a career as a winemaker. Halfway through the journey, he made national headlines when an explosion at Drayton Family Wines in the Hunter Valley killed two others and left William with serious burns to 70% of his body, his life hanging by a thread and a two-year recovery ahead. His first job as winemaker had been at Canobolas Smith in Orange, and after interludes in Bordeaux, Mudgee and the Hunter, he returned to Orange in '11. Together with wife Kimberley (and their two young daughters) he began small batch contract winemaking in '15, and bought land at 1040m the following year, planting chardonnay and pinot noir. He has plans underway for a winery and cellar door (with 'killer views'). He clearly has an innate feel for making Chardonnay and Pinot Noir, and the future is bright. Watch this space.

♟♟♟♟♟ Black Label Orange Chardonnay 2016 Hand-picked, whole-bunch pressed, wild-fermented on full juice solids in French barriques (25% new), matured for 10 months. A best barrel selection that distinguishes itself with an extra level of intensity and complexity that draws out the length of the finish. Screwcap. 12.6% alc. **Rating** 95 **To** 2024 $55

Black Label Orange Pinot Noir 2016 Clones 114, 667 and MV6, wild-fermented with 33% whole bunches, matured in French barriques (40% new). A barrel selection of the best of vintage, the style is very similar to its varietal sibling, the difference lying in the length of the palate and power of its aftertaste. Screwcap. 13.7% alc. **Rating** 95 **To** 2029 $65

Orange Chardonnay 2016 Flawless winemaking, coupled with high quality grapes. An elegant wine, with very good balance between fruit, acidity and oak. Flows across the mouth, reaching every part. Screwcap. 12.7% alc. **Rating** 94 **To** 2022 $30 ○

Orange Pinot Noir 2016 Light, faintly turbid colour; a pinot with personality and punch to its mix of fresh red and sour cherries; has very good line and length. Screwcap. 13.7% alc. **Rating** 94 **To** 2027 $40

Orange Shiraz 2016 The light, bright ruby colour and fragrant bouquet have a pinotesque note, as does the lifted, juicy finish of the palate. Striking wine. Screwcap. 13.9% alc. **Rating** 94 **To** 2029 $50

Rileys of Eden Valley

PO Box 71, Eden Valley, SA 5235 **Region** Eden Valley
T (08) 8564 1029 **www**.rileysofedenvalley.com.au **Open** Not
Winemaker Peter Riley, Jo Irvine (Consultant) **Est.** 2006 **Dozens** 2000 **Vyds** 11.24ha

Rileys of Eden Valley is owned by Terry and Jan Riley with son Peter, who, way back in 1982, purchased 32ha of a grazing property that they believed had potential for quality grape production. The first vines were planted in that year and now extend to over 12ha. In '98 Terry retired from his position (professor of mechanical engineering) at the University of SA, allowing him to concentrate on the vineyard, and, more recently, winemaking activities, but the whole family (including granddaughter Maddy) have been involved in the development of the property. It had always been intended that the grapes would be sold, but when not all the grapes were contracted in '06, the Rileys decided to produce some wine and they've not looked back.

🍷🍷🍷🍷🍷 **Jump Ship Shiraz 2015** Just into full-bodied territory, with both red- and black-berried fruit flavours and a generous coating of coffee-cream oak. This is simultaneously soft, eager-to-please and well structured, with plenty of flavour gushing through the finish. Perfect red for a winter's evening. Screwcap. 14.5% alc. **Rating** 94 **To** 2028 $30 CM ✪

🍷🍷🍷🍷🍷 **Cabernet Sauvignon 2016 Rating** 93 **To** 2030 $30 CM
Museum Release Family Riesling 2010 Rating 90 **To** 2019 $30 CM

Riposte ★★★★★
PO Box 256, Lobethal, SA 5241 **Region** Adelaide Hills
T (08) 8389 8149 **www**.timknappstein.com.au **Open** Not
Winemaker Tim Knappstein **Est.** 2006 **Dozens** 11 000
It's never too late to teach an old dog new tricks, particularly when the old dog in question is Tim Knappstein. With 50+ years of winemaking and more than 500 wine show awards under his belt, Tim started another new wine life in 2006 with Riposte. This business is owned and run by Tim, wife Dale and son Nick, and has annually produced wines of quality and style at prices that are mouthwatering. The wines are sold through select retailers and restaurants across Australia, and exported to various international markets. Exports to the UK, the US, Switzerland, Denmark, Indonesia and China.

🍷🍷🍷🍷🍷 **Reserve Adelaide Hills Pinot Noir 2016** The second Reserve release, and lives up to expectations. It is supremely elegant, yet has power partially hidden in the folds of the cape. The hue is bright crimson-purple, and the flavour and structure meld intense cherry fruit with fine-spun, persistent tannins. Screwcap. 13.5% alc. **Rating** 96 **To** 2031 $80
The Dagger Adelaide Hills Pinot Noir 2017 Full colour. The dagger has only just been drawn as at September '17, but will underwrite the development of a wine that has much to offer. It has considerable depth and complexity to its plum and dark cherry fruit. A foresty/earthy subtext adds another dimension. Screwcap. 13.5% alc. **Rating** 94 **To** 2025 $20 ✪

🍷🍷🍷🍷🍷 **The Katana Adelaide Hills Chardonnay 2016 Rating** 93 **To** 2021 $28 CM

Rise Vineyards ★★★★
PO Box 7336, Adelaide, SA 5000 **Region** Clare Valley
T 0419 844 238 **www**.risevineyards.com.au **Open** Not
Winemaker Matthew McCulloch **Est.** 2009 **Dozens** 1200
Rise is very much a busman's holiday for Grant Norman and Matthew McCulloch. The two are a close-knit team, Grant looking after the business and Matt the wine. Matt spent more than a decade in the UK wine trade. In 2006 Matt and wife Gina moved to the Clare Valley, where he was responsible for sales and marketing at Kirrihill Wines, of which Grant, an Australian wine industry veteran, was general manager. The move to Clare enabled Matt and Gina to realise a long-held dream of owning their own vineyard, growing the grapes and making the wine, with the help of Grant and his wife Alice. Having spent 11 years on the road, working with more than 70 winemakers in 13 countries, Matt was convinced the focus of Rise should be on making small-scale, terroir-driven Riesling, Cabernet Sauvignon, Grenache and Shiraz, reflecting the unique vineyard sites from which they come. Exports to China.

ŢŢŢŢŢ **Watervale Riesling 2017** Kaffir lime and lemon-scented bath salts kick start the steely engine, forceful despite the wine's light to mid-weighted composure. Bristling across high-wired, mineral cylinders, the wine careens to a finish of pumice and talc. This is a liquid postcard for Watervale. The range is vegan and vegetarian-friendly to boot, indicating the avoidance of malign fining agents. Screwcap. 11.5% alc. **Rating** 93 **To** 2027 $23 NG ✪

Clare Valley Shiraz 2016 This is very good regional shiraz, with the Clare's black to blue-fruited generosity and mint billowing across gentle oak seams; nicely hewn tannins, pulpy and moreish. A lesson in generosity meets restraint, this mid to full-weighted wine is eminently drinkable sans any overt reductive notes. Others take heed! Screwcap. 14.5% alc. **Rating** 93 **To** 2022 $25 NG ✪

Clare Valley Grenache 2016 Vines dating from the mid-'60s, planted on loam over an ironstone substrata, have delivered a delicious mid-weight grenache. The wine is lithe in its delivery of cherry kirsch notes and there's a spurt of dried herb across a jangle of cranberry acidity. Screwcap. 14.5% alc. **Rating** 92 **To** 2020 $22 NG ✪

Clare Valley Cabernet Sauvignon 2016 A gentle cabernet, striking the chord of judicious extraction shared among the other wines in the range. In this case, though, a bit more extraction may have imparted some welcome tannic respite to the gentle currant, kirsch and leafy notes, growing sweeter with each sip. The oak, as always, is sensibly dished up. Screwcap. 14% alc. **Rating** 92 **To** 2022 $25 NG ✪

Risky Business Wines   ★★★★

PO Box 6015, East Perth, WA 6892 **Region** Various
T 0457 482 957 **www**.riskybusinesswines.com.au **Open** Not
Winemaker Andrew Vesey, Gavin Berry, Michael Kerrigan **Est.** 2013 **Dozens** 4000
The name Risky Business is decidedly tongue-in-cheek, for the partnership headed by Rob Quenby has neatly side-stepped any semblance of risk. First up, the grapes come from vineyards in Great Southern and Margaret River that are managed by Quenby Viticultural Services. Since the batches of wine are very small (150–800 dozen), the partnership is able to select grapes specifically suited to the wine style and price. So there is no capital tied up in vineyards, nor in a winery – the wines are contract-made. Exports to Japan and China.

ŢŢŢŢŢ **Margaret River Cabernet Sauvignon 2015** Offers the joy of Margaret River cabernet, a reasonable price, and a larger make (550 dozen) – it's all a win for wine consumers. Medium in weight, dusted with chocolate, fresh with blackcurrant and lifted by mint/gum leaf notes. It slinks softly through the palate, seducing as it travels. Screwcap. 14.5% alc. **Rating** 93 **To** 2028 $25 CM ✪

Margaret River Shiraz Grenache Tempranillo 2015 It brings flavour, texture and personality to the table and, for that, it's a most welcome visitor. It presents a mixture of black/red berried fruit flavours with sandy/spicy/smoky inputs and feels lively and eager throughout. Spot-on for drinking now. Screwcap. 14.5% alc. **Rating** 92 **To** 2023 $25 CM ✪

Margaret River Cabernet Sauvignon 2016 Bright; attractive scents of currant, blueberry, dried sage and olive. The palate is full, but savoury, twirled around a carapace of ambitious oak and acidity – a bit incendiary in the wine's youth. It should age well in the medium term. **Rating** 92

White Knuckle Margaret River Chardonnay 2016 A good Margaret River chardonnay, with layers of ripe white peach, nectarine and fig fruit doing all the heavy lifting. Oak adds its weight in a controlled fashion, but is the least risky. Already drinking well. Screwcap. 13% alc. **Rating** 91 **To** 2022 $25

King Valley Pinot Gris 2017 250 dozen. Fresh as a daisy, clean as a whistle, soft as a baby's coo. I said coo. Apple and nashi pear flavours slide through the palate in a most pleasant fashion. Screwcap. 13% alc. **Rating** 90 **To** 2018 $25 CM

King Valley Prosecco NV It sits light on the tongue, but there's a bite of citrus-shot flavour to the finish; it swings easily through the palate and then gives you something to hold onto as you swallow. They've done pretty well here. Crown seal. 10% alc. **Rating** 90 **To** 2019 $25 CM

ŢŢŢŢ **Pinot Noir Rose 2017 Rating** 89 **To** 2019 $25 CM

Rivergate Wines

★★★

580 Goornong Road, Axedale, Vic 3551 **Region** Bendigo
T (03) 5439 7367 **www.rivergatewines.com.au Open** By appt
Winemaker Andrew Kotlarz, Geoff Kerr **Est.** 1999 **Dozens** 500 **Vyds** 2.2ha
Rivergate Wines is the Kerr family business, producing intense-flavoured, full-bodied wines at
Axedale, midway between Bendigo and Heathcote. They specialise in growing and producing
Shiraz, from low-yielding, hand-tended estate vines. The wines are matured in French and
American oak barriques for 12 months. When seasonal conditions permit, a small amount of
Reserve Shiraz is made.

    Bendigo Shiraz 2013 The colour is deep for its age; the black fruits powerful,
with a strong savoury backbone; the tannins still banging the drum. The wine
spent twice as long in barrel, the oak French, but boisterous. Screwcap. 14.8% alc.
Rating 89 **To** 2033 $30
Reserve Bendigo Shiraz 2008 A tribute to the screwcap just for starters, the
colour of a wine half its age. It's medium-bodied, its flavours very ripe and slightly
stewed, likely attractive to as many consumers as it deters. 15% alc. **Rating** 89
To 2023 $35

Riversdale Estate

★★★★☆

222 Denholms Road, Cambridge, Tas 7170 **Region** Southern Tasmania
T (03) 6248 5555 **www.riversdaleestate.com.au Open** 7 days 10–5
Winemaker Nick Badrice **Est.** 1991 **Dozens** 9000 **Vyds** 37ha
Ian Roberts purchased the Riversdale property in 1980 while a university student, and says
he paid a record price for the district. The unique feature of the property is its frontage to the
Pittwater estuary, which acts as a buffer against frost, and also moderates the climate during
the fruit's ripening phase. It is a large property, with 37ha of vines and one of the largest olive
groves in Tasmania, producing 50 olive-based products. Five families live permanently on
the estate, providing all the labour for the various operations, which also include four 5-star
French Provincial cottages overlooking the vines. A cellar door and French bistro opened
in '16. Wine quality is consistently good, and can be outstanding.

🍷🍷🍷🍷🍷 **Pinot Noir 2016** A complex pinot from the first whiff through to the sweet,
juicy fruit on the aftertaste. Spicy notes bounce off dark cherry/berry fruit on the
long palate, silky tannins providing structure. Tasmanian pinot is as Tasmanian pinot
does. Screwcap. 12.7% alc. **Rating** 95 **To** 2026 $38
Centaurus Pinot Noir 2016 Strong colour; a powerful rose with dark cherry/
plum fruit and tannins (just) sufficient to provide balance. Screwcap. 13.5% alc.
Rating 94 **To** 2026 $48

🍷🍷🍷🍷♀ **Crater Chardonnay 2016 Rating** 93 **To** 2024 $50

Rob Dolan Wines

★★★★☆

21–23 Delaneys Road, South Warrandyte, Vic 3134 **Region** Yarra Valley
T (03) 9876 5885 **www.robdolanwines.com.au Open** 7 days 10–5
Winemaker Rob Dolan, Mark Nikolich **Est.** 2010 **Dozens** 20 000 **Vyds** 25ha
Rob Dolan has been making wine in the Yarra Valley for over 20 years, and knows every
nook and cranny there. In 2011 he was able to purchase the Hardys Yarra Burn winery at
an enticing price. It is singularly well equipped, and in addition to making the excellent
Rob Dolan wines there, he conducts an extensive contract winemaking business. Business is
booming, production having doubled, with exports driving much of the increase. Exports to
the UK, the US, Canada, Malaysia, Singapore, Hong Kong and China.

    White Label Yarra Valley Cabernet Sauvignon 2016 Trophy Best Cabernet,
Yarra Valley Wine Show '17. It's an elegant wine but it's the seamless combination
of fruit and oak that really lifts your heart rate. Blackcurrant, bay leaf, cedar wood
and black olive flavours swoosh through the palate in confident style; mint and

boysenberry notes keeping the conversation flowing and fresh. Everything here is dotted and crossed; it's immaculate. Screwcap. 14% alc. **Rating** 95 **To** 2036 $35 CM ✪

ŢŢŢŢ♀ **White Label Pinot Gris 2017 Rating** 93 **To** 2019 $30 CM
White Label Shiraz 2016 Rating 93 **To** 2025 $35 CM
True Colours Field Blend 2016 Rating 92 **To** 2019 $24 CM ✪
True Colours Sauvignon Blanc 2017 Rating 90 **To** 2019 $24 CM

Rob Hall Wines   ★★★★★

157 Pine Avenue, Healesville, Vic 3777 (postal) **Region** Yarra Valley
T 0448 224 003 **www**.robhallwine.com.au **Open** Not
Winemaker Rob Hall **Est.** 2013 **Dozens** 2000 **Vyds** 3ha
Rob Hall has had considerable experience in making Yarra Valley chardonnay and pinot noir, previously at Mount Mary, and thereafter at Kellybrook. His business took several steps forward in 2015. First, he acquired the 3ha vineyard on the property where he grew up. It was planted in 1996 by his parents (in particular, mother Harriet, hence Harriet's Vineyard). Next, he leased the Limbic winery at Pakenham Upper. It has an underground barrel room, making it ideal for maturation, and also enabling much cellar work to be conducted using gravity. It is well equipped with a sorting table, Bucher crusher/destemmer, and a Bucher press.

ŢŢŢŢŢ **Harriet's Vineyard Yarra Valley Pinot Noir 2017** This follows the '15; none was made in '16 (the quality was not there). 90% destemmed, 10% whole bunches, 60% matured in 1yo French puncheons, the remainder in used hogsheads. It has a deep well of cherry fruit within the savoury/spicy envelope of superfine tannins. Screwcap. 13.5% alc. **Rating** 96 **To** 2027 $40 ✪
Yarra Valley Cabernets 2017 49% cabernet sauvignon, 48% merlot, 3% malbec. The time Rob Hall spent at Mount Mary with John Middleton comes through loud and clear with this elegant and immaculately balanced wine. It is smooth as silk, with cassis fruit in the vanguard; fine tannins are there, but don't interrupt the conversation. Screwcap. 12.5% alc. **Rating** 96 **To** 2037 $26 ✪
Yarra Valley Chardonnay 2017 The grapes come from 3 Lower and Upper Valley vineyards. It's a very interesting group and it works well. 70% whole-bunch pressed to barrel with full solids, 20% destemmed with 24 hours skin contact, 10% destemmed and fermented on skins for 7 days, matured in French oak (10% new). The bouquet is complex, as too is the palate; tangy, and with a long life ahead. Screwcap. 13% alc. **Rating** 95 **To** 2027 $26 ✪
Harriet's Vineyard Yarra Valley Chardonnay 2016 90% whole-bunch pressed to barrel with full solids, 10% destemmed and fermented on skins for 5 days, matured in new and used French oak. This has seriously good texture and structure; the aftertaste, too, is incredibly persistent. The flavours aren't so much in the grapefruit spectrum, as Meyer lemon. Bred to stay the distance. Screwcap. 13% alc. **Rating** 95 **To** 2026 $40
Yarra Valley Pinot Noir 2017 Hand-picked in small batches from multiple vineyards, most destemmed, 10% of the batches fermented with 100% whole bunches, typically 10 days on skins (a few batches for 1 month); matured in French oak (10% new). This shares its elegance with Harriet's Vineyard, and also a balanced web of spicy, savoury tannins. Rob Hall didn't miss the opportunities of the '17 vintage. Screwcap. 13.5% alc. **Rating** 95 **To** 2024 $26 ✪

Robert Channon Wines   ★★★★

32 Bradley Lane, Amiens, Qld 4352 **Region** Granite Belt
T (07) 4683 3260 **www**.robertchannonwines.com **Open** Mon, Tues & Fri 11–4, w'ends 10–5
Winemaker Paola Cabezas **Est.** 1998 **Dozens** 2500 **Vyds** 8ha
Peggy and Robert Channon have established verdelho, chardonnay, pinot gris, shiraz, cabernet sauvignon and pinot noir under permanent bird protection netting. The initial cost of

installing permanent netting is high, but in the long term it is well worth it: it excludes birds and protects the grapes against hail damage. Also, there is no pressure to pick the grapes before they are fully ripe. Exports to NZ.

♀♀♀♀♀ **Reserve Granite Belt Shiraz 2016** There is rich, spicy berry character all through this wine, with elements of red and black fruit, and some vanillan sweetness which may be the American oak in play. The texture is supple and there's length of flavour on the palate, with well executed tannin pulling through the finish. Screwcap. 14% alc. **Rating** 94 **To** 2024 $30 SC ✪

Reserve Granite Belt Cabernet Sauvignon 2016 It's the variety clearly on show here, with aromas of very pure blackcurrant fruit, supported by black olive, cedar, and some perfectly valid green, grassy/herbal notes. The palate is elegant but flavoursome, of typically medium-to-full cabernet weight, finishing strongly. Screwcap. 14% alc. **Rating** 94 **To** 2024 $30 SC ✪

♀♀♀♀♀ **Chopin Granite Belt Chardonnay 2016 Rating** 91 **To** 2020 $30 SC
Reserve Granite Belt Pinot Noir 2016 Rating 90 **To** 2021 $35 SC
Reserve Granite Belt Malbec 2016 Rating 90 **To** 2021 $35 SC

Robert Oatley Vineyards   ★★★★★

Craigmoor Road, Mudgee, NSW 2850 **Region** Mudgee
T (02) 6372 2208 **www**.robertoatley.com.au **Open** 7 days 10–4
Winemaker Larry Cherubino, Rob Merrick **Est.** 2006 **Dozens** NFP **Vyds** 440ha
Robert Oatley Vineyards is the venture of the Oatley family, previously best known as the owners of Rosemount Estate until it was sold to Southcorp. Sandy Oatley is chairman, following the death of father Bob in 2016. Wild Oats, as anyone with the remotest interest in yachting and the Sydney–Hobart Yacht Race will know, has been the name of Bob's racing yachts. The family has long owned vineyards in Mudgee, but the new business was rapidly expanded by the acquisition of the Montrose winery and the Craigmoor cellar door and restaurant. The recruitment of Larry Cherubino as a winemaker has been a major factor in the radical reshaping of the overall business, with most of the best wines now coming from WA. While there is a plethora of wines, the portfolio is easy to understand: at the bottom, Pocketwatch; next Wild Oats; Robert Oatley Signature Series; Robert Oatley Finisterre; and at the top, Robert Oatley The Pennant. The Cornucopia wines are a joint project with Larry Cherubino. Exports to the UK, the US and other major markets (including China).

♀♀♀♀♀ **Robert Oatley The Pennant Margaret River Chardonnay 2013** Hand-picked, whole-bunch pressed direct to new French oak, wild-fermented, matured for 10 months, no racking or batonnage, 6 barrels made. This is an exceptional wine, showing that doing less can be the hardest. References to Burgundy irritate some, so I tend to stay away unless I feel strongly, as I do here. This is Australia's answer to Montrachet, and a convincing one at that. This is going up to the house. Screwcap. 13% alc. **Rating** 97 **To** 2025 $70 ✪

Robert Oatley The Pennant Frankland River Cabernet Sauvignon 2013 From the Justin vineyard, matured for 12 months in new and 1yo French oak, 6 barrels made. Purple-crimson hue; the bouquet doesn't dilly dally in nailing its colours to the mast, the racy, lithe palate in hot pursuit, the finishing line far distant. Screwcap. 14% alc. **Rating** 97 **To** 2037 $80 ✪

Robert Oatley The Pennant Margaret River Cabernet Sauvignon 2012 Excellent hue; the super-fragrant and expressive bouquet doesn't prepare you for the unadulterated power of the palate, putting this in the class of the super-cabernets that are the flagship wines of the First Families in Margaret River. It has tiers of fruit – the tannins there in respectful attendance – giving rise to perfect balance. Screwcap. **Rating** 97 **To** 2044 $80 ✪

Robert Oatley The Pennant Frankland River Cabernet Sauvignon 2012 The colour is deep crimson-purple, and the bouquet waves a warning that this isn't to be taken lightly. Despite all its power and drive, the wine is superbly balanced and focused: blackcurrant fruit is framed by impeccably trimmed tannins, cedary oak is equally poised. A great cabernet. Screwcap. 14.5% alc. **Rating** 97 To 2037 $80 ⚙

🍷🍷🍷🍷🍷 **Four in Hand Barossa Shiraz 2015** The bright purple-crimson colour sits well with the modest alcohol (slightly less than 14%). The wine bursts with juicy fruits, more red than black, the tannins perfectly weighted. Gold medals Melbourne and National Wine Shows '17, and winner of the Great Australian Shiraz Challenge '17. Screwcap. **Rating** 96 To 2030 $25 ⚙

Robert Oatley Finisterre Margaret River Cabernet Sauvignon 2015 This is looking pretty good, and very Margaret River. There is a pattern of flavours, and a pattern of textures from cedar and smoke, from purple to black fruits, from cassis to bay leaf. 24 hours later this wine was, by a small margin but enough to reflect in points, the best. Screwcap. **Rating** 96 To 2032 $40 ⚙

Robert Oatley Finisterre McLaren Vale Shiraz 2016 Essence of McLaren Vale shiraz; medium to full-bodied, but in a carefully tailored suit to give shape in the right places. While dark chocolate has a role, it's the intense black fruits that provide the drive and balance, aided and abetted by a savoury twitch of licorice. Screwcap. 14% alc. **Rating** 95 To 2036 $40

Robert Oatley Finisterre Great Southern Syrah 2015 Strong crimson-purple; a luxuriant cool-grown shiraz, spice/pepper sprinkled on the dark cherry robes of the fruit. Medium-bodied, with great overall balance, and a pleasantly savoury finish. Screwcap. 13.5% alc. **Rating** 95 To 2030 $40

Robert Oatley Finisterre Margaret River Cabernet Sauvignon 2016 The difference between this and its Great Southern sibling is profound. The colour is a slightly different shade, but it's the bouquet and the wine in the mouth that march to the tune of their own drum. This is more textured, and more nuanced in its palette. The corollary lies in the obvious question – is the Great Southern more pure? Screwcap. 14% alc. **Rating** 95 To 2036 $40

Robert Oatley Finisterre Great Southern Cabernet Sauvignon 2016 Deep, bright crimson-purple; kid gloves cabernet, every aspect from the first whiff of the bouquet through to the aftertaste of the palate is exactly proportioned and polished. Too well groomed? Natural wine lovers would hate it because it's a really lovely cabernet. Note to the natural camp: the only additive is a minimal amount of SO_2. Screwcap. 14% alc. **Rating** 95 To 2036 $40

Robert Oatley Finisterre Great Southern Cabernet Sauvignon 2015 Identical vinification to the '16. Imperceptibly lighter in colour, likewise in body. Which would I prefer to drink tonight? This wine. Which do I think is the better wine? The '16, by the barest margin, but 24 hours later it's this wine (by the same margin). Screwcap. 14% alc. **Rating** 95 To 2035 $40

Robert Oatley The Pennant Margaret River Chardonnay 2014 Very youthful for a 4yo chardonnay. A complex wine, with paths in different directions until they all come together at the finish. Screwcap. 13% alc. **Rating** 94 To 2023 $70

Robert Oatley The Pennant Margaret River Cabernet Sauvignon 2013 The balance is good, and the still tightly furled tannins present no problem – all the wine needs to do is put half a dozen Sydney to Hobart races under its belt. Screwcap. 13.5% alc. **Rating** 94 To 2038 $80

🍷🍷🍷🍷🍷 **Montrose Black Mudgee Shiraz 2016** Rating 92 To 2028 $35 JF
Wild Oats Sauvignon Blanc 2017 Rating 90 To 2019 $18 JF ⚙
Montrose Stony Creek Chardonnay 2016 Rating 90 To 2021 $23 JF
Wild Oats Mudgee Rose 2017 Rating 90 To 2018 $18 JF ⚙
Four in Hand Barossa Shiraz 2016 Rating 90 To 2024 $27

Robert Stein Vineyard

Pipeclay Lane, Mudgee, NSW 2850 **Region** Mudgee
T (02) 6373 3991 **www**.robertstein.com.au **Open** 7 days 10–4.30
Winemaker Jacob Stein **Est.** 1976 **Dozens** 20 000 **Vyds** 18.67ha

While three generations of the family have been involved since Robert (Bob) Stein established the vineyard, the winemaking pedigree stretches even further back, going to Bob's great-great-grandfather, Johann Stein, who was brought to Australia in 1838 by the Macarthur family to supervise the planting of the Camden Park Vineyard. Bob's son Drew and grandson Jacob have now taken over winemaking responsibilities. Jacob worked vintages in Italy, Canada, Margaret River and Avoca, and, more particularly, in the Rheingau and Rheinhessen regions of Germany. Since his return, one success has followed another. Exports to Germany, Hong Kong, Singapore and China.

🍷🍷🍷🍷🍷 **Reserve Mudgee Riesling 2017** Fermented wild in old oak. No oak flavour at all, but highly textural and fluid; the flavours of lime, mineral, orange peel and slate pull as one towards a long, velvety finish. This is a class act from the start, but the curl of extra flavour through the finish ices it. Screwcap. 12% alc. **Rating** 96 To 2027 $50 CM ✪

Mudgee Riesling 2017 Grown on 40yo vines at 580m above sea level. It's hard to know where to start: the texture, the intensity of flavour, the purity or indeed the effortless high-toned style. It shimmies and shines and yet it feels effortless; you find yourself uttering the word 'Germanic' even when you'd sworn not to. In any case it's a standout wine. Screwcap. 11.5% alc. **Rating** 95 To 2025 $30 CM ✪

The Kinnear Mudgee Shiraz 2015 Shiraz at its most svelte; chocolate and caramel notes sliding through blackberry, earth, undergrowth and sweet spice, tannin idling in the background. Tang, cream, flecks of herbs – every time you look, you find more. Screwcap. 14% alc. **Rating** 95 To 2034 $80 CM

Reserve Mudgee Chardonnay 2016 Straw-yellow. A powerful wine, loaded with ripe peach-like fruit flavour and smoothed over with creamy oak. Bran, lees and flint notes add complex edges. It deserves to be served in large-bowled glassware; there's more than a little of fanfare to this wine. Screwcap. 13.5% alc. **Rating** 94 To 2024 $40 CM

🍷🍷🍷🍷🍷 **Museum Release Reserve Riesling 2010** Rating 93 To 2024 $80 CM
Gewurztraminer 2017 Rating 93 To 2021 $20 CM ✪
Mudgee Shiraz 2015 Rating 93 To 2027 $25 CM ✪
Reserve Mudgee Shiraz 2015 Rating 93 To 2032 $50 CM
Half Dry Mudgee Riesling 2017 Rating 92 To 2022 $35 CM
Aged Release Mudgee Semillon 2017 Rating 91 To 2022 $25 CM

Robin Brockett Wines   ★★★★★

43 Woodville St, Drysdale, Vic 3222 (postal) **Region** Geelong
T 0418 112 223 **Open** Not
Winemaker Robin Brockett **Est.** 2013 **Dozens** 400

Robin Brockett is chief winemaker at Scotchmans Hill, a position he has held for over 30 years, and where he has consistently made very good wines, through the ebbs and flows of climate. In 2013 he took the first steps towards the realisation of a 35-year dream of making and selling wines under his own label. He put in place an agreement to buy grapes from the Fenwick (2ha) and Swinburn (1ha) vineyards, and in '13 made the first wine, venturing into the unknown with the Amphora Syrah. In '16 he made Pinots from each of the two vineyards, and a Fenwick Shiraz, but left it until January '16 to come out, as it were, announcing the business and the wines available for sale.

🍷🍷🍷🍷🍷 **Swinburn Vineyard Bellarine Peninsula Pinot Noir 2015** Open-fermented with 15% whole bunches, hand-plunged for 2 weeks, matured for 12 months in used French oak. This has compelling depth to its delicious layers of plum fruits. Made in precisely the same way as its Fenwick vineyard pinot noir sibling, yet is totally different. The dark cherry and plum fruit are pure pinot, and it's a wine that can be enjoyed right now or in 15+ years to come. Screwcap. 13% alc. **Rating** 96 To 2030 $38 ✪

Fenwick Vineyard Bellarine Peninsula Shiraz 2015 Densely coloured and lusciously rich, it tastes radically different, with a dense forest of blackberry, licorice and spice, yet remains relatively light on its feet, an achievement born of long practice in Geelong winemaking. Screwcap. 14.5% alc. **Rating** 96 **To** 2045 $38 ✪

Amphora Bellarine Peninsula Syrah 2014 10% whole bunches (and 5% viognier whole bunches), the balance destemmed on top, wild-fermented in amphorae, hand-plunged daily, basket-pressed and returned to amphorae for 4 months maturation. Fascinating vinification; the decision for no filtration was particularly brave given its path from vine to bottle (fully justified by the wisdom of hindsight). It has a unique legacy of warm spices, tangy red and black fruits and papery tannins. Natural wine depends on who made it. Screwcap. 14.5% alc. **Rating** 95 **To** 2029 $45

🍷🍷🍷🍷🍷 **Fenwick Vineyard Pinot Noir 2015 Rating** 93 **To** 2025 $38

Rochford Wines

878-880 Maroondah Highway, Coldstream, Vic 3770 **Region** Yarra Valley
T (03) 5957 3333 **www.**rochfordwines.com.au **Open** 7 days 9–5
Winemaker Marc Lunt **Est.** 1988 **Dozens** 16000 **Vyds** 23.2ha

This Yarra Valley property was purchased by Helmut Konecsny in 2002; he had already established a reputation for Pinot Noir and Chardonnay from the family-owned Romsey Park vineyard in the Macedon Ranges. Since '10, Helmut has focused on his Yarra Valley winery and vineyards. Winemaker Marc Lunt had a stellar career as a Flying Winemaker over a six-year period in Bordeaux and Burgundy; in the latter region he worked at Armand Rousseau and Domaine de la Romanée-Conti. The property also has a large restaurant and cafe, cellar door, retail shop, expansive natural amphitheatre and observation tower. It is a showpiece in the region, hosting a series of popular summer concerts. Exports to China.

🍷🍷🍷🍷🍷 **Premier Yarra Valley Pinot Noir 2017** Bright, clear crimson; a great pinot noir with almost freakish mouthwatering power and intensity. It's a narrative that fills all the senses: plums, cherries and berries woven through with fine, suspended tannins, and spices that will develop continuously over time. Screwcap. 13% alc. **Rating** 98 **To** 2037 $130 ✪

Premier Yarra Valley Chardonnay 2017 From the Swallowfield vineyard at Gembrook, crushed and pressed direct to French oak (20% new), wild-fermented, mlf, matured for 10 months. The mlf seems obvious on the bouquet; has grapefruit up front, continuing through the mid-palate; richer and rounder, the most complete. Screwcap. 13.4% alc. **Rating** 97 **To** 2027 $100 ✪

🍷🍷🍷🍷🍷 **Terre Yarra Valley Chardonnay 2017** Clones I10V1, 76 and 96 from the Swallowfield vineyard, hand-picked 27 Mar; the only Rochford Chardonnay not to undergo mlf. Greater purity, but, counterintuitively, has softer acidity. Screwcap. 13% alc. **Rating** 96 **To** 2026 $60 ✪

L'Enfant Unique Yarra Valley Pinot Noir 2017 The colour is markedly younger than Dans les Bois, as are the flavours, clone MV6 to the fore. Here the whole-bunch component (20%) is simply part of a much bigger and enduring bouquet and palate of very high quality; it's flush with varietal fruit, filling a framework of texture and structure. Screwcap. 13.3% alc. **Rating** 96 **To** 2035 $85

Isabella's Vineyard Yarra Valley Chardonnay 2017 From Block 2 of the Briarty Hill Vineyard, the site protected from wind and frost, hand-picked 23 Feb, identical vinification to its Chardonnay siblings. Fragrant bouquet, higher acidity clamps the fruit; will evolve. Screwcap. 13% alc. **Rating** 95 **To** 2024 $75

Dans les Bois Yarra Valley Chardonnay 2017 Hand-picked from a vineyard at Gembrook, crushed and pressed direct to French oak (20% new) for wild fermentation and 10 months maturation on lees. Bright straw-green; moutherwateringly bright and intense, grapefruit and lemon, yet ripe. Has all the expected length and drive. Screwcap. 13% alc. **Rating** 95 **To** 2049 $49

Dans les Bois Yarra Valley Pinot Noir 2017 Pale red colour, but there's nothing pale about the impact of the bouquet and palate. The 50% whole-bunch component drives the wine, with scant respect for observers; at once spicy, tangy and buzzing with red fruits Screwcap. 13% alc. **Rating** 95 **To** 2032 $54

Estate Yarra Valley Pinot Noir 2017 Fuller, richer and more conventional, the whole bunches have less impact on the colour, the aromas and flavours; here black cherry and plum beat the pinot drum with gay abandon. Very good now, even better to come. Screwcap. 13.5% alc. **Rating** 95 **To** 2032 $38

Yarra Valley Pinot Noir 2017 Counterintuitively, has the deepest and brightest colour; a rich powerhouse that has no right to be as good as it is. Perfectly pitched spices illuminate both the bouquet and palate, whole bunches playing a role, as do tannins. Screwcap. 13.5% alc. **Rating** 95 **To** 2032 $30 **☉**

Estate Yarra Valley Chardonnay 2017 Multiple batches hand-picked in Feb and Mar, standard Rochford Chardonnay vinification. Grapefruit, white peach and green apple do all the heavy lifting, oak playing a backdrop role. Lacks the drive of the best. Screwcap. 13.2% alc. **Rating** 94 **To** 2023 $38

Latitude Yarra Valley Pinot Noir 2017 From 20yo vines, open-fermented with 20% whole bunches, matured for 10 months in barrel (20% new). The whole bunch signature sits demurely in the corner, letting the destemmed fruit have its say. The flavours are long lasting, and very well balanced. Screwcap. 13.5% alc. **Rating** 94 **To** 2025 $22 **☉**

🍷🍷🍷🍷🍷 **Yarra Valley Chardonnay 2017 Rating** 93 **To** 2023 $30 **☉**
Yarra Valley Pinot Gris 2017 Rating 93 **To** 2025 $30
Pinot Noir Gamay 2017 Rating 92 **To** 2024 $35
Latitude Yarra Valley Chardonnay 2017 Rating 91 **To** 2023 $22 **☉**
Isabella's Vineyard Yarra Valley Blanc de Blanc 2015 Rating 91 $54

🍇 Rock of Wisdom   ★★★★

24 Roenfeldt Drive, Tanunda, SA 5352 **Region** Barossa Valley
T 0419 802 246 **www.**rockofwisdom.com.au **Open** By appt
Winemaker Peter Hiscock, Sofi Hiscock **Est.** 2013 **Dozens** 900

Rock of Wisdom has been established by the husband and wife team of Peter (Rock) and Sofi (Wisdom) Hiscock. Peter has an impressive CV given the small size of the business. He has a degree in oenology and viticulture from Adelaide University, has spent 18 years in domestic wineries in various capacities including cellarhand, vineyard management, biodynamics and wholesale trade, working for wineries such as Torbreck and Penfolds. He has also undertaken vintage in Sonoma, California, and Chateauneuf du Pape. Sofi has had 10+ years in operations and business development. The names of the wines, the packaging and some of the aphorisms on the back labels seem to put in question the seriousness of the business, but the wine quality is undeniable.

🍷🍷🍷🍷🍷 **Barossa Valley Shiraz Viognier 2016** 'Shiraz viognier is all about bringing sexy back.' 7% viognier skins added during fermentation, matured for 12 months in used French oak; 7% viognier is a substantial addition, and could easily have been too much, but the shiraz hasn't succumbed. It's a rich tapestry with velvet cushions, mouthfilling, but with the balance to develop and shed some of its puppy fat. Screwcap. 14.4% alc. **Rating** 94 **To** 2031 $28 **☉**

🍷🍷🍷🍷🍷 **SuperFly Barossa Valley Rose 2017 Rating** 91 $20 **☉**

RockBare   ★★★★★

62 Brooks Road, Clarendon, SA 5157 **Region** South Australia
T (08) 8388 7155 **www.**rockbare.com.au **Open** 7 days 11–5
Winemaker Shelley Torresan **Est.** 2000 **Dozens** 10 000 **Vyds** 29ha

The RockBare journey, which began in late 2000, last year took a new direction, when two multi-generational wine families came together in partnership: the Jackson family from California and the Melbourne-based Valmorbida family. Their combined focus is on giving a distinctive expression to the diverse wine regions across SA and those varieties that make them famous. Winemaker Shelley Torresan heads a team that sources grapes from family-owned vineyards and well-regarded growers. Many of these loyal growers have been involved with RockBare for the past 18 years, committed to representing the very best of South Australia and being part of the now bigger RockBare family. Exports to most major markets.

🍷🍷🍷🍷🍷 **Barossa Babe Shiraz 2015** From a single vineyard in Marananga, 3 days cold soak, open-fermented, matured for 18 months in French and American hogsheads (30% new). Great colour; a particularly good example of single vineyard Barossa Valley shiraz, picked before any sign of overripeness, thus taking full advantage of the great vintage. The oak handling was just where it should be. Screwcap. 14.5% alc. **Rating** 95 **To** 2040 $50

2017 Tideway McLaren Vale Grenache Grenache so pure and delicate it borders on angelic (or celestial, if you prefer). The gentlest touch, and the effective expulsion of oak, has given you a picture of grenache at its prettiest. Screwcap. 13.5% alc. **Rating** 95 **To** 2024 $25 ✪

McLaren Vale Shiraz 2016 From several vineyards in McLaren Vale; fermented in stainless steel, matured for 14 months in French and American hogsheads (20% new). Archetypal McLaren Vale shiraz, generous black fruits/berries with a constant quiet background of dark chocolate, rounded tannins and integrated oak. Screwcap. 14.5% alc. **Rating** 94 **To** 2031 $26 ✪

🍷🍷🍷🍷🍷 **The Clare Valley Riesling 2017** **Rating** 92 **To** 2027 $22 ✪
Tideway McLaren Vale Shiraz Roussanne 2017 **Rating** 90 **To** 2027 $25

Rockcliffe ★★★★★

18 Hamilton Road, Denmark, WA 6333 **Region** Denmark
T (08) 9848 2622 **www**.rockcliffe.com.au **Open** 7 days 11–5
Winemaker Michael Ng **Est.** 1990 **Dozens** 15 000 **Vyds** 10ha
The Rockcliffe winery and vineyard business, formerly known as Matilda's Estate, is owned by citizen of the world Steve Hall. Over the years, Rockcliffe has won more than its fair share of trophies, gold and silver medals in wine shows. Exports to Canada, Malaysia, Singapore and China.

🍷🍷🍷🍷🍷 **Single Site Denmark Chardonnay 2017** Hand-picked, chilled, whole-bunch pressed to French oak for fermentation and maturation. When the grapes are of this quality, the function of the winemaker is that of a quality control operator. Tasted when recently bottled, it will develop well, its length and balance guarantors. In the meantime, there is succulent white peach to enjoy. Screwcap. 13.5% alc. **Rating** 95 **To** 2028 $45

Single Site Denmark Pinot Noir 2017 The vinification is broadly similar to that of Third Reef, but the wine is clearly superior, despite its also recent bottling. This demonstrates the old aphorism that great wine has to show its greatness from the moment of its birth, and it does here with its purity, elegance and length. Screwcap. 13.5% alc. **Rating** 95 **To** 2029 $45

Single Site Frankland River Shiraz 2016 The intense, deep colour heralds an equally dense and deep wine on the bouquet; black fruits, spice, pepper and licorice play tag on the long palate. Despite its power, the balance leans more to medium-bodied than full-bodied. Screwcap. 14.5% alc. **Rating** 95 **To** 2041 $45

Single Site Frankland River Cabernet Sauvignon 2016 Has a distinguished track record based on a distinguished vineyard. It has a fragrant, cassis-lined bouquet and a medium-bodied palate, dripping with juicy cassis, the finish long and eminently satisfying. Screwcap. 14% alc. **Rating** 95 **To** 2036 $45

Single Site Mount Barker Riesling 2017 The freshness and purity achieved by the vinification takes this wine out of the ruck. The bouquet is of lime and lemon blossom, leading the way for the delicate, long and perfectly balanced palate. Screwcap. 12.5% alc. **Rating** 94 **To** 2032 $35

Third Reef Great Southern Chardonnay 2017 Whole-bunch pressed direct to French oak for wild fermentation (no mlf). An attractive, well made wine, with above average texture to its white-fleshed stone fruit and pink grapefruit, the finish long, well balanced and cleansing. Screwcap. 13.5% alc. **Rating** 94 **To** 2027 $30 ✪

🍷🍷🍷🍷🍷 **Third Reef Riesling 2017** **Rating** 93 **To** 2027 $28
Third Reef Cabernet Sauvignon 2016 **Rating** 93 **To** 2028 DB
Third Reef Sauvignon Blanc 2017 **Rating** 92 **To** 2020 $22 ✪

Third Reef Rose 2017 Rating 91 To 2020 $22 ✪
Third Reef Pinot Noir 2017 Rating 90 To 2025 $30
Third Reef Shiraz 2016 Rating 90 To 2036 DB
Quarram Rocks Shiraz Cabernet 2016 Rating 90 To 2029 $21 ✪

Rockford   ★★★★★

131 Krondorf Road, Tanunda, SA 5352 **Region** Barossa Valley
T (08) 8563 2720 **www.**rockfordwines.com.au **Open** 7 days 11–5
Winemaker Robert O'Callaghan, Ben Radford **Est.** 1984 **Dozens** NFP
Rockford can only be described as an icon, no matter how overused that word may be. It has a devoted band of customers who buy most of the wine through the cellar door or mail order (Rocky O'Callaghan's entrancing annual newsletter is like no other). Some wine is sold through restaurants, and there are two retailers in Sydney, and one each in Melbourne, Brisbane and Perth. Whether they will have the Basket Press Shiraz available is another matter; it is as scarce as Henschke Hill of Grace (but less expensive). Ben Radford, whom I first met in South Africa some years ago, has been entrenched as Rocky's right-hand man, and is destined to take over responsibility for winemaking when the time comes for Rocky to step back from an active role. Exports to the UK, Canada, Switzerland, Russia, Vietnam, Singapore, Japan, Hong Kong, Fiji and NZ.

🍷🍷🍷🍷🍷 **Basket Press Barossa Shiraz 2014** Quintessential Basket Press, bowing to no passing fad or fancy: the high-shouldered, brown bottle with Rockford Wines embossed on its base, and the distinctive label that will never change because it's so perfect. It's a manifestation of the wine it contains always very good, this vintage outstanding. I taste over 5000 wines per year for the *Wine Companion*, and am seldom tempted to swallow during a day-long tasting session – well, this wine was the exception to prove the rule. Its balance, mouthfeel and silky purple and black fruits are perfect. Cork. 13.8% alc. **Rating** 99

🍷🍷🍷🍷🍷 **Black Shiraz NV** Disgorged Aug '17. The price of the wine is irrelevant, the challenge is to find a bottle for sale – it disappears into starless black nights the moment it's released (on strict allocation). Liqueur plums and cherries for openers, then Swiss chocolate with the highest cacao content to provide a momentary flavour balance, then a cupboard full of spices, rose petals and biscotti. This release is magically fresh and light on its feet. It's a national treasure. Cork. 13.5% alc. **Rating** 96
Rifle Range Barossa Valley Cabernet Sauvignon 2015 This is Rocky speaking from his heart. It's powerful but pure; any slight roughness around the edges is certain to smooth out to velvet with 5-10 years more in bottle. It is what it is, needing no apology, especially to those Rockford devotees with multiple vintages of Rocky's core red wines (this and the Shiraz) in their cellars stretching back 20-30 years. '15 was a great vintage, and Rockford hit the bullseye. Cork. 13.8% alc. **Rating** 95 To 2035
Hand Picked Eden Valley Riesling 2015 The delicacy and flavour spectrum have been enhanced substantially by the skin contact, the future of the wine extended by an even greater length. It's a revelation. Screwcap. 12.5% alc. **Rating** 94 To 2030

🍷🍷🍷🍷🍷 **Rod & Spur Shiraz Cabernet 2015** Rating 92 To 2030
Moppa Springs Grenache Mataro Shiraz 2014 Rating 92 To 2021

🍂 Rocky Vale Vineyard   ★★★★

PO Box 332, Tanunda, SA 5352 **Region** Barossa Valley
T 0438 133 239 **Open** Not
Winemaker Ryan Johns **Est.** 2015 **Dozens** 150 **Vyds** 2ha
This is the ultimate accidental vineyard. When David and Vanessa Rochford purchased a small property between Vine Vale and Rocky Valley on the slopes of the Barossa Ranges in 2013, the plan was to clear the land (including the vines) and have a few acres to run a couple of

sheep and plant some trees. A friend suggested the quality of the grapes was such that there was a real opportunity to sell them and make money from the venture. So, the decision was taken to see what might happen in '15. They made what they termed a 'small estimation error' and in late March that year had a tonne of grenache hanging on the vine. Step in a couple of great mates, and the first wine was made. A similar small error was made in '16, hand-picking shiraz on a 38°C day in late February, with the pickers leaving 2t of shiraz on the vine that missed the delivery time. Once again, mates came to the rescue, and given that surplus grapes seemed to be happening all too often, Rocky Vale winery was born.

♟♟♟♟♟ **Barossa Valley Grenache 2015** This shows a confident approach to old vine grenache that allows the variety to reach physiological ripeness and with that, an apogee of hedonistic aromas and textures here: kirsch, cranberry, bramble and whole-cluster led cardamom, anise and spiky tannin. Despite the alcohol (15.3%) noted and no details, the Afghan bazaar of spice sublimates the sweetness into a confident whole, with plenty of swagger. Screwcap. **Rating** 94 **To** 2024 $30 NG ✪

Rogers & Rufus

PO Box 10, Angaston, SA 5353 **Region** Barossa Valley
T (08) 8561 3566 **www**.rogersandrufus.com **Open** Not
Winemaker Sam Wigan **Est.** 2009 **Dozens** NFP
This is a decidedly under the bedcover partnership between Robert Hill-Smith and his immediate family, and Rupert and Jo Clevely. Rupert was the former Veuve Clicquot director in Australia, but now runs the gastro pub group Geronimo Inns in London. Late in 2008 the Hill-Smiths and Clevelys decided (in their words) 'to do something fun together, with a serious dip at Euro styled dry and savoury delicate rose using three site specific, old, low-yielding, dry-grown grenache sites from the Barossa floor'. Most of the production is sold in the US, with a small allocation marketed in Australia by Samuel Smith & Son.

♟♟♟♟♟ **Grenache of Barossa Rose 2017** Very pale, almost translucent pink. Not a lot of flavour; some watermelon and rind, and a dash of Angostura bitters; more texture with lemon zest, and a neat crispness on the finish from lemon-sherbet acidity. Screwcap. 12% alc. **Rating** 90 **To** 2019 $22 JF

Rolf Binder

Cnr Seppeltsfield Road/Stelzer Road, Tanunda, SA 5352 **Region** Barossa Valley
T (08) 8562 3300 **www**.rolfbinder.com **Open** Mon–Sat 10–4.30, Sun on long weekends
Winemaker Rolf Binder, Christa Deans, Harry Mantzarapis **Est.** 1955 **Dozens** 28 000
Vyds 90ha
A winery steeped in family tradition and Barossa history. Rolf Binder and sister Christa Deans are following their father's philosophy, using primarily estate-grown fruit from their own vineyards located in various districts of the Barossa. A recent vineyard acquisition in the Vine Vale area has provided the family with centenarian shiraz vines planted in the 1890s, in fact parent vines to the Hanisch Shiraz. The winemaking team of Rolf, Christa and Harry Mantzarapis has been in place for many years, with wide acclaim for their work with shiraz, mataro, grenache and riesling. The Vinify BV The Vineyard Architect wines are a joint venture between Rolf and exporter Rob Bull, the wine named in honour of Barossa Valley viticulturist Vic Kraft. Exports to all major markets.

♟♟♟♟♟ **Heysen Barossa Valley Shiraz 2015** An integrated 50/50% blend of American (50% new) and French oak, aged for 22 months, adds a frame to this single vineyard wine, and there's plenty of stuffing, too. A complex, rich mix of black-red fruits flecked with licorice, new leather and warm earth fragrant with iron. There's real composure to this, thanks to its fine-grained tannins and persistence on the finish. Screwcap. 14% alc. **Rating** 96 **To** 2037 $70 JF ✪
Eden Valley Riesling 2017 Riesling from the Eden Valley is an elixir for the soul. This has texture, length and a lick of sweetness cut with requisite zesty acidity. More regional expression and lift come from florals of citrus blossom and

roses, with a hint of baked quince plus lemon-lime juiciness. Screwcap. 12.5% alc. Rating 95 To 2030 $25 JF ✪

RHB Reserve Barossa Shiraz 2015 It's really polished and glossy with an array of red and blue fruits mingling with licorice, mocha and oak; full-bodied yet restrained, with plush tannins and a lingering finish. Complex, balanced and while in the zone now, it will reward the patient. Screwcap. 14% alc. **Rating** 95 **To** 2030 $35 JF ✪

Hanisch Barossa Valley Shiraz 2015 The flagship wine that's a picture of concentration. Flavours of coconut husk and raw cedar abound, but the fruit is taking it all in its stride. The full-bodied palate overflows with intense blackberries and currants, dark chocolate and freshly roasted coffee, with sturdy tannins. Yet it all comes together, gliding along to a decisive conclusion, just a touch of warmth on the finish. Cork. 14.8% alc. **Rating** 95 **To** 2030 $110 JF

Vinify BV The Vineyard Architect Shiraz Mataro 2016 Concentrated red and black berried fruit; touches of reduction; sweet herbs and toasty, coconut cream-like notes. This is rich, plush, robust and velvety textured all at once. Satisfying and then some. Screwcap. 14.5% alc. **Rating** 95 **To** 2036 $45 CM

RHB Reserve Barossa Shiraz 2016 Deep garnet-purple-black – amazing hue; packed with flavour, a bounty of dark fruit, warm spices, chocolate and espresso coffee, plus sweet cedary oak. There are plenty of savoury tones on the palate helping to offset the oak flavours, which should recede in time; ripe, plump tannins and structure will ensure this has some way to go. Screwcap. 14% alc. **Rating** 94 **To** 2030 $35 JF

Vinify BV The Vineyard Architect Barossa Valley Mataro Grenache 2016 55/45% blend of mataro/grenache, matured in 50/50% American/French oak. Complexity is its middle name. This isn't your standard fare. Graphite and leather, blackberry and anise, a touch of wood smoke. It's generous in proportion but the flavours go off on various tangents, in a positive sense. It will keep drinkers on their toes. Screwcap. 14.5% alc. **Rating** 94 **To** 2027 $45 CM

ⵢⵢⵢⵢⵢ **Bull's Blood Barossa Valley Shiraz Mataro Pressings 2015** Rating 93 To 2030 $55 JF

Heinrich Barossa Valley Shiraz Mataro Grenache 2016 Rating 93 To 2024 $35 JF

Eden Valley Montepulciano 2016 Rating 93 To 2021 $40 JF

Stephanie Barossa Valley Shiraz 2015 Rating 92 To 2024 $40 JF

The Rude Mechanicals Three Monkeys Barossa Valley Grenache Shiraz Mourvedre 2016 Rating 91 To 2023 $20 CM ✪

JJ Hahn Homestead Barossa Valley Cabernet Sauvignon 2016 Rating 91 To 2022 $25 JF

Tramino Frizzante Moscato 2017 Rating 91 To 2018 $20 JF ✪

Barossa Valley Shiraz 2016 Rating 90 To 2025 $25 JF

Eden Valley Shiraz 2015 Rating 90 To 2024 $30 JF

JJ Hahn Reginald Barossa Valley Shiraz Cabernet 2016 Rating 90 To 2022 $25 JF

Romney Park Wines   ★★★★★

116 Johnsons Road, Balhannah, SA 5242 **Region** Adelaide Hills
T (08) 8398 0698 **www.**romneyparkwines.com.au **Open** By appt
Winemaker Rod and Rachel Short **Est.** 1997 **Dozens** 500 **Vyds** 2.8ha
Rod and Rachel Short planted chardonnay, shiraz and pinot noir in 1997. Yields are limited to 3.7–5t per ha for the red wines, and 2–3t for the chardonnay. The vineyard is managed organically, with guinea fowl cleaning up the insects, all vines hand-picked and hand-pruned. In every way the set-up (including the wines) has the beauty of a hand-painted miniature. Exports to China.

ⵢⵢⵢⵢⵢ **Gloria Adelaide Hills Chardonnay 2016** Attractive style with a satisfying edge to the bouquet and palate giving a stamp of authority to the wine. Pink grapefruit and nectarine flavours do most of the work, allied with fresh (natural) acidity. It all works very well. Diam. 13.1% alc. **Rating** 95 **To** 2023 $50

Adelaide Hills Pinot Noir 2015 A most attractive and well made pinot that keeps its focus and line from the first whiff, through the length of the palate and into the aftertaste. It's only just into medium-bodied territory, but its red cherry/ berry fruits, spice and soft fruit and oak tannins all sing the same song. May go on longer than I suggest. Diam. 14% alc. **Rating** 95 **To** 2023 $14 ✪

Adelaide Hills Blanc de Blancs 2010 Has thrived with 7 years on lees, and if there was any sweetness in the liqueur d'expedition, it's not easy to see, so perfect is the balance and overall length in its gently creamy palate. The third disgorgement of this wine. Crown seal. 12.5% alc. **Rating** 95 $65

♟♟♟♟♟ **Adelaide Hills Shiraz 2015** **Rating** 90 **To** 2027 $45

Ros Ritchie Wines

Magnolia House, 190 Mount Buller Road, Mansfield, Vic 3722 **Region** Upper Goulburn
T 0448 900 541 **www.**rosritchiewines.com **Open** See website
Winemaker Ros Ritchie **Est.** 2008 **Dozens** 2000 **Vyds** 7ha
Ros Ritchie was winemaker at the Ritchie family's Delatite winery from 1981 to 2006, but moved on to establish her own winery with husband John in '08 on a vineyard near Mansfield. They became shareholders in Barwite Vineyards in 2012 (planted to chardonnay, pinot noir, riesling and pinot gris), and in '14 established their new winery there. Apart from gewurztraminer (grown at Dead Man's Hill Vineyard), they work with local growers, foremost the Kinlock, McFadden, Timbertop and Baxendale vineyards, the last planted by the very experienced viticulturist Jim Baxendale (and wife Ruth) high above the King River Valley. All vineyards are managed with minimal spray regimes. The cellar door is loacted at historic Magnolia House in Mansfield and is open on select weekends, as well as hosting seasonal wine dinners and special events.

♟♟♟♟♟ **Dead Man's Hill Vineyard Gewurztraminer 2017** It offers flavour and – of course – fragrance, but it does so in a neat and controlled way. That's why it's impressive. It tastes of green and red apples, citrus rind, rose water and assorted florals, a snip of reduction working to absolute positive effect. Ros Ritchie continues her long-term love affair with gewurztraminer. Screwcap. 13% alc. **Rating** 95 **To** 2025 $25 CM ✪

Barwite Vineyard Riesling 2017 This is its usual floral self, underwritten by citrus juice and rind, a kind of chalkiness at play through the finish, but it just has that little something extra this year. Really excels though sheer intensity of flavour from the outset. Screwcap. 12% alc. **Rating** 94 **To** 2025 $25 CM ✪

♟♟♟♟♟ **Baxendale's Vineyard Sauvignon Blanc 2017** **Rating** 92 **To** 2020 $25 CM ✪

Baxendale's Vineyard Cabernet Sauvignon 2016 **Rating** 92 **To** 2028 $28 CM

McFadden's Vineyard Pinot Gris 2017 **Rating** 90 **To** 2019 $25 CM

Timbertop Vineyard Merlot 2016 **Rating** 90 **To** 2026 $28 CM

Rosabrook Margaret River Wine

1390 Rosa Brook Road, Rosa Brook, WA 6285 **Region** Margaret River
T (08) 9368 4555 **www.**rosabrook.com.au **Open** Not
Winemaker Brian Fletcher **Est.** 1980 **Dozens** 12 000 **Vyds** 25ha
The original Rosabrook estate vineyards were established between 1984 and '96. In 2007 Rosabrook relocated its vineyard to the northwestern end of the Margaret River wine region, overlooking Geographe Bay and the Indian Ocean. Warm days and cool nights, influenced by the ocean, result in slow, mild-ripening conditions. Exports to the UK, Sweden, Dubai, Hong Kong and China.

ΨΨΨΨΨ **Sauvignon Blanc Semillon 2017** If you need to understand how terroir shapes the flavour and texture of a wine (or explain it to others), cold-fermented, early bottled Margaret River SBS (or SSB) is a great example. The maritime climate works as well as the same blend from Bordeaux. The wines open with intense flavour, pause to build citrus and mineral notes on the mid-palate, then finish long and dry. And while great young, they are certain to build creamy/toasty characters over the next 5++ years. Screwcap. 12.5% alc. **Rating** 92 **To** 2022 $20 ❂

Cabernet Sauvignon 2016 Full colour; a generous, plush medium-bodied wine with gently ripe cassis fruit, not needing to defend its status in the pantheon of Margaret River cabernets. It pushes near to offering too much, but is promptly pulled back by earthy tannins and quality oak. Screwcap. 14.5% alc. **Rating** 92 **To** 2029 $25 ❂

Rosby   ★★★☆

122 Strikes Lane, Mudgee, NSW 2850 **Region** Mudgee
T (02) 6373 3856 **www**.rosby.com.au **Open** W'ends 11–4, or by appt
Winemaker Tim Stevens **Est.** 1996 **Dozens** 1500 **Vyds** 9ha
Gerald and Kay Norton-Knight have 4ha of shiraz, 2ha of cabernet sauvignon, and 1ha of riesling, chardonnay and sangiovese established on what is truly a unique site in Mudgee. Many vignerons like to think that their vineyard has special qualities, but in this instance the belief is well founded. Rosby is situated in a small valley, with unusual red basalt over a quartz gravel structure, encouraging deep root growth and making the use of water far less critical than normal. Tim Stevens of Huntington Estate has purchased some of the ample production, and makes the Rosby wines.

ΨΨΨΨΨ **Mudgee Cabernet Sauvignon 2015** One is tempted to call the wine rough-hewn, but right or wrong, it is layered with dark earth and brambly, blackcurrant fruit. In its own way, it is balanced, and will certainly benefit from extended maturation. Screwcap. 14.3% alc. **Rating** 91 **To** 2029

Rosenthal Wines   ★★★★★

24 Rockford Street, Denmark, WA 6333 **Region** Great Southern
T 0432 312 918 **www**.rosenthalwines.com.au **Open** Not
Winemaker Luke Eckersley, Coby Ladwig **Est.** 2001 **Dozens** 20 000 **Vyds** 17ha
The original Rosenthal Vineyard (Springfield Park) was established in 1997 just north of Manjimup by Dr John Rosenthal. In 2012, Coby Ladwig and Luke Eckersley acquired the business and relocated it to Mount Barker. Both winemakers have a sound knowledge of vineyards throughout the southwest of WA. The fruit for Rosenthal wines is sourced from their own leased vineyard in Mount Barker, plus growers in Frankland River and Pemberton. Coby and Luke have partnered with an importer/distributor in China, and in 2018 will open and office/showroom in Shanghai. Exports to the UK, India and China.

ΨΨΨΨΨ **Collector Mount Barker Cabernet Sauvignon 2016** Deep crimson-purple; thanks to (rather than in spite of) the modest alcohol, this is uncompromisingly full-bodied. Tannins make themselves evident from the word go, but they don't grow and cause gridlock – they're just there. They set the scene for deep-seated blackcurrant fruit, framed by quality French oak on the long palate. Despite the fact the wine is perfectly balanced, it simply has to be respected and given more time. Screwcap. 13.9% alc. **Rating** 96 **To** 2036 $75 ❂

Richings Mount Barker Riesling 2017 Hand-picked, chilled, gently pressed; free-run juice cool-fermented with neutral yeast in stainless steel; 3 months on lees. This is, of course, in the first stage of its life, with many years in front of it, but with a slight edge already, with lime juice starting to lick the tongue. Screwcap. 12.1% alc. **Rating** 95 **To** 2027 $33 ❂

Richings Great Southern Shiraz 2016 Bright crimson-purple; the wine starts with a burst of black/purple berries and spices, moving into a more savoury mode on the fore-palate, then changing pace and direction back into expressive

red berries and dark cherries on the finish. Screwcap. 14.5% alc. **Rating** 95
To 2030 $42

Richings Frankland River Cabernet Sauvignon 2016 Bright crimson-purple; the wine has a particular juicy palate all of its own, which flows between beacons of exotic spices, satsuma plum, sweet earth, cigar box and fine-spun tannins. It moves with ease, and can be enjoyed any time, with a long window of opportunity. Screwcap. 14.2% alc. **Rating** 95 To 2029 $42

Collector Mount Barker Chardonnay 2016 Has developed more colour than expected, but wasn't bottled until Jun '17. Its acidity has high-tensile wire impact, and while the wine has much to enjoy, you need to have tolerance for it. Screwcap. 12.9% alc. **Rating** 94 To 2025 $75

 Garten Series Pemberton Chardonnay 2017 Rating 93 To 2025 $25 ✪
Garten Series Great Southern Cabernet Sauvignon 2016 Rating 93 To 2026 $25 ✪

Rosenvale Wines   ★★★★

467 Research Road, Nuriootpa, SA 5355 **Region** Barossa Valley
T 0407 390 788 **www**.rosenvale.com.au **Open** By appt
Winemaker James Rosenzweig, Philip Leggett **Est.** 1999 **Dozens** 3000 **Vyds** 100ha
The Rosenzweig family vineyards, some old and some new, are planted to riesling, semillon, chardonnay, grenache, shiraz, merlot and cabernet sauvignon. Most of the grapes are sold to other producers, but some are retained and vinified for release under the Rosenvale label.

 Reserve Barossa Valley Shiraz 2015 This is a lovely shiraz. James Rosenzweig has seized the opportunity of the '15 vintage with both hands, and with clever winemaking has produced an elegant wine, with some characters normally from cooler climates. There are spicy notes, and lifted fruit courtesy of a ride on the back of fine tannins. Diam. 15% alc. **Rating** 95 To 2035 $39

Barossa Valley Rose 2017 Rating 90 To 2019

Rosily Vineyard   ★★★★★

871 Yelverton Road, Wilyabrup, WA 6284 **Region** Margaret River
T (08) 9755 6336 **www**.rosily.com.au **Open** 7 days Dec–Jan 11–5
Winemaker Mick Scott **Est.** 1994 **Dozens** 5500 **Vyds** 12.28ha
Ken Allan and Mick Scott acquired the Rosily Vineyard site in 1994, and the vineyard was planted over three years to sauvignon blanc, semillon, chardonnay, cabernet sauvignon, merlot, shiraz, grenache and cabernet franc. The first crops were sold to other makers in the region, but by '99 Rosily had built its own 120t capacity winery. It has gone from strength to strength, all of its estate-grown grapes being vinified under the Rosily Vineyard label, substantially over-delivering for their prices.

Margaret River Chardonnay 2017 Another wine of exceptional value from Rosily, sourced from leaner gravels which, with reductive handling, imparts flinty tension to effusive notes of peach, quince, apricot, citrus and measured vanilla-pod oak. The ferment was initiated with ambient yeast, before a 'pied de cuve' of a more robust strain kicked it through to dryness. An intelligent approach given the sweetness on many 'wild' ferments. Mid-weighted, layered and thrillingly long. Screwcap. 13.5% alc. **Rating** 96 To 2025 $27 NG ✪

Reserve Margaret River Cabernet Sauvignon 2014 From 20yo vines at the highest elevation on the Rosily vineyard at Wilyabrup. Matured for 24 months in French oak, 40% new, 60% 1yo. A beautifully composed wine from start to finish. Complexity of variety, region and oak on display, with blackcurrant, black olive, bay leaf, tobacco and cedar all in the mix. Deeply flavoured and firmly structured, it feels completely unforced and already in balance though its peak is still years away. Super impressive. Screwcap. 14% alc. **Rating** 96 To 2034 $50 SC ✪

Reserve Margaret River Chardonnay 2016 Hailing from the exulted alluvials across the Wilyabrup district, this breaks out all the contemporary bells and whistles with gusto: reductive mineral-clad flint, wild yeast, truffled macadamia and glimpses of stone fruits and oak as an adjunct, rather than a scream across the wine's bow. The finish is tensile, tactile and palate-staining. Screwcap. **Rating** 95 **To** 2024 $50 NG
Margaret River Cabernet Sauvignon 2016 This superlative value wine displays a sensitive winemaking hand. The oak (16 months, 40% new French) is well positioned to chaperone a flow of red and blackcurrant notes, dried sage, bay leaf and olive, along a bed of gravely bitter chocolate tannins, moreish and ripe. Mid to full-weighted, with an accent on savoury rather than overt fruit, the finish is nicely firm. Screwcap. 14% alc. **Rating** 95 **To** 2028 $27 NG ✪

ɤɤɤɤɤ **Margaret River Sauvignon Blanc 2017 Rating** 93 **To** 2019 $20 SC ✪
The Cartographer 2013 Rating 93 **To** 2024 $25 NG ✪
Cellar Release Margaret River Semillon Sauvignon Blanc 2012 Rating 92 **To** 2020 $25 ✪
Margaret River Shiraz 2015 Rating 92 **To** 2023 $25 NG ✪
Margaret River Semillon Sauvignon Blanc 2017 Rating 91 **To** 2027 $20 ✪
Other Side of the Moon Margaret River Grenache Shiraz 2016 Rating 90 **To** 2021 $20 NG ✪

Ross Hill Wines   ★★★★★
134 Wallace Lane, Orange, NSW 2800 **Region** Orange
T (02) 6365 3223 **www**.rosshillwines.com.au **Open** 7 days 10.30–5
Winemaker Phil Kerney **Est.** 1994 **Dozens** 25000 **Vyds** 18.2ha
Peter and Terri Robson planted chardonnay, merlot, sauvignon blanc, cabernet franc, shiraz and pinot noir on north-facing slopes of the Griffin Road vineyard in 1994. In 2007, their son James and his wife Chrissy joined the business, and the Wallace Lane vineyard (pinot noir, sauvignon blanc and pinot gris) was planted. The vines are now mature, and the winery was NCOS Certified Carbon Neutral in 2013. The Barrel & Larder School of Wine and Food operates from the extended cellar door. Exports to Germany, Singapore, Bali, Hong Kong and China.

ɤɤɤɤɤ **Pinnacle Series Wallace Lane Vineyard Orange Pinot Noir 2016** MV6, wild yeast–open fermented with 15% whole bunches, matured for 18 months in new and used French oak. Very good colour and bouquet. Excellent palate, bright red cherry and damson plum flavours supported by integrated French oak and long, whispering tannins. Screwcap. 14.1% alc. **Rating** 95 **To** 2026 $45
Pinnacle Series Griffin Road Vineyard Orange Shiraz 2016 Hand-picked and sorted, wild-fermented with 30% whole bunches in small open fermenters, matured for 18 months in French barriques. The colour isn't deep, but the medium-bodied palate has attractive red fruit flavours that join with the aromatic bouquet. Its length builds significantly on the second and third tastings. Screwcap. 14.4% alc. **Rating** 95 **To** 2030 $45
The Griffin 2014 The flagship wine of Ross Hill; 50% cabernet sauvignon, 35% merlot and 15% cabernet franc, a blended best barrel selection matured for 34 months in new French oak. A rare wine, not really ready for drinking now, but of undoubted quality, and will progressively pull the oak back from centre stage over the next 5-10 years. Screwcap. 14.5% alc. **Rating** 95 **To** 2044 $95
Pinnacle Series Griffin Road Vineyard Orange Cabernet Sauvignon 2016 Hand-picked, wild yeast–open fermented, matured for 18 months in new and used French oak. An elegant, medium-bodied cabernet with good use of oak to build texture and structure. There is an annoying whisper of jammy fruit that isn't a deal-breaker, but can't be entirely ignored. Screwcap. 14% alc. **Rating** 94 **To** 2031 $45

ɤɤɤɤɤ **Jack's Lot Orange Shiraz 2016 Rating** 93 **To** 2023 $25 SC ✪
Pinnacle Series Griffin Road Vineyard Orange Sauvignon Blanc 2017 Rating 92 **To** 2019 $30 SC

Pinnacle Series Griffin Road Vineyard Orange Chardonnay 2016 Rating 92 **To** 2022 $35
Pinnacle Series Wallace Lane Vineyard Orange Pinot Gris 2017 Rating 90 **To** 2023 $30
Isabelle Orange Cabernet Franc Merlot 2016 Rating 90 **To** 2024 $25 SC

Rouleur ★★★★★

150 Bank Street, South Melbourne, Vic 3205 (postal) **Region** Yarra Valley/McLaren Vale
T 0419 100 929 **www**.rouleurwine.com **Open** Not
Winemaker Matthew East **Est.** 2015 **Dozens** 2000

Owner Matt East's interest in wine began at an early age, growing up in the Yarra Valley and watching his father plant a vineyard in Coldstream. Between 1999 and 2015 his day job was in sales and marketing, culminating in his appointment in '11 as national sales manager for Wirra Wirra. He lives in Melbourne, with the Yarra in easy striking distance, and together he and Rob Hall source fruit and make the wines. Matt's time with Wirra Wirra in McLaren Vale set the wheels in motion for Rouleur, and he also makes wine there, using the facilities at Dennis Winery, drawing on the expertise/assistance of winemaking friends when needed. Back in Melbourne he is transforming a dilapidated milk bar in North Melbourne into the inner-city cellar door for Rouleur.

🍷🍷🍷🍷🍷 **McLaren Vale Shiraz 2017** From two vineyards at Blewitt Springs; open-fermented with varying percentages of whole bunches, 11 months in French puncheons (15% new). Exceptional power and complexity, yet retains nigh on perfect balance and structure. The combination of Blewitt Springs and '17 provides shiraz that will be remembered with awe for years to come. Super-fragrant spices and flowers leap from the glass, the glazed shiraz rounded and succulent yet not cloying. Screwcap. 14% alc. **Rating** 97 **To** 2040 $32 ✪

🍷🍷🍷🍷🍷 **Issy's Macclesfield Yarra Valley Chardonnay 2017** 80% whole-bunch pressed to used French puncheons, wild-fermented, no mlf, 20% open-fermented on skins for 7 days, matured for 10 months on lees before blending. The complexity of the wine in the glass is a direct reflection of the complexity of the vinification. Bright straw-green, it is super-intense and focused, keeping its shape through to the long finish, grapefruit riding on the back of white peach. Diam. 12.9% alc. **Rating** 96 **To** 2027 $43 ✪

Yarra Valley Chardonnay 2017 From two vineyards in Woori Yallock and Macclesfield; hand-picked, 90% whole-bunch pressed to barrel, 10% fermented on skins, 10% mlf, matured for 9 months on lees in French oak (15% new). Until the finish you think this is simply a good Yarra Valley chardonnay, then the power of the finish and aftertaste hits you. Great stuff. Screwcap. 12.9% alc. **Rating** 95 **To** 2025 $32 ✪

🍷🍷🍷🍷 **Ronda McLaren Vale Nero d'Avola 2017 Rating** 91 **To** 2023 $32
McLaren Vale Grenache 2017 Rating 90 **To** 2021 $32

Rowlee ★★★★★

19 Lake Canobolas Road, Nashdale, NSW 2800 **Region** Orange
T (02) 6365 3047 **www**.rowleewines.com.au **Open** 7 days 11–5
Winemaker Nicole Samodol, James Manny **Est.** 2000 **Dozens** 3000 **Vyds** 8ha

The Samodol family established Rowlee vineyard in 2000. The 8ha vineyard sits in ancient volcanic soils, 950m above sea level, exposed to the cool climate and unique topography of the Orange region. Plantings include arneis, chardonnay, gewurztraminer, pinot gris, riesling, sauvignon blanc, nebbiolo and pinot noir. Rowlee's single vineyard wines are harvested by hand and crafted in small batches, the aim to make 'delicious' wine under a philosophy of minimal intervention and sustainable methods. Winemaking commenced in 2013 in conjunction with viticulturalist, Tim Esson and winemaker, PJ Charteris. Nicole Samodol and her partner James Manny came onboard full-time in '17, collaborating with experienced local winemakers Chris Derrez and Lucy Maddox.

ΨΨΨΨΨ **Single Vineyard Orange Chardonnay 2016** One of the finds of the year. An outstanding chardonnay, with as much power as finesse. Grapefruit, white peach, custard, apple and flint, a hum of cedar-spice oak only serving to amplify what is a gorgeous expression of the variety. The deal is completely sealed on the finish. A wowee wine from Rowlee, you might say. Deserved trophy winner at the Orange Wine Show. Screwcap. 13.5% alc. **Rating** 97 **To** 2024 $40 CM ✪

ΨΨΨΨΨ **R-Series Orange Nebbiolo 2016** Pallid ruby and stamped with nebbiolo's DNA of brisk, saline acidity and spindly marked tannins. This savoury wine's firm structural carapace is nicely buffered by sour cherry, sassafras and wood smoke notes, expanding across the midriff and tucked into vanillan oak seams. Definitively nebbiolo – a strong domestic showing augurs well for the future at this estate. Screwcap. 14% alc. **Rating** 94 **To** 2024 $60 NG

ΨΨΨΨΨ **Single Vineyard Orange Nebbiolo 2016 Rating** 93 **To** 2027 $40 CM
Orange Arneis 2017 Rating 90 **To** 2020 $30 NG

Rudderless   ★★★★★

Victory Hotel, Main South Road, Sellicks Beach, SA 5174 **Region** McLaren Vale
T (08) 8556 3083 **www**.victoryhotel.com.au **Open** 7 days
Winemaker Charlie Seppelt **Est.** 2004 **Dozens** 450 **Vyds** 2ha
It's a long story how Doug Govan, owner of the Victory Hotel (circa 1858), came to choose the name Rudderless for his vineyard. The vineyard is planted on two levels (in 1999 and 2003) to a complex mix of shiraz, graciano, grenache, malbec, mataro and viognier, surrounding the hotel, which is situated in the foothills of the Southern Willunga escarpment as it falls into the sea. The wines are mostly sold through the hotel, where the laid-back Doug keeps a low profile.

ΨΨΨΨΨ **Sellicks Hill McLaren Vale Grenache 2015** From the estate planting of 538 grenache vines. The colour is bright and clear, the hue headed towards magenta; this is yet another wonderful wine from Doug Govan (and winemaker Charlie Seppelt). It is an exercise in seemingly effortless purity, its bevy of red fruits linking like cow bells on Swiss pastures. Screwcap. 14.5% alc. **Rating** 97 **To** 2029

ΨΨΨΨΨ **Sellicks Hill McLaren Vale Grenache Mataro Graciano 2015** The wine is fabulously opulent and rich, with red and purple fruits, spice, dark chocolate and velvety tannins. The ultimate in each-way enjoyment – tonight or in 10 years. Screwcap. 14% alc. **Rating** 96 **To** 2030 $35 ✪
Sellicks Hill McLaren Vale Shiraz 2015 From the estate's planting of 1500 vines of shiraz. The colour is deep, and the seemingly effortless power of the wine is a tribute to the vineyard. The fruits are all black and inky, with licks of licorice and an airbrush of oak leaving no room for others at this stage. It's full-bodied, but not extractive, and most certainly not tannic. Screwcap. 14.5% alc. **Rating** 95 **To** 2045 $35 ✪
Sellicks Hill McLaren Vale Shiraz Malbec 2016 60/40% blend, and what a colour – deep, dark purple-garnet; these two gems, one a stalwart of the Vale, malbec less well known, work in unison. Expect a fragrance of black shoe polish, dark plums, chocolate and a wave of ripe and pliable tannins crossing the length of the full-bodied palate. Add raspberry-fresh acidity and there's a wine of distinction. Screwcap. 13.8% alc. **Rating** 95 **To** 2030 $35 JF ✪
Sellicks Hill McLaren Vale Grenache 2016 When grenache finds its groove, it rocks. Aside from its vibrancy and raspberry-like acidity racing across the medium-bodied palate, this takes in spiced cherry fruit, star anise and red licorice. Definitely not confection, it's wonderfully savoury, earthy and immensely pleasurable. Screwcap. 14.5% alc. **Rating** 95 **To** 2026 $35 JF ✪
Sellicks Hill McLaren Vale Grenache Mataro Graciano 2016 A harmonious 44/38/18% blend, unencumbered by new oak (9 months in old French barrels). The freshness and purity of fruit shines through like a light beam. While it has pretty aromas and flavours of raspberries, sweet red cherries and red licorice,

they're pared back by its fine, sandy tannins. Unlikely one glass will suffice.
Screwcap. 14% alc. **Rating** 95 **To** 2032 $35 JF ✪

Sellicks Hill McLaren Vale Malbec 2016 The malbec adds up to a mere 487
vines on the site. There's no denying the quality, and while it has the variety's
telltale dark plum and plummy character, it's beautifully restrained and fresh. Hints
of black shoe polish on new leather, exotic spices and plush tannins fall into place.
Screwcap. 13.8% alc. **Rating** 95 **To** 2028 $35 JF ✪

Sellicks Hill McLaren Vale Malbec 2015 Malbec usually has good colour,
and this has it in spades. It also has a Cherry Ripe bouquet, joining region and
variety to each other at the hip. This is a seriously good malbec, its structure and
texture without fault on the medium to full-bodied palate. Screwcap. 14.5% alc.
Rating 95 **To** 2035 $35 ✪

🍷🍷🍷🍷♀ **Sellicks Hill McLaren Vale Shiraz 2016 Rating** 93 **To** 2030 $35 JF

Ruggabellus

PO Box 32, Stockwell, SA 5355 **Region** Barossa Valley
T 0412 773 536 **www**.ruggabellus.com.au **Open** Not
Winemaker Abel Gibson **Est.** 2009 **Dozens** 1000
Abel Gibson arrived in the Barossa Valley as a 2-year-old in 1975, his father on the way to
becoming senior viticulturist for Penfolds. It was almost inevitable that Abel absorbed the
150-year-old history of the Valley. Between 1990 and '92, he flirted with university studies
(including wine science at Roseworthy), then decided he wanted nothing more to do with it.
Between '93 and 2000 he spent winters skiing and snowboarding, and did a serious amount
of travelling. In '01 he took a vintage job at Penfolds, then had a position at Rockford. An '03
vintage in Spain at Campo de Borja was followed by the '04 vintage with Charles Melton,
before joining his father's winery over the next three years. The next decisive step was a
three-year stint at Spinifex, cementing all of the pieces of his prior experience into a coherent
whole, and laying the ground for his small-batch winemaking, linked to specific plots of old
vines. Exports to the UK, US and Japan.

🍷🍷🍷🍷🍷 **Archaeus 2016** It's stonkingly good. Deep, dark garnet hue; perfumed with
florals, spiced cherries and pips; all the flavours seem to float across the more
medium-bodied palate. There's texture from detailed, filigreed tannins. Never
thought I'd say that of a Barossa syrah, but it is elegant and beautifully composed.
Alas, a mere 672 bottles produced. Screwcap. 14.3% alc. **Rating** 96 **To** 2030 $60
JF ✪

Solumodo 2015 What struck me tasting through the Ruggabellus 'whites', is
why they aren't on skins longer than a few weeks; it's like hedging your bets.
Then comes Solumodo – 71% semillon, 21% riesling and 8% muscat – 1 year on
skins, aged 10 months in seasoned French oak hogsheads, with 7 months in bottle.
It's the most complete and detailed of the Ruggabellus whites. A bright copper-
orange; smells of pomander, Middle Eastern spices and panforte. Tastes of toffee
apple, tart apples too; phenolics are well handled, grippy but ultra-refreshing. For
fans of the style; only 690 bottles made. Screwcap. 13.3% alc. **Rating** 95 **To** 2028
$45 JF

Efferus 2016 Mataro leads with 71%, plus 17% syrah, 10% grenache and a splash
of cinsaut; 29% whole-bunches in the ferment, then aged 10 months in seasoned
French oak puncheons. This is mighty good. While there's so much flavour of
aniseed, charcuterie, warm earth, satsuma plums and umeboshi, everything is pulled
into place by fresh acidity and defined tannins across its tight, just-mid-weighted
palate. Delicious drinking now, and will continue to unfurl for a few years yet.
Screwcap. 13.8% alc. **Rating** 95 **To** 2028 $45 JF

Timaeus 2016 Grenache makes up 76%, then 12% syrah, 7% mataro and
5% cinsaut. Heady aromatics of florals, red licorice, plums and Middle Eastern
spices like sumac. Super savoury. It's light on its feet, yet has complexity: juicy,
vibrant and layered, with textural tannins and a buoyancy. This just feels effortless.
Screwcap. 13.6% alc. **Rating** 95 **To** 2026 $45 JF

♟♟♟♟♟ Sallio 2015 Rating 92 To 2023 $27 JF
Quomodo 2015 Rating 92 To 2024 $45 JF
Fluus 2016 Rating 92 To 2024 $27 JF

Rusty Mutt   ★★★★
26 Columbia Avenue, Clapham, SA 5062 (postal) **Region** McLaren Vale
T 0402 050 820 **www**.rustymutt.com.au **Open** Not
Winemaker Scott Heidrich **Est.** 2009 **Dozens** 1000
Scott Heidrich has lived in the shadow of Geoff Merrill for 20 years, but has partially emerged into the sunlight with his virtual micro-winery. Back in 2006, close friends and family (Nicole and Alan Francis, Stuart Evans, David Lipman and Phil Cole) persuaded Scott to take advantage of the wonderful quality of the grapes that year and make a small batch of Shiraz. The wines are made at a friend's micro-winery in McLaren Flat. The name Rusty Mutt comes from Scott's interest in Chinese astrology, and feng shui; Scott was born in the year of the dog, with the dominant element being metal, hence Rusty Mutt. What the ownership group doesn't drink is sold through fine wine retailers and selected restaurants, with a small amount exported to the UK and China.

♟♟♟♟♟ **Rocky Ox McLaren Vale Grenache Shiraz Mataro 2016** Attractive aromas here with blood plum, candied orange rind and raspberry liqueur. Old vinous grenache scents surge across a rich mid-palate, held close to the chest by the arsenal of mataro tannins, ferruginous, grippy and bloody. There is clear American oak influence here, with its bourbon-sappiness, but it all works well in a classical regional vein. Screwcap. 14.5% alc. **Rating** 93 To 2026 $27 NG ✪
Original McLaren Vale Shiraz 2015 This is as honest a postcard for McLaren Vale shiraz as one could hope for. A blend of fruit from McLaren Flat, Willunga and Blewitt Springs, before 12 months ageing in a combination of French and American oak. There is ample black fruit, Christmas cake spice and some bourbon-soused vanillans to keep the hedonist in us all happy. Powerful, but relaxed. Screwcap. 14.5% alc. **Rating** 92 To 2023 $27 NG
Vermilion Bird McLaren Vale Shiraz 2014 There is more pushin' to this wine than the others in the swag. It is a take-no-prisoners sort of wine, that on one hand, I suppose, is inimitably South Australian. On the other it is a bit over the top, with 3 years spent in spanking new French oak, delivering plenty of cedar and vanilla-clad tannins to bridle the gushing dark fruit and menthol notes. Cork. 14.5% alc. **Rating** 91 To 2024 $75 NG

Rutherglen Estates   ★★★★
Tuileries, 13 Drummond Street, Rutherglen, Vic 3685 **Region** Rutherglen
T (02) 6032 7999 **www**.rutherglenestates.com.au **Open** 7 days 10–5.30
Winemaker Marc Scalzo **Est.** 1997 **Dozens** 70 000 **Vyds** 26.5ha
Rutherglen Estates is one of the larger growers in the region. The focus of the business has changed: it has reduced its own fruit intake, while maintaining its contract processing. Production has turned to table wine made from parcels of fruit hand-selected from five Rutherglen vineyard sites. Rhône and Mediterranean varieties such as durif, viognier, shiraz and sangiovese are a move away from traditional varieties, as are alternative varieties including zinfandel, fiano and savagnin. Exports to Singapore, Thailand and China.

♟♟♟♟♟ **Renaissance Viognier Roussanne Marsanne 2016** A 54/33/13% blend; matured in 56% new French hogsheads and puncheons – everything has come together well. There's texture, a slipperiness, flavours of poached stone fruit with ginger cream, plus a savoury twist. Full-bodied and with a touch of richness, without it getting lost. Screwcap. 14% alc. **Rating** 93 To 2021 $32 JF
Renaissance Durif 2015 This already powerful wine spends 20 months in French, American and Hungarian hogsheads, 55% new. The quality and freshness of the fruit is holding the oak flavours convincingly, the sturdy, drying tannins behaving and tempered by an appealing mix of black fruit, iodine, dark chocolate and squid ink. Screwcap. 14.5% alc. **Rating** 93 To 2025 $50 JF

Single Vineyard Arneis 2017 It turns grip to its advantage. Stone fruit, pear and honeysuckle flavours burst from the blocks, but remain safely within their lanes; the result is one of controlled power. A real zip to the back half has this wine in a good place. Screwcap. 13.8% alc. **Rating** 92 **To** 2020 $24 CM ◐

Single Vineyard Fiano 2016 Oak has added weight to a clean, floral wine with grapefruit and sweet pear flavours in good measure. It's not just fun and fruity, though it is that; there's an extra gravity to this. Screwcap. 13.7% alc. **Rating** 92 **To** 2018 $24 CM ◐

Classic Muscat NV 375ml. Hard not to admire both the freshness and (related) drinkability of this. It has all the flavours you might hope for – raisins, peanut brittle, toffee and cream – but it swings almost juicily through the palate, the wine's overt sweetness not harming the wine's momentum in any way. Great buying. Screwcap. 17% alc. **Rating** 92 $22 CM ◐

Shelley's Block Marsanne Viognier Roussanne 2016 You get aroma, you get flavour, you get texture and you get balance. It's a hard wine to argue with but an easy one to drink. Floral aromatics, stone fruit flavours and a subtle-but-important waxiness to the texture. The value is just as clear-cut. Screwcap. 14.1% alc. **Rating** 91 **To** 2020 $19 CM ◐

Single Vineyard Marsanne 2016 Matured in French puncheons over 10 months. Fresh with fruit and well weighted, it's succulent throughout too. The influence of oak is clear, but the wine's balance is never called into question. Screwcap. 14.1% alc. **Rating** 90 **To** 2021 $24 CM

Single Vineyard Durif 2015 Inky-purple hue; a hearty wine laden with blackberries and plums, sweet vanillan oak and an overlay of warm earth. Full-bodied with furry tannins, yet with a bit of give; it's not all brute force. However, best to drink sooner, as the very ripe to overripe flavours – as in currants, prunes and blackstrap licorice – are to the fore. Screwcap. 14.5% alc. **Rating** 90 **To** 2022 $24 JF

♥♥♥♥ **Single Vineyard Shiraz 2015** Rating 89 To 2022 $24 JF
Sparkling Shiraz Durif 2014 Rating 89 $28 CM

Rymill Coonawarra ★★★★★

Riddoch Highway, Coonawarra, SA 5263 **Region** Coonawarra
T (08) 8736 5001 www.rymill.com.au **Open** Mon–Sat 11–5, Sun 12–5
Winemaker Federico Zaina, Joshua Clementson **Est.** 1974 **Dozens** 40000 **Vyds** 137ha
The Rymills are descendants of John Riddoch, and long owned some of the finest Coonawarra soil, upon which they grew grapes since 1970. In 2016 the Rymill family sold the winery, vineyards and brand to a Chinese investor. The management, vineyard and winery teams have remained in place and new capital has financed moves to improve the vineyards and winery. Josh Clementson (winemaker and vineyard manager) has been joined by Argentinean-born Frederico Zaina. The winery building also houses the cellar door and art exhibitions, which, together with viewing platforms over the winery, make it a must-see destination for tourists. Exports to all major markets.

♥♥♥♥♥ **Cabernet Sauvignon 2015** A statuesque cabernet brimful of bold, curranty fruit and with all the complexity and structure you could hope for. This is an absolute beauty. Tobacco, cloves, smoky oak and a range of ripe, dark-berried fruit. When Coonawarra cabernet is good, it's exceptional. Screwcap. 14.5% alc. Rating 96 To 2042 $32 CM ◐

The Surveyor Cabernet Sauvignon 2015 Best barrels of cabernet from the estate 35yo vines. 100% new French oak. It's remarkably elegant despite its heft: blackberry, boysenberry and blackcurrant all combine with tobacco, mint and creamy/smoky oak to create a gorgeous expression of the variety. The only 'problem' with this wine is that the estate's 'standard' release is its equal. Cork. 14.5% alc. Rating 96 To 2040 $90 CM

♥♥♥♥♡ **Shiraz 2015** Rating 93 To 2029 $32 CM
Cabernet Sauvignon 2014 Rating 93 To 2030 $32 SC

The Dark Horse Cabernet Sauvignon 2016 Rating 92 To 2026 $23 CM ❂
Maturation Release Cabernet Sauvignon 2012 Rating 92 To 2025 $45 SC
GT Gewurztraminer 2017 Rating 90 To 2019 $20 CM ❂
The Yearling Sauvignon Blanc 2017 Rating 90 To 2019 $16 CM ❂
The Yearling Coonawarra Rose 2017 Rating 90 To 2018 $15 CM ❂

Saddler's Creek   ★★★★☆

Marrowbone Road, Pokolbin, NSW 2320 **Region** Hunter Valley
T (02) 4991 1770 **www**.saddlerscreek.com **Open** 7 days 10–5
Winemaker Brett Woodward **Est.** 1989 **Dozens** 6000 **Vyds** 10ha
Saddler's Creek is a boutique winery that is little known outside the Hunter Valley, but has
built a loyal following of dedicated supporters. It came onto the scene over 25 years ago with
some rich, bold wines, and maintains this style today. Fruit is sourced from the Hunter Valley
and Langhorne Creek, with occasional forays into other premium regions.

🍷🍷🍷🍷🍷 Bluegrass Langhorne Creek Cabernet Sauvignon Shiraz 2015 Fruit is
from two reputable Langhorne Creek vineyards: Follet and River's End. This
is a seamless blend; the tannins precise, well alloyed and showing great balance,
length and composure. Milk chocolate, oak, currant, blueberry, anise, bush leaves
and a herbal potpourri meld across a long, easy glide down the throat. Screwcap.
14.5% alc. **Rating** 95 To 2030 $40 NG
Bluegrass Shiraz 2015 A blend of fruit from Mudgee and Langhorne Creek.
Purple florals blend with blueberry, anise, iodine and deli meats. The flow of
mocha tannins is detailed, precise and well managed. Large-framed and a bit old
fashioned, this has meritorious poise and glide. Screwcap. 14.5% alc. **Rating** 94
To 2028 $40 NG

🍷🍷🍷🍷♀ Allessandro Reserve Shiraz 2015 Rating 93 To 2030 $65 NG
Ryan's Reserve Langhorne Creek Cabernet Shiraz 2015 Rating 93
To 2025 $40 NG
Ryan's Reserve Hunter Valley Semillon 2017 Rating 92 To 2031 $36 NG
Allessandro Reserve Chardonnay 2017 Rating 92 To 2025 $36 NG
Alluvia Shiraz 2015 Rating 92 To 2024 $22 NG ❂
Bluegrass Langhorne Creek Cabernet Sauvignon 2015 Rating 92
To 2032 $40 NG
Alluvia Cabernet Sauvignon 2014 Rating 92 To 2024 $22 NG ❂
Reserve Riesling 2016 Rating 91 To 2024 $36 NG
Hunter Valley Semillon 2017 Rating 91 To 2029 $26 NG
Alluvia Semillon 2013 Rating 91 To 2024 $22 NG ❂
Allessandro Reserve Cabernet Sauvignon 2015 Rating 91 To 2032
$65 NG
Botrytis Semillon 2015 Rating 91 To 2023 $36 NG
Alluvia Sauvignon Blanc 2017 Rating 90 To 2019 $22 NG

Sailor Seeks Horse   ★★★★★

102 Armstrongs Road, Cradoc, Tas 7109 **Region** Southern Tasmania
T 0418 471 120 **www**.sailorseekshorse.com.au **Open** Not
Winemaker Paul and Gilli Lipscombe **Est.** 2010 **Dozens** 1200 **Vyds** 6.5ha
While I was given comprehensive information about the seriously interesting careers of Paul
and Gilli Lipscombe, and about their vineyard, I am none the wiser about the highly unusual
and very catchy name. The story began in 2005 when they resigned from their (unspecified)
jobs in London, did a vintage in Languedoc, and then headed to Margaret River to study
oenology and viticulture. While combining study and work, their goal was to learn as much
as possible about pinot noir. They worked in large, small, biodynamic, conventional, minimum
and maximum intervention vineyards and wineries – Woodlands, Xanadu, Beaux Freres,
Chehalem and Mt Difficulty. By 2010 they were in Tasmania, working for Julian Alcorso's
Winemaking Tasmania, and found a derelict vineyard that had never cropped, having been
abandoned not long after being planted in '05. It was in the Huon Valley, the coolest district

in Tasmania, and precisely where they had aimed to begin. They are working as winemakers for celebrated Home Hill wines and manage Jim Chatto's vineyard in Glaziers Bay. Exports to the US and Singapore.

🍷🍷🍷🍷🍷 **Chardonnay 2016** It feels as though it floats lightly – and brightly – through the palate but the finish is intense. This is a beautiful chardonnay; good now but with better days to come, its flavours of lemon curd and white peach, brine and sweet spice gorgeous to behold. Screwcap. 12.9% alc. **Rating** 96 **To** 2026 $50 CM ✪
Pinot Noir 2016 A beautiful pinot noir, as much nerve as verve. Its fresh, frisky disposition is supported by well powered fruit, its sweetness of both spice and roasted nuts offset by the wine's savoury heart. In short, it smells, tastes and feels fantastic, and has the balance and structure to embrace bottle age with open arms. Screwcap. 13.4% alc. **Rating** 95 **To** 2026 $50 CM

St Hallett ★★★★★

St Hallett Road, Tanunda, SA 5352 **Region** Barossa
T (08) 8563 7000 **www**.sthallett.com.au **Open** 7 days 10–5
Winemaker Toby Barlow, Shelley Cox, Darin Kinzie **Est.** 1944 **Dozens** 210 000
St Hallett sources all grapes from within the Barossa GI, and is synonymous with the region's icon variety, shiraz. Old Block is the ultra-premium leader of the band (using old vine grapes from Lyndoch and Eden Valley), supported by Blackwell (Greenock, Ebenezer and Seppeltsfield). The winemaking team headed by Toby Barlow continues to explore the geographical, geological and climatic diversity of the Barossa, manifested through individual processing of all vineyards and single-vineyard releases. In 2017 it was acquired by Accolade. Exports to all major markets.

🍷🍷🍷🍷🍷 **Eden Valley Riesling 2017** Puts a smile on the face as its purity and freshness come through without the least hesitation. Distilled Eden Valley lemon-lime and mineral notes all hunt together, and end any discussion about the quality (and exceptional value) of this label. Screwcap. 12% alc. **Rating** 96 **To** 2032 $23 ✪

🍷🍷🍷🍷🍷 **Barossa Touriga Nacional 2016 Rating** 93 **To** 2023 $25 JF ✪

St Huberts ★★★★★

Cnr Maroondah Highway/St Huberts Road, Coldstream, Vic 3770 **Region** Yarra Valley
T (03) 5960 7096 **www**.sthuberts.com.au **Open** 7 days 10–5
Winemaker Greg Jarratt **Est.** 1966 **Dozens** NFP **Vyds** 20.49ha
The St Huberts of today has a rich 19th-century history, not least in its success at the 1881 Melbourne International Exhibition, which featured every type of agricultural and industrial product. The wine section alone attracted 711 entries. The Emperor of Germany offered a Grand Prize, a silver gilt epergne, for the most meritorious exhibit in the show. A St Huberts wine won the wine section, then competed against objects as diverse as felt hats and steam engines to win the Emperor's Prize, featured on its label for decades thereafter. Like other Yarra Valley wineries, it dropped from sight at the start of the 20th century, was reborn in 1966, and after several changes of ownership, became part of what today is TWE. The wines are made at Coldstream Hills, but have their own, very different, focus. St Huberts is dominated by Cabernet and the single vineyard Roussanne. Its grapes come from warmer sites (part owned and part under contract), particularly the valley floor.

🍷🍷🍷🍷🍷 **Yarra Valley Chardonnay 2016** '16 was a very warm vintage in the Yarra. Vineyard management and with that, picking windows and expediency were often key determinants of quality wines. Leading off with a bumptious note of stone fruits, this medium-bodied wine strings it all together with a gentle pillar of crunchy acidity, tangy mineral and vanillan-cashew oak, sensibly appointed in acknowledgement that the vintage is looser of structure, forward of fruit and more approachable than usual. Screwcap. 13% alc. **Rating** 93 **To** 2022 $27 NG ✪
Yarra Valley Pinot Noir 2016 There is more mettle and gristle to this cuvee than the other pinots in the range. Firm, savoury tannins serve as a guiding light to

a cavalry of ripe bing cherry, mulch and clove. Tangy and bright of fruit, vanillan oak and anchored by a call of the earth, this is solid pinot and very Yarra at that. Screwcap. 13.5% alc. **Rating** 93 **To** 2024 $33 NG

Yarra Valley Cabernet Merlot 2016 A flavourful, medium-bodied cabernet blend, drawing on the currant of the mainstay, the plumminess of the merlot and a potpourri of herb-soused tannins, melded with coconut roughed oak. A bit trop, but plenty of effort in the mix. Screwcap. 14% alc. **Rating** 92 **To** 2024 $27 NG

Yarra Valley Roussanne 2017 As far as I am concerned, this needs to be riper. Roussanne is a brilliant variety per se, with brimstone kindling on these shores. Yet it is quintessentially Mediterranean, melding an ample viscosity with an uncanny vibrancy, at its best. Lemon oil, quince, nashi pear and rooibos. The tangy acidity is a little obtuse. This shows great promise. Let it out, rather than reining it in! Screwcap. 12% alc. **Rating** 91 **To** 2022 $30 NG

The Stag Yarra Valley Pinot Noir 2017 A light ruby, verging into crimson. This is a featherweight pinot, that explores wet forest floor, camp fire, camphor and a cardamom and clove-soused spindle of tannin, presumably due to the inclusion of some stems in the ferment. An honest Yarra reference point. Screwcap. 13.5% alc. **Rating** 91 **To** 2023 $24 NG

The Stag Cool Climate Shiraz 2016 There's some pretty good fruit in this wine given its price, with black cherry, blackberry and plum all involved. The texture, too, is good, the oak treatment likewise. Made for drinking here and now, but will go the distance. Screwcap. 14.5% alc. **Rating** 90 **To** 2026 $20 ○

🍷🍷🍷🍷 **The Stag Chardonnay 2017** Rating 89 **To** 2021 $20 NG
The Stag Heathcote Shiraz 2017 Rating 89 **To** 2023 $24 NG

St Hugo   ★★★★★

2141 Barossa Valley Way, Rowland Flat, SA 5352 **Region** Barossa Valley
T (08) 8115 9200 **www**.sthugo.com **Open** 7 days 10.30–4.30
Winemaker Daniel Swincer **Est.** 1983 **Dozens** NFP **Vyds** 57ha
This a standalone business within the giant bosom of Pernod Ricard, focused on the premium and ultra-premium end of the market, thus differentiating it from Jacob's Creek. It is presumably a substantial enterprise, even though no information about its size or modus operandi is forthcoming. Exports to the UK, Singapore, NZ and China.

🍷🍷🍷🍷🍷 **Eden Valley Riesling 2017** A striking multifaceted riesling that starts asking questions (and providing answers in due course) from the moment it enters the mouth. Lemon, lime, lime zest and pith, and minerally acidity pull the palate onwards, taking no prisoners. A very good riesling. Screwcap. 10.5% alc. **Rating** 96 **To** 2032 $40 ○

Cellar Collection Barossa Shiraz 2012 Good quality cork, well inserted. Fully reflects the great vintage; the slow march to maturity has only just begun, but the cadenced black fruits, spices, quality oak and polished tannins are in perfect harmony. 14.3% alc. **Rating** 96 **To** 2032 $99

Coonawarra Cabernet Sauvignon 2015 Destemmed, not crushed, open and closed fermenters, 12–21 days on skins, matured for 16 months in a majority of French oak (70% new). Good colour; a medium-bodied palate with clear cassis and mulberry varietal character, oak and tannins in support roles. Gold medal Limestone Coast Wine Show '17. Screwcap. 14.6% alc. **Rating** 95 **To** 2030 $58

Cellar Collection Coonawarra Cabernet Sauvignon 2012 From vines planted in 1995. Machine-harvested, cultured yeast, 22 days on skins, matured for 23 months in new oak (94% French, 6% American). A very good cabernet with a long future ahead. The bottling line was set up correctly, the high quality cork perfectly inserted. Cassis flows liberally across the mouth, with balanced tannins and oak in respectful support. 14.8% alc. **Rating** 95 $99

🍷🍷🍷🍷🍷 **Barossa Shiraz 2015** Rating 93 **To** 2030 $58
Private Collection Marananga Barossa Shiraz 2013 Rating 90 **To** 2020 $65

St John's Road

1468 Research Road, St Kitts, SA, 5356 **Region** Barossa Valley
T (08) 8362 8622 **www**.stjohnsroad.com **Open** Not
Winemaker Phil Lehmann, Charlie Ormsby, James Lienert **Est.** 2002 **Dozens** 20 000
Vyds 20ha

St John's Road is now part of WD Wines Pty Ltd, which also owns Hesketh Wine Company and Parker Coonawarra Estate. It brings together a group of winemakers with an intimate knowledge of the Barossa Valley, and a fierce pride in what they do. Curiously, each obtained their first degree in other disciplines: Phil Lehmann as an electrical engineer, Charlie Ormsby as a librarian with a Bachelor of Arts and James Lienert with a Bachelor of Science (organic and inorganic chemistry) from the University of Adelaide. Others in the ownership group have extensive sales and marketing expertise. Exports to all major markets.

The Evangelist Old Vine Barossa Shiraz 2016 38% ex 57yo Eden Valley vines, 62% ex 82yo bushvines at Stone Well, fermented separately, 8–9 days on skins, matured for 18 months in French hogsheads (50% new). A remarkable achievement in the light of the chaotic '16 vintage, the freshness imbued by the modest alcohol. A truly lovely wine, flowing red and black fruits the key. Screwcap. 13.5% alc. **Rating** 96 **To** 2036 $58 ✪

Gee Whiz Tram Driver Eden Valley Dry Traminer Riesling 2017 A 57/43% blend from two vineyards, 80% fermented with full solids in stainless steel, 20% in barrel. No effort was spared in increasing the complexity of the wine, and the result is as good as can have been expected. It has considerable texture and depth to the palate, yet isn't the least bit heavy. The flavours are predominantly citrus, but with spice and talc nuances adding yet more interest. Screwcap. 12% alc. **Rating** 94 **To** 2027 $18 ✪

Block 8 Maywald Clone Resurrection Vineyard Barossa Valley Shiraz 2016 Delicate shiraz of great, fragrant charm. You could say that it tiptoes through the palate but that would undersell its deliberate footprints of spice, earth, red cherry and anise. It's both snappy and precise. The impression it makes goes well beyond its light to medium weight; indeed it's fast becoming a champion of the less-is-more movement in Australian red wine. Bravo. Screwcap. 12.9% alc. **Rating** 94 **To** 2026 $38 CM

The Evangelist Old Vine Barossa Shiraz 2015 It saw 50% new (French) oak, but highly scented fruit is the principal player, this wine proving that you can be rich and ripe and still maintain a fresh, vibrant disposition. Cranberry and plum, coffee-cream and port-wine jelly, all studded with clove and star anise. It feels confident from start to finish; it makes quality look easy. Screwcap. 14.5% alc. **Rating** 94 **To** 2032 $58 CM

Prayer Garden Selection Resurrection Vineyard Barossa Valley Grenache 2016 The aromas run free but the strain gauge is tight. This is a good drink now but it's going nowhere in a hurry; tannin and acid have the leash pulled tight. Foresty berries, violets, subtle herb notes, orange rind; it tastes like wine plucked from a garden. The St John's Road range is a treasure trove at present. Screwcap. 14% alc. **Rating** 94 **To** 2024 $30 CM ✪

The Prophet Resurrection Vineyard Barossa Shiraz 2016 Rating 93 To 2036 $30
The Resilient Barossa Grenache 2017 Rating 93 To 2024 $22 CM ✪
Peace of Eden Riesling 2017 Rating 92 To 2027 $22 ✪
PL Wild Yeast Reversed Ferment Eden Valley Chardonnay 2016 Rating 91 To 2021 $30 CM
Motley Bunch Barossa Valley GMS 2016 Rating 91 To 2023 $22 ✪
Line & Length Barossa Cabernet Sauvignon 2016 Rating 90 To 2025 $22 CM

St Leonards Vineyard

St Leonards Road, Wahgunyah, Vic 3687 **Region** Rutherglen
T 1800 021 621 **www.**stleonardswine.com.au **Open** Thurs–Sun 10–5
Winemaker Nick Brown, Chloe Earl **Est.** 1860 **Dozens** 5000 **Vyds** 12ha
An old favourite, relaunched in late 1997 with a range of premium wines, cleverly marketed through an attractive cellar door and bistro at the historic winery on the banks of the Murray. It is run by Eliza Brown (CEO), sister Angela (online communications manager) and brother Nick (vineyard and winery manager). They are perhaps better known as the trio who fulfil the same roles at All Saints Estate. Exports to the UK and the US.

ΨΨΨΨΨ **Durif 2015** Damson plums and blackstrap licorice, cedary and laced with cinnamon. While full-bodied, the ripe tannins are sandy, and overall, it's not a big wine. A whiff of dusty old oak, in an old cellar, is pleasing. And there's freshness to this, making it immediately accessible. Screwcap. 14.3% alc. **Rating** 93 **To** 2025 $28 JF

Shiraz 2016 Vibrant dark crimson; briary fruit with spiced plums, quite tangy and noticeable lemony acidity streaking across the tight palate. While aged in a mix of seasoned French and American oak for 18 months, it makes its presence felt both in flavour, and a cedary and coconut character. A pleasingly balanced wine. Screwcap. 13.9% alc. **Rating** 92 **To** 2023 $32 JF

Cabernet Franc 2016 Pale-mid garnet-purple; some aniseed, cake baking spices and panforte flavours mingle with the dark cherries and plums. It's ripe but the tannins, and body are lithe; while it tapers off to a dry finish, it is easy to enjoy. Screwcap. 13% alc. **Rating** 92 **To** 2021 $32 JF

Durif 2016 Very good colour; sweetly-fruited and supple with a fragrance of licorice, warm earth, cedary oak and new leather. Full-bodied with furry big tannins, but in sync and, overall, very satisfying. Screwcap. 14% alc. **Rating** 91 **To** 2025 $32 JF

Classic Rutherglen Muscat NV Mid-mahogany with a ruby rim; it's rich and balanced thanks to the acidity and its 15+ years ageing in old barrels, so while there's an impression of sweetness, it's not cloying. Tastes of candied peel, raisins in caramel fudge and a lemony note. 375ml. Screwcap. 18% alc. **Rating** 91 $35 JF

Saint Oaks Estate Vineyard

PO Box 40, Oakbank, SA 5243 **Region** Adelaide Hills
T 0487 886 888 **www.**saintoaksestate.com.au **Open** Not
Winemaker Simon Greenleaf **Est.** 2016 **Dozens** 1450 **Vyds** 16.1ha
In 1996 real estate agent Chris Weston and wife Sue purchased a block of land, with prime dual frontage to Beasley and Wenzel Roads in Oakbank that had been in family ownership for three generations. Three years later the Westons planted 4.7ha of pinot noir, 4.7ha of sauvignon blanc and 2.9ha of shiraz. The grapes were sold, their quality leading to the planting of 3.8ha of French clone chardonnay on adjacent land acquired in '15. Simon Greenleaf, small-batch wine specialist at Lobethal, makes shiraz, pinot noir and sauvignon blanc from a small part of the crop withheld from sale.

ΨΨΨΨΨ **Adelaide Hills Pinot Noir 2016** This ticks all the boxes: the colour is good, the bouquet fresh, and the palate better still. It is 50/50% dark cherry and plum, with pleasing texture ex fine, ripe tannins and some new oak. The length is admirable, the balance and texture likewise. Has 8–10 years in front of it. Screwcap. 13.5% alc. **Rating** 94 **To** 2028

ΨΨΨΨΨ **Adelaide Hills Shiraz 2016 Rating** 92 **To** 2029
Weston Adelaide Hills Sauvignon Blanc 2017 Rating 91 **To** 2021 $15 ✪
Adelaide Hills Sauvignon Blanc 2016 Rating 90 **To** 2019

Salo Wines

28 Dorothy Street, Healesville, Vic 3777 (postal) **Region** Yarra Valley
T (03) 5962 5331 **www**.salowines.com.au **Open** Not
Winemaker Steve Flamsteed, Dave Mackintosh **Est.** 2008 **Dozens** 250
Business partners Steve Flamsteed and Dave Mackintosh say that Salo means dirty and a little
uncouth, which, with the Australian sense of humour, can be used as a term of endearment.
They wish to keep their wines a little dirty by using hands-off, minimal winemaking, except
for a few strange techniques to make more gritty, textured wines. Quantities are unfortunately
minuscule, with 150 dozen bottles of Chardonnay and 100 dozen of Syrah. Exports to
Hong Kong.

Yarra Valley Chardonnay 2015 Grown on the Full Moon Vineyard at
Gladysdale. No new oak. Style takes a back seat to pure fruit flavour, the
chardonnay grape on open display. It tastes of white peach and mineral, melon and
grapefruit, the wine's final crackle of energetic flavour placing an emphasis on its
quality. The body of flavour here is substantial and yet it hones beautifully through
the finish. Screwcap. 13% alc. **Rating** 94 **To** 2022 $40 CM

Salomon Estate

17 High Street, Willunga, SA 5171 **Region** Southern Fleurieu
T 0447 808 243 **www**.salomonwines.com **Open** Not
Winemaker Bert Salomon, Simon White **Est.** 1997 **Dozens** 6500 **Vyds** 12.1ha
Bert Salomon is an Austrian winemaker with a long-established family winery in the Kremstal
region, not far from Vienna. He became acquainted with Australia during his time with import
company Schlumberger in Vienna; he was the first to import Australian wines (Penfolds) into
Austria, in the mid-1980s, and later became head of the Austrian Wine Bureau. He was so
taken by Adelaide that he moved his family there for the first few months each year, sending
his young children to school and setting in place an Australian red winemaking venture. He is
now a full-time travelling winemaker, running the family winery in the northern hemisphere
vintage, and overseeing the making of the Salomon Estate wines at Chapel Hill. Salomon
Estate now shares a cellar door with Hither & Yon, just a few steps away from the Saturday
farmers market in Willunga. Exports to all major markets.

Finniss River Sea Eagle Vineyard Fleurieu Peninsula Shiraz 2015 Estate-
grown, matured for 18 months in French barriques (33% new). Finniss River
is adjacent to McLaren Vale, but has its own site climate and soil that doesn't,
however, turn its back on dark chocolate as one of its flavours. The wine is
medium to full-bodied, with succulent black fruits and licorice, French oak
and velvety tannins completing a particularly enjoyable palate. Cork. 14.5% alc.
Rating 96 **To** 2040 $38
Alttus Southern Fleurieu Shiraz 2010 As a 7yo, it's just starting to soften.
There's ample brood and bulk here, but the mellow of age has opened the
drinking door. It tastes of creamy vanilla, spearmint and powerful blue/black
berried fruit, a semblance of fresh leather in the aftertaste. For all its might, it still
manages some finesse, particularly via its detailed lines of tannin. Many years yet
ahead of it. Cork. 14.5% alc. **Rating** 95 **To** 2025 $110 CM
Aestatis Grenache Shiraz Mourvedre 2010 The grenache came from 90yo
bushvines in Blewitt Springs, matured for 21 months in French hogsheads (20%
new). Has stood the test of time very well indeed. The wine was given 94 points
when tasted Jan '13, and has more than fulfilled the promise it then showed. This
is a delicious, silky grenache blend, ready tonight or in another 13 years. Screwcap.
15% alc. **Rating** 95 **To** 2030 $45
Dark Pearl Fleurieu Peninsula Cabernet SFM 2016 Matured for 18 months
in French barriques, mainly used. Bright crimson-purple hue; a medium-bodied
blend of cabernet sauvignon, cabernet franc and merlot; supple, smooth and — in a
word — delicious. Screwcap. 14.5% alc. **Rating** 95 **To** 2026 $28

Alttus Southern Fleurieu Shiraz 2003 Museum release. Beefy and substantial even as a 14yo. Leather, blackberry, plum, honey and saltbush notes get a good chatter of flavour going, all within a soft/mellow context. It won't fall over in a hurry but there's unlikely to be any positive development from here. Drinking quite beautifully now. Cork. 14.5% alc. **Rating** 94 **To** 2022 $120 CM

ΨΨΨΨΨ Wildflower Fleurieu Peninsula Syrah-V 2016 Rating 93 To 2029 $28
The Verve Free Red 2016 Rating 91 To 2023 $29

Saltram ★★★★★

Murray Street, Angaston, SA 5353 **Region** Barossa Valley
T (08) 8561 0200 **www**.saltramwines.com.au **Open** 7 days 10–5
Winemaker Alex MacKenzie, Richard Mattner **Est.** 1859 **Dozens** 150 000
There is no doubt that Saltram has taken strides towards regaining the reputation it held 30 or so years ago. Grape sourcing has come back to the Barossa Valley for the flagship wines. The red wines, in particular, have enjoyed great show success over the past decade, with No. 1 Shiraz and Mamre Brook leading the charge. Exports to all major markets.

ΨΨΨΨΨ The Journal Centenarian Old Vine Shiraz 2015 From vines c1900 grown in the Eden Valley. What a wine this is – for its complexity, depth of flavour and its sheen. Vivid purple; layers of dark fruit lifted with a heady fragrance of lavender and violets, a sprinkling of licorice and wood spices lead onto a full-bodied palate. No shortage of tannins, yet there's this bright acid lift on the finish: both ensure this will be long-lived. Screwcap. 14.5% alc. **Rating** 96 **To** 2040 $175 JF
Pepperjack Porterhouse Graded Langhorne Creek Shiraz 2016 This basks in its regionality with distinctive flavours of black plums dipped in chocolate and cinnamon, with a raspberry lift. Fuller-bodied, the palate smooth and glossy with pillow-soft tannins; the overall feel is of a balanced wine offering immediate drinking pleasure. Screwcap. 14.5% alc. **Rating** 95 **To** 2028 $50 JF
No. 1 Barossa Shiraz 2015 No shortage of colour, flavour, density and tannins. And sure, there's a certain muscularity, but it's not excessive. There's a freshness, a buoyancy making this appear ready now, even if its best days are yet to come. The usual dark fruits, woodsy spices and savoury nuances are in abundance. Impressive. Screwcap. 14.5% alc. **Rating** 95 **To** 2035 $100 JF
Pepperjack Certified Shiraz Cabernet 2016 Excellent dark purple hue; well composed with one variety not outdoing the other; offers a mix of cassis, black plums, licorice and a generous slather of oak and spices. What makes one take notice is the glossy texture and ripe, plush, determined tannins. For fans of big reds and steak. Screwcap. 14.5% alc. **Rating** 95 **To** 2028 $30 JF ✪

ΨΨΨΨΨ Limited Release Winemaker's Selection Barossa Valley Shiraz Tempranillo 2016 Rating 93 To 2026 $50 JF
Mr Pickwick's Limited Release Particular Tawny NV Rating 93 $75 JF
Limited Release Winemaker's Selection Fiano 2017 Rating 92 To 2020 $25 JF ✪
Limited Release Winemaker's Selection Old Vine Barossa Valley Grenache 2016 Rating 92 To 2024 $35 JF
Limited Release Winemaker's Selection Barossa Valley Sangiovese 2016 Rating 92 To 2024 $35 JF
Pepperjack Barossa Valley Sparkling Shiraz NV Rating 92 $35 JF
Mamre Brook Eden Valley Riesling 2017 Rating 91 To 2027 $23 JF ✪
Pepperjack Barossa Shiraz Cabernet 2015 Rating 90 To 2025 $30 CM
Pepperjack Barossa Shiraz Grenache Mourvedre 2016 Rating 90 To 2025 $30 JF
Pepperjack Premium Cut Cabernet Shiraz 2016 Rating 90 To 2028 $38 JF

Sam Miranda of King Valley ★★★★

1019 Snow Road, Oxley, Vic 3678 **Region** King Valley
T (03) 5727 3888 **www**.sammiranda.com.au **Open** 7 days 10–5
Winemaker Sam Miranda **Est.** 2004 **Dozens** 25 000 **Vyds** 55ha
Sam Miranda, grandson of Francesco Miranda, joined the family business in 1991, striking out on his own in 2004 after Miranda Wines was purchased by McGuigan Simeon. The Myrrhee Estate vineyard is at 450m in the upper reaches of the King Valley. This is where the varieties for Sam Miranda's Signature Range of wines are sourced, each with the name of the nearest town or named district. In 2016 Sam Miranda purchased the Oxley Estate vineyard on Snow Road, with 40ha of vines to be reworked over coming years. Exports to the UK, Fiji and China.

♟♟♟♟♟ **Sangiovese 2016** A morass of sassafras, tomato leaf, bitter herb and dark cherry notes across the attack. The feel is mid-weighted and versatile. The tannins crackle and bite reassuredly, in that Italian structured vein. Acidity and brightness, too. Yet the structural pillars are a bit fuzzy and tweaked. Not effortless enough to merit a higher score. Screwcap. 13% alc. **Rating** 91 **To** 2026 $60 NG

Prosecco NV I like prosecco as a spirited ode to all that is visceral in wine. Its fruit and froth can be thirst-slaking and joyous when done well, with no reason to compare the style to, for example, Champagne. It is a completely different wine! This hits all the right notes: apple and pear gelato sluiced by a gentle bead of fizz and sherbety acidity. Fresh, flavourful and palpably dry. Bravo. Crown seal. 11% alc. **Rating** 91 **To** 2019 $20 NG ⊙

Arneis 2017 A Piedmontese staple that has a strong track record in the similarly inclined sub-alpine climate of the King Valley. Stone and orchard fruits mingle across gentle ginger spice and raw almond bite. This is a standout among the estate's whites, melding dutiful richness with a cool-climate air of freshness. Screwcap. 12% alc. **Rating** 90 **To** 2019 $20 NG ⊙

Barbera 2015 Blueberries and violets on display. Punchy and mid-weighted, with plenty of sass. The generosity of this lies in stark contrast to its dolcetto brethren, with barbera's code of highly strung acidity towing this along. There is a whiff of barnyard rusticity. Slightly drying. Technocratic tasters may take umbrage, but at this level of charge it is a welcome respite from monotonous fruit. Very Italian on a guttural level. Screwcap. 13.4% alc. **Rating** 90 **To** 2020 $35 NG

Samson Tall ★★★★

219 Strout Road, McLaren Vale, SA 5171 **Region** McLaren Vale
T 0488 214 680 **www**.samsontall.com.au **Open** 7 days 10–5
Winemaker Paul Wilson **Est.** 2016 **Dozens** 500
This is the venture of Paul Wilson and partner Heather Budich. They purchase grapes from local growers in McLaren Vale, and make the wine in the small pug church, built in 1854 in the grounds of the house. The winery and church are surrounded by gardens and vineyard, and an historic local cemetery. Paul Wilson has learnt his craft as a winemaker well, all of the wines being well made, the grapes well chosen.

♟♟♟♟♟ **Grenache Rose 2017** The evocative label has many allusions, but the wine inside the bottle is firmly anchored to the red fruits of the bouquet and palate It's quite a wine, catching you unawares. Screwcap. 13% alc. **Rating** 92 **To** 2023 $25 ⊙

Shiraz 2016 Deep crimson-purple; speaks as eloquently of its place as its variety. A supple medium-bodied shiraz with plum, blackberry and dark chocolate all on display, and no tannins to assuage. Screwcap. 14.2% alc. **Rating** 92 **To** 2031 $30

Grenache 2016 Bright crimson; a fresh, light to medium-bodied grenache with considerable tenacity and length. Far removed from the high alcohol (15+%) and dead fruit flavours of traditional grenache. Attractive wine. Screwcap. 14.5% alc. **Rating** 92 **To** 2025 $30

♟♟♟♟ **Tempranillo 2016** **Rating** 89 **To** 2023 $30

Samuel's Gorge   ★★★★

193 Chaffeys Road, McLaren, SA 5171 **Region** McLaren Vale
T (08) 8323 8651 **www**.gorge.com.au **Open** 7 days 11–5
Winemaker Justin McNamee **Est.** 2003 **Dozens** 3500 **Vyds** 10ha
After a wandering winemaking career in various parts of the world, Justin McNamee
became a winemaker at Tatachilla in 1996, where he remained until 2003, leaving to found
Samuel's Gorge. He has established his winery in a barn built in 1853, part of the old Seaview
Homestead. The historic property was owned by Sir Samuel Way, variously Chief Justice
of the South Australian Supreme Court and Lieutenant Governor of the state. The grapes
come from small contract growers spread across the ever-changing (unofficial) subregions of
McLaren Vale, and are basket-pressed and fermented in old open slate fermenters lined with
beeswax. Exports to the US, Canada, Hong Kong and NZ.

ΨΨΨΨΨ **McLaren Vale Shiraz 2015** Trademark blend of dense, sweet fruit and earth-
like savouriness. Pen and pencil style; inky fruit finely inscribed with spice, shaved
dark chocolate and clove-studded leather. Super supple and super drinkable as a
result, almost suede-like. Beautiful red wine. Cork. 14.5% alc. **Rating** 94 **To** 2025
$40 CM

ΨΨΨΨΨ **McLaren Vale Mourvedre 2015** **Rating** 92 **To** 2025 $40 CM

Sandalford   ★★★★★

3210 West Swan Road, Caversham, WA 6055 **Region** Margaret River
T (08) 9374 9374 **www**.sandalford.com **Open** 7 days 9–5
Winemaker Hope Metcalf **Est.** 1840 **Dozens** 60 000 **Vyds** 105ha
Sandalford is one of Australia's oldest and largest privately owned wineries. In 1970 it moved
beyond its original Swan Valley base, purchasing a substantial property in Margaret River
that is now the main source of its premium grapes. Wines are released under the Element,
Winemakers, Margaret River and Estate Reserve ranges, with Prendiville Reserve at the top.
Exports to all major markets.

ΨΨΨΨΨ **Estate Reserve Margaret River Verdelho 2017** Gives the '17 Mandoon
Verdelho a run for its money, and would have Jack Mann and his butcher's mincer
primed to go. The usual throwaway phrase of tropical fruit salad has no place in
the flavours of this wine. Screwcap. 12.5% alc. **Rating** 95 **To** 2025 $25
Margaret River Cabernet Merlot 2016 Estate-grown, matured in new French
oak. Cassis, plum and leaf on the bouquet are replicated in the opening stanzas on
the palate. It's not until the finish that the tannins appear, and lock onto the taste
buds, allied with bay leaf and black olive. Demands patience. Screwcap. 14% alc.
Rating 94 **To** 2046 $20 ●

ΨΨΨΨΨ **Classic Dry White Margaret River Semillon Sauvignon Blanc 2017**
Rating 92 **To** 2023 $22
Estate Reserve Margaret River Sauvignon Blanc Semillon 2017
Rating 91 **To** 2020 $25

Sandhurst Ridge   ★★★★

156 Forest Drive, Marong, Vic 3515 **Region** Bendigo
T (03) 5435 2534 **www**.sandhurstridge.com.au **Open** 7 days 11–5
Winemaker Paul Greblo **Est.** 1990 **Dozens** 3000 **Vyds** 7.3ha
The Greblo brothers (Paul is the winemaker, George the viticulturist), with combined
experience in business, agriculture, science, and construction and development, began the
establishment of Sandhurst Ridge in 1990, planting the first 2ha of shiraz and cabernet
sauvignon. Plantings have increased to over 7ha, principally cabernet and shiraz, but also a
little merlot, nebbiolo and sauvignon blanc. As the business has grown, the Greblos have
supplemented their crush with grapes grown in the region. Exports to Norway, Malaysia,
Taiwan and China.

ŸŸŸŸ♀ **Reserve Bendigo Shiraz 2015** A concentrated, full-bodied shiraz, more so after 19 months in French and Hungarian barrels (80% new). It has a ball of intense dark red fruits laden with sweet oak, green walnut, flavours of dried goji berries and prunes, star anise and licorice. The full-bodied palate has massive yet glossy tannins, and it's just tipping in the too-ripe spectrum with its warm finish. Fans of bigger-styled reds rejoice. Screwcap. 15% alc. **Rating** 93 **To** 2025 $50 JF

ŸŸŸŸ **Bendigo Shiraz Cabernet 2016 Rating** 89 **To** 2022 $22 JF

Sanguine Estate ★★★★★

77 Shurans Lane, Heathcote, Vic 3523 **Region** Heathcote
T (03) 5433 3111 **www**.sanguinewines.com.au **Open** W'ends & public hols 10–5
Winemaker Mark Hunter **Est.** 1997 **Dozens** 10 000 **Vyds** 21.57ha
The Hunter family – parents Linda and Tony, and their children Mark and Jodi, with their respective partners Melissa and Brett – have 20ha of shiraz, with a 'fruit salad block' of chardonnay, viognier, merlot, tempranillo, petit verdot, cabernet sauvignon and cabernet franc. Low-yielding vines and the magic of the Heathcote region have produced a shiraz of exceptional intensity, which has received rave reviews in the US, and led to the 'sold out' sign being posted almost immediately upon release. With the ever-expanding vineyard, Mark has become full-time vigneron and winemaker, and Jodi has taken over from her father as CEO and general manager. Exports to Singapore and China.

ŸŸŸŸŸ **D'Orsa Heathcote Shiraz 2014** The flag-bearer for Sanguine Estate, and rightly so. It is in the full-bodied arena of almost all of Sanguine's Shirazs, but its opulence is polished and supple, black berries, plums and currants supported by balanced tannins. The good quality, properly inserted and wax-sealed cork should do its job for the 20+ years needed for this wine to complete its journey. 15% alc. **Rating** 95 **To** 2035

ŸŸŸŸ♀ **Robo's Mob Heathcote Shiraz 2016 Rating** 93 **To** 2029
Progeny Heathcote Shiraz 2016 Rating 92 **To** 2032
Wine Club Heathcote Shiraz 2016 Rating 91
Music Festival Heathcote Shiraz 2016 Rating 91 **To** 2030
D'Orsa Heathcote Shiraz 2015 Rating 90 **To** 2025
Heathcote Cabernets 2016 Rating 90 **To** 2026

Santa & D'Sas ★★★★

2 Pincott Street, Newtown, Vic 3220 **Region** Various
T 0417 384 272 **www**.santandsas.com.au **Open** Not
Winemaker Andrew Santarossa, Matthew Di Sciascio **Est.** 2014 **Dozens** 7000
Andrew Santarossa and Matthew Di Sciascio met while studying for a Bachelor of Applied Science (wine science) and the business is a collaboration between their two families. Wines are released under the Valentino label (Fiano, Sangiovese and Shiraz), dedicated to Matthew's father; the remaining wines simply identify the region and variety. Exports to China.

ŸŸŸŸŸ **King Valley Pinot Grigio 2017** This is exceptional as far as grigio goes on these shores, with a stream of mineral melded to juicy acidity, towing jasmine scents and nashi pear to apple gelato flavours, long and brisk. Crunchy, lightweighted but brimming with flavour. A pumice-like pucker, too, for good effect at the conclusion of the narrative. Screwcap. 12% alc. **Rating** 95 **To** 2019 $24 NG

ŸŸŸŸ♀ **Heathcote Shiraz 2016 Rating** 92 **To** 2024 $40 NG
Valentino Heathcote Sangiovese 2016 Rating 92 **To** 2024 $45 NG
King Valley Rosato 2017 Rating 91 **To** 2019 $24 NG
King Valley Nuovo Rosso 2017 Rating 91 **To** 2021 $24 NG
King Valley Prosecco NV Rating 91 **To** 2019 $24 NG
Valentino King Valley Fiano 2017 Rating 90 **To** 2022 $45 NG
D'Sas King Valley Prosecco 2017 Rating 90 **To** 2019 $32 CM

Santolin Wines

c/- 21–23 Delaneys Road, South Warrandyte, Vic 3134 **Region** Yarra Valley
T 0402 278 464 **www**.santolinwines.com.au **Open** Not
Winemaker Adrian Santolin **Est.** 2012 **Dozens** 1000
Adrian Santolin grew up in Griffith, NSW, and has worked in the wine industry since he was
15. He moved to the Yarra Valley in 2007 with wife Rebecca, who has worked in marketing
roles at various wineries. Adrian's love of pinot noir led him to work at wineries such as
Wedgetail Estate, Rochford, De Bortoli, Sticks and Rob Dolan Wines. In '12 his dream came
true, when he was able to buy 2t of pinot noir from the Syme on Yarra vineyard, increasing
production in '13 to 4t, split between chardonnay and pinot noir. The Boy Meets Girl wines
are sold through www.nakedwines.com.au. Exports to the UK, the US and Hong Kong.

🍷🍷🍷🍷🍷 **Gladysdale Yarra Valley Chardonnay 2016** From the Willowlake Vineyard
in the Upper Yarra. 250 dozen. More than a little majesty to this release. Fantastic
concentration of fruit flavour, the full complement of toasty oak, a significant burst
of stone fruit, and a creamy/nougat character to the finish. The aftertaste then just
goes on. Powerhouse of a chardonnay. Screwcap. 13.7% alc. **Rating** 96 **To** 2024
$35 CM ○

Cosa Nostra Pinot Gris 2017 160 dozen. It cracks straight into spice and pear
flavours, adding a textural element for good measure. Taut through the finish but
there's a riot of flavour at its core. Super. Screwcap. 13.5% alc. **Rating** 94 **To** 2019
$25 CM ○

Gladysdale Yarra Valley Pinot Noir 2016 From the Willowlake Vineyard.
15% whole bunch, 30% new oak. 250 dozen made. It has that light Upper Yarra
colour, and indeed persona, though there's a fair amount of meat on its bones.
It's a wine of broody, spicy character; the fruit stewed over leaf matter; the finish
sinewy and dry. You'd bet on it developing well. Screwcap. 14.2% alc. **Rating** 94
To 2025 $42 CM

Syme on Yarra Vineyard Yarra Valley Pinot Noir 2016 Wild ferment, 15%
whole bunch, 30% new oak, unfined and unfiltered. 250 dozen. It's a cranberried
wine with spice notes aplenty and tight strings of tannin. It's one of those pinots
you just want to sit and smell all evening: the perfume of red berries, so redolent
of summer; those woodsy spices, like opening a window to a wooded field. Fair to
say this wine is in a good place. Screwcap. 13% alc. **Rating** 94 **To** 2024 $42 CM

🍷🍷🍷🍷🍷 **Family Reserve Yarra Valley Chardonnay 2016** Rating 93 To 2022 $32 CM
Yarra Valley A Rose By Any Other Name 2017 Rating 91 To 2019 CM
Family Reserve Pinot Noir 2016 Rating 91 To 2023 $32 CM
A&R Shiraz Viognier 2016 Rating 91 To 2031 $14 ○

Saracen Estates ★★★☆

342 Murray Street, Perth, WA 6000 **Region** Margaret River
T (08) 9486 9410 **www**.saracenestates.com.au **Open** Mon–Fri 9–5
Winemaker Clive Otto **Est.** 1998 **Dozens** 5000
The sale of the Saracen Estate property has left a cloud of uncertainty over how the business
intends to operate into the future. Maree Saraceni and her brother Dennis Parker are running a
virtual winery operation through their Perth office, employing contract winemaker Clive Otto.

🍷🍷🍷🍷🍷 **Maree 2010** 80% chardonnay, 20% pinot noir. The chardonnay does the heavy
lifting, giving the wine line and length, citrus in the driving seat. Someone who
has a real understanding of sparkling wine made the calls on this, the dosage
perfectly judged after 6.5 years on lees. Diam. 12% alc. **Rating** 91 $38

🍷🍷🍷🍷 **Margaret River Shiraz 2016** Rating 89 To 2022 $35

Sassafras Wines

20 Grylls Crescent, Cook, ACT 2614 (postal) **Region** Canberra District
T 0476 413 974 **www**.sassafraswines.com.au **Open** Not
Winemaker Paul Starr, Hamish Young **Est.** 2015 **Dozens** 300

Paul Starr and Tammy Braybrook brought unusual academic knowledge with them when they established Sassafras Wines. Tammy has a science degree, has worked as an economist, and is now an IT professional and part-time florist. Paul has a PhD in cultural studies and intended to be an academic in humanities, before a detour into environment work in government. Tammy knew Mark Terrell, of Quarry Hill, and the pair ended up working in the Terrell Vineyard with pruning and vintage work, leading to local college courses in winemaking. Paul worked at Eden Road cellar door on weekends for four years. History is an interest for both, and when thinking of heading in an altogether new wine direction, they read of what they describe as the ancestral method of making sparkling wine, using the original yeast and fermentable sugar to create the mousse, bypassing disgorgement altogether.

Chardonnay Savagnin Ancestral 2017 Among the best examples of the style in Australia. The ancestral method, aka 'Pet Nat', refers to a gentle sparkling expression for which the first fermentation is finished in bottle, leaving varying degrees of sweetness married to a soft, frothy bead of fizz. Scrumptious cider-like aromas of bosc pear and red apple are coaxed across a light body of frothy freshness, by a gentle fizz and leesy nourishment. This hits the right balance between dryness, texture, weight and energy. Delicious. Crown seal. 12% alc. Rating 96 $30 NG ◐

Hilltops Fiano 2017 Rating 93 To 2021 $30 NG

Savitas Wines

Level 8, 420 King William Street, Adelaide, SA 5000 (postal) **Region** Barossa Valley
T 0417 895 200 **www**.savitaswines.com **Open** Not
Winemaker Matt O'Leary **Est.** 2015 **Dozens** 3000 **Vyds** 13.6ha

The business seems to have a single purpose in life, namely, the export of its wines to China. But it does have a vineyard that substantially pre-dates its 2015 establishment date. The earliest shiraz vines were planted in 1970, additional plantings continuing until '07. Grenache was planted in '71, and later vines planted in '98. The vineyard is located on the eastern side of the Valley at the foot of the Barossa Range near Menglers Hill. With the exception of the very experienced winemaker, Matt O'Leary, the business has a distinct corporate feel to it with CEO Chris Insanally, John Erskine as chairman and Aaron Read as CFO. The quality is a little variable, but the top end is a very good Reserve Shiraz.

Insignis Green's Vineyard Reserve Barossa Valley Shiraz 2014 From the oldest plantings of the vineyard, the dry grown vines planted in '70; matured in new and used French oak for 18 months. A best barrel selection, more supple and elegant than its sibling, but it has a 30-year future cupped in its hands. Screwcap. 14.5% alc. Rating 94 To 2029 $90

Insignis Green's Vineyard Barossa Valley Shiraz 2014 Rating 89 To 2034 $45
Insignis Green's Vineyard Barossa Valley Shiraz Grenache Mataro 2015 Rating 89 To 2023 $36

SC Pannell

60 Olivers Road, McLaren Vale, SA 5171 **Region** McLaren Vale
T (08) 8323 8000 **www**.scpannell.com.au **Open** 7 days 11–5
Winemaker Stephen Pannell **Est.** 2004 **Dozens** 20 000 **Vyds** 22ha

The only surprising piece of background is that it took (an admittedly still reasonably youthful) Steve Pannell and wife Fiona so long to cut the painter from Constellation/Hardys and establish their own winemaking and consulting business. Steve radiates intensity, and extended experience has resulted in wines of the highest quality, right from the first vintage.

The Pannells have two vineyards in McLaren Vale, the first planted in 1891 with a precious 3.6ha of shiraz. A second property was purchased in 2014, lifting the estate vineyards to a total of 22ha. The future for the Pannells is limitless, the icon status of the label already established. Exports to the UK.

ＹＹＹＹＹ **Adelaide Hills Syrah 2016** Hand-picked, open-fermented with 30% whole bunches, 10 months in large French oak vats and puncheons. A very smart wine. The bouquet offers a combination of black fruits and stern spices, plus a waft of oak. The medium-bodied palate seamlessly picks up the theme in a star dust of spicy/peppery flavours and texture. It is at once powerful, yet calmly insistent. Screwcap. 14% alc. **Rating** 96 **To** 2036

Tempranillo Touriga 2016 57% tempranillo, 29% touriga, 14% tinta cao from McLaren Vale and the Barossa Valley; open-fermented, matured for 7 months in French puncheons (20% new). This doesn't rely on tannin to become full-bodied, just the ongoing drum rolls of black and glace cherries, panforte, an old drawer of spices, the tannins so sneakily firm that you may miss them the first time around, but not the second. Whether you go back to the bouquet or just the palate, there are constant discoveries awaiting you. Screwcap. 14% alc. **Rating** 96 **To** 2036

Adelaide Hills Nebbiolo Rose 2017 Single vineyard, hand-picked, crushed, chilled, 8 hours on skins. The palest possible pink. A heady perfume of rose petals and scented talc, the palate of extraordinary power and intensity, soaring through to maximum impact on the aftertaste, forest fruits lurking in the shadows. Screwcap. 14% alc. **Rating** 95 **To** 2022

Adelaide Hills Barbera 2016 Bright, deep crimson-purple; the strident messbag of berries of every description is quintessentially Italian, its absence of drying tannins equally varietal. Steve Pannell has waved his magic wand over this wine, making you reluctant to spit it out. Any Italian restaurant will make you love it more. Screwcap. 14% alc. **Rating** 95 **To** 2026

Arido McLaren Vale Grenache Rose 2017 Machine-harvested, no extended skin contact. Very pale pink; a highly scented bouquet, the palate playing hopscotch between edgy acidity and raspberry/wild strawberry fruits. Not your usual rose. Screwcap. 13.5% alc. **Rating** 94 **To** 2021

McLaren Vale Grenache Shiraz Touriga 2016 Hand-picked, crushed, open-fermented, matured in 2800l French vats for 7 months. Good colour; interesting texture, partly juicy, part slightly savoury/sandy, but carries the flavours well, with an unexpected hint of licorice along with cherry/raspberry. Screwcap. 14% alc. **Rating** 94 **To** 2023

The Vale 2016 70% grenache (74yo vines), 30% shiraz, fermented and matured separately, blended Jun '17 and returned to vats and hogsheads for 4 months before bottling. A complex bouquet with the black fruits, licorice and spice of shiraz outgunning the red fruits of grenache, but it's a neat blend all up, grenache not unhappy with its lot. Screwcap. 14.5% alc. **Rating** 94 **To** 2023

Dead End McLaren Vale Tempranillo 2016 10 days in small open fermenters, matured for 12 months in large-format French and Hungarian vats and puncheons (20% new). The varietal red and black cherry trademark of tempranillo pours out of the glass as soon as you give it even a cursory swirl. Then comes the palate, leaving little more to say, which is just as well when the tannins jump on you for a free ride to the finish, brushing off any complaints with a Spanish flick of the wrist. Screwcap. 14% alc. **Rating** 94 **To** 2029

ＹＹＹＹＹ **Basso McLaren Vale Garnacha 2017** **Rating** 91 **To** 2022

Scarborough Wine Co ★★★★☆

179 Gillards Road, Pokolbin, NSW 2320 **Region** Hunter Valley
T (02) 4998 7563 **www.**scarboroughwine.com.au **Open** 7 days 9–5
Winemaker Ian Scarborough, Jerome Scarborough **Est.** 1985 **Dozens** 25 000 **Vyds** 14ha
Ian Scarborough honed his white winemaking skills during his years as a consultant, and has brought all those skills to his own label. He makes three different styles of chardonnay: the

Blue Label is a light, elegant, chablis style for the export market; a richer barrel-fermented wine (Yellow Label) is primarily aimed at the Australian market; the third is the White Label, a cellar door-only wine made in the best vintages. The Scarborough family also acquired a portion of the old Lindemans Sunshine vineyard (after it lay fallow for 30 years) and planted it with semillon and (quixotically) pinot noir. Exports to the UK and the US.

ŸŸŸŸŸ **The Obsessive The Cottage Vineyard Hunter Valley Semillon 2017**
Fruit is from The Cottage vineyard, characterised by deep, free-draining, very fine sand. A pale but glowing brassy green – gold hue in the glass is inviting. Classic Hunter semillon aromas of freshly cut hay, lemon curd and old-fashioned soap lead the way, the palate brisk and racy, refreshing as cool water on a hot day. Years of development ahead of course, and all this at 10% alcohol. Screwcap. **Rating** 95 To 2030 $30 SC ❂

ŸŸŸŸŸ **The Obsessive Ogilvie's View Vineyard Hunter Valley Chardonnay 2016**
Rating 92 To 2019 $40 SC
Yellow Label Chardonnay 2015 Rating 90 To 2020 $28 SC

Schild Estate Wines   ★★★★★

1095 Barossa Valley Way, Lyndoch, SA 5351 **Region** Barossa Valley
T (08) 8524 5560 **www**.schildestate.com.au **Open** By appt
Winemaker Scott Hazeldine **Est.** 1998 **Dozens** 40 000 **Vyds** 163ha
Ed Schild is a Barossa Valley grapegrower, who first planted a small vineyard at Rowland Flat in 1952, steadily increasing his vineyard holdings over the next 50 years to their present level. The flagship wine is made from 170-year-old shiraz vines on the Moorooroo vineyard. Exports to all major markets.

ŸŸŸŸŸ **Moorooroo Barossa Valley Shiraz 2015** From four rows of vines planted in 1847 by the Jacob brothers, saved in 1984 by Ed Schild from the jaws of the Vine Pull Scheme. A Leviathan bottle to end all comparisons. Best of all is the wine's elegance and balance, the fruits purple and black, the tannins fine and gently persistent, the oak a means to an end. This is only the start of the story for a wine of this stature, which will take its next huge step in 2047. Cork. 14.5% alc. **Rating** 99 To 2055 $125 ❂

ŸŸŸŸŸ **Pramie Barossa Valley Shiraz 2015** From the estate Liebich Vineyard, providing the best wine of the vintage. It has the full tapestry of the aromas and flavours that shiraz can provide: black fruits, licorice, dark chocolate and savoury tannins. Cork. 14.5% alc. **Rating** 95 To 2040 $70
Ben Schild Reserve Single Vineyard Barossa Valley Shiraz 2013 Machine-harvested, destemmed, open-fermented with cultured yeast, 21 days on skins, matured in French, American and Hungarian oak (30% new) for 24 months. Deluxe heavyweight bottle and matching label design. A luscious, full-throated, full-bodied Barossa shiraz, that adroitly evades any alcohol heat or heavy extract. It's still very young, the colour a bright crimson-purple. A class act in the context of the style. Screwcap. 14.5% alc. **Rating** 95 To 2033 $40
Ben Schild Reserve Single Vineyard Barossa Valley Shiraz 2014 There's plenty of oomph to the fruit but it comes ripped with tannin and feels well toned in general. This sits squarely at the richer, warmer end of the shiraz spectrum, with asphalt and saltbush flavours mixed in with the mainstay of blackberry, plum and toast. It gives its muscles a good flex but it doesn't tear its shirt in the process; it keeps things neat in the context of bulk. Screwcap. 14.5% alc. **Rating** 94 To 2030 $40 CM
Edgar Schild Reserve Old Bush Vines Barossa Valley Grenache 2016 From the Kleeman Vineyard planted 1915 and '16, destemmed, open-fermented, matured in new and used French hogsheads for 12 months. A very rich traditional style with lusciously ripe fruit, and the impression of higher alcohol than 14.5%. On the other side, there's no confectionary flavours to complain about. The history alone is worth far more than the cost. Screwcap. **Rating** 94 To 2046 $40

ŸŸŸŸŸ Barossa Valley Grenache Shiraz Mourvedre 2015 Rating 91 To 2023
$18 CM ✪
Barossa Valley Cabernet Sauvignon 2015 Rating 90 To 2024 $22 CM

Schubert Estate ★★★★★

26 Kensington Road, Rose Park, SA 5067 **Region** Barossa Valley
T (08) 8562 3375 **www**.schubertestate.com **Open** Mon–Fri 11–5
Winemaker Steve Schubert **Est.** 2000 **Dozens** 4200 **Vyds** 14ha
Steve and Cecilia Schubert are primarily grapegrowers, with 12.8ha of shiraz and 1.2ha of
viognier. They purchased the 25ha property in 1986, when it was in such a derelict state
that there was no point trying to save the old vines. Both were working in other areas, so
it was some years before they began replanting, at a little under 2ha per year. Almost all
the production is sold to Torbreck. In 2000 they decided to keep enough grapes to make a
barrique of wine for their own (and friends') consumption. They were sufficiently encouraged
by the outcome to venture into the dizzy heights of two hogsheads a year (since increased to
four or so). The wine is made with wild yeast–open fermentation, basket pressing and bottling
without filtration. In 2016 Schubert Estate opened a cellar door in Adelaide in a renovated
stone villa. Exports to Germany, Malaysia, Hong Kong and China.

ŸŸŸŸŸ **Goose-yard Block Barossa Valley Shiraz 2015** Estate-grown, open-
fermented, basket-pressed, barrel-matured for 20 months. Holding hue well;
marries complexity with style, power with finesse, blackberry with dark chocolate,
and plum with licorice. Diam. 15% alc. **Rating** 96 To 2040 $69 ✪
The Gosling Single Vineyard Barossa Valley Shiraz 2016 Deep, intense
crimson-purple, holding its colour through to the rim. While I'd love to be able to
taste this wine at 14% (or even 14.5%) alcohol, I'll roll over and acknowledge the
black fruit flavour is so powerful it makes light work of the alcohol. It has all the
packaging attributes, and all the wine signature of wines in the $80–$100 price
range. Diam. 15% alc. **Rating** 95 To 2036 $28 ✪
The Sentinel Barossa Valley Shiraz 2015 Hand-picked, destemmed into
small open fermenters, 6–8 days on skins, pumped over twice daily, matured for
18 months in used French barriques. A very good example of full-bodied Barossa
Valley shiraz from the Marananga district, crammed full of black fruits, licorice,
oak and tannins, all in balance. This really deserves cellaring, as it carries its alcohol
without effort. Diam. 15% alc. **Rating** 94 To 2035 $56

ŸŸŸŸŸ The Hatchling Barossa Valley Shiraz 2016 Rating 93 To 2030 $25 ✪

Schwarz Wine Company ★★★★★

PO Box 779, Tanunda, SA 5352 **Region** Barossa Valley
T 0417 881 923 **www**.schwarzwineco.com.au **Open** At Artisans of Barossa
Winemaker Jason Schwarz **Est.** 2001 **Dozens** 4500
The economical name is appropriate for a business that started with 1t of grapes, making two
hogsheads of wine in 2001. Shiraz was purchased from Jason Schwarz's parents' vineyard in
Bethany, the vines planted in 1968; the following year half a tonne of grenache was added,
once again purchased from the parents. In 2005, grape sale agreements with another (larger)
winery were terminated, freeing up 1.8ha of shiraz and 0.8ha of grenache. From this point on
things moved more quickly: in '06 Jason formed a partnership (Biscay Road Vintners) with
Peter Schell of Spinifex, giving them total control over production. Exports to the US, France,
Singapore and China.

ŸŸŸŸŸ **The Schiller Single Vineyard Barossa Valley Shiraz 2015** Made from a mere
400 vines, planted in 1881. It's a hearty, deep-set, seductive wine with freshness
kept paramount. It slinks along the tongue in satiny fashion, runs with the flavours
of redcurrant, blackberry, coal and caramel, and trails impressively out through an
extended finish. Barossa shiraz in all its glory. Straps of flavour-drenched tannin
will help ensure a very long future. Screwcap. 14.5% alc. **Rating** 96 To 2035
$75 CM ✪

Thiele Road Single Vineyard Barossa Valley Grenache 2016 Hand-picked from the family block in Bethany, vines planted '41. Open-fermented with 20% whole bunches, foot-stomped at the end of fermentation and left on skins for a further 15 days; basket-pressed to used French puncheons and a small tank, bottled Oct '17. Very light, clear crimson; this is Barossa Valley grenache on its best behaviour, with a glorious abundance of sweet red fruits in a gossamer net of the finest tannins. It emphatically doesn't show any sign of underripe fruit. A wine for rejoicing. Screwcap. 13.5% alc. **Rating** 96 **To** 2026 $43 ✪

Meta Barossa Valley Shiraz 2016 Hand-picked from Stone Well, Moppa (Barossa Valley) and the Eden Valley; wild-fermented with 25% whole bunches, not fined or filtered. Highly aromatic, with spicy/tangy whole bunch aromas; the full-bodied palate ticks all the boxes, with powdery tannins dusting the seductive black fruits. Overall line, length and balance spot on. Screwcap. 14.3% alc. **Rating** 95 **To** 2036 $35 ✪

Nitschke Block Single Vineyard Barossa Valley Shiraz 2016 The vineyard was planted in '68 by Jason Schwarz's parents in the Bethany district. Wild-fermented with 25% whole bunches, lengthy maceration, basket-pressed, matured in French oak (25% new). The bouquet is compelling, with a spice and fresh leather overlay to the black fruits. It is medium-bodied, fresh and lively, the oak and whole bunches introducing elements not common in the Barossa Valley, and protected by modest alcohol. A good outcome for the vintage. Screwcap. 14% alc. **Rating** 95 **To** 2030 $43

Meta Barossa Valley Mataro 2017 Hand-picked, wild-fermented with 20% whole bunches, unfined and unfiltered. 177 dozen made. Shows how much flavour can be achieved at lower than conventional alcohol levels, resulting in fresh, vibrant varietal fruit, a juicy mix of raspberry and blood plum, the tannins sufficient but no more. Screwcap. 13.8% alc. **Rating** 95 **To** 2025 $35 ✪

♟♟♟♟♟ **Barossa Valley Shiraz 2016** Rating 93 To 2026 $30
Barossa Valley GSM 2016 Rating 93 To 2025 $30 CM
Barossa Valley Rose 2017 Rating 90 To 2019 $25 SC
Meta Barossa Valley Grenache 2017 Rating 90 To 2021 $35

Scion Vineyard & Winery   ★★★★☆

74 Slaughterhouse Road, Rutherglen, Vic 3685 **Region** Rutherglen
T (02) 6032 8844 **www.**scionvineyard.com **Open** 7 days 10–5
Winemaker Rowly Milhinch **Est.** 2002 **Dozens** 1650 **Vyds** 3.2ha
Scion Vineyard was established by retired audiologist Jan Milhinch, who is a great-great-granddaughter of GF Morris, founder of the most famous Rutherglen wine family. Jan has now handed the baton to son Rowland (Rowly), who continues to manage the vineyard – planted on a quartz-laden red clay slope to durif, viognier, brown muscat and orange muscat – and make the wines.

♟♟♟♟♟ **Rutherglen Durif Viognier 2015** Winemaker Rowly Milhinch grows powerful durif but his grand goal is to give it an elegant turn. Here he hits pay dirt. This release boasts a churning complexity: deep, dark fruit, smoky peppery notes and firm but ultra-fine tannin. It will keep the faithful fans of Rutherglen Durif happy and also help win over a new audience; it takes muscular fruit and lands it softly on the palate. This is the wine Scion has been striving for. 193 dozen made. Screwcap. 13.2% alc. **Rating** 96 **To** 2033 $42 CM ✪

Rutherglen Syrah 2016 It's mostly made with fruit grown on the rejuvenated Terravinia Vineyard, located in the Gooramadda district, 9km northeast of Scion at Rutherglen. It saw 10% stalks, 1% viognier and 20% new French oak. It combines elegance and power, its dark, tar-laden, blackberried fruit studded with spice, wood smoke, rust and saltbush notes. There's plenty going on and yet it works simply as a mouthful of flavour, too. Viognier shows on the finish more than it does on the nose; it sends the wine merrily on its way. Screwcap. 13.7% alc. **Rating** 94 **To** 2028 $35 CM

Rutherglen Durif 2015 A fine mesh of tannin is woven through deep, dark fruit; chocolate, blackberry, kirsch and iodine flavours the most obvious. The '15 season was clearly a watershed for Scion and its durif; this wine is clean, powerful, immaculately well balanced and – ultimately – authoritative. Tannin here is al dente and so the wine can be enjoyed now, but it will respond well to the passage of time. Screwcap. 13.7% alc. **Rating** 94 **To** 2032 $42 CM

♀♀♀♀♀ **Rutherglen Rose 2017 Rating** 92 **To** 2018 $28 CM
Rutherglen Viognier 2016 Rating 91 **To** 2018 $32 CM

Scorpo Wines ★★★★★

23 Old Bittern-Dromana Road, Merricks North, Vic 3926 **Region** Mornington Peninsula
T (03) 5989 7697 **www**.scorpowines.com.au **Open** By appt
Winemaker Paul Scorpo **Est.** 1997 **Dozens** 3500 **Vyds** 17.3ha
Paul Scorpo has a background as a horticulturist/landscape architect, working on major projects ranging from private gardens to golf courses in Australia, Europe and Asia. His family has a love of food, wine and gardens, all of which led to their buying a derelict apple and cherry orchard on gentle rolling hills between Port Phillip and Westernport bays. They have established pinot noir (10.4ha), pinot gris and chardonnay (3.2ha each) and shiraz (0.5ha). Exports to Singapore and Hong Kong.

♀♀♀♀♀ **Eocene Single Vineyard Chardonnay 2015** When you combine fruit power with this kind of complexity, and add finesse to the equation, then you go straight into the elite class. This drives home its case with flavours of peach, nougat, flint and a variety of barrel-worked complexities. One sip and you feel caught in its headlights; there's so much going on, its hard not to become fixated. Screwcap. 13.5% alc. **Rating** 96 **To** 2023 $60 CM ✪
Mornington Peninsula Pinot Noir 2016 Rich and svelte at once, its cherry-berried flavours, cedar wood and sweet spice notes entirely seductive both in isolation and in team. This is the way to combine the swishness of oak, the sweet-sour tang of varietal fruit, and studs of spice and leaves. The statement it makes on quality is clear. Screwcap. 13.5% alc. **Rating** 95 **To** 2026 $60 CM
Mornington Peninsula Shiraz 2016 Wild with florals and undergrowth, game, and black cherry. There's a power of spice and garden herb complexity here though the delivery is silken, the fruit ripe and fleshy. It smells sensational, tastes it too, the tannin and finish yet to resolve properly but it will. Screwcap. 13.5% alc. **Rating** 95 **To** 2028 $45 CM

♀♀♀♀♀ **Mornington Peninsula Pinot Gris 2017 Rating** 93 **To** 2021 $35 CM
Bestia Mornington Peninsula Pinot Grigio 2016 Rating 93 **To** 2020 $45 CM
Noirien Mornington Peninsula Pinot Noir 2017 Rating 93 **To** 2024 $32 CM

Scotchmans Hill ★★★★★

190 Scotchmans Road, Drysdale, Vic 3222 **Region** Geelong
T (03) 5251 3176 **www**.scotchmans.com.au **Open** 7 days 10.30–4.30
Winemaker Robin Brockett, Marcus Holt **Est.** 1982 **Dozens** 50 000 **Vyds** 40ha
Established in 1982, Scotchmans Hill has been a consistent producer of well made wines under the stewardship of long-term winemaker Robin Brocket and assistant Marcus Holt. The wines are released under the Scotchmans Hill, Cornelius, Jack & Jill and Swan Bay labels. A change of ownership in 2014 has resulted in significant vineyard investment. Exports to Asia.

♀♀♀♀♀ **Bellarine Peninsula Chardonnay 2016** Estate-grown and made with unrelenting attention to detail. A beautifully weighted and composed wine, with pink grapefruit and white peach sharing the fruit message, which is given equal support by integrated oak and crisp acidity. It has exceptional length. Screwcap. 13.5% alc. **Rating** 97 **To** 2029 $35 ✪

ŸŸŸŸŸ **Cornelius Single Vineyard Bellarine Peninsula Sauvignon 2016** The drive, focus and intensity of this sauvignon are immediate and mouthwatering. Pink grapefruit, white flowers, lemon preserve, orange blossom – the list is endless, the wine just lovely. Screwcap. 13.5% alc. **Rating** 96 **To** 2021 $30 ●

Sutton Vineyard Bellarine Peninsula Chardonnay 2010 Penfolds P58 clone, hand-picked, whole-bunch pressed, the juice run straight to barrel for wild fermentation and 16 months maturation. It's bursting with pink grapefruit and white peach flavours, and an insistent drive through the length of the palate. For the record, I did suggest '19 when I first tasted the wine in Mar '13. Screwcap. 13.5% alc. **Rating** 96 **To** 2023 $50 ●

Cornelius Armitage Vineyard Bellarine Peninsula Pinot Noir 2015 Excellent colour; Robin Brockett and Marcus Holt don't know how to make indifferent wine. The only variable is just how good it will be – so, in this golden vintage it was preordained to be very good indeed. It's not built on power, but on carefully considered tannin and spice, which have earned their place alongside red cherry and damson plum fruit. Screwcap. 13.5% alc. **Rating** 96 **To** 2027 $50 ●

Cornelius Norfolk Vineyard Bellarine Peninsula Pinot Noir 2015 Good colour; a complex, layered pinot with a seductive crosscut of spices and fine-grained tannins, the palate with a very long, mouthwatering red fruit finish. Screwcap. 13% alc. **Rating** 95 **To** 2028 $50

Bellarine Peninsula Shiraz 2016 Whole berries and 15% whole bunches cold soaked for 5 days, after 7 days on skins; pressed and matured in new and used French oak for 16 months. The distinctively spicy, peppery bouquet is the overture for a powerful palate, rippling tannins at the feet of black fruits, oak adding to the all-up complexity. Screwcap. 14.5% alc. **Rating** 95 **To** 2031

Cornelius Strathallan Vineyard Bellarine Peninsula Syrah 2015 Nuances of spice, licorice and black fruits are replayed with high fidelity on the medium to full-bodied palate, combining finesse with length and power. Screwcap. 14% alc. **Rating** 95 **To** 2035 $60

Swan Bay Bellarine Peninsula Pinot Noir Rose 2017 An interesting saline edge to the fruit rises and falls like gentle waves reaching a beach at night; here salinity and strawberry fruit are the taste players. A rose with great character. Screwcap. 12.5% alc. **Rating** 94 **To** 2020 $22 ●

Armitage Vineyard Bellarine Peninsula Pinot Noir 2010 It presents a mix of truffle, sour cherry, undergrowth and sweet spice flavours, all aspects pulling as a team, all in delicious working order. Tangy, tasty and lengthy. Perfect for drinking right now. Screwcap. 14% alc. **Rating** 94 **To** 2021 $50 CM

Bellarine Peninsula Pinot Noir 2016 Good depth to the colour; intense fruit, with black cherry/plum running as a stream between savoury, spicy banks. A good outcome for the '16 vintage. Screwcap. 13.5% alc. **Rating** 94 **To** 2025

Norfolk Vineyard Bellarine Peninsula Pinot Noir 2010 Remarkable retention of colour, still with no sign of onion skin. The red fruits are held in a spicy savoury basket with a long finish and aftertaste. Screwcap. 14% alc. **Rating** 94 **To** 2022 $50

Cornelius Spray Farm Vineyard Bellarine Peninsula Syrah 2015 Youthful crimson; a fragrant bouquet with purple fruit aromas introduces a medium–bodied palate that brings spicy/savoury nuances to add complexity. Screwcap. 14.5% alc. **Rating** 94 **To** 2030 $60

ŸŸŸŸŸ **Cornelius Sutton Vineyard Chardonnay 2015** **Rating** 93 **To** 2026 $50
Jack & Jill Shiraz 2017 **Rating** 93 **To** 2022 SC
Riesling 2017 **Rating** 92 **To** 2025
Cornelius Airds Vineyard Chardonnay 2015 **Rating** 92 **To** 2025 $50
Jack & Jill Pinot Noir Rose 2017 **Rating** 91 **To** 2020 SC
Jack & Jill Sauvignon Blanc 2017 **Rating** 90 **To** 2020
Swan Bay Sauvignon Blanc 2017 **Rating** 90 **To** 2019
Cornelius Kancardine Chardonnay 2015 **Rating** 90 **To** 2021 $50
Jack & Jill Pinot Gris 2017 **Rating** 90 **To** 2020

Scott

102 Main Street, Hahndorf, SA 5245 **Region** Adelaide Hills
T (08) 8388 7330 **www.**scottwines.com.au **Open** 1st w'end of the month 11–5
Winemaker Sam Scott **Est.** 2009 **Dozens** 4000

Sam Scott's great-grandfather worked in the cellar for Max Schubert, and passed his knowledge down to Sam's grandfather. It was he who gave Sam his early education. Sam enrolled in business at university, continuing the casual retailing with Booze Brothers, which he'd started while at school, picking up the trail with Baily & Baily. Next came wine wholesale experience with David Ridge, selling iconic Australian and Italian wines to the trade. This led to a job with Michael Fragos at Tatachilla in 2000, and since then he has been the 'I've been everywhere man', working all over Australia and in California. He moved to Bird in Hand winery at the end of '06, where Andrew Nugent indicated that it was about time he took the plunge on his own account, and this he has done. Exports to the UK and Singapore.

🍷🍷🍷🍷🍷 **The Denizen Adelaide Hills Chardonnay 2016** A complex bouquet, with a hint of reductive funk that's chased by some winemakers in both hemispheres, and by some such as French oenologist Emile Paynaud (who simply treated reduction as the opposite of oxidation), knowing it could be remedied in a flash with the addition of SO_2. Here we see whole-bunch pressing and passive oxidation of full solids, with wild yeast in used (3-6yo) French oak for fermentation and maturation. The wine has remarkable lightness, yet packs a decidedly dangerous punch. Screwcap. 13.5% alc. **Rating** 95 **To** 2029 $26 ✪

La Prova Adelaide Hills Fiano 2017 Scott nails it again: a wine with precision and power, texture and acidity. Lemon pith and zest draw out the saliva, lengthening the palate as they do so; then you find yet more flavour, like the good part of durian. It's a full-fledged assault on the senses. Fiano at its most convincing. Screwcap. 13.5% alc. **Rating** 95 **To** 2023 $26 ✪

Piccadilly Valley Chardonnay 2016 Zero information on the charcoal back label. It's super-elegant and fresh, and there's no problem with the vinification. The only question is about the marginally light fruit weight/intensity. Screwcap. 13.5% alc. **Rating** 94 **To** 2026 $45

La Prova Sangiovese 2016 This is fast moving into topnotch territory. Red cherry slips into boysenberry; floral notes turn to spice; fruit flesh makes way for flavour-drenched tannin. There's a ferrous note too; indeed all manner of flavours and scents put their name forward as it breathes. Track this down. Screwcap. 14.1% alc. **Rating** 94 **To** 2022 $25 CM ✪

La Prova Langhorne Creek Montepulciano 2016 Matured for 7 months in used oak. Bright crimson hue – and crimson fruits. Montepulciano doesn't need the distraction of new oak, its perfume guaranteeing the pretty flavours, its fine, sandy tannins providing structure. Screwcap. 13.2% alc. **Rating** 94 **To** 2026 $25 ✪

🍷🍷🍷🍷🍷 **La Prova Adelaide Hills Pinot Grigio 2017** Rating 93 **To** 2023 $25 ✪
La Prova Adelaide Hills Pinot Nero 2016 Rating 93 **To** 2024 $26 CM ✪
La Prova Adelaide Hills Aglianico Rosato 2017 Rating 92 **To** 2018 $25 ✪
La Prova Barossa Valley Nero d'Avola 2016 Rating 92 **To** 2023 $25 CM ✪
La Prova McLaren Vale Nero d'Avola 2016 Rating 90 **To** 2032 $25

Seabrook Wines

1122 Light Pass Road, Tanunda, SA 5352 **Region** Barossa Valley
T 0427 224 353 **www.**seabrookwines.com.au **Open** Thurs–Mon 11–5
Winemaker Hamish Seabrook **Est.** 2004 **Dozens** 3000 **Vyds** 10.1ha

Hamish Seabrook is the youngest generation of a proud Melbourne wine family once involved in wholesale and retail distribution, and as leading show judges of their respective generations. Hamish, too, is a wine show judge, but was the first to venture into winemaking, working with Best's and Brown Brothers in Vic before moving to SA with wife Joanne. In 2008 Hamish set up his own winery, on the family property in Vine Vale, having previously made the wines at Dorrien Estate and elsewhere. Here they have shiraz (4.4ha), cabernet sauvignon (3.9ha), and mataro (1.8ha), and also continue to source small amounts of shiraz from the Barossa, Langhorne Creek and Pyrenees. Exports to Hong Kong and China.

🍷🍷🍷🍷🍷 **The Judge Eden Valley Riesling 2017** Every variety of apple seems to explode across a juicy beam of limy acidity. This is high-tensile riesling, its origins unmistakable. Most impressive is its lack of rasp or grate. The flavours flow and the acidity nourishes, drawing one back for another glass. Screwcap. 11.5% alc. Rating 95 To 2029 $23 NG ✪

🍷🍷🍷🍷🍷 **The Chairman Great Western Shiraz 2014** Rating 93 To 2026 $32 NG
The Founder Mataro 2015 Rating 93 To 2030 $29
Le Maitre de Cave Marsanne 2017 Rating 92 To 2021 $25 NG ✪
The Merchant Shiraz 2014 Rating 92 To 2026 $35 NG
The Broker Cabernet Sauvignon Shiraz 2015 Rating 92 To 2030 $29

Sedona Estate

182 Shannons Road, Murrindindi, Vic 3717 **Region** Upper Goulburn
T (03) 9730 2883 **www.**sedonaestate.com.au **Open** Wed–Sun & public hols 11–5
Winemaker Paul Evans **Est.** 1998 **Dozens** 3500 **Vyds** 5.5ha
Sedona Estate, established by Paul Evans (a trained commercial pilot) and Sonja Herges (from Germany's Mosel Valley), is located in the picturesque Yea Valley, gateway to Victoria's high country. The unique combination of abundant sunshine, cool nights and low rainfall in this elevated wine region provides a true cool climate for growing premium-quality fruit. Sangiovese (the vines sourced from Yarra Yering) and carmenere were added to the existing plantings of cabernet sauvignon, merlot and shiraz in 2017. Exports to China.

🍷🍷🍷🍷🍷 **Reserve Yea Valley Shiraz 2015** The vintage and the fruit are the prime movers here, the medium to full-bodied palate with an abundance of dark fruits ranging from plum to blackberry and a sweetness ex the vanillan oak. No hint of any green fruits. The overall length and balance are very good. Screwcap. 14% alc. Rating 95 To 2030 $35 ✪

🍷🍷🍷🍷🍷 **Yea Valley Sangiovese 2016** Rating 90 To 2026 $30

See Saw Wines

Annangrove Park, 4 Nanami Lane, Cargo, NSW 2800 **Region** Orange
T (02) 6364 3118 **www.**seesawwine.com **Open** By appt
Winemaker Contract **Est.** 1995 **Dozens** 4000 **Vyds** 171ha
Justin and Pip Jarrett have established one of the largest vineyards in the Orange region. Varieties include chardonnay (51ha), sauvignon blanc (28ha), shiraz and merlot (22ha each), pinot gris (15ha), cabernet sauvignon (14ha), pinot noir (11ha), gewurztraminer and prosecco (3ha each), and marsanne (2ha). They also provide management and development services to growers of another 120ha in the region. A substantial part of the annual production is sold to others. One of the purchasers of Jarretts' grapes was See Saw, a venture then owned by Hamish MacGowan (of Angus the Bull) and Andrew Margan. In 2014 Hamish and Andrew decided to concentrate on other wine activities, and the Jarretts were the logical purchasers. Exports to the UK.

🍷🍷🍷🍷🍷 **Orange Pinot Noir Rose 2017** This is a bang on rose. Vibrant, pale tea-rose pink. Bright, fresh strawberry and redcurrant fruit, with hints of green spice that flood the palate. By whole-bunch pressing without skin contact, the phenolics are beautifully managed, giving the wine both delicacy and elegance. Screwcap. 13% alc. Rating 94 To 2018 DB

🍷🍷🍷🍷 **Orange Prosecco 2017** Rating 89 To 2018 DB

 Sellicks Hill ★★★★☆

3737 Main South Road, Sellicks Hill, SA 5174 **Region** McLaren Vale
T (08) 8556 3000 **www**.sellickshillwines.com **Open** Fri–Mon 10.30–5
Winemaker Paul Petagna **Est.** 2004 **Dozens** 1000 **Vyds** 7.1ha
Paul Petagna lays it on the line thus: 'I never went to university, I've never been to Europe
for vintage, my science knowledge extends to bucket measurements, I don't even have a wine
rack let alone a cellar, I drive a beat-up old faithful land cruiser called "the pig" … All I have
is a shovel, a small basket press, great advisers, and a bag full of passion. I'm just an average
Aussie bloke making wine in his shed …' His introduction to wine was, to put it mildly,
unusual. It came about during his time working at Magill Estate for Southcorp, Penfolds et al,
as an in-house IT trainer. His summary of their first days picking for backyard winemaking is
equally catching – 'We drove the well and truly overloaded old HZ ute down the hill, with the
back end swaying and tyres bulging along, with a floating steering wheel that didn't seem to be
of much assistance at times.' His winemaking back up at that stage, and continuing for many
years thereafter, was Modestino 'Steve' Piombo. It was he who, together with Paul, oversaw
the first red wine fermentation taking place. It was his family that purchased (as bare land)
what was to become Sellicks Hill vineyard. Paul explains, 'Once the property was purchased,
I settled in as the resident "human tractor", used for laying out kilometres of wire, dripper
hose, posts, plumbing and all the other paraphernalia used to construct a vineyard. We literally
built the vineyard and began working it without a tractor and/or much equipment at all'. This
is part of a true Australian Story, but space prevents the telling more of it.

🍷🍷🍷🍷🍷 **GSM McLaren Vale Grenache Shiraz Mourvedre 2013** Good colour, both
depth and hue; has balance and length to its medium to full-bodied palate, red and
purple fruits framed by firm tannins. Needs more time for all its potential to be
realised. Screwcap. 14% alc. **Rating** 90 **To** 2028 $20 ○

🍷🍷🍷🍷 **McLaren Vale Shiraz 2013 Rating** 89 **To** 2020 $20

Semprevino ★★★★☆

271 Kangarilla Road, McLaren Vale, SA 5171 **Region** McLaren Vale
T 0417 142 110 **www**.semprevino.com.au **Open** Not
Winemaker Russell Schroder **Est.** 2006 **Dozens** 1000
Semprevino is the venture of Russell Schroder and Simon Doak, who became close friends
while at Monash University in the early 1990s – studying mechanical engineering and
science respectively. The prime mover is Russell, who, after working for CRA/Rio Tinto
for five years, left on a four-month trip to Western Europe and became captivated by the
life of a vigneron. Returning to Australia, he enrolled in part-time wine science at CSU,
obtaining his wine science degree in 2005. Between '03 and '06 he worked vintages in Italy
and Victoria, coming under the wing of Stephen Pannell at Tinlins (where the Semprevino
wines are made).

🍷🍷🍷🍷🍷 **McLaren Vale Shiraz 2015** You don't have to go past the full colour and
bouquet to find a wine screaming about its variety and place. Dark chocolate
coats its deep cherry and blood plum fruit; tannins and oak join the party with
enthusiasm, underscoring the quality of the vintage and its long-term potential.
Screwcap. 14.3% alc. **Rating** 95 **To** 2040 $28 ○

🍷🍷🍷🍷🍷 **McLaren Vale GSM 2016 Rating** 92 **To** 2018 $24 ○

Sentio Wines ★★★★★

23 Priory Lane, Beechworth, Vic 3437 (postal) **Region** Various Victoria
T 0433 773 229 **www**.sentiowines.com.au **Open** Not
Winemaker Chris Catlow **Est.** 2013 **Dozens** 800
This is a winery to watch. Owner/winemaker Chris Catlow was born and raised in
Beechworth, and says, 'A passion for wine was inevitable'. He drew particular inspiration from
Barry Morey of Sorrenberg, working there in his late teens. He completed a double-major

in viticulture science and wine science at La Trobe University, working with Paringa Estate, Kooyong and Portsea Estate from 2006–13. Here Sandro Mosele led him to his fascination with the interaction between place and chardonnay, and he in turn worked with Benjamin Leroux in Burgundy during vintage '13, '14 and '16.

🍷🍷🍷🍷🍷 **Yarra Valley Chardonnay 2016** It pours on the flavour and covers it in velvet, all the while keeping something in reserve for the finish. It's a beautiful Yarra Valley chardonnay, thoroughly harmonious and boasting totally convincing length. Screwcap. 13% alc. **Rating** 96 **To** 2025 $45 CM ✪

Beechworth Chardonnay 2016 There's an effortless flow to this wine and better still, it carries with it armloads of delicious flavour. This is the power of Beechworth chardonnay, cut to an elegant pattern. Peach, grapefruit, cedar wood and almond flavours drive through the palate in emphatic style. Honeysuckle notes add an extra layer. Screwcap. 13.1% alc. **Rating** 95 **To** 2024 $42 CM

Macedon Chardonnay 2016 This chardonnay is singing. It's juicy and flavoursome, yet long and stylish. Everything about this wine seems to be happy with its lot: the white peach flavour, the pears, the grapefruit, the steely backbone of acidity, the kiss of cedar wood oak. Very good. Screwcap. 12.7% alc. **Rating** 94 **To** 2024 $45 CM

Beechworth Pinot Noir 2016 Body, texture and length. There's a surliness to the mid-palate, where macerated cherry flavours reside, but aromatically it's expressive and it pulls through nicely on the finish too. It takes complexity (assorted florals and spices) in its stride and, indeed, feels impeccable from start to finish. Screwcap. 13.3% alc. **Rating** 94 **To** 2025 $39 CM

🍷🍷🍷🍷🍷 **Beechworth Blanc 2016 Rating** 92 **To** 2022 $30 CM

Seppelt   ★★★★★
36 Cemetery Road, Great Western, Vic 3377 **Region** Grampians
T (03) 5361 2239 **www**.seppelt.com.au **Open** 7 days 10–5
Winemaker Adam Carnaby **Est.** 1851 **Dozens** NFP **Vyds** 500ha

Seppelt once had dual, very different, claims to fame. The first was as Australia's leading producer of both white and red sparkling wine; the former led by Salinger, the latter by Show Sparkling and Original Sparkling Shiraz. The second claim, even more relevant to the Seppelt of today, was based on the small-volume superb red wines made by Colin Preece from the 1930s through to the early '60s. These were ostensibly Great Western–sourced, but – as the laws of the time allowed – were often region, variety and vintage blends. Two of his labels (also of high quality) were Moyston and Chalambar, the latter recently revived. Preece would have been a child in a lolly shop if he'd had today's viticultural resources to draw on, and would be quick to recognise the commitment of the winemakers and viticulturists to the supreme quality of today's portfolio. Ararat businessman Danial Ahchow has leased the cellar door and surrounds, including the underground drives. Exports to the UK, Europe and NZ.

🍷🍷🍷🍷🍷 **Drumborg Vineyard Riesling 2017** An utterly beautiful riesling, the scented bouquet soars upwards from the glass, the flavour instantaneously filling the mouth with flavour-sweet (not sugar-sweet) lime and lemon fruit, and finishes with an oxymoron of quietly emphatic acidity. In a word, ravishing. Screwcap. 11% alc. **Rating** 98 **To** 2037 $40 ✪

Show Sparkling Limited Release Shiraz 2007 A whole berry ferment precedes 12 months maturation in a large, old French vat, and 8 years on lees before disgorgement. Winemaker Adam Carnaby has threaded the needle with precisely the right amount of dosage, making a unique and great Australian red wine. Crown seal. 13% alc. **Rating** 97 $100 ✪

🍷🍷🍷🍷🍷 **St Peters Grampians Shiraz 2016** At this stage still quite closed. Nothing leaps out of the glass, and what you find with exploration is given up reluctantly. Deep and brooding, there are aromas of charcuterie, red and black fruits, and a suggestion of the countryside – freshly mown hay and dust. The palate is dense but it feels medium-bodied, with ripe but slightly tart-edged fruit buried in a surreptitiously enveloping cloak of tannin that builds and builds. This wine will take you on an intriguing journey if you have the time to follow it. Screwcap. 14.5% alc. **Rating** 96 **To** 2046 $80 SC

Great Western Riesling 2017 Selectiv'-harvested, crushed, fermented in tank, minimum time on lees. A label with a long history. It was early picked, with high acidity balanced by similarly high titratable acidity. This is the Mosel Valley speaking, and I'm an all-day sucker when it comes to wines like this. Screwcap. 10% alc. **Rating** 95 **To** 2032 $27 **☉**

Drumborg Vineyard Henty Chardonnay 2016 Hand-picked, whole-bunch pressed, fermented in French oak (25% new), 10% mlf, matured for 8 months. Layered, textured flavours flaunt their wares as they stroll across the palate, leaving nothing to the imagination. History shows this wine will age superbly, even if a little more quickly than in the cool years. Balance is the key to the glory box. Screwcap. 12% alc. **Rating** 95 **To** 2030 $40

Drumborg Vineyard Henty Pinot Noir 2016 Hand-picked, open-fermented with 30% whole bunches, matured for 8 months in French oak (30% new). Bright, clear colour; the bouquet is fragrant and true to the variety. An elegant palate, once again with red cherry varietal fruit; oak in support, no more; good length and balance. Screwcap. 12.5% alc. **Rating** 95 **To** 2030 $45

Chalambar Grampians Heathcote Shiraz 2016 Seems to be showing a stronger Heathcote influence with this release, or perhaps it's the warmer vintage expressing itself. In any case, it's quite an open and accessible wine; spicy and sweet-fruited, although there is a gamey, savoury element. Finished with a smooth veneer of oak, it's a well rounded package and continues to deliver genuine value for money. Screwcap. 14.5% alc. **Rating** 94 **To** 2028 $27 SC **☉**

Moyston Cabernet Sauvignon 2016 Selectiv'-harvested, whole berries fermented in static and open fermenters, matured in 20% new oak; includes 13% shiraz. Moyston has come full circle since its glory days in the '50s and early '60s. This comes entirely from the Grampians, and would stand right up to the wines made by winemaker cult hero Colin Preece. And it's such a bargain. Screwcap. 14% alc. **Rating** 94 **To** 2036 $27 **☉**

ΨΨΨΨΨ **Limited Release Drumborg Vineyard Pinot Meunier 2016** Rating 92 To 2022 $36
Salinger Premium Cuvee NV Rating 91 $25
Original Sparkling Shiraz NV Rating 90 $27

Seppeltsfield   ★★★★★

730 Seppeltsfield Road, Seppeltsfield, SA 5355 **Region** Barossa Valley
T (08) 8568 6200 **www**.seppeltsfield.com.au **Open** 7 days 10.30–5
Winemaker Fiona Donald, Matthew Pick **Est.** 1851 **Dozens** 10 000 **Vyds** 1300ha
This historic Seppelt property and its bounty of old fortified wines was purchased by Janet Holmes à Court, Greg Paramor and Kilikanoon Wines in 2007, from Foster's Wine Estates (now TWE). Foster's kept the Seppelt brand for table and sparkling wines, mostly produced at Great Western, Victoria (see separate entry). In '09 Warren Randall (ex sparkling winemaker for Seppelt at Great Western in the 1980s) acquired 50% of Seppeltsfield and became managing director; in February '13, he increased his shareholding to over 90%. The change also marks a further commitment to the making of table wine, as well as more focused marketing of the fortified wines. In March '17 Seppeltsfield acquired the Ryecroft winery (with a production capacity of around 30 000t) from TWE, together with 40ha of adjoining vineyard and water licences. Yet another similar acquisition of the historic Clare Valley Quelltaler Estate was announced in October '17. It included the 1000t winery and 365ha of owned/leased vineyards. Exports to Hong Kong and China.

ΨΨΨΨΨ **100 Year Old Para Liqueur 1918** This utterly unique wine is a flavour (and bouquet) black hole in space. It comes to you with speed and intensity more akin to a rocket, rather than any wine or spirit you have dreamt of. The smallest sip reaches every tastebud in your mouth as you watch the remaining wine on the sides of the glass apply a near-waterproof coat of dark, burnt umber colour to the sides. If the searing intensity of the flavour, the bottle, the presentation box, and my 100-point rating (it's the only wine I accord this score) is not enough, then let me say there is no other vintage wine in the world released annually after 100 years in barrel, 100% of the given age. Over time, it has lost 66% of its original volume, hence the concentration. It is sold in a specially designed and made 100ml bottle in its hinged wooden box. Cork. 21.6% alc. **Rating** 100 $700

ᵵᵵᵵᵵᵵ **Para Rare Tawny NV** Minimum average age 18 years. Lighter colour than the '97 Para Tawny. The game changes here, with a near-doubling of the age of the Grand Para and far greater intensity and complexity in the rainbow of spice, Christmas cake, liqueur cumquats and rancio (the essential quasi-acid lance that provides balance). Screwcap. 20.9% alc. **Rating** 96 $75 ❍
Para Tawny 1997 Luscious, rich – more so than the NVs, but less rancio – it is the easiest to drink. James Godfrey, the one-time steward of Seppeltsfield's treasure trove of fortified wines (dating back to 1878) analysed the changes in baume, acidity, alcohol and volatile acidity. These reached their peak between 50 and 75 years after vintage, so this has decades to go as long as it's left in cask. Once bottled, all (desirable) development stops. Screwcap. 21.2% alc. **Rating** 96 $88
Grand Para NV Minimum average age 10 years. The colour shows the age, with no hint of red remaining. Lots of spice, almost into pepper; dried fruits (raisins and prunes) abounding. It has attitude to spare, its price a reflection of the refusal of the broader drinking public to acknowledge the quality and provenance (and cost of production) of this wine. Screwcap. 20.5% alc. **Rating** 94 $38

ᵵᵵᵵᵵᵧ **Barossa Vermentino 2017** Rating 92 To 2021 $23 ❍
Barossa Shiraz 2016 Rating 90 To 2031 $25

Serafino Wines   ★★★★★

Kangarilla Road, McLaren Vale, SA 5171 **Region** McLaren Vale
T (08) 8323 0157 **www**.serafinowines.com.au **Open** Mon–Fri 10–4.30, w'ends & public hols 10–4.30
Winemaker Charles Whish **Est.** 2000 **Dozens** 30 000 **Vyds** 121ha
After the sale of Maglieri Wines to Beringer Blass in 1998, Maglieri founder Serafino (Steve) Maglieri acquired the McLarens on the Lake complex originally established by Andrew Garrett. The operation draws upon over 40ha each of shiraz and cabernet sauvignon, 7ha of chardonnay, 2ha each of merlot, semillon, barbera, nebbiolo and sangiovese, and 1ha of grenache; part of the grape production is sold. Serafino Wines has won a number of major trophies in Australia and the UK, and Steve Maglieri was awarded a Memeber of the Order of Australia in 2018. Exports to the UK, the US, Canada, Hong Kong, Malaysia and NZ.

ᵵᵵᵵᵵᵵ **Sharktooth McLaren Vale Shiraz 2015** 30% new American oak, 20% new French oak. It delivers flavour with a baseball bat. It's thick, heavy, dense and strong. It tastes of resin and toasted wood, coffee-cream and blackberry. There are musky violet-like notes but the strong fruit-and-oak barges through. For all its heavy-handedness, though, the concentration here is excellent, the ripe and fine-grained nature of the tannin likewise, and the length completely convincing. Screwcap. 14.5% alc. **Rating** 95 To 2035 CM
McLaren Vale Shiraz 2016 Estate-grown, made from the best rows of the best blocks, ripened quickly and early by the hot, dry vintage. Given this background it is an impressive wine, with blackberry, Cherry Ripe, chocolate and licorice flavours, the shape of the wine in the mouth the most admirable. Screwcap. 14.5% alc. **Rating** 94 To 2029 $28 ❍
Goose Island McLaren Vale Shiraz 2016 Estate-grown. Deep, but bright crimson; a high quality McLaren Vale shiraz with lively red cherry and choc-mint nuances, moving onto plum on the palate. Attractive regional wine. Screwcap. 14% alc. **Rating** 94 To 2031 $18 ❍

Malpas Vineyard McLaren Vale Shiraz 2016 Aged in 3yo French oak. The oak wasn't new, but it's infused the wine with a smoky, cedary flavour, the effect both measured and clear at once; it works a treat. The fruit here is fresh and substantial enough – blackberry and plum, but with brighter, redder edges, peppercorns too. In the Serafino range this is arguably the best balanced wine of the lot. Screwcap. 14% alc. **Rating** 94 To 2034 CM

Terremoto Single Vineyard McLaren Vale Syrah 2015 Open-fermented, French oak. Fluid and soft for the most part, though the finish turns appropriately firm. Plums, saltbush, an influx of smoky oak, orange rind, roses in bloom. It certainly has power, but it floats lightly through the mouth. Seductive to say the least. Screwcap. **Rating** 94 To 2032 CM

🍷🍷🍷🍷🍷 **McLaren Vale Cabernet Sauvignon 2016** Rating 93 To 2036 $28
Bellissimo Nebbiolo 2015 Rating 93 To 2025 $20 ✪
Sharktooth Wild Ferment McLaren Vale Chardonnay 2016 Rating 91 To 2023 SC
Bellissimo Fiano 2017 Rating 91 To 2023 $20 ✪
Magnitude McLaren Vale Shiraz 2014 Rating 91 To 2028 $45 CM
Bellissimo Sangiovese 2016 Rating 91 To 2022 $22 CM ✪
Bellissimo Vermentino 2017 Rating 90 To 2022 $20 ✪
Sorrento McLaren Vale Shiraz 2017 Rating 90 To 2024 $20 CM ✪
Bellissimo McLaren Vale Tempranillo 2017 Rating 90 To 2021 CM
Bellissimo Montepulciano 2017 Rating 90 To 2021 $22 CM
Bellissimo Lagrein 2016 Rating 90 To 2025 $20 ✪
Bellissimo Quattuor 2016 Rating 90 To 2022 CM

Serrat   ★★★★★

PO Box 478, Yarra Glen, Vic 3775 **Region** Yarra Valley
T (03) 9730 1439 **www.serrat.com.au Open** Not
Winemaker Tom Carson **Est.** 2001 **Dozens** 1000 **Vyds** 3.1ha
Serrat is the family business of Tom Carson (after a 12-year reign at Yering Station, now running Yabby Lake and Heathcote Estate for the Kirby family) and wife Nadege Suné. They have close-planted (at 8800 vines per hectare) 0.8ha each of pinot noir and chardonnay, 0.4ha of shiraz, and a sprinkling of viognier. Most recent has been the establishment of an esoteric mix of 0.1ha each of malbec, nebbiolo, barbera and grenache. As well as being a consummate winemaker, Tom has one of the best palates in Australia, and a deep understanding of the fine wines of the world, which he and Nadege drink at every opportunity (when they aren't drinking Serrat). Viticulture and winemaking hit new heights with the 2014 Yarra Valley Shiraz Viognier named *Wine Companion* 2016 Wine of the Year (from a field of 8863 wines). Exports to Singapore and Hong Kong.

🍷🍷🍷🍷🍷 **Yarra Valley Pinot Noir 2017** Destemmed, wild-fermented in small open fermenters with 20% whole bunches, 12 days on skins, 11 months in French puncheons (25% new). Very good colour; it's difficult to tear yourself away from the infinitely complex bouquet to begin the tasting process, to find a whirling dervish of spicy, savoury red and blue fruits on an exceptionally long palate. It's hard to nominate single fruit influences because of the purity and singularity of this gloriously fresh wine. $90 a bottle would be a fair price. Screwcap. 13.5% alc. **Rating** 98 To 2032 $44 ✪

Yarra Valley Shiraz Viognier 2017 Open-fermented with 5% whole bunches and 5% viognier, 12 days on skins, matured for 11 months in French puncheons (25% new). Deep crimson; fascinating bouquet – I don't always find the violets that others talk about, but here they go close to challenging the dark cherry/ blackberry fruits, and the spiced cracked pepper. The finish is simultaneously slippery, yet gently tactile, refusing to let go. Screwcap. 13.5% alc. **Rating** 98 To 2037 $44 ✪

Yarra Valley Chardonnay 2017 Whole-bunch pressed, wild-fermented in French puncheons (25% new) on full solids, no mlf, matured for 11 months.

The clarity of expression of this wine is outstanding. White peach holds front of stage, leaving grapefruit/citrus/apple nuances to follow, with a mere shadow of oak. The balance is utterly exceptional. Screwcap. 12.5% alc. **Rating** 97 **To** 2027 $44 ✪

ŸŸŸŸŸ **Yarra Valley Grenache Noir 2017** Wild-fermented with 10% whole bunches, 14 days on skins, 11 months in used French oak. Clean, bright crimson; highly fragrant; bright red fruits – cherry to the fore, raspberry close behind – reach the back-palate, tannins simply a farewell kiss. Welcome cool-climate grenache. Screwcap. 13.5% alc. **Rating** 96 **To** 2030 $44 ✪

Fourre-Tout 2017 46% barbera, 31% malbec, 9% nebbiolo, 7% pinot noir and 7% grenache, fermented and matured separately in used French oak for 11 months. If this proves that Tom Carson has the golden touch (and it does) I'm happy. If it means he was simply having a bit of fun, I'm likewise all for it. Think of the practical jokes by great classical wine composers, players and singers. It's simply bloody delicious, although '17 may have set a very high bar. Screwcap. 13% alc. **Rating** 95 **To** 2026 $30 ✪

Yarra Valley Nebbiolo 2017 Close-planted, destemmed, wild, open fermentation, 11 months in a 10yo French barrique. Nebb, as contemporary wine-speak among young wine professionals would have it, is not ever a laughing matter. This is varietally correct, and I'm impressed, but I still don't want to drink it. Screwcap. 13.5% alc. **Rating** 94 **To** 2025 $44

Sevenhill Cellars   ★★★★★

111C College Road, Sevenhill, SA 5453 **Region** Clare Valley
T (08) 8843 5900 **www**.sevenhill.com.au **Open** 7 days 10–5
Winemaker Liz Heidenreich **Est.** 1851 **Dozens** 25 000 **Vyds** 95.8ha
One of the historical treasures of Australia; the oft-photographed stone wine cellars are the oldest in the Clare Valley, and winemaking remains an enterprise within the Jesuit Province of Australia. All the wines reflect the estate-grown grapes from old vines. Notwithstanding the difficult economic times, Sevenhill Cellars has increased its vineyard holdings from 74ha to 95ha, and, naturally, production has risen. Exports to the UK, Switzerland, Indonesia, Malaysia, Vietnam, Japan, Hong Kong and Taiwan.

ŸŸŸŸŸ **St Francis Xavier Single Vineyard Riesling 2017** From the Weikert Vineyard planted in the '70s. Less than a hectare in size, the Geisenheim clone, loam-over-shale soil, and sheltered aspect are considered ideal for producing outstanding riesling. The aromas and flavours are overwhelmingly grapefruit and lime juice, and the acidity is piercing, but there's no trace of hardness. Screwcap. 12% alc. **Rating** 95 **To** 2037 $35 SC ✪

Brother John May Reserve Shiraz 2012 This celebrates the 31-year contibution of the universally loved Sevenhill winemaker Brother John May, his role theoretically ending in '03, but continuing as 'winemaker emeritus' for a decade thereafter. The wine itself is a rock of ages, with layer upon layer of dark berry fruits, savoury tannins and sweet oak entirely consistent with the style and balancing the savoury notes. Screwcap. 15.5% alc. **Rating** 95 **To** 2035 $95

ŸŸŸŸŸ **Museum Release St Francis Xavier Single Vineyard Riesling 2011** **Rating** 93 **To** 2021 $40
Inigo Clare Valley Riesling 2017 **Rating** 92 **To** 2025 $22 SC ✪
Inigo Clare Valley Rose 2017 **Rating** 90 **To** 2020 $24 SC
Inigo Clare Valley Cabernet Sauvignon 2015 **Rating** 90 **To** 2035 $28 SC

Seville Estate   ★★★★★

65 Linwood Road, Seville, Vic 3139 **Region** Yarra Valley
T (03) 5964 2622 **www**.sevilleestate.com.au **Open** 7 days 10–5
Winemaker Dylan McMahon **Est.** 1972 **Dozens** 8000 **Vyds** 12ha

Seville Estate was founded by Dr Peter and Margaret McMahon in 1972. It underwent several changes in ownership up to 2006, when wealthy Chinese businessman Yiping Wang, with a background of wine shops in China, acquired outright ownership. Throughout the changes, Peter McMahon's grandson Dylan McMahon remained as winemaker, and has been appointed general manager/winemaker. Significant investments have been made, including the purchase of the neighbouring vineyard and property (formerly Ainsworth Estate), which has lifted the property size to 20ha, with 12ha under vine. The extra land has allowed for replanting original vine material grafted onto rootstock, in an effort to preserve the original 1972 clones and safeguard the future of the precious property. Seville Estate also has luxury accommodation, with the original homestead and three self-contained apartments. Exports to the US, Canada and China. *Wine Companion* 2019 Winery of the Year.

ΨΨΨΨΨ **Old Vine Reserve Yarra Valley Pinot Noir 2017** Vines planted '72; 70% whole berry/30% whole bunches, wild yeast–open ferment, 23 days on skins, matured in French oak (30% new) for 10 months. Vivid crimson-purple; a majestic pinot, unrolling its beautiful tapestry of wild strawberry and forest berries, accompanied by feather-light, but persistent, tannins. I checked its quality by swallowing some at 8.30am. Screwcap. 13.8% alc. **Rating** 99 **To** 2032 $70 ❂

Dr McMahon Yarra Valley Shiraz 2015 Vines planted '72, scrupulously hand-picked, selecting only the best; 100% whole-bunch fermented in two new French puncheons, 60 days on skins, matured for 10 months. Guigal comes to the Yarra Valley. Intensely aromatic and equally intensely flavoured oak and fruit, fruit and oak. It's like a frog transfixed by a snake – you just want to drink it – forget deconstruction. Screwcap. 13.5% alc. **Rating** 99 $125 ❂

Reserve Yarra Valley Chardonnay 2017 Fruit from the heart of the estate plantings is the key, the other difference is 25% new French hogsheads and puncheons. The very obvious difference between this and its two siblings is the Montrachet-like density of this in the mouth. It's a show stopper, as it moves from white peach to melon, then swaggers around limey/lemony acidity. Screwcap. 13.5% alc. **Rating** 98 **To** 2030 $70 ❂

Old Vine Reserve Yarra Valley Shiraz 2016 Vines planted '72, hand-picked and vineyard-sorted, wild yeast–open fermented, 28 days on skins, 10 months in used French oak. The old vines invest this with lusciousness, yet keep it light on its feet. The array of red and black berry fruits, cracked pepper, licorice, spice and oak are lined up with the precision of a Chinese army parade. Screwcap. 13.5% alc. **Rating** 98 **To** 2046 $70 ❂

Yarra Valley Chardonnay 2017 Estate-grown, fermented and matured in French hogsheads, puncheons and foudres (2200l). Employs the not broken/don't fix vinification techniques that so brilliantly capture the terroir of the Yarra Valley and its districts – here back to the Upper Yarra. This floats and dances in the mouth with the delicacy of a fairy – a beautiful fairy – with gossamer intensity. That'll do nicely. Screwcap. 13.5% alc. **Rating** 97 **To** 2035 $40 ❂

Yarra Valley Pinot Noir 2017 Vines planted '72, hand-picked and sorted in the vineyard, 70% whole berry/30% whole bunches, wild yeast–open ferment, 23 days on skins, matured in French oak (30% new) for 10 months. A meltingly beautiful pinot, reflecting the vintage and vineyard inputs. Right from the outset, it offers a spray of red flowers and spices (bouquet), and red fruits plus spices and a spider web of ultra-fine tannins (palate). This is an exercise in the purity of pinot noir at a high level, perfect to drink tonight or in a decade hence. Screwcap. 13.5% alc. **Rating** 97 **To** 2029 $40 ❂

ΨΨΨΨΨ **Yarra Valley Shiraz 2016** Vines planted '76, 65% whole berry/35% whole bunches, wild yeast–open fermented, 28 days on skins, 10 months in used French oak. An extremely expressive bouquet with black cherry, spice, pepper and oak all clamouring for attention. The medium-bodied palate also throws in a stick of black licorice and educated tannins to the hotpot of delicious cool-climate shiraz. Screwcap. 13.8% alc. **Rating** 96 **To** 2040 $40 ❂

Old Vine Reserve Yarra Valley Cabernet Sauvignon 2016 Winemaker Dylan McMahon can do no wrong; this is yet another great within the current release. It is the polished sterling silver that delineates the varietal cassis fruit, and the managing of the wine during fermentation, that nullifies any raw edge to young cabernet tannins found in otherwise fine wines. This is a cabernet that pinot lovers have to admire. Screwcap. 13.8% alc. **Rating** 96 $70 ✪

Sewn Yarra Valley Chardonnay 2017 Clone I10V1, hand-picked, whole-bunch pressed, wild-fermented and matured for 10 months in French oak (10% new). From 'selected' vineyards, it sings from the rooftops of the vintage and the purity this has instilled, over and above the effortless length of Yarra chardonnay. I'm disinclined to glorify this wine – go buy a bottle (better still, six bottles) and taste it for yourself. Screwcap. 13.5% alc. **Rating** 95 **To** 2027 $24 ✪

Sewn Yarra Valley Pinot Noir 2017 Vines planted '96, MV6, hand-picked and sorted in the vineyard, 70% whole berry/30% whole bunches, wild yeast–open ferment, 15 days on skins, matured in French oak (10% new) for 10 months. A glorious entry point wine, red fruits at the core, countered by savoury/spicy flavours and texture; a long, balanced finish and aftertaste. Screwcap. 13.5% alc. **Rating** 95 **To** 2027 $24 ✪

Sewn Yarra Valley Shiraz 2017 Great colour. This is so fresh it is jumping out of its skin, with vibrant raspberry, blueberry and red cherry fruits filling the light to medium-bodied palate. While (rightly) most will be enjoyed soon, any bottle forgotten in the corner of the cellar could spring a major surprise in a blind tasting. Screwcap. 13.5% alc. **Rating** 94 **To** 2023 $24 ✪

🍷🍷🍷🍷🍷 **Sewn Yarra Valley Rose 2017** **Rating** 93 **To** 2019 $24 ✪
The Barber Yarra Valley Shiraz 2016 **Rating** 91 **To** 2022 $24

Sew & Sew Wines ★★★★

PO Box 1924, McLaren Flat, SA 5171 **Region** Adelaide Hills
T 0419 804 345 **www**.sewandsewwines.com.au **Open** Not
Winemaker Jodie Armstrong **Est.** 2004 **Dozens** 630

Winemaker and viticulturist Jodie Armstrong has worked in the wine industry for more than 20 years. She sources grapes from the vineyards that she manages, her in-depth knowledge of these vineyards allowing her to grow and select premium fruit. She makes the wines in friends' wineries, 'where collaboration is a source of inspiration'. Exports to Denmark.

🍷🍷🍷🍷🍷 **Contour Series Adelaide Hills Chardonnay 2017** I10V5 clone from Kuitpo; crushed, pressed, settled, fermented in stainless steel, matured in French oak (40% new) for 10 months on lees. Struck match/gunflint, call it what you will, but it's one of the virtues of this wine (and its Burgundian nuances). The length and balance are also on the money. Screwcap. 13.5% alc. **Rating** 94 **To** 2025

Sashiko Series Adelaide Hills Chardonnay 2017 From Kuitpo; crushed, pressed, settled, fermented in stainless steel, matured in French oak (10% new). Melon, white peach, green apple, grapefruit. Any more takers for the fruit ride? I don't think so, nor is there much oak influence to talk about, just a touch of the struck match of its '17 Contour stablemate. Screwcap. 13.5% alc. **Rating** 94 **To** 2026

🍷🍷🍷🍷🍷 **Sashiko Series Adelaide Hills Fiano 2017** **Rating** 93 **To** 2022
Sashiko Series McLaren Vale Shiraz 2016 **Rating** 93 **To** 2029
Contour Series Adelaide Hills Syrah 2016 **Rating** 92 **To** 2026
Sashiko Series Adelaide Hills Sauvignon Blanc 2017 **Rating** 90 **To** 2020
Contour Series Adelaide Hills Pinot Noir 2016 **Rating** 90 **To** 2025

Shadowfax ★★★★★

K Road, Werribee, Vic 3030 **Region** Geelong/Macedon Ranges
T (03) 9731 4420 **www**.shadowfax.com.au **Open** 7 days 11–5
Winemaker Alister Timms **Est.** 2000 **Dozens** 12 000

Shadowfax is part of an awesome development at Werribee Park, a mere 20 minutes from Melbourne. The truly striking winery, designed by Wood Marsh Architects and built in 2000, is adjacent to the extraordinary private home built in the 1880s by the Chirnside family and known as The Mansion – the centrepiece of a 40 000ha pastoral empire. The equally magnificent gardens were part of the reason for the property being acquired by Parks Victoria in the early 1970s. The Mansion is now The Mansion Hotel, with 92 rooms and suites. The 10ha Werribee Minnow vineyard (eight varieties including 5ha of shiraz) was planted in 1999, the Little Hampton vineyard in 2003 with 5ha of close-planted pinot noir, 5ha of chardonnay and 1ha of pinot gris. Little Hampton is one of the highest vineyards in the Macedon Ranges. Exports to the UK, the US and China

ŶŶŶŶŶ **Macedon Ranges Chardonnay 2016** Gold medal Macedon Wine Show. Gleaming straw-green – considerable depth, but very bright. A powerful and intense wine with excellent varietal character, balance and length, handsomely ticking all the boxes. Continues a history of success by Shadowfax, with verve and style. Screwcap. 13% alc. **Rating** 96 **To** 2026 $36 ✪

Macedon Ranges Pinot Gris 2017 A great example of pinot gris, made with integrity and intent. It's full of flavour and texture without being heavy. A mix of poached pears, clotted cream dipped in ginger spice, with some pippy/apricot kernel savoury nuances. Lovely. Screwcap. 13% alc. **Rating** 95 **To** 2023 $28 JF ✪

Little Hampton Pinot Noir 2016 The bouquet is very fragrant, with rose petal and violets, the palate a delicate but perfectly balanced peacock's tail display. The individual pieces of this silk tapestry may be small, but they combine to create a picture of total harmony. Screwcap. 13% alc. **Rating** 95 **To** 2031 $65

Macedon Ranges Pinot Noir 2016 Its full crimson-purple hue is far deeper and brighter than its Little Hampton sibling. It's a wine of power, not persuasion, but isn't extractive or brutish – give it 5++ years and you'll be mightily pleased with yourself. Screwcap. 13% alc. **Rating** 94 **To** 2033 $36

ŶŶŶŶŶ **Geelong Riesling 2017** **Rating** 93 **To** 2025 $28 JF
Minnow Rose 2017 **Rating** 92 **To** 2020 $26
Minnow 2016 **Rating** 91 **To** 2021 $30
Adelaide Hills Sauvignon Blanc 2017 **Rating** 90 **To** 2020 $24 JF

Sharmans   ★★★★☆

175 Glenwood Road, Relbia, Tas 7258 **Region** Northern Tasmania
T (03) 6343 0773 **www**.sharmanswines.com.au **Open** 7 days 10–4
Winemaker Jeremy Dineen, Ockie Myburg **Est.** 1986 **Dozens** 2500 **Vyds** 7ha
When Mike Sharman planted the first vines at Relbia in 1986, he was the pioneer of the region, and he did so in the face of a widespread belief that it was too far inland, and frost-prone. He proved the doomsayers wrong, helped by the slope of the vineyard draining cold air away from the vines. In 2012 the property was acquired by local ophthalmologist Ian Murrell and his wife Melissa, a Launceston-based interior designer. The grounds and vineyards have been developed and renovated, the original residence now a cellar door and al fresco area, the picturesque grounds enhanced by award-winning landscaper Chris Calverly.

ŶŶŶŶŶ **Pinot Noir 2015** The aromatics in Tasmanian pinot noir are something else and the 20% whole bunches in the ferment has added extra perfume and lift. A heady mix of dark and red cherries, orange peel, woodsy spices and a dash of pepper. More medium-bodied, the oak integrated as the fine tannins move effortlessly across the supple palate. Screwcap. 13.6% alc. **Rating** 95 **To** 2023 $35 JF ✪

ŶŶŶŶŶ **Shiraz 2015** **Rating** 90 **To** 2023 $35 JF

Shaw + Smith   ★★★★★

136 Jones Road, Balhannah, SA 5242 **Region** Adelaide Hills
T (08) 8398 0500 **www**.shawandsmith.com **Open** 7 days 11–5
Winemaker Martin Shaw, Adam Wadewitz **Est.** 1989 **Dozens** NFP **Vyds** 56ha
Cousins Martin Shaw and Michael Hill Smith MW already had unbeatable experience when they founded Shaw + Smith as a virtual winery in 1989. In '99 Martin and Michael purchased

the 36ha Balhannah property, building the superbly designed winery in 2000 and planting more sauvignon blanc, shiraz, pinot noir and riesling. It is here that visitors can taste the wines in appropriately beautiful surroundings. The 20ha Lenswood vineyard, 10km northwest of the winery, is mainly planted to chardonnay and pinot noir. Exports to all major markets.

ΨΨΨΨΨ **Lenswood Vineyard Adelaide Hills Chardonnay 2016** A compelling wine; exudes power with lots of flavour, but doesn't appear overworked or too big. Kicks off with ginger flower – more stone fruit this vintage – citrus (especially mandarin), and complex leesy notes with creamed honey. Deep, with a luscious palate of woodsy spices and balanced oak. Complex, yet keeps a lightness of touch. Screwcap. 13% alc. **Rating** 97 **To** 2026 $85 JF ✪
Lenswood Vineyard Adelaide Hills Pinot Noir 2016 Inaugural release. Light hue, but it's the perfume that stops you in your tracks, an ethereal mix of spice, warm earth, dried herbs and florals. A hint of cherries and raspberries, but this is savoury through and through. Sealing the deal is the ultra-fine palate, medium-bodied with gossamer-like tannins, yet a tensile force. Screwcap. 13% alc. **Rating** 97 **To** 2027 $85 JF ✪
Adelaide Hills Shiraz 2016 Seduces with swathes of dark cherries dipped in kirsch, florals, ferrous and woodsy spices, with toasty oak sewn to the shape of the fuller-bodied palate. Everything is in its place, creating an immaculate whole – the fine-grained tannins, the length, the freshness and detail. It's polished and totally convincing. Screwcap. 14.5% alc. **Rating** 97 **To** 2028 $46 JF ✪

ΨΨΨΨΨ **Adelaide Hills Sauvignon Blanc 2017** This is a dignified sauvignon blanc that continuously reveals itself, as you move from the bouquet through to the aftertaste of the palate. Initially it has classic restraint, but by the time you pick up the sweet fruit (not sugar) you realise it's the product of a vintage designed for sauvignon blanc. Screwcap. 12% alc. **Rating** 96 **To** 2020 $27 ✪
Adelaide Hills Riesling 2017 While it holds all the delight of the variety – florals, lemon-lime juice and freshness – it steps up a notch thanks to its texture. A smidge of lime curd on toast and Bickford's lemon barley cordial, with chalky acidity. Feels effortless, and is certainly effortless to drink. Screwcap. 11.5% alc. **Rating** 95 **To** 2027 $30 JF ✪
M3 Adelaide Hills Chardonnay 2016 So much flavour is packed into this chardonnay, but it never loses focus or detail. Pristine and perfectly ripe fruit, a mix of stone fruit and citrus folded into creamy lees, and ginger notes with a liberal seasoning of integrated French oak spice. A fuller bodied palate, texture and complexity with ultra-refreshing acidity. No point waiting. Screwcap. 13% alc. **Rating** 95 **To** 2024 $46 JF
Adelaide Hills Pinot Noir 2016 Pale red with a watery rim. Cool fruit origins – fragrant red fruits, brown spice and potpourri. Balance is the key, with a web of filigreed tannins and a fine line of acidity complementing the red fruited nature of the wine. Ethereal. Screwcap. 13% alc. **Rating** 95 **To** 2022 DB

Shaw Family Vintners ★★★★☆

369 Myrtle Grove Road, Currency Creek, SA 5214 **Region** Currency Creek/McLaren Vale **T** (08) 8555 4215 **www.**shawfamilyvintners.com **Open** Mon–Fri 10–5
Winemaker Brooke Blair **Est.** 2001 **Dozens** 70 000 **Vyds** 414ha
Shaw Family Vintners was established in the early 1970s by Richard and Marie Shaw and sons Philip, Nathan and Mark, when they planted shiraz at McLaren Flat. Extensive vineyards were acquired and developed in McLaren Vale (64ha) and Currency Creek (350ha), and a winery at Currency Creek. In April 2017 the winery, vineyards, stock and brands were purchased by Casella Family brands, and are now managed by the next generation of Casella and Shaw families. Exports to the UK, the US, Canada and China.

ΨΨΨΨΨ **The Ballaster McLaren Vale Cabernet Sauvignon 2013** 65yo estate vines, matured for 2 years in French hogsheads. Comes in a massively heavy black glass bottle (like The Encounter). The wine in the bottle is very different, its colour bright crimson-purple, and it is indeed well balanced, even if full-bodied. It has plenty going for it. Cork. 14.5% alc. **Rating** 95 **To** 2038 $100

The 9N Single Vineyard McLaren Vale Shiraz 2014 It takes a little time for this to open its doors for inspection. It is fresh for its age, and has red and purple fruits allied with firm tannins. Just when you think the tannins are too obvious, tangy fruits take control of the finish and aftertaste. Cork. 14.5% alc. **Rating** 94 **To** 2027 $40

ŸŸŸŸŸ **The Encounter Currency Creek Cabernet Sauvignon 2014** Rating 90 **To** 2039 $100

Shaw Vineyard Estate

34 Isabel Drive, Murrumbateman, NSW 2582 **Region** Canberra District
T (02) 6227 5827 **www.**shawvineyards.com.au **Open** Wed–Sun & public hols 10–5
Winemaker Graeme Shaw, Jeremy Nascimben **Est.** 1999 **Dozens** 12 000 **Vyds** 33ha
Graeme and Ann Shaw established their vineyard (cabernet sauvignon, merlot, shiraz, semillon and riesling) in 1998 on a 280ha fine wool–producing property established in the mid-1800s and known as Olleyville. It is one of the largest privately owned vineyard holdings in the Canberra area. Their children are fully employed in the family business, Michael as viticulturist and Tanya as cellar door manager. Shaw Vineyard Estate have their wines in a number of retail outlets in China, including Suntay Wines in Hainan and 1919 wine stores in Shanghai and Guangzhou. Exports to Vietnam, Singapore, Thailand, the Philippines, South Korea and Hong Kong.

ŸŸŸŸŸ **Isabella Reserve Canberra District Riesling 2017** 8g/l residual. Sweet red apple, orange and zippy lime flavours set this wine off to a flying start. We're onto a good one here. It builds a delicious volume of flavour but keeps the pace up throughout, eventually bursting out through the finish. Brilliant now, but will cellar. Screwcap. 10.5% alc. **Rating** 95 **To** 2025 $40 CM

Estate Canberra Riesling 2017 Exceptionally pale colour but with a slight green tinge. It's a floral, buoyant wine with slate and citrus flavours slashing through the palate. It's clean, it's pure, it's long. Its dry style works beautifully with the floral lift. It is, in short, in fine form. Screwcap. 12.5% alc. **Rating** 94 **To** 2026 $30 CM ☉

Canberra District Cabernet Shiraz 2015 77/23% blend. Bold blackcurrant, gum leaf, dark chocolate and ripe plum flavours make a strong impression. Bay leaf notes make sure we're all aware that cabernet holds the tiller. This is a quality red wine. Tannin has both firmness and finesse on its side. There's a gentle bitterness to the aftertaste but it's not a negative. This should mature handsomely. Screwcap. 14.5% alc. **Rating** 94 **To** 2030 $30 CM ☉

ŸŸŸŸŸ **Estate Canberra Shiraz 2015** Rating 93 **To** 2026 $34 CM

 # Sherrah Wines

19 St Marys Street, Willunga, SA 5172 (postal) **Region** McLaren Vale
T 0403 057 704 **www.**sherrahwines.com.au **Open** Not
Winemaker Alex Sherrah **Est.** 2016 **Dozens** 800
Alex Sherrah's career started with a bachelor of science in organic chemistry and pharmacology, leading him to travel the world, returning broke, and in need of a job. He became a cellar rat at Tatachilla for the vintage, and followed this by completing a graduate diploma in oenology at Waite University while working Fridays at Tatachilla, earning the nickname Boy Friday – turning up each Friday in time to do some work and then enjoy the weekly barbecue. Two vintages of Tatachilla were followed by a job in the Napa Valley, where he worked at Kendall Jackson's crown jewel, Cardinale, making ultra premium Bordeaux blend wines. Before returning to Australia, he'd arranged a job with Knappstein in the Clare Valley, where he worked for two years before moving to O'Leary Walker. While there he was able to complete vintages in Burgundy and Austria. At the end of 2011 he moved to McLaren Vale and Coriole, where he became senior winemaker in '12, remaining there for six years,

before moving on to head up winemaking at Haselgrove, his present day job. Along the way, his girlfriend became his wife, and two children ensued. I cannot help but pass on some of his words of wisdom (and I'm not being sarcastic). 'Wine to me is not about tasting blackcurrant and cigar box but how the wine "feels" to drink. Flavour is obviously a big part of this, but how does the wine flow from front to back palate? It should transition effortlessly from first smell and sip to swallow, aftertaste and lingering influence of tannin and acid. I believe in balance, a great wine should have no sharp edges, it should have beautiful smooth curves from front to back.' Small wonder he makes such wonderful wines.

ΨΨΨΨΨ **Red et Al McLaren Vale Grenache Shiraz Nero 2016** A 60/25/15% blend, fermented and matured separately. Complexity with a capital C is the order of the day with the carefully planned and executed vinification. It keeps you on your toes, different facets showing on each visit to the wine. In the end, it's the purity of the fruit line that holds sway, earthy complexity ever present, but unable to take control of the palate. Screwcap. 14.5% alc. **Rating** 96 **To** 2029 $30 ✪
McLaren Vale Shiraz 2016 Selectiv'-harvested (with an on-board destemmer/sorter), open-fermented, hand-plunged for 14 days, matured in French oak (10% new) for 10 months. There's a wealth of flavour and texture here, held together by a silken web of tannins and regional earth and savoury dark chocolate trimmings. Given its vinification (genuine whole berries) its structure is impressive. Screwcap. 14.5% alc. **Rating** 95 **To** 2036 $30 ✪

ΨΨΨΨΩ **McLaren Vale Nero d'Avola 2017 Rating** 90 **To** 2022 $30

Shingleback   ★★★★★

3 Stump Hill Road, McLaren Vale, SA 5171 **Region** McLaren Vale
T (08) 8323 7388 **www.**shingleback.com.au **Open** 7 days 10–5
Winemaker John Davey, Dan Hills **Est.** 1995 **Dozens** 150 000 **Vyds** 120ha
Brothers Kym and John Davey planted and nurture their family-owned and sustainably managed vineyard on land purchased by their grandfather in the 1950s. Shingleback has been a success story since its establishment. Its 120ha of estate vineyards are one of the keys to that success, which includes winning the Jimmy Watson Trophy 2006 for the '05 D Block Cabernet Sauvignon. The well made wines are rich and full-flavoured, but not overripe (and, hence, not excessively alcoholic). Exports to the UK, the US, Canada, Cambodia, Vietnam, China and NZ.

ΨΨΨΨΨ **The Gate McLaren Vale Shiraz 2016** If you want heft then you've come to the right place. This lays it on and does so in excellent style. Chocolate and blackberry, ripe plum and toast. Peppercorns too. It's svelte and rugged at once – it's a mouthful. Tannin comes in from a long run and rumbles through the finish. Screwcap. 14.5% alc. **Rating** 95 **To** 2035 $35 CM ✪
Unedited McLaren Vale Shiraz 2016 It's dark with molasses and malt-like flavours, not to mention blackberry, licorice and saltbush, and yet it's not weighed down or (too) heavy; it almost feels like sleight of hand. It's a substantial red wine with both softness and heartiness attended to, and a significant surge of flavour and tannin to close. A powerhouse. Screwcap. 14% alc. **Rating** 95 **To** 2035 $80 CM
Davey Estate McLaren Vale Cabernet Sauvignon 2016 It's a dusty number, but it's a good one. Indeed the value meter sets off an alert straight away. It tastes of boysenberry and dry licorice, dust and dry herbs. It has enough volume to satisfy, enough length to impress, and the shape to age well. Screwcap. 14% alc. **Rating** 94 **To** 2030 $25 CM ✪
D Block Reserve McLaren Vale Cabernet Sauvignon 2016 It's very good. It's fresh with boysenberry, but tapped with blackcurrant. It shows spearmint-like highlights and elements of florals, though there's a kind of blackberry pie character here too. Of course it's ripe and solid, but a light hand has been applied. Cork. 14.5% alc. **Rating** 94 **To** 2030 $55 CM

ΨΨΨΨΩ **Aficionado Rose 2017 Rating** 93 **To** 2019 $15 DB ✪
Davey Estate McLaren Vale Shiraz 2016 Rating 93 **To** 2028 $25 CM ✪

D Block Reserve McLaren Vale Shiraz 2014 Rating 93 To 2028 $55 CM ·
Kiss me Kate Adelaide Hills Chardonnay 2016 Rating 91 To 2022
$25 CM
Haycutters McLaren Vale Shiraz 2016 Rating 90 To 2023 $18 CM ✪
Red Knot McLaren Vale Grenache Shiraz Mourvedre 2017 Rating 90
To 2022 $15 CM ✪

Shining Rock Vineyard   ★★★★☆

165 Jeffrey Street, Nairne, SA 5252 **Region** Adelaide Hills
T 0448 186 707 **www**.shiningrock.com.au **Open** By appt
Winemaker Con Moshos, Darren Arney **Est.** 2000 **Dozens** 1200 **Vyds** 14.4ha
Agronomist Darren Arney and psychologist wife Natalie Worth had the opportunity to
purchase the Shining Rock Vineyard from Lion Nathan in 2012. It had been established
by Petaluma in '00, and until '15 the grapes were sold to various premium wineries in the
Adelaide Hills. Darren graduated from Roseworthy Agricultural College in the late 1980s,
and saw the vineyard as the opportunity of a lifetime to produce top quality grapes from a
very special vineyard. They hit the ground running with the inaugural vintage of '15 made by
Peter Leske (Revenir), but since '16 Con Moshos has taken over the task in conjunction with
Darren. It hardly need be said that the wines reflect the expertise of those involved, with the
éminence grise of Brian Croser in the background.

♀♀♀♀♀ **Adelaide Hills Shiraz 2016** Hand-picked, co-fermented with 2% viognier,
no whole bunches this vintage, matured in French puncheons (25% new) for
15 months. An interesting follow-on to the '15, that vintage giving rise to many
very good wines. The '16 takes its time in asserting its character and quality, which
it does so handsomely on the back-palate and finish. Here spicy, savoury notes
are allied with terrific tannins, fine, yet persistent. Screwcap. 14% alc. **Rating** 95
To 2031 $35 ✪
Adelaide Hills Sangiovese 2016 Hand-picked Matura 6 and 7 clones, matured
for 15 months in French barriques (10% new). Excellent colour; this is a pretty
smart sangio, the red cherry fruits within a filigree of tannins, part satin, part spicy.
The oak maturation has worked well, shaping texture more than flavour. Screwcap.
14% alc. **Rating** 94 To 2026 $30 ✪

Shirvington   ★★★★★

PO Box 220, McLaren Vale, SA 5171 **Region** McLaren Vale
T (08) 8323 7649 **www**.shirvington.com **Open** Not
Winemaker Kim Jackson **Est.** 1996 **Dozens** 950 **Vyds** 23.8ha
The Shirvington family began the development of their McLaren Vale vineyards in 1996
under the direction of viticulturist Peter Bolte, and now have almost 24ha under vine,
the majority to shiraz and cabernet sauvignon, with small additional plantings of grenache
and mataro. A substantial part of the production is sold as grapes, the best reserved for the
Shirvington wines. Exports to the UK and the US.

♀♀♀♀♀ **McLaren Vale Shiraz 2015** Bright crimson-purple; an elegant and very well-
balanced shiraz, with a fragrant black fruit and spice bouquet and a deliciously
lively palate, tasting like 13.5% alcohol rather than 14.5%. French oak adds another
dimension simply because it's so well integrated. Delicious now or in a decade.
Screwcap. **Rating** 95 To 2030 $28 ✪
The Redwind McLaren Vale Cabernet Sauvignon 2015 Uncompromisingly
full-bodied, but in no way extractive, let alone alcoholic. The power of the fruit is
awesome, and stands upright in the face of 90% new French oak. It's a three barrel
selection, so how can you arrive at a 90/10% new and used oak split? Screwcap.
14% alc. **Rating** 95 To 2035 $55
The Redwind McLaren Vale Shiraz 2015 Similar colour to its '15 varietal
sibling, but that's where the similarity stops. This is an altogether fuller bodied and
more complex wine, but doesn't go over the top. The black cherry and blackberry

fruits have a streak of dark chocolate and rather more cedary French oak. Simply needs more time for higher points. Screwcap. 14% alc. **Rating** 94 To 2035 $55

ŢŢŢŢ♀ McLaren Vale Cabernet Sauvignon 2015 Rating 93 To 2029 $28
Row X Row McLaren Vale Grenache 2017 Rating 91 To 2023 $30

Shoofly | Frisk ★★★☆

PO Box 119, Mooroolbark, Vic 3138 **Region** Various
T 0405 631 557 **www.**shooflywines.com **Open** Not
Winemaker Ben Riggs, Garry Wall, Mark O'Callaghan **Est.** 2003 **Dozens** 15 000
This is a far-flung, export-oriented business. It purchases a little over 620t of grapes each vintage; the lion's share (surprisingly) riesling (250t), followed by shiraz (200t) and chardonnay (50t); the remainder is made up of pinot noir, gewurztraminer, merlot, dolcetto and muscat gordo blanco. Ben Riggs makes Shoofly Shiraz and Chardonnay at Vintners McLaren Vale. The Frisk and Prickly Lane Riesling is made by Garry Wall at King Valley Wines. The bulk of exports go to the US, Canada and Ireland.

ŢŢŢŢ♀ Shoofly Shiraz 2016 Blimey Charlie, this is an outstanding bargain. It's packed with warm black fruits decorated with spicy stars from the cooler-grown shiraz (the wine is a blend of SA regions), the flavours hold together like magnets, the finish as compelling as the opening stanza. Don't hesitate to tuck away a bottle or more in a dark place. Screwcap. 14.5% alc. **Rating** 90 To 2031 $15 ❂

Shottesbrooke ★★★★★

Bagshaws Road, McLaren Flat, SA 5171 **Region** McLaren Vale
T (08) 8383 0002 **www.**shottesbrooke.com.au **Open** Mon–Fri 10–4.30, w'ends & public hols 11–5
Winemaker Hamish Maguire **Est.** 1984 **Dozens** 25 000 **Vyds** 30.64ha
Shottesbrooke is a proudly family-owned and managed business with second-generation Hamish Maguire chief winemaker and general manager. Before taking the reins at Shottesbrooke, Hamish completed two vintages in France and one in Spain, giving him a personal knowledge of the world of wine. The investment of time and money over the past 33 years have taken Shottesbrooke to the position where it can embark on the next major step and undertake major improvements in the size and operation of its winery. The central theme is the investment in state-of-the-art equipment, allowing more gentle fermentation, pressing, movement and maturation of the wines. Thus there has been a 25% increase in the temperature-controlled main barrel storage areas, sufficient to hold an additional 600 barrels. Once bottled and packaged, the wines are held in a purpose-built air-conditioned storage facility until shipped to customers in refrigerated containers to ensure quality and consistency throughout the entire process. Exports to all major markets, most importantly, China.

ŢŢŢŢŢ Eliza Reserve McLaren Vale Shiraz 2014 Holding hue well, with no hint of change; a distillation of McLaren Vale shiraz, full-bodied yet so perfectly balanced that you don't hesitate to taste it several times. Savoury, spicy notes come first, but are promptly upstaged by the bow wave of blackberry fruit, dark chocolate a cultured farewell. Screwcap. 14.5% alc. **Rating** 97 To 2039

ŢŢŢŢŢ Single Vineyard Tom's Block Blewitt Springs McLaren Vale Shiraz 2015 Superb crimson-purple hue, deep and brilliant. If I were to start again (I'm not) in McLaren Vale, there is only one place I'd choose to plant shiraz – Blewitt Springs. The wines have a unique structure, texture, flavour and style, elegant yet highly aromatic and effortlessly flavoured. Spice, black fruits, licorice and dark chocolate all play a role, finishing with savoury tannins on the long finish. 480 dozen made. Screwcap. 14.5% alc. **Rating** 96 To 2030
Single Vineyard Bush Vine McLaren Vale Grenache 2016 A neat and convincing example of the lead that McLaren Vale's grenaches have over those of other regions, exceptions such as Turkey Flat's Jimmy Watson winner agreed. This single vineyard has a deep sand over clay soil, and has gully breezes that produce

a beautifully light to medium-bodied wine, with highly spiced red fruits and silky tannins. If you don't have pinot noir to hand at your local Chinese restaurant, this should do the trick to perfection. Screwcap. 14.5% alc. **Rating** 95 **To** 2023

Langhorne Creek Cabernet Sauvignon 2016 While not particularly deep, the hue is youthful, and the fragrant eucalyptus nuances that accompany the fresh cassis of the palate are regional (and shared with Coonawarra). The finely spun tannins are a feature of a medium-bodied cabernet made to be drunk whenever the idea pleases you. Screwcap. 14.5% alc. **Rating** 95 **To** 2030

Single Vineyard Adelaide Hills Chardonnay 2016 From a steep, south-facing vineyard at 540m, between Meadows and Macclesfield; 30% unsulphured and wild-fermented in new French hogsheads. Notably pale colour; very different from (and better than) its Estate Series sibling (tasted at the same time): this is vibrant and fresh, grapefruit joining forces with stone fruit on the feline, juicy palate and long aftertaste. Screwcap. 13% alc. **Rating** 94 **To** 2022 $33

Estate Series McLaren Vale Shiraz 2015 Medium crimson-purple; an elegant medium-bodied shiraz, sending a crystal clear message of its place and variety. The blackberry/black cherry fruits are dipped in dark chocolate, then finished with superfine tannins that draw out the long finish. Screwcap. 14.5% alc. **Rating** 94 **To** 2025

ΨΨΨΨΩ **Estate Series McLaren Vale Cabernet Sauvignon 2016** Rating 93 To 2029
Punch Reserve McLaren Vale Cabernet Sauvignon 2014 Rating 93 To 2029
Estate Series McLaren Vale GSM 2016 Rating 91 To 2026
The Proprietor Reserve Series 2014 Rating 91 To 2021

Shut the Gate Wines   ★★★★★

8453 Main North Road, Clare, SA 5453 **Region** Clare Valley
T 0488 243 200 **www**.shutthegate.com.au **Open** 7 days 10–4.30
Winemaker Contract **Est.** 2013 **Dozens** 6000
Shut the Gate is the venture of Richard Woods and Rasa Fabian, which took shape after five years' involvement in the rebranding of Crabtree Watervale Wines, followed by 18 months of juggling consultancy roles. During this time Richard and Rasa set the foundations for Shut the Gate, with striking and imaginative labels (and parables) catching the eye. The engine room of the business is located at the Clare Valley, where the wines are contract-made and the grapes for many of the wines are sourced. They have chosen their grape sources and contract winemakers with considerable care.

ΨΨΨΨΨ **For Hunger Single Site Clare Valley Shiraz 2014** From 120yo vines. Matured in all-French oak for 24 months. Brilliant with flavour. Deep, ripe, fresh, long, structured – the works. Blood plum, blackberry, gum leaf, wood smoke and sweet spices. A wave of tannin, flavour running with it. Excellent from every angle. Screwcap. 14.8% alc. **Rating** 96 **To** 2034 $45 CM ✪

For Love Single Site Wrattonbully Tempranillo 2014 Intense flavours of raspberry, blueberry, spearmint and cola come touched by a healthy serve of smoky/cedary oak. There's a volume of tannin too, but it's well disguised by its ripe, velvety texture. Both quality and value here are right up there. Screwcap. 14.5% alc. **Rating** 95 **To** 2025 $25 CM ✪

ΨΨΨΨΩ **For Freedom Polish Hill River Riesling 2017** Rating 93 To 2025 $25 CM ✪
For Love Watervale Riesling 2017 Rating 93 To 2027 $25 CM ✪
Fur Elise Clare Valley Grenache Rose 2017 Rating 93 To 2020 $20 CM ✪
For Hunger Single Site Adelaide Hills Pinot Noir 2016 Rating 93 To 2025 $28 CM
Rosie's Patch Watervale Riesling 2017 Rating 91 To 2023 $20 CM ✪
For Hunger Single Site Clare Valley Grenache 2015 Rating 90 To 2023 $25 CM

Side Gate Wines ★★★★

57 Rokeby Street, Collingwood, Vic 3066 **Region** South East Australia
T (03) 9417 5757 **www.**sidegate.com.au **Open** Mon–Fri 8–5
Winemaker Josef Orbach **Est.** 2001 **Dozens** 50 000
Side Gate is a Melbourne-based multiregional producer, specialising in cool-climate reds and whites. Founder Josef Orbach lived and worked in the Clare Valley from 1994 to '98 at Leasingham, and completed a winemaking degree at the University of Melbourne in 2010. Side Gate is a classic négociant business, buying grapes and/or wines from various regions. Their wines may be either purchased in bulk, then blended and bottled by Orbach, or purchased as cleanskins. Exports to Canada, Thailand, Singapore and China.

ΨΨΨΨΨ **Adelaide Hills Pinot Noir 2017** The colour is light and may well develop quickly, but in the meantime the fruit catches attention with its nervous energy and long palate. Oak is incidental, but does its job. Screwcap. 12.9% alc. **Rating** 91 To 2025 $25

Adelaide Hills Pinot Grigio 2017 Fresh and lively, with nashi pear in a sea of crisp citrus fruits. Lithe and long. Screwcap. 12% alc. **Rating** 90 **To** 2019 $15 ✪

ΨΨΨΨ **Clare Valley Cabernet Sauvignon 2014 Rating** 89 **To** 2027 $18 ✪

Sidewood Estate ★★★★★

Maximillian's Restaurant, 15 Onkaparinga Road, Oakbank, SA 5245 **Region** Adelaide Hills
T (08) 8389 9234 **www.**sidewood.com.au **Open** Wed–Sun 11–5
Winemaker Darryl Catlin **Est.** 2004 **Dozens** NFP **Vyds** 93ha
Sidewood Estate is part vineyard, and part horse stables and racehorse training. Owned by Owen and Cassandra Inglis since 2004, both aspects of the business are flourishing. Sidewood Estate lies in the Onkaparinga Valley, with the vines weathering the coolest climate in the Adelaide Hills. Significant expenditure on regeneration of and increase in the size of the vineyards was already well underway when Sidewood obtained a South Australian State Regional Government Fund grant of $856 000. This contributed to a $3.5 million expansion of the winery capacity from 500t to 2000t each vintage. The expansion includes new bottling and canning facilities capable of handling 400 000 bottles of wine and cider annually. Wines are released under the Sidewood Estate, Stable Hill and Mappinga labels, as well as the Reserve range. Exports to the UK, the US, Canada, Malaysia, Singapore, Japan and China.

ΨΨΨΨΨ **Adelaide Hills Shiraz 2016** Whole berry/carbonic maceration ferment, matured in French barriques for 16 months. This hits like a thunderstorm after you have navigated the fragrant bouquet and taken the first sip. Blackberry, red and black cherries, and plum flood the fore- and mid-palate, after which the whirlwind of black pepper, spice, licorice and dark chocolate take command before the fine, persistent tannins on the long finish and aftertaste. Screwcap. 14.5% alc. **Rating** 96 To 2041 $26 ✪

Adelaide Hills Shiraz 2015 Has a highly fragrant bouquet, verging on outright perfume; spicy notes are part climate, part whole bunch-derived, and the multi-clone backdrop provides a beautifully poised palate. Very good value. Screwcap. 14.7% alc. **Rating** 96 To 2030 $25 ✪

Mappinga Shiraz 2015 Shares the striking bouquet of its Estate sibling, and follows on the bulkier '13 which won a trophy at the Decanter Wine Awards (no '14 was released). It has a spicy/juicy palate with a carpet of red fruits framed by fine-spun tannins. Classy wine. Screwcap. 14.7% alc. **Rating** 96 To 2032 $65 ✪

Adelaide Hills Sauvignon Blanc 2017 Quite an achievement winning a gold medal in the bastion of sauvignon blanc, the Perth Wine Show. A wine made in the vineyard, with multiple pickings over 2 weeks, row by row, with earlier canopy management and fruit dropping reducing the yield. Winemaker Darryl Catlin opted for cool fermentation in tank with 4 months' lees contact. Perfectly ripened fruit midway between citrus and tropical are neatly balanced by acidity. Screwcap. 12% alc. **Rating** 95 To 2018 $20 ✪

Adelaide Hills Chardonnay 2016 Wild-fermented in French barriques, matured for 10 months. The intensity and length of the fruit is exceptional, and has swallowed up the French oak without even blinking. The accent is slightly more on the citrus (grapefruit) side than the stone fruit (nectarine, white peach), the finish as fresh as a spring day. Value++. Screwcap. 12.5% alc. **Rating** 95 To 2024 $22 ✪

Owen's Adelaide Hills Chardonnay 2016 Part whole bunch, part whole berry wild fermentation, and partial mlf and maturation for 10 months in new and used French oak all point to attention to detail. A total production of 85 dozen. As smooth as silk. Screwcap. 12.5% alc. **Rating** 95 To 2026 $50

Mappinga Chardonnay 2016 The best parcels of fruit from the vineyard, whole-bunch pressed, the free-run juice wild-fermented and matured for 10 months in new and used French oak. Three gold medals in '17 – in NZ and Spain, and at the Royal Adelaide Wine Show – is an interesting trifecta. More important is the sheer quality, purity and length of a beautifully crafted (and grown) wine. It hasn't put a foot wrong at any point along the way, instead conjuring up a combination of crisp acidity and softness. Screwcap. 12.5% alc. **Rating** 95 To 2024 $35 ✪

Owen's Adelaide Hills Chardonnay 2015 Offers a complex, gently funky bouquet, very much à la mode. The tangy, juicy palate is very long, drawing on its lively acidity, sustained by a deft touch of French oak. Screwcap. 13.4% alc. **Rating** 95 To 2024 $50

Mappinga Chardonnay 2015 An opulent style, very different from its 2015 Owen sibling which struck gold at several shows. This has a lively mouthfeel, full of white peach, grapefruit and cashew, with the oak handling being particularly good. Screwcap. 12.8% alc. **Rating** 95 To 2025 $35 ✪

Adelaide Hills Tempranillo Rose 2017 Hand-picked, chilled for 24 hours, destemmed and crushed, 3 hours skin contact, the free-run juice pressed to used French oak for wild fermentation and 8 months maturation on lees. Pale, bright magenta; the fragrant, expressive bouquet alerts you that this isn't your average rose. It is vibrant and crisp, with wild strawberry, crunchy apple skin and cranberries. The palate is dry – very dry – but has excellent texture, mouthfeel and length. Screwcap. 12% alc. **Rating** 95 To 2021 $22 ✪

777 Adelaide Hills Pinot Noir 2016 Clone 777, hand-picked, wild yeast–open fermented with 30% whole bunches, 8 months in French oak. The light colour is no indication of the elegance and precision of the palate, nor the highly fragrant cherry blossom bouquet. The long, lingering palate rests on a bed of wild strawberries, the tannins as fine as silk. Screwcap. 12.5% alc. **Rating** 95 To 2031 $35 ✪

Adelaide Hills Pinot Noir 2016 The clonal mix (Oberlin, Abel and 777) gives complexity through the bouquet, palate and finish. Notes of plum join the red fruits of its 777 clone sibling. Has excellent line, length and balance, the 30% whole bunch inclusion pefect. Screwcap. 12.5% alc. **Rating** 95 To 2032 $30 ✪

Adelaide Hills Pinot Gris 2017 Rating 94 To 2021 $22 ✪

Adelaide Hills Isabella Rose Methode Traditionelle 2013 Rating 94 $30 ✪

ΨΨΨΨΨ **Fume Blanc 2015 Rating** 93 To 2019 $35

Adelaide Hills Chloe Cuvee Methode Traditionelle 2014 Rating 92 $30

Adelaide Hills Pinot Blanc 2017 Rating 91 To 2019 $22 ✪

Sieber Road Wines ★★★★

Sieber Road, Tanunda, SA 5352 **Region** Barossa Valley
T (08) 8562 8038 **www**.sieberwines.com **Open** 7 days 11–4
Winemaker Tony Carapetis **Est.** 1999 **Dozens** 4500 **Vyds** 18ha
Richard and Val Sieber are the third generation to run Redlands, the family property, traditionally a cropping/grazing farm. They have diversified into viticulture, with shiraz (14ha) occupying the lion's share, the remainder split between viognier, grenache and mourvedre. Son Ben Sieber is the viticulturist. Exports to Canada and China.

ΨΨΨΨΨ **Abigail Rose 2017** 100% shiraz, crushed and destemmed, held in the press until colour achieved (4 days), the juice clarified and fermented until dry. Early picked shiraz bequests pretty red fruits. Screwcap. 12.5% alc. **Rating** 90 **To** 2020 $18 ○
Barossa Valley Shiraz Grenache 2015 A 62/38% blend, matured in 2yo French and American oak for 18 months before blending. This is a better wine than its Shiraz Mataro sibling. The fruit is fresh, the palate supple and well balanced, and the finish is long. Screwcap. 15% alc. **Rating** 90 **To** 2022 $20 ○

Signature Wines

31 King Street, Norwood, SA 5067 **Region** Adelaide Hills/Barossa Valley
T (08) 8568 1757 **www**.signaturewines.com.au **Open** Mon–Fri 9–5, w'ends by appt
Winemaker Warwick Billings (Contract) **Est.** 2011 **Dozens** 15000 **Vyds** 16ha
Signature Wines, owned by Daniel Khouzam and family, has formed a special relationship with core growers in the Adelaide Hills and the greater Barossa region. Daniel has been in the industry for over 20 years, and during that time has slowly developed Signature Wines's export markets. It operates out of the one-time Penfolds winery in the Eden Valley. Exports to the UK, Malaysia, Singapore, Hong Kong, China and NZ.

ΨΨΨΨΨ **Reserve Adelaide Hills Sauvignon Blanc 2017** It delivers varietal flavour in sure, certain fashion, but it simultaneously feels strict and well-structured. It's a very good release. Lemongrass, passionfruit and lime leaf characters lead a disciplined charge. Screwcap. 12% alc. **Rating** 93 **To** 2020 $27 CM ○

ΨΨΨΨ **Co-ordinates Range Adelaide Hills Sauvignon Blanc 2017** Rating 89 To 2019 $30 CM
Chardonnay Pinot Noir NV Rating 89 $25 CM

Silkman Wines

c/- The Small Winemakers Centre, McDonalds Road, Pokolbin, NSW 2320
Region Hunter Valley
T 0414 800 256 **www**.silkmanwines.com.au **Open** 7 days 10–5
Winemaker Shaun Silkman, Liz Silkman **Est.** 2013 **Dozens** 3500
Winemaking couple Liz (née Jackson; one-time dux of the Len Evans Tutorial) and Shaun Silkman were both born and raised in the Hunter Valley. They worked many vintages (both in Australia and abroad) before joining forces at First Creek Wines, which is owned and run by Shaun's father, Greg, and is where Liz is senior winemaker. This gives them the opportunity to make small quantities of the three classic varieties of the Hunter Valley: semillon, chardonnay and shiraz. Unsurprisingly, the wines released so far have been of outstanding quality. Exports to the US.

ΨΨΨΨΨ **Reserve Hunter Valley Semillon 2017** The highly expressive bouquet has layers far more often found in red than white wines, and the palate is just short of electrifying, instantly reaching every corner of the mouth. I seldom give points of this magnitude to a 1yo semillon, but this is no ordinary wine. Its glittering acidity throws off sparks of lemon, lime and crushed green leaves/grasses. Screwcap.
Rating 97 **To** 2037 $35 ○
Reserve Shiraz Pinot 2017 Silkman was, as far as I know, the first to explore this blend since the death of Maurice O'Shea. It raises a question with no real answer – why did the blend take so long to gain currency afresh? It is the ultimate now or later style, brilliant in its flavour profile, and in the synergy discovered by O'Shea. Screwcap. **Rating** 97 **To** 2030 $50 ○

ΨΨΨΨΨ **Reserve Hunter Valley Semillon 2014** The bouquet is perfumed, the wine flying on the wings of a butterfly, so delicate yet detailed is its overall mouthfeel and flavour. Hunter Valley winemakers gave this semillon faint praise in '14, but they would be only too happy now to be told to drink this vintage by way of penitence. Screwcap. 11% alc. **Rating** 96 **To** 2034

Single Vineyard Blackberry Hunter Valley Semillon 2014 Fulfils most of the expectations held for it as a 1yo when tasted by Campbell Mattinson in Feb '15. It's more robust and complex than its Reserve sibling, with hints of grapefruit along with the more usual lemon. Both have time to go, but this is the wine I would drink tonight. Screwcap. 11% alc. **Rating** 96 **To** 2030

SILK Chardonnay 2017 To some degree the richest and most complex of the trio of Silkman 2017 chardonnays tasted here. That richness might be ascribed to the warm/hot climate, but that doesn't make sense. This is fruit selection, and a cautious addition of new oak. Or is it? No winemaking details received. Screwcap. **Rating** 96 $80

Single Vineyard Blackberry Hunter Valley Semillon 2017 Clearly a very well-made wine from a great vintage, with intensity, line and exceptional length. Does enough to keep your hand near the glass, but much more is around the corner for what will be a great wine. Screwcap. **Rating** 95 **To** 2032 $35 ✪

Maluna Vineyard Chardonnay 2017 No details, but clearly barrel-fermented. Elegant and fine to the point of being an outright delicacy, but is ripe. White peach, nectarine, some cashew; perfect balance and length. Screwcap. **Rating** 95 **To** 2023 $65

Reserve Hunter Valley Shiraz 2017 There is more flavour here, seemingly more oak (even though integrated) and maximum fruit sorting/selection, but the same black hole in information as its sibling. Either or both of these wines would have received higher points if information had been received, especially for the extra layer of plum and black berry fruits here. Screwcap. **Rating** 95 **To** 2047 $50

Hunter Valley Semillon 2017 Rating 94 **To** 2027
Reserve Chardonnay 2017 Rating 94 $50
Hunter Valley Shiraz 2017 Rating 94 **To** 2037 $30 ✪

♀♀♀♀♀ **Reserve Hunter Valley Shiraz 2015 Rating** 93 **To** 2029

Silver Spoon Estate ★★★★

503 Heathcote-Rochester Road, Heathcote, Mount Camel, Vic 3523 **Region** Heathcote
T 0412 868 236 **www.**silverspoonestate.com.au **Open** W'ends 11–5, or by appt
Winemaker Peter Young **Est.** 2008 **Dozens** 1500 **Vyds** 22ha
When Peter and Tracie Young purchased an existing shiraz vineyard on the top of the Mt Camel range in 2008, they did not waste any time. They immediately planted a second vineyard, constructed a small winery, and in '13 acquired a neighbouring vineyard. The estate name comes from the Silver Spoon fault line that delineates the Cambrian volcanic rock from the old silver mines on the property. Peter became familiar with vineyards when working in the 1970s as a geologist in the Hunter Valley, and he more recently completed the Master of Wine Technology and Viticulture degree at the University of Melbourne.

♀♀♀♀♀ **The Hallmark Heathcote Shiraz 2015** Hand-picked, basket-pressed, matured for 18 months in French oak, neither fined nor filtered. Deep, dense colour suggests a ripe wine that manages to walk around its alcohol level without missing a beat. There are positively juicy dark fruits that linger on the finish without losing their shape or appeal. Screwcap. 15.2% alc. **Rating** 94 **To** 2035 $55

The Ensemble Heathcote Shiraz Viognier 2015 A 95/5% co-fermented blend, matured for 18 months in French barriques. At the absolute extreme of power for this style; anise, pepper and licorice emanate from the bouquet, black fruits line up in military precision providing support (if needed). A challenging style that will greatly appeal to more than a few. Screwcap. 14.7% alc. **Rating** 94 **To** 2035 $32

♀♀♀♀♀ **Cambrian Gold Heathcote Viognier 2016 Rating** 93 **To** 2020 $35
The Third Man Heathcote Mourvedre 2015 Rating 92 **To** 2030 $28

Simão & Co

PO Box 231, Rutherglen, Vic 3685 **Region** North East Victoria
T 0439 459 183 **www**.simaoandco.com.au **Open** Not
Winemaker Simon Killeen **Est.** 2014 **Dozens** 800
'Simão' is Portuguese for Simon, an inspiration far from Rutherglen where Simon Killeen
was born and bred. He grew up with vines all around him, and knew from an early age he
was going to become a winemaker. After working in wineries across Australia, France and
Portugal, he returned home to establish Simão & Co in 2014. It leaves time for him, by one
means or another, to watch every minute of every game played by the Geelong Cats and hunt
down the ruins of ghost wineries around Rutherglen.

King Valley Sauvignon Blanc 2017 From a cool site in the King Valley, so
this is steely yet textural, flavoursome yet reined-in with bath salts–like acidity. It's
mouth-watering with a nod to passionfruit pith and lemon zest, then branches
out to include kaffir lime, nettles and pine needles alongside a slatey, lemony-saline
sensation on the palate. Judicious and balanced oak influence make it hard to stop
at one glass. Screwcap. 12.5% alc. **Rating** 95 **To** 2021 $24 JF ✪

Ugni Blanc 2017 Simon Killeen has a deep love of wine history – from 98yo
vines in Glenrowan and 'based on great-grandpa's old notes of 1924, I'm trying to
make a wine as close to what he would have done'. This modern take is textural
and grippy thanks to skin contact, full mlf and lees stirring, yet fresh as it stays
in tank for 3 months. While the variety's natural acidity is paramount, flavours
of honeycomb, preserved lemons, stone fruit and tangy pickled quince abound.
It's also super dry, savoury, smoky, phenolic, flavoursome, complex, detailed and
delicious. Screwcap. 12.8% alc. **Rating** 95 **To** 2022 $32 JF ✪

Beechworth Shiraz 2016 About 40% whole bunches with the remainder whole
berries, on skins 3 weeks, pressed to French puncheons and barriques (30% new),
aged for 10 months. Bright mid-garnet; the wine balances savouriness with
ripe fruit. Fuller-bodied but not big, juicy fruit but not sweet, tannins perfectly
poised and oak seamlessly integrated. It also incorporates dark red fruit, star anise
and cinnamon, some Chinese five-spice and dried herbs. Mouth-watering and
delicious. Screwcap. 13.8% alc. **Rating** 95 **To** 2025 $32 JF ✪

Alpine Valleys Tempranillo 2016 There's a hint of cool alpine herbs, menthol-
like and appealing as it blends in with plum compote and wafts of ripe fruit, yet
the palate is lively and savoury and refreshing acidity the key. It's a lighter framed
wine, earthy with a hint of sarsaparilla, and the supple tannins indicate it's best
enjoyed young. Screwcap. 13.5% alc. **Rating** 94 **To** 2021 $32 JF

Nebbiolo Rose 2017 Rating 93 **To** 2019 $24 JF ✪
Alpine Valleys Nebbiolo 2015 Rating 93 **To** 2024 $37 JF
Branca Verdelho NV Rating 92 $27 JF

Simon Whitlam & Co

PO Box 1108, Woollahra, NSW 1350 **Region** Hunter Valley
T (02) 9007 5331 **Open** Not
Winemaker Edgar Vales (Contract) **Est.** 1979 **Dozens** 3000
My association with the owners of Simon Whitlam – Andrew and Hady Simon, Nicholas
and Judy Whitlam, and Grant Breen – dates back to the late 1970s, at which time I was a
consultant to the Simon's leading wine retail shop in Sydney, the Camperdown Cellars. The
association continued for a time after I moved to Melbourne in '83, but ceased altogether
in '87 when Camperdown Cellars was sold (it was later merged with Arrowfield Wines).
The Simon Whitlam label was part of the deal, and it passed through a number of corporate
owners until 20 years later, when the original partners regained control of the business.

Hunter Valley Semillon 2012 Estate-grown, 6yo Hunter Valley semillon at
this price makes winemakers cry and customers jump for joy. Relatively little
change since first tasted in Jan '16; lemongrass/acidity still the driver, and will

remain, so another decade should be a doddle. Screwcap. 11.7% alc. **Rating** 96
To 2032 $22 **○**

❦❦❦❦❦ Hunter Valley Semillon Sauvignon Blanc 2012 Rating 93 To 2020 $24 **○**
Hunter Valley Chardonnay 2012 Rating 92 To 2023 $22 **○**
Hunter Valley Verdelho 2011 Rating 90 To 2020 $24

Sinapius Vineyard ★★★★★

4232 Bridport Road, Pipers Brook, Tas 7254 **Region** Northern Tasmania
T 0417 341 764 **www**.sinapius.com.au **Open** Jun–Aug Thur–Mon 12–5
Winemaker Vaughn Dell **Est.** 2005 **Dozens** 1500 **Vyds** 4.07ha
Vaughn Dell and Linda Morice purchased the former Golders Vineyard in 2005 (planted
in 1994). More recent vineyard plantings include 13 clones of pinot noir and eight clones
of chardonnay, as well as a small amount of gruner veltliner. The vineyard is close-planted,
ranging from 5100 vines per hectare for the gruner veltliner, to 10 250 vines per hectare
for the pinot noir and chardonnay. The wines are made with a minimalist approach: natural
ferments, basket pressing, extended lees ageing, and minimal fining and filtration.

❦❦❦❦❦ Home Vineyard Chardonnay 2016 Tasmania and chardonnay – a perfect
marriage. The gamut of varietal/regional/winemaking flavours manifest in white
stone fruit, citrus, creamy soft lemon curd, with subtle oak influence. It is is almost
linear thanks to the line of natural acidity, and yet there's a bounty of flavour
within. Screwcap. 13% alc. **Rating** 95 To 2025 $55 JF
Vintage Extra Brut 2006 This is 100% chardonnay; the mid straw–pale gold
hue hardly surprising given this has spent 10 years on lees, disgorged in Jan '17.
It is still so fresh and tightly wound thanks to electrifying, racy acidity. There's a
powerful thread wound around citrus notes with lemon curd and clotted cream,
plus some savoury, complex, lees-ageing characters in its midst, especially of
buttered toast with Vegemite. Cork. 12.5% alc. **Rating** 95 $80 JF

❦❦❦❦❦ La Clairiere Close Planted Pinot Noir 2016 Rating 93 To 2024 $68 JF
Clem Blanc 2017 Rating 92 To 2022 $38 JF
The Enclave Close Planted Pinot Noir 2016 Rating 92 To 2025 $80 JF
Esme Rouge Gamay 2017 Rating 90 To 2019 $38 JF

Sinclair's Gully ★★★☆

288 Colonial Drive, Norton Summit, SA 5136 **Region** Adelaide Hills
T (08) 8390 1995 **www**.sinclairsgully.com **Open** Aug–June Sun & public hols 12–4
Winemaker Contract **Est.** 1998 **Dozens** 900 **Vyds** 1ha
Sue and Sean Delaney purchased their property at Norton Summit in 1997. The property had
a significant stand of remnant native vegetation, with a state conservation rating, and much
energy has been spent on restoring 8ha of pristine bushland, home to 130 species of native
plants and 66 species of native birds, some recorded as threatened or rare. Their adoption of
biodynamic viticulture has coincided with numerous awards for their protection of the natural
environment and, more recently, ecotourism. Sinclair's operates the only ECO-certified cellar
door in the Adelaide Hills, and has won innumerable ecological and general tourism awards.
Sparkling wine disgorgement demonstrations are a particular attraction.

❦❦❦❦❦ Rubida 2008 Despite 6 years on lees, there is no colour development. Here
the colour is fresh straw, the dosage of 8g/l just within bounds. Diam. 13% alc.
Rating 92 $40

❦❦❦❦ Cheeky Little Bastard Unwooded Grenache 2015 Rating 89 To 2020 $25
Grumpy Old Bastard McLaren Flat Grenache 2014 Rating 89 $32

Singlefile Wines

90 Walter Road, Denmark, WA 6333 **Region** Great Southern
T 1300 885 807 **www.**singlefilewines.com **Open** 7 days 11–5
Winemaker Mike Garland, Coby Ladwig **Est.** 2007 **Dozens** 8000 **Vyds** 3.75ha
In 1968 geologist Phil Snowden and wife Viv moved from South Africa to Perth, where they developed their successful multinational mining and resource services company, Snowden Resources. Following the sale of the company in 2004, they turned their attention to their long-held desire to make and enjoy fine wine. In '07 they bought an established vineyard (planted in 1989) in the beautiful Denmark subregion. They pulled out the old shiraz and merlot vines, kept and planted more chardonnay, and retained Larry Cherubino to set up partnerships with established vineyards in Frankland River, Porongurup, Denmark, Pemberton and Margaret River. The cellar door, tasting room and restaurant are strongly recommended. The quality consistency of their Singlefile wines is outstanding, as is their value for money. Exports to the US, Singapore, Japan, Hong Kong and China.

🍷🍷🍷🍷🍷 **The Vivienne Denmark Chardonnay 2015** Picked across three passes through the vineyard focusing on separate plots, forming a beautifully crafted chardonnay, irrepressible and delicious to drink, despite its undoubted ageability. Toasted hazelnuts, almond croissant and truffle notes override the underlying creamy peachiness. A visceral mineral thrust pushes it long, with the oak buried beneath the sheer concentration of flavour. As a whole, seamless. If I tasted this blind on a good day, I may think it a fine producer's meursault from a top site. Screwcap. 13% alc. **Rating** 98 To 2029 $80 NG ✪

The Philip Adrian Frankland River Cabernet Sauvignon 2015 Extended pre-fermentation cold soak. Good crimson-purple; an unambiguously full-bodied cabernet, laden to the gills with all things cabernet. Blackcurrant, black olive, earth, tar and tannins genuflecting to no one, new French oak (60%) and 18 months in barrel all provide the answers to the secrets of this majestic wine. Screwcap. 14.5% alc. **Rating** 97 To 2049 $80 ✪

🍷🍷🍷🍷🍷 **Single Vineyard Mount Barker Riesling 2017** From Pearse vineyard grapes from the site of the first planting of riesling in the Great Southern. The hand-picked grapes show the innate power old vines can produce. The bouquet is scented with nuances of bath powder, spice and blossom, the linear drive of the palate striking like a bolt of lightning; minerally citrus fruits with perfect balance and texture. Screwcap. 12.3% alc. **Rating** 96 To 2037 $30 ✪

Run Free Great Southern Riesling 2017 This is the obverse of its line-priced sibling. The fruit impact is immediate in the bouquet and palate, with a lime infusion and a long, flowing palate. Despite all this, it is refined and genteel in its demeanour, ready to welcome you tonight or in 5-10 years. Screwcap. 12.1% alc. **Rating** 95 To 2027 $25 ✪

Family Reserve Denmark Chardonnay 2017 Whole-bunch pressed to Frnch oak (40% new) and the remainder to single passed oak – all French. This is a powerful chardonnay of rapier-like intensity and precision with an oaky carapace that needs time to shed. The cinnamon and nutmeg choir is the oak speaking, meshing with a mineral riff to shepherd stone fruit allusions, toasted nuts and nougat into a long finish and an even longer future. Screwcap. 13.2% alc. **Rating** 95 To 2028 $50 NG

Single Vineyard Frankland River Shiraz 2016 Deep colour; the bouquet is immediately and intensely complex with cedar, cigar box, licorice and spice notes woven through black fruits, the palate is away and racing from the first sip. It's very savoury and spicy, its power threatening through to the mid-palate, but (happily) backs off on the finish and aftertaste thanks to fine-spun tannins. Screwcap. 14.5% alc. **Rating** 95 To 2036 $37

Clement V 2016 A blend of 52% shiraz, 30% grenache, 18% mourvedre fermented separately, matured in barriques (30% new) for 10 months. The majority of GSMs are made for early consumption, but this wine is most definitely in the minority – while its balance and structure mean you can drink it now, its development potential is written in capital letters. Shiraz will always be the blend master, in particular with its black fruits and licorice, but both it and the grenache have so much more to say than that. Great value. Screwcap. 14.5% alc. **Rating** 95 To 2030 $30 ◯

Great Southern Cabernet Sauvignon Merlot 2016 Comprising 79% cabernet and 21% merlot, cold soaked in small fermenters for 12 days for aroma and colour, before undergoing fermentation and further maceration to polymerise the tannins. While 40% of the wine was matured in new barriques, the remainder was in used wood for 10 months. The result is a savoury meld of damson plum, redcurrant and bay leaf tannins, firmly meshed with vanilla, graphite and cedar. They are firm enough to direct the ship, while sufficiently pliant to breach at a younger stage. Great value. Screwcap. 14.3% alc. **Rating** 95 To 2025 $25 NG ◯

Single Vineyard Frankland River Cabernet Sauvignon 2016 From the Riversdale Vineyard, 10 days cold soak, 8 days post-ferment maceration, matured for 16 months in Bordeaux barrels (40% new). Good colour. In the line of prior releases, with flavour coming from every direction you look. Blackcurrant/cassis flavours are first up; high quality French oak still settling in for the journey, a contributor both now and later; the tannins were well managed/massaged. Screwcap. 14.5% alc. **Rating** 95 To 2036 $37

ŶŶŶŶŶ **Great Southern Riesling 2017** Rating 93 To 2032 $25 ◯
Denmark Blanc de Blancs 2011 Rating 93 $80
Chardonnay Pinot Noir NV Rating 93 $30 NG
Great Southern Semillon Sauvignon Blanc 2017 Rating 92 To 2022 $25 NG ◯
Run Free Cabernet Shiraz 2015 Rating 92 To 2022 $25 NG ◯
Run Free Pinot Noir 2017 Rating 91 To 2023 $25 NG
Run Free Shiraz 2016 Rating 91 To 2022 $25 NG
Denmark Pinot Chardonnay 2011 Rating 90 $80

Sirromet Wines   ★★★★

850–938 Mount Cotton Road, Mount Cotton, Qld 4165 **Region** Granite Belt
T (07) 3206 2999 **www**.sirromet.com **Open** 7 days 9–4.30
Winemaker Adam Chapman, Jessica Ferguson **Est.** 1998 **Dozens** 55 000 **Vyds** 98.7ha
This ambitious venture has succeeded in its aim of creating Queensland's premier winery. The founding Morris family retained a list of skilled proessionals: a leading architect to design the striking state-of-the-art winery; the state's foremost viticultural consultant to plant three major vineyards (in the Granite Belt); and the most skilled winemaker practising in Queensland, Adam Chapman, to make the wine. Sirromet has a 200-seat restaurant, a wine club, and is firmly aimed at the tourist market, taking advantage of its situation halfway between Brisbane and the Gold Coast. Exports to Sweden, South Korea, Papua New Guinea, Hong Kong, China and Japan.

ŶŶŶŶŶ **Elezo x Sirromet Wild Ferment Granite Belt Tasmania Pinot Noir 2016** A blend of 59% Granite Belt, 41% Coal River Valley. The first such blend, and one can only hope there will be more. This wine could not possibly be made in the Granite Belt alone, but that part of its DNA still shows. The two components were fermented and matured separately, ultimately blended after 6 months in French oak. Savoury/spicy elements on the one hand, plum and black cherry on the other; no new oak and minimal tannins throw the accent onto the fruit. Screwcap. 14.3% alc. **Rating** 94 To 2023 $45

Saint Jude's Road Grand Reserve Monopole Granite Belt Cabernet Sauvignon 2014 By sheer accident (serendipitously), this wine contains a part of every one of the '16 estate cabernet blocks, and 3050l was the total make (388 dozen). It's an elegant wine with excellent balance and length, and clear varietal expression. Screwcap. 14% alc. **Rating** 94 To 2029 $300

2016 Granite Belt Late Harvest The fermentation was stopped with 105g/l of residual sugar. Pale orange-pink; this is an exceptional achievement – yes it's luscious and sweet, but it's so much more than that. It is long, balanced and has exotic flavours of guava, pears flambéed then bottled, and burnt spices. Screwcap. 9.2% alc. **Rating** 94 **To** 2023 $47

ㅇㅇㅇㅇㅇ **Signature Collection Terry Morris Granite Belt Shiraz Viognier 2016**
Rating 90 **To** 2024 $36 SC
Signature Collection Terry Morris Granite Belt Shiraz Viognier 2015
Rating 90 **To** 2029 $36

Sister's Run ★★★★

PO Box 382, Tanunda, SA 5352 **Region** Barossa
T (08) 8563 1400 **www**.sistersrun.com.au **Open** Not
Winemaker Elena Brooks **Est.** 2001 **Dozens** NFP
Sister's Run is owned by noted Barossa Valley vignerons Carl and Peggy Lindner (also owners of Langmeil), directly employing the skills of Elena Brooks as winemaker, and, indirectly, the marketing know-how of husband Zar Brooks. The stiletto and boot on the label are those of Elena, and their motto – 'The truth is in the vineyard, but the proof is in the glass' – is, I would guess, the work of Zar Brooks. Exports to all major markets.

ㅇㅇㅇㅇㅇ **Epiphany McLaren Vale Shiraz 2016** Cloves, roasted plums, touches of graphite and peppercorn. This is a wine of richness and style, the value high, the enjoyment likewise. Feel and flavour at a very tasty price. Screwcap. 14.5% alc. **Rating** 93 **To** 2025 $22 CM ✪
Calvary Hill Lyndoch Shiraz 2016 A juicy, jammy wine with sweet berry flavours filling the palate before more savoury, herbal, woody characters move into focus. Nicely done. Screwcap. 14.5% alc. **Rating** 91 **To** 2024 $22 CM ✪
Sunday Slippers Lyndoch Barossa Chardonnay 2017 A flash of fresh fruit, citrus as much as stone fruit, washes juicily through the palate. Nicely handled and presented. Screwcap. 12% alc. **Rating** 90 **To** 2021 $20 CM ✪

Sittella Wines ★★★★★

100 Barrett Street, Herne Hill, WA 6056 **Region** Swan Valley
T (08) 9296 2600 **www**.sittella.com.au **Open** Tues–Sun & public hols 11–5
Winemaker Colby Quirk, Yuri Berns **Est.** 1998 **Dozens** 8000 **Vyds** 10ha
Simon and Maaike Berns acquired a 7ha block (with 5ha of vines) at Herne Hill, making the first wine in 1998 and opening a most attractive cellar door facility. They also own the Wildberry Estate vineyard in Margaret River. Consistent and significant wine show success has brought well-deserved recognition for the wines. Exports to Japan and China.

ㅇㅇㅇㅇㅇ **Reserve Wilyabrup Margaret River Chardonnay 2017** We've got a live one here. It's a wine of intensity, length, texture and beauty. It announces itself on the nose, charges across the palate, and bursts out through the finish. Flint, stone fruits, the sizzle of citrus. It's a super wine. Screwcap. 13% alc. **Rating** 96 **To** 2025 $33 CM ✪
Berns Reserve 2016 A blend of 93% cabernet sauvignon, 5% malbec, 2% petit verdot; 40% new French oak. It's elegant for the most part, but it's stern and tannic to close. This isn't going anywhere in a hurry. Boysenberry, bay leaf and leather notes before blackcurrant and mint. There's a toasty cedar wood character about the edges, but for the most part oak doesn't add much to the flavour profile. It's still really finding its feet but it would be hard to go wrong here as a cellaring prospect. Screwcap. 14% alc. **Rating** 95 **To** 2034 $58 CM
Single Vineyard Margaret River Cabernet Malbec 2016 It's a chocolatey expression of this blend – and it's a fine one. Here's the quick summary: power and balance. It tastes of blackcurrant, bay and dark chocolate, and throughout it feels both confident and at ease. Very good. Screwcap. 14% alc. **Rating** 94 **To** 2032 $28 CM ✪

Avant-Garde Series Margaret River Malbec 2016 Leather laced with blackberry and cedar wood. It sounds like a lyric; it tastes like a song. There's a softness to the texture, a richness to the fruit, and a firm dryness to the finish. It doesn't put a foot wrong. Screwcap. 14% alc. **Rating** 94 **To** 2025 $38 CM

♥♥♥♥♡ **Field Blend Avant-Garde Series Margaret River Pinot Gris Pinot Noir 2017** Rating 93 To 2021 $28 CM
Coffee Rock Swan Valley Shiraz 2016 Rating 93 To 2027 $55 CM
Avant-Garde Series Swan Valley Grenache 2016 Rating 93 To 2024 $38 CM
Avant-Garde Series Swan Valley Tempranillo 2017 Rating 93 To 2023 $38 CM
Methode Traditionnelle Cuvee Blanc NV Rating 93 $29 CM
Tinta Rouge Shiraz Tempranillo Petit Verdot Grenache 2017 Rating 92 To 2023 $19 CM ❂
Methode Traditionnelle Chenin Blanc NV Rating 92 $22 CM ❂
The Wild One Margaret River Sauvignon Blanc 2017 Rating 91 To 2020 $22 CM ❂
The Calling Single Vineyard Swan Valley Verdelho 2017 Rating 91 To 2021 $19 CM ❂
Marie Christien Lugten Grand Vintage Methode Traditionelle 2013 Rating 91 $36 CM
Blanc de Blancs NV Rating 91 $32 CM
Swan Valley Shiraz 2016 Rating 90 To 2024 $27 CM

Six Acres ★★★★

20 Ferndale Road, Silvan, Vic 3795 **Region** Yarra Valley
T 0408 991 741 **www**.sixacres.com.au **Open** W'ends 10–4, or by appt
Winemaker Ralph Zuccaro **Est.** 1999 **Dozens** 470 **Vyds** 1.64ha
Nestled in the southern hills of the Yarra Valley, Six Acres boutique winery and vineyard is owned and worked by the Zuccaro family. Planted in 1999 by Ralph and Lesley Zuccaro, the vineyard (pinot noir, cabernet sauvignon and merlot) is dry grown in deep red volcanic soil, with yields kept low to encourage balance and concentration within the grapes. Currently biologically farmed, the family's goal is to move towards organic/sustainable grapegrowing. The small size of the property means that the whole family is involved in the minimal intervention winemaking process. A visit to Six Acres will likely involve being greeted by a Zuccaro family member as they emerge from the rows of vines or from the barrel shed.

♥♥♥♥♡ **Yarra Valley Chardonnay 2016** There are clearly good things going on at this estate when all fruit is hand-harvested, crafted with such precision across the range and sold for a song! This was gently crushed by feet, too, releasing ample flavour and texture; peach, nectarine and oatmeal lees imparting detail and breadth. Creamy oak rims and some wild yeast funk at the core. A mid-weighted, plump chardonnay loaded with flavour and drinkability. Screwcap. 12.5% alc. **Rating** 93 **To** 2022 $25 NG ❂

Yarra Valley Pinot Noir 2016 Red berry fruits and candied orange peel are coaxed to a sensation of amaro bitterness by spindle-laced tannins brushed with clove and other whole-bunch goodness. This is a sassy, light to gently mid-weighted pinot, handled with aplomb. The minimally intervened deck is on show, mitigating fruit sweetness while conferring structure, yet not to the expense of regional nuance, poise and deliciousness. Screwcap. 13.5% alc. **Rating** 93 **To** 2022 $30 NG

Yarra Valley Rose 2017 A delicious, lip-smacking rose with a refined pale hue, crunchy strawberry and raspberry CO_2 pop across the palate, with some garden herb strewn about too, helping to tidy things up in the name of savour over sweetness. Not short on flavour. Screwcap. 13.5% alc. **Rating** 92 **To** 2019 $22 NG ❂

Blue Label Yarra Valley Pinot Noir 2016 This has Yarra pinot's stamp of sapid red fruit flavours strung over a mosaic of whole-cluster spikiness, gentle in its rasp, with the cardamom, clove and nutmeg notes that ensue, all tailing across a sappy, expansive finish. Lots of flavour and sophistication stuffed into a well-priced package. Screwcap. 13.5% alc. **Rating** 91 **To** 2021 $22 NG ○

Skillogalee

Trevarrick Road, Sevenhill via Clare, SA 5453 **Region** Clare Valley
T (08) 8843 4311 **www.**skillogalee.com.au **Open** 7 days 7.30–5
Winemaker Dave Palmer, David King **Est.** 1970 **Dozens** 15000 **Vyds** 50.3ha
David and Diana Palmer have fully capitalised on the exceptional fruit quality of the Skillogalee vineyards. All the wines are generous and full-flavoured, particularly the reds. In 2002 the Palmers purchased Waninga Vineyards their next-door neighbour, with 30ha of 30yo vines, allowing an increase in production without any change in quality or style. Exports to the UK, Denmark, Switzerland, Malaysia, Thailand and Singapore.

🍷🍷🍷🍷🍷 **Basket Pressed Clare Valley The Cabernets 2014** With 85% cabernet sauvignon, 9% malbec, 6% cabernet franc; open-fermented, matured in predominantly French hogsheads for 24 months. The blend and vinification have had the synergistic outcome doubtless hoped for. The wine is lusciously full-bodied, with the components knitted together by the tannins and French oak. These Skillogalee releases stand outside – indeed above – the normal borders of the Clare Valley red wine style. Screwcap. 14% alc. **Rating** 95 **To** 2034 $33 ○
Basket Pressed Clare Valley Shiraz 2015 From dry-grown vines surrounding the Skillogalee homestead, open-fermented, matured in French and American hogsheads. A wine that has benefited in no uncertain terms from the vintage. It is medium-bodied, with a velvety softness encompassing the fruit, tannins and oak. It's hardly necessary to say its balance is nigh on perfect. Screwcap. 14% alc. **Rating** 94 **To** 2035 $33

🍷🍷🍷🍷🍷 **Clare Valley Riesling 2017** Rating 91 To 2027 $25
Trevarrick Single Contour Clare Valley Riesling 2015 Rating 91 To 2035 $52
Clare Valley Gewurztraminer 2016 Rating 90 To 2023 $27
Take Two Basket Pressed Clare Valley Shiraz Cabernet 2015 Rating 90 To 2028 $24

Small Island Wines

Drink Co, Shop 10, 33 Salamanca Place, Hobart, Tas 7004 **Region** Southern Tasmania
T 0414 896 930 **www.**smallislandwines.com **Open** Mon–Sat 10–8
Winemaker James Broinowski **Est.** 2015 **Dozens** 3500 **Vyds** 3ha
Tasmanian-born James Broinowski completed his Bachelor of Viticulture and Oenology at the University of Adelaide in 2013. He was faced with the same problem as many other young graduates wanting to strike out on their own: cash. While others in his predicament may have found the same solution, his is the first wine venture to successfully seek crowdfunding. The first year ('15) allowed him to purchase pinot noir from Glengarry in the north of the island, making 2100 bottles of pinot noir that won a gold medal at the Royal International Hobart Wine Show '16, and 200 bottles of rose that sold out in four days at the Taste of Tasmania Festival '15. In '16 he was able to buy pinot from the highly rated Gala Estate on the east coast, and back up the '15 purchase from the Glengarry Vineyard with a '16 purchase. It looks very much like a potential acorn to oak story, for the quality of the wines is seriously good.

🍷🍷🍷🍷🍷 **Single Vineyard North Pinot Noir 2016** A total of 80 dozen made. From the Glengarry Vineyard. Bottled unfined and unfiltered. It's a powerhouse wine with the perfume to give it a prettiness. This steps you straight into 'knock your socks off' territory. Undergrowth, mint, plum, cranberry and assorted twigs and spices. Wood smoke. Reduction. There's a great deal going on, a wide spread of tannin too, but the inherent depth of the palate and the full fan of the finish shoot this straight to the top of the quality pile. Screwcap. 14.5% alc. **Rating** 96 **To** 2028 $50 CM ○

Single Vineyard East Pinot Noir 2016 It fits into the perfumed steamroller category. It's light but powerful, pretty but not at the expense of substance. It looks as though Small Island Wines is a star in the making. Crisp red berries, undergrowth, woody spices, a svelte impersonation of plum, florals. Billboards of savouriness line the road of fruit. It's a brilliant wine. Screwcap. 13% alc. **Rating** 96 **To** 2028 $50 CM ○

Black Label Pinot Noir 2016 Made using grapes from both the Gala (east) and Glengarry (north) vineyards with 180 dozen produced. Perfumed and pretty on the one hand, stewy and a little grumpy on the other. It rushes up to greet you but then holds you in a moody stare. Cranberry, forest berries, florals, sweet dry spices. It has all the basics covered, but it then adds some flare. You'd bet on this developing well. Screwcap. 13.5% alc. **Rating** 94 **To** 2025 CM

♥♥♥♥♡ **Single Vineyard South Riesling 2017 Rating** 93 **To** 2026 $35 CM
Patsie's Blush Rose 2017 Rating 92 **To** 2020 $30 CM

Smallfry Wines ★★★★★

13 Murray Street, Angaston, SA 5353 **Region** Barossa Valley
T (08) 8564 2182 **www.**smallfrywines.com.au **Open** By appt (0412 153 243)
Winemaker Wayne Ahrens **Est.** 2005 **Dozens** 6500 **Vyds** 27ha
The engagingly named Smallfry Wines is the venture of Wayne Ahrens and partner Suzi Hilder. Wayne is from a fifth-generation Barossa family; Suzi is the daughter of well-known Upper Hunter viticulturist Richard Hilder and wife Del, former partners in Pyramid Hill Wines. Both Wayne and Suzi have degrees from CSU, and both have extensive experience – Suzi was a consultant viticulturist, and Wayne's track record includes seven vintages as a cellar hand at Orlando Wyndham and other smaller Barossa wineries. Their vineyards in the Eden Valley (led by cabernet sauvignon and riesling) and the Vine Vale area of the Barossa Valley (shiraz, grenache, semillon, mourvedre, cabernet sauvignon and riesling) are certified biodynamic/organic. Exports to the UK, the US, Canada, the Philippines, Singapore, Hong Kong, Japan and China.

♥♥♥♥♥ **Eden Valley Riesling 2017** Hand-picked, whole-bunch pressed, fermentation stopped with 4.5g/l residual sugar remaining, filling the bouquet with the scents from a garden of flowers. The balance and mouthfeel are quite exceptional, coating the mouth with citrus fruits held tight by livewire acidity. Screwcap. 10.5% alc. **Rating** 95 **To** 2027 $28 ○

El Grande Barossa Shiraz 2012 Hand-picked, crushed and destemmed, open-fermented with 4% muscadelle, matured in a new French hogshead for 40 months. It's important to remember that while the oak was new when the wine went into it, by the time it came out was over 3yo. The co-fermentation of muscadelle (a blend invented by the late Peter Lehmann 30 years or so before the arrival of viognier) has done its job very well with the still-bright colour. Juicy black fruits from a great fruit vintage and the time investment have been well worth it. Screwcap. 14.8% alc. **Rating** 95 **To** 2027 $48

Barossa Shiraz 2016 Hand-picked, crushed and destemmed, open-fermented, some whole bunches, matured for 18 months in used French and American oak. The medium-bodied palate runs easily between the banks of red and black fruits on either side, the fluid nature of the palate enhanced by the quiescent tannin and oak inputs. Takes a while to work its way into full perspective. Screwcap. 14.5% alc. **Rating** 94 **To** 2032 $36

♥♥♥♥♡ **Eden Valley Cabernet Sauvignon 2015 Rating** 93 **To** 2030 $36
Barossa Joven 2017 Rating 90 **To** 2020 $28

Smidge Wines

150 Tatachilla Road, McLaren Vale, SA 5171 **Region** McLaren Vale
T 0419 839 964 **www**.smidgewines.com **Open** By appt
Winemaker Matt Wenk **Est.** 2004 **Dozens** 5000 **Vyds** 4.1ha

Smidge Wines is owned by Matt Wenk and wife Trish Callaghan, and was for many years an out-of-hours occupation for Matt; his day job was as winemaker for Two Hands Wines and Sandow's End. In 2013 he retired from Two Hands, and plans to increase production of Smidge to 8000 dozen over the next few years. His retirement meant the Smidge wines could no longer be made at Two Hands, and the winemaking operations have been moved to McLaren Vale, where Smidge is currently leasing a small winery. Smidge owns the vineyard in Willunga, which provides the grapes for all their cabernet sauvignon releases and some of the McLaren Vale shiraz. The vision is to build a modern, customised facility on the Willunga property in the not-too-distant future. Exports to the UK, the US, South Korea and China.

Houdini McLaren Vale Shiraz 2016 From one estate vineyard plus other vineyards across McLaren Vale, crushed/destemmed, 11 months on French oak (11% new). An extremely interesting medium-bodied wine that immediately captures attention with the energy and focus of its plum and blackberry fruits which marry intensity with elegance, heightened further by silky tannins. Fantastic value, and ready when you are. Screwcap. 14.5% alc. **Rating** 96 To 2026 $23 **○**

Magic Dirt Menglers Hill Eden Valley Shiraz 2015 From 12yo vines planted by long-term growers, the Mattschoss family; matured in 3yo French barriques for 30 months, not fined or filtered. The vineyard elevation of 480m gives a distinct cool-grown edge to the dark cherry and bramble flavours of the elegant, medium-bodied palate and its compliant tannins. Screwcap. 13.9% alc. **Rating** 96 To 2035 $100

Pedra Branca Adelaide Hills Tempranillo 2016 The back label states without equivocation, 'made in very small quantities'. From this point on the utterances are determinedly Delphic. The colour is a superb crimson, the tannins mouthwatering, red fruits a silver bullet. Its texture might well have come from an egg, but the cedary oak says French oak. This is one smart wine. Screwcap. 13.5% alc. **Rating** 96 To 2025 $45 **○**

Magic Dirt Penrice Barossa Valley Shiraz 2015 This isn't a best barrels series, it's a selection of the barrel from a particular vineyard that most truly reflects the terroir of the vineyard. Here 40yo vines on a west-facing slope at 360m, grown by six generations, matured in 3yo French barriques for 30 months. Exotic black fruits, spices, licorice aromas and flavours. A full-bodied wine of power and intensity, the tannins akin to built-in cupboards. Screwcap. 14.2% alc. **Rating** 95 To 2040 $100

Grand Rutherglen Muscat NV The addition of a small amount of fresh material with each release has had all the right consequences. Very complex; plum pudding, burnt toffee and spice flavours, then cleansing rancio on the finish. Cork. 18% alc. **Rating** 95 $85

Pedra Branca Adelaide Hills Sauvignon Blanc 2016 Part wild-fermented with cloudy juice in 1yo barriques, part fermented in tank – this used to top the barriques monthly, 10 months on lees with monthly batonnage. A pretty nice wine from 25yo vines. It has a one-track citrus mind, lemon and grapefruit the protagonists. Screwcap. 12.1% alc. **Rating** 94 To 2020 $45

Houdini McLaren Vale Grenache Rose 2017 Hand-picked from a 70yo block, 24 hours cold soak, wild-fermented, 4 months on lees. A striking wine, bone dry, with a savoury/spicy framework for the juicy sour cherry palate. Screwcap. 12% alc. **Rating** 94 To 2020 $23 **○**

S Barossa Valley Shiraz 2015 This wine is 58% from Moppa, 29% Penrice foothills and 13% Menglers Hills, matured for 30 months in 3yo French barriques. Barrels with more complexity were chosen for inclusion, the volume turned up well into medium to full-bodied territory. Black fruits reign without serious challenge, stern tannins their lieutenants. Screwcap. 14.1% alc. **Rating** 94 To 2040 $65

La Grenouille McLaren Vale Cabernet Sauvignon 2015 Estate-grown near Willunga, matured for 22 months in (predominantly) used French oak. Variety and region come through with equal strength, reaffirming the region's maritime climate's suitability for quality cabernet. While no more than medium-bodied, the wine has the patrician mark of cabernet, savoury and tending austere, but shouldering arms on the long, well-balanced finish. Screwcap. 14.5% alc. Rating 94 To 2029 $30 ☻

ΨΨΨΨ   **The Ging McLaren Vale Shiraz 2015** Rating 89 To 2025 $30

Snake + Herring   ★★★★★

PO Box 918, Dunsborough, WA 6281 **Region** South West Australia
T 0419 487 427 **www.**snakeandherring.com.au **Open** Not
Winemaker Tony Davis **Est.** 2010 **Dozens** 7000
Tony ('Snake') Davis and Redmond ('Herring') Sweeny both started their university degrees before finding that they were utterly unsuited to their respective courses. Having stumbled across Margaret River, Tony's life changed forever; he enrolled at the University of Adelaide, thereafter doing vintages in the Eden Valley, Oregon, Beaujolais and Tasmania, before three years at Plantagenet, next at Brown Brothers, then at a senior winemaking role at Yalumba; a six-year stint designing Millbrook Winery in the Perth Hills; and four years with Howard Park in Margaret River. Redmond's circuitous course included a chartered accountancy degree and employment with an international accounting firm in Busselton, and the subsequent establishment of Forester Estate in 2001, in partnership with Kevin McKay. Back on home turf Redmond is the marketing and financial controller of Snake + Herring. Exports to China.

ΨΨΨΨΨ   **Hallelujah Porongurup Chardonnay 2016** Gleaming straw-green; pink grapefruit, white nectarine and peach, nutty oak. Has the iron fist in a velvet glove power of Porongurup – never obvious, but always there. Screwcap. Rating 96 To 2027 $45 ☻
Cannonball Margaret River Cabernet Sauvignon Merlot Petit Verdot 2015 Makes it look easy. This fills the mouth with flavour, seduces as it lays it all on, and reaches out authoritatively through the finish. Every inch of it feels classic. The hit of blackcurrant, the bay leaf lift, the pencilly oak, the dark chocolate, the way boysenberry notes hurry the inkiness along, the way spice and tobacco characters look quite happy ensconced in the dark-but-fresh folds of fruit. Screwcap. 14% alc. Rating 96 To 2035 $45 CM ☻
Perfect Day Margaret River Sauvignon Blanc Semillon 2017 Beautiful wine. Ever so textural. More than enough fruit too, showing both weight and push-ahead power. Gravel and grasses, gooseberry and anise. Excellent. Screwcap. 12% alc. Rating 95 To 2022 $24 CM ☻
Corduroy Margaret River Chardonnay 2016 Excellent intensity and palate weight and length. This leaves no room for question marks over its quality. It tastes of sweet, ripe peach, lemon, toasty oak and flint, and while there's plenty to hold on to, it's a wine of charm rather than obviousness. That said, it's a quintessential Margaret River chardonnay. Screwcap. 13% alc. Rating 95 To 2023 $45 CM ☻
Redemption Great Southern Shiraz 2015 Sourced entirely from Mount Barker, and used three small 1t open fermenters, all with wild yeast; one with 100% whole bunches, one with 20% and the remainder crushed and destemmed, the third with 100% whole berries; 12 months in new and used puncheons. It is as vibrant and fresh as expected, with spiced red berries on the bouquet and palate alike, ranging from raspberry to red cherry, the tannins fine and spicy. Screwcap. Rating 95 To 2030 $24 ☻

ΨΨΨΨΨ   **Dirty Boots Cabernet Sauvignon 2015** Rating 93 To 2029 $24 CM ☻
2016 Vamos Tempranillo Rating 93 To 2025 $24 ☻
Tough Love Chardonnay 2017 Rating 92 To 2021 $24 ☻
Tough Love Chardonnay 2016 Rating 92 To 2021 $24 CM ☻

Bizarre Love Triangle Frankland River Pinot Gris Gewurztraminer
Riesling 2017 Rating 92 To 2021 $29 CM
Bizarre Love Triangle Frankland River Pinot Gris Gewurztraminer
Riesling 2016 Rating 91 To 2019 $29 CM
Wide Open Road Pinot Noir 2017 Rating 91 To 2023 $24
Redemption Shiraz 2014 Rating 90 To 2023 $24 CM

Snobs Creek Wines   ★★★☆

486 Goulburn Valley Highway, via Alexandra, Vic 3714 **Region** Upper Goulburn
T (03) 9596 3043 **www.**snobscreekvineyard.com.au **Open** W'ends 11–5
Winemaker Marcus Gillon **Est.** 1996 **Dozens** 1500 **Vyds** 5ha
In the 1860s, well-respected West Indian shoemaker 'Black' Brookes occupied a cottage
at the bridge over Cataract Creek. After he passed away in the late 1880s the creek was
renamed Snobs Creek, 'snob' being an old English term for cobbler (shoe repairer), and the
last that shapes the toe end of the shoe. The vineyard is situated where Snobs Creek joins the
Goulburn River, 5km below the Lake Eildon wall. The varieties grown are shiraz (2.5ha),
sauvignon blanc (1.5ha) and chardonnay (1ha); all manage to produce no more than 7.4t per
hectare. It's described as a 'cool-climate vineyard in a landscaped environment'.

♆♆♆♆♀ The Artisan Heathcote Shiraz 2016 A full-bodied shiraz with texture and
structure wrapped around a rich fruit core of black fruits. Needs time. Screwcap.
14.2% alc. **Rating** 91 To 2036

♆♆♆♆ Cordwainer Chardonnay 2016 Rating 89 To 2022

Solitaire Estate

PO Box 486, Echunga, SA 5153 **Region** Adelaide Hills
T 0432 787 041 **www.**solitairestate.com.au **Open** Not
Winemaker Simon White **Est.** 2007 **Dozens** 1500 **Vyds** 18.6ha
The Solitaire Estate vineyard has a rich history. It was once part of a much larger property
originally owned by one of South Australia's viticultural pioneers, John Barton Hack. He
grew grapes on his Echunga property in the 1840s, and even sent a sample of his 'hock' to
Queen Victoria, following in the footsteps of Walter Duffield, who had earlier sent Queen
Victoria a case of 1844 white, and was promptly prosecuted for making wine without the
requisite licence. Re-establishment of the vineyard began in 1999 (by former owner Jock
Calder and family), with sauvignon blanc, shiraz and riesling planted. The vineyard was
purchased by Paul Freer and Dennis Clift in 2007, who have increased the plantings. Exports
to Singapore and China.

♆♆♆♆♀ Adelaide Hills Cabernet Sauvignon 2014 Solid citizen of a wine. Steady
flavours of blackcurrant, creamy vanilla and violet, overtones of eucalyptus adding
lift. There's a juiciness, a freshness to this, though it has depth covered. Not a
hiccup in sight; it's a nice wine. Screwcap. 13.8% alc. **Rating** 91 To 2026 CM
Adelaide Hills Shiraz 2014 Sweet blackberry and plum flavours come gently
topped with milk chocolate. Just over medium in weight, but its smooth, syrupy
aspect helps to give it an impression of 'size'. There's a tangy, almost tomato-like
character in the background, but the wine takes it in its stride. Screwcap. 14.5% alc.
Rating 90 To 2024 CM

♆♆♆♆ The Pinnacle Shiraz 2013 Rating 89 To 2025 CM

Sons & Brothers Vineyard

Spring Terrace Road, Millthorpe, NSW 2798 (postal) **Region** Orange
T (02) 6366 5117 **www.**sonsandbrothers.com.au **Open** Not
Winemaker Dr Chris Bourke **Est.** 1978 **Dozens** 300 **Vyds** 2ha
Chris and Kathryn Bourke do not pull their punches when they say, 'Our vineyard has had
a chequered history, because in 1978 we were trying to establish ourselves in a nonexistent
wine region with no local knowledge, and limited personal knowledge of grapegrowing and

winemaking. It took us about 15 years of hits and misses before we started producing regular supplies of appropriate grape varieties at appropriate ripeness levels for sale to other New South Wales wineries.' Chris has published two fascinating papers on the origins of savagnin in Europe; he has also traced its movements in Australia after it was one of the varieties collected by James Busby – and moved just in time to save the last plantings in New South Wales of Busby's importation.

🍷🍷🍷🍷🍷 **Cabernet of Millthorpe 2016** Co-fermented with 2% savagnin in 780l open pots, matured for 10 months in tank with French oak staves (10% new). Particularly given the alternative vinification methods imposed by the single-wine winery, this is the best Sons & Brothers cabernet I can remember. The purity of the cassis fruit, enhanced by the slow, cool ferment, is striking, and the ideal vintage weather (warm and dry) also played its part. Crown seal. 13.4% alc. Rating 96 To 2030 $30 ✪

Sons of Eden   ★★★★★

Penrice Road, Angaston, SA 5353 **Region** Barossa
T (08) 8564 2363 **www**.sonsofeden.com **Open** 7 days 11–6
Winemaker Corey Ryan, Simon Cowham **Est.** 2000 **Dozens** 9000 **Vyds** 60ha
Corey Ryan and Simon Cowham both learnt and refined their skills in the vineyards and cellars of Eden Valley. Corey is a trained oenologist with over 20 vintages under his belt, having cut his teeth as a winemaker at Henschke. Thereafter he worked in Coonawarra for Rouge Homme and Penfolds, backed up by winemaking stints in the Rhône Valley, and in 2002 he took the opportunity to work in NZ for Villa Maria Estates. In '07 he won the Institute of Masters of Wine scholarship. Simon has had a similarly international career, covering such diverse organisations as Oddbins, UK, and the Winemakers' Federation of Australia. Switching from the business side of things to grapegrowing when he qualified as a viticulturist, Simon worked for Yalumba as technical manager of the Heggies and Pewsey Vale vineyards. With this background, it comes as no surprise to find that the estate-grown wines are of outstanding quality, nor that in '13 they were awarded the title of Barossa Winemaker of the Year by the Barons of Barossa. Exports to the UK, the US, Germany, Switzerland, Hong Kong, the Philippines, Taiwan and China.

🍷🍷🍷🍷🍷 **Remus Old Vine Eden Valley Shiraz 2015** Flirtations of a floral nature. This is primed with red and black berries, and with woody spice notes too, but floral overtones add another dimension – an intoxicating one too. Anise, mint and clove characters have their own version of events, but no matter which angle you look at this, it's fabulous. Rich shiraz fruit, smoky oak, incredibly fine tannin and silken mouthfeel. Caution: it may induce swooning. Screwcap. 14.5% alc. Rating 96 To 2035 $80 CM

Cirrus Single Vineyard High Eden Valley Riesling 2017 From an 18yo vineyard growing at 550m. It's soft and searing at once. Grapefruit, lime rind, lemon sorbet and then a mix of minerals and florals. It floats through the palate and then roars through the finish. Will cellar of course, but ever-so-gorgeous right now. Screwcap. 12% alc. Rating 95 To 2028 $56 CM

Romulus Old Vine Barossa Valley Shiraz 2015 Glorious Barossa Valley shiraz. Thick with both oak and fruit, but fine-grained through to the finish and polished to the nth degree. As seductive as they come. Blackberry, coal, toast, nougat and dill. A substantial spread of flavour. Length to match. Black satin. Screwcap. 14.5% alc. Rating 95 To 2035 $80 CM

Zephyrus Barossa Shiraz 2016 Sourced from eight vineyards across the Barossa and Eden valleys. Indeed 19 individual parcels were used, 48% from the Eden Valley and 52% Barossa. It sees a limited inclusion of whole bunches and 35% new French oak. It's dark and dense, but soft and mellifluous. Blackberry jam, the sweeter side of boysenberry, flings of dry spice and no shortage of florals. You wouldn't call it overly complex, but you would call it a pleasure dome. Screwcap. 14.5% alc. Rating 94 To 2028 $50 CM

Kennedy Barossa Valley Grenache Shiraz Mourvedre 2016 Grenache introduces raspberry and redcurrant flavours to meaty blackberry, plum and sweet spice. It feels a little sophisticated, a lot textural, and has the pitch of weight, tannin and acid exactly right. This is an exquisitely crafted red wine. Indeed the word 'intricate' is apt. This Sons of Eden range is in remarkable shape. Screwcap. 14.5% alc. **Rating** 94 **To** 2026 $33 CM

Selene Barossa Valley Tempranillo 2015 A latticework of a wine. The fine detail of spice, the web of tannin, the way red and darker berried fruits beaver away at the treble and bass; the ultimate wash of coffee, unsweetened cola character through the finish. Oak seems to be at play, but the fruit is the thing. A wine in beautiful form. Screwcap. 14.5% alc. **Rating** 94 **To** 2028 $54 CM

ᵧᵧᵧᵧᵧ **Freya Eden Valley Riesling 2017** Rating 93 To 2029 $30
Marschall Barossa Valley Shiraz 2016 Rating 93 To 2036 $33
Pumpa Eden Valley Cabernet Sauvignon Shiraz 2015 Rating 90
To 2030 $33

Soul Growers

218–230 Murray Street, Tanunda, SA 5352 **Region** Barossa Valley
T 0410 505 590 **www.**soulgrowers.com **Open** By appt
Winemaker Paul Heinicke, Stuart Bourne **Est.** 1998 **Dozens** 5000 **Vyds** 4.85ha
In January 2014 Paul Heinicke (one of the four founders of the business) purchased the shares previously held by David Cruickshank, and James and Paul Lindner. Mainly situated on hillside country in the Seppeltsfield area, the vineyards comprise shiraz, cabernet sauvignon, grenache and chardonnay (the most important varieties), and lesser plantings of mataro and black muscat. There are then pocket-handkerchief blocks of shiraz at Tanunda, mataro at Nuriootpa and a 1.2ha planting of grenache at Krondorf. Exports to the US, Canada, Singapore, Hong Kong and China.

ᵧᵧᵧᵧᵧ **Gobell Single Vineyard Barossa Valley Shiraz 2016** From 150yo vines in Marananga, the usual 10-day, whole berry open fermentation with two cultured yeasts at 22–25°C. A single barrel 100% new French oak, matured for 18–19 months. Has old-vine super intensity, yet has the balance needed for a 20–40 year maturation depending on cork. Black fruits, touches of licorice and tar, very firm, but ripe, tannins. An organoleptic comment is that the format means oak plays a large part in these single-barrel flagship wines, this one fighting back with the depth of its full-bodied palate. 14.5% alc. **Rating** 97 **To** 2041 $150 ✪

Hoffman 100 Year Old Block Single Vineyard Barossa Valley Shiraz 2016 From 100+yo vines from the Ebenezer district; the usual 50% new/50% used French hogsheads. Seductive, opulent flavours with dark chocolate, soft tannins and a juicy aftertaste. This is the most instantaneously attractive wine of the group; when new oak is done well, it is done very well. Cork. 14.5% alc. **Rating** 97 **To** 2056 $150 ✪

106 Vines Barossa Valley Mourvedre 2016 Whole berry–open fermented, 7–10 days on skins, basket-pressed, matured for 19 months in used French hogsheads, 60 dozen made. Made from 106 100+yo vines (has a good ring to it), and the wine celebrates its ongoing life with a spring in its step. Atypical freshness and elegance can also be attributed to its very modest alcohol. Its essence is silky plum fruit flavours, superfine tannins and exceptional balance. Cork. 13.5% alc. Rating 97 To 2046 $110 ✪

ᵧᵧᵧᵧᵧ **Kroehn Single Vineyard Eden Valley Shiraz 2016** Made from 20+yo vines from the Eden Valley township. Slightly lighter colour, and likewise body, the result is an elegant style. Juicy black fruits flow across the palate in convincing style. Eden Valley is key for me. Cork. 14% alc. **Rating** 96 **To** 2041 $150

Defiant Barossa Valley Mataro 2016 From old vines in Marananga and Vine Vale, whole berry–open fermented, 7–10 days on skins, basket-pressed, matured for 19 months in used French hogsheads. Very good colour, full and bright; spicy forest berries on the bouquet lead into a medium-bodied palate that has remarkable drive, precision and freshness to its dark berry/cherry fruits and ripe tannins. Cork. 14% alc. **Rating** 96 **To** 2036 $60 ✪

Single Vineyard Eden Valley Riesling 2017 From a single 72yo vineyard. Pale quartz-green, the wine has a tactile grip that grows on you each time you taste it, taking the idea of minerally acidity onto centre stage. It is dazzlingly fresh, 'minerally', the reflection of a white wine with low pH, but not exactly one that has any mineral content. Screwcap. 12% alc. **Rating** 95 **To** 2031 $25 ✪

Hampel Single Vineyard Barossa Valley Shiraz 2016 A single barrel made from 16yo vines from Kalimna. Superb colour; very high quality fruit flavours, but needing time for the oak to integrate. These vines must be stars on a weight for age measure. The palate has an almost slinky length, and you lose the oak on retasting (or rather, multiple retastings). Cork. 14% alc. **Rating** 95 **To** 2041 $150

Slow Grown Barossa Shiraz 2016 Rating 94 **To** 2036 $60

Persistence Barossa Valley Grenache 2016 Rating 94 **To** 2029 $60

Barossa Valley El Major 2016 Rating 94 **To** 2046 $110

♟♟♟♟♟ **Soul Sister Barossa Valley Rose 2017 Rating** 92 **To** 2020 $25 ✪

Soumah

18 Hexham Road, Gruyere, Vic 3770 **Region** Yarra Valley
T (03) 5962 4716 **www.**soumah.com.au **Open** 7 days 10–5
Winemaker Scott McCarthy **Est.** 1997 **Dozens** 12000 **Vyds** 19.47ha

It was a voyage of discovery unravelling the story behind the exotically named Soumah, and its strikingly labelled Savarro (reminiscent of 19th-century baroque design). 'Soumah' is in fact an abbreviation of 'South of Maroondah (Highway)', and 'Savarro' is an alternative name for savagnin. This is the venture of Brett Butcher, who has international experience in the hospitality industry as CEO of the Langham Group, and a long involvement in retailing wines to restaurants in many countries. Tim Brown is viticultural director. The many varieties planted have been clonally selected and grafted onto rootstock with the long-term future in mind, although some of the sauvignon blanc is already being grafted over to bracchetto. Exports to the UK, Canada, Denmark, South Korea, Singapore, Hong Kong, Japan and China.

♟♟♟♟♟ **Equilibrio Single Vineyard Yarra Valley Chardonnay 2017** Fonts in a tiny size running every which way on the busy, large front and back labels allowed me to ascertain that the clone used is Mendoza. This wine does full justice to the excellent vintage; with white peach and grapefruit – a familiar but ever enjoyable repartee between them. Screwcap. 13.1% alc. **Rating** 96 **To** 2029 $77

U. Ngumby Single Vineyard Yarra Valley Chardonnay 2017 The richest of the Soumah range, but doesn't rely on sweetness (there is none) nor extraction. The balance and length are both exceptional, the pure varietal expression courtesy of grapefruit and zesty acidity. Will flourish with more time in bottle. Screwcap. 12.7% alc. **Rating** 95 **To** 2027 $40

Equilibrio Single Vineyard Yarra Valley Pinot Noir 2016 Equilibrio is a best barrel selection focusing on harmony and balance. This wine is wild-fermented and matured in French oak (35% new). The flavours are bright red, the mouthfeel slippery and delicious, the finish long and supported by fine tannins. Screwcap. 12.5% alc. **Rating** 95 **To** 2030 $77

Hexham Single Vineyard Yarra Valley Chardonnay 2017 Clones 95, 76 and Mendoza wild-fermented in French oak (22% new), matured for 8 months. A highly energetic and crisp wine that asks the question whether it was picked a little too early, but leaves room for many different answers. Screwcap. 12.8% alc. **Rating** 94 **To** 2022 $40

Select Vineyard Yarra Valley Chardonnay d'Soumah 2017 Hundreds of words on the front and back labels tell you the wine is predominantly fermented and matured for 8 months in French oak. A snappy, fresh chardonnay born of the cool '17 vintage and steep vineyard hills, part undergoing mlf! Bargain hunters ahoy. Screwcap. 13% alc. **Rating** 94 **To** 2025 $27 ✪

Hexham Single Vineyard Yarra Valley Viognier 2017 Aromas sit firmly in the stone fruit realm with apricot leading the way, and a touch of skins character providing a more savoury element. Displays the typically textured mouthfeel of the variety, the flavours ripe but not sweet, and a juicy, mouthwatering acidity running through the palate. Screwcap. 13% alc. **Rating** 94 To 2021 $38 SC

🍷🍷🍷🍷🍷 Hexham Yarra Valley Pinot Grigio 2017 **Rating** 93 To 2019 $27 SC ⊙
Hexham Yarra Valley Savarro 2017 **Rating** 93 To 2020 $29 SC
Hexham Yarra Valley Syrah 2016 **Rating** 93 To 2024 $38 SC
Hexham Yarra Valley Cabernet Sauvignon 2016 **Rating** 93 To 2028 $40 SC
Yarra Valley Ai Fiori 2017 **Rating** 92 To 2019 $27 SC
Equilibrio Yarra Valley Syrah 2015 **Rating** 92 To 2030 $77 SC

Souter's Vineyard   ★★★★

390 Happy Valley Road, Rosewhite, Vic 3737 **Region** Alpine Valleys
T (03) 5752 1077 **www**.happyvalley75.com.au/soutersvineyard/ **Open** Fri–Sun 10–4, 7 days in Jan
Winemaker Various contract **Est.** 1983 **Dozens** 150 **Vyds** 2ha
Professional Melbourne couple Kay and Allan Souter acquired the former Rosewhite Vineyard in late 2003. The vineyard, one of the oldest in the Alpine Valleys region, had been significantly run-down due to the age and ill health of the former owners. The Souters have invested much time and effort in rehabilitating, re-trellising and regrafting the vineyard to more suitable varieties.

🍷🍷🍷🍷🍷 Alpine Valleys Gewurztraminer 2016 Winemaker Jo Marsh takes
gewurztraminer off Souter's 30yo vines and weaves her magic. The wine bursts with aroma and flavour, provokes just enough interest and remains disciplined throughout. Made in tiny quantities, but worth a shot if you see it. Screwcap. 13.5% alc. **Rating** 92 To 2019 $25 CM ⊙
Alpine Valleys Cabernet Sauvignon 2015 Excellent dark fruit intensity comes well matched to clovey/smoky oak. This doesn't put a foot wrong. Balance is arguably its strongest suit, though all aspects here are pulling as one. Diam. 14.5% alc. **Rating** 92 To 2025 $30 CM

Spence   ★★★★★

760 Burnside Road, Murgheboluc, Vic 3221 **Region** Geelong
T (03) 5265 1181 **www**.spencewines.com.au **Open** 1st Sun each month
Winemaker Peter Spence, Scott Ireland **Est.** 1997 **Dozens** 1300 **Vyds** 3.2ha
Peter and Anne Spence were sufficiently inspired by an extended European holiday, which included living on a family vineyard in Provence, to purchase a small property and establish a vineyard and winery. They have planted 3.2ha on a north-facing slope in a valley 7km south of Bannockburn with the lion's share planted to three clones of shiraz (1.83ha), the remainder to chardonnay, pinot noir and fast-diminishing cabernet sauvignon (it is being grafted over to viognier for use in the Shiraz). The vineyard attained full organic status in 2008, and since then have used only biodynamic practices.

🍷🍷🍷🍷🍷 Geelong Chardonnay 2016 Geelong chardonnays have great depth and power
even when young, making them particularly ageworthy as they move slowly and deliberately, like some of the well-known winemakers of the region. More stone fruit on parade, citrus making its presence felt in conjunction with acidity. Screwcap. 13.3% alc. **Rating** 95 To 2031 $30 ⊙
Geelong Shiraz 2016 From 20yo vines (a mix of clones), co-fermented with 3% viognier, 20% whole bunches, 10% of the juice run off, 20 days on skins, matured for 16 months in French oak (10% new). This approach simply builds further on the propensity of the Geelong region to produce full-bodied shiraz with spice and licorice partners to the fruit. Screwcap. 13.8% alc. **Rating** 95 To 2040 $30 ⊙
Geelong Viognier 2016 Whole-bunch pressed, wild-fermented in amphorae and stainless steel barrels, 8 months on lees. Interesting wine; the percentage of amphorae not known. What is known/obvious is the tighter texture and lower

alcohol of most viogniers (a thoroughly good thing), with a flash of ginger on the finish as a cleansing agent. All up, a pretty smart wine. Screwcap. 13.5% alc. **Rating** 94 To 2021 $30 ✪

ŢŢŢŢ   Geelong Pinot Noir 2016 **Rating** 89 To 2023 $35

Spinifex   ★★★★★

PO Box 511, Nuriootpa, SA 5355 **Region** Barossa Valley
T (08) 8564 2059 **www**.spinifexwines.com.au **Open** At Artisans of Barossa
Winemaker Peter Schell **Est.** 2001 **Dozens** 6000
Peter Schell and Magali Gely are a husband-and-wife team from NZ who came to Australia in the early 1990s to study oenology and marketing at Roseworthy Agricultural College. They have spent four vintages making wine in France, mainly in the south, where Magali's family were vignerons for generations near Montpellier. The focus at Spinifex is on the red varieties that dominate in the south of France: mataro (more correctly, mourvedre), grenache, shiraz and cinsaut. The wines are made in open fermenters, basket-pressed, with partial wild (indigenous) fermentation and relatively long post-ferment maceration. This is a very old approach, but nowadays it's à la mode. Exports to the UK, Canada, Belgium, Singapore, Hong Kong, China and NZ.

ŢŢŢŢŢ   **Barossa Valley Syrah 2017** It's a massive distance between Yarra Valley pinot and Barossa Valley shiraz, yet this '17 vintage has kissed them both, with lower alcohol levels, producing wines of great intensity, length and balance. The Barossa Valley seldom has spice and licorice as first up aromas and flavours, but it does that here in spades, with a glorious rendition on the palate. It borders on full-bodied, but to leave or reduce any part of what is here would be vinocide. Screwcap. 14% alc. **Rating** 97 To 2042 $30 ✪

ŢŢŢŢŢ   **Luxe 2017** A blend of 51% mataro, 38% grenache, 11% cinsaut. Brighter colour and different blend percentages than its sibling; the heady aromas of a field of wild and cultivated flowers in spring on a cloudless spring day, lead into red berries skipping along the palate before a bone-dry finish. High quality rose. Screwcap. 13% alc. **Rating** 96 To 2021 $35 ✪

Bête Noir 2015 From 70yo vines, matured in French oak (20% new) for 16 months. A medium-bodied shiraz with flavours of dark berries and plums framed by a complex web of savoury spices, forest floor and tannins. Exceptional length, beautiful wine. Screwcap. 14.5% alc. **Rating** 96 To 2040 $40 ✪

Esprit 2015 A blend of 58% grenache, 40% mataro, 2% cinsaut, matured for 14 months in used French oak. This is still at the dawn of its life; the colour brilliant, but deep; the bouquet simply directing traffic to the medium-bodied palate that has so much to say. Red and dark fruits come first, spice, herbs and earth next, frisky tannins on the finish. Screwcap. 14.9% alc. **Rating** 96 To 2030 $35 ✪

Garcon 2016 From 80yo vines; 70% is matured for 8 months in used French oak, 30% in tank. Light colour, typical of grenache; red fruits and elastic tannins play hopscotch on the supple palate and long finish. Hard to visualise a table that wouldn't welcome this wine. Screwcap. 14% alc. **Rating** 95 To 2026 $40

Barossa Valley Rose 2017 A blend of 54% grenache, 28% mataro, 18% cinsaut, part destemmed and crushed, part crushed bunches, wild-fermented, 8 months on lees in tank and old French oak. Spinifex can't hide the skill with which this light pink rose has been made. It has a deliciously spicy/savoury array of flavours that carry the wine into a long fruit-sweet, dry finish. Screwcap. 13% alc. **Rating** 94 To 2020 $28 ✪

Papillon 2017 Comprising 58% grenache, 42% cinsaut, from 90yo vines. Light hue; a fragrant bouquet of wild herbs, dusty earth and diminutive red berry aromas is followed by a fresh, lively, spicy palate. 'Drink me', it says, 'but don't talk about me'. Hard not to – it's so fresh. Screwcap. 13% alc. **Rating** 94 To 2023 $26 ✪

ŢŢŢŢŢ   Lola 2017 **Rating** 90 To 2027 $28

Springington Hills Wines ★★★★

41 Burnbank Grove, Athelstone, SA 5076 (postal) **Region** Eden Valley
T (08) 8337 7905 www.springtonhillswines.com.au **Open** Not
Winemaker John Ciccocioppo **Est.** 2001 **Dozens** 3000 **Vyds** 12ha
The Ciccocioppo family migrated from central Italy in the 1950s. As is so often the case, wine
was in their veins. In 2001, second-generation John and wife Connie purchased a grazing
property at Springton, and began the planting of shiraz and riesling. Each year they increased
the shiraz and riesling blocks, but also added smaller amounts of cabernet sauvignon and
grenache, and a smaller amount still of montepulciano. The wines are available for tasting at
Urban Wine Room, 33–37 Wright Street, Adelaide. Good label design and packaging.

🍷🍷🍷🍷🍷 **La Cosa Nostra Eden Valley Montepulciano 2015** Enticing, dark purple-
crimson; a concentrated, more serious style, yet there's so much to like – from the
dark spiced satsuma plums, wafts of licorice and menthol to the savoury Italianate
tannin structure. It's full-bodied, but not at all heavy, with a tangy, almost Campari
twist to the finish. Screwcap. 13.7% alc. **Rating** 93 **To** 2023 $38 JF

Squitchy Lane Vineyard ★★★★☆

Medhurst Road, Coldstream, Vic 3770 **Region** Yarra Valley
T (03) 5964 9114 www.squitchylane.com.au **Open** W'ends 11–5
Winemaker Robert Paul **Est.** 1982 **Dozens** 2000 **Vyds** 5.75ha
Mike Fitzpatrick acquired a taste for fine wine while a Rhodes scholar at Oxford University
in the 1970s. Returning to Australia he guided Carlton Football Club as captain to two
premierships, then established Melbourne-based finance company Squitchy Lane Holdings.
The wines of Mount Mary inspired him to look for his own vineyard, and in '96 he found
a vineyard of sauvignon blanc, chardonnay, pinot noir, merlot, cabernet franc and cabernet
sauvignon, planted in '82, just around the corner from Coldstream Hills and Yarra Yering.

🍷🍷🍷🍷🍷 **Yarra Valley Cabernet Sauvignon Cabernet Franc Merlot 2016** This
estate-grown blend comes together with deceptively easy harmony. It's already a
complete wine, with an almost velvety flow. Fruit of this quality doesn't need oak
or tannins to fill holes or paper over the cracks, so I'm not stressing about having
no knowledge of the oak treatment. Screwcap. 13.5% alc. **Rating** 95 **To** 2036
Yarra Valley Chardonnay 2016 Be careful when you pick the bottle up – it's
as heavy as any red wine battleship. It's a paradox then, that the wine should be
so fresh and breezy, with an acidity that sticks to the gums and requires repeated
removal work. Pink grapefruit and Granny Smith apple have snuck into the grapes
and survived fermentation, with oak not getting in the way. Screwcap. 13% alc.
Rating 94 **To** 2030 $30 ◐

🍷🍷🍷🍷🍷 **Yarra Valley Cabernet Sauvignon 2016 Rating** 93 **To** 2036
Yarra Valley Fume Blanc 2015 Rating 92 **To** 2021 $30
Yarra Valley Rose 2017 Rating 90 **To** 2021 $25

Stage Door Wine Co ★★★★★

22 Whibley Street, Henley Beach, SA 5022 (postal) **Region** Eden Valley
T 0400 991 968 www.stagedoorwineco.com.au **Open** Not
Winemaker Graeme Thredgold **Est.** 2013 **Dozens** 2500 **Vyds** 32.3ha
It took a long time for Graeme Thredgold to establish this still-embryonic wine business.
Having been a successful professional musician for 15 years during the 1980s and '90s, he
developed vocal nodules in the early '90s, putting an end to his musical career. Having spent
so much time working in hotels and night clubs, a new playing field stared him in the face:
the liquor industry. In '92 he began working for Lion Nathan as a sales representative, then
spent five years with South Australian Brewing Company, and in '98 ventured into the world
of wine as national sales manager for Andrew Garrett. Around 2000 he moved on to the
more fertile pasture of Tucker Seabrook as state sales manager for South Australia. Further
roles with Barossa Valley Estate and Chain of Ponds Wines (as general manager) added to an

impressive career in sales and marketing before he made his final move to Eden Hall Wines as general manager. Eden Hall Wines is owned by his sister and brother-in-law, David and Mardi Hall. Grapes are sourced mainly from the family vineyard, plus contract-grown fruit. Exports to Canada.

ŶŶŶŶŶ **Eden Valley Shiraz 2016** Matured for almost 2 years in French hogsheads (40% new). An impressive follow-on from its '15 sibling, with an unusual lacquered palate of a panoply of black fruits and spices. It flows evenly and without hurry along toasty oak, without a breath of alcohol heat; the cedary aromas and flavours of the French oak slotting into the finish and aftertaste. This wine has balance from the word go, and its long term future, gold-plated. Screwcap. 14.5% alc. **Rating** 97 To 2046 $50 **○**

ŶŶŶŶŶ **The Green Room Eden Valley Riesling 2017** From the Avon Brae vineyard, the vines planted in '96, free-run juice fermented with cultured yeast. Combines purity and intensity with length and power, but you have to focus on the finish and aftertaste to unlock the vault holding the lime, lemon and passionfruit flavours that led to its gold medal at the Canberra International Riesling Challenge '17. This has a long future awaiting those who are patient. Screwcap. 12.5% alc. **Rating** 95 To 2032 $25 **○**
White Note Wild Ferment Eden Valley Gruner Veltliner 2017 From the Avon Brae vineyard, hand-picked, free-run juice wild-fermented, 3 months on lees in used French barriques. Its gold medals from the Australian Alternative Varieties Wine Show and Winewise Small Vigneron Awards in '17 were doubtless recognition of the textural complexity and the urgency of the drive on the palate – the zesty, dry finish yet another virtue. Screwcap. 12.1% alc. **Rating** 95 To 2027 $25 **○**
Eden Valley Cabernet Sauvignon 2016 A single vineyard release, machine-harvested, open-fermented with cultured yeast, matured in French barriques (40% new). The bouquet is loaded with fragrant cassis fruit and you wonder whether the wine will be over the top. Well, never fear: it's full-bodied, with impressive line and length, which will see it safely through the decades to come. Screwcap. 14.5% alc. **Rating** 95 To 2041 $50
Full House Barossa Cabernet Sauvignon 2016 From two blocks on the Avon Brae vineyard in the Eden Valley and a single vineyard in the Barossa Valley, open-fermented, matured in French barriques (15% new) for almost 2 years before blending. The Reynell clone has for many, many years been regarded as awesome when used with French oak, and this wine is one of innumerable examples. The wine is very complex, with a suite of flavours inching to the spice/licorice of cool-grown shiraz. A snap at the price. Screwcap. 14.5% alc. **Rating** 94 To 2036 $25 **○**

ŶŶŶŶŷ **Front and Centre Barossa Shiraz 2016 Rating** 93 To 2031 $25 **○**

Stanton & Killeen Wines   ★★★★★
440 Jacks Road, Murray Valley Highway, Rutherglen, Vic 3685 **Region** Rutherglen
T (02) 6032 9457 **www**.stantonandkilleen.com.au **Open** Mon–Sat 9–5, Sun &
public hols 10–5
Winemaker Andrew Drumm, Joe Warren **Est.** 1875 **Dozens** 12 000 **Vyds** 34ha
In 2020 Stanton & Killeen will celebrate its 145th anniversary. The business is owned and run by seventh-generation vigneron Natasha Killeen, and her mother and CEO, Wendy Killeen. Fortifieds are a strong focus for the winery, with around half of its production dedicated to this style. Their vineyards comprise 14 varieties, including seven Portuguese cultivars used for both fortified and table wine production – with two additional Portuguese varieties planned for future planting. A vineyard rejuvenation program has been implemented since 2014, focusing on sustainable and environmentally friendly practices. The rating has been maintained; a representative range of wines was not received for this edition. Exports to the UK, Switzerland, Hong Kong and China.

🍷🍷🍷🍷🍷 **Classic Rutherglen Muscat NV** The colour is a nutty mahogany without a scintilla of red remaining; you get your money's worth here and then some. It abounds with raisins, plum pudding, burnt toffee, exotic spices – and the all-important rancio. 500ml. Screwcap. 18% alc. **Rating** 93 $35

Stargazer Wine ★★★★★

37 Rosewood Lane, Tea Tree, Tas 7017 **Region** Tasmania
T 0408 173 335 **www**.stargazerwine.com.au **Open** By appt
Winemaker Samantha Connew **Est.** 2012 **Dozens** 1000 **Vyds** 1ha

Samantha 'Sam' Connew has racked up a series of exceptional achievements, commencing with Bachelor of Law and Bachelor of Arts degrees, majoring in political science and English literature, from the University of Canterbury, NZ. But her future direction showed when she obtained a postgraduate diploma of oenology and viticulture from Lincoln University, NZ. Sam moved to Australia, undertaking the advanced wine assessment course at the Australian Wine Research Institute in 2000. She was chosen as a scholar at the '02 Len Evans Tutorial, won the George Mackey Trophy for the best wine exported from Australia in '04. In '07 she was named Red Winemaker of the Year at the International Wine Challenge in London. After a highly successful and lengthy position as chief winemaker at Wirra Wirra, Sam moved to Tasmania (via the Hunter Valley) to make the first wines for her own business, something she said she would never do. The emotive name (and label) of Stargazer is in part a tribute to Abel Tasman, the first European to sight Tasmania before proceeding to the South Island of NZ, navigating by the stars. Exports to the UK, the US and Singapore.

🍷🍷🍷🍷🍷 **Coal River Valley Riesling 2017** Hand-picked, destemmed, 8 hours skin contact, gentle pressing, wild-fermented; 75% in stainless steel, 10% in a ceramic egg, the remainder in used oak; weekly lees stirring until bottling on 22 Aug; 7.9g/l residual sugar, 7.7g/l titratable acidity. This is absolutely not your usual Tasmanian riesling, but the complex vinification hasn't been an exercise in eg(g)omania. The result is a delicate, yet intense (yes, oxymoron), and long palate, balance is its supreme virtue. Top-flight German makers of riesling would instantly recognise what is going on here. Screwcap. 11.6% alc. **Rating** 96 **To** 2032 $35 ❂

Coal River Valley Chardonnay 2016 Hand-picked, whole-bunch pressed, wild-fermented in French puncheons (20% new), 100% mlf, matured for 8 months, no lees stirring. The nutty edge to the bouquet is as likely from mlf as from oak, but given the grapes were picked at 11.8° baume, mlf would have been imperative. Melon and white peach cut a clean path through the long palate, balancing the key. Screwcap. 12.5% alc. **Rating** 95 **To** 2026 $45

Coal River Valley Pinot Noir 2016 The first Stargazer wine from the Palisander Vineyard purchased in '16, wild yeast–open fermented with 40% whole bunches, matured in French puncheons (20% new) for 8 months. Star-bright, clear crimson; a seriously attractive wine, the red fruits of the bouquet setting much of the agenda with its burst of fragrance. It is light-bodied, but has exceptional tenacity and length, the red fruits embraced by sunbeam notes of dried herb, the finest tannins drawing out the finish and aftertaste. Screwcap. 13.5% alc. **Rating** 95 **To** 2024 $50

Tupelo 2017 Pinot gris (45%) and gewurztraminer (17%) from the Tamar Valley, co-fermented with riesling (38%) from the Derwent Valley, the blend inspired by the Alasatian Gentil style; fermented in stainless steel (45%), used oak (40%) and a ceramic egg (15%), weekly lees stirring until bottled in Aug. Exotic and highly expressive on the bouquet, doubling up on that start with pear and wild strawberry flavours, the phenolics positive. Screwcap. 12.9% alc. **Rating** 94 **To** 2022 $35

🍷🍷🍷🍷 **Rada 2017 Rating** 89 **To** 2021 $35

Steels Creek Estate ★★★☆

1 Sewell Road, Steels Creek, Vic 3775 **Region** Yarra Valley
T (03) 5965 2448 **www**.steelscreekestate.com.au **Open** Fri–Mon & public hols 10–6
Winemaker Simon Peirce **Est.** 1981 **Dozens** 400 **Vyds** 1.7ha

The Steels Creek vineyard, family-operated since 1981, is located in the picturesque Steels Creek Valley, with views towards the Kinglake National Park. All the wines are made onsite by owner and winemaker Simon Peirce, following renovations to the winery. The vineyard has chardonnay, shiraz, cabernet sauvignon, cabernet franc and colombard.

ŶŶŶŶŶ Single Vineyard Yarra Valley Cabernet Sauvignon 2016 Mid-crimson and bright; a light to medium-bodied frame; fragrant cassis and redcurrant fruit mingling with some woodsy spices, lavender bath salts and leafy freshness − not green though. There's a flick of volatility and slight astringency to the acidity on the finish. Diam. 13.5% alc. **Rating** 90 **To** 2024 $35 JF

Steels Gate
★★★☆

227 Greenwoods Lane, Steels Creek, Vic 3775 (postal) **Region** Yarra Valley
T 0419 628 393 **www**.steelsgate.com.au **Open** Not
Winemaker Aaron Zuccaro **Est.** 2010 **Dozens** 500 **Vyds** 2ha
Brad Atkins and Matthew Davis acquired a 2ha vineyard of 25–30yo dry-grown chardonnay and pinot noir in 2009. For reasons unexplained, the owners have a particular love of gates, and as the property is at the end of Steels Creek, the choice of 'Steels Gate' was obvious. The next step was to engage French designer Cecile Darcy to create the Steels Gate logo.

ŶŶŶŶŶ Yarra Valley Chardonnay 2015 The packaging and, particularly, the label are striking, which would suggest $100 a bottle, not $25. The wine is riveting, fresh and bright thanks to lemony acidity that some consumers won't be able to deal with. I'm acid-tolerant, and it tested me, but I couldn't stop liking the good part of the curate's egg. Screwcap. 12.8% alc. **Rating** 91 **To** 2029 $25

ŶŶŶŶ Yarra Valley Pinot Noir Rose 2017 Rating 89 **To** 2019 $22

Stefani Estate
★★★★★

122 Long Gully Road, Healesville, Vic 3777 **Region** Yarra Valley/Heathcote
T (03) 9570 8750 **www**.stefaniestatewines.com.au **Open** By appt
Winemaker Peter Mackey **Est.** 1998 **Dozens** 6800 **Vyds** 30ha
Stefano Stefani came to Australia in 1985. Business success has allowed Stefano and wife Rina to follow in the footsteps of Stefano's grandfather, who had a vineyard and was an avid wine collector. The first property they acquired was at Long Gully Road in the Yarra Valley, planted to pinot grigio, cabernet sauvignon, chardonnay and pinot noir. The next property they acquired was in Heathcote, adjoining that of (ex–Mount Mary) Mario Marson. On this, they built a winery and established 14.4ha of shiraz, cabernet sauvignon, merlot, cabernet franc, malbec and petit verdot. In 2003 a second Yarra Valley property named The View, reflecting its high altitude, was acquired and Dijon clones of chardonnay and pinot noir were planted. In addition, 1.6ha of sangiovese have been established, using scion material from the original Stefani vineyard in Tuscany. Exports to China.

ŶŶŶŶŶ Barrel Selection Heathcote Vineyard Shiraz 2016 A barrel selection that evidently started in the vineyard, given its riper fruit and higher alcohol. It is richer and deeper, its dark fruits nestled on quality oak and ripe tannins. It is notably supple, and immediately enjoyable. Clearly the best Stefani Estate wine from '16, and will give enjoyment for many years. Diam. 14.5% alc. **Rating** 96 **To** 2036 $65 **☉**
Vigna Stefani Yarra Valley Chardonnay 2017 Extraordinarily pale colour, but there is nothing light or inconsequential about the intensity and length of the wine nor its varietal expression, which, of course, are the cornerstones of Yarra Valley chardonnay. Barrel ferment characters are present, but oak per se isn't obvious; the wine gaining intensity and grip as it is retasted, and as it finishes. Screwcap. 13.5% alc. **Rating** 95 **To** 2029 $30 **☉**
Heathcote Vineyard Merlot 2015 Estate-grown grapes were whole-bunch sorted into open fermenters, hand-plunged, matured in new and used French oak. The varietal expression is impressive, traversing cassis, plum, bay leaf and spice.

Overall medium-bodied, but long, and particularly well balanced, with oak and tannins simply doing traffic control. Diam. 14% alc. **Rating** 95 **To** 2030
The View Yarra Valley Vineyard Chardonnay 2015 Hand-picked, bunch-sorted, pressed, fermented in French oak, matured for 12 months. Still bright straw-green, it is an elegant, albeit very long and complex, wine. In true Yarra fashion, it will continue to develop slowly. Diam. 13.5% alc. **Rating** 94 **To** 2023
Heathcote Vineyard Shiraz 2016 Hand-picked and sorted into open fermenters, hand-plunged, pressed to new and used French oak for 12 months maturation. Has a complex texture; juicy red and black cherry/berry fruits with spice and pepper nuances backed up by fine, persistent, tannins. Screwcap. 14% alc. **Rating** 94 **To** 2029
Vigna Stefani Heathcote Malbec 2017 Bright crimson hue; a malbec that greets you with open arms and a warm hug. The supple fruit has cascades of red-fleshed plums and a splash of raspberry. Tannin, acidity and oak are all spot on. Screwcap. 13.5% alc. **Rating** 94 **To** 2023 $30 ✪

🍷🍷🍷🍷 **Vigna Stefani Yarra Valley Arneis 2017** **Rating** 92 **To** 2023
The Gate Yarra Valley Shiraz 2015 **Rating** 90 **To** 2028
Boccallupo Yarra Valley Sangiovese 2017 **Rating** 90 **To** 2022 $40

Stefano de Pieri ★★★☆

27 Deakin Avenue, Mildura, Vic 3502 **Region** Murray Darling
T (03) 5021 3627 **www**.stefano.com.au **Open** Mon–Fri 8–6, w'ends 8–2
Winemaker Sally Blackwell, Stefano de Pieri **Est.** 2005 **Dozens** 25 000
Stefano de Pieri decided to have his own range of wines that reflect his Italian spirit and the region he lives in. Mostly hand-picked, the fruit comes from a variety of Mildura vineyards, including the highly respected Chalmers Nurseries. They are intended to be fresh and zesty, deliberately aiming at lower alcohol; to retain as much natural acidity as possible, designed to go with food; and to be inexpensive and easy to enjoy, reflecting Stefano's philosophy of generosity and warmth. The emphasis is on the Italian varieties, from arneis to aglianico, including a frizzante pinot grigio and the innovative blend of moscato gialla, garganega and greco, while retaining some local workhorses such as cabernet and chardonnay.

Stefano Lubiana ★★★★★

60 Rowbottoms Road, Granton, Tas 7030 **Region** Southern Tasmania
T (03) 6263 7457 **www**.slw.com.au **Open** Wed–Sun 11–4 (closed Jul)
Winemaker Steve Lubiana, Thomas New **Est.** 1990 **Dozens** NFP **Vyds** 25ha
Monique and Steve Lubiana moved in 1990 from the hot, brown inland Australia to the beautiful banks of the Derwent River to pursue Steve's dream of making high quality sparkling wine. The sloping site allowed them to build a gravity-fed winery, and his whole winemaking approach has since been based on attention to detail within a biodynamic environment. Their first sparkling wines were made in 1993 from the first plantings of chardonnay and pinot noir. Over the years they have added riesling, sauvignon blanc, pinot gris and merlot. The Italian-inspired Osteria restaurant is based on their own biodynamically produced vegetables and herbs, the meats (all free-range) are from local farmers, and the seafood is wild-caught. In 2016 the Lubianas purchased the Panorama Vineyard, first planted in 1974, in the Huon Valley. Exports to the UK, Singapore, Indonesia, South Korea, Japan, Taiwan, Hong Kong and China.

🍷🍷🍷🍷🍷 **Riesling 2017** In tight flying formation at supersonic speed, lime blossom aromas and zesty/pithy lime juice fly in the lead, not relinquishing that position on the long palate and aftertaste. Screwcap. 12.5% alc. **Rating** 95 **To** 2037
Collina Chardonnay 2014 A best barrels selection from the estate hillside block ('collina' means 'little hill'). Full straw-green; is now starting to move towards maturity with hints of cashew and fig, joining stone fruit and citrus. Oak has been a means, not an end. Screwcap. **Rating** 95 **To** 2023
Sasso Pinot Noir 2016 A best barrels selection produced in only the best years from low-yielding estate vines. This is classic full-bodied Tasmanian breeding stock,

dark in its fruit expression and needing ample time to relax and unveil the beauty within. Cork. 13.5% alc. **Rating** 95 **To** 2024
Primavera Chardonnay 2016 Pale but bright straw-green; a wine with elegance and length, not burdened by oak or use of endless additions from the vineyard or winery. Its balance is perfect, and the marriage of pink grapefruit, Granny Smith apple and white peach is likewise perfect. Screwcap. 13.5% alc. **Rating** 94 **To** 2024

♀♀♀♀♀ **Estate Pinot Noir 2016 Rating** 91 **To** 2030

Stella Bella Wines   ★★★★★

205 Rosabrook Road, Margaret River, WA 6285 **Region** Margaret River
T (08) 9758 8611 **www**.stellabella.com.au **Open** 7 days 10–5
Winemaker Luke Jolliffe, Michael Kane **Est.** 1997 **Dozens** 40 000 **Vyds** 55.7ha
This enormously successful winemaking business produces wines of true regional expression, with fruit sourced from the central and southern parts of Margaret River. The company owns and operates six vineyards, and also purchases fruit from small contract growers. Substantial quantities of wine covering all styles and price points make Stella Bella Wines an important producer for Margaret River. Exports Stella Bella, Suckfizzle and Skuttlebutt labels to all major markets.

♀♀♀♀♀ **Suckfizzle Margaret River Sauvignon Blanc Semillon 2015** Always a regional tour de force, this has high quality Graves written all over it. Not merely fermented in French oak (60% new), but aged (40% new) as well for 14 months, with incremental batonnage to amplify the compelling textural detail. A citrus choir with the focus on lemon: lemon grass, lemon curd and ripe Meyer, all soaring along a balancing beam of vanilla cream oak. This is world class, transcending the general malaise when it comes to these oft-abused varieties. Screwcap. 13% alc. **Rating** 97 **To** 2024 $40 NG ✪

♀♀♀♀♀ **Margaret River Sauvignon Blanc 2017** Man alive, the bouquet is positively humming with a potent cocktail of all things tropical! Led by passionfruit, guava, gooseberry and pineapple, and this transitions into the opening stanza of the palate, before a veil of lime, orange and mandarin citrus comes over the top to calm things down. Screwcap. 12.5% alc. **Rating** 95 **To** 2020 $25 ✪
Margaret River Semillon Sauvignon Blanc 2017 This has it all, the X-factor in high relief. The cradle of multifaceted tropical fruits and the bundle of herbs, grass and citrus are perfectly balanced, and they surge on the finish and aftertaste without any congestion. Lovely now, and will be different – but still lovely – in 5+ years. Great value. Screwcap. 12.5% alc. **Rating** 95 **To** 2023 $25 ✪
Serie Luminosa Margaret River Chardonnay 2016 A surprisingly subtle chardonnay for the region, with fermentation in oak followed by settling in tank. Stone fruit hints, wild yeast pungency and crisp mineral energy. A swathe of vanillan oak, barely detectable. The beauty here is in the detail, vinosity and compelling length. Screwcap. 11.7% alc. **Rating** 95 **To** 2025 $65 NG
Skuttlebutt Margaret River Sauvignon Blanc Semillon 2017 This wine has it both ways: tropical fruits of all kinds headed by sauvignon blanc's passionfruit on the bouquet, palate and finish, and semillon's firmer hand on the tiller throughout the journey providing shape and texture. Great value, of course. Screwcap. 12% alc. **Rating** 94 **To** 2019 $18 ✪
Margaret River Cabernet Sauvignon 2015 This is benchmark proprietary cabernet. Mid to full-weighted, it exudes regional pastille and olive DNA, melded effortlessly to currant, plum and bay leaf notes. The tannins are palpable, albeit massaged to the gentler side in the name of mid-tern ageability and savour. Screwcap. 14% alc. **Rating** 94 **To** 2025 $38 NG

♀♀♀♀♀ **Suckfizzle Margaret River Cabernet Sauvignon 2015 Rating** 93 **To** 2025 $55 NG
Margaret River Shiraz 2016 Rating 92 **To** 2024 $32 NG

Margaret River Cabernet Merlot 2016 Rating 92 To 2022 $25 NG ✪
Margaret River Sangiovese Cabernet Sauvignon 2016 Rating 90 To 2022
$32 NG
Margaret River Tempranillo 2016 Rating 90 To 2021 $32 NG

Steve Wiblin's Erin Eyes ★★★★★

58 Old Road, Leasingham, SA 5452 (postal) **Region** Clare Valley
T (08) 8843 0023 **www.**erineyes.com.au **Open** Not
Winemaker Steve Wiblin **Est.** 2009 **Dozens** 2500
Steve Wiblin became a winemaker accidentally when he was encouraged by his mentor at
Tooheys Brewery, who had a love of fine art and fine wine. This was 38 years ago, and because
Tooheys owned Wynns and Seaview, Steve's change in career from beer to wine was easy. He
watched the acquisition of Wynns and Seaview by Penfolds, and then Seppelt, before moving
to Orlando, US. He moved from the world of big wineries to small when he co-founded
Neagles Rock in 1997. In 2009 he left Neagles Rock and established Erin Eyes, explaining,
'in 1842 my English convict forebear John Wiblin gazed into a pair of Erin eyes. That gaze
changed our family make-up and history forever. In the Irish-influenced Clare Valley, what
else would I call my wines but Erin Eyes?'

🍷🍷🍷🍷🍷 **Pride of Erin Single Vineyard Reserve Clare Valley Riesling 2017** A high
quality wine by any standards, fully reflecting the vineyard and the vintage – the
hand of the winemaker simply respecting the quality of the grapes. There is a core
of juicy citrus, flanked on either side by minerally acidity that gives the wine its
structure and length. Screwcap. 12% alc. **Rating** 95 To 2032 $35 ✪
Ballycapple Clare Valley Cabernet Sauvignon 2016 From 35yo vines,
matured for 20 months in French oak. Excellent deep crimson–purple hue; the
bouquet suggests what the palate confirms. This is the best Erin Eyes Cabernet
Sauvignon made to date in a region that does little more than tolerate cabernet.
It is rich in blackcurrant/cassis, with tannins assisting rather than quarrelling with
the fruit, oak a finishing touch. Screwcap. 14.5% alc. **Rating** 95 To 2031

🍷🍷🍷🍷🍷 **Emerald Isle Clare Valley Riesling 2017** Rating 91 To 2030 $24
Shamrock Clare Valley Malbec 2015 Rating 91 To 2029 $30
Blarney Stone Clare Valley Shiraz 2016 Rating 90 To 2036

Sticks Yarra Valley | Rising ★★★★

206 Yarraview Road, Yarra Glen, Vic 3775 (postal) **Region** Yarra Valley
T (03) 9224 1911 **www.**sticks.com.au **Open** Not
Winemaker Tom Belford, Travis Bush **Est.** 2000 **Dozens** 25 000
Sticks produces cool-climate wines that embody the regional characteristics and diversity of
the Yarra Valley. The winemaking team is headed by Tom Belford, who has been with Sticks
for over 10 years and knows the valley intimately. Fruit is sourced from the renowned Rising
Vineyard at Christmas Hills, as well as from other growers across the valley. Their Rising label
was released in 2017; the wines made with minimal intervention from premium parcels of
fruit exclusively from the Rising Vineyard.

🍷🍷🍷🍷🍷 **Rising Chardonnay 2017** The wine label must set a record for being the most
boring, seemingly dirty (it's not), devoid of any pretence of useful information.
The wine in the mouth is a different story; strongly varietal, and reminiscent of
Rising Vineyard, when I made one of Coldstream Hills' most awarded wines back
in '88. Screwcap. 13% alc. **Rating** 93 To 2026 $30
Pinot Noir 2016 From vineyards in Dixon's Creek, Yarra Glen and Coldstream,
separately vinified with different techniques and temperatures, matured in barrel and
tank for 10 months. Deep, clear crimson, it is brimful of spicy red and purple fruit
flavours offering rich rewards to those who drink half (mandatory at this mind-
bending price) and cellar half. Screwcap. 13.5% alc. **Rating** 93 To 2028 $20 ✪
Rising Gamay 2017 This wine is unlike the accidental/minimalist labels for the
Rising series. Light, bright crimson; don't be fooled for a second by the colour,

this has a wealth of sauteed strawberry and raspberry flavours. Sweet on the palate, dry on the finish and aftertaste. Best now/soonish with its fruits in full flower. Screwcap. 12.5% alc. **Rating** 92 **To** 2022 $30

Cabernet Sauvignon 2016 The warmth of the vintage offers opportunities and traps. This nailed it at a beggar's price, the fruit draped over the shoulders of the wine, cassis, palate and bramble all contributing. Screwcap. 14% alc. **Rating** 92 **To** 2031 $20 **❍**

Rising Shiraz 2017 There's no information about the fermentation techniques used, but there has to be a whole-bunch component. The bouquet has spiced barnyard aromas against a background of luscious dark fruits and soft tannins. Screwcap. 12.5% alc. **Rating** 91 **To** 2032 $30

Rising Pinot Noir 2017 Crimson-purple; the difference between this wine and its Gamay sibling is substantial in every way, summarised by the savoury nature of this wine. Blossom-like plum aromas set the scene for spicy/savoury plum flavours that finish short. Screwcap. 12.5% alc. **Rating** 90 **To** 2022 $30

Stockman's Ridge Wines   ★★★★

21 Boree Lane, Lidster, NSW 2800 **Region** Orange
T (02) 6365 6512 **www**.stockmansridge.com.au **Open** Thurs–Mon 1105
Winemaker Jonathan Hambrook **Est.** 2002 **Dozens** 2000 **Vyds** 3ha
Stockman's Ridge Wines, founded and owned by Jonathan Hambrook, started its wine life in Bathurst, before relocating to its present vineyard on the northwest slopes of Mt Canobolas, at an elevation of 800m. Jonathan has planted 1.2ha of pinot noir and 1ha of gruner veltliner. His next door neighbour is the Booree Lane Vineyard, owned by Bob Clark, who has 21.6ha of shiraz, merlot, cabernet franc, chardonnay and gewurztraminer. Exports to the US and China.

♥♥♥♥♥ Handcrafted Central Ranges Savagnin 2015 A settled, composed, gently developed white wine with fruit power aplenty and the texture to match. Honeysuckle, crisp green apples, poached pears, crushed dry fennel and citrus. Lots of torque to this wine's motor. Drink it soonish and you'll be in clover. Screwcap. 11.6% alc. **Rating** 93 **To** 2021 $30 CM

Handcrafted Central Ranges Pinot Noir 2015 Completely different beast to the Rider Pinot Noir of the same vintage. This is tangier, fresher, wilder and awash with undergrowth-like characters. Sour cherry rather than stewed/sweet, fistfuls of fresh herbs rather than dry, and with stringy, twiggy tannin pulling through on the finish. This is more authentic to the variety; the Rider is the safer version. Screwcap. 13.2% alc. **Rating** 91 **To** 2023 $30 CM

Rider Orange Sauvignon Blanc 2016 Smoke and nettle notes marshal forces before the cavalry of tropical fruit arrives. It has texture and power, both aided by a smidgen of fruit sweetness, though it finishes dry and with no shortage of finesse. Tasty. Screwcap. 12.5% alc. **Rating** 90 **To** 2019 $25 CM

Rider Central Ranges Pinot Gris 2016 Straw-coloured with the slightest tinge of pink. There's plenty of fruit here and a good crackle of spice too, the show continuing faithfully through to a warmish but satisfying finish. Keep it nicely chilled. Screwcap. 13.7% alc. **Rating** 90 **To** 2019 $25 CM

♥♥♥♥   Rider Central Ranges Pinot Noir 2015 Rating 89 **To** 2022 $25 CM

Stomp Wine   ★★★★

504 Wilderness Road, Lovedale, NSW 2330 **Region** Hunter Valley
T 0409 774 280 **www**.stompwine.com.au **Open** Thurs–Mon 10–5
Winemaker Michael McManus **Est.** 2004 **Dozens** 1000
After a seeming lifetime in the food and beverage industry, Michael and Meredith McManus moved to full-time winemaking. They have set up Stomp Winemaking, a contract winemaker designed to keep small and larger parcels of grapes separate through the fermentation and maturation process, thus meeting the needs of boutique wine producers in the Hunter Valley. The addition of their own Stomp label is a small but important part of their business.

♥♥♥♥♡ **Limited Release Orange Sauvignon Blanc 2017** Sophisticated sauvignon blanc from a site lying at 900m in Orange. A light-bodied palate promotes greengage, nettle and snow pea, underlain by soused-guava acidity, gently pungent, yet fruity enough to mitigate sauvignon's tendencies towards excessive herbaceousness. Screwcap. 13% alc. **Rating** 92 **To** 2019 $23 NG ◐

Hunter Valley Verdelho 2017 Cold-fermented in stainless steel to retain primary fruit freshness; in this wine lie the usual culprits of pulpy grapefruit, quince, guava, nashi pear and candied citrus rind. The acidity is gentle and seemingly natural, promoting an easy-going drinkability. Screwcap. 13% alc. **Rating** 91 **To** 2019 $21 NG ◐

Vivre Sparkling Verdelho NV Fermented a second time in pressurised tank, this is fruity, frothy and built for guzzling with a good chill. Guava, orchard fruits, sherbet, and all. This is done well. Very. I hesitate to say it, but this is among the more salacious, yet enjoyable, verdelho I have tasted. The fizz, chill and acidity are all vehicles to corral any cloyingness, especially given the dollop of residual sugar (16g/l). They are applied with a deft touch. Crown seal. 12.5% alc. **Rating** 90 $25 NG

Stone Bridge Wines   ★★★★

Section 113 Gillentown Road, Clare, SA 5453 **Region** Clare Valley
T (08) 8843 4143 **www.**stonebridgewines.com.au **Open** Thurs–Mon 10–4
Winemaker Craig Thomson, Angela Meaney **Est.** 2005 **Dozens** 3500 **Vyds** 34ha
'From little things, big things grow' is certainly true for Craig and Lisa Thomson, who planted 0.6ha of shiraz in 1997 and now own 34ha in three locations in the Clare Valley. They crush around 150t, more than 10 times their first batch in '05, when they launched the Stone Bridge Wines label and cellar door. They make grenache, riesling, shiraz, malbec, pinot gris and sangiovese, along with sparkling wines made in the traditional method. Their winery is also a contract processing plant for local and interstate wine labels. Visitors to the rammed earth cellar door can enjoy pizza (May–Sept) from the wood-fired oven made by Craig, a baker by trade. Exports to Canada, Denmark, Singapore and China.

♥♥♥♥♥ **Clare Valley Riesling 2017** An altogether riveting example of the '17 vintage, with great drive and intensity. No Meyer lemon here – instead in its place, green lime and grapefruit zest, and no sweetening. It's so mouthwatering; it's so great now, its undoubted future is of little interest to most purchasers. Screwcap. 12.2% alc. **Rating** 94 **To** 2027

Clare Valley Grenache Mataro 2016 A surprise packet, bright colour first up setting the scene for a lively red berry/cherry bouquet, the flavours speaking of perfectly ripened fruits, natural acidity and freshness its calling card. Ready now. Screwcap. 14% alc. **Rating** 94 **To** 2029

♥♥♥♥♡ **Clare Valley Pinot Gris 2017 Rating** 90 **To** 2019

Stonefish   ★★★★

24 Kangarilla Road, McLaren Vale, SA 5171 (postal) **Region** Various
T (02) 9668 9930 **www.**stonefishwines.com.au **Open** Not
Winemaker Contract, Peter Papanikitas **Est.** 2000 **Dozens** 10 000
Peter Papanikitas has been involved in various facets of the wine industry for the past 30+ years. His contact was initially with companies that included Penfolds, Lindemans and Leo Buring, then he spent five years working for Cinzano, gaining experience in worldwide sales and marketing. In 2000 he established Stonefish, a virtual winery operation, in partnership with various grapegrowers and winemakers, principally in the Barossa Valley and Margaret River, who provide the wines. The value for money has never been in doubt, but Stonefish has moved to another level with its Icon and Reserve wines. Exports to China, Thailand, Vietnam, Hong Kong, Indonesia, the Philippines, the Maldives, Singapore and Fiji.

♥♥♥♥♡ **Nero Old Vines Barossa Valley Shiraz 2014** This is sumptuous, with any hard edges seamlessly buried by waves of silken textures and ripe fruit flavours: purple and black fruit allusions. Violet lift on the nose. Olive and pepper grind too. This is warm-climate shiraz glimpsing a cool-climate idiom, with the stuffing and vinosity of older vine material. Well done. Cork. 14.5% alc. **Rating** 93 **To** 2026 $43 NG

Nero Margaret River Cabernet Sauvignon 2015 The attention to detail across this wine's vinification leaves little doubt as to quality aspirations. Top French oak too (50% new), for 15 months of maturation. Yet the fruit is machine-harvested, suggesting this may well have something to do with the wine's coarse underbelly. Still, typical cabernet astringency drips with sapid currant flavours and a wine gum juiciness. A potpourri of dried, exotic herbs in the mix too. In all, this screams variety and region. Screwcap. 14% alc. **Rating** 93 **To** 2028 $37 NG

Icon Barossa Valley Shiraz 2014 This vermilion, potent-looking shiraz was hand-picked 14 days or so prior to fermentation followed by 24 months in French oak (60% new). Coffee-grind, oaky tannins mosey with blueberry, black cherry and dried plum, leaving one with the impression of needing a plate of Peking duck to tame it all! Remorseless! This is drying, but will please those who like it a bit over the top. Cork. 15% alc. **Rating** 91 **To** 2025 $80 NG

Reserve Margaret River Cabernet Sauvignon 2016 Textbook Margaret River cabernet, with cassis, sage and tea leaf astringency melding with quality French oak tannins. An undercarriage of green olive mitigates any sweetness. Mid-weighted and highly savoury, and this is just on the more brittle side than most. Screwcap. 14.5% alc. **Rating** 91 **To** 2026 $33 NG

Reserve Margaret River Chardonnay 2015 Barrel-fermented before spending 6 months in French barrels (40% new), this is a rich, bumptious chardonnay. Billows of vanillan oak tie in a wave of peach, caramelised apple tart and nectarine. The acidity is tangy and pushes it all along, yet the oak needs time to nestle. A bit over the top at the moment. Screwcap. 13.2% alc. **Rating** 90 **To** 2021 $33 NG

♀♀♀♀ **Reserve Barossa Valley Shiraz 2016 Rating** 89 **To** 2024 $33 NG

Stonehurst Cedar Creek   ★★★☆

1840 Wollombi Road, Cedar Creek, NSW 2325 **Region** Hunter Valley
T (02) 4998 1576 www.stonehurst.com.au **Open** 7 days 10–5
Winemaker Tamburlaine **Est.** 1995 **Dozens** 4000 **Vyds** 6.5ha
Stonehurst Cedar Creek has been established by Daryl and Phillipa Heslop on a historic 220ha property in the Wollombi Valley, underneath the Pokolbin Range. The vineyards (planted to chambourcin, semillon, chardonnay and shiraz) are organically grown. A substantial part of the business, however, is the six self-contained cottages on the property. Exports to all major markets.

♀♀♀♀♀ **Reserve Hunter Valley Chardonnay 2014** Hand-picked, 70% tank-fermented and matured, 30% in new French oak. It comes together well, the wine looking more youthful than its '17 sibling, with stone fruit foremost, some citrussy acidity, the oak subtle. Screwcap. 13% alc. **Rating** 90 **To** 2020 $25

Stoney Rise   ★★★★★

96 Hendersons Lane, Gravelly Beach, Tas 7276 **Region** Northern Tasmania
T (03) 6394 3678 www.stoneyrise.com **Open** Thurs–Mon 11–5
Winemaker Joe Holyman **Est.** 2000 **Dozens** 2000 **Vyds** 7.2ha
The Holyman family had been involved in vineyards in Tasmania for 20 years, but Joe Holyman's career in the wine industry, first as a sales rep, then as a wine buyer, and more recently working in wineries in NZ, Portugal, France, Mount Benson and Coonawarra, gave him an exceptionally broad-based understanding of wine. In 2004 Joe and wife Lou purchased the former Rotherhythe Vineyard, which had been established in 1986, and set about restoring it to its former glory. There are two ranges: the Stoney Rise wines, focusing on fruit and early drinkability; and the Holyman wines, with more structure, more new oak

and the best grapes, here the focus is on length and potential longevity. Exports to the UK, the Netherlands, Singapore and Japan.

ΨΨΨΨΨ Holyman Chardonnay 2016 Straw with bright green hues. Classic cool-climate white flowers and grapefruit presentation cantilevered with spicy/toasty oak and yeast-derived complexity. The palate is pure, textured and long. A lovely line of acidity adding length and dimension. Hard to fault, although some will quibble over the oak level. Screwcap. 12.5% alc. **Rating** 95 **To** 2025 $55 DB
Holyman Project X Pinot Noir 2015 The big broody wine of the Holyman stable. The dark purple-red colour indicative of what is to come – ripe black cherry, blue fruits and plum, sweet vanilla from 100% new oak, Chinese five-spice from whole bunches. The lot, really. Despite the aromatic intensity, it's surprisingly elegant and light on its feet (only 12.5% alcohol) with fine, persistent tannin and a taut cranberry acidity that adds both line and length. One for the cellar to let the oak become one. Screwcap. **Rating** 95 **To** 2030 $90 DB
Holyman Pinot Noir 2016 Bright cherry red with a pale hue. Lovely, pristine red fruit – redcurrant, alpine strawberry, cherry and perhaps pomegranate. Oak is a player on the palate adding both spice and grainy tannins, and leaving a chalky aftertaste. Will doubtless evolve well over time given its inherent depth of fruit and structure. Screwcap. 12.5% alc. **Rating** 94 **To** 2026 $55 DB

ΨΨΨΨΨ Pinot Noir 2016 Rating 92 **To** 2023 $30 DB
Trousseau 2017 Rating 92 **To** 2018 $40 DB

Stonier Wines   ★★★★★
Cnr Thompson's Lane/Frankston-Flinders Road, Merricks, Vic 3916
Region Mornington Peninsula
T (03) 5989 8300 **www**.stonier.com.au **Open** 7 days 11–5
Winemaker Michael Symons, Will Byron, Luke Burkley **Est.** 1978 **Dozens** 35 000
Vyds 17.6ha
This may be one of the most senior wineries on the Mornington Peninsula, but that does not stop it moving with the times. It has embarked on a serious sustainability program that touches on all aspects of its operations. It is one of the few wineries in Australia to measure its carbon footprint in detail, using the officially recognised system of the Winemaker's Federation of Australia. It is steadily reducing its consumption of electricity; it uses rainwater, collected from the winery roof, for rinsing and washing in the winery, as well as for supplying the winery in general; it has created a balanced ecosystem in the vineyard by strategic planting of cover crops and reduction of sprays; and it has reduced its need to irrigate. All the Stonier wines are estate-grown and made with a mix of wild yeast (from initiation of fermentation) and cultured yeast (added towards the end of fermentation to ensure that no residual sugar remains), and almost all are destemmed to open fermenters. All have a two-stage maturation – always French oak and variable use of barriques and puncheons for the first stage. Exports to all major markets.

ΨΨΨΨΨ W-WB Mornington Peninsula Pinot Noir 2016 From 0.5ha of vines trained lower to the ground on the Windmill Vineyard in '11; 100% whole bunches, then a multi-stage French oak maturation and selection. The colour is good, the bouquet and palate with more verve and complexity than the other wines in the Stonier '16 release, the whole bunches investing the wine with lovely forest floor and spice notes grafted onto the cherry plum base. Screwcap. 14.5% alc. **Rating** 96 **To** 2029 $85
Gainsborough Park Vineyard Mornington Peninsula Chardonnay 2016 Fermented in French puncheons (25% new), 100% mlf. After 6 months, selected barrels were blended and matured for a further 2 months in used puncheons. Bright quartz-green; the wine must have had very high acidity before it went through mlf, for neither it (mlf) nor the blending and further oak maturation have blurred the fruit profile. Grapefruit and Granny Smith apple fruit flavours at 14% alcohol are another deviation from accepted wisdom. Altogether interesting. Screwcap. 14% alc. **Rating** 95 **To** 2024 $45

Reserve Mornington Peninsula Chardonnay 2016 From the KBS (50%), Thompson (25%), Lyncroft and Jimjoca vineyards, whole-bunch pressed, fermented in French puncheons (25% new), 70% mlf, blended after 7 months. Blending by no means guarantees synergy, but it has been achieved here, with the KBS and Thompson components doing most of the heavy lifting. There is good tactile grip, the flavours tipped towards grapefruit, the length very good. Screwcap. 14% alc. **Rating** 95 **To** 2029 $48

KBS Vineyard Mornington Peninsula Chardonnay 2016 Fermented in French puncheons (25% new), 50% mlf, blended after 6 months, and returned to used puncheons for a further 5 months. A bright, light, fresh colour, bouquet and palate – but well it's not quite that simple. The fruit/acid/oak balance is very good, the flavours fine and grapefruit-driven, albeit with a backing of white peach and apple. Harmony is its ace in the hole. Screwcap. 13.5% alc. **Rating** 95 **To** 2027 $50

Thompson Vineyard Mornington Peninsula Chardonnay 2016 Fermented in French puncheons, no mlf, blended after 6 months, matured for a further 5 months in a new puncheon. Has the most intensity and drive of the Stonier Chardonnays, and takes no prisoners. This is love it or leave it, far from the comfort of sitting room chairs accorded by most of its siblings. Zero mlf was a huge call, and one I agree with, leaving white and pink grapefruit free to range at will. Before the jury can deliver its verdict, 5+ years are needed. Screwcap. 13.5% alc. **Rating** 95 **To** 2031 $55

Reserve Mornington Peninsula Pinot Noir 2016 From six vineyards in almost equal proportions, matured separately in French oak (16% new) for 7 months before blending, and a further 4 months in barrel. Clear crimson hue; lifts the ante with a fragrant and pure mix of cherry and plum, then a seamless transition to the delicious, fresh and finely pitched palate. The inclusion of 15% whole bunches gives the wine the X-factor that separates it from its similarly priced siblings. Screwcap. 14.5% alc. **Rating** 95 **To** 2027 $60

Windmill Vineyard Mornington Peninsula Pinot Noir 2016 Fermented in five French barriques (20% new; one barrique with 100% whole bunches), matured for 7 months, then blended and matured for a further 2 months. The combination of 20% whole-bunch fermentation and new barriques has imprinted the winemakers' thumbprints firmly on the wine, taking it in a direction different to all of its siblings. Vive la difference, for there is the depth of fruit to respond well to the vinification. Screwcap. 14.5% alc. **Rating** 95 **To** 2030 $65

Windmill Vineyard Mornington Peninsula Pinot Noir 2015 Bright, clear crimson; complex bouquet, obvious oak first up then other fruit-based notes come forward. The palate has fruit/acid drive that is transfixing, the finish particularly so. Fascinating. Very good wine, the outcome of some audacious winemaking. Screwcap. 14.5% alc. **Rating** 95 **To** 2023 $65

Lyncroft Vineyard Mornington Peninsula Chardonnay 2016 Rating 94 To 2028 $35

Lyncroft Vineyard Mornington Peninsula Pinot Noir 2016 Rating 94 To 2026 $55

Merron's Vineyard Mornington Peninsula Pinot Noir 2016 Rating 94 To 2026 $60

Stonier Family Vineyard Mornington Peninsula Pinot Noir 2016 Rating 94 To 2028 $85

♀♀♀♀♀ **Jimjoca Vineyard Pinot Noir 2016** Rating 93 To 2025 $45
Chardonnay 2016 Rating 91 To 2021 $30 CM
Pinot Noir 2016 Rating 91 To 2023 $28 CM
Jack's Ridge Vineyard Pinot Noir 2016 Rating 91 To 2023 $50

Stormflower Vineyard

3503 Caves Road, Wilyabrup, WA 6280 **Region** Margaret River
T (08) 9755 6211 **www**.stormflower.com.au **Open** 7 days 11–5
Winemaker Stuart Pym **Est.** 2007 **Dozens** 2500 **Vyds** 9ha

Stormflower Vineyard is owned by David Martin, Howard Cearns and Nic Trimboli, three friends better known as co-founders of Little Creatures Brewery in Fremantle. They thought the location of the property (and the vineyard on it that had been planted in the mid-'90s) was ideal for producing high quality wines. But whether they knew that storms hit the property on a regular basis, with hail and wind impacting the crop in most seasons, isn't known. What is known, however, is the investment they have made in the vineyard by pulling out one-third of the vines planted in the wrong way, in the wrong place, leaving the present 9ha of cabernet sauvignon, shiraz, chardonnay, sauvignon blanc, semillon and chenin blanc in place. The driving force in the vineyard is David Martin, who has a family background in agriculture. They have moved the management focus towards organic compost and natural soil biology, gaining an 'In Conversion to Organic' certificatation awarded by NASAA (National Association for Sustainable Agriculture, Australia) in '15.

Margaret River Cabernet Shiraz 2016 Mouthfilling, rich and generous; brimming with luscious purple and black fruits; the tannins soft; the oak a means to an end, not an end in itself. Screwcap. 14.5% alc. **Rating** 92 **To** 2029 $27
Margaret River Semillon Sauvignon Blanc 2017 A blend of 51% semillon, 35% sauvignon blanc, 14% chardonnay fermented separately (two different yeasts); 30% finishing fermentation in French oak (40% new) before being returned to tank where it remained for 3 months on lees before blending. The thought and effort that went into the vinification of this wine have been repaid handsomely. It's not a giant-killer, it's a seductress. Screwcap. 13% alc. **Rating** 91 **To** 2021 $25
Margaret River Shiraz 2014 Has held its hue very well; a full-bodied shiraz that speaks clearly of its variety, but not so much of its place. It's well made, with plum and blackberry fruit driving the wine, the new French oak totally integrated. Nice shiraz. Screwcap. 14.5% alc. **Rating** 91 **To** 2029 $28

Studley Park Vineyard

5 Garden Terrace, Kew, Vic 3101 (postal) **Region** Port Phillip
T (03) 9254 2777 **www**.studleypark.com.au **Open** Not
Winemaker Llew Knight (Contract) **Est.** 1994 **Dozens** 250 **Vyds** 0.5ha

Geoff Pryor's Studley Park Vineyard is one of Melbourne's best-kept secrets. It is situated on a bend of the Yarra River barely 4km from the Melbourne CBD, on a 0.5ha block once planted to vines, but for a century was used for market gardening, and then replanted with cabernet sauvignon. A spectacular aerial photograph shows that immediately across the river, and looking directly to the CBD, is the epicentre of Melbourne's light industrial development, while on the northern and eastern boundaries are suburban residential blocks.

Rose 2017 Bright orange-crimson in colour and it puts on a pretty distinctive turn in the mouth too. Blood orange, sweet red cherry, cooked apple, dust and spice flavours run juicily throughout, offering a decent amount of pleasure as they do. Light-ish, but it's not bad at all. Screwcap. 13% alc. **Rating** 90 **To** 2019 CM
Rose 2016 Made from cabernet sauvignon. Bright, light crimson; vibrant red and morello cherry aromas switch to fresh cassis on the palate. Perfect fruit weight, balance and mouthfeel. It won't fade away, but will just become even more complex. Great value. Screwcap. 13% alc. **Rating** 90 **To** 2020 $15 ✪

Stumpy Gully

1247 Stumpy Gully Road, Moorooduc, Vic 3933 **Region** Mornington Peninsula
T 1800 STUMPY (788679) **www**.stumpygully.com.au **Open** Thurs–Sun 10–5
Winemaker Wendy Zantvoort, Frank Zantvoort, Michael Zantvoort **Est.** 1988
Dozens 12 000 **Vyds** 40ha

Frank and Wendy Zantvoort began planting their first vineyard in 1988; Wendy, having enrolled in the oenology course at CSU, subsequently graduated with a Bachelor of Applied Science in Oenology. In addition to the original vineyard, they have deliberately gone against prevailing thinking with their Moorooduc vineyard, planting it solely to red varieties, predominantly cabernet sauvignon, merlot and shiraz. They believe they have one of the warmest sites on the Peninsula, and that ripening should present no problems to late-ripening varieties such as shiraz and sangiovese. Exports to all major markets.

🍷🍷🍷🍷♀ **Mornington Peninsula Sangiovese 2016** Good depth to the colour; a wine that steps out well from the first whiff, and keeps the conversation flowing until the last sip. The full cherry tribe – savoury, red, black, morello and whatever you would like to nominate – are there to be had. Ironic, given the difficulty of growing and making good sangiovese. Screwcap. 13.6% alc. **Rating** 92 **To** 2024

Magic Black Zantvoort Reserve Pinot Noir 2016 Wild yeast–open fermented on skins for 10 days. Matured for 9 months in new French oak, which has inevitably impacted the bouquet and palate. However, its deep crimson colour and a generous assemblage of dark cherry and plum fruit should push the oak off the stage in a few years. Good outcome for a challenging vintage. Screwcap. 13.8% alc. **Rating** 91 **To** 2026

Mornington Peninsula Pinot Grigio 2017 Has been carefully made from estate-grown fruit. The varietal character is good, and the wine has both concentration and length. Needs food to go with it, but should match most you try. Screwcap. 13.8% alc. **Rating** 90 **To** 2019

Peninsula Panorama Shiraz 2015 An estate-grown shiraz that handsomely over-delivers in the context of its price. Lashings of spice and pepper are threaded through the dark fruits of this fresh, medium-bodied wine. It won't overwhelm food, and will instead form a synergistic bond with venison or game protein. Screwcap. 13.8% alc. **Rating** 90 **To** 2024 $20 ✪

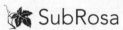

SubRosa ★★★★★

PO Box 181, Ararat, Vic 3377 **Region** Grampians/Pyrenees
T 0478 072 259 **www.**wubrosawine.com.au **Open** Not
Winemaker Adam Louder **Est.** 2013 **Dozens** 400
SubRosa is one of the best new wineries in this *Wine Companion*, and is created by two high performance partners in life and in this new exceptional winery. The 37yo Adam Louder had completed 31 vintages in the Grampians, Pyrenees, Margaret River, Bordeaux and the Napa Valley, most with famous names. He met Gold Coast–born partner Nancy Panter in the Napa Valley in 2011 while she was working for Visa on projects that included the Olympic Games, FIFA World Cup and NFL. After the '12 London Olympics, she and Adam split their time between the US and Australia, returning permanently to Australia in '15, after having laid the ground work for SubRosa in '13. This is a business that will win gold medals galore should it enter wine shows.

🍷🍷🍷🍷🍷 **Pyrenees Shiraz 2015** Grown by the John family at Malakoff Estate, matured for 16 months in French barriques. Its deeper crimson-purple colour and medium to full-bodied palate are in continuing contrast for the two SubRosa shirazs, but not in the skill of the winemaker. If 'balance' is said to be the one word to describe a great wine, then this wine personifies balance. This exudes velvety black cherry at every turn. Cedary oak nuances and persistent, pliable tannins complete the picture. Screwcap. 15% alc. **Rating** 96 **To** 2040 $45 ✪

Grampians Shiraz 2015 Estate-grown, matured for 16 months in French barriques, neither fined nor filtered. Bright in colour and light in body (by Grampians standards). Its mouthfeel, balance and studied length are on another level, with vibrant red fruits, spices and feather-light tannins. Screwcap. 14% alc. **Rating** 95 **To** 2030 $45

Pyrenees Nebbiolo 2015 From the Malakoff Estate, matured for 12 months in used French barriques. Well, it's like jumping into the surf thinking it's going to be very cold, only to find it's perfect. Coming to the end of the day's tasting, nebbiolo tannins can fill the mouth like fast-drying cement. This is a high quality wine by any standards, complete with violets on the bouquet, sumptuous dark fruits and millimetre perfect tannins. Screwcap. 13.5% alc. **Rating** 95 **To** 2029 $30 ○

♟♟♟♟♟ Viognier 2015 **Rating** 92 **To** 2023 $30

Summerfield ★★★★★

5967 Stawell-Avoca Road, Moonambel, Vic 3478 **Region** Pyrenees
T (03) 5467 2264 **www**.summerfieldwines.com **Open** Mon–Sat 10–5, Sun 10–3
Winemaker Mark Summerfield **Est.** 1979 **Dozens** 4000 **Vyds** 18.2ha
Founder Ian Summerfield handed over the winemaker reins to son Mark several years ago. Mark has significantly refined the style of the wines with the introduction of French oak, and by reducing the alcohol without compromising the intensity and concentration of the wines. If anything, the longevity of the wines produced by Mark will be even greater than that of the American-oaked wines of bygone years. Exports to Japan and China.

♟♟♟♟♟ Sahsah Shiraz 2016 Mark Summerfield prefers to leave the wines – and in particular alcohol levels – unchanged, but the fast and furious Trump-like vintage resulted in levels above the comfort zone, so he used reverse osmosis to reduce the alcohol of this wine by 0.5%. It has resulted in a wine of limitless energy, allowing a complex array of spices to decorate the fruitcake richness of the palate, and no heat whatsoever on the finish. Screwcap. 14.7% alc. **Rating** 96 **To** 2040 $75 ○
Reserve Pyrenees Shiraz 2016 Open-fermented with 20% whole bunches, hand-plunged, matured for 18 months in French and American oak (30% new). A distinctive and attractive bouquet brings dark chocolate, blackberry, black cherry, satsuma plum and spices into play, the texture of the palate providing a nuanced array of varietal fruit flavours, the tannins ripe and also playing a part in achieving gently savoury balance. Screwcap. 14.9% alc. **Rating** 96 **To** 2039 $63 ○
Pyrenees Shiraz 2016 Deep colour; in rich and bold Summerfield style, which sees voluminous blackberry and cherry fruits improbably retain elegance, freshness and juiciness. A wine that has the best of all possible roles. Screwcap. 14.6% alc. **Rating** 95 **To** 2031 $39
Taiyo Cabernet Sauvignon 2016 Here there are real surprises in the form of 50% whole bunches and 18 months in French oak (30% new). There's no doubting the fundamental differences imposed by the oak type and whole bunches, my answer to the question of quality to be found in the points – they are the same. Screwcap. 13.7% alc. **Rating** 95 **To** 2041 $75
Pyrenees Cabernet Sauvignon 2016 Mark has long been at peace with his vines and his wines, so there's little or no point in asking rhetorical questions about the matching of American oak and cabernet, any more than you would of Penfolds and Bin 707. And with its ripe blackcurrant and its relatively soft tannins, there's no denying the quality of this full-bodied cabernet. Screwcap. 14.7% alc. **Rating** 95 **To** 2036 $36
Saieh Shiraz 2016 As with its Sahsah sibling, reverse osmosis was used to reduce the alcohol level by 1.5%, the original 16.3% a direct consequence of yields of 1.25t/ha. Its dense, deep colour leaves little doubt about the rapidity of the ripening in this early vintage. The tannins interrupt the story, but the cure (aggressive fining) may well have been worse than the illness. Screwcap. 14.8% alc. **Rating** 94 **To** 2030 $75

♟♟♟♟♟ Back Block Sparkling Shiraz 2015 **Rating** 90 $40

Summit Estate ★★★★

291 Granite Belt Drive, Thulimbah, Qld 4377 **Region** Granite Belt
T (07) 4683 2011 **www**.summitestate.com.au **Open** 7 days 10–4.30
Winemaker Mike Hayes **Est.** 1997 **Dozens** 2000 **Vyds** 4.01ha
Summit Estate, at 925m, is planted to chardonnay, marsanne, viognier, verdelho, muscat, pinot noir, shiraz, merlot, tempranillo, mourvedre, grenache, malbec, petit verdot and cabernet sauvignon, and they have set up a small, specialised contract winemaking facility.

ΨΨΨΨΨ **Granite Belt Viognier 2016** An interesting and challenging variety to make, but Mike Hayes has pulled it off here. It's got positive varietal fruit throughout, and while the finish exerts its hold on the palate, it doesn't slam the door shut. Drink soon. Screwcap. 13.5% alc. **Rating** 93 **To** 2020

QC Granite Belt Queensland Cabernet 2016 A blend of 85% cabernet sauvignon and carmenere, 10% merlot, 5% petit verdot. In the Summit Estate pattern – light colour, light body, and elegant balance and mouthfeel to its exotic mix of blackcurrant, blueberry and spices galore. The modest alcohol has also contributed. Screwcap. 14% alc. **Rating** 92 **To** 2025

Reserve Granite Belt Tempranillo 2016 Rich and medium to full-bodied on first acquaintance, but smoothes out with a supple and lingering finish. Tannins rather than oak provide texture and structure. Screwcap. 12% alc. **Rating** 91 **To** 2026

ΨΨΨΨ **Wild Ferment Granite Belt Syrah 2016 Rating** 89 **To** 2019

Sunshine Creek

350 Yarraview Road, Yarra Glen, Vic 3775 (postal) **Region** Yarra Valley
T (03) 9818 5142 **www**.sunshinecreek.com.au **Open** Not
Winemaker Chris Lawrence **Est.** 2009 **Dozens** 7000 **Vyds** 100ha
Packaging magnate James Zhou has a wine business in China and, over the years, has worked with an A–Z of distinguished Australian winemakers, including Grant Burge, Philip Shaw, Phillip Jones, Pat Carmody and Geoff Hardy, in bringing their wines to China. It was a logical extension to produce Australian wine of similar quality, and James commissioned Mario Marson to find an appropriate existing vineyard. They discovered Martha's Vineyard, which was planted in the 1980s by Olga Szymiczek. The site was a particularly good one, which compensated for the need to change the existing spur-pruned vineyard (for mechanisation) to vertical shoot position (VSP) for increased quality and hand-picking. At the same time, an extensive program of grafting was undertaken and new clones were planted. In 2011 Andrew Smith (formerly of Lusatia Park Vineyard) was appointed vineyard manager to change the focus of management to sustainability and minimal interference. In '14 winemaker Chris Lawrence joined the team, and an onsite winery (capable of handling 275t) was completed prior to the '16 vintage. In '17 there was a changing of the guard in the winery as Mario decided to concentrate solely on his Vinea Marson brand, and Chris took on the role of chief winemaker. Exports to Hong Kong, Japan and China.

ΨΨΨΨΨ **Yarra Valley Chardonnay 2015** What a difference a year makes, because the '15 is a replica of the previous vintage in terms of winemaking: hand-picked, whole-bunch pressed with wild and inoculated yeasts, matured in French oak (30% new) for 10 months. Here is a fresh, flavoursome yet composed wine with just the right amount of citrus, stone fruit, creamy leesy notes and oak spices for the bright acidity to carry through to the persistent finish. Diam. 13.5% alc. **Rating** 93 **To** 2023 $45 JF

Heathcote Shiraz 2015 No shortage of flavours here: spiced black plums, new leather, menthol, bay leaves, wood smoke and scorched earth. The wine spends 1 year in French barrels (30% new), and aside from cedary wood spices, the fruit has soaked up the oak. There is a ripeness to this and, while the tannins have a firm hold, drink it sooner rather than later. Diam. 14.5% alc. **Rating** 93 **To** 2025 $45 JF

Yarra Valley Cabernets 2015 A 70/9/8/7/6% blend of cabernet sauvignon, malbec, merlot, petit verdot and cabernet franc, aged 1 year in French barrels (30% new); lots of leafy freshness, dried and fresh herbs mingle with blackcurrants, mulberries and sharper cranberries. Medium-bodied, juicy, tart and tangy with firm tannins and cedary oak spice; rather bracing acidity makes it feel as if it is still coming together. Diam. 14% alc. **Rating** 91 **To** 2025 $45 JF

Yarra Valley Pinot Noir 2015 Vibrant, light ruby; deeply aromatic – florals, cherries, woodsy spices and earthy; full-bodied with a bounty of flavours from sweet dark cherries macerated in kirsch, dried herbs to prosciutto, all meeting up with raspy tannins before the wine tapers off with cranberry-tart acidity. While it's aged in French barrels (25% new) for just 10 months, there's a rawness to the oak tannins, giving this quite a bit of grunt. Time might help. Diam. 13.5% alc. **Rating** 90 **To** 2023 $45 JF

Surveyor's Hill Vineyards ★★★★

215 Brooklands Road, Wallaroo, NSW 2618 **Region** Canberra District
T (02) 6230 2046 **www**.survhill.com.au **Open** W'ends & public hols
Winemaker Brindabella Hills (Dr Roger Harris), Greg Gallagher (sparkling) **Est.** 1986
Dozens 1000 **Vyds** 10ha
Surveyor's Hill Vineyards is on the slopes of the eponymous hill, at 550–680m above sea level. It is on an ancient volcano, producing granite-derived, coarse-structured (and hence well-drained) sandy soils of low fertility. This has to be the ultimate patchwork-quilt vineyard, with 1ha each of chardonnay, shiraz and viognier; 0.5ha each of roussanne, marsanne, aglianico, nero d'Avola, mourvedre, grenache, muscadelle, moscato giallo, cabernet franc, riesling, semillon, sauvignon blanc, touriga nacional and cabernet sauvignon.

♟♟♟♟♟ **Hills of Hall Cabernets 2015** Cabernet sauvignon, cabernet franc and a little merlot fill the bouquet and palate in fine style following maturation in French oak. While only medium-bodied, the wine has considerable presence thanks to the purity of the fruit, picked at optimal ripeness. Screwcap. 14.5% alc. **Rating** 94 **To** 2030 $28 ✪

♟♟♟♟♟ **Hills of Hall Shiraz 2016** Rating 91 To 2029 $25
Hills of Hall Cabernet Franc Rose 2017 Rating 90 To 2021 $20 ✪

Sussex Squire ★★★★

293–295 Spring Gully Road, Gillentown, SA 5453 **Region** Clare Valley
T 0458 141 169 **www**.sussexsquire.com.au **Open** 7 days 11–5
Winemaker Daniel Wilson, Mark Bollen **Est.** 2014 **Dozens** 1500 **Vyds** 6ha
There's a long family history attached to this embryonic wine business, starting with Walter Hackett (1827–1914), a Sussex farmer; next came Joseph Hackett (1880–1958), followed by Joseph Robert Hackett (1911–98), and now fourth-generation Mark and Skye Bollen. Over the generations, the family had worked in a successful major grain and seed business, then established the Nyora grazing property near Mintaro and Wyndham Park near Sevenhill, which is still farmed today with herds of black and red Angus cattle. Mark and Skye returned to the Clare Valley after spending 25 years working on other pursuits – Mark in wine sales and marketing, Skye in five-star hotels for a decade before embarking on a successful career in recruitment. In 1998 Mark and Skye planted 6ha of dry-grown, organically managed shiraz, and in lieu of Angus cattle, have a flock of Black Suffolk sheep that roam the vineyard during winter to provide natural weed control and to fertilise the soil.

♟♟♟♟♟ **The Hungry Sheep Single Vineyard Clare Valley Mataro 2016** From a dry-grown vineyard in Penwortham, open-fermented, matured in French oak (30% new) for 12 months, named after the sheep that roam the vineyard in the winter months. Sussex Squire really nailed this wine, getting the picking date at the right moment, and making no mistakes in either vinification or maturation. It's full-flavoured yet fresh, with no cooked fruit characters whatsoever. The oak has been absorbed, leaving the finish clear and bright. Screwcap. 14% alc. **Rating** 94 **To** 2030 $30 ✪

♟♟♟♟♟ **Thomas Block Single Vineyard Clare Valley Shiraz 2016** Rating 93 To 2031 $30
The Partnership Clare Valley Shiraz Mataro 2016 Rating 93 To 2031 $35
Samuel Block Single Vineyard Clare Valley Cabernet Sauvignon 2016 Rating 93 To 2031 $30
The Raging Bull Single Vineyard Clare Valley Malbec 2016 Rating 92 To 2032 $30

Sutherland Estate   ★★★★★

2010 Melba Highway, Dixons Creek, Vic 3775 **Region** Yarra Valley
T 0402 052 287 **www.**sutherlandestate.com.au **Open** W'ends & public hols 10–5
Winemaker Cathy Phelan, Angus Ridley, Rob Hall **Est.** 2000 **Dozens** 1500 **Vyds** 4ha
The Phelan family established Sutherland Estate in 2000 when they purchased a mature
2ha vineyard at Dixons Creek. Further plantings followed. The plantings now consist of 1ha
each of chardonnay and pinot noir, and 0.5ha each of gewurztraminer, cabernet sauvignon,
tempranillo and shiraz. Ron Phelan designed and built the cellar door, which enjoys
stunning views over the Yarra Valley, while daughter Cathy studied Wine Science at CSU.
The sparkling wines are made by Phil Kelly, the reds by Cathy and partner Angus Ridley,
and Chardonnay by Rob Hall.

♥♥♥♥♥ **Daniel's Hill Vineyard Yarra Valley Pinot Noir 2017** Comprising 75%
whole berries, 25% whole bunches wild yeast–open fermented, matured in new
and used French oak. Deeply coloured, and no less deeply flavoured, reflecting
the exceptionally cool vintage. Black cherry flavours have a backdrop of spices
of many hues, tannins in balance with the power of the fruit, oak simply a frame
for the picture. A long and prosperous life ahead. Screwcap. 13.1% alc. **Rating** 95
To 2029 $30 ❍
Yarra Valley Pinot Noir Chardonnay 2012 Made in the traditional method
(i.e. fermented in this bottled) and spent 5 years on tirage/lees. Has exceptional
depth of flavour, with notes of brioche alongside generous fruit. It hits the nail
on the head with the acidity on the finish and lingering aftertaste. Crown seal.
12.5% alc. **Rating** 95 $35 ❍

♥♥♥♥ **Wildcat Unwooded Chardonnay 2017 Rating** 89 To 2020 $18 ❍

Swan Wine Group   ★★★★

218 Murray Street, Tanunda, SA 5352 **Region** Barossa Valley
T (02) 8203 2239 **www.**auswancreek.com.au **Open** Wed–Sun 10–5
Winemaker Ben Riggs **Est.** 2008 **Dozens** 30 000 **Vyds** 12ha
Swan Wine Group was formed through the merger of Inspire Vintage and Australia Swan
Vintage. The jewel in the business is a 10ha vineyard in Angaston – 1.7ha of shiraz planted in
1908 and 0.86ha planted in the '60s; 5.43ha of younger shiraz; 1.76ha of cabernet sauvignon;
and 1.26ha of grenache. The 2ha cellar door and winery vineyard in Tanunda provide the
home base. The major part of the production comes from grapes purchased from growers
across SA, and the wines are released under the Auswan Creek and Red Deer Station labels.
The focus is on exports to Singapore, Thailand and China.

♥♥♥♥♡ **Red Deer Station S.J's Blend Barossa Valley Grenache Shiraz
Mourvedre 2015** A split of 42/38/20%. Being under screwcap has made all
the difference, given the predilection for cork with the other Auswan wines.
This is altogether brighter, fresher and livelier. It's also savoury with red plums,
cherries and red licorice, and a layer of woodsy spices that follow through on the
fuller-bodied palate. Grainy tannins, raspberry-like acidity; a lot to like. 14.5% alc.
Rating 93 To 2024 $35 JF
Red Deer Station 100 Royal Reserve Cabernet Sauvignon 2015 Dusty,
earthy and tarry aromas mingle with the core of sweet blackberries and currants;
there's power here in structure and fruit weight, given a touch of relief from poppy
acidity. The freshest of the trio of high-end reds. Cork. 14.5% alc. **Rating** 91
To 2028 $120 JF
Auswan Creek Discovery Clare Valley Shiraz Viognier 2016 Dark garnet-
black; the fruit just stops short of being too ripe, given some edge by the spices,
mint and acidity. Full-bodied, ripe tannins and glossy across the palate. Cork.
14.8% alc. **Rating** 90 To 2024 $35 JF

Sweetwater Wines   ★★★★★

PO Box 256, Cessnock, NSW 2325 **Region** Hunter Valley
T (02) 4998 7666 **www.**sweetwaterwines.com.au **Open** Not
Winemaker Bryan Currie **Est.** 1998 **Dozens** NFP **Vyds** 13.5ha

Sweetwater Wines is in the same ownership as Hungerford Hill, and wouldn't normally have a separate winery entry in the *Wine Companion*. But its substantial vineyard is unusual, with back vintages of shiraz particularly impressive. They were made by Andrew Thomas from 2003 to '16 and all stored in a temperature-controlled underground wine cellar that is part of the very large ornate house and separate guest accommodation built on the property. The reason for the seemingly unusual focus on cabernet sauvignon (second to shiraz) is the famed red volcanic soil over limestone. The shiraz and cabernet sauvignon are supplemented by contract-grown semillon.

🍷🍷🍷🍷🍷 **Hunter Valley Shiraz 2004** The cork is in pretty good shape, and so is the wine. Supple black fruits, spice, earth, leather, on lees – all intertwined; soft but persistent tannins holding the ship of state in fine trim. Cork. 13.4% alc. **Rating** 96 To 2024 $90
Hunter Valley Shiraz 2010 Estate-grown, matured in a 60/40% mix of French and American oak. Still has good colour, and the bouquet and palate are developing in good spirits; blackberry and plum with some regional earth and leather notes to underline the place. Screwcap. 14% alc. **Rating** 95 To 2025 $90
Single Vineyard Hunter Valley Semillon 2017 Precisely judged vinification from start to finish. The flavours, while very young, have already taken shape and will build into the classic lemon/lemongrass/lemon curd/honey over the next 7 years. Screwcap. 11.5% alc. **Rating** 94 To 2025 $27 ○

🍷🍷🍷🍷🍷 **Hunter Valley Cabernet Sauvignon 2007** Rating 91 To 2029 $90

Swinging Bridge   ★★★★★

701 The Escort Way, Orange, NSW 2800 **Region** Orange
T 0409 246 609 **www.**swingingbridge.com.au **Open** Tues–Wed by appt
Winemaker Tom Ward **Est.** 1995 **Dozens** NFP **Vyds** 6ha

Swinging Bridge estate was established in 1995 by the Ward and Payten families. In 2008, having been involved from the start, Tom and Georgie Ward took the helm and have since evolved Swinging Bridge into a premium supplier of cool-climate wines from Orange. The label had its founding in Canowindra with initial plantings of chardonnay and shiraz, and named after the historic wooden pedestrian bridge that traverses the Belubula River at the foot of the vineyard. Today, Swinging Bridge has a variety of ranges on offer, including a number of Reserve wines, the Experimental Series, Winemaker Series and Estate Series. Tom and Georgie searched for a number of years for the perfect place to call home in Orange, both for their family and Swinging Bridge. Tom's pursuit of premium grapes resulted in a number of wines made from grapes grown on Peter and Lee Hedberg's Hill Park Vineyard (planted in 1998). Hill Park Vineyard is now the permanent home of Swinging Bridge, Tom and Georgie able to realise their move when this outstanding property became available. Tom was a Len Evans scholar in 2012 and has been president of New South Wales Wine since '13.

🍷🍷🍷🍷🍷 **Mrs Payten Orange Region Chardonnay 2015** Nabbed the trophy in the '15 and older class at Orange Wine Show '17, and it's easy to see why: it balances the riper fruit profile of white peach and pear with ginger nut biscuit, yet contains itself within a lighter frame and tight palate, thanks to a thrust of fresh acidity piercing its way through the middle. Savoury, moreish and mouth-watering. Screwcap. 12.8% alc. **Rating** 95 To 2025 $32 JF ○
Block D Orange Chardonnay 2015 An impressive wine – it's slinky, lithe with gossamer acidity, but there are layers of flavour. Predominantly working off a citrus theme, includes a saline-lemon sherbet sensation with stone fruit and oak spice, some creamy nougat too. The palate is tight, linear and oh-so-right. Terrific length and energy. Screwcap. 12.9% alc. **Rating** 95 To 2025 $58 JF

Tom Ward #004 2017 A barrel-fermented pinot noir rose with a cherry pink hue and utterly delicious writ large. While it has a fragrance of wild strawberries, cherry pips and watermelon, it's spicy and ultimately has a savoury style. It has texture thanks to some lees stirring and a certain depth of flavour and complexity with an appealing Campari-bitter-twang on the finish matched to mouth-watering acidity. Screwcap. 13.2% alc. **Rating** 95 **To** 2020 $30 JF ✪

Tom Ward #006 Tempinot 2016 Part of Tom Ward's experimental series, it's a 61/39% blend of tempranillo and pinot noir. This has come together exceptionally well with its dark crimson hue; red-berried fruits, Middle Eastern spices and pomegranate-like acidity, yet definitely savoury in outlook. Medium-bodied, with neatly pitched textural tannins. Screwcap. 13.2% alc. **Rating** 95 **To** 2025 $35 JF ✪

Tom Ward M.A.W. Orange Region Pinot Noir 2016 Pale ruby; gorgeous aromas of rose petals, Sichuan pepper, sweet wild strawberries, ripe cherries and pips, and all that belies the palate. While medium-bodied at best, it's quite tannic, but the textural savoury tannins are grippy and bolstered by bright acidity. Convincing nonetheless, just needs more time to settle. Trophy for Best Pinot Noir at the Orange Wine Show '17. Screwcap. 13.2% alc. **Rating** 94 **To** 2024 $38 JF

🍷🍷🍷🍷 **Block D Orange Chardonnay 2016** **Rating** 93 **To** 2024 $58 JF

Mrs Payten Orange Region Chardonnay 2016 **Rating** 92 **To** 2022 $32 JF

Swings & Roundabouts ★★★★☆

2807 Caves Road, Yallingup, WA 6232 **Region** Margaret River

T (08) 9756 6640 **www**.swings.com.au **Open** 7 days 10–5

Winemaker Brian Fletcher **Est.** 2004 **Dozens** 20 000 **Vyds** 5ha

The Swings & Roundabouts name comes from the expression used to encapsulate the eternal balancing act between the various aspects of grape and wine production. Swings aims to balance the serious side with a touch of fun. Their wines are released under the Swings & Roundabouts and Backyard Stories labels. The arrival of Brian Fletcher as winemaker will, without question, underwrite the quality of the wines. Brian has never been far from the wine headlines, with 35 years of experience making wine all over the world. Exports to the US, China, Canada and Japan.

🍷🍷🍷🍷🍷 **Backyard Stories Margaret River Chardonnay 2017** Barrel-fermented with lees stirring. A chardonnay with exceptional power and drive even in the context of the Margaret River. The fruit honours are divided equally between white peach/nectarine and grapefruit. You know there's oak there, but it's not obvious. Very good chardonnay. Screwcap. 13% alc. **Rating** 95 **To** 2027 $45

Backyard Stories Margaret River Rose 2017 Crafted from a single parcel of sangiovese, cold-settled and pressed to French barrels for wild fermentation. At its conclusion a small amount of stainless steel-fermented sangiovese was blended in, successfully creating a rose with crisp red fruits running through to a bone dry finish. Screwcap. 13% alc. **Rating** 94 **To** 2021 $34

Backyard Stories Margaret River Cabernet Sauvignon 2016 A blend of 90% cabernet sauvignon, 5% malbec, 5% merlot, assembled from several small batch parcels. As usual, a very fine, pure expression of Margaret River cabernet with this release. Redolent of cassis, cedar wood and bay leaf, it's no more than medium-bodied; finely tuned, the emphasis is more on elegance than power, with fruit, oak and tannin all in accord. Screwcap. 14% alc. **Rating** 94 **To** 2028 $55 SC

🍷🍷🍷🍷 **Backyard Stories Margaret River Chardonnay 2016** **Rating** 93 **To** 2024 $39 JF

Novus Margaret River Malbec 2017 **Rating** 91 **To** 2025 $24

Margaret River Rose 2017 **Rating** 90 **To** 2019 $24 CM

Swinney Vineyards ★★★★★

325 Frankland-Kojonup Road, Frankland River, WA 6396 (postal) **Region** Frankland River

T (08) 9200 4483 **www**.swinneyvineyards.com.au **Open** Not

Winemaker Peter Dawson, Tony Davis **Est.** 1998 **Dozens** 2500 **Vyds** 160ha

The Swinney family (parents Graham and Kaye, and son and daughter Matt and Janelle) has been resident on their 2500ha property since it was settled by George Swinney in 1922. In the '90s they decided to diversify, and now have 160ha of vines across four vineyards, including the Powderbark Ridge vineyard in Frankland River (planted in '98, purchased in partnership with former Hardys winemaker Peter Dawson). The lion's share goes to shiraz (67ha) and cabernet sauvignon (48ha), followed by riesling, semillon, pinot gris, gewurztraminer, viognier, vermentino and malbec. They also pushed the envelope by establishing grenache, tempranillo and mourvedre as bushvines, a rarity in this part of the world. Exports to the UK and Singapore.

ΨΨΨΨΨ **Tirra Lirra Syrah 2016** Hand-picked 20yo vines in Frankland River, crushed, open-fermented with 20% whole bunches, matured in large-format French oak (40% new). Bright crimson-purple; a suave, supple wine with every part of its journey through the fermenter, barrel and bottle carefully planned and executed. This is only medium-bodied, but it has that relaxed, unhurried attitude that paradoxically leads you on to another glass after the next. Screwcap. 14% alc. **Rating** 95 **To** 2036 $38

Tirra Lirra Syrah Mourvedre Grenache 2016 Light, bright, clear crimson-purple; it's amazing that the late ripening varieties of mourvedre and grenache should perform as well as they do in this vibrantly fresh wine. Its quality comes from the intensity and purity of the fruit, not tannins or oak; the bushvine architecture is the key to unlock the puzzle. I really like this wine. Screwcap. 14% alc. **Rating** 95 **To** 2031 $43

Tirra Lirra Tempranillo Cabernet Sauvignon Grenache 2016 Comprising 38% tempranillo, 28% cabernet sauvignon, 25% grenache, 9% malbec, blended after fermentation, matured in French and Hungarian oak (25% new). This is playing hopscotch on a pogo stick while blindfolded. How could you plan the outcome? It has to have come after the event, as it were, but (obviously) shortly before bottling so the fine-tuning of the parts could be finalised. Here you have an ever-turning circle of every red and purple fruit you could imagine. Screwcap. 14% alc. **Rating** 94 **To** 2030

🍇 Switch Wines   ★★★

PO Box 1426, Nairne, SA 5252 **Region** South Australia
T 0433 886 634 **www.**switchwine.com.au **Open** Not
Winemaker Vanessa Altmann **Est.** 2010 **Dozens** 800
Owner/winemaker Vanessa Altmann has been making wines throughout Adelaide Hills, Barossa, Langhorne Creek and the Riverland since 2010. With a focus on sustainable and organic winemaking, she began making small batch wines under the Switch label in '10, purchasing organically grown grapes, and working closely with growers and friends. Vanessa says her winemaking style is 'strung together by the ethos that outstanding wines come not only from great vineyards, but from people who love what they do'. Exports to the US and Singapore.

ΨΨΨΨ **Village Botanist Langhorne Creek Merlot 2017** The fact that the wine was made using the Italian Ripasso technique (the wine spent 3 days on cabernet skins from anther ferment) isn't mentioned anywhere on the label. It's a juicy red fruit job, with pretty good varietal expression, and good balance. Screwcap. 13.8% alc. **Rating** 89 **To** 2025 $22

Symphonia Wines   ★★★★☆

1699 Boggy Creek Road, Myrrhee, Vic 3732 **Region** King Valley
T (02) 4952 5117 **www.**symphoniafinewines.com.au **Open** By appt
Winemaker Lilian Carter **Est.** 1998 **Dozens** 1500 **Vyds** 28ha
Peter Read and his family are veterans of the King Valley, commencing the development of their vineyard in 1981. After extensive trips to both western and eastern Europe, Peter embarked on an ambitious project to trial a series of grape varieties little known in this country. Current owners Peter and Suzanne Evans are committed to continuing Peter Read's

pioneering legacy, making arneis, petit manseng, pinot grigio, savagnin, tannat, tempranillo and saperavi.

🍷🍷🍷🍷🍷 **La Solista King Valley Tempranillo 2015** A sprightly, tangy and lighter-framed tempranillo with pretty aromatics of raspberry, cranberries and red licorice, and more intriguing notes of curry leaves and red peppers. It's juicy, the tannins barely perceptible. Definitely a red for summer. Screwcap. 13.1% alc. **Rating** 91 **To** 2019 $24 JF

Symphony Hill Wines   ★★★★★

2017 Eukey Road, Ballandean, Qld 4382 **Region** Granite Belt
T (07) 4684 1388 **www**.symphonyhill.com.au **Open** 7 days 10–4
Winemaker Mike Hayes **Est.** 1999 **Dozens** 6000 **Vyds** 3.5ha
Ewen Macpherson purchased an old table grape and orchard property in 1996. A partnership with his parents, Bob and Jill Macpherson, led to development of the vineyard, while Ewen completed his Bachelor of Applied Science in viticulture (2003). The vineyard (now much expanded) was established using state-of-the-art technology; vineyard manager/winemaker Mike Hayes is a third-generation viticulturist in the Granite Belt region, and became an equal co-owner of Symphony Hill in '14. He also has impressive academic achievements, with a degree in viticulture, followed by a Masters of Professional Studies (Viticulture), and was awarded a Churchill Fellowship in '12 to study alternative wine grape varieties in Europe. Exports to China.

🍷🍷🍷🍷🍷 **Gewurztraminer 2017** Gold medal Qld Wine Award '17; trophy for Best Alternative White Wine at the National Wine Show '17. The highly aromatic/fragrant bouquet has musk, spice and rose petal aromas, the palate building on that start. Its expression of flavour is not achieved by phenolics, but simply by its balance, length and tenacity of the lychee and peach varietal expression on the finish and aftertaste. Screwcap. 12.7% alc. **Rating** 96 **To** 2023 $45 ✪
Barrel Fermented Gewurztraminer 2016 Fermented and matured (6 months) in new French hogsheads. Mike Hayes must have relied on his experience of this vineyard's gewurztraminer, and the higher alcohol of the wine, in deciding to barrel ferment it. The strength of the wine lies in its complex texture and structure rather than the exotic varietal aromas and flavours. Gold medals at the Sydney and Qld wine shows '17. Screwcap. 13.9% alc. **Rating** 95 **To** 2022 $45
Reserve Granite Belt Cabernet Sauvignon 2016 From 17yo vines, hand-picked, destemmed, crushed, 21 days cold soak, fermented with wild and cultured yeasts, matured for 12 months in French oak (30% new). Good depth and clarity to a distinguished and clearly articulated cabernet sauvignon. It has blackcurrant/cassis as its powerful engine, the aromas expansive and seductive, the palate with ripe, but not overripe, dark berry fruits. The marriage with ripe tannins and French oak is the icing on the cake, making light of the alcohol level. Screwcap. 14.8% alc. **Rating** 95 **To** 2041 $65
Reserve Granite Belt Shiraz 2016 The symphonic back label sets the record for its duration without venturing any description of the vinification. It explodes with flavour; rivulets of juicy blackcurrant and blackberry running through to the end of the palate. It seems ripe with 14.9% alcohol, yet there's a hint of green. Screwcap. 14.9% alc. **Rating** 94 **To** 2026 $95
Inspiration Range Reserve Barossa Shiraz 2016 Good colour; luscious blackberry fruit takes pride of place, augmented by spice, ripe, fine tannins and just enough oak on the finish. Carries its alcohol level well. Screwcap. 14.8% alc. **Rating** 94 **To** 2031 $65
Reserve Nero d'Avola 2015 From 10yo vines grown in Heathcote, hand-picked, destemmed and crushed, 14 days cold soak, fermented with wild and cultured yeasts, matured for 12 months in 1–2yo oak. The colour lightens on the rim, which is not surprising. Here there is a courteous dialogue between place, winemaker, length and typicity as the wine reveals its spicy, red fruits at the centre of the palate. Screwcap. 13.9% alc. **Rating** 94 **To** 2025 $65

🍷🍷🍷🍷🍷 Fiano 2017 Rating 93 To 2023 $45
Reserve Granite Belt Sangiovese 2015 Rating 92 To 2022 $65
Reserve Riverland Lagrein 2016 Rating 91 To 2031 $95
Tempranillo 2015 Rating 90 To 2025 $30
Reserve Organic Saperavi 2016 Rating 90 To 2026 $95
Reserve Heathcote Lagrein 2016 Rating 90 To 2023 $95

Syrahmi   ★★★★☆

2370 Lancefield–Tooborac Road, Tooborac, Vic 3523 **Region** Heathcote
T 0407 057 471 **www.**syrahmi.com.au **Open** Not
Winemaker Adam Foster **Est.** 2004 **Dozens** 2000
Adam Foster worked as a chef in Victoria, Australia and London, UK, before moving to the front of house and becoming increasingly interested in wine. He then worked as a cellar hand with the who's who of wine in Australia and France, including Torbreck, Chapoutier, Mitchelton, Domaine Ogier, Heathcote Winery, Jasper Hill and Domaine Pierre Gaillard. He became convinced that the Cambrian soils of Heathcote could produce the best possible shiraz, and since 2004 has purchased grapes from the region, using the full bag of winemaking techniques. Exports to the US, Japan and Hong Kong.

🍷🍷🍷🍷🍷 Garden of Earthly Delights Pinot Noir 2015 Macedon Ranges; hand-picked,
sorted, 75% whole berry/25% whole bunches, wild yeast–open fermented, 26 days on skins, matured for 15 months in French oak (50% new). This isn't a heavy hitter, and was never intended to be. Every part is precisely shaped and weighted, red fruits and silky tannins the main protagonists, elegance and finesse its bywords. Screwcap. 13.6% alc. **Rating** 95 To 2027 $50
Granite Heathcote Shiraz 2015 Hand-picked and sorted in vineyard and winery, wild yeast–open fermented, 85% whole bunches, 32 days on skins, matured in a 2800l used French demi-muid. Elegant, highly spiced bouquet, the palate medium-bodied with the stalky/savoury/purple fruit profile that whole bunches create. This has length and finesse. Will please most, but not all. Screwcap. 13.5% alc. **Rating** 94 To 2030 $55

🍷🍷🍷🍷🍷 Demi Heathcote Mourvedre Rose 2017 Rating 90 To 2019

T'Gallant   ★★★☆

1385 Mornington–Flinders Road, Main Ridge, Vic 3928 **Region** Mornington Peninsula
T (03) 5931 1300 **www.**tgallant.com.au **Open** 7 days 9–5
Winemaker Adam Carnaby **Est.** 1990 **Dozens** NFP **Vyds** 8ha
Husband-and-wife winemakers Kevin McCarthy and Kathleen Quealy carved out such an important niche market for the T'Gallant label that in 2003, after protracted negotiations, it was acquired by Beringer Blass (now part of TWE). The acquisition of a 15ha property and the planting of 8ha of pinot gris gave the business a firm geographic base, as well as providing increased resources for its signature wine.

🍷🍷🍷🍷🍷 Pinot Grigio 2016 For decades T'Gallant was one of the leaders of the pinot
grigio pack, and the wines are as good as ever. Nashi pear, ginger, apple and citrus skin join hands to dance around the maypole of the bottle. Screwcap. 12.5% alc. **Rating** 92 To 2020 $19

🍷🍷🍷🍷 Pinot Grigio 2017 Rating 89 To 2019 SC

Tahbilk   ★★★★★

254 O'Neils Road, Tabilk, Vic 3608 **Region** Nagambie Lakes
T (03) 5794 2555 **www.**tahbilk.com.au **Open** Mon–Sat 9–5, Sun 11–5
Winemaker Alister Purbrick, Neil Larson, Alan George **Est.** 1860
Dozens 120 000 **Vyds** 221.5ha
A winery steeped in tradition (with National Trust classification). It makes wines – particularly red wines – utterly in keeping with that tradition. It should be visited at least once by every

wine-conscious Australian. The essence of that heritage comes in the form of their tiny quantities of Shiraz made from vines planted in 1860. The quality of the 2012 and '13 wines continued to underwrite the reputation of Tahbilk. A founding member of Australia's First Families of Wine. *Wine Companion* 2016 Winery of the Year. Exports to all major markets.

ΨΨΨΨΨ **1860 Vines Shiraz 2014** This was the first iconic wine that I ever tasted. I still recall parting with my pocket money with glee! This is as of red fruit notes as it is of black. Yet at this nascent stage, a herbal potpourri is slathered across a carapace of oak cedars, impeccably wrought slinky tannins and dutiful acidity. A seamless sheath! The wine's pulse is forceful and the finish long, although it is far from heavy in any way. The fruit will unravel in time, yet it is not to be rushed. Screwcap. 13.3% alc. **Rating** 96 **To** 2040 $325 NG

1927 Vines Marsanne 2012 From the sole 90yo plot of marsanne in the country and, in fact, one of the oldest marsanne sites in the world, this is a compelling wine released after just enough bottle age to bestow the beginnings of corpuscular complexity. Honeysuckle, orange blossom and apricot await the virtues of time, framed by brilliant acidity. Screwcap. 11% alc. **Rating** 95 **To** 2031 $46 NG

Old Vines Cabernet Shiraz 2015 Reminiscent of the wines I enjoyed in my early 20s. It is nice to still enjoy them! After all, everything moves in circles, and this is viscerally Australian. Blue, red and black fruit allusions, with tar, anise and a whiff of Aussie scrub billowing across the wine's stern. Cabernet's stern genetics and its authoritative chalky tannins placate the avalanche of fruit. This will age very well. Screwcap. 14% alc. **Rating** 95 **To** 2035 $46 NG

Marsanne 2017 Honeysuckle, beeswax and wisteria on the bouquet, then firm, racy mineral and Meyer lemon on the palate, gaining velocity and depth of fruit flavour. Screwcap. 12% alc. **Rating** 94 **To** 2030 $20 ✪

Shiraz 2015 The colour isn't particularly deep, but the hue is bright. The wine, too, is fresher and livelier than those of yore. The flavours span blackberry, plum and cherry, and the tannins are ripe and balanced in a medium-bodied palate. Large oak vats and smaller French and American barrels were used for maturation. Screwcap. 14.5% alc. **Rating** 94 **To** 2040 $26 ✪

Eric Stevens Purbrick Shiraz 2014 A bit lofty of alcohol; Tahbilk's calling card of impeccably manicured tannins stave off any overt sweetness. Plenty fresh with bouncy blue fruits, eucalyptus and licorice splashing across the mid-palate. Softer of weave than the 1860 Vines, making for a wine that drinks well today, as it will in 20 years' time Screwcap. 14.4% alc. **Rating** 94 **To** 2035 $72 NG

Cabernet Sauvignon 2015 Unimpeachable varietal expression from the first whiff of the bouquet to the finish of the medium-bodied palate. A fusion of cassis/blackcurrant, black olive, bay leaf and savoury tannins. As is usual, oak plays a minor role in shaping flavour. Screwcap. 14% alc. **Rating** 94 **To** 2035 $26 ✪

Eric Stevens Purbrick Cabernet Sauvignon 2014 A bright cabernet with a savoury, herbal midriff, neatly defined by delineated, fine-boned tannins for a brisk bite and definition. A beam of dark currant, piercing the wine from attack to lilting finish, scatters a potpourri of herbs across the mouth – sage, dried tea and eucalyptus are all there; a paean to strait-laced, elegant domestic cabernet. Good it is, too. Screwcap. 13.6% alc. **Rating** 94 **To** 2024 $72 NG

ΨΨΨΨΨ **Grenache Mourvedre Rose 2017** Rating 93 To 2018 $21 ✪
Cane Cut Marsanne 2014 Rating 93 To 2024 $25 NG ✪
Museum Release Marsanne 2012 Rating 92 To 2024 $26 NG
Roussanne Marsanne Viognier 2016 Rating 92 To 2019 $26

Talbots Block Wines   ★★★★★

62 Possingham Pit Road, Sevenhill, SA 5453 **Region** Clare Valley
T 0402 649 979 **www**.talbotsblock.com.au **Open** By appt
Winemaker Contract **Est.** 2011 **Dozens** 900 **Vyds** 5ha
Thanks to careers in government and the oil industry, Alex and Bill Talbot started their journey to wine in 1997 while working and living at Woomera in the South Australian desert.

They purchased land in the Sevenhill area of the Clare Valley, having fallen in love with the place, and dreamed of some day making wine for their friends. They then moved to various places in Asia, including Kuala Lumpur, Jakarta and Singapore, their minds always returning to their Sevenhill vineyard. They now live in the house they built high on the block, which gives views across the vineyard, and have the opportunity to tend the vines whenever they please. Initially the grapes were sold, but since 2012 they have kept enough of the production to have 1000 dozen made across their two distinctly different Shiraz styles. The labels are striking and evocative.

🍷🍷🍷🍷🍷 **The Sultan Clare Valley Shiraz 2015** The best fruit from the higher east-facing western slope of the vineyard is reserved for The Sultan, producing sumptuously rich grapes, ideal for more oak exposure. The wine spent 21 months in French (35% new) and American hogsheads, and yes, this layered and rich full-bodied wine reflects the site and the great '15 vintage. Screwcap. 14.9% alc. **Rating** 96 To 2040 $36 ✪

The Prince Clare Valley Shiraz 2016 Estate-grown, matured for 10 months in used French and American oak. This is indeed an exceptional year (better than the original evaluations of the winemakers) in the Clare Valley and elsewhere in South Australia. It's a full-bodied wine with a luscious, velvety mouthfeel, the flavours of fresh blackberry, with some jammy nuances adding to the flavour, structure and length. Screwcap. 14.2% alc. **Rating** 95 To 2036 $26 ✪

Talisman Wines ★★★★★

Evedon Park Bush Retreat, 205 Lennard Road, Burekup, WA 6227 **Region** Geographe
T 0401 559 266 **www**.talismanwines.com.au **Open** Wed–Sun 11–3
Winemaker Peter Stanlake **Est.** 2009 **Dozens** 2700 **Vyds** 9ha
Kim Robinson and wife Jenny began the development of their vineyard in 2000, and now have cabernet, shiraz, malbec, zinfandel, chardonnay, riesling and sauvignon blanc. Kim says that 'after eight frustrating years of selling grapes to Evans & Tate and Wolf Blass, we decided to optimise the vineyard and attempt to make quality wines'. The measure of their success has been consistent gold medal performance (and some trophies) at the Geographe Wine Show. They say this could not have been achieved without the assistance of vineyard manager Victor Bertola and winemaker Peter Stanlake. Exports to the UK and China.

🍷🍷🍷🍷🍷 **Geographe Riesling 2017** A wine of effusive scents offset by a tight, mineral-clad palate of precision and tension, unwinding with air like a metronome's systemic ticks: rose, musk and green toffee apple; lemon peel, lime and spa salts. This is light, but intense in flavour. Balletic, even, as it tiptoes an ascetic acid line. Dry. Very. But not harsh. Screwcap. 11% alc. **Rating** 95 To 2027 $23 NG ✪

Geographe Merlot 2016 Meritorious merlot. Hallelujah! Let's work our way back to the fruit, because the tannin appropriation is superb, defining all that is and will be to this scented, mid- to fully flared merlot. A raft of tannins: defined and basted with bitter chocolate to malty vanilla detail. These chaperone plum, spice and dried tobacco leaf notes, neither soprano nor baritone, to a long, savoury finish. Juicy acidity, too. This sits on the palate in a wholesome, appetising way. Nothing too forced. Screwcap. 14.5% alc. **Rating** 95 To 2024 $35 NG ✪

Barrique Geographe Sauvignon Blanc Fume 2016 The type of sauvignon that transcends the bang-in-bang-out type of tropical potions, while evoking fine white Bordeaux and sending the message that this oft-maligned variety can be highly complex, of place and versatile on these shores too. Wild yeast pungent. Spicy. Greengage, durian and tangerine shimmer across vibrant acidity, creamy oak and leesy detail, melding as a long bridge from fore to aft. Screwcap. 12.7% alc. **Rating** 94 To 2022 $27 NG ✪

Gabrielle Geographe Chardonnay 2016 Hand-picked and whole-bunch pressed to barrel, before undergoing a wild yeast ferment; this is a buxom, fully flavoured chardonnay with finely tuned acid-restraining devices and vanillan oak bulwarks. The end result is all stone fruits and vanilla pod, meshed with a creamy core of toasted hazelnuts and truffle cream. Of flavour and sophistication. Just a bit of heat detracts. Screwcap. 13.8% alc. **Rating** 94 To 2024 $37 NG

Geographe Zinfandel 2014 Another wine of interest, drawing one back to the glass to revel in zinfandel's eccentric personality. This is founded on the grape's intrinsic melody of erratic ripening within bunches. Thus, the sweet/sour harmony. The richness, albeit, the freshness. The power, but in this case, a sleigh of gentle pucker and bright acidity to keep it on the drier side of the straight and narrow. Very good, with the high alcohol a mere note on the tech sheet. Screwcap. 15% alc. **Rating** 94 **To** 2022 $42 NG

 Aged Release Geographe Riesling 2009 Rating 93 To 2023 $29 NG
Arida 2017 Rating 91 To 2019 $20 NG ✪
Geographe Zinfandel 2015 Rating 90 To 2021 $42 NG

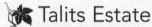 ## Talits Estate ★★★

722 Milbrodale Road, Broke, NSW 2321 **Region** Hunter Valley
T 0404 841 700 **www.**talitsestate.com.au **Open** Not
Winemaker Daniel Binet **Est.** 2008 **Dozens** 800 **Vyds** 4ha
Gayle Meredith is the owner of this small 4ha vineyard in the Broke Fordwich subregion of the Hunter Valley. The prime function of the property is luxury accommodation, and the house sits on 20ha of meticulously maintained gardens, olive trees and the estate merlot and shiraz vines. Daniel Binet is the winemaker, and has had a distinguished career in the region over the past 17 years. I'm not at all sure I understand why the wines should not be better than they are; perhaps it's just early days.

Tallavera Grove | Carillion ★★★★★

749 Mount View Road, Mount View, NSW 2325 **Region** Hunter Valley
T (02) 4990 7535 **www.**tallaveragrove.com.au **Open** Thurs–Mon 10–5
Winemaker Andrew Ling **Est.** 2000 **Dozens** 6000 **Vyds** 148ha
In 2000, the Davis family decided to select certain parcels of fruit from their 28ha Tallavera Grove vineyard in the Hunter Valley, along with the family's other vineyards in Orange (the 30ha Carillion Vineyard) and Wrattonbully (the 90ha Stonefields Vineyard), to make wines that are a true expression of their location. To best reflect this strong emphasis on terroir, the resulting wines were categorised into three labels, named after their respective vineyards. In recent years, Tim Davis has taken over the reins from his father John, and brought these selected brands under the banner of Davis Premium Vineyards. He also launched the Lovable Rogue range of wines, which highlights his keen interest in alternative grape varieties (particularly Italian), as well as in exploring innovative and experimental winemaking methods.

 Carillion Single Barrel Orange Chardonnay 2016 One 500l puncheon. Bernard (95) clone chardonnay, wild-fermented. It was part of the make for the Crystals release but stood out and was bottled separately. Straw-yellow, rich, zesty, fresh and compelling. White peach and vanilla custard; lime and fennel; flint and cooked apples. A generous mid-palate but a sizzling finish. Screwcap. 13.5% alc. **Rating** 95 **To** 2024 $70 CM
Stonefields Block 22 Wrattonbully Cabernet Sauvignon 2015 A statuesque cabernet with blackcurrant, cedar wood, mint and wood smoke flavours pouring through to a strong, sustained finish. Sweet red licorice notes play prettily about the edges. It has firmness, balance and pure fruit power all on its side. Screwcap. 14% alc. **Rating** 95 **To** 2038 $50 CM
Carillion The Feldspars Orange Shiraz 2016 It's more about personality than depth, but what a personality it is. Game, milk coffee, black pepper and tobacco notes add ample interest to the core of black cherry. Spice bomb. Fine fingers of tannin. Impressive in its own way. Screwcap. 14% alc. **Rating** 94 **To** 2026 $40 CM
Carillion The Volcanics Orange Cabernet Sauvignon 2016 It somehow manages to take tomato bush aromatics and bold/sweet-fruited flavours and combine them into a wine that seems at one with itself. This wine is an exercise in cohesion, against the odds, partly because it doesn't push too hard in any given direction, and partly because it's just so well balanced. Screwcap. 14% alc. **Rating** 94 **To** 2032 $50 CM

ΤΤΤΤΩ Carillion Orange Riesling 2017 Rating 93 To 2032 $25 **☉**
Tallavera Grove Hunter Valley Semillon 2017 Rating 93 To 2029
$25 CM **☉**
Tallavera Grove Hunter Valley Shiraz 2016 Rating 93 To 2032 $30 CM
The Feldspars Single Vineyard Orange Shiraz Viognier 2017 Rating 93
To 2023 $75 CM
Stonefields Arbitrage Wrattonbully Cabernet Merlot Shiraz 2015
Rating 92 To 2035 $40 CM
Carillion Orange Cabernet Merlot Petit Verdot 2016 Rating 90 To 2025
$30 CM

Taltarni ★★★★★

339 Taltarni Road, Moonambel, Vic 3478 **Region** Pyrenees
T (03) 5459 7900 www.taltarni.com.au **Open** 7 days 11–5
Winemaker Robert Heywood, Peter Warr, Ben Howell **Est.** 1969 **Dozens** 80 000
Vyds 78.5ha
The American owner and founder of Clos du Val (Napa Valley), Taltarni and Clover Hill (see
separate entry) has brought the management of these three businesses and Domaine de Nizas
(Languedoc) under the one roof, forming the group known as Goelet Wine Estates. Taltarni is
the largest of the Australian ventures, its estate vineyards of great value and underpinning the
substantial annual production. Insectariums are established in permanent vegetation corridors,
each containing around 2000 native plants that provide a pollen and nectar source for the
beneficial insects, reducing the need for chemicals and other controls of the vineyards. In
recent years Taltarni has updated its winemaking techniques, and in 2017 celebrated 40 years
of winemaking. Exports to all major markets.

ΤΤΤΤΤ Estate Pyrenees Cabernet Sauvignon 2016 From vines planted in '69.
Includes 10% merlot. It's back to its sturdy self – the tannin firm and sure, the fruit
ripe and bold. The length of the finish takes care of itself. Dark berries and dark
chocolate, Aussie bush characters, a hint of florals. It's a wine of impact, but it's not
without elegance and it's all been polished just so. Screwcap. 14.5% alc. **Rating** 95
To 2036 $40 CM

ΤΤΤΤΩ Shiraz Mourvedre 2015 Rating 93 To 2030 SC
Old Block Estate Pyrenees Cabernet Sauvignon 2015 Rating 93
To 2030 SC
Brut 2013 Rating 93 $26 CM **☉**
Old Vine Estate Shiraz 2016 Rating 92 To 2032 $45 CM
Reserve Pyrenees Shiraz Cabernet 2015 Rating 92 To 2035 SC
Cuvee Rose 2013 Rating 92 $26 CM
Tache 2013 Rating 92 $26 CM
Heathcote Shiraz 2016 Rating 91 To 2025 $35 CM
Merlot 2016 Rating 91 To 2024 $26 CM
Estate Pyrenees Cabernet Sauvignon 2015 Rating 91 To 2025 SC
Nebbiolo 2016 Rating 91 To 2024 $26 CM
Blanc de Blancs 2013 Rating 91 $26 CM
Victoria & Tasmania Chardonnay 2016 Rating 90 To 2020 SC

Tamar Ridge | Pirie ★★★★★

1A Waldhorn Drive, Rosevears, Tas 7277 **Region** Northern Tasmania
T (03) 6330 0300 www.tamarridge.com.au **Open** 7 days 10–5
Winemaker Tom Wallace **Est.** 1994 **Dozens** 14 000 **Vyds** 120ha
In August 2010 Brown Brothers purchased Tamar Ridge from Gunns Limited for
$32.5 million. While Dr Andrew Pirie has retired from his former position of CEO and chief
winemaker, he points out that the end of his five-year tenure happened to coincide with
the acquisition. Tasmania is the one region of Australia with demand for grapes and wine
exceeding supply. Tamar Ridge was well managed during the seven years it was owned by
Gunns, avoiding the financial meltdown of Gunns. Exports to all major markets.

ŶŶŶŶŶ **Pirie Traditional Method 2011** An amplified glass of fizz, with compelling autolytic depth and the toast, brioche and iodine notes that come with it. Flavours of citrus and orchard fruits find harmony. These are sprung to a long, creamy finish across an accelerator of cool-climate acidity and a controlling throttle of pungent truffled mineral. A whiff of acacia infers some oak handling. Very smart. Cork. 12.5% alc. **Rating** 95 $40 NG

Pirie Traditional Method Rose 2010 Superb rose with pinot-centric crunchy red fruit allusions on full beam across the nose and palate. Expansive, with brioche and clotted cream doused rails of mineral crunch and juicy acidity, pulling it all long. Poised. Highly complex. Weightless, yet powerful – the dichotomy at the heart of all fine wine. Cork. 12% alc. **Rating** 95 $48 NG

Tamar Ridge Reserve Pinot Noir 2015 A light crimson, with a carnal nose of forest floor, cardamom, clove and wood smoke wafting about a core of sweet cherry, keeping it all on the savoury side of the tracks. Enticing stuff, with applaudable intensity of flavour corseted by a mosaic of firm, spindly tannins (whole-bunch, surely), nestled oak and crunchy acidity. Long and tactile. Screwcap. 13% alc. **Rating** 94 To 2024 $65 NG

ŶŶŶŶŶ **Tamar Ridge Pinot Gris 2017** Rating 93 To 2021 $28 NG
Tamar Ridge Sauvignon Blanc 2017 Rating 91 To 2019 $28 NG
Tamar Ridge Pinot Noir 2016 Rating 91 To 2022 $34 NG
Tamar Ridge Riesling 2017 Rating 90 To 2025 $28 NG
Pirie Traditional Method NV Rating 90 $30 NG

Tambo Estate   ★★★★☆

96 Pages Road, Tambo Upper, Vic 3885 **Region** Gippsland
T (03) 5156 4921 **www.tambowine.com.au Open** Thurs–Sun 11–5, 7 days Dec–Jan
Winemaker Alastair Butt **Est.** 1994 **Dozens** 1380 **Vyds** 5.11ha
Bill and Pam Williams returned to Australia in the early 1990s after seven years overseas, and began the search for a property which met the specific requirements for high quality table wines established by Dr John Gladstones in his masterwork *Viticulture and Environment*. They chose a property in the foothills of the Victorian Alps on the inland side of the Gippsland Lakes, with predominantly sheltered, north-facing slopes. They planted a little over 5ha of chardonnay (the lion's share of the plantings at 3.4ha), sauvignon blanc, pinot noir, cabernet sauvignon and a splash of merlot. They are mightily pleased to have secured the services of Alastair Butt (one-time winemaker at Seville Estate).

ŶŶŶŶŶ **Gippsland Lakes Sauvignon Blanc 2015** Whole-bunch pressed, wild yeast barrel-fermented, matured for 5 months on gross lees. You know there's lots of complex flavour there, but it's like a python: slow to move, but then folding itself around you inexorably – here with a happier end. Screwcap. 12.8% alc. **Rating** 94 To 2017 $26 ✪

ŶŶŶŶŶ **Gippsland Lakes Cabernet Sauvignon 2013** Rating 92 To 2028 $26

Tamburlaine Organic Wines   ★★★★

358 McDonalds Road, Pokolbin, NSW 2321 **Region** Hunter Valley
T (02) 4998 4200 **www.tamburlaine.com.au Open** 7 days 9.30–5
Winemaker Mark Davidson, Ashley Horner, Remi Loirat **Est.** 1966 **Dozens** 60 000
Vyds 205ha
A thriving business that sold over 90% of its wine through the cellar door and by mailing list (with an active tasting club members' cellar program) – that is until exports started to grow significantly. The maturing of the estate-owned Orange vineyard led to the introduction of reserve varietals across the range. The Hunter Valley and Orange vineyards are all now certified organic. Exports to Finland, Nepal, South Korea, the Philippines, Malaysia, Japan and China.

ŶŶŶŶŶ **Single Vineyard Borenore Orange Chardonnay 2016** Solids fermentation, partial wild yeast, and maturation in new and used French oak. Has character and complexity, greater than most in the large current range of wines; toasty/savoury bouquet, some funk; slows down on the finish, needing a jab of acidity for gold medal points. Screwcap. 13.7% alc. **Rating** 94 **To** 2022 $25 **✪**

Single Vineyard Bellview Orange Pinot Noir 2017 Estate-grown, hand-picked, open-fermented with 30% whole bunches, 9 days on skins, matured in French oak, some new. Has marked intensity and length; satsuma and blood plum fruits, savoury spices; good length. Could flower with age. Screwcap. 13.3% alc. **Rating** 94 **To** 2029 $25 **✪**

Single Vineyard Borenore Orange Malbec 2016 There's no question this vineyard and its organic management leave you with complexity to both the bouquet and medium-bodied palate. There's almost a velvety mouthfeel, and with pinches of spice and pepper its Reserve sibling lacks. All up a very worthwhile malbec. Screwcap. 14.3% alc. **Rating** 94 **To** 2024 $25 **✪**

♟♟♟♟♟ **Reserve Hunter Valley Semillon 2017** Rating 91 To 2023 $33
Reserve Orange Riesling 2017 Rating 90 To 2023 $33
Reserve Orange Fume Blanc 2017 Rating 90 To 2019 $33
Reserve Orange Syrah 2016 Rating 90 To 2036 $44

Tapanappa   ★★★★★

15 Spring Gully Road, Piccadilly, SA 5151 **Region** Adelaide Hills
T (08) 7324 5301 **www.**tapanappa.com.au **Open** Thurs–Mon 11–4
Winemaker Brian Croser **Est.** 2002 **Dozens** 2500 **Vyds** 16.7ha

Tapanappa came home in many ways in 2015. It has the original Petaluma winery back, and a cellar door at the picturesque Tiers Vineyard. Equally importantly, it is now wholly owned by Brian and Ann Croser, albeit with the involvement of daughter Lucy and son-in-law Xavier Bizot. The business-as-usual components are the Whalebone Vineyard at Wrattonbully (planted to cabernet sauvignon, shiraz and merlot over 30 years ago), the Tiers Vineyard at Piccadilly in the Adelaide Hills (chardonnay), and the Foggy Hill Vineyard (pinot noir) on the southern tip of the Fleurieu Peninsula. Exports to the UK, France, Sweden, the United Arab Emirates, South Korea, Singapore, Hong Kong and China.

♟♟♟♟♟ **Tiers Vineyard 1.5m Piccadilly Valley Chardonnay 2016** The vineyard was replanted in '03 with Bernard clones 76 and 95. Bright straw-green; a powerful, distinguished chardonnay with almond, cashew and white stone fruit on the bouquet that flow through to the palate, joined by some grapefruit notes. Fruit, not oak or artefact, drives this wine. Screwcap. 13.8% alc. **Rating** 96 **To** 2029 $55 **✪**

Piccadilly Valley Chardonnay 2016 Gleaming straw-green; this is a beautifully cadenced chardonnay, with white peach, nectarine and fig lanced by a rivulet of citrussy acidity. Barrel fermentation (33% new French oak) was, of course, employed. Screwcap. 13.8% alc. **Rating** 96 **To** 2026 $39 **✪**

Fleurieu Peninsula Pinot Noir 2015 Light, bright crimson; a beautifully fragrant wine, the use of 30% whole bunches a master stroke for a supremely elegant and pure red-berried pinot strongly reminiscent of Volnay, Burgundy. This wine has transformed itself over the past 12 months. Screwcap. 13.4% alc. **Rating** 96 **To** 2024 $39 **✪**

Whalebone Vineyard Wrattonbully Cabernet Shiraz 2014 Dark red and even at 3yo, still purple-edged and bright. A function of 30yo vines and painfully low cropping at 2.5t/ha. Cabernet takes the central role (85%) with its dusty black fruit and fine, long tannins; shiraz (15%) seemingly adding flesh and spice to add additional depth and complexity. Period of 20 months in oak has only added a sturdy platform for the future. Cork. 14.5% alc. **Rating** 96 **To** 2037 $55 DB **✪**

Tiers Vineyard Piccadilly Valley Chardonnay 2016 Hand-picked, chilled overnight, whole-bunch pressed, matured for 10 months in French oak (30% new), mlf prevented. The complex, but clean, bouquet hints at the layers of flavour that duly appear on the palate ranging through stone fruit, fig and a hint of honey, the finish with crisp acidity. Screwcap. 13.8% alc. **Rating** 95 **To** 2026 $79

Whalebone Vineyard Wrattonbully Merlot Cabernet Franc 2014
Two-thirds merlot, one-third franc from 40yo vines. Historically low-yielding, but crops reduced even further by poor flowering conditions. Dark brick-red, brooding ripe fruit, earth scents and cigar box from 60% new oak. It's surprisingly light on its feet, medium-bodied with grainy tannins and a pleasing acid line that gives it a real flourish on the finish. Cork. 14.4% alc. **Rating** 95 **To** 2032 $79 DB
Foggy Hill Vineyard Fleurieu Peninsula Pinot Noir 2016 From the warmest vintage since 1947, matured in French hogsheads (30% new) made by Dargaud & Jaegle, bottled Apr 2017. It is a very powerful pinot that demands time in bottle, preferably 5+ years, for the tannins to soften and for spicy, secondary flavours to emerge. Definitely in the warrior class of pinot noir. Cork. 13.5% alc. **Rating** 94 **To** 2030 $55

Tar & Roses   ★★★★☆

61 Vickers Lane, Nagambie, Vic 3608 **Region** Heathcote
T (03) 5794 1811 **www**.tarandroses.com.au **Open** 1st w'end each month 10–4 (closed Jan)
Winemaker Narelle King **Est.** 2006 **Dozens** 18 000
Tar & Roses produces wines inspired by the classic Mediterranean varietals, and was named after the signature characteristics of nebbiolo. The name also ties back to the winemaking team behind the venture, the legendary Don Lewis and his winemaking partner Narelle King. Narelle is carrying on the Tar & Roses tradition after Don's passing in 2017. Exports to the UK, the US, Canada, Switzerland, Singapore, Japan, China and NZ.

♀♀♀♀♀   **The Rose Heathcote Shiraz 2014** Beautiful tannin and structure with this
full-bodied shiraz, all the regional flavours at play – dark fruits, satsuma plums, blueberries, bay leaves and graphite/ironstone/the smell of Heathcote soil. There's plenty of spice and oak, but it's stitched well into the fabric of this impressive wine. Screwcap. 15% alc. **Rating** 96 **To** 2030 $60 JF ❂

♀♀♀♀♀   **Lewis Riesling 2017 Rating** 93 **To** 2025 $27 JF ❂
Central Victoria Pinot Grigio 2017 Rating 93 **To** 2020 $22 JF ❂
Heathcote Shiraz 2016 Rating 92 **To** 2025 $22 CM ❂
Heathcote Nebbiolo 2016 Rating 90 **To** 2027 $50 JF

Tarrahill.   ★★★★★

340 Old Healesville Road, Yarra Glen, Vic 3775 **Region** Yarra Valley
T (03) 9730 1152 **www**.tarrahill.com **Open** By appt
Winemaker Jonathan Hamer, Geof Fethers **Est.** 1992 **Dozens** 700 **Vyds** 6.5ha
Owned by Jonathan Hamer, former partner at Mallesons law firm and wife Andrea, former doctor and also daughter of Ian Hanson, who made wine for many years under the Hanson-Tarrahill label. Ian had a 0.8ha vineyard at Lower Plenty, but needed at least 2ha to obtain a vigneron's licence. In 1990 the Hamers purchased a property in the Yarra Valley and planted the requisite vines (the pinot noir was ultimately destroyed by the 2009 bushfires). Jonathan and company director/friend Geof Fethers worked weekends in the vineyard, and in '04 decided that they would undertake a wine science degree at CSU; they graduated in '11. In '12 Jonathan retired from law and planted more vineyards (cabernet sauvignon, cabernet franc, merlot, malbec and petit verdot) and Ian (aged 86) retired from winemaking. Andrea has also contributed with a second degree (horticulture); she is a biodynamics advocate.

♀♀♀♀♀   **Shiraz 2016** The inky depths of the colour, of the smoking bouquet, the endless
layers of the omnibus of black fruits, licorice, the voluminous but soft folds of tannins are exceptional. You need to give it a bare minimum of 20 years to lose its puppy fat, another decade for its adolescence and then you will have 30 years to enjoy the mature wine that awaits. Buy some for your grand- or godchildren, and hope to nick a glass when they aren't looking. Screwcap. 14.2% alc. **Rating** 97 **To** 2078 $35 ❂

♀♀♀♀♀   **Le Savant Cabernets 2016** Includes 2% shiraz, matured in French oak
(25% new) for 12 months. Densely coloured; comes from the same school as the

Shiraz with its densely packed black fruit flavours and ripe tannins joining hands on the long, even, velvety palate. This is natural fruit, not extracted. A unique wine in the context of the Yarra Valley, but has to have time – 10+ years. Screwcap. 13.8% alc. **Rating** 96 To 2046 $80

ΨΨΨΨΨ Pinot Noir 2016 Rating 91 To 2031 $40
Le Batard 2016 Rating 90 To 2030 $30

TarraWarra Estate ★★★★★

311 Healesville-Yarra Glen Road, Yarra Glen, Vic 3775 **Region** Yarra Valley
T (03) 5962 3311 **www.**tarrawarra.com.au **Open** Tues–Sun 11–5
Winemaker Clare Halloran, Adam McCallum **Est.** 1983 **Dozens** 12 000 **Vyds** 28.98ha
TarraWarra is, and always has been, one of the top tier wineries in the Yarra Valley. Founded by Marc Besen AO and wife Eva, it has operated on the basis that quality is paramount, cost a secondary concern. The creation of the TarraWarra Museum of Art (twma.com.au) in a purpose-built building provides another reason to visit; indeed, many visitors come specifically to look at the ever-changing displays in the Museum. Changes in the vineyard include the planting of shiraz and merlot, and in the winery, the creation of a four-tier range: the deluxe MDB label made in tiny quantities and only when the vintage permits; the single vineyard range; a Reserve range; and the 100% estate-grown varietal range. Exports to France, Vietnam and China.

ΨΨΨΨΨ Reserve Yarra Valley Chardonnay 2016 Elegance is really the keynote here, with the subtlety of each element contributing to that. The aromas and flavours are built around white-fleshed stone fruit with a complexity of creamy lees texture and lightly spicy oak, the acidity softly persistent and long through the finish. Fine and composed now, a little more bottle age will add depth and richness. Screwcap. 13% alc. Rating 95 To 2024 SC

ΨΨΨΨΨ Yarra Valley Roussanne Marsanne Viognier 2016 Rating 93 To 2025 $30 SC
Yarra Valley Pinot Noir 2016 Rating 93 To 2023 SC
South Block Yarra Valley Chardonnay 2016 Rating 92 To 2021 SC
Yarra Valley Chardonnay 2016 Rating 92 To 2022 SC
Yarra Valley Roussanne Marsanne Viognier 2017 Rating 92 To 2027 SC
Yarra Valley Pinot Noir Rose 2017 Rating 92 To 2019 $25 SC ✪
Yarra Valley Barbera 2016 Rating 92 To 2021 SC
Yarra Valley Nebbiolo 2015 Rating 92 To 2022 SC

Tatachilla ★★★★☆

151 Main Road, McLaren Vale, SA 5171 (postal) **Region** McLaren Vale
T (08) 8563 7000 **www.**tatachillawines.com.au **Open** Not
Winemaker Jeremy Ottawa **Est.** 1903 **Dozens** 43 000 **Vyds** 12.4ha
Tatachilla was reborn in 1995, but has had a tumultuous history going back to 1903. Between then and '61, the winery was owned by Penfolds; it was closed in '61 and reopened in '65 as Southern Vales Cooperative. In the late '80s it was purchased and renamed The Vales but did not flourish; in '93 it was purchased by local grower Vic Zerella and former Kaiser Stuhl chief executive Keith Smith. After extensive renovations, the winery was officially reopened in '95 and won a number of tourist awards and accolades. It became part of Banksia Wines in 2001 which was in turn acquired by Lion Nathan in '02. In '17 it (along with all wine brands owned by Lion Nathan) was acquired by Accolade. Exports to all major markets.

ΨΨΨΨΨ Drops on Tide McLaren Vale Cabernet Sauvignon 2016 From the estate Clarendon and Tatachilla vineyards, matured for 14 months in French oak (20% new) before blending. Trophy McLaren Vale Wine Show '17. Well balanced, medium-bodied, cassis and dried herbs flavours. Screwcap. 14% alc. Rating 95 To 2029 $25 ✪

ΨΨΨΨΨ Foundation McLaren Vale Shiraz 2014 Rating 93 To 2034 $60
Burnt Souls McLaren Vale Shiraz 2015 Rating 92 To 2025 $25 ✪

Taylor Ferguson   ★★★★

Level 1, 62 Albert Street, Preston, Vic 3072 (postal) **Region** South East Australia
T (03) 9487 2599 **www.**alepat.com.au **Open** Not
Winemaker Norman Lever **Est.** 1996 **Dozens** 40 000

Taylor Ferguson is the much-altered descendant of the business of that name, established
in Melbourne in 1898. A connecting web joins the winery with Alexander & Paterson
(1892) and the much more recent distribution business of Alepat Taylor, formed in 1996.
The development of the Taylor Ferguson wines has been directed by winemaker Norman
Lever, using grapes sourced from various regions, but mainly from Coonawarra, Langhorne
Creek and the Riverina. Exports to Germany, Iraq, Singapore, Malaysia, Vietnam, Taiwan
and China.

ΨΨΨΨΨ **Fernando The First Barossa Valley Cabernet Sauvignon 2015** Includes a
splash of shiraz for good measure; it's really fresh given it's under cork, so that's just
luck. Deep garnet; swathes of cassis, satsuma plums and soy sauce; it's big, densely
oaked with lemony acidity and an astringent finish. 14.5% alc. **Rating** 91 **To** 2023
$45 JF
Fernando The First Barossa Valley Shiraz 2015 While the label states
it's a shiraz sourced from 80yo vines in the Barossa Valley, it also has 10% durif
and 4% cabernet sauvignon, which explains the depth of colour and its inky, leafy
notes. Nothing shy here – it's full-bodied and glossy, with expansive yet smooth
tannins; ripe, sweet fruit compote doused in lots of oak flavour and Middle Eastern
spices. Cork. 14.5% alc. **Rating** 90 **To** 2023 $45 JF

Taylors   ★★★★★

Taylors Road, Auburn, SA 5451 **Region** Clare Valley
T (08) 8849 1111 **www.**taylorswines.com.au **Open** Mon–Fri 9–5, w'ends 10–4
Winemaker Adam Eggins, Phillip Reschke, Chad Bowman **Est.** 1969 **Dozens** 250 000
Vyds 400ha

The family-founded and -owned Taylors continues to flourish and expand – its vineyards are
now by far the largest holding in the Clare Valley. There have also been changes in terms of
the winemaking team and the wine style and quality, particularly through the outstanding
St Andrews range. With each passing vintage, Taylors is managing to do for the Clare Valley
what Peter Lehmann did for the Barossa Valley. Recent entries in international wine shows
have resulted in a rich haul of trophies and gold medals for wines at all price points. A
founding member of Australia's First Families of Wine. Exports (under the Wakefield brand
due to trademark reasons) to all major markets.

ΨΨΨΨΨ **St Andrews Clare Valley Riesling 2017** Very interesting: Taylors says the
grapes are harvested, pressed and chilled below 10°C within 15 minutes of harvest.
That's some sort of speed record, even if the vineyard is adjacent to the winery.
Opens quietly then rapidly gains flavour and length as it moves towards the lovely,
juicy, lime-infused finish. Screwcap. 12.5% alc. **Rating** 95 **To** 2032 $40
St Andrews Clare Valley Cabernet Sauvignon 2015 Coaxing Clare Valley
cabernets to behave well in public isn't easy, but it was achieved here. Destemmed,
5 days cold soak, fermented with specialist cabernet yeast, extended skin contact
before pressing to French oak (40% new), matured for 18 months. The oak, in
particular, has tamed the fruit: the choice of yeast likewise important. Cassis, tar,
olive, earth and quality oak all emerge once the bouquet and palate have been
revisited several times. Screwcap. 14.5% alc. **Rating** 95 **To** 2035 $70
St Andrews Clare Valley Shiraz 2015 Fermented in open-topped barrels, and
then transferred back to American oak after pressing. Subsequent maturation for
20 months prior to bottling. It's ripe-fruited and American-oaked, but there's no
denying the quality here. Aromatic and spicy on the bouquet, the sweetly, edged
flavour on the palate is generous but refined, likewise the finely grained tannin.
Screwcap. 14.5% alc. **Rating** 94 **To** 2027 $70 SC

ŢŢŢŢŲ **TWP Taylors Winemaker's Project McLaren Vale Nero d'Avola 2016**
Rating 93 To 2026 $25 ✪
St Andrews Clare Valley Chardonnay 2016 Rating 92 To 2021 $40 SC
Taylor Made Adelaide Hills Pinot Noir Rose 2017 Rating 92 To 2020
$25 ✪
Jaraman Clare Valley McLaren Vale Shiraz 2016 Rating 92 To 2028
$30 SC
Taylor Made American Oak Clare Valley Malbec 2016 Rating 91 To 2024
$25 SC
Clare Valley Riesling 2017 Rating 90 To 2027 $20 ✪
Clare Valley Cabernet Sauvignon 2016 Rating 90 To 2026 $20 SC ✪

Telera   ★★★★

Arthurs Seat Road, Red Hill, Vic 3937 (postal) **Region** Mornington Peninsula
T 0407 041 719 **www**.telera.com.au **Open** Not
Winemaker Michael Telera **Est.** 2006 **Dozens** 45 **Vyds** 0.4ha
Telera was established by Michael and Susanne (Lew) Wynne-Hughes, who planted the
vines in 2000, naming the venture MLF Wines. In '11 Michael Telera leased the vineyard,
and, following the death of Michael Wynne-Hughes in that year, the name was changed to
Telera. He has learnt the trade through six vintages as a cellar hand/assistant winemaker at
Dr George Mihaly's Paradigm Hill winery, and produces shiraz sourced from other growers
on the Peninsula. He plans to plant 12 rows of pinot noir on the leased property, making the
total 20 rows of pinot noir and nine rows of sauvignon blanc. Production is increased with
small amounts of contract-grown sauvignon blanc.

ŢŢŢŢŲ **Pernella Mornington Peninsula Fume Sauvignon Blanc 2017** Barrel-
fermented sauvignon blanc, held on lees for 6 months. This is similar to its Itana
brethren with the exception of the wild-yeast ferment (or at least as far as I can
tell). This has punch and moxie! A narrative of nettle, greengage and lemon zest.
There is a hint of tropical fruit but thankfully, not much. The acidity is crunchy
and refreshing. The physiological ripeness of the fruit suits this approach more
than the Itana. Screwcap. 12.4% alc. **Rating** 92 **To** 2022 $29 NG
Rae Margaret River Shiraz 2016 Reductive handling at its best, tightening
up a sumptuous, mid-weighted palate of violet, sassafras, clove, anise, iodine and
vanilla to blueberry notes. The finish is long and slinky, with a well-judged bite of
peppery acidity and tannic grit; just a bit drying. Screwcap. 13.4% alc. **Rating** 92
To 2024 $39 NG
Su Mar Mornington Peninsula Pinot Noir 2016 A clonal blend, wild-
fermented in open-top vessels before 12 months of ageing in an assortment of
French oak; this is a lightweighted frisky pinot, playing the carnal undergrowth
card, while embracing a riot of maraschino cherry and stemmy root spice flavours,
kissing the finish with an amaro bite. A good drink, on the cooler side. Screwcap.
13.2% alc. **Rating** 91 **To** 2024 $55 NG
Itana Mornington Peninsula Fume Sauvignon Blanc 2017 This is barrel-
fermented sauvignon (under the aegis of ambient yeast), with some lees work for
additional crunch and breadth. It works well enough, although given the attention
to detail and breadth across the palate, it would have benefited from a later picking
window. This has a whiff of sophistication, melded to the usual culprits of guava,
greengage and sherbet acidity. Screwcap. 12.4% alc. **Rating** 90 **To** 2022 $39 NG

Tellurian   ★★★★☆

408 Tranter Road, Toolleen, Vic 3551 **Region** Heathcote
T 0431 004 766 **www**.tellurianwines.com.au **Open** W'ends 11–4.30, or by appt
Winemaker Tobias Ansted **Est.** 2002 **Dozens** 6000 **Vyds** 21.87ha
The vineyard is situated on the western side of Mt Camel at Toolleen, on the red Cambrian
soil that has made Heathcote one of the foremost regions in Australia for the production of
shiraz ('Tellurian' means 'of the earth'). Viticultural consultant Tim Brown not only supervises

the Tellurian estate plantings, but also works closely with the growers of grapes purchased under contract for Tellurian. Further Rhône red and white varieties were planted on the Tellurian property in 2011. Exports to the UK, Canada, Singapore and China.

🍷🍷🍷🍷🍷 **Tranter Heathcote Shiraz 2014** While a case could still be mounted for reducing the amount of new oak and time spent in barrel (50% new, 17 months in 90/10% French/American oak), more time in bottle has helped this Tranter to settle. Dark garnet-purple; a mix of dark plums covered in licorice, spice, dried herbs especially bay leaves. A brightness to the raspberry-like acidity, working across the fuller bodied structured palate and incorporating supple, furry tannins and all the oak. Screwcap. 14.5% alc. **Rating** 95 To 2024 $40 JF

🍷🍷🍷🍷🍷 **Heathcote Marsanne 2016** Rating 93 To 2022 $28 JF
Pastiche Heathcote Shiraz 2016 Rating 93 To 2025 $28 JF
Heathcote Nero d'Avola 2016 Rating 93 To 2021 $28 JF
GMS Heathcote Grenache Mourvedre Shiraz 2016 Rating 91 To 2022 $28 JF
Heathcote Rose 2017 Rating 90 To 2019 $24 JF

Temple Bruer

Cnr Broke Road/McDonalds Road, Pokolbin, NSW 2320 **Region** Langhorne Creek
T (08) 8537 0203 **www.**templebruer.com.au **Open** Mon–Fri 9.30–4.30
Winemaker Kate Wall, Verity Cowley **Est.** 1980 **Dozens** 35 000 **Vyds** 123ha
Temple Bruer was in the vanguard of the organic movement in Australia and was the focal point for the formation of Organic Vignerons Australia. Part of the production from its estate vineyards is used for its own label, part sold. Winemaker-owner David Bruer also has a vine propagation nursery, likewise run on an organic basis. Exports to the UK, the US, Canada, Sweden, Japan and China.

🍷🍷🍷🍷🍷 **Organic Preservative Free Cabernet Sauvignon Merlot 2017** Good colour sends an automatic alert, and indeed this McLaren Vale/Langhorne Creek blend has very attractive fruits, wearing its McLaren Vale component on its sleeve. It has blackcurrant fruit dipped in chocolate along with red and black cherry, the tannins soft. A must-try for those needing preservative-free wine. Screwcap. 14.5% alc. **Rating** 92 To 2021

🍷🍷🍷🍷 **Organic Preservative Free Shiraz Malbec 2017** Rating 89 To 2022

Tempus Two Wines

Broke Road, Pokolbin, NSW 2321 **Region** Hunter Valley
T (02) 4993 3999 **www.**tempustwo.com.au **Open** 7 days 10–5
Winemaker Andrew Duff **Est.** 1997 **Dozens** 55 000
Tempus Two is a mix of Latin ('tempus' is Latin for time) and English. It has been a major success story, production growing from 6000 dozen in 1997 to 55 000 dozen today. Its cellar door, restaurant complex (including the Oishii Japanese restaurant) and small convention facilities are situated in a striking building. The design polarises opinion; I like it. Exports to all major markets.

🍷🍷🍷🍷🍷 **Uno Hunter Valley Semillon 2014** It's fair to baulk at the price but the quality is arresting. Developed notes make a gentle play, but the main game is super-intense citrus, wax and lemongrass flavours. It bursts and rolls from start to finish in captivating fashion. It's a thing of beauty. Screwcap. 10.5% alc. **Rating** 96 To 2024 $75 CM ✪
Uno Hunter Valley Semillon 2015 There's a ripe sweetness to the fruit here, almost a candied aspect, and it gives the wine a puppy-dog eagerness. One sip and it's all over you, hoping to please. Lime, lemon and honeysuckle with a gentle waxiness to the texture. Intensity is very good. Sheer enjoyment and quality, in one. Screwcap. 11.5% alc. **Rating** 94 To 2024 $75 CM

ㅇㅇㅇㅇㅇ Pewter Hunter Valley Semillon 2017 Rating 93 To 2025 $40 CM
Copper Series Hunter Valley Shiraz 2017 Rating 92 To 2023 $35 CM
Pewter Hunter Valley Chardonnay 2017 Rating 91 To 2021 $45 CM
Uno Hunter Valley Shiraz Pinot 2017 Rating 91 To 2030 $75 CM
Copper Series Semillon 2017 Rating 90 To 2022 $30 CM

Ten Minutes by Tractor ★★★★★

1333 Mornington-Flinders Road, Main Ridge, Vic 3928 **Region** Mornington Peninsula
T (03) 5989 6455 **www.**tenminutesbytractor.com.au **Open** 7 days 11–5
Winemaker Sandro Mosele, Martin Spedding **Est.** 1999 **Dozens** 12000 **Vyds** 35.9ha
The energy, drive and vision of Martin Spedding have transformed Ten Minutes by Tractor
since he acquired the business in early 2004. In mid-'06 Ten Minutes By Tractor purchased
the McCutcheon Vineyard; it also has long-term leases on the two other original home
vineyards, the Judd and Wallis vineyards, thus having complete control over grape production.
Three new vineyards have been added in recent years: the one at the cellar door and
restaurant site is organically certified and is used to trial organic viticultural practices that are
progressively being employed across all the vineyards; the Coolart Road Vineyard in the north
of the Peninsula was purchased in '09; the Spedding Vineyard in Main Ridge purchased in
'15. There are now three ranges of wines. Single Vineyard – from the Judd, McCutcheon,
Wallis and Coolart vineyards; Estate – the best blend of pinot and of chardonnay from their
vineyards; and finally 10X – from other estate-owned Mornington Peninsula vineyards. At
3:30pm on Sunday February 25 2018, a fire erupted in a storage facility adjacent to the
kitchen serving the '18 winery restaurant. Half a million dollars' worth of bottled wines were
lost, including the wines for what was one of the finest wine lists for a winery restaurant,
the majority of the wines destroyed from the greatest wineries of France. (One bottle of
Romanée-Conti was a rare survivor amongst the 16000 bottles lost.) The facility also housed
a collection of vintage trucks and tractors. In all, 12 pallets of Ten Minutes by Tractor wines,
including magnums of back vintages, were lost. The tragedy is magnified by the irreplaceable
nature of so much history. A temporary cellar door was opened in March, and rebuilding of
the restaurant was underway, which is to be opened for business in Sept/Oct '18. Exports to
the UK, the US, Canada, Sweden, Switzerland, Hong Kong and China.

ㅇㅇㅇㅇㅇ **Wallis Mornington Peninsula Chardonnay 2016** Stunning chardonnay.
Fireworks in a glass. Sunny peaches and cream, blasts of wood smoke, crackles
of mineral and bangs of spice. Flint notes too. It's simultaneously obvious and
sophisticated. It's big on flavour, but long through the finish, and for good measure
the texture has a satiny quality. A 'wow' wine. Screwcap. 14% alc. **Rating** 97
To 2024 $68 CM ✪

Wallis Mornington Peninsula Pinot Noir 2016 In fantastic form. The flavours
roam far and wide through the backyard of the palate before finally running away
from home through the finish. Class A pinot noir. Dry, spicy, tannic, awash with
sweet-sour fruit and rose petals, earthen, as complex as you'd like and as persistent
too. Drinking it is a thrill. Screwcap. 13.5% alc. **Rating** 97 To 2026 $78 CM ✪

ㅇㅇㅇㅇㅇ **Judd Vineyard Chardonnay 2016** It's elegant and pure and the finish goes on
for just about ever. Or so it seems. This does everything it can not to smack you
between the eyes, but it still leaves you dazed by the finish. Grapefruit, figs, flint,
cashews and cream. Wonderful wine, with a future. Screwcap. 14% alc. **Rating** 96
To 2025 $68 CM ✪

Coolart Road Mornington Peninsula Pinot Noir 2016 It's the beefiest of the
10X individual releases but it still presents in silken style. A cake-and-eat-it wine.
Black cherries, rhubarb, fresh acidity, smoky oak and assorted dry spices. It has
both might and complexity on its side. Spot on. Screwcap. 13.5% alc. **Rating** 95
To 2024 $78 CM

Judd Mornington Peninsula Pinot Noir 2016 Its best days are well in front
of it, but the current brooding power of this is enough to have you whetting your
lips. It carries highlights of fresh strawberries, but the heart is pure plum, earth and
sweet spice, effectively transitioning into chicory, smoky oak and undergrowth

characters that contribute to a complex impression. It should develop beautifully. Screwcap. 13.5% alc. **Rating** 95 **To** 2025 $78 CM

McCutcheon Mornington Peninsula Chardonnay 2016 Straw-yellow colour. Quite rich, quite flavoursome, but with plenty of thrust. It doesn't muck about. Lime, nuts, peaches and nectarine, layers of cedar wood and oak-spice. Very good wine if not an outstanding one. Screwcap. 14% alc. **Rating** 94 **To** 2024 $68 CM

10X Mornington Peninsula Rose 2017 Made with pinot noir and so delicious it's ridiculous. Copper in colour, textural in manner, alive with blood orange, sweet spice and strawberry-like flavour, and wonderfully refreshing. The fruit suggests sweetness, but really this is herbal, savoury and dry. Served chilled, it's a terrific pick-me-up. Screwcap. 13.5% alc. **Rating** 94 **To** 2019 $28 CM ❂

Estate Mornington Peninsula Pinot Noir 2016 A slightly stricter release than previous and, in this case, a positive step. The seamless integration of strawberry-plum fruit with creamy oak; the way acidity exposes autumn leaf characters to the sun; the way tartness makes fruit sweetness seem sophisticated. It's a wine in excellent form. Screwcap. 13.5% alc. **Rating** 94 **To** 2024 $48 CM

♀♀♀♀♀ **10X Mornington Peninsula Sauvignon Blanc 2017 Rating** 93 **To** 2020 $28 CM

Estate Mornington Peninsula Chardonnay 2016 Rating 93 **To** 2025 $44 CM

Wallis Tasmania Mornington Peninsula Pinot Noir 2016 Rating 93 **To** 2025 $78 CM

McCutcheon Mornington Peninsula Pinot Noir 2016 Rating 93 **To** 2025 $78 CM

10X Mornington Peninsula Pinot Gris 2016 Rating 92 **To** 2019 $28 CM

10X Mornington Peninsula Pinot Noir 2016 Rating 92 **To** 2023 $28 CM

Blanc de Blancs NV Rating 92 $68 CM

Tenafeate Creek Wines   ★★★★

1071 Gawler-One Tree Hill Road, One Tree Hill, SA 5114 **Region** Adelaide
T (08) 8280 7715 **www**.tcw.com.au **Open** Fri–Sun & public hols 11–5
Winemaker Larry Costa, Michael Costa **Est.** 2002 **Dozens** 3000 **Vyds** 1ha
Larry Costa, a former hairdresser, embarked on winemaking as a hobby in 2002. The property, with its 1ha of shiraz, cabernet sauvignon and merlot, is situated on the rolling countryside of One Tree Hill in the Mount Lofty Ranges. The business grew rapidly, with grenache, nebbiolo, sangiovese, petit verdot, chardonnay, semillon and sauvignon blanc purchased to supplement the estate-grown grapes. Michael, Larry's son, has now joined his father as co-owner of the business. Michael has 17 vintages under his belt, mainly in the Barossa Valley, with Flying Winemaker stints in southern Italy and Provence. The red wines have won many medals over the years.

♀♀♀♀♀ **Basket Press Adelaide Hills Pinot Noir 2016** Youthful colour; a surprise packet, particularly given the warm vintage; it has generous red cherry/berry fruits, with a balancing thrust of faintly citrussy acidity adding to both balance and length. The aftertaste backs up all that has gone before. Screwcap. 13.5% alc. **Rating** 94 **To** 2026 $28 ❂

Vincenzo 2014 A blend of 70% shiraz, 30% cabernet sauvignon; co-fermented, matured in new French hogsheads for 24 months; named in honour of Michael's late grandfather who migrated to Australia during the early 1900s; 66 dozen made. The colour is very good, and the fruit hasn't drowned in the new French oak, indeed far from it – the black fruits hold their ground on the medium to full-bodied palate and through to the aftertaste, with attractive savoury edges encompassing licorice and cedar. It has years in front of it. Screwcap. 14.5% alc. **Rating** 94 **To** 2034 $55

♀♀♀♀♀ **Adelaide Hills Sauvignon Blanc 2017 Rating** 92 **To** 2018 $20 ❂

Basket Press Shiraz 2015 Rating 90 **To** 2030 $28

Judgement Shiraz 2014 Rating 90 **To** 2039 $100

Terindah Estate

90 McAdams Lane, Bellarine, Vic 3223 **Region** Geelong
T (03) 5251 5536 **www.**terindahestate.com **Open** 7 days 10–4
Winemaker Tim Byrne **Est.** 2003 **Dozens** 3000 **Vyds** 5.6ha

Retired quantity surveyor Peter Slattery bought the 48ha property in 2001, intending to plant the vineyard, make wine and develop a restaurant. He has achieved all of this (with help from others, of course), planting shiraz, pinot noir, pinot gris, picolit, chardonnay and zinfandel. Picolit is most interesting: it is a highly regarded grape in northern Italy, where it makes small quantities of high quality sweet wine. It has proven very temperamental here, as in Italy, with very unreliable fruit set. Terindah makes classic wines of very high quality from classic grape varieties – not wines for sommeliers to drool over because they're hip.

🍷🍷🍷🍷🍷 **Single Vineyard Bellarine Peninsula Rose 2017** From 100% MV6 pinot noir; trophy at the Geelong Wine Show '17. Light pink; a highly aromatic and spicy bouquet ushers in a perfectly balanced and delineated palate with juicy plum and red berry fruits. No vinification tricks, it's all in the fruit. Screwcap. 13% alc. Rating 95 To 2021 $30 ❂

🍷🍷🍷🍷🍷 **Single Vineyard Bellarine Peninsula Pinot Grigio 2017** Rating 91 To 2021

Terra Felix

52 Paringa Road, Red Hill South, Vic 3937 (postal) **Region** Central Victoria
T 0419 539 108 **www.**terrafelix.com.au **Open** Not
Winemaker Willy Lunn **Est.** 2001 **Dozens** 12 000 **Vyds** 7ha

Long-term industry stalwarts Peter Simon and John Nicholson, with an involvement going back well over 30 years, have built on the estate plantings of pinot noir (5ha) and chardonnay (2ha) through purchases from Coonawarra, McLaren Vale, Barossa Valley, Langhorne Creek, Yarra Valley and Strathbogie Ranges. Terra Felix exports 70% of its production to Hong Kong, Nepal and China.

🍷🍷🍷🍷🍷 **Yarra Valley Pinot Noir 2016** Crushed into open fermenters, matured in French oak for 12 months. This is an extremely expressive pinot with aromas of spiced red berries and red flowers. The palate is seriously good, its length and balance opening the way for dark fruits, earthy spices and a surge of plummy fruit on the finish and aftertaste. Screwcap. 13% alc. Rating 96 To 2029 $25 ❂
Yarra Valley Cabernet Sauvignon 2012 From a steep, north-facing slope in Coldstream and a 40yo vineyard; open-fermented, matured in French barriques for 16 months. The price has risen from $40, but it is well worth it. Instead of starting to lighten off since last tasted 4 years ago, it has built presence and complexity. Diam. 13.7% alc. Rating 95 To 2025 $50

🍷🍷🍷🍷🍷 **Heathcote Shiraz 2016** Rating 90 To 2026 $25

Terre à Terre

PO Box 3128, Unley, SA 5061 **Region** Wrattonbully/Adelaide Hills
T 0400 700 447 **www.**terreaterre.com.au **Open** At Tapanappa
Winemaker Xavier Bizot **Est.** 2008 **Dozens** 4000 **Vyds** 8ha

It would be hard to imagine two better-credentialled owners than Xavier Bizot (son of the late Christian Bizot, of Bollinger fame) and wife Lucy Croser (daughter of Brian and Ann Croser). 'Terre à terre' is a French expression meaning 'down to earth'. The close-planted vineyard is on a limestone ridge, adjacent to Tapanappa's Whalebone Vineyard. Terre à Terre's vineyard area has increased (3ha each of cabernet sauvignon and sauvignon blanc, and 1ha each of cabernet franc and shiraz), leading to increased production. In 2015, Terre à Terre secured the fruit from one of the oldest vineyards in the Adelaide Hills, the Summertown Vineyard. With this, we will see greater quantities of Daosa, and a Piccadilly Valley pinot noir. Wines are released under the Terre à Terre, Down to Earth, Sacrebleu and Daosa labels. Exports to the UK, Singapore, Taiwan and Hong Kong.

🍷🍷🍷🍷🍷 **Daosa Blanc de Blancs 2012** Burgundy chardonnay clones 76 and 95 form the Bizot Vineyard at 500m in the Piccadilly Valley, planted '95-96. This is a very attractive blanc de blancs, immaculately made by the traditional method from high quality clones, tiraged for 5 years on lees. It's fresh, long and the 6g/l dosage was right on the bull's eye. Diam. 12.4% alc. **Rating** 96 $55 ✪

Down to Earth Wrattonbully Sauvignon Blanc 2017 Made from 36% whole-bunch pressed and fermented in two foudres (3000l and 2000l) and 600l demi-muids, the balance crushed and destemmed, and cool-fermented in tank, then matured on lees for 7 months before blending. Citrus and white stone fruit flavours are built into the texture, and form part of a continuum that also brings French oak and cleansing acidity to the long palate. Won't bite you if you cellar it for some years. Screwcap. 13.5% alc. **Rating** 95 **To** 2023 $26 ✪

Crayeres Vineyard Wrattonbully Cabernet Sauvignon 2015 A blend of 44% shiraz, 36% cabernet sauvignon, 20% cabernet franc; fermentation and maceration for 29 days; pressed to French barrels (35% new) for 8 months, then to a 1yo foudre for 14 months. Here the complex vinification has worked well, the wine at the savoury end of the spectrum is in part thanks to the lengthy time in oak. The palate is long, the tannins firm but balanced, the oak integrated. Cork. 14.5% alc. **Rating** 95 **To** 2035 $40

Crayeres Vineyard Wrattonbully Cabernet Franc 2015 Hand-picked, 75% wild-fermented with 20% whole bunches, the remainder destemmed, matured for 22 months in French barriques (25% new). The vinification has worked well, and the grapes were picked ripe, not overripe. Juicy red and black cherry fruits are framed by persistent fine tannins, oak assisting not interfering. Elegant. Full of fruit. Screwcap. 14.5% alc. **Rating** 95 **To** 2030 $40

🍷🍷🍷🍷🍷 **Rouge 2015 Rating** 93 **To** 2029 $32 CM
Rouge 2015 Rating 93 **To** 2029 $32
Piccadilly Valley Rose 2017 Rating 90 **To** 2021 $30

Tertini Wines   ★★★★

Kells Creek Road, Mittagong, NSW 2575 **Region** Southern Highlands
T (02) 4878 5213 **www.tertiniwines.com.au Open** 7 days 10–5
Winemaker Jonathan Holgate **Est.** 2000 **Dozens** 5000 **Vyds** 7.9ha
When Julian Tertini began the development of Tertini Wines in 2000, he was following in the footsteps of Joseph Vogt 145 years earlier. History does not relate the degree of success that Joseph had, but the site he chose then was, as it is now, a good one. Tertini has pinot noir and riesling (1.8ha each), cabernet sauvignon and chardonnay (1ha each), arneis (0.9ha), pinot gris (0.8ha), merlot (0.4ha) and lagrein (0.2ha). Winemaker Jonathan Holgate, who is responsible for the outstanding results achieved at Tertini, presides over High Range Vintners, a contract winemaking business also owned by Julian Tertini. Exports to Asia.

🍷🍷🍷🍷🍷 **Tasmania Riesling 2017** Grown in the Coal River Valley. A long, cool ferment was followed by 2 months on fine lees prior to fining, filtering and bottling. Shows the perfumed, lifted floral characters that typify Tasmanian riesling, with underlying citrus zestiness on the bouquet and palate. Residual sugar adds weight and richness, and linear, sherbet-like acidity provides the focus and balance. Screwcap. 12.5% alc. **Rating** 93 **To** 2025 $40 SC

Southern Highlands Riesling 2016 Bright straw-green; fresh, brisk lime/lemon zest aromas and flavours; good length and overall mouthfeel. Screwcap. 11.1% alc. **Rating** 93 **To** 2025 $24 ✪

Private Cellar Collection Southern Highlands Arneis 2016 Produced from the oldest arneis vines on the Yaraandoo vineyard, fermented in two French oak hogsheads, one new and one 4yo, bottled after 4 months maturation. Deep in colour, the oak has made its presence felt, but the fruit has matched it, with grilled nuts, milky almonds and spicy pear all in the mix. Has character. Screwcap. 12.9% alc. **Rating** 93 **To** 2023 $38 SC

Southern Highlands Blanc de Blancs 2012 Chardonnay sourced from the Central Highlands. Bottle-fermented and aged on lees for 36 months. The deep golden colour sets the scene for the wine's rich and full-flavoured style. The toasty, nutty lees-aged characters are imposing on the bouquet, but apple and citrus fruit flavours reign on the palate, riding the wave of the energetic mousse and bracing acidity. Diam. 12% alc. **Rating** 93 $48 SC

Private Cellar Collection Southern Highlands Riesling 2016 Fruit from the Yaraandoo Vineyard. Spent 3 months on lees post ferment. Just beginning to show a little honeyed development on the bouquet, with the fruit reminiscent of lime and red apple. An impression of slight sweetness as the wine enters the mouth, but the citrus-like acidity quickly kicks in and becomes quite dominant. Screwcap. 11.1% alc. **Rating** 92 To 2028 SC

Hilltops Nebbiolo 2016 Grown on the Mullany vineyard near Young at 500m, where warm days and cool nights are well suited to this variety. This is nebbiolo in a gentle vein, with red-berried fruit that shows both ripe and savoury sides, complemented by a sweet spiciness on the bouquet and palate. The tannin is moderate, firm enough without being intrusive. Screwcap. 13.9% alc. **Rating** 91 To 2024 $28 SC

ŶŶŶŶ **Southern Highlands Arneis 2016** Rating 89 To 2020 $30 SC
Southern Highlands Pinot Noir 2016 Rating 89 To 2021 $48 SC

Teusner ★★★★★

95 Samuel Road, Nuriootpa, SA 5355 **Region** Barossa Valley
T (08) 8562 4147 **www**.teusner.com.au **Open** By appt
Winemaker Kym Teusner, Matt Reynolds **Est.** 2001 **Dozens** 30 000
Teusner is a partnership between former Torbreck Vintners winemaker Kym Teusner and her brother-in-law Michael Page, and is typical of the new wave of winemakers determined to protect very old, low-yielding, dry-grown Barossa vines. The winery approach is based on lees ageing, little racking, no fining or filtration, and no new American oak. As each year passes, the consistency, quality (and range) of the wines increase; there must be an end point, but it's not easy to guess when, or even if, it will be reached. Exports to the UK, the US, Canada, the Netherlands, Malaysia, Singapore, Japan, Hong Kong and China.

ŶŶŶŶŶ **Joshua 2017** A blend of 55% grenache, 35% mataro and 10% shiraz; no new oak so it's all about the quality of fruit shining through and how well it has amalgamated into a holistic blend. The jubey brightness of grenache leads at first, then it envelopes the savoury, meaty components of mataro and the pepper spice of shiraz; the end result supple and vibrant – it's one of those wines you just keep coming back to for another sip, another glass. Screwcap. 14.5% alc. **Rating** 96 To 2027 $35 JF ❂

Avatar 2015 The trio of great Barossa reds (grenache 55%, mataro 25% and shiraz 25%) come together to spend 18 months in seasoned oak before unfurling into a complete, compelling wine – GMS at its best. Light on its feet, with svelte tannins, plenty of substance and depth, though with buoyant flavours of cherries and raspberries, pips and spice, prosciutto and pepper. Glorious. Screwcap. 14.5% alc. **Rating** 96 To 2028 $45 JF ❂

Empress Eden Valley Riesling 2017 Pale straw and bright; a fusion of lemon and lime juice, plus zest, white florals, pristine fruit, and talc-lemony acidity, so lively it's almost thirst-quenching. Ticks all the riesling boxes. Screwcap. 12.5% alc. **Rating** 95 To 2029 $23 JF ❂

The Bilmore Barossa Valley Shiraz 2016 Everything about this is just right: its colour a dark purple-red; the core of ripe black fruits dipped in licorice, dark chocolate and woodsy spices and the suppleness of the silky tannins leading on to the medium to fuller-bodied palate. It's so easy to drink and great value. Screwcap. 14.5% alc. **Rating** 95 To 2028 $27 JF ❂

Big Jim Barossa Valley Shiraz 2015 An impenetrable dark purple hue; moves into bigger, bolder, riper territory without falling over, with shades of satsuma, black and tart plums, currants, savoury notes of hot bitumen and roasted coffee beans, all completely absorbing the oak while adding a layer of sweet, cedary flavours. Full-bodied, tannins and acid the key – velvety yet powerful, refreshing and uplifting. Screwcap. 14.5% alc. **Rating** 95 **To** 2030 $65 JF

The Dog Strangler 2016 It's mataro through and through, yet not as you know it. It has come together so well and with an underlying restraint. It's savoury, with dried Mediterranean herbs mingling with dark fruit, a sprinkle of spice and that tinny-ferrous note of the variety, which is utterly appealing. Hovers over a medium-weighted palate, tannins ripe with some grip, the finish powerful but not overwrought. Screwcap. 14.5% alc. **Rating** 95 **To** 2029 $35 JF ✪

Righteous Barossa Valley Mataro 2015 This is reined in, the sweet fruit expressive, a floral lift and a touch of eucalyptus with savoury layers across the full-bodied palate of salumi, coffee grounds, wood smoke and iron. Certainly, it is rich and ripe, but holds its 15% alcohol well; everything integrated. Cork. **Rating** 95 **To** 2025 $90 JF

Righteous FG Barossa Valley Shiraz 2014 This is somewhat dialled up – the bottle absurdly hefty, weighing close to 2kg, the wine not shy with 15% alcohol (and shows with warm on the finish), and the oak adds a cedary-sweet layer to the already richly fruited wine. That said, it has appeal, depth and a savoury tone with persuasive tannins and length. Cork. **Rating** 94 **To** 2028 $160 JF

The Independent Barossa Valley Shiraz Mataro 2016 There's a flurry of bright, juicy fruit; earthy, warm spices rolling onto the palate, just shy of full-bodied. There's a succulence here with lithe tannins, and there's depth and structure; it's absolutely commendable to make a wine of this quality and deliciousness. Screwcap. 14.5% alc. **Rating** 94 **To** 2024 $27 JF ✪

ᵨᵨᵨᵨᵨ **Woodside Sauvignon Blanc 2017** Rating 93 To 2019 $23 JF ✪
Salsa Rose 2017 Rating 93 To 2020 $23 JF ✪
The Riebke Shiraz 2016 Rating 93 To 2030 $27 JF ✪
The Wark Family Shiraz 2016 Rating 93 To 2025 $30 JF
The Gentleman Cabernet 2016 Rating 93 To 2027 $27 JF ✪
The Playground Dr Frank's Big Black One 2014 Rating 93 To 2023 $38 JF

The Alchemists ★★★★

PO Box 74, Cowaramup, WA 6284 **Region** Margaret River
T (08) 9755 5007 **www**.alchemistswines.com.au **Open** Not
Winemaker Dave Johnson (Contract) **Est.** 2009 **Dozens** 3000 **Vyds** 13.6ha
Brad and Sarah Mitchell were metallurgists for 15 and 20 years respectively, working on gold and hydro-metallurgical plants, having studied metallurgy and chemistry at university. Now they're more alchemists, changing grapes into wine. When they purchased the vineyard in 2007 it was already 11 years old, the prior owners having sold the grapes to various well-known Margaret River wineries. Since taking control of the vineyard, Brad and Sarah have removed vines on unsuitable soil, and grafted others. These are moves that have paid dividends, and allowed contract winemaker Dave Johnson (Credaro Family Estate) to make a series of wines that have been consistent medal winners at significant wine shows.

ᵨᵨᵨᵨᵨ **Reserve Elixir Margaret River Semillon Sauvignon Blanc 2016** Expansive tropical fruit flavours make this a joy to drink, its edges of lemongrass/thistle and wood smoke/gravel lending it a certain sophistication. The spread, the run, the feel. A most enjoyable white wine. Screwcap. 12.5% alc. **Rating** 93 **To** 2018 $28 CM

Margaret River Sauvignon Blanc Semillon 2016 Bursting with tropical fruit flavour and slung with apple-like acidity. Pitched and flavoured just right. Screwcap. 13% alc. **Rating** 91 **To** 2018 $19 CM ✪

Twin Cellars Margaret River Shiraz 2014 Well cut, well polished. Black cherry and sweet red berry flavours pour through the palate, with anise, spearmint and woody herb notes as inflections. Velvety texture sure doesn't hurt. Screwcap. 14.1% alc. **Rating** 91 **To** 2021 $19 CM ✪

Margaret River Cabernet Merlot 2014 It sits on the light side of medium weight and has juicy drinkability all sewn up. Plum, redcurrant and hints of blackcurrant show the way. Gentle infusions of briar-bush and sweet herbs keep simplicity at bay. Screwcap. 14.5% alc. **Rating** 90 **To** 2022 $19 CM ✪

The Bridge Vineyard ★★★★

Shurans Lane, Heathcote, Vic 3552 **Region** Heathcote
T (03) 5441 5429 **www.**thebridgevineyard.com.au **Open** Select w'ends
Winemaker Lindsay Ross **Est.** 1997 **Dozens** 1000 **Vyds** 4.75ha
This is the venture of former Balgownie Estate winemaker Lindsay Ross and wife Noeline, and is part of a broader business known as Winedrops, which acts as a wine production and distribution network for the Bendigo wine industry. The wines are sourced from long-established vineyards, providing shiraz (4ha), malbec (0.5ha) and viognier (0.25ha). The viticultural accent is on low cropping, thus the concentrated flavours; the winemaking emphasis on finesse and varietal expression.

🍷🍷🍷🍷🍷 **Shurans Lane Heathcote Shiraz 2014** Hand-picked fruit, 20% whole bunch, open-fermented with wild yeast, 25 days on skins. Three years in oak. Excellent balance carries the day for this wine. Aromas and flavours show warmth and generosity without being overripe; dark plum skin, sweet blackberries, spice and licorice all in the mix, with the oak pronounced but not overbearing. Full-bodied in weight, it moves surprisingly easily along the palate, the fruit, oak and tannin all neatly in sync, and the finish something of a highlight with real quality in its depth and persistence. Diam. 14.5% alc. **Rating** 94 **To** 2026 $45 SC

🍷🍷🍷🍷🍷 **Shurans Lane Heathcote Viognier 2017 Rating** 93 **To** 2020 $25 SC ✪
Shurans Lane Heathcote Shiraz Malbec 2014 Rating 93 **To** 2024 $30 SC

 # The Collective Wine Company ★★★★☆

Unit 2/20–28 Ricketty Street, Mascot, NSW 2020 (postal) **Region** Eden Valley
T (02) 9955 2009 **www.**thecollectivewinecompany.com.au **Open** Not
Winemaker Simon Gilbert **Est.** 2013 **Dozens** 20 000
The business has two vineyards, one (45ha) in the Eden Valley, the second (5ha) in the Barossa Valley. It also has an unexplained link with Mudgee via winemaker Simon Gilbert, yet the winery's address is in South Australia. The website contains images, but almost no facts.

🍷🍷🍷🍷🍷 **Artiste Eden Valley Riesling 2016** It's obvious the vineyard source(s) is of considerable merit. The wine is fresh and lively, looking as much like a '17 as it would a '16, and has way above average intensity, and clarity in its Meyer lemon and lime fruit. Take a second taste and your eyes will likely open agog – this is special stuff. Screwcap. 12.5% alc. **Rating** 96 **To** 2037 $24 ✪

🍷🍷🍷🍷🍷 **The Masterpiece Eden Valley Chardonnay 2014 Rating** 93 **To** 2021 $30
Millon Estate The Impressionist Eden Valley Shiraz 2015 Rating 91 **To** 2027 $15 ✪
Artiste Eden Valley Pinot Grigio 2017 Rating 90 **To** 2019 $24

The Deanery Vineyards ★★★☆

PO Box 1172, Balhannah, SA 5242 **Region** Adelaide Hills
T (08) 8390 1948 **Open** Not
Winemaker Duncan Dean (Sangiovese), Phil Christiansen (Shiraz), Petaluma (Sauvignon Blanc) **Est.** 1995 **Dozens** 500
The Dean family – Pat and Henry, and sons Duncan, Nick and Alan – purchased a 30ha dairy farm in Balhannah in late 1994, and planted 6.5ha of chardonnay, sauvignon blanc and semillon in the spring of '95, subsequently adding 0.67ha of shiraz. Pinot noir and a tiny block of sangiovese were also planted at a property at Piccadilly. A further 8ha are now being developed on a third property, adjacent to the original Balhannah holding. Alan

Dean, a CSU-trained viticulturist and former Petaluma vineyard manager, is in charge of the vineyards, working alongside brother Duncan. The primary aim of the business is contract grapegrowing, and their purchasers include some high profile names.

🍷🍷🍷🍷🍷 **Bull Paddock Adelaide Hills Shiraz 2013** Whichever way you look at it, this has a lot to offer for its price. There is a wealth of plum fruit, and oak (just) stays within bounds. Why it is only $19 isn't quite obvious, but remember – don't look a gift-horse in the mouth. Screwcap. 13.8% alc. **Rating** 90 **To** 2019 $19 ✪

The Hairy Arm ★★★☆
18 Plant Street, Northcote, Vic 3070 **Region** Sunbury/Heathcote
T 0409 110 462 **www.**hairyarm.com **Open** By appt
Winemaker Steven Worley **Est.** 2004 **Dozens** 1000 **Vyds** 3ha
Steven Worley graduated as an exploration geologist, then added a Master of Geology degree, followed by a postgraduate Diploma in Oenology and Viticulture. Until December 2009 he was general manager of Galli Estate Winery. The Hairy Arm started as a university project in '04. It has grown from a labour of love to a commercial undertaking. Steven has an informal lease of 2ha of shiraz at Galli's Sunbury vineyard, which he manages, and procures 1ha of nebbiolo from the Galli vineyard in Heathcote. Exports to Canada.

🍷🍷🍷🍷🍷 **Heathcote Nebbiolo 2015** Wild-yeast fermented with 40% whole bunches, 45 days on skins and aged 2 years in used French puncheons. Given all that considered extraction, it's surprisingly light on its feet. The tannins are abundant, chalky with some grip, but the palate is medium-weighted and bouncy with sweet and sour red cherries, pips, wood smoke and spice; fresh acidity on the finish keeps everything in check. Screwcap. 14.5% alc. **Rating** 93 **To** 2028 $45 JF

The Islander Estate Vineyards ★★★★★
78 Gum Creek Road, Cygnet River, SA 5223 **Region** Kangaroo Island
T (08) 8553 9008 **www.**iev.com.au **Open** Thurs–Tues 12–6
Winemaker Jacques Lurton **Est.** 2000 **Dozens** 7000 **Vyds** 10ha
Established by one of the most famous Flying Winemakers in the world, Bordeaux-born and -trained, and part-time Australian resident Jacques Lurton. He has established a close-planted vineyard; the principal varieties are cabernet franc, shiraz and sangiovese, with lesser amounts of grenache, malbec, semillon and viognier. The wines are made and bottled at the onsite winery in true estate style. After several vintages experimenting with a blend of sangiovese and cabernet franc, Jacques has settled on cabernet franc as the varietal base of the signature wine, The Investigator. Exports to the UK, the US, Canada, France, Germany, Malta, Hong Kong, Taiwan and China.

🍷🍷🍷🍷🍷 **Reserve Bark Hut Road 2014** Estate-grown shiraz and cabernet franc. Deep, youthful colour, the bouquet and palate yodelling black fruits that glide through the mouth on ball-bearing skates, shiraz surely by far the dominant partner. A striking wine with endless layers of fruit, yet isn't the least extractive. Screwcap. 14% alc. **Rating** 96 **To** 2029 $50 ✪

🍷🍷🍷🍷 **The Red Kangaroo Island Shiraz 2016 Rating** 89 **To** 2028 $20

The Lake House Denmark ★★★★★
106 Turner Road, Denmark, WA 6333 **Region** Denmark
T (08) 9848 2444 **www.**lakehousedenmark.com.au **Open** 7 days 10–5
Winemaker Harewood Estate (James Kellie) **Est.** 1995 **Dozens** 8000 **Vyds** 5.2ha
Garry Capelli and Leanne Rogers purchased the property in 2005 and have restructured the vineyard to grow varieties suited to the climate – chardonnay, pinot noir, semillon and sauvignon blanc – incorporating biodynamic principles. They also manage a couple of small family-owned vineyards in Frankland River and Mount Barker, with a similar ethos. Wines are released in three tiers: the flagship Premium Reserve range, the Premium Block range, and the

quirky He Said, She Said easy-drinking wine range. The combined cellar door, restaurant and gourmet food emporium is a popular destination. Exports to Singapore and China.

🍷🍷🍷🍷🍷 **Premium Reserve Single Vineyard Denmark Riesling 2017** This takes the best of the flavours of its Premium Block sibling, tunes some up, some down, ending up with a masterclass in a glass. Here, pure Rose's lime juice flavours set for the mouthwatering reactions to soar, and resutling in a convulsed grab for the glass to be sure everything is as good as it seems to be – and it is. Screwcap. 12% alc. **Rating** 96 **To** 2032 $40 ✪

Premium Reserve Single Vineyard Frankland River Shiraz 2015 Matured for 24 months in French oak (40% new). The fragrant bouquet has plenty to say, with red and black cherry/berry fruits standing over the French oak, a dominance continuing into and through the length of the juicy palate until the aftertaste – when it does take its place. Screwcap. 14.5% alc. **Rating** 95 **To** 2035 $45

Premium Reserve Premium Selection Cabernet Sauvignon 2015 Matured for 24 months in French oak (40% new). The finest of fine print on the label does say the wine is from the Great Southern region (not Denmark), which is simply the name of the business. It's got the depth and the strength of good cabernet from the region, framed by quality French oak, finishing with good tannins. Screwcap. 14.5% alc. **Rating** 95 **To** 2035 $55

Premium Block Selection Riesling 2017 The impact of this wine in the mouth is amazing, so rich you momentarily look for a statement regarding oak, putting other eastern Australian rieslings of this price into rapid retreat. It is layered with luscious tropical and citrus fruits, needing no cellaring, just open throat consumption. Screwcap. 12% alc. **Rating** 94 **To** 2027 $25 ✪

Premium Reserve Single Vineyard Semillon Sauvignon Blanc 2017 A 51/49% blend, matured in French oak for 3 months (25% new). The game changes radically here, thanks in no small measure to the barrel fermentation and maturation. The difference in the blend proportions from the Premium Block Selection almost certainly points to serious fruit selection of better parcels. Screwcap. 12% alc. **Rating** 94 **To** 2023 $35

Premium Reserve Single Vineyard Chardonnay 2016 Matured for 10 months in French oak (50% new). Has had little difficulty in meeting the 50% new oak on its own terms and hasn't blinked. It's luscious and rich, the accent on ripe stone fruit tempered only by citrussy acidity; the finish is as long as it is clean. A candidate for drinking, not cellaring or talking about. Screwcap. 13% alc. **Rating** 94 **To** 2026 $40

Premium Block Selection Shiraz 2015 Matured for 12 months in French oak (25% new). Good depth and hue, paradoxically a touch better than the Reserve. It has lively, medium-bodied, cool-grown black cherry with a generous sprinkling of spice, French oak intersecting with the fruit from start to finish. Over-delivers in this price bracket, typical Lake House, fine tannins. Screwcap. 14.5% alc. **Rating** 94 **To** 2035 $25 ✪

🍷🍷🍷🍷 **Single Vineyard Selection Great Southern Pinot Noir 2015** **Rating** 90 **To** 2023 $25

The Lane Vineyard ★★★★★

Ravenswood Lane, Hahndorf, SA 5245 **Region** Adelaide Hills
T (08) 8388 1250 **www**.thelane.com.au **Open** 7 days 10–4.30
Winemaker Michael Schreurs, Martyn Edwards **Est.** 1993 **Dozens** 25 000 **Vyds** 75ha

After 15 years at The Lane Vineyard, Helen and John Edwards, and sons Marty and Ben, took an important step towards realising their long-held dream – to grow, make and sell estate-based wines that have a true sense of place. In 2005, at the end of the (now discontinued) Starve Dog Lane joint venture with Hardys, the Edwards commissioned a state-of-the-art 500t winery, bistro and cellar door overlooking their vineyards on picturesque Ravenswood Lane. The Vestey Group (UK; headed by Lord Samual Vestey and the Right Honourable Mark Vestey) have aquired a significant shareholding in The Lane Vineyard, having previously invested in Delatite, and earlier before that in the established Coombe Farm in the Yarra Valley. The remaining shares are owned by Martyn Edwards and Ben Tolstoshev. Exports to all the UK, the US, Canada, the Netherlands, Belgium, UAE, Hong Kong and China.

ŸŸŸŸŸ **Block 5 Adelaide Hills Shiraz 2016** Deep crimson; medium-bodied shiraz that combines elegance with considerable depth and complexity. Black cherry fruit, spice, pepper and licorice sit comfortably in a chair of oak, tannins providing the seat. The postscript is a dash of cleansing acidity. Screwcap. 13.5% alc. **Rating** 95 To 2031 $25 **○**

Block 14 Single Vineyard Basket Press Adelaide Hills Shiraz 2016 10% whole bunch. It's a floral, lifted, spicy shiraz with beautiful, fluid fruit running sweetly throughout. It's medium in weight, but it feels generous; an infusion of bacony/toasty oak adding positively to the impression. Tip top. Screwcap. 13.5% alc. **Rating** 95 To 2030 $39 CM

Reginald Germein Single Vineyard Adelaide Hills Chardonnay 2014 Fermented wild in 100% new French oak. No mlf, 9 months in oak only. Strong with peach, cedar wood, cider apple and custard cream flavours, its heart beating full and strong, the sweetness of both its fruit and oak tempered by sure citrussy acidity. It would be easy to argue that there's too much oak here, but truth is the fruit is right up there with it. Screwcap. 12.5% alc. **Rating** 94 To 2024 $100 CM

Reunion Single Vineyard Adelaide Hills Shiraz 2015 More than enough oomph, but with spice and herb notes aplenty. This is a cake-and-eat-it style in the most positive of ways. It tastes of black cherries and plums, woody spices, toasty oak and blossomy herbs. Tannin curls ably through the finish. It feels soft throughout. It's a very good offering. Screwcap. 13.5% alc. **Rating** 94 To 2027 $65 CM

ŸŸŸŸŸ **Adelaide Hills Rose 2017** Rating 93 To 2019 $25 CM **○**

19th Meeting Single Vineyard Adelaide Hills Cabernet Sauvignon 2015 Rating 93 To 2027 $65 CM

Gathering Single Vineyard Adelaide Hills Sauvignon Blanc Semillon 2017 Rating 92 To 2020 $35 CM

Single Vineyard John Crighton Adelaide Hills Shiraz Cabernet Sauvignon 2013 Rating 92 To 2026 $110 CM

Cuvee Helen Adelaide Hills Blanc de Blancs 2010 Rating 92 $55 CM

Block 10 Single Vineyard Adelaide Hills Sauvignon Blanc 2017 Rating 91 To 2020 $25 CM

Lois Adelaide Hills Brut Rose NV Rating 91 $25 CM

Gathering Single Vineyard Adelaide Hills Sauvignon Semillon 2016 Rating 90 To 2018 $30

Beginning Single Vineyard Adelaide Hills Chardonnay 2016 Rating 90 To 2024 $39

Block 2 Single Vineyard Adelaide Hills Pinot Gris 2017 Rating 90 To 2019 $25 CM

Lois Adelaide Hills Blanc de Blancs NV Rating 90 $23 CM

The Old Faithful Estate ★★★★☆

281 Tatachilla Road, McLaren Vale, SA 5171 **Region** McLaren Vale
T 0419 383 907 **www.**oldfaithful.com.au **Open** By appt
Winemaker Nick Haselgrove, Warren Randall **Est.** 2005 **Dozens** 2000 **Vyds** 5ha
This is a joint venture of Nick Haselgrove (see separate entry) and Warren Randall (of Seppeltsfield and other major holdings in every aspect of making and selling Australian wine). Old Faithful's shiraz, grenache and mourvedre come from old, single site blocks in McLaren Vale. Exports to the US, Canada, Hong Kong and China.

ŸŸŸŸŸ **Cafe Block McLaren Vale Shiraz 2014** From a vineyard planted in the early '50s. It sees all-French oak, 25% new. This is a voluptuous release, rich in blackberried flavour and polished with smoky, cedary oak. Notes of iodine, raspberry jam and dark chocolate struggle to get a word in edgeways; this wine sets a rich tone of dark-berried fruit early and there's no shoving it aside. Full-bodied red wine, done well. Diam. 14.5% alc. **Rating** 94 **To** 2034 $70 CM

The Other Wine Co ★★★☆

136 Jones Road, Balhannah, SA 5242 **Region** South Australia
T (08) 8398 0500 **www.theotherwineco.com Open** At Shaw + Smith
Winemaker Martin Shaw, Adam Wadewitz **Est.** 2015 **Dozens** 1000
This is the venture of Michael Hill Smith and Martin Shaw, established in the shadow of Shaw + Smith, but with an entirely different focus and separate marketing. The two wines produced are a McLaren Vale Grenache and an Adelaide Hills Pinot Gris, both intended for casual consumption, the whole focus being freshness combined with seductive mouthfeel. The concept of matching variety and place is one without any particular limits, and there may well be other wines made by The Other Wine Co in years to come. Exports to the UK, Canada and Germany.

🍷🍷🍷🍷 **McLaren Vale Grenache 2017** Light, bright purple-red. Fragrant, ripe red fruit, black cherry and whole-bunch-like brown spice notes. It's reductive and slightly pongy, but that is part of its charm. On the palate, its all crunchy acidity and tight pippy fruit. A really refreshing bar wine that is good to go. Screwcap. 13% alc. **Rating** 93 **To** 2020 $26 DB ⊙

🍷🍷🍷🍷 **Adelaide Hills Pinot Gris 2017 Rating** 89 **To** 2018 $26 DB

The Pawn Wine Co. ★★★★☆

10 Banksia Road, Macclesfield, SA 5153 **Region** Adelaide Hills
T 0438 373 247 **www.thepawn.com.au Open** Not
Winemaker Tom Keelan **Est.** 2002 **Dozens** 5000 **Vyds** 54.92ha
This is a partnership between Tom and Rebecca Keelan, and David and Vanessa Blows. Tom was for some time manager of Longview Vineyard at Macclesfield in the Adelaide Hills, and consulted for the neighbouring vineyard, owned by David and Vanessa. In 2004 Tom and David decided to make some small batches of petit verdot and tempranillo at the Bremerton winery, where Tom is now vineyard manager. The wines are sourced from grapes grown on their Macclesfield vineyards; the remainder of the grapes supply brands such as Shaw + Smith, Penfolds, Orlando and Scott Winemaking.

🍷🍷🍷🍷🍷 **Jeu de Fin Adelaide Hills Shiraz 2016** A mix of four clones Selectiv'-harvested, whole berries open-fermented, matured in French oak (25% new) for 12 months. Speaks clearly of its place, the climate perfect for shiraz, with the accent on elegance while still delivering abundant dark cherry and blackberry flavours. The bouquet is fragrant, the palate long and persistent. Screwcap. 14.5% alc. **Rating** 95 **To** 2036 $36
El Desperado Adelaide Hills Pinot Noir 2017 Multiple clones, whole berries wild-fermented in 3t open stainless steel fermenters, matured in French oak (25% new) for 6 months. A pinot made equally in the vineyard and in the winery. A rose petal and spice bouquet, the precise palate replete with red and black cherry fruit decorated with fine, savoury/earthy tannins running through to a long finish. The price is barely believable. Screwcap. 14% alc. **Rating** 94 **To** 2027 $19 ⊙

🍷🍷🍷🍷 **Jeu de Fin Adelaide Hills Fume Blanc 2017 Rating** 92 **To** 2020 $36
The Austrian Attack Adelaide Hills Gruner Veltliner 2017 Rating 92 **To** 2027 $24 ⊙
The Gambit Adelaide Hills Sangiovese 2016 Rating 92 **To** 2020 $24 ⊙

The Trades ★★★☆

13/30 Peel Road, O'Connor, WA 6163 (postal) **Region** Margaret River
T (08) 9331 2188 **www.terrawines.com.au Open** Not
Winemaker Bruce Dukes (Contract) **Est.** 2006 **Dozens** 770

Thierry Ruault and Rachel Taylor have run a wholesale wine business in Perth since 1993, representing a group of top end Australian and foreign producers. The wines they offered to their clientele were well above $20 per bottle, but they have since decided to fill the price gap with a contract-made Shiraz and Sauvignon Blanc from Margaret River.

🍷🍷🍷🍷🍷 **Margaret River Sauvignon Blanc 2017** Typical Bruce Dukes' effortless mastery, bonding 92% sauvignon blanc, 8% semillon and 20% barrel fermentation into a single seamless stream of tangy citrus, gooseberry, lychee and green apple. Made to be enjoyed now, but can be cellared. Great value. Screwcap. 12% alc. **Rating** 91 **To** 2020 $20 ✪

The Vintner's Daughter   ★★★★

5 Crisps Lane, Murrumbateman, NSW 2582 **Region** Canberra District
T (02) 6227 5592 **www**.thevintnersdaughter.com.au **Open** W'ends 10–4
Winemaker Stephanie Helm **Est.** 2014 **Dozens** 1000 **Vyds** 3ha
The Vintner's Daughter is Stephanie Helm, daughter of Ken Helm. She made her first wine when she was nine, and won her first trophy when she was 14. On finishing school she enrolled in an arts/law degree at the Australian National University (ANU), thereafter pursuing a career outside the wine industry until 2011, when she began her wine science degree at CSU. Along the way, while she was at ANU, she met a young bloke, Ben Osborne, from Lightning Ridge at a pub, and introduced him to the world of wine. It wasn't too long before he became vineyard manager (with his background as a qualified horticulturist and landscaper) for Ken Helm. In late '14 everything came full circle when a vineyard, originally planted in 1978 with gewurztraminer, crouchen and riesling, extended to 3ha in '99, came on the market. It was in an immaculate position between Clonakilla and Eden Road, and they purchased it in a flash and set about some urgently needed rejuvenation of the vineyard. Stephanie (and Ben) waltzed into the trophy arena at the Canberra International Riesling Challenge '15, winning Best Canberra District Riesling, and for good measure, also won Best Riesling at the Winewise Small Vigneron Awards '15. Gewurztraminer is also part of the estate-based portfolio. And yes, Stephanie and Ben are life partners.

🍷🍷🍷🍷🍷 **Canberra District Gewurztraminer 2017** This is an elegant wine that successfully plies gewurztraminer's spice-lycheee-rosewater exuberance and slippery viscosity, all across a gentle beam of phenolic grip and a waft of acidity. Despite the moderate alcohol (11.5%), this is neither green, stringy nor mean, as so many are in Australia. The fruit is of impeccable ripeness, the wine of a balletic gait and posture. Screwcap. **Rating** 94 **To** 2021 $26 NG ✪

🍷🍷🍷🍷🍷 **Canberra District Riesling 2017 Rating** 93 **To** 2028 $30 NG

The Willows Vineyard   ★★★★★

310 Light Pass Road, Light Pass, Barossa Valley, SA 5355 **Region** Barossa Valley
T (08) 8562 1080 **www**.thewillowsvineyard.com.au **Open** Wed–Mon 10.30–4.30
Winemaker Peter Scholz, Michael Scholz **Est.** 1989 **Dozens** 6000 **Vyds** 42.74ha
The Scholz family have been grapegrowers for generations, and they have over 40ha of vineyards, selling part of the crop. Current-generation winemakers Peter and Michael Scholz make rich, ripe, velvety wines under their own label, some marketed with some bottle age. Exports to the UK, Canada, Switzerland, China and NZ.

🍷🍷🍷🍷🍷 **Bonesetter Barossa Shiraz 2015** Made from small patches of The Willows' oldest vineyard, the wine matured in high quality French barriques. A powerful, layered and concentrated wine, its black fruits with an insistent savoury drum beat, tannins evenly distributed through the length of the palate. Cork. 14.8% alc. **Rating** 95 **To** 2040 $60
The Doctor Sparkling Red NV Tirage bottled and left on yeast lees for 19 months. This is towards the upper end of the Barossa Valley sparkling shirazs, which is led by Rockford's Black Shiraz. This sparkling red has depth, complexity

and great balance, mouthfeel, all the black fruits doing the work, not the high dosage. Diam. 14.2% alc. **Rating** 95

🍷🍷🍷🍷🍷 Barossa Valley Shiraz 2015 Rating 93 To 2030 $28

Thick as Thieves Wines ★★★★☆

355 Healesville-Kooweerup Road, Badger Creek, Vic 3777 **Region** Yarra Valley
T 0417 184 690 **www.tatwines.com.au Open** By appt
Winemaker Syd Bradford **Est.** 2009 **Dozens** 1800 **Vyds** 1ha
Syd Bradford is living proof that small can be beautiful, and that an old dog can learn new tricks. A growing interest in good food and wine might have come to nothing had it not been for Pfeiffer Wines giving him a vintage job in 2003. In that year he enrolled in the wine science course at CSU; he moved to the Yarra Valley in '05. He gained experience at Coldstream Hills (vintage cellar hand), Rochford (assistant winemaker), Domaine Chandon (cellar hand) and Giant Steps/Innocent Bystander (assistant winemaker). In '06 Syd achieved the Dean's Award for Academic Excellence at CSU, and in '07 he was the sole recipient of the A&G Engineering Scholarship. At 35, he was desperate to have a go at crafting his own 'babies', and in '09 when he came across a small parcel of arneis from the Hoddles Creek area, Thick as Thieves was born. The techniques used to make his babies could only come from someone who has spent a long time observing and thinking about what he might do if he were calling the shots. Exports to Japan and Singapore.

🍷🍷🍷🍷🍷 **Single Barrel Project #1 Yarra King Valley Pinot Noir Gamay 2017**
Pinot noir from the Yarra Valley, gamay from the King Valley, wild yeast–open fermented separately with 50% whole bunches, a short maturation in used French oak. Perhaps I've fallen for a pea and thimble trick, but this wine does have that missing depth of the others. It's got red fruits of all flavours, and there's a whole-bunch (I assume) component adding to the texture and length. Diam. 13.1% alc.
Rating 95 **To** 2024 $80
Another Bloody Yarra Valley Chardonnay 2017 Comprising 50% Upper Yarra, 50% Briarty Hill; whole-bunch pressed, wild-fermented in French puncheons (50% new), 100% mlf, bottled in Dec. It's the one and only chardonnay made by Syd Bradford. The 100% mlf hasn't emasculated the flavour and complexity, and there's every reason to be impatient and polish it off as soon as possible. Screwcap. 13.4% alc. **Rating** 94 **To** 2019 $35
The Aloof Alpaca Yarra Valley Arneis 2017 From the Murramong Vineyard, whole-bunch stomped, 24 hours skin contact, pressed to used puncheons for wild fermentation, no mlf, lees stirring. There are contradictions in the vinification which make it hard to explain/understand what's going on here. I also find the textural pucker a high point (as did Ned Goodwin last year) in a wine that says so many things at the same time. Screwcap. 13.5% alc. **Rating** 94 **To** 2023 $25

🍷🍷🍷🍷🍷 Plump Yarra Valley Pinot Noir 2017 Rating 92 To 2025 $35
Pocco Rosso King Valley Nebbiolo 2015 Rating 92 To 2025 $40
La Vie Rustique Yarra Valley Pinot Noir Rose 2017 Rating 91 To 2022 $25
Driftwood Yarra King Valley Pinot Noir Gamay 2017 Rating 91
To 2021 $30
Purple Prose King Valley Gamay 2017 Rating 90 To 2022 $35

Thistledown Wines ★★★★★

c/- Revenir, Peacock Road North, Lenswood, SA 5240 **Region** South Australia
T +44 7778 003 959 **www.thistledownwines.com Open** Not
Winemaker Peter Leske, Giles Cooke MW, Fergal Tynan MW **Est.** 2010 **Dozens** 4000
Giles Cooke and Fergal Tynan are based in Scotland, and have a collective experience of 40+ years in buying and selling Australian wines. They have been friends since 1998, when they met over a pint of beer on the evening before the first Master of Wine course they were to embark on. In 2006 they established Alliance Wine Australia, which purchases Australian wines for distribution in the UK; they took the process one step

further when Alliance began the Thistledown Wines venture. This focuses on Barossa Valley shiraz, McLaren Vale grenache, and smaller amounts of chardonnay from the Adelaide Hills. The wines are made under Peter Leske's direction at his small-batch Revenir winery in the Adelaide Hills. Giles says he has particular affection for grenache, and is precisely right (in my view) when he says, 'McLaren Vale grenache is world class, and it best expresses itself when made in the mould of pinot noir'. Exports to the UK, the US, Canada, Ireland, the Netherlands, Czech Republic, South Korea, Singapore, China and NZ.

Bachelor's Block Ebenezer Barossa Valley Shiraz 2016 Deluxe packaging is the start, the vinification precisely reflected in the dark berries of the bouquet and the supple, medium-bodied palate. By both whole-bunch/berry fermentation and French oak maturation, the tannins are relegated to the sidelines and told to keep quiet. An opulent wine in opulent packaging – no expense spared. Cork. 14.5% alc. **Rating** 97 **To** 2046 $70 🟡

Silken Beastie Nor'wester Barossa Valley Shiraz 2015 Comprising 90% Barossa shiraz from Kalimna/Koonuga/Ebenezer, and 10% old bushvine grenache from Blewitt Springs. Deep, although bright, crimson-purple; delicious red and black cherry, plum and blackberry fruits are handsomely framed by fine, ripe tannins and quality French oak. At the moment that oak needs to pull in its horns, but a couple of years will give it no alternative but to do just that. Screwcap. **Rating** 96 **To** 2035 $50 🟡

The Vagabond Old Vine Blewitt Springs McLaren Vale Grenache 2017 From old bushvines at Blewitt Springs, matured in a concrete egg and French puncheons (10% new). Ah, take one look at the crystal clear crimson hue and you'll know the wine comes from old vines in McLaren Vale. What is truly remarkable is the way the wine has soaked up the new French oak without raising a sweat. This is lovely. Screwcap. 14.5% alc. **Rating** 96 **To** 2037 $50 🟡

Sands of Time Old Vine Single Vineyard Blewitt Springs McLaren Vale Grenache 2017 From 80yo vines, matured in French puncheons (25% new). A high class wine begging to be given as long as possible before a blind tasting with Chateau Rayas et al. It has the power and depth to its red and blue fruits, tamed by oak, set to develop another leg or two over the next 20 years. Classy tannins. Great package. Diam. 14.5% alc. **Rating** 96 **To** 2037 $70 🟡

Suilven Adelaide Hills Chardonnay 2016 Ultra-deluxe packaging, Leviathan bottle, high quality cork (well, it costs more than a screwcap), and then my bête noire: the grey-black label with red font reads 'Bottle no. 313'. Of 314 or 5000 bottles? Stuff it, I do love the moody label. The wine? I'm very acid-tolerant, and always have been. This trembles on the brink. 13% alc. **Rating** 95 **To** 2026 $70

Our Fathers Barossa Shiraz 2016 Deep crimson-purple; many of the thumbprints of Bachelor's Block are repeated here, but with a lighter/scaled-down matrix. You don't need any encouragement to buy the wine, and the profits are donated to health charities (details from www.ourfathers.co.uk). This is an elegant Barossa shiraz in every respect, the balance perfect. Cork. 14% alc. **Rating** 95 **To** 2036 $50

Silken Beastie Nor'wester Barossa Valley Shiraz 2016 You get a lot of expensive wine in your mouth, so rich it seems viscous, with liqueur cherry (which isn't sweet) and finishes bright and fresh (like an Amontillado sherry, which likewise isn't sweet). And glory be, there's no sweet alcohol to deal with. Screwcap. 14.5% alc. **Rating** 95 **To** 2036 $50

Advance Release Schuller Rd Blewitt Springs McLaren Vale Grenache 2017 From 80yo dry-grown bushvines, 400 numbered bottles made. Very good bright purple-crimson hue; it is uninhibitedly juicy, flush with all the red berries you'd care to name. For the record, the wine is not the least reduced. Screwcap. 14.5% alc. **Rating** 95 **To** 2027 $50

She's Electric Old Vine Single Vineyard McLaren Vale Grenache 2017 A fragrant, pure bouquet and palate, both sending the same message – they're the starting point for this beautifully detailed wine. It's actually quite firm on the palate, but it comes from the fruit not tannins, so it can be missed. The length and finish reveal just how complex the wine is. Screwcap. 13.5% alc. **Rating** 95 **To** 2030 $60

Our Fathers Barossa Shiraz 2015 An impressively packaged and made shiraz; the 40% whole bunch component has heightened the spicy elements of the wine whilst operating in tandem with the shiraz fruit flavours and quality oak. Cork. 14.5% alc. **Rating** 94 **To** 2030 $50

Advance Release Smart Vineyard Clarendon McLaren Vale Grenache 2017 Has a darker fruit range than the Schuller Road, and some tannins in the mix. Very good wine, but with a slightly less bright welcome mat. Screwcap. 14% alc. **Rating** 94 **To** 2027 $50

Thorny Devil Barossa Valley Grenache 2017 Very impressive. Still has power at 14% alcohol, and a consequent clarity of flavour in a full red and blue spectrum. No cosmetics, nor Turkish delight. Well made. Screwcap. **Rating** 94 **To** 2027 $30 ✪

🍷🍷🍷🍷🍷 **Great Escape Adelaide Hills Chardonnay 2017** **Rating** 90 **To** 2019 $25

Thomas Vineyard Estate ★★★★

PO Box 490, McLaren Vale, SA 5171 **Region** McLaren Vale
T 0419 825 086 **www**.thomasvineyard.com.au **Open** Not
Winemaker Mike Farmilo **Est.** 1998 **Dozens** 500 **Vyds** 5.26ha

Merv and Dawne Thomas thought long and hard before purchasing the property on which they have established their vineyard. It is 3km from the coast of the Gulf of St Vincent on the Fleurieu Peninsula, with a clay over limestone soil known locally as Bay of Biscay soil. They had a dream start to the business when the 2004 Shiraz won the trophy for Best Single Vineyard Wine (red or white) at the McLaren Vale Wine Show '05, with the Reserve Shiraz also winning a gold medal.

🍷🍷🍷🍷🍷 **McLaren Vale Shiraz 2016** It's inky, concentrated and thick in all manner of ways. A mass of black fruits injected with licorice, woodsy spices and eucalyptus, yet it goes off on a savoury tangent. Expansive yet surprisingly giving, tannins glide across the full-bodied palate. It's very much a concocted style and some folks will love it. Screwcap. 14.5% alc. **Rating** 90 **To** 2023 $25 JF

Estate Reserve McLaren Vale Shiraz 2016 There's no pretence as to what this is because the back label says 'Big Red'. It sure is, with a wall of concentration of all ripe black and red fruits, lava-like chocolate, black strap licorice and lashings of oak. While there's a plumpness on the full-bodied palate, the tannins are particularly drying and it feels warmer and riper than 14.5% alcohol. Saved, somewhat, by a freshness with the acidity. Screwcap. **Rating** 90 **To** 2024 $50 JF

Thomas Wines ★★★★★

28 Mistletoe Lane, Pokolbin, NSW 2320 **Region** Hunter Valley
T (02) 4998 7134 **www**.thomaswines.com.au **Open** 7 days 10–5
Winemaker Andrew Thomas, Scott Comyns **Est.** 1997 **Dozens** 10 000 **Vyds** 6ha

Andrew Thomas came to the Hunter Valley from McLaren Vale to join the winemaking team at Tyrrell's Wines. After 13 years, he left to undertake contract work and to continue the development of his own label. He makes individual-vineyard wines, underlining the subtle differences between the various subregions of the Hunter. Plans for the construction of an estate winery have been abandoned for the time being, and for the foreseeable future he will continue to lease the James Estate winery on Hermitage Road. The major part of the production comes from long-term arrangements with growers of semillon (15ha) and shiraz (25ha); an additional 3ha of shiraz is leased. The quality of the wines and the reputation of Andrew Thomas have never been higher. The appointment of Scott Comyns as winemaker was also a significant step; but the acquisition of Braemore Vineyard in December 2017 was even more significant, giving Thomas Wines a long-term supply of grapes from one of the Hunter Valley's most distinguished vineyards. Exports to the US, Japan and China.

🍷🍷🍷🍷🍷 **Braemore Individual Vineyard Hunter Valley Semillon 2017** Braemore is one of the best vineyards in the Hunter Valley, and Thomas hasn't missed the mark here. This wine is capable of out-riesling riesling in the lemon/lime stake as a young wine. There's nothing inscrutable here, just joyous citrus/lemongrass and succulent acidity. Screwcap. 10.7% alc. **Rating** 96 **To** 2037 $33 ✪

The O.C. Individual Vineyard Hunter Valley Semillon 2017 'O.C.' stands for Oakey Creek, where this vineyard was planted in '82. It's a wine seeking to have the best of both worlds, accessible when young with elevated levels of citrus-accented fruit reflected by the slightly higher alcohol than some, yet able to work the magic transformation of semillon over a 10–20-year timeframe. Screwcap. 11.3% alc. **Rating** 96 **To** 2032 $26 ✪

Cellar Reserve Braemore Individual Vineyard Hunter Valley Semillon 2012 Still a fresh-faced baby, but don't ignore the doubling of the price here. So either buy lots of the '17 Braemore Semillon, cellar some and drink some, or buy both the young and mature versions. Screwcap. 10.3% alc. **Rating** 96 **To** 2029 $65 ✪

Murphy's Individual Vineyard Hunter Valley Semillon 2017 From 50yo vines planted on the sandy soils adjacent to Black Creek, an area the famous Lindemans wines used to come from; hand-picked and whole-bunch pressed. It's super lively, the high-tensile acidity underpinning the citrus/grapefruit/grass notes of the fruit. Screwcap. 10.8% alc. **Rating** 95 **To** 2030 $26 ✪

Kiss Limited Release Hunter Valley Shiraz 2016 Always a pleasure to taste this wine, the flagship Hunter shiraz of the formidable Andrew Thomas stable. Sourced from the oldest vines on the esteemed Pokolbin Estate, planted in '69. Typically at the fuller end of medium-bodied, there's an extra dimension here; a bit more depth of fruit, a bit more oak, finer tannin – just more complexity and class all around really. Screwcap. 14.2% alc. **Rating** 95 **To** 2036 $75 SC

Synergy Vineyard Selection Hunter Valley Semillon 2017 Composed from individual parcels of old vine grapes spread across the Valley. Relatively speaking, it's light-bodied, but is no wimp. The acidity is, of course, present and important, but doesn't overshadow the deliberate lemony/grassy flavours that build steadily right from the word go. Screwcap. 11.3% alc. **Rating** 94 **To** 2029 $20 ✪

The Dam Block Individual Vineyard Hunter Valley Shiraz 2016 Only the second release from this tiny (0.8ha) vineyard, so it's still developing its identity somewhat. Geographically it's closest to Kiss and seems to share some of that site's qualities. Blueberry fruit is prominent on the bouquet with a savoury background, the palate providing impressive depth and length of favour in an elegant framework, the acidity finishing decisively. Screwcap. 14% alc. **Rating** 94 **To** 2028 $40 SC

Sweetwater Individual Vineyard Hunter Valley Shiraz 2016 Good Hunter Valley things here, with sweet, spicy and savoury elements all on display. Juicy red and black berry aromas and flavours are at the core, surrounded by subtle earthiness and spice, the palate medium-bodied but multilayered and supple, building as it goes along. The lively acidity kicks in late after swallowing, providing some serious length. Screwcap. 14.5% alc. **Rating** 94 **To** 2028 $35 SC

Elenay Barrel Selection Hunter Valley Shiraz 2016 Typically comprising a selection of barrels from across vineyards in the Thomas Hunter portfolio. Rich and full (in a Hunter context), with blackberry and dark plum fruit imposing itself on the bouquet and contributing to the plushness of texture on the palate. Around that there are touches of sweet spice, oak and earth, with ripe, velvety tannin to finish. Screwcap. 14.5% alc. **Rating** 94 **To** 2030 $50 SC

🍷🍷🍷🍷🍷 **Synergy Vineyard Selection Hunter Valley Shiraz 2016** **Rating** 93 **To** 2026 $25 SC ✪

Two of a Kind Shiraz 2016 **Rating** 92 **To** 2021 SC

Fordwich Hill Individual Vineyard Hunter Valley Semillon 2017 **Rating** 91 **To** 2027 $26

Thompson Estate

299 Tom Cullity Drive, Wilyabrup, WA 6284 **Region** Margaret River
T (08) 9755 6406 **www**.thompsonestate.com **Open** 7 days 11–5
Winemaker Bob Cartwright, Paul Dixon **Est.** 1994 **Dozens** 10 000 **Vyds** 28.63ha
Cardiologist Peter Thompson planted the first vines at Thompson Estate in 1997, inspired by his and his family's shareholdings in the Pierro and Fire Gully vineyards, and by visits to many of the world's premium wine regions. The vineyard is planted to cabernet sauvignon, cabernet franc, merlot, chardonnay, sauvignon blanc, semillon, pinot noir and malbec. Thompson Estate wines are made by Bob Cartwright (former Leeuwin Estate winemaker) at its state-of-the-art winery. Exports to Canada, Singapore, Hong Kong and China.

The Specialist Margaret River Cabernet Sauvignon 2014 There's such a power to this wine. That can come from nowhere else but its strong regional stamp, there's also a certain level of elegance and an almost-restraint. A balanced blend of mulberries, blackberries and plums lightly spiced, the oak integrated, the fuller-bodied palate comfortable, and the chiselled tannins and acid line will ensure this lasts for quite some time. Screwcap. 14.5% alc. **Rating** 96 **To** 2034 JF
Margaret River Cabernet Merlot 2016 An ever-reliable blend with cabernet sauvignon leading with its refinement and restraint, a mix of cassis and pips, dried herbs and really fine-grained tannins. The merlot, with splashes of malbec and cabernet franc, are supporting acts and add another dimension. Just a tad drying on the finish. Screwcap. 14.5% alc. **Rating** 94 **To** 2027 $35 JF

SSB Semillon Sauvignon Blanc 2017 Rating 92 **To** 2023 $35 JF
The Specialist Chardonnay 2014 Rating 92 **To** 2020 $75 JF

Thorn-Clarke Wines

Milton Park, 266 Gawler Park Road, Angaston, SA 5353 **Region** Barossa Valley
T (08) 8564 3036 **www**.thornclarkewines.com.au **Open** Mon–Fri 9–5, w'ends 11–4
Winemaker Peter Kelly **Est.** 1987 **Dozens** 90 000 **Vyds** 268ha
Established by David and Cheryl (née Thorn) Clarke, and son Sam, Thorn-Clarke is one of the largest family-owned estate-based businesses in the Barossa Valley. Their winery is close to the border between the Barossa and Eden valleys, and three of their four vineyards are in the Eden Valley: the Mt Crawford vineyard is at the southern end of the Eden Valley, while the Milton Park and Sandpiper vineyards are further north in the Eden Valley. The fourth vineyard is at St Kitts at the northern end of the Barossa Range. In all four vineyards careful soil mapping has resulted in matching of variety and site, with all the major varieties represented. The quality of grapes retained for the Thorn-Clarke label has resulted in a succession of trophy- and gold medal–winning wines at very competitive prices. Exports to all major markets.

Sandpiper Eden Valley Riesling 2017 Estate-grown and skilfully made to preserve the flowery, citrus fruits of the bouquet and palate. It is from the velvet-glove-and-steel-hand school, offering great varietal fruit now and long into the future. It has the tactile acidity found in a few young rieslings. Grows on you each time it is retasted. Screwcap. 11% alc. **Rating** 95 **To** 2027 $20 ❂
Shotfire Barossa Quartage 2015 A Bordeaux blend that has often exceeded expectations, both with the quality of the estate-grown fruit, the way the components are handled in the winery, and the blending process. Everything about the wine defies the normal yawn that greets Barossa Valley Bordeaux blends with its bright mouthfeel and cedary fruit flavours. Screwcap. 14.5% alc. **Rating** 95 **To** 2029 $27 ❂
Barossa Trail St Kitts Block 9 Shiraz 2016 From the St Kitts Vineyard in the far north of the Barossa, destemmed, open-fermented with cultured yeast, pressed 10 days after crushing to French oak for 12 months' maturation. Deep, bright colour, bright and clear; a seductively fragrant and salubriously rich shiraz that keeps moving despite – or due to – its peacock's tail of aromas and flavours ranging from dark chocolate and licorice to stewed plum and blackberries. Screwcap. 14.5% alc. **Rating** 94 **To** 2031 $35

William Randell Barossa Shiraz 2015 Right in the wheelhouse for those who like full-flavoured Barossa shiraz. Sweet, generous fruit is the dominant theme, with plum, blackberry and blueberry all involved, and freshness to be found despite the apparent ripeness. Smoky oak and a tarry regional twang are an easy fit, as is the ample but round-edged tannin. Well crafted. Screwcap. 14.5% alc. **Rating** 94 **To** 2030 $50 SC

William Randell Eden Valley Cabernet Sauvignon 2015 French oak (40% new) matured for 18 months. A selection of the best barrels only included in the final blend. Solid, chunky, dusty cabernet, which is clearly going to do well in the cellar. Plenty of familiar varietal elements all through, with blackcurrant, mint, herb and just a touch of licorice. Oak plays its part with a cedary, chocolate overlay, and while the tannins are quite firm they're in tune with the wine overall. Screwcap. 14.5% alc. **Rating** 94 **To** 2035 $50 SC

♟♟♟♟♟ **Sandpiper Eden Valley Pinot Gris 2017** Rating 93 To 2019 $20 ✪
Shotfire Barossa Shiraz 2016 Rating 93 To 2030 $27 DB ✪
Eden Trail Riesling 2017 Rating 92 To 2030 $24 SC ✪
Barossa Trail Saleyards Road Grenache 2016 Rating 91 To 2026 $35
Sandpiper Barossa Cabernet Sauvignon 2016 Rating 90 To 2026 $20 ✪

Three Dark Horses   ★★★★★
49 Fraser Avenue, Happy Valley, SA 5159 **Region** McLaren Vale
T 0405 294 500 **www.3dh.com.au Open** Not
Winemaker Matt Broomhead **Est.** 2009 **Dozens** 5000
Three Dark Horses is the project for former Coriole winemaker Matt Broomhead. After vintages in southern Italy (2007) and the Rhône Valley, he returned to McLaren Vale in late 2009 and, with his father Alan, started buying quality grapes, thanks to the long experience they have both had in the region. The third dark horse is Matt's grandfather, a vintage regular. But things are changing. In Nov '17 the business acquired a 5ha vineyard in McLaren Vale, and will build an onsite winery in time for the '19 vintage. They are expanding the plantings with grenache blanc, clairette and touriga nacional, and reworking some of the shiraz vines planted in 1964. Part of the vineyard is sand soil-based interspersed with ironstone, a highly desirable mix for shiraz and cabernet sauvignon. Exports to NZ and China.

♟♟♟♟♟ **McLaren Vale Mataro 2016** A whole-berry wild ferment, matured in used French oak for 15 months. Its deep, dense colour translates into a deep, dense, velvety palate of exceptional quality. How Matt Broomhead manages to secure grapes of sufficient quality to make his wines is an Australian Story. Screwcap. 14% alc. **Rating** 96 **To** 2036 $25 ✪
Frank Ernest McLaren Vale Shiraz 2015 Wild-fermented with 20% whole bunches, matured in French oak (50% new) for 22 months. Frank Ernest Broomhead was still helping every vintage at 92yo in '15, and this is a mighty tribute to him, coming from the old Renmano vineyard. The intense crimson-purple hue signals a medium-bodied shiraz that has finesse, focus and length to its black cherry/berry fruits and spicy tannins. Quite simply, a lovely wine. Screwcap. 14.5% alc. **Rating** 95 **To** 2040 $50
Langhorne Creek Touriga 2017 Destemmed, wild-fermented, matured in old puncheons for 12 months. You have to simultaneously juggle the variety, the exceptionally cool vintage and the unknown. This is, as it should be, very different from all the other horses in the current release, which makes it doubly important. Screwcap. 14% alc. **Rating** 94 **To** 2029 $25 ✪

♟♟♟♟♟ **Grenache 2017** Rating 93 To 2037 $25 ✪
The Bandy Cabernet Sauvignon 2016 Rating 93 To 2036 $20 ✪
Grenache + Touriga 2017 Rating 92 To 2023 $25 ✪
Grenache Rose 2017 Rating 91 To 2019 $20 ✪
Shiraz 2016 Rating 91 To 2029 $25

3 Drops ★★★★★

PO Box 1828, Applecross, WA 6953 **Region** Mount Barker
T (08) 9315 4721 **www**.3drops.com **Open** Not
Winemaker Robert Diletti (Contract) **Est.** 1998 **Dozens** 5000 **Vyds** 21.5ha

3 Drops is the name given to the Bradbury family vineyard at Mount Barker. The name stands for three elements: wine, olive oil and water, all of which come from the substantial property. The vineyard is planted to riesling, sauvignon blanc, semillon, chardonnay, cabernet sauvignon, merlot, shiraz and cabernet franc, and irrigated by a large wetland on the property. 3 Drops also owns the 14.7ha Patterson's vineyard, planted in 1982 to pinot noir, chardonnay and shiraz. Exports to South Korea, Hong Kong and China.

ⵟⵟⵟⵟⵟ **Riesling 2017** Impossible not to admire this wine's intensity, purity and length. It has a pleasing textural element too. Lime leaf, juice and blossom characters are the delicious drivers. Length of the finish is quite something. Screwcap. 12% alc. **Rating** 95 **To** 2030 $25 CM **◐**

Pinot Noir 2017 This pinot noir, like its '16 sibling, is full of varietal character and complexity – no pussyfooting around here. It has dark cherry and forest berry flavours, then some whole bunch/forest floor adding yet more to a pinot that offers tip-top cellaring options as its aftertaste offers yet more to the mix. Screwcap. 13% alc. **Rating** 95 **To** 2025 $32 **◐**

Chardonnay 2016 This darts through the mouth with grapefruit, green apple and oak-spice flavours, the finish sailing close to chalk territory. Strong argument to suggest that time is required, underlined by the wine's keen acidity. Struck-match characters add another dimension. The longer you sit with this the more impressed you become. Screwcap. 12.5% alc. **Rating** 94 **To** 2025 $26 CM **◐**

Merlot 2017 It's no surprise that the wine should be well made, likewise that the climate is to merlot's liking. It's the precision of every aspect here, and the absence of most in other regions/wineries, that makes you do a double-take. Blackcurrant/redcurrant/bay leaf/tapenade – they're all here. Great bargain. Screwcap. 14.5% alc. **Rating** 94 **To** 2025 $25 **◐**

Cabernets 2016 This isn't deep or brooding, having everything in the right place, and in appropriate measure, gives it a presence beyond the sum of its parts. It tastes of bay leaves and blackcurrant, woodsy herbs and ground coffee, a gentle tang helping to keep it all afloat. The good form of this wine continues unchecked. Screwcap. 13.5% alc. **Rating** 94 **To** 2032 $25 CM **◐**

ⵟⵟⵟⵟⵙ **Nebbiolo Rose 2017** Rating 93 To 2019 $25 CM **◐**
Shiraz 2015 Rating 93 To 2027 $25 CM **◐**
Sauvignon Blanc 2017 Rating 90 To 2020 $22
Chardonnay 2017 Rating 90 To 2020 $25

Three Kangaroos ★★★★★

Level 3, 242–244 Franklin Street, Adelaide, SA 5000 (postal) **Region** Barossa Valley
T (08) 8212 0459 **www**.threekangaroos.com.au **Open** Not
Winemaker Janelle Badrice (Consultant) **Est.** 2014 **Dozens** NFP

What a surprise, and what a pleasure. A virtual wine business that owns neither vineyard nor winery, with its primary business exporting its wines to Vietnam, Japan and China. There is nothing unusual in this business strategy, but it's rare for such wines to be of high quality. Owners Easan Liu and Tally Gao had previous successful business ventures in real estate and telecommunications, and in 2012 began an international wine distribution business, expanding this by establishing Three Kangaroos.

ⵟⵟⵟⵟⵟ **Hill Side Barossa Valley Cabernet Sauvignon Shiraz 2016** A blend of 58% cabernet sauvignon from Stone Well and 42% shiraz from Light Pass; matured for 18 months in French and American oak. This has power to burn, yet is elegant from start to finish. There are ripples of muscle interspersed with the calm of contentment; the fruit is foremost, but oak and tannins all play an important role in this classy wine. All the corks used have been of high quality, perfectly inserted, and should allow the wines to complete their journey. 14% alc. **Rating** 97 **To** 2046 $60 ✪

🍷🍷🍷🍷🍷 **Full Moon Old Vine Barossa Valley Shiraz 2016** From 65yo vines at Light Pass, matured for 18 months in French hogsheads, 200 dozen made. Massively rich and concentrated, oozing and dripping succulent black fruits. Of its style, well orchestrated. Cork. 15% alc. **Rating** 95 **To** 2036 $70

Double Barrels Barossa Valley Shiraz 2015 From a vineyard in Marananga, matured for 30 months in oak. Has a savoury edge from the fruit and possibly oak. That does serve to slightly diminish the impact of the double barrel shotgun. The same comment/question as that for its Full Moon sibling. Cork. 15.5% alc. **Rating** 95 **To** 2040 $60

3 Oceans Wine Company ★★★★

Cnr Boundary Road/Bussell Highway, Cowaramup, WA 6284 **Region** Margaret River
T (08) 9756 5656 **www**.3oceanswine.com.au **Open** 7 days 10–5
Winemaker Jonathan Mettam **Est.** 1999 **Dozens** 160 000

After a period of spectacular growth and marketing activity, Palandri Wine went into voluntary administration in February 2008. In June of that year the Ma family, through their 3 Oceans Wine Company Pty Ltd, acquired the Palandri winery, its Margaret River vineyard and 347ha of the Frankland River vineyards. In October '08 3 Oceans also acquired the Palandri and Baldivis Estate brands. There is a strong focus on the emerging markets of the Asia Pacific region, but no neglecting of the domestic market. Given the size of production, the quality of the wines is impressive. Exports to the UK, Singapore, Japan and China.

🍷🍷🍷🍷🍷 **The Explorers Sauvignon Blanc Semillon 2013** Estate-grown fruit from the Frankland River, fermented in new French barriques, matured for 9 months with lees stirring. Its glowing, green-yellow hue is a sign of a fully mature wine, but may see out a year or so before reaching its drink to date. Screwcap. 12.9% alc. **Rating** 94 **To** 2020 $30 ✪

🍷🍷🍷🍷 **The Explorers Margaret River Chardonnay 2015** **Rating** 93 **To** 2025 $30
The Estates Chardonnay 2014 **Rating** 93 **To** 2021 $22 ✪
The Explorers Margaret River Chardonnay 2013 **Rating** 93 **To** 2022 $30
Vita Novus Frankland River Shiraz 2012 **Rating** 92 **To** 2022 $30
The Estates Frankland River Shiraz 2014 **Rating** 90 **To** 2020 $22

Tidswell Wines ★★★★

14 Sydenham Road, Norwood, SA 5067 **Region** Limestone Coast
T (08) 8363 5800 **www**.tidswellwines.com.au **Open** By appt
Winemaker Ben Tidswell, Wine Wise Consultancy **Est.** 1994 **Dozens** 4000 **Vyds** 136.4ha

The Tidswell family (Andrea and Ben Tidswell) has two large vineyards in the Limestone Coast zone near Bool Lagoon; the lion's share is planted to cabernet sauvignon and shiraz, with smaller plantings of merlot, sauvignon blanc, petit verdot, vermentino and pinot gris. Tidswell Wines is a fully certified member of Winemaker's Federation of Australia environmental sustainability program. Wines are released under the Jennifer, Heathfield Ridge and The Publicans labels. Exports to Singapore, Japan and China.

🍷🍷🍷🍷 **Heathfield Limestone Coast Cabernet Sauvignon 2014** A plush cabernet with abundant currant, black plum and licorice notes embedded in a carapace of well-massaged grape tannins, vanilla chocolate oak (30% French) and a skein of jangly acidity. Plenty to like here. Screwcap. 14.5% alc. **Rating** 92 **To** 2022 $28 NG

Heathfield Limestone Coast Vermentino 2014 A shiraz with few rough edges, allusions of dark fruits of all descriptions are interwoven with clove, anise, cedar and mocha, following handling in a combination of French and American oak. The finish is warm and easy to nestle up to. Screwcap. 14.5% alc. **Rating** 91 **To** 2022 $28 NG

Tilbrook Estate

1856 Lobethal Road, Lobethal, SA 5241 **Region** Adelaide Hills
T (08) 8389 5318 **www.**tilbrookestate.com.au **Open** Fri–Sun & public hols 11–5
Winemaker James Tilbrook **Est.** 1999 **Dozens** 1000 **Vyds** 3.97ha

James and Annabelle Tilbrook have almost 5ha of multi-clone chardonnay and pinot noir, plus sauvignon blanc and pinot gris, at Lenswood. English-born James came to Australia in 1986, aged 22, but a car accident led to his return to England. Working for Oddbins and passing the WSET diploma set his future course. He returned to Australia, met Annabelle, purchased the vineyard and began planting it in '99. After 15 years of operating their cellar door from the old woollen mill at Lobethal, 'it was time to move out of town and into the vineyard'. The Tilbrooks have since established a winery and began construction of their cellar door, in the meantime operating a 'pop-up' cellar door at the property.

ŶŶŶŶŶ Lenswood Adelaide Hills Chardonnay 2015 Straw-coloured and powerfully built. Fresh cedar wood, yellow stone fruit and menthol flavours combine to create a wine of real oomph without, importantly, losing shape or control. As delicious as it is distinctive. Screwcap. 13.5% alc. **Rating** 93 **To** 2022 $35 CM

Adelaide Hills Syrah 2016 A perfumed, expressive red with black cherry and overt florals dancing across both the nose and palate. It attacks well before settling into more modest territory. Tannin is both fine and firm. There are savoury spice notes here, but they're well integrated with the fruit. It's trim, neat and attractive. Screwcap. 14% alc. **Rating** 91 **To** 2026 $25 CM

Adelaide Hills Shiraz Cabernet 2014 Shiraz from the Adelaide Hills, cabernet sauvignon from the Eden Valley. It's a pretty smooth operator. It tastes of leather and raisins, blackcurrant and blonde tobacco, a subtle shift of cedar wood helping to shuffle it all together. Gently developed, in a good way. Ready to drink any time from now. Screwcap. 14% alc. **Rating** 91 **To** 2024 $25 CM

ŶŶŶŶ Lenswood Sauvignon Blanc 2017 **Rating** 89 **To** 2019 $25 CM
Adelaide Hills Pinot Gris 2017 **Rating** 89 **To** 2019 $25 CM

Tim Adams

156 Warenda Road, Clare, SA 5453 **Region** Clare Valley
T (08) 8842 2429 **www.**timadamswines.com.au **Open** Mon–Fri 10.30–5, w'ends 11–5
Winemaker Tim Adams, Brett Schutz **Est.** 1986 **Dozens** 60 000 **Vyds** 145ha

Tim Adams and partner Pam Goldsack preside over a highly successful business. Having expanded the range of estate plantings with tempranillo, pinot gris and viognier, in 2009 the business took a giant step forward with the acquisition of the 80ha Leasingham Rogers Vineyard from Constellation Wines Australia, followed in '11 by the purchase of the Leasingham winery and winemaking equipment (for less than replacement cost). The winery is now a major contract winemaking facility for the region. Exports to the UK, the Netherlands, Sweden, South Korea, Hong Kong, China and NZ.

ŶŶŶŶŶ Reserve Clare Valley Riesling 2011 Made from free-run juice (500l/t), and shows its class from the outset. Bright and minerally, it has citrus juice flavours without a hint of sweetness, and is starting to build light toast and honey notes. Screwcap. 10.5% alc. **Rating** 95 **To** 2026 $29 **✪**

Clare Valley Semillon 2015 This is always a great expression of semillon that glimpses fine Graves, while being so very different from the featherweight, high-acid norm of the Hunter. The toasty oak plays a huge role in toning white fig, nettle and lemon drop candy notes, bridled to a lively undercarriage of acidity that is juicy rather than forced. It ages beautifully. Screwcap. 12.7% alc. **Rating** 95 **To** 2028 $24 NG **✪**

Clare Valley Cabernet Malbec 2014 A 70/30% blend from four vineyards, fermented separately, matured in new and used French oak for 24 months. A very well-made wine based on a Clare Valley special blend with a long lineage, this wine is absolutely in the centre of that line. Cabernet provides the structure, malbec the fruit to fill the spaces. Retasting underlines the balance of a wine destined for a long future. Screwcap. 14.5% alc. **Rating** 95 **To** 2034 $25 **○**

Clare Valley Riesling 2017 Direct, linear riesling best suited for the cellar, yet so crisp and refreshing that it'll be hard to keep your mitts off it in its youth. Lemon, lemongrass, grapefruit and talc-like flavours bullet through the palate and through the finish. Impeccable. Screwcap. 11.5% alc. **Rating** 94 **To** 2027 $22 CM **○**

Reserve Clare Valley Cabernet Malbec 2012 Straight as a gun barrel despite the softening effect of some bottle age, this is a plush, avuncular cabernet stamped with cassis, sage, bay leaf and a strong genetic line of graphite tannins, melded to cocoa oak. Spearmint, sarsaparilla, capsicum and violet, too. This is a full-bodied, quintessentially regional wine with thrust, mettle and pointed length. It will age very well. Screwcap. 14.5% alc. **Rating** 94 **To** 2028 $45 NG

♀♀♀♀♀ **Clare Valley Pinot Gris 2017** Rating 93 **To** 2019 $22 CM **○**

Tim Gramp   ★★★★

1033 Mintaro Road, Watervale, SA 5452 **Region** Clare Valley
T (08) 8843 0199 **www.**timgrampwines.com.au **Open** W'ends 12–4
Winemaker Tim Gramp **Est.** 1990 **Dozens** 6000 **Vyds** 16ha
Tim Gramp has quietly built up a very successful business, and by keeping overheads to a minimum provides good wines at modest prices. Over the years the estate vineyards (shiraz, riesling, cabernet sauvignon and grenache) have been expanded significantly. Exports to Malaysia, Taiwan and China.

♀♀♀♀♀ **Watervale Riesling 2017** All the hallmarks of Watervale are highlighted from white blossom, spice, bath salts to its slatey, cool palate. Plenty of lemon and lime juice freshness driven by its bright acidity seal the deal. Screwcap. 12% alc. **Rating** 93 **To** 2023 $21 JF **○**

Basket Pressed Watervale Cabernet Sauvignon 2014 Matured in a mix of French and American oak, none of it new. Only 317 dozen produced. Freshness is the key here. It bursts into life with boysenberry and blackcurrant flavours, the fruit sweet and jellied, but well tempered by notes of peppercorn and gum leaf. This is frisky with flavour, in the most positive of ways. Screwcap. 14.5% alc. **Rating** 92 **To** 2024 $22 CM **○**

♀♀♀♀ **Basket Pressed Watervale Shiraz 2014** Rating 89 **To** 2020 $30 JF

Tim McNeil Wines   ★★★★★

71 Springvale Road, Watervale, SA 5452 **Region** Clare Valley
T (08) 8843 0040 **www.**timmcneilwines.com.au **Open** Fri–Sun & public hols 11–5
Winemaker Tim McNeil **Est.** 2004 **Dozens** 1500 **Vyds** 2ha
When Tim and Cass McNeil established Tim McNeil Wines, Tim had long since given up his teaching career, graduating with a degree in oenology from the University of Adelaide in 1999. He then spent 11 years honing his craft at important wineries in the Barossa and Clare valleys. In Aug 2010 Tim McNeil Wines became his full-time job. The McNeils' 16ha property at Watervale includes mature dry-grown riesling. The cellar door overlooks the riesling vineyard, with panoramic views of Watervale and beyond. Exports to Canada.

♀♀♀♀♀ **Reserve Watervale Riesling 2018** Deliciously archetypal. Classic lemon and lime flavours, zippy as all get out, with floral lifts and energy to burn. Dry, long, intense; it's firing on all cylinders. Screwcap. 12.5% alc. **Rating** 95 **To** 2027 $24 CM **○**

Reserve Clare Valley Riesling 2017 It's not more intense than its Watervale sibling, but it's more textural. The flavours slow down and linger as they roll through your mouth. Lime, lemon blossom and fennel seed flavours. Excellent extension through the finish. A class act. Screwcap. 12.5% alc. **Rating** 95 **To** 2024 $32 CM **○**

♀♀♀♀♀ **Clare Valley Shiraz 2014** Rating 91 **To** 2025 $35 CM

Tintilla Wines

725 Hermitage Road, Pokolbin, NSW 2320 **Region** Hunter Valley
T (02) 6574 7093 **www**.tintilla.com.au **Open** 7 days 10.30–6
Winemaker James Lusby, Robert Lusby **Est.** 1993 **Dozens** 3500 **Vyds** 6.5ha
The Lusby family has established shiraz (2.2ha), sangiovese (1.6ha), merlot (1.3ha), semillon (1.2ha) and cabernet sauvignon (0.2ha) on a northeast-facing slope with red clay and limestone soil. Tintilla was the first winery to plant sangiovese in the Hunter Valley (in 1995). The family has also planted an olive grove producing four different types of olives, which are cured and sold from the estate.

Museum Release Angus Hunter Valley Semillon 2011 A bright, light straw-gold with a green tinge; plenty of racy acidity and flavour from lemongrass to lemon zest and pith. A touch herbal, but attractive and more in the basil spectrum, some aged notes coming through as toasty as a marshmallow over an open fire. Screwcap. 10.9% alc. **Rating** 94 **To** 2024 $40 JF

Patriarch Hunter Valley Syrah 2016 Rating 93 **To** 2028 $60 JF
Pebbles Brief Hunter Valley Chardonnay 2016 Rating 91 **To** 2024 $30 JF
Angus Hunter Semillon 2016 Rating 90 **To** 2025 $30 JF
Reserve Hunter Valley Shiraz 2015 Rating 90 **To** 2023 $40 JF

Tobin Wines

34 Ricca Road, Ballandean, Qld 4382 **Region** Granite Belt
T (07) 4684 1235 **www**.tobinwines.com.au **Open** 7 days 10–5
Winemaker Adrian Tobin **Est.** 1964 **Dozens** 1500 **Vyds** 5.9ha
In the early 1960s the Rica family planted table grapes, followed by shiraz and semillon in '64–'66: these are said to be the oldest vinifera vines in the Granite Belt region. The Tobin family (headed by Adrian and Frances) purchased the vineyard in 2000 and has increased the plantings, which now consist of shiraz, cabernet sauvignon, merlot, tempranillo, semillon, verdelho, chardonnay, muscat and sauvignon blanc.

Jacob Tempranillo 2016 Incredibly supple for a tempranillo, and medium-bodied with just the telltale acidity cutting through. And with no new oak influence, aged 1 year in seasoned barrels, the fruit can shine through – a mix of dark plums and cherries. It's very much in the savoury spectrum and ultimately satisfying. Screwcap. 13.5% alc. **Rating** 92 **To** 2024 $55 JF
Max Shiraz Block Two 2016 Excellent dark red hue; a more complete wine than its Block One sibling, this having more flesh on its bones. A mix of pulpy red and black fruits, and while aged in older oak, it's adding woodsy spices and slightly drying tannins. Fuller bodied, plenty of acidity dancing across the palate to keep this lively. Screwcap. 13.9% alc. **Rating** 91 **To** 2026 $55 JF

Charlotte Barrel Fermented Granite Belt Sauvignon Blanc 2016
Rating 89 **To** 2020 $45 JF

 Tocco Wines

5 Wilcox Street, Preston, Vic 3072 (postal) **Region** Barossa Valley/McLaren Vale
T (03) 8529 9023 **www**.toccowines.com.au **Open** By appt
Winemaker Contract **Est.** 2015 **Dozens** 10 000
You may guess, the moment you see the labels, that the wines are destined for the greater China market, or for specialised niche outlets in Australia. The wines are from a virtual winery, Tocco owning neither vineyards nor winery, and based in Preston, Victoria. They share what might be termed an artisanal quality. Exports to China.

Block 1889 Old Vine McLaren Vale Soul Shiraz 2014 There's no indication on the bottle of who owns the block of vines planted in McLaren Vale in 1889, or who might have made the wine, but I'm prepared to disregard the uncertainties and say the alcohol, while substantial, tastes lower than that of the Five Generations wine. This McLaren Vale wine is impressive, the packaging is striking, and underpriced – it should be at least twice as expensive as Five Generations. Cork. 16% alc. **Rating** 89 **To** 2022 $25

Vine Pedigree Reserve Barossa Valley Shiraz 2013 Better balanced; full-bodied, of course, but there's some attractive plum and dark cherry fruit, blackberry also in the flavour mix. The packaging makes it unsaleable in Australia to a normal audience. Cork. 15% alc. **Rating** 89 **To** 2028 $40

Tokar Estate ★★★★★

6 Maddens Lane, Coldstream, Vic 3770 **Region** Yarra Valley
T (03) 5964 9585 **www**.tokarestate.com.au **Open** 7 days 10.30–5
Winemaker Martin Siebert **Est.** 1996 **Dozens** 4000 **Vyds** 12ha
Leon Tokar, a very successful businessman, and wife Rita dreamed of a weekender and hobby farm, and it was largely by chance that in 1995 they found a scruffy paddock fronting onto Maddens Lane. By the end of the day, they had signed a contract to buy the property, following in the footsteps of myself and wife Suzanne ten years earlier when we also signed a contract to purchase what became Coldstream Hills on the day we first set foot on it (albeit several years after we first saw it). The Tokars wasted no time, and by '99 they had planted their 12ha vineyard, and built a Mediterranean-inspired cellar door and restaurant. Martin Siebert has been winemaker for many years, making consistently good wines, and with son Daniel Tokar as general manager, has full responsibility for the day-to-day management of the business.

🍷🍷🍷🍷🍷 **Yarra Valley Shiraz 2016** From estate vines planted in '96, hand-picked, foot-stomped to leave 50% whole bunches, wild-fermented, matured in French oak. An exceptionally intense wine with great length born of that intensity. French and American oak has joined with firm tannins to provide some of the texture and structure of this remarkable wine. Screwcap. 14.7% alc. **Rating** 96 **To** 2046 $35 **۞**

Yarra Valley Cabernet Sauvignon 2016 Small batches crushed and destemmed, wild-fermented and matured in new and used French oak for 15 months. Tokar Estate has forged a reputation for its cabernet, and this follows the pattern of long and well-balanced wines. Screwcap. 14.5% alc. **Rating** 95 **To** 2036 $45

Yarra Valley Chardonnay 2016 Classy chardonnay. Flint threaded through stone fruit. It breaks quartz open and splatters sparks of mineral and spice through the palate. Fresh, lively, fine and sophisticated. Screwcap. 13.5% alc. **Rating** 94 **To** 2022 $35 CM

Yarra Valley Rose 2017 A shiraz rose made from the ground up (half the estate block was picked 2 weeks earlier than the main shiraz harvest specifically for this wine). The edge of salmon to the colour is a fact, its cause debatable, especially in the context of 50/50% barrel/tank fermentation. Both the mouthfeel and flavour are yet another face of the glorious vintage. Screwcap. 13.2% alc. **Rating** 94 **To** 2021 $25 **۞**

🍷🍷🍷🍷🍷 **Tempranillo 2016** Rating 93 **To** 2029 $35
Carafe & Tumbler Pinot Shiraz 2016 Rating 92 **To** 2025 $25 CM **۞**
Pinot Noir 2016 Rating 92 **To** 2023 $40 CM
Carafe & Tumbler Tempranillo 2016 Rating 92 **To** 2023 $25 CM **۞**

Tolpuddle Vineyard ★★★★★

37 Back Tea Tree Road, Richmond, Tas 7025 **Region** Southern Tasmania
T (08) 8155 6003 **www**.tolpuddlevineyard.com **Open** At Shaw + Smith
Winemaker Martin Shaw, Adam Wadewitz **Est.** 1988 **Dozens** 1800 **Vyds** 20ha
If ever a winery was born with blue blood in its veins, Tolpuddle would have to be it. The vineyard was established in 1988 on a continuous downhill slope facing northeast, and in 2006 won the inaugural Tasmanian Vineyard of the Year Award. Michael Hill Smith MW and Martin Shaw are joint managing directors. David LeMire looks after sales and marketing;

Adam Wadewitz, one of Australia's brightest winemaking talents, is senior winemaker. Vineyard manager Carlos Souris loses nothing in comparison, with over 30 years of grapegrowing in Tasmania under his belt, and has an absolutely fearless approach to making a great vineyard even greater. Exports to the US, the UK, Canada, Denmark, China, Japan and Singapore.

🍷🍷🍷🍷🍷 **Pinot Noir 2015** Bright, clear crimson; a very complex bouquet with perfumed and alluring fruits, charcuterie and red flowers, reflecting whole berry/whole bunch vinification. Amazing power and length to the palate, the spicy tannins pure class. Wow. Screwcap. 13.5% alc. **Rating** 97 **To** 2028 $78 **○**

🍷🍷🍷🍷🍷 **Chardonnay 2016** A warm and drier than average season has resulted in richer and more intense flavours of stone fruit, ginger flower and preserved lemon. More complexity and depth from winemaking inputs such as whole-bunch pressed and fermented and 9 months in French oak. Yet this never feels besieged, as the natural acidity glides across the palate reining everything in. A pleasure to drink. Screwcap. 13% alc. **Rating** 96 **To** 2025 $70 JF **○**

Pinot Noir 2016 A wine that explains the love at first sight when the Tolpuddle partners saw the vineyard. It comes flying through the weather of the vintage that trapped others with a highly perfumed red flower bouquet and into a layered palate, reflecting the whole-bunch/whole-berry fermentation; spicy, savoury, foresty notes form a laurel wreath on the fruit, the oak integrated. Screwcap. 13% alc. **Rating** 95 **To** 2026 $70

Tomboy Hill ★★★★★

204 Sim Street, Ballarat, Vic 3350 (postal) **Region** Ballarat
T (03) 5331 3785 **Open** Not
Winemaker Scott Ireland (Contract) **Est.** 1984 **Dozens** 600 **Vyds** 3.6ha

Former schoolteacher Ian Watson seems to be following the same path as Lindsay McCall of Paringa Estate (also a former schoolteacher) in extracting greater quality and style than any other winery in their respective regions. Since 1984 Ian has patiently built up a patchwork quilt of small plantings of chardonnay and pinot noir. In the better years, single vineyard Chardonnay and/or Pinot Noir are released; Rebellion Chardonnay and Pinot Noir are multi-vineyard blends, but all 100% Ballarat. After difficult vintages in 2011 and '12, Tomboy Hill has been in top form since '15.

🍷🍷🍷🍷🍷 **The Tomboy Chardonnay 2016** A flamboyant wine of compelling richness hewn to sensitive oak and lees handling, imparting restraint and textural intrigue. Toasted hazelnut, *pain grillé*, truffle and vanilla pod mingle with peach and apricot flavours, all melding effortlessly to rumble far and wide across the palate, towed by a stream of mineral notes. A wine of power and precision, strongly reminiscent of a fine meursault. Screwcap. 13.2% alc. **Rating** 96 **To** 2028 $50 NG **○**

The Tomboy Ballarat Pinot Noir 2016 Bright, tangy aromas of persimmon, sarsaparilla, candied orange rind and red berries leap from the glass, underlain by a souk of cardamom, clove and anise. The influence of whole clusters in the fermentation is clear, imparting too a spider web of tannins expanding nicely across the long, sappy finish. This is a bit shins and elbows at the moment, but the fruit and structural attributes will integrate across a bright future. Screwcap. 12.7% alc. **Rating** 95 **To** 2026 $75 NG

Rebellion Ballarat Chardonnay 2016 A richly endowed chardonnay, despite the controlled alcohol (12.7%) and early picking window of the vintage. Nougat, gingerbread, truffle and cashew flood the senses. There is plenty of stone fruit in the mix, as well, but the indelible impression is one of ample flavour and creamy detail. Screwcap. 12.7% alc. **Rating** 94 **To** 2025 $35 NG

Tomich Wines ★★★★☆

87 King William Road, Unley, SA 5061 **Region** Adelaide Hills
T (08) 8299 7500 **www.tomich.com.au** **Open** Mon–Sat 11–4
Winemaker Randal Tomich **Est.** 2002 **Dozens** 60 000 **Vyds** 180ha

Patriarch John Tomich was born on a vineyard near Mildura, where he learnt firsthand the skills and knowledge required for premium grapegrowing. He went on to become a well-known Adelaide ear, nose and throat specialist. Taking the wheel full circle, he completed postgraduate studies in winemaking at the University of Adelaide in 2002, and embarked on the Master of Wine revision course from the Institute of Masters of Wine. His son Randal is a cutting from the old vine, having invented new equipment and techniques for tending the family's vineyard in the Adelaide Hills, resulting in a 60% saving in time and fuel costs. Exports to the US, Singapore and China.

ŸŸŸŸŸ **Single Vineyard Adelaide Hills Chardonnay 2016** Hand-picked at dawn, wild-fermented, partial mlf, matured in French barriques. An elegant wine, zesty stone fruit and grapefruit rippling along a light-bodied palate. Chablis? Why not. Screwcap. 13% alc. **Rating** 94 **To** 2023 $25 ✪

Tomich Hill Hilltop Adelaide Hills Pinot Noir 2016 No questions to be asked about this deeply coloured pinot and its imperious palate, still with years in front of it. Plum and black cherry fruit sweet through the mouth, latent spices still to break free. Screwcap. 13.5% alc. **Rating** 94 **To** 2026 $28 ✪

ŸŸŸŸŸ **Single Vineyard Pinot Noir 2016 Rating** 92 **To** 2025 $30
Woodside Vineyard Riesling 2017 Rating 90 **To** 2023 $25
Woodside Park Sauvignon Blanc 2017 Rating 90 **To** 2019 $22
Single Vineyard Gruner Veltliner 2017 Rating 90 **To** 2021 $25

Toolangi Vineyards ★★★★★

PO Box 9431, South Yarra, Vic 3141 **Region** Yarra Valley
T (03) 9827 9977 **www**.toolangi.com **Open** Not
Winemaker Various contract **Est.** 1995 **Dozens** 7000 **Vyds** 12.2ha
Garry and Julie Hounsell acquired their property in the Dixons Creek area of the Yarra Valley, adjoining the Toolangi State Forest, in 1995. The primary accent is on pinot noir and chardonnay, accounting for all but 2.7ha, which is predominantly shiraz and a little viognier. Winemaking is by Yering Station (Willy Lunn), Giaconda (Rick Kinzbrunner), Hoddles Creek Estate (Franco D'Anna), Andrew Fleming (Coldstream Hills) and Oakridge (David Bicknell), as impressive a quintet of winemakers as one could wish for. Exports to the UK, Hong Kong, Singapore, Japan and China.

ŸŸŸŸŸ **Block F Yarra Valley Chardonnay 2015** Both this and its '16 sibling were made by Rick Kinzbrunner at Giaconda in identical fashion (wild-fermented in French Sirugue barrels, 50% new, matured for 18 months). Thus the vintage is the key (and an extra year's development for this wine). It was a great vintage, full ripeness at a lower alcohol level, the length prodigious. Screwcap. 13.8% alc. **Rating** 96 **To** 2027 $100

Block D Yarra Valley Shiraz 2015 Hand-picked, whole berries wild yeast–open fermented, matured for 14 months in French oak (30% new). Bright crimson-purple; highly fragrant and flowery, cool-grown shiraz aromas set their own agenda, deftly opening the doors to allow the discussion to start. Sweet red cherry fruit, with a hint of forest strawberry, are given the floor, freed by the 13.5% alcohol, no heat, no eye-popping, just beautiful shiraz, unforced by new French oak. Screwcap. 13.8% alc. **Rating** 96 **To** 2035 $60 ✪

Block F Yarra Valley Chardonnay 2016 Hand-picked Mendoza clone, crushed and pressed, wild-fermented, matured for 18 months in French Sirugue oak (50% new). Full of vibrant youth, largely circumventing the rapid-fire vintage. Exceeds expectations. Screwcap. 14.5% alc. **Rating** 95 **To** 2025 $100

Estate Yarra Valley Pinot Noir 2016 Identical vinification to its Yarra Valley sibling, except for 20% new oak rather than 10%. Although no mention is made, it seems certain that some fruit selection was made before delivery to the winery. This has a somewhat deeper colour than its sibling, and deeper fruit flavour, red cherry to the fore, fine tannin to finish. Screwcap. 14% alc. **Rating** 95 **To** 2026 $45

Yarra Valley Pinot Noir 2016 MV6, hand-picked, destemmed, wild yeast–open fermented, matured for 10 months in French barriques (10% new). Light, clear red-purple; bright, fresh red fruits on the fragrant bouquet and palate alike; light to medium-bodied; has good length and mouthfeel. Excellent value. Screwcap. 13.8% alc. **Rating** 94 **To** 2029 $28 **O**

♥♥♥♥♀ **Yarra Valley Chardonnay 2016** Rating 93 To 2024 $28
Yarra Valley Shiraz 2016 Rating 91 To 2031 $26

Top Note

546 Peters Creek Road, Kuitpo, SA 5172 **Region** Adelaide Hills
T 0406 291 136 **www**.topnote.com.au **Open** W'ends 11–4 (closed Aug–May)
Winemaker Nick Foskett **Est.** 2011 **Dozens** 800 **Vyds** 17ha
Computer chip designer Nick Foskett and opera singer Cate Foskett were looking for a lifestyle property in the Adelaide Hills after full-on careers in their very different occupations. By chance they came across a 24ha property planted to five varieties, all mainstream except for 0.5ha of a rare mutation of semillon, which turns the skin red. They say, 'Despite the small hurdles of our not knowing much about anything and none of the grapes being under contract, we sold our city house, enrolled in postgraduate viticulture and winemaking at the Waite Campus, University of Adelaide, and became grapegrowers'. Two years on, Cate became possibly the only qualified operatic viticulturist in the world, and still works as a singer between harvests, managing the vineyard and sales.

♥♥♥♥♀ **Adelaide Hills Cabernet Shiraz 2016** It was a difficult season, but they've made a decent fist of it. Creamy oak helps matters, but redcurrant fruit and gently candied aspects keep the palate alive and well, savoury notes are also there. Screwcap. 14% alc. **Rating** 90 **To** 2024 $35 CM

Topper's Mountain Wines ★★★★☆

13420 Guyra Road, Tingha, NSW 2369 **Region** New England
T 0411 880 580 **www**.toppers.com.au **Open** By appt
Winemaker Mike Hayes **Est.** 2000 **Dozens** 1500 **Vyds** 9.79ha
Topper's Mountain is named after brothers Edward and William Topper, who were employees of George Jr and Alwyn Wyndham (sons of George Wyndham, founder of Wyndham Estate). They previously owned New Valley Station, which included the present-day Topper's Mountain. These days, Topper's Mountain is owned by Mark Kirkby. Planting began in the spring of 2000, with the ultimate fruit salad trial of 15 rows each of innumerable varieties and clones. The total area planted was made up of 28 separate plantings, many of these with only 200 vines in a block. As varieties proved unsuited, they were grafted over to those that held the most promise. Thus far, the Gewurztraminer and Sauvignon Blanc hold most promise among their white wines, with the Mediterranean reds doing better than their French cousins. The original 28 varieties are now down to 16; chardonnay, gewurztraminer, sauvignon blanc, tempranillo, shiraz and merlot are the commercial varieties, the remainder in the fruit salad block still under evaluation. Integrated pest management has been successfully adopted throughout the vineyard. Exports to Germany.

♥♥♥♥♥ **Gewurztraminer 2016** This estate-grown wine would cause any Alsace winemaker to nod in appreciation. Its heady musk and rose petal aromas pick up a dash of lychee on the palate. There are phenolics on the finish, but they add to the appeal with their spicy bite. No tricks in the vinification: this is the vintage speaking. Screwcap. 13.9% alc. **Rating** 95 **To** 2023 $35 **O**

♥♥♥♥♀ **Barrel Ferment Gewurztraminer 2016** Rating 91 To 2022 $35

Torbreck Vintners

Roennfeldt Road, Marananga, SA 5352 **Region** Barossa Valley
T (08) 8562 4155 **www**.torbreck.com **Open** 7 days 10–6
Winemaker Ian Hongell, Scott McDonald **Est.** 1994 **Dozens** 55 000 **Vyds** 150ha

Torbreck Vintners was already one of Australia's best-known high quality red wine makers when, in September 2013, wealthy Californian entrepreneur and vintner Peter Kight (of Quivira Vineyards) acquired 100% ownership of the business. The brand structure is led by the ranges The Laird (single vineyard shiraz), RunRig (shiraz/viognier), The Factor (shiraz), Descendant (shiraz/viognier) and The Pict (mataro). In March 2018 Torbreck purchased renowned pinot noir producer Escarpment (Martinborough, NZ), with founder Larry McKenna staying on as winemaker. Exports to all major markets.

ΨΨΨΨΨ **The Struie 2016** Deep crimson; the wine is of typical Torbreck style, sweeping away all before its flavours of blackberry, licorice, spice, tar and oak click in, the alcohol just part of the scenery, as are the ripe tannins. Cork. 15% alc. **Rating** 97 To 2036

RunRig 2015 One of the classic Torbreck wines, with the added benefits of the '15 vintage. It is a gorgeously deep pool of supple, mouthfilling/watering fruit flavours (impossible, I know, but it is). Seduction clinically confronts and comforts the consumer. Black fruits, licorice and a shaft of dark chocolate, plus oak, do the business. Cork. 15% alc. **Rating** 97 To 2035

The Factor 2015 Dense, inky colour; it is, of course, gloriously rich, the Torbreck DNA and touch found whatever part of the wine you are analysing (or simply drinking and enjoying). Once again, the '15 vintage imposes its will. Cork. 15% alc. **Rating** 97 To 2035

The Laird 2012 Astonishingly vibrant colour for a 5yo wine. The intensity of this 100% shiraz burns like an arc light across the senses, catching every nuance of the panoply of the purple and black fruits at the core of this remarkable wine. The balance and length are awesome, making a mockery of its alcohol. Cork. 15.5% alc. **Rating** 97 To 2047 $750

Descendant 2015 By Torbreck standards this wine is medium-bodied, but by normal standards full-bodied. There is more textural give and take, presumably from the viognier. At the end of the day it doesn't matter, the lilt on the finish brings you back to where you began. Cork. 15% alc. **Rating** 97 To 2035

Descendant 2014 Vivid crimson-purple; this is a glorious wine from a less than glorious vintage, its juicy red and black fruits beating a tattoo on both the bouquet and palate. The use of second-fill French oak has provided a perfect framework for the fruit. Cork. 14.5% alc. **Rating** 97 To 2044 $125 ✪

ΨΨΨΨΨ **The Steading 2016** This is wholly traditional, and also very good. Its complexity and richness have energy, focus and freshness; an ever-changing cast of flavours crossing the palate on their way to the finish. The alcohol in no way imposes itself on you. Cork. 15% alc. **Rating** 96 To 2036 $38 ✪

Barossa Valley Roussanne 2017 What a vintage to let loose with the Rhône varieties – and with screwcaps. The bouquet is of white flowers and faint spices, the palate absolutely stacked with honey and crushed leaves, and skins of citrus as a minerally offset. Screwcap. 13% alc. **Rating** 95 To 2025

The Factor 2014 An ultra-full-bodied shiraz with a velvety mouthfeel; supple, round and long, it needs decades to slim down, or in the short-term, be matched with a kilo of rib eye on the bone. If you are going to use a cork for long-term ageing, use Torbreck as a benchmark for high quality cork. 15% alc. **Rating** 95 To 2044 $125

The Loon 2016 Right in the centre of the Torbreck shiraz style, with all encompassing flavours from the word go, assisted (if indeed possible) by the inclusion of roussanne. Blackberry, licorice and spice have a savoury (one is tempted to say tarry) background, tannin and oak playing junior roles. Screwcap. 14% alc. **Rating** 95 To 2036

Harris Barossa Valley Grenache 2016 From bushvines planted in '02, matured in used French hogsheads for 12 months. It is a full-bodied grenache notwithstanding the alcohol, and it will be fascinating to see what comes along with the '17 vintage. Screwcap. 14.5% alc. **Rating** 95 To 2036

Woodcutter's Barossa Valley Semillon 2017 Rating 94 To 2034
Woodcutter's Barossa Valley Rose 2017 Rating 94 To 2023

The Struie 2015 Rating 94 To 2030 $50
RunRig 2014 Rating 94 To 2040 $260

ŢŢŢŢŢ The Steading 2015 Rating 93 To 2025 $40
The Steading Blanc 2017 Rating 91 To 2024
Hillside Vineyard Barossa Valley Grenache 2016 Rating 91 To 2036
Woodcutter's Barossa Valley Roussanne Viognier Marsanne 2017
Rating 90 To 2022

Torzi Matthews Vintners ★★★★

Cnr Eden Valley Road/Sugarloaf Hill Road, Mt McKenzie, SA 5353 **Region** Eden Valley
T 0412 323 486 **www.torzimatthews.com.au Open** By appt
Winemaker Domenic Torzi **Est.** 1996 **Dozens** 3000 **Vyds** 10ha
Domenic Torzi and Tracy Matthews, former Adelaide Plains residents, searched for a number
of years before finding a block at Mt McKenzie in the Eden Valley. The block they chose is
in a hollow; the soil is meagre, but they were in no way deterred by the knowledge that it
would be frost-prone. The result is predictably low yields, concentrated further by drying the
grapes on racks, thus reducing the weight by around 30% (the Appassimento method is used
in Italy to produce amarone-style wines). Newer plantings of sangiovese and negro amaro,
and an extension of the original plantings of shiraz and riesling, have seen their wine range
increase. Exports to the UK and Denmark.

ŢŢŢŢŢ **Frost Dodger Eden Valley Riesling 2017** Pristine apple and lime with a lilt
of talc through the finish. Delicate, but not underpowered. Archetypal Eden Valley
riesling, yet it still manages a personality of its own. Slatey aftertaste. Very good.
Screwcap. 12.5% alc. **Rating** 93 **To** 2027 $25 CM ✪
Schist Rock Single Vineyard Barossa Shiraz 2016 Schist Rock Shiraz rides
again. The power of dark-berried fruit, the complex array of deli meat and dried
herb flavour, the slinky texture, the great wash of flavour through the finish. It's
bright and rich at once, the flavours flowing freely, aniseed a delicious finishing
touch. It will cellar, but there's no real need. Screwcap. 14.5% alc. **Rating** 93
To 2026 $22 CM ✪
Vigna Cantina Barossa Rosato di Sangiovese 2017 Pale crimson in colour.
A soft centre of raspberried fruit comes marshalled by savouriness, mostly in the
form of dry/dusty spice, but with crackles of dried leaves too. It's a crunchy wine,
dry and serious, but that centre of sweet fruit flavour has more than a little 'come
hither' about it. Screwcap. 13.5% alc. **Rating** 92 **To** 2019 $25 CM ✪

Totino Estate ★★★★

982 Port Road, Albert Park, SA 5014 (postal) **Region** Adelaide Hills
T (08) 8349 1200 **www.totinowines.com.au Open** Not
Winemaker Don Totino, Damien Harris **Est.** 1992 **Dozens** 15 000 **Vyds** 29ha
Don Totino migrated from Italy in 1968, and at the age of 18 became the youngest barber in
Australia. He soon moved on into general food importing and distribution. Festival City, as the
business is known, has been highly successful, recognised by a recent significant award from the
Italian government. In 1998 he purchased a rundown vineyard at Paracombe in the Adelaide
Hills, and has since extended the plantings to 29ha of chardonnay, pinot grigio, sauvignon
blanc, sangiovese and shiraz. Various family members, including daughter Linda, are involved
in the business. Exports to Italy and China.

ŢŢŢŢŢ **Francesco Reserve Shiraz 2014** There's a concern that the cork had severe
leakage right through, given its youth. The wine has integrity, but the colour is
advanced. There's a flurry of dark fruits, and all manner of woodsy spices, mocha
and menthol. Full-bodied, very supple, velvety tannins and while by no means a
wallflower, there's a savouriness keeping this well contained. 14.5% alc. **Rating** 92
To 2022 $55 JF
SSC Adelaide Hills Sangiovese Shiraz Cabernet 2015 This is a bonza
blend, with tangy morello cherry and plums, some cabernet-esque leafy freshness

and currants, pepper and sprightly sangiovese acidity. It all comes together to make a balanced, savoury wine and, with the price, I'd take that as part of a good deal. Screwcap. 14% alc. **Rating** 92 **To** 2021 $22 JF ✪

Adelaide Hills Pinot Grigio 2016 Mid-straw and bright; opens up to offer some florals, ginger spice and crisp pears. While there's a lick of sweetness and texture softening the edges, this is tight with brisk lemony acidity. Refreshing, definitely. Screwcap. 12% alc. **Rating** 90 **To** 2018 $20 JF ✪

Traviarti   ★★★★

39 Elgin Road, Beechworth, Vic 3747 **Region** Beechworth
T 0439 994 075 **www**.traviarti.com **Open** By appt
Winemaker Daniel Balzer, Simon Grant **Est.** 2011 **Dozens** 450 **Vyds** 0.43ha
After 15 years in the wine trade, first as a buyer in retail, followed by sales and marketing roles for producers, Simon Grant and partner Helen spent several years looking for the right place to grow nebbiolo, the wine which had the greatest appeal for them. When they moved to Beechworth to run a grapegrowers' co-operative, they found the site and planted both nebbiolo and tempranillo in 2011. At around 600m on the red decomposed shale and mudstone soils just above the town of Beechworth, they have planted multiple clones on a combination of rootstocks and their own roots. Until these vines come into bearing, they source cabernet sauvignon and tempranillo from Mark Walpole's Beechworth vineyard.

🍷🍷🍷🍷♀ **Rosso 2016** A vivid blend of nebbiolo, cabernet and barbera, this is a mid-weighted wine, threaded through a spindle of edgy tannin; vigour aplenty, embedded in the acid energy that tows it joyously along. Red berries, amaro orange rind and chinotto, strewn with a herb or three. Dangerous, devilish! This is meritorious – based on poise and my desire for another glass alone! Among the country's best Italo-blends. **Rating** 93 **To** 2021 NG
Beechworth Tempranillo 2016 A jubey, licorice expression of the variety, impacted modestly by spicy/coffeed oak, the back half of the wine as sure-footed as it is soft. Tannin is integrated, harmony is paramount, drinkability is a given. Screwcap. 13.8% alc. **Rating** 91 **To** 2021 $35 CM

Treasury Wine Estates   ★★★★★

The Atrium, 58 Queensbridge Street, Southbank, Vic 3006 (postal) **Region** Various
T 1300 651 650 **www**.tweglobal.com **Open** Not
Winemaker Numerous **Est.** 2011 **Dozens** NFP **Vyds** NFP
Treasury Wine Estates (TWE), the renamed wine division of Foster's Group Limited, was fully separated from Foster's via a separate listing on the Australian Securities Exchange in May 2011. TWE has the full range of wine businesses: from those with a dedicated winery or wineries, household brand names and long-term grape supply from owned vineyards or contract arrangements, through to brands that have been stripped of their wineries and vineyards, but continue to have a significant brand presence in the marketplace. Those who fall into the dedicated winery/estate vineyards pattern are Penfolds, Wynns Coonawarra Estate, Seppelt, Devil's Lair, St Huberts and Coldstream Hills. Other brands include Annie's Lane, Heemskerk, Ingoldby, Jamiesons Run, Leo Buring, Lindemans, Rosemount Estate, Saltram, Tollana, Wolf Blass and Yellowglen. The rating is simply a recognition of the array of great brands that make up the vinous treasury of the group. All of this said, Penfolds is the ultimate jewel in the crown, with a greater brand value than all of the other brands combined. Exports to all major markets.

Trentham Estate   ★★★★

6531 Sturt Highway, Trentham Cliffs, NSW 2738 **Region** Murray Darling
T (03) 5024 8888 **www**.trenthamestate.com.au **Open** 7 days 10–5
Winemaker Anthony Murphy, Shane Kerr, Kerry Morrison **Est.** 1988 **Dozens** 70 000
Vyds 50.17ha
Remarkably consistent tasting notes across all wine styles from all vintages attest to the expertise of ex-Mildara winemaker Tony Murphy, a well-known and highly regarded

producer. Estate vineyards are on the Murray Darling. With an eye to the future, but also to broadening the range of the wines in offer, Trentham Estate is selectively buying grapes from other regions with a track record for the chosen varieties. The value for money is unfailingly excellent. Exports to the UK, China and other major markets.

🍷🍷🍷🍷🍷 **Estate Sauvignon Blanc 2017** The special yeast selected from wild yeast strains has undoubtedly played a critical role in the expression of tropical fruits, ranging from lychee to guava and passionfruit. Detailed attention in the vineyard and winery has added to the outcome. Screwcap. 12.5% alc. **Rating** 90 **To** 2019 $18 ⚪
Estate Chardonnay 2017 Only Tony Murphy knows how to conjure up wines, particularly white, of this quality from the Murray Darling, and I'm sure he's not about to tell. What's more, he does it again and again, not missing the opportunity in years like '17. White peach, crisp acidity and an inflection of French oak all fall into place. Screwcap. 13.5% alc. **Rating** 90 **To** 2021 $18 ⚪
Reserve Tumbarumba Chardonnay 2017 Hand-picked, whole-bunch pressed, fermentation commenced in stainless steel, completed in French oak, matured for 6 months. It seems obvious that the oak was used, and equally obvious that new oak would have suffocated what is an elegant wine, length its strong point. Screwcap. 13% alc. **Rating** 90 **To** 2025 $26
Reserve Heathcote Shiraz 2015 Good wine made from good grapes is a no-brainer, even when it's an eager-to-please variety. This is an elegant light to medium-bodied wine that takes full advantage of the '15 vintage. Screwcap. 14.5% alc. **Rating** 90 **To** 2025 $26

🍷🍷🍷🍷 **The Family Sanglovese Rose 2017** **Rating** 89 **To** 2018 $15 ⚪
Estate Shiraz 2016 **Rating** 89 **To** 2026 $16 ⚪

Trevelen Farm ★★★★★

506 Weir Road, Cranbrook, WA 6321 **Region** Great Southern
T 0418 361 052 **www.**trevelenfarm.com.au **Open** By appt
Winemaker Harewood Estate (James Kellie) **Est.** 1993 **Dozens** 3500 **Vyds** 6.5ha
In 2008 John and Katie Sprigg decided to pass ownership of their 1300ha wool, meat and grain-producing farm to son Ben and wife Louise. However, they have kept control of the 6.5ha of sauvignon blanc, riesling, chardonnay, cabernet sauvignon and merlot planted in 1993. When demand requires, they increase production by purchasing grapes from growers in the Frankland River subregion. Riesling remains the centrepiece of the range. Exports to the US, Japan and China.

🍷🍷🍷🍷🍷 **Aged Release Riesling 2010** Gleaming, light straw-green; has developed in its own little world, calmly and unhurried. Its balance is the key, with its citrus fruit an armchair of soft, but ample, acidity. Back releases of semillon and riesling are on a well-deserved upwards spiral. This is a beautiful wine to drink tonight. Screwcap. 12% alc. **Rating** 96 **To** 2025 $50 ⚪
The Tunney Cabernet Sauvignon 2015 A wonderfully rich and complex cabernet with layers of varietal fruit, cassis/blackcurrant, plump tannins and quality French oak. It's juicy and spicy, lightening its load to medium-bodied status. Screwcap. 14% alc. **Rating** 96 **To** 2040 $25 ⚪
Sauvignon Blanc Semillon 2017 A 70/30% blend. The fruit in the wine is so sweet it could be mistaken for residual sugar, but I'll run with the idea that it's dry. There's a wealth of complementary flavours, lemongrass/lemon from the semillon, moving through stone fruit to tropical notes ex the sauvignon blanc. Screwcap. 12.5% alc. **Rating** 95 **To** 2022 $18 ⚪
Frankland Reserve Shiraz 2015 How to make a full-bodied shiraz look like medium-bodied or less? Good question, because usually it's the other way around, and, secondly, I don't know the answer. Here there's an abundance of plum and blackberry fruit, with a scatter of spice and pepper. It never slows its movement in the mouth, never cloys for a moment, and isn't weighed down by oak or tannin. Screwcap. 14.5% alc. **Rating** 95 **To** 2038 $30 ⚪

Estate Chardonnay 2016 Bright straw-green; an elegant wine with the accent firmly on the seamless fusion of fruit, oak and energising acidity; exemplary length. Screwcap. 14% alc. **Rating** 94 **To** 2025 $25

 Estate Riesling 2017 **Rating** 93 **To** 2032 $25

 # Trinchini Estate Wines ★★★★

6 Noble Street, Anglesea, Vic 3230 (postal) **Region** Geelong
T 0411 205 044 **www.trinchini.com.au Open** Not
Winemaker Marcus Trinchini **Est.** 2014 **Dozens** 1500

Marcus Trinchini was born in December 1975, after his father came from Italy to Australia when he was 21 years old. He had always made wine, like his father and his grandfather before him. From a childhood interest in everything about wine, in 2006 Marcus started working with wines and wineries. He moved to Victoria with his wife, and in '12 started working with a small winery on the surf coast. This allowed him to begin the search for the perfect location for his first vineyard, which he found in Heathcote. He also found the old Pettavel winery in Geelong, and was underway by '14, making his own wine, sourcing fruit from Heathcote, Geelong and the Yarra Valley. No machinery is used at any stage, and while this is no doubt true of the crushing and pressing of the grapes, one assumes pumps are used to move the wine around the winery. Marcus certainly learnt his craft well. The four wines submitted for this edition are all of good quality. Marcus says, 'With almost 15 years of experience working in wineries and/or vineyards, I continue to enjoy my craft, strive to master it, making a better piece of art each time so that one day I will craft a Mona Lisa of wine'. Exports to China.

Black Label Heathcote Shiraz 2014 Oak and fruit are happily married, length is good and the spread of (integrated) tannin is impressive. This shows some signs of development, both in its mellow feel and flavour profile, and it's to positive effect. Blackberry, leather, dark chocolate and mint flavours have this humming along nicely. Screwcap. 14% alc. **Rating** 93 **To** 2025 $45 CM

Green Label Heathcote Shiraz 2016 Well balanced, sweet fruited, generous and enjoyable. This hits the spot well. Wood smoke, cloves, sandalwood and black cherry, easing into blackberry. It's all about sweet dark fruit, but it has some charisma too. A creamy veneer of oak keeps it all running smoothly. Screwcap. 14.5% alc. **Rating** 92 **To** 2026 $25 CM ○

Black Label Heathcote Shiraz 2015 It's called Black Label, though the label is predominantly white. It's fermented with 20% whole bunches and sees both French and American oak. It's toasty and blackberried, earthen and sweet. It's a hefty shiraz, full-bodied, stacked through the mid-palate and sheeted with oak. Tannin clamps on the finish, but warm fruit flavour remains raring to go. Screwcap. 14.5% alc. **Rating** 91 **To** 2027 $45 CM

Green Label Heathcote Shiraz 2015 Resiny character to both the texture and flavour, but there's good dark-berried fruit here and it's satisfying, if warm, carrying through to the finish. It's a big-ish, hearty style, but it's not ill-mannered. Screwcap. 14.5% alc. **Rating** 90 **To** 2024 $25 CM

tripe.Iscariot ★★★★★

74 Tingle Avenue, Margaret River, WA 6285 **Region** Margaret River
T 0414 817 808 **www.tripeiscariot.com Open** Not
Winemaker Remi Guise **Est.** 2013 **Dozens** 250

This has to be the most way out winery name of the century. It prompted me to email South African-born and trained winemaker/owner Remi Guise asking to explain its derivation and/ or meaning, and he courteously responded with a reference to Judas as 'the greatest black sheep of all time', and a non-specific explanation of 'tripe' as 'challenging in style'. He added, 'I hope this sheds some light, or dark, on the brand'. The wines provide a better answer, managing to successfully harness highly unusual techniques at various points of their élevage. His day job as winemaker at Naturaliste Vintners, the large Margaret River contract winemaking venture of Bruce Dukes, provides the technical grounding, allowing him to throw the 'how to' manual out of the window when the urge arises. His final words on his Marrow Syrah Malbec are: 'So, suck the marrow from the bone, fry the fat, and savour the warm, wobbly bits'.

ŦŦŦŦŦ Absolution Wilyabrup Margaret River Chenin Blanc 2017 A complex mix of sun-bleached hay, dried saltbush, smoky, baked quinces, lots of texture yet tangy with a line of lemon zest, and is ultra dry. Persimmon-like tannins, as this is fermented on skins for 9 days and aged 9 months in seasoned barrels. Very detailed and an excellent savoury chenin. Fruity is not in its vocabulary. Screwcap. 12.8% alc. **Rating** 95 **To** 2025 $30 JF ✪

Aspic Margaret River Grenache Rose 2015 Barrel aged for 9 months and with lees stirring has created a textural, savoury rose, but it doesn't lose its fresh spine-tingling appeal. Pale pastel pink-bronze; watermelon and rind, really spicy and savoury with ginger cream; zesty lemon, talc-like acidity. Textural yet dry, and dangerously delicious. Screwcap. 12.8% alc. **Rating** 95 **To** 2020 $30 JF ✪

Absolution Karridale Grenache Noir Syrah Viognier Malbec 2017 A blend of mostly grenache, about 74%, then syrah and malbec, and 5% all up of skin-fermented chenin blanc and marsanne, the latter two not added to complicate matters, says Remi Guise, but to add a tannic and textural drive the grenache lacked and the blend needed. Well, it worked. This is gorgeous. Wafts of black pepper and fennel linked to a core of red fruits – think cherries and raspberries, and yet there's a savoury thread. It has grip and drive. Perfectly composed with crunchy acidity, fine sandpaper-like tannins with a freshness, a vibrancy that makes you want another glass. Screwcap. 12.8% alc. **Rating** 95 **To** 2025 $30 JF ✪

ŦŦŦŦŢ Absolution Karridale Chenin Blanc 2017 Rating 93 **To** 2024 $30 JF
Absolution Danse Macabre 2017 Rating 93 **To** 2021 $24 JF ✪
Marrow Syrah Malbec 2016 Rating 93 **To** 2024 $40 JF

Tuck's Ridge ★★★★★

37 Shoreham Road, Red Hill South, Vic 3937 **Region** Mornington Peninsula
T (03) 5989 8660 **www**.tucksridge.com.au **Open** Wed–Sun 11–5
Winemaker Simon Black **Est.** 1985 **Dozens** 6000 **Vyds** 3.4ha
Tuck's Ridge has changed focus significantly since selling its large Red Hill vineyard, but it has retained the Buckle Vineyard with the chardonnay and pinot noir that consistently provide outstanding grapes (and wine). In late 2017 Tuck's Ridge was purchased by John and Wendy Mitchell of neighbouring Montalto. They have revamped the cellar door and restaurant, keeping Tuck's Ridge as a separate operation. Exports to the US and Hong Kong.

ŦŦŦŦŦ Buckle Pinot Noir 2016 An impressive, classy wine. Such is the quality of fruit that comes together beautifully with wafts of dark cherries, florals and woodsy spices. Flavours build on the palate, the tannins assertive, ripe and savoury, fleshy fruit and great persistence. Screwcap. 13.5% alc. **Rating** 96 **To** 2026 JF

Buckle Chardonnay 2016 Even in a riper vintage, this has morphed so very well into an excellent wine of great refinement. Everything in its place from the stone fruit, figs, the dash of citrus to the leesy, creamy texture and fresh acidity. Moreish, savoury and ready now. Screwcap. 13.6% alc. **Rating** 95 **To** 2025 JF

Mornington Peninsula Pinot Gris 2017 No forthcoming information, as with the other Tuck's Ridge wines, but I'm assuming this has some barrel ferment as there's lovely, creamy texture and a depth of flavour that doesn't get lost among the rich pear and ginger spice. A bright lemony acidity reins everything in. Screwcap. 13.5% alc. **Rating** 95 **To** 2022 JF

Mornington Peninsula Pinot Noir 2016 It starts with aromas of dark cherries, cinnamon, cedary oak and florals. The palate is full-bodied, sweetly fruited and textured with pliable tannins, as more complex, savoury flavours and aromas take hold; think forest floor and earthy notes. There is a brightness too and, overall, it's delicious. Screwcap. 13.5% alc. **Rating** 95 **To** 2026 JF

ŦŦŦŦŢ Mornington Peninsula Sauvignon Blanc 2017 Rating 90 **To** 2020 JF

Tulloch

★★★★★

Glen Elgin, 638 De Beyers Road, Pokolbin, NSW 2321 **Region** Hunter Valley
T (02) 4998 7580 **www**.tullochwines.com **Open** 7 days 10–5
Winemaker Jay Tulloch, First Creek **Est.** 1895 **Dozens** 40 000 **Vyds** 80ha
The Tulloch brand continues to build success on success. Its primary grape source is estate
vines owned by part-shareholder Inglewood Vineyard in the Upper Hunter Valley. It also
owns the JYT Vineyard, which was established by Jay Tulloch in the mid-1980s at the foot of
the Brokenback Range, right in the heart of Pokolbin. Contract-grown fruit is also sourced
from other growers in the Hunter Valley and futher afield. With Christina Tulloch a livewire
marketer, skilled winemaking by First Creek Winemaking Services has put the icing on the
winemaking cake. Exports to Belgium, the Philippines, Singapore, Hong Kong, Malaysia,
Thailand, Japan and China.

🍷🍷🍷🍷🍷 **Limited Release Julia Hunter Valley Semillon 2017** While the appeal of
youthful Hunter semillon can be a mystery to the uninitiated, after 5 years or
so, the wines take on a luminescence of hue and lanolin, and this grows into
an alchemical complexity within a decade or more. This is an exceptional wine
boasting compelling vinosity underlain with saliva-inducing acidity and a filigreed
transparency that will, I promise, transform the elemental citrus notes into truffle,
lanolin and lemon drop glory. Screwcap. 10.3% alc. **Rating** 96 **To** 2042 $30
NG ✪
Limited Edition G3 Hunter Valley Semillon 2013 The apogee of Hunter
semillon's strict line and length, perhaps, but what I like about this wine is the
uncanny juiciness of the acidity rather than the battery acid norm. Lemon drop,
talc, grapefruit and a lick of something herbal. This hails from a single, assiduously
selected parcel. The result is vinous and effortless, yet still lying within the strict
Hunter paradigm of highly ageable, dry whites. Screwcap. 11.1% alc. **Rating** 95
To 2035 $40 NG
Cellar Door Release Orange Vermentino 2017 This wine is a paean to
a texturally intriguing and pungently aromatic variety, which sees its apogee in
Sardinia and Liguria. Examples such as this suggest Australia is not too far behind.
Peach, Meyer lemon and a whiff of fennel curl their way across an attractively
unctuous palate, brought to life by juicy acidity, mineral and some unresolved
spritz for lift. An exceptional vermentino. Screwcap. 13.5% alc. **Rating** 95 **To** 2021
$22 NG ✪
Hunter River White Semillon 2017 As true to the region and its reputation for
age-worthy dry semillon as any top example. Candied lemon rind, talc, menthol,
hay and a sprig of herbal notes careen along a beam of bright acidity. The finish is
punchy and very long, auguring a great life ahead. Screwcap. 10.1% alc. **Rating** 94
To 2032 $25 NG ✪
Limited Release EM Hunter Valley Chardonnay 2017 EM is produced only
in exceptional years. This is a no-brainer style. A generously flavoured chardonnay
that will sate those in the boardroom as much as those whose tastes lean towards
more streamlined, crunchy styles. The oak purrs across the wine's peachy rims,
impeccably appointed. A core of cashew cream and nougat infuses the wine
with a paradoxical generosity, given just how fresh and supple the overall style is.
Screwcap. 12.5% alc. **Rating** 94 **To** 2025 $35 NG
Cellar Door Release Hilltops Barbera 2016 Among the most food-friendly
varieties of all, barbera's origins lie in the subalpine Piedmont. The mind's eye can
easily equate this with New South Wales's high Hilltops country, whence this wine
hails. This is a sappy wine, with a curled lip of acidity setting notes of raspberry,
black cherry, sarsaparilla and a lick of anise scurrying to a bright, persistent
finish. Impeccably extracted. This is a very good rendition! Screwcap. 13.4% alc.
Rating 94 **To** 2021 $26 NG ✪

🍷🍷🍷🍷🍸 **Limited Edition G4 Chardonnay 2017 Rating** 93 **To** 2029 $55 NG
Cellar Door Release Limited Edition Hilltops Cabernet Sauvignon 2016
Rating 93 **To** 2028 $50 NG

Vineyard Selection Chardonnay 2017 Rating 92 To 2022 $20 NG ✪
Cellar Door Release Viognier 2017 Rating 92 To 2021 $22 NG ✪
JYT Selection Shiraz 2016 Rating 92 To 2031 $40 NG
Cellar Door Release Pinot Gris 2017 Rating 91 To 2020 $22 NG ✪
Pokolbin Dry Red Shiraz 2016 Rating 91 To 2026 $30 NG
Cellar Door Release Hilltops Sangiovese 2017 Rating 91 To 2022 $26 NG

Tumblong Hills ★★★★

PO Box 38, Gundagai, NSW 2722 **Region** Gundagai
T 0408 684 577 **www**.tumblonghills.com **Open** Not
Winemaker Paul Bailey **Est.** 2009 **Dozens** 10 000 **Vyds** 202ha
This large winery was established by Southcorp Wines in the 1990s as part of Project Max, an initiative to honour Max Schubert of Penfolds Grange fame. In 2009 the winery was acquired by business partners Danny Gilbert, Peter Leonard and Peter Waters. They were able to secure the services of viticulturist and general manager Simon Robertson, who knew the vineyard like the back of his hand, although his experience stretches far wider than that, over most of New South Wales. In '11 close friends of Danny Gilbert, investors Wang Junfeng and Handel Lee, came onboard to strengthen Tumblong Hills' presence in Australia and foster a strong relationship with the Chinese premium wine market, where most of the wine goes. Winemaker Paul Bailey is also a key figure; as a graduate from Roseworthy College he initially worked in the Barossa Valley, and in '04 was awarded Best Red Wine at the International Wine and Spirit Competition's Great Australian Shiraz Challenge. He has also worked in Bordeaux for one of the most high profile winemakers in that region, Michel Rolland. While shiraz and cabernet sauvignon remain the two most important varieties in the vineyard, plantings now include nebbiolo, barbera, sangiovese and pinot noir. Exports to China.

🍷🍷🍷🍷🍷 **Single Vineyard Gundagai Premiere Cuvee Syrah 2015** There's little difference in colour to the Flash Jack, but in every other respect this is a bigger and richer wine, with the quality, branded cork suggesting a foreign shore. The increased intensity from 0.5% more alcohol is striking, giving the wine vigour and a greater range of flavours in a black fruit, licorice and spice spectrum. The tannins are firmer, but balanced. 14.5% alc. **Rating** 94 **To** 2035 $40
Table of Plenty Sangiovese 2017 Light, bright crimson-purple; another '17 victory, a sangiovese with bright red cherry and raspberry fruits, and then a long palate with silky tannins to conclude. Seriously delightful. Screwcap. 14% alc.
Rating 94 **To** 2025 $20 ✪

🍷🍷🍷🍷🍷 **Regional Characters Flash Jack Gundagai Shiraz 2015** Rating 91 To 2025 $25
Table of Plenty Barbera 2016 Rating 90 To 2031 $20 ✪

Turkey Flat ★★★★★

Bethany Road, Tanunda, SA 5352 **Region** Barossa Valley
T (08) 8563 2851 **www**.turkeyflat.com.au **Open** 7 days 11–5
Winemaker Mark Bulman **Est.** 1990 **Dozens** 20 000 **Vyds** 47.83ha
The establishment date of Turkey Flat is given as 1990, but it might equally have been 1870 (or thereabouts) when the Schulz family purchased the Turkey Flat vineyard, or 1847 when the vineyard was first planted to the very old shiraz that still grows there today and the 8ha of equally old grenache. Plantings have since expanded significantly, now comprising shiraz (24ha), grenache (10.5ha), cabernet sauvignon (5.9ha), mourvedre (3.7ha), and smaller plantings of marsanne, viognier and dolcetto. The business is run by sole proprietor Christie Schulz. Exports to the UK, the US and other major markets.

🍷🍷🍷🍷🍷 **Barossa Valley Shiraz 2016** The price of this classic estate-grown wine has been increased, but not by much, leaving this as underpriced as it is a beautifully crafted wine with a history of its own. It has power and presence, and above all, a purity of taste and structure. The black fruits have waves and cross-currents of flavour and texture, the finish long and balanced. Screwcap. 14.2% alc. **Rating** 98 To 2051 $50 ✪

🍷🍷🍷🍷🍷 **Barossa Valley Grenache 2016** Here the cherries are red, the raspberries dark, and fine tannins run throughout the palate. It is an iconic wine, and while the yields are less than those from younger vines, the quality is markedly consistent from year to year, with none of the confection that is common in the Barossa Valley. This is a grandstand bargain; winner of the Jimmy Watson Trophy '17. Screwcap. 15% alc. **Rating** 96 **To** 2031 $30 ✪

Butchers Block Barossa Valley Shiraz 2016 Fermented with 15% whole bunches, and matured in used oak to throw the emphasis on the fruit. The Turkey is in full flight here, with delicious cherry and satsuma plum fruit given context by persistent, but rounded, tannins (and oak maturation). Screwcap. 14% alc. **Rating** 95 **To** 2029 $25 ✪

Barossa Valley Mataro 2017 Open-fermented with 20% whole bunches, matured for 6 months in French oak (50% new). Altogether elegant, likewise fresh and vibrantly juicy. The whole-bunch inclusion has worked very well, bringing a note of spice that will increase in the years ahead. Attention to detail is one of the many strengths of Turkey Flat. Screwcap. 13.3% alc. **Rating** 95 **To** 2027 $32 ✪

The Last Straw 2015 Partially dried on straw mats, and follows (in tiny amounts) the practice used in the Rhône Valley. It's beautifully balanced, the marsanne fruit hand in glove with oak, residual sugar and acidity. It will thrive with decades in bottle. Screwcap. 11.5% alc. **Rating** 95 **To** 2045 $35 ✪

Barossa Valley Rose 2017 Pale salmon-crimson. Bursting to impress on both the nose and in the mouth. Raspberries, strawberries, anise and dried spice, a cut of apple-like acidity ramping the freshness further. No doubt 100% Barossa Valley, 100% delicious. They could give a money-back guarantee on this and never have to refund a cent. Screwcap. 13% alc. **Rating** 94 **To** 2018 $21 CM ✪

Butchers Block Red 2016 A shiraz/grenache/mourvedre blend, part sourced from some of the oldest (1865) vines on the Turkey Flat vineyard. A warm and spicy bouquet introduces a medium-bodied palate with red and black berries, plus good mouthfeel and length. Oak plays little or no part in framing the palate, fine tannins doing the trick instead. Screwcap. 14% alc. **Rating** 94 **To** 2030 $21 ✪

Turner's Crossing Vineyard ★★★★☆

747 Old Bridgewater-Serpentine Road, Serpentine, Vic 3517 **Region** Bendigo
T 0427 843 528 **www.**turnerscrossingwine.com **Open** Not
Winemaker Sergio Carlei **Est.** 1999 **Dozens** 4000 **Vyds** 42ha
This outstanding, mature vineyard was named to remember the original landholder, Thomas Turner. During the 1800s, farmers and gold rush prospectors crossed the Loddon River beside the property, at what became known as Turners Crossing. During the Gold Rush period, European settlers in the area started to plant vineyards, trusting that Bendigo's terroir would reveal itself as a suitable site on which to grow grapes. And they were right to be so confident. Its Mediterranean climate and alluvial composition of rich limestone soils make it a happy home for viticulture in particular. Turners Crossing Vineyard now spans 42ha of mature vines. The vineyard is virtually pesticide and chemical free; warm days and cool nights allow the grapes to ripen during the day and the vines to recover overnight. The vineyard bears shiraz, cabernet sauvignon, viognier and picolit, a rare white Italian variety. Exports to the UK, the US, Canada, Vietnam and China.

🍷🍷🍷🍷🍷 **The Crossing Shiraz 2008** Whole berries open-fermented, 40–50 days on skins, matured for 2 years in French oak (15% new). Typical deep colour – and full-bodied. Despite the Diam closure, these wines still need to shed some of their awesome power, which in the style of surrogate Barossa, biggest-is-best wines. This is in a role reversal with the '10, meeting the softening with age criteria. Diam. 14.9% alc. **Rating** 95 **To** 2027 $65

Bendigo Shiraz 2015 In the best Turner's Crossing style, with great colour; a generous and rich wine with a strong sense of place not diluted by the co-fermentation of viognier. It layers the tongue and cheeks with succulent cassis and blackcurrant conserve, ripe tannins on the finish. Diam. 14.5% alc. **Rating** 94 **To** 2035 $26 ⚫

The Crossing Shiraz 2010 A barrel release (barrel no. 34). The colour is still deep, as are the black fruits and tannins of a full-bodied wine, with another 8 years to run before it starts to enter a plateau of full development. Diam. 14.5% alc. **Rating** 94 **To** 2030 $65

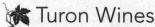 # Turon Wines

1760 Lobethal Road, Lobethal, SA 5241 (postal) **Region** Adelaide Hills
T 0423 956 480 **www.**turonwines.com.au **Open** Not
Winemaker Turon White **Est.** 2013 **Dozens** 550 **Vyds** 5ha

This is the thoroughly impressive venture of Turon White and his fiancée Alex Daniel, and with their marriage planned for October 2019. Working for several small wineries while studying at university, Turon realised the potential of the ever-varying site climates within the Adelaide Hills. His overseas winemaking experience while completing his degree was appropriately lateral, with vintage winemaking at Argyle in Oregon, US, and at Kovac Nimrod in Eger, Hungary. Out of this has come a minimal intervention approach to winemaking, being confident enough to stand back and let the wine develop and be itself, but being equally prepared to intervene if need be. Selecting the right site, soil and mesoclimate within the region is, Turon believes, crucial in allowing the wines to reach their full potential. That said, experimentation of method is also of prime importance in understanding the potential of terroir and variety. One could go on about the philosophical side, but there is also a practical element. They have built a new winery at their property in Lenswood, and turned it into a co-operative winery from the outset, where young winemakers can work together, share equipment, resources and knowledge. They called the venture Hills Handcrafted Collective, with wines to be released from the Collective a bit further down the track. With the quality of the wines release under the Turon Wines label, one is tempted to say the sky's the limit. As it is, it is one of the best three new wineries in this *Wine Companion*.

🍷🍷🍷🍷🍷 **Limited Single Vineyard Single Barrel Piccadilly Valley Pinot Noir 2016** This wine starts where its varietal sibling finished. The red cherry fruits are firm and pay little attention to spice and forest notes. Nonetheless, everything in this wine is in balance. Screwcap. 13.7% alc. **Rating** 95 **To** 2026 $45

Limited Single Vineyard Single Barrel Lobethal Syrah 2016 Matured in a single French hogshead for 15 months. Doesn't seem it was a new hogshead, but likely 1yo. The colour is excellent, the wine a compelling mix of luscious dark fruits, finely tuned tannins and oak (which provides texture and balance). Screwcap. 12.5% alc. **Rating** 95 **To** 2036 $45

Artist Range Forreston Adelaide Hills Shiraz 2015 Brightly hued, this has a perfumed, spicy bouquet, the medium-bodied palate vibrating with its intensity and mouthwatering suite of fruit and spice flavours, the tannins tailored down to the last micron. It's the sort of wine you'd drink, not just sip. Screwcap. 13.5% alc. **Rating** 95 **To** 2030 $30 ⚫

Adelaide Hills Shiraz 2014 This is a beautiful wine, peppered with spice, a touch meaty, ripped with black cherry and fresh with boysenberry and fennel root. It serves a savoury meal, but keeps succulent fruit on the pour. Length and tannin management are exemplary. Screwcap. 13% alc. **Rating** 95 **To** 2029 $30 CM ⚫

Artist Range Adelaide Hills Field Blend 2017 A 50/50% combination of chardonnay and sauvignon blanc, hand-picked, fermented on skins for 7 days, whole-bunch pressed, 3 months on lees. There's no attempt to carbon-fine the wine or apologise for its light brassy gold colour from fermentation on skins. The decision to press the skins while the fermentation was still protecting against oxidation or other issues makes perfect sense, the wine ending up with great texture and fresh flavours. Screwcap. 12% alc. **Rating** 94 **To** 2022 $25 ⚫

🍷🍷🍷🍷🍷 **Piccadilly Valley Chardonnay 2015** **Rating** 93 **To** 2020 $30 CM
Artist Range Adelaide Hills Rose 2017 **Rating** 90 **To** 2019 $25

Artist Range Piccadilly Valley Pinot Noir 2016 Rating 90 To 2025 $30
Adelaide Hills Pinot Noir 2014 Rating 90 To 2019 $30 CM

Twinwoods Estate ★★★★★

Brockman Road, Cowaramup, WA 6284 (postal) **Region** Margaret River
T 0419 833 122 **www**.twinwoodsestate.com **Open** Not
Winemaker Deep Woods Estate (Julian Langworthy), Aldo Bratovic **Est.** 2005
Dozens 2500 **Vyds** 8.5ha

This is a winery that was always bound to succeed. It is owned by the Jebsen family, for
many years a major player in the importation and distribution of fine wine in Hong Kong,
and more recently expanded into China. Fifteen years ago Jebsen invested in a NZ winery,
following that with the acquisition of this vineyard in Margaret River in 2005. It brings
together senior Jebsen managing director, Gavin Jones, and peripatetic winemaker Aldo
Bratovic, who began his career decades ago under the tutelage of Brian Croser. The winery's
widespread distribution is interesting, not all the eggs are put into the Hong Kong/China
baskets. It commenced selling wine in Australia in 2014, with Terroir Selections its Australian
partner – another intersection with Brian Croser. Exports to Denmark, Germany, Singapore,
Taiwan, Hong Kong, China and NZ.

🍷🍷🍷🍷🍷 **Margaret River Shiraz 2014** Estate-grown, 3 days cold soak, fermented with
two pumpovers per day, matured for 12 months in French oak (33% new).
A particularly elegant and finely etched wine, its still bright hue attesting to its
quality and potential longevity. The fruits are primarily in red and purple robes,
the tannins super fine, the finish long and harmonious. Screwcap. 13.5% alc.
Rating 95 To 2029
Margaret River Cabernet Sauvignon 2014 Full crimson-purple, holding
its hue very well. A classic Margaret River cabernet in every sense of that term.
It has a degree of austerity from its firm tannins, yet is only medium-bodied. Its
core lies in the purity of its fruit, complemented by the handling of its significant
proportion (40%) of new French oak. Screwcap. 14% alc. **Rating** 95 To 2034

🍷🍷🍷🍷🍷 **Optivus Reserve Cabernet Sauvignon 2013** Rating 90 To 2033

Two Hands Wines ★★★★★

273 Neldner Road, Marananga, SA 5355 **Region** Barossa Valley
T (08) 8562 4566 **www**.twohandswines.com **Open** 7 days 10–5
Winemaker Ben Perkins **Est.** 2000 **Dozens** 55 000 **Vyds** 15ha

The 'hands' in question are those of SA businessmen Michael Twelftree and Tim Hower,
Michael in particular having extensive experience in marketing Australian wine in the US
(for other producers). On the principle that if big is good, bigger is better, the style of the
wines has been aimed squarely at the palate of Robert Parker Jr and Wine Spectator's Harvey
Steiman. Grapes are sourced from the Barossa Valley, McLaren Vale, Clare Valley, Langhorne
Creek and Padthaway. The emphasis is on sweet fruit and soft tannin structure, all signifying
the precise marketing strategy of what is a very successful business. At the end of 2015, Two
Hands embarked on an extensive planting program, using vines propagated from a number of
vineyards (including Prouse's Eden Valley, Wendouree's 1893, Kaesler's Alte Reben, Penfolds'
Modbury, Kay's Block 6 and Kalimna's 3C). This includes a high-density 1.4ha clos (i.e. a
walled vineyard), with the vines trained in the goblet style of the northern Rhône Valley.
Exports to all major markets.

🍷🍷🍷🍷🍷 **Holy Grail Single Vineyard Seppeltsfield Barossa Valley Shiraz 2015**
Matured in French puncheons and hogsheads (18% new) for 19 months. Deep,
dense colour; the striking bouquet exudes savoury pipe tobacco and smoke
aromas, spices also seeking airplay. The full-bodied palate features a titanic struggle
between the plethora of black fruits and insistent high quality tannins – evident
from the first sip all the way through to the aftertaste. Remarkable wine. Diam.
14.8% alc. **Rating** 97 To 2040 $100 ❂

🍷🍷🍷🍷🍷 **The Boy Eden Valley Riesling 2017** Pristine and pure, yet is a riesling that pulses so strongly with its flavour profile of fresh and preserved lemons, bath salt-like acidity, mineral and a Murray River-long finish. Just gorgeous. Screwcap. 12.6% alc. **Rating** 96 **To** 2030 $25 JF ✪

Yacca Block Single Vineyard Mengler Hill Road Eden Valley Shiraz 2016 There's just something about this wine that makes it stand tall. It's partly the perfectly ripe fruit, the spice in between, the succulence, the detail, the savouriness, the surprisingly filigreed tannins and a certain degree of structure with its exceptional length. It has presence and poise in equal measure. Diam. 14.4% alc. **Rating** 96 **To** 2036 $100 JF

Holy Grail Single Vineyard Seppeltsfield Barossa Valley Shiraz 2016 There's no denying its Seppeltsfield stamp as this is a whorl of satisfying flavours, and yet a perfectly composed wine. Expect dark fruit, red fruit, florals, layers of spice and savoury notes of tar and warm earth. Full-bodied, to be sure, with sweet tannins the texture of raw silk. Diam. 14.5% alc. **Rating** 96 **To** 2036 $100 JF

Coach House Block Single Vineyard Greenock Barossa Valley Shiraz 2015 The deep, dense colour tells you a full body awaits, and doesn't deceive. Its power is implacable, yet the nigh-on perfect balance of its blackberry, plum fruit, cedary oak and ripe tannins make it eminently possible to drink it tonight, even though it will richly repay 20 years in bottle. Diam. 14.5% alc. **Rating** 96 **To** 2035 $100

The Boy Eden Valley Riesling 2016 A seriously good Eden Valley riesling with great regional and varietal typicity. The highly floral bouquet opens the door to a palate charged with citrus fruits strung along a high tension wire of acidity. Top flight value, offering much now, but even more in the future. Screwcap. 12% alc. **Rating** 95 **To** 2030 $25 ✪

Dave's Block Single Vineyard Blythmans Road Blewitt Springs Shiraz 2016 It's far from shy as it has all the flavours a shiraz from this region can muster – think black fruits, chocolate, licorice, dried herbs, charry notes and a truck-load of spice. Yet everything is in its place and balanced accordingly. Full-bodied with ripe savoury and velvety tannins, and a sweet fruit kick on the finish. Diam. 14.3% alc. **Rating** 95 **To** 2030 $100 JF

Bella's Garden Barossa Valley Shiraz 2016 Dark, inky red and oozes the same coloured fruit into a matrix of spice with blackstrap licorice and curranty essence, leading onto a full-bodied, decisive palate. Tannins – an abundance of them, flavour through and through, and yet this is contained, never straying into the too big territory. Diam. 14.2% alc. **Rating** 95 **To** 2036 $60 JF

Charlie's Garden Eden Valley Shiraz 2016 While this shines the spotlight on the fruit, there's certainly oak flavours and tannin seeping through to the wine but just the right amount. Also in the mix are blackberry essence, plum compote, molasses and savoury, persimmon-like tannins. Diam. 14.2% alc. **Rating** 95 **To** 2036 $60 JF

Harriet's Garden Adelaide Hills Shiraz 2016 Heady aromatics are the first enticement; all floral, peppery and spicy as it moves on to a medium-bodied palate, with chorus of crunchy red fruits with a savoury lift, chalky-raspberry acidity and fine sandpaper tannins. It has gluggability written all over it. Diam. 13.5% alc. **Rating** 95 **To** 2027 $60 JF

Fields of Joy Clare Valley Shiraz 2016 Oozing all the charm of the Clare Valley starting with its dark purple hue, its fragrance of Chinese five-spice, graphite and menthol with tangy black plums, currants and tart tamarind acidity. The well-composed palate incorporates finely chiselled savoury tannins and plenty of joy in between. Screwcap. 14% alc. **Rating** 95 **To** 2028 $27 JF ✪

Secret Block Single Vineyard Wildlife Road Moppa Hills Shiraz 2016 Sensational deep purple colour. The fruit is vibrant, offering flavours of red plums and black cherries, and a succulence too; plenty of spice, a fistful of dried herbs all flowing on to a full-bodied but composed palate. Savoury, powerful tannins on a structured palate, with fresh acidity to close. Diam. 13.8% alc. **Rating** 95 **To** 2030 $100 JF

Bella's Garden Barossa Valley Shiraz 2015 Full crimson-purple hue; the quality of the fruit is obvious from the first whiff. Its warm spices open proceedings, building with a touch of licorice before expansive black fruits fill every corner of the mouth, aided and abetted by graphite tannins on the long finish and aftertaste. Diam. 14.2% alc. **Rating** 95 **To** 2030 $60

Ares Barossa Valley Shiraz 2015 It's big. It's bold. It's Barossa shiraz. Expect deep red and black fruits spiced with licorice root, nutmeg and cinnamon with lashings of quality French oak flavours. Full-bodied with expansive tannins, and yet what underpins it all is a thread of fresh raspberry-lemony acidity so it remains on an even keel. Impressive for the style. Oh, and you could do some damage with the bottles in the flagship series, weighing in at a whopping 1975g. Diam. 14.8% alc. **Rating** 95 **To** 2035 $165 JF

Twelftree Greenock Ebenezer Barossa Valley Grenache Mourvedre 2014 Good colour; a really attractive and fresh array of raspberry, cherry and plum fruit, an exception (there are quite a few) to the common Barossa rule, with a vibrant and juicily fresh finish. Screwcap. 13.5% alc. **Rating** 95 **To** 2027 $50

Coach House Block Single Vineyard Greenock Barossa Valley Shiraz 2016 Laden with blackberry and ripe plum dipped in aged and unctuous balsamic vinegar, licorice a given, and an earthy note too. Charry oak (35% new French hogsheads, aged for 18 months) still lingers, but the finish is resolute. Diam. 14.4% alc. **Rating** 94 **To** 2030 $100 JF

Gnarly Dudes Barossa Valley Shiraz 2016 A highly expressive medium-bodied shiraz full of black cherry and blackberry fruit. Despite the intensity of its flavours (mirroring the bouquet), it is light on its feet thanks to its restrained extract and controlled alcohol. Screwcap. 13.8% alc. **Rating** 94 **To** 2029 $27 **○**

Max's Garden Heathcote Shiraz 2016 While unencumbered by new oak (spends 19 months in used French hogsheads), this is a rich and intensely concentrated wine, full-bodied yet quite evenly balanced. No shortage of red fruits and blackberries; a spice shop full of fragrance, bay leaves and chocolate. Diam. 14.1% alc. **Rating** 94 **To** 2030 $60 JF

Max's Garden Heathcote Shiraz 2015 There is an intriguing hint of lavender behind the gently spicy plum and blackberry fruits of the bouquet. The medium-bodied palate is fresh, vibrant and full of charm before classy, savoury tannin brings down the curtain on a wine open for business any time. Diam. 14.2% alc. **Rating** 94 **To** 2030 $60

Samantha's Garden Clare Valley Shiraz 2015 A complex full-bodied shiraz packed full of red, purple and black aromas and flavours that constantly shift in a kaleidoscopic fashion each time it is swirled; savoury tannins the one (needed) constant. Diam. 14.5% alc. **Rating** 94 **To** 2030 $60

Brave Faces Barossa Valley Grenache Mourvedre Shiraz 2015 A 60/35/5% blend. This hums with the freshness of its bounteous array of red fruits (raspberry, strawberry and cherry), the finish as bright as a spring day. Screwcap. 14% alc. **Rating** 94 **To** 2023 $27 **○**

ＹＹＹＹＹ The Wolf Clare Valley Riesling 2017 Rating 93 To 2027 $25 JF **○**
Angels' Share McLaren Vale Shiraz 2016 Rating 93 To 2025 $27 CM **○**
Lily's Garden McLaren Vale Shiraz 2016 Rating 93 To 2030 $60 JF
Windmill Block Single Vineyard Stonewell Road Barossa Valley Shiraz 2016 Rating 93 To 2030 $100 JF
Aerope Barossa Valley Grenache 2015 Rating 93 To 2026 $90 JF
Aerope Barossa Valley Grenache 2014 Rating 93 To 2029 $90
Twelftree Greenock Grenache Mataro 2015 Rating 93 To 2025 $45 JF
Brave Faces Barossa Valley GSM 2016 Rating 93 To 2020 $27 JF **○**
Samantha's Garden Clare Valley Shiraz 2016 Rating 92 To 2028 $60 JF
Angels' Share McLaren Vale Shiraz 2015 Rating 92 To 2029 $27
Aphrodite Cabernet Sauvignon 2015 Rating 92 To 2029 $165 JF
Heartbreak Hill Single Vineyard Roach Road White Hut Clare Valley Shiraz 2016 Rating 91 To 2026 $100 JF
Twelftree Sturt Road Grenache 2015 Rating 91 To 2023 $55 JF

2 Mates

160 Main Road, McLaren Vale, SA 5171 (postal) **Region** McLaren Vale
T 0411 111 198 **www.2mates.com.au Open** Not
Winemaker Matt Rechner, Mark Venable **Est.** 2003 **Dozens** 500 **Vyds** 20ha
The two mates are Mark Venable and David Minear, who say, 'Over a big drink in a small
bar in Italy a few years back, we talked about making our perfect Australian Shiraz'. The
wine was duly made in 2005, and won a silver medal at the Decanter World Wine Awards
in London, among exalted company. Eleven years on they have hit the rarefied height of 97
points for their $35 The Perfect Ten McLaren Vale Shiraz.

🍷🍷🍷🍷🍷 **The Perfect Ten McLaren Vale Shiraz 2016** The disproportionate impact
of a 20% proportion of 150yo vines is obvious, though we do not know the
age of the remaining 80%. The colour is superb, the bouquet and palate secure
in the knowledge of the quality of the blackberry, plum and licorice flavours.
Tannins and oak are in the mix, but are merely custodians of the fruit. The price
is ludicrously cheap. Screwcap. 14.9% alc. **Rating** 97 **To** 2051 $35 ✪

Two Rivers

2 Yarrawa Road, Denman, NSW 2328 **Region** Hunter Valley
T (02) 6547 2556 **www.tworiverswines.com.au Open** 7 days 11–4
Winemaker Liz Silkman **Est.** 1988 **Dozens** 10 000 **Vyds** 67.5ha
A significant part of the viticultural scene in the Upper Hunter Valley, with 67.5ha of
vineyards, and involves an investment of several million dollars. Part of the fruit is sold
under long-term contracts, and part is kept for Two Rivers' winemaking and marketing
operations. Their emphasis is on chardonnay and semillon with most rated at 95 or 96
points. Two Rivers is also a partner in the Tulloch business, together with the Tulloch and
Angove families, and supplies grapes to the Tulloch label. A contemporary cellar door adds
significantly to the appeal of the Upper Hunter Valley as a wine tourist destination. The
appointment of immensely talented winemaker Liz Silkman has had an immediate impact.

🍷🍷🍷🍷🍷 **Museum Release Stone's Throw Semillon 2013** Four trophies, including
the Hunter Valley Wine Show '14, and six gold medals collected between '14 and
'17 is impressive. If Two Rivers has sufficient stock to keep entering this wine in
shows it will go on its merry way – it's gloriously vibrant and fresh, and the acidity
is friend, not foe. Screwcap. 11.6% alc. **Rating** 96 **To** 2023 $45 ✪
Stone's Throw Semillon 2017 Trophy and five gold and silver medals from
small maker shows set the scene for the skills of contract winemaker Liz Jackson.
Lemon zest, lemon curd and glitzy acidity drive the long palate and aftertaste, the
mouthfeel correspondingly fresh. Screwcap. 10.5% alc. **Rating** 95 **To** 2030 $20 ✪
Yarrawa Road Hunter Valley Chardonnay 2017 This comes from the Upper
Hunter Valley, making its provenance surprising – almost all those of great quality
have come from the Lower Hunter. The wine is medium-bodied, the flavours
classic, and has had no problem absorbing its French oak. Screwcap. 13% alc.
Rating 94 **To** 2027 $45

🍷🍷🍷🍷🍷 **Vigneron's Reserve Chardonnay 2017 Rating** 93 **To** 2025 $26 ✪
Lightning Strike Chardonnay 2017 Rating 90 **To** 2022 $20 ✪

Tynan Road Wines

185 Tynan Road, Kuitpo, SA 5172 (postal) **Region** Adelaide Hills
T 0413 004 829 **www.tynanroadwines.com.au Open** Not
Winemaker Duane Coates **Est.** 2015 **Dozens** 150 **Vyds** 10.25ha
This is the venture of Heidi Craig, a lawyer who wanted a pretty outlook and tolerates
the grapegrowing and winemaking folly of her gastroenterologist husband, Sandy Craig.
Living in Kuitpo made the folly eminently reasonable, and they have gone the whole way
with building an onsite winery and securing the services of the very good and experienced
winemaker Duane Coates.

ᵀᵀᵀᵀᵀ **Kuitpo Adelaide Hills Shiraz 2016** The '16 was a vintage that came under the shadow of the very high quality '15. With a longer perspective, it's clear that what '16 might have lacked in finesse, it made up in concentration and power. What's more, this wine has excellent length and balance to its array of gently spicy, anise-accented palate. Screwcap. 14% alc. **Rating** 94 **To** 2036 $30 ✪

ᵀᵀᵀᵀᵀ **Kuitpo Adelaide Hills Sauvignon Blanc 2017 Rating** 90 **To** 2021 $20 ✪

Tynan Wines   ★★★☆
PO Box 164, Wickham, NSW 2293 **Region** Various
T 0402 442 614 **www.tynanwines.com.au Open** Not
Winemaker Mark Tynan **Est.** 2009 **Dozens** 500
Mark Tynan, founder and owner of this eponymous business, is currently studying for a Master of Viticulture and Oenology at CSU. He is sharing winemaking facilities with a couple of Hunter Valley winemakers, and is preparing to establish his own winery. There he will make varietal wines sourced from various parts of New South Wales.

Tyrrell's Wines   ★★★★★
1838 Broke Road, Pokolbin, NSW 2321 **Region** Hunter Valley
T (02) 4993 7000 **www.tyrrells.com.au Open** Mon–Sat 9–5, Sun 10–4
Winemaker Andrew Spinaze, Mark Richardson **Est.** 1858 **Dozens** 220 000
Vyds 158.22ha
One of the most successful family wineries, it was a humble operation in its first 110 years, but has since grown beyond recognition in the past 40 years. Their Vat 1 Semillon is one of the most dominant wines in the Australian show system, and their Vat 47 Chardonnay is one of the pacesetters for its variety. The winery has an awesome portfolio of single vineyard Semillons released when 5–6 years old. Its estate plantings are over 116ha in the Hunter Valley, 15ha in the Limestone Coast and 26ha in Heathcote. In December 2017 Tyrrell's purchased the 13.5ha Stevens Old Hillside Vineyard on Marrowbone Road from the family; 6.11ha are planted to shiraz, including a 1.1ha block planted in 1867, the balance planted in 1963, notably to shiraz and semillon. There are 11 blocks of vines older than 100 years in the Hunter Valley, and the Tyrrell family owns seven of them. A founding member of Australia's First Families of Wine. Exports to all major markets.

ᵀᵀᵀᵀᵀ **Museum Release Vat 1 Hunter Semillon 2013** The Emperor, shy but strident, wearing a myriad of citrus and orchard colours and a tensile sash of calm and poise. This majestic wine's light weight belies its sheer stretch of flavours across the palate. Energetic and gently grippy; tightly wound, but bristling with mineral intent. Bottle age has softened this ever so slightly. Nothing more. An Australian classic in the making! Screwcap. 11.5% alc. **Rating** 97 **To** 2033 $85 NG ✪
Vat 9 Hunter Shiraz 2016 A gleaming chassis of redcurrant, satsuma plum, Chinese herb and the Hunter's signature whiff of creamy leather – all driven by cylinders of high quality French oak, gentle acidity and firm tannins of a ferrous sheen, nestled as a whisper behind the fruit, but increasingly apparent as the wine expands in the glass. Screwcap. 13% alc. **Rating** 97 **To** 2043 $85 NG ✪

ᵀᵀᵀᵀᵀ **Johnno's Semillon 2017** Basket-pressed with limited juice clarification adds to the textural quality. It succeeds, although it might be partly ascribed to the ancient vines, as it has an intense citrus/minerally acidity drive to the palate. It will live for many decades. Screwcap. 10.3% alc. **Rating** 96 **To** 2057 $60 ✪
Single Vineyard Belford Hunter Valley Semillon 2013 The aromas are already enticing with dried hay, lemongrass, allusions of citrus and a glimpse of riper stone fruits reeling across the nostrils. The palate is one of precision, detail and tightly coiled energy, auguring a bright future based on the wine's vinosity and tenacity of length alone. Limpid, febrile and punchy as is de rigueur, this will ease into a majestic utopia. Screwcap. 11.5% alc. **Rating** 96 **To** 2028 $35 NG ✪
Museum Release Vat 1 Hunter Semillon 2012 Tasted in '12 after 5 years in bottle – the magic moment when the first phase of moving to maturity is

completed. This magic moment sees the palate swelling with toast and honey components clasped to the bosom by minerally acidity – the wine will never lose. It's a great match for rich seafood dishes. Screwcap. 10.5% alc. **Rating** 96 To 2032 $80

Vat 47 Hunter Chardonnay 2014 Always delicious, this is as bright of stone fruit aromas as its Belford sibling, albeit more tightly bound to cylinders of leesy mineral crunch, vanillan oak and ginger to toasted hazelnut flavours, with the benefit of some bottle age imparting further textural intrigue. A superb Vat 47, from a superlative vintage. Screwcap. 13.5% alc. **Rating** 96 To 2028 $75 NG ✪

4 Acres Hunter Valley Shiraz 2016 A deceiving light- to mid-ruby, this shiraz has the youthful allure and aroma of high quality pinot, once called 'Hunter River Burgundy'. Soaring bing cherry and wild strawberry notes, scented further with lilac and creamy kirsch, belie the gentle hue. Medium weight, precise detail and yet imperious vinosity and length, this makes for a compelling contrast to the Vat 9. From plantings dating back to 1879. Screwcap. 13% alc. **Rating** 96 To 2041 $90 NG

Single Vineyard Stevens Hunter Valley Semillon 2013 While there is no doubting the oft-used quip 'length and line' of any of Tyrrell's Single Vineyard Semillons, the key in this one is in the texture and persistence. This is Meyer lemon, poached quince, apricot, buttered toast and citrus marmalade, all ricocheting along a beam of pumice and crunch. The most exuberant of the top tier. Screwcap. 11.5% alc. **Rating** 95 To 2028 $35 NG ✪

Special Release Hunter Valley Gamay 2017 From the 40yo vines planted by Len Evans at the family house he called Loggerheads. This wine is enough to raise Len from his grave to taste and praise this utterly delicious wine with its crunchy, fresh cherry flavours, picked and fermented within days of harvest, all the right levers pulled in the vinification process. Screwcap. 12.9% alc. **Rating** 95 To 2020 $30 ✪

Single Vineyard Pokolbin Hills Hunter Valley Semillon 2017 Youthful. Zesty. Punchy. As filigreed of talcy acidity and as fine boned as the rest of the crew. This is guava, lemongrass and sherbet, teeming along a line of candied citrus chew. The wine will blossom in the medium term, but will not shy away from some aged furrows and complexity. Screwcap. 12% alc. **Rating** 94 To 2029 $35 NG

Single Vineyard Belford Hunter Valley Chardonnay 2016 While semillon is the postcard of the region, Tyrrell's chardonnays, too, are Hunter benchmarks. This is bright and energetic, exuding white peach, nectarine and truffled curd, wrapped around a creamy core of nougat, vanillan oak and cashew. Screwcap. 13% alc. **Rating** 94 To 2025 $45 NG

ᵠᵠᵠᵠᵠ Single Vineyard Stevens Shiraz 2016 Rating 93 To 2026 $45 NG
Shiraz 2016 Rating 93 To 2026 $25 NG ✪
Special Release Gewurztraminer 2017 Rating 92 To 2020 $25 NG ✪
Single Vineyard Old Hut Shiraz 2016 Rating 92 To 2024 $45 NG
Lunatiq Shiraz 2016 Rating 92 To 2025 $40 NG
Semillon 2017 Rating 91 To 2023 $23 CM ✪
Chardonnay 2017 Rating 91 To 2021 $25 NG
Special Release Pinot Noir 2017 Rating 91 To 2021 $30 NG
Brookdale Semillon 2016 Rating 90 To 2022 $25
Beyond Broke Road Sauvignon Blanc 2016 Rating 90 To 2020 $19 ✪

Ubertas Wines ★★★★

790 Research Road, Light Pass, SA 5355 **Region** Barossa Valley
T (08) 8565 7820 **www**.ubertaswines.com.au **Open** By appt
Winemaker Wine Wise, Philip Liu **Est.** 2013 **Dozens** 2500 **Vyds** 12ha
Brothers Phil and Kevin Liu followed their father from Taiwan to mainland China, working for their father's car component factory. In 2006 they made a life-changing decision to migrate to Australia, and saw an opportunity to start a wine export business to China, and named their business Rytor. It succeeded, and over the following years they both obtained

masters degrees – Phil in oenology from the University of Adelaide, Kevin in marketing from the University of South Australia. By 2014 they had taken another major step, building and managing their own winery at Light Pass in the Barossa Valley, and in '17 were in the process of creating a cellar door. Exports to Japan, Taiwan and China.

ᵀᵀᵀᵀᵀ **Single Vineyard Barossa Valley Shiraz Cabernet Sauvignon 2016** The wine has the hallmark depth and hue of Ubertas's red wines. This has much to offer, with blackberry and blackcurrant fruit, firm but not aggressive tannins, and well-balanced and integrated oak. Will repay cellaring for 5–10 years and beyond. Cork. 14.5% alc. **Rating** 94 **To** 2036 $30 ❂

ᵀᵀᵀᵀᵀ **Barossa Valley Shiraz 2016 Rating** 90 **To** 2041 $50

Ulithorne   ★★★★★

211 Kays Road, McLaren Vale, SA 5171 **Region** McLaren Vale
T 0411 024 014 **www.ulithorne.com.au Open** By appt
Winemaker Matthew Copping **Est.** 1971 **Dozens** 2500 **Vyds** 7.2ha
Ulithorne produces small quantities of red wines from selected parcels of grapes from its estate vineyard in McLaren Vale, planted in 1950 by Bob Whiting. The small batch of high quality wines are influenced by Ulithorne's associate Laurence Feraud, owner of Domaine du Pegau, of Chateauneuf du Pape. Exports to the UK, the US, Canada, Sweden, Malaysia, Hong Kong and China.

ᵀᵀᵀᵀᵀ **Frux Frugis McLaren Vale Shiraz 2015** The bouquet makes me think of the River Styx, dark and impenetrable; the full-bodied palate's power and liquid intensity coming as a shock. No light touch here, and why should there be? It is a remarkable wine of very high quality, piling on the flavour as its length extends inexorably. Bottle no. 3635. Cork. 14.5% alc. **Rating** 97 **To** 2040 $100 ❂

ᵀᵀᵀᵀᵀ **Avitus McLaren Vale Shiraz 2015** You are greeted by a bouquet shrieking of its regional origin, the palate more calmly sending the same message. The tannin management is a feature of the medium to full-bodied weight of the wine, delivering structure in a civilised fashion. Screwcap. 14.5% alc. **Rating** 96 **To** 2035 $75 ❂
Unicus McLaren Vale Shiraz 2015 Bright, deep hue; this is a full-bodied wine that nonetheless has a certain lightness of touch. Licorice, dark chocolate and spice form a garland around the vibrant dark fruits. Tannins and oak are in play, but of far lesser importance. Screwcap. 14.5% alc. **Rating** 96 **To** 2035 $75 ❂
Familia McLaren Vale Shiraz 2016 Distinctly deeper in colour than its Dona sibling. Fruit selection is part of the story, but so too is the making. This is intense, yet barely medium-bodied, dusty tannins interacting with dark berry fruits and regional dark chocolate. Screwcap. 14% alc. **Rating** 95 **To** 2031 $40
Paternus McLaren Vale Cabernet Sauvignon 2015 Dense, deep purple; you might expect this to be ultra-full-bodied and dense with ripe fruit flavours – the reality is very different: dark and swarthy, with black olive tapenade flavours and a latticework of tannins. Unusual for McLaren Vale, but very worthwhile and long. Cork. 14.5% alc. **Rating** 95 **To** 2035 $85

ᵀᵀᵀᵀᵀ **Dona Shiraz 2016 Rating** 93 **To** 2025 $27 ❂
Chi Shiraz Grenache 2016 Rating 93 **To** 2026 $40
Specialis Tempranillo Grenache 2016 Rating 91 **To** 2022 $32
Dona Blanc 2017 Rating 90 **To** 2018 $27
Dona GSM 2016 Rating 90 **To** 2028 $27

Ulupna Winery   ★★★☆

159 Crawfords Road, Strathmerton, Vic 3641 **Region** Goulburn Valley
T (03) 9533 8831 **www.ulupnawinery.com.au Open** By appt
Winemaker Vio Buga, Viviana Ferrari **Est.** 1999 **Dozens** 16 700 **Vyds** 22ha

Ulupna started out as a retirement activity for Nick and Kathy Bogdan. The vineyard on the banks of the Murray River is planted to shiraz (50%), cabernet sauvignon (30%) and chardonnay (20%), the plantings allowing for expansion in the years ahead. The wines are made under the direction of Vio Buga, who also designed and planted the vineyard. Exports are primarily directed to China, followed by Hong Kong, South Korea and Singapore.

ΨΨΨΨΨ **Royal Phoenix Cabernet Sauvignon 2016** Matured in 100% new French oak for 18 months. It's a sweet expression of the variety, but it flows well and has satisfying persistence. Boysenberry and redcurrant flavours are only lightly dressed by cedar wood and peanut-like notes from the oak. It won't go anywhere in a hurry, but it's arguably best consumed youngish. Screwcap. 15% alc. **Rating** 90 To 2024 $55 CM

ΨΨΨΨ **Royal Phoenix Single Vineyard Shiraz 2016** Rating 89 To 2024 $55 CM

Umamu Estate

PO Box 1269, Margaret River, WA 6285 **Region** Margaret River
T (08) 9757 5058 **www.umamuestate.com** **Open** Not
Winemaker Bruce Dukes (Contract) **Est.** 2005 **Dozens** 1800 **Vyds** 16.8ha
Chief executive Charmaine Saw explains, 'My life has been a journey towards Umamu. An upbringing in both eastern and western cultures, graduating in natural science, training as a chef, combined with a passion for the arts and experience as a management consultant have all contributed to my building the business creatively yet professionally'. The palindrome 'Umamu', says Charmaine, is inspired by balance and contentment. In practical terms this means an organic approach to viticulture and a deep respect for the terroir. The plantings, dating back to 1978, include cabernet sauvignon, chardonnay, shiraz, semillon, sauvignon blanc, merlot and cabernet franc. Exports to Hong Kong, Malaysia, Indonesia and the Philippines.

ΨΨΨΨΨ **Shiraz 2015** Bright crimson hue; it is the first time shiraz has been included in its red seal collection. The bouquet is wondrously complex, with a collection of exotic spices establishing its quality before it is tasted, and when that occurs it simply validates the promise of the bouquet. While there is a lot of oak on the mid-palate in particular, it breaks free on the long finish. Screwcap. 13.8% alc. Rating 96 To 2035 $54 ❂
Cabernet Sauvignon 2015 This is a a pretty smart Margaret River cabernet, playing fruit, tannins and oak off against each other right from the word go. The cassis, cedar and bay leaf aromas have a silken whisper, growing and evolving on the medium-bodied palate, superfine tannins bowing to the grace and richness of the long palate. Screwcap. 13.8% alc. **Rating** 96 To 2030 $64 ❂

ΨΨΨΨΨ **Margaret River Chardonnay 2015** Rating 91 To 2024 $51

Underground Winemakers

1282 Nepean Highway, Mt Eliza, Vic 3931 **Region** Mornington Peninsula
T (03) 9775 4185 **www.ugwine.com.au** **Open** 7 days 10–5
Winemaker Peter Stebbing **Est.** 2004 **Dozens** 10 000 **Vyds** 12ha
Owned by Adrian Hennessy, Jonathon Stevens and Peter Stebbing. Each has made wine in Alsace, Burgundy, Northern Italy and Swan Hill, and each has extensive experience in the vineyards and wineries of the Mornington Peninsula. Their first step, in 2004, was to lease a small winery at Mt Eliza that had closed years earlier, but still had a vineyard with some of the oldest plantings of pinot noir, pinot gris and chardonnay on the peninsula. Their portfolio is nothing if not eclectic: pinot gris, pinot noir and chardonnay from the Mornington Peninsula, and durif, moscato, cabernet merlot and shiraz from Northern and Central Victoria. The San Pietro wines are made according to the philosophy of traditional Italian winegrower San Pietro, who has vineyards in the hills south of Benalla and in the Mornington Peninsula (more information at www.sanpietrowine.com).

ΨΨΨΨΨ **Mornington Peninsula Pinot Noir 2017** Affordable $20 cool-climate pinot noirs used to be as rare as hen's teeth – they're not common now, but they're there for those on the lookout. This is a good wine, with a complex array of red fruits and a savoury overcoat, and will improve with limited cellaring. Screwcap. 13.5% alc. **Rating** 91 **To** 2022 $20 ✪

𝍢𝍢𝍢𝍢 **San Pietro Shiraz 2012 Rating** 89 **To** 2020 $30

Upper Reach   ★★★★

77 Memorial Avenue, Baskerville, WA 6056 **Region** Swan Valley
T (08) 9296 0078 **www**.upperreach.com.au **Open** 7 days 11–5
Winemaker Derek Pearse **Est.** 1996 **Dozens** 4000 **Vyds** 8.45ha
This 10ha property on the banks of the upper reaches of the Swan River was purchased by Laura Rowe and Derek Pearse in 1996. The original 4ha vineyard was expanded, and plantings now include chardonnay, shiraz, cabernet sauvignon, verdelho, semillon, merlot, petit verdot and muscat. All wines are estate-grown. Several years ago they leased the restaurant area to Anthony and Annalis Broad, who now run Broads Restaurant at Upper Reach; the restaurant is encased by full-length glass doors and surrounded by a deck overlooking the vineyard. They have integrated the cellar door with the restaurant, the glass walls bringing vineyard views into the cellar door, where wines are tasted in Riedel glasses. Next they constructed a deck where visitors can relax and enjoy a glass or two, resulting in *Gourmet Traveller WINE* choosing Upper Reach as the Star Cellar Door in the Swan Valley.

𝍢𝍢𝍢𝍢𝍢 **Reserve Margaret River Cabernet Sauvignon 2015** Fruit from Wilyabrup, which explains the intense boysenberry/mulberry aromas, and waves of menthol, new leather and aniseed. Full-bodied, lots of new French oak (50% and the rest aged for 1 year) that has yet to be integrated, but is likely to do so given the rich fruit weight. A slight sweet-sour edge to the finish, but still youthful and needs more time in bottle. Screwcap. 14% alc. **Rating** 93 **To** 2030 $55 JF
Reserve Swan Valley Shiraz 2015 A powerhouse of a wine, from the dark purple-black colour to the density of ripe fruit. Concentrated flavours of blackstrap licorice, blackberry jubes mingling with coriander seeds and cloves. It's full-bodied, very rich with sweet oak flavours dominating, as do the wood tannins. Screwcap. 14.5% alc. **Rating** 90 **To** 2027 $39 JF

Vasarelli Wines   ★★★

164 Main Road, McLaren Vale, SA 5171 **Region** McLaren Vale
T (08) 8323 7980 **Open** 7 days 8–5
Winemaker Nigel Dolan (Contract) **Est.** 1995 **Dozens** 18 000 **Vyds** 33ha
Pasquale (Pat) and Vittoria (Vicky) Vasarelli moved with their parents from Melbourne to McLaren Vale in 1976. They began the establishment of their vineyard, and over the succeeding years increased the area under vine to over 30ha, planted to semillon, sauvignon blanc, chardonnay, pinot gris, vermentino, shiraz, cabernet sauvignon and merlot. Until '95 the grapes were sold to other producers, but in that year they joined Cellarmaster Wines and the Vasarelli brand was born. In a reverse play of the usual pattern, they opened a cellar door in 2009 on a small property they had purchased in '92.

𝍢𝍢𝍢𝍢 **Estate Grown McLaren Vale Shiraz 2015** Sourced from the Home and Seaview Blocks. At 15% alcohol it's inevitably a full-blooded, robust offering. There's plenty of flavour, with typically regional blackberry, plum and chocolate running through the palate, and while there's some warmth on the finish, the tannin has been well managed, providing a sound and solid structure without being dominating. Screwcap. 15% alc. **Rating** 89 **To** 2025 $28 SC

Vasse Felix   ★★★★★

Cnr Tom Cullity Drive/Caves Road, Cowaramup, WA 6284 **Region** Margaret River
T (08) 9756 5000 **www**.vassefelix.com.au **Open** 7 days 10–5
Winemaker Virginia Willcock **Est.** 1967 **Dozens** 150 000 **Vyds** 232ha
Vasse Felix was the first winery to be built in the Margaret River. Owned and operated by the Holmes à Court family since 1987, Vasse Felix has undergone extensive changes and expansion.

Chief winemaker Virginia Willcock has energised the winemaking and viticultural team with her no-nonsense approach and fierce commitment to quality. The estate vineyards contribute to all but a small part of the annual production, and are scrupulously managed, quality the sole driver. Wines include top of the range Tom Cullity (a cabernet blend) and Heytesbury Chardonnay; as well as the premier range of mainly varietal wines – Filius Chardonnay and Filius Cabernet Merlot; and Classic Dry White and Classic Dry Red. Limited quantities of specialty wines include Cane Cut Semillon and Blanc de Blancs. Exports to all major markets.

ΨΨΨΨΨ **Heytesbury Margaret River Chardonnay 2016** A wine all about finesse and length – extreme length. The inexorable drive and logic of the bouquet and (in particular) the palate leaves little room for argument, but plenty for discussion. Pink grapefruit, pear, nectarine and a satin bow of oak are all as one. Screwcap. 13% alc. **Rating** 97 **To** 2030 $85 ✪

Tom Cullity Margaret River Cabernet Sauvignon Malbec 2014 The ship slowly turns and sets sail for the future. It's not the deepest or darkest of wines at first, but give it time to breathe and the reach and power is something to behold. It tastes of blackcurrant and camphor, bay leaves and black olives, smoky oak applied as an infusion rather than as anything terribly overt. Flavour – most certainly. Tannic power – oh, yes. Explosive length – most definitely. Screwcap. 14.5% alc. **Rating** 97 **To** 2039 $180 CM

ΨΨΨΨΨ **Margaret River Shiraz 2015** This is a medium to full-bodied shiraz that has such pinpoint clarity it is able to tread lightly. It's all about high quality fruit that has been given the oak support it needs, but not one iota more. Its texture and structure are admirable, the black fruits with a slightly savoury twist by the carefully extracted tannins. Screwcap. 14% alc. **Rating** 96 **To** 2035 $37 ✪

Margaret River Chardonnay 2016 Has the intensity, complexity and drive expected of Vasse Felix, with layers of white peach, pear and sotto voce grapefruit paired with the all-important acidity. There's an argument to be made – this offers the best value of the three '16 Vasse Felix Chardonnays. Screwcap. 13% alc. **Rating** 95 **To** 2027 $39

Margaret River Cabernet Sauvignon 2015 A medium-weight cabernet to show more bulkier renditions a clean set of heels. This is a slashing way to present cabernet. Energetic and bright, yet fluid and soft. It boasts just enough weight and power to build good momentum through the palate, but at no point does it press too hard, or for too much. Bay leaf, black olive and blackcurrant flavours are the main conveyors here. Tannin is a light sheet through the back half of the wine. The touch is light, the effect dramatic. Screwcap. 14% alc. **Rating** 95 **To** 2035 $47 CM

Margaret River Sauvignon Blanc Semillon 2017 Stamped with class. The texture, the intensity of flavour, the acceleration of the finish. Indeed it's difficult – and pointless – to single out individual flavours because it all seems so unified. It's an excellent white wine from all angles, with elegance included. Screwcap. 12.5% alc. **Rating** 94 **To** 2023 $24 CM ✪

ΨΨΨΨΨ **Margaret River Classic Dry White 2017 Rating** 93 **To** 2021 $19 ✪
Filius Margaret River Cabernet Merlot 2016 Rating 92 **To** 2029 $28
Filius Margaret River Chardonnay 2016 Rating 90 **To** 2021 $28
Margaret River Classic Dry Red 2016 Rating 90 **To** 2022 $19 CM ✪

Verdun Park Wines   ★★★☆

14 Sandow Road, Verdun, SA 5245 (postal) **Region** Adelaide Hills
T (08) 8388 7357 **www**.verdunparkwines.com.au **Open** Not
Winemaker Michael Sykes **Est.** 2009 **Dozens** 300 **Vyds** 2ha
Verdun Park is owned by Sandy and Bob Voumard (with backgrounds in education and accountancy) and run with the assistance of their daughter Danielle and son-in-law Shaun McBeath (viticulturist). The initial release, 2009 Lyla Sauvignon Blanc, was made from specifically selected contract-grown grapes, which went on to win a gold medal at the fiercely contested (for sauvignon blanc) Adelaide Hills Wine Show '09.

ŸŸŸŸŸ **Lyla Adelaide Hills Sauvignon Blanc 2016** It's fresh and vibrant, full of tropical fruit, yet tempered by some lemongrass, ginger and basil; a touch of sweetness on the finish adds to the mouthfeel. Screwcap. 11.5% alc. **Rating** 90 **To** 2018 $22 JF

Vickery Wines   ★★★★☆

28 The Parade, Norwood, SA 5067 **Region** Clare Valley/Eden Valley
T (08) 8362 8622 **www**.vickerywines.com.au **Open** Not
Winemaker John Vickery, Phil Lehmann **Est.** 2014 **Dozens** 4000 **Vyds** 12ha
It must be a strange feeling for John Vickery to begin at the beginning again, 60 years after his first vintage, in 1951. His interest in, love of, and exceptional skills with riesling began with Leo Buring in '55 at Chateau Leonay. Over the intervening years he became the uncrowned but absolute monarch of riesling makers in Australia until, in his semi-retirement, he passed the mantle on to Jeffrey Grosset. Along the way he had (unsurprisingly) won the Wolf Blass Riesling Award at the Canberra International Riesling Challenge 2007, and had been judged by his peers as Australia's Greatest Living Winemaker in a survey conducted by *The Age* Epicure in '03. His new venture has been undertaken in conjunction with Phil Lehmann, with 12ha of Clare and Eden valleys' riesling involved, and wine marketer Jonathan Hesketh moving largely invisibly in the background. The coded wine makes are easy to decipher when it comes to EVR (Eden Valley Riesling) and WVR (Watervale Riesling), but thereafter the code strikes. The numerics are the dates of harvest, thus '103' is '10 March', '172' is '17 February'. The initials that follow are even more delphic, standing for the name of the vineyard or those of the multiple owners. Exports to the UK, EU and Canada.

ŸŸŸŸŸ **Eden Valley Riesling 2017** EVR 604 MZR. Made of slightly sterner stuff than its Watervale stablemate, but just as attractive as a young wine. Pure aromas and flavours, fruit sweetness harnessed by the gently firm acidity. Like many '17 SA rieslings, excellent each-way drinking; highly enjoyable now and with great ageing potential. Screwcap. 12.5% alc. **Rating** 95 **To** 2037 $27 SC ●
Watervale Riesling 2017 WVR 143 CBK. Inviting bouquet, with citrus fruit, citrus flowers and the bath salts aromas, which are all so typical. Lovely balance through the palate, the flavours fresh and quite delicate. The natural acidity which is real characteristic of this vintage comes into play as well, with distinctive softness and very fine, subtle persistence on the finish. Screwcap. 13% alc. **Rating** 94 **To** 2037 $23 SC ●

Victory Point Wines   ★★★★★

4 Holben Road, Cowaramup, WA 6284 **Region** Margaret River
T 0417 954 655 **www**.victorypointwines.com **Open** By appt
Winemaker Mark Messenger (Contract) **Est.** 1997 **Dozens** 2000 **Vyds** 12.9ha
Judith and Gary Berson have set their sights high. They established their vineyard without irrigation, emulating those of the Margaret River pioneers (including Moss Wood). The fully mature plantings comprise 4.2ha chardonnay and 0.5ha of pinot noir, the remainder of Bordeaux varieties, with cabernet sauvignon (6.2ha), cabernet franc (0.5ha), malbec (0.8ha) and petit verdot (0.7ha).

ŸŸŸŸŸ **Margaret River Chardonnay 2014** Gin Gin (63%) and Dijon clones 277, 76 and 95, fermented in French oak (40% new), matured on lees for 9 months. An exciting chardonnay that portrays the synergy between the clones and the place, purity and elegance in a symbiotic union that opens new doors every time you come back to it. Screwcap. 13.5% alc. **Rating** 96 **To** 2030 $45 ●
Margaret River Cabernet Sauvignon 2014 Doing what comes easily in the Margaret River, other regions looking on enviously. Bright, full colour; the fragrant, cassis and dried bay leaf aromas and flavours sit comfortably in a medium-bodied, textured palate of great elegance and length. Great now, but will breeze through the next 20 years. Screwcap. 14% alc. **Rating** 95 **To** 2037 $45

Margaret River Malbec 2014 One of those distinguished, albeit small, producers of malbec in the Margaret River that throw down the gauntlet to Langhorne Creek and Clare Valley. The Mediterranean climate of the Clare Valley is shared with Langhorne Creek, but the soil is very different in the Margaret River, giving the wine a freshness and juicy precision to its dark plum fruit. Screwcap. 14% alc. **Rating** 95 To 2029 $35 ❂

ŶŶŶŶŶ **Margaret River Rose 2017 Rating** 93 To 2020 $23 ❂

View Road Wines ★★★★★

Peacocks Road, Lenswood, SA 5240 **Region** Adelaide Hills
T 0402 180 383 **www.**viewroadwines.com.au **Open** Not
Winemaker Josh Tuckfield **Est.** 2011 **Dozens** 500
View Road Wines sources prosecco, arneis, chardonnay, sangiovese, merlot, sagrantino and syrah from Adelaide Hills vineyards; shiraz, aglianico and sagrantino from McLaren Vale vineyards; and nero d'Avola and fiano from the Riverland. All of the wines are wild-yeast fermented, and matured in used oak.

ŶŶŶŶŶ **Piccadilly Valley Chardonnay 2015** All class. A remarkably sophisticated wine. Glowing yellow in colour with struck match, white peach, grapefruit and cooked apple flavours motoring through the palate with energy and impact. Spicy, smoky oak sits in complete agreement with the fruit, the finish long and complex. Mesmerising. Screwcap. 13.5% alc. **Rating** 96 To 2024 $37 CM ❂
McLaren Vale Shiraz 2015 From Blewitt Springs. It's all about the vineyard and the grapes it grows – and it shows. The fragrance here is dramatic, the flavour drastic in its freshness, its buoyancy. It's virtually impossible not to like or enjoy this. Blueberry and black cherry, woodsy spices, wild fennel and lavender. In short, it's gorgeous from start to finish; there's no reason not to enjoy it young. Screwcap. 14.2% alc. **Rating** 96 To 2030 $37 CM ❂

Vigena Wines ★★★★★

210 Main Road, Willunga, SA 5172 (postal) **Region** McLaren Vale
T 0433 966 011 **Open** Not
Winemaker Ben Heide **Est.** 2010 **Dozens** 20000 **Vyds** 15.8ha
The principal business of Vigena Wines is exports to Singapore, Hong Kong and China. In recent years the vineyard has been revitalised, with one significant change: chardonnay being grafted to shiraz, giving the business a 100% red wine focus.

ŶŶŶŶŶ **McLaren Vale Shiraz Grenache 2016** A 55/45% blend matured for 18 months in French puncheons (60% new). A shiraz/grenache blend like no other, so deep in colour, so powerful and complex, the savoury palate long and well balanced. Cork. 14.5% alc. **Rating** 96 To 2045 $49 ❂
Limited Edition McLaren Vale Shiraz 2016 The deep crimson-purple colour serves notice of the depths of the black berry/charry fruit flavours that immediately take ownership of the bouquet and palate. It is medium to full-bodied, yet the tannins play a minimal role in establishing the commanding profile. Instead it comes from high quality estate-grown fruit and hints of dark chocolate. Cork. 14.5% alc. **Rating** 95 To 2036 $79
Gran Reserve McLaren Vale Shiraz 2015 It's strange that a Gran Reserve from a great vintage should be less expensive than its younger Limited Edition sibling – it's all in a name, I suppose, neither with any official meaning in Australia. It's also true that this wine has an extra degree of complexity, but less luscious fruit and a shorter anticipated life. Cork. 14.5% alc. **Rating** 94 To 2035 $59
McLaren Vale Cabernet Sauvignon Shiraz 2016 Dark colour; in the hyper-concentrated Vigena style, luscious and bold, and tailor-made for their intended markets, a high quality cork and heavy bottle all part of the story. Cork. 14% alc. **Rating** 94 To 2036 $55

Vigna Bottin   ★★★★☆

147 Plains Road, Sellicks Hill, McLaren Vale, SA 5171 **Region** McLaren Vale
T 0414 562 956 **www**.vignabottin.com.au **Open** By appt
Winemaker Paolo Bottin **Est.** 2006 **Dozens** 1500 **Vyds** 15.22ha
The Bottin family migrated to Australia in 1954 from Treviso in northern Italy, where they
were grapegrowers. The family began growing grapes in McLaren Vale in '70, focusing on
mainstream varieties for sale to wineries in the region. When son Paolo and wife Maria made
a trip back to Italy in '98, they were inspired to do more. Paolo says, 'My love for barbera and
sangiovese was sealed during a vintage in Pavia. I came straight home to plant both varieties in
our family plot. My father was finally happy!' They now trade with the catchy phrase 'Italian
Vines, Australian Wines'.

🍷🍷🍷🍷🍷 **Sangiovese 2015** A warm climate expression, bringing to mind the forceful,
chocolatey wines of the Maremma, in coastal Tuscany. This was finished in
French wood for 14 months, the aspirations of the approach embedded in a finely
groomed piste of oak-melded tannins, ripe cherry to plummy scents, and a gentle
waft of herb, root spice and acidity across the back end. A very smart, potent and
highly modern sangiovese. Screwcap. 14.5% alc. **Rating** 95 **To** 2025 $28 NG ✪

🍷🍷🍷🍷🍷 **Vermentino 2017 Rating** 93 **To** 2020 $24 NG ✪
Fiano 2017 Rating 92 **To** 2019 $24 NG ✪
McLaren Vale Versecco NV Rating 92 $35 NG
Rosato 2017 Rating 91 **To** 2019 $24 NG

Vignerons Schmolzer & Brown   ★★★★

39 Thorley Road, Stanley, Vic 3747 **Region** Beechworth
T 0411 053 487 **www**.vsandb.com.au **Open** By appt
Winemaker Tessa Brown **Est.** 2014 **Dozens** 500 **Vyds** 2ha
Winemaker/viticulturist Tessa Brown graduated from CSU in the late 1990s with a
degree in viticulture, and undertook postgraduate winemaking studies at the University of
Adelaide in the mid-2000s. Her self-description of being 'reasonably peripatetic' covers her
winemaking in Orange in '99, and Canberra, SA, Strathbogie Ranges, Rioja (Spain) and
Central Otago (NZ), before joining Kooyong and Port Phillip Estate in '08. In '09 Mark
Walpole showed Tess and architect partner Jeremy Schmolzer a property he described as 'the
jewel in the crown of Beechworth'. When it came onto the market unexpectedly in '12, they
were in a position to jump. The property (named Thorley) was 20ha, and cleared; they have
since planted chardonnay, shiraz, riesling and nebbiolo. By sheer chance, just across the road
from Thorley was a tiny vineyard, a bit over 0.4ha, with dry-grown pinot and chardonnay
around 20 years old. When they realised it was not being managed for production, they struck
up a working relationship with the owners, getting the vineyard into shape, and made their
first (very good) wines in '14.

🍷🍷🍷🍷🍷 **Pret-a-Rose 2017** Made with shiraz from Whorouly South (Alpine Valleys) and
pinot noir from Stanley and Everton Upper (Beechworth). Dry, savoury, perfumed,
a belly of red fruits, hair of spice. It's a dry, structured rose with plenty going on; if
there's a lull in the lunch table conversation this could easily re-ignite it. Screwcap.
13% alc. **Rating** 94 **To** 2019 $28 CM ✪

🍷🍷🍷🍷🍷 **Brunnen Beechworth Chardonnay 2016 Rating** 93 **To** 2025 CM
Pret-a-Rouge 2014 Rating 92 **To** 2021 $28 CM
Pret-a-Blanc 2017 Rating 91 **To** 2020 $26 CM

Vinaceous Wines   ★★★★☆

49 Bennett Street, East Perth, WA 6004 (postal) **Region** Various
T (08) 9221 4666 **www**.vinaceous.com.au **Open** Not
Winemaker Gavin Berry, Michael Kerrigan **Est.** 2007 **Dozens** 25 000
This is the somewhat quirky venture of Nick Stacy (wine marketer), Michael Kerrigan
(winemaker/partner Hay Shed Hill) and Gavin Berry (winemaker/partner West Cape

Howe). The fast-moving and fast-growing brand was originally directed at the US market, but has changed direction due to the domestic demand engendered (one might guess) by the decidedly exotic/erotic labels and, more importantly, by the fact that the wines are of seriously good quality and equally good value. Margaret River provides over half of the production, the remainder from McLaren Vale and the Adelaide Hills. Yet more labels, ranges and wines are in the pipeline; the website is the best method of keeping up to date. Exports to the UK, the US, Canada, South America, Denmark, Finland, Indonesia, the Philippines, Thailand, Singapore and Hong Kong.

ΨΨΨΨΨ **Clandestine Vineyards #1 McLaren Vale Grenache 2016** From a single vineyard planted in 1923 as bushvines in the hills above Clarendon. Light, bright colour; a full-bodied, savoury grenache unique to Clarendon with its structure and mouthfeel (but not its flavours); as robust as shiraz. It deserves a minimum of 5 years for the spices (presently locked up) to burst forth. Screwcap. 14.5% alc. **Rating** 96 **To** 2031 $40 **☺**

Right Reverend V Mount Barker Riesling 2017 The name may be quirky, but the wine isn't. It's a classic Mount Barker riesling, with a juicy mid-palate given shape and strength by crunchy acidity on the way through to the finish. This calls for more time. Screwcap. 12% alc. **Rating** 94 **To** 2035 $25 **☺**

Right Reverend V Mount Barker Syrah 2016 It is with increasing trepidation that I taste much cooler-climate Australian syrah, fearing the clench of overt reduction. But this makes me a believer! Attractive florals lead one to a buoyant, medium-bodied palate redolent of blue and black fruits held aloft by a reverberating palate of juicy acidity, sensitive oak and a long, energetic finish smeared with olive tapenade, pepper grind and a whiff of mortadella. Phew! Screwcap. 14% alc. **Rating** 94 **To** 2024 $25 NG **☺**

ΨΨΨΨΩ **Right Reverend V WBX SSB 2016 Rating** 93 **To** 2020 $25 NG **☺**
Right Reverend V Chardonnay 2016 Rating 93 **To** 2026 $25 **☺**
Right Reverend V Cabernet Sauvignon 2016 Rating 93 **To** 2026 $25 NG **☺**
Right Reverend V Pinot Rose 2017 Rating 92 **To** 2018 $25 **☺**
Voodoo Moon Malbec 2016 Rating 91 **To** 2022 $25 NG
Clandestine Vineyards #2 Pinot Gris 2017 Rating 90 **To** 2020 $28

Vinden Estate ★★★★★

138 Gillards Road, Pokolbin, NSW 2320 **Region** Hunter Valley
T (02) 4998 7410 **www.**vindenestate.com.au **Open** Wed–Sun 10–5
Winemaker Angus Vinden, Daniel Binet **Est.** 1998 **Dozens** 4000 **Vyds** 5ha
Vinden Estate is now under the guidance of second-generation winemaker Angus Vinden, who took over the business from parents Sandra and Guy in 2015. Angus has maintained the original traditional Hunter wines, and has also introduced newer styles. All wines are Hunter Valley-sourced, mainly from the estate vineyard (2ha alicante bouschet, 1.25ha shiraz, 1ha mourvedre, 0.75ha gamay), and local old vines sites, in particular the Somerset Vineyard in Pokolbin where Angus was mentored under eighth-generation grower Glen Howard.

ΨΨΨΨΨ **The Vinden Headcase Hunter Valley Nouveau Shiraz 2017** In terms of Hunter shiraz, this wine is lighter framed, juicy and very fresh. Setting the scene is a heady fragrance of raspberries and blueberries, red licorice, warm earth, violets and roses. Soft, gentle tannins and reviving acidity ensure this is purely and simply a joyful drink. Screwcap. 13% alc. **Rating** 95 **To** 2022 $30 JF **☺**

The Vinden Headcase Charmless Man Shiraz 2017 This is a blend of 60% pinot noir and 40% alicante bouschet and it is charming. Entices with its bright purple-red as much as with the flavour of succulent fruit – a mix of raspberries, blueberries and cherries. Lighter framed with a very juicy palate. Screwcap. 13% alc. **Rating** 95 **To** 2021 $30 JF **☺**

The Vinden Headcase Hunter Valley Shiraz 2016 Single barrel of shiraz from the Somerset Vineyard, transferred between new French (3 months), old French (6 months) and new American (1 month) during its maturation. A curious approach. The end result shows ample toast and sweet oak spice, but the fruit, tannin and swashbuckling finish have this wine headed for a special place. Give it time, it will be worth the wait. Diam. 14% alc. **Rating** 95 **To** 2030 $60 CM

The Vinden Single Barrel Hunter Valley Shiraz 2016 Richly flavoured, full-bodied and deep, the oak flavour has slipped through, adding some spice and a touch of sweetness. There's lavender, plums, new leather, giving tannins with some hold. All in all, a composed wine. Diam. 14% alc. **Rating** 95 **To** 2026 $50 JF

The Vinden Headcase Hunter Valley Semillon 2017 Aside from the usual citrus bent of young semillon, with juice, pith and zest, this has more unusual and appealing aromatics, including curry leaves, white pepper and wet stones. Crisp acidity works its way across the linear palate, but it's not so tightly coiled that it can't be enjoyed now as there's an openness as well. Screwcap. 10.5% alc. **Rating** 94 **To** 2028 $30 JF ❂

ΨΨΨΨΨ   **The Vinden Semillon 2017 Rating** 93 **To** 2028 $30 JF
Reserve Semillon 2016 Rating 93 **To** 2030 $40 JF
The Vinden Headcase Tempranillo 2016 Rating 93 **To** 2023 $40 CM
The Vinden Basket Press Shiraz 2016 Rating 92 **To** 2023 $40 JF
The Vinden Back Block Shiraz 2013 Rating 91 **To** 2021 $60 JF
The Vinden Headcase Rose 2017 Rating 90 **To** 2019 $30 JF
The Vinden Headcase Nouveau Shiraz 2016 Rating 90 **To** 2022 $30 CM

Vinea Marson   ★★★★☆

411 Heathcote-Rochester Road, Heathcote, Vic 3523 **Region** Heathcote
T 0430 312 165 **www**.vineamarson.com **Open** W'ends
Winemaker Mario Marson **Est.** 2000 **Dozens** 2500 **Vyds** 7.12ha
Owner-winemaker Mario Marson spent many years as winemaker/viticulturist with the late Dr John Middleton at the celebrated Mount Mary estate. Mario has over 35 years of experience in Australia and overseas, having undertaken vintages at Isole e Olena in Tuscany and Piedmont, and Domaine de la Pousse d'Or in Burgundy. There he was inspired to emulate the multi-clonal wines favoured by these producers, pioneered in Australia by John Middleton. In 1999 Mario and wife Helen purchased the Vinea Marson property on the eastern slopes of the Mt Camel Range, and have planted shiraz and viognier, plus Italian varieties sangiovese, nebbiolo, barbera and refosco dal peduncolo. Marson also sources northeastern Italian varietals from Porepunkah in the Alpine Valleys. Exports to China.

ΨΨΨΨΨ   **Rose 2015** Pale, bright pink; still as fresh as a daisy, perhaps in part due to the cool vintage, but impressive nonetheless, with drive through to the finish. Lovely wine, better than its '16 sibling. Screwcap. 13.5% alc. **Rating** 94 **To** 2021
Shiraz Viognier 2014 An elegant 98/2% blend, lifted red fruits reflecting the influence of the viognier; medium-bodied, supple and long, extended maceration works well, imparting length yet is not extractive. Diam. 14% alc. **Rating** 94 **To** 2029

ΨΨΨΨΨ   **Sangiovese 2014 Rating** 92 **To** 2024
Viognier 2015 Rating 91 **To** 2020

Vinifera Wines   ★★★☆

194 Henry Lawson Drive, Mudgee, NSW 2850 **Region** Mudgee
T (02) 6372 2461 **www**.viniferawines.com.au **Open** Mon–Sat 10–5, Sun 10–4
Winemaker Jacob Stein **Est.** 1997 **Dozens** 1200 **Vyds** 12ha
Having lived in Mudgee for 15 years, Tony McKendry (a regional medical superintendent) and wife Debbie succumbed to the lure of winemaking; they planted their small (1.5ha) vineyard in 1995. In Debbie's words, 'Tony, in his spare two minutes per day, also decided to start Wine Science at CSU in 1992'. She continues, 'He's trying to live 27 hours per day (plus we have four kids!). He fell to pieces when he was involved in a severe car smash in 1997. Two months in hospital stopped his full-time medical work, and the winery dreams became inevitable'. Financial compensation finally came through and the small winery was built. The now-expanded vineyard includes 3ha each of chardonnay and cabernet sauvignon, and 1.5ha each of semillon, tempranillo and grenache, as well as smaller plantings of graciano and monastrell.

ΨΨΨΨΨ **Organic Semillon 2017** Sure, it's light, but it flits through the mouth in lovely style; its lines are straight, its aim true. It drinks well now, and should also mature well over the next handful of years. Screwcap. 12% alc. **Rating** 90 **To** 2024 $24 CM

Vinrock   ★★★★

1/25 George Street, Thebarton, SA 5031 (postal) **Region** McLaren Vale
T (08) 8408 8900 **www**.vinrock.com **Open** Not
Winemaker Michael Fragos **Est.** 1998 **Dozens** 13 000 **Vyds** 30ha
Owners Don Luca, Marco Iannetti and Anthony De Pizzol all have backgrounds in the wine industry, but none more than Don, a former board member of Tatachilla. Don also planted the Luca vineyard in 1998 (21ha of shiraz, 5ha grenache and 4ha cabernet sauvignon). The majority of the grapes are sold, but steadily increasing quantities of wine have been made from the best blocks in the vineyard, with many of these wines at tempting prices.

ΨΨΨΨΨ **Block 19 McLaren Vale Shiraz 2016** A whirl of dark sweet fruit encases rich flavours of dark chocolate, hoisin sauce, eucalyptus and vanillan oak, and all are amalgamated. The frame is full-bodied, dense with substantial tannins, yet the wine glides across the palate with ease. Screwcap. 14.3% alc. **Rating** 92 **To** 2026 $40 JF
McLaren Vale Grenache 2016 Open the windows and feel the syrupy soft flavours billow in. This is pure, delicious, grenache-to-a-tee fruit, all raspberry and redcurrant, with warm, sweet spice and anise laid on. Joyous wine. Screwcap. 14.5% alc. **Rating** 92 **To** 2024 $25 CM ✪
McLaren Vale Grenache Shiraz Mourvedre 2016 It's all hung on a thread of ripe raspberry. It works like a guiding light, shining sweetness and brightness into folds of spice, leather and earth. Salty tannin works as a counterbalance; everything here feels balanced, and it drinks well as a result. Screwcap. 14.5% alc. **Rating** 91 **To** 2024 $25 CM
McLaren Vale Shiraz 2016 It pours sweet berried flavour in generous measure, but goes easy on the chocolate overtones – always an attractive combination. It feels loose and free-flowing, and that's exactly why it will be enjoyed by many. Richness is in this wine's favour. Screwcap. 14.5% alc. **Rating** 90 **To** 2024 $25 CM
Terra Mia McLaren Vale Grenache Shiraz Mataro 2016 A 54/40/6% blend that spends 12 months in used French oak, and it's a neat combo of spiced plums, raspberries, green walnuts (and of all things salted) and dried umeboshi plums. Full-bodied, sandy tannins, and ripe for your next barbecue. Screwcap. 14.1% alc. **Rating** 90 **To** 2021 $25 JF

Virago Vineyard   ★★★★

40 Boundary Road, Everton Upper, Vic 3678 **Region** Beechworth
T 0411 718 369 **www**.viragobeechworth.com.au **Open** By appt
Winemaker Karen Coats, Rick Kinzbrunner **Est.** 2007 **Dozens** 175 **Vyds** 1ha
Karen Coats was a tax accountant, but has now completed the Bachelor of Wine Science at CSU. It was her love of nebbiolo and the Beechworth region that made Virago Vineyard her new office of choice. Prue Keith is an orthopaedic surgeon, but devotes her free time (whatever is not occupied by mountain biking, skiing and trekking to the peaks of mountains) to Virago Vineyard. The vines had been removed from the property long before Karen and Prue purchased it, but the existing terracing, old posts and broken wires laid down a challenge that was easily accepted, although the planting of nebbiolo was not so easy. The one and only Rick Kinzbrunner has a more than passing interest in nebbiolo, so it was inevitable that he would be the consultant winemaker.

ΨΨΨΨΨ **Beechworth Nebbiolo 2014** It all hones towards the finish. Sweet-sour cherries, plums, leather and anise characters take on notes of decaying roses and mint, a flash of blood orange too. It's varietally true, sheeted with tannin and – most impressively – has plenty to carry on through to the finish. It's a good'un. Due for release Sept '18. Diam. 14% alc. **Rating** 94 **To** 2026 $45 CM

Voyager Estate

Lot 1 Stevens Road, Margaret River, WA 6285 **Region** Margaret River
T (08) 9757 6354 **www.**voyagerestate.com.au **Open** 7 days 10–5
Winemaker Steve James, Travis Lemm **Est.** 1978 **Dozens** 40 000 **Vyds** 110ha
The late mining magnate Michael Wright pursued several avenues of business and agriculture before setting his sights on owning a vineyard and winery. It was thus an easy decision in 1991 when he was able to buy what was then called Freycinet Estate from founder and leading viticulturist Peter Gherardi. Peter had established the vineyard in '78, and it was significantly expanded by Michael over the ensuing years. Apart from the Cape Dutch- style tasting room and vast rose garden, the signpost for the estate is the massive Australian flag pole – after Parliament House in Canberra, it is the largest flag pole in Australia. Michael's daughter, Alexandra Burt, has been at the helm of Voyager Estate for many years, and is supported by general manager Chris Furtado and long-serving, committed staff. Michael is remembered as a larger-than life character, more at home in his favourite work pants and boots than in a suit, and never happier than when trundling around the estate on a four-wheeler or fixing a piece of machinery. Exports to the UK, the US, Canada, Germany, Indonesia, East Africa, Malaysia, Singapore, Japan, Hong Kong and China.

🍷🍷🍷🍷🍷 **Broadvale Block 5 Margaret River Chardonnay 2016** Hand-picked, chilled overnight, whole-bunch pressed, wild-fermented in French oak (17% new), matured for 11 months. The highly regarded Gin Gin clone didn't require mlf for balance. Complex and rich, but is never in danger of losing its line or balance; has the greatest volume of stone fruit on the finish, and citrussy acidity on the aftertaste. Screwcap. 13.5% alc. **Rating** 96 **To** 2026

Tom Price Margaret River Cabernet Sauvignon 2014 Estate-grown, 50% from the Old Block, 50% from Block 12, matured in French oak (15% new) for 18 months, a barrel selection returned to oak for a further 6 months. Exceptional colour; a supple rendition of pure cassis/blackcurrant, with a resounding finish. Clearly the best wine. Screwcap. **Rating** 96 **To** 2034

Margaret River Chardonnay 2016 Dijon clones 76, 95 and 96, and Gin Gin clone; chilled overnight, whole-bunch pressed, fermented in French oak (36% new), 25% mlf, matured for 11 months. The greatest fruit weight and mouthfeel of the Voyager Chardonnays, with a complex array of white peach, nectarine and cashew/oak surroundings. Screwcap. 13.5% alc. **Rating** 95 **To** 2030

Old Block V9 Margaret River Cabernet Sauvignon 2014 Includes 5% petit verdot, matured for 18 months in French oak. An elegant medium-bodied wine; fragrant bouquet; long palate with superfine tannins, blackcurrant a recurring taste theme. Screwcap. 14% alc. **Rating** 95 **To** 2029

Tom Price Margaret River Chardonnay 2016 The second Tom Price Chardonnay to be released. Feels quite restrained at this stage, with latent depth and complexity not fully on show. A subtle, almost subdued bouquet, with aromas of white peach and pear with a touch of marzipan and a minerally, oyster shell element. Shows intensity and focus on a palate that will surely become more layered and expansive with time as the citrus and stone fruit characters evolve. Screwcap. 13.5% alc. **Rating** 94 **To** 2028 SC

Broadvale Block 6 Margaret River Chardonnay 2016 Whole-bunch pressed, Dijon clone 95, wild fermentation, 100% mlf, 11 months maturation in French oak (39% new). Exceedingly fine and pure, with overall delicacy; green apple, lemon curd and a constant whisper of enlivening grapefruity acidity. Screwcap. 12.5% alc. **Rating** 94 **To** 2025

Project Margaret River Rose 2017 Comprising 53% shiraz, 42% merlot, 5% cabernet sauvignon; free-run juice cool-fermented separately, 3 weeks on lees before blending; the shiraz grown specifically for this wine. Light, bright crimson; the bouquet and palate alike with juicy red fruits; the finish long, satisfying and fresh. Screwcap. 13% alc. **Rating** 94 **To** 2021 $24 ♥

Margaret River Shiraz 2016 This is like an iron fist in a velvet glove. Its immediate inclusion of black fruits, spice, French oak and tannins all have a stately quality, yet the whole is greater than the sum of its parts. This is a new-generation

Margaret River shiraz that has moved on from being a bit experimental to the stage where it can stand up to Margaret River cabernet. Screwcap. 14% alc. Rating 94 To 2031

North Block U12 Margaret River Cabernet Sauvignon 2014 Includes 5% petit verdot. Towards the lighter side of medium-bodied, the fruit intensely focused but needing to relax and fatten up somewhat – the edge on the finish likewise. Screwcap. 14% alc. **Rating** 94 To 2029

ŸŸŸŸŸ **Margaret River Sauvignon Blanc Semillon 2017** Rating 92 To 2020 SC
Girt by Sea Margaret River Cabernet Merlot 2016 Rating 92 To 2036

🍇 Walsh & Sons ★★★★★

4/5962 Caves Road, Margaret River, WA 6285 **Region** Margaret River
T (08) 9758 8023 www.walshandsons.com.au **Open** Not
Winemaker Ryan Walsh, Freya Hohnen **Est.** 2014 **Dozens** 1500 **Vyds** 20ha

The name Walsh & Sons has a Burgundian twist, the only difference is that Walsh & Sons would be Walsh et Fils. The analogy continues: the sons Roi and Hamish (Ryan Walsh and Freya Hohnen their parents), who in turn are from McHenry Hohnen, of Margaret River blue blood wine aristocracy. Ryan and Freya have had a Burgundian family association making wine for McHenry Hohnen from 2004 to '12, and over that time visiting/working for wineries in France, Spain, Switzerland and the US. At the present time, part of the crop from their 11ha Burnside Vineyard (where they base themselves) and the Walsh 7ha Osmington Vineyard is sold to McHenry Hohnen, Yalumba and Domain & Vineyards. They make an impressive start in the *Wine Companion* 2019, and the only thing they dream of is their own cellar door on the Burnside Vineyard, which would allow a greater production under their own label. Exports to the US.

ŸŸŸŸŸ **Burnside Margaret River Chardonnay 2017** From the Burnside Vineyard
planted in '81, hand-picked, pressed straight to barrel (30% new French oak)
for wild fermentation and maturation. Fascinating wine, with grippy acidity
and phenolics suggesting very low yield. The tension the wine creates between
the extremes of grapefruit and nutty nougat from mlf is remarkable. Screwcap.
13.5% alc. **Rating** 95 To 2027 $50
Burnside Margaret River Chardonnay 2016 This wine has some of
the tension of the '17 but not the startling grip, just refreshing acidity as the
centrepiece of a complex palate. Screwcap. 13.5% alc. **Rating** 95 To 2023 $50
Roi Margaret River Cabernet Sauvignon 2016 From the Osmington district,
20% hand-picked whole bunches into a concrete vat with 80% machine-harvested,
2 days later tipped and on top (no crushing or destemming), pressed to French oak
(80% new) for 12 months maturation. A very powerful, sombre black-fruited wine
with savoury herbal notes and pushy tannins on a long palate. Cork. 13.5% alc.
Rating 94 To 2036 $45

ŸŸŸŸŸ **Lola Red 2016** Rating 93 To 2029 $26 ✪
Little Poppet White 2017 Rating 91 To 2023 $24
Little Poppet White 2016 Rating 91 To 2022 $24

Walter Wines ★★★★

179 Tinja Lane, Mudgee, NSW 2850 **Region** Mudgee
T 0419 251 208 www.walterwines.com.au **Open** Fri–Sat 10.30–4.30, Sun 10–2
Winemaker Lisa Bray (Contract) **Est.** 2005 **Dozens** 1000 **Vyds** 17ha

Lynn and Paul Walter had been keen observers of Mudgee and its wines for 15 years before deciding to take the plunge and plant a 17ha vineyard. It was the mid-1990s, and all the portents were good. As competition increased, and prices for grapes decreased, they realised that their original business plan of simply being growers was not going to be financially viable, even though they thought the downturn would prove to be a temporary one.

🍷🍷🍷🍷🍷 Federation Hill Reserve Mudgee Cabernet Sauvignon 2014
The propensity of Mudgee mud and cabernet is strongly manifest in this wine.
Full-bodied, yet of impeccably balanced proportions: a cavalcade of blackcurrant,
bay leaf, menthol, bitter chocolate; well-appointed oak vanillas, French and
American, palpably buried beneath the extract and gauntlet of juicy, well-extracted
grape tannins, almost pulpy. This is very long and expansive, boding well for
further cellaring. Screwcap. 14% alc. **Rating** 94 **To** 2028 $33 NG

🍷🍷🍷🍷🍷 Federation Hill Reserve Mudgee Chardonnay 2017 **Rating** 93 **To** 2025
$25 NG ⊘
Federation Hill Mudgee Shiraz 2013 **Rating** 93 **To** 2026 $25 NG ⊘
Federation Hill Mudgee Chardonnay 2017 **Rating** 91 **To** 2022 $20 NG ⊘
Federation Hill Mudgee Merlot 2016 **Rating** 91 **To** 2022 $22 NG ⊘

Wangolina   ★★★★☆
8 Limestone Coast Road, Mount Benson, SA 5275 **Region** Mount Benson
T (08) 8768 6187 **www**.wangolina.com.au **Open** 7 days 10–4
Winemaker Anita Goode **Est.** 2001 **Dozens** 4000 **Vyds** 11ha
Four generations of the Goode family have been graziers at Wangolina Station, but now Anita
Goode has broken with tradition by becoming a vigneron. She has planted sauvignon blanc,
shiraz, cabernet sauvignon, semillon and pinot gris.

🍷🍷🍷🍷🍷 Single Vineyard Mt Benson Syrah 2015 Perfect balance plus silken texture
results in a beautiful wine. This is a joy to drink. Ample red/black-berried
fruit, slips of fennel, peppercorns and florals; everything here is in a good place,
including well-finessed tannin, and extension through the finish the natural
consequence. A beauty. Screwcap. 14% alc. **Rating** 95 **To** 2030 $30 CM ⊘

🍷🍷🍷🍷🍷 Limestone Coast Lagrein 2016 **Rating** 93 **To** 2023 $22 CM ⊘
Single Vineyard Cabernet Sauvignon 2015 **Rating** 92 **To** 2026 $30 CM
Spectrum Syrah 2015 **Rating** 91 **To** 2026 $50 CM
Limestone Coast Tempranillo 2016 **Rating** 91 **To** 2023 $22 CM ⊘
Limestone Coast Pinot Gris 2017 **Rating** 90 **To** 2019 $20 CM ⊘

Warner Glen Estate   ★★★★☆
PO Box 383, Mount Barker, WA 6324 **Region** Margaret River
T 0457 482 957 **Open** Not
Winemaker Various **Est.** 1993 **Dozens** 6000 **Vyds** 34.6ha
The primary fruit source for Warner Glen Estate is its Jindawarra Vineyard, located south
of Karridale. With north-facing slopes and soils of gravelly loams, it is the ideal site for high
quality grapes. Planted in 2000, the vines are mature, balanced, and of moderate vigour. The
vineyard is only 6km from the Southern Ocean and 4km from the Indian Ocean, and avoids
extreme high temperatures as a result of the cooling sea breezes. Plantings are of shiraz,
chardonnay, sauvignon blanc, pinot noir, viognier and pinot gris. Cabernet sauvignon is
sourced from the Warner Glen-managed vineyard at Wilyabrup.

🍷🍷🍷🍷🍷 Cabernet Sauvignon 2016 Full-bodied red of depth and stature. This lays its
cards all out on the table. Blackcurrant and bay, gum leaf and chocolate. Rippling
muscles of tannin. It doesn't taste anything like a $20 wine, and I mean that in the
most positive of ways. Screwcap. 14.5% alc. **Rating** 95 **To** 2031 $20 CM ⊘
Margaret River Chardonnay 2016 Has changed since first tasted in Mar '17,
the bouquet is complex and notably fragrant, the palate joining white peach,
nectarine and pink grapefruit. Despite barrel fermentation, the oak isn't obvious,
let alone assertive. Very good value. Screwcap. 13% alc. **Rating** 94 **To** 2020 $20 ⊘

🍷🍷🍷🍷🍷 Frog Belly Pinot Grigio 2017 **Rating** 90 **To** 2018 $13 ⊘

Warramate

27 Maddens Lane, Gruyere, Vic 3770 **Region** Yarra Valley
T (03) 5964 9267 **www**.warramatewines.com.au **Open** Not
Winemaker Sarah Crowe **Est.** 1970 **Dozens** 3000 **Vyds** 6.6ha

A long-established and perfectly situated winery reaping the full benefits of its 48-year-old vines; recent plantings have increased production. All the wines are well made, the Syrah providing further proof (if even needed) of the suitability of the variety to the region. In 2011 Warramate was purchased by the partnership that owns the adjoining Yarra Yering. The Warramate brand is kept as a separate operation, and uses the existing vineyards. Exports to the UK, the US, Singapore, Hong Kong and China.

🍷🍷🍷🍷🍷 **Yarra Valley Syrah 2016** A stellar expression of Yarra syrah. Blueberry fruit, a gentle whiff of violet-scented tension, star anise, cracked pepper and a sensitive winemaking hand that has opted for real extraction and poised tannic mettle, rather than excessive reductive handling to confer tension. This is a much more rewarding option. The palate juicy; the fruit pulpy; the tannins firm, conferring a gentle scrape of authority. Screwcap. 14% alc. **Rating** 95 **To** 2023 $30 NG ✪
Yarra Valley Chardonnay 2017 Clearly in the Warramate mould across its relaxed gait, unencumbered by excessive additions and winemaking; admirable in lieu of the fruit intensity conferred by a commitment to dry growing sans irrigation. Bravo! Melon, nectarine and judicious vanillan oak communicate across a creamy core of cashew and leesy detail. Nothing wrong with this as it brims with flavour and a glimpse of mineral-clad tension, without excess of any sort. Screwcap. 13% alc. **Rating** 94 **To** 2023 $30 NG ✪

🍷🍷🍷🍷♀ **Yarra Valley Pinot Noir 2017** Rating 93 To 2022 $30 NG
Yarra Valley Cabernet 2016 Rating 92 To 2022 $30 NG

Warramunda Estate

860 Maroondah Highway, Coldstream, Vic 3770 **Region** Yarra Valley
T 0412 694 394 **www**.warramundaestate.com.au **Open** Fri 10–5, w'ends 10–6
Winemaker Ben Haines **Est.** 1998 **Dozens** 2000 **Vyds** 19.2ha

In 1975 Ted Vogt purchased the original Warramunda property, on which a cattle and sheep stud known as 'Warramunda Station' was run, then extended the property by 320 acres in '80. A large dam was built in '81, and the property now supports three vineyards and some grazing land. The Magdziarz family acquired Warramunda from the Vogt family in 2007. The Magdziarz family have built on the existing solid foundations with a deep respect for the surrounding landscape, and a vision for terroir-driven wines. Exports to China.

🍷🍷🍷🍷🍷 **Coldstream Yarra Valley Syrah 2016** From its fragrance – a heady mix of red fruits, woodsy spices and florals, to the supple, velvety tannins on the medium to fuller-bodied palate, this is equally delightful and delicious. It's not fruity, as the savoury aspect comes through clearly and everything just falls into place. Great composure. Diam. 13.5% alc. **Rating** 96 **To** 2030 $45 JF ✪
Coldstream Yarra Valley Marsanne 2017 Everything about this is finely tuned: delicate florals of lemon blossom, honeysuckle and lavender; the right amount of spice – ginger especially and lemon flavours with zest and curd. Very tight, almost linear, and while enchanting in its youth, it will reward more with bottle age. Diam. 12% alc. **Rating** 95 **To** 2032 $35 JF ✪
Coldstream Yarra Valley Marsanne 2016 A classy wine with its white blossom and ginger flower fragrance, wafts of grilled nuts and buttered toast. It's not a heavy wine at all; neatly played phenolics and texture are there, but it's graceful and fresh as a spring day. Screwcap. 12.7% alc. **Rating** 95 **To** 2030 $35 JF ✪

🍷🍷🍷🍷♀ **Coldstream Cabernet Sauvignon 2015** Rating 93 To 2026 $48 JF
Coldstream Pinot Noir 2016 Rating 92 To 2023 $45 JF
Coldstream Viognier 2017 Rating 90 To 2022 $35 JF

Warrenmang Vineyard & Resort   ★★★☆

188 Mountain Creek Road, Moonambel, Vic 3478 **Region** Pyrenees
T (03) 5467 2233 www.warrenmang.com.au **Open** 7 days 10–5
Winemaker Greg Foster **Est.** 1974 **Dozens** 10 000 **Vyds** 32.1ha
Luigi and Athalie Bazzani continue to watch over Warrenmang; a new, partially underground barrel room with earthen walls has been completed, wine quality remains high, and the accommodation for over 80 guests, plus a restaurant, underpin the business. Over the 40 years that Luigi and Athalie have been at Warrenmang, a very loyal clientele has been built up. The business was sold before going to press, but no details were available. Exports to Denmark, the Netherlands, Poland, Taiwan, Singapore, Malaysia and China.

🍷🍷🍷🍷 **Estate Chardonnay 2016** Simple but effective. Fresh pear and peach with a
gentle kiss of sweet cedar wood. Pleasant and pleasing all the way along the palate.
Screwcap. 13% alc. **Rating** 89 **To** 2022 CM

Warwick Billings   ★★★★

c/- Post Office, Lenswood, SA 5240 (postal) **Region** Adelaide Hills
T 0405 437 864 www.wowique.com.au **Open** Not
Winemaker Warwick Billings **Est.** 2009 **Dozens** 600
This is the venture of Warwick Billings and partner Rose Kemp. Warwick was a cider maker in the UK who came to study at Roseworthy, and got diverted into the wine world. He completed a postgraduate oenology degree at the University of Adelaide in 1995, and worked for Miranda Wine, Orlando and Angove Family Winemakers from 2002 to '08, along the way moonlighting in France and Spain for 12 vintages. Warwick's approach to his eponymous label is self-deprecating, beginning with the name Wowique, and saying, 'Occasionally a vineyard sings to the winemaker. [We] have taken one of these songs and put it into a bottle'. The vineyard in question is planted to an unusual clone of chardonnay and nurtured on a sloping hilltop site in Mt Torrens. Warwick's final word on all of this is, 'The winemaking is unashamedly inspired by Burgundy, but care is taken to acknowledge that the soil is different, the clones are often different, the climate is definitely different, and the end consumer is usually different'.

🍷🍷🍷🍷🍷 **Wowique Single Vineyard Lenswood Sauvignon Blanc 2017** There is an
air of confidence across this lightweighted wine; an aura of restraint. Dry. There is
no need need to shout with this sort of swagger across the midriff: pungent tones
of greengage, lemongrass and citrus peel, with no tropical release points. Herbal
and nicely coiled across a phenolic pinbone. Eminently enjoyable. Screwcap.
11.5% alc. **Rating** 93 **To** 2021 $25 NG
Wowique Single Vineyard Adelaide Hills Chardonnay 2016 A heavily
stylised, light to mid-weighted contemporary chardonnay, drawing stone fruit
flavours across a bow of mealy oatmeal, cashew and pungent mineral-meld
oak. Proportionately, this is just right. Long, crunchy and punchy. Tight, with
the flavours unravelling nicely and effortlessly, the tension sustained. Screwcap.
13.5% alc. **Rating** 92 **To** 2022 $30 NG
Wowique Lenswood Pinot Noir 2016 The tannins are a a spider web spindle;
an edgy brush across tangy red fruits and vermouth-like bitterness. The oak, a bit
too much perhaps, given the light shade to the fruit. Like the other wines in the
range, this walks a fine line between fruit and structural bristle, laden with whole
cluster clove and cardamom across the crunchy, dry finish. Screwcap. 12.5% alc.
Rating 90 **To** 2022 $35 NG

Water Wheel   ★★★★

Bridgewater-on-Loddon, Bridgewater, Vic 3516 **Region** Bendigo
T (03) 5437 3060 www.waterwheelwine.com **Open** Mon–Fri 9–5, w'ends 12–4
Winemaker Bill Trevaskis, Amy Cumming **Est.** 1972 **Dozens** 30 000 **Vyds** 136ha
Peter Cumming, with more than two decades of winemaking under his belt, has quietly
built on the reputation of Water Wheel year by year. The winery is owned by the Cumming

family, which has farmed in the Bendigo region for more than 50 years, with horticulture and viticulture the special areas of interest. Over half the vineyard area is planted to shiraz (75ha), followed by chardonnay, sauvignon blanc (15ha each), cabernet sauvignon, malbec (10ha each), and smaller plantings of petit verdot, semillon, roussanne and grenache. Water Wheel continues to make wines that over-deliver at their modest prices. Exports to the UK, the US, Canada and China.

ㅸㅸㅸㅸㅸ **Baringhup Bendigo Shiraz 2015** Dense crimson-purple; this is heaven for those looking for a full-bodied shiraz that will repay with cellaring. It ticks each and every box for that purpose, with clear-cut varietal character at the warm end of the spectrum – blackberry, licorice and pepper braced by ripe tannins. Terrific value. Screwcap. 14.5% alc. **Rating** 94 ✪

ㅸㅸㅸㅸㅸ **Bendigo Viognier 2015 Rating** 90 **To** 2019 $20 ✪

Watershed Premium Wines ★★★★★

Cnr Bussell Highway/Darch Road, Margaret River, WA 6285 **Region** Margaret River
T (08) 9758 8633 **www**.watershedwines.com.au **Open** 7 days 10–5
Winemaker Severine Logan, Conrad Tritt **Est.** 2002 **Dozens** 100 000 **Vyds** 137ha
Watershed Wines has been set up by a syndicate of investors, with no expense spared in establishing the substantial vineyard and striking cellar door, with a 200-seat cafe and restaurant. Situated towards the southern end of the Margaret River region, its neighbours include Voyager Estate and Leeuwin Estate. The vineyard development occurred in three stages (in 2001, '04 and '06), the last in Jindong, well to the north of stages one and two. The first stage of the winery was completed prior to the '03 vintage, with a capacity of 400t, increased the following year to 900t, then another expansion in '05 to 1200t. March '08 saw the crush capacity reach 1600t; wine storage facilities have increased in lockstep with crush capacity, lifted by a further 170 000 kilolitres. Exports to Germany, Indonesia, Fiji, Thailand, Papua New Guinea, Singapore, Hong Kong and China.

ㅸㅸㅸㅸㅸ **Awakening Single Block A1 Margaret River Chardonnay 2016**
The soaring intensity and precision of the wine obliterates any comment about the oak. It is one of those uncommon chardonnays that demands you give it time – the more the merrier. Grapefruit is the masthead, but it gathers around it a suite of flavours that keep its energy and drive on track. Screwcap. 13% alc.
Rating 98 **To** 2034 $47 ✪

ㅸㅸㅸㅸㅸ **Awakening Margaret River Cabernet Sauvignon 2014** Laden with gold medals, this bottle incites heady expectations! Thankfully, it doesn't disappoint. Graphite, cassis, pencil lead and bouquet garni set the aromas alight. A sinuous, mid-weighted frame. Bay leaf and black olive confer a more savoury chord. The oak serves as a conduit for the intensity of fruit, dishing up a gentle bit of roughage across the finely wrought beam of grape tannins. Will age well. Screwcap. 14% alc. **Rating** 96 **To** 2029 $90 NG
Senses Margaret River Cabernet Merlot 2015 An 81/19% blend matured in new and used French oak for 18 months. Fragrant blackcurrant/cassis aromas set the compass for a medium-bodied wine that has a delicious juicy stream of cassis and plum running down the middle of the palate with no need to even think about interference from tannins. Screwcap. 14% alc. **Rating** 94 **To** 2030 $30 ✪

ㅸㅸㅸㅸㅸ **Shades Margaret River Sauvignon Blanc Semillon 2017 Rating** 91
To 2019 $20 NG ✪
Senses Margaret River Chardonnay 2017 Rating 91 **To** 2023 $30 NG
Senses Margaret River Viognier 2011 Rating 91 **To** 2020 $30 NG
Shades Margaret River Merlot 2016 Rating 91 **To** 2024 $20 NG ✪

Waterton Hall Wines ★★★★☆

61 Waterton Hall Road, Rowella, Tas 7270 **Region** Northern Tasmania
T 0417 834 781 **www**.watertonhall.com.au **Open** By appt
Winemaker Winemaking Tasmania (Glenn James) **Est.** 2006 **Dozens** 750 **Vyds** 2.5ha
Waterton Hall has a rich history dating back to the 1850s, when the homestead that is today
the home of Waterton Hall Wines was built. Originally a private residence, it was modified
extensively in 1901 by a well-known neo-gothic architect Alexander North, and ultimately
passed into the ownership of the Catholic church from '49–'96. Together with various
outbuildings it was variously used as a school, a boys' home and a retreat. In 2002 it was
purchased by Jennifer Baird and Peter Cameron, and in '15 passed into the family ownership
of 'one architect, one farmer, one interior designer, one finance director and one labradoodle'.
Their real names are David and Susan Shannon (brother and sister), who are based in SA,
and John Carter and Belinda Evans, who are based in Sydney. Planting is underway under the
guidance of Glenn James, and this will see the current 2.5ha progressively extended to 10ha.

🍷🍷🍷🍷🍷 **Tamar Valley Shiraz 2016** Estate-grown vines planted in '99 and '13, hand-
picked, wild-fermented, matured in French oak for 12 months. Very interesting
wine; it's fragrant and juicy, yet also intense and very long on the palate, with no
hint of green/vegetal notes. It looks as if it has waltzed its way to its alcohol, and
is happy in its own skin. Impressive, and demands you to crack the screwcap here
and now. Screwcap. 14.4% alc. **Rating** 95 **To** 2029 $42

🍷🍷🍷🍷 **Tamar Valley Riesling 2016 Rating** 89 **To** 2024 $28
Tamar Valley Viognier 2016 Rating 89 **To** 2021 $39

WayWood Wines ★★★★☆

67 Kays Road, McLaren Vale, SA 5171 **Region** McLaren Vale
T (08) 8323 8468 **www**.waywoodwines.com **Open** Tues–Fri 12–4, w'ends &
public hols 11–5
Winemaker Andrew Wood **Est.** 2005 **Dozens** 1500 **Vyds** 3ha
This is the culmination of Andrew Wood and Lisa Robertson's wayward odyssey. Andrew left
his career as a sommelier in London and retrained as a winemaker, working in Portugal, the
UK, Italy and the Granite Belt (an eclectic selection), and settling in McLaren Vale in early
2004. Working with Kangarilla Road winery over the succeeding six years, all the while
making small quantities of shiraz, cabernets and tempranillo from purchased grapes, led them
to nebbiolo, montepulciano and shiraz. Lisa's business, Luscious Red, offers food at the cellar
door. Exports to Canada and China.

🍷🍷🍷🍷🍷 **McLaren Vale Cabernet Sauvignon 2015** Strong fruit, strong frame, strong
finish. This pumps out currant, earth, chocolate, dust and garden mint flavours in
serious volume, then ties them all firmly together with ropes of tannin. Balance
keeps it drinkable, even though it's young and tailor-made for the cellar. Screwcap.
14.5% alc. **Rating** 94 **To** 2035 $28 CM ❂

🍷🍷🍷🍷🍷 **McLaren Vale Shiraz 2016 Rating** 93 **To** 2031 $25 CM ❂
Quattro Vini 2015 Rating 91 **To** 2025 $25 CM

Wendouree ★★★★★

Wendouree Road, Clare, SA 5453 **Region** Clare Valley
T (08) 8842 2896 **Open** Not
Winemaker Tony Brady **Est.** 1895 **Dozens** 2000 **Vyds** 12ha
An iron fist in a velvet glove – this best describes Wendouree's extraordinary wines. They are
fashioned with commitment from the very old vineyard (shiraz, cabernet sauvignon, malbec,
mataro and muscat of alexandria), with its unique terroir, by Tony and Lita Brady, who rightly
see themselves as custodians of a priceless treasure. The 100+-year-old stone winery is virtually
unchanged from the day it was built; this is in every sense a treasure beyond price. Wendouree
has never made any comment about its wines, but the subtle shift from the lighter end of
full- bodied to the fuller end of medium-bodied seems to be a permanent one (though always

subject to the dictate of the vintage). The best news of all is that I will drink some of the Wendourees I have bought over the past 10 years before I die, and not have to rely on my few remaining bottles from the 1970s (and rather more from the '80s and '90s).

ㅇㅇㅇㅇㅇ **Shiraz 2015** This is 100% shiraz from the Central vineyard bushvines planted in 1893, and the Eastern vineyard planted in 1919. The colour isn't particularly dark, but the flavours are very, very deep, complex and positively mouthwatering. You'd have no hope of understanding this wine without repeated visits to the glass. Texture, flavour and structure intermingle on the palate; purple and black fruits are but part of the story of a great vintage with magnificent longevity. Screwcap. 14.3% alc. **Rating** 98 **To** 2050

Shiraz Mataro 2015 An 80/20% blend from 1893 (Central vineyard), 1919 (Eastern), and 1920 (Eastern) bushvines. Purely in terms of weight, and not flavour, this has a lighter body than the Shiraz or Cabernet Malbec. The youngest vines were 95yo at the time of vintage, and all the vines producing any grapes incorporated in Wendouree's wines are in prime condition for such ancient vines. There's a silky patina on entry into the mouth, then there is a relentless build-up of purple and black fruits, and the rippling muscle of tannins. Great wine from a great vintage. Screwcap. 14.2% alc. **Rating** 97 **To** 2043

ㅇㅇㅇㅇㅇ **Cabernet Malbec 2015** Cabernet sauvignon, malbec and shiraz from 1919 and '75 plantings on the Eastern and Central vineyards. A nigh-on perfect vintage for this blend, particularly the two headline components, the shiraz falling into line without even a hint of displeasure. The result is a medium-bodied wine, with cassis and red berries offset by some blackberry building complexity and complementing the cabernet tannins. Screwcap. 14% alc. **Rating** 95 **To** 2045

West Cape Howe Wines ★★★★★

Lot 14923 Muir Highway, Mount Barker, WA 6324 **Region** Mount Barker
T (08) 9892 1444 **www**.westcapehowewines.com.au **Open** 7 days (various hours)
Winemaker Gavin Berry, Andrew Vasey, Caitlin Gazey **Est.** 1997 **Dozens** 60 000
Vyds 310ha

West Cape Howe is owned by a partnership between four West Australian families, including winemaker/managing partner Gavin Berry and viticulturist/partner Rob Quenby. Grapes are sourced from estate vineyards in the Mount Barker and Frankland River regions. The Langton vineyard (Mount Barker) has 100ha planted to cabernet sauvignon, shiraz, ricsling, sauvignon blanc, chardonnay and semillon, and the Russell Road vineyard (Frankland River) has 210ha planted. West Cape Howe also sources select parcels of fruit from valued contract growers. West Cape Howe was named Best Value Winery in *Wine Companion* 2016. Exports to the UK, the US, Denmark, Switzerland, South Korea, Singapore, Japan, Hong Kong and China.

ㅇㅇㅇㅇㅇ **King Billy Mount Barker Cabernet Sauvignon 2013** Bottled in Oct '14 but not released until May '18. The softness of its texture and general cuddliness of the fruit help disguise the stern face of the finish; this wine is beautifully equipped for the future. It's floral, dusty, ripped with succulent red and black currants, and it's ever so slightly minty. Every sip reveals powerful positives. One for the long haul. Screwcap. **Rating** 96 **To** 2042 CM

King Billy Mount Barker Cabernet Sauvignon 2012 Only four barriques made of this flag-bearer for West Cape Howe. The colour shows little sign of development, setting the scene for a cabernet made from old vines, and stamps its personality on the bouquet and full-bodied palate alike. Classic is a word debased by excessive use (I'm sure I offend), but is the most appropriate for this classy wine. Blackcurrant, graphite, bay leaf (fresh or dried) and carefully manicured tannins all surge through to the long finish. Screwcap. 14.5% alc. **Rating** 96 **To** 2042 $50 ❂

Two Steps Mount Barker Shiraz 2015 From the pick of the crop of West Cape Howe's most mature vineyards in Mount Barker. This has class written all over it; blackberry, black cherry and pepper aromas and flavours first up, then incisive cedary tannins on the finish and aftertaste. Right now it needs either protein or further time in bottle, but have no fear about its long-term future. Screwcap. 14.5% alc. **Rating** 95 **To** 2035 $28 **☺**

Book Ends Mount Barker Cabernet Sauvignon 2015 A selection of the best parcels of grapes from West Cape Howe's oldest vineyards in Mount Barker, matured for 18 months in French oak. The bright colour and purity of the fruit on the bouquet set the antennae waving, the palate cast in the same mould, with purity its middle name. Red and black currant fruits provide the full menu for first class entertainment. Screwcap. 14.5% alc. **Rating** 95 **To** 2030 $28 **☺**

Hannah's Hill Mount Barker Frankland River Cabernet Malbec 2016 From estate vineyards in Mount Barker and Frankland River. Bright, clear crimson hue; achieves the impossible result of elegance and finesse in the midst of luxuriant cabernet's cassis and malbec's plum jam. The undeniably silky tannins manipulated by an unseen puppet master create the magic. Screwcap. 14% alc. **Rating** 95 **To** 2031 $20 **☺**

Styx Gully Mount Barker Chardonnay 2016 Largely from West Cape Howe's Langton vineyard. A complex bouquet is followed by a complex, barrel-ferment palate; it has scads of tree-ripened peach and nectarine fruit, acid that accommodates and braces the generosity of the fruit, and a positive role for oak. Screwcap. 13% alc. **Rating** 94 **To** 2026 $28 **☺**

Tempranillo Rose 2017 Clear, vivid crimson; has the detail, freshness, balance and length missing from the lesser wines from '17. It has controlled drive and power, with sparkling acidity cleansing and lengthening the finish. High quality rose at the right price raring to go. Screwcap. 13% alc. **Rating** 94 **To** 2019 $17 **☺**

Frankland River Shiraz 2016 Matured in new and used French oak – not much at this price, and no more needed. It has bright, fresh flavours of plum, black cherry and blackberry, with a liberal sprinkle of black pepper and spice, tannins a feature of a wine worth twice the price. Screwcap. 14.5% alc. **Rating** 94 **To** 2036 $20 **☺**

♥♥♥♥♀ **Mount Barker Riesling 2017 Rating** 92 **To** 2026 $22 CM **☺**
Mount Barker Pinot Noir 2016 Rating 92 **To** 2023 CM
Cabernet Merlot 2016 Rating 92 **To** 2025 $17 CM **☺**
Semillon Sauvignon Blanc 2017 Rating 91 **To** 2021 $17 **☺**
Frankland River Perth Hills Tempranillo 2016 Rating 91 **To** 2026 $20 **☺**
Mount Barker Sauvignon Blanc 2017 Rating 90 **To** 2018 $20 **☺**
Chardonnay 2017 Rating 90 **To** 2020 $17 CM **☺**
Old School Mount Barker Frankland Chardonnay 2017 Rating 90 **To** 2020 $20 CM **☺**

Westlake Vineyards   ★★★★☆

Diagonal Road, Ebenezer, SA 5355 **Region** Barossa Valley
T 0428 656 208 **www.**westlakevineyards.com.au **Open** By appt
Winemaker Darren Westlake **Est.** 1999 **Dozens** 500 **Vyds** 36.2ha

Darren and Suzanne Westlake tend 22ha of shiraz, 6.5ha of cabernet sauvignon, 2ha of viognier, and smaller plantings of petit verdot, durif, mataro, grenache and graciano planted on two properties in the Koonunga area of the Barossa Valley. They do all the vineyard work themselves, and have a long list of high profile winemakers queued up to buy the grapes, leaving only a small amount for production under the Westlake label. Suzanne is a sixth-generation descendant of Johann Georg Kalleske, who came to SA from Prussia in 1838; the 717 Convicts label draws on the history of Darren's ancestor Edward Westlake, who was transported to Australia in 1788.

♥♥♥♥♥ **Albert's Block Barossa Valley Shiraz 2016** Limited production (50 dozen) yet generous in flavour; this oozes blueberry, mulberry and molten raspberry liqueur notes slung across a gauze of toasty oak vanillans. The intensity is admirable, the vinosity, compelling. While the pulpy tannins are – as with the wines across the range – juicy and addictive, this is a strutter of a wine; a behemoth pushing the envelope. It works. Screwcap. 15% alc. **Rating** 94 **To** 2031 $25 NG **☺**

The Caretaker Barossa Valley Shiraz 2013 From select parcels of older vines, with fruit gently and minimally intervened with, as is de rigueur at this address. Whole berries, plunged in open-top fermenters; a lashing of pressings to bolster the tannins before 18 months in French wood. Pulpy purple fruits tee off, beamed along violet scents reverberating from nose to palate. Seductive tannins yet again, once the olfactories acclimatise to the oak. Anise and five-spice linger. The alcohol is testy, but far from obtuse. Cork. 15% alc. **Rating** 94 **To** 2035 $80 NG

🍷🍷🍷🍷 **717 Convicts The Felon Barossa Valley Shiraz 2016 Rating** 92 **To** 2022 $20 NG ✪
717 Convicts The Warden Barossa Valley Shiraz 2016 Rating 92 **To** 2024 $30 NG

Whicher Ridge

200 Chapman Hill East Road, Busselton, WA 6280 **Region** Geographe
T (08) 9753 1394 **www.**whicherridge.com.au **Open** Thurs–Mon 10–5
Winemaker Cathy Howard **Est.** 2004 **Dozens** 1500 **Vyds** 5ha
It is hard to imagine a founding husband-and-wife team with such an ideal blend of viticultural and winemaking experience accumulated over a combined 40+ years. Cathy Howard (née Spratt) was a winemaker for 16 years at Orlando and St Hallett in the Barossa Valley, and at Watershed Wines in the Margaret River. She not only has her own winemaking consulting business covering the southwest regions of WA, but also makes the Whicher Ridge wines. Neil's career as a viticulturist began in the Pyrenees region with Taltarni vineyards and Blue Pyrenees Estate; then he moved to Mount Avoca as vineyard manager for 12 years. When he moved to the west, he managed the Sandalford vineyard in Margaret River for several years, then developed and managed a number of smaller vineyards throughout the region. Whicher Ridge's Odyssey Creek vineyard at Chapman Hill has sauvignon blanc, cabernet sauvignon and viognier planted. The Howards have chosen the Frankland River subregion of the Great Southern to supply shiraz and riesling, and they also buy grapes from the Margaret River.

🍷🍷🍷🍷🍷 **Long Road Frankland River Shiraz 2014** Machine-harvested, 4.5 hours to the winery, crushed, open-fermented with cultured yeasts, various cap management techniques, matured in 90% French oak, 10% American oak (15% new), with 3–4% younger Frankland Shiraz blended in. The convoluted fermentation process (and thereafter maturation) is married to high quality shiraz; Frankland River deserves recognition as one of the best shiraz regions in Australia. The colour is deep and youthful, the bouquet and intense, medium to full-bodied palate going down the same path. Screwcap. 13.8% alc. **Rating** 96 **To** 2044 $34 ✪
The Jetty Geographe Shiraz 2016 Standard Whicher Ridge (read: complicated) shiraz vinification, matured in tank on French oak boards for 9 months. The bright crimson-purple hue announces a totally delicious medium-bodied wine made from high quality grapes and vinified with considerable attention to detail. The flavours come from a Catherine wheel of red, purple and black fruits, with bursts of pepper and spice. Juicy acidity then flows to bring peace and order to a wine that is a steal at this price. Screwcap. 13.5% alc. **Rating** 95 **To** 2031 $21 ✪
Elevation Geographe Cabernet Sauvignon 2014 Named Elevation due to its (relatively) higher vineyard site, and its status as Whicher Ridge's flagship wine. Similar vinification to shirazs, open-fermented, complex cap management, matured for 2 years in French barriques (25% new). Excellent colour, still holding the purple-crimson of youth; an elegant cabernet with distinct cool-climate characteristics from its continental climate. It is fresh, positively lively, the cassis with dried herb notes alongside the cedar of the French oak. Will be long-lived. Screwcap. 13.8% alc. **Rating** 95 **To** 2049 $40
Mademoiselle V Geographe Viognier 2016 Hand-picked, destemmed, crushed, 3–4 hours skin contact, basket-pressed, wild fermentation initiated in tank and completed in used French oak with cultured yeast, matured on lees for 12 months. This is a very good viognier. It has juicy peach and apricot fruit kept

fresh and lively by gentle citrus nuances to its crisp acidity. Screwcap. 13.7% alc. **Rating** 94 To 2020 $32

🍷🍷🍷🍷🍷 **Henry Road Margaret River Chardonnay 2016** Rating 93 To 2025 $34
Elevage Geographe Sauvignon Blanc 2016 Rating 92 To 2020 $28
The Jetty Geographe Sauvignon Blanc Semillon 2017 Rating 90 To 2020
$20 ⚫

Whimwood Estate Wines   ★★★★

PO Box 250, Nannup, WA 6275 **Region** Blackwood Valley
T 0417 003 235 **www**.whimwoodestatewines.com.au **Open** Not
Winemaker Bernie Stanlake **Est.** 2011 **Dozens** 700 **Vyds** 1.2ha
Maree Tinker and Steve Johnstone say they fell in love with the property at first sight in 2011, without even knowing that it had a vineyard. The name draws on the region's past timber milling history, where horse-drawn whims were used for hauling logs. The vineyard had been planted in 2004 to chardonnay, with an agreement in place for the purchase of the grapes by a local winemaker. The grape shortage of '04 had turned into a grape surplus by '11, and it was left to Maree and Steve to remove 6000 of the 8000 chardonnay vines, and increase the handful of shiraz vines originally planted by grafting onto chardonnay rootstock. They now have 0.7ha of chardonnay and 0.5ha of shiraz. Exports to the UK and Sweden.

🍷🍷🍷🍷🍷 **Blanc de Blanc 2016** Cream and lees characters add softness and variation to the inherent peachiness of the fruit. Tart, lemony acidity helps keep the lines taut. It's young and fresh, but there's much to admire here. Diam. 10.4% alc. **Rating** 91 $30 CM

Whispering Brook   ★★★★★

Rodd Street, Broke, NSW 2330 **Region** Hunter Valley
T (02) 6579 1386 **www**.whispering-brook.com **Open** W'ends 11–5, Fri by appt
Winemaker Susan Frazier, Adam Bell **Est.** 2000 **Dozens** 2000 **Vyds** 3ha
It took some time for partners Susan Frazier and Adam Bell to find the property on which they established their vineyard 15 years ago. It has a combination of terra rossa loam soils on which the reds are planted, and sandy flats for the white grapes. The partners have also established an olive grove and accommodation for 10–18 guests in the large house set in the vineyard and offer vineyard and winery tours. Exports to Canada and Japan.

🍷🍷🍷🍷🍷 **Single Vineyard Hunter Valley Semillon 2017** Feather-light, yet more ample and textural than the regional norm, notes of citrus peel, dried straw and flint all beam along a laser of crunchy acidity and tangy minerality. Hewn of dry-grown fruit from centurion vines, there is impressive pump and depth to this as it expands across the palate. Screwcap. 12% alc. **Rating** 96 To 2032 $28 NG ⚫
Museum Release Basket Pressed Hunter Valley Shiraz 2011 Hand-picked, given a cold soak before a relatively cool fermentation and a gentle extraction regime, then to barrel for 14 months. This engaging, mid-weighted wine exhibits a whiff of aged complexity while holding plenty more cards up its sleeve. Bitter chocolate and coffee grind tannins unravel notes of hoisin sauce, anise and old leather, mingling with the primary dark fruit tones still clinging to their youth. Diam. 14% alc. **Rating** 95 To 2030 $70 NG
Single Vineyard Hunter Valley Shiraz 2016 This new school of fresher, gulpable Hunter shiraz is on full display across reductive floral scents, deli meats and dark plum flavours, all polished by some smart oak; the wine glimpses the region's past across a swathe of savoury, dusty tannins and a whiff of varnish. Screwcap. 14.6% alc. **Rating** 94 To 2036 $30 NG ⚫

Whispering Hills

580 Warburton Highway, Seville, Vic 3139 **Region** Yarra Valley
T (03) 5964 2822 **www**.whisperinghills.com.au **Open** 7 days 10–6
Winemaker Murray Lyons, Darcy Lyons **Est.** 1985 **Dozens** 800 **Vyds** 5ha
Whispering Hills is owned and operated by the Lyons family (Murray, Audrey and Darcy). Murray and Darcy are responsible for the winemaking, while Audrey takes care of the cellar door and distribution. The vineyard was established in 1985 with further plantings in '96 and some grafting in 2003, and now consists of cabernet sauvignon (2ha), riesling, chardonnay and pinot noir (1ha each). Exports to Sweden and Japan.

Quartz Block Bendigo Shiraz 2015 From 22yo vines, crushed, destemmed, wild yeast–open fermented, 3 weeks on skins, matured in a French and American hogshead (25% new). A powerhouse shiraz reflecting its single vineyard/single block heritage, and the vinification, in particular the 3 weeks on skins. This is absolutely full-bodied, the only thing we don't know is how long it spent in oak. It is balanced despite its build, and simply asks for time – lots of it. Screwcap. 14% alc. **Rating** 91 **To** 2031

Seville Yarra Valley Cabernet Sauvignon 2016 **Rating** 89 **To** 2024

Whistler Wines

Seppeltsfield Road, Marananga, SA 5355 **Region** Barossa Valley
T (08) 8562 4942 **www**.whistlerwines.com **Open** 7 days 10.30–5
Winemaker Josh Pfeiffer **Est.** 1999 **Dozens** 6500 **Vyds** 14.2ha
Whistler was established in 1999 by brothers Martin and Chris Pfeiffer, but has recently undergone a major change for the better, thanks to the next generation. With Josh Pfeiffer at the helm since 2013, the estate vineyards have been converted to organic and biodynamic practices, and the wines have all gone through a facelift in both labelling and wine style. The wines now being produced are designed to be fun and easy to drink, with a drink-now approach to a lot of them. Josh has maintained the Estate Range of wines, being the more traditional straight varietals that are made in a cellar-worthy style. Exports to the UK, Denmark, Mauritius, Singapore, Hong Kong and China.

Stacks On Barossa Valley GSM 2017 A blend of 34% 16yo grenache vines, 34% 20yo shiraz and 32% 30yo bushvine mataro; wild yeast–open fermented with 17% whole bunches, 12 days on skins, matured for 6 months in used French oak; the grenache in puncheons, the shiraz in hogsheads and the mataro in barriques. It is extraordinary how the fruit flavours are ripe with such a low alcohol for this blend; this meets McLaren Vale on equal terms. Totally delicious wine. Screwcap. 12.5% alc. **Rating** 95 **To** 2023 $35 ✪
Shiver Down My Spine Barossa Valley Shiraz 2016 From vines 20–23yo, various clones; 80% Selectiv'-harvested, 20% hand-picked by mailing list customers; wild-fermented with 20% whole bunches in old open concrete fermenters, matured in used French oak for 16 months before blending. You have to grin at Josh Pfeiffer's cunning – he ends up with a seriously good wine, club members delighted to give their labour free in providing the 20% whole bunch component, and then have the opportunity to buy the succulent and rich wine. Screwcap. 14% alc. **Rating** 94 **To** 2036 $35
Get in my Belly Barossa Valley Grenache 2017 Single vineyard, mostly destemmed (7% whole bunches), wild yeast–open fermented, 15 days on skins, matured for 6 months in used French puncheons. Light, bright crimson; the vinification has captured all the varietal fruit with a slinky approach that has worked very well, with no cosmetic notes. Screwcap. 12.5% alc. **Rating** 94 **To** 2025 $35

Dry as a Bone Barossa Valley Rose 2017 **Rating** 90 **To** 2019 $25

Whitlocks Vineyard ★★★★

PO Box 467, Maldon, Vic 3463 **Region** Bendigo
T 0439 031 075 **www**.whitlocksvineyard.com.au **Open** Not
Winemaker Cameron Leith **Est.** 2012 **Dozens** 240 **Vyds** 1ha
Emily Girdwood and partner Simon Smith moved from Melbourne to the country in 2011
so that their children could enjoy the freedom, space and safety of country life. The property
they purchased overlooks Lake Cairn Curran, and to the east out to Mt Tarrengower. Historic
Maldon is the closest town. It just so happened the property had a 1ha vineyard of largely
20yo shiraz, and they cleverly gained the services of Cameron Leith to make the wines. Emily
and Simon are in charge of the vineyard, although at times vineyards are in charge of their
carers. Good luck!

🍷🍷🍷🍷🍷 **Smiths Paddock Shiraz 2015** Hand-picked from 20+yo vines, matured for
10 months in French oak. The wine rises above the drought conditions; the grapes
were picked at the right time. Concentrated and focused, with mouthwatering
fresh red and black fruits dotted with spice and pepper, fine tannins on the finish
sealing the deal. Screwcap. 13.9% alc. **Rating** 94 **To** 2030 $30 ✪

Wicks Estate Wines ★★★★★

21 Franklin Street, Adelaide, SA 5000 (postal) **Region** Adelaide Hills
T (08) 8212 0004 **www**.wicksestate.com.au **Open** Not
Winemaker Leigh Ratzmer **Est.** 2000 **Dozens** 20 000 **Vyds** 53.96ha
Tim and Simon Wicks had a long-term involvement with orchard and nursery operations at
Highbury in the Adelaide Hills prior to purchasing their property at Woodside in 1999. They
planted sauvignon blanc, shiraz, chardonnay, pinot noir, cabernet sauvignon, tempranillo and
riesling. Wicks Estate has won more than its fair share of wine show medals over the years,
the wines priced well below their full worth. Exports to the US, Singapore, Hong Kong
and China.

🍷🍷🍷🍷🍷 **Eminence Adelaide Hills Shiraz 2015** The outcome of a grand plan to
make the absolute best shiraz from the estate, where cost is no consideration.
The best ferments (batches 5 and 8) selected, matured for 2 months in French
oak (50% new). Its intensity is almost shocking. I'm not sure I understand the
choice of bottle shape, but I'm sure that they were expensive. Screwcap. 14.5% alc.
Rating 97 **To** 2035 $100 ✪

🍷🍷🍷🍷🍷 **C.J. Wicks Adelaide Hills Shiraz 2015** From 17yo vines, multiple clones
open-fermented separately, 20 days on skins, matured for 20 months in French
oak (60% new). Deep crimson-purple; a stunningly rich, layered and complex
wine; a conga line of aromas, flavours, French oak and ripe tannins. All in all,
absurdly cheap at $45, particularly if you want to lay down the odd dozen or so
for an offspring having a big birthday in '30, '35 or '40. Better buy several cases.
Screwcap. 14.5% alc. **Rating** 96 **To** 2040 $45 ✪
C.J. Wicks Adelaide Hills Cabernet Sauvignon 2015 From 16yo vines,
Selectiv'-harvested, 75% crushed/destemmed, 25% whole berries open-fermented,
22 days on skins matured for 20 months in French oak (75% new). An extremely
rich and intense cabernet, all the components of fruit, oak and tannins
reflecting the individual block choice, the quality of the French oak, and tannins
from the vineyard and winery. The oak has been entirely absorbed, the power of
the fruit there for all to see. Screwcap. 14.5% alc. **Rating** 95 **To** 2035 $45
Adelaide Hills Shiraz 2016 Multiple clones open-fermented separately,
14–17 days on skins, matured for 12 months in French oak (20% new). Deep,
bright crimson-purple; the Adelaide Hills has nothing to prove about the
suitability of most districts to produce elegant, medium-bodied shirazs that
welcome French oak, but can live without it. Spice, pepper and licorice all play
hide and seek within the lithe frame of the wine. This really is a wonderful drink
at its price. Screwcap. 14.5% alc. **Rating** 94 **To** 2031 $25 ✪

ρρρρ♀ Adelaide Hills Sauvignon Blanc 2017 Rating 93 To 2018 $20 CM ✪
Adelaide Hills Chardonnay 2017 Rating 93 To 2023 $25 ✪
Adelaide Hills Riesling 2017 Rating 92 To 2023 $20 ✪
Adelaide Hills Cabernet Sauvignon 2016 Rating 92 To 2031 $25 ✪
Adelaide Hills Pinot Rose 2017 Rating 90 To 2021 $20 ✪
Adelaide Hills Pinot Noir 2017 Rating 90 To 2023 $25
Pamela Adelaide Hills Chardonnay Pinot Noir 2013 Rating 90 $30

Willem Kurt Wines ★★★★★

Croom Lane, Beechworth, Vic 3747 (postal) **Region** Beechworth
T 0428 400 522 **www**.willemkurtwines.com.au **Open** Not
Winemaker Daniel Balzer **Est.** 2014 **Dozens** 500 **Vyds** 1.2ha
This is the venture of Daniel Balzer and Marije van Epenhuijsen, he with a German background, she Dutch. The name of the winery is drawn from the middle names of their two children: Willem (Dutch) and Kurt (German), in each instance reflecting long usage in the two families. Daniel moved into the wine industry in 1998, working first at Yarra Ridge (including a vintage in Germany) before joining Gapsted Wines in 2003. He then completed his Bachelor of Wine Science at CSU the following year. Seven years were given over to contract winemaking for smaller producers, and it was inevitable that sooner or later Daniel and Marjie would start making wine for their own brand. They currently lease a vineyard in Beechworth, and buy select parcels of fruit. Beechworth is the region they know and love best, and began planting their own vineyard in 2017 with 0.6ha of chardonnay, and 0.6ha of shiraz following in '18. The quality of the wines made to date suggests it should succeed.

ρρρρρ Chardonnay 2016 Powerful chardonnay. Weighty, fruit-rich, splashed with oak, and persistent. It's fresh and buoyant, but there's no mistaking its amplitude. This would stand tall alongside wines at twice or thrice the price. Screwcap. 13.2% alc. **Rating** 95 To 2023 $34 CM ✪
Shiraz 2015 As much elegance as power but the real quality markers are in its length and overall complexity. The Willem Kurt wares have found an extra gear it would seem. Black pepper, complex spice, boysenberry and black cherry, a nutty/chocolatey/smoky oak-derived overlay sitting neatly with the fruit. Top-notch shiraz in anyone's language. Screwcap. 14% alc. **Rating** 95 To 2029 $36 CM

ρρρρ♀ Alpine Valleys Shiraz 2015 Rating 93 To 2029 $32
Alpine Valleys Vermentino 2017 Rating 92 To 2022 $26

Willoughby Park ★★★★★

678 South Coast Highway, Denmark, WA 6333 **Region** Great Southern
T (08) 9848 1555 **www**.willoughbypark.com.au **Open** 7 days 10–5
Winemaker Michael Ng **Est.** 2010 **Dozens** 13 000 **Vyds** 19ha
Bob Fowler, who comes from a rural background and had always hankered for a farming life, stumbled across the opportunity to achieve this in early 2010. Together with wife Marilyn, they purchased the former West Cape Howe winery and surrounding vineyard that became available when West Cape Howe moved into the far larger Goundrey winery. In '11 Willoughby Park purchased the Kalgan River vineyard and business name, and winemaking operations transferred to Willoughby Park. There are now three labels: Kalgan River single vineyard range (Kalgan River Ironrock from single sites within the Kalgan River vineyard); Willoughby Park, the Great Southern brand for estate-grown and purchased grapes; and Jamie & Charli, a sub-$20 Great Southern range of wines. Exports to China.

ρρρρρ Ironrock Kalgan River Albany Shiraz 2015 This is mid to full-weighted: highly aromatic shiraz toys with the reductive card for tension without playing its hand too heavily, leaving on full display a full deck of blue pulpy fruits flecked with violet scents, iodine and shiraz's peppery DNA. Juicy, well-appropriated tannin handling. Easy to drink due to its inherent poise and sensible winemaking. Right on the money! Screwcap. 14.5% alc. **Rating** 96 To 2024 $55 NG ✪

Ironrock Kalgan River Albany Riesling 2017 This is good. Very! Hewn of fruit from a premium, single vineyard, this juicy effort ascribes to welcome trends of less angular acidity and more free-flowing flavour. Grapefruit pulp, spa salts, fennel and talcy mineral draw the saliva and induce a grasp for the next glass across a long, dry finish. Screwcap. 12.5% alc. **Rating** 95 **To** 2027 $35 NG ☻

Ironrock Kalgan River Albany Cabernet Sauvignon 2015 Clearly, there is ambition asunder here. Piercing aromas of red and black currants are flecked with mint, strewn herb and oak vanillans. The sheer soprano pitch of the nose is reflective of Chilean cabernet. Sappy length soused with bouquet garni notes. Screwcap. 14.5% alc. **Rating** 95 **To** 2023 $55 NG

Kalgan River Albany Cabernet Sauvignon 2015 A classic cool climate cabernet, laden with black olive, strewn herb, currant and anise. Dutifully ripe, expansive and growing plusher and sweeter with each sip, the streamlined pencil lead tannins and sensitive oak do their job, buffering the flow of fruit while directing it across the palate and into a bright future ahead. Screwcap. 14.2% alc. **Rating** 94 **To** 2027 $30 NG ☻

☲☲☲☲☱ **Kalgan River Albany Riesling 2017** **Rating** 93 **To** 2025 $27 NG ☻
Kalgan River Albany Chardonnay 2017 **Rating** 92 **To** 2025 $30 NG
Kalgan River Albany Pinot Noir 2017 **Rating** 91 **To** 2023 $30 NG

Willow Bridge Estate   ★★★★★

178 Gardin Court Drive, Dardanup, WA 6236 **Region** Geographe
T (08) 9728 0055 **www.**willowbridge.com.au **Open** 7 days 11–5
Winemaker Kim Horton **Est.** 1997 **Dozens** 25 000 **Vyds** 59ha
Jeff and Vicky Dewar have followed a fast track in developing Willow Bridge Estate since acquiring the spectacular 180ha hillside property in the Ferguson Valley. Chardonnay, semillon, sauvignon blanc, shiraz and cabernet sauvignon were planted, with merlot, tempranillo, chenin blanc and viognier following. Many of its wines offer exceptional value for money. On 22 March 2015, Willow Bridge's 44-year-old senior winemaker, Simon Burnell, died in a windsurfing accident off the coast of Margaret River. Kim Horton, with extensive experience in WA, most recently as senior winemaker at Ferngrove, was appointed to take Simon's place. Exports to the UK, China and other major markets.

☲☲☲☲☲ **Black Dog Geographe Shiraz 2013** The colour is still deep and fresh; a very good shiraz, with high quality estate-grown grapes: the vinification steps are all well-conceived and -executed. The fruits cover plum, blackberry and red cherry, all with a juicy disposition. Impressive wine. Screwcap. 13.4% alc. **Rating** 96 **To** 2033 $65 ☻

Solana Geographe Tempranillo 2015 Excellent colour; the signature dark cherry fruit doesn't blink, the tannins totally in tune and balanced, the finish fresh. Screwcap. 13.9% alc. **Rating** 95 **To** 2030 $28 ☻

Dragonfly Geographe Sauvignon Blanc Semillon 2017 A portion was barrel-fermented to add texture and structure to the richly endowed palate, with its array of ripe tropical fruits of guava, ripe pineapple and passionfruit, Meyer lemon juice providing a counterpoint. Screwcap. 12.3% alc. **Rating** 94 **To** 2018 $20 ☻

Dragonfly Geographe Shiraz 2016 You'd have to travel a long way to find a better turned out red at this price level. It's so well balanced, fruited and polished; it draws you in immediately and holds your interest throughout. This should go straight onto your shopping list. It offers a juicy flush of berried flavour, perhaps some graphite, a touch of anise and then into peppercorn. But dissecting the flavours isn't necessary here. It tastes good, it's expertly shaped, and it impresses without tipping into try-hard territory. Screwcap. 13.9% alc. **Rating** 94 **To** 2026 $20 CM ☻

Dragonfly Geographe Cabernet Sauvignon Merlot 2016 Composure is key. This delivers mid-weighted, curranty fruit flavour in unruffled fashion, its dry spice and clove-like notes allowed to trill harmoniously about the edges. Its tannin is ripe, fine and integrated; its mix of sweet fruit and savoury/earthen/spice characters tuned just so. This is 'take a bow' territory for the wine team behind this label; it's 'buy a case' territory for the rest of us. Screwcap. 13.8% alc. **Rating** 94 To 2028 $20 CM ○

🍷🍷🍷🍷🍷 **Dragonfly Geographe Chardonnay 2017** Rating 93 To 2020 $20 ○
Rosa de Solana Geographe Tempranillo Rose 2017 Rating 92
To 2018 $25 ○

Willow Creek Vineyard ★★★★★

166 Balnarring Road, Merricks North, Vic 3926 **Region** Mornington Peninsula
T (03) 5931 2502 **www.**rarehare.com.au **Open** 7 days 11–5
Winemaker Geraldine McFaul **Est.** 1989 **Dozens** 4000 **Vyds** 11ha
Significant changes have transformed Willow Creek over the past decade. In 2008, winemaker Geraldine McFaul, with many years of winemaking in the Mornington Peninsula under her belt, was appointed, and worked with viticulturist Robbie O'Leary to focus on minimal intervention in the winery – in other words, to produce grapes in perfect condition. In '13 the Li family arrived from China and expanded its portfolio of hotel and resort properties in Australia by purchasing Willow Creek, and developing the luxury 46-room Jackalope Hotel, the Rare Hare and Doot Doot Doot restaurants, as well as a cocktail bar and tasting room.

🍷🍷🍷🍷🍷 **Mornington Peninsula Chardonnay 2016** This is a pretty snappy chardonnay, pulsating with life, yet never getting in your face, happy to let you come to your own conclusion. It's hard to split the flavours; the individual components allow space for each other in the most harmonious way, and all from the very centre of the chardonnay hymn book. Screwcap. 13% alc. **Rating** 95 To 2028 $45
Rare Hare Mornington Peninsula Rose 2017 A 60/40% blend of pinot noir and cabernet sauvignon, made with attention to detail, and a strategic plan that has delivered the goods. It is juicy, vibrant and spicy on entrance to the mouth, gaining power and traction from the rose petal/red berry fruits and an intriguing citrus edge to the finish. Screwcap. 13% alc. **Rating** 95 To 2020 $30 ○
Mornington Peninsula Pinot Gris 2017 Very pale pink; the complex, spicy bouquet aromas flow sweetly into the delicious palate ('sweetly' a figure of speech). Lychee, pear, strawberry and spice intermingle, a twist of acidity keeping the finish focused on its job. Great stuff. Screwcap. 13.5% alc. **Rating** 94 To 2022 $35
Mornington Peninsula Pinot Noir 2016 Bright crimson-purple; fragrant and flowery aromas, with a soupçon of spice, are the signposts for a bright, lively and long palate that opens with bright red cherry/berry fruits, then veers towards a more savoury palate with a breezy finish. Screwcap. 13.5% alc. **Rating** 94 To 2026 $45
Mornington Peninsula Brut 2013 This is 100% pinot noir D5V12, 4 years on lees, 3g/l dosage. The low dosage was doubtless inspired by the time on lees, and is right on the money. An oddity is the relative absence of mousse in the glass even when swirled, yet it is very active in the mouth. The flavours are a mix of small berries and dominant citrus, the length and balance very good. Diam. 12.8% alc. **Rating** 94 $50

🍷🍷🍷🍷🍷 **Rare Hare Shiraz Grenache 2016** Rating 93 To 2031 $30
Rare Hare Sparkling NV Rating 90 $35

Willunga 100 Wines ★★★★☆

PO Box 2427, McLaren Vale, SA 5171 **Region** McLaren Vale
T 0414 419 957 **www.**willunga100.com **Open** Not
Winemaker Tim James, Mike Farmilo **Est.** 2005 **Dozens** 10 000
Willunga 100 is solely owned by Liberty Wines (UK), sourcing its grapes from McLaren Vale and Adelaide Hills (pinot gris and a portion of its viognier). The winemaking team these days is decidedly high powered, with the hugely experienced Tim James and Mike Farmilo the conductors of the band. The focus is on the diverse districts within McLaren Vale and dry-grown bushvine grenache. Exports to the UK, Canada, Singapore, Hong Kong and NZ.

¶¶¶¶¶ **The Hundred McLaren Vale Grenache 2016** Pale-mid ruby; ridiculously aromatic verging on pretty, with raspberries and wild strawberries mingling with violets, lavender, basil and red licorice. On a lighter frame, but certainly not wimpy; the pomegranate-like acidity, as cutting as a scythe, makes its way through, stopping just for the fine, sandy tannins to make their mark. Very pure. Screwcap. 14.5% alc. **Rating** 95 **To** 2024 $35 JF ✪

¶¶¶¶¶ **McLaren Vale Shiraz Viognier 2016 Rating** 93 **To** 2028 $25 JF ✪
McLaren Vale Shiraz Grenache 2016 Rating 93 **To** 2028 $25 JF ✪
The Tithing Grenache 2016 Rating 93 **To** 2028 $45 JF
McLaren Vale Grenache Rose 2017 Rating 92 **To** 2019 $18 JF ✪

Wilson Vineyard ★★★★★
Polish Hill River, Sevenhill via Clare, SA 5453 **Region** Clare Valley
T (08) 8822 4050 **www**.wilsonvineyard.com.au **Open** W'ends 10–4
Winemaker Daniel Wilson **Est.** 1974 **Dozens** 3000 **Vyds** 11.9ha
In 2009 the winery and general operations were passed on to son Daniel Wilson, the second generation. Daniel, a graduate of CSU, spent three years in the Barossa with some of Australia's largest winemakers before returning to the Clare Valley in '03. Parents John and Pat Wilson still contribute, but in a limited way, content to watch developments in the business they created. Daniel continues to follow John's beliefs about keeping quality high, often at the expense of volume, and rather than talk about it, believes the proof is in the bottle.

¶¶¶¶¶ **Polish Hill River Riesling 2017** A wine of exceptional intensity, purity and length that counterintuitively hides its power in a velvet glove. Its citrus is unsweetened lemon, acidity riding shotgun on the long finish. A great riesling from a great vintage. Screwcap. 12.5% alc. **Rating** 96 **To** 2040 $29 ✪
DJW Clare Valley Riesling 2017 Gold medals at the Canberra Riesling Challenge '17, Brother John May Trophy for Wine of Provenance Clare Valley Wine Show '17 (together with the '06 and '10). An enduring marriage between the small patch on the 20yo estate vineyard that is succoured by a subsoil winter stream of water, vine vigour and bunch weights not impinging on the power of the Polish Hill River district. The wine has a sour lemon sherbet flavour that is mouthwatering and very long. Screwcap. 12.5% alc. **Rating** 96 **To** 2037 $24 ✪
Watervale Riesling 2017 This is 85% machine-harvested, 15% hand-picked from a single vineyard, destemmed, chilled to 3°C before pressing. Vibrantly fresh and juicy; insouciantly flows through the palate concealing tropical fruit in the background. A tribute to the unique 100% limestone subsoil, 40 years of experience and a great vintage. A snap at this price. Screwcap. 12% alc. **Rating** 94 **To** 2027 $19 ✪

Windance Wines ★★★★★
2764 Caves Road, Yallingup, WA 6282 **Region** Margaret River
T (08) 9755 2293 **www**.windance.com.au **Open** 7 days 10–5
Winemaker Tyke Wheatley **Est.** 1998 **Dozens** 4000 **Vyds** 7.25ha
Drew and Rosemary Brent-White founded this family business, situated 5km south of Yallingup. Cabernet sauvignon, shiraz, sauvignon blanc, semillon and merlot have been established, incorporating sustainable land management and organic farming practices where possible. The wines are exclusively estate-grown. Daughter Billie and husband Tyke Wheatley now own the business: Billie, a qualified accountant, was raised at Windance, and manages the business and the cellar door, and Tyke (with winemaking experience at Picardy, Happs and Burgundy) has taken over the winemaking and manages the vineyard.

¶¶¶¶¶ **Margaret River Cabernet Sauvignon 2016** This is a shining chassis of pure cabernet currency: blackcurrant, mint, strewn herbs, graphite and cigar box; driven by an engine of stiff upper-lipped, gravelly tannins, bright acidity and sensitively applied oak. The extraction levels have upped the ante, delivering a wine that lacks the eminent joy of the Cabernet Merlot, but albeit one that will have its time in the sun. Bury this in the cellar or decant for an hour. Screwcap. 14% alc. **Rating** 96 **To** 2035 $32 NG ✪

Margaret River Cabernet Merlot 2016 A pointed cabernet blend that meshes an effortless drinkability in its youth with the potential for real staying power. The extraction of currant, sage and bay leaf notes is gentle and on point. The application of French oak is sensible, rather than overly ambitious. This said, a carapace of detailed tannins impeccably bound to pencil and iron shavings augur for a joyous life ahead. Bravo! Screwcap. 14% alc. **Rating** 95 **To** 2028 $24 NG ✪

 Glen Valley Margaret River Blanc de Blancs 2016 Rating 92 $34 NG
Reserve Margaret River Chardonnay 2016 Rating 91 To 2025 $38 NG
Margaret River Shiraz 2016 Rating 91 To 2024 $24 NG
Glen Valley Margaret River Rose 2017 Rating 90 To 2019 $24 NG

Windfall Wine Estate ★★★★☆

7 Dardanup West Road, North Boyanup, WA 6237 **Region** Geographe
T 0408 930 332 **www.**windfallwines.com.au **Open** Fri–Sun 12–5
Winemaker Luke Eckersley **Est.** 1996 **Dozens** 2500 **Vyds** 3ha

Julie and Phil Hutton put their money where their hearts are, electing to plant a merlot-only vineyard in 1996. Presumably knowing the unpredictable habits of merlot when planted on its own roots, they began by planting 3500 Swartzman rootstock vines, and then 12 months later field-grafted the merlot scion material. Small wonder their backs are still aching. I don't doubt for a millisecond the sincerity of their enthusiasm for the variety when they say, 'Fruity, plummy, smooth and velvety. Hints of chocolate too. If you're new to wine and all things merlot, this is a wonderful variety to explore'. The previous name of the venture, Bonking Frog, was fun, but became wildly unsuited to what has become a serious player in the Geographe region.

 Estate Ivor Merlot 2014 This is an utterly delicious, elegant and supple merlot; the bright, clear colour an early signal of the quality of the wine. It fills the mouth gently with red fruit flavours, sending signals to the brain – 'don't spit this out, it's too lovely'. Screwcap. 13.5% alc. **Rating** 96 **To** 2034 $38 ✪

Frog Song Great Southern Shiraz 2016 Rating 91 To 2026
Single-Handed Geographe Merlot 2016 Rating 90 To 2031

Windowrie Estate ★★★★

Windowrie Road, Canowindra, NSW 2804 **Region** Cowra
T (02) 6344 3234 **www.**windowrie.com.au **Open** By appt
Winemaker Antonio D'Onise **Est.** 1987 **Dozens** 30 000 **Vyds** 240ha

Windowrie Estate was established by the O'Dea family in 1987 on a grazing property at Canowindra, 30km north of Cowra. A portion of the grapes is sold to other makers, but increasing quantities are being made for the Windowrie Estate and The Mill labels. The winery is certified organic, and the substantial vineyard (mostly certified organic or in conversion) is planted to chardonnay, sauvignon blanc, semillon, verdelho, chenin blanc, shiraz, tempranillo, sangiovese, petit verdot, cabernet sauvignon and merlot. Exports to Canada, China, Japan and Singapore.

Central Ranges Merlot 2015 It saw both French and American oak and, while that's not always a good thing, it's helped turn out a beauty here. Oak spice, sweet red berries, cedar wood and liquorice flavours swirl deliciously through the palate and faithfully on through the finish. Even if merlot isn't your usual choice this is worth a punt; say you're Buying it For A Friend – do what you have to do. The wine is very good. Screwcap. 14% alc. **Rating** 93 **To** 2024 $20 CM ✪

Windows Estate ★★★★★

4 Quininup Road, Yallingup, WA 6282 **Region** Margaret River
T (08) 9756 6655 **www**.windowsestate.com **Open** 7 days 10–5
Winemaker Chris Davies **Est.** 1996 **Dozens** 3500 **Vyds** 6.3ha
Chris Davies planted the Windows Estate vineyard (cabernet sauvignon, shiraz, chenin blanc, chardonnay, semillon, sauvignon blanc and merlot) in 1996 at the age of 19, and has tended the vines ever since. Initially selling the grapes, Chris moved into winemaking in 2006 and has had considerable show success for the consistently outstanding wines. Exports to Germany, Singapore and Taiwan.

🍷🍷🍷🍷🍷 **Petit Lot Chardonnay 2015** Hand-picked 19yo dry-grown Mendoza and 95 clones, whole-bunch pressed, wild-fermented in French barriques (75% new), matured for 12 months with batonnage. Right in the slot of the extreme intensity and complexity of the Windows style, and retaining shape, balance and precision as the exceptional length of the wine unrolls and reveals itself. The varietal fruit flavours are equally exceptional. Screwcap. 13% alc. **Rating** 97 **To** 2030 $60 ✪

🍷🍷🍷🍷🍷 **Estate Grown Margaret River Sauvignon Blanc 2017** Two clones from two vineyard blocks, F4V6 whole berries chilled for 24 hours prior to pressing, H5V10 chilled and whole-bunch pressed, the free-run juice part fermented in tank, part in used barriques. A compelling sauvignon that is a nod to the Loire Valley style of the late Didier Dagueneau, but is less flamboyant – and more precise in its intensity. The fruit flavours coast through tropical to citrus, resulting in a wine of real class. Screwcap. 12% alc. **Rating** 95 **To** 2022 $24 ✪
Estate Grown Margaret River Semillon Sauvignon Blanc 2017 The aromas and flavours of the blend are in high relief, but it's the tactile quality of the wine – linked to Meyer lemon and subtle barrel ferment nuances – that set it apart with its own personality. Screwcap. 12% alc. **Rating** 95 **To** 2022 $28 ✪
Margaret River Chardonnay 2016 In the elegant style that owner/winemaker Chris Davies prefers. The fragrant flower and blossom-scented bouquet leads into a perfectly balanced palate, stone fruit cradled by subtle barrel ferment oak. It is here that the length of the wine becomes obvious (but not bombastic). Screwcap. 12.8% alc. **Rating** 95 **To** 2026 $44
Petit Lot Petit Verdot 2014 Micro-vinification with a single 1t fermenter (around 22 dozen bottles), matured for 18 months in used French oak. Deep colour, vivid and bright; the bouquet and palate are loaded with blackcurrant/cassis, dark forest floor and dried herbs providing a very well-judged counterpoint. Striking wine. Screwcap. 14% alc. **Rating** 95 **To** 2039 $45
Petit Lot Malbec 2014 Petit lot indeed – only 50 dozen made, matured in new and used French oak for 18 months. In full-blooded and bodied style, rich and layered, black fruits, savoury dried herbs and gravelly tannins settling down to a decades-long discussion about the order of importance of each component. Screwcap. 14% alc. **Rating** 95 **To** 2039 $45

🍷🍷🍷🍷 **Basket Pressed Margaret River Syrah 2015 Rating** 89 **To** 2023 $36

🍇 Wine Movement ★★★★☆

314 Glen Osmond Road, Myrtle Bank, SA 5064 (postal) **Region** McLaren Vale
T 0423 006 348 **www**.winemovement.com.au **Open** Not
Winemaker Seamus O'Fathartaigh, Aggie Janusz **Est.** 2011 **Dozens** NFP
This is the venture of Seamus O'Fathartaigh and Aggie Janusz, both with impressive knowledge and experience in very different aspects of wine. Indeed, it's hard to imagine a more perfect fit. Seamus was first out of the blocks when he entered the world of bulk wine brokerage, having previously attained a Bachelor of Science degree followed by a Graduate Diploma in viticulture from the University of Adelaide. He worked with wineries large and small (all highly reputed), gaining invaluable experience in the entire wine supply chain from vineyards to retailers. Aggie completed a PhD and Post Doctoral Fellowship, both focused on wine flavour. Almost as an afterthought (so it would seem), she also gained a Graduate

Diploma in oenology from the University of Adelaide. After a diversion to the brewing industry, she turned back to wine, joining Wine Movement as a business and life partner.

🍷🍷🍷🍷🍷 **Latarenka McLaren Vale Shiraz 2016** This has a truly interesting and mouthwatering, flavour wheel. There are spicy dark chocolate notes, but they are welded together along with a dusting of dried berries. The mouthfeel is so supple it moves into velvet before integrated acidity and tannins provide the other face of the wine. All in all, compelling. Screwcap. 14.5% alc. **Rating** 95 **To** 2026

🍷🍷🍷🍷🍷 **Latarenka McLaren Vale Aglianico 2016** **Rating** 93 **To** 2026
Latarenka McLaren Vale Nero d'Avola 2016 **Rating** 93 **To** 2023

Wine Unplugged ★★★★☆
2020 Upton Road, Upton Hill, Vic 3664 (postal) **Region** Various Victoria
T 0432 021 668 **www**.wineunplugged.com.au **Open** Not
Winemaker Callie Jemmeson, Nina Stocker **Est.** 2010 **Dozens** 5000 **Vyds** 14ha
Nina Stocker and Callie Jemmeson believe that winemaking doesn't have to have barriers – what it does need is quality, focus and a destination. With a strong emphasis on vineyard selection and a gentle approach to their small-batch winemaking, the wines are a true reflection of site. The wines are released under the pacha mama, La Vie en Rose and Cloak & Dagger labels.

🍷🍷🍷🍷🍷 **pacha mama Heathcote Shiraz 2016** Pachamamma is an Incan earth goddess. The wine has all the richness that comes from Heathcote soil, and has stolen another level of richness from McLaren Vale (not actually part of the wine, of course). The end result is a gloriously luscious shiraz for now or later, for humans or gods. Screwcap. 14.6% alc. **Rating** 95 **To** 2036

🍷🍷🍷🍷🍷 **pacha mama Yarra Valley Chardonnay 2016** **Rating** 90 **To** 2023
The Dagger Pinot Grigio 2017 **Rating** 90 **To** 2020

Wine x Sam ★★★★
69–71 Anzac Avenue, Seymour, Vic 3660 **Region** Strathbogie Ranges
T 0403 059 423 **www**.winebysam.com.au **Open** 7 days 9–4
Winemaker Sam Plunkett, Matt Froude **Est.** 2013 **Dozens** 60 000 **Vyds** 10.2ha
Since 1991 Sam Plunkett and partner Bron Dunwoodie have changed shells as often as a lively hermit crab. 1991 – first estate vineyard established and mud-brick winery built. 2001 – created a new winery at Avenel. 2004 – purchased the large Dominion Wines in partnership with the Fowles family. 2011 – Fowles purchased the Plunkett family's shareholding, except 7ha of shiraz and 3.2ha of chardonnay. Winemaking moved to the Taresch family's Elgo Estate winery. Within two years the Plunkett interests had leased the entire Elgo winery, now making the Elgo wines as well as their own brands. A large contract make for Naked Wines saw production increase to 20 000 dozen, and in a few blinks of the eye later production is 60 000. Exports to the UK, the US and China.

🍷🍷🍷🍷🍷 **Single Vineyard Series Whitegate Vineyard Strathbogie Ranges Pinot Noir 2017** The attractive label design catches your attention from the outset. The cool vintage has given the wine bell-clear varietal character, with red and black cherries from the word go, gaining further from the texture of the long palate. Screwcap. 13.5% alc. **Rating** 94 **To** 2027

🍷🍷🍷🍷🍷 **The Victorian Strathbogie Ranges Pinot Grigio Rose 2017** **Rating** 91 **To** 2020

Wines by Geoff Hardy ★★★★★
327 Hunt Road, McLaren Vale, SA 5171 **Region** South Australia
T (08) 8383 2700 **www**.winesbygeoffhardy.com.au **Open** 7 days 11–5
Winemaker Geoff Hardy, Shane Harris **Est.** 1980 **Dozens** 90 000 **Vyds** 43ha

Geoff Hardy's great-great-grandfather, the original Thomas Hardy, first planted grapes in SA in the 1850s and was one of the founding fathers of the Australian wine industry. In 1980 together with wife Fiona, Geoff left the then family company Thomas Hardy & Sons to make his own way in all sectors of the Australian wine business. Wines by Geoff Hardy is made up of three ventures/brands founded by Geoff: Pertaringa in McLaren Vale, K1 by Geoff Hardy in the Adelaide Hills (Tynan Rd, Kuitpo) and Hand Crafted by Geoff Hardy, sourced from a variety of premium regions across South Australia. Exports to Canada, the UK, Germany, Sweden, Finland, India, Malaysia, South Korea, Indonesia, Japan, Singapore, Taiwan, Hong Kong and China.

ŸŸŸŸŸ **Geoff Hardy GMH Meritage 2016** Crafted from select parcels across better SA sites, this is a Bordeaux-inspired blend under an oft-used American moniker. And good it is, too. Milk chocolate tannins are slathered with blackcurrant, blueberry and damson plum notes, all pierced with a high-toned whiff of mint and dried tobacco. Quality oak is a mere adjunct, buried in the sheer extract. Great value. Cork. 14.5% alc. **Rating** 95 To 2034 $20 NG ✪

Pertaringa Cabernet Sauvignon 2016 A satin velour of crushed currant and blackberries transitions to a structural riff of gritty, bitter chocolate tannins and finely handled oak. Mint lifts the package, imparting freshness and the clear cut voice of cabernet across the wine's savoury aft. Great value for enjoyment now and future development. Cork. 14.5% alc. **Rating** 94 To 2032 $20 NG ✪

GMH Cabernet Sauvignon 2016 From South Australian regional holdings, this is sophisticated fare. Amped up with generosity and the usual cavalcade of red to black fruit notes, what sets this wine apart is its impeccably wrought sinew of tannin. It is on this that everything else hinges. A herbaceous lick of piment, too, gives lift. Cork. 14.5% alc. **Rating** 94 To 2032 $20 NG ✪

ŸŸŸŸ︎ **Pertaringa Scarecrow Adelaide Sauvignon Blanc 2017** Rating 93 To 2019 $22 NG ✪

Pertaringa Cabernet Sauvignon 2016 Rating 93 To 2026 $35 NG

Pertaringa Red Meritage 2016 Rating 93 To 2028 $20 NG ✪

Hand Crafted by Geoff Hardy Teroldego 2016 Rating 93 To 2026 $30

Pertaringa Lakeside Moscato 2017 Rating 93 To 2019 $20 NG ✪

K1 by Geoff Hardy Adelaide Hills Autumn Harvest 2017 Rating 93 To 2026 $25 NG ✪

Pertaringa Sauvignon Blanc 2017 Rating 92 To 2021 $30 NG

K1 by Geoff Hardy Shiraz 2016 Rating 92 To 2024 $25 NG ✪

Pertaringa Undercover Shiraz 2016 Rating 92 To 2024 $22 NG ✪

Pertaringa Stage Left Merlot 2016 Rating 92 To 2022 $22 NG ✪

Pertaringa Understudy Cabernet 2016 Rating 92 To 2030 $22 NG ✪

Pertaringa Cabernet Sauvignon 2016 Rating 92 To 2026 $35 NG

Hand Crafted by Geoff Hardy Nero d'Avola 2016 Rating 92 To 2026 $30

Pertaringa Gruner Veltliner 2017 Rating 91 To 2023 $30 NG

Hand Crafted by Geoff Hardy Arneis 2017 Rating 91 To 2021 $25 NG

Pertaringa Shiraz 2017 Rating 91 To 2025 $20 NG ✪

Pertaringa Shiraz 2015 Rating 91 To 2021 $35 NG

Wines by KT   ★★★★★

20 Main North Road, Watervale, SA 5452 **Region** Clare Valley
T 0419 855 500 **www**.winesbykt.com **Open** By appt
Winemaker Kerri Thompson **Est.** 2006 **Dozens** 1400
'KT' is winemaker Kerri Thompson. Kerri graduated with a degree in oenology from Roseworthy Agricultural College in 1993, and thereafter made wine in McLaren Vale, Tuscany, Beaujolais and the Clare Valley, becoming well known as the Leasingham winemaker in the Clare Valley. She left Leasingham in 2006 after seven years at the helm, and after a short break became winemaker at Crabtree. Here she is also able to make Wines by KT, sourcing the grapes from two local vineyards – one biodynamic, the other farmed with sulphur and copper sprays only. Exports to the UK.

ŸŸŸŸŸ **Churinga Vineyard Watervale Riesling 2017** Arguably the most detailed Churinga to date reaching lofty heights with its clarity and whorl of citrus from mandarin blossom, to lemon juice and pith, with flavours building along the palate. Its frame is linear and elegant, and the acidity has laser precision right through to the long finish. Screwcap. 12.5% alc. **Rating** 97 **To** 2033 $33 JF ✪

Peglidis Vineyard Watervale Riesling 2017 Peglidis presents itself as a wine of intensity and depth with complex flavours that are quite savoury in outlook. Coriander seeds, lemon salt, aspirin and wet slate. Of course, there's excellent fruit and acid balance, both key to its vibrancy, detail and potential age-worthiness. On song. Screwcap. 12% alc. **Rating** 97 **To** 2033 $38 JF ✪

ŸŸŸŸŸ **5452 Riesling 2017** Once the two single rieslings are assembled (Peglidis and Churinga), what doesn't make that top tier goes into this easy-to-drink and stylish riesling. Backed up by florals, especially lemon blossom and fennel flowers, with a smidge of baked ricotta. There's some texture and succulence with lemon barley water and fine natural acidity to close. Screwcap. 12.5% alc. **Rating** 95 **To** 2027 $25 JF ✪

5452 Watervale Grenache Mataro 2016 It's all about the quality of the fruit – a 60/40% split, with the grenache bush vines planted in the 1930s – meeting unfussy winemaking. This is light on its feet from the pale ruby hue to the delicacy of the fruit, but has plenty of energy and flavour. A mix of red berries, musk sticks, warm earth and rhubarb compote that meet exceptionally fine-sandpaper and savoury tannins; quite lithe with a touch of tamarind acidity. Screwcap. 14% alc. **Rating** 94 **To** 2023 $25 JF ✪

ŸŸŸŸŸ **Bianca Clare Valley Vermentino 2016 Rating** 93 **To** 2020 $25 JF ✪
Pazza Unfiltered Wild Fermented Riesling 2015 Rating 92 **To** 2019 $30 JF

 # Wines of Merritt

PO Box 1122, Margaret River, WA 6285 **Region** Margaret River
T 0438 284 561 **www**.winesofmerritt.com.au **Open** Not
Winemaker Nick James-Martin **Est.** 2017 **Dozens** 600

Nick James-Martin grew up in a tiny Riverland town, spending his early working life in some of Adelaide's better restaurants, helping his family establish a vineyard in McLaren Vale. Two years working for *WINE Magazine* in London offered him the opportunity of travelling through France, Spain, Portugal and Italy, immersing himself in wine in those countries. He then studied wine marketing and oenology at the University of Adelaide, sitting for a masters degree. He worked at Rosemount, Vasse Felix and Stella Bella, plus on overseas vintages in Hawke's Bay, NZ, and Languedoc, France. Sarah James-Martin is a hospitality professional, and prior to moving to Margaret River she ran the acclaimed Salopian Inn in McLaren Vale, and worked for other wineries in the region. She's currently learning the art of cheesemaking at Yallingup Cheese Company. I have always said that if I see a natural wine, I will pay attention if I know the winemaker is able to make commercial wines without the natural hook. I haven't tasted any of Nick's wines made using conventional methods, but there's no doubt that he could if he so wished.

ŸŸŸŸŸ **Single Vineyard Small Batch Chenin Blanc 2017** Natural winemaking made easy, from a close-planted vineyard (double normal density) planted in the mid-'80s opposite Cullen, 75% cloudy juice wild-fermented in old French oak (50% mlf), 25% open-fermented on skins and upwards from that no acid additions, no fining, no filtration, no plating to check yeast population, no cold stabilisation. Diam. 12% alc. **Rating** 90 **To** 2022 $40

ŸŸŸŸ **Single Vineyard Small Batch Vermentino 2017 Rating** 89 **To** 2023 $35

Wirra Wirra

463 McMurtrie Road, McLaren Vale, SA 5171 **Region** McLaren Vale
T (08) 8323 8414 **www**.wirrawirra.com **Open** Mon–Sat 10–5, Sun & public hols 11–5
Winemaker Paul Smith, Tom Ravech, Kelly Wellington **Est.** 1894 **Dozens** 150 000
Vyds 51.31ha

Long respected for the consistency of its white wines, Wirra Wirra has now established an
equally formidable reputation for its reds. The wines are of exemplary character, quality and
style; The Angelus Cabernet Sauvignon and RSW Shiraz battling each other for supremacy,
with The Absconder Grenache one to watch. Long may the battle continue under the
direction of managing director Andrew Kay and the winemaking team of Paul Smith and Tom
Ravech, who forge along the path of excellence first trod by the late (and much loved) Greg
Trott, the pioneering founder of modern-day Wirra Wirra. Its acquisition of Ashton Hills in
2015 added a major string to its top quality bow. Exports to all major markets.

🍷🍷🍷🍷🍷 **Chook Block Shiraz 2016** The Chooks are hand-raised from the outset with
the first birth in '08, and only six vintages have been reared and released. The vines
were planted in '60, the wine matured in French oak (40% new). The texture
is freakishly good, the juicy black fruits with a crosscut of superfine tannins and
cedary French oak. It is only medium-bodied, but has a nigh-on unlimited future.
Screwcap. 14.5% alc. **Rating** 97 **To** 2056 $130 **☉**

🍷🍷🍷🍷🍷 **RSW McLaren Vale Shiraz 2016** From a range of vineyards across McLaren
Vale, each vinified and matured for 15 months in French oak separately prior to
blending. The ultimate in glass bottle packaging, with 'RSW' boldly engraved on
the glass. The second the wine enters the mouth it booms like a foghorn on a
liner from years gone by, with a tinge of dark chocolate from Switzerland. The
taste doesn't change much: black fruits, earth, spice, oak and tannins are also part of
the DNA of this painstakingly made wine. Screwcap. **Rating** 96 **To** 2039 $70 **☉**
The Absconder McLaren Vale Grenache 2016 Open-fermented, basket-
pressed, matured for 10 months in French oak. Bright crimson hue; this is one of a
number of outstanding grenaches from '16 with the structure and texture of shiraz
or cabernet sauvignon. The bouquet and palate have struck a deal to mirror each
other identically; this luxury-packaged wine has the certainty of a long, happy life.
Screwcap. 14.5% alc. **Rating** 96 **To** 2031 $70 **☉**
The Lost Watch Adelaide Hills Riesling 2017 A wine with one cardinal
quality: its purity. This comes from the way citrus and apple are fused into a single
stream by crystalline acidity, all ending as a single character. This is a deadset stayer.
Screwcap. 12.5% alc. **Rating** 95 **To** 2037 $24 **☉**
Hiding Champion Single Vineyard Adelaide Hills Sauvignon Blanc 2017
Reflects the cool, late vintage that came as a relief after '16's fast and furious
antics. Hand-picked from the Yandra Vineyard, it has intensity, focus and
length – uncommon qualities for sauvignon blanc, as are the mineral and citrus
heartstrings on the palate. It's lipsmackingly good. Screwcap. 12.5% alc. **Rating** 95
To 2020 $24 **☉**
The 12th Man Adelaide Hills Chardonnay 2017 Whole-bunch pressed, free-
run juice wild-fermented in French puncheons (33% new), mlf, matured on lees.
Given every opportunity to take to the field, and not remain on the boundary
rope – even if the field trip was simply to carry the drinks. It has a lovely burst
of grapefruit juice rising over more sedate stone fruit and controlled French oak.
Screwcap. 12.5% alc. **Rating** 95 **To** 2027 $35 **☉**
The Angelus McLaren Vale Cabernet Sauvignon 2016 From old vine
vineyards across McLaren Vale, each parcel vinified separately, matured for
15 months in French oak (30% new) before barrel selection and blending. The
alcohol was unknown at the time of tasting, but seems moderate. The super-
fragrant bouquet is full of red flowers and red fruits that positively dance on the
tongue as you start to assess the palate. Freshness and length are the keys to this
very elegant cabernet. Screwcap. **Rating** 95 **To** 2041 $70

ΨΨΨΨ️ **Catapult McLaren Vale Shiraz 2016** Rating 93 To 2031 $25 ✪
Woodhenge Basket-Pressed McLaren Vale Shiraz 2016 Rating 93
To 2028 $35 SC
Mrs Wigley McLaren Vale Grenache Rose 2017 Rating 92 To 2018 $20 ✪
Amator Biodynamic Vineyards McLaren Vale Shiraz 2016 Rating 92
To 2024 $30 SC
Amator Biodynamic Vineyards McLaren Vale Cabernet Sauvignon 2016
Rating 92 To 2024 $30 SC
Sparrow's Lodge McLaren Vale Shiraz 2016 Rating 91 To 2031 $30

Wirrega Vineyards ★★★

PO Box 94, Mundulla, SA 5270 **Region** Limestone Coast
T (08) 8743 4167 www.wirregavineyards.com **Open** Not
Winemaker Tom O'Donnell **Est.** 1993 **Dozens** 4500 **Vyds** 163ha
This is the venture of what might kindly be called wine village elders, as they have an
awesome amount of knowledge about every aspect of the wine industry. In 1993 they
formed a partnership to develop this large vineyard which, until 2013, was content to stick
to its knitting supplying grapes to some of the partners' own enterprises and businesses
as large as Pernod Ricard. For the record, the partners are Scott Collett, Rocco Melino,
Roger Oakeshott, Grant Tilbrook, John Younger and Guido Zuccoli. The Lilliputian
production could skyrocket if the partners so wish, for the quality is obvious. Exports to
the UK, Ireland, Switzerland, Malaysia and China.

ΨΨΨΨ **Sfera Limestone Coast Shiraz 2014** Made, so we are told, with a small
amount of oak and extended time on skins after fermentation. The Sfera range
represents the best of each varietal base in the winery. This is juicy and rich on the
fore-palate, turning strongly savoury on the finish. Will make the grade with the
help of protein. Screwcap. 14.5% alc. **Rating** 89 **To** 2024 $20
Sfera Limestone Coast Dolcetto 2015 Made using the appassimento
technique. It works well within its style; dolcetto may not have delivered the same
depth, even with the benefit of small berries to start with. It's been achieved without
bitterness, and the red and black cherry, licorice and dark chocolate flavours come
together to create a supple finish. Screwcap. 14.5% alc. **Rating** 89 **To** 2023 $20

Wise Wine ★★★★☆

237 Eagle Bay Road, Eagle Bay, WA 6281 **Region** Margaret River
T (08) 9750 3100 www.wisewine.com.au **Open** 7 days 11–5
Winemaker Andrew Siddell, Matt Buchan, Larry Cherubino (Consultant) **Est.** 1986
Dozens 10 000 **Vyds** 2.5ha
Wise Wine, headed by Perth entrepreneur Ron Wise, has been a remarkably consistent
producer of high quality wine. The vineyard adjacent to the winery (2ha of cabernet sauvignon
and shiraz, and 0.5ha of zinfandel) in the Margaret River is supplemented by contract-grown
grapes from Pemberton, Manjimup and Frankland River. The value for money of many of the
wines is extraordinarily good. Exports to Switzerland, the Philippines and Singapore.

ΨΨΨΨΨ **Lot 80 Margaret River Cabernet Sauvignon 2016** This is a barrel selection,
aged for 18 months in French oak barriques, the amount of new oak not specified,
but all integrated. A convincing wine with its currants, mulberries and spiced fruit
compote notes all layered with bay leaves, cedar and cloves. Fuller-bodied, detailed
savoury tannins and complete. Ready to pour. Screwcap. 14.2% alc. **Rating** 95
To 2026 $45 JF

ΨΨΨΨ️ **Leaf Margaret River Cabernet Sauvignon 2016** Rating 93 To 2023 $28 JF
Leaf Margaret River Cabernet Malbec 2016 Rating 93 To 2027 $28 JF
Eagle Bay Margaret River Chardonnay 2016 Rating 92 To 2022 $45 JF
Sea Urchin Mazza Block Margaret River Shiraz 2016 Rating 92 To 2026
$20 JF ✪
Margaret River Botrytis Semillon 2017 Rating 90 To 2020 $28 JF

Witches Falls Winery ★★★★★

79 Main Western Road, Tamborine Mountain, Qld 4272 **Region** Queensland
T (07) 5545 2609 **www**.witchesfalls.com.au **Open** Mon–Fri 10–4, w'ends 10–5
Winemaker Jon Heslop, Arantza Milicua Celador **Est.** 2004 **Dozens** 12 000 **Vyds** 0.4ha
Witches Falls is the venture of Jon and Kim Heslop. Jon has a deep interest in experimenting
with progressive vinification methods in order to achieve exceptional and interesting results.
He has a degree in applied science (oenology) from CSU, and experience working in the
Barossa and Hunter valleys as well as at Domaine Chantel Lescure, Burgundy, and with a
Napa-based winegrower. Witches Falls' grapes are sourced from the Granite Belt (other than
its 0.4ha of estate durif), and it is one of the consistently good performers in that context.
Exports to the US, Norway, Taiwan and China.

♟♟♟♟♟ **Wild Ferment Granite Belt Viognier 2016** A burst of fruit, a layer of oak,
sparks of spice and florals. This puts a host of runs on the board, and quickly. You
have to admire the verve of this. It captures your attention and refuses to let go.
Screwcap. 13.5% alc. **Rating** 95 **To** 2020 $34 CM ✪
Prophecy Granite Belt Cabernet Sauvignon 2016 Medium-weight is
classy. Or so this wine would convince you. Boysenberry fruit flavour with well
integrated cedar wood oak; fresh mint infused through cassis; floral overtones.
It tastes of money, except the oak, but it's seamless, juicy and long. Screwcap.
13.2% alc. **Rating** 95 **To** 2030 $51 CM
Wild Ferment Granite Belt Sauvignon Blanc 2016 Barrel-fermented (wild)
and then whipped straight off lees after ferment; 10 months in (100% used) French
oak. It's not your average sauvignon blanc. It's all smoke and flint, peat and cut
grass, the impact of the wine bedded down entirely by the richness and ripeness
of the fruit. It's not to be messed with; it's a statuesque white wine. Screwcap.
13.1% alc. **Rating** 94 **To** 2021 $34 CM
Wild Ferment Granite Belt Fiano 2016 Tremendously delicious. Lemon
blossom, honeysuckle, candied citrus, almonds, fennel. It's all going on. It bursts,
it shakes, it blooms. It was matured in (old) oak but it's not heavy at all; it's thirst
quenching. It just makes you want to come back for more and more. Screwcap.
12.8% alc. **Rating** 94 **To** 2019 $34 CM

♟♟♟♟♟ **Wild Ferment Granite Belt Viognier 2017** Rating 93 To 2021 $34 CM
Wild Ferment Granite Belt Verdelho 2016 Rating 92 To 2020 $34 CM
Granite Belt Cabernet Sauvignon 2016 Rating 92 To 2026 $28 CM
Granite Belt Syrah 2016 Rating 91 To 2025 $28 CM
Granite Belt Verdelho 2017 Rating 90 To 2019 $24 CM

Witchmount Estate ★★★★

557 Leakes Road, Plumpton, Vic 3335 **Region** Sunbury
T (03) 9747 1055 **www**.witchmountestatewinery.com.au **Open** Wed–Sun 11–5
Winemaker Steve Goodwin **Est.** 1991 **Dozens** 8000 **Vyds** 25.5ha
Witchmount Estate, with its restaurant and function centre, is only 30 minutes from
Melbourne, in the Sunbury region. The vineyard is planted to shiraz (12ha), cabernet
sauvignon (6ha) and chardonnay (2ha), with lesser amounts of sauvignon blanc, pinot gris,
merlot, tempranillo and barbera. The quality of the wines has been consistent, the prices very
modest. Exports to China.

♟♟♟♟♟ **Chardonnay 2016** The vinification decisions have all realised expectations;
early(ish) picking and moving the wine to barrel well after fermentation started
were timed with precision, 13% alcohol hits the centre of the fruit flavour bullseye.
Screwcap. **Rating** 94 **To** 2023 $32
Shiraz 2016 The vineyard and winery pool their resources to come up with this
wine. The colour is convincing, the mouthfeel really attractive, supple and smooth,
the new French oak absorbed, the tannins fine. Screwcap. 14% alc. **Rating** 94
To 2031 $32

Cabernet Franc 2017 There's an uncommon consistency in the winemaking at Witchmount regardless of the region and the variety (the logistics involved would prove too much for some to handle, different varieties likewise), and there's also consistency in the value for money. This Sunbury-grown cabernet franc exemplifies all the foregoing with its display of juicy red and purple fruits, the freshness of the palate excellent. Diam. 12.6% alc. **Rating** 94 **To** 2030 $32

🍷🍷🍷🍷 **Shiraz 2015 Rating** 92 **To** 2030 $32

Wolf Blass   ★★★★★
97 Sturt Highway, Nuriootpa, SA 5355 **Region** Barossa Valley
T (08) 8568 7311 **www**.wolfblasswines.com **Open** 7 days 10–4.30
Winemaker Chris Hatcher, Steve Frost, Marie Clay, Clare Dry, John Ashwell **Est.** 1966
Dozens NFP
Although merged with Mildara and now under the giant umbrella of TWE, the brands (as expected) have been left largely intact. The Wolf Blass wines are made at all price points, ranging through Red, Yellow, Gold, Brown, Grey, Sapphire, Black, White and Platinum labels, at one price point or another covering every one of the main varietals. In 2016 a new range of wines labelled BLASS was introduced. The style and range of the wines continue to subtly evolve under the leadership of chief winemaker Chris Hatcher. Exports to all major markets.

🍷🍷🍷🍷🍷 **Black Label Cabernet Shiraz Malbec 2015** The 43rd vintage of this wine, and is imperious. Impeccably made. Sumptuous black and blue fruit allusions stain a satin chassis of grape and oak tannins, the former massaged into a textural sheen; the latter still evident and needing time. Floral and forceful. Sumptuous and beguiling. This is a keeper. Screwcap. 14.5% alc. **Rating** 96 **To** 2038 $130 NG
Platinum Label Medlands Vineyard Barossa Shiraz 2014 A wine for those who like 'em soft, molten and rich. Vanilla-mocha-caramel brittle oak leads off. A swathe of vanilla and blueberry too, segueing to sweet, raisiny tannins. There is some herbal complexity providing respite to the power and fruit sweetness, while platforming an impressive strut across a very long finish. Screwcap. 14.7% alc. **Rating** 95 **To** 2038 $200 NG
BLASS Reserve Barossa Shiraz 2016 This label offers startling value across contemporary, tighter expressions of high quality regional fruit. While Barossan of intensity, the style is crunchy, appetising and more mid-weighted than the norm, with floral lilac scents segueing to blue fruits, anise and a melody of spice. The finish is long and as reliant on a smart card of reductive tension as it is on the peppery acid glide and gentle oak pillars. Very smart. Screwcap. 14% alc. **Rating** 94 **To** 2023 $22 NG ✪

🍷🍷🍷🍷 **BLASS Reserve Langhorne Creek Cabernet Sauvignon 2016 Rating** 93 **To** 2023 $22 NG ✪
Gold Label Eden Valley Riesling 2017 Rating 92 **To** 2027 $28 NG
White Label Adelaide Hills Chardonnay 2017 Rating 92 **To** 2024 $34 NG
Brown Label Classic Shiraz 2016 Rating 92 **To** 2026 $50 NG
Grey Label McLaren Vale Shiraz 2016 Rating 92 **To** 2031 $45 NG
Gold Label Coonawarra Cabernet Sauvignon 2016 Rating 92 **To** 2025 $28 NG
Grey Label Langhorne Creek Cabernet Shiraz 2016 Rating 92 **To** 2036 $45 NG
Gold Label Adelaide Hills Sauvignon Blanc 2017 Rating 91 **To** 2020 $28 NG
Altitude Limestone Coast Sauvignon Blanc 2017 Rating 90 **To** 2019 $20 NG ✪
Yellow Label Shiraz 2016 Rating 90 **To** 2021 $18 NG ✪

Wood Park

263 Kneebones Gap Road, Markwood, Vic 3678 **Region** King Valley
T (03) 5727 3778 **www**.woodparkwines.com.au **Open** At Milawa Cheese Factory
Winemaker John Stokes **Est.** 1989 **Dozens** 7000 **Vyds** 16ha
John Stokes planted the first vines at Wood Park in 1989 as part of a diversification program
for his property at Bobinawarrah, in the hills of the Lower King Valley, east of Milawa. The
vineyard is managed with minimal chemical use, winemaking a mix of modern and traditional
techniques (what wine isn't?). The reach of Wood Park has been expanded with Beechworth
Pinot Noir and Chardonnay and a mix of mainstream and alternative varieties, all well made.
It also has a cellar door in Ford St, Beechworth. Exports to Taiwan, Singapore and China.

🍷🍷🍷🍷🍷 **Beechworth Chardonnay 2016** Hand-picked, destemmed and crushed, settled,
transferred to French barriques (33% new). Has that distinctive Beechworth
weight and generosity to its fruit, with cashew and fig notes alongside nectarine
and white peach. Screwcap. 13.5% alc. **Rating** 95 **To** 2022 $30 ✪
Reserve King Valley Zinfandel 2016 From 25yo vines on the home block,
wild yeast–open fermented, 23 months in new American oak. How utterly
remarkable: very good hue, no feel of warmth, plush/velvet red berry/cherry fruit,
no spikes of green – just supple and seductive. Screwcap. 15.2% alc. **Rating** 95
To 2026 $40
The Tuscan 2016 An Uncle Tom Cobbly and all blend of cabernet sauvignon,
shiraz, sangiovese, petit verdot and colorino, with the cabernet and shiraz doing
the heavy lifting. It's a very attractive medium-bodied wine with blackberry, black
cherry and blackcurrant flavours meshing very well with each other; the tannins
are soft, the acidity ditto. Screwcap. 14.2% alc. **Rating** 94 **To** 2029 $28 ✪

🍷🍷🍷🍷🍷 **Reserve Cabernet Sauvignon 2016 Rating** 93 $40
Monument Lane Roussanne 2016 Rating 90 **To** 2023 $28
Monument Lane Cabernet Shiraz 2016 Rating 90 **To** 2026 $28

Woodhaven Vineyard

87 Main Creek Road, Red Hill, Vic 3937 **Region** Mornington Peninsula
T 0421 612 178 **www**.woodhavenvineyard.com.au **Open** By appt
Winemaker Lee and Neil Ward **Est.** 2003 **Dozens** 200 **Vyds** 1.6ha
Woodhaven is the venture of Lee and Neil Ward, both qualified accountants for 30 years in
Melbourne, albeit working in different fields. They spent two years looking for a suitable
site on the Mornington Peninsula, ultimately finding one high on Red Hill. Bringing the
venture to the point of production has been a slow and, at times, frustrating business. They
decided from the outset to be personally responsible for all aspects of growing the grapes
and making the wines, relying on the advice readily given to them by George and Ruth
Mihaly of Paradigm, David and (the late) Wendy Lloyd of Eldridge, John and Julie Trueman
of Myrtaceae and Nat and Rose White, formerly of Main Ridge. They also decided to grow
the vines organically and biodynamically, and it took eight years to produce their first two
barrels of wine, in 2010. In '13 the 0.8ha each of pinot noir and chardonnay finally produced
more than one barrel of each wine.

Woodlands

3948 Caves Road, Wilyabrup, WA 6284 **Region** Margaret River
T (08) 9755 6226 **www**.woodlandswines.com **Open** 7 days 10–5
Winemaker Stuart Watson **Est.** 1973 **Dozens** 15 500 **Vyds** 26.58ha
Founders David Watson and wife Heather had spectacular success with the Cabernets he
made in 1979 and the early '80s. Commuting from Perth on weekends and holidays, as well
as raising a family, became all too much, and for some years the grapes from Woodlands were
sold to other Margaret River producers. With the advent of sons Stuart and Andrew (Stuart
primarily responsible for winemaking), the estate has bounced back to pre-eminence. The
wines come in four price bands, the bulk of the production under the Chardonnay and
Cabernet Merlot varietals, then a series of Reserve and Special Reserves, then Reserve de la

Cave, and finally Cabernet Sauvignon. The top-end wines primarily come from the original Woodlands vineyard, where the vines are over 40 years old. Exports to the UK, the US, Sweden, the Netherlands, Indonesia, Malaysia, the Philippines, Singapore, Japan and China.

ΨΨΨΨΨ **Reserve de la Cave Margaret River Cabernet Franc 2016** Demand and supply are the twin forces that make the price of this wine more than double that of Emily and Clementine. Cabernet franc of this quality is very rare – this is by far the best of the handful made in Australia, and can stand toe to toe with the best of St Emillion. It is beautifully cadenced, supple and pure, with cassis, cedar and a whiff of tobacco leaf. Screwcap. 13.5% alc. **Rating** 97 **To** 2041 $98 ✪

ΨΨΨΨΨ **Clementine 2016** A blend of 55% cabernet sauvignon, 16% malbec, 15% merlot, 14% petit verdot. This, like all the Woodlands wines, is a reflection of a great site, meticulous viticulture and unrelenting attention to detail in the winery. Its majority percentage of cabernet means it is firmer than Emily, but it's a question of degree: first the tannins are perfectly ripe, and secondly, the other varieties are juicy and plush, the tannins very soft. Screwcap. 13.5% alc. **Rating** 96 **To** 2036 $39 ✪
Emily 2016 Cabernet franc, merlot, malbec, cabernet sauvignon and petit verdot. This takes all the inputs of Clementine, but alters the varietal components. It's strange, but this early in its life it has a precision, a lightness of foot, that places it in a category of its own. Screwcap. 13.5% alc. **Rating** 96 **To** 2041 $39 ✪
Chloe 2016 In the opulent, rich, complex style of Chloe. It coats the mouth with its ripe citrus and stone fruit parade, yet doesn't cloy. Drink tonight or by '20 to gain maximum pleasure. Screwcap. 13.5% alc. **Rating** 95 **To** 2020 $98
Reserve de la Cave Margaret River Malbec 2016 The Woodlands Reserve de la Cave wines are like angels painted on a pinhead. What's more, they are normally two of the most challenging varieties, providing that X-factor simply because they are so uncommon. This has untold depths of various plums, bolstered by tannins and acidity on a calibrated finish. Screwcap. 13.5% alc. **Rating** 95 **To** 2036 $98

ΨΨΨΨΨ **Wilyabrup Valley Cabernet Sauvignon Merlot 2015** **Rating** 93 **To** 2025 $28

Woods Crampton   ★★★★★

PO Box 417, Hamilton, NSW 2303 **Region** Barossa Valley
T 0417 670 655 **www**.woods-crampton.com.au **Open** Not
Winemaker Nicholas Crampton, Aaron Woods **Est.** 2010 **Dozens** 30 000
This is one of the most impressive ventures of Nicholas Crampton (his association with McWilliam's is on a consultancy basis) and winemaking friend Aaron Woods. The two make the wines at the Sons of Eden winery with input advice from Igor Kucic. The quality of the wines, and the enticing prices, has seen production soar from 1500 to 30 000 dozen, with every expectation of continued success. Exports to the UK, Canada, Denmark, Hong Kong and China.

ΨΨΨΨΨ **Phillip Patrick Old Vines Single Vineyard Eden Valley Shiraz 2015** It is, of course, a massive, full-bodied wine, crammed with blackberry, pepper and anise fruit that has ridden roughshod over 70% new oak. The tannins on the finish are ripe, and are necessary to guarantee the 50-year future of the wine. Cork. 14.7% alc. **Rating** 97 **To** 2065 $125 ✪

ΨΨΨΨΨ **Michael John Centenarian Vines Single Vineyard Barossa Valley Shiraz 2015** Unmistakably regional, varietal and quite compelling. Dark red with purple hues, and while ripe, it is fresh fruited with a ribbon of red fruit. Strong but balanced oak support and soft, silky tannins. Not a hair out of place. Cork. 14.7% alc. **Rating** 96 **To** 2040 $125 DB
Old Vine Single Vineyard Eden Valley Shiraz 2016 Bright purple-red. Very primary – blackcurrant and bramble fruit, with a ribbon of spice and herbs woven through the succulent fruit tannins. Bright, fresh and long. Excellent value. Screwcap. 14.5% alc. **Rating** 95 **To** 2032 $21 DB ✪

Old John Barossa Shiraz 2016 Comprising 86% 55–60yo shiraz and 14% 75yo bonvedro, matured in French barrels (large and small). Deeply coloured, full-bodied and richly robed, with liqueured black fruits, licorice, bitter chocolate and superfine tannins. Screwcap. 14.3% alc. **Rating** 95 **To** 2041 $24 ✪

Old Vine Moculta Single Vineyard Eden Valley Shiraz 2016 This and its two single vineyard siblings make a fascinating trio, each has its strong points. This is medium+-bodied, and derives both flavour and texture from the new French oak component, coupled with the more elegant Eden Valley fruit. Screwcap. 14.5% alc. **Rating** 95 **To** 2036 $45

Old Vine Angaston Single Vineyard Barossa Shiraz 2016 Matured for 18 months in used Russian oak. Black fruits are the order of the day, starting with the bouquet, and progressively building power and impact as a potent, full-bodied savoury/spicy edge clicks in, changing the flavour profile (for the better). Screwcap. 14.5% alc. **Rating** 95 **To** 2041 $45

Old Vine Single Vineyard Barossa Valley Mataro 2016 Hand-picked form the 80yo Marshall Vineyard; 95% mataro, 5% grenache. The Woods Crampton vinification bible focuses on old, single vineyards, open fermentation in 2t fermenters, significant whole bunch inclusion and maturation in used oak. It works very well indeed, adding to the complexity and mouthfeel, and giving the fruit a plushness that is most attractive. Screwcap. 14.5% alc. **Rating** 95 **To** 2036 $28 ✪

🍷🍷🍷🍷♀ **Old Vine Barossa Shiraz 2016** Rating 93 **To** 2031
The Primrose Path McLaren Vale Shiraz 2016 Rating 93 **To** 2030 $30
Pedro Barossa Valley Grenache Shiraz Mourvedre 2017 Rating 93 **To** 2019 $24 DB ✪
Take it to the Grave Pale & Dry Rose 2017 Rating 92 **To** 2019 $18 ✪
South Australia Pinot Noir 2016 Rating 92 **To** 2020 $18 CM ✪
The Big Show Shiraz Mataro 2016 Rating 92 **To** 2031 $24 ✪
Take it to the Grave Coonawarra Cabernet Sauvignon 2016 Rating 92 **To** 2022 $18 CM ✪
Eden Valley Dry Riesling 2017 Rating 90 **To** 2023 $21 DB ✪
Third Wheel Barossa Valley Rose 2017 Rating 90 **To** 2020 $24 DB
Speak No Evil Organic Shiraz 2017 Rating 90 **To** 2019 $18 DB ✪
Five Horses Barossa Valley Shiraz 2016 Rating 90 **To** 2026
Sleeping Dogs Barossa Valley Red Blend 2017 Rating 90 **To** 2019 $24

Woodside Park Vineyards   ★★★★

27 Croydon Road, Keswick, SA 5035 (postal) **Region** Adelaide Hills
T (08) 7070 1401 **www.cloudbreakwines.com.au Open** Not
Winemaker Simon Greenleaf, Randal Tomich **Est.** 1998 **Dozens** 22 000 **Vyds** 76ha
Woodside Park Vineyards is a joint venture between Randal Tomich and Simon Greenleaf, who share a friendship of over 20 years. Woodside specialises in cool-climate wines (released under the Cloudbreak label), grown on the Tomich family's Woodside Park Vineyard. Simon has been producing wines from the Tomich vineyards since 2005, and has a strong understanding of the site and fruit quality. Randal has had more than 20 years' experience in winemaking, specialising in vineyard development, and plants vineyards for brands across Australia and California, US. The vineyards comprise chardonnay (22ha), sauvignon blanc (18ha), pinot noir (15ha), gruner veltliner (6ha), and riesling, gewurztraminer and shiraz (5ha each).

🍷🍷🍷🍷♀ **Adelaide Hills Chardonnay 2016** Bursts out of the block with clearly delineated varietal fruit that hits the G-spot; pink grapefruit, white peach and nectarine have excellent drive and acid balance, oak relegated to observer status. Screwcap. 13.5% alc. **Rating** 93 **To** 2024 $22 ✪
Winemakers Reserve Adelaide Hills Sauvignon Blanc 2017 A fresh, vibrant wine with a range of tropical fruits woven through notes of green pea. The finish is in the same mode, acidity in fine fettle ex the cool vintage. Screwcap. 13% alc. **Rating** 90 **To** 2021 $22

Woodsoak Wines

9 Woolundry Road, Robe, SA 5276 (postal) **Region** Robe
T 0437 681 919 **www**.woodsoakwines.com.au **Open** Not
Winemaker Peta Baverstock, Don Berrigan **Est.** 2010 **Dozens** 1450 **Vyds** 22ha
The Woodsoak farming property has been in the Legoe family for over 60 years, used for grazing cattle and sheep. In 1998 Will and Sonia Legoe diversified into grapegrowing, followed (inevitably) by a small batch of wine made in 2006 for family and friends – and finally the commercial establishment of Woodsoak Wines in '10. The vineyard includes cabernet sauvignon, shiraz, merlot and pinot noir; the Cabernet, Shiraz and Rose are named after their three children, and the Pyaar Pinot Noir after the Hindi word for love. The Legoes say, 'We ran out of children, and there was no call for more'.

ŢŢŢŢŢ **Methode Traditionnelle Blanc de Noirs 2015** While Robe pinot noir makes up 90% of this blanc de noirs, there's actually 10% chardonnay from Mount Gambier, too. Pale straw and bright; all citrus nuanced and really zesty. There's a touch of toasty complexity with the lemon sorbet acidity keeping this tight, and the 6g/l dosage is well placed. Plenty of bead and enjoyment. Disgorged Oct '17. Diam. 12.5% alc. **Rating** 91 $40 JF
Pyaar Robe Pinot Noir 2016 A pretty wine from the pale garnet hue to the raspberry and strawberry aromatics, and well matched to its light frame. Sweet fruit and such faint tannins, a mere hint of pinosity and best enjoyed in its youth. Screwcap. 13% alc. **Rating** 90 **To** 2022 $19 JF ✪

Woodstock ★★★★☆

215 Douglas Gully Road, McLaren Flat, SA 5171 **Region** McLaren Vale
T (08) 8383 0156 **www**.woodstockwine.com.au **Open** 7 days 10–5
Winemaker Ben Glaetzer **Est.** 1905 **Dozens** 22 000 **Vyds** 18.44ha
The Collett family is among the best known in McLaren Vale; the late Doug Collett AM for his World War II exploits flying Spitfires and Hurricanes with the RAF and RAAF, returning to study oenology at Roseworthy Agricultural College, and rapidly promoted to take charge of South Australia's largest winery, Berri Co-operative. In 1973 he purchased the Woodstock estate, built a winery, and in '74 he crushed its first vintage. Son Scott Collett, once noted for his fearless exploits in cars and on motorcycles, became winemaker in '82, and has won numerous accolades. Equally importantly, he purchased an adjoining shiraz vineyard planted circa 1900 (now the source of The Stocks Shiraz) and a bushvine grenache vineyard planted in '30. In '99, he joined forces with Ben Glaetzer, passing responsibility for winemaking to Ben, but retaining responsibility for the estate vineyards. Exports to most major markets.

ŢŢŢŢŢ **The OCTOgenarian McLaren Vale Grenache 2015** Sourced from 90+yo vines grown in sandy soils. Dark garnet-red and concentrated looking. More savoury than sweet on both nose and palate – dry earth and brown spice, then layers of poached plum, mulberry preserve and cranberry sauce. Tannins are fine and smooth, and woven through an uncluttered palate. Maturation without barrels a master stroke. Screwcap. 14.5% alc. **Rating** 95 **To** 2026 $32 DB ✪

ŢŢŢŢŢ **The Stocks Single Vineyard Shiraz 2015 Rating** 93 **To** 2030 $80 DB
The OCTOgenarian McLaren Vale Grenache Tempranillo 2014 Rating 92 **To** 2030 $32 DB
McLaren Vale Cabernet Sauvignon 2015 Rating 91 **To** 2026 $25 DB
Collett Lane Single Vineyard McLaren Vale Cabernet Sauvignon 2015 Rating 90 **To** 2030 $45 DB

Woody Nook ★★★★★

506 Metricup Road, Wilyabrup, WA 6280 **Region** Margaret River
T (08) 9755 7547 **www**.woodynook.com.au **Open** 7 days 10–4.30
Winemaker Neil Gallagher, Craig Dunkerton **Est.** 1982 **Dozens** 7500 **Vyds** 14.23ha
Woody Nook, with a backdrop of 18ha of majestic marri and jarrah forest, doesn't have the high profile of the biggest names in Margaret River, but has had major success in wine shows

over the years. It was purchased by Peter and Jane Bailey in 2000, and major renovations have transformed it, with a new winery, a gallery tasting room for larger groups and an alfresco dining area by the pond. A link to the past is Neil Gallagher's continuing role as winemaker, viticulturist and minority shareholder (Neil is the son of founders Jeff and Wynn Gallagher). Exports to the UK, the US, Canada, Bermuda, Hong Kong and China.

🍷🍷🍷🍷🍷 **Single Vineyard Margaret River Chardonnay 2016** Bright straw-green, the bouquet is initially slightly muffled, but the palate throbs with intensity, drawing saliva, and imperiously imposing grapefruit, stone fruit and minerally acidity. No room for argument, this is a very good wine. Screwcap. 13% alc. **Rating** 95 To 2024 $35 ✪
Gallagher's Choice Margaret River Cabernet Sauvignon 2015 A potent, serious wine from start to finish. Something like a young, expensive Bordeaux as you nose it, the dark cassis character and oak engaged in a battle for supremacy. Deeply flavoured but closed, a hint of sweet fruit just a teaser. Demands bottle age. Diam. 14% alc. **Rating** 95 To 2030 $65 SC

🍷🍷🍷🍷🍷 **Single Vineyard Margaret River Shiraz 2015** **Rating** 93 To 2030 $35
Limited Release Margaret River Merlot 2015 **Rating** 93 To 2020 $26 ✪

Word of Mouth Wines   ★★★★☆

42 Wallace Lane, Orange, NSW 2800 **Region** Orange
T 0429 533 316 **www.**wordofmouthwines.com.au **Open** 7 days 10.30–5
Winemaker David Lowe, Liam Heslop **Est.** 1999 **Dozens** 1250 **Vyds** 2.5ha
Peter Gibson has been the one constant figure in Word of Mouth – his involvement dating back to 1999 when he established Pinnacle Wines with an early planting of pinot gris. Word of Mouth was formed when Pinnacle amalgamated with neighbouring Donnington Vineyard. In 2013 the Donnington parcel was sold, and has since become Colmar Estate. Peter retained his original block, and continues under the Word of Mouth label.

🍷🍷🍷🍷🍷 **Orange Chardonnay 2016** Made by Will Rikard-Bell, wild-fermented in French oak (20% new), matured for 12 months on lees. High quality grapes have been picked when ripe, and then well made, a slightly funky bouquet adding to the complexity (and pleasure) of the wine. The flavour spectrum offers nectarine and white peach, citrus, Granny Smith apple and a toasty/grilled nut subtext. Screwcap. 12.5% alc. **Rating** 95 To 2025 $30 ✪

🍷🍷🍷🍷🍷 **Orange Petit Manseng 2017** **Rating** 91 To 2025 $30
Orange Petit Manseng 2016 **Rating** 90 To 2025 $30
Fluffy 2013 **Rating** 90 $50
1k high Riesling 2017 **Rating** 90 To 2024 $40

Wykari Wines   ★★★★

PO Box 905, Clare, SA 5453 **Region** Clare Valley
T (08) 8842 1841 **www.**wykariwines.com.au **Open** Not
Winemaker Neil Paulett **Est.** 2006 **Dozens** 1200 **Vyds** 20ha
'Wykari' is an indigenous word meaning 'windy hill'. Local Clare families Rob and Mandy Knight and Peter and Robyn Shearer own two vineyards, one to the north, the other to the south of Clare. The vineyards were first planted in 1974, and are dry-grown and hand-pruned. In all there are shiraz, riesling, cabernet sauvignon and chardonnay.

🍷🍷🍷🍷🍷 **Windy Hill Riesling 2016** Very different in style to the Naughty Boy Riesling, with a vibrantly fresh bouquet and palate. Many tasters would simply enjoy the purity of the fruit expression and long finish, not realising the skill of winemaker Neil Paulett in retaining a little residual sugar (0.63g/l) hidden by the acidity of 6.97g/l and low pH. Screwcap. 12% alc. **Rating** 94 To 2025 $22 ✪

🍷🍷🍷🍷🍷 **Single Vineyard Shiraz 2014** **Rating** 92 To 2027 $28
Single Vineyard Cabernet Sauvignon 2014 **Rating** 90 To 2027 $26

Wynns Coonawarra Estate ★★★★★

Memorial Drive, Coonawarra, SA 5263 **Region** Coonawarra
T (08) 8736 2225 **www**.wynns.com.au **Open** 7 days 10–5
Winemaker Sue Hodder, Sarah Pidgeon **Est.** 1897 **Dozens** NFP

Large-scale production has not prevented Wynns (an important part of TWE) from producing excellent wines covering the full price spectrum – from the bargain-basement Riesling and Shiraz through to the deluxe John Riddoch Cabernet Sauvignon and Michael Shiraz. Even with steady price increases, Wynns offers extraordinary value for money. Investments in rejuvenating and replanting key blocks, under the direction of Allen Jenkins, and skilled winemaking by Sue Hodder, have resulted in wines of far greater finesse and elegance than many of their predecessors. Exports to the UK, the US, Canada and Asia.

ŸŸŸŸŸ **The Gables Cabernet Sauvignon 2016** Blood plum, currant and anise scents are sheathed in a smooth veneer of detailed, gravelly and yet, impeccably massaged tannins. Together with juicy acidity, these serve as a welcome signpost to the fruit while conferring authority and a welcome savouriness. The finish is long and saline, laying bay leaf and strewn herb across the gums while expanding the flavours across the palate. This is a fine, highly refined cabernet with compelling vinosity and sap. Sue Hodder is a cabernet wunderkind with wines firmly stamped with a regional footprint. Screwcap. 13.5% alc. **Rating** 97 **To** 2038 $35 NG ✪

ŸŸŸŸŸ **Messenger Shiraz 2015** This vineyard has been drawn on only twice, prior to this vintage: '05 and '10. Dry grown across the deeper terra rossa zones, the beauty of this loaded expression is as much the power, as the palate-whetting tannins, drawing the saliva across the mouth and making one hanker for the next bite and sip. Currant, olive, fennel, bracken and strewn herb, with an accent on sage. This is statuesque yet restrained; focused and genetically imbued with Coonawarra's finest accents. Screwcap. 13.8% alc. **Rating** 96 **To** 2038 $150 NG

Michael Shiraz 2015 Coonawarra shiraz is an interesting conversation. A dialogue between cool-climate precision, mid-palate warmth and a certain austerity that is far from, say, the exuberant floral persuasion of Beechworth, Yarra or the Canberra region. This wine more than compensates with a skein of energetic peppery acidity threading liquorice, thyme and black and blue fruit all with a fine boned tannic needle. There is plenty of oak, but ample intensity and concentration of fruit, too, reassuring the drinker that all will gel effortlessly with patience. **Rating** 96 **To** 2035 NG

Black Label Cabernet Sauvignon 2015 Selected from the upper branches of Wynn's Coonawarra Estate's immense tree of cabernet, benefiting from all the investment made in reviving and/or replanting parts of lesser-performing plots. This is a top class Black Label, fully deserving this price. It is plush and pliant, with varietal character oozing from its blackcurrant fruit, balanced tannins and oak. Screwcap. 13.8% alc. **Rating** 96 **To** 2045 $45 ✪

Black Label Cabernet Sauvignon 2016 This is sumptuous, savoury cabernet at a ridiculous price. The tannins are pristine and tight of grain; the acidity fresh and juicy; the oak embellishing rather than smothering; the fruit, an effortless flow of currant, leaf, mint, bitter chocolate and a punctuation of bay leaf and a herbal potpourri, staining the long finish. Screwcap. 13.8% alc. **Rating** 95 **To** 2031 $45 NG

V&A Lane Cabernet Shiraz 2016 A superlative example of this archetypal Australian blend, with the blue-fruited pulp and violet aromatics of the shiraz, melding effortlessly with a blackcurrant-herbal astringency of the cabernet. Olive, sage and bracken, too. The structural carapace is fascinating: a pepper twinge of acidity and firmer, more stolid tannins. As juicy and exuberant as it is stiff-upper-lipped. Long and compelling. Screwcap. 13.4% alc. **Rating** 95 **To** 2028 $60 NG

ŸŸŸŸŸ **Black Label Shiraz 2016 Rating** 93 **To** 2025 $45 NG
V&A Lane Shiraz 2016 Rating 93 **To** 2028 $60 NG
Cabernet Shiraz Merlot 2016 Rating 93 **To** 2027 $25 NG ✪
Riesling 2017 Rating 92 **To** 2026 $25 NG ✪

Shiraz 2016 Rating 92 To 2024 $25 NG ☺
The Siding Cabernet Sauvignon 2016 Rating 91 To 2024 $25 NG

Xabregas ★★★★☆

Spencer Road, Mount Barker, WA 6324 (postal) **Region** Mount Barker
T (08) 6389 1382 **www.xabregas.com.au Open** Not
Winemaker Luke Eckersley **Est.** 1996 **Dozens** 8000 **Vyds** 80ha
The Hogan family have five generations of Western Australia history, and family interests in sheep grazing and forestry in the Great Southern, dating back to the 1860s. Terry Hogan, founding Xabregas chairman, felt the Mount Barker region was 'far too good dirt to waste on blue gums', and vines were planted in 1996. The Hogan family concentrates on the region's strengths – shiraz and riesling. Exports to the US, Japan and China.

ΨΨΨΨΨ **Mount Barker Riesling 2016** It's not easy to create an impression of generosity as the flavours dart through the mouth, plushness and speed rarely going together, and yet this riesling manages it. Jellied lime, apple, talc and assorted citrus blossom notes make for both delicious and dramatic drinking. Screwcap. 12.3% alc. **Rating** 95 **To** 2026 $25 CM ☺
Mount Barker Riesling 2017 Ever so succulent. Ripe lime meets lemon rind meets stony mineral. It begins juicy and generous but soon turns dry and steely. At every step, it's delicious. Screwcap. 11.5% alc. **Rating** 94 **To** 2015 $22 CM ☺
Artisan Syrah 2012 Co-fermented with whole-bunch viognier in large vats. The treatment has certainly had an impact, with orange-like acidity and floral notes bursting out of a mass of squished dark berries. It threatens to run fast and loose, but volleys of black pepper and cloves tie savouriness to the mast. Superfine tannin trims the sails. Not a heavy wine in any sense but it hums along. Screwcap. 14.4% alc. **Rating** 94 **To** 2030 $35 CM

ΨΨΨΨΨ **X by Xabregas Figtree Riesling 2017 Rating** 93 **To** 2024 $38 CM
Mount Barker Rose 2017 Rating 93 **To** 2021 $22 ☺
Mount Barker Cabernet Sauvignon 2013 Rating 92 **To** 2027 $25 CM ☺
X by Xabregas SR Sparkling Riesling 2014 Rating 91 $38 CM
Mount Barker Sauvignon Blanc 2017 Rating 90 **To** 2018 $22 CM

Xanadu Wines ★★★★★

Boodjidup Road, Margaret River, WA 6285 **Region** Margaret River
T (08) 9758 9500 **www.xanaduwines.com Open** 7 days 10–5
Winemaker Glenn Goodall **Est.** 1977 **Dozens** 70000 **Vyds** 109.5ha
Xanadu Wines was established in 1977 by Dr John Lagan. In 2005 it was purchased by the Rathbone family, and together with Glenn Goodall's winemaking team they have significantly improved the quality of the wines. The vineyard has been revamped via soil profiling, precision viticulture, improved drainage and reduced yields. The quality of the wines made since the acquisition of the Stevens Road Vineyard in '08 has been consistently outstanding. Exports to most major markets.

ΨΨΨΨΨ **Reserve Margaret River Chardonnay 2016** Gin Gin clone from Lagan Estate, whole-bunch pressed, wild-fermented in French barriques (30% new), no mlf, 9 months with lees stirring. It's not hard to see why Xanadu has had such show success and critical praise for its Chardonnays. This is resplendent in its generosity, yet also maintains perfect balance with its grapefruit wrapped in thin gauge beeswax and honey, acidity and oak precisely where they should be. Screwcap. 13% alc. **Rating** 97 **To** 2030
Stevens Road Margaret River Chardonnay 2016 Gin Gin clone, from 20 rows of Block 2 on the Stevens Road Vineyard, whole-bunch pressed, wild-fermented in French barriques (25% new), no mlf, matured for 9 months. The Reserve Chardonnay has a complexity that this adroitly sidesteps, holding its own ground with feline grace, every part of its body precisely shaped and weighted, leaving the palate with an airy freshness that will never tire you. Screwcap. 13% alc. **Rating** 97 **To** 2031

🍷🍷🍷🍷🍷 **DJL Margaret River Sauvignon Blanc Semillon 2017** A gold and trophy winner at the Sydney Wine Show '17. Partial barrel ferment has undoubtedly been the crux of the texture and structure that led to its trophy, of course — it is in any event a wine at which Margaret River excels. Here tropical and grassy/herbal components are on even terms. Screwcap. 13% alc. **Rating** 96 **To** 2021 $24 ✪

Margaret River Chardonnay 2016 Gin Gin clone estate-grown in Wallcliffe, whole-bunch pressed, wild-fermented in French oak (25% new), no mlf, matured for 9 months. Brings all the desired aspects into play from the first taste. It positively hums with energy and complexity, stone fruits leading, citrussy acidity and oak on a harmonious back-palate and finish. All the steps that should have been taken, and all those to be avoided, were precisely positioned. Screwcap. 13% alc. **Rating** 96 **To** 2036 $39 ✪

DJL Margaret River Shiraz 2015 Deep crimson; continuing a line of distinguished wines at bargain basement prices, it is elegant, full of life, and brings together a stream of juicy black cherry fruit, balanced and integrated tannins, and some cleverly handled oak inputs. It is of particularly exceptional value. Screwcap. 14% alc. **Rating** 96 **To** 2035 $24 ✪

Margaret River Cabernet Sauvignon 2015 This is 88% cabernet sauvignon, 7% petit verdot, 5% malbec, crushed and destemmed, fermented with 33% left on skins for 4 weeks, matured for 14 months in French oak (40% new). This wine has a scented, spicy nuance to the cassis base that adds a dimension to the flavour, yet leaves the wine not even medium-bodied, giving it grace and not making demands on the consumer. Superfine tannins complete the deal. Screwcap. 13.5% alc. **Rating** 96 **To** 2035 $39 ✪

Exmoor Margaret River Rose 2017 Pale salmon pink; predominantly shiraz, but also has a splash of graciano; lees stirring adding to the mouthfeel. A striking palate offers red fruits, citrus nuances and spice, the texture exceptional, the length likewise. Screwcap. 13% alc. **Rating** 95 **To** 2018 $18 ✪

Stevens Road Margaret River Cabernet Sauvignon 2015 From Block 3 of the vineyard that Xanadu knows like the back of its hand. Static fermented, 28 days post-ferment maceration, matured for 14 months in French barriques (40% new). Combines elegance with length, intensity and balance. Blackcurrant, earth, black olive and cabernet tannins all chime in on the heavy lifting — this at 14% alcohol tells it all. Screwcap. **Rating** 95 **To** 2030

Stevens Road Margaret River Malbec 2014 From a tiny 11-row block, crushed/destemmed, open-fermented, matured for 14 months in French oak (40% new) before the best barrels were blended and returned to oak for a further 2 months; 100 dozen made. This has flown under the radar, but it's the third release (normally blended with cabernet). It is supple and juicy, yet also has depth and power, and justifies its price. Screwcap. 14% alc. **Rating** 95 **To** 2039 $60

DJL Margaret River Cabernet Sauvignon 2015 Beautifully balanced medium-weight cabernet. The bouquet is full of blackcurrant, floral perfume and chocolate; the palate is sweetly fruited and supple, with fine, melting tannin that provides a lingering freshness on the finish. Either happily drink now or cellar. Screwcap. 13.5% alc. **Rating** 94 **To** 2027 SC

🍷🍷🍷🍷🍷 **DJL Margaret River Chardonnay 2017** Rating 93 To 2022 $24 ✪
Exmoor Margaret River Chardonnay 2016 Rating 93 To 2021 $18 ✪
Exmoor Margaret River Chardonnay 2017 Rating 92 To 2022 SC
Stevens Road Margaret River Graciano 2014 Rating 92 To 2026 SC
Exmoor Margaret River Cabernet Sauvignon 2015 Rating 90 To 2022 SC

🍇 XO Wine Co ★★★★

13 Wicks Road, Kuitpo, SA 5172 (postal) **Region** Adelaide Hills
T 0402 120 680 **www**.xowineco.com.au **Open** Not
Winemaker Greg Clack, Kate Horstmann **Est.** 2015 **Dozens** 299
Clackers is dead, long live XO Wine Co. Greg Clack has been in the wine industry for 14 years, the first 11 in McLaren Vale with Haselgrove Wines. In 2014 he took himself to the

Adelaide Hills as chief winemaker at Chain of Ponds – this remains his day job, nights and days here and there devoted to the then Clackers Wine Co. But when he met Kate Horstmann mid-'16, its name, its owners and its mission statement all changed to a lesser or greater degree, with the name change to XO Wine Co the most obvious. Its raison d'être still revolves around small-batch, single vineyard wines chiefly made from grenache, barbera, chardonnay and gamay. All winemaking was brought onto the site, minimising wine movements and protecting freshness.

🍷🍷🍷🍷🍷 **Small Batch Adelaide Hills Chardonnay 2016** Whole-bunch pressed directly to used French oak, 25% mlf, matured for 18 months. A complex wine reflecting the complexity of cultivation and vinification and the unusually long time in oak. No harm whatsoever has come from that, the wine fresh, detailed and crisp, the flavour suite taking in Granny Smith apple and pear alongside the more usual duo of white peach and grapefruit. Screwcap. 13% alc. **Rating** 94 **To** 2023 $32

🍷🍷🍷🍷🍷 **Single Vineyard Small Batch Barbera 2017 Rating** 93 **To** 2022 $32
Small Batch Sauvignon Blanc 2017 Rating 92 **To** 2020 $24 ✪

Yabby Lake Vineyard ★★★★★

86–112 Tuerong Road, Tuerong, Vic 3937 **Region** Mornington Peninsula
T (03) 5974 3729 **www**.yabbylake.com **Open** 7 days 10–5
Winemaker Tom Carson, Chris Forge **Est.** 1998 **Dozens** 3350 **Vyds** 50.8ha
This high profile wine business was established by Robert and Mem Kirby (of Village Roadshow), who had been landowners in the Mornington Peninsula for decades. In 1998 they established Yabby Lake Vineyard, under the direction of vineyard manager Keith Harris. The vineyard is on a north-facing slope, capturing maximum sunshine while also receiving sea breezes. The main focus is the 25ha of pinot noir, 14ha of chardonnay and 8ha of pinot gris; 3ha of shiraz, merlot and sauvignon blanc take a back seat. The arrival of the hugely talented Tom Carson as Group Winemaker has added lustre to the winery and its wines, making the first Jimmy Watson Trophy-winning Pinot Noir in 2014, and continuing to blitz the Australian wine show circuit with Single Block Pinots. Exports to the UK, Canada, Sweden, Singapore, Hong Kong and China.

🍷🍷🍷🍷🍷 **Single Block Release Block 6 Mornington Peninsula Chardonnay 2017** Mendoza clone, crushed, pressed, wild-fermented on solids in tight grain French puncheons, no mlf, matured on lees for 11 months. The complex, tangy, faintly funky, bouquet leads into an intense palate, grapefruit very much to the fore, and driving the long, very tightly bound, finish and aftertaste. The natural acidity, coupled with the absence of mlf, will mean a slow boat to China – but what an enjoyable one. Screwcap. 13% alc. **Rating** 98 **To** 2037 $95 ✪
Single Block Release Block 6 Mornington Peninsula Pinot Noir 2017 D4V2 clone, hand-sorted, destemmed into French oak open fermenters, 4 days cold soak, wild-fermented, 17 days on skins, matured for 11 months in French puncheons. Can't get away from the iron fist in a velvet glove. Dark cherry and plum fruit are riddled with spices, the texture and balance perfect, juicy fruits both a present and future bank for Bitcoin miners – it's equally magical. Screwcap. 13.5% alc. **Rating** 97 **To** 2032 $95 ✪

🍷🍷🍷🍷🍷 **Single Vineyard Mornington Peninsula Pinot Noir 2017** A mix of clones, open-fermented with a small percentage of whole bunches (less than 5%), 15 days on skins, matured for 11 months in French puncheons (20% new). Bright, clear crimson; more immediately accessible than Block 6, and likely to remain so. It's floral and fragrant, with bright red fruits running smoothly like a stream, pebbles (aka tannins) on its bed in no way breaking the flow. Screwcap. 13% alc. **Rating** 96 **To** 2029 $60 ✪
Single Vineyard Mornington Peninsula Chardonnay 2017 A distinguished clonal mix from Tuerong, crushed, pressed, matured in French puncheons (20% new), matured on lees for 11 months. Having been in a sold out sign for several months before this wine came onto the market, the return this offers

consumers must have been welcomed by all concerned. This isn't a sarcastic or backhanded swipe, far from it. It's a lovely chardonnay, white-fleshed stone fruit and grapefruity acidity are totally synergistic, the palate long and balanced, the 20% new oak barely perceptible. Screwcap. 12.5% alc. **Rating** 95 **To** 2029 $45

Single Vineyard Mornington Peninsula Pinot Gris 2017 Hand-picked solely from Block 2, whole-bunch pressed, part fermented in used French puncheons. The aromas of the bouquet are positively heady with floral cherry blossom, then a textured and intense palate with far more to say for itself than all but a few of its combatants. Screwcap. 13% alc. **Rating** 95 **To** 2022 $33 ✪

Pink Claw Heathcote Grenache Rose 2017 Complex vinification has been repaid by the softly insistent texture and the floral tones of grenache, red berries front and centre, the sum of the parts captured on the finish and aftertaste. A thinking person's rose, complete in itself. Screwcap. 12.5% alc. **Rating** 94 **To** 2021 $27 ✪

Single Vineyard Mornington Peninsula Cuvee Nina 2012 Chardonnay, pinot noir and pinot meunier. Retains remarkable freshness after 4 years on lees, white peach and nectarine joined with strawberry fruits, the dosage precise, the length admirable. Diam. 12.5% alc. **Rating** 94 $45

🍷🍷🍷🍷🍷 **Red Claw Chardonnay 2017** Rating 93 To 2024 $27 ✪
Red Claw Pinot Noir 2017 Rating 92 To 2021 $30

Yal Yal Estate ★★★★

15 Wynnstay Road, Prahran, Vic 3181 (postal) **Region** Mornington Peninsula
T 0416 112 703 **www**.yalyal.com.au **Open** Not
Winemaker Sandro Mosele **Est.** 1997 **Dozens** 2500 **Vyds** 2.63ha
In 2008 Liz and Simon Gillies acquired a vineyard planted in 1997 to 1.6ha of chardonnay and a little over 1ha of pinot noir.

🍷🍷🍷🍷🍷 **Yal Yal Rd Mornington Peninsula Chardonnay 2016** Wild-fermented in French oak, no mlf, no fining, 10 months maturation. Subtle complexity is the hallmark here. Fruit and oak mesh seamlessly through the bouquet and palate, with aromas and flavours of citrus, white peach, creamy lees and cashew. A wine of finesse more than great intensity, and length is more of a feature than depth at this stage. Screwcap. 13.5% alc. **Rating** 93 **To** 2022 $30 SC

Yal Yal Rd Mornington Peninsula Pinot Gris 2016 Whole-bunch pressed, wild yeast, 50% tank- and 50% French oak–fermented, aged on lees for 9 months without stirring. A very attractive expression of one of this region's signature varieties. Subtle aromas of pear and apple are indicative of the grape, with the influence of skins, lees and oak providing a savoury complexity. The freshness, texture, and a really juicy vinosity on the palate are a winning combination. Screwcap. 14% alc. **Rating** 92 **To** 2020 $30 SC

Yal Yal Rd Mornington Peninsula Pinot Noir 2016 Cold soak, then wild-fermented in tank. 12 months maturation in French oak. Fragrant pinot aromas in the bouquet, red-fruit/strawberry, with notes of sweet spice and vanilla. Just on the light side of medium-bodied, there's a core of both ripe and savoury varietal flavours including cherry and cranberry overlaid with a wash of gently persistent tannin. Screwcap. 13.5% alc. **Rating** 92 **To** 2024 $30 SC

Yalumba ★★★★★

40 Eden Valley Road, Angaston, SA 5353 **Region** Eden Valley
T (08) 8561 3200 **www**.yalumba.com **Open** 7 days 10–5
Winemaker Louisa Rose (chief), Kevin Glastonbury, Natalie Cleghorn **Est.** 1849
Dozens 930 000 **Vyds** 180ha
Family-owned and run by Robert Hill-Smith, Yalumba has a long commitment to quality and great vision in its selection of vineyard sites, new varieties and brands. It has always been a serious player at the top end of full-bodied (and full-blooded) Australian reds, and was a pioneer in the use of screwcaps. While its estate vineyards are largely planted to mainstream

varieties, it has taken marketing ownership of viognier. However, these days its own brands revolve around the Y Series and a number of stand-alone brands across the length and breadth of South Australia. A founding member of Australia's First Families of Wine. Exports to all major markets.

ΨΨΨΨΨ The Caley Coonawarra Barossa Cabernet Shiraz 2013 Stained/spongy cork. A beautiful wine in all respects, its heart soft and generous, its head stern and serious, the combination as complete as it is complex. It tastes of an assortment of red and black berries, tobacco and cloves, with tremendously well-integrated smoky oak and plenty of tang, tannin, flavour and run through the finish. An exhibition in both power and elegance. Cork permitting, it will mature gloriously. Cork. 13.5% alc. **Rating** 97 **To** 2043 $349 CM

ΨΨΨΨΨ Steeple Vineyard Light Pass Barossa Valley Shiraz 2014 Class of the highest order. It has sex appeal where it needs to and modesty where it doesn't. It's balanced perfectly, is ripped with blackcurrant and plum, shows hints of mint and boysenberry, and is all wrapped up in smoky, bacony, cedary oak. Tannin is assertive, al dente, and at one with the fruit. It's quite beautiful. Cork. 13.5% alc. **Rating** 96 **To** 2040 $75 CM ○

FDR1A Cabernet Shiraz 2013 There's a spread to this wine that is beyond the norm. It hits and flows, in a satisfying way, but when it hits what might be the finish it fans out impressively. That extra kick of flavour – you could simply call it 'quality' – that we're all hoping for but rarely receive; it's on beautiful display here. Cork. 13.5% alc. **Rating** 96 **To** 2040 $50 CM ○

The Virgilius Eden Valley Viognier 2016 Elegance is as much in favour as flavour, though so too is complexity. This is a fine wine, slender, flinty, spicy, kissed with wood smoke, carried by stone fruit. It darts in many different directions, but ultimately it zeroes in long through the finish. Screwcap. 12.5% alc. **Rating** 95 **To** 2022 $52 CM

The Octavius Old Vine Barossa Shiraz 2014 You have to admire the way this combines mouthfilling flavour with freshness, elegance and indeed beauty. This packs prettiness into its power. It's as much about boysenberry as blackberry, as much violets and mint as sweet, soft plums. There's a glide of smoky, chocolatey oak, but no more than that. Oak here just taps the fruit into line, and adds to the texture. It's quite a beauty. Cork. 14% alc. **Rating** 95 **To** 2040 $130 CM

Block 2 Barossa Valley Grenache Rose 2017 From 100+yo vines, wild yeast, 5 months in old oak. Pale copper. Incredibly dry and direct. Mouthwatering in the extreme. Raspberry, spice, earth and steel, with wood spice and florals adding their own versions of bass and treble respectively. Stunning in its own way. Screwcap. 12.5% alc. **Rating** 94 **To** 2021 $40 CM

The Cigar The Menzies Vineyard Cabernet Sauvignon 2014 It's a strict, rigid cabernet with fragrant herb, currant and black olive characters running straight and true through the palate, the (tannic) finish is all muscle and bone. It needs time. It has the necessary requirements. Coiled power is the phrase. Cork. 13.5% alc. **Rating** 94 **To** 2040 $35 CM

ΨΨΨΨΨ Eden Valley Viognier 2016 **Rating** 93 **To** 2019 $24 CM ○
Samuel's Garden Collection Eden Valley Roussanne 2016 **Rating** 93 **To** 2022 $24 CM ○
Hand Picked Eden Valley Shiraz + Viognier 2015 **Rating** 93 **To** 2030 $39 CM
Samuel's Garden Collection Old Bush Vine Barossa Grenache 2016 **Rating** 93 **To** 2022
The Scribbler Cabernet Sauvignon Shiraz 2014 **Rating** 93 **To** 2026 $23 CM ○
FSW8B Wrattonbully Botrytis Viognier 2017 **Rating** 93 **To** 2023 $29 CM
FSW8B Wrattonbully Botrytis Viognier 2015 **Rating** 93 **To** 2024 $30
Samuel's Garden Collection Triangle Block Eden Valley Shiraz 2014 **Rating** 92 **To** 2026 $24 CM ○

Y Series Barossa Riesling 2017 Rating 91 To 2023 $15 JF ✪
Y Series Sangiovese Rose 2017 Rating 90 To 2018 $15 JF ✪
The Strapper Barossa Grenache Shiraz Mourvedre 2015 Rating 90
To 2023 $22 CM

Yangarra Estate Vineyard ★★★★★

809 McLaren Flat Road, Kangarilla, SA 5171 **Region** McLaren Vale
T (08) 8383 7459 www.yangarra.com.au **Open** 7 days 10–5
Winemaker Peter Fraser, Shelley Torresan **Est.** 2000 **Dozens** 15000 **Vyds** 89.3ha
This is the Australian operation of Jackson Family Wines, one of the leading premium
wine producers in California, which in 2000 acquired the 172ha Eringa Park vineyard
from Normans Wines (the oldest vines dated back to 1923). The renamed Yangarra Estate
Vineyard is the estate base for the operation, and is moving to certified organic status with its
vineyards. Peter Fraser has taken Yangarra Estate to another level altogether with his innovative
winemaking and desire to explore all the possibilities of the Rhône Valley red and white styles.
Thus you will find grenache, shiraz, mourvedre, cinsaut, carignan, tempranillo and graciano
planted, and picpoul noir, terret noir, muscardin and vaccarese around the corner. The white
varieties are roussanne and viognier, with grenache blanc, bourboulenc and picpoul blanc
planned. Then you see ceramic eggs being used in parallel with conventional fermenters. In
2015 Peter was named Winemaker of the Year at the launch of the *Wine Companion* 2016.
Exports to the UK, the US and other major markets.

🍷🍷🍷🍷🍷 **High Sands McLaren Vale Grenache 2015** For many devotees of McLaren
Vale grenache, Yangarra Estate High Sands is the king. It's not for idle dalliance
as is young grenache that is focused on freshness and purity of red fruit flavours,
this has power and depth, the oak simply softening an edge or two here and
there, most assuredly not about imparting oak flavour. Red and black fruits both
contribute without cutting across the power of the other. Screwcap. 14.5% alc.
Rating 98 To 2045 $140 ✪
McLaren Vale Shiraz 2016 This is profoundly exciting, another masterpiece
from Peter Fraser. It's not often I'm tempted to sneakily swallow half a mouthful of
a wine (it's almost as if an unseen force refuses to let me actually drink a little). The
wine is spicy, textured, with a rainbow of dark fruit flavours – bloody gorgeous.
Screwcap. 14.5% alc. **Rating** 97 To 2036 $30 ✪
Ironheart McLaren Vale Shiraz 2015 A distilled essence of shiraz from two
blocks within a single estate vineyard. It's in no way overdone, but it does have
some of the authoritarian stance of top flight cabernet. The black fruits speak in
one voice of the ironstone soil in which the vines are planted. Great vintage, great
wine. Screwcap. 14.5% alc. **Rating** 97 To 2045 $105 ✪

🍷🍷🍷🍷🍷 **Ovitelli McLaren Vale Grenache 2016** Fermented in two 675l ceramic eggs,
remaining on skins post fermentation for 140 days, no oak maturation. Peter Fraser
says he can't explain why eggs perform as they do, and of course nor can I. But I
am sure you could not bypass oak in favour of stainless steel tanks. The eggs give
the wine texture akin to tight-grain oak, and no reduced character whatsoever.
Screwcap. 14.5% alc. **Rating** 96 To 2036 $72 ✪
McLaren Vale Grenache Shiraz Mourvedre 2016 Magical, deep crimson; as
devotees of Chateau Rayas, and others from the Rhône Valley will attest, grenache
has many faces, the most admired in that part of France, its serious, long-lived,
complex and structured single varietal pose. But it's usually in a blend, and in
Australia usually with shiraz and mourvedre, and this is a compelling example
of all the individual flavours of its components. Screwcap. 14.5% alc. **Rating** 95
To 2041 $32 ✪
McLaren Vale Roussanne 2017 It all sees oak, though only 10% of it is new.
This just has that something extra; it carries along in competent style but the sparks
really fly on the finish. It's slippery and textural, though not oily, fresh with fruit, and
then wild with dry spice, roasted nuts, fennel, fruit and mineral to close. You want
more? It gives it to you. Screwcap. 13% alc. **Rating** 94 To 2021 $35 CM

Roux Beaute McLaren Vale Roussanne 2016 It's incredible that so little evidence of wild, way out winemaking has produced a bright straw-green wine, that truly tastes of roussanne, a non-aromatic variety. The only sign is a touch of heat or ginger (I don't know which) that flickers every now and then. Screwcap. 13.5% alc. **Rating** 94 **To** 2026 $72

McLaren Vale Grenache Rose 2017 Pale copper-crimson, gorgeously aromatic, spotlessly clean and a delight to drink. Echoes of redcurrant and spice, dried herbs and cherries. Dry and racy, but not anaemic or underdone. Everything here, price included, is in alignment. Screwcap. 12.5% alc. **Rating** 94 **To** 2019 $25 CM ✪

Old Vine McLaren Vale Grenache 2016 Very good colour; rich, full predominantly red fruits supported by fine tannins. No hint at all of confection or jam. The finish simply reinforces the depth and the freshness of the fruit from 70yo vines. Bargain. Screwcap. 14.5% alc. **Rating** 94 **To** 2026 $35

McLaren Vale Mourvedre 2016 Matured for 10 months in used French oak. Normally this goes into the GSM, in exceptional years made as a single varietal. This is high quality mourvedre, with luscious purple and black fruits with a markedly juicy palate and aftertaste. Screwcap. 14.5% alc. **Rating** 94 **To** 2031 $35

♟♟♟♟♟ **Small Pot McLaren Vale Clairette 2017** Rating 93 To 2020 $30 CM
PF McLaren Vale Shiraz 2017 Rating 92 To 2019 $25 SC ✪

Yarra Burn   ★★★★

4/19 Geddes Street, Mulgrave, Vic 3170 (postal) **Region** Yarra Valley
T 1800 088 711 www.yarraburn.com.au **Open** Not
Winemaker Ed Carr **Est.** 1975 **Dozens** NFP
At least in terms of name, this is the focal point of Accolade's Yarra Valley operations. However, the winery was sold, and the wines are now made elsewhere. The Upper Yarra vineyard largely remains. The lack of interest in the brand and its quality is as sad as it is obvious.

♟♟♟♟♟ **Premium Cuvee Brut NV** No details supplied so the vintage base is unknown other than a blend of pinot noir and chardonnay. However, it is fresh with lemon blossom and zest meeting up with some crisp apple. Not overly complex but hits the spot at this price point. Cork. 12.5% alc. **Rating** 90 $17 JF ✪

Yarra Yering   ★★★★★

Briarty Road, Coldstream, Vic 3770 **Region** Yarra Valley
T (03) 5964 9267 www.yarrayering.com **Open** 7 days 10–5
Winemaker Sarah Crowe **Est.** 1969 **Dozens** 5000 **Vyds** 26.37ha
In September 2008, founder Bailey Carrodus died, and in April '09 Yarra Yering was on the market. It was Bailey Carrodus's clear wish and expectation that any purchaser would continue to manage the vineyard and winery, and hence the wine style, in much the same way as he had done for the previous 40 years. Its acquisition in June '09 by a small group of investment bankers has fulfilled that wish. The low-yielding, unirrigated vineyards have always produced wines of extraordinary depth and intensity. Dry Red No. 1 is a cabernet blend; Dry Red No. 2 is a shiraz blend; Dry Red No. 3 is a blend of touriga nacional, tinta cao, tinta roriz, tinta amarela, alvarelhao and souzao; Pinot Noir and Chardonnay are not hidden behind delphic numbers; Underhill Shiraz (planted in 1973) is from an adjacent vineyard purchased by Yarra Yering in 1987. Sarah Crowe was appointed winemaker after the '13 vintage. She has made red wines of the highest imaginable quality right from her first vintage in '14, and to the delight of many, myself included, has offered all the wines with screwcaps. For good measure, she introduced the '14 Light Dry Red Pinot Shiraz as a foretaste of that vintage, and an affirmation of the exceptional talent recognised by her being named Winemaker of the Year in the *Wine Companion* 2017. The '16 Yarra Yerings are an absolute triumph. Exports to the UK, the US, Singapore, Hong Kong, China and NZ.

ΤΤΤΤΤ **Carrodus Cabernet Sauvignon 2016** Restored my sanity after tasting a long string of green, miserable merlots and cabernets. Every aspect of this wine from vineyard to bottle is faultless, encouraging repeated visits to the glass making sure it is as good as it is. There is a cavalcade of perfectly ripe blue and black fruits running between rounded tannins, touches of leaf, herb and olive tapenade. Perfect balance at this stage is a rare thing with cabernet. Screwcap. 14% alc. **Rating** 99 To 2041 $250 ✪

Dry Red No. 1 2015 This is a superlative, tightly furled Bordeaux blend of pedigree, age-worthiness and a sapid quiver of blackcurrant to herbal notes: crushed, dried and strewn about the palate, all tightly guarded by gravelly tannins and juicy natural acidity. A blend of 67% cabernet sauvignon, 16% merlot, 13% malbec and a mere seasoning of petit verdot synergise to make an imperious, beautiful wine with a long, long life ahead. Screwcap. 14% alc. **Rating** 99 **To** 2040 $100 ✪

Carrodus Shiraz 2016 Exceptional vivid colour; the calm bouquet is driven by dark fruits, the oak not assertive. The full-bodied palate is a revelation, plush and deep flavours of blackberry and plum on entry, the tannins and oak on the mid- to back-palate and supple finish. The magic comes in the aftertaste, where spicy red fruits burst into song. Screwcap. 14.5% alc. **Rating** 98 **To** 2051 $250

Light Dry Red Pinot Shiraz 2017 Brilliant hue; 50% pinot noir/50% shiraz. It's wholly remarkable how the flavours and aromas of these two very different varieties flow sinuously into each other, red fruits the epicentre of a wine that has launched a thousand ships. Its balance is perfect, the length prodigious, the texture ... Well, just taste it. Screwcap. 13.5% alc. **Rating** 97 **To** 2032 $92 ✪

Pinot Noir 2016 A Winston Churchill figure in Yarra Valley's pinot noirs, standing higher than all others. It has layer upon layer of flavours derived from the fruit, unique fermentation, tannins, oak, and X-factor from vines nearing 50yo. It has no need to advertise its quality or style as it glides through the length of the medium-bodied palate. Screwcap. 14% alc. **Rating** 97 **To** 2036 $100 ✪

Dry Red No. 2 2016 Comprising 95% shiraz, 2% viognier, 2% mataro, 1% marsanne. The most highly aromatic bouquet with perfumed fruits and spices dancing on forest floor, the palate a liquid expression of the bouquet. Alive with juicy, gently savoury tannins beating a beautiful tattoo, the finish drawn out by the peacock's tail of the multifaceted aftertaste. Screwcap. 14.2% alc. **Rating** 97 **To** 2041 $100 ✪

Dry Red No. 1 2016 Made of 66% cabernet sauvignon, 16% merlot, 15% malbec, 3% petit verdot, matured separately in French oak (40% new) for 15 months. Profoundly juicy and rich, yet kept under tight control by the web of ripe tannins, oak part of the structure and texture but not flavour per se. It is a wine that you can sit with for a prolonged examination and discussion, and still not cover all its characteristics or ask all the questions. Screwcap. 14% alc. **Rating** 97 **To** 2041 $100 ✪

Dry Red No. 3 2016 Consists of 45% touriga nacional, 28% tinta cao, 9% tinta roriz, 7% tinta amarela, 7% avarelhao, 4% sousao, foot-stomped in traditional Portuguese lagar fashion, matured in old oak for 10 months. You have to wait for this blend to work its magic, for it is a wine of quite remarkable finesse and aromatic qualities. Its length, too, is beyond the ordinary. Screwcap. 14% alc. **Rating** 97 **To** 2030 $100 ✪

Malbec 2016 At one time I had several bottles of the '78 in my cellar, serving Bailey Carrodus a bottle decanted at my home (he was one of our closest neighbours). It was a nice old wine, but not in the same league as the '16, its luscious plum and black cherry flowing in all directions (unbidden) in the mouth, velvety tannins giving the fruit an armchair ride. Screwcap. 14% alc. **Rating** 97 **To** 2041 $100 ✪

ΤΤΤΤΤ **Underhill 2016** Bright, deep colour; right from the outset, very different from the other wines in the release, with more spring in its step, more stalky/spice flavours behind black fruits, peppery notes inlaid into the broader mosaic of a constantly changing colour. Screwcap. 14% alc. **Rating** 96 **To** 2036 $100

Agincourt Cabernet Malbec 2016 An 80/20% blend. As with all the red wines in the Yarra Yering range, it has excellent colour, deep in the centre, vivid on the rim. In other respects it strikes out on its own, highly aromatic and tightly strung, with savoury, spicy notes. The tannins are supple and pliable, so it greets the taster with an elegant bow, the finish a flourish of juicy essence. Screwcap. 14.5% alc. **Rating** 96 **To** 2036 $100

Chardonnay 2016 The estate's dry-grown vines, planted in '69, are among the oldest in the Yarra Valley. There's something about the Yarra Yering site that always delivers richer wine than any other in the Valley. Of course, vine age is exceptional, as is the gentle north-facing slope, and this also imparts a unique honeyed richness. Lest you think it's all too much, wait for the lovely citrussy acidity that lingers long after the wine has been swallowed. Screwcap. 13.5% alc. **Rating** 95 **To** 2023 $100

Carrodus Viognier 2016 From the oldest viognier vines in Australia, only two barrels made. Sarah Crowe has managed to have the best of both worlds, making a viognier with varietal flavour, without a lumpy phenolic finish. The decision to block mlf was a saviour. Screwcap. 15% alc. **Rating** 94 **To** 2022 $160

♟♟♟♟♟ **Dry White No. 1 2016** Rating 93 To 2022 $55

Yarrabank

38 Melba Highway, Yarra Glen, Vic 3775 **Region** Yarra Valley
T (03) 9730 0100 **www**.yering.com **Open** 7 days 10–5
Winemaker Michel Parisot, Willy Lunn **Est.** 1993 **Dozens** 5000 **Vyds** 4ha

Yarrabank is a highly successful joint venture between Yering Station and the French Champagne house Devaux, established in 1993. Until '97 the Yarrabank Cuvee Brut was made under Claude Thibaut's direction at Domaine Chandon, but thereafter the entire operation has been conducted at Yarrabank. There are 4ha of dedicated vineyards at Yering Station (planted to pinot noir and chardonnay); the balance of the intake comes from growers in Yarra Valley and southern Victoria. Exports to all major markets.

♟♟♟♟♟ **Cuvee 2012** Comprising 51% chardonnay, 49% pinot noir, 5 years on lees, 12% reserve wine kept in a 5500l foudre, 4.g/l dosage. Yellow-straw; complex wine, nashi pear and biscuit on the bouquet leads into a rich palate with peach and nectarine fruit; creamy mouthfeel. Diam. 13% alc. **Rating** 95 $38

Late Disgorged 2007 58% pinot noir, 42% chardonnay, 10 years on lees, 15% reserve wine kept in a 5500l foudre, zero dosage. An unbelievably complex wine, demonstrated by zero dosage when bottled. Length, elegance and a complex matrix of berry fruits, aromas and flavours. Diam. 12.5% alc. **Rating** 94 $55

Yarradindi Wines

1018 Murrindindi Road, Murrindindi, Vic 3717 **Region** Upper Goulburn
T 0438 305 314 **www**.mrhughwine.com **Open** Not
Winemaker Hugh Cuthbertson **Est.** 1979 **Dozens** 90 000 **Vyds** 70ha

The former Murrindindi Vineyards was established by Alan and Jan Cuthbertson as a minor diversification of their cattle property. Son Hugh, with a long and high profile wine career, took over the venture and in 2015 rebranded the business as Yarradindi Wines. The main focus is now export to China, with distribution organisations in Hangzhou, shipping 1 million bottles annually.

♟♟♟♟♟ **Mr Hugh Blue Range Estate Vineyard Mornington Peninsula Chardonnay 2015** Bright straw-green; it's fine and delicate, and if mlf has been used, it is not obvious. The oak treatment is subtle, leaving the stone fruit, apple and grapefruit aromas and flavours free to play on the senses without indifference. Diam. 13.5% alc. **Rating** 94 **To** 2028 $50

♟♟♟♟♟ **Mr Hugh McLaren Vale Shiraz 2014** Rating 93 To 2034 $50
Family Reserve Yea Valley Shiraz 2013 Rating 93 To 2028 $35
Yarradindi Family Reserve Yarra Valley Cabernet Sauvignon Merlot 2015 Rating 93 To 2035 $35

Yarran Wines

178 Myall Park Road, Yenda, NSW 2681 **Region** Riverina
T (02) 6968 1125 www.yarranwines.com.au **Open** Mon–Sat 10–5
Winemaker Sam Brewer **Est.** 2000 **Dozens** 8000 **Vyds** 30ha

Lorraine Brewer and late husband John were grapegrowers for over 30 years, and when son Sam completed a degree in wine science at CSU, they celebrated his graduation by crushing 1t of shiraz, fermenting the grapes in a milk vat. The majority of the grapes from the estate plantings are sold, but each year a little more has been made under the Yarran banner; along the way a winery with a crush capacity of 150t has been built. Sam worked for Southcorp and De Bortoli in Australia, and also overseas (in the US and China), but in 2009 decided to take the plunge and concentrate on the family winery with his parents. The majority of the grapes come from the family vineyard, but some parcels are sourced from growers, including Lake Cooper Estate in the Heathcote region. It is intended that the portfolio of regions will be gradually increased, and Sam has demonstrated his ability to make silk purses out of sow's ears, and sell them for the price of the latter. Exports to Singapore and China.

🍷🍷🍷🍷⚲ **A few words Montepulciano Rose 2017** Yarran crafts admirable wines offering real value, none more than this thirst-slaking dry, highly attractive rose. The nose, crushed strawberry, jasmine and Mediterranean allusions. The wine rides along a vein of skinsy crunch and further textural detail following a fermentation kicked off by wild yeast, partly in barrel, some of it new. Stirring has imparted breadth and a gravitas belying the price. Screwcap. 13% alc. **Rating** 93 **To** 2019 $17 NG **❶**

B Series Heathcote Shiraz 2016 This is an old but good-school shiraz, coating the mouth with blue and dark fruit flavours, boozy fruit cake spice, mocha and bourbon vanilla tones from an arsenal of American oak. This said, the alcohol feels digestible and the tannins coat the gums rather than rasping them. Forceful in personality and length. Comforting, if far from prosaic, like sagging into a comfy chair. Screwcap. 14.4% alc. **Rating** 92 **To** 2022 $25 NG **❶**

B Series Yenda Durif 2016 A wine for those who like to be bludgeoned rather than caressed, attesting to the veracity of the back label schtick: a 'true heavy wine drinker's friend.' Blue and black berry flavours ooze across a beam of toasty oak, while anise and tobacco pouch notes impart a herbal lift. The sheer extract stains the palate and fills the senses. A satisfying, powerful red. Screwcap. 14.5% alc. **Rating** 91 **To** 2025 $22 NG **❶**

Cuvee Blanc NV Crafted from a select batch of chardonnay, baked apple, dried pineapple, a hint of toast and a persuasive mushroom note – all linger from fore to aft, indicating some lees handling. The fizz is frothy and gentle. While the acidity plays a refreshment card, it is far from cool climate-high. Another top value proposition across a spritz or straitlaced. Cork. 11% alc. **Rating** 90 $12 NG **❶**

Yarrh Wines

440 Greenwood Road, Murrumbateman, NSW 2582 **Region** Canberra District
T (02) 6227 1474 www.yarrhwines.com.au **Open** Fri–Sun 11–5
Winemaker Fiona Wholohan **Est.** 1997 **Dozens** 2000 **Vyds** 6ha

Fiona Wholohan and Neil McGregor are IT refugees, and both now work full-time running the Yarrh Wines vineyard and making the wines. Fiona undertook the oenology and viticulture course at CSU, and has also spent time as an associate judge at wine shows. They say they spent five years moving to a hybrid organic vineyard, with composting, mulching, biological controls and careful vineyard floor management. The vineyard includes cabernet sauvignon, shiraz, sauvignon blanc, riesling, pinot noir and sangiovese. They have recently tripled their sangiovese plantings with two new clones. Yarrh was the original Aboriginal name for the Yass district.

🍷🍷🍷🍷🍷 **Canberra District Riesling 2017** Quartz-white; this is a pretty nifty wine, yet another example of the terroir and its welcome embrace of riesling. Its faintly floral bouquet will build with time, the palate already well down the track with its intensity, and purity of the citrus fruits encompassed by crunchy acidity. Screwcap. 11.5% alc. **Rating** 94 To 2027 $25 **✪**

♀♀♀♀♀ **Canberra District Cabernet Sauvignon 2015** Rating 93 To 2040 $30
Canberra District Sangiovese 2016 Rating 90 To 2022 $30

Yeates Wines ★★★☆

138 Craigmoor Road, Mudgee, NSW 2850 **Region** Mudgee
T 0427 791 264 **www.**yeateswines.com.au **Open** By appt
Winemaker Jacob Stein **Est.** 2010 **Dozens** 420 **Vyds** 16ha
In 2010 the Yeates family purchased the 16ha Mountain Blue Vineyard in Mudgee from Fosters, planted in 1968 by the late Robert (Bob) Oatley. The vines have since been reinvigorated and cane-pruned, with the grapes now being hand-picked. In 2013 the use of chemicals and inorganic fertiliser were eliminated and organic management practices introduced, in an effort to achieve a more sustainable ecological footprint. The vines and wines have flourished under this new management regimen.

♀♀♀♀ **The Gatekeeper Reserve 2016** Predominantly shiraz with some cabernet sauvignon. Brighter colour than its Shiraz sibling, and keeps its shape until the finish and aftertaste, when the alcohol and extract make their presence felt. It's a glass half full, and does have overall presence. For the patient. Screwcap. 15% alc. **Rating** 89 To 2031

Yelland & Papps ★★★★★

279 Nuraip Road, Nuriootpa, SA 5355 **Region** Barossa Valley
T (08) 8562 3510 **www.**yellandandpapps.com **Open** Mon–Sat 10–4
Winemaker Michael Papps **Est.** 2005 **Dozens** 5000 **Vyds** 1ha
Michael and Susan Papps (née Yelland) set up this venture after their marriage in 2005. It is easy for them to regard the Barossa Valley as their home, for Michael has lived and worked in the wine industry in the Barossa Valley for more than 20 years. He has a rare touch, with his wines consistently excellent, but also pushing the envelope; as well as using a sustainable approach to winemaking with minimal inputs, he has not hesitated to challenge orthodox approaches to a number of aspects of conventional fermentation methods.

♀♀♀♀♀ **Barossa Valley Vermentino 2017** Smells of lemon blossom and the sea. It tastes zesty with grapefruit pith, neat phenolics and saline-lemon flavours with a smidge of dried Mediterranean herbs. Must be vermentino. It's spot-on. Screwcap. 12.3% alc. **Rating** 95 To 2020 $28 JF **✪**
Second Take Barossa Valley Shiraz 2017 As with all the Second Take wines, there's immediate drinkability and enjoyment. Shiraz is the star of the reds in this vintage, with a deep, purple-noir hue. A neat combo of dark fruits and spice (especially licorice) with some warm earth and pepper. Very savoury, tangy with firm but giving tannins. Screwcap. 13.8% alc. **Rating** 95 To 2028 $40 JF
Second Take Barossa Valley Vermentino 2017 Wild-fermented with a whopping 231 days on skins in tank. Quite phenolic with a bitter-radicchio finish and racy acidity. In the midst it has gorgeous aromatics and flavours – quince paste, lemon barley water, rose petals and exotic spices. Savoury and moreish. Needs food as its friend. Screwcap. 11.6% alc. **Rating** 94 To 2021 $40 JF
Second Take Barossa Valley Grenache 2017 A pale-mid ruby; way too easy to drink this, as it's on a lighter frame full of bright, juicy fruit, a hint of red licorice and confection. Crisp acidity keeps it lively. It's not complex, ready now and wouldn't last long during lunch. Screwcap. 13.9% alc. **Rating** 94 To 2023 $40 JF

♀♀♀♀♀ **Vin de Soif 2016** Rating 93 To 2026 $25 **✪**
Second Take Barossa Valley Roussanne 2017 Rating 92 To 2024 $40 JF
Second Take Barossa Valley Mataro 2017 Rating 92 To 2024 $40 JF
Barossa Valley Shiraz 2016 Rating 90 To 2024 $25 JF

Yering Station

38 Melba Highway, Yarra Glen, Vic 3775 **Region** Yarra Valley
T (03) 9730 0100 **www**.yering.com **Open** 7 days 10–5
Winemaker Willy Lunn, Brendan Hawker **Est.** 1988 **Dozens** 60 000 **Vyds** 112ha

The historic Yering Station (or at least the portion of the property on which the cellar door sales and vineyard are established) was purchased by the Rathbone family in 1996 and is also the site of the Yarrabank joint venture with French Champagne house Devaux. A spectacular and very large winery was built, handling the Yarrabank sparkling and the Yering Station table wines, immediately becoming one of the focal points of the Yarra Valley, particularly as the historic Chateau Yering, where luxury accommodation and fine dining are available, is next door. Willy Lunn, a graduate of Adelaide University, has more than 25 years of cool-climate winemaking experience around the world, including at Petaluma, Shaw + Smith and Argyle Winery (Oregon). Exports to all major markets.

ᵀᵀᵀᵀᵀ **Scarlett Pinot Noir 2015** A wine that achieves more by doing less. Its light colour is deceptive, for it has rare intensity and power. Its bouquet has violets and rose petals (a rare double) and exotic spices, and the very long palate has immaculate tannins sewn through the predominantly red fruits. This wine honours Nathan Scarlett (1975–2013) who developed the precision viticulture at Yering Station that pinpointed the tiny patch of exceptional vines that give rise to this great pinot. Screwcap. 13% alc. **Rating** 97 **To** 2028 $250

Reserve Yarra Valley Shiraz Viognier 2015 Co-fermented with 3% viognier, aged in French barriques (35% new) for 18 months. The powerful, resplendent black cherry and plum fruits have touches of pepper and spice as well as that of the near-unseen viognier. French oak and tannins are in their due place. Screwcap. 13.8% alc. **Rating** 97 **To** 2045 $120 ✪

ᵀᵀᵀᵀᵀ **Yarra Valley Chardonnay 2016** Straw-yellow. In the zone for flavour, texture and length. Peach, pear, grapefruit and spice notes generate excellent power but it's the mouthfeel and overall class that really seal the deal. It's complex at every turn but inviting and accessible too. A top example of modern Australian chardonnay. Screwcap. 13% alc. **Rating** 95 **To** 2023 CM

Yarra Valley Shiraz Viognier 2015 On its own, the colour might seem good, and it is, but nowhere near the hue of the Reserve. The black fruits of the bouquet have notes of licorice, pepper and spice, and swing into full power mode on the long palate. Likewise there is a palisade of tannins to keep any attack on the fruit at bay – they are a natural antioxidant. Screwcap. 13.8% alc. **Rating** 95 **To** 2035 $40

Village Yarra Valley Rose 2017 So juicy. So moreish. Red cherry and pomegranate flavours come flecked with anise. It's bursting with life. It's just a cracking rose, basically, and begs to be consumed with (responsible) gusto. Screwcap. 12% alc. **Rating** 94 **To** 2020 CM ✪

Yarra Valley Pinot Noir 2016 Get a smell of this. This draws you straight in, the nose so exquisitely turned out, the palate following straight on, the finish letting no one down. Undergrowth, spice notes, cherries, plums, folds of satin, wafts of wood smoke. Oak certainly contributes here, but the fruit has its back. One highly seductive pinot noir. Screwcap. 13.4% alc. **Rating** 94 **To** 2026 $40 CM

Village Yarra Valley Shiraz Viognier 2015 With 2% viognier. In fine form, both balance and fruit intensity are key markers of its quality. Black cherry and licorice flavours come stitched with cloves and spice. Toasty oak plays a role, but a minor one. Spice-shot tannin spreads its wings through the back half of the wine. Good from every angle. Screwcap. 13.5% alc. **Rating** 94 **To** 2032 $24 CM ✪

ᵀᵀᵀᵀᵀ **Village Yarra Valley Marsanne Viognier 2017 Rating** 91 **To** 2027
Yarra Valley Cabernet Sauvignon 2015 Rating 90 **To** 2030 $40

Yeringberg

Maroondah Highway, Coldstream, Vic 3770 **Region** Yarra Valley
T (03) 9739 0240 **www**.yeringberg.com.au **Open** By appt
Winemaker Sandra de Pury **Est.** 1863 **Dozens** 1500 **Vyds** 3.66ha
Guill de Pury and daughter Sandra, with Guill's wife Katherine in the background, make wines for the new millennium from the low-yielding vines re-established in the heart of what was one of the most famous (and infinitely larger) vineyards of the 19th century. In the riper years, the red wines have a velvety generosity of flavour rarely encountered, while never losing varietal character; the long-lived Marsanne Roussanne takes students of history back to Yeringberg's fame in the 19th century. Exports to the US, Switzerland, Hong Kong and China.

ϘϘϘϘϘ **Yarra Valley Shiraz 2015** Excellent dark purple hue, thanks to a splash of viognier. It's a glorious, perfectly pitched, cool-climate shiraz with a lot packed into it, yet retains an elegance on its medium-bodied palate. Heady aromas of dark and red fruits, black pepper, some pine needles/garrigue notes and a fleck of charry-wood spices from the otherwise integrated oak. There's a suppleness, juiciness on the palate, and a savoury note that tempers the fruit; the tannin's fine and detailed with the acidity, like a refreshing squirt of raspberry juice. Screwcap. 14% alc. **Rating** 96 **To** 2030 $85 JF
Yeringberg 2015 The wine has presence, charm and elegance in equal measure. A blend of 66% cabernet sauvignon, 13% cabernet franc and splashes of merlot, petit verdot and malbec, all of which has created a medium-bodied wine. Expect a mix of red berries and leafy freshness, some menthol and spice with super fine tannins and excellent length. It's a contemplative wine to savour. Screwcap. 14% alc. **Rating** 96 **To** 2038 $98 JF
Yarra Valley Chardonnay 2016 Hand-picked fruit, destemmed and crushed, aged in French barrels (30% new) for 11 months with 30% mlf. Always a flavoursome, fuller bodied chardonnay with stone fruit, figs and leesy, creamy notes. Yet it keeps a well-formed frame with bright acidity helping. Screwcap. 13% alc. **Rating** 95 **To** 2024 $66 JF
Yarra Valley Marsanne Roussanne 2016 A 59/41% split, spends 10 months on lees in seasoned barrels and it's a mighty wine for its depth and precision. Flavour-wise, it's perfectly proportioned with whispers of stone fruit, honeysuckle, creamed honey and fine acidity. **Rating** 95 **To** 2030 $66 JF
Yarra Valley Pinot Noir 2015 A bright, sparkling crimson-purple, this is an enticing wine with aromas of florals, red fruits and some woodsy spices, the oak perfectly integrated. It's deceptive at first as it feels effortless and lighter bodied, which it is, but it builds additional layers of fine tannin, more fruit and cleansing acidity. Screwcap. 13.5% alc. **Rating** 95 **To** 2028 $98 JF

ϘϘϘϘϘ **Yeringberg 2016 Rating** 93 **To** 2021 $36 JF

Yes said the Seal

1251–1269 Bellarine Highway, Wallington, Vic 3221 **Region** Geelong
T (03) 5250 6577 **www**.yessaidtheseal.com.au **Open** 7 days 10–5
Winemaker Darren Burke **Est.** 2014 **Dozens** 1000 **Vyds** 2ha
This is a new venture for David and Lyndsay Sharp, long-term vintners on Geelong's Bellarine Peninsula. The 2ha of estate vineyard were planted to shiraz in 2010; other varieties are purchased from growers on the Bellarine Peninsula. It is situated onsite at the Flying Brick Cider Co's Cider House in Wallington.

ϘϘϘϘϘ **The Bellarine Pinot Noir 2016** Right from the outset this wine proclaims its varietal character in an elegant, relaxed, yet pure, manner. The colour is good, the varietal character on the spicy red fruit bouquet unfolding on the palate with striking silky mouthfeel, and flavours of red berries. Screwcap. 12.8% alc. **Rating** 96 **To** 2031 $45 ❂
The Bellarine Chardonnay 2016 Matured in French oak (25% new) for 10 months with lees stirring. The mouthfeel provides the first and last highlights of a beautifully made chardonnay; it's impossible to criticise the wine because the

fruit line through the mid-palate was maintained. Screwcap. 13.5% alc. **Rating** 95
To 2026 $33 ✪

The Bellarine Shiraz 2016 Matured for 10 months in French oak (10% new).
This is as close to the ultimate in juicy, cool-climate shiraz as you are likely to
encounter. It's stacked with red and purple fruits, and enough oak and tannin
to provide shape and a medium-bodied depth. Screwcap. 14% alc. **Rating** 95
To 2036 $33 ✪

The Bellarine Sauvignon Blanc 2017 From two vineyards, 'one for the
richness, the other for thrill and acidity', 100% fermented in French oak
(20% new), 8 months on lees. This takes sauvignon blanc into Loire Valley territory
as much as Margaret River. There's one taste compartment for citrus and tropical
fruits, and another for toasty/biscuity notes. A split personality at this stage, but
likely deliberately so. Screwcap. 13.2% alc. **Rating** 94 To 2025 $27 ✪

The Bellarine Rose 2017 100% shiraz. Bright, clear crimson; a rose very nearly
intruding into light, dry red space, but because of its length, depth and balance
there aren't likely to be any complaints about the lingering red fruit flavours.
Screwcap. 12.8% alc. **Rating** 94 To 2021 $25 ✪

Z Wine ★★★★★

Shop 3, 109–111 Murray Street, Tanunda, SA 5352 **Region** Barossa Valley
T (08) 8563 3637 **www.**zwine.com.au **Open** Mon–Wed 10–5, Thurs–Sun 10–late
Winemaker Janelle Zerk **Est.** 1999 **Dozens** 10 000 **Vyds** 1ha
Z Wine is the partnership of sisters Janelle and Kristen Zerk, whose heritage dates back
five generations at the Zerk vineyard in Lyndoch. Vineyard resources include growers that
supply old vine shiraz, old bushvine grenache and High Eden Valley riesling. Both women
have completed degrees at Adelaide University (Janelle in winemaking and Kristen in wine
marketing). Janelle also has vintage experience in Puligny Montrachet, Tuscany and Sonoma
Valley. Wines are released under the Z Wine, Rustica and Section 3146 labels. In 2017
Z Wine opened a cellar door in the main street of Tanunda. Exports to the US, Singapore,
NZ, Taiwan, Hong Kong and China.

🍷🍷🍷🍷🍷 **Poole Old Vine Barossa Valley Shiraz 2016** From 64yo vines in the Light
Pass district. Open-fermented before being pressed into (50% new) French
oak. Total of 94 dozen made. Heavy with both fruit and oak, but it feels sturdy,
composed and complete. Saturated plums, mint, bitumen, cedar wood and violets.
A heady, sweet-fruited wine and a controlled one. Cork. 14.5% alc. **Rating** 96
To 2040 $120 CM

Hein Ancestor Vine Barossa Valley Shiraz 2016 Production of 60 dozen,
in 50% new French oak from 140yo vines (Langmeil). Extreme concentration of
fruit. Happy marriage to smoky oak. Velvety. Sumptuous but firm. One sip and
you can rattle off its qualities rapid-fire; everything here is abundant and clear.
Cork. 14.5% alc. **Rating** 95 To 2040 $300 CM

Roman Barossa Valley Grenache Shiraz Mourvedre 2016 51/33/16%
blend. It sees no new oak. The grenache component (the mainstay of the
blend) is from 90yo vines. It's in fabulous form. Rich, bright, sweet, and smoky,
with a glorious burst of fruit to both the nose and palate, and ample reductive
complexities besides. It lets rip, and it works. No need to wait; tuck in now.
Screwcap. 14.5% alc. **Rating** 95 To 2025 $35 CM ✪

Aveline Barossa Valley Rose 2017 Made off 70yo grenache vines. 5% sees
new French oak. Spice, fruit, acidity and a firmness to the finish. Even in rose
form it showcases its variety, and maybe even its vine age too. Spicy style, but not
at the expense of home-base flavour. Screwcap. 13.5% alc. **Rating** 94 To 2020
$20 CM ✪

Section 3146 Barossa Valley Shiraz 2015 Ample oak and ample fruit team
up to create a big-flavoured red with smoothness (of texture) on its side. Integrated
tannin is another keen, and key, feature. Orange-like acidity and coffee notes about
the edges help get a real hum going. Everything here makes a positive impression.
Screwcap. 14.5% alc. **Rating** 94 To 2030 $35 CM

🍷🍷🍷🍷♀ Julius Barossa Valley Shiraz 2015 Rating 93 To 2030 $60 CM
Section 3146 Barossa Valley Cabernet Sauvignon 2015 Rating 93
To 2027 $35 CM
Plowman Dry Grown Barossa Valley Shiraz 2016 Rating 92 To 2036
$120 CM
Rustica Reserve Barossa Valley Shiraz 2015 Rating 91 To 2028 $34 CM
Hedley Barossa Valley Shiraz 2015 Rating 91 To 2027 $35 CM
Audrey Barossa Valley Cabernet Sauvignon 2015 Rating 91 To 2026
$35 CM
Rustica Barossa Valley Shiraz 2015 Rating 90 To 2024 $20 CM ✪

Zema Estate

14944 Riddoch Highway, Coonawarra, SA 5263 **Region** Coonawarra
T (08) 8736 3219 www.zema.com.au **Open** Mon–Fri 9–5, w'ends & public hols 10–4
Winemaker Greg Clayfield **Est.** 1982 **Dozens** 20000 **Vyds** 61ha
Zema is one of the last outposts of hand pruning in Coonawarra, with members of the Zema
family tending the vineyard set in the heart of Coonawarra's terra rossa soil. Winemaking
practices are straightforward; if ever there was an example of great wines being made in the
vineyard, this is it. Exports to the UK, Vietnam, Hong Kong, Japan, Singapore and China.

🍷🍷🍷🍷🍷 Cluny Coonawarra Cabernet Merlot 2014 Comprising 65% cabernet
sauvignon, 25% merlot, and 5% each cabernet franc and malbec. It's one of
relatively few cabernet–merlot blends in Coonawarra, and makes you wonder why
there aren't more. If there are green or minty notes, I can't see them; instead there
are supple, sweet cassis, redcurrant and dried herb flavours supported by fine, ripe
tannins and French oak. Screwcap. 13.5% alc. Rating 95 To 2034 $26 ✪

🍷🍷🍷🍷♀ Coonawarra Cabernet Sauvignon 2015 Rating 92 To 2025 $30 DB
Coonawarra Shiraz 2015 Rating 90 To 2032 $26 DB

Zerella Wines

182 Olivers Road, McLaren Vale, SA 5171 **Region** McLaren Vale
T (08) 8323 8288/0488 929 202 www.zerellawines.com.au **Open** Thurs–Mon 11–4
Winemaker Jim Zerella **Est.** 2006 **Dozens** 2500 **Vyds** 58ha
In 1950 Ercole Zerella left his native Campania in southern Italy to seek a better life in
South Australia. With a lifetime of farming and grapegrowing, the transition was seamless.
Ercole's son Vic followed in his father's footsteps, becoming an icon of the farming and wine
industries in South Australia. Vic founded Tatachilla, where his son Jim began as a cellar
hand, eventually controlling all grape purchases. While working there, Jim purchased land in
McLaren Vale and, with help from family and friends, established what is now the flagship
vineyard of Zerella Wines. He also established a vineyard management business catering to
the needs of absentee owners. When Tatachilla was purchased by Lion Nathan in 2000, Jim
declined the opportunity of continuing his role there, and by 2006 had purchased two more
vineyards and become a shareholder in a third. These all now come under the umbrella of
Zerella Wines, with its 58ha of vines. The winemaking techniques used are thoroughly à la
mode, and definitely not traditional Italian. Exports to Canada.

🍷🍷🍷🍷🍷 Workhorse McLaren Vale Shiraz 2015 Matured for 18 months in French
oak (30% new). A pure thoroughbred, far from a workhorse. Has unlimited
horsepower, however, with tension between black fruits, bitter chocolate, licorice
and tannins. Top class wine. Screwcap. 14.5% alc. Rating 96 To 2040 $30 ✪
La Gita McLaren Vale Arneis 2016 Bright pale green; this has been very
well made, with a strong textural feel running alongside zesty citrus pith flavours.
4.64ha of pinot noir were grafted to arneis in '11 – absolutely the right call.
Screwcap. 13.5% alc. Rating 95 To 2022 $30 ✪
Packing Shed McLaren Vale Grenache Mataro Shiraz 2015 Comprising
47% grenache, 28% mataro, and 25% shiraz, and matured in used French oak for
15 months. Ah, McLaren Vale, ah, 13.5% alcohol, ah, used French oak. Such is

the frame around the elegant, medium-bodied palate, with its gently spicy but fresh red fruits, given context by perfectly weighted tannins. Screwcap. **Rating** 95 To 2030 $30 ✪

Oliveto Single Vineyard McLaren Vale Mataro 2016 Matured in used oak for 8 months. A sumptuously rich medium to full-bodied wine, true to both its variety and its place. Plum and blackberry fruits fill the mouth, and fine, ripe tannins underpin its length. Screwcap. 14.5% alc. **Rating** 95 To 2031 $50

La Gita McLaren Vale Nero d'Avola 2015 The vintage allowed this nero to express itself with elan. The medium crimson-purple hue isn't particularly striking, but the wine is supple, smooth and seductive, with exotic spicy aromas, and fine, distinctly savoury tannins adding to the dark fruitcake flavour. Screwcap. 14% alc. **Rating** 95 To 2025 $35 ✪

La Gita McLaren Vale Fiano 2017 Fills the mouth from start to finish, seductive and full of mysteries. How is it possible to have so much flavour without extraction or high alcohol? Its layer upon layer of laminated flavour texture are also on the march. Then there's the acidity. Screwcap. 13.5% alc. **Rating** 94 To 2027 $30 ✪

4056 McLaren Vale Cabernet Sauvignon 2015 Classic McLaren Vale cabernet with masses of blackcurrant fruit studded with earth, dark chocolate and ripe tannins, the finish replete with cedary oak that adds substantially to a cleverly made wine. There's a lot of value in the $30 price tag. Screwcap. 14.5% alc. **Rating** 94 To 2030 $30 ✪

Zig Zag Road ★★★★

201 Zig Zag Road, Drummond, Vic 3446 **Region** Macedon Ranges
T (03) 5423 9390 **www**.zigzagwines.com.au **Open** Thurs–Mon 10–5
Winemaker Eric Bellchambers, Llew Knight **Est.** 1972 **Dozens** 700 **Vyds** 4.5ha
In 2002 Eric and Anne Bellchambers became the third owners of this vineyard, planted by Roger Aldridge in 1972. The Bellchambers have extended the plantings with riesling and merlot, supplementing the older, dry-grown plantings of shiraz, cabernet sauvignon and pinot noir.

🍷🍷🍷🍷🍷 **Macedon Ranges Pinot Grigio 2017** Yellow to amber in hue. Attractively ripe on the nose, brimming with Bosc pear, red apple cider, grilled nuts, candied ginger and marzipan. This is more a gris than a grigio, but who cares? Richly textured too, with a volatile spike for lift at the tail of a long finish, massaged with skinsy phenolics. Nourishing and saline. Screwcap. 13% alc. **Rating** 93 To 2021 $24 NG ✪

Macedon Ranges Sauvignon Blanc 2017 Distinctly turbid, chunky and pulpy across the palate. Clearly made with minimal messing about in the winery. Lemon oil, curd, honeydew melon and a curious cucumber note splay across a tonic water freshness, as reliant on the moderate acidity for verve as it is on a rail of well-handled phenolics for brio. Screwcap. 12.5% alc. **Rating** 91 To 2021 $24 NG

Macedon Ranges Riesling 2017 An intriguing riesling, with moreish acidity beaming from fore to aft. Crunchy. Granny Smith apple. White flower. Finishes tangy and doused with talc and sherbet meandering about its phenolic curves. Screwcap. 12% alc. **Rating** 90 To 2025 $24 NG

Macedon Ranges Cabernet Sauvignon 2015 There is fluidity to this, presumably because cabernet's physiognomy of tannic mettle manages to meld more readily with the oak choice. Currant, anise, eucalyptus and the usual herbal potpourri are slung across the verdant-scented oak. Chunky. Should age in an interesting way. Screwcap. 14.5% alc. **Rating** 90 To 2028 $24 NG

Zilzie Wines ★★★★

544 Kulkyne Way, Karadoc, Vic 3496 (postal) **Region** Murray Darling
T (03) 5025 8100 **www**.zilziewines.com **Open** Not
Winemaker Hayden Donohue **Est.** 1999 **Dozens** NFP **Vyds** 572ha

The Forbes family has been farming since the early 1990s. Zilzie is currently run by Ian and Ros Forbes, with sons Steven and Andrew, and the diverse range of farming activities includes grapegrowing from substantial vineyards. Having established a dominant position as a supplier of grapes to Southcorp, Zilzie formed a wine company in '99 and built a winery in 2000, expanding it in '06 to its current capacity of 45000t. The wines consistently far exceed expectations, given their enticing prices, that consistency driving the production volume to 200000 dozen (the last known publicised amount) – this in an extremely competitive market. The business includes contract processing, winemaking and storage. Exports to the UK, Canada, Hong Kong and China.

ŢŢŢŢŢ **Selection 23 Rose 2017** A lolly shop of flavours from musk, strawberry jubes, passionfruit, pear and kiwi fruit essence. Certainly lively with lemony acidity, which is much needed to cut through the sweetness, yet ends up balanced enough and refreshing. Screwcap. 11.5% alc. **Rating** 90 **To** 2018 $13 JF ✪
Regional Collection Barossa Shiraz 2016 A bright mid-garnet colour, its appeal is immediate with florals, red fruits and a dash of woodsy spices. It's fleshy with ripe, plump fruit on the palate, pliable tannins and a price matched accordingly. Screwcap. 14.5% alc. **Rating** 90 **To** 2021 $20 JF ✪
Regional Collection King Valley Prosecco NV A racy prosecco with lemon-sorbet acidity driving right through the middle then to a snappy finish. In between, crunchy pears and red apples, a dab of ginger spice and refreshingly dry. Crown seal. 12% alc. **Rating** 90 **To** 2018 $22 JF

ŢŢŢŢ **Regional Collection Adelaide Hills Pinot Gris 2017** Rating 89 To 2019 $20 JF
Estate Merlot 2017 Rating 89 To 2020 $12 JF ✪
Estate Cabernet Sauvignon 2017 Rating 89 To 2020 $12 JF ✪
Regional Collection Coonawarra Cabernet Sauvignon 2016 Rating 89 To 2020 $20 JF
MCMXI Cabernet Sauvignon 2015 Rating 89 To 2022 $50 JF

Zitta Wines   ★★★★

3 Union Street, Dulwich, SA 5065 (postal) **Region** Barossa Valley
T 0419 819 414 **www.zitta.com.au Open** Not
Winemaker Angelo De Fazio **Est.** 2004 **Dozens** 3000 **Vyds** 26.3ha
Owner Angelo De Fazio says that all he knows about viticulture and winemaking came from his father (and generations before him). It is partly this influence that has shaped the label and brand name. 'Zitta' is Italian for 'quiet' and this is reflected on their wine bottle label; 'Zitta' is printed boldly and clearly, accompanied by what seems to be its surface reflection, but is really the word 'Quiet' creatively set upside down. The Zitta vineyard dates back to 1864, with a few vines remaining from that time, and a block planted with cuttings taken from those vines. Shiraz dominates the plantings (22ha), with the balance made up of chardonnay, grenache and a few mourvedre vines. Only a small amount of the production is retained for the Zitta label. The property has two branches of Greenock Creek running through it, and the soils reflect the ancient geological history of the site – in part with a subsoil of river pebbles, reflecting the course of a long-gone river. Exports to Denmark and China.

ŢŢŢŢŢ **Single Vineyard Greenock Barossa Valley Shiraz 2015** Being the first Zitta produced, it is regarded as the pinnacle in the range. And while it can stand proud, the alcohol makes its presence felt, disrupting the finish. The fruit is ripe but not too ripe, with dark plums and blackberry flavours, loads of oak spice and a power thrust of tannin across the full-bodied palate. And yet, it retains a freshness. Screwcap. 15.1% alc. **Rating** 92 **To** 2025 $60 JF
Single Vineyard Bernardo Greenock Barossa Valley Shiraz 2015 While this is at the riper, sweeter end of the shiraz spectrum, and given its 2 years in French and American oak, it holds its own and fans of big, bolshie reds will go for it. Fleshy ripe fruit, currants and plum pudding notes; definitely full-bodied with expansive tannins. Screwcap. 14.8% alc. **Rating** 91 **To** 2030 $45 JF

▼▼▼▼ Single Vineyard 1864 Greenock Barossa Valley GSM 2015 Rating 89
To 2024 $45 JF

Zonte's Footstep ★★★★☆

The General Wine Bar, 55A Main Road, McLaren Flat, SA 5171 **Region** McLaren Vale
T (08) 8383 2083 **www**.zontesfootstep.com.au **Open** 7 days 10–5
Winemaker Ben Riggs **Est.** 2003 **Dozens** 20 000 **Vyds** 214.72ha
Zonte's Footstep has been very successful since a group of long-standing friends, collectively
with deep knowledge of every aspect of the wine business, decided it was time to do
something together. Along the way there has been some shuffling of the deck chairs, but all
achieved without any ill feeling from those who moved sideways or backwards. The major
change has been a broadening of the regions (Langhorne Creek, McLaren Vale, the Barossa
and Clare valleys, and elsewhere) from which the grapes are sourced. Even here, however, most
of the vineyards supplying grapes are owned by members of the Zonte's Footstep partnership.
Exports to the UK, the US, Canada, Finland, Sweden, Denmark, Thailand and Singapore.

▼▼▼▼▼ Blackberry Patch Fleurieu Cabernet 2016 Cabernet sauvignon (95%),
tempranillo (5%). All French oak, 10% new. Squeaky clean, brightly fruited,
moreish. All manner of positives, not to mention value. It tastes of boysenberries,
violets, fragrant/blossomy herbs and kirsch, and if you can stop at one glass then
you're better than I am. It's absolutely ready to rip right now. Screwcap. 14.5% alc.
Rating 95 **To** 2026 $25 CM ◎
Z-Force 2015 Shiraz (90%), petite sirah (10%). Matured in both French and
American oak, 30% new, for 18 months. It's a Z-Force of nature. This is a brute
of a red; its dark leather, tar, blackberry and boysenberry flavours roaring through
the palate in confident, if not authoritative, style. A swagger of tannin tops it all off.
Screwcap. 14.5% alc. **Rating** 94 **To** 2035 $55 CM

▼▼▼▼♀ Baron Von Nemesis Single Site Barossa Shiraz 2016 Rating 93 To 2030
$35 CM
Violet Beauregard Langhorne Creek Malbec 2016 Rating 93 To 2027
$25 CM ◎
Dawn Patrol Adelaide Hills Pinot Noir 2016 Rating 92 To 2023 CM
Chocolate Factory Shiraz 2016 Rating 92 To 2028 $25 CM ◎
Doctoressa Di Lago Adelaide Hills Pinot Grigio 2017 Rating 91 To 2018
$20 CM ◎
Scarlet Ladybird Rose 2017 Rating 91 To 2018. $18 CM ◎
Lake Doctor Langhorne Creek Shiraz 2016 Rating 91 To 2026 $25 CM
Love Symbol McLaren Vale Grenache 2016 Rating 91 To 2023 $25 CM
Canto di Lago Fleurieu Peninsula Sangiovese Barbera Lagrein 2016
Rating 91 To 2023 $25 CM

Zonzo Estate ★★★☆

957 Healesville-Yarra Glen Road, Yarra Glen, Vic 3775 **Region** Yarra Valley
T (03) 9730 2500 **www**.zonzo.com.au **Open** Wed–Sun 12–4
Winemaker Kate Goodman, Caroline Mooney **Est.** 1998 **Dozens** 2075 **Vyds** 18.21ha
This is the new iteration of Train Trak, best known by Yarra Valley locals for the quality of its
wood fired–oven pizzas. The vineyard was planted in 1995, with the first wines made from the
1998 vintage. The business was acquired by Rod Micallef in 2016. It's open for lunch from
Wed–Sun, dinner Fri–Sun.

▼▼▼▼ Rose 2017 A pale pastel pink; it's refreshingly dry and flavoured with watermelon,
spiced cherries and just enough texture to add more interest. Screwcap. 13% alc.
Rating 89 **To** 2018 JF

Index

	Cellar door sales
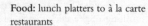	Food: lunch platters to à la carte restaurants
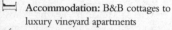	Accommodation: B&B cottages to luxury vineyard apartments
	Music events: monthly jazz in the vineyard to spectacular yearly concerts

Coonawarra (SA)

Cowra (NSW)

Kangaroo Island (SA)